T0320937

The Oxford Handbook of the
Psychology of Competition

OXFORD LIBRARY OF PSYCHOLOGY

OXFORD LIBRARY OF PSYCHOLOGY

The Oxford Handbook of the Psychology of Competition

Edited by

Stephen M. Garcia, Avishalom Tor, and Andrew J. Elliot

OXFORD
UNIVERSITY PRESS

OXFORD
UNIVERSITY PRESS

Oxford University Press is a department of the University of Oxford. It furthers
the University's objective of excellence in research, scholarship, and education
by publishing worldwide. Oxford is a registered trade mark of Oxford University
Press in the UK and certain other countries.

Published in the United States of America by Oxford University Press
198 Madison Avenue, New York, NY 10016, United States of America.

Library of Congress Control Number: 2023949095

ISBN 978–0–19–006080–0

DOI: 10.1093/oxfordhb/9780190060800.001.0001

Printed by Integrated Books International, United States of America

CONTENTS

List of Contributors   ix

I · Introduction

1. What Is the Psychology of Competition?   3
   Stephen M. Garcia, Avishalom Tor, and *Andrew J. Elliot*
2. Competition in Psychology and Experimental Economics   9
   Uriel Haran and *Yoella Bereby-Meyer*

II · Biological Approaches

3. Examination of the Potential Functional Role of
   Competition-Induced Testosterone Dynamics   39
   Tracy-Lynn Reside, Brittney A. Robinson, and *Justin M. Carré*
4. Biological Sex Differences and Competition   55
   Alicia Salvador, Vanesa Hidalgo, Raquel Costa, and
   Esperanza González-Bono
5. Psychobiology of Competition: A Review of Men's Endogenous
   Testosterone Dynamics   101
   Brian M. Bird, Lindsay Bochon, Yin Wu, and *Samuele Zilioli*
6. Neuroscience and Competitive Behavior   117
   Michela Balconi and *Laura Angioletti*
7. The Evolution of Competition: A Darwinian Perspective   134
   Ben Winegard and *David Geary*

III · Motivational and Emotional Approaches

8. Competitive Arousal: Sources, Effects, and Implications   163
   Gillian Ku and *Marc T. P. Adam*
9. Motivational Dynamics Underlying Competition: The Opposing
   Processes Model of Competition and Performance   189
   Kou Murayama, Andrew J. Elliot, and *Mickaël Jury*
10. Competition and Goal Pursuit: A Temporally Dynamic
    Model   210
    Szu-chi Huang and *Stephanie Lin*

11. Intrinsic Motivation, Psychological Needs, and Competition:
A Self-Determination Theory Analysis 240
Richard M. Ryan and *Johnmarshall Reeve*

12. Envy: A Prevalent Emotion in Competitive Settings 265
Ronit Montal-Rosenberg and *Simone Moran*

IV · Cognitive and Decision-Making Approaches

13. Judgmental Biases in the Perception of Competitive Advantage: On Choosing
the Right Race to Run 287
David Dunning

14. Social Dilemmas: From Competition to Cooperation 305
Poonam Arora, Tamar Kugler, and *Francesca Giardini*

15. Self-Evaluation in Competition Pools 332
Mark D. Alicke, Yiyue Zhang, Nicole B. Stephenson, and *Ethan Zell*

16. On Predicting and Being Predicted: Navigating Life in a Competitive Landscape
Full of Mind Readers 350
Oscar Ybarra, Kimberly Rios, Matthew C. Keller, Nicholas Michalak, Iris Wang,
and *Todd Chan*

17. Competition and Risk-Taking 373
Sandeep Mishra, Cody Fogg, and *Jeff Deminchuk*

V · Social-Personality and Organizational Approaches

18. Social Comparison and Competition: General Frameworks, Focused Models,
and Emerging Phenomena 401
Stephen M. Garcia and *Avishalom Tor*

19. Psychology of Rivalry: A Social-Cognitive Approach to Competitive
Relationships 422
Benjamin A. Converse, David A. Reinhard, and *Maura M. K. Austin*

20. The Psychology of Status Competition within Organizations: Navigating
Two Competing Motives 444
Sarah P. Doyle, Sijun Kim, and *Hee Young Kim*

21. Social Identity and Intergroup Competition 476
Sucharita Belavadi and *Michael A. Hogg*

22. Benefits and Drawbacks of Trait Competitiveness 496
Craig D. Parks

23. Gender Differences in the Psychology of Competition 514
Kathrin J. Hanek

VI · Competition in Context

24. Ready, Steady, Go: Competition in Sport   545
    Maria Kavussanu, Andrew Cooke, and *Marc Jones*
25. Competition in Education   569
    Fabrizio Butera, Wojciech Świątkowski, and *Benoît Dompnier*
26. Mindfulness, Competition, and Sports Psychology: A Phenomenological
    Perspective   598
    Ramaswami Mahalingam
27. Hide a Dagger Behind a Smile: A Review of How Collectivistic Cultures
    Compete More Than Individualistic Cultures   611
    Kaidi Wu and *Thomas Talhelm*

Index   643

CONTRIBUTORS

Marc T. P. Adam
Associate Professor in Computing and IT, School of Information and Physical Sciences, University of Newcastle

Mark D. Alicke
Professor of Psychology, Ohio University

Laura Angioletti
Post-Doctoral Researcher, International Research Center for Cognitive Applied Neuroscience (IrcCAN), Department of Psychology, Catholic University of the Sacred Heart

Poonam Arora
Associate Dean and Professor of Management, Quinnipiac University

Maura M. K. Austin
Graduate Student, Department of Psychology, University of Virginia

Michela Balconi
Professor of Psychophysiology and Cognitive Neuroscience, Director of International Research Center for Cognitive Applied Neuroscience (IrcCAN), Head of the Research Unit in Affective and Social Neuroscience, Department of Psychology, Catholic University of the Sacred Heart

Sucharita Belavadi
Assistant Professor, Jindal Institute of Behavioural Sciences, O. P. Jindal Global University

Yoella Bereby-Meyer
Professor of Psychology, Department of Psychology, Ben-Gurion University of the Negev

Brian M. Bird
Simon Fraser University

Lindsay Bochon
PhD Candidate, Psychology Department, Simon Fraser University

Fabrizio Butera
Professor of Social Psychology, Institute of Psychology, University of Lausanne

Justin M. Carré
Professor of Psychology, Nipissing University

Todd Chan
PhD Candidate, University of Michigan

Benjamin A. Converse
Associate Professor of Public Policy and Psychology, University of Virginia

Andrew Cooke
Senior Lecturer in Performance Psychology, Institute for the Psychology of Elite Performance (IPEP), School of Human and Behavioural Sciences, Bangor University

Raquel Costa
Lecturer, Department of Psychobiology, Faculty of Psychology and Speed Therapy, University of Valencia

Jeff Deminchuk
Graduate Student, University of Regina

Benoît Dompnier
Senior Lecturer, Institute of Psychology, University of Lausanne

Sarah P. Doyle
Assistant Professor of Management and Organizations, University of Arizona Eller College of Management

David Dunning
Professor of Psychology, University of Michigan

Andrew J. Elliot
Professor of Psychology, University of Rochester

Cody Fogg
Department of Psychology, University of Regina

Stephen M. Garcia
Professor of Organizational Behavior, Graduate School of Management, University of California, Davis

David Geary
Curators' Distinguished Professor, Psychological Sciences, University of Missouri

Francesca Giardini
Associate Professor of Sociology, Department of Sociology, University of Groningen

Esperanza González-Bono
Professor of Psychobiology, Psychobiology Department, Psychology Faculty, University of Valencia

Kathrin J. Hanek
Associate Professor of Management, Department of Management and Marketing, University of Dayton

Uriel Haran
Senior Lecturer of Organizational Behavior, Department of Management, Ben-Gurion University of the Negev

Vanesa Hidalgo
Associate Professor of Psychobiology, Psychology and Sociology Department, University of Zaragoza

Michael A. Hogg
Professor of Social Psychology, Claremont Graduate University

Szu-chi Huang
Associate Professor of Marketing and R. Michael Shanahan Faculty Scholar, Stanford Graduate School of Business, Stanford University

Marc Jones
Professor of Psychology, Department of Psychology, Manchester Metropolitan University

Mickaël Jury
Assistant Professor of Social Psychology of Education, INSPé, Université Clermont-Auvergne

Maria Kavussanu
School of Sport, Exercise and Rehabilitation Sciences, University of Birmingham

Matthew C. Keller
Professor, Psychology & Neuroscience, University of Colorado

Hee Young Kim
Associate Professor, Management Department, Rider University

Sijun Kim
Assistant Professor, Department of Management, Texas A&M University

Gillian Ku
Professor of Organisational Behaviour, London Business School

Tamar Kugler
Associate Professor of Management and Organizations, University of Arizona

Stephanie Lin
Assistant Professor of Marketing, INSEAD

Ramaswami Mahalingam
Barger Leadership Institute Professor, Department of Psychology, University of Michigan

Nicholas Michalak
PhD Candidate, University of Michigan

Sandeep Mishra
Associate Professor of Management, Lang School of Business and Economics, University of Guelph

Ronit Montal-Rosenberg
Postdoctoral Fellow, The Federmann School of Public Policy, The Hebrew University of Jerusalem

Simone Moran
Associate Professor, Department of Management, Guilford Glazer Faculty of Business and Management, Ben-Gurion University of the Negev

Kou Murayama
Professor, Hector Research Institute of Education Sciences and Psychology, University of Tübingen

Craig D. Parks
Professor of Psychology, Washington State University

Johnmarshall Reeve
Professor, Institute for Positive Psychology and Education, Australian Catholic University

David A. Reinhard
University of Massachusetts Amherst

Tracy-Lynn Reside
Nipissing University

Kimberly Rios
Professor of Psychology, Ohio University

Brittney A. Robinson
Nipissing University

Richard M. Ryan
Professor, Institute for Positive Psychology and Education, Australian Catholic University

Alicia Salvador
Professor of Psychology, University of Valencia

Nicole B. Stephenson
Ohio University

Wojciech Świątkowski
University of Lausanne

Thomas Talhelm
Associate Professor of Behavioral Science, University of Chicago Booth School of Business

Avishalom Tor
Professor of Law and Director, Notre Dame Program on Law and Market Behavior, Notre Dame Law School (ND LAMB)

Iris Wang
Graduate Student, University of Michigan

Ben Winegard
Assistant Professor of Psychology, Hillsdale College

Kaidi Wu
Postdoctoral Scholar, University of California, San Diego, Rady School of Management

Yin Wu
Associate Professor, Department of Applied Social Sciences, Shenzhen University

Oscar Ybarra

Professor of Business Administration,
University of Illinois

Ethan Zell

Associate Professor of Psychology,
UNC Greensboro

Yiyue Zhang

Graduate Research, Department of
Psychology, Ohio University

Samuele Zilioli

Associate Professor, Department of
Psychology, Wayne State University

PART I

Introduction

What is the Psychology of Competition?

Stephen M. Garcia, Avishalom Tor, *and* Andrew J. Elliot

Abstract

Common definitions of competition tend to emphasize its objective features, which produce a zero-sum interaction whereby the outcome establishes winners and losers based on more than mere chance. The psychological study of competition, however, is primarily concerned with individuals' behavior and their subjective feelings, perceptions, motivations, and intentions. As such, this chapter defines competition more broadly to include all manifestations of individual competitive behavior or competitive psychological state, even when they occur outside of overtly competitive institutional arrangements or explicitly competitive interactions. The authors then outline the chapters in this volume to showcase the study of competition across the broad spectrum of psychology.

Key Words: competition, competitive behavior, biopsychology, motivation, emotion, cognitive psychology, decision making, social psychology, personality psychology, organizational psychology

Competition is a powerful and prevalent presence in daily life, and this volume focuses on the psychology of this important topic. While the psychological perspective on competition overlaps with perspectives from other fields, particularly economics (see Haran & Bereby-Meyer, this volume), it also differs substantially, as the psychological experience of competition is an individual and subjective one. This introductory chapter addresses definitional issues regarding competition and provides an overview of this volume that showcases the study of competition across the broad spectrum of psychology, including biopsychology, evolutionary psychology, neuroscience, motivation, emotion, cognitive psychology, decision making, social psychology, personality psychology, organizational psychology, educational psychology, sports psychology, and more. While the psychological study of competition was initiated several generations ago (Triplett, 1898; Deutsch, 1949; Festinger, 1954; Greenberg, 1932), it has more recently garnered new and vigorous attention (e.g., Dunning et al., 2003; Garcia et al., 2006; Kilduff et al., 2010; Murayama & Elliot, 2012; Schurr & Ritov, 2016; Stanne et al., 1999). This volume seeks to advance the psychological study of competition further by bringing together and organizing the literature in a first-of-its-kind anthology.

What is Competition from a Psychological Perspective?

"Competition" is a widely used term, bearing a broad range of potential meanings, with typical dictionary definitions focusing on the act or process of individuals vying for outcomes, or, alternatively, on its institutional setting that pits competitors against one another (Garcia et al., 2020). Common definitions of competition thus tend to emphasize its objective features, which produce a zero-sum interaction whereby the outcome establishes winners and losers (Bronson & Merryman, 2014; Roth, 2016) based on more than mere chance. Given the overt nature of such competitions, moreover, the individuals or groups involved usually perceive themselves as engaging in a competition. This common form of competition includes myriad and varied institutional arrangements, such as sports leagues and other athletic contests, online games, school admissions, job markets, promotion and salary pools, elections, bids, auctions, resource dilemmas, and more.

The psychological study of competition, however, is primarily concerned with individuals' behavior and their subjective feelings, perceptions, motivations, and intentions. For this reason, this handbook defines competition more broadly to include all manifestations of individual competitive behavior or competitive psychological state, even when they occur outside of overtly competitive institutional arrangements or explicitly competitive interactions. After all, people can feel competitive or act competitively in circumstances that are not inherently, structurally competitive. For instance, people with a shared history of rivalry may view as competitive routine interactions and situations that are objectively non-competitive—that is, circumstances in which their respective outcomes are not negatively linked (e.g., Garcia & Tor, this volume).

At other times, one party may be competitive towards another, engaging in one-upmanship to achieve a superior outcome or experiencing subtle positional concerns (Graf-Vlachy et al., 2012), even when the perceived competitor is wholly unaware that a competition is taking place. To illustrate, imagine two guests staying in a high-rise hotel with a scenic view entering the same elevator. While one may perceive the elevator merely as a means for getting to the desired floor, the other guest may see the elevator ride as a competition to determine who is staying on a higher, supposedly more prestigious, floor. Such positional concerns may be idiosyncratic, and occasionally limited to single instances (e.g., competing to get a better parking spot at the mall). But an important marker of these implicit competitions is their highly subjective nature that is capable of converting even an explicitly non-competitive situation into a perceived competition (Reese et al., 2022).

Finally, irrespective of its cause, perceived competition can manifest in a variety of behavioral and psychological outcomes. Some of these manifestations are obvious, as when one tackles an opponent in football or tries to run faster than one's competitors in a relay race. Yet other forms of competitive behavior are more stealthy or difficult to identify, such as when an actor dissembles (e.g., arguing that a particular job candidate is superior to another while holding the opposite belief; Garcia et al., 2010) or when seemingly cooperative behavior is driven more by a desire to signal one's competitive advantage (Greenberg, 1932). In short, competition is not only ubiquitous but is also rich with variety and complexity, and so is its psychological study.

The Psychological Study of Competition

Following our more expansive, psychologically driven definition of competition and its manifestations, the present volume provides a broad, even comprehensive, view of competition across the field of psychology, dividing the literature into four groups: Biological Approaches, Motivation and Emotion Approaches, Cognitive and Decision-Making Approaches, and Social-Personality and Organizational Approaches. In the final section, we also provide a psychological perspective on competition in specific domains, including sports, education, and culture.

We begin with *Biological Approaches* because biological processes affect the psychology of competition in the most physical, basic ways. While psychology generally reflects the relationship between brain and behavior, the biological approach highlights how the physical processes of the brain affect competitive behaviors. For example, Reside, Robinson, and Carré examine the social neuroendocrinological underpinnings of human competition, showing how competitive situations trigger increases in testosterone, which in turn is linked to competitive, aggressive behavior and risk-taking processes. Bird, Bochon, Wu, and Zilioli further chart the cyclical effects of testosterone in competition, reviewing the literature showing that testosterone is both a precursor and consequence of a wide variety of competitive processes among men. Salvador, Hidalgo, Costa, and González-Bono further unpack the biological sex differences in competition, linking brain structures, neurotransmitters, and the neuro-endocrine-immune system to sex differences across a variety of competitive behaviors.

Offering a neuroscience perspective on competition, Balconi and Angioletti explain how advances in hyperscanning areas of the brain and other methodological techniques have begun to shed light on how various brain regions are associated with different forms of competitive behavior. Finally, Winegard and Geary use an evolutionary perspective on the psychology of competition to explicate how early humankind's primordial challenges of survival and propagation shaped the kinds of competitive behavior observed today.

Building upon these biological approaches, the volume next explores *Motivational and Emotional Approaches* toward understanding the psychology of competition. Ku and Adam explore the basic influence of arousal on a host of competitive behaviors, including its origins and downstream consequences. Murayama, Elliot, and Jury then present an opposing processes model of competition and performance, showing how competition can induce both approach motivation and avoidance motivation, which have different influences on performance outcomes. Huang and Lin review the well-established literature on goals and competition, as well as present the most recent advances in this field. Ryan and Reeve examine the relationship between intrinsic motivation and competition and use self-determination theory to explain the seeming paradox that competition can invoke yet also undermine intrinsic motivation. Finally, Montal-Rosenberg and Moran explore the role of envy as determinants and consequences of competitive feelings and behavior.

The psychology of competition can also be understood through *Cognitive and Decision Making Approaches*. For example, Dunning reviews biases that individuals have when judging their own performance relative to others, including better-than-average effects in general and the Dunning-Kruger Effect specifically. Focusing on the interdependent decisions to cooperate versus compete, Arora, Kugler, and Giardini explore mixed-motives in social dilemma games and offer a framework for understanding contextual and norm-based influences on decisions to cooperate. Alicke, Zhang, Stephenson, and Zell then offer an analysis of how competitors evaluate themselves in competition pools, including how local comparisons carry more weight than broader and larger comparisons, even if the latter are more diagnostically useful to the self. Ybarra, Rios, Keller, Michalak, Wang, and Chan then review how competitors become more or less predictable to others depending on whether the social landscape is cooperative or competitive. Finally, Mishra, Fogg, and Deminchuk review the topic of competition and risk-taking, addressing the question of how competition motivates risk-taking behavior.

Building upon the biological, motivational, and cognitive perspectives, *Social-Personality and Organizational Approaches* to competition broadly emphasize how individual competitive behavior depends on the person and the situation. Parks provides a comprehensive review of competitiveness as a personality trait, while Garcia and Tor explore the relationship between social comparison and competition, reviewing two general models in this area, and showing how these models both help organize a large and diverse literature and highlight promising hypotheses for further study. Converse, Reinhard, and Austin then offer a focused social-cognitive model on the psychology of rivalry that distinguishes rivals from mere competitors and explains both the antecedents of rivalry and its psychological consequences. Doyle, S. Kim, and H. Y. Kim contribute to the social and organizational approach by reviewing the literature on status competition in groups and they link these status competitive processes to broader status hierarchies. Through the lens of social identity and self-categorization theories, Belavadi and

Hogg review the intergroup competition literature, which has particularly deep roots in the study of social and organizational psychology. Finally, Hanek examines gender as an individual difference factor, reviewing how women and men differ in their competitive preferences and behavior across social and organizational contexts.

The final section examines the psychology of competition in specific contexts. Kavussanu, Cook, and Jones review the competition literature in sports, defining different types of competition and discussing factors that affect a host of outcome measures, including performance, enjoyment, anxiety, choking, and pro- and anti-social behaviors. Similarly, Butera, Świątkowski, and Dompnier present a perspective on competition in education, highlighting the benefits, drawbacks, and unanswered questions regarding competitive processes and various aspects of the learning experience. Offering a complementary mindfulness perspective, Mahalingam explains how mindfulness can be incorporated into competitive processes, showing that it can be used to reap the positive benefits of competitiveness. Last, taking an even wider perspective on the psychology competition, Wu and Talhelm review key differences in the construal, meaning, and manifestation of competitive processes across broad swaths of Eastern versus Western cultures.

We believe that this compilation of chapters represents an important contribution to the literature by providing a one-stop, comprehensive, resource for all those interested in the psychology of competition, researchers, and practitioners alike. Our hope is that this *Oxford Handbook of the Psychology of Competition* will advance this burgeoning multidisciplinary area and inspire even more scholars to join the highly promising efforts of extant researchers in this field.

References

Bronson, P., & Merryman, A. (2014). *Top dog: The science of winning and losing.* Twelve Books.

Deutsch, M. (1949). An experimental study of the effects of co-operation and competition upon group process. *Human Relations 2*(3), 199–231.

Dunning, D., Johnson, K., Ehrlinger, J., & Kruger, J. (2003). Why people fail to recognize their own competence. *Current Directions in Psychological Science 12*, 83–87.

Festinger, L. (1954). A theory of social comparison processes. *Human Relations 7*(2), 117–140.

Garcia, S. M., Reese, Z., & Tor, A. (2020) Social comparison before, during, and after the competition. In J. Sul, L. Wheeler, and R. Collins (Eds.), *Social comparison, judgment and behavior* (pp. 105–142). Oxford University Press.

Garcia, S.M., Song, H., & Tesser, A. (2010). Tainted recommendations: The social comparison bias. *Organizational Behavior and Human Decision Processes 113*, 97–101.

Garcia, S. M., Tor, A., & Gonzalez, R. (2006). Ranks and rivals: A theory of competition. *Personality and Social Psychology Bulletin 32*(7), 970–982. https://doi.org/10.1177/0146167206287640.

Graf-Vlachy, L., König, E., & Hungenberg, H. (2012). Debiasing competitive irrationality: How managers can be prevented from trading off absolute for relative profit. *European Management Journal 30*, 386–403.

Greenberg, P. J. (1932). Competition in children: An experimental study. *American Journal of Psychology 44*, 221–248.

Kilduff, G. J., Elfenbein, H. A., & Staw, B. M. (2010). The psychology of rivalry: A relationally dependent analysis of competition. *Academy of Management Journal 53*(5), 943–969.

Murayama, K., & Elliot, A. J. (2012). The competition–performance relation: A meta-analytic review and test of the opposing processes model of competition and performance. *Psychological Bulletin 138*(6), 1035–1070.

Reese, Z. A., Garcia, S. M., & Edelstein, R. S. (2022). More than a game: Trait competitiveness predicts motivation in minimally competitive contexts. *Personality and Individual Differences 185*, 111262.

Roth, A. (2016). *Who gets what—and why: The new economics of matchmaking and market design.* Eamon Dolan/Mariner Books

Schurr, A., & Ritov, I. (2016). Winning a competition predicts dishonest behavior. *Proceedings of the National Academy of Sciences 113*(7), 1754–1759. https://doi.org/10.1073/pnas.1515102113.

Stanne, M. B., Johnson, D. W., & Johnson, R. T. (1999). Does competition enhance or inhibit motor performance: A meta-analysis. *Psychological Bulletin 125*, 133–154.

Triplett, N. (1898). The dynamogenic factors in pacemaking and competition. *American Journal of Psychology 9*, 507–533.

Competition in Psychology and Experimental Economics

Uriel Haran *and* Yoella Bereby-Meyer

Abstract

Competition is a fundamental phenomenon in human behavior and a key topic of interest for psychologists and economists alike. Both psychology and economics strive to better understand behavior in competitive environments, but they differ in their research objectives, theoretical perspectives, and empirical methods. Economics typically adopts a normative approach, assuming that agents make rational decisions that balance the tradeoff between the costs of competing and the benefits associated with winning. Economists view competition as a class of incentive structures and investigate the effects of comparative reward schemes on behavior and performance. Psychology adopts a more descriptive approach. Psychologists are interested in the cognitive, affective, and motivational processes that affect decision making. They examine the interpersonal effects of competition and compare them with other social situations. In this chapter, the authors review selected literature on competition in experimental economics and psychology, exploring two common research areas. One is rank-order, effort-based tournaments, by which experimental economists study the effects of various incentive structures on effort and performance, whereas social psychologists examine processes of social comparison. The second is common value auctions and the winner's curse. The authors discuss how research in economics and psychology examine the winner's curse, explanations for the phenomenon, and recommendations to overcome it. Finally, the authors outline possible directions for mutual enrichment for scholars interested in competition. Psychologists can benefit from the precise definitions present in economic experiments, whereas economists can use the insights on the underlying processes of competitive attitudes and behavior offered by research in psychology.

Key Words: competition, experimental economics, social psychology, winner's curse, common value auction, social comparison, tournaments

The study of social behavior involves various scientific disciplines, including psychology, sociology, political science, and anthropology, among others. These disciplines address similar social issues by applying different foci of interest, theoretical approaches, and methodological tools. Competition is no different. It is inherently a social behavior which involves decision making on the part of two or more actors who need to consider the choices of their actions in view of their conficting interests. In this chapter, we refer to competition as encompassing both the process of competitive behavior and the institutional setting in which a competitive situation takes place (Garcia et al., 2020).

The two main disciplines in the social sciences that study competitive behavior are psychology and economics. In this chapter, we consider the questions these two disciplines ask in their attempt to understand behavior in competition, and the different ways in which they address these questions. The approaches adopted by psychology and economics are similar in certain respects, but they differ in some fundamental parts. Understanding these differences can help researchers in each discipline appreciate the contributions of the other, use its insights to complement their work, and achieve a synthesis of the knowledge gained in each.

Conceptualizing Competition

Competition is as basic and important a phenomenon in human behavior as it is ubiquitous. Animals compete for food and shelter. Firms compete for market share. People compete for land, prestige, and power. Academics compete for grants and publication space. Students compete for scholarships and class ranking. Competition seems to be inseparable from almost every facet of human experience.

Brown et al. (1998) proposed three ways to conceptualize competition. The first is structural competition, referring to situations in which two or more people compete for rewards. The rewards can be either tangible or intangible, as long as they are sufficiently scarce to prevent everyone from enjoying them equally (Kohn, 1992). For one person to win and enjoy a greater share of rewards, another must lose and settle for less. The second conceptualization is trait competitiveness, an aspect of one's personality that increases the enjoyment of competing, the desire to win, and the ambition to be better than others (Spence & Helmreich, 1983). Finally, perceived environmental competition refers to the feeling that one is competing with another, even if no formal competitive structure is in place. In the present chapter, we focus primarily on structural competition and on social comparison processes that are integral to behavior in a competitive structure.

Competition is an important topic in both psychology and economics, but the two disciplines diverge on several essential attributes. Specifically, they differ in their objectives, theoretical perspectives, and the empirical methodologies they use to address their questions about behavior in competitive settings. This chapter aims to demonstrate the differences between experimental economics and psychology in their research on competition, and to highlight the features and insights that scholars in the two disciplines can gain from each other.

Fundamental Differences and Commonalities between Psychology and Economics

The relation between economics and psychology has been the topic of discussion for a long time (e.g., Simon, 1986; Rabin, 1998; Ariely & Norton, 2007). Both seek to understand human behavior, but they do so from different perspectives, and have different assumptions about how people act. As Rabin (1998) pointed out, economics "has conventionally assumed that individuals have stable and coherent preferences, and that they rationally maximize those preferences. Given a set of options and probabilistic beliefs, a person is assumed to maximize the expected value of a utility function, U(x)." For economists, the essential elements to be abstracted are derived from some general normative theory based on the assumption that behavior is driven by utility maximization. Economists, therefore, emphasize the incentive structure of the situation (i.e., the costs and benefits of different outcomes that apply to various participants in the situation) and the information available to participants that is relevant to their decisions. Psychology, on its part, seeks to develop descriptive models of human behavior. To this end, it focuses on the cognitive, motivational, and affective factors that help gain a better understanding of the underlying mechanisms of decision making and behavior.

Unlike economics, social psychology is not committed to a normative model, and its experiments often do not examine concrete predictions derived from such a model. Psychologists investigate people's decisions in given situations; therefore, they often use cover stories, confederates, and even deception to simulate real-life conditions as closely as possible. The requirements in economic research are somewhat different, and the important criterion is the correspondence to a theoretical, normative model or to the incentive structure of the environment. Great stress is placed on the need to control for any factor that can affect behavior, according to the theoretical model. Therefore, there is strong reluctance in economics research to employ any form of deception. This reluctance stems from the assumption that if participants in experiments believe that the information they receive is not valid, their responses might be limited to their beliefs regarding the experiment, rather than to what the incentive structure of the experiment represents in real life (Ariely & Norton, 2007).

In the last three decades, a new branch of economics has evolved, known as behavioral economics. Research in this field concerns the concrete actions carried out in situations involving multiple interacting players. Behavioral economics expands analytical game theory by adding to it emotions, mistakes, limited foresight, conjectures about others' intelligence, and learning. It uses psychological regularities to suggest ways to weaken rationality assumptions and to extend theory (Camerer, 2003).

How Psychology and Experimental Economics Study Competition

Competition in economics is mainly about markets. A market, in the broadest sense of the term, refers to any context in which goods, services, and any other type of resource are exchanged (Pearce, 1994). Competition functions as a mechanism and a set of rules that can allow the market to operate efficiently, by enabling the allocation of productive resources to their most highly valued uses. Sellers compete to attract favorable offers from prospective buyers, potential buyers compete to obtain good offers from suppliers, and workers try to outperform each other in the pursuit of prizes, promotions, and recognition.

Research in the field of industrial organization (IO) in economics tended to deal mainly with market deviations from idealized conditions of perfect competition (Einav & Levin, 2010). Experimental studies examine competitions through auctions, lotteries, and tournaments. A subfield of experimental economics deals with experimental studies related to IO. The detailed review of the IO literature is beyond the scope of the present chapter, where we focus on common-value auctions, and in particular, on the winner's curse phenomenon, and on rank-order tournaments.

Auctions are a common mechanism for setting the price of a commodity or service. Economic approaches to auctions are based on a large theoretical and experimental literature that compares different kinds of items (e.g., private value vs. common value) and mechanisms (e.g., English, Dutch, first-price, and second-price sealed-bid auctions) with respect to the revenue they generate (for a review, see Kagel, 1995; Ku et al., 2005). One way of studying competition in experimental economics is through auction games, where individuals compete by investing monetary resources to buy a commodity (i.e., to win a prize). Tournaments compare competitors on such dimensions as effort, output, and performance. The theoretical components they test often have to do with the incentives provided to players for doing their work (e.g., different prize structures, rank orders, and pay dispersions). Psychological research on competition uses similar mechanisms to those discussed above. Studies use auction settings to investigate cognitive biases and other phenomena in judgment and decision making, and tournaments to explore motivation, self-assessment, social cognition, and affect.

To date, the study of competition in social psychology and in experimental economics appears to have been conducted in parallel, with too few points of contact. Although parallel research of the same questions in different disciplines may create redundancies, many of the findings in the two disciplines are complementary, and most insights from one discipline prove useful for the other. In general, psychology has a broader view of competition, and considers factors beyond market structure, incentive types, effort, and outcomes. It is sensitive to affective, motivational, and perceptual processes that can explain behavior and competitive outcomes but are often overlooked in economics. At the same time, psychologists can learn from the economists' precise and profound understanding of competitive structures. Most studies in psychology operationalize competition by simply setting a goal of outperforming an individual or a subset of other participants. By contrast, economic experiments carefully formalize the rules and incentive structure of the competition, recognizing a wide range of types of competition, which can then be systematically tested. Understanding the principles of each discipline can greatly enhance the understanding of competition and open the door to higher-quality research in both psychology and economics. The current chapter discusses two main areas of research on competition common to economics and psychology: tournaments and common value auctions. We discuss the differences between the structure-oriented approach of experimental economics and the mechanism-oriented approach of social psychology, as well as the shared themes between the two disciplines in these two common areas of research.

Rank-Order Tournaments and Effort-Based Competitions

Many organizational, educational, gaming, and sports settings involve tournaments—competitions that are based on comparative effort and rank-order incentives. Competition takes the form of an incentive system that links players' rewards to their rank among competitors on a focal dimension, rather than to their absolute performance or result on that dimension. The differences in approach between psychology and economics, discussed at the beginning of this chapter, are clearly apparent in their research on tournaments.

Studies in psychology typically compare only competitive (e.g., rank-order) incentives with non-competitive ones (i.e., piece-rate or fixed pay), whereas studies in experimental economics are sensitive to the more nuanced attributes of competitive incentive structures. Economic experiments examine factors such as the dispersion of prize value awarded to different ranks (e.g., Harbring & Irlenbusch, 2011), prize distribution among multiple winners (e.g., Amaldoss et al., 2000), and the relation between effort levels observed in competition and theoretical equilibrium levels (e.g., Bull et al., 1987).

Extensive research in economics on behavior in tournaments began with Lazear and Rosen's (1981) tournament theory. A tournament setting is one in which two or more actors invest effort or resources to win a prize, which is awarded based on relative rank (Lazear, 1989). An actor's chance to win the prize is a function of both the actor's willingness and ability to compete, and of the number and qualities of other competitors. This structure mirrors that of an all-pay auction (Hillman & Riley, 1989; Baye et al., 1996).

Tournament theory explains how relative rank-order prizes are better at motivating multiple actors than are individual pay-for-performance incentives. According to the theory, performance motivation is higher when the prize for success is not contingent on one's absolute result, but is rather determined by identifying the best result among participants. The increased motivation is driven by the prospect of generating large differences in rewards by even small differences in performance, which induces individuals to keep striving to do better. This argument has received ample empirical support (e.g., Bull et al., 1987; Eisenkopf & Teyssier, 2013; Orrison et al., 2004; Schotter & Weigelt, 1992). For example, Bull et al. (1987) conducted a series of lab experiments comparing various competitive incentive structures to piece-rate incentives and measured the costs participants were willing to bear to defeat their competitors (these costs represented effort levels). They found that players who competed with others often exerted greater effort than their theoretic equilibrium levels (i.e., at which the value of their costs is equal to the expected value of their gains), and were considerably more likely to do so than players working in a piece-rate system. Other research found that competitive effort may at times reach a level that is counterproductive, for example, when players choose to compete even when opting out of the competition offers higher expected value (Niederle & Vesterlund, 2007). Later studies found that the effects of relative incentive schemes on players' behavior become even more pronounced when the players choose their incentive scheme rather than having it assigned to them (Agranov & Tergiman, 2013; Camerer & Lovallo, 1999; Eriksson et al., 2009).

Social psychology has also paid a great deal of research attention to rank-order competitions. Whereas economics studies competition from a formalistic, structural perspective, research in social psychology views rank-order competition through the prism of the cognitive, motivational, and affective processes elicited by the competitive setting, and it has therefore been able to explain deviations in competitors' behavior from the predictions of economic models, such as excess entry and overbidding in auctions (Cain et al., 2015; Ku et al., 2005). The central theoretical construct in the psychological study of competition is social comparison. According to social comparison theory (Festinger, 1954), people are motivated by the desire to outperform others, achieve higher status than others, or compare favorably to them. Comparing favorably to others improves individuals' self-esteem (Taylor & Lobel, 1989), reduces their negative affect (Wills, 1981), and increases their optimism about the future. For example, in response to a win by their favorite sports team, fans report a more positive mood, higher self-esteem, and greater life satisfaction (Hirt et al., 1992; Schwarz et al., 1987).

Psychological research has regarded competition as a manifestation of social comparison. Information about social comparison serves as a source of self-evaluation, making it a necessary component of competition (Ames & Ames, 1984; Garcia et al., 2013). Competitive motivation has also been equated with the motivation to compare favorably with others, while competitive behavior is the investment of effort or resources to prevail in these comparisons. Competitive settings, markets, and reward structures are structural factors that highlight and enhance social comparison (Murayama & Elliot, 2012), directing the attention of participants to comparative information and cues. They focus competitors' attention on social comparison information even when competitors do not have any prior interest in such information (Ames & Ames, 1984). As a result, goals based on relative performance encourage greater levels of task effort and persistence than individual achievement goals (Haran, 2019). In the next section we discuss the attributes of competition that affect people's behavior, and which have been of particular interest to social psychology and experimental economics.

Determinants of Behavior in Competitions

Research on tournaments in both experimental economics and psychology examines variables related to the players' willingness to invest effort or resources to achieve their goals. At times, the two disciplines even use the same constructs and measures. For example, opting in vs. out of tournaments serves as a measure of competitive behavior both in economic (e.g., Gneezy et al., 2009) and in psychological research (e.g., Haran et al., 2021). In all these studies, participants completed a task and chose the way they preferred to be compensated for their performance. One alternative was based on their individual performance; the other involved comparing their performance with that of another participant and rewarding them based on their relative success. Although the economic studies focused on tournament structure whereas the psychological ones on emotional antecedents of competitive behavior, they all used the same dependent variable. Nevertheless, differences remain in theoretical foci between the two disciplines and they are also observed in the research questions they strive to answer. The variables of interest for economists are structural, namely the size of the competitive field and the prize spread—the difference between the prize awarded to the winner(s) and that awarded to the loser(s). Social psychology, while also studying these factors, is interested primarily in how competitive incentives affect people's motivation and in the downstream consequences of competing with others on various psychological outcomes, including future motivation, self-evaluation, and affect.

In economics, tournament theory makes two foundational predictions (Knoeber & Thurman, 1994): (a) that players' level of effort, investment, or performance is determined by how that effort, investment, or performance affects their probability of winning (similarly to expectancy theory, which makes the same proposition in the context of employee motivation; Vroom, 1964); and (b) that players care more about the differences between the winner's and loser's payouts than about the absolute size of those payouts (Knoeber & Thurman, 1994). Thus, according to the theory, tournaments can help competitors achieve optimal output levels by accurately determining the prize spread. To achieve these optimal output levels, the spread should be high enough to encourage players to exert high levels of effort, but not high enough for production to exceed need (Knoeber, 1989; Lazear & Rosen, 1981).

In light of these predictions, research on tournaments in experimental economics has dealt primarily with the number of participants included in them and with ways of distributing prizes to contestants (Harbring & Irlenbusch, 2003). To psychologists, this focus may seem nuanced and of limited scope, but it offers highly precise definitions and operationalizations of incentive structures and prize distribution systems, which studies in psychology typically do not attain. Orrison et al. (2004) varied tournament size and prize distribution using a task similar to that employed by Bull et al. (1987), in which participants' effort was determined by the price they were willing to pay to win. They varied tournament size using two-person, four-person, and six-person tournaments, and varied the number of winners, or competitors who can receive a prize, between two and four winners in a six-person contest. They found that effort levels are higher in small competitions than in large ones, and that effort is higher in competitions that offer a few prizes of high value than in those that offer many prizes. Sheremeta (2011) varied the number of players in a lottery contest and found that the effort participants were willing to invest decreases as the number of contestants rises, from 33 percent of the prize value in a two-player contest to 25 percent of the prize value in a four-player contest.

Studies of all-pay auctions revealed similar trends.[1] Similarly to tournaments, in which all players exert effort but only the player with the highest performance wins, all-pay auctions require that all players pay their bids but only the highest-bidding player wins the prize with certainty. An example of such an auction is the bidding process to host the Olympic games. Before the International Olympic Committee awards one city the right to host the event, all candidate cities must each submit a bid, which typically costs between $50 million and $150 million to prepare (McBride, 2018). Most studies of all-pay auctions find significant overbidding relative to the Nash equilibrium prediction, with some bidders submitting very low bids and others very high ones (Dechenaux et al., 2015). Overbidding becomes even more rampant when the competitive field is smaller. As cost-minded bidders drop out and fewer competitors are left, remaining bidders tend to become more competitive by bidding past their limits, and the likelihood of individual bidders dropping out of the auction at the later stages decreases (Gneezy & Smorodinsky, 2006; Ku et al., 2005). Ku et al. (2005) argued that an affective state of competitive arousal, which they describe as "an adrenaline rush that accompanies individuals' desires to win," occurs when there are few, rather than many, bidders in the auction, when the auction is nearing its end, and when bidders feel that they are under time pressure. The affective state intensifies further when the bidding is public, before an audience, placing the individual in the spotlight, and when bidding against a rival (see section on rivalry below). Competitive arousal, like other pressure-related states, impairs systematic decision making and leads to irrational choices, such as overbidding. Fong et al., (2020) examined whether personality traits and individual differences in competitiveness can explain this behavior. They found that extraversion was positively related to competitiveness, whereas agreeableness predicted both lower self-reported competitiveness and less competitive auction bidding.

Tournament theory stresses two main structural variables, competition size and prize spread, but experimental economists have studied other structural characteristics of competitions as well. One such characteristic is the difference in competitors' abilities, or their *a priori* likelihood to win. Several studies (e.g., Baik, 1994; Gradstein, 1995; Stein, 2002) suggested that high variation in abilities between players creates a discouragement effect. The high effort required to compete and the low likelihood of defeating superior players deters weaker players, and leads to a reduction of their investment in pursuit of the goal. This makes the competition easier for the stronger players, for whom investing high resources to win becomes unnecessary. Economists are also interested in the number of stages in the competition (i.e., whether the competition is a static, one-shot decision game or a dynamic situation with sequential rounds of resource investment), the focal point of the competitive goal (winning vs. avoiding elimination), and the number of contests competitors engage in simultaneously (Dechenaux et al., 2015), among other issues.

Some research in psychology also varied structural factors and measured their influence on competitive behavior. Garcia and Tor (2009) argued that social comparison processes, and, consequently, competitive behaviors, are more emphasized when the competitive landscape includes fewer actors, whereas a multitude of targets for social comparison diffuses these processes and reduces their effects. In their study, participants exhibited willingness to work harder and completed tasks significantly faster when they competed against a few others than when they competed against many. This effect was resistant against possible sampling error by competitors, and persisted even when competitors estimated their chances of winning accurately (Tor & Garcia, 2010).

The interest of psychology in competitive behavior is manifested in research on social comparison and its effects on behavior in rank-order competitions. The empirical evidence suggests that, similarly to relative incentive structures, evaluation of oneself through social comparison exerts a stronger influence on people's judgment, feelings, and behavior than do evaluations of one's performance in absolute terms. Strickhouser and Zell (2015) asked participants to take a quantitative test and a verbal test, then informed them of their rank in both tests, before measuring their self-evaluated ability in the two domains, as well as their emotional responses to their results. The comparison with other people had a significantly greater influence on how participants assessed their performance and ability and on how they felt than did inter-domain comparisons.

As the underlying psychological process of competition, social comparison determines competitive motivation and behavior. Even the decision to compete in the first place is influenced primarily by comparative self-assessment, and this influence seems to be stronger than that of perceptions of one's own skill. Cain et al. (2015) studied the phenomenon of excess market entry, which research on entrepreneurship attributes to overconfidence (Koellinger et al., 2007). Although self-evaluations of ability and performance tend to display underconfidence in easy domains and overconfidence in difficult ones (Moore & Healy, 2008), people prefer entering markets in easy domains over more difficult ones. Cain et al. (2015) discovered that in the markets of easy domains, entrants were overconfident about their rank relative to other market players, which predicted their entry choices.

Social comparison increases not only individuals' desire to compete, but also competitors' desire to win. Locke (2007) surveyed race runners, who reported running faster when comparing themselves to another participant in the race whom they knew well than when their targets of comparison were other runners in general. A similar result was obtained in lab studies of competing dyads. Haran and Ritov (2014) applied a minimal intervention to increase the salience of a social comparison target by manipulating its identifiability. In half the dyads, competitors were unspecified to each other, knowing only that their opponent was "another participant in the study," and in the other half they were identified by a participant ID number. Participants exerted greater effort to defeat an identified counterpart than an unspecified one. These increases in competitiveness correlated with a similarly increased concern participants had about losing to their counterparts, highlighting the role of social comparison in encouraging competitive behavior.

The findings discussed above highlight the interest of psychologists in the affective and cognitive variables that influence competitive behavior through social comparison. Because social comparison and competition are embedded in an interpersonal context, they are naturally affected by relational factors. The psychological literature focuses primarily on two factors: (1) the similarity between the actor and the target and (2) the closeness of their relationship. Research on social comparison finds that people are more likely to compare themselves with others who are similar to them than with others who are not (Festinger, 1954), and with people who are closer to them than with more distant targets (Tesser & Campbell, 1982). Furthermore, similarity and closeness increase social comparison even when they are unrelated to the domain on which the counterparts are competing (Miller et al., 1988). For example, after an exam, we may engage in comparing our potential score to that of the person who sat next to us during the exam, but given a chance, we would also compare the model of our car to that person's.

Perhaps the most salient example of how the similarity and closeness between competitors affect their relationship is rivalry. Rivalries are subjective competitive relationships between actors that entail increased psychological involvement and perceived stakes, independent of the objective characteristics of the situation (Kilduff et al., 2010). Rivalries lead individuals, teams, and organizations to display higher motivation, invest greater resources, and even engage in more unethical behavior to defeat a rival than when competing with non-rival counterparts (Converse & Reinhard, 2016; Hsieh et al., 2014; Kilduff, 2014; Kilduff et al., 2016). Rivalries form when actors perceive themselves as similar to each other and their relationship as competitive. Repeated opportunities to compete further develop and enhance rivalries. Thus, actors who are similar or close to each other in their location or their attributes are likely to become rivals. For example, US collegiate sports teams are more likely to form a rivalry the closer they are to each other geographically. Similarities in other attributes, unrelated to sports, such as academic quality and the number of enrolled students, also contribute to the emergence of rivalries (Kilduff et al., 2010). These findings show that the mechanisms that affect the competitive behavior of individuals are influential at the team level as well.

Team Competitions: Collaborate in Order to Compete

A key question pertaining to competitive motivation concerns the effect of competition-related factors on the performance of groups and teams.[2] Although competition between groups is prevalent, competing groups depend on the willingness of their individual members to forgo their immediate objectives, cooperate with each other, and contribute costly resources for the sake of their team's higher objectives (Sheremeta, 2018). For example, in the Tour de France, individual cyclists undertake tough assignments, which often slow them down, to help the team captain win the race, so that team success then depends on its individual members sacrificing their own competitive goals.

From the perspective of pure self-interest, team competitions present a clear disincentive for individual team members to contribute to the team. First, the negative effect of one's contribution on one's own outcome is almost always greater than the positive effect of that contribution on the team as a whole (Halevy et al., 2008). Furthermore, the benefits gained from winning, or being part of the winning team, are often available to all team members regardless of their individual contributions. As a result, one can theoretically contribute very little, or even nothing, to the collective effort of the team and still enjoy part of the collective gain (Bornstein, 1992, 2003; Rapoport & Bornstein, 1987). Nevertheless, empirical findings suggest that group competition increases the level of effort individuals expend to help their team win. Erev et al. (1993) conducted a field experiment with orange pickers, who were each paid according to one of three incentive schemes. In one condition, pickers were paid according to their individual output; in another condition, they were assigned to teams and received an equal share of the team's total pay; and a third condition presented a competitive incentive structure, where groups of participants were compared with each other, and participants received a bonus if their group outperformed the competing group. Worker output was highest in the group competition condition, and its advantage over the two other incentive schemes even increased over time.

Both social psychology and experimental economics have attempted to explain the puzzle of group competition, but their approaches to the solution have focused on different factors. Research in psychology finds that intergroup competition increases the importance of the group's relative standing and decreases the importance of its overall welfare (Turner et al., 1979). Members of competing groups are willing to sacrifice absolute gains, both for themselves and for their group, to maximize their group's relative gains vis-à-vis other groups. Thus, increased prosociality and cooperation between team members result in more competitive behavior by the team as a whole (McCallum et al., 1985).

The heightened competitive motivation in group competition appears to be related to social comparison: when individuals were distributing money between themselves and members of a relevant comparison group, they displayed greater in-group favoritism than when the group to which their counterparts belonged was not relevant for social comparison. Tamir and Nadler (2007) found the same effect for group similarity: participants in their study displayed more competitive behavior in allocating resources between members of their own group and those of an outgroup when the outgroup was similar to their own than when the groups were different from each other.

Other research found that competition enhances factors that contribute to individuals' commitment to the team, such as norms of altruism and members' prosocial goals (Hardy & Van Vugt, 2006). Competing teams emphasize and enforce norms of altruism more actively than do teams that are not in a competitive situation (Goette et al., 2012), and some have argued that intergroup competition played a role in the evolution of altruism in humans (Bowles, 2006). Research findings provide ample support for the idea that intergroup competition is conducive to enhancing cooperation between group members (Bornstein & Erev, 1994; Burton-Chellew et al., 2010; Erev et al., 1993). In a study of behavior in a public goods game, Burton-Chellew et al. (2010) assigned participants to groups and varied whether or not the groups were competing with each other. They found that group competition increased not only individuals' willingness to contribute to the group, but also the extent to which they viewed other members of their group as collaborators, rather than as competitors.

Economists studying group performance focus on group incentives and their role in determining the output of groups. These studies generally find that the factors that enhance individual performance do the same for groups. Similarly to individuals, groups are more sensitive to incentives that reward high relative performance than to those based on individual targets and they tend to respond to competitive incentives with investing more resources to win those incentives than they normatively should (Brookins et al., 2015). In one study, Nalbantian and Schotter (1997) organized participants in groups of six members each, all of them contributing resources from their individual endowments to their group's collective pool. Team performance was defined as the sum of all individual contributions within the group. Some groups were rewarded based on their own performance, whereas others competed with other groups, with the goal of outperforming the competitor to receive the reward. The authors found that the competitive incentive scheme resulted in higher levels of contribution and less free riding by group members. Other research has found that competitive incentives are more effective in increasing the effort of groups than of individuals, although both groups and individuals respond to competitive incentives with expenditures that are higher than the level predicted by the Nash equilibrium (Abbink et al., 2010).

Experimental economists are interested not only in the type of reward the group receives, but also in how that reward is distributed within the group. In real-life competitions, there is variation in the individual rewards that individual team members receive. For example, when a band's song climbs to number one in the charts, the increased royalties may be shared equally among all members or be awarded mainly (or even exclusively) to the members who wrote the song. Despite the prevalence of this variation in real life, psychological studies of group competition have not paid much attention to it, and most of the insight regarding its effects comes from economics. The general finding is that incentive structures that reward group members based on their own individual performance elicit higher effort than egalitarian prize sharing structures (e.g., Amaldoss et al., 2000; Gunnthorsdottir & Rapoport, 2006). Amaldoss et al. (2000) compared team performance in a competition between two profit-sharing systems. One allocated profits equally, each member of the winning team receiving the same portion of the prize as the others; the other was a proportional profit-sharing system, where players' rewards were based on their individual investments. The results showed that linking the reward to a player's contribution increased players' willingness to commit resources for the good of the group.

In sum, both social psychology and experimental economics are interested in the effect of competition on groups and on the behavior of individual group members, and both disciplines reach similar conclusions regarding ultimate performance, namely that group competition enhances intra-group cooperation and competitive behavior of the group as a whole. The disciplines diverge along the expected lines with regard to their interests beyond effort and performance, with economics aiming to understand the nuanced effects of incentive structures and psychology exploring the emotional and interpersonal effects of group competition.

The Dark Side of Competition: How Competitive Incentives Encourage Harmful Behavior

In the previous sections of this chapter we discussed the many advantages of competition for motivation and performance that studies in psychology and economics have documented. But the effects of competitive structure and incentives are not uniformly positive. Studies in both disciplines report similar findings regarding the possible drawbacks of competitive settings, and the differences between psychology and economics in empirical approach and variables of interest make their findings complementary. Numerous studies have shown that competition can inhibit rather than enhance motivation and effort, and may create adversarial relationships between competitors, leading to harmful and at times unethical behaviors.

WHEN COMPETITION REDUCES MOTIVATION

Research in experimental economics, which focuses mostly on competitors' material welfare and investment of effort, found that competition can have a negative effect on these outcomes. For example, some studies have reported that competition can reduce rather than increase effort. Van Dijk et al. (2001) conducted a real-effort experiment, in which one group of participants worked individually for a piece-rate payment, another group was divided into pairs which were paid according to their collective performance, and a third group included pairs of competing participants who were paid based on a competitive, rank-order incentive scheme. Although the highest average effort level was observed in the competition condition, this condition also displayed the highest variability in effort, with more workers exerting low effort levels in the competition than in the other work settings. Another negative outcome of competition was that the hardest-working competitors were undercompensated for their high levels of effort. Lazear (1989) argued that the structure of rank-order incentives makes it beneficial to look for competitions populated by low-quality players, with whom achieving a favorable comparison is easier and more likely, thus benefiting from a favorable comparison to them. Similarly, Van Dijk et al. (2001)

demonstrated that attempting to achieve superior performance by maximizing effort may be a suboptimal strategy.

Another negative effect of competition on motivation has been observed on individuals' desire to compete. Competitive incentive structures can at times be perceived as a deterrent, rather than an enticing opportunity. Fershtman and Gneezy (2011) compared levels of tournament rewards as part of 10th grade gym class activities on students' behavior and performance. They found that increasing the competitive incentive increased participants' likelihood to drop out of the competitive activity and effectively forgo the pursuit of their goal altogether. Rather than promote higher effort, competition resulted in higher rates of quitting.

Studies in psychology have also reported cases in which competitive incentives resulted in lower task effort, but their focus was on the psychological underpinnings of the reduction in motivation. For example, competition presents an inevitable conflict between the motivation to achieve one's personal goal and the desire to maintain good relationships with others (Haran, 2019). When the maintenance of interpersonal relationships is important, with their counterparts in particular or with others generally, competitors experience an internal conflict that can harm their desire to achieve their goal and taint the good feeling brought about by winning. Exline and Lobel (1999) found that the perception of oneself as a target for upward social comparison often makes people uncomfortable. When they believe that others are making envious comparisons with them, people feel uneasiness, distress, or sorrow. Feelings of guilt, an emotion generally associated with high motivation for goal-achievement, lead to lower motivation and performance in the pursuit of competitive goals. Consequences of this emotional state include lower task motivation in a competition (Haran, 2019) and preferences for more cooperative and altruistic outcomes, such as diminishing the significance of the outcome or sharing the winner's reward (Zell & Exline, 2010).

WHEN COMPETITION BECOMES COUNTERPRODUCTIVE AND HARMFUL

An inevitable consequence of competitions and tournaments is that they create inequality and hierarchy between people. They emphasize a certain goal or outcome that is pursued by multiple individuals or groups but can be attained only by one. A favorable comparison of one person over another cannot be attained by both; the same is true for victory in a competition. Naturally, this inherent conflict adds difficulties to maintaining a mutually beneficial relationship between competitors (Danziger et al., 2017; Exline & Lobel, 1999). Social comparison makes people perceive their targets of comparison as possessing lower integrity and as more hostile, and the emotional bonds between themselves and their targets as weaker. As a result, people's willingness to trust their counterparts is lower when engaging in social comparison (Dunn et al., 2012). Similarly, competing with others makes attitudes toward them more negative: after playing a competitive game, players remember their counterparts' faces as more aggressive than do participants who played a cooperative version of the same game, and evaluate competitors who have defeated them as more hostile (Balas & Thomas, 2015; Salovey & Rodin, 1984). These negative attitudes ultimately reduce individuals' willingness to help their competitors and their propensity to inflict punishment upon each other increases (Tesser & Smith, 1980; Yip et al., 2017).

Studies in both economics and psychology have found that rank-order competition encourages unethical behavior. Research in psychology has reported that situations that highlight social comparison increase people's likelihood of cheating on tasks. This phenomenon occurs both among those who compare unfavorably and those who enjoy a favorable comparison. John et al. (2014) had participants complete a series of tasks for variable wages, with some participants being paid more than others for the same level of performance. Cheating, by submitting falsified performance reports, was more prevalent among underpaid participants than among those who had been treated favorably, but only when the pay of their overpaid counterparts was made known. Schurr and Ritov (2016) found that winning could also result in cheating. Following a contest from which they emerged as either winners or losers, participants privately rolled a pair of dice to determine their monetary payoffs in the experiment, and self-reported the results. Winners reported higher outcomes of the die-roll, claiming greater pay than did losers. The authors argued that increased social comparison, combined with the favorable result and the claimed winner status, induced a sense of entitlement in winners, which encouraged their unethical behavior.

Research in economics has also reported a link between competitive incentives and unethical, counterproductive behavior. Although tournaments are designed to enhance competitors' efforts toward improving their performance, at times they encourage competitors to aim their efforts at harming other participants or the competitive field as a whole. Collusion, for example, occurs when contestants coordinate with each other to collectively reduce effort levels to prevent competitive escalation. Although this cooperative behavior may benefit the individual parties to this relationship, it typically harms the overall field by creating unfair advantages and market failures, and it is often in violation of laws and regulations designed to protect competitors and other stakeholders (e.g., consumers). Harbring (2006) demonstrated the risk of collusion by providing competitors the ability to communicate with each other by chat. Participants who used the chat feature in a collaborative team compensation scheme displayed higher effort than other groups, but when the incentive scheme was competitive, free communication between contestants resulted in lower overall effort. Lugovskyy et al., (2010) found that collusion can develop even without communication by simply letting contestants play against each other repeatedly over time. In a repeated all-pay auction experiment, participants who were matched with the same counterparts for the duration of the study ended up bidding lower amounts than those whose counterparts changed from round to round.

Tournament settings may also encourage sabotaging the work of others to make it less favorable in comparison to one's own performance. Evidence of sabotaging behavior has been found in experimental studies by Harbring and Irlenbusch (2008, 2011). In one study, participants had the opportunity to determine both their productive and destructive efforts vis-à-vis their competitors. Wider spreads between prizes awarded to the winner and to the loser were associated with higher investment by players in sabotaging the output of their competitors. This effect was resistant to variations in the size of the competitive field. Carpenter et al., (2010) demonstrated just how counterproductive these behaviors can be. Their study varied both participants' incentive scheme (piece-rate vs. tournament) and possibility of sabotage. Although the highest performance was observed in the tournament where sabotage was not possible, whenever it was possible, sabotage was popular among contestants and resulted in the lowest total output.

To summarize, behavior in tournaments is studied by both experimental economists and social psychologists, who are interested in many common questions pertaining to this type of competition. Whereas economists are interested primarily in structural factors and in direct effects on behaviors and outcomes, psychologists study the cognitive, motivational, and affective processes that are invoked by assigning competitive achievement goals, and how these processes shape competitors' motivation and goal-directed behavior.

The Winner's Curse and Common Value Auction

Auctions are a prevalent form of competition used in various circumstances, and they have been studied extensively in both psychology and economics. Works of art, antique furniture, artisanal wines, real estate, used cars, and the radio spectrum are all commonly objects of auctions. The most common types of auctions are the English and the Dutch. In an English auction, bidders adjust their bids upward, and the highest bid wins the auction. The Dutch auction is a descending one: the auctioneer starts with a high price and adjusts it downward until a bidder stops the auction and claims the good for the price that was declared at the moment of the action. There are first-price auctions, in which the highest bidder claims the object for the amount of the bid, and second-price auctions, which are awarded to the highest bidder, but the winner pays only the amount of the second highest bid. Auction theory makes different predictions about the prices that rational bidders will pay for an object, based on precise assumptions about the rules of the auction and the way in which bidders value the object (Camerer, 2003). Experimental economists then test these predictions in the lab. Issues such as risk aversion, uncertainty, collusion, learning, and the number of bidders have played large roles in this research (Ku et al., 2005). In this section we focus on common value auctions; that is, auctions in which the value of the auctioned items is equal for all bidders. We review experiments conducted on the winner's curse phenomenon, which has been widely studied by both economists and psychologists, and discuss the differences between the goals, perspectives, and methods of the two disciplines in studying this phenomenon.

What Are Common Value Auctions?

In common value auctions, the value of the auctioned item is the same for all bidders, as for example, in the case of drilling rights for oil. The amount of oil a certain location can yield is assumed to be the same for all companies. However, because it is difficult to estimate the exact value of the item, estimates of its value can vary substantially between bidders. In most cases, the bidder with the highest estimate of the value of the item makes the highest offer for it and wins the auction. Because high estimates are usually not based on better information, the winner most likely overpays for the item. This is an example of an *adverse selection* problem, which, if not taken into account by bidders before submitting their bids, can result in suboptimal or even negative profits for winners. The winner's curse refers to the fact that to win in a common value auction, the winner is likely to have overestimated the value of the item. Consequently, the winner is likely to gain less than expected and may even lose (i.e., is said to be "cursed"). Indeed, research has shown that "winning bidders" often find that they have overpaid for the acquired commodities (e.g., Kagel & Levin, 1986).

Standard economic theory does not predict the effect of the winner's curse, which is not expected from rational bidders. It was first discovered by Capen et al. (1971), who studied field data from oil field auctions. The authors pointed out that, on average, firms that acquired oil fields in auctions fell prey to the winner's curse and sustained a loss. If all bidders are rational and adjust their bids to account for adverse selection, the winner's curse cannot materialize, therefore evidence for the phenomenon in market settings indicates an anomaly. Economists are doubtful about this finding because it demonstrates an out-of-equilibrium phenomenon (Roth, 1995).

The Winner's Curse Is Real (Psychologists and Economists Agree)

Laboratory experiments in economics that have examined the winner's curse, tested the robustness of the phenomenon and determined the features of the auction to which it may respond. Bazerman and Samuelson (1983) were the first to explore the winner's curse in an experimental setting. The study was conducted on MBA students who participated in a sealed-bid auction for collections of various objects, including coins, paper clips, etc., contained in a jar with a total value of $8. Participants were told that the highest bidder would receive the value of the jar minus their bid. The authors varied the number of bidders and the contents of the jar. They also asked bidders in addition to their bids to estimate the value of the jar and to give their 90 percent confidence intervals around these estimates. Although participants underestimated the value of the objects in the jar, providing a mean value estimate of $5.13, the mean winning bid was $10.01, higher than both the bidders' own value estimates and the actual value of the jar. Thus, winners incurred a loss of $2.01, on average, at these auctions. The authors found that the size of the winner's curse increased with the number of bidders and with uncertainty about the value of the jar.

Subsequent experiments involving the winner's curse, especially those conducted by economists, implemented the common value auction in a more formal way. This enabled researchers to manipulate more precisely factors that were important from an economic theoretical perspective, such as the number of bidders, the uncertainty regarding the value of the good, and the type of auction.

The perspective of experimental economics with regard to the winner's curse is neatly demonstrated by Kagel and Levin (1986), who engaged participants in several auctions. In each auction, the value of the auctioned good, x_0, was randomly chosen from a uniform distribution and was the same for all bidders. Each bidder received a private information signal, x_i, drawn from a uniform distribution on $[x_0 - \varepsilon, x_0 + \varepsilon]$, with ε known to participants. Because economists assume that bidders are rational, lab experiments provide participants with optimal conditions to reveal their rationality, especially with respect to experience and feedback. Participants in the Kagel and Levin (1986) study received an initial cash endowment, and those who lost their entire endowment in the auction were declared bankrupt and prevented from further bidding. After each auction, participants received extensive feedback about their bid, the value of the winning bid, the true value of the good, and the performance of other participants in the auction. Participants were able to observe the earnings of the winning bidders and of the others, and learn from their experience. Despite this meticulous experimental design, the winner's curse persisted. The authors also found a more pronounced bias in large auctions than in ones that included a small group of bidders. Participants in large auctions bid more aggressively than in small ones, whereas rationally, they should have bid more conservatively as more bidders participated in the auction. Experience, however, helped reduce the winner's curse, but does not eliminate it.

A common criticism of economic findings, especially when they fail to agree with economic theory, concerns the subject pool, and argues that the students who composed the subject pool may not be representative of people who voluntarily join auctions and bid in real life. But the results regarding the winner's curse seem to be consistent across various populations, including MBA students (Bazerman and Samuelson, 1983; Kagel and Levin, 1986), talented undergraduates (Lind and Plott, 1991), and construction firm managers (Dyer et al., 1989).

Theoretical Explanations of the Winner's Curse

Nash equilibrium in common value auctions requires complicated calculations of the best response to other bidders' actions that involve beliefs about others' rationality and strategic uncertainty. The robustness of the winner's curse observed in the lab for inexperienced bidders motivated theorists to explain the phenomenon within a normative Nash bidding model with fewer assumptions, which permits a more relaxed belief system (Kagel & Roth, 2015). Eyster and Rabin (2005) assumed that the bidders accurately predict the distribution of others' bids and know how to best respond to it, but do not correctly perceive how these other bids depend on other bidders' information. Crawford and Iriberri (2007) explained the winner's curse by different levels of "sophistication" or "k-level reasoning." They demonstrated that the majority of players can be classified as level-0 players who chose randomly between possible actions or level-1 players who plan their response to the expected behavior of level-0 players. The relative lack of players with higher levels of sophisticated planning explains the high prevalence of the winner's curse. Thus, both studies allow for a more relaxed belief system while maintaining assumptions about rational players making the best response in accordance with their (relaxed) belief structure.

The Underlying Mechanism of the Winner's Curse, as Demonstrated by the Acquiring
a Company Problem

To understand the cognitive process that accounts for the winners' curse, psychologists have used mostly the Acquiring a Company task, in which the optimal behavior does not depend on beliefs regarding the rationality of other players. The task, an adaptation of Akerlof's (1970) market for lemons problem by Samuelson and Bazerman (1985), models bargaining under asymmetric information. The Acquiring a Company task describes a company that considers acquiring another. The seller, who owns the target company, knows its exact value, v, but the buyer knows only that v is a value taken from a uniform distribution ranging between zero and 100 monetary units. Both parties know that if purchased, the value of the company to the buyer will increase by 50 percent to $1.5v$. In these circumstances, what final offer should the buyer make for the company?

Because the seller knows the value of the company, the seller agrees to sell the company only for the price of v or more. This selective acceptance of offers by the seller leads to a negative expected profit for any accepted bid. Thus, any offer greater than zero has a negative expected profit and is therefore not profitable.

Despite the simplicity of this game, which removes many of the complications embodied in a multiplayer auction context, players still suffer from not recognizing the adverse selection effect of winning and succumb to the winner's curse. Participants typically bid somewhere between the expected value to the seller of 50 monetary units and the ex-ante expected value to the acquirer of 75. Carroll et al. (1988) sought to understand this non-optimal behavior of the buyers. Using a classic method of experimental social psychology, they asked participants to think aloud while performing the task. They found that participants simplified their decision task by ignoring the selective acceptance of the seller, treating the problem as if the seller had the same limited information they had. The authors suggested that this simplification is a special case of individuals' more general tendency to make simplifying and potentially biased assumptions when trying to incorporate knowledge about future contingent events. Accordingly, they showed that performance did not improve when changing the cover story from a bidding scenario to an individual decision-making task.

Similarly, Charness and Levin (2009) transformed the Acquiring a Company task to an individual decision-making problem in which there is no responding seller or any mention of such a role. Their objective was to examine the normative models suggested by Eyster and Rabin (2005) and by Crawford and Iriberri (2007) using a winner's curse task in which avoiding the winner's curse does not depend on beliefs about other bidders' actions. Despite this simplification of the winner's curse task, no convergence to the optimal bid was found. Charness and Levin's results rule out both models as an explanation for the winner's curse because there are no other players whose actions must be taken into account. The authors suggested that the suboptimal performance reflects people's difficulty performing contingent reasoning on future events. Recently, Koch and Penczynski (2018) also examined the cognitive processes involved in the winner's curse from an economic perspective, and assessed whether the phenomenon is driven predominantly by conditional reasoning or by belief formation, that is, by ignoring the selective acceptance of the bid or by beliefs that do not take into account others' bidding. In the modified auction setting that requires neither conditional reasoning nor belief formation for optimal behavior, the authors observed bids that are close to equilibrium. Unlike psychologists, they proposed to relate deviations from equilibrium play to objective game complexities rather than to focus on people's behavior and on the way they think about complex games.

Learning to Overcome the Winner's Curse

The winner's curse demonstrates the bidders' inability to take into account the other's perspective and its resulting choice when determining their bids. One explanation provided by economists to this behavioral pattern is participants' inexperience with the task. According to the mainstream economic argument (e.g., Thaler, 1992), although people can be deceived once or twice by such a problem, with experience they figure out the principles and traps inherent in the task. Psychologists agree that experience can help people learn to attenuate biases, but they do not share the economists' optimism that all biases can be overcome with sufficient experience. Research in psychology aims to understand the cognitive process that leads to the bias and provide feedback based on this process. By contrast, economists incorporate the learning process into a theoretical model to test the conditions under which behavior converges to its theoretical economic equilibrium.

Ball et al. (1991) examined learning in the Acquiring a Company task. They let participants complete 20 trials of the task, with financial incentives and full feedback, but did not observe any learning or gradual decrease in the bids. In a second experiment, the researchers allowed participants to reverse roles to make the asymmetry of information more salient to the buyers. For the group that switched roles, the rate of learners (defined as participants who bid zero at any particular trial and continue to do so until the end of the experiment) increased from nine percent to 37 percent. At the same time, the mean offer decreased only slightly for those not defined as learners. A limitation of the learning in this study was that participants could learn only from their own experience. They received no information about others' losses or their own potential for losses if their bids had been accepted. Foreman and Murnighan (1996) addressed this limitation by giving participants ample feedback and experience, as is customary in experimental economics. Over a period of four weeks, participants participated in two Acquiring a Company tasks and four common value auctions, and were encouraged to reflect on their bids between sessions. One group received full feedback on their and others' bids and outcomes, which enabled them to learn from their own experience as well as from that of others. Despite this optimal learning environment, experience had little effect on bidding, and although the additional feedback reduced overbidding to some extent, it never extinguished the winner's curse. Note that the experiment was conducted on students with no real incentives, which may have attenuated learning.

Economists Selten et al. (2005) also studied learning in the Acquiring a Company task. Approaching the task from an economic perspective, they showed that a simple directional learning model can capture the behavior in this task. Participants completed 100 trials of the task, compared with 20 in the Ball et al. (1991) paradigm, to address the possibility that the lack of convergence to the optimum in the prior study was due to an insufficient number of rounds. They also experimented the task with different minimum values, so as not to restrict the study to conditions under which the optimum is extreme. Despite these changes, no apparent convergence toward the optimum was observed.

Unlike in psychology, studies in experimental economics are careful to design the incentive structures in a way that participants are paid according to their performance. Bereby-Meyer and Grosskopf (2008) suggested that one factor that may account for the slow learning in the Acquiring a Company task is the noise in the feedback; that is, the variance in participants' ultimate payoff. The task used by Ball et al. (1991) had a large gain-loss variance, so that the same offer could potentially end up with a profit of 50 percent or with a significant loss. These sources of variability result in choices and outcomes that are only partly correlated, therefore sub-optimal choices may have high positive payoffs. Indeed, one-third of the time participants gain positive amounts of money while bidding and acquiring a company, which makes it difficult for participants to reject the hypothesis that it is good to bid. Bereby-Meyer and Grosskopf (2008) showed in an experiment that when the variance in the feedback was reduced, bids decreased and performance improved significantly. The susceptibility of learning to feedback variance suggests that economists may be right in arguing that biases can be eliminated with experience, but this effect may be restricted to environments with low amounts of noise. This highlights the importance of conducting experiments that test learning in noisy environments that better reflect real-life situations.

Research has found that decision makers failed to perform optimally in competitive settings because they paid attention and focused only on their own thoughts and actions, and failed to incorporate a clear understanding of the rules of the game and their interaction with their competitors' behaviors (e.g., Carroll et al., 1988; Tor & Bazerman, 2003). Using protocol analysis, Tor and Bazerman (2003) showed that the interactions between the parties and the rules of the game were the most important predictors of success. They suggested that the difference between successful and unsuccessful decision makers was not necessarily how much they thought about the different aspects of the competitive situation, but how they thought about the decisions of others and the rules of the game. They found that the same errors existed and predicted failure across three seemingly different tasks: the Acquiring a Company problem, the Monty Hall problem, and the Multiparty Ultimatum game.

Idson et al. (2004) proposed a cognitive intervention to overcome the winner's curse. Inspired by the findings of Tor and Bazerman (2003), as well as by research on analogical reasoning in negotiation (Loewenstein et al., 1999; Thompson et al., 2000), they explored whether participants can learn by understanding differences in seemingly similar task problems, versions of the Monty Hall problem (Nalebuff, 1987; Friedman, 1998) and the Multiparty Ultimatum game (Messick et al., 1997; Tor & Bazerman, 2003), to focus more accurately on other parties' decisions and the rules of the game. The analogical training was found to be successful in focusing participants on the rules of the games and consequently overcoming the winner's curse. A similar active approach was adopted by Grosskopf et al. (2007), who added cognitive feedback to the Acquiring a Company task, as suggested in the psychology literature. They presented participants with different parameters of the task, asking them to compare and contrast the different parameters (see Idson et al., 2004 for a similar manipulation). Participants received full feedback on the history of their choices and the resulting outcomes, and were allowed to interact with a human opponent instead of a computer program. None of these manipulations led to a better understanding of the task. The bias in participants' behavior proved persistent and was impervious to these learning interventions.

In sum, although economics and psychology use different approaches to the winner's curse, the conclusions from the research are similar: the winners' curse is a robust bias that is difficult to overcome, even with ample experience and feedback, and it involves complex cognitive learning procedures. It may be attenuated, but it is difficult to eliminate.

Conclusion

In his paper, "Rationality in Psychology and Economics" (1986), Herbert Simon wrote that "economics has almost uniformly treated human behavior as rational. Psychology, on the other hand, had always been concerned with both the irrational and the rational aspects of behavior." In this chapter, we propose that this distinction between the two disciplines is also apparent in the way they have studied competition. But the approach of economics to the study of competition also reflects the changes in the way it has viewed rationality over the last two decades; that is, taking into account mistakes, doubts about how smart others are, and learning the normative models of competition. Experimental economists aim to develop rational models and strive to capture a better understanding of agents' bounded rationality, given the complexity of the environment. The field of economics can continue enriching its models by incorporating insights from psychological studies on cognition, emotions, and motivation into their theories of competition.

Social psychology, in turn, has also evolved in its approach to competition. We have witnessed a transition from scenario-based research to incentivized experiments of real behavior, including the provision of extensive feedback. Still, psychologists can further enrich their research on competition by adopting some principles of experimental economics. Psychology would be well served by aiming to develop formal models that more precisely abstract the social context to include the different agents in the situation, such as buyers and sellers in the Acquiring a Company task, rather than trying to achieve simplification. This may be a challenging task, however, given the goal of understanding cognitive processes without losing internal validity.

To conclude, we find the increase in multidisciplinary research on competition in social psychology and experimental economics an encouraging trend. The high level of openness and mutual enrichment between the two disciplines suggests that the two may be moving closer to each other, and that they are better able to learn from one another and to collaborate in developing a rich understanding of this fascinating human behavior.

Notes

1. We discuss auctions in the second part of the chapter, but we describe all-pay auctions in this part because of their structural similarity to tournaments.
2. Some studies refer to groups and others to teams. Here we use the two terms interchangeably.

References

Abbink, K., Brandts, J., Herrmann, B., & Orzen, H. (2010). Intergroup confict and intra-group punishment in an experimental contest game. *American Economic Review 100* (1), 420–447. https://doi.org/10.1257/aer.100.1.420.

Agranov, M., & Tergiman, C. (2013). Incentives and compensation schemes: An experimental study. *International Journal of Industrial Organization 31* (3), 238–247. https://doi.org/10.1016/j.ijindorg.2012.06.001.

Akerlof, G. (1970). The market for lemons: Qualitative uncertainty and the market mechanism. *Quarterly Journal of Economics 89*, 488–500.

Amaldoss, W., Meyer, R. J., Raju, J. S., & Rapoport, A. (2000). Collaborating to compete. *Marketing Science 19* (2), 105–126.

Ames, C., & Ames, R. (1984). Systems of student and teacher motivation: Toward a qualitative definition. *Journal of Educational Psychology 76* (4), 535–556. https://doi.org/10.1037/0022-0663.76.4.535.

Ariely D., & Norton M. I. (2007). Psychology and experimental economics: A gap in abstraction. *Current Directions in Psychological Science 16*, 336–339.

Baik, K. H. (1994). Effort levels in contests with two asymmetric players. *Southern Economic Journal 61* (2), 367–378. https://doi.org/10.2307/1059984.

Balas, B., & Thomas, L. E. (2015). Competition makes observers remember faces as more aggressive. *Journal of Experimental Psychology: General 144* (4), 711–716. https://doi.org/10.1037/xge0000078.

Ball, S., Bazerman, M., & Carroll, J. (1991). An evaluation of earning in the bilateral winner's curse. *Organizational Behavior and Human Decision Processes 48*, 1–22.

Baye, M. R., Kovenock, D., & De Vries, C. G. (1996). The all-pay auction with complete information. *Economic Theory 8* (2), 291–305. https://doi.org/10.1007/BF01211819.

Bazerman, M. H., & Samuelson, W. F. (1983). I won the auction but don't want the prize. *Journal of Conflict Resolution 27*, 618–634

Bereby-Meyer, Y., & Grosskopf, B. (2008). Overcoming the winner's curse: An adaptive learning perspective. *Journal of Behavioral Decision Making 21* (1), 15–27.

Bornstein, G. (1992). The free-rider problem in intergroup conflicts over step-level and continuous public goods. *Journal of Personality and Social Psychology 62* (4), 597–606. https://doi.org/10.1037/0022-3514.62.4.597.

Bornstein, G. (2003). Intergroup conflict: Individual, group, and collective interests. *Personality and Social Psychology Review 7* (2), 129–145. https://doi.org/10.1207/S15327957PSPR0702_129-145.

Bornstein, G., & Erev, I. (1994). The enhancing effect of intergroup competition on group performance. *International Journal of Conflict Management 5* (3), 271–283. https://doi.org/10.1108/eb022905.

Bowles, S. (2006). Group competition, reproductive leveling, and the evolution of human altruism. *Science 314* (5805), 1569–1572. https://doi.org/10.1126/science.1134829.

Brookins, P., Lightle, J. P., & Ryvkin, D. (2015). An experimental study of sorting in group contests. *Labour Economics 35*, 16–25. https://doi.org/10.1016/j.labeco.2015.03.011.

Brown, S. P., Cron, W. L., & Slocum, J. W., Jr. (1998). Effects of trait competitiveness and perceived intra-organizational competition on salesperson goal setting and performance. *Journal of Marketing 62*, 88–98.

Bull, C., Schotter, A., & Weigelt, K. (1987). Tournaments and piece rates: An experimental study. *Journal of Political Economy 95* (1), 1–33. https://doi.org/10.1086/261439.

Burton-Chellew, M. N., Ross-Gillespie, A., & West, S. A. (2010). Cooperation in humans: competition between groups and proximate emotions. *Evolution and Human Behavior 31* (2), 104–108. https://doi.org/10.1016/j.evolhumbehav.2009.07.005.

Cain, D. M., Moore, D. A., & Haran, U. (2015). Making sense of overconfidence in market entry. *Strategic Management Journal 36* (1), 1–18. https://doi.org/10.1002/smj.2196.

Camerer, C. (2003). *Behavioral game theory: Experiments on strategic interaction.* Princeton University Press.

Camerer, C., & Lovallo, D. (1999). Overconfidence and excess entry: An experimental approach. *The American Economic Review 89* (1), 306–318.

Capen, E. C., Clapp, R. V. & Campbell. W. M. (1971). Competitive bidding in high-risk situations. *Journal of Petroleum Technology 23*, 641–653.

Carpenter, J., Matthews, P., & Schirm, J. (2010). Tournaments and office politics: Evidence from a real effort experiment. *The American Economic Review 100* (1), 504–517.

Carroll, J. S., Bazerman, M. H., & Maury, R. (1988). Negotiator cognitions: A descriptive approach to negotiators' understanding of their opponents. *Organizational Behavior and Human Decision Processes 41*, 352–370.

Charness, G., & Levin, D. 2009. The origin of the winner's curse: A laboratory study. *American Economic Journal: Microeconomics 1*, 207–236.

Converse, B. A., & Reinhard, D. A. (2016). On rivalry and goal pursuit: Shared competitive history, legacy concerns, and strategy selection. *Journal of Personality and Social Psychology 110* (2), 191–213. https://doi.org/10.1037/pspa0000038.

Crawford, V., & Iriberri. N. (2007). Level-k auctions: Can boundedly rational strategic thinking explain the winner's curse? *Econometrica 75*, 1721–1770.

Danziger, S., Disatnik, D., & Shani, Y. (2017). Remembering friends as not so friendly in competitive and bargaining social interactions. *Journal of Behavioral Decision Making 30* (4), 987–998. https://doi.org/10.1002/bdm.2019.

Dechenaux, E., Kovenock, D., & Sheremeta, R. M. (2015). A survey of experimental research on contests, all-pay auctions and tournaments. *Experimental Economics 18* (4), 609–669. https://doi.org/10.1007/s10683-014-9421-0.

Dunn, J., Ruedy, N. E., & Schweitzer, M. E. (2012). It hurts both ways: How social comparisons harm affective and cognitive trust. *Organizational Behavior and Human Decision Processes 117* (1), 2–14. https://doi.org/10.1016/j.obhdp.2011.08.001.

Dyer, D., & Kagel. J. H. & Levin, D. (1989). A comparison of naive and experienced bidders in common value offer auctions: A laboratory analysis. *The Economic Journal 99*, 108–115.

Eisenkopf, G., & Teyssier, S. (2013). Envy and loss aversion in tournaments. *Journal of Economic Psychology 34*, 240–255. https://doi.org/10.1016/j.joep.2012.06.006.

Einav, L. & Levin, J (2010). Empirical industrial organization: A progress report. *Journal of Economic Perspectives 24*, 145–162.

Erev, I., Bornstein, G., & Galili, R. (1993). Constructive intergroup competition as a solution to the free rider problem: A field experiment. *Journal of Experimental Social Psychology 29*, 463–478. https://doi.org/10.1006/jesp.1993.1021.

Eriksson, T., Teyssier, S., & Villeval, M. C. (2009). Self-selection and the efficiency of tournaments. *Economic Inquiry 47* (3), 530–548. https://doi.org/10.1111/j.1465-7295.2007.00094.x.

Exline, J. J., & Lobel, M. (1999). The perils of outperformance: Sensitivity about being the target of a threatening upward comparison. *Psychological Bulletin 125* (3), 307–337. https://doi.org/10.1037/0033-2909.125.3.307.

Eyster, E., &. Rabin. M. (2005). Cursed equilibrium. *Econometrica 73*, 1623–72.

Fershtman, C., & Gneezy, U. (2011). The tradeoff between performance and quitting in high power tournaments. *Journal of the European Economic Association 9* (2), 318–336. https://doi.org/10.1111/j.1542-4774.2010.01012.x.

Festinger, L. (1954). A theory of social comparison processes. *Human Relations 7*, 117–140. https://doi.org/10.1177/001872675400700202.

Fong, M., Zhao, K., & Smillie, L. D. (2020). Personality and competitiveness: Extraversion, agreeableness, and their aspects, predict self-reported competitiveness and competitive bidding in experimental auctions. *Personality and Individual Differences 169*, 109907. https://doi.org/10.1016/j.paid.2020.109907.

Foreman, P., & Murnighan, J. K. (1996). Learning to avoid the winner's curse. *Organizational Behavior and Human Decision Processes 67*, 170–180.

Friedman, D. (1998). Monty Hall's three doors: Construction and deconstruction of a choice anomaly. *American Economic Review 88*, 933–946.

Garcia, S. M., & Tor, A. (2009). The N-effect: More competitors, less competition. *Psychological Science 20* (7), 871–877. https://doi.org/10.1111/j.1467-9280.2009.02385.x.

Garcia, S. M., Reese, Z. A., & Tor, A. (2020). Social comparison before, during, and after the competition. In J. Suls, R. L. Collins, & L. Wheeler (Eds.), *Social comparison, judgment, and behavior* (pp. 105–142). Oxford University Press. https://doi.org/10.1093/oso/9780190629113.003.0005.

Garcia, S. M., Tor, A., & Schiff, T. M. (2013). The psychology of competition: A social comparison perspective. *Perspectives on Psychological Science 8*, 634–650. https://doi.org/10.1177/1745691613504114.

Gneezy, U., & Smorodinsky, R. (2006). All-pay auctions-an experimental study. *Journal of Economic Behavior and Organization 61* (2), 255–275. https://doi.org/10.1016/j.jebo.2004.09.013.

Gneezy, U., Leonard, K. L., & List, J. A. (2009). Gender differences in competition: Evidence from a matrilineal and a patriarchal society. *Econometrica 77* (5), 1637–1664. https://doi.org/10.3982/ecta6690.

Goette, L., Huffman, D., Meier, S., & Sutter, M. (2012). Competition between organizational groups: Its impact on altruistic and antisocial motivations. *Management Science 58* (5), 948–960. https://doi.org/10.1287/mnsc.1110.1466.

Gradstein, M. (1995). Intensity of competition, entry and entry deterrence in rent seeking contests. *Economics and Politics 7* (I), 79–91.

Grosskopf, B., Bereby-Meyer, Y., & Bazerman, M. (2007). On the robustness of the winners' curse phenomenon. *Theory and Decision 63*, 389–418.

Gunnthorsdottir, A., & Rapoport, A. (2006). Embedding social dilemmas in intergroup competition reduces free-riding. *Organizational Behavior and Human Decision Processes 101* (2), 184–199. https://doi.org/10.1016/j.obhdp.2005.08.005.

Halevy, N., Bornstein, G., & Sagiv, L. (2008). "In-group love" and "out-group hate" as motives for individual participation in intergroup conflict: A new game paradigm. *Psychological Science 19* (4), 405–411.

Haran, U. (2019). May the best man lose: Guilt inhibits competitive motivation. *Organizational Behavior and Human Decision Processes 154*, 15–33. https://doi.org/10.1016/j.obhdp.2019.07.003.

Haran, U., & Ritov, I. (2014). Know who you're up against: Counterpart identifiability enhances competitive behavior. *Journal of Experimental Social Psychology 54*, 115–121. https://doi.org/10.1016/j.jesp.2014.04.009.

Haran, U., Van Dijk, D., Barina, M., Krief, M., & Rosenzweig, S. (2021). *Winning isn't everything: The effect of guilt proneness on competitive goal pursuit.* Unpublished manuscript.

Harbring, C. (2006). The effect of communication in incentive systems—An experimental study. *Managerial and Decision Economics 27* (5), 333–353. https://doi.org/10.1002/mde.1266.

Harbring, C., & Irlenbusch, B. (2003). An experimental study on tournament design. *Labour Economics 10* (10), 443–464. https://doi.org/10.1016/S0927-5371(03)00034-4.

Harbring, C., & Irlenbusch, B. (2008). How many winners are good to have? On tournaments with sabotage. *Journal of Economic Behavior and Organization 65*, 682–702. https://doi.org/10.1016/j.jebo.2006.03.004.

Harbring, C., & Irlenbusch, B. (2011). Sabotage in tournaments: Evidence from a laboratory experiment. *Management Science 57* (4), 611–627. https://doi.org/10.1287/mnsc.1100.1296.

Hardy, C. L., & Van Vugt, M. (2006). Nice guys finish first: The competitive altruism hypothesis. *Personality and Social Psychology Bulletin 32* (10), 1402–1413. https://doi.org/10.1177/0146167206291006.

Hillman, A. L., & Riley, J. G. (1989). Politically contestable rents and transfers. *Economics and Politics 1* (1), 17–39. https://doi.org/10.1111/j.1468-0343.1989.tb00003.x.

Hirt, E. R., Zillmann, D., Erickson, G. A., & Kennedy, C. (1992). Costs and benefits of allegiance: Changes in fans' self-ascribed competencies after team victory versus defeat. *Journal of Personality and Social Psychology 63* (5), 724–738. https://doi.org/10.1037/0022-3514.63.5.724.

Hsieh, K.-Y., Tsai, W., & Chen, M.-J. (2014). If they can do it, why not us? Competitors as reference points for justifying escalation of commitment. *Academy of Management Journal 58* (1), 38–58. https://doi.org/10.5465/amj.2011.0869.

Idson, L. C., Chugh, D., Bereby-Meyer, Y., Moran, S., Grosskopf, B., & Bazerman, M. (2004). Overcoming focusing failures in competitive environment. *Journal of Behavioral Decision Making 17*, 159–172.

John, L. K., Loewenstein, G., & Rick, S. I. (2014). Cheating more for less: Upward social comparisons motivate the poorly compensated to cheat. *Organizational Behavior and Human Decision Processes 123* (2), 101–109. https://doi.org/10.1016/j.obhdp.2013.08.002.

Kagel, J. H. (1995). Auctions: A survey of experimental research. In J. H. Kagel, & A. E. Roth (Eds.), *The handbook of experimental economics* (pp. 501–536). Princeton University Press.

Kagel, J. H., & Levin, D. (1986). The winner's curse and public information in common value auctions. *American Economic Review 76*, 894–920.

Kagel, J. H., & Roth, A. E. (2015). *The handbook of experimental economics, volume 2*. Princeton University Press.

Kilduff, G. J. (2014). Driven to win: Rivalry, motivation, and performance. *Social Psychological and Personality Science 5* (8), 944–952. https://doi.org/10.1177/1948550614539770.

Kilduff, G. J., Anger Elfenbein, H., & Staw, B. M. (2010). The psychology of rivalry: A relationally dependent analysis of competition. *Academy of Management Journal 53* (5), 943–969.

Kilduff, G. J., Galinsky, A. D., Gallo, E., & Reade, J. J. (2016). Whatever it takes: Rivalry and unethical behavior. *Academy of Management Journal 59* (5), 1508–1534. https://doi.org/10.5465/amj.2014.0545.

Knoeber, C. R. (1989). A real game of chicken: Contracts, tournaments, and the production of broilers. *Journal of Law, Economics, & Organization 5* (2), 271–292.

Knoeber, C. R., & Thurman, W. N. (1994). Testing the theory of tournaments: An empirical analysis of broiler production. *Journal of Labor Economics 12* (2), 155–179.

Koch, C., &. Penczynski, S. P. (2018). The winner's curse: Conditional reasoning and belief formation. *Journal of Economic Theory 174*, 57–102.

Koellinger, P., Minniti, M., & Schade, C. (2007). "I think I can, I think I can": Overconfidence and entrepreneurial behavior. *Journal of Economic Psychology 28* (4), 502–527. https://doi.org/10.1016/j.joep.2006.11.002.

Kohn, A. (1992), *No contest: The case against competition*. Houghton-Mifflin.

Ku, G., Malhotra, D., & Murnighan, J. K. (2005). Towards a competitive arousal model of decision-making: A study of auction fever in live and Internet auctions. *Organizational Behavior and Human Decision Processes 96* (2005), 89–103. https://doi.org/10.1016/j.obhdp.2004.10.001.

Lazear, E. (1989). Pay equality and industrial politics. *Journal of Political Economy 97* (3), 561–580.

Lazear, E. P., & Rosen, S. (1981). Rank-order tournaments as optimum labor contracts. *Journal of Political Economy 89* (5), 841–864. https://doi.org/10.1086/261010.

Lind, B., & Plott, C. R. (1991). The winner's curse: Experiments with buyers and with sellers. *American Economic Review 81*, 335–346.

Lugovskyy, V., Puzzello, D., & Tucker, S. (2010). An experimental investigation of overdissipation in the all pay auction. *European Economic Review 54* (8), 974–997. https://doi.org/10.1016/j.euroecorev.2010.02.006.

Locke, K. D. (2007). Personalized and generalized comparisons: Causes and consequences of variations in the focus of social comparisons. *Personality & Social Psychology Bulletin 33* (2), 213–225. https://doi.org/10.1177/0146167206293492.

Loewenstein, J., Thompson, L., & Gentner, D. (1999). Analogical encoding facilitates knowledge transfer in negotiation. *Psychonomic Bulletin and Review* 6, 586–597.

McBride, J. (2018). *The economics of hosting the Olympic Games.* Council on Foreign Relations. https://www.cfr.org/backgrounder/economics-hosting-olympic-games.

McCallum, D. M., Harring, K., Gilmore, R., Drenan, S., Chase, J. P., Insko, C. A., & Thibaut, J. (1985). Competition and cooperation between groups and between individuals. *Journal of Experimental Social Psychology 21* (4), 301–320. https://doi.org/10.1016/0022-1031(85)90032-0.

Messick, D. M., Moore, D. A., & Bazerman, M. H. (1997). Ultimatum bargaining with a group: underestimating the importance of the decision rule. *Organizational Behavior and Human Decision Processes 69,* 87–101.

Miller, D. T., Turnbull, W., & McFarland, C. (1988). Particularistic and universalistic evaluation in the social comparison process. *Journal of Personality and Social Psychology 55* (6), 908–917. https://doi.org/10.1037/0022-3514.55.6.908.

Moore, D. A., & Healy, P. J. (2008). The trouble with overconfidence. *Psychological Review 115* (2), 502–517. https://doi.org/10.1037/0033-295X.115.2.502.

Murayama, K., & Elliot, A. J. (2012). The competition-performance relation: A meta-analytic review and test of the opposing processes model of competition and performance. *Psychological Bulletin 138* (6), 1035–1070. https://doi.org/10.1037/a0028324.

Nalbantian, B. H. R., & Schotter, A. (1997). Productivity under group incentives: An experimental study. *American Economic Review 87* (3), 314–341.

Nalebuff, B. (1987). Puzzles: Choose a curtain, duelity, two point conversions, and more. *Journal of Economic Perspectives 1,* 157–163.

Niederle, M., & Vesterlund, L. (2007). Do women shy away from competition? Do men compete too much?: A (failed) replication. *Quarterly Journal of Economics 122* (3), 1067–1101.

Orrison, A., Schotter, A., & Weigelt, K. (2004). Multiperson tournaments: An experimental examination. *Management Science 50* (2), 268–279. https://doi.org/10.1287/mnsc.1030.0128.

Pearce, D.W., ed. 1994. *The MIT Dictionary of Modern Economics.* 4th Ed. MIT Press.

Rabin, M. (1998). Psychology and economics. *Journal of Economic Literature 36,* 11–46.

Rapoport, A., & Bornstein, G. (1987). Intergroup competition for the provision of binary public goods. *Psychological Review 94* (3), 291–299. https://doi.org/10.1037/0033-295X.94.3.291.

Roth, A. E. (1995). *Handbook of experimental economics,* edited by John Kagel and Alvin E. Roth. Princeton University Press.

Salovey, P., & Rodin, J. (1984). Some antecedents and consequences of social-comparison jealousy. *Journal of Personality and Social Psychology 47* (4), 780–792.

Samuelson, W. F., & Bazerman, M. H. (1985). Negotiation under the winner's curse. In V. Smith (Ed.), *Research in experimental economics* (Vol. III, pp. 38–105). JAI Press.

Schotter, A., & Weigelt, K. (1992). Asymmetric tournaments, equal opportunity laws, and affirmative action: Some experimental results. *Quarterly Journal of Economics 107* (2), 511–539.

Schurr, A., & Ritov, I. (2016). Winning a competition predicts dishonest behavior. *Proceedings of the National Academy of Sciences 113* (7), 1754–1759. https://doi.org/10.1073/pnas.1515102113.

Schwarz, N., Strack, F., Kommer, D., & Wagner, D. (1987). Soccer, rooms, and the quality of your life: Mood effects on judgments of satisfaction with life in general and with specific domains. *European Journal of Social Psychology 17* (1), 69–79. https://doi.org/10.1002/ejsp.2420170107.

Selten, R., Abbink, K., & Cox, R. (2005). Learning direction theory and the Winner's Curse. *Experimental Economics 8,* 5–20.

Sheremeta, R. M. (2011). Contest design: An experimental investigation. *Economic Inquiry 49* (2), 573–590. https://doi.org/10.1111/j.1465-7295.2009.00274.x.

Sheremeta, R. M. (2018). Behavior in group contests: A review of experimental research. *Journal of Economic Surveys 32* (3), 683–704. https://doi.org/10.1111/joes.12208.

Simon, H. A. (1986). Rationality in psychology and economics. *The Journal of Business 59,* S209–S224.

Spence, J. T., & Helmreich, R. L. (1983). Achievement related motives and behavior. In J. T. Spence (Ed.), *Achievement and achievement motives: Psychological and sociological dimensions* (pp. 7–74). Freeman.

Stein, W. E. (2002). Asymmetric rent-seeking with more than two contestants. *Public Choice 113* (3–4), 325–336. https://doi.org/10.1023/A:1020877410243.

Strickhouser, J. E., & Zell, E. (2015). Self-evaluative effects of dimensional and social comparison. *Journal of Experimental Social Psychology 59*, 60–66. https://doi.org/10.1016/j.jesp.2015.03.001.

Tamir, Y., & Nadler, A. (2007). The role of personality in social identity: Effects of field-dependence and context on reactions to threat to group distinctiveness. *Journal of Personality 75* (5), 927–954. https://doi.org/10.1111/j.1467-6494.2007.00461.x.

Taylor, S. E., & Lobel, M. (1989). Social comparison activity under threat: Downward evaluation and upward contacts. *Psychological Review 96* (4), 569–575.

Tesser, A., & Campbell, J. (1982). Self-evaluation maintenance and the perception of friends and strangers. *Journal of Personality 50* (3), 261–279. https://doi.org/10.1111/j.1467-6494.1982.tb00750.x.

Tesser, A., & Smith, J. (1980). Some effects of task relevance and friendship on helping: You don't always help the one you like. *Journal of Experimental Social Psychology 16*, 582–590.

Thaler, R. H. (1992). *The winner's curse: Paradoxes and anomalies of economic life.* Free Press.

Thompson, L., Gentner, D., & Loewenstein, J. (2000). Analogical training more powerful than individual case training. *Organizational Behavior and Human Decision Processes 82*, 60–75.

Tor, A., & Bazerman, M. H. (2003). Focusing failures in competitive environments: Explaining decision errors in the Monty Hall game, the Acquiring a Company problem, and Multiparty Ultimatums. *Journal of Behavioral Decision Making 16*, 353–374.

Tor, A., & Garcia, S. M. (2010). The n-effect: Beyond probability judgments. *Psychological Science 21* (5), 748–749. https://doi.org/10.1177/0956797610368813.

Turner, J. C., Brown, R. J., & Tajfel, H. (1979). Social comparison and group interest in ingroup favouritism. *European Journal of Social Psychology 9* (2), 187–204. https://doi.org/10.1002/ejsp.2420090207.

Van Dijk, F., Sonnemans, J., & Van Winden, F. (2001). Incentive systems in a real effort experiment. *European Economic Review 45* (2), 187–214. https://doi.org/10.1016/S0014-2921(00)00056-8.

Vroom, V. (1964). *Work and motivation.* Wiley & Sons.

Wills, T. A. (1981). Downward comparison principles in social psychology. *Psychological Bulletin 90* (2), 245–271. https://doi.org/10.1037/0033-2909.90.2.245.

Yip, J. A., Schweitzer, M. E., & Nurmohamed, S. (2017). Trash-talking: Competitive incivility motivates rivalry, performance, and unethical behavior. *Organizational Behavior and Human Decision Processes 144*, 125–144. https://doi.org/10.1016/j.obhdp.2017.06.002.

Zell, A. L., & Exline, J. J. (2010). How does it feel to be outperformed by a "good winner"? Prize sharing and self-deprecating as appeasement strategies. *Basic and Applied Social Psychology 32*, 69–85. https://doi.org/10.1080/01973530903540125.

PART II

Biological Approaches

PART II

Biological Approaches

Examination of the Potential Functional Role of Competition-Induced Testosterone Dynamics

Tracy-Lynn Reside, Brittney A. Robinson, *and* Justin M. Carré

Abstract

Across the animal kingdom, testosterone levels change rapidly within the context of competitive and/or mating related interactions. It has been speculated that such acute changes in testosterone concentrations may ultimately function to regulate ongoing and future behaviors, such as aggression, competitiveness, mate-seeking, and risk-taking. In this chapter, the authors review the growing body of evidence suggesting that competition-induced changes in testosterone positively map onto competitive, aggressive, risk-taking, and mating-related psychological and behavioral processes. The authors also review evidence from single dose pharmacological challenge studies that attempt to draw more substantial causal claims concerning testosterone's role in promoting these psychological and behavioral processes.

Key Words: testosterone, behaviour, competition, risk-taking, aggression, mate-seeking, testosterone reactivity, social neuroendocrinology

The HPG Axis and Testosterone Physiology

The hypothalamic-pituitary-gonadal (HPG) axis regulates human reproductive physiology and behavior. It is a neuroendocrine network that coordinates endogenous and exogenous signals to orchestrate the physiological processes related to reproduction and sex hormones. For the purposes of understanding testosterone and its links to human competition, this brief overview will focus strictly on the HPG axis and testosterone regulation.

The HPG axis undergoes three separate activation processes, the first two occurring during the fetal and neonatal development and the second during puberty. Fetal activation has critical influences on the normal development of the reproductive system, including the development of reproductive organs (testes, uterus, ovaries) and external genitalia (Kuiri-Hänninen et al., 2014). The more familiar activation of the HPG axis occurs during puberty, when we see the development of secondary sex characteristics. During this period, the hypothalamus begins the pulsatile release of gonadotropin-releasing hormone (GnRH), which travels directly through the hypophyseal portal to the anterior pituitary gland; this, in turn, causes the anterior pituitary to release a suite of stimulating hormones, including follicle-stimulating hormone (FSH) and luteinizing hormone (LH), as well as thyroid-stimulating hormone, adrenocorticotropin, and growth hormone (Clavijo & Hsiao, 2018). LH and FSH are vital components in regulating estrogen and progesterone production in the female menstrual cycle and together are involved in promoting and maintaining spermatogenesis in males. Although women, in general, have much less testosterone than men, they do produce it in the ovaries, adrenal glands, and peripheral tissues. In men, LH travels through the bloodstream and stimulates the Leydig cells of the testes to synthesize and release testosterone (Selvaraj & Koganti, 2018). In peripheral tissues, testosterone can be converted into estradiol via aromatase in both sexes (Azcoitia et al., 2011). Regulation occurs primarily through a negative feedback loop involving testosterone, estradiol, and inhibin (produced by the Sertoli cells in the testes) to reduce the production of GnRH, LH, and FSH in the hypothalamus and anterior pituitary (Molnar & Gair, 2019).

One of the major players in the human endocrine system, testosterone is an essential hormone in male and female human physiology. Once secreted, testosterone can interact with receptors in various tissues to influence physiological and behavioral processes critical to survival and reproduction. Importantly, hormone–behavior associations are bidirectional, whereby hormones may modulate social behavior, and social behavior may feedback to influence hormone concentrations. Social neuroendocrine research and testosterone have been dominated by studies on mating behaviors, aggression, and competitive interactions (see Bos et al., 2012 for review), with theoretical models focusing on hormone changes and social behavior in men (Carré & Olmstead, 2015). Testosterone, however, is also a critical hormone within the female endocrine system with physiological actions mediated directly and via aromatization to estradiol in numerous tissues and systems throughout the body. There is also growing evidence for its role in female social behaviors (see Casto & Prashad, 2017 for review).

Testosterone Dynamics and Human Behavior

Human competition is used to gain favor and, ultimately, status and resources. In the animal kingdom, competition plays a crucial role in survival and reproduction with success in competition allowing for a greater number of resources and mating opportunities. Notably, testosterone is known to modulate psychological and behavioral processes related to both survival and reproduction (Ketterson & Nolan, 1992).

There is a wealth of evidence demonstrating that testosterone concentrations change rapidly in the context of human competitive interactions. Meta-analytic evidence indicates that the outcome of competitive interactions modulates the pattern of testosterone release, with winners experiencing larger increases in testosterone concentrations relative to losers (see Geniole et al., 2020). Theoretical models (e.g., Mazur, 1985; Wingfield et al., 1990) have postulated that such acute changes in testosterone may serve to modulate ongoing and/or future behavior. In the next section, we review studies examining associations between testosterone dynamics, competitive motivation, aggression, risk-taking, mating psychology, and athletic performance.

Competitive Behavior

Recent work has examined whether acute changes in testosterone during competition predict future behavior—particularly competitive motivation, or the willingness to approach a competitive interaction. The first experiment to demonstrate this effect was conducted by Mehta and Josephs (2006). In this study, men (n = 64) were randomly assigned to either win or lose a series of rigged competitive interactions against each other. Saliva samples were obtained immediately prior and 15 minutes after the competitive interaction. After the competition, participants were given a choice between competing again against the same opponent or completing a questionnaire on food and music preferences. Participants who demonstrated a rise in testosterone were more likely to compete again relative to individuals who demonstrated a decrease in testosterone during the competitive interaction. Notably, this effect was most pronounced among individuals who lost the competitive interaction. Building on this finding, Carré and McCormick (2008) used the Point Subtraction Aggression Paradigm (PSAP) to assess aggressive behavior within a competition, changes in testosterone, and subsequent motivation to compete in a relatively small sample of young men (n = 38). The PSAP task involves earning points, stealing points, and protecting one's own points from an opponent. All points earned during the PSAP are later converted to real-world money. Participants are told that they are playing the game with another person, but it is a computer task programmed to provoke participants by stealing points at random intervals during the game.

The PSAP is a well-validated measure of reactive aggression (see Geniole, MacDonell, et al., 2017 for review). The PSAP itself is not a competition; however, anecdotal reports from participants suggest that they view the task as a competition to earn more money than their game partner. Carré and McCormick (2008) found that testosterone changes during the PSAP positively predicted men's willingness to choose a competitive versus non-competitive option. Further, studies have investigated how contextual factors moderate the relationship between changes in testosterone and future competitive motivation. Mehta et al. (2014) had male participants (n = 62) compete in a cognitive task with a predetermined outcome; either a close victory or a decisive victory over a male confederate. After the victory, they were asked if they wanted to compete against the same opponent, a different opponent, or participate in a non-competitive task. This study showed that an increase in testosterone after victory predicted willingness to compete again, but only for decisive victories. In contrast, after a close victory, a rise in testosterone predicted willingness to participate in a non-competitive task. In the context of the biosocial model of status, these results support the theory that increases in testosterone predict the motivation to compete again (gain further status) but only after a decisive victory, representing an explicit gain in status but not indeterminate status gains (close victory). Other evidence in healthy young men (n = 165) indicates that changes in testosterone during a competitive interaction are positively correlated with self- and observer-perceived personality traits such as dominance and confidence (Kordsmeyer & Penke, 2019). In another study, Zilioli and Watson (2014) had a sample of young men (n = 84) compete on a game of Tetris in which the outcome of the contest was manipulated, and saliva samples collected pre- and post-competition. Results indicated that winners had elevated testosterone relative to losers. Remarkably, the change in testosterone during the task positively predicted performance gains on a second Tetris competition performed 24 hours later.

Most of the research examining change in testosterone and its effect on future competitive behavior has been conducted with samples of men; however, several recent studies have used female samples. In athletic competition, Casto and Edwards (2016a) conducted a study using female soccer players (n = 30), finding that elevated testosterone after a competition positively correlated with the individual's willingness to reconcile with their opponent, regardless of whether they won or lost. Also, in a sample of men and women (n = 190), Casto et al. (2020) found that competitive will performance (one's willingness to endure physical pain to win a competition) was positively correlated with testosterone reactivity patterns during the task. Collectively, these studies indicate that testosterone reactivity during competition may play a role in the decision to engage in future competitive behaviors and potentially impact perceived social status and state personality traits after competitive interactions.

Aggressive Behavior

Our lab has investigated the extent to which acute changes in testosterone map onto aggressive behavior in people. In earlier work, participants were asked to provide a saliva sample before completing the PSAP and 10 minutes afterwards. Results revealed that men who responded the most aggressively in the PSAP task also experienced the largest increase in testosterone from pre- to post-competitive interaction. One limitation of this work is that changes in testosterone and aggressive behavior were assessed simultaneously, raising questions as to whether a rise in testosterone promoted aggressive behavior, or whether aggressive behavior promoted a rise in testosterone (see Geniole & Carré, 2018). Of course, pharmacological challenge work could help to resolve this issue, but carefully designed correlational studies could assist in ruling out the role of aggression in promoting a rise in testosterone. Klinesmith et al. (2006) were one of the first groups to test the effects of an acute rise in testosterone on subsequent aggressive behavior. In order to assess the impact of aggressive stimuli on testosterone levels, the authors first had male participants (n = 30) interact with either a fake gun or a board game. The presence of a weapon has been associated with increases in aggressive thoughts and behaviors (see Bettencourt & Kernahan, 1997, for meta-analysis; Berkowitz & Lepage, 1967), so although the gun in the experiment was fake, it was chosen to look and feel as though it was a real gun. After interacting with the item, participants were given a cup of water to add as much or as little hot sauce as they desired, later to be consumed by another participant who reported disliking spicy foods. This hot sauce paradigm was developed by Lieberman et al. (1999) to minimize potential harm when experimentally measuring aggression. They derived the use of hot sauce as a form of aggression from previous research in which participants were more aggressive towards individuals who had given them some form of noxious substance (Baron & Richardson, 1994; Geen, 1990) as well as being a familiar form of aggression in the media. Results indicated that participants who had interacted with the fake gun demonstrated a significant rise in testosterone and were more aggressive relative to men who interacted with the board game. Notably, testosterone reactivity mediated the effect of interacting with a gun on subsequent aggressive behavior.

In other work, Carré et al. (2009) had participants (n = 99, 60 percent women) engage in a rigged competitive interaction whereby participants were randomly assigned to win or lose a number of competition interactions. Saliva samples were collected pre- and post-competition. After providing the second saliva samples, participants played three rounds of the PSAP against the same person they previously competed against. This design feature ensured that changes in testosterone were recorded prior to the assessment of aggressive behavior, enabling the authors to rule out reverse causality (i.e., that aggressive behavior promoted a rise in testosterone). Results revealed that a rise in testosterone in response to the competitive interaction was positively correlated with subsequent aggression assessed using the PSAP, an effect that was found in men, but not women. In a conceptual replication of this work, and using a larger sample of men and women (n = 237, 52 percent women), Carré et al. (2013) randomly assigned participants to win or lose a series of rigged video games of either boxing or volleyball. Men (but not women) who experienced a series of victories showed elevated testosterone levels as well as increased aggressive behavior relative to men assigned to experience a series of defeats. Furthermore, among men, changes in testosterone mediated the effect of winning on subsequent aggressive behavior. That is, male winners were more aggressive than male losers, in part because they demonstrated a more robust increase in testosterone during the competitive interaction. There is also longitudinal evidence in which "at-risk" students received social-cognitive-behavioral therapy or no therapy (Carré et al., 2014). A sample of 63 male kindergarten students was randomly assigned to receive a 10-year behavioral intervention (n = 34) or to a control group (n = 29). Participants were then tested after 20 years at a mean age of 26. Results indicated that individuals in the treatment condition showed a diminished testosterone response to social provocation as well as less aggressive behaviors in the PSAP task. Notably, dampened testosterone reactivity in the intervention group mediated the effect of the intervention on aggressive behavior. This suggests that psychosocial interventions in childhood may be effective in diminishing aggressive behaviors partially due to an enduring biological mechanism. Collectively, the evidence reviewed in this section suggests that acute changes in testosterone concentrations positively predict subsequent aggressive behavior in men, but not women. Consistent with these findings, our recent meta-analysis on this topic indicates that acute changes in testosterone positively map onto aggressive behavior in men ($r = .16$), but not women ($r = .01$; see Geniole et al., 2020).

Risk-Taking

Similar to research on aggression, a growing body of work indicates a relatively weak, positive correlation ($r = .12$) between baseline testosterone concentrations and risk-taking behavior (see Kurath & Mata, 2018 for review). Risk-taking can be defined as choosing activities and behaviors that are potentially rewarding and come with a significant chance of loss or harm. Testosterone has emerged in research as a potential biomarker for predicting increased risk-taking in response to competition. As with other similar behavioral traits, correlations between risk-taking and basal testosterone levels have been mixed in the literature (Apicella et al., 2008; Sapienza et al., 2009; Stanton et al., 2011).

A few studies have investigated the extent to which competition-induced changes in testosterone map onto future risk-taking behavior. Apicella et al. (2013) had male participants ($n = 49$) engage in a competitive interaction (15 rounds of rock, paper, scissors) where they won or lost a financial reward. They found a rise in testosterone in 73 percent of participants, with winners seeing a significantly larger increase in testosterone than losers. Also, they found that an increase in testosterone during the competition predicted decreased risk aversion. Building on this, researchers have also begun to consider other factors that might impact this relationship between testosterone dynamics and risk-taking behavior. Welker et al. (2017) investigated the relationship between testosterone changes and risk-taking behaviors among men ($n = 165$) while also considering individual differences in self-construal. Self-construal is the extent to which an individual considers the self as connected with others. People with an independent self-construal consider themselves relatively independent of others, whereas people with an interdependent self-construal consider themselves relatively connected to others. Results indicated that a rise in testosterone predicted increased risk-taking behavior but only among winners who scored relatively high in independent self-construal.

Mating Psychology and Behavior

In addition to competition, several studies have now demonstrated that testosterone levels rise rapidly in the context of interactions with potential mates. Roney and colleagues (2003) examined testosterone's response to potential mates using male participants ($n = 39$) assigned to one of two conditions: interaction with a male confederate or interaction with an attractive female confederate. The authors reported that testosterone levels increased by 30 percent among men interacting with the female, but not the male confederate. Moreover, the authors reported that the female confederate's ratings of the men's courtship behaviors were positively correlated with men's testosterone responses during the interaction. In a larger sample of men ($n = 99$), Roney et al. (2007) reported that men experienced a rise in testosterone concentrations when interacting with women. Furthermore, female confederates' ratings of men's extraversion and self-disclosure were positively correlated with changes in testosterone concentrations. In more recent work, Simmons and Roney (2011) demonstrated that variability in the number of cytosine-adenine-guanine (CAG) repeats within the androgen receptor (AR) gene explained variability in testosterone reactivity patterns observed in men interacting with an attractive woman. They found that men with fewer CAG repeats within the AR demonstrated a larger increase in testosterone when interacting with an attractive woman. Notably, in vitro experimental work suggests that increasing the number of CAG repeats within the AR gene (or increasing the length of the polyglutamine tract of the AR protein) leads to a reduction in the androgen receptor's transcriptional efficiency (Chamberlain et al., 1994). Examining the role of competition on subsequent mate-seeking, Van der Meij et al. (2012) had male same-sex dyads ($n = 84$) compete using a rigged computer task – 50 percent of participants were winners and 50 percent losers. After the competitive interaction, participants interacted with a male or female confederate for five minutes. Men who experienced a larger increase in testosterone during the competitive interaction smiled more, presented themselves better and made more eye contact with the female confederates, suggesting that a rise in testosterone during competition may positively modulate men's mating effort. Further, male varsity athletes ($n = 42$) from the UK competed in a rigged head-to-head indoor rowing competition—again experimentally generating winners and losers (Longman et al., 2018). Participants filled out several questionnaires, including assessments of sexual attitudes and behaviors, as well as willingness to approach different individuals, including attractive women. Individuals who experienced a rise in testosterone following a manipulated victory in the rowing competition self-reported a greater likelihood of approaching attractive women, as well as a higher self-reported propensity toward casual sex. Although research involving testosterone reactivity and behavior primarily focuses on men, some evidence suggests that women may also experience a rise in testosterone to facilitate courtship behaviors (Lopez et al., 2009). In one sample of healthy young women ($n = 120$)—70 naturally cycling and 50 taking contraceptives—were randomly selected to watch a 20-minute video clip in one of four conditions. The experimental condition involved a physically attractive man, with several attractive behavioral traits, courting a woman. The non-experimental conditions involved a nature documentary, an unattractive older man courting a woman (male control) and an attractive woman without a man (female control). Women who were naturally cycling experienced a rapid rise in testosterone when watching the experimental video, but not any of the control videos. The extent to which such rapid endogenous elevations in testosterone may facilitate female mating psychology and behavior is not yet known.

Athletic Performance

In addressing another aspect of the biosocial model of status, there is also a growing body of work exploring acute changes in testosterone during competitive events and how those changes might influence future athletic performance. Research has established that testosterone fluctuations occur in connection to competitive interactions in both males and females. There is consistent evidence showing that short-term increases in testosterone occur in anticipation of competitive events (see Casto & Edwards, 2016b for review). In addition, research suggests that testosterone fluctuations occur when measured before and after competitions, particularly sporting competitions, and that these fluctuations vary in direction and magnitude depending on the context and outcome of the competition. In relationship to competition and social status outcomes, a recent meta-analysis of this work indicated that there was a significant effect of contest outcome on testosterone changes, with winners showing more significant increases than losers (Cohen's $d = 0.20$, Geniole, Bird et al., 2017). This effect was most robust (Cohen's $d = 0.43$) for competitions that occurred outside the lab (i.e., sports competitions) compared to studies conducted in a laboratory setting (Cohen's $d = 0.08$). Recent studies have also investigated whether such acute changes in testosterone may map onto subsequent athletic performance and physical strength. Crewther and Cook (2012a) found that professional rugby players ($n = 12$) who received positive feedback from their coaches prior to a competitive interaction experienced an increase in testosterone concentrations and, subsequently, had better athletic performance. In a separate study, the authors reported that watching motivational and aggressive video clips increased testosterone concentrations and improved subsequent physical strength (in a squat performance test) (Crewther & Cook, 2012b).

Pharmacological Challenge

The previous section reviewed the evidence that competition-induced changes in testosterone may modulate future behavior. However, a limitation of this work is that it is correlational, preventing researchers from making strong claims about the causal role of testosterone in modulating such processes. Pharmacological challenge paradigms have been designed which acutely elevate testosterone concentrations to assess the extent to which such short-term changes in neuroendocrine function have any impact on human competitive, aggressive, risk-taking, and mating psychology and behavior.

Competitive Behavior

Correlational evidence reviewed previously suggests that acute fluctuations in testosterone may promote competitive motivation. Similar to the aggression work, these findings are limited by their correlational approach. Recent work has investigated the extent to which testosterone promotes competitive motivation in people using a causal approach. In one experiment with a sample of healthy young women ($n = 54$), Mehta et al. (2015) reported that administration of testosterone decreased willingness to compete after a loss, but increased willingness to compete after a victory, but only for women scoring high in trait dominance. The latter finding is consistent with correlational work in which a rise in testosterone after a victory predicted increased aggressive behavior, but only among men scoring high in trait dominance (Carré et al., 2009). In another study using a within-subject, crossover design (n = 118 men), Geniole, Proietti, et al. (2019) examined the effect of a single dose of testosterone on competitive resource division. In this task, participants had to propose how to split a separate 10 dollars for each of 20 fictitious male responders, whose faces were manipulated to appear relatively high, or low, in threat value. Participants were told that responders could either accept the proposal—in which case each player would be paid their corresponding amounts—or reject the offer—in which case each player would receive nothing (zero dollars). Participants were told their goal was to make as much money as possible, which could be achieved by offering the lowest amount to each responder, without having the offer rejected. Consistent with previous work (Geniole, MacDonell, et al., 2017), results indicated that participants ceded more resources to high vs. low threat faces, a phenomenon dubbed the "threat premium." However, testosterone reduced this threat premium by 57 percent. The results suggest that testosterone modulates competitive decision-making by recalibrating the integration of threat into the decision-making process. Also, a recent study in a sample of healthy men (n = 115) suggests that context and variability in the steroid hormone cortisol may impact the effect of testosterone on competitive behavior (Knight et al., 2022. Testosterone treatment coupled with high cortisol levels was associated with an increased preference to compete against females and to re-compete against lower status opponents (prior losers), whereas testosterone treatment coupled with low cortisol levels was associated with a preference to compete against males and to re-compete against higher status opponents (prior winners). Finally, Vermeer et al. (2020) reported that the effect of testosterone on men's competitive effort depending on the stability of the status hierarchy. Specifically, testosterone boosted competitive effort, but only when there was an opportunity to improve one's social status.

Aggressive Behavior

Testosterone's link to aggressive behavior is relatively weak and inconsistent (r = .05, see Geniole et al., 2020 for meta-analysis). However, the evidence previously discussed in this chapter suggests that acute, competition-induced changes in testosterone positively map onto future aggressive behavior in men (r = .16; see Geniole et al., 2020 for meta-analysis). Recent single-dose pharmacological challenge experiments have begun to investigate whether testosterone promotes aggression. In one experiment, a single dose of transdermal testosterone, which increased levels to the high-normal range, had a relatively weak positive effect (Cohen's d = .30) on aggression in young men (n = 120, Carré et al., 2017). Notably, in the same study, we reported that individual differences in trait dominance and self-control moderated the effect of testosterone on aggression. Specifically, testosterone increased aggressive behavior, but only among men scoring relatively high in trait dominance and/or low in self-control (Carré et al., 2017). More recently, our lab replicated and extended these findings in a larger sample (n = 308) of healthy young men. Similar to our earlier experiment, testosterone had a relatively weak positive effect on aggression. Again, we found that a single dose of testosterone increased aggressive behavior, but only in men with risky personality traits (dominant, impulsive, independent; Geniole, Procyshyn, et al., 2019). Notably, this drug x personality interaction was further moderated by variability in the number of CAG repeats within the androgen receptor. Specifically, the potentiating effects of testosterone among men with risky personality traits occurred among men with fewer CAG repeats within the AR (Geniole, Procyshyn, et al., 2019). In another experiment (n = 103), aggressive behavior was assessed in a competitive reaction time task in which participants were able to subtract money from the opponent after winning a trial. The authors reported that a single dose of testosterone did not increase aggressive behavior. However, the authors found that testosterone strengthened the effect of provocation on subsequent aggressive behavior. That is, it appeared that testosterone promoted more of a tit-for-tat strategy during the game (Wagels et al., 2018). Finally, in another experiment using a non-social provocation task indexing "implicit aggression," the authors found that a single dose of testosterone to young men (n = 90) increased self-reported anger in response to provocation. Moreover, testosterone exerted an indirect effect on implicit aggression through its effects on participants' anger. Testosterone increased state anger, which, in turn, promoted increased aggressive behavior (Panagiotidis et al., 2017).

Risk-Taking

A number of studies have investigated the role of testosterone in promoting risk-taking. In one of the earliest studies, van Honk et al. (2004) used a within-subject crossover design to demonstrate that a single dose of testosterone to women (n = 12) increased sensitivity to reward and decreased sensitivity to punishment as measured using the Iowa Gambling Task. Another experiment in women (within-subject, crossover design, n = 26), Wu et al. (2016) found that testosterone increased risk-taking behavior by reducing loss-chasing. Research in the area of financial decision-making has reported that testosterone increased economic optimism (n = 41 men; Cueva et al., 2015) and increased asset bubbles in trading markets (n = 140 men; Nadler et al., 2018). Despite these findings, other pharmacological challenge studies with both women and men have failed to document consistent effects of testosterone on various indices of risk-taking behaviors (e.g., Ortner et al., 2013; Goudriaan et al., 2010; Boksem et al., 2013; Zethraeus et al., 2009; Stanton et al., unpublished). Interestingly, one recent unpublished experiment with a sample of men (n = 166) reported that testosterone altered risk preferences for gains and losses in social rank, but not for monetary gains and losses. In particular, for high status (but not low status) men, testosterone increased risk-taking behavior to increase social rank (Vermeer et al., unpublished). The latter findings strengthen the idea that testosterone's effects on behavioral outcomes are highly dependent upon social context.

Mating Psychology and Behavior

As discussed, competition-induced changes in testosterone were positively correlated with men's mating psychology and behavior (van der Meij et al., 2012; Longman et al., 2018). Pharmacological challenge work suggests that acutely elevating testosterone may rapidly modulate men's mating psychology. For instance, across two experiments (n = 24, within-subject design; n = 93 between-subject design), Bird et al. (2016) reported that testosterone increased men's preference for feminized female faces in a short-term versus long-term relationship context. Similar work in Chinese men (n = 140) reported that testosterone increased preferences for feminized female faces (Han et al., 2020). In a recent experiment (Geniole et al., 2022) testosterone's effects on men's ratings of female facial attractiveness were modulated by relationship status and the attractiveness of the stimulus faces. Specifically, in a within-subject crossover paradigm, male participants (n = 106) received testosterone or placebo (counter-balanced) and rated emotionally neutral Caucasian female faces on attractiveness using a Likert scale (1 = not at all attractive, 7 = extremely attractive). For single men, testosterone increased ratings of attractiveness for relatively low (but not high) attractive stimulus faces. In contrast, for paired men, testosterone increased ratings of attractiveness for relatively high (but not low) attractive stimulus faces.

Summary

Collectively, the evidence reviewed in this chapter indicates that acute, competition-induced changes in testosterone may play an important role in fine-tuning ongoing and/or future behavioral outcomes, including competitiveness, aggression, risk-taking, mating psychology, and athletic performance. The single-dose pharmacological challenge work provides some (albeit mixed) evidence for the causal role of testosterone in modulating these psychological and behavioral processes.

Acknowledgement

Tracy-Lynn Reside and Brittney A. Robinson contributed equally to the preparation of this chapter.

References

Apicella, C. L., Dreber, A., & Mollerstrom, J. (2013). Salivary testosterone change following monetary wins and losses predicts future financial risk-taking. *Psychoneuroendocrinology 39*, 58–64. doi:10.1016/j.psyneuen.2013.09.025.

Apicella, C. L., Dreber, A., Campbell, B., Gray, P. B., Hoffman, M., & Little, A. C. (2008). Testosterone and financial risk preferences. *Evolution and Human Behavior 29*(6), 384–390. doi:10.1016/j.evolhumbehav.2008.07.001.

Azcoitia, I., Yague, J. G., & Garcia-Segura, L. M. (2011). Estradiol synthesis within the human brain. *Neuroscience 191*, 139–147. doi:10.1016/j.neuroscience.2011.02.012.

Baron, R. A., & Richardson, D. R. (1994). *Human aggression*. 2nd ed. Plenum Press.

Berkowitz, L., & Lepage, A. (1967). Weapons as aggression-eliciting stimuli. *Journal of Personality and Social Psychology 7*(2, Pt.1), 202–207. doi:10.1037/h0025008.

Bettencourt, B. A., & Kernahan, C. (1997). A meta-analysis of aggression in the presence of violent cues: Effects of gender differences and aversive provocation. *Aggressive Behavior 23*(6), 447–456. doi:10.1002/(SICI)1098-2337(1997)23:6<447::AID-AB4>3.0.CO;2-D.

Bird, B. M., Welling, L. L. M., Ortiz, T. L., Moreau, B. J. P., Hansen, S., Emond, M., . . . Carré, J. M. (2016). Effects of exogenous testosterone and mating context on men's preferences for female facial femininity. *Hormones and Behavior 85*, 76–85. doi:10.1016/j.yhbeh.2016.08.003.

Boksem, M. A. S., Mehta, P. H., Van den Bergh, B., van Son, V., Trautmann, S. T., Roelofs, K., . . . Sanfey, A. G. (2013). Testosterone inhibits trust but promotes reciprocity. *Psychological Science 24*(11), 2306–2314. doi:10.1177/0956797613495063.

Bos, P. A., Panksepp, J., Bluthé, R. M., & Honk, J. V. (2012). Acute effects of steroid hormones and neuropeptides on human social-emotional behavior: A review of single administration studies. *Frontiers in Neuroendocrinology 33*, 17–35. doi:10.1016/j.yfrne.2011.01.002.

Carré, J. M., & McCormick, C. M. (2008). Aggressive behavior and change in salivary testosterone concentrations predict willingness to engage in a competitive task. *Hormones and Behavior 54*(3), 403–409. doi:10.1016/j.yhbeh.2008.04.008.

Carré, J. M., & Olmstead, N. A. (2015). Social neuroendocrinology of human aggression: Examining the role of competition-induced testosterone dynamics. *Neuroscience 286*, 171–186. doi:10.1016/j.neuroscience.2014.11.029.

Carré, J. M., Campbell, J. A., Lozoya, E., Goetz, S. M. M., & Welker, K. M. (2013). Changes in testosterone mediate the effect of winning on subsequent aggressive behaviour. *Psychoneuroendocrinology 38*(10), 2034–2041. doi:10.1016/j.psyneuen.2013.03.008.

Carré, J. M., Geniole, S. N., Ortiz, T. L., Bird, B. M., Videto, A., & Bonin, P. L. (2017). Exogenous testosterone rapidly increases aggressive behavior in dominant and impulsive men. *Biological Psychiatry 82*(4), 249–256. doi:10.1016/j.biopsych.2016.06.009.

Carré, J. M., Iselin, A. R., Welker, K. M., Hariri, A. R., & Dodge, K. A. (2014). Testosterone reactivity to provocation mediates the effect of early intervention on aggressive behavior. *Psychological Science 25*(5), 1140–1146. doi:10.1177/0956797614525642.

Carré, J. M., Putnam, S. K., & McCormick, C. M. (2009). Testosterone responses to competition predict future aggressive behaviour at a cost to reward in men. *Psychoneuroendocrinology 34*(4), 561–570. doi:10.1016/j.psyneuen.2008.10.018.

Casto, K. V., & Edwards, D. (2016a). Testosterone and reconciliation among women: After-competition testosterone predicts prosocial attitudes towards opponents. *Adaptive Human Behavior and Physiology 2*(3), 220–233. doi:10.1007/s40750-015-0037-1.

Casto, K. V., & Edwards, D. A. (2016b). Testosterone, cortisol, and human competition. *Hormones and Behavior 82*, 21–37. doi:10.1016/j.yhbeh.2016.04.004.

Casto, K. V., & Prasad, S. (2017). Recommendations for the study of women in hormones and competition research. *Hormones and Behavior 92*, 190–194. doi:10.1016/j.yhbeh.2017.05.009.

Casto, K. V., Edwards, D. A., Akinola, M., Davis, C., & Mehta, P. H. (2020). Testosterone reactivity to competition and competitive endurance in men and women. *Hormones and Behavior 123*, 104665. doi:10.1016/j.yhbeh.2019.104665.

Chamberlain, N. L., Driver, E. D., & Miesfeld, R. L. (1994). The length and location of CAG trinucleotide repeats in the androgen receptor N-terminal domain affect transactivation function. *Nucleic Acids Research 22*(15), 3181–3186. doi:10.1093/nar/22.15.3181.

Clavijo, R. I., & Hsiao, W. (2018). Update on male reproductive endocrinology. *Translational Andrology and Urology 7*(S3), S367–S372. doi:10.21037/tau.2018.03.25.

Crewther, B. T., & Cook, C. J. (2012)a. Effects of different post-match recovery interventions on subsequent athlete hormonal state and game performance. *Physiology & Behavior, 106*(4), 471–475. doi:10.1016/j.physbeh.2012.03.015

Crewther, B. T., & Cook, C. J. (2012)b. Changes in salivary testosterone concentrations and subsequent voluntary squat performance following the presentation of short video clips. *Hormones and Behavior, 61*(1), 17–22. doi:10.1016/j.yhbeh.2011.09.006

Cueva, C., Roberts, R. E., Spencer, T., Rani, N., Tempest, M., Tobler, P. N., . . . Rustichini, A. (2015). Cortisol and testosterone increase financial risk taking and may destabilize markets. *Scientific Reports 5*(1), 11206. doi:10.1038/srep11206.

Geen, R. G. (1990). *Human aggression.* Thomson Brooks/Cole Publishing Co.

Geniole, S. N., Bird, B. M., McVittie, J. S., Purcell, R. B., Archer, J., & Carré, J. M. (2020). Is testosterone linked to human aggression? A meta-analytic examination of the relationship between baseline, dynamic, and manipulated testosterone on human aggression. *Hormones and Behavior 123*, 104644. doi:10.1016/j.yhbeh.2019.104644.

Geniole, S. N., Bird, B. M., Ruddick, E. L., & Carré, J. M. (2017). Effects of competition outcome on testosterone concentrations in humans: An updated meta-analysis. *Hormones and Behavior 92*, 37–50. doi:10.1016/j.yhbeh.2016.10.002.

Geniole, S. N., MacDonell, E. T., & McCormick, C. M. (2017). The threat premium in economic bargaining. *Evolution and Human Behavior 38*(5), 572–582. doi:10.1016/j.evolhumbehav.2016.12.004.

Geniole, S. N., Procyshyn, T. L., Marley, N., Ortiz, T. L., Bird, B. M., Marcellus, A. L., Carré, J. M. (2019). Using a psychopharmacogenetic approach to identify the pathways through which—and the people for whom—testosterone promotes aggression. *Psychological Science 30*(4), 481–494. doi:10.1177/0956797619826970.

Geniole, S. N., Proietti, V., Bird, B. M., Ortiz, T. L., Bonin, P. L., Goldfarb, B., Carré, J. M. (2019). Testosterone reduces the threat premium in competitive resource division. *Proceedings of the Royal Society B: Biological Sciences 286*(1903), 20190720. doi:10.1098/rspb.2019.0720.

Geniole, S. N., Proietti, V., Robinson, B. A., Bird, B. M., Watson, N. V., Bonin, P. L., Goldbarb, B., & Carré, J. M. (2022). Relatively rapid effects of testosterone on men's ratings of female attractiveness depend on relationship status and the attractiveness of stimulus faces. *Hormones and Behavior*, 142. doi: 10.1016/j.yhbeh.2022.105174.

Geniole, S. N., & Carré, J. M. (2018). Human social neuroendocrinology: review of the rapid effects of testosterone. *Hormones and behavior, 104*, 192–205.

Goudriaan, A. E., Lapauw, B., Ruige, J., Feyen, E., Kaufman, J., Brand, M., & Vingerhoets, G. (2010). The influence of high-normal testosterone levels on risk-taking in healthy males in a 1-week letrozole administration study. *Psychoneuroendocrinology 35*(9), 1416–1421. doi:10.1016/j.psyneuen.2010.04.005.

Han, C., Zhang, Y., Lei, X., Li, X., Morrison, E. R., & Wu, Y. (2020). Single dose testosterone administration increases men's facial femininity preference in a Chinese population. *Psychoneuroendocrinology 115*, 104630. doi:10.1016/j.psyneuen.2020.104630.

Ketterson, E. D., & Nolan Jr., V. (1992). *Hormones and life histories: An integrative approach.* University of Chicago Press.

Klinesmith, J., Kasser, T., & McAndrew, F. T. (2006). Guns, testosterone, and aggression: An experimental test of a mediational hypothesis. *Psychological Science 17*(7), 568–571. doi:10.1111/j.1467-9280.2006.01745.x.

Kordsmeyer, T. L., & Penke, L. (2019). Effects of male testosterone and its interaction with cortisol on self- and observer-rated personality states in a competitive mating context. *Journal of Research in Personality 78*, 76–92. doi:10.1016/j.jrp.2018.11.001.

Kuiri-Hänninen, T., Sankilampi, U., & Dunkel, L. (2014). Activation of the hypothalamic-pituitary-gonadal axis in infancy: Minipuberty. *Hormone Research in Paediatrics 82*(2), 73–80. doi:10.1159/000362414.

Knight, E.L., MNorales, P.J., Christian, C.B., Prasad, S., Harbaugh, W.T., Mehta, P.J., & Mayr, U (2022). The causal effect of testosterone on men's competitive beavior is moderated by basal cortisol and cues to an opponent's status: Evidence for a context-dependent dural-hormone hypothesis. *Journal of Personality and Social Psychology 123* (4), 693–716. doi: 10.1037/pspa0000305.

Kurath, J., & Mata, R. (2018). Individual differences in risk taking and endogeneous levels of testosterone, estradiol, and cortisol: A systematic literature search and three independent meta-analyses. *Neuroscience & Biobehavioral Reviews 90*, 428–446. doi:10.1016/j.neubiorev.2018.05.003.

Lieberman, J. D., Solomon, S., Greenberg, J., & McGregor, H. A. (1999). A hot new way to measure aggression: Hot sauce allocation. *Aggressive Behavior 25*(5), 331–348. doi:10.1002/(SICI)1098-2337(1999)25:5<331::AID-AB2>3.0.CO;2-1.

Longman, D. P., Surbey, M. K., Stock, J. T., & Wells, J. C. K. (2018). Tandem androgenic and psychological shifts in male reproductive effort following a manipulated "win" or "loss" in a sporting competition. *Human Nature 29*(3), 283–310. doi:10.1007/s12110-018-9323-5.

López, H. H., Hay, A. C., & Conklin, P. H. (2009). Attractive men induce testosterone and cortisol release in women. *Hormones and Behavior 56*(1), 84–92. doi:10.1016/j.yhbeh.2009.03.004.

Mazur, A. (1985). A biosocial model of status in face-to-face primate groups. *Social Forces 64*(2), 377–402. doi:10.2307/2578647.

Mehta, P. H., & Josephs, R. A. (2006). Testosterone change after losing predicts the decision to compete again. *Hormones and Behavior 50*(5), 684–692. doi:10.1016/j.yhbeh.2006.07.001.

Mehta, P. H., Snyder, N. A., Knight, E. L., & Lassetter, B. (2014). Close versus decisive victory moderates the effect of testosterone change on competitive decisions and task enjoyment. *Adaptive Human Behavior and Physiology 3*(1), 291–311. doi:10.1007/s40750-014-0014-0.

Mehta, P. H., van Son, V., Welker, K. M., Prasad, S., Sanfey, A. G., Smidts, A., & Roelofs, K. (2015). Exogenous testosterone in women enhances and inhibits competitive decision-making depending on victory-defeat experience and trait dominance. *Psychoneuroendocrinology 60*, 224–236. doi:10.1016/j.psyneuen.2015.07.004.

Molnar, C., & Gair, J. (2019). Section 24.4: Hormonal control of human reproduction. In C. Molnar and J. Gair (Eds.), Concepts of Biology. 1st Cdn ed. BCcampus Open Publishing. https://opentextbc.ca/biology/chapter/24-4-hormonal-control-of-human-reproduction/.

Nadler, A., Jiao, P., Johnson, C., Alexander, V., & Zak, P. J. (2018). The bull of wall street: Experimental analysis of testosterone and asset trading. *Management Science 64*(9), 4032–4051. https://doi.org/10.1287/mnsc.2017.2836.

Ortner, G. R., Wibral, M., Becker, A., Dohmen, T., Klingmüller, D., Falk, A., & Weber, B. (2013). No evidence for an effect of testosterone administration on delay discounting in male university students. *Psychoneuroendocrinology 38*(9), 1814–1818. doi:10.1016/j.psyneuen.2012.12.014.

Panagiotidis, D., Clemens, B., Habel, U., Schneider, F., Schneider, I., Wagels, L., & Votinov, M. (2017). Exogenous testosterone in a non-social provocation paradigm potentiates anger but not behavioral aggression. *European Neuropsychopharmacology: The Journal of the European College of Neuropsychopharmacology 27*(11), 1172–1184. doi:10.1016/j.euroneuro.2017.07.006.

Roney, J. R., Lukaszewski, A. W., & Simmons, Z. L. (2007). Rapid endocrine responses of young men to social interactions with young women. *Hormones and Behavior 52*(3), 326–333. doi:10.1016/j.yhbeh.2007.05.008.

Roney, J. R., Mahler, S. V., & Maestripieri, D. (2003). Behavioral and hormonal responses of men to brief interactions with women. *Evolution and Human Behavior 24*(6), 365–375. doi:10.1016/S1090-5138(03)00053-9.

Sapienza, P., Zingales, L., & Maestripieri, D. (2009). Gender differences in financial risk aversion and career choices are affected by testosterone. *Proceedings of the National Academy of Sciences of the United States of America 106*(36), 15268–15273. doi:10.1073/pnas.0907352106.

Selvaraj, V., & Koganti, P. P. (2018). Eat, drink, and be merry: Leydig cell autophagy in testosterone production. *Biology of Reproduction 99*(6), 1113–1115. doi:10.1093/biolre/ioy153.

Simmons, Z. L., & Roney, J. R. (2011). Variation in CAG repeat length of the androgen receptor gene predicts variables associated with intrasexual competitiveness in human males. *Hormones and Behavior 60*(3), 306–312. doi:10.1016/j.yhbeh.2011.06.006.

Stanton, S. J., Liening, S. H., & Schultheiss, O. C. (2011). Testosterone is positively associated with risk taking in the Iowa gambling task. *Hormones and Behavior 59*(2), 252–256. doi:10.1016/j.yhbeh.2010.12.003.

Stanton, S. J., Welker, K. M., & Carré, J. M. (unpublished). The effects of testosterone on economic risk-taking and temporal discounting.

van der Meij, L., Almela, M., Buunk, A. P., Fawcett, T. W., & Salvador, A. (2012). Men with elevated testosterone levels show more affiliative behaviours during interactions with women. *Proceedings of the Royal Society. B, Biological Sciences 279*(1726), 202–208. doi:10.1098/rspb.2011.0764.

van Honk, J., Schutter, Dennis J. L. G., Hermans, E. J., Putman, P., Tuiten, A., & Koppeschaar, H. (2004). Testosterone shifts the balance between sensitivity for punishment and reward in healthy young women. *Psychoneuroendocrinology 29*(7), 937–943. doi:10.1016/j.psyneuen.2003.08.007.

Vermeer, A. L., Boksem, M., Gausterer, C., Eisenegger, C., & Lamm, C. (unpublished). Testosterone increases risk-taking for status but not for money. *PsyArXiv*. 10.31234/osf.io/eu8jm.

Vermeer, A. L., Krol, I., Gausterer, C., Wagner, B., Eisenegger, C., & Lamm, C. (2020). Exogenous testosterone increases status-seeking motivation in men with unstable low social status. *Psychoneuroendocrinology 113*, 104552.

Wagels, L., Votinov, M., Kellermann, T., Eisert, A., Beyer, C., & Habel, U. (2018). Exogenous testosterone enhances the reactivity to social provocation in males. *Frontiers in Behavioral Neuroscience 12*, 37. doi:10.3389/fnbeh.2018.00037.

Welker KM, Norman RE, Goetz SMM, Moreau BJP, Kitayama S & Carré JM (2017). Preliminary evidence that testosterone's association with aggression depends on self-construal. *Hormones and Behavior, 92*, 117–127.

Wingfield, J. C., Hegner, R. E., Dufty, A. M., & Ball, G. F. (1990). The "challenge hypothesis": Theoretical implications for patterns of testosterone secretion, mating systems, and breeding strategies. *The American Naturalist 136*(6), 829–846. doi:10.1086/285134.

Wu, Y., Liu, J., Qu, L., Eisenegger, C., Clark, L., & Zhou, X. (2016). Single dose testosterone administration reduces loss chasing in healthy females. *Psychoneuroendocrinology 71*, 54–57. doi:10.1016/j.psyneuen.2016.05.005.

Zethraeus, N., Kocoska-Maras, L., Ellingsen, T., von Schoultz, B., Hirschberg, A. L., & Johannesson, M. (2009). A randomized trial of the effect of estrogen and testosterone on economic behavior. *Proceedings of the National Academy of Sciences—PNAS 106*(16), 6535–6538. doi:10.1073/pnas.0812757106.

Zilioli, S., & Watson, N. V. (2014). Testosterone across successive competitions: Evidence for a "winner effect" in humans? *Psychoneuroendocrinology 47*, 1–9. doi:10.1016/j.psyneuen.2014.05.001.

Biological Sex Differences and Competition

Alicia Salvador, Vanesa Hidalgo, Raquel Costa, *and* Esperanza González-Bono

Abstract

There is evidence of the existence of biological differences between males and females at multiple levels. Sex differences are shown in both genotypic and phenotypic dimensions in almost all species. Body differences are apparent, but differences in many other systems, including the neuro-endocrine-immune system, are also very important and related to evolutionary aims. Brain differences have been reported in recent decades in numerous structures, neurotransmitters, pathways, etc. These differences are reflected in behavioral and other cognitive and affective processes that have attracted considerable attention from researchers and the general public. Some of the clearest behavioral differences are aggressive and violent behavior, spatial orientation, mathematics and language skills, and other differences related to reactivity to stress. Agonistic or competitive behavior has been studied for decades, particularly in males in many different species, including humans, although more recently interest in female intrasexual competition has increased. Several differences in the competitive behavior of men and women, as well as in the underlying mechanisms, have begun to be established, mainly related, at least partially, to biological and social dimensions. In this chapter, the authors will review results found in the research on the biological basis of sex differences and its impact on competition.

Key Words: seuxal selection, sex differentiation, sexual dimorphism, sex hormones, competition effect, winner effect, cognitive appraisal, attribution, self-efficacy

This chapter explores the biological bases of sex differences and their impact on competitive behavior. In recent decades, the importance of sex differences has increasingly been recognized in both research and social contexts. The different prevalence rates of many serious diseases (cardiovascular, cancer, autoimmune, and neurodegenerative, among others) and affective and mental disorders (such as depression or schizophrenia) have probably played an important role. Thus, physical and mental health differences stemming from being a man or a woman are now socially acknowledged. Hence, there is a need to study these sex differences, not only to gain basic knowledge, but also for purposes of diagnosis and treatment, as in the case of pharmacological interventions. Consequently, there is a strong movement to study sex differences in both animals and humans, as well as several criteria for research funding and publishing (Lee, 2018).

Striking differences between males and females of the same species are commonplace in nature. Here we focus our attention on the biological basis of sex differences in humans. It is necessary to consider the presence and complex measurement of these differences, but also their origin and evolution. Furthermore, we have to keep in mind that sex differences and their underlying biological mechanisms are developed throughout the life span due to physical and social influences. Thus, it is worth noting that sex differences are the result of both evolutionary and ontogenetic forces acting on each individual. Due to the complexity of human social structures and the importance of the community and culture, it is necessary to think about these differences as gender differences. However, although human cultural history and social rules add many elements to these differences, they are built on basic biological mechanisms similar to those of other species. Here we focus particularly on the biological bases, but without forgetting the importance of the social and cultural influences or the fact that sex differences suffer dramatic changes across the life cycle.

The chapter is organized in six parts. The first three are more generally about sex differences susceptible to modifying psychological aspects associated with competitive behavior. First, we will address the reasons for these differences and their evolutionary meaning. Second, we will briefly present the process and the main hormones that contribute to sexual differentiation and then consider some different changes across the life cycle. Third, we will describe the organizational and activational effects of hormones, as well as the critical periods for sexual differentiation. Fourth, we will review the brain features as well as the main cognitive, affective, and behavioral differences resulting from sexual differentiation. Fifth, we will mention the main results obtained by our research group and other research groups using contests such as sports competitions and laboratory studies as a model for social behavior, focusing on the sex of the participants. Finally, we will provide a summary of the main ideas and conclusions about this topic.

Introduction

Competition plays a central role in the evolutionist approach to understanding human life. From this theoretical perspective, natural selection can be characterized as competition between phenotypes, with those able to best adapt to the changing environmental conditions prevailing. Competition is also a key concept in understanding the organization of social species that usually face scarce resources. It is closely related to social dominance, hierarchy, and status, with different types of behaviors displayed by individuals of different sexes.

Sex differences are ultimately the product of evolution. Evolutionary advantages of sexual reproduction mainly stem from their contribution to genetic variation, increasing the possibility of adapting to changing circumstances. In fact, *natural selection* depends on the relationship between this variation, resulting in part from genetic mutations and sexual reproduction, and the chances of surviving to adulthood and successfully reproducing. Differences among individuals in traits relevant for survival or reproduction are influenced by genetic factors and subjected to evolutionary dynamics within micro- and macro-evolutionary processes.

In addition to natural selection, Darwin (1871) proposed the concept of *sexual selection* to explain the evolutionary origins of sex differences. Darwin argued that fundamental differences in the reproductive interests of the sexes result in sharp differences in the strength and direction of both sexual and natural selection in males and females. These arguments were later elaborated on by Bateman (1948), Trivers (1972), and others. Their contributions resulted in a paradigmatic view of the evolution of sexual dimorphism rooted in *anisogamy*, which implies the union or fusion of two gametes that differ in size and/or form. According to this view, the divergent gamete investment strategies that define the sexes directly affect divergent degrees of mating, competition, parental care, and other aspects of life, leading to sex differences in the selection that promote the evolution of *sexual dimorphism*. Thus, sexual selection is considered a major source driving the sexual dimorphism observed in behavioral, morphological, physiological, and life history traits (Hedrick & Temeles, 1989). The *Darwin–Bateman–Trivers Paradigm* has had a great impact on scientific research, as well as on social and cultural contexts. We will briefly review some important aspects of this paradigm.

In *The Descent of Man and Selection in Relation to Sex*, Darwin (1871) presented the main principles of *sexual selection* to explain the evolution of some "secondary" sexual characteristics as a result of intrasexual competition. Darwin divided sexual selection into two processes: male–male competition and female choice. He also argued that males are typically eager to copulate, whereas females are choosy about who to mate with (known as the "ardent male–coy female hypothesis"). Several decades later, Bateman (1948) proposed the ultimate reasons for this sex difference in mating propensity. He demonstrated that, in fruit flies, reproductive fitness and mating success are more variable in males than in females ("Bateman's principle," as it was called by Wilson, 1975). In contrast, the fertility of females showed little increase as a function of the number of copulations (the "Bateman gradient"). Bateman suggested that the greater action of sexual selection on males was due to sex differences in the cost of producing gametes. The "*variability hypothesis*" or "*greater male variability hypothesis*" has been widely supported and often discussed with regard to several traits, including cognitive function.

As mentioned above, Darwin described sexual selection based on two principles: males tend to compete, and females tend to be choosy. Nearly 100 years later, Trivers (1972) proposed that the bias toward competition or choice is linked to the parental investment in each sex. Thus, the sex that provides more than his or her share of parental investment is an important reproductive resource for members of the opposite sex. The result is competition among members of the lower-investing sex (typically males) over the parental investment of members of the higher-investing sex (typically females). Because sexual selection is believed to act more strongly in males, some characteristics (such as size, health, and strength) would be more important for reproductive success in males than in females. Thus, Trivers expanded the theoretical framework by implicating the relative parental investment of the sexes as the driving force in sexual selection.

The Darwin–Bateman–Trivers paradigm is extensively invoked to explain conventional sex roles; however, it has also been recognized that sex differences are more complex than initially suggested (Dewsbury, 2005). It has been claimed that the procedure of sexual selection and, particularly, the intrasexual competition in females, deserves more research attention (Clutton-Brock, 2007). In fact, some strong criticisms have been made by some evolutionary biologists, such as Joan Roughgarden, in her article "Challenging Darwin's Theory of Sexual Selection" (2007), who proposed that *social selection* should replace sexual selection. However, other researchers defend Darwin's concept of conventional sex roles as accurate, and they refute criticisms of sexual selection theory (Janicke et al., 2016). Thus, although this paradigm forms the cornerstone of modern sexual selection theory, at least several aspects are being debated, particularly since 2004 (Hoquet, 2020).

Some relevant criticisms come from studies on primates because the Darwin–Bateman–Trivers paradigm focused on species in which sexual activity is tightly linked to female fertility and limited behavioral flexibility. In primates, there is a decoupling of sex and fertility, and most females accept costs, such as lengthy gestation and prolonged periods of lactation and infant dependency. Male primates display behaviors related to protecting, adopting, carrying, playing with, and grooming infants, which are very different from those shown by males of other species. Furthermore, a clear distinction between male competition and female choice is more difficult due to the complex social organization. Because both sexes display dominance hierarchies, social status is likely to confer reproductive benefits to both males and females. In addition, social dynamics often include cooperative behaviors and even coalitions to compete for resource control or social influence (West-Eberhard, 1983). In their review, Drea (2005) highlighted numerous disparities between the sex behavioral differences predicted by the Darwin–Bateman paradigm and the actual sex roles displayed in primates.

In any case, the Darwin–Bateman–Trivers paradigm explained that both sexes are subject to different selection pressures that lead to conventional *sex roles*. The subsequent evolution of sex differences leads to improving the survival of species whose members are organized in groups, with the distribution of roles among individuals depending on their sex and status. Thus, the relevance of *social selection* pressures has gradually been recognized. For instance, competition among members of the same species can result in selection acting on traits that facilitate this competition, to the extent that these traits are evolvable and influence survival or reproductive prospects.

An important perspective stems from emerging work on the importance of ecology in mediating evolutionary conflicts between the sexes, the role of sex differences, and the importance of competition as an evolutionary driver of phenotypic diversity. Ecological sexual dimorphisms are thought to be a by-product of either sexual selection and divergent gamete investment or of competition-driven niche partitioning between the sexes (*ecological character displacement, ECD theory*). From this point of view, sexual dimorphism in ecologically relevant traits can evolve purely through competition between the sexes for a shared resource (*resource competition*). Recently, De Lisle (2019) argued that embracing the non-exclusivity of causal models of sexual dimorphism may provide insight into the evolution of sex differences. He defended the idea that integrating the two models of sexual dimorphism may be the key to fully understanding the origins and consequences of ecological differences between the sexes. Thus, currently, the idea that resource competition-driven, sexually antagonistic selection may align with other sources of sex-biased selection, such as sexual selection, may have important implications for studies of sexual dimorphism at higher levels of biological organization.

Finally, it is important to note that distal evolutionary mechanisms, such as sexual selection, parental investment, or resource competition, and more proximate and malleable biosocial and sociocultural factors, are not mutually exclusive. Complementing these positions, therefore, *the life history theory* (Hawley, 1999) explains the intermediate mechanisms governing the evolution and manifestation of gender relations in various ecological and social environments. Overall, theories of sexual selection, social selection, and organization, as well as theories of life history, state that evolution has shaped the male and female brain, body, and behavior differently to make them good competitors. However, it is also important to take into account that sex-role flexibility may differ in different species and in different circumstances within species. Therefore, re-evaluation of previous knowledge is important and likely to yield a more complex and comprehensive perspective.

From genetic and hormonal bases involved in the early development of individual and group behavior, multiple factors influence each stage and have overlapping effects. In the next section, we will look at these first levels briefly.

Characteristics and Functioning of the Sex Hormones

The study of competitive behavior from a psychobiological perspective has focused mainly on sexual hormones. Endocrine effects on tissues and behaviors are based on and conditioned by chemical properties and multiple regulation levels. This section contains a brief description of sex hormones, from chemical features, the hormone axis, and receptors to biological effects and functions.

Sex hormone is a functional label that comprises two families of steroid hormones especially involved in the development of secondary sexual characteristics and behaviors of sexually dimorphic species: in females, the estrogens, and in males, the androgens. This classical conception of a single correspondence between a hormone and a function is not realistic in light of current knowledge. Adequate levels of different hormones are needed for the optimal development of a function in both sexes. Furthermore, a hormone contributes to different processes, and a process should be influenced by several hormones, with complex interactions among them. Sex hormones, for example, contribute to neural development, phenotypic sex determination, behavior, and private processes such as cognition and emotion.

This variety of effects at different levels is mainly possible due to cellular actions and chemical properties that sex hormones share with other steroid hormones. Thus, a brief overview of steroid hormones is necessary to understand the mechanisms involved in the trajectory between hormones and functions.

Steroid hormones are important regulators of sex differences, among other processes such as metabolism, development, physiology, and behavior. In mammalians, they are families of hormones that can be classified as estrogens, androgens, progestins, mineralocorticoids, glucocorticoids, and vitamin D, including their metabolites. Thus, briefly, progestins are essential for reproduction; mineralocorticoids regulate renal sodium; glucocorticoids exert effects on carbohydrate metabolism and are related to stress processes; and the vitamin-D hormone is important for the regulation of calcium and phosphorus homeostasis, bone growth, and development. Finally, androgens and estrogens will be the focus of this chapter.

Steroid hormones receive this label due to their common chemical composition, esters, usually derived from an acid in which at least one –OH group is replaced by an –O-alkyl group. Their common precursor is cholesterol (with 27 carbon atoms), and they differ in the pattern of bonds within the rings and side chains through chemical alterations, such as isomerization, aromatization, dehydrogenation, and fission in the ring structure, and modifications such as hydroxylation in the side chains of the cholesterol. Cholesterol is converted to pregnenolone in the mitochondria of secretory cells in endocrine glands, catalyzed by the CYP11A1 enzyme, which is the immediate precursor of the synthesis of all the steroids. The following reactions, until the origin of each steroid, are catalyzed by specific enzymes present in the endocrine gland that synthesizes each steroid, such as lyases, dehydrogenases and isomerases, aromatase enzyme, and hydroxylases.

In the case of the androgens (19 carbon atoms), they are mainly synthesized by the testes in males and, to a lesser degree, but not less important, by the adrenal cortex in both males and females. Female androgens can also proceed from the ovaries, from the placenta, and from peripheral conversion, although the total circulating concentration of androgens is much lower than in men. In the order of androgenic activity, androgens are 5α-dihydrotestosterone (5α-DHT), testosterone (T), androstanediol, androstenedione, androsterone, and dehydroepiandrosterone (DHEA). Testes are composed of convoluted tubes, called seminiferous tubules, and connective tissue. Seminiferous tubules include two types of cells, Sertoli and Leydig cells. Sertoli cells are involved in spermatogenesis and secretion of 5α-DHT. Leydig cells are responsible for T production from cholesterol, which is converted into pregnenolone in their cellular mitochondria. Afterward, pregnenolone will suffer successive conversions into progesterone and androstenedione before the T secretion that will diffuse out of the Leydig cells to interstitial space and peripheral circulation.

In the case of the estrogens (18 carbon atoms), they include estradiol, estriol, and estrone and are mainly synthesized in the ovarian follicle, but also the corpus luteum and the fetal-placental system, and the adrenal cortex can produce them in lower quantities. In the ovarian follicle, the theca cells express the enzymes to convert cholesterol into androgens, which are aromatized (conversion catalyzed by the aromatase enzyme) to estradiol by the granulose cells. This production involves more than 95 percent of the circulating estradiol and explains the fact that the blood concentration of this hormone in females is much higher than in males. In males, the estrogens proceed from the adrenal cortex, which can also generate small quantities of estrone from androstenedione (an androgen) in both males and females and through aromatization of androgens.

To produce sex hormones, the most important endocrine glands, testes in males and ovaries in females, are stimulated by specific peptide hormones called gonadotropins: luteinizing hormone (LH) and follicle-stimulating hormone (FSH). In turn, these peptides are secreted into the blood circulation by the adenohypophysis when it is stimulated by pulsatile secretion of the hypothalamic gonadotropin-releasing hormone (GnRH) every 60 to 90 minutes. The frequency of the pulses determines the ratio of production of LH and FSH. Although gonads of both sexes are the main target organs of the gonadotropins, the mechanisms of steroidogenesis present certain particularities in the testes and the ovaries. In the testes, the target cells of LH are Leydig cells, which, in response to the stimulation, secrete T, whereas Sertoli cells are the target of FSH. In the ovaries, LH facilitates the conversion of cholesterol to androgens in the theca cells, whereas FSH favors the aromatization of androgens (androstenedione and T) to estrogens (estrone and estradiol) in the granulosa cells (Neal, 2016).

Once in the bloodstream, like all steroids, sex hormones are insoluble in an aqueous medium such as plasma. Thus, approximately 97 to 98 percent of the hormone is transported bound to plasma proteins, called hormone-binding globulins. The other two to three percent of the hormones can circulate freely as the biologically active portion of hormones with the capability of going into the cells. The use of binding globulins to transport hormones provides their itinerant storage, which hampers oscillations in the free hormonal concentration. For sex hormones, the binding globulins used as a carrier are nonspecific, as in the case of albumin, and specific to sex hormones, called the sex hormone-binding globulin (SHBG). SHBG is produced by the liver and binds approximately 44 percent of total T, dihydrotestosterone, and approximately 20 percent of total estradiol (Bikle, 2021). Different conditions could affect SHBG levels, including other hormones and proinflammatory cytokines of the immune system. Recent research suggests that SHBG has a more relevant role than that of a carrier because its levels have been related to diseases in the male and female reproductive system (Wang et al., 2020; Zhu et al., 2019, respectively).

The circulation of hormones in the bloodstream provides them with the possibility of having a wide range of effects. Overall, sex hormones promote four types of effects: (a) growth and differentiation of reproductive organs; (b) anabolic effects on skeletal, muscle, subcutaneous fat distribution, and sexual organs; (c) development of male and female secondary sexual characteristics, from the growth of external genitalia to hair distribution; and (d) actions in the central nervous system differentiating the cortex, neural tissue, and initiation of puberty. For the development of these functions, hormonal actions reach cells and tissues of the whole organism, but they only exert their effects on cells and tissues with specific receptors for that hormone, the target cells and tissues of this hormone.

The steroid receptors are soluble proteins with molecular weights ranging between 50 and 94 kDa. Their main functional characteristic is that they are located inside the target cells, in the cellular cytoplasm and nucleus. There are two types of sex hormone receptors for estrogens, estrogen receptor alpha (ERα) and beta (ERβ), and one type for androgens (AR). The lipophilic nature of the sex hormones means that, when they have been liberated from their carrier protein, they easily diffuse throughout the cellular membranes, both external and nuclear membranes, searching for unoccupied receptors in the cytoplasm or, if not, in the nucleus. Inside the cell, they bond to their specific receptor, forming an active hormone-receptor complex that interacts with DNA. The outcome of this interaction is the transcription of mRNA, which provokes the synthesis of new proteins in the cellular cytoplasm to produce a biological response. Thus, a hormone may modulate around 300 genes in the organism, although, in a specific cell, only a few genes can be regulated (Wierman, 2007). This classical model of cell action of steroids was referred to as "genomic action." However, more recent research suggests that steroids can also exert so-called "non-genomic actions" on cells. This idea was supported by the findings for other receptors that can also be involved in correct transcriptional activation or repression. Among them, receptors of other hormones have been proposed as mediators, the class II receptors (e.g., vitamin D and thyroid hormone receptors) as well as orphan receptors (e.g., steroidogenic factor-1 and estrogen-related receptor), although the action mechanisms have not been completely clarified (Wierman, 2007). Once the effects take place, inactivation of the steroids occurs mainly in the liver, and metabolites are excreted by the urine.

Apart from the biological effects of circulating hormones on the tissues, endocrine levels contribute to maintaining the subtle equilibrium of secretions acting as key agents in hormonal regulation through down-to-up mechanisms. In males, circulating T exerts a negative feedback loop, inhibiting LH release by the hypophysis and the hypothalamic GnRH. Curiously, this inhibitory effect is mediated by estradiol. The regulation of FSH release is mainly performed by the inhibin secreted in Sertoli cells, as an inhibitory factor, and the activin, as a stimulating factor. In females, estradiol enhances the release of LH and inhibits FSH secretion along with inhibins. However, this pattern of influences changes throughout the menstrual cycle because high levels of progesterone, characteristic of the post-ovulation phase, inhibit LH secretion but favor FSH production. Inhibin production by granulosa cells of the mature follicles also contributes to the modulation of

FSH, provoking oscillations in the levels of this gonadotropin between the follicular and luteal phases (Molina, 2013).

Classically, androgens have been labeled "male" hormones and estrogens "female" hormones. However, in light of the current knowledge, this is a very simplistic view. Recent research in patients with deficiencies in the androgen or estrogen hormone and the development of animal models provide evidence of complex, but not completely clear, interactions between the two types of hormones in a promising field of study. Men and women need optimal levels of both androgens and estrogens to regulate critical biological and pathological processes, albeit in different quantities (Hammes & Levin, 2019). This supply is ensured by biochemical reactions, mainly aromatization, and it has important implications for the receptor actions on cells and functions. Aromatization is the irreversible conversion of androgen into estrogen, catalyzed by the aromatase enzyme. This enzyme belongs to the cytochrome P450 enzyme superfamily and is expressed in the human testis, ovary, placenta, adipose tissue, skin, and brain (Kaymak & Yıldırım, 2020). In the human brain, nuclei of both men and women that are especially critical in the expression of aromatase are located in the pons, thalamus, hypothalamus, and hippocampus (Sasano et al., 1998).

Androgen and estrogen receptors are also present in target cells of both sexes, in crosstalk between androgenic and estrogenic effects. In men, T binds to AR in the interior of the cells. A portion of this T is converted to DHT by 5α-reductase, which also binds to AR, and a portion is converted to estradiol by aromatase, which binds to ER. The activation of AR and ER produces crosstalk between androgenic and estrogenic effects, with the activation of gene transcription as the outcome. In women, androgen and estrogen secretions are parallel throughout the menstrual cycle. T in women proceeds from adrenal secretion, but also from the conversion of androstenedione (another androgen) by 17-hydroxysteroid dehydrogenase. However, virilization is prevented by higher levels of SHBG than in men, which keeps the hormone inactive, and by aromatization of androgens to estrogens (Molina, 2013). Additionally, the ovaries produce estrogen, but in a process that involves androgens. Locally, theca cells of the dominant follicle synthesize androstenedione and T, whereas granulosa cells of the mature follicle convert them to estradiol and estrone.

Functionally, the equilibrium between androgens and estrogens in both men and women is a critical condition of health (Hammes & Levin, 2019). In men, androgenic actions on AR, but also estrogenic action on ERα in the brain, are required in the negative feedback that regulates LH and FSH. In women, androgens may also play a role in the maintenance of pregnancy, especially concerning parturition. Although evidence mainly comes from animal models, the activation of AR favors the expression of collagenase in the cervix, and, in animals and humans, AR levels are high in myometrial cells early in pregnancy but reduced by parturition (Molina, 2013). Moreover, increasing evidence suggests that alterations in the equilibrium between androgens and estrogens in both men and women seem to promote certain aspects of disease. In men, deficiencies in aromatase activity that prevent estrogen production generate abnormalities in bone formation, metabolic syndrome, and alterations in tract development, impairing fertility. In women, androgen excess could impair fertility; however, androgen levels at physiological doses are needed for follicle growth, probably mediating FSH action. Finally, it is worth noting that the brain is a target organ for estrogens in both men and women, especially via aromatization. This leads to the idea that estradiol production in critical regions, such as the hypothalamus and hippocampus, could mediate aggressive and sexual behaviors (Hammes & Levin, 2019), as well as cognitive processes. However, more research is needed in controlled trials with human samples to find out to what extent findings from animal models can be extrapolated to human processes and behaviors.

In sum, sexual steroids belong to a family of hormones with common chemical and physiological properties whose main functions are involved in sexual development and behavior, but also other behaviors. Although hormonal profiles are different in men and women, common pathways lead to regulating parallel processes across the life span.

Sex Determination and Differentiation at Morphological and Physiological Levels

Humans are a sexodimorphic species. Across the life span, sex hormones have dramatic effects on the nervous system and, therefore, on affect, cognition, and behavior, acting to promote differences between men and women. These differences play an important role in their social adaptation, which includes establishing hierarchies and competitive behavior. A description of these basic effects is presented in this section.

In the adult age, our bodies present a wide variety of forms that, independently of the social context, sexual identity, or beliefs, usually show evident male or female characteristics. These phenotypical signs are the outcome of complex processes at different stages of development, which include genetic and hormonal changes. Sex determination is performed by gene expression, and related to this, hormonal levels favor the differentiation of sexual organs and characteristics. Moreover, our brain is sensitive to this differentiation process, which overlaps with learning-related plasticity in the early stages of development. The confluence of these interactions between neural differentiation and learning affects sexual behaviors in humans in a different manner. The set of behaviors associated with sex, highly influenced by the social and cultural environment, is called the sex or gender role. Here, sex determination and differentiation of sexual characteristics will be briefly described, whereas brain differentiation and sexual dimorphism will be addressed afterward.

In this setting, it is worth remembering the classical classification of hormonal effects on behavior into two categories: organizational and activational effects (Phoenix et al., 1959). Organizational effects of hormones are referred to as the set of endocrinologically regulated processes that provoke permanent structural changes in organs and tissues during critical periods of development. An alteration in hormonal levels during the critical period of an organ or tissue has irreversible effects on the organism. However, the integrity of an organ does not ensure the optimal deployment of behavior related to that organ. For example, in male birds, certain T levels are needed for the adequate development of the singing brain nuclei in pre-born stages. However, the bird does not sing immediately after birth; this behavior is initiated in the young bird when T increases in pubertal stages. These latter effects are classically referred to as activational effects because certain hormonal levels are needed to "activate" a certain behavior, regardless of whether previously required organs and tissues had an optimal development. An alteration in hormonal levels at this point has less serious consequences than alterations during organizational effects because the consequences are reversible.

Organizational effects occur earlier in development than activational effects. The starting point of the conversion to a specific sex occurs at the moment of conception, when the genetic sex is established. Combining the genetic material of the progenitors, all the nuclei of each cell of the human fetus will contain 23 pairs of chromosomes—22 pairs of autosomes, and one pair of sex chromosomes. In this latter pair, if the combination of sex chromosomes is XX, the fetus will be genetically female, whereas it will be genetically male if the outcome is XY. The Y-chromosome contains the SrY gene, which is especially relevant for later development because, at the seventh to eighth week of gestation, the existence of the Y gene will provoke a cascade of endocrine events whose effects will strongly condition the gonadal sex of the future individual (Bakker, 2018).

Thus, the period between the seventh to eighth week of gestation and birth is considered critical for the organizational effects of hormones on reproductive organs of the future individual or, in other words, for the gonadal sex. Until this critical point, the human fetus can potentially become either the male or female form, like the rest of the mammals, because internal and external sexual organs are unisexual and undifferentiated until the seventh to eighth week of gestation. During this period, precursors of internal sexual organs (Wolf and Müller systems for male and female organs, respectively) coexist. Externally, fetal genital protuberances can potentially develop male or female external sexual characteristics. Thus, although the typical development assumes a coherence between genetic and gonadal sex, if the hormonal function is altered in this critical period, cases of discrepancies between genetic and gonadal sex can occur.

As a corollary, female sexual differentiation occurs in the absence of androgens and/ or the absence of androgen action on the AR. In this regard, the Jost Hypothesis states that androgens are necessary for male sexual differentiation (Jost, 1953, 1972). Thus, the existence of the SrY gene will induce the formation of testes, which will secrete androgens. Three androgens are especially relevant in this critical period. First, the T, secreted by the testicular Leydig cells, will produce the development of the Wolffian ducts (such as the epididymis, the vas deferens, and the seminal vesicles); second, the anti-Müllerian hormone, secreted by the testicular Sertoli cells, will cause regression of the female-typical

Müllerian ducts; and third, the dihydrotestosterone, formed from the reduction in T by the 5α-reductase enzyme, will favor the development of the penis and scrotum. T is first detected in the human fetus at nine weeks, increasing until it reaches a peak at 15 to 18 weeks of fetal life and then declines, independently of the interactions between receptor of luteinizing and human chorionic gonadotropin hormones (Swerdloff et al., 2002). According to the Jost Hypothesis, in females, the absence of the SrY gene will promote the development of the undifferentiated gonads into ovaries. As a result, the absence of testes and androgens will favor the Müllerian ducts that develop into the uterus, fallopian tubes, and the distal portion of the vagina, whereas the Wolffian ducts will regress and disappear (Bakker, 2018). Accordingly, fetal genital protuberances will lead to clitoris and labia. The total development of the external genital protuberances will conform to the external sexual organs if the absence of hormonal influence remains.

Some considerations are needed at these stages of development. First, the phenotypical gonadal sex will condition the sexual identity in most cases. However, in some cases, the individual does not feel that the phenotypical sex is coherent, and may even be contradictory, with his/her perception of his/her sex. These discrepancies emphasize the need to distinguish between sex and gender. Thus, sex is reserved for chromosomal and gonadal differences, whereas gender refers more to social roles, including sexual identity. Second, the latter findings of Jost's paradigm reveal that not only are the sex chromosomes involved in the sex determination, but autosomes could also play a relevant role in this process (Blecher & Erickson, 2007). Third, the strategic location of the androgen receptors, as well as the estrogen receptors, in the human genital tubercle can condition the appropriate development of sexual organs because the human penis and clitoris express both types of receptors (Baskin et al., 2020). Fourth, T levels continue to increase during intrauterine life and the neonatal period during approximately the first three months of life. It has been suggested that these secretory episodes during intrauterine life are critical for genital sexual differentiation, whereas intrauterine and neonatal increases may be relevant for gender-associated differences in behavior and cognition (Swerdloff et al., 2002). Finally, the potential role of interactions between sex steroids and other hormones, such as cortisol, thyroid hormones, or the growth hormone, for instance, cannot be ignored. Certain levels of these hormones are necessary for optimal development, but deep fluctuations could also alter the androgen levels during these critical processes.

Although sexual organs have been organized by hormonal actions, they are not prepared to exhibit sexual behavior in the childhood stage. Activational effects of hormones are required, and they are mainly conformed before (adrenarche and menarche for boys and girls, respectively) and during puberty, when the person is first capable of sexual reproduction. Until these new critical periods, any contact of the baby with its genitalia is just one more exploratory play activity, but not sexual behavior.

In boys, adrenarche occurs at approximately seven or eight years of age, when the secondary sexual characteristics start to appear. Although the definition of hormonal factors that induce the adrenarche is not complete after decades of research, it is assumed that the onset of adrenarche is caused by adrenal androgen production (Dumontet & Martinez, 2021). Thus, the hormonal mechanism to induce adrenarche seems to be independent from the control of LH and FSH because the main hormonal candidate is the adrenocorticotropic hormone (ACTH), which stimulates the zona reticularis, the innermost region of the adrenal cortex. The outcome of this stimulation is the synthesizing and secretion of adrenal androgens, mainly DHEA and its sulfated derivative (DHEAS). The conversion of these androgens to T and DHT mediates the prepubertal growth spurt and the early development of pubic and axillary hair. In this setting, puberty is initiated in the brain before 13.5 years of age and will be completed in 4.5 years, with increases in the pulsatile pattern of the GnRH hypothalamic factor. These increases reduce the negative feedback that low levels of T were exerting on pituitary LH and FSH levels until this moment. As the outcome, concentrations of gonadal steroids progressively increase, and T or its metabolites (mainly DHT) favor spermatogenesis in the intratesticular space, the growth of the penis, scrotum, and testes, and other secondary characteristics such as deepening of the voice and hair distribution on the face, axillar, chest, abdomen, thigh, and pubic zones. In height development, T is also responsible for the closure of the bone epiphyses and the increase in bone mass, probably through estradiol mediation (Swerdloff et al., 2002). The T peak will be reached in early adulthood and begin to decline as early as 30 years of age.

In girls, menstruation is the landmark of pubertal development. However, menarche occurs quite late compared to other pubertal changes such as breast development or peak height velocity. Adrenal T has been associated with body hair distribution and sexual desire. On the first day of menstruation, estrogen and progesterone levels are low while GnRH is secreted in a pulsatile fashion from the hypothalamus, stimulating the secretion of FSH and LH from the pituitary. The secretion increase in the FSH levels stimulates estrogen secretion by the ovarian follicles, which contributes to the negative feedback on FSH release from the pituitary. One of the follicles will reach a higher stage of maturation (follicle of Graff) and contribute to the secretion of estrogen. The secretion increase in the LH levels provokes ovulation (expulsion of the egg from the follicle) 35 to 44 hours after the onset of the LH increases. After this follicular phase, the LH stimulation favors that the remains of the ovarian follicle (corpus luteum) secrete progesterone and estradiol, which marks the onset of the luteal phase. If the egg is not fertilized, the corpus luteum atrophies, and menstruation takes place within 12 to 16 days of ovulation. During the last days of the luteal phase, estradiol levels decrease, reducing the negative feedback on FSH secretion. As a consequence, FSH levels will rise and initiate the next menstrual cycle.

Puberty initiates the fertile period of the individual's life. From young to late adulthood, both the hormonal patterns and physiological processes involved in reproduction progressively become less efficient. However, the way the fertile period ends and the profile of hormonal senescence are different depending on the sex. For men, gonadal hormone secretion suffers a gradual decline from young adult ages. For instance, bio-available T declines at an increasing rate in each decade after 40 years old. However, this decline is also extended to pituitary hormones and GnRH pulses, along with a loss of the responsiveness of LH and FSH to GnRH stimulation and alterations in the negative feedback signals. Additionally, these changes also affect the subtle equilibrium with other hormones, such as the decline in the levels of adrenal androgens (DHEA and DHEAS) and immune function. Although there are broad individual differences, hormonal senescence is accompanied by loss of energy, libido, and muscle mass and strength, depressed mood, erectile dysfunction, osteoporosis, and increased fat mass, which could lead to age-associated metabolic syndrome. For women, the fertile period is associated with an abrupt cessation of gonadal hormone secretion in menopause at approximately 50 years old, although hormonal alterations are observed five years earlier as a transition to meno-pause (perimenopause). During this period, lower ovarian inhibin secretion reduces nega-tive feedback at hypothalamic and pituitary levels. As a result, GnRH and FSH secretion are enhanced, whereas the ovarian estradiol secretion could be normal or even elevated, with occasional episodes of normal cycling. When estrogen levels are lower, fewer ovu-latory cycles will occur, and hypogonadism will extend until menstruation withdrawal. Changes in estradiol and progesterone will affect other hormones such as T or growth factors (Swerdloff et al., 2002).

In summary, hormonal patterns differ by sex, but general aspects of the critical peri-ods for sexual differentiation, reproduction, and behavior are common to women and men. These critical periods are the prenatal stage, the first months of birth, puberty, and senescence. All the main events of these periods are initiated and regulated by the brain. Thus, their appropriate development will have relevant implications in all the spheres of life of the individual.

Sex Differences and Dimorphism

Evolution has favored the use of different strategies by each sex in striving for resources. Both sexes benefit from attaining a higher status because natural resources are usually scarce and frequently organized according to status derived from social hierarchies. Therefore, it is reasonable that biological responses to competition were necessary in order to survive in ancient times, resulting in sex differences. Different physiological, behavioral, and cogni-tive characteristics have been described from early childhood. For example, boys are more likely than girls to engage in rough-and-tumble play. Later, puberty promotes the develop-ment of physical features related to physical dominance and dimensions related to moti-vation and status. Thus, sex differences in competitive behavior could be influenced by sex hormones, mainly testosterone. Moreover, hormonal levels and aggressive/competitive behavior interact and vary across the life span. In turn, environmental and experiential factors influence hormonal functioning.

In this section, we will review the brain features as well as the main cognitive, affective, and behavioral differences resulting from sexual differentiation. This leads to viewing a wide variety of constructs, such as abilities, affect and its relationship with social behavior (including cooperation and aggression), neuropsychiatric disorders, and response to stress.

Sex Differences in Brain Structure and Function

There are differences in the brain structures and functions of males and females across species of the animal kingdom. Studies mainly carried out in rats show that there are differences between male and female brains in the size, number, and connectivity of the neurons of some brain regions. In humans, these structural differences are not as obvious as in animals, but they also occur. In both animals and humans, these sexually dimorphic brain areas are located around the anterior hypothalamus, that is, the third ventricle, and they are involved in sexual and parental behavior, which are two dimorphic behaviors. In addition, according to McCarthy (2008), sex differences can be connective, consisting of differences in the type or number of synapses or the size of a specific projection or volumetric related to size differences in specific brain regions or nuclei between the two sexes. These brain differences, in addition to social and cultural aspects, can explain some behavioral sex differences.

In animals, we can distinguish volumetric sexual differences in several brain areas. In the mammalian brain, the most characteristic difference is the *sexually dimorphic nucleus of the preoptic area* (SDN-POA). This nucleus is within the anterior hypothalamus, a brain region implicated in reproductive behaviors such as copulation in male rats and the estrous cycle in female rats. The SDN-POA can be as much as five to eight times larger in male rats than in female rats. Evidence indicates that differences in perinatal exposure to androgens levels could explain this structural sexual difference. In addition, the aromatization of testosterone seems to be involved in the masculinization of this nucleus. Accordingly, in female rats treated with androgens early in life, a SDN-POA size similar to that of male rats has been observed, whereas the size of the SDN-POA in castrated males resembles that of females. Sexual dimorphism has been found in other brain structures, such as the *bed nucleus of the stria terminals* (BNST) and the *anteroventral periventricular nucleus* (AVPV). The BNST is a limbic forebrain structure involved in autonomic, neuroendocrine, and behavior responses, and it is around 20 percent larger in males than in females. In contrast to the BNST, the AVPV is larger in female rats than in male rats, although this size difference is visible from puberty. This nucleus is involved in the regulation of ovulation and endocrine responses. The number of neurons in this brain nucleus is similar in female and male rats after testosterone administration in females or castration in male neonates. It is important to point out that testosterone or its metabolites can have opposite effects on apoptosis, and a clear example is what occurs in two of the brain nuclei mentioned. Thus, testosterone (or its metabolites) inhibits apoptosis in the SDN-POA, but it promotes apoptosis in the AVPV. The *bulbocavernous spinal nucleus* (BSN), at the motor system level, is also sexually dimorphic. This nucleus consists of a small set of motor neurons involved in the control of penile erection and the external anal sphincter through the bulbocavernous muscles located at the base of the penis in males and around the opening of the vagina in females. In male rats, the BSN has a larger size and a greater number of cells. However, in females, there is a regression of this nucleus and atrophy of the muscle. Thus, although both sexes are born with neurons in the BSN, after the first week of life, these neurons only remain in males due to the action testosterone exerts on pelvic muscles to promote survival, but they disappear in females. In addition, at the sensory level, the *vomeronasal organ* is different in males and females. This structure presents a greater volume and a larger number of neurons in males than in females. Both the sexual differentiation phase, which takes place during early development, and its permanence into adulthood depend on the level of sex hormones such as testosterone. Finally, testosterone exposure in females during the postnatal period causes an increase in the size of the *vocal control regions*. In addition, if an androgenized rat is administered more testosterone, the size of these regions will increase even more. Regarding this set of nuclei, a clear example of sex differences in species is the song behavior in the bird kingdom. This behavioral difference is due to neural dimorphism. In birds, there is an organ that controls song, called the syrinx, whose muscles respond to the cranial nerve II or hypoglossal nerve, controlled by vocal control regions. These regions are at least five times larger in males than in females. The song behavior in birds seems to require both the organizing and activating effect of androgens.

As animals, humans also present differences in their brains according to sex, but they are less numerous than those found in animals. Overall, men have brains that are around 15 percent larger than women's brains. However, the greater complexity of folds in the cortex of the frontal and parietal lobes observed in women (Luders et al., 2004) could compensate for this size difference. In humans, the corresponding SDN-POA is called *interstitial nuclei of the anterior hypothalamus* (INAH), and it consists of four regions (e.g., INAH-1, INAH-2, INAH-3, and INAH-4) of neuronal cell bodies in both the anterior hypothalamus and preoptic area in humans. Actually, the INAH-1 is considered more clearly equivalent to the SDN-POA in rats. However, sex differences have been reported in INAH-2 and INAH-3, given that they are larger in men than in women, although these sex differences in INAH-2 volume have not been found in all studies. In addition, in these two regions, the number of neurons is higher in men than in women. Structural differences have been reported in the *suprachiasmatic nucleus* (SCN) of the hypothalamus depending on the sexual orientation of the person. Thus, this nucleus has more neurons in homosexual men than in heterosexual men. It is possible that these differences could be due to the action of androgens and/or estrogens in early development because this nucleus has receptors for them. Another brain structure that presents sex-related differences is *Onuf's nucleus*, which is the corresponding nucleus to the BSN in humans. Onuf's nucleus is located in the sacral spinal cord and divided into ventrolateral and dorsomedial cells, with the ventrolateral cells being more numerous in men than in women. In addition to differences in general brain size and specific regions, sex differences have been observed in the degree of brain asymmetry. Thus, in men, compared to women, it has been observed that it is more common to find asymmetry in the *planum temporale* (greater in the left hemisphere) and greater asymmetry in the Silvio fissure, and the asymmetry in the parietal plane (greater in the right hemisphere) is approximately twice as large. In contrast, women have more inter-hemispheric connections. Finally, neuroimaging studies maintain that brain activity is more asymmetric in men than in women, especially related to linguistic tasks.

Focusing on specific brain regions and correcting for the relative size of the brain compared to the rest of the body, differences between the two sexes are observed, on average, in the population, and they are summarized in Table 4.1.

Finally, it is important to note that there are few dimorphisms in the human brain structure, and they alone cannot explain the possible different behaviors of the two sexes. To determine why men and women display sexually dimorphic behavior, other factors should be taken into consideration, such as the patterns of neural connections, the

Table 4.1 Main neuro-anatomical differences between the two human sexes

Men

- Higher mean volume:
  - SDN-POA
  - Interstitial nucleus of the anterior hypothalamus-3 (INAH-3)
  - Bed nucleus of the stria terminals (BNST)
  - Medial frontal and cingulate areas
  - Amygdala and hippocampus
  - Global white matter
  - Cerebral ventricles
  - Right *planum temporale*
- Higher number of motor neurons in Onuf's nucleus
- Higher global number of neurons

Women

- Higher mean volume:
  - Dorsolateral prefrontal cortex
  - Superior temporal gyrus
  - Anterior commissure
  - Massa intermedia of thalamus
  - Brain regions involved in language, medial paralimbic regions, and some frontal regions
  - Relative gray matter
- More elongated suprachiasmatic nuclei (SCN)
- More symmetrical left and right *planum temporale*
- More bulbous corpus callosum (posterior portion)
- Higher neuronal density in *planum temporale*
- More dendrites and axons

Note: SND-POA sexually dimorphic nucleus of the preoptic area.

neurochemistry of the brain, and the influence of sex-related hormones on neural development and function. Moreover, studies about sex differences are frequently carried out postmortem or using clinical samples, which means the conclusions have to be considered with caution. Additionally, data about sex differences in the size of brain structures and cognitive capabilities are usually offered as a mean of men or women. However, the high variability among individuals of each sex, which is probably underestimated, could overlap some similarities in these characteristics between sexes.

Cognitive Sex Differences

Although sexual differences are not as obvious at a structural level in humans, they do appear to exist at the cognitive level. They have been found in different cultures, which would indicate that sex steroid hormones could be the cause. These cognitive abilities include senso-perceptive, verbal, mathematical reasoning, and visuospatial abilities.

Regarding *senso-perceptive abilities*, sex differences have been found, specifically, in pain, olfaction, taste, audition, and vision. Thus, women have lower thresholds and, therefore, show less tolerance to pain than men, especially cutaneous and visceral pain. The activational effects of sex steroids would seem to underlie sex differences in pain perception. Thus, women display a higher response to pain because their opioid system activation is lower than men's and dependent on the levels of estrogen. In addition, it is important to note that pain perception could be influenced by cultural factors. In this regard, according to gender roles, men are expected to tolerate pain more than women. Sex differences have also been reported in olfactory sensitivity and odor identification. For example, women are more sensitive to musk-like and amyl acetate odors, and they outperform men on chemosensory detection. This olfactory acuity is generalizable to all ages and across cultures. Sex steroid hormones influence olfactory sensitivity, as shown in studies throughout the menstrual cycle, during pregnancy, and with clinical endocrine disorder patients; however, it is not clear how hormones affect olfactory sensitivity. On average, women are superior to men on taste perception tasks, especially in naming and discriminating tastes and bitter tastes. These sex differences are more pronounced after puberty, during pregnancy, and in the follicular phase of the menstrual cycle, and they decline after menopause, suggesting that sex steroid hormones could explain these differences. In addition, animal studies have demonstrated sex differences in taste preference, showing females' preference for sweet tastes, depending on the estrogen levels. Finally, women are more sensitive to sound than men, but the latter have greater visual acuity than the former. From an early age, girls respond preferentially to auditory stimuli and boys to visual stimuli.

According to Doreen Kimura (1999), sexual differences are also observed at the cognitive and motor levels. Although no sex differences in the intelligence quotient have been reported, men and women present, on average, better performance in some cognitive domains than in others. Men outperform women on tests of mathematical reasoning, whereas women have a greater advantage on calculation tasks. Given that these differences are observed before puberty, the activational effects of hormones would not explain them. Regarding spatial analysis, although there is indeed a belief that men tend to perform better than women, this is only true for some spatial tasks. Thus, men perform better on tasks involving mental rotation of objects and spatial navigation, whereas women do better on spatial memory tasks. These visuospatial differences between the sexes are present after puberty, indicating a possible influence of sex hormones on them. In contrast, women outperform men on verbal tasks, especially women who present better language comprehension, faster language acquisition, and better spelling, verbal fluency grammar skills, and verbal memory than males. Importantly, language is the cognitive domain where the greatest hemispheric specialization occurs, with the left hemisphere being the most specialized in this function, although the right hemisphere is responsible for the prosody of language. At a functional level, a study indicates that sexual differences are found, instead, in *inter- and intra-hemispheric connectivity*. Thus, the smallest brains show greater inter-hemispheric connectivity, and larger brains have greater intra-hemispheric connectivity. In addition, on average, women have smaller brains than men (Martínez et al., 2017). Moreover, sex differences have been reported in decision making (a complex cognitive domain included in executive functions), which could be related to sex differences in brain circuitry on prefrontal-basal ganglia circuits (van den Bos et al., 2013) and laterality (Reber & Tranel, 2016). Men usually choose the long-term advantageous option involving global information, whereas women tend to obtain more information by choosing a more detailed way. This difference in strategies currently leads to better performance in men (van den Bos et al., 2013). Recently, we also found that young women showed greater sensitivity to losses than to wins during a decision-making task, reflected in greater amplitude for losses than wins in the feedback-related negativity component, an event-related potential component that is associated with earlier feedback processing in the medial frontal cortex (Garrido-Chaves et al., 2021).

There is growing evidence of sex differences in social cognition that seem to be biologically associated with females' chromosomal karyotype, specifically in hemispheric lateralization for face processing, facial expression encoding, face gender encoding, interest in social scenes and human faces, emotional response to negative affective information, empathy for pain, understanding gestures, body language and intentions, and parental response to the baby schema (see review Proverbio, 2021).

Cognitive sex differences are usually explained from an evolutionary perspective. Thus, men present higher performance on these abilities than women, which stems from managing the environment when they assumed the role of hunters. In this line, men outperform women on map reading, maze learning, mathematical reasoning, and mental rotation of object tasks, with these sexual differences being more evident in the latter skill. In contrast, women show better performance than men on social and verbal abilities because they were involved in caring for the offspring. From childhood, women report greater comprehension and writing skills than men. Specifically, women outperform men on tasks such as naming objects of the same color, listing words beginning with the same letter, and verbal memory.

One possible explanation for cognitive dimorphism is the different hormonal levels of men and women. According to this idea, in women, a negative correlation has been found between spatial reasoning performance and estrogen levels. In addition, in older men with lower testosterone levels, the administration of this hormone improves spatial performance. However, although hormones can affect cognition, this statement should be viewed with caution because the association between performance on spatial or verbal tasks and hormone levels is not clear. Results of other studies point to the influence of prenatal testosterone exposure on cognitive and motor abilities. Thus, women with CAH have shown higher accuracy when throwing balls and darts at targets (a result that was not due to muscle strength) and mental rotation performance, but this latter result has not always been reported. In addition, it has been suggested that this population reported impaired fine motor performance, which is a form of female-typical behavior. In men with CAH, poorer visuo-spatial task performance has been found on tasks such as on mental rotation and others. Individuals (men and women) with CAH have shown alterations only in mathematical ability, a skill on which men excel, but not on abilities on which women excel, such as verbal fluency or perceptual speed. Thus, men and women with CAH reported lower arithmetic and mathematical test performance and no changes in verbal fluency or perceptual speed performance. Given these results, it is possible that prenatal testosterone exposure only significantly affects motor abilities and not cognitive functions (Hines, 2011).

Despite this, there are a few issues that should be taken into consideration in cognitive dimorphism. For example, sexual differences are not found in all studies. In addition, although there are larger differences in large groups of both sexes, in reality, the differences are found after comparing individuals, and so they are not sex-related differences. Finally, it is important to note that this cognitive dimorphism could be due to exposure to different experiences in men and women that can affect their performance on some abilities and, in turn, their neural circuitry. It has been suggested that social and cultural aspects could be underlying cognitive sex differences. In support of this, sexual differences in some cognitive abilities, such as mathematical skills, disappear over time. Moreover, in mathematical and science performance, differences are greater depending on the nation rather than on the sex. Thus, sex-related differences on mathematical tasks depend on the nation because in nations where men and women have a similar representation in the legislature, the mathematics ability is quite similar in both sexes.

Affective Sex Differences

There is some evidence that men and women are also different at the affective level. These differences are already found in the way men and women process the same stimuli, in terms of their level of threat (Clarkson et al., 2021), and in their cognitive control, given that the relationship between anxiety and error monitoring (i.e., a core component of cognitive control) is higher in women than in men.

Affective sex differences have been studied through different neuropsychiatric disorders. There is a clear sex effect on the prevalence, risk, age of onset, course, and symptomatology of some neuropsychiatric disorders. For example, men are more susceptible to suffering a neurodevelopmental disorder (i.e., intellectual disability, autism spectrum disorder, and attention-deficit activity disorder), schizophrenia, and dopamine system-related deficits (i.e., Parkinson's disease) than women. In contrast, women usually present a higher response to negative emotional stimuli, leading them to have an increased risk of developing affective neuropsychiatric disorders. Some results in this line are presented below.

Sex differences have also been found in bipolar and monopolar disorders. In women, it is more common to see a greater prevalence of bipolar disorder II, hypomania, comorbid phobia, panic disorder, posttraumatic stress disorder, eating disorders, borderline personality disorder, and suicidal behavior. Women with bipolar disorder show lower recognition of surprise and fear prosody and increased sensorimotor gating in comparison with healthy women. In contrast, men have a greater prevalence of mania. Men with bipolar disorder present more comorbid conduct and substance use disorders, worse verbal memory performance and recognition of happy prosody, and lower sensorimotor gating performance compared to healthy men. Regarding treatments, women are more frequently treated with antidepressants, electroconvulsive therapy, and psychotherapy than men, whereas men are more often lithium users than women. Jogia et al. (2012) suggested that there are structural and functional sex-related differences in the limbic and prefrontal subcortical and cortisol regions involved in the appearance of bipolar disorder. During social-cognitive tasks, women with bipolar disorders present a non-usual neural engagement of the caudate and prefrontal cortex, in contrast to control women. Men with bipolar disorder show a lower volume of medial prefrontal cortex grey matter when compared with control men. In addition, a reduced left parahippocampal gyrus and left/right hippocampal volume has been found in people with bipolar disorder, as well as less volume of the right hippocampus in women with bipolar disorder than in men (Shi et al., 2018). Women in early adolescence have twice the possibility of experiencing depressive symptoms than men, a difference that is maintained across the life span. According to Nolen-Hoeksema et al. (1999), the female triad of vulnerabilities to depressive symptoms could be at the base of this sex difference. Thus, women with depression more frequently experience more chronic strain, a greater tendency to ruminate when distressed, and a lower sense of control over their lives.

Another disorder almost twice as prevalent in women as in men is posttraumatic stress disorder (PTSD), probably because of a different reactivity to trauma in women and men, regardless of the type of trauma (Blanco et al., 2018). Another possible explanatory mechanism would be that women, in response to stress and with a similar cortisol response to the stressor as men, present greater negative memory consolidation than men (Felmingham et al., 2012). Accordingly, women respond better to PTSD-related treatment than men (Gogos et al., 2019). A relationship between exposure to trauma and reduced hippocampal volume has been found, and it is more significant in the right hemisphere in women (Karl et al., 2006). According to a recent review (Gogos et al., 2019), there is evidence that low levels of the hormones estradiol and, to a lesser extent, progesterone are related to a higher probability of having PTSD and bipolar disorder and greater symptom severity.

Although there are no sex differences in the incidence of obsessive-compulsive disorder (OCD), some differences are observed in the expression and age of onset of the symptoms and the course and response to treatment. Thus, the first symptoms are observed earlier in men, specifically in puberty, whereas in women they appear after the age of 20, coinciding with pregnancy and childbirth. In addition, men present more tics, greater severity, and a worse prognosis, and women present more compulsions about cleaning and checking. It seems that these differences could be explained by hormonal and genetic mechanisms. Regarding the hormonal influence, Alexander and Peterson (2004) found that males with tic disorders (i.e., OCD and Tourette Syndrome) presented a behavioral profile similar to that of children who were exposed to elevated prenatal androgen levels (i.e., increased masculine play preference, a positive relationship between this preference and the severity of the tic symptoms, and relative impairment in mental rotation ability). In addition, changes in the symptoms of women diagnosed with OCD have been described in the premenstrual/menstrual phase and after pregnancy and menopause (Lochner et al., 2004). A genetic predisposition to OCD has been reported. In this regard, the down-regulation of the catechol-O-methyl-transferase contributes to a predisposition to OCD only in men, although these results are not conclusive (Pooley et al., 2007; Wang et al., 2009). Recently, two genes (GRID2 and GPR135) have been identified in women, but not in men (Khramtsova et al., 2019).

Despite sex differences in neuropsychiatric disorders, in both experimental and clinical studies, it is necessary to attend to the sex of the patients and the phase of the menstrual cycle in women to better understand the role of gonadal hormones in these disorders and their potential therapeutic implications. For instance, although there is a similar prevalence of epilepsy in men and women, there is one gender-specific type of epilepsy, that is, catamenial epilepsy, characterized by seizures most often around the premenstrual or periovulatory period in adult women.

In sum, epidemiological data suggest a higher prevalence of monopolar and bipolar affective disorders. Other neuropsychiatric pathologies do not show clear differences between the sexes in their prevalence, although a certain sex effect is observed when the subtypes, symptoms, onset, and course of the disorders are examined.

Behavior Sex Differences

As the perspective moves from genetic or physiological aspects to behavior, the results with humans present a greater degree of variability. These discrepancies are due, at least in part, to the contribution of other explanatory variables, such as learning and the social context. The influence of these aspects throughout the life span includes social conventions and biases in the behavior displayed by the individual, which is highly dependent on culture and could overlap with sex differences.

The influence of the gonadal hormones on human development is shown in several behaviors, with studies on childhood play being the main resource of evidence of the effect of hormones on early development. Thanks to these studies, we know that, although boys and girls tend to choose playmates of their own sex, boys usually prefer to play with vehicles, in contrast to girls, who prefer dolls, and boys spend more time on rough-and-tumble play in comparison with girls. Thus, we can say that boys and girls tend to have different toys, playmates, and activity preferences (Hines, 2010). In addition, other types of studies where children are exposed to high androgen levels prenatally, such as studies of girls with CAH or children with mothers with androgenic progestin treatment during pregnancy, have supported this evidence. In both cases, increased male-typical toys and activities have been shown. Studies with nonhuman primates (Alexander & Hines, 2002; Hassett et al., 2008) support the idea that these childhood-play sex differences could be explained independently of social and cognitive processes involved in the gender development of the children. Other adult behaviors, such as *sexual orientation* and *core gender identity*, could also be affected by prenatal exposure to testosterone. For example, a reduced heterosexual interest and identification with people of their own sex have been reported in women with CAH.

Focusing on social behavior, which is a type of behavior where two or more individuals interact and one or more of them benefits, sex differences have been reported in a wide range of behaviors, such as aggression, cooperativeness, empathy, leadership, and the stress response, among others.

Overall, men tend to express more aggressive behavior than women, and this sex difference appears at very early ages. This tendency could be explained by three hypotheses that are not mutually exclusive (Nelson & Kriegsfeld, 2017). According to these hypotheses, it is possible that men are more aggressive than women because they have higher blood concentrations of androgens, have been exposed to higher levels of androgens prenatally, leading to a brain organization that facilitates the expression of this behavior, or are more encouraged by their social network to carry out this behavior, compared to women. In line with the first argument of prenatal androgen exposure, studies have found that girls and adult women with CAH and children exposed to androgenic progestins show increased physical aggression. Moreover, in young men, we found that those who scored higher on aggressive behavior had a 2D:4D more masculine ratio, that is, a lower ratio (van der Meij et al., 2012). This ratio is an indirect index of prenatal exposure to androgens.

It is important to note that, although overall aggressive behavior is related to the male sex, there are also aggressive behaviors expressed by women. They are more subtle than those shown by men, but they are also performed to achieve their own survival and that of their descendants. Other individual characteristics related to aggressive behavior, such as dominance or assertiveness, despite being higher in men than women, do not seem to be affected by prenatal testosterone exposure because no differences have been found, for example, in women with CAH (Hines, 2011).

Overall, women are more sensitive to social stimuli than men. Thus, in women, a higher activation of brain regions related to emotion has been reported during cooperativeness, in comparison with men, as well as more empathy and a predisposition to use behaviors based on empathy (Moya-Albiol et al., 2010; Yamasue et al., 2008). From an evolutionary perspective, these sex-related differences could be due to a different function of social brain regions in demands such as caring for children. Empathy, the ability to understand and share the internal status of others, is a personality trait that might be related to prenatal testosterone exposure. Thus, although women in general present higher scores on empathy than men, reduced empathy has been reported in women with CAH. Accordingly, after testosterone administration, a reduction in empathy has been reported in both men (Hermans et al., 2006) and women (Bos et al., 2010; van Honk et al., 2011). In addition, a negative association between empathy and testosterone levels in amniotic fluid was found in children of both sexes (Chapman et al., 2006).

The different patterns of leadership have also been associated with hormone levels. In this regard, some studies have related testosterone to gender and sex roles. Thus, higher testosterone levels have been reported in women lawyers in comparison with athletes, nurses, or teachers. Women with higher testosterone levels had an uninhibited personality, self-confidence, and action orientation, whereas those with lower testosterone levels were defined as conventional, socialized, and having a caring attitude (Baucom et al., 1985). In addition, a positive relationship has been described between the testosterone levels and the perception of improved status and assertiveness in women students, on the one hand, and androstenedione levels and the tendency to express their competitive feelings through verbal aggression, on the other (Cashdan, 2003). However, higher testosterone levels have been associated with lower-status professions in men (Dabbs, 1992).

Finally, sex differences have been reported in the way men and women respond to stress, although the results are far from homogeneous. Thus, although the prototypic physiological and behavioral response to stress is the *fight-or-flight* response, Taylor et al. (2000) proposed that, at the behavioral level but not at the physiological level, women's response to stress is characterized by a pattern of *tend-and-befriend*, in contrast to men, who display the *fight-or-flight* strategy. Physiologically, the *fight-or-flight* strategy consists of sympathetic nervous system activation, resulting in the secretion of catecholamines into the bloodstream. Behaviorally, following this strategy, if people believe that they can successfully cope with the situation, they will fight, but if they think they do not have the necessary resources, they will flee. However, the *tend-and-befriend* strategy consists of a combination of affiliation (formation and maintenance of a small group of interpersonal relationships with other women) and protection and care of offspring. According to these authors, women's responses to stress are aimed at maximizing their probability of survival and that of their offspring.

One model of social behavior widely used by our research group is competitive behavior in two settings: sports competitions and laboratory studies, attending to the sex of the participants. In the next section, we provide an extensive review of the main results found by our group and other research groups in this line of research.

Sex Differences in Competitive Contexts

In this section, we are going to examine sex differences in the psychobiological response to competition, focusing on hormonal, emotional, and psychological variables. Competitive and aggressive behavior has predominantly been associated with males who, throughout evolution, have been placed in the main fight-or-flight settings, although social competition is present in both sexes (Clutton-Brock & Huchard, 2013; Costa et al., 2016). It is usually assumed that the male brain has been shaped to compete, and that morphological (e.g., higher muscle mass) and physiological (e.g., aerobic capacity) differences could help males to be more effective competitors than females. However, competitive contexts are not exclusive to men, although they are probably somewhat different in women. In fact, the main theories on competition have defended the possibility of applying them to females as well as to males. Furthermore, competition for limited resources drives natural, sexual, and social selection. However, even though both men and women can compete, the nature of their competition may differ, especially in response to environmental variations (Van Anders & Watson, 2006). Nevertheless, currently in Western societies, competitive settings are fairly common in both sexes because men and women share academic or intellectual tasks or even sports events, and so competition on these tasks could be fairly similar for both (Cashdan, 1998).

The initial theoretical framework was based on observation and studies in different contexts and species: the Biosocial Status Hypothesis (Mazur, 1985) in primates and the Challenge Hypothesis (Wingfield et al., 1990) in monogamous birds. The Biosocial Status Hypothesis defended a relationship between dominance and T levels. Primates compete for status in agonistic encounters whose outcomes produce different T changes: victory would lead to increases in T levels, whereas defeat would lead to decreases. Subsequently, winners are prone to engaging in future encounters by showing dominant behaviors; in contrast, losers would develop submissive signs. The Challenge Hypothesis pointed out the role of adaptive T changes in spring, which favors agonistic behavior related to territoriality, dominance, and protection of offspring. Later, this hypothesis was extrapolated to human competition (Archer, 2006; Carré & Archer, 2018).

Based on findings from animal research, several studies were carried out in men in competitive sports settings, due to their parallelism with agonistic encounters (Salvador, 2005). However, from the first studies, humans' psychobiological response to competition showed a more complex scenario than in animal investigations, making it necessary to pay attention to previous experience, mood, and psychological dimensions of the opponents, as well as the physical effort exerted (Salvador et al., 1987, 1990). The challenge of relating hormonal changes to behavior has been difficult because the hormonal response to competition is not always directly related to winning or losing; instead, it is modulated by complex psychological and cognitive processes.

In this framework, we proposed that the psychobiological response to competition would be better understood within a more general stress model. From this perspective, the Coping Competition Model (CCM) established that psychological factors such as motivation to win and appraisal are core variables in explaining psychobiological responses to competition (Salvador, 2005; Salvador & Costa, 2009). With this model, we distinguished three phases: pre-competition, competition, and post-competition. First, it is worth noting that motivation to compete is a necessary condition to elicit the psychobiological changes related to competition and outcome. The pre-competition phase begins before the start of the competition, with a clear anticipatory nature. Then, there is a quick estimation of the contest (conscious or unconscious), and the individual appraises the situation, deciding whether there is an imbalance between the demands and the perceived resources to cope with the situation. Both distal factors, such as a history of previous competitions or personality, and proximal factors, such as motivation, expectancies, perceived self-efficacy, the possible change in status (increase or decrease), or the opponent's characteristics, influence the cognitive evaluation of the specific situation that leads to a final appraisal of threat or challenge. When the individual perceives the situation as important and controllable, the probability of a challenge appraisal increases, along with the use of an active coping strategy characterized by the fight response with high levels of T, SNS increases, and increments in positive mood. The active coping strategy increases the probability of winning. However, when the individual perceives an imbalance between the demands and resources, the situation can be perceived as threatening, eliciting a more passive coping strategy. The psychobiological response to this situation is characterized by lower T and SNS responses, as well as an increase in C and negative mood. Passive coping is related to a high probability of defeat. Finally, in the post-competition phase (after the competition), the CCM model also points out that cognitive evaluations can moderate the psychobiological response. For example, both causal attributions of the outcome obtained, and the behavior displayed, will affect satisfaction, mood, and hormonal recovery. Likewise, cognitive appraisals also influence proximal and distal factors affecting future competitions. Figure 4.1 depicts the main phases and variables of the model. Although the CCM is the most detailed model, the aforementioned models are not incompatible or exclusive in explaining the way men and women face competitive

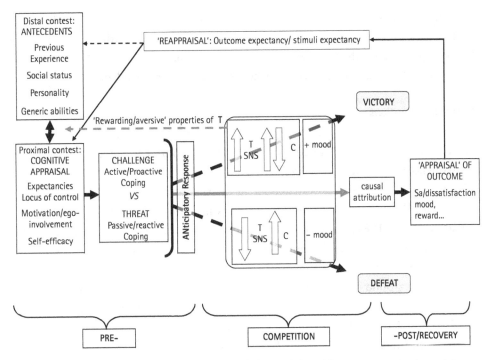

Figure 4.1 The *Coping Competition Model* (CCM) defends that psychological factors are core to understand the responses to competition (modified from Salvador & Costa, 2009). Used with permission from Elsevier.

contests and their outcomes. It is worth noting that all these hypotheses outline the bidirectional relationship between hormones and behavior.

Psychobiological responses to competitive contexts were initially studied in men, and, although the theories and hypotheses also apply to females, the first studies analyzed the results in men and overgeneralized them to women. However, from an evolutionary perspective, the nature of competition, motivation to compete, cognitive appraisal, and physiological responses can be the same in both sexes, or different depending on the context, as we mentioned previously. Most of the investigation on competition has focused on T. Without a doubt, there are sex differences in T levels and functions. A remarkable point is the capability of social situations such as sports competitions or laboratory studies to elicit hormonal changes in men and women. This can be called the *"competition effect"* to differentiate it from the *"winner effect"* associated with the outcome obtained in the competition. Geniole et al. (2017), in their meta-analysis, reported a *winner effect* in men, and no analyses were carried out on *the competition effect*.

The aim of the subsequent sections is to provide an overview of the psychobiological responses to competition and the outcome, focusing on sex differences. The first section is dedicated to sports competitions, and the second one to laboratory competitions. The third section focuses on cognitive and psychological variables that are affecting psychobiological responses in both sexes, before and after competition, in sports and laboratory settings. Finally, some long-term consequences will be analyzed. Direct sex-difference studies are scarce, especially in sports competitions. In laboratory settings, more research has been published with mixed-sex samples, although analyses separated by sex were not always carried out, and so additional investigations have been included.

Sports Competitions

The sports context allows a high degree of ecological validity because measurements can be obtained in real competitions where the outcome has short- and long-term consequences. Moreover, there is a relationship between effort, performance, and (usually) outcome. Initial studies carried out in men reported that T changes were associated with the outcome obtained in sports, as in tennis (Mazur & Lamb, 1980) or wrestling (Elias, 1981), with increments in winners and decreases in losers (*winner effect*). Subsequent studies did not reflect these differences in individual sports, such as judo (Salvador et al., 1987; Suay et al., 1999), or in team sports, such as basketball (González-Bono et al., 1999, 2000), although a "*competition effect*" was found. In addition, these studies emphasized the relevance of motivation to win and the causal attributions related to the outcome in understanding the T changes. More recent studies have confirmed the *competition effect* associated with heightened T levels (Casto & Edwards, 2016b).

The first studies in women began 20 years later than those in men, and they mainly analyzed hormonal responses in team sports. Bateup et al. (2002) were the first to confirm T changes in real competitive situations involving five rugby league matches with high physical and psychological implications, but these changes were not related to the outcome or performance self-assessments. Hamilton et al. (2009) reported significant T increases unrelated to the outcome in wrestling, pointing to a link between individual head-to-head competition and T in women. As in men's studies, a *competition effect* was mostly reported (Bateup et al., 2002; Edwards & Casto, 2013; Edwards & Kurlander, 2010; Edwards et al., 2006). However, a "*winner effect*" was found in a final soccer competition, a situation with high personal involvement where the outcome involved a change of status (Oliveira et al., 2009). In all these cases, women belonged to a specific group: they were young and usually varsity sportswomen with considerable previous experience and an enhanced physical condition. Furthermore, some of these sports require considerable physical effort and a high level of fitness (e.g., rugby, soccer, and wrestling). All these conditions had been emphasized in our previous studies in men (González-Bono et al., 1999; Salvador et al., 1990; Serrano et al., 2000; Suay et al., 1999).

Although the ideal way to examine sex differences in competition is to include men and women and compare them directly, mixed-sex sample studies in competitive settings are scarce (see Table 4.2). In addition, there are several limitations in sports studies: (a) lack of mixed-sex competitions due to physiological sex differences, (b) the small number

Table 4.2 Mixed-sex sample studies in competitive settings

Author (year)	Sample	Experimental situation	Hormones & main variables	Main results
Kivlighan et al. (2005)	23 M 23 F	Rowing ergometer competitive	T & C: (1) resting day (2) before, (3) 20 min after, (4) 40 min after Performance Mental state and experience Bonding, dominance–competitiveness	M→ ↑T in winners & losers F → ↑C in winners & losers
Edwards et al. (2006)	22 M 18 F	Soccer competition M: 1 Won (13 played) F: 1 Won (15 played)/1 Lost (10 played on booth)	T & C: (1) 1 hour before, (2) 20 min after Player rating scale (PRS)	M→ ↑T & ↑C in winners F → ↑T & ↑C in winners & losers M→ T after & T change +CORR PRS F → T before +CORR PRS
Filaire et al. (2009)	8 M 8 F	Tennis competition	C: Resting day: (1) 08:00 hs, (2) 20:00 hs Compet: (3) 08:00 hs, (3) 1 hour before, (5) 10 min before, (6) 10 min after, (7) 1 hour after, (8) 20:00 hs Anxiety	M & W* → ↑C in losers Anticipatory C: ↑ competition day F >M → somatic anxiety F <M → self-confidence
Jiménez et al. (2012)	27 M 23 F	Badminton elite competition	T & C: (1) 40 min before (2) 40 min after competition	M & F → ↑T in winners M & F → ↑C in losers
Le Panse et al. (2012)	8 M 11 F	World powerlifting championship	T & C: Basal: (1) 1 day before competition Compet: (2) during the weighing, (3) 1 hour after competition Performance	M→ ↑T afterM & F → ↑C M→ performance - CORR T after F → performance + CORR C after
Casto et al. (2014)	10 M 15 F 15 M 20 F	Cross country competition 2 races	T & C: (1) Before warm-up, (2) after warm-up, (3) after competition Performance	M & F → ↑T & ↑C after Not related to performance

Abbreviations: T = testosterone, C = cortisol, M = men, F = women, PRS = player rating scale, CORR = correlation

*no sex differences analyzed

of participants in team sports, (c) difficulties in obtaining homogeneous samples in individual sports, (d) the number of sports people in individual tournaments, (e) the fact that outcome is a rank (not just winning-losing) in most individual sports competitions, and (f) organizational opposition to assessment in official sports competition because the sample recruitment compromises participants' routines. Hereinafter, we summarize the main results of the studies, highlighting sex similarities and differences and the main variables analyzed.

Based on the Biosocial Model of Status, Jiménez et al. (2012) assessed men and women in an elite badminton competition. These authors found a T increase in winners and a drop in losers of both sexes, and they found the opposite in C, with increases in losers and decreases in winners (*winning effect*). In this case, participants were very motivated to win, with a social and economic incentive related to a T rise in winners. In the same line, in team sports, Edwards et al. (2006) analyzed T and C changes in one soccer match in men (ended in victory) and in two matches in women (victory and defeat), reporting increments in T and C after competition in all matches regardless of sex and outcome (in the case of women). The authors pointed out the functional significance of these T increases, relating them to dominant behavior, physical risks, and better reaction time and spatial memory. In cross-country runner teams, men and women increased their T and C levels, although these changes were not associated with performance (Casto et al., 2014). In tennis, the same C response and a relationship between anxiety and anticipatory C levels in men and women were found, although no sex differences depending on outcome were analyzed (Filaire et al., 2009).

However, other studies that compared mixed samples in sports competitions pointed out certain sex differences in the hormonal and emotional response to competition. In a powerlifting championship, a T increase was reported only in men, and a C increase in both men and women. Moreover, performance was negatively related to T in men, but positively associated with C in women (Le Panse et al., 2012). Likewise, in competitive ergometer rowing, Kivlighan et al. (2005) described a pattern of complex sex differences on a university crew team, finding a T rise in men (*competition effect*), associated with performance only in varsity men, but not in novices. This result contrasted with T reductions in women and a negative relationship between T and performance. In addition, during the recovery period, T elevations remained in varsity men, whereas women and novice men followed with low T levels. This study confirmed the importance of experience and sex in explaining the psychobiological response to competition.

In sum, sports competitions would elicit increases in T in both men and women, but in women, the results are more divergent than in men. The sources of these differences are still unclear. It is possible that psychological variables such as mood, anxiety, bonding, or experience modulate the T response, and sex differences in the perception of competition may also be a source of variability. The next section will focus on laboratory competitions, where more psychological variables have been studied.

Laboratory Competitions

Despite the ecological validity of sports competitions, laboratory studies have several advantages. They allow greater control over all the variables and a larger number of measurements. In this case, competitiveness is usually promoted through task instructions, credits, and/or a monetary reward. In laboratory settings, more personal factors (psychological, emotional), contextual variables, and possible moderating variables have been deeply analyzed. Moreover, the possibility of carrying out more complex statistical analyses, due to the larger size samples recruited, has been useful for advancing the knowledge. For these reasons, most of the research has been moved to the laboratory. However, more inconsistent results have been described in the laboratory. Geniole et al. (2017), in their meta-analyses, found a weak *winning effect* in laboratory studies. In this section, the main results of laboratory competition will be discussed, focusing once more on sex differences.

Laboratory competitions have usually studied the *winning effect* in rigged competition, removing the effect of physical effort and analyzing hormonal and emotional patterns to competition. In men, the first published study took into account whether the outcome was due to personal effort or to luck. Mazur and Lamb (1980) found no T responses on a luck task (lottery) and concluded that T increases would only appear in situations involving personal effort (such as tennis). However, years later, McCaul et al. (1992) reported T increases in winners and decreases in losers on a task whose outcome was due to luck. This was an open question, hardly studied, except regarding causal attribution. We studied this point in a laboratory competition (Salvador et al., 2017) by manipulating task attribution (merit vs. chance task) and outcome (winning vs. losing). In this study, we found a *competition effect*, with T rises on the merit task when subjects appraised the outcome internally, but no differences were found depending on the outcome. In this same line, previously, a *competition effect* was found on a laboratory computer task competition (van der Meij et al., 2010). All these studies were carried out with young men.

Laboratory studies in women began with a mixed-sex sample participating in a videogame competition, and the results did not show significant hormonal changes in men and women (Mazur et al., 1997). Subsequently, in a face-to-face competition, Costa and Salvador (2012) found both *competition* and *winner effects*, along with increments in T and positive mood, in young women. Winners also showed higher motivation to compete than losers. It is worth noting that the contest was manipulated to increase competitive cues by including an economic reward and feedback on partial scores, and the outcome was directly related to real performance against a competitor (not manipulated). Moreover, a psychobiological pattern related to active coping was found, supporting the CCM model. This investigation revealed a psychobiological response to competition in women in laboratory settings. Subsequently, we found that the higher the self-efficacy, the higher the T levels throughout the experimental procedure, including baseline, along with positive mood, suggesting that self-efficacy affected the psychobiological experience of competing. In addition, self-efficacy was positively related to performance, suggesting that efficacy beliefs affected women's effort, strength, and motivation to compete (Costa et al., 2016b).

On the one hand, laboratory studies with mixed samples that include outcomes that are not manipulated are scarce (Abad-Tortosa et al., 2019; Casto et al., 2020; van Anders & Watson, 2007). The advantage is that a direct relationship can be reported between outcome and performance, but, at the same time, the disadvantage is that winning can be either a cause or a consequence of T changes. On the other hand, studies with a rigged competition are the ideal situation to study the effect of the outcome (without considering the effort or the participant's real performance) on emotional and hormonal responses. Therefore, manipulation of the outcome makes it possible to study the causality of winning on T levels.

This differentiation between real and rigged competition leads to the question of whether there are sex differences in a competition directly related to effort compared to a rigged competition. van Anders & Watson (2007) carried out two studies in men and women who completed a competitive computer-based vocabulary task through their own ability (Study 1) or by chance (Study 2). In the first study, all the participants showed a significant (or nearly significant) decrease in T over time, except for male winners, further suggesting that winning attenuated a decrease in T in men. In the second experiment, there were no T differences between winners and losers. Therefore, the direct relationship between performance and outcome seems relevant, but only in male winners. Even so, participants were not aware of the difference between the ability task and the chance task because they were asked about causal attribution of the outcome and a similar distribution of internal (ability) and external (luck) attributions was found in both studies. The authors concluded that winning due to their own ability elicited T increments or attenuated T decreases; therefore, neither good performance nor external recognition alone could mediate the *competition effect* in men. In another study, the importance of performance and T and C responses was assessed in instructors of dogs participating in an agility competition. They had to move and give orders efficiently. The authors found different patterns depending on sex: high basal T men dropped C after winning but increased C after defeat, whereas low basal T men showed no C changes. These results support the idea that high basal T men are motivated to gain status. Women winners diminished their C levels in comparison with losers (Mehta et al., 2008).

More recently, we analyzed hormonal and emotional changes associated with competition with real outcomes using a dyadic approach in young men and women (Abad-Tortosa et al., 2019). No differences in T or C responses appeared, although C was consistently related to competition (the previous C explained subsequent C levels) in women, but not in men. Women showed a stable emotional state, regardless of the outcome, whereas winner men increased their emotional valence (feelings of happiness, pleasure, satisfaction, and optimism) predicted by pre-task levels. In addition, loser men's post-task emotional valence was predicted by competition-valence. Furthermore, after competition, T levels moderated men's emotional valence, but not women's. In other words, higher basal T in men was related to higher negative mood after defeat, suggesting that high T men experienced the defeat as more threatening. T and mood have been inversely related in other investigations in women. Thus, Zilioli et al. (2014), in a competition characterized by uncertainty, that is, without feedback during the competition, found that the more surprised the women were about losing, the greater the T changes. It is possible that in a lower dominance position (narrow defeat), T increases may encourage dominance-seeking behaviors in women.

Casto et al. (2020) studied endurance (holding a weight) competitions with three conditions: (a) individual, (b) in dyads of same and mixed-sex pairs, or (c) in teams (without the presence of the other team). They reported no T outcome effect in men or women, but T reactivity was associated with task performance in both sexes when competing alone or in dyads. Focusing on dyads, the T response was different depending on the sex and outcome. T reactivity was positively related to performance in winner men and loser women. However, in the team condition, T reactivity positively predicted performance in men, but not in women. The authors concluded that, in men, transient changes in T influenced persistence (task performance) with the purpose of enhancing social status.

Threatened status has been studied by Maner et al. (2008) through social anxiety in a rigged competition, finding T decreases after defeat in high anxiety men, but not in winner men or women. Therefore, it is possible that these T decreases reflected social submission in threatening situations. Carré et al. (2009) reported no outcome effect on the same rigged competition task. However, basal T was predicted by trait dominance. This result was corroborated by Carré et al. (2013), who reported high T in men winners, but not in women or loser men. Overall, research relates basal T to dominance and status, but mainly in men.

Schultheiss et al. (2005) studied implicit power motivation, a measure of dominance, in two studies, the first in men and the second in women. It was assessed with a picture story that distinguished between assertive attempts to control, influence, dominate, or persuade others (indicative of power motivation) with an altruistic, socialized component. Subsequently, participants competed in a computerized serial task (manipulated outcome). High power motivation was related to T. In addition, sex differences appeared: power motivation predicted T increases in winner men and decreases in loser men, whereas in women, power motivation predicted T increases in losers. Moreover, winners showed increments in hedonic tone, and losers showed decreases (not related to T).

The CCM argues that cognitive appraisal has an influence during competition. In this section, it has been pointed out that psychological and emotional variables contribute to explaining sex differences in the response to competition. The next section is going to focus on cognitive appraisal and moderating variables in the response to competition and its outcome. Therefore, both field and laboratory investigations are included.

Cognitive Appraisal and Moderating Variables

Divergence or coincidence in the results can be partially explained by several moderating variables. First of all, theoretical reviews and meta-analyses (Casto & Edwards, 2016a; Geniole et al., 2017) have pointed out that *allocation* is a clear moderating variable because the literature shows a higher outcome effect in field competitions than in laboratory competitions. The rationale for this result is that in field studies there are other factors beyond the competition's outcome. For example, outside the laboratory: (a) the outcome is determined naturally (and is more relevant for sports people); (b) pre-competition T is usually collected earlier, even a day before (not just 10 minutes before competition, as in most laboratory studies); (c) current competition is real, and so participants are motivated and more engaged; and (d) their investment is higher (usually they are real sports competitions with consequences), among others. It is possible that current laboratory designs do not elicit T and C changes in the same way as sports competitions do (Abad-Tortosa et al., 2019), and there may be lower task involvement.

Other relevant moderating variables are related to individual differences. In the CCM, we highlight the role of individual differences in the perception of the contest, related to short- and long-term variables such as personality, competitiveness, or previous history of victory and defeat (Salvador, 2005; Salvador & Costa, 2009). Recently, the need for a more in-depth study of individual variations has also been pointed out (Casto & Edwards, 2021). Initial investigations on responses to competition and the outcome analyzed them from a biological point of view. However, from the beginning, competition stands out as involving changes in psychological variables, including emotional and cognitive processes (Ehrlesnpiel & Strahler, 2012). Therefore, understanding the way the individual interprets stimuli and his/her own capabilities or those of the opponent elicits a psychobiological response pattern (Salvador, 2012). There is a need to assess and consider the role of psychological variables and the response to competition and the outcome along with the biological variables, resulting in facilitator or detrimental effects on performance and outcome and increasing (or decreasing) the probability of victory.

Hence, before the competition, *motivation* is necessary to obtain involvement (and response to competition), but most studies have not assessed it directly. In real sports competition situations, such as a World Wrestling Competition (Le Panse et al., 2012) or a soccer league final game (Oliveira et al., 2009), motivation must be high. The importance of the situation for the individual is going to influence his/her perception. For example, Jiménez et al. (2020) found a T rise in men in a soccer competition, but not in friendly matches, regardless of the sports category; that is, regardless of whether the contest was perceived as challenging (or threatening), the stimuli were not sufficient to elicit T changes. Likewise, the *self-efficacy* perception (one's own or the opponent's) before competition acts as a moderator of the effort and resources invested to win the competition in both men (van der Meij et al., 2010) and women (Costa et al., 2016).

Another important factor is the *opponent*. A study by van der Meij et al. (2010) related T increases in men to the opponent's perceived self-efficacy, pointing out that the adversary is an essential element in making competition challenging, producing T changes. Thus, T administration in men promoted men's competitive persistence even in a low control context and against a stronger opponent (Kutlikova et al., 2021). In mixed-sex samples, C during a competition was related to the opponent's C; perhaps there were non-verbal clues during the competition that could give information to the opponent (Abad-Tortosa et al., 2019). In contrast, T predicted a prosocial attitude toward the opponent (Casto & Edwards, 2016c), pointing to the affiliative tendency in women. In sum, these results highlight the importance of the opponent's perceived characteristics; in addition, the presence of the opponent can be perceived differently by men and women. In this regard, men perceived their own capacity as higher and their opponent's capacity as lower, compared to women, although there were no differences in objective performance in the competition, suggesting that there were sex differences in the appraisal (Abad-Tortosa et al., 2017). In men, the presence of a women or the possibility of a date with a women increased T in dominant men, and a T rise during same-sex competition showed more affiliative behaviors when interacting with women (Borráz-León et al., 2018; van der Meij et al., 2008, 2011). Moreover, T increases may suppress affiliative processes to improve social status.

In team sports, where team success relies on players' complementing and cooperating, *bonding and connectedness* with teammates is a relevant variable that has been analyzed in relation to steroid hormones. In a soccer match, men's T changes after the game were positively related to bonding and status with teammates, whereas in women this relationship was with T levels before the game, and C was not associated with bonding (Edwards et al., 2006). This result has also been described in studies in women, where pre-competition T levels have been related to connectedness or bonding with teammates in rugby (Bateup et al., 2002), providing evidence of a relationship between connectedness, status or dominance, and T in female team sports. Likewise, in mixed-sex rowing teams, C was positively associated with bonding in women, but not in men, along with competition, but T did not show significant relationships (Kivlighan et al., 2005). This pattern of relationships agrees with the *tend-and-befriend* strategy (Taylor, 2006).

After the competition, the individual appraises the competition and the outcome, yielding outcome attributions, satisfaction with the outcome, and a mixture of emotions and physiological responses. The first moderating variable studied in the literature was positive mood in winners. In general, a robust outcome effect has been reported, with increases in positive mood or the emotional valence in winners compared to losers (Abad-Tortosa et al., 2019). In the case of outcome attributions, sex differences have been reported. Higher internal attributions in winners in sports (González-Bono et al., 1999) and laboratory competitions (Salvador et al., 2017) and higher external attributions in losers (González-Bono et al., 2000) have been found in men. However, in women, higher external attributions have been found in winners compared to losers, and it is possible that this result was related to social bias (Costa & Salvador, 2012). Regarding other emotional changes after the competition, both positive and negative emotional states seem to predict performance in competitions (Beedie et al., 2000). In several studies, participants were asked how they perceived the contest (in terms of difficulty or frustration, among others), and no sex differences were found (Carré et al., 2013), although winners showed less frustration (Carré et al., 2013; Costa & Salvador, 2012; van der Meij et al., 2010). In sports, higher pre-competition negative emotions, such as anger, depression, or fatigue, have been found in losers in comparison with winners (González-Bono et al., 1999), and higher satisfaction with the result has been described in winners (Suay et al., 1999). Finally, higher anxiety has been reported in women than in men, and in general, it has been related to losing and C increases (Filaire et al., 2009). In sum, sex differences could modulate the emotional response and individual appraisal after the competition.

Other important variables related to the distal contest are dimensions of *personality*, *personal history of success* (or defeat), and *experience*. Competitiveness is defined as the desire to engage and win in situations of interpersonal competitivity, and the will to be better than the others (or the best) has been studied. In general, men showed higher scores than women (Gladue & Bailey, 1995), and high T levels have been associated with dominance, the tendency to fight, or extraversion in men, and to action goals, self-confidence, and dominance in women (Cashdan, 1995). In competition settings, competitiveness has been related to T and C in men and women (Crewther & Cook, 2018; Kivlighan et al., 2005). Studies have shown that highly dominant individuals are usually in high-status positions, and that women are less prone to being involved in status-ranking. Evidence in animals and humans suggests that T promotes status-seeking and social dominance motivation and, thus, plays an important role in social status hierarchies (Eisenegger et al., 2011; Losecaat Vermeer et al., 2020; Salvador & Hidalgo, 2021).

Therefore, both emotional and personality variables affect coping with competition, and the research reveals that men and women appraise it somewhat differently. We have stated that, when the situation is important and the individual perceives that he/she has the resources to deal with it efficiently (Lazarus & Folkman, 1984), there is a high probability of facing it as a challenge (Salvador, 2005; Salvador & Costa, 2009). This challenge is going to affect the individual's effort and perception of control. Competition *per se* elicits higher responses than the same task carried out in a non-competitive way (i.e., higher performance in winners than in the control group, Abad-Tortosa et al., 2017). In competitions, men invest more effort and show T responses under certain circumstances, whereas women seem less dependent on the contest. In addition, there is a tendency for women to perceive competition as more threatening than men, possibly because men are more competitive and self-confident and have approach attitudes toward competition (Niederle & Vesterlund, 2011). Different competitive strategies have been described in the quest for status between the sexes. Men actively attempt to become the best in face-to-face interactions, interfering with opponents and seeking high status. In this process, coalitions increase the probability of winning against other groups, a strategy called *contest competition*. In contrast, women currently engage in solitary self-improvements, competing for status but avoiding direct competition by using a wide range of tactics, a strategy called *scramble competition* (Benenson & Abadzi, 2020).

Finally, it is worth noting that other possible sources of differences between men and women are changes in the sex hormones associated with the menstrual cycle. Although the menstrual cycle has not been controlled in general (except for Costa & Salvador, 2012), changes in T during the menstrual cycle in sports have been reported, with higher T levels around ovulation associated with changes in competitiveness and training motivation (Crewther & Cook, 2018). In contrast, in the early follicular phase, low T levels were related to less proneness to express competitive feelings, and estrogen was related to less competitive athletic interactions (Cashdan, 2003) and fewer choices to compete, although gender differences disappeared with performance feedback (Wozniak et al., 2014). An anticipatory estradiol response was found in soccer players (Casto & Edwards, 2016a). Furthermore, lower baseline T in women OC users has been described, although results show that it does not affect the T response to competition (Casto et al., 2014, 2020; Edwards & O'Neal, 2009). In addition, in the luteal phase, women are as likely as men to enter a competition (Wozniak et al., 2014).

Short- and Long-Term Effects of Competition

Several laboratory studies have investigated the effects of outcome (winning vs. losing) and the hormone response, beyond focusing on short competition effects on cognition, learning, or decision-making. In this context, Schultheiss et al. (2005) reported that, in men and women, power motivation predicted enhanced learning after winning a competition, whereas it impaired learning in losers, even though it was implicit learning. Employing the same procedure, Wirth et al. (2006) found that C after the competition was associated with high power motivation in losers and low power motivation in winners. Although no sex differences were analyzed, it is worth noting that losing a competition did not activate the hypothalamic-pituitary-adrenal axis; instead, C increases appeared in participants who strived for dominance and lost, but also in those with low dominance who won. These results are consistent with higher stress in situations of threatened status, that is, in mismatch situations where there is an incongruence between the desired level of status and the actual status. In this regard, Josephs et al. (2006) analyzed the condition of mismatch in rigged competition, dividing a mixed sample into high or low basal T levels (positively related to status), and its effects on a subsequent cognitive task. These authors reported that losers in the mismatch condition showed high T levels and worse performance on the posterior cognitive task. Mehta et al. (2009) studied basal T in a mixed-sex sample that completed a set card game; subsequently, participants competed under individual or group conditions. They found that basal T was positively related to performance in individual competition, but negatively related to performance in intergroup competition. Based on the former studies, it seems more likely that T levels could serve as a biological marker for an individual's motivation to increase (or maintain) status. In situations of mismatch, individuals strove for status, and low T individuals were more motivated to cooperate. However, no sex comparisons were carried out in these studies (Josephs et al., 2006; Mehta et al., 2009; Wirth et al., 2006).

In addition, the T response to context is related to subsequent situations. Thus, after a competition, T responses predicted the willingness to engage in future reactive aggression in men, but not in women, and so T reactivity was positively associated with higher subsequent aggressive behavior and T decreases with more passive behavior (Carré et al., 2009, 2013). Alacreu-Crespo et al. (2019) reported that T changes after competition predicted risky decision-making in men, but only when C was low, whereas high T and C were related to less risky decisions in women. In sum, high basal T were able to induce more risk-taking and reward-seeking, but only when C was low; moreover, hormonal situational variations can be related to daily choices, with a different impact on long-term outcomes in men and women.

The CCM asserts that the competitive context also has long-term effects. These long-term changes are difficult to study, due to the difficulty in collecting data from longitudinal studies. As explained above, investigations have tried to analyze changes after competition, pointing out that T may influence memory processes, improving motor skills to increase performance in future competitions (Wright et al., 2012). However, repeated-measures designs have been used less frequently. In this line, Zilioli and Watson, (2014) reported that T responses on one day predicted task performance on a second day, emphasizing long-term effects on learning and memory. Winning one competition promotes future competitiveness, enhancing the effort in future competitions and, therefore, increasing the future probability of winning (Losecaat Vermeer et al., 2016). In addition, competing implies choosing the best action in a particular situation that has some degree of uncertainty; that is, competition also involves decision-making that affects performance directly (and the outcome). Furthermore, considering that a person faces competitive situations throughout the life span, it is possible that circulating T would affect brain functioning, modifying cognitive and affective processes. Sex differences in information processing have been described, for example, in emotional memory or perception processing. Brain structures such as the amygdala, hippocampus, and lateralization underlie these differences (Ycaza Herrera et al., 2019). In fact, androgens are involved in brain shaping during the life span, with organizational and activational effects on the brain's structures, circuits, and receptors linked to emotion, social processing, learning, and decision-making.

Conclusions

Animal research emphasizes the existence of social competition in both sexes. In group-living animals, males compete for territories and mates, and females compete for reproductive opportunities, membership in breeding groups (and social status within them), and breeding sites. Inter-group competition is also common, with different breeding individuals competing for resources and space. The reasons for social competition are similar in both sexes, and differences are more quantitative than qualitative (Clutton-Brock & Huchard, 2013). Intrasexual competition for reproductive opportunities can occur in both sexes (Clutton-Brock, 2007). Therefore, there is sufficient evidence that evolution has shaped men and women to become effective competitors. A *competition effect* appears in both sexes when various circumstances and conditions exist, whereas a *winner effect* is more supported by studies employing sports competitions and mainly in men. Further research in women analyzing hormonal and psycho-social dimensions more in-depth is necessary to better understand these effects.

The sex differences shown in the literature may be a consequence of divergent features, such as sex-dimorphic physiological development through genetic and hormonal influences that are subsequently activated in childhood and adolescence in interactions with behavior and the environment. In this context, androgens have dramatic effects on the brain, also affecting behavior and competitiveness. T is related to rank, dominant behavior, and status. In addition, estrogen and progesterone have also been related to different competitivity during the menstrual cycle, also interfering with other hormones. Hence, noticeable sex differences in cognitive, emotional, and affective disorders have been described. Eventually, steroid effects on the brain may have spillover effects that enable sex differences in situational appraisal.

An important point is that, although men and women strive for status, the motivations to compete can be different. More importantly, the routes through which humans achieve status are diverse and unequal between the sexes, and dominance in the social context can be achieved indirectly (e.g., achieve a position or marry someone in a higher social position). In addition, men are willing to become the best in direct interactions, whereas women prefer indirect competitions. There are different patterns of social interactions depending on sex (Costa et al., 2017; Salvador & Hidalgo, 2021). In addition, it is worth noting that competition is not just winning or losing. In fact, several moderating variables, such as positive mood, self-efficacy, causal attributions, the opponent, influence competition responses, and several others are somewhat different in men and women.

In sum, the study of sex differences in the response to competition still has some unresolved questions and methodological issues that should be addressed to understand which variables are related to winning or losing a competition, as well as the different incidence of some disorders in men and women.

References

Abad-Tortosa, D., Alacreu-Crespo, A., Costa, R., Salvador, A., & Serrano, M. A. (2017). Sex differences in autonomic response and situational appraisal of a competitive situation in young adults. *Biological Psychology 126*, 61–70. https://doi.org/10.1016/j.biopsycho.2017.04.008.

Abad-Tortosa, D., Costa, R., Alacreu-Crespo, A., Hidalgo, V., Salvador, A., & Serrano, M. A. (2019). Hormonal and emotional responses to competition using a dyadic approach: Basal testosterone predicts emotional state after a defeat. *Physiology and Behavior 206*, 106–117. https://doi.org/10.1016/j.physbeh.2019.03.025.

Alacreu-Crespo, A., Costa, R., Abad-Tortosa, D., Hidalgo, V., Salvador, A., & Serrano, M. A. (2019). Hormonal changes after competition predict sex-differentiated decision-making. *Journal of Behavioral Decision Making 32*(5), 550–563. https://doi.org/10.1002/bdm.2128.

Alexander, G. M., & Hines, M. (2002). Sex differences in response to children's toys in nonhuman primates (Cercopithecus aethiops sabaeus). *Evolution and Human Behavior 23*(6), 467–479. https://doi.org/10.1016/S1090-5138(02)00107-1.

Alexander, G. M., & Peterson, B. S. (2004). Testing the prenatal hormone hypothesis of tic-related disorders: Gender identity and gender role behavior. *Development and Psychopathology 16*(2), 407–420. https://doi.org/10.1017/S095457940404458X.

Archer, J. (2006). Testosterone and human aggression: An evaluation of the challenge hypothesis. *Neuroscience and Biobehavioral Reviews 30*(3), 319–345. https://doi.org/10.1016/j.neubiorev.2004.12.007.

Bakker, J. (2018). The Sexual Differentiation of the Human Brain: Role of Sex Hormones Versus Sex Chromosomes. *Current Topics in Behavioral Neurosciences, 43*, 45–67. https://doi.org/https://doi.org/10.1007/7854_2018_70.

Baskin, L., Cao, M., Sinclair, A., Li, Y., Overland, M., Isaacson, D., & Cunha, G. R. (2020). Androgen and estrogen receptor expression in the developing human penis and clitoris. *Differentiation 111*, 41–59. https://doi.org/10.1016/j.diff.2019.08.005.

Bateman, A. J. (1948). Intra-sexual selection in drosophila. *Heredity 2*(3), 349–368.

Bateup, H. S., Booth, A., Shirtcliff, E. A., & Granger, D. A. (2002). Testosterone, cortisol, and women's competition. *Evolution and Human Behavior 23*(3), 181–192. https://doi.org/10.1016/S1090-5138(01)00100-3.

Baucom, D. H., Besch, P. K., & Callahan, S. (1985). Relation between testosterone concentration, sex role identity, and personality among females. *Journal of Personality and Social Psychology 48*(5), 1218.

Beedie, C. J., Terry, P. C., & Lane, A. M. (2000). The profile of mood states and athletic performance: Two meta-analyses. *Journal of Applied Sport Psychology 12*(1), 49–68. https://doi.org/10.1080/10413200008404213.

Benenson, J. F., & Abadzi, H. (2020). Contest versus scramble competition: sex differences in the quest for status. *Current Opinion in Psychology 33*, 62–68. https://doi.org/10.1016/j.copsyc.2019.07.013.

Bikle, D. D. (2021). The free hormone hypothesis: When, why, and how to measure the free hormone levels to assess vitamin D, thyroid, sex hormone, and cortisol status. *JBMR Plus 5*(1), 1–10. https://doi.org/10.1002/jbm4.10418.

Blanco, C., Hoertel, N., Wall, M. M., Franco, S., Peyre, H., Neria, Y., Helpman, L., & Limosin, F. (2018). Toward understanding sex differences in the prevalence of posttraumatic stress disorder: Results from the National Epidemiologic Survey on Alcohol and Related Conditions. *The Journal of Clinical Psychiatry 79*(2), 16m11364. https://doi.org/10.4088/JCP.16m11364.

Blecher, S. R., & Erickson, R. P. (2007). Genetics of sexual development: A new paradigm. *American Journal of Medical Genetics, Part A 143A*, 3054–3068. https://doi.org/10.1002/AJMG.A.32037.

Borráz-León, J. I., Cerda-Molina, A. L., Rantala, M. J., & Mayagoitia-Novales, L. (2018). Choosing fighting competitors among men: Testosterone, personality, and motivations. *Evolutionary Psychology 16*(1), 1–10. https://doi.org/10.1177/1474704918757243.

Bos, P. A., Terburg, D., & Van Honk, J. (2010). Testosterone decreases trust in socially naïve humans. *Proceedings of the National Academy of Sciences of the United States of America 107*(22), 9991–9995. https://doi.org/10.1073/pnas.0911700107.

Carré, J. M., & Archer, J. (2018). Testosterone and human behavior: The role of individual and contextual variables. *Current Opinion in Psychology 19*, 149–153. https://doi.org/10.1016/j.copsyc.2017.03.021.

Carré, J. M., Campbell, J. A., Lozoya, E., Goetz, S. M. M., & Welker, K. M. (2013). Changes in testosterone mediate the effect of winning on subsequent aggressive behaviour. *Psychoneuroendocrinology 38*(10), 2034–2041. https://doi.org/10.1016/j.psyneuen.2013.03.008.

Carré, J. M., Putnam, S. K., & McCormick, C. M. (2009). Testosterone responses to competition predict future aggressive behaviour at a cost to reward in men. *Psychoneuroendocrinology 34*(4), 561–570. https://doi.org/10.1016/j.psyneuen.2008.10.018.

Cashdan, E. (1995). Hormones, sex, and status in women. *Hormones and Behavior 29*(3), 354–366. https://doi.org/https://doi.org/10.1006/hbeh.1995.1025.

Cashdan, E. (1998). Are men more competitive than women? *British Journal of Social Psychology 37*(2), 213–229. https://doi.org/10.1111/j.2044-8309.1998.tb01166.x.

Cashdan, E. (2003). Hormones and competitive aggression in women. *Aggressive Behavior 29*(2), 107–115. https://doi.org/10.1002/ab.10041.

Casto, K. V., & Edwards, D. A. (2016a). Before, during, and after: How phases of competition differentially affect testosterone, cortisol, and estradiol levels in women athletes. *Adaptive Human Behavior and Physiology 2*(1), 11–25. https://doi.org/10.1007/s40750-015-0028-2.

Casto, K. V., & Edwards, D. A. (2016b). Testosterone, cortisol, and human competition. *Hormones and Behavior 82*, 21–37. https://doi.org/10.1016/j.yhbeh.2016.04.004.

Casto, K. V., & Edwards, D. A. (2016c). Testosterone and reconciliation among women: After-competition testosterone predicts prosocial attitudes towards opponents. *Adaptive Human Behavior and Physiology 2*(3), 220–233. https://doi.org/10.1007/s40750-015-0037-1.

Casto, K. V., & Edwards, D. A. (2021). Individual differences in hormonal responsiveness to social encounters: Commentary on Félix et al., 2020 and review of pertinent issues. *Hormones and Behavior 129*(September 2020). https://doi.org/10.1016/j.yhbeh.2020.104921.

Casto, K. V., Edwards, D. A., Akinola, M., Davis, C., & Mehta, P. H. (2020). Testosterone reactivity to competition and competitive endurance in men and women. *Hormones and Behavior 123*, 104665. https://doi.org/10.1016/j.yhbeh.2019.104665.

Casto, K. V., Elliott, C., & Edwards, D. A. (2014). Intercollegiate cross country competition: Effects of warm-up and racing on salivary levels of cortisol and testosterone. *International Journal of Exercise Science 7*(4), 318–328. http://digitalcommons.wku.edu/ijes/vol7/iss4/8/.

Chapman, E., Baron-Cohen, S., Auyeung, B., Knickmeyer, R., Taylor, K., & Hackett, G. (2006). Fetal testosterone and empathy: Evidence from the empathy quotient (EQ) and the "reading the mind in the eyes" test. *Social Neuroscience 1*(2), 135–148. https://doi.org/10.1080/17470910600992239.

Clarkson, T., Karvay, Y., Quarmley, M., & Jarcho, J. M. (2021). Sex differences in neural mechanisms of social and non-social threat monitoring. *Developmental Cognitive Neuroscience 52*, 101038. https://doi.org/10.1016/j.dcn.2021.101038.

Clutton-Brock, T. (2007). Sexual selection in males and females. *Science 318*, 1882–1885. http://www.ncbi.nlm.nih.gov/pubmed/18096798.

Clutton-Brock, T., & Huchard, E. (2013). Social competition and selection in males and females. *Philosophical Transactions of the Royal Society B 368*, 1–14. https://doi.org/10.1098/rstb.2013.0074.

Costa, R., & Salvador, A. (2012). Associations between success and failure in a face-to-face competition and psychobiological parameters in young women. *Psychoneuroendocrinology 37*(11), 1780–1790. https://doi.org/10.1016/j.psyneuen.2012.03.012.

Costa, R., Serrano, M. A., & Salvador, A. (2017). Psychobiological Responses to Competition in Women. In M. L. Fisher (Ed.), *The Oxford handbook of women and competition* (pp. 1–30). Oxford University Press. https://doi.org/10.1093/oxfordhb/9780199376377.013.21.

Costa, R., Serrano, M. A., & Salvador, A. (2016). Importance of self-efficacy in psychoendocrine responses to competition and performance in women. *Psicothema 28*(1), 66–70. https://doi.org/10.7334/psicothema2015.166.

Crewther, B. T., & Cook, C. J. (2018). A longitudinal analysis of salivary testosterone concentrations and competitiveness in elite and non-elite women athletes. *Physiology and Behavior 188*, 157–161. https://doi.org/10.1016/j.physbeh.2018.02.012.

Dabbs Jr, J. M. (1992). Testosterone and occupational achievement. *Social Forces 70*(3), 813–824. https://doi.org/https://doi.org/10.1093/sf/70.3.813.

Darwin, C. (1871). *The descent of man, and selection in relation to sex* (J. T. Bonner & R. M. May (Ed.), 1st issue. Princenton Universitiy Press.

De Lisle, S. P. (2019). Understanding the evolution of ecological sex differences: Integrating character displacement and the Darwin–Bateman paradigm. *Evolution Letters 3*(5), 434–447. https://doi.org/10.1002/evl3.134.

Dewsbury, D. A. (2005). The Darwin–Bateman paradigm in historical context. *Integrative and Comparative Biology 45*, 831–837. http://isi1.isiknowledge.com/portal.cgi/wos.

Drea, C. M. (2005). Bateman revisited: The reproductive tactics of female primates. *Integrative and Comparative Biology 45*, 915–923. https://academic.oup.com/icb/article/45/5/915/624509.

Dumontet, T., & Martinez, A. (2021). Adrenal androgens, adrenarche, and zona reticularis: A human affair? *Molecuar and Cellular Endocrinology 528*, 111239. https://doi.org/https://doi.org/10.1016/j.mce.2021.111239.

Edwards, D. A., & Casto, K. V. (2013). Women's intercollegiate athletic competition: Cortisol, testosterone, and the dual-hormone hypothesis as it relates to status among teammates. *Hormones and Behavior 64*(1), 153–160. https://doi.org/10.1016/j.yhbeh.2013.03.003.

Edwards, D. A., & Kurlander, L. S. (2010). Women's intercollegiate volleyball and tennis: Effects of warm-up, competition, and practice on saliva levels of cortisol and testosterone. *Hormones and Behavior 58*(4), 606–613. https://doi.org/10.1016/j.yhbeh.2010.06.015.

Edwards, D. A., & O'Neal, J. L. (2009). Oral contraceptives decrease saliva testosterone but do not affect the rise in testosterone associated with athletic competition. *Hormones and Behavior 56*(2), 195–198. https://doi.org/10.1016/j.yhbeh.2009.01.008.

Edwards, D. A., Wetzel, K., & Wyner, D. R. (2006). Intercollegiate soccer: Saliva cortisol and testosterone are elevated during competition, and testosterone is related to status and social connectedness with teammates. *Physiology and Behavior 87*(1), 135–143. https://doi.org/10.1016/j.physbeh.2005.09.007.

Ehrlesnpiel, F., & Strahler, K. (2012). *Psychoneuroendocrinology of sport and exercise: Foundations, markers, trends*. 1st ed. Routledge. https://doi.org/https://doi.org/10.4324/9780203133743.

Eisenegger, C., Haushofer, J., & Fehr, E. (2011). The role of testosterone in social interaction. *Trends in Cognitive Sciences 15*(6), 263–271. https://doi.org/10.1016/j.tics.2011.04.008.

Elias, M. (1981). Serum cortisol, testosterone, and testosterone-binding globulin responses to competitive fighting in human males. *Aggressive Behavior 7*(3), 215–224. https://doi.org/10.1002/1098-2337(1981)7:3<215::AID-AB2480070305>3.0.CO;2-M.

Felmingham, K. L., Tran, T. P., Fong, W. C., & Bryant, R. A. (2012). Sex differences in emotional memory consolidation: The effect of stress-induced salivary alpha-amylase and cortisol. *Biological Psychology 89*(3), 539–544. https://doi.org/10.1016/j.biopsycho.2011.12.006.

Filaire, E., Alix, D., Ferrand, C., & Verger, M. (2009). Psychophysiological stress in tennis players during the first single match of a tournament. *Psychoneuroendocrinology 34*(1), 150–157. https://doi.org/10.1016/j.psyneuen.2008.08.022.

Garrido-Chaves, R., Perez-Alarcón, M., Perez, V., Hidalgo, V., Pulopulos, M. M., & Salvador, A. (2021). FRN and P3 during the Iowa gambling task: The importance of gender. *Psychophysiology 58*(3). https://doi.org/10.1111/psyp.13734.

Geniole, S. N., Bird, B. M., Ruddick, E. L., & Carré, J. M. (2017). Effects of competition outcome on testosterone concentrations in humans: An updated meta-analysis. *Hormones and Behavior 92*, 37–50. https://doi.org/10.1016/j.yhbeh.2016.10.002.

Gladue, B. A., & Michael Bailey, J. (1995). Aggressiveness, competitiveness, and human sexual orientation. *Psychoneuroendocrinology 20*(5), 475–485. https://doi.org/https://doi.org/10.1016/0306-4530(94)00073-J.

Gogos, A., Ney, L. J., Seymour, N., Van Rheenen, T. E., & Felmingham, K. L. (2019). Sex differences in schizophrenia, bipolar disorder, and post-traumatic stress disorder: Are gonadal hormones the link? *British Journal of Pharmacology 176*(21), 4119–4135). https://doi.org/10.1111/bph.14584.

González-Bono, E., Salvador, A., Ricarte, J., Serrano, M. A., & Arnedo, M. (2000). Testosterone and attribution of successful competition. *Aggressive Behavior 26*(3), 235–240. https://doi.org/10.1002/(SICI)1098-2337(2000)26:3<235::AID-AB3>3.0.CO;2-L.

González-Bono, E., Salvador, A., Serrano, M. A., & Ricarte, J. (1999). Testosterone, cortisol, and mood in a sports team competition. *Hormones and Behavior 35*(1), 55–62. https://doi.org/10.1006/hbeh.1998.1496.

Hamilton, L. D., Van Anders, S. M., Cox, D. N., & Watson, N. V. (2009). The effect of competition on salivary testosterone in elite female athletes. *International Journal of Sports Physiology and Performance 4*, 538–542. https://doi.org/10.1123/ijspp.4.4.538.

Hammes, S. R., & Levin, E. R. (2019). Impact of estrogens in males and androgens in females. *Journal of Clinical Investigation 129*(5), 1818–1826. https://doi.org/10.1172/JCI125755.

Hassett, J. M., Siebert, E. R., & Wallen, K. (2008). Sex differences in rhesus monkey toy preferences parallel those of children. *Hormones and Behavior 54*(3), 359–364. https://doi.org/10.1016/j.yhbeh.2008.03.008.

Hawley, P. H. (1999). The ontogenesis of social dominance: A strategy-based evolutionary perspective. *Developmental Review 19*(1), 97–132. http://linkinghub.elsevier.com/retrieve/pii/S0273229798904701.

Hedrick, A. V, & Temeles, E. J. (1989). The evolution of sexual dimorphism in animals: Hypotheses and tests. *Trends in Ecology & Evolution 4*(5), 136–138. https://doi.org/https://doi.org/10.1016/0169-5347(89)90212-7.

Hermans, E. J., Putman, P., & van Honk, J. (2006). Testosterone administration reduces empathetic behavior: A facial mimicry study. *Psychoneuroendocrinology 31*(7), 859–866. https://doi.org/10.1016/j.psyneuen.2006.04.002.

Hines, M. (2010). Gendered behavior across the life span. In R. M. Lerner, M. E. Lamb, & A. Freund (Ed.), *The handbook of life-span development* (Vol II: pp. 341–378). John Wiley & Sons. https://doi.org/https://doi.org/10.1002/9780470880166.hlsd002010.

Hines, M. (2011). Gender development and the human brain. *Annual Review of Neuroscience 34*, 69–88. https://doi.org/10.1146/annurev-neuro-061010-113654.

Hoquet, T. (2020). Bateman (1948): Rise and fall of a paradigm? *Animal Behaviour 164*, 223–231. https://doi.org/10.1016/j.anbehav.2019.12.008.

Janicke, T., Häderer, I. K., Lajeunesse, M. J., & Anthes, N. (2016). Darwinian sex roles confirmed across the animal kingdom. *Science Advances 2*, e1500983. https://doi.org/10.1126/sciadv.1500983.

Jiménez, M., Aguilar, R., & Alvero-Cruz, J. R. (2012). Effects of victory and defeat on testosterone and cortisol response to competition: Evidence for same response patterns in men and women. *Psychoneuroendocrinology 37*(9), 1577–1581. https://doi.org/10.1016/j.psyneuen.2012.02.011.

Jiménez, M., Alvero-Cruz, J. R., Solla, J., García-Bastida, J., García-Coll, V., Rivilla, I., Ruiz, E., García-Romero, J., Carnero, E. A., & Clemente-Suárez, V. J. (2020). Competition seriousness and competition level modulate testosterone and cortisol responses in soccer players. *International Journal of Environmental Research and Public Health 17*(1), 350. https://doi.org/10.3390/ijerph17010350.

Jogia, J., Dima, D., & Frangou, S. (2012). Sex differences in bipolar disorder: A review of neuroimaging findings and new evidence. *Bipolar Disorders 14*(4), 461–471. https://doi.org/10.1111/j.1399-5618.2012.01014.x.

Josephs, R. A., Sellers, J. G., Newman, M. L., & Mehta, P. H. (2006). The mismatch effect: When testosterone and status are at odds. *Journal of Personality and Social Psychology 90*(6), 999–1013. https://doi.org/10.1037/0022-3514.90.6.999.

Jost, A. (1953). Problems of fetal endocrinology: The gonadal and hypophyseal hormones. *Recent Progress in Hormone Research 8*, 379–418.

Jost, A. (1972). A new look at the mechanisms controlling sex differentiation in mammals. *The Johns Hopkins Medical Journal 130*(1), 38–53.

Karl, A., Schaefer, M., Malta, L. S., Dörfel, D., Rohleder, N., & Werner, A. (2006). A meta-analysis of structural brain abnormalities in PTSD. *Neuroscience and Biobehavioral Reviews 30*(7), 1004–1031. https://doi.org/10.1016/j.neubiorev.2006.03.004.

Kaymak, E., & Yıldırım, A. B. (2020). Aromatase, estrogen and male reproduction: A review. *Experimental and Applied Medical Science 1*(3), 100–108. https://doi.org/10.46871/eams.2020.13.

Khramtsova, E. A., Heldman, R., Derks, E. M., Yu, D., Davis, L. K., & Stranger, B. E. (2019). Sex differences in the genetic architecture of obsessive–compulsive disorder. *American Journal of Medical Genetics, Part B: Neuropsychiatric Genetics 180*(6), 351–364. https://doi.org/10.1002/ajmg.b.32687.

Kimura, D. (1999). *Sex and cognition*. MIT Press.

Kivlighan, K. T., Granger, D. A., & Booth, A. (2005). Gender differences in testosterone and cortisol response to competition. *Psychoneuroendocrinology 30*(1), 58–71. https://doi.org/10.1016/j.psyneuen.2004.05.009.

Kutlikova, H. H., Geniole, S. N., Eisenegger, C., Lamm, C., Jocham, G., & Studer, B. (2021). Not giving up: Testosterone promotes persistence against a stronger opponent. *Psychoneuroendocrinology 128*, 105214. https://doi.org/10.1016/j.psyneuen.2021.105214.

Lazarus, R. S., & Folkman, S. (1984). *Stress, appraisal, and coping*. Springer.

Le Panse, B., Labsy, Z., Baillot, A., Vibarel-Rebot, N., Parage, G., Albrings, D., Lasne, F., & Collomp, K. (2012). Changes in steroid hormones during an international powerlifting competition. *Steroids 77*(13), 1339–1344. https://doi.org/10.1016/j.steroids.2012.07.015.

Lee, S. K. (2018). Sex as an important biological variable in biomedical research. *BMB Reports 51*(4), 167–173. https://doi.org/10.5483/BMBRep.2018.51.4.034.

Lochner, C., Hemmings, S. M. J., Kinnear, C. J., Moolman-Smook, J. C., Corfield, V. A., Knowles, J. A., Niehaus, D. J. H., & Stein, D. J. (2004). Gender in obsessive-compulsive disorder: Clinical and genetic findings. *European Neuropsychopharmacology 14*(2), 105–113. https://doi.org/10.1016/S0924-977X(03)00063-4.

Losecaat Vermeer, A. B., Krol, I., Gausterer, C., Wagner, B., Eisenegger, C., & Lamm, C. (2020). Exogenous testosterone increases status-seeking motivation in men with unstable low social status. *Psychoneuroendocrinology 113*, 104552. https://doi.org/10.1016/j.psyneuen.2019.104552.

Losecaat Vermeer, A. B., Riečanský, I., & Eisenegger, C. (2016). Competition, testosterone, and adult neurobehavioral plasticity. *Progress in Brain Research 229*, 213–238. https://doi.org/10.1016/bs.pbr.2016.05.004.

Luders, E., Narr, K. L., Thompson, P. M., Rex, D. E., Jancke, L., Steinmetz, H., & Toga, A. W. (2004). Gender differences in cortical complexity. *Nature Neuroscience 7*(8), 799–800. https://doi.org/10.1038/nn1277.

Maner, J. K., Miller, S. L., Schmidt, N. B., & Eckel, L. A. (2008). Submitting to defeat: Social anxiety, dominance threat, and decrements in testosterone. *Psychological Science 19*(8), 764–768. https://doi.org/10.1111/j.1467-9280.2008.02154.x.

Martínez, K., Janssen, J., Pineda-Pardo, J. Á., Carmona, S., Román, F. J., Alemán-Gómez, Y., Garcia-Garcia, D., Escorial, S., Quiroga, M. Á., & Santarnecchi, E. (2017). Individual differences in the dominance of interhemispheric connections predict cognitive ability beyond sex and brain size. *NeuroImage 155*, 234–244. https://doi.org/https://doi.org/10.1016/j.neuroimage.2017.04.029.

Mazur, A. (1985). A biosocial model of status in face-to-face primate groups. *Social Forces 64*(2), 377–402. https://doi.org/https://doi.org/10.2307/2578647.

Mazur, A., & Lamb, T. A. (1980). Testosterone, status, and mood in human males. *Hormones and Behavior 14*(3), 236–246. https://doi.org/10.1016/0018-506X(80)90032-X.

Mazur, A., Susman, E. J., & Edelbrock, S. (1997). Sex difference in testosterone response to competition in a video game. *Evolution and Human Behavior 18*, 317–326. https://doi.org/https://doi.org/10.1016/S1090-5138(97)00013-5.

McCarthy, M. M. (2008). Estradiol and the developing brain. *Physiological Reviews 88*(1), 91–124. https://doi.org/10.1152/physrev.00010.2007.

McCaul, K. D., Gladue, B. A., & Joppa, M. (1992). Winning, losing, mood, and testosterone. *Hormones and Behavior 26*(4), 486–504. https://doi.org/10.1016/0018-506X(92)90016-O.

Mehta, P. H., Jones, A. C., & Josephs, R. A. (2008). The social endocrinology of dominance: Basal testosterone predicts cortisol changes and behavior following victory and defeat. *Journal of Personality and Social Psychology 94*(6), 1078–1093. https://doi.org/10.1037/0022-3514.94.6.1078.

Mehta, P. H., Wuehrmann, E. V., & Josephs, R. A. (2009). When are low testosterone levels advantageous? The moderating role of individual versus intergroup competition. *Hormones and Behavior 56*(1), 158–162. https://doi.org/10.1016/j.yhbeh.2009.04.001.

Molina, P. E. (2013). *Endocrine physiology*. 4th ed. McGraw Hill Medical.

Moya-Albiol, L., Herrero, N., & Bernal, M. C. (2010). The neural bases of empathy. *Revista de Neurologia 50*(2), 89–100. https://doi.org/https://doi.org/10.33588/rn.5002.2009111.

Neal, J. M. (2016). *How the endocrine system works*. 2nd ed. John Wiley & Sons.

Nelson, R. J., & Kriegsfeld, L. J. (2017). *An introduction to behavioral endocrinology*. 5th ed. Sinauer Associates, Inc. Publishers.

Niederle, M., & Vesterlund, L. (2011). Gender and competition. *Annual Review of Economics 3*(1), 601–630. https://doi.org/10.1146/annurev-economics-111809-125122.

Nolen-Hoeksema, S., Larson, J., & Grayson, C. (1999). Explaining the gender difference in depressive symptoms. *Journal of Personality and Social Psychology 77*(5), 1061–1072. https://doi.org/10.1037/0022-3514.77.5.1061.

Oliveira, T., Gouveia, M. J., & Oliveira, R. F. (2009). Testosterone responsiveness to winning and losing experiences in female soccer players. *Psychoneuroendocrinology 34*(7), 1056–1064. https://doi.org/10.1016/j.psyneuen.2009.02.006.

Phoenix, C. H., Goy, R. W., Gerall, A. A., & Young, W. C. (1959). Organizing action of prenatally administered testosterone propionate on the tissues mediating mating behavior in the female guinea pig. *Hormones and Behavior 504*, 369–382. https://doi.org/https://doi.org/10.1210/endo-65-3-369.

Pooley, E. C., Fineberg, N., & Harrison, P. J. (2007). The met158 allele of catechol-O-methyltransferase (COMT) is associated with obsessive-compulsive disorder in men: Case-control study and meta-analysis. *Molecular Psychiatry 12*(6), 556–561. https://doi.org/10.1038/sj.mp.4001951.

Proverbio, A. M. (2021). Sex differences in the social brain and in social cognition. *Journal of Neuroscience Research*. https://doi.org/10.1002/jnr.24787.

Reber, J., & Tranel, D. (2016). Mini-review sex differences in the functional lateralization of emotion and decision making in the human brain. *Journal of Neuroscience Research 95*, 270–278. https://doi.org/10.1002/jnr.23829.

Roughgarden, J. (2007). Challenging Darwin's theory of sexual selection. *Daedalus 136*(2), 23–36.

Salvador, A. (2005). Coping with competitive situations in humans. *Neuroscience and Biobehavioral Reviews 29*(1), 195–205. https://doi.org/10.1016/j.neubiorev.2004.07.004.

Salvador, A. (2012). Steroid hormones and some evolutionary-relevant social interactions. *Motivation and Emotion 36*(1), 74–83. https://doi.org/10.1007/s11031-011-9265-2.

Salvador, A., & Costa, R. (2009). Coping with competition: Neuroendocrine responses and cognitive variables. *Neuroscience and Biobehavioral Reviews 33*(2), 160–170. https://doi.org/10.1016/j.neubiorev.2008.09.005.

Salvador, A., Costa, R., Hidalgo, V., & González-Bono, E. (2017). Causal attribution and psychobiological response to competition in young men. *Hormones and Behavior 92*, 72–81. https://doi.org/10.1016/j.yhbeh.2017.04.004.

Salvador, A., & Hidalgo, V. (2021). Diferencias en los patrones conductuales de hombres y mujeres en las interacciones sociales. In M. R. Edinete & S. V. Puliese (Ed.), *Múltiples facetas de la violencia en Latinoamérica* (pp. 22–46). Edufes.

Salvador, A., Simón, V., Suay, F., & Llorens, L. (1987). Testosterone and cortisol responses to competitive fighting in human males: A pilot study. *Aggressive Behavior 13*(1), 9–13. https://doi.org/10.1002/1098-2337(1987)13:1<9::AID-AB2480130103>3.0.CO;2-4.

Salvador, A., Suay, F., & Cantón, E. (1990). Efectos del resultado de una competición y de la categoría deportiva sobre los cambios en la testosterona y el cortisol séricos. *Actas Del II Congreso Nacional Del Colegio Oficial de Psicólogos 49*–54.

Sasano, H., Takahashi, K., Satoh, F., Nagura, H., & Harada, N. (1998). Aromatase in the human central nervous system. *Clinical Endocrinology 48*(3), 325–329. https://doi.org/10.1046/j.1365-2265.1998.00390.x.

Schultheiss, O. C., Wirth, M. M., Torges, C. M., Pang, J. S., Villacorta, M. A., & Welsh, K. M. (2005). Effects of implicit power motivation on men's and women's implicit learning and testosterone changes after social victory or defeat. *Journal of Personality and Social Psychology 88*(1), 174–188. https://doi.org/10.1037/0022-3514.88.1.174.

Serrano, M. A., Salvador, A., González-Bono, E., Sanchís, C., & Suay, F. (2000). Hormonal responses to competition. *Psicothema 12*, 440–444. https://reunido.uniovi.es/index.php/PST/article/view/7615.

Shi, J., Guo, H., Fan, F., Fan, H., An, H., Wang, Z., Tan, S., Yang, F., & Tan, Y. (2018). Sex differences of hippocampal structure in bipolar disorder. *Psychiatry Research—Neuroimaging 273*, 35–41. https://doi.org/10.1016/j.pscychresns.2017.11.011.

Suay, F., Salvador, A., González-Bono, E., Sanchís, C., Martínez, M., Martínez-Sanchis, S., Simón, V., & Montoro, J. B. (1999). Effects of competition and its outcome on serum testosterone, cortisol and prolactin. *Psychoneuroendocrinology 24*(5), 551–566. https://doi.org/10.1016/S0306-4530(99)00011-6.

Swerdloff, R. S., Wang, C., & Sinha Hikim, A. P. (2002). Hypothalamic-pituitary-gonadal axis in men. In D. W. Pfaff, A. P. Arnold, S. E. Fahrbach, A. M. Etgen, & R. T. Rubin (Ed.), *Hormones, brain and behavior* (pp. 1–36). Academic Press. https://doi.org/https://doi.org/10.1016/B978-012532104-4/50085-8.

Taylor, S. E. (2006). Tend and befriend: Biobehavioral bases of affiliation under stress. *Current Directions in Psychological Science 15*(6), 273–277. https://doi.org/https://doi.org/10.1111/j.1467-8721.2006.00451.x.

Taylor, S. E., Klein, L. C., Lewis, B. P., Gruenewald, T. L., Gurung, R. A. R., & Updegraff, J. A. (2000). Biobehavioral responses to stress in females: Tend-and-befriend, not fight-or-flight. *Psychological Review 107*(3), 411–429. https://doi.org/10.1037//0033-295X.107.3.411.

Trivers, R. L. (1972). Parental investment and sexual selection. In B. G. Campbell (Ed.), *Sexual selection and the descent of man* (pp. 136–179). Routledge.

van Anders, S. M., & Watson, N. V. (2007). Effects of ability- and chance-determined competition outcome on testosterone. *Physiology and Behavior 90*(4), 634–642. https://doi.org/10.1016/j.physbeh.2006.11.017.

Van Anders, S. M., & Watson, N. V. (2006). Social neuroendocrinology effects of social contexts and behaviors on sex steroids in humans. *Human Nature 17*(2), 212–237. https://doi.org/10.1007/s12110-006-1018-7.

van den Bos, R., Homberg, J., & de Visser, L. (2013). A critical review of sex differences in decision-making tasks: Focus on the Iowa Gambling Task. *Behavioural Brain Research 238*(1), 95–108. https://doi.org/10.1016/j.bbr.2012.10.002.

van der Meij, L., Almela, M., Buunk, A. P., Dubbs, S., & Salvador, A. (2012). 2D:4D in men is related to aggressive dominance but not to sociable dominance. *Aggressive Behavior 38*, 208–212. https://doi.org/10.1002/ab.21422.

van der Meij, L., Almela, M., Buunk, A. P., Fawcett, T. W., & Salvador, A. (2011). Men with elevated testosterone levels show more affiliative behaviours during interactions with women. *Proceedings of the Royal Society B: Biological Sciences 279*(1726), 202–208. https://doi.org/10.1098/rspb.2011.0764.

van der Meij, L., Buunk, A. P., Almela, M., & Salvador, A. (2010). Testosterone responses to competition: The opponent's psychological state makes it challenging. *Biological Psychology 84*(2), 330–335. https://doi.org/10.1016/j.biopsycho.2010.03.017.

van der Meij, L., Buunk, A. P., van de Sande, J. P., & Salvador, A. (2008). The presence of a woman increases testosterone in aggressive dominant men. *Hormones and Behavior 54*(5), 640–644. https://doi.org/10.1016/j.yhbeh.2008.07.001.

van Honk, J., Schutter, D. J., Bos, P. A., Kruijt, A.-W., Lentjes, E. G., & Baron-Cohen, S. (2011). Testosterone administration impairs cognitive empathy in women depending on second-to-fourth digit ratio. *Proceedings of the National Academy of Sciences 108*(8), 3448–3452. https://doi.org/10.1073/PNAS.1011891108.

Wang, S. C., Chen, Y. C., Chen, S. J., Lee, C. H., & Cheng, C. M. (2020). Alcohol addiction, gut microbiota, and alcoholism treatment: A review. *International Journal of Molecular Sciences 21*(17), 1–11. https://doi.org/10.3390/ijms21176413.

Wang, Y., Samuels, J. F., Chang, Y. C., Grados, M. A., Greenberg, B. D., Knowles, J. A., McCracken, J. T., Rauch, S. L., Murphy, D. L., Rasmussen, S. A., Cullen, B., Hoehn-Saric, R., Pinto, A., Fyer, A. J., Piacentini, J., Pauls, D. L., Bienvenu, O. J., Riddle, M., Shugart, Y. Y., . . . Nestadt, G. (2009). Gender differences in genetic linkage and association on 11p15 in obsessive-compulsive disorder families. *American Journal of Medical Genetics, Part B: Neuropsychiatric Genetics 150*(1), 33–40. https://doi.org/10.1002/ajmg.b.30760.

West-Eberhard, M. J. (1983). Sexual selection, social competition, and speciation. *The Quarterly Review of Biology 58*(2), 155–183. http://www.jstor.org/stable/2828804.

Wierman, M. E. (2007). Sex steroid effects at target tissues: Mechanisms of action. *Advances in Physiology Education 31*(1), 26–33. https://doi.org/10.1152/advan.00086.2006.

Wilson, E. O. (1975). *Sociobiology: The new synthesis.* Harvard University Press.

Wingfield, J. C., Hegner, R. E., Dufty Jr, A. M., & Ball, G. F. (1990). The "challenge hypothesis": Theoretical implications for patterns of testosterone secretion, mating systems, and breeding strategies. *The American Naturalist 136*(6), 829–846. https://www.jstor.org/stable/2462170.

Wirth, M. M., Welsh, K. M., & Schultheiss, O. C. (2006). Salivary cortisol changes in humans after winning or losing a dominance contest depend on implicit power motivation. *Hormones and Behavior 49*(3), 346–352. https://doi.org/10.1016/j.yhbeh.2005.08.013.

Wozniak, D., Harbaugh, W. T., & Mayr, U. (2014). The menstrual cycle and performance feedback alter gender differences in competitive choices. *Journal of Labor Economics 32*(1), 161–198.

Wright, N. D., Edwards, T., Fleming, S. M., & Dolan, R. J. (2012). Testosterone induces off-line perceptual learning. *Psychopharmacology 224*, 451–457. https://doi.org/10.1007/s00213-012-2769-y.

Yamasue, H., Abe, O., Suga, M., Yamada, H., Rogers, M. A., Aoki, S., Kato, N., & Kasai, K. (2008). Sex-linked neuroanatomical basis of human altruistic cooperativeness. *Cerebral Cortex 18*(10), 2331–2340. https://doi.org/10.1093/cercor/bhm254.

Ycaza Herrera, A., Wang, J., & Mather, M. (2019). The gist and details of sex differences in cognition and the brain: How parallels in sex differences across domains are shaped by the locus coeruleus and catecholamine systems. *Progress in Neurobiology 176*, 120–133. https://doi.org/10.1016/j.pneurobio.2018.05.005.

Zhu, J. Ling, Chen, Z., Feng, W. Jie, Long, S. Lian, & Mo, Z. C. (2019). Sex hormone-binding globulin and polycystic ovary syndrome. *Clinica Chimica Acta 499*, 142–148. https://doi.org/10.1016/j.cca.2019.09.010.

Zilioli, S., & Watson, N. V. (2014). Testosterone across successive competitions: Evidence for a "winner effect" in humans? *Psychoneuroendocrinology 47*, 1–9. https://doi.org/10.1016/j.psyneuen.2014.05.001.

Zilioli, S., Mehta, P. H., & Watson, N. V. (2014). Losing the battle but winning the war: Uncertain outcomes reverse the usual effect of winning on testosterone. *Biological Psychology 103*(1), 54–62. https://doi.org/10.1016/j.biopsycho.2014.07.022.

Psychobiology of Competition: A Review of Men's Endogenous Testosterone Dynamics

Brian M. Bird, Lindsay Bochon, Yin Wu, *and* Samuele Zilioli

Abstract

Competition is a defining feature of most living organisms. Among humans, the engagement in, and the associated outcomes of, competition (i.e., win or loss) can hold important consequences for survival, individual and group status, and mating-related opportunities. As such, considerable research efforts have been devoted to identifying and delineating the factors that influence human competitive decision-making. The steroid hormone testosterone, in particular, has been identified as one such factor, not only influencing competitive decision-making and behavior, but also responding flexibly to competitive cues and outcomes to then feedback to ongoing pursuits. Growing evidence suggests that the extent to which testosterone exerts its effects may depend on variables across a number of domains, such as individual preferences or dispositions, social cues, and other hormones. This chapter provides an overview of such competitive biopsychology with a focus on men's testosterone dynamics. The authors provide a brief introduction to testosterone, and a summary of some of the key theoretical approaches to understanding testosterone dynamics in humans, followed by an overview of correlational and experimental studies that examine the independent and interactive effects of testosterone on competition and competition-related variables.

Key Words: testosterone reactivity, life history, competition, aggression, mating

Testosterone

The discovery of the steroid hormone testosterone is often linked to the seminal experiments of Arnold Berthold (1849). In his work, he demonstrated that castrating roosters would suppress the typical development of their secondary sexual characteristics, crowing, and aggression toward other roosters. Further, he found that by re-implanting one testis into the body cavity of each bird, with severed vascular and neural connections, that typical secondary sexual characteristics and behaviors reemerged. The natural conclusion from his observations was that the testes secreted a chemical messenger that influenced morphology and behavior.

Testosterone is produced in men and, to a much lesser degree, women. In men, the pulsatile release of gonadotropin-releasing hormone (GnRH) from the hypothalamus stimulates the secretion of the luteinizing hormone from the anterior pituitary gland, which, in turn, is responsible for the pulsatile release of testosterone from the Leydig cells in the testes. In women, testosterone secretion happens primarily in the ovaries from cells that are similar to those in the testes. Testosterone subsequently acts via one of two mechanisms. In the first, called a genomic mechanism, unbound testosterone binds to the androgen receptor and ultimately activates or represses gene transcription. Testosterone can also be converted to other sex hormones, such as estradiol via the enzyme aromatase. The genomic mechanisms are considered "slow," generally taking longer than 30 minutes, up to as long as days. In the second, called a non-genomic mechanism, testosterone does not induce gene transcription but instead rapidly (generally less than 30 minutes) interacts with cell membrane receptors, such as $GABA_A$ (Foradori et al., 2008).

The extant literature on testosterone and competition primarily focuses on men, perhaps because early findings and theoretical accounts were based on the observations of males, and because studies incorporating men and women have generally found effect sizes to be larger among men (e.g., Geniole et al., 2017, 2019a). We focus our review here on men's testosterone dynamics, but agree with other researchers that testosterone may also be relevant for aspects of women's competition (e.g., perceptions of personal success in competition; Casto et al., 2017; for a review, see Casto & Edwards, 2016; see Casto & Prasad, 2017 for recommendations on the inclusion of women in hormones and competition research). Future work with female or mixed populations will help increase our understanding of the relationship between testosterone and competition in both sexes.

Key Theories and Findings on Testosterone and Competition

The Challenge Hypothesis

The challenge hypothesis (Wingfield et al., 1990) was originally developed to explain seasonal variation in testosterone and aggression among migratory avian species. Some of the key findings from this work included that males' testosterone levels (a) were lowest in the nonbreeding season; (b) rose at the start of the breeding season; (c) reached a physiological maximum during male-to-male competitive interactions, subsequently facilitating territorial or aggressive behavior; and (d) showed temporary decreases during the expression of paternal care.

Since this work, the challenge hypothesis has shown applicability to a wide variety of species (e.g., California mouse; see Fuxjager et al., 2017 for review; see also Marler & Trainor, 2019), including humans (for a review of the past 30 years of relevant research in humans, see Gray et al., 2019). Indeed, human research has found that testosterone can increase in anticipation of, during, and in response to direct competitive interactions (Archer, 2006; Casto & Edwards, 2016; Geniole et al., 2017), and that testosterone responsivity is found in both athletic (e.g., Cook & Crewther, 2012a) and non-athletic competitions (e.g., laboratory; Carré et al., 2009). As one example, participants who were shoulder bumped in the hallway and then insulted (presumably indicating some form of competitive challenge) showed significantly greater increases in testosterone relative to those in a control condition, who were not insulted (Cohen et al., 1996).

The Biosocial Model of Status

The biosocial model of status (Mazur & Booth, 1998) is a theoretical model that is conceptually similar to the challenge hypothesis, with the additional prediction that testosterone concentrations vary according to the competition outcome. Specifically, it suggests that winners will show a rise in testosterone and losers will show a decrease in testosterone, with the argument that competition winners potentially face additional status challenges, and thus an acute rise in testosterone can help promote behavior to adaptively defend or further promote one's own status. For competition losers, it may be more adaptive to retreat to avoid a further loss of status, and thus decreased testosterone may function to promote such behavior.

Research over several decades has tested the predictions of this model in humans, and recent meta-analytic findings show that on the whole, competition winners show larger increases in testosterone than losers ("the winner–loser effect"; Geniole et al., 2017). Moreover, research has found that a competition-induced increase in testosterone predicts outcomes relevant for competition, such as competitive motivation (Carré & McCormick, 2008; Mehta & Josephs, 2006), physical strength (Cook & Crewther, 2012b), and aggression (see Geniole et al., 2019a for meta-analysis; for reviews, see Carré & Olmstead, 2015; Zilioli & Bird, 2017; see Carré, Robinson, & Reside, this volume for a more detailed description of these findings). The winner–loser effect shows significant heterogeneity in effects, however, suggesting the presence of moderators for the relationship between competition and testosterone change (Geniole et al., 2017).

Life History Theory and Integrated Models

Life History Theory

In the struggle to maximize reproductive fitness, there are inherent tradeoffs between finite resources (e.g., energy, time, nutrients), such that when resources are invested into one fitness-promoting trait, there are necessarily less resources available for other traits. Some of the physiological (e.g., immune function), morphological (e.g., muscle growth and maintenance), and behavioral processes (e.g., copulation and courtship) important for life-history trade-offs are thought to be mediated by testosterone.

Perhaps one of the most studied trade-offs in the context of competition is between mating effort and parenting effort. In prioritizing mating effort, there are increased needs and risks for competition with intrasexual rivals; thus, mating strategies are often characterized by an increase in related behaviors, such as aggression and risk-taking. In contrast, more energy dedicated to parenting effort entails a greater focus on long-term romantic relationships, child-rearing, and provisioning. Testosterone is hypothesized to flexibly coordinate the mating versus parenting trade-off by increasing behaviors relevant to mating and decreasing behaviors relevant to parenting. Indirect evidence is supportive in finding, for example, that men with higher testosterone reported greater mating success (Peters et al., 2008) and, among dominant men, showed greater courtship behavior in the laboratory (Slatcher et al., 2011). With respect to parenting effort and investment in long-term relationships, a highly cited longitudinal study found that the largest declines in testosterone over approximately five years were observed in men who were married and had a child (Gettler et al., 2011); further, those men with the greatest levels of childcare investment showed the lowest levels of testosterone. Recent meta-analytic findings similarly showed that pair-bonded men had lower testosterone than unpaired men, and fathers had lower testosterone than men without children (Grebe et al., 2019b).

Integrated Models

Testosterone not only responds to context over longer periods of time (e.g., decreasing over time in a committed relationship), but it also fluctuates quite rapidly in response to environmental inputs. Recent theoretical review papers have hypothesized that these rapid fluctuations serve to modulate cognition, physiology, and behavior, including competition, that is relevant for survival and reproduction (Geniole & Carré, 2018; Zilioli & Bird, 2017).

The findings in the social neuroendocrinology literature have led to the development of integrated models to explain the contexts in which testosterone changes are expected, the behaviors it propels, and the motivational, situational, and physiological variables expected to modulate effects. For instance, the conceptual model of testosterone response to social stimuli in Zilioli and Bird (2017) suggests that evolutionarily salient social contexts that are directly or indirectly involved in mating effort (e.g., interaction with a mate, intrasexual competition) are generally associated with an increase in testosterone, whereas contexts involving parenting effort (e.g., interactions with offspring) are generally associated with a testosterone decline. Changes in testosterone have subsequent downstream effects by promoting ongoing domain-specific behaviors (e.g., competition, risk-taking, aggression). These relationships, however, are often qualified by moderators, such as situational outcomes (e.g., winning vs. losing a competition), motivation (e.g., personality), and physiology (e.g., other hormones). Similarly, the fitness model of testosterone dynamics (Geniole & Carré, 2018) suggests that testosterone rises rapidly in response to social challenge, or when there are opportunities that either threaten or enhance fitness. Testosterone surges subsequently activate a general "fitness protection" system that promotes relevant behaviors (e.g., aggression, competition). In turn, these behaviors and associated outcomes feedback to modulate testosterone and the probability of encountering subsequent fitness-related challenges. Again, such relationships often depend on the presence of individual differences and context-specific variables, which are described in the next section.

Moderators of Testosterone Reactivity to Competition

Competition is one of several relevant contexts within the overarching framework of life history theory, encapsulating the predictions of the challenge hypothesis (Archer, 2006) and the biosocial model of status (Mazur, 1985; Mazur & Booth, 1998). Under this framework, reproductive fitness is enhanced by intrasexual competition that can involve aggressive, hostile, and confrontational behavior toward same-sex rivals. Testosterone is not only responsive to competitive cues, but also to the socially relevant outcome of the conflict, thus facilitating future competitiveness to enhance status and fitness. Testosterone reactivity to competition, as seen in the winner–loser effect, has recently been examined by meta-analyses (Archer, 2006; Geniole et al., 2017), the results from which showed significant heterogeneity in effect sizes. Methodological factors resulting in more robust effects for real-world competitive contexts than for laboratory experiments may contribute to this heterogeneity. However, situational, motivational, and physiological factors are also highly relevant moderators of testosterone release, and may reflect evolutionarily salient features of the social and environmental context that contribute to competition-induced testosterone release.

Situational Moderators

CHARACTERISTICS OF THE COMPETITION

Previous research has found that the location in which a competition takes place can affect testosterone concentrations, with higher pre-competition levels in male soccer (Neave & Wolfson, 2003), ice-hockey (Carré et al., 2006), and basketball players (Arruda et al., 2014; but see Cunniffe et al., 2015) who competed at home versus away. Post-competition testosterone is also higher following a victory at home rather than at an opponent's venue (Carré, 2009), and when a victory is determined by ability rather than chance (van Anders & Watson, 2007). Spectators of winning teams (Bernhardt et al., 1998; Carré & Putnam, 2010; Pound et al., 2009; but see van der Meij et al., 2012b) and supporters of successful political campaigns (Stanton et al., 2009) experience a testosterone increase, while their losing counterparts experience a decrease, suggesting that physical involvement in a competition is not a necessary component of the winner–loser effect. Characteristics of the opponent can also influence testosterone release, such that hormonal increases are greater when opponents appear more capable and confident (van der Meij et al., 2010), aggressive (Carré et al., 2010), and when they are members of an outgroup (Flinn et al., 2012; Oxford et al., 2010).

STABILITY OF THE HIERARCHY

Hierarchical instability may be particularly stressful for high-status individuals because it implies potential status changes or the need to defend a high-status position. Testosterone release is, therefore, amplified in high-status individuals (Knight & Mehta, 2017) and across multiple competitions (Zilioli & Watson, 2014) when the hierarchy is unstable.

The status instability hypothesis (Zilioli et al., 2014) suggests that narrow victories and defeats may result in a reversal of the typical winner–loser effect, namely because such close outcomes render the hierarchy unstable. Wu et al. (2017) found that a close victory on a Tetris-based competitive task resulted in decreased testosterone, particularly among participants with high basal cortisol. Such testosterone decrease following a narrow win may facilitate avoidance of further competition, a preferable behavioral strategy in the context of an unstable hierarchy. Decisive victories, on the other hand, should follow predictions outlined by the biosocial model of status because such clear victories model stable hierarchies. In line with this, testosterone increase and the decision to compete again are more likely following a decisive rather than a close victory (Mehta et al., 2015a), reflecting a dominance strategy associated with gaining and maintaining high status.

REPRODUCTIVE OPPORTUNITIES

Men experience rapid increases in testosterone in response to reproductively relevant stimuli. A brief social interaction with an attractive woman, for example, increased testosterone concentrations in young men above those who interacted with another man or who sat by themselves (Roney et al., 2007). This result was later found to be particularly accentuated among men with aggressive-dominant personalities (van der Meij et al., 2008). Given that intrasexual competition often results in reproductive benefits for the winners, hormonal and behavioral changes are likely to reflect the reproductive potential of any particular competition. Elevated testosterone, for example, resulted in greater risk-taking among participants of a skateboarding demonstration (Ronay & von Hippel, 2010a), as well as increased affiliative behavior (van der Meij et al., 2012a) when in the presence of a woman. For example, in van der Meij et al.'s study (2012a), testosterone elevations, which were induced by having male participants compete against each other, were found to positively correlate with men's courtship behaviors towards a female confederate. Similarly, Miller et al. (2012) found increased testosterone among competitors of an ultimate frisbee match in response to a larger ratio of opposite-sex to same-sex spectators, suggesting that testosterone is also responsive to the relative proportions of eligible mating partners present at a competition.

The brief period of mammalian peak fertility immediately surrounding the day of ovulation results in a limited window for male reproductive success. Accordingly, ability to detect cues of ovulation is an adaptive advantage for males. Empirical evidence suggests that males are, in fact, able to reliably detect such cues (Gildersleeve et al., 2012), demonstrated by increased ratings of female attractiveness, and increased aggression and hostility towards rival males during this high fertile window (Fales et al., 2014). Elevated testosterone during this period may facilitate intersexual interaction to enable mating, while intrasexual competition may serve as a form of mate guarding. In line with this, male partners were found to have higher testosterone concentrations when exposed to rival males at high- relative to low-levels of fertility in their female partner's ovulatory cycle. Exposure to a non-competitive male, however, did not result in elevated testosterone (Fales et al., 2014). The fertility status of female partners, therefore, appears to moderate male intra-sexual competitiveness at a time when competition loss may be reproductively costly.

Such reproductive effort is often theorized to be at odds with parental behaviors, and is delineated as involving opposing effects on testosterone (van Anders et al., 2011). However, divergent testosterone responses to various parental contexts may be understood as deriving from situations that are nurturant as opposed to protective. As such, a paradoxical increase in testosterone is seen in the case of offspring defense (van Anders et al., 2011), which may be more appropriately categorized as a challenge situation, more akin to a competitive rather than a nurturant context. In support of this, van Anders et al. (2012) found that testosterone decreased when men were able to provide nurturant responses to the cries of a baby. However, testosterone increased when men were prevented from performing such nurturant behavior, suggesting that this situation may represent an evolutionary relevant challenge context associated with protective parental care.

Motivational Moderators

PERSONALITY FACTORS

Power motivation denotes the degree to which individuals implicitly wish to exert power and influence over others and find others having power over them to be aversive (Stanton & Schultheiss, 2009). Individuals high in implicit power motivation are more likely to be successful in leadership positions (McClelland & Boyatzis, 1982), are more sexually promiscuous (Schultheiss et al., 2003), more likely to engage in spousal abuse (Mason & Blankenship, 1987), and more likely to have higher baseline testosterone (Stanton & Schultheiss, 2009). Furthermore, testosterone reactivity in power motivated individuals is associated with implicit learning of instrumental behaviors that are associated with successful competition (Schultheiss et al., 2005; Schultheiss & Rohde, 2002). Schultheiss and Rohde (2002) proposed that the testosterone response associated with winning augments dopaminergic transmission in the nucleus accumbens, suggesting that behaviors associated with victory were reinforced through the rewarding properties of this neurotransmitter.

Other personality factors thought to moderate testosterone reactivity to competition include social anxiety (Maner et al., 2008; but see, Norman et al., 2015), attachment and coping style (Koolhaas et al., 2007; Salvador, 2005), and aggressiveness (Carré & McCormick, 2008). For example, Maner et al. (2008) reported that social anxiety—the degree to which individuals perceive social situations as uncomfortable—was negatively associated with testosterone responses to a competitive task.

APPRAISAL

The degree to which individuals attribute the outcome of a contest to their own ability and performance is another moderator of competition-related endocrine responses. Victories that are internally attributed, as an outcome of one's own merit and performance, result in higher testosterone release than those that are attributed to external factors, such as luck (Gonzalez-Bono et al., 2000; Salvador et al., 2017; Trumble et al., 2012). Furthermore, individual differences in baseline testosterone influence how hierarchical positions are perceived, as well as the behavioral consequences of this perception. For example, Ronay and von Hippel (2010b) found that when men were instructed to imagine a scenario in which they had low power, individuals with higher testosterone took more risks than those with lower testosterone. When primed with high power, however, high testosterone individuals were less likely to take risks. Risk-taking, then, may come as a function of the perceived mismatch between current status and desired status, and might be a functional strategy for high-testosterone, low-power individuals to pursue social status (Maner et al., 2007). Upon achieving the desired social status, however, desire to maintain this position of power may make these individuals risk-averse.

Physiological Moderators

ANDROGEN RECEPTOR POLYMORPHISM

Transcriptional activity of the androgen receptor is stimulated by testosterone binding, and varies with the number of CAG codon repeats in the androgen receptor gene (Chamberlain et al., 1994; Eisenegger et al., 2017; Zitzmann & Nieschlag, 2003). Polymorphisms in the androgen receptor gene substantially influence the receptor's capacity to enhance or reduce the activity of androgen-dependent genes. A lower number of CAG repeats is associated with enhanced transcriptional activity (Chamberlain et al., 1994) and greater phenotypic androgenicity—the degree to which traits typically associated with androgen exposure are expressed (Zitzmann & Nieschlag, 2003). Given the enhanced efficiency of testosterone that is associated with a lower number of CAG repeats, Simmons and Roney (2011) have suggested that CAG repeats might calibrate the expression of fitness-relevant traits that are associated with energy allocation towards mating and survival effort. In other words, androgen-dependent allocation of energy investment towards pursuing and competing for mates versus survival-related outcomes, such as the capacity to mount an immune response (Muehlenbein & Bribiescas, 2005), is associated with shorter CAG repeat length (Simmons & Roney, 2011). In line with this suggestion, lower CAG repeats in men from the polygynous Datoga of Tanzania were associated with higher levels of aggressive competition and number of offspring (Butovskaya et al., 2015). CAG number was also negatively associated with upper body strength, as well as self-reported prestige and dominance (Simmons & Roney, 2011), confidence during a competition (Eisenegger et al., 2017), amygdala reactivity to threat-related cues (Manuck & Marsland, 2010), and testosterone reactivity to interactions with a female (Roney et al., 2010). Various lines of indirect evidence, therefore, point to the likely moderation of testosterone reactivity to competition by CAG polymorphism length.

PHYSICAL CONDITION

Immunological activation to disease is an energetically costly response whose efficiency depends upon energy allocation directed towards either reproduction or immunocompetence—a physiological trade-off determined by relative concentrations of testosterone (Muehlenbein & Bribiescas, 2005). Energy allocation towards muscle anabolism and behaviors that are instrumental to reproduction are enhanced in the presence of testosterone, and are adaptive only to the extent that environmental conditions are favorable. Environments with increased energetic demands, such as those characterized by high levels of disease, favor reduced testosterone concentrations due to the associated immunosuppressive and increased metabolic demands (Muehlenbein et al., 2010). Such trade-offs are reflected in a reduction in baseline testosterone as a result of pathogen exposure (Muehlenbein et al., 2010), influenza vaccination (Simmons & Roney, 2009), and in non-industrial populations living in energetically stressful environments that are characterized by high pathogen load (Trumble et al., 2012). Sleep deprivation (Leproult & Van Cauter, 2011; Cote et al., 2013) and fasting (Trumble et al., 2010) represent additional homeostatic challenges in which basal, and potentially reactive, testosterone concentrations are reduced.

HORMONAL INFLUENCES

In their seminal work, Mehta and Josephs (2010) proposed the dual-hormone hypothesis, which posits that the relationship between testosterone and competitive behavior, and between basal testosterone and testosterone reactivity to competition is buffered by glucocorticoids released by the hypothalamic-pituitary-adrenal (HPA) axis, particularly cortisol. In their original study, Mehta and Josephs (2010) found that the decision to re-challenge a competitor following a defeat was positively associated with pre-competition testosterone levels, but only among those with low pre-competition cortisol levels. Glucocorticoid inhibition of the hypothalamic-pituitary-gonadal (HPG) axis may be an evolutionary functional mechanism that inhibits metabolically costly behaviors, such as those involved in reproduction and status-seeking, during times of environmental stress (Carré & Mehta, 2011; Zilioli & Watson, 2012; Hamilton et al., 2015). Only during times of relative quiescence, indicated by low cortisol concentrations, would testosterone promote status-seeking and reproduction-related behaviors.

A number of studies have found dual-hormone associations with competition-related variables. For example, high basal testosterone and low basal cortisol have been associated with the attainment of leadership positions (Mehta & Josephs, 2010; Sherman et al., 2016), popularity within social networks (Ponzi et al., 2016), group performance (Akinola, et al., 2016), reduced friendliness (Lozza et al., 2017), risk-taking (Mehta et al., 2015c), antisocial behavior (Dabbs et al., 1991; Pfattheicher et al., 2014; Popma et al., 2007), chronic status-seeking tendencies (Pfattheicher, 2017), costly overbidding in an economic game (van den Bos et al., 2013), and increased testosterone in winners of a competition (Zilioli & Watson, 2012). Several recent systematic reviews and meta-analyses (Dekkers et al., 2019; Grebe et al., 2019a), however, indicate that caution is warranted when considering the dual-hormone hypothesis. The authors of these studies reported that the overall effect size of testosterone-cortisol interaction on several status-relevant outcome measures (including status, dominance, risk-taking, aggression, and psychopathy) was significant but small ($r = -.061$, $p = .026$; Dekkers et al., 2019), and none of the outcome measures were significant on their own.

Exogenous Testosterone and Competition

The studies reviewed so far have focused on the natural fluctuation of testosterone in response to competitive interactions, how this relationship is moderated by intrapersonal (i.e., motivational and physiological) and contextual (i.e., situational) factors, and the extent to which competition-induced testosterone fluctuations feedback into competitive behaviors. Studies on the latter topic are, by definition, correlational in nature. A more direct approach to investigate the causal effects of rapid testosterone increases on competition is through testosterone administration (i.e., exogenous testosterone). This topic is covered more in-depth in Carré, Robinson, & Reside, this volume; however, here we provide a short primer to this topic.

Testosterone administration studies offer an advantage by allowing the random assignment of participants to receive testosterone or placebo. Compared to contest-fluctuations in endogenous testosterone (see Carré & Olmstead, 2015 for a review), testosterone administration is more reliable, robust, and less prone to individual differences. Typical testosterone administration methods include injection (Dreher et al., 2016), sublingual administration (Tuiten et al., 2000), gel administration (Bird et al., 2016; Eisenegger et al., 2013), and nasal spray administration (Bird et al., 2019; Geniole et al., 2019b).

A well-developed line of research has combined testosterone administration with decision-making in economic games. One of the most commonly used tasks is the Ultimatum Game, during which two players—a proposer and a responder—are asked to split a fixed amount of money. The responder can either accept or reject offers from the proposer. Rejection of unfair offers has been interpreted as an index of reactive aggression (Güth et al., 1982; Mehta & Beer, 2010). Previous research has shown that higher endogenous testosterone is associated with increased rejection rates of unfair offers (Burnham, 2007; Mehta & Beer, 2010). Testosterone administration studies further corroborated these findings by showing that exogeneous testosterone increased the punishment of proposers that made unfair offers (Dreher et al., 2016). Nevertheless, findings from this literature are mixed and include null results (Cueva et al., 2017; Eisenegger et al., 2010; Zethraeus et al., 2009), with one study reporting a trend-level increase in the propensity to accept unfair offers after testosterone administration (Kopsida et al., 2016). These inconsistent findings seem to suggest that important moderators at the sample (e.g., gender difference) and research design level (e.g., method of testosterone delivery) might modulate the link between exogenous testosterone and performance on the Ultimatum Game.

Rejections and punishments in the Ultimatum Game (Dreher et al., 2016) can be considered as competitive strategies that participants engage in to protect their social status. However, they are still indirect measures of competitive behavior. To date, only a handful of studies have tested the direct impact of testosterone administration on competitive behavior (Mehta et al., 2015b; Vermeer et al., 2020; Knight et al., 2022 preprint). For example, Mehta et al. (2015b) found that testosterone administration increased willingness to engage in a competition among participants who recently won a competition and those who reported high levels of dominance. More recently, Vermeer et al. (2020) found similar effects, with the additional caveat that hierarchy stability and CAG repeats acted as additional moderators of the testosterone-competitive behavior link. Lastly, in a yet to be published study, Knight et al. (2022 preprint) found that high baseline cortisol participants receiving testosterone were more willing to compete against losers of a recent competition and avoided competition with winners of a recent competition, while the opposite was true for low baseline cortisol participants. As this field of research moves forward, more work on the effects of exogenous testosterone on competitive behaviors across contexts is necessary.

Conclusion

This chapter provided an overview of the key theories and findings that relate primarily to men's endogenous testosterone dynamics and competitive behavior. In sum, testosterone appears to fluctuate rapidly in anticipation of, during, and following competition, and these dynamic changes appear to modulate cognition, physiology, and behavior—including competition—that are relevant for survival and reproduction. A host of situational, motivational, and physiological factors have been identified as relevant modulators of both the direction of testosterone response (e.g., rise or drop) and the extent to which such dynamic testosterone changes map onto subsequent behavioral action. The complex bi-directional relationships between testosterone and behavior can be understood through studies that examine the natural testosterone response to contextual stimuli (e.g., competition win or loss), in addition to pharmacological challenge paradigms that attempt to isolate potential causal effects of testosterone on behavior.

References

Akinola, M., Page-Gould, E., Mehta, P. H., & Lu, J. G. (2016). Collective hormonal profiles group performance. *Proceedings of the National Academy of Sciences of the United States of America 113* (35), 9774–9779.

Archer, J. (2006). Testosterone and human aggression: An evaluation of the challenge hypothesis. *Neuroscience & Biobehavioral Reviews 30* (3), 319–345.

Arruda, A. F. S., Aoki, M. S., Freitas, C. G., Drago, G., Oliviera, R., Crewther, B. T., & Moreira, A. (2014). Influence of competition playing venue on the hormonal responses, state anxiety, and perception of effort in elite basketball athletes. *Physiology & Behavior 130*, 1–5.

Bernhardt, P. C., Dabbs, Jr. J. M., Fielden, J. A., & Lutter, C. D. (1998). Testosterone changes during vicarious experiences of winning and losing among fans at sporting events. *Physiology & Behavior 65* (1), 59–62.

Berthold, A. A. (1849). Transplantation der hoden [Transplantation of the testes]. *Archiv für Anatomie, Physiologie und wissenschaftliche Medicin 16*, 42–46.

Bird, B. M., Geniole, S. N., Procyshyn, T. L., Ortiz, T. L., Carré, J. M., & Watson, N. V. (2019). Effect of exogenous testosterone on cooperation depends on personality and time pressure. *Neuropsychopharmacology, 44*(3), 538–545.

Bird, B. M., Welling, L. L., Ortiz, T. L., Moreau, B. J., Hansen, S., Emond, M., . . . & Carré, J. M. (2016). Effects of exogenous testosterone and mating context on men's preferences for female facial femininity. *Hormones and Behavior, 85*, 76–85.

Burhman, T. C. (2007). High-testosterone men reject low ultimatum game offers. *Proc. R. Soc. B. 274*, 2327–2330.

Butovskaya, M. L., Lazebny, O. E., Vasilyev, V. A., Dronova, D. A., Karelin, D. V., Mabulla, A. Z. P., . . . & Ryskov, A. P. (2015). Androgen receptor gene polymorphism, aggression, and reproduction in Tanzanian foragers and pastoralists. *PLoS ONE 10* (8), 1–12.

Carré, J. M. (2009). No place like home: Testosterone responses to victory depend on game location. *American Journal of Human Biology 21* (3), 392–394.

Carré, J. M. Gilchrist, J. D., Morrissey, M. D., & McCormick, C. M. (2010). Motivational and situational factors and the relationship between testosterone dynamics and human aggression during competition. *Biological Psychology 84* (2), 346–353.

Carré, J. M., & McCormick, C. M. (2008). Aggressive behavior and change in salivary testosterone concentrations predict willingness to engage in a competitive task. *Hormones and Behavior 54* (3), 403–409.

Carré, J. M., & Mehta, P. H. (2011). Importance of considering testosterone-cortisol interactions in predicting human aggression and dominance. *Aggressive Behavior 37* (6), 489–491.

Carré, J. M., Muir, C., Belanger, J., & Putnam, S. K. (2006). Pre-competition hormonal and psychological levels of elite hockey players: Relationship to the 'home advantage'. *Physiology and Behavior 89* (3), 392–398.

Carré, J. M., & Olmstead, N. A. (2015). Social neuroendocrinology of human aggression: examining the role of competition-induced testosterone dynamics. *Neuroscience 286*, 171–186.

Carré, J. M., & Putnam, S. K. (2010). Watching a previous victory produces an increase in testosterone among elite hockey players. *Psychoneuroendocrinology 35* (3), 475–479.

Carré, J. M., Putnam, S. K., & McCormick, C. M. (2009). Testosterone responses to competition predict future aggressive behaviour at a cost to reward in men. *Psychoneuroendocrinology, 34*(4), 561–570.

Casto, K. V., & Edwards, D. A. (2016). Testosterone, cortisol, and human competition. *Hormones and Behavior, 82*, 21–37.

Casto, K. V., & Prasad, S. (2017). Recommendations for the study of women in hormones and competition research. *Hormones and Behavior 92*, 190–194.

Casto, K. V., Rivell, A., & Edwards, D. A. (2017). Competition-related testosterone, cortisol, and perceived personal success in recreational women athletes. *Hormones and Behavior 92*, 29–36.

Chamberlain, N. L., Driver, E. D., Miesfeld, R. L. (1994). The length and location of CAG trinucleotide repeats in the androgen receptor N-terminal domain affect transactivation function. *Nucleic Acids Research 22* (15), 3181–3186.

Cohen, D., Nisbett, R. E., Bowdle, B. F., & Schwarz, N. (1996). Insult, aggression, and the southern culture of honor: An "experimental ethnography." *Journal of Personality and Social Psychology 70* (5), 945.

Cook, C. J., & Crewther, B. T. (2012a). The effects of different pre-game motivational interventions on athlete free hormonal state and subsequent performance in professional rugby union matches. *Physiology & Behavior 106* (5), 683–688.

Cook, C. J., & Crewther, B. T. (2012b). Changes in salivary testosterone concentrations and subsequent voluntary squat performance following the presentation of short video clips. *Hormones and Behavior 61* (1), 17–22.

Cote, K. A., McCormick, C. M., Geniole, S. N., Renn, R. P., & MacAulay, S. D. (2013). Sleep deprivation lowers reactive aggression and testosterone in men. *Biological Psychology 92* (2), 249–256.

Cueva, C., Roberts, R. E., Spencer, T. J., Rani, N., Tempest, M., Tobler, P. N., . . . & Rustichini, A. (2017). Testosterone administration does not affect men's rejections of low ultimatum game offers or aggressive mood. *Hormones and Behavior 87*, 1–7.

Cunniffe, B., Morgan, K. A., Baker, J. S., Cardinale, M., & Davies, B. (2015). Home versus away competition: Effect on psychophysiological variables in elite rugby union. *International Journal of Sports Physiology and Performance 10* (6), 687–694.

Dabbs, J. M., Jurkovic, G. J., & Frady, R. L. (1991). Salivary testosterone and cortisol among late adolescent male offenders. *Journal of Abnormal Child Psychology 19* (4), 469–478.

Dekkers, T. J., Agelink van Rentergem, J. A., Meijer, B., Popma, A., Wagemaker, E., & Huizenga, H. M. (2019). A meta-analytical evaluation of the dual-hormone hypothesis: Does cortisol moderate the relationship between testosterone and status, dominance, risk taking, aggression, and psychopathy? *Neuroscience and Biobehavioral Reviews 96*, 250–271.

Dreher, J. C., Dunne, S., Pazderska, A., Frodl, T., Nolan, J. J., & O'Doherty, J. P. (2016). Testosterone causes both prosocial and antisocial status-enhancing behaviors in human males. *Proceedings of the National Academy of Sciences of the United States of America 113* (41), 11633–11638.

Eisenegger, C., Kumsta, R., Naef, M., Gromoll, J., & Heinrichs, M. (2017). Testosterone and androgen receptor gene polymorphism are associated with confidence and competitiveness in men. *Hormones and Behavior 92*, 93–102.

Eisenegger, C., Neaf, M., Snozzi, R., Heinrichs, M., & Fehr, E. (2010). Prejudice and truth about the effect of testosterone on human bargaining behaviour. *Nature 463*, 356–359.

Eisenegger, C., von Eckardstein, A., Fehr, E., & von Eckardstein, S. (2013). Pharmacokinetics of testosterone and estradiol gel preparations in healthy young men. *Psychoneuroendocrinology 38* (2), 171–178.

Fales, M. R., Gildersleeve, K. A., & Haselton, M. G. (2014). Exposure to perceived male rivals raises men's testosterone on fertile relative to nonfertile days of their partner's ovulatory cycle. *Hormones and Behavior 65*, 454–460.

Flinn, M. V., Ponzi, D., & Muehlenbein, M. P. (2012). Hormonal mechanisms for regulation of aggression in human coalitions. *Human Nature 23* (1), 68–88.

Foradori, C. D., Weiser, M. J., & Handa, R. J. (2008). Non-genomic actions of androgens. *Frontiers in Neuroendocrinology 29* (2), 169–181.

Fuxjager, M. J., Trainor, B. C., & Marler, C. A. (2017). What can animal research tell us about the link between androgens and social competition in humans? *Hormones and Behavior 92*, 182–189.

Geniole, S. N., Bird, B. M., Ruddick, E. L., & Carré, J. M. (2017). Effects of competition outcome on testosterone concentrations in humans: An updated meta-analysis. *Hormones and Behavior 92*, 37–50.

Geniole, S. N., Bird, B. M., McVittie, J. S., Purcell, R. B., Archer, J., & Carré, J. M. (2019a). Is testosterone linked to human aggression? A meta-analytic examination of the relationship between baseline, dynamic, and manipulated testosterone on human aggression. *Hormones and Behavior 123*, 104644. doi: 10.1016/j.yhbeh.2019.104644.

Geniole, S. N., & Carré, J. M. (2018). Human social neuroendocrinology: Review of the rapid effects of testosterone. *Hormones and Behavior 104*, 192–205.

Geniole, S. N., Procyshyn, T. L., Marley, N., Ortiz, T. L., Bird, B. M., Marcellus, A. L., . . . & Carré, J. M. (2019b). Using a pharmacogenetic approach to identify the pathways through which—and the people for whom—testosterone promotes aggression. *Psychological Science 30* (4), 481–494.

Gettler, L. T., McDade, T. W., Feranil, A. B., & Kuzawa, C. W. (2011). Longitudinal evidence that fatherhood decreases testosterone in human males. *Proceedings of the National Academy of Sciences 108* (39), 16194–16199.

Gildersleeve, K. A., Haselton, M. G., Larson, C. M., & Pillsworth, E. G. (2012). Body odor attractiveness as a cue of impending ovulation in women: Evidence from a study using hormone-confirmed ovulation. *Hormone and Behavior 61*, 157–166.

Gonzalez-Bono, E., Salvador, A., Ricarte, J., Serrano, M. A., & Arnedo, M. (2000). Testosterone and attribution of successful competition. *Aggressive Behavior 26*, 235–240.Gray, P. B., Straftis, A. A., Bird, B. M., McHale, T. S., & Zilioli, S. (2019). Human reproductive behavior, life history, and the Challenge Hypothesis: A 30-year review, retrospective and future directions. *Hormones and Behavior 123*, 104530. doi: 10.1016/j.yhbeh.2019.04.017.

Grebe, N. M., Del Giudice, M., Emery Thompson, M., Nickels, N., Ponzi, D., Zilioli, S., . . . & Gangestad, S. W. (2019a). Testosterone, cortisol, and status-striving personality features: A review and empirical evaluation of the Dual Hormone hypothesis. *Hormones and Behavior 109*, 25–37.

Grebe, N. M., Sarafin, R. E., Strenth, C. R., & Zilioli, S. (2019b). Pair-bonding, fatherhood, and the role of testosterone: A meta-analytic review. *Neuroscience & Biobehavioral Reviews 98*, 221–233.

Güth, W., Schmittberger, R., & Schwarze, B. (1982). An experimental analysis of ultimatum bargaining. *Journal of Economic Behavior & Organization 3* (4), 367–388.

Hamilton, L. D., Carré, J. M., Mehta, P. H., Olmstead, N., & Whitaker, J. D. (2015). Social neuroendocrinology of status: A review and future directions. *Adaptive Human Behavior and Physiology 1* (2), 202–230.

Knight, E. L., & Mehta, P. H. (2017). Hierarchy stability moderates the effect of status on stress and performance in humans. *Proceedings of the National Academy of Sciences of the United States of America 114* (1), 78–83.

Knight, E. L., Morales, P., Christian, C., Prasad, S., Harbaugh, W. T., Mehta, P. H., & Mayr, U. (2022). The Causal Effect of Testosterone on Men's Competitive Behavior is Moderated by Basal Cortisol and Cues to an Opponent's Status: Evidence for a Context-Dependent Dual Hormone Hypothesis. *Journal of Personality and Social Psychology.* Advance online publication. https://doi.org/10.1037/pspa0000305.

Koolhaas, J. M., de Boer, S. F., Buwalda, B., & van Reenen, K. (2007). Individual variation in coping with stress: A multidimensional approach of ultimate and proximate mechanisms. *Brain Behav. Evol. 70,* 218–226.

Kopsida, E., Berrebi, J., Petrovic, P., & Ingvar, M. (2016). Testosterone administration related differences in brain activation during the ultimatum game. *Front. Neurosci. 10*(66), 1–11.

Leproult, R., & Van Cauter, E. (2011). Effect of 1 week of sleep restriction on testosterone levels in young healthy men. *JAMA 305* (21), 2172–2173.

Lozza, N., Spoerri, C., Ehlert, U., Hubmann, P., Kesselring, M., Farahmand, F., . . . & La Marca, R. (2017). Predicting social behavior: Basal and dynamic joint effects of testosterone and cortisol. *Adaptive Human Behavior and Physiology 3,* 255–274.

Maner, J. K., Gailliot, M. T., Butz, D. A., & Peruche, B. M. (2007). Power, risk taking, and the status quo: Does power promote riskier or more conservative decision making. *PSPB 33* (4), 451–462.

Maner, J. K., Miller, S. L., Schmidt, N. B., & Eckel, L. A. (2008). Submitting to defeat: Social anxiety, dominance threat, and decrements in testosterone. *Psychol. Sci. 19*(8), 764–768.

Manuck, S. B., Marsland, A. L. (2010). Salivary testosterone and a trinucleotide (CAG) lengthpolymorphism in the androgen receptor gene predict amygdala reactivity in men. *Psychoneuroendocrinology 35* (1), 94–104.

Marler, C. A., & Trainor, B. C. (2019). The challenge hypothesis revisited: Focus on reproductive experience and neural mechanisms. *Hormones and Behavior 123,* 104645. https://doi.org/10.1016/j.yhbeh.2019.104645.

Mason, A., & Blankenship, V. (1987). Power and affiliation motivation, stress, and abuse in intimate relationships. *Journal of Personality and Social Psychology 52* (2), 203–210.

Mazur, A., 1985. A biosocial model of status in face-to-face primate groups. *Soc. Forces 64,* 377–402.

Mazur, A., & Booth, A. (1998). Testosterone and dominance in men. *Behavioral and Brain Sciences 21* (3), 353–363.

McClelland, D. C., & Boyatzis, R. E. (1982). Leadership motive pattern and long-term success in management. *Journal of Applied Psychology 67* (6), 737–743.

Mehta, P. H., & Beer, J. (2010). Neural mechanisms of the testosterone-aggression relation: The role of orbitofrontal cortex. *Journal of Cognitive Neuroscience 22* (10), 2357–2368.

Mehta, P. H., & Josephs, R. A. (2006). Testosterone change after losing predicts the decision to compete again. *Hormones and Behavior 50* (5), 684–692.

Mehta, P. H., & Josephs, R. (2010). Testosterone and cortisol jointly regulate dominance: evidence for a dual-hormone hypothesis. *Hormones and Behavior 58* (5), 898–906.

Mehta, P. H., Snyder, N. A., Knight, E. L., & Lassetter, B. (2015a). Close versus decisive victory moderates the effect of testosterone change on competitive decisions and task enjoyment. *Adaptive Human Behavior and Physiology 1* (3), 291–311.

Mehta, P. H., von Son, V., Welker, K. M., Prasad, S., Sanfey, A. G., Smidts, A., & Roelofs, K. (2015b). Exogenous testosterone in women enhances and inhibits competitive decision-making depending on victory-defeat experience and trait dominance. *Psychoneuroendocrinology 60,* 224–236.

Mehta, P. H., Welker, K. M., Zilioli, S., & Carré, J. M. (2015c). Testosterone and cortisol jointly modulate risk-taking. *Psychoneuroendocrinology 56,* 88–99.

Miller, S. L., Maner, J. K., & McNulty, J. K. (2012). Adaptive attunement to the sex of individuals at a competition: The ratio of opposite- to same-sex individuals correlates with changes in competitors' testosterone levels. *Evolution and Human Behavior 33,* 57–63.

Muehlenbein, M. P., & Bribiescas, R. G. (2005). Testosterone-mediated immune functions and male life histories. *American Journal of Human Biology 17,* 527–558.

Muehlenbein, M. P., Hirschtick, J. L., Bonner, J. Z., & Swartz, A. M. (2010). Towards quantifying the usage costs of human immunity: Altered metabolic rates and hormone levels during acute immune activation in men. *American Journal of Human Biology 22*, 546–556.

Neave, N., & Wolfson, S. (2003). Testosterone, territoriality, and the 'home advantage'. *Physiology & Behavior 78* (2), 269–275.

Norman, R. E., Moreau, B. J. P., Welker, K. M., & Carré, J. M. (2015). Trait anxiety moderates the relationship between testosterone responses to competition and aggressive behavior. *Adaptive Human Behavior and Physiology 1* (3), 312–324.

Oxford, J., Ponzi, D., & Geary, D. C. (2010). Hormonal responses differ when playing violent video games against an ingroup and outgroup. *Evolution and Human Behavior 31* (3), 201–209.

Peters, M., Simmons, L. W., & Rhodes, G. (2008). Testosterone is associated with mating success but not attractiveness or masculinity in human males. *Animal Behaviour 76* (2), 297–303.

Pfattheicher, S. (2017). Illuminating the dual-hormone hypothesis: About chronic dominance and the interaction of cortisol and testosterone. *Aggressive Behavior 43* (1), 85–92.

Pfattheicher, S., Landhäuber, A., & Keller, J. (2014). Individual differences in antisocial punishment in public goods situations: The interplay of cortisol with testosterone and dominance. *Journal of Behavioral Decision Making 27*, 340–348.

Ponzi, D., Zilioli, S., Mehta, P. H., Maslov, A., & Watson, N. V. (2016). Social network centrality and hormones: The interaction of testosterone and cortisol. *Psychoneuroendocrinology 68*, 6–13.

Popma, A., Vermeiren, R., Geluk, C. A. M. L., Rinne, T., van den Brink, W., Knol, D. L., . . . & Doreleijers, T. A. H. (2007). Cortisol moderates the relationship between testosterone and aggression in delinquent male adolescents. *Biol Psychiatry 61* (3), 405–411.

Pound, N., Penton-Voak, I. S., & Surridge, A. K. (2009). Testosterone responses to competition in men are related to facial masculinity. *Proc. R. Soc. B. 276*, 153–159.

Ronay, R., & von Hippel, W. (2010a). The presence of an attractive women elevates testosterone and physical risk taking in young men. *Social Psychological and Personality Science 1* (1), 57–64.

Ronay, R., & von Hippel, W. (2010b). Power, testosterone, and risk-taking. *Journal of Behavioral Risk Taking 23*, 473–482.

Roney, J. R., Lukaszewski, A. W., & Simmons, Z. L. (2007). Rapid endocrine responses of young men to social interactions with young women. *Hormones and Behavior 52* (3), 326–333.

Roney, J. R., Simmons, Z. L., & Lukaszewski, A. W. (2010). Androgen receptor gene sequence and basal cortisol concentrations predict men's hormonal responses to potential mates. *Proc. R. Soc. B. 277*, 57–63.

Salvador, A., 2005. Coping with competitive situations in humans. *Neurosci. Biobehav. Rev. 29*, 195–205.

Salvador, A., Costa, R., Hidalgo, V., & González-Bono, E. (2017). Causal attribution and psychobiological response to competition in young men. *Hormones and Behavior 92*, 72–81.

Schultheiss, O. C., Dargel., A., Rohde, W. (2003). Implicit motives and sexual motivation and behavior. *Journal of Research in Personality 37* (3), 224–230.

Schultheiss, O. C., & Rohde, W. (2002). Implicit power motivation predicts men's testosterone changes and implicit learning in a contest situation. *Hormones and Behavior 41* (2), 195–202.

Schultheiss, O. C., Wirth, M. M., Torges, C. M., Pang, J. S., Villacorta, M. A., & Welsh, K. M. (2005). Effects of implicit power motivation on men's and women's implicit learning and testosterone changes after social victory or defeat. *Journal of Personality and Social Psychology 88* (1), 174–188.

Sherman, G. D., Lerner, J. S., Josephs, R. A., Renshon, J., & Gross, J. J. (2016). The interaction of testosterone and cortisol is associated with attained status in male executives. *Journal of Personality and Social Psychology 110* (6), 921–929.

Simmons, Z. L., & Roney, J. R. (2009). Androgens and energy allocation: Quasi-experimental evidence for effects of influenza vaccination on men's testosterone. *American Journal of Human Biology 21*, 133–135.

Simmons, Z. L., & Roney, J. R. (2011). Variation in CAG repeat length of the androgen receptor gene predicts variables associated with intrasexual competitiveness in human males. *Hormones and Behavior 60* (3), 306–312.

Slatcher, R. B., Mehta, P. H., & Josephs, R. A. (2011). Testosterone and self-reported dominance interact to influence human mating behavior. *Social Psychological and Personality Science 2* (5), 531–539.

Stanton, S. J., Beehner, J. C., Saini, E. K., Kuhn, C. M., LaBar, K. S. (2009). Dominance, politics, and physiology: Voters' testosterone changes on the night of the 2008 United States presidential election. *PLoSONE 4* (10), e7543, 7510.1371/journal.pone.0007543.

Stanton, S. J., & Schultheiss, O. C. (2009). The hormonal correlates of implicit power motivation. *Journal of Research in Personality 43*, 942–949.

Trumble, B. C., Brindle, E., Kupsik, M., & O'Connor, K. A. (2010). Responsiveness of the reproductive axis to a single missed evening meal in young adult males. *American Journal of Human Biology 22*, 775–781.

Trumble, B. C., Cummings, D., von Rueden, C., O'Connor, K. A., Smith, E. A., Gurven, M., & Kaplan, H. (2012). Physical competition increases among Amazonian forager-horticulturists: a test of the "challenge hypothesis". *Proc. R. Soc. B. 279*, 2907–2912.

Tuiten, A., Van Honk, J., & Koppeschaar, H. (2000). Time course of effects of testosterone administration on sexual arousal in women. *Arch. Gen. Psychiatry 57* (2), 149–153.

van Anders, S. M., Goldey, K. L., & Kuo, P. X. (2011). The steroid/peptide theory of social bonds: Integrating testosterone and peptide responses for classifying social behavioral contexts. *Psychoneuroendocrinology 36* (9), 1265–1275.

van Anders, S. M., Tolman, R. M., & Volling, B. L. (2012). Baby cries and nurturance affect testosterone in men. *Hormones and Behavior 61* (1), 31–36.

van Anders, S. M., & Watson, N. V. (2007). Effects of ability- and chance-determined competition outcome on testosterone. *Physiology & Behavior 90* (4), 634–642.

van den Bos, W., Golka, P. J. M., Effelsberg, D., & McClure, S. M. (2013). Pyrrhic victories: The need for social status drives costly competitive behavior. *Frontiers in Neuroscience 7* (189), 1–11

van der Meij, L., Almela, M., Buunk, A. P., Fawcett, T. W., & Salvador, A. (2012a). Men with elevated testosterone levels show more affiliative behaviors during interactions with women. *Proc. R. Soc. B. 279*, 202–208.

van der Meij, L., Almela, M., Hidalgo, V., Villada, C., Ijzerman, H., van Lange, P. A. M., & Salvador, A. (2012b). Testosterone and cortisol release among Spanish soccer fans watching the 2010 world cup final. *PLoS One 7* (4): e34814.

van der Meij, L., Buunk, A. P., Almela, M., & Salvador, A. (2010). Testosterone responses to competition: The opponent's psychological state makes it challenging. *Biological Psychology 84* (2), 330–335.

van der Meij, L., Buunk, A. P., van den Sande, J., & Salvador, A. (2008). The presence of a women increases testosterone in aggressive dominant men. *Hormones and Behavior 54* (5), 640–644.

Vermeer, A. B. L., Krol, I., Gausterer, C., Wagner, B., Eisenegger, C., & Lamm, C. (2020). Exogenous testosterone increases status-seeking motivation in men with unstable low social status. *Psychoneuroendocrinology 113*, 104552.

Wingfield, J. C., Hegner, R. E., Dufty Jr., A. M., & Ball, G. F. (1990). The "challenge hypothesis": Theoretical implications for patterns of testosterone secretion, mating systems, and breeding strategies. *The American Naturalist 136* (6), 829–846.

Wu, Y., Eisenegger, C., Zilioli, S., Watson, N. V., & Clark, L. (2017). Comparison of clear and narrow outcomes on testosterone levels in social competition. *Hormones and Behavior 92*, 51–56.

Zethraeus, N., Kocoska-Maras, L., Ellingsen, T., von Schoultz, B., Hirschberg, A. L., & Johannesson, M. (2009). A randomized trial of the effect of estrogen and testosterone on economic behavior. *PNAS 106* (16), 6535–6538.

Zilioli, S., & Bird, B. M. (2017). Functional significance of men's testosterone reactivity to social stimuli. *Frontiers in Neuroendocrinology 47*, 1–18.

Zilioli, S., Mehta, P. H., & Watson, N. V. (2014). Losing the battle but winning the war: Uncertain outcomes reverse the usual effect of winning on testosterone. *Biological Psychology 103*, 54–62.

Zilioli, S., & Watson, N. V. (2012). The hidden dimensions of the competition effect: Basal cortisol and basal testosterone jointly predict changes in salivary testosterone after social victory in men. *Psychoneuroendocrinology 37* (11), 1855–1865.

Zilioli, S., & Watson, N. V. (2014). Testosterone across successive competitions: Evidence for the "winner effect" in humans? *Psychoneuroendocrinology 47*, 1–9.

Zitzmann, M., & Nieschlag, E. (2003). The CAG repeat polymorphism within the androgen receptor gene and maleness. *International Journal of Andrology 26* (2), 76–83.

Neuroscience and Competitive Behavior

Michela Balconi *and* Laura Angioletti

Abstract

Cognitive and social neuroscience may provide a wide range of neuroscientific tools and paradigms for the research on competitive behavior. Specifically, hyperscanning is a relatively new paradigm in neuroscience that involves capturing the brain activity of two or more participants engaged in a joint task, such as a competitive game, simultaneously. A brief overview of hyperscanning studies on competition and the intra-brain and inter-brain functional connectivity analysis have been here described. Taking inspiration from previous hyperscanning protocols, this chapter suggests that the neuroscientific study of competitive behavior could also be fruitfully explored in other real-life contexts, such as the educational field, the peer group, the sports field, and the organizational context.

Key Words: competition, social neuroscience, hyperscanning, functional connectivity, fNIRS, EEG, autonomic indices

Hyperscanning as a Social Neuroscience Paradigm to Study Competition

Cognitive and social neuroscience may provide a wide range of tools and paradigms for the research on competitive behavior. However, the relatively new possibility provided by technology that allows for simultaneous recording of the activity of the brains of two or more people has paved the way for the development of a new paradigm known as "hyperscanning."

Hyperscanning is a relatively new paradigm in neuroscience that involves capturing the brain activity of two or more participants engaged in interactive activities at the same time (Balconi & Vanutelli, 2017). This metric allows researchers to look at the interpersonal brain systems that are triggered by social interactions.

Through the use of hyperscanning, the application of neuroscientific tools can be also provided on two individuals in a natural interaction context or during shared task performance. Indeed, by simultaneously recording two interacting subjects' cerebral activity, it represents an optimal technique for understanding the competitive or cooperative joint strategy of two interacting brains (Balconi & Vanutelli, 2016, 2017). Former studies have shown that reciprocal adaptation of two interacting brains leads to brain synchronization, and cooperative activities are one of the greatest examples of such applications. As a result, single-subject recordings are unable to capture these processes (Balconi & Vanutelli, 2017).

The ability to sustain a competitive behavior to obtain a result is regulated by perceptual-motor processes, but also by cognitive and affective mechanisms that coordinate the carrying out of specific strategies readable when observing a social interaction. Moreover, as suggested by evidence from hyperscanning research (Konvalinka & Roepstorff, 2012), it is the presence of a real interlocutor in the experimental setting that may especially affect the inter-brain responsiveness and cognitive outcomes.

Paradigms used to explore interpersonal dynamics and to investigate the neural responses of two individuals involved in a social interaction typically focus on the structures that coordinate the performance of a joint task. This joint task can be computerized or face-to-face, but, for both cases, it requires individuals to coordinate intentionally or spontaneously to achieve a specific result and a common but unique specific goal. Given these preliminary methodological considerations, the hyperscanning approach has been shown to be effective in emphasizing the brain synchronization of two interacting participants during joint activities such as cooperation and competition. These two behaviors can be measured through different experimental tasks requiring for instance:

1) paradigms that used rhythm, music, and motor synchronization;
2) card tasks taken from the Game Theory;
3) computerized tasks; and
4) possible real-life applications (Balconi & Vanutelli, 2017).

Neuroscience-Based Experimental Task and Measures

In this second section, we will first describe an experimental joint task recently developed to investigate social dynamics and that was mainly adopted for cooperation and competition research in the neuroscientific field.

Then, we emphasize how the integration of multiple neuroscientific methods during task execution is an approach that allows us to grasp the complexity of competitive behavior at multiple levels: with neural (electrophysiological and hemodynamic), physiological (electrodermal and cardiovascular indices), behavioral, and self-reported measures. Thanks to this methodological approach, it is also possible to evaluate the implicit (automatic) and explicit (controlled) cognitive and emotional factors that characterize competitive behavior.

The Sustained Selective Attention Joint Task

In a series of recent experimental paradigms on competition, we used a new joint task that can artificially induce competition during an interpersonal game by providing specific feedback to the members of the dyads, in order to investigate the role of behavioral, peripheral, and neural components in competition (Balconi, Crivelli, et al., 2017; Balconi & Pagani, 2014, 2015; Balconi, Pezard, et al., 2017; Balconi, Gatti, et al., 2018a, 2018b, 2018c; Balconi, Vanutelli, et al., 2018; Balconi & Vanutelli, 2016, 2017, 2017a, 2017b, 2017c, 2017d 2018a, 2018b, 2018c).

More specifically, participants were told that some cognitive attentional measures were used to evaluate the subjective skills and, to reinforce their motivation, that these measures were usually applied as a screening to test their future professional career success (teamwork capabilities). In addition, the competitive nature of the task was stressed: participants were told that the scoring was based on the capacity to produce a better performance than the competitor, in terms of accuracy (number of errors: Error Rate, ER) and response times (RTs). They were seated side-by-side but separated by a black screen in a way that they could not see each other.

The cognitive task consisted of a sustained selective attention task. Participants were required to select a target stimulus between non-targets, based on four different options of shape/color: the stimuli might interchangeably be a triangle or a circle, colored in red or green. They were required to distinguish between target/non-target by focusing attention on each stimulus. The target was displayed on the video (indicated as the target for selection) and the successive stimuli were presented one after another. The target stimulus features changed every 25 trials. The subjects were instructed to make a two-alternative forced-choice response by pressing a left/right button. After each trial, composed of three stimuli, subjects received a feedback: two up-arrows for a high score; a dash for a mean performance; or two down-arrows for a low score.

The task was composed of two sessions: the first which did not include specific general feedback to performance (four blocks before the feedback, 100 trials), and a second one which included specific positive feedback to performance (four blocks with the feedback, 100 trials) Halfway, in fact, participants received a general evaluation of their performance. Both trial feedbacks and the general feedback were artificially managed. The feedback order (two sessions) was counterbalanced across subjects. Regarding the general feedback, participants were told that they had an outcome "well above" their competitor's one and were encouraged to maintain their performance level, during the second part of the experiment ("*The measures recorded till now reveal that your performance is very good. Your response profile is well superior to your competitor's one. If you want to win, keep going like this in the following part*").

Across the task, after an initial mean performance, subjects were constantly reinforced about their good performance by presenting the up-arrows in 70 percent of cases, while the dash or the down-arrows appeared only in 30 percent of cases (mainly at the beginning of the task) to make the task more credible and plausible. In addition, after each block of 25 trials, subjects were required to evaluate their performance and efficacy in terms of their ranking on a 7-point Likert scale (from 1 = most decreased ranking due to performance, to 7 = most improved ranking due to performance). Finally, a post-session questionnaire explored the following aspects: degree of their engagement in the task; trust in the received feedback; relevance of task for their social status perception; perceived improving ranking position (Balconi & Vanutelli, 2016).

The Integration of Multiple Neuroscientific Methods

Between the neuroscientific measures, neuroimaging techniques (such as functional Magnetic Resonance Imaging [fMRI] and functional Near Infrared Spectroscopy [fNIRS]) and electrophysiological methods (such as electroencephalogram [EEG]) are valid methods to explore central nervous system (CNS) responses reflecting cognitive and emotional factors of competition. Instead, autonomic measures can provide information on the activity of the autonomic nervous system (ANS), and the psychophysiological (peripheral) emotional response of the individuals (Balconi et al., 2015), including facial displays through electromyography (EMG) (Balconi & Canavesio, 2013).

To gather the complexity of the phenomenon, together with neural (electrophysiological and hemodynamic), physiological (electrodermal and cardiovascular indices), and behavioral parameters, self-report measures were acquired during the task. Indeed, the integration of multiple neuroscientific methods allows for assessing the cognitive and emotional factors featuring competitive behavior and the different levels of the experience, from the implicit levels (automatic), up to the more explicit levels (controlled).

Indeed, for grasping participants' full experience, former studies in the field of competition integrated neural indices with tasks' behavioral performance and self-report measures such as questionnaires investigating working memory, cognitive demand, and workload (such as the NASA Task Load Index; see Hart & Staveland, 1988); individual differences in approach and avoidance attitude (by administering the BIS/BAS questionnaire; see Carver & White, 1994); cognitive and emotional empathy (Interpersonal Relational Index [IRI]; see Davis, 1980); and Balanced Emotional Empathy Scale (BEES; see Albiero et al., 2009) (Balconi & Bortolotti, 2012; Balconi & Canavesio, 2013; Wang et al., 2014). Following this methodological approach, other recent applied research integrated self-report measures in physiological protocols and developed the assessment of three concrete constructs related to emotional processes in competitive contexts: the desire to win, the fear of losing, and the "competitive arousal" which stems from the thrill of beating competitors (Adam et al., 2015)

Multi-method study designs have been shown to be a viable approach for grasping the cognitive and emotional assumptions and consequences of competition at the neurophysiological, psychophysiological, behavioral, and self-report levels. Furthermore, the use of the previously described task allowed us to undertake multiple orders of analysis (from a single person to the two-person perspective) to get insight into the neurological, physiological, behavioral, and psychological correlates of competitive behavior in each dyad.

Hyperscanning Studies Applied to Competitive Behavior

The underlying neural mechanisms of competition and cooperation, especially from an interpersonal perspective, have not been fully explored yet.

According to a vast corpus of prior studies, the increase in neural connectivity patterns (related with physiological linkage and interpersonal tuning) that happens when individuals are participating in cooperative dynamics is one of the most fascinating neurophysiological evidence in the field of cooperation studies (for further evidence and understanding, see Astolfi et al., 2011; Balconi, Crivelli, et al., 2017, 2019; Balconi & Salati, 2017; Balconi, Fronda, et al., 2019; Balconi, Gatti, et al., 2018a, 2018b; Balconi, Pezard, et al., 2017; Balconi, Fronda, et al., 2020; Balconi & Vanutelli, 2018b; Vanutelli et al., 2017; Venturella et al., 2017). Instead, to date, a smaller number of studies have focused on the neural dynamics of competition by exploiting the hyperscanning paradigm.

The most interesting evidence deriving from hyperscanning studies conducted to explore the neural and psychophysiological correlates of competitive behavior are reported below.

fNIRS-Based Hyperscanning Studies

We begin with the most significant evidence derived from hyperscanning studies using the fNIRS instrument to investigate the hemodynamic brain correlates of competitive behavior. Indeed, the perception of competition has an impact on one's subjective self-evaluation and can result in increased cerebral cortex activity in some prefrontal regions, which can in turn alter performance results. Cui et al. (2012) used fNIRS to examine the prefrontal cortex (PFC) activations of pairs of individuals during concurrent cooperation and competition. Due to the demands of modeling our own behavior on others' behaviors in cooperative interactions, the participant pairs demonstrated enhanced inter-brain neural synchronization (INS) in their right superior frontal cortices during cooperation (but not during competition). The authors suggested there may be little INS in competitive interactions.

Differently, in Liu et al.'s (2017) work, fNIRS data demonstrated significant INS across participant pairs' right posterior superior temporal sulcus (pSTS) in both the cooperation and competition conditions (at a computerized turn-taking disk-game on a computer), and the competition condition also involved significant INS in the right inferior parietal lobule (IPL). Due to task demands of shared attention and intention comprehension, the right pSTS may be engaged in both cooperation and competition, whereas the right IPL may be more relevant for competition due to extra requirements of mentalizing resources in competitive settings. Second, empathy among participants may enhance INS in the bilateral IFG between competitors, and, as a result, affect their competitive performance.

During competitive tasks, a significant increase in PFC activity, particularly in the medial Prefrontal Cortex (mPFC), which might reflect increased executive processing demands, was previously reported (Decety et al., 2004). Previously, it was shown that the processing load associated with competitive social dynamics is linked to increased PFC activation, as evidenced by EEG and hemodynamic measures (by fNIRS), which showed a decrease in alpha power and an increase in blood oxygenation, respectively, when compared to the other brain regions studied (Balconi and Vanutelli, 2016, 2017a, 2017b). As a result, overall competition would seem to impose a higher cognitive load.

In a previous study, we found that when subjects were informed about their efficient interaction (during the experimentally manipulated feedback condition) and specifically for positive feedback (vs negative or pre-feedback condition), the PFC was significantly more responsive (increased oxygenated hemoglobin response), implying a central role for the PFC in the case of a positive self-perception (i.e., "to be a good performer") in a social condition where the competitive dynamics is significant and stressful. This "enhanced brain effect" was followed by significant improvements in cognitive and behavioral abilities (decreased ER and RTs) (Balconi and Vanutelli, 2016, 2017, 2017a).

Interestingly, in competitive situations, the inherent link between conduct and social representation may in fact reflect the reciprocal effect between PFC and self-perception, as well as the PFC and the cognitive task, as two sides of the same coin. In this sense, a sort of "circular effect" may be suggested. On the one hand, the social significance of a subject's performance for the social hierarchy appears to be crucial in balancing the subjects' performance across the task (with a consistent and parallel increase in social ranking perception and subjective performance), which is modulated by the PFC, which may support the social perception process (accurate self-knowledge and self-improvement). On the other hand, the sharp rise in cognitive outcomes may have an impact on self-perception of ranking position, with advantages for subjective social status representation. Also, in this second case, the PFC may support the reciprocal link between cognitive performance and social representation, reinforcing the "social value" of the PFC (Freeman et al., 2009; Koslov et al., 2011; Liu et al., 2015; Marsh et al., 2009).

As for other brain areas, while Decety et al. (2004) interpreted the right inferior parietal activity as processing the distinction between self and other, both dorsolateral (DLPFC) and ventrolateral (VLPFC) cortices have been shown to be engaged during ranking considerations (Balconi & Pagani, 2014, 2015; Chiao et al., 2009). The activation of these brain regions during social interactions that include assessment of social performance is likely to be connected with higher-level top-down processes over emotional responses. It is possible that when it comes to social status, such systems are designed to control acceptable behavioral reactions. These brain networks might be engaged to elicit socio-emotional reactions and behavioral inhibition associated with dominance and submission, as a prior study has shown (Marsh et al., 2009).

Paired participants in competition had a greater inter-brain homologous response, in terms of INS, after the feedback condition in the previously described selective attention task (Balconi & Vanutelli, 2017a). When individuals were artificially alerted and thought to have performed better, the two brains exhibited a homologous and comparable brain response, with more coherent PFC activity within the pair. Even though the task was competitive, the respondents' self-perceived efficacy created a type of "glue" between participants' brains, directing them in the same direction and perhaps generating a parallel strategy. Current findings provide preliminary evidence for the hypothesis of a significant inter-brain effect during competitive tasks, as well as recommendations for future research into the extent to which competition between two brains is selectively related to improved cognitive joint performance for the two inter-agents (Balconi & Vanutelli, 2017a).

EEG-Based Hyperscanning Research

We can also look at EEG-based research with hyperscanning, whereby EEG is measured simultaneously from the brains of two or more people. For example, pair of participants involved in a recent EEG research played a turn-based computer game in which the intensity of competition was systematically adjusted between cooperation and competition (Spapé et al., 2013). Increased beta and gamma EEG frequency band power was observed in the central and parietal brain regions in this study, particularly when individuals competed against one another (both individually and interpersonally), accordingly, these electrophysiological responses were therefore linked to social competition.

Cui et al. (2016) also found that the processing load associated with the competitive condition resulted in increased cortical activity, as assessed by high-alpha EEG power, across all brain areas studied, suggesting competition increased the cognitive load. Furthermore, there was a significant increase in cortico-cortical connection, with increased communication between all non-motor regions and the strategy planning region, which is located in the prefrontal areas.

Other research in the fields of rhythm, music, and motor synchronization employed rhythmic synchronization to measure the ability to cooperate or not with one another using a leader-follower test. In a recent leader–follower dynamics, a recent finger-tapping experiment used an asymmetric pattern between two members (Konvalinka et al., 2014). The authors found that frontal alpha suppression, which is a reduction of the presence of alpha band power, may be used as an indicator to distinguish roles, being more evident in leaders than followers. Alpha suppression is typically seen as the consequence of excitatory input from either bottom-up or top-down inputs (Bauer et al., 2012; De Lange et al., 2008), and therefore considered to reflect an increase of neural activity (for instance, over the sensorimotor cortex during production of movements). In the current study, the decrease of alpha power would thus suggest that leaders allocated more attentional resources to self-processing to monitor their own rhythm, while followers could have been monitoring the output of their partner.

However, in a later study, it was discovered that for competitive dyads, there was a progressive decrease in INS functional EEG connectivity of delta and theta band in prefrontal regions over time, especially in a post-feedback condition compared to control condition (Balconi & Vanutelli, 2018b). This effect was mainly consistent for delta frequency band, previously linked to high-arousal and emotionally-connoted stimuli and deeper emotional engagement (Balconi et al., 2015; Knyazev et al., 2009) and theta band, connoting strategic control and conflict monitoring (Billeke et al., 2013; Cristofori et al., 2013). Thus, showing that the motivational and attentional value of ongoing competitive social dynamics and processing of key social-affective signals may be linked to the specific modulation of theta and delta band power. In other words, the difference between cooperation and competition is that in competitive situations, the emotional and motivational components might diverge.

Regarding the emotional and motivational correlates of competition, in a previous EEG–fNIRS study, individuals with a high Behavioural Activation System (high-BAS) scale score displayed a strong hemisphere lateralization effect during competitive conditions, with a left lateralized PFC activation in concomitance to positive feedback (Balconi & Vanutelli, 2016). In addition, high-BAS showed better behavioral performance than low-BAS (low RT and ER). The left hemispheric effect was shown to be one of the most important outcomes, explaining both hemodynamic and cortical EEG modulations. The fact that this left cortical "unbalance" occurred in response to positive reinforcing conditions, such as competition to achieve a higher social position, and was also accompanied by superior performance and increased social efficacy during ranking attribution, may suggest an underlying link between left cortical activity, external social ranking representation (the perception of being a better performer), and competition. In support of this interpretation, previous research has shown that strong social power perception is linked to more left frontal brain activity than is low social power perception (Boksem et al., 2012).

On the other hand, regardless of BAS levels, a significant right hemisphere has been found to be more engaged than the left hemisphere in post-feedback condition (Balconi & Vanutelli, 2017a). This apparently counterintuitive finding can be explained by considering PFC's social role and the lateralized evidence observed in prior works (such as Balconi et al., 2012): a greater right hemisphere reactivity can indeed be correlated to an increase in negative and avoidance feelings toward the rival, which is linked to the competitive situation. The right PFC is supporting the aversive circumstances where the subjects are required to manage the conflictual and potential divergent goals (Balconi et al., 2012). As a result, the task's individualistic and competitive goals may create a sort of "negative echo" for the individuals, resulting in a substantial rise in withdrawal attitudes in terms of emotional behavior.

Using a traditional motion-sensing tennis game, recently Liu et al. (2021) investigated the brain correlates of both competition and cooperation within the same ecological paradigm using an EEG-based hyperscanning approach. The intra-brain spectral power as well as the inter-brain coupling (inter-brain amplitude correlation and inter-brain phase-locking) were investigated. Only the inter-brain amplitude correlation revealed a clear distinction between competition and cooperation, with distinct spatial patterns in the theta, alpha, and beta frequency bands. Cooperation and competition elicited distinct inter-brain coupling patterns: cooperation elicited positive inter-brain amplitude correlation at the delta and theta bands in extensive brain regions, whereas competition elicited negative occipital inter-brain amplitude correlation at the alpha and beta bands. These findings add to our understanding of the electrophysiological correlates of competition and indicate the need of investigating the neurophysiological underpinnings of social interaction in ecological situations from an inter-brain stance.

Autonomic Indices for Measuring Physiological Linkage

A very easy and less expensive method to investigate competitive dynamics consists of the application autonomic measures recording for the physiological linkage (PL) calculation of multiple subjects. Psychophysiological autonomic measurements (such as skin conductance, heart rate, blood pressure, and skin temperature) are commonly used in neuroscience-based studies for assessing arousal modulation. Arousal is described as the neurophysiological substrate underpinning all activities in the human organism, with a special function for emotional behavior regulation. Especially skin conductance is a reliable and sensitive indication that responds to even the slightest changes in phasic arousal, which is the behavioral reaction to a specific stimulus emotional valence (Balconi et al., 2012).

Starting from a single subject's study on auctions with varying social competition circumstances, Adam et al. (2015) assessed skin conductance response (SCR) and heart rate (HR) as objective proxies for bidders' arousal and immediate emotions, respectively. They had the strongest arousal reactions when they were competing against other human bidders, as opposed to when there was no social rivalry (computer condition). This finding not only demonstrated the impact of competition on autonomic indices but also the importance of knowledge in human interactions for bidders to feel compelled to outbid their competitors. This sets the basis for the use of paradigms in experimental settings that account for real-world human interactions and that can collect the PL between the two individuals.

As has already been stated, PL would capture the intensity of social interactions particularly when conflict is at hand (Järvelä et al., 2014). Indeed, marital interactions have been linked to higher PL during conflicting dialogues than neutral ones, as well as in couples who have expressed dissatisfaction with their relationships (Saxbe & Repetti, 2010). Kaplan et al. (1964) found similar results in two studies comparing PL within members of small groups consisting of persons who liked or hated each other, revealing greater correlations in skin conductance within the "dislike" group. Similar effects were also observed in the patient-therapist interaction, with higher PL when conflict is expected (DiMascio et al., 1957) or in friends' dyads during an issue disclosure (Fritz et al., 2003). Finally, during intergroup interactions between persons primed with dissimilarity, the occurrence of PL and affiliative behaviors was found (Danyluck & Page-Gould, 2018).

A recent study adopted autonomic indices to measure competition during the hyper-scanning paradigm, and increased skin conductance level (SCL), SCR, and HR in dyads, implying higher arousal conditions and improved behavioral performance were found during a joint competitive interactive task (Vanutelli et al., 2018). Furthermore, the inter-subject analysis indicated enhanced PL following positive feedback, resulting in higher SCR and HR synchronization in this study.

Intra-Brain and Inter-Brain Functional Connectivity Analysis: A Brief Methodological Note

By shifting from a basic study of each subject's brain response during joint tasks and its relationship with behavioral performance to more complex computations, the above-mentioned hyperscanning studies allow to greatly enhanced neuroscientific research analyzing competitive dynamics (Babiloni & Astolfi, 2012). Indeed, thanks to this approach it is feasible to explore *if* and *how* one's brain activity is connected to that of another interacting partner who is being recorded concurrently (synchrony analysis).

Moving from the single-brain analysis perspective to a second-person approach (in which the functioning of two brains is considered simultaneously), more complex analyses related to concomitant and joint neurophysiological data have been discussed and developed, in both the time and frequency domains. It is crucial for future research to define and interpret the significance of the occurrence of such "hyperlinks" by using evidence-based theoretical models to comprehend and explain neuronal parameter co-modulation. The potential of EEG-, fNIRS-, and autonomic-based hyperscanning techniques should however be better framed in future studies that translate the competition in human-to-human interactions into brain-to-brain interactions.

As Crivelli and Balconi (2017) point out, major issues have been raised in the endeavor to answer the research questions about the appropriate statistical technique to construct particular indices reflecting the strength of such a hyperlink. Indeed, in the literature on hyperscanning several approaches for analyzing and interpreting concurrent data and cal-culating inter-brain synchronization, or functional connectivity, have been devised.

Taking a step back, interpersonal-brain synchronization is the relationship between neural activity arising from different brain regions or, in the case of hyperscanning, from distinct, separated brains. Before, interpersonal coordination was described as "the degree to which the behaviors in an interaction are non-random, patterned or synchronized in both timing (and) form" (Bernieri & Rosenthal, 1991, p. 403). It follows that when dealing with both the neurophysiological data underlying such joint behaviors, the time course is of primary interest. In fact, when assessing inter-cerebral connectivity, the fun-damental aim is to determine if the two (or more) time series are consistent throughout time (Balconi, Pezard, et al., 2017; Crivelli & Balconi, 2017; Vanutelli et al., 2016). Depending on the neuroscientific methodology and technique, several analyses are used to determine synchronization. However, the first main distinction concerns time-domain and frequency-domain analyses.

Time-Domain Data

For time-domain procedures, correlational indices are often computed to examine temporal consistency between two biological occurrences, data point by data point (functional hyperconnectivity). Various correlational indicators have been utilized before.

For instance, Balconi and Vanutelli (2017a) used the joint attentive tasks as described in the previous paragraph, and applied this type of analysis for exploring inter-brain and cognitive strategies similarities during competitive interactions.

Multiple steps of analysis can be carried out in this regard:

1) The first stage is to observe all of the brain regions that are engaged in the task by looking at each one separately.
2) The second step is aimed at assessing intra-brain connectivity.
3) The assessment of inter-brain connectivity is the third stage. Partial correlation indices, which are a measure of the linear dependency of two random variables, may be used to investigate intra-brain and inter-brain connectivity (for the formula see: Balconi, Pezard, et al., 2017).
4) The fourth step was introduced to compute a new coefficient "ConIndex" to calculate the effects related to the inter-brain synchrony net to the effects related to intra-brain synchrony. In a study on cooperation, the ConIndex modulation was explored across the different blocks of the task (Balconi, Pezard, et al., 2017). This research is an excellent illustration of how concurrent data may be used from simple to complex computations.

Granger causality is a statistical procedure for assessing whether one-time series may predict another and is a viable alternative to basic correlational methods. This procedure tests the relationship of dependency, which is assessed by determining the ability of one-time series to predict the future values of another. As a result, it can generate an effective hyperconnectivity index. Because the hemodynamic response is not uniform across various brain regions, this approach is generally applied to neuroelectrical signals (Babiloni & Astolfi, 2012).

Frequency-Domain Data

For frequency-domain studies, coherence measures have been proposed to investigate the presence of a combined trend of various frequency components inside oscillating signals (Crivelli & Balconi, 2017). The analysis may only be performed on two data series at a time in this case.

Pan et al. (2017), which involved a cooperative task, applied such a procedure of analyses; nevertheless, it would be interesting to extend frequency-domain data analyses to ecological competitive situations.

Future Areas of Interest for the Neuroscientific Study of Competitive Behavior

So far, it has been discussed how hyperscanning has been used to further the study of competition in the following fields: basic research on empathy (Liu et al., 2017), emotions (Balconi & Vanutelli, 2017a), and game theory (Astolfi et al., 2011, 2012, 2010). However, taking inspiration from a few examples of protocols developed thanks to the hyperscanning approach, we believe that competitive dynamics could also be fruitfully explored in other contexts, such as the educational field, the peer group, the sports field, and the organizational context.

For instance, to investigate prosocial behavior in a cooperative dynamic, the influence of a gift donation on a cooperative task was recently explored on a sample of healthy young adults by using a multimethod EEG–fNIRS hyperscanning paradigm (Balconi, Fronda, et al., 2019, 2020). Prosocial behavior was found to enhance perceived self-efficacy, cognitive capacities, and social relationships. Similarly, this basic research could also be developed in the context of competitive behavior to explore the effects of prosocial behavior in a competitive condition, with applicative implications that could be interesting for teamwork dynamics for sport, business companies, and organizations, and for the educational field.

In addition, the emerging discipline of neuromanagement offers potential interesting insights for competition research. For example, hyperscanning studies have made it possible to explore real-time communication between managers with different leadership styles and employees and observe points of success, where communication is successful, or fractures (Balconi, Cassioli, et al., 2019).

In a first neuromanagement hyperscanning study, leaders and employees addressed issues pertaining to the firm, the workgroup, and their own personal growth and change, while couples' neural and autonomic reactions were monitored to explore neurophysiological brain and body synchrony as an indication of interpersonal tuning (Venturella et al., 2017).

When discussing personal transformation and business goals, leaders showed a higher brain electrophysiological response than employees, evidence, that together with the self-report information, was interpreted as an indicator of the attitude to act, face challenges and propose solutions based on personal knowledge and commitment. Furthermore, when participants were asked to describe past episodes in which they were directly engaged in managing a situation aimed at company improvement (during the discussion of personal change), leaders who adopted an authoritative style showed higher autonomic activity (i.e., HR), a marker of increased arousal, than leaders who adopted a cooperative style.

In parallel, employees displayed an overall higher emotional activation, with increased SCL values, regardless of the manager's leadership style, perhaps due to the unusual situation. Nonetheless, when the employee was confronted with an authoritative boss and his unidirectional communication style, especially when the employee's personal change topic was discussed, SCR showed a rise in arousal. On the other hand, when employees had to deal with a participative leader, they showed higher SCR values when the leader was participating in the personal change topic discussion (Venturella et al., 2017). In this last case, the leader's involvement may have succeeded in qualifying the employees' genuine response.

As a result, the leader may positively communicate to the employee his tendency to engage in new challenges, promoting positive transformation and, as a result, the company's success. In contrast, an employee's prolonged long-term level of arousal (increased SCR) might cause a physiological and psychological discomfort cycle of distress. This is consistent with prior research that shows charismatic and transformative leadership are linked to lower levels of employee stress, whereas authoritarian leadership is linked to higher levels of employee stress (De Hoogh & Den Hartog, 2008).

Also, in the perspective of social hierarchy, the effect of a unidirectional *versus* reciprocal feedback (provided only by the leader or by leader and employee), as well as the assignment of a quantitative or just a qualitative assessment during a job interview was recently explored (Balconi, Venturella, Fronda, & Vanutelli, 2019; Balconi, Venturella, Fronda, De Filippis, et al., 2019).

These studies are just an example of a large body of research exploring how to manage leadership in cooperative and competitive terms in ecological contexts (Balconi & Salati, 2017; Rock, 2008). However, they could be a starting point for further considerations on the application of neuroscience on competitive behavior in real-life ecological contexts and may bring out some research questions that have not yet been answered.

If leaders with higher emotional intelligence can empathize more effectively with their employees' emotions and exhibit more emotionally appropriate interactions and behaviors (Mayer et al., 2008), what could be the consequences of constantly adopting competitive behaviors in one's leadership style (both in symmetrical and asymmetrical working relationships)? What are the neural markers highlighting a competitive attitude in leaders and managers? Needless to say, studying competition through the lens of neuroscience, equipped with methodologies such as hyperscanning, researchers can undoubtedly contribute to our understanding of competition and competitive behavior, especially in organizational contexts, as we perennially grapple with issues ranging from management and leadership to intra- and intergroup processes.

References

Adam, M. T. P., Krämer, J., & Müller, M. B. (2015). Auction Fever! How time pressure and social competition affect bidders' arousal and bids in retail auctions. *Journal of Retailing 91* (3), 468–485. https://doi.org/10.1016/j.jretai.2015.01.003.

Albiero, P., Matricardi, G., Speltri, D., & Toso, D. (2009). The assessment of empathy in adolescence: A contribution to the Italian validation of the "Basic Empathy Scale." *Journal of Adolescence 32* (2), 393–408. https://doi.org/10.1016/j.adolescence.2008.01.001.

Astolfi, L., Toppi, J., Borghini, G., Vecchiato, G., He, E. J., Roy, A., Cincotti, F., Salinari, S., Mattia, D., He, B., & Babiloni, F. (2012). Cortical activity and functional hyperconnectivity by simultaneous EEG recordings from interacting couples of professional pilots. *Proceedings of the Annual International Conference of the IEEE Engineering in Medicine and Biology Society, EMBS*, 4752–4755. https://doi.org/10.1109/EMBC.2012.6347029.

Astolfi, L., Toppi, J., Cincotti, F., Mattia, D., Salinari, S., De Vico Fallani, F., Wilke, C., Yuan, H., He, B., & Babiloni, F. (2011). Methods for the EEG hyperscanning. Simultaneous recordings from multiple subjects during social interaction. *International Conference on Bioelectromagnetism, NFSI and ICBEM 2011*, 5–8. https://doi.org/10.1109/NFSI.2011.5936807

Astolfi, L., Toppi, J., De Vico Fallani, F., Vecchiato, G., Salinari, S., Mattia, D., Cincotti, F., & Babiloni, F. (2010). Neuroelectrical hyperscanning measures simultaneous brain activity in humans. *Brain Topography 23* (3), 243–256. https://doi.org/10.1007/s10548-010-0147-9.

Babiloni, F., & Astolfi, L. (2012). Social neuroscience and hyperscanning techniques: past, present and future. *Neuroscience & Biobehavioral Reviews 44*, 76–93. https://doi.org/10.1016/j.neubiorev.2012.07.006.

Balconi, M., & Bortolotti, A. (2012). Resonance mechanism in empathic behavior. BEES, BIS/BAS and psychophysiological contribution. *Physiology and Behavior 105* (2), 298–304. https://doi.org/10.1016/j.physbeh.2011.08.002.

Balconi, M., & Canavesio, Y. (2013). Emotional contagion and trait empathy in prosocial behavior in young people: The contribution of autonomic (facial feedback) and Balanced Emotional Empathy Scale (BEES) measures. *Journal of Clinical and Experimental Neuropsychology 35* (1), 41–48. https://doi.org/10.1080/13803395.2012.742492.

Balconi, M., & Pagani, S. (2014). Personality correlates (BAS-BIS), self-perception of social ranking, and cortical (alpha frequency band) modulation in peer-group comparison. *Physiology and Behavior 133*, 207–215. https://doi.org/10.1016/j.physbeh.2014.05.043.

Balconi, M., & Pagani, S. (2015). Social hierarchies and emotions: Cortical prefrontal activity, facial feedback (EMG), and cognitive performance in a dynamic interaction. *Social Neuroscience 10* (2), 166–178. https://doi.org/10.1080/17470919.2014.977403.

Balconi, M., & Salati, M. (2017). Cervelli e corpi in hyperscanning. Le strategie di sintonizzazione nei processi di valutazione. *Harvard Business Review Italia*, 94–94. https://doi.org/10807/119855.

Balconi, M., & Vanutelli, M. E. (2016). Competition in the brain: The contribution of EEG and fNIRS modulation and personality effects in social ranking. *Frontiers in Psychology 7*, 1–14. https://doi.org/10.3389/fpsyg.2016.01587.

Balconi, M., & Vanutelli, M. E. (2017). Cooperation and competition with hyperscanning methods: Review and future application to emotion domain. *Frontiers in Computational Neuroscience 11*, 1–6. https://doi.org/10.3389/fncom.2017.00086.

Balconi, M., & Vanutelli, M. E. (2017a). Brains in competition: Improved cognitive performance and inter-brain coupling by hyperscanning paradigm with functional near-infrared spectroscopy. *Frontiers in Behavioral Neuroscience 11* (August), 1–10. https://doi.org/10.3389/fnbeh.2017.00163.

Balconi, M., & Vanutelli, M. E. (2017b). Cooperation and competition with hyperscanning methods: Review and future application to emotion domain. *Frontiers in Computational Neuroscience 11* (September), 1–6. https://doi.org/10.3389/fncom.2017.00086.

Balconi, M., & Vanutelli, M. E. (2017c). Interbrains cooperation: Hyperscanning and self-perception in joint actions. *Journal of Clinical and Experimental Neuropsychology 39* (6), 607–620. https://doi.org/10.1080/13803395.2016.1253666.

Balconi, M., & Vanutelli, M. E. (2017d). When cooperation was efficient or inefficient. Functional Near-Infrared Spectroscopy evidence. *Frontiers in Systems Neuroscience 11*, 1–10. https://doi.org/10.3389/fnsys.2017.00026.

Balconi, M., & Vanutelli, M. E. (2018a). Alpha brain oscillations, approach attitude, and locus of control affect self-perception of social efficacy in cooperative joint-action. *Frontiers in Life Science 11* (1), 11–25. https://doi.org/10.1080/21553769.2018.1465858.

Balconi, M., & Vanutelli, M. E. (2018b). EEG hyperscanning and behavioral synchronization during a joint action. *Neuropsychological Trends 24*, 23–47. https://doi.org/10.7358/neur-2018-024-balc.

Balconi, M., & Vanutelli, M. E. (2018c). Functional EEG connectivity during competition. *BMC Neuroscience 19* (1), 1–11. https://doi.org/10.1186/s12868-018-0464-6.

Balconi, M., Cassioli, F., Fronda, G., & Vanutelli, M. E. (2019). Cooperative leadership in hyperscanning. Brain and body synchrony during manager-employee interactions. *Neuropsychological Trends 2* (26), 23–44. https://doi.org/10.36830/ijcam.2(1).

Balconi, M., Crivelli, D., & Vanutelli, M. E. (2017). Why to cooperate is better than to compete: Brain and personality components. *BMC Neuroscience 18* (1), 1–15. https://doi.org/10.1186/s12868-017-0386-8.

Balconi, M., Falbo, L., & Conte, V. A. (2012). BIS and BAS correlates with psychophysiological and cortical response systems during aversive and appetitive emotional stimuli processing. *Motivation and Emotion 36*(2), 218–231. https://doi.org/10.1007/s11031-011-9244-7.

Balconi, M., Fronda, G., & Vanutelli, M. E. (2019). Donate or receive? Social hyperscanning application with fNIRS. *Current Psychology 38*, 991–1002. https://doi.org/10.1007/s12144-019-00247-4.

Balconi, M., Fronda, G., & Vanutelli, M. E. (2020). A gift for gratitude and cooperative behavior: brain and cognitive effects. *Social Cognitive and Affective Neuroscience, 14*(12), 1–11. https://doi.org/10.1093/scan/nsaa003.

Balconi, M., Gatti, L., & Vanutelli, M. E. (2018a). Cooperate or not cooperate EEG, autonomic, and behavioral correlates of ineffective joint strategies. *Brain and Behavior 8* (2), 1–12. https://doi.org/10.1002/brb3.902.

Balconi, M., Gatti, L., & Vanutelli, M. E. (2018b). EEG functional connectivity and brain-to-brain coupling in failing cognitive strategies. *Consciousness and Cognition 60* (February), 86–97. https://doi.org/10.1016/j.concog.2018.03.001.

Balconi, M., Gatti, L., & Vanutelli, M. E. (2018c). When cooperation goes wrong: brain and behavioural correlates of ineffective joint strategies in dyads. *International Journal of Neuroscience 128* (2), 155–166. https://doi.org/10.1080/00207454.2017.1379519.

Balconi, M., Grippa, E., & Vanutelli, M. E. (2015). What hemodynamic (fNIRS), electrophysiological (EEG) and autonomic integrated measures can tell us about emotional processing. *Brain and Cognition 95*, 67–76. https://doi.org/10.1016/j.bandc.2015.02.001.

Balconi, M., Pezard, L., Nandrino, J.-L., & Vanutelli, M. E. (2017). Two is better than one: The effects of strategic cooperation on intra- and inter-brain connectivity by fNIRS. *PLOS ONE 12* (11), e0187652. https://doi.org/10.1371/journal.pone.0187652.

Balconi, M., Vanutelli, M. E., & Gatti, L. (2018). Functional brain connectivity when cooperation fails. *Brain and Cognition 123* (February), 65–73. https://doi.org/10.1016/j.bandc.2018.02.009.

Balconi, M., Venturella, I., Fronda, G., & Vanutelli, M. E. (2019). Who's boss? Physiological measures during performance assessment. *Managerial and Decision Economics 40* (2), 213–219. https://doi.org/10.1002/mde.2997.

Balconi, M., Venturella, I., Fronda, G., De Filippis, D., Salati, E., & Vanutelli, M. E. (2019). To rate or not to rate autonomic response and psychological well-being of employees during performance review. *Health Care Manager 38* (2), 179–186. https://doi.org/10.1097/HCM.0000000000000257.

Bauer, M., Kennett, S., & Driver, J. (2012). Attentional selection of location and modality in vision and touch modulates low-frequency activity in associated sensory cortices. *Journal of Neurophysiology 107* (9), 2342–2351. https://doi.org/10.1152/jn.00973.2011.

Bernieri, F. J., & Rosenthal, R. (1991). Interpersonal coordination: behavioral matching and interactional synchrony. In R. S. Feldman & B. Rimé (Eds.), *Fundamentals of nonverbal behavior* (pp. 401–432). Cambridge University Press.

Billeke, P., Zamorano, F., Cosmelli, D., & Aboitiz, F. (2013). Oscillatory brain activity correlates with risk perception and predicts social decisions. *Cerebral Cortex (New York, N.Y.: 1991) 23*(12), 2872–2883. https://doi.org/10.1093/cercor/bhs269.

Boksem, M. A. S., Smolders, R., & De Cremer, D. (2012). Social power and approach-related neural activity. *Social Cognitive and Affective Neuroscience 7* (5), 516–520. https://doi.org/10.1093/scan/nsp006.

Carver, C. S., & White, T. L. (1994). Behavioral inhibition, behavioral activation, and affective responses to impending reward and punishment: The BIS/BAS scales. *Journal of Personality and Social Psychology 67* (2), 319–333. https://doi.org/10.1037/0022-3514.67.2.319.

Chiao, J. Y., Harada, T., Oby, E. R., Li, Z., Parrish, T., & Bridge, D. J. (2009). Neural representations of social status hierarchy in human inferior parietal cortex. *Neuropsychologia 47* (2), 354–363. https://doi.org/10.1016/j.neuropsychologia.2008.09.023.

Cristofori, I., Moretti, L., Harquel, S., Posada, A., Deiana, G., Isnard, J., Mauguière, F., & Sirigu, A. (2013). Theta signal as the neural signature of social exclusion. *Cerebral Cortex 23* (10), 2437–2447. https://doi. org/10.1093/cercor/bhs236.

Crivelli, D., & Balconi, M. (2017). Near-infrared spectroscopy applied to complex systems and human hyperscanning networking. *Applied Sciences 7* (9), 922. https://doi.org/10.3390/app7090922.

Cui, F., Zhu, X., Duan, F., & Luo, Y. (2016). Instructions of cooperation and competition influence the neural responses to others' pain: An ERP study. *Social Neuroscience 11* (3), 289–296. https://doi.org/10.1080/ 17470919.2015.1078258.

Cui, X., Bryant, D. M., & Reiss, A. L. (2012). NIRS-based hyperscanning reveals increased interpersonal coherence in superior frontal cortex during cooperation. *NeuroImage 59* (3), 2430–2437. https://doi.org/ 10.1016/j.neuroimage.2011.09.003.

Danyluck, C., & Page-Gould, E. (2018). Intergroup dissimilarity predicts physiological synchrony and affiliation in intergroup interaction. *Journal of Experimental Social Psychology 74*, 111–120. https://doi.org/ 10.1016/j.jesp.2017.08.001.

Davis, M. H. (1980). A multidimensional approach to individual differences in empathy. *Journal of Personality and Social Psychology 10*, 85–104. https://doi.org/10.1037/0022-3514.44.1.113.

Decety, J., Jackson, P. L., Sommerville, J. A., Chaminade, T., & Meltzoff, A. N. (2004). The neural bases of cooperation and competition: An fMRI investigation. *NeuroImage 23* (2), 744–751. https://doi.org/ 10.1016/j.neuroimage.2004.05.025.

De Hoogh, A. H. B., & Den Hartog, D. N. (2008). Ethical and despotic leadership, relationships with leader's social responsibility, top management team effectiveness and subordinates' optimism: A multi-method study. *Leadership Quarterly 19* (3), 297–311. https://doi.org/10.1016/j.leaqua.2008.03.002.

De Lange, F. P., Jensen, O., Bauer, M., & Toni, I. (2008). Interactions between posterior gamma and frontal alpha/beta oscillations during imagined actions. *Frontiers in human neuroscience 2*, 7. https://doi.org/ 10.3389/neuro.09.007.2008.

DiMascio, A., Boyd, R. W., & Greenblatt, M. (1957). Physiological correlates of tension and antagonism during psychotherapy; a study of interpersonal physiology. *Psychosomatic Medicine 19* (2), 99–104. https:// doi.org/10.1097/00006842-195703000-00002.

Freeman, J. B., Rule, N. O., Adams, R. B., & Ambady, N. (2009). Culture shapes a mesolimbic response to signals of dominance and subordination that associates with behavior. *NeuroImage 47* (1), 353–359. https:// doi.org/10.1016/j.neuroimage.2009.04.038.

Fritz, H. L., Nagurney, A. J., & Helgeson, V. S. (2003). Social interactions and cardiovascular reactivity during problem disclosure among friends. *Personality and Social Psychology Bulletin 29* (6), 713–725. https://doi. org/10.1177/0146167203029006004.

Hart, S. G., & Staveland, L. E. (1988). Development of NASA-TLX (Task Load Index): Results of empirical and theoretical research. *Advances in Psychology 52*, 139–183. https://doi.org/10.1016/ S0166-4115(08)62386-9.

Järvelä, S., Kivikangas, J. M., Kätsyri, J., & Ravaja, N. (2014). Physiological linkage of dyadic gaming experience. *Simulation and Gaming 45* (1), 24–40. https://doi.org/10.1177/1046878113513080.

Kaplan, H. B., Burch, N. R., & Bloom, S. W. (1964). Physiological covariation and sociometric relationships in small peer groups. In P. Leiderman & D. Shapiro (Eds.), *Psychobiological approaches to social behavior* (pp. 92–109). Stanford University Press.

Knyazev, G. G., Slobodskoj-Plusnin, J. Y., & Bocharov, A. V. (2009). Event-related delta and theta synchronization during explicit and implicit emotion processing. *Neuroscience 164* (4), 1588–1600. https://doi.org/ 10.1016/j.neuroscience.2009.09.057.

Konvalinka, I., Bauer, M., Stahlhut, C., Hansen, L. K., Roepstorff, A., & Frith, C. D. (2014). Frontal alpha oscillations distinguish leaders from followers: Multivariate decoding of mutually interacting brains. *NeuroImage 94*, 79–88. https://doi.org/10.1016/j.neuroimage.2014.03.003.

Konvalinka, I., & Roepstorff, A. (2012). The two-brain approach: how can mutually interacting brains teach us something about social interaction? *Frontiers in Human Neuroscience 6* (July), 1–10. https://doi.org/ 10.3389/fnhum.2012.00215.

Koslov, K., Mendes, W. B., Pajtas, P. E., & Pizzagalli, D. A. (2011). Asymmetry in resting intracortical activity as a buffer to social threat. *Psychological Science 22* (5), 641–649. https://doi.org/10.1177/095679761 1403156.

Liu, T., Saito, G., Lin, C., & Saito, H. (2017). Inter-brain network underlying turn-based cooperation and competition: A hyperscanning study using near-infrared spectroscopy. *Scientific Reports 7* (8684), 1–12. https://doi.org/10.1038/s41598-017-09226-w.

Liu, T., Saito, H., & Oi, M. (2015). Role of the right inferior frontal gyrus in turn-based cooperation and competition: A near-infrared spectroscopy study. *Brain and Cognition 99*, 17–23. https://doi.org/10.1016/j.bandc.2015.07.001.

Liu, H., Zhao, C., Wang, F., & Zhang, D. (2021). Inter-brain amplitude correlation differentiates cooperation from competition in a motion-sensing sports game. *Social cognitive and affective neuroscience, 16*(6), 552–564. https://doi.org/10.1093/scan/nsab031

Marsh, A. A, Blair, K. S., Jones, M. M., Soliman, N., & Blair, R. J. R. (2009). Dominance and submission: The ventrolateral prefrontal cortex and responses to status cues. *Journal of Cognitive Neuroscience 21* (4), 713–724. https://doi.org/10.1162/jocn.2009.21052.Dominance.

Mayer, J. D., Salovey, P., & Caruso, D. R. (2008). Emotional intelligence: New ability or eclectic traits? *American Psychologist 63* (6), 503–517. https://doi.org/10.1037/0003-066X.63.6.503.

Pan, Y., Cheng, X., Zhang, Z., Li, X., & Hu, Y. (2017). Cooperation in lovers: an f NIRS-based hyperscanning study. *Human brain mapping, 38*(2), 831–841. https://doi.org/10.1002/hbm.23421

Rock, D. (2008). *The neuroscience of leadership*. Middlesex University Research.

Saxbe, D., & Repetti, R. L. (2010). For better or worse? Coregulation of couples' cortisol levels and mood states. *Journal of Personality and Social Psychology 98* (1), 92–103. https://doi.org/10.1037/a0016959.

Spapé, M. M., Kivikangas, J. M., Järvelä, S., Kosunen, I., Jacucci, G., & Ravaja, N. (2013). Keep your opponents close: Social context affects EEG and fEMG linkage in a turn-based computer game. *PLoS ONE 8* (11), 1–9. https://doi.org/10.1371/journal.pone.0078795.

Vanutelli, M. E., Gatti, L., Angioletti, L., & Balconi, M. (2017). Affective synchrony and autonomic coupling during cooperation: A hyperscanning study. *BioMed Research International 2017*, 1–9. https://doi.org/10.1155/2017/3104564.

Vanutelli, M. E., Gatti, L., Angioletti, L., & Balconi, M. (2018). May the best joint-actions win: Physiological linkage during competition. *Applied Psychophysiology Biofeedback, 43*(3), 227–237. https://doi.org/10.1007/s10484-018-9402-8.

Vanutelli, M. E., Nandrino, J. L., & Balconi, M. (2016). The boundaries of cooperation: Sharing and coupling from ethology to neuroscience. *Neuropsychological Trends 19* (1), 80–104. https://doi.org/10.7358/neur-2016-019-vanu.

Venturella, I., Gatti, L., Vanutelli, M. E., & Balconi, M. (2017). When brains dialogue by synchronized or unsynchronized languages. Hyperscanning applications to neuromanagement. *Neuropsychological Trends 21* (1), 35–51. https://doi.org/10.7358/neur-2017-021-vent.

Wang, Y., Yuan, B., Roberts, K., Wang, Y., Lin, C., & Simons, R. F. (2014). How friendly is a little friendly competition? Evidence of self-interest and empathy during outcome evaluation. *International Journal of Psychophysiology 91* (3), 155–162. https://doi.org/10.1016/j.ijpsycho.2013.10.009.

The Evolution of Competition: A Darwinian Perspective

Ben Winegard *and* David Geary

Abstract

Human competition is, at least partially, responsible for some of the transcended achievements of the species (walking on the moon, the polio vaccine, etc.), but the forces unleashed by competition have also led to profound human suffering (warfare, domination of one group by another group, etc.). In this article, the authors approach competition from an evolutionary perspective, applying Darwin's theories of natural and sexual selection to understand better the nature of human competition. From the perspective of evolutionary psychology, humans engage in competition to gain resources, including status, food, and mating opportunities. Males tend to engage in more overt and aggressive forms of competition than females, but both sexes desire access to material and cultural goods associated with reproductive fitness. In the last roughly seventy years, the nature of men's competition has transformed dramatically leading to declines in both within and between-group violence. As developed societies have succeeded in suppressing more overt and destructive forms of male–male competition, men attempt to gain status through occupational success, cognitive sophistication, moral signaling, and other relatively nonviolent behaviors. In this sense, men's and women's competition is more similar than it was a century ago. However, women's competition is still less visible and relies on more indirect mechanisms (e.g., spreading gossip, subtle use of body language). For this reason, female–female competition has attracted less study than male–male competition. Fortunately, in the last decade, psychologists have partially redressed this imbalance.

Key Words: natural selection, sexual selection, WEIRD, status, intrasexual competition, intersexual competition, coalition, prestige, dominance

Introduction

In game seven of the 2016 NBA finals, the Cleveland Cavaliers, led by LeBron James, found themselves tied with the heavily favored Golden State Warriors. With 1:56 to play, Andre Iguodala of the Warriors appeared to have an open layup, when suddenly, out of nowhere, a streaking LeBron James leapt into air and swatted the ball against the backboard—a play that became known simply as "the block" (McMenamin, 2016). The Cavaliers went on to win the game and the NBA championship. It was the first time in fifty-two years that a Cleveland team had won a major sports championship.

Sports often represent the very best of the human competitive spirit, creating memories that millions of fans remember for their entire lives and lifting the mood and finances of cities and even nations. It is difficult to believe that the same cognitive and affective systems that are responsible for such transcendent moments such as "the block" are also responsible for unspeakable brutality and horror: from Stalin's gulags to the daily violence that claims thousands of lives each year in the cities of the United States. Clearly, the desire to compete with conspecifics and gain status is a powerful universal human drive (Anderson et al., 2015). And as many communist nations discovered in the middle of the twentieth century, the human drive toward self-interest and competition is impossible to extinguish without simultaneously extinguishing freedom.

In the following chapter, we approach competition from an evolutionary perspective. First, we provide the theoretical background needed to fully understand human competition and do so using Darwin's theories of natural and sexual selection. We then apply these theories to men's competition in traditional and early historical societies. We note that men's competition throughout our species' history has caused tremendous destruction and suffering. We next turn to women's competition, which is often neglected because it is not as conspicuous as the behaviors associated with men's competition. Finally, we discuss the historical shift in the nature of men's competition that slowly emerged during human history. A transformation that has resulted in massive declines in both within- and between-group violence as well as myriad lesser forms of aggression and coercion. We believe that this chapter demonstrates the power of the Darwinian paradigm to shed light on human nature and the interactive nature of biology, culture, and society.

Natural, Sexual, and Social Selection

In order to make sense of the benefits and historical trajectory of competition in humans, it's important to understand how evolutionary selection works. Natural selection is of course well known and can occur whenever there is heritable variation in traits (e.g., plumage camouflage) that influence survival prospects (Darwin, 1859; Mayr, 1977). Darwin's (1871) theory of sexual selection and West-Eberhard's (1979, 1983) theory of social selection are not as well-known, but are often more potent evolutionary processes than natural selection. This is especially true for sexual selection, whereby the associated competition for mates or control of reproductively-related resources (e.g., nesting sites) creates selection pressures that are about twice as intense as those associated with natural selection (Janicke et al., 2016). Sexual and social selections are thus important for fully understanding the evolution of all sexually reproducing species and especially so for humans, given our highly complex social dynamics (Geary, 2021).

Sexual Selection
Sexual selection refers to social dynamics that influence variation in reproductive rather than survival outcomes (Anderson, 1994; Kuijper et al., 2012). Darwin (1859)

introduced sexual selection in his masterwork and greatly elaborated two years later (Darwin, 1871). One goal was to account for elaborate and exaggerated "ornaments" or "armaments" such as antlers, plumage, canines, and body size that are found in one sex and often difficult to understand as a result of selection for survival (Rico-Guevara & Hurme, 2019).

The principle components of sexual selection, *intersexual choice* (appealing directly to members of the other sex) and *intrasexual competition* (competing with members of one's own sex), have been thoroughly studied and are firmly established as potent evolutionary forces that influence competition across species (Anderson, 1994). Generally speaking, sexual selection operates more strongly on males than females due to sex differences in minimal obligatory parental investment (Clutton-Brock, 1991; Janicke et al., 2016; Trivers, 1972; Williams, 1966). This is because the reproductive success of members of the lower investing sex (typically males) is more strongly influenced by the number of mates that can be found than by investing in the well-being of individual offspring. The reproductive success of members of the higher investing sex (typically females) is more strongly influenced, in most cases, by investment in offspring than by competing for mates. The greater investment in offspring makes them attractive to the opposite sex and thereby reduces the need to compete for mates.

Intersexual Choice

In most species, female investment in parenting makes the female a valuable reproductive resource over which males compete. Male competition in turn typically results in females' choice, that is, that ability to select among the competing males (Andersson, 1994; Darwin, 1871; Trivers, 1972). Males can also be choosey in some species, especially when they invest in parenting, but they are typically less exacting than females. Whoever is making the choices, the evolutionary result is the exaggeration of the traits on which the mate choices are made. Well-studied examples include the elaborate plumage coloration of male birds in many species and the length and symmetry of their tail feathers (e.g., Loyau et al., 2005), as shown in Figure 7.1.

In many species, elaborate traits may serve as indicators of the physical or genetic health of the individual, or serve as an indicator of the ability (e.g., vigor in searching for food) to provide parental investment (Andersson, 1994; Zahavi, 1975). These traits provide the chooser with important information about the health and vitality of the prospective mate because such traits serve as difficult to fake signals of underlying physical and genetic fitness (Geary, 2015; Hamilton & Zuk, 1982; Hill, 2014; von Schantz et al., 1999). The choosing sex has evolved to be sensitive to these traits because prospective mates who possess them pass better adapted (e.g., to local parasites) genes to offspring, thus increasing offspring viability and fitness. This is known as selection for indirect benefits because the benefits accrue to offspring in terms of attractiveness and viability (Kotiaho & Puurtinen, 2007).

Figure 7.1 Female and male hummingbirds (*Spathura underwoodi*) from *The descent of man, and selection in relation to sex*, Vol. II, by C. Darwin, 1871, London, John Murray, p. 77. The large tail feathers of the male are a sexually selected trait and likely to be an honest indicator of the males' health but may compromise escape from predators.

In many species, from birds to humans, organisms also select mates on the basis of direct benefits. These include benefits, such as nuptial gifts, territory, and parental care that immediately benefit the chooser and typically their offspring (Jones & Ratterman, 2009). For example, in passerine birds, females often chose males on the basis of territory quality (Slagsvold, 1986). Related research suggests that female barn swallows (*Hirundo rustica*) select and invest more (e.g., provision their offspring more frequently) in males who possess high parental quality, as measured by nest-building ability (Soler et al., 1998). Sexual selection based on direct benefits is widespread in the animal kingdom and leads to competition among the selected sex to provide the resources needed by the other sex to successfully reproduce (Anderson, 1994).

Intrasexual Competition

Intrasexual competition among males often involves physical threats and overt fights over access to females or for control of the territory and resources that females need to raise offspring (Anderson, 1994; Darwin, 1871). As with intersexual choice, the result is the evolutionary exaggeration of the traits that facilitate competitive ability, as shown in Figure 7.2. Generally, this competition is one-on-one, but in certain species, including humans, it involves groups or coalitions (McDonald et al., 2012). Typically, in one-on-one intrasexual selection, the more robust and aggressive males are able to defeat weaker rivals in contest competitions and monopolize resources, including females. This leads to high reproductive skew—a few males have many offspring, while the majority have few or none—and, therefore, results in the evolution of sex differences in biological armaments, aggressiveness, and physical size (Rico-Guevara & Hurme, 2019).

In some species, male–male competition takes place within and between coalitions (Wrangham, 1999). In these species, males jockey for status within their coalition, often through physical fighting and aggressive display, but they also form complex, hierarchical coalitions that then compete with other male coalitions (Goodall, 1986; Mitani, 2009). In chimpanzees, such coalitional conflict is often deadly and has been compared to primitive human warfare (Feldblum et al., 2018). There is good evidence that this lethal intergroup aggression can lead to territorial expansion and associated reproductive benefits (Mitani et al., 2010).

The development and maintenance of coalitions is a complex social endeavor that requires a sophisticated balancing act: coalitions need to be large and coordinated to be competitive, but if they are too large, the associated reproductive costs of shared mating outweigh the benefits (de Waal, 2000; Packer et al., 1991). Further, within coalitions, males form dominance hierarchies that are complex and often involve shifting alliances (Goodall, 1986). Therefore, coalitional competition often selects for cognitive and affective traits such as intelligence and gregariousness that allow more complex social organizations, including multilevel social systems (Grueter et al., 2012).

Social Selection

Many animals compete for resources other than mates that impact reproductive success, including resources for offspring or high-status allies. West-Eberhard (1979, 1983) proposed that such competition is a form of social selection but does not fall under traditional definitions of sexual selection; in fact, sexual selection can be seen as a subset of

Figure 7.2 The male kudu (*Tragelaphus strepsiceros*) from *The descent of man, and selection in relation to sex*, Vol. II, by C. Darwin, 1871, London, John Murray, p. 255. Males compete by locking horns and pulling and pushing each other as a display of physical strength and stamina. Females are hornless.

social selection. This broader perspective provides a framework for better understanding female–female competition than is possible with only consideration of sexual selection, that is, competition for mates. Indeed, female–female competition is common across species and is more likely to be over control of high-quality resources than over mates (Tobias et al., 2012). Successful females and their offspring are typically in better health relative to lower-status females and their offspring, and the offspring of higher-status females are more likely to survive and reproduce in adulthood. Thus, social selection allows us to understand the presence of elaborated female traits and intense female–female competition that is quite common across species, even when females do not directly compete for mates (Stockley & Bro-Jorgensen, 2011). Even so, the overall influence of sexual and social selection is generally stronger in males than females, with the exception of species in which males provide most or all of the parental care (Janicke et al., 2016).

As an example of social selection, consider the Soay sheep (*Ovis aries*), a polygynous ungulate that inhabits the British Isles. Dominant male Soay sheep engage in one-on-one contest competitions over access to females and have evolved horns that facilitate this competition, as with the horns of the Kudu shown in Figure 7.2 (Clutton-Brock & Pemberton, 2004). Generally, the larger males with longer horns win such contests and leave more offspring than their smaller conspecifics (Preston et al., 2003). However, some female Soay sheep also grow horns and use these to compete for ecological resources, not access to mates. The horns function as an adaptation that allows females to better compete with other females for access to food and position in social groups that reduce predation risks. Females also use their horns to protect their offspring by intimidating or defeating rival females in antagonistic interactions (Robinson & Kruuk, 2007). Social selection is likely an important force in human evolution for myriad reasons. First, humans are an extremely social species, relying on complex relationships with extended kin and alliances with non-kin (Nowak, 2012). Second, children require extreme parental care, including copious paternal investment in most societies. Third, humans can transfer status and wealth intergenerationally (Borgerhoff Mulder et al., 2009; Shenk et al., 2010).

Human Competition

As in other species, human social competition is fundamentally about achieving social influence and some level of control over culturally important resources. This is the case for both sexes, but manifests differently in men and women (Geary, 2021). Men have evolved to attempt to organize their social world and life trajectory in ways that increase their social status and influence within the wider communities in which they live, and to attempt to gain access to and control of culturally important resources. Women have evolved to attempt to create networks of social relationships that provide them and their children with social and emotional support and that enhance their access to and control of culturally important resources. As we document below, these basic differences, which are the result of sexual and social selection, lead to divergent forms of competition in men and women.

Male–Male Competition

The ways in which men compete can vary substantively from one context to another, but underneath this variation is a very real and often times deadly struggle for social influence and control of culturally important resources (Betzig, 1986; Daly, 2016; Scheidel, 2017). Irons' (1979) concept of cultural success pulls together all of these different ways of competing and ties them to the underlying motive to achieve social status and resource control vis-à-vis that of other men in their communities (Betzig, 2012; Hopcroft, 2006; Scheidel, 2017). One useful way to think about the dimensions along which men compete is dominance and prestige (Henrich & Gil-White, 2001). Prestige is based on the acquisition of culturally important competencies (e.g., hunting skills and hunting returns) that can contribute to the well-being of others who then freely confer status to the individual with these competencies (Anderson et al., 2015). Dominance is simply the use of force or threat of force to coerce others into relinquishing their property or doing as one wishes, whether or not it is in these others' best interest.

The relative balance of dominance- or prestige-based forms of competition depends on a number of cultural (e.g., third part resolution of disputes), psychological (e.g., empathy, need for cooperation), and economic factors, and ranges from Genghis Khan's rampage through Asia to Picasso's creation of novel art forms (Winegard et al., 2014). Dominance is the ancestral form of male–male competition (Boehm, 2012) and, as elaborated below, is common in traditional contexts and reached a historical peak during the age of empires (Betzig, 2012). As was argued by Hobbes (1651) some time ago, the gradual suppression of dominance-related strategies for enhancing status or resolving conflicts, along with economic diversification and other historic changes (e.g., socially impose monogamy), changed the nature of social dynamics and, for that matter, altered the course of human evolution.

Importantly, in addition to competing as individuals, men also compete in large, complex coalitions. However, the logic of coalitional competition is similar to individual-level competition: groups compete over important cultural resources and broader social influence, resources that are then distributed among members of successful coalitions (Mann, 2012). For example, the Los Angeles Lakers (NBA basketball team)—a prestige-based form of individual and group-level competition—compete to defeat opposing teams and, ultimately, to win the NBA championship. If successful, the Lakers gain in prestige and, at least among some people, social influence, as well as gain economic resources that are shared between players and other members of the Lakers coalition (e.g., the Chief Executive Officer, the Team Physical, the Chief Legal Officer). Similarly, members of the Lakers coalition compete with each other for influence and status (prestige) on the team. In general, the members of a coalition that contribute the most value to the team also gain the most status and recognition from other members of the coalition (Winegard et al., 2016).

This competition, as noted, is based on relative status and, therefore, leads to evolutionary arms races. The extra $20 million bonus earned by a Wall Street executive does not enhance his ability to survive or produce viable offspring. Rather, today the drive to earn additional money and control more resources is an expression of the relative nature of status and health, as higher relative status is consistently associated with better health and a longer lifespan (Marmot, 2004). Before the suppression of dominance-related competition, the accumulation of wealth often preceded the formation of regional armies and attempts to use them to gain control of a nation-state or to expand into the territories of other groups (Turchin, 2007). Whatever the context, there is often no absolute standard for gauging success: Amazon must increase its competitiveness and market share as a corporation to survive because hundreds of other corporations are attempting to outcompete it. The result is an evolved disposition to engage in social comparisons that are focused on relative status accumulation and social control, not simply a desire to achieve sufficient resources for survival and reproduction (Alexander, 1989; Flinn et al., 2005; Geary, 2005).

Traditional Societies

Good indicators of a dominance-based evolutionary history of male–male competition are larger, stronger, and behaviorally more aggressive males than females. These are species in which dominant males mate polygynously and submissive ones fail to reproduce. Humans fit this general pattern in terms of sex differences in physical size and aggressiveness (Daly & Wilson, 1988; Tanner, 1990), and in terms of dominant men mating polygynously when social and ecological conditions do not prevent them from doing so (Betzig, 2012; Murdock, 1981).

Generally, polygyny in traditional societies results from the possession of social power rather than extreme skew in material resources. The Yanomamö (Venezuela, Brazil) are a classic and well-studied example of social power polygyny in a hunter-gatherer society (Chagnon, 1997, 2013). Among the Yanomamö, within-group aggression often results from conflicts over sexual relationships and takes the form of club and machete fights to chest-pounding and verbal intimidation. While such aggression is generally not deadly, the fights often lead to serious physical injury and reputational loss for the loser.

In addition to these one-on-one dominance-related contests, Yanomamö men form complex coalitions and engage in between-group competition including, in the extreme, the raiding of neighboring villages. These between-village raids are often deadly and related to blood feuds (retaliating for harm to kin) and at times bride capture (Chagnon, 1979, 1988). Men who participate in successful raids, those leading to the death of a man from the other village, gain prestige and are considered fierce warriors. In the Yanomamö villages studied by Chagnon (1997), two out of five men have participated in at least one such killing. These men marry sooner and more often. They have two-and-a-half times as many wives as men who have not participated in a killing and three times as many children. The Yanomamö are not unusual, as roughly one out of four men died during raids of rival villages across precontact South American (Walker & Bailey, 2013).

The pattern of male-on-male coalitional violence found in South America is a common feature across hunter-gatherer, horticultural, pastoral, and agricultural societies more generally (Kissel & Kim, 2019). In a large survey of traditional societies, Keeley (1996) estimated that roughly 30 percent of men died from raids, ambushes, and more organized forms of coalitional conflict (see also Gat, 2006, 2019). In more than 70 percent of the traditional societies surveyed, some form of between-group conflict is continuous or nearly so (Ember 1978; Ember & Ember, 1994; White & Burton, 1988). The motivations for such conflict are varied but often include revenge, economic gains, taking of women, desire for prestige, and the fear of perceived rivals. While the outcome is much deadlier, the motives are similar to those that propel a corporate CEO to work fourteen-hour days in an attempt to out-compete rivals and gain market share.

Early Empires

The development of large-scale agriculture supported larger populations than those found in traditional cultures and helped to keep famine at bay or at least reduced its frequency. At the same time, the additional calories produced by these initially small agricultural communities and the ability to store them (e.g., grains, livestock) created a tempting source of wealth for the taking (Hirschfeld, 2015; Turchin, 2007). The details are not critical here, but the gist is a historical cycle of increasingly large intergroup raids, especially at the frontiers between nomadic groups and agricultural communities. The dynamic increased the gains to cooperation within communities and among neighboring communities, either to enhance the size and effectiveness of raiding parties or defend ones' community from such parties (Currie et al., 2020). The theft of these communities' resources by raiders created benefits for the formation of larger agricultural communities. To counter the defensive advantage of these larger communities, smaller nomadic groups had to unite in order to continue their raiding. This type of cycle appears to have occurred in many parts of the world, aided by advances in military technology (e.g., chariot), and eventually led to the formation of early empires (Turchin, 2007; Turchin et al., 2013), and the out-sized influence of war and coalitional male-male competition.

The key point for us is that the formation of larger states and ultimately empires was achieved and maintained by an increase in the level of male-on-male violence and resulted in a substantial increase in the level of polygyny and reproductive and material inequality among men and their families (Betzig, 1986, 2012; Raffield et al., 2017; Scheidel, 2017). In hunter-gatherer societies, would-be despots are kept in check by coalitions of other men, but this is no longer effective in these larger groups (Boehm, 2012). The result is the potential for despots and their allies to emerge and to exert control over other people with force or threat of force, and this is what happened. In these societies, coalitions of men practiced a combination of social power and resource-based polygyny.

Betzig (1986, 1993), in fact, argued that in each of the first human six civilizations (ancient Mesopotamia, Egypt, Aztec [Mexico], Inca [Peru] and imperial India and China), "powerful men mate with hundreds of women, pass their power on to a son by one legitimate wife, and take the lives of men who get in their way" (Betzig, 1993, p. 37). The historical record and population genetic studies confirm that these social dynamics have occurred many times during human history, in many parts of the world, and must have altered the path of human evolution (e.g., Zeng et al., 2018).

Reproductive Skew

The core factor that drives the evolution of competition is variation in reproductive success (Janicke et al., 2016). Across species, dominant males sire more offspring than their less-competitive peers, resulting in reproductive skew and the evolutionary elaboration of the traits that enhance competitive ability. The same is true for men in traditional societies. For the Yanomamö group studied by Chagnon (1979, 2013), the most successful man—nicknamed Shinbone—had eleven wives and forty-three children, as compared to fourteen children for the single most successful women. Shinbone's father "had 14 children, 143 grandchildren, 335 great grandchildren and . . . 401 great-great grandchildren" (Chagnon, 1979, p. 380): the two latter estimates are low because many of the descendants of Shinbone's father are still in their reproductive years. At the same time, many low-status Yanomamö men never marry or reproduce (Jaffe et al., 1993).

More typically, the reproductive differences across men in societies with social power polygyny are not this extreme, but can still be substantial and evolutionarily significant. There are, of course, individual differences in the number of children that women successfully raise to adulthood, but the differences are consistently larger among men than among women (Archer, 2009; Betzig, 2012). An example is proved by the Xavante of Brazil (Salzano et al., 1967). In this traditional society, women had on average 3.6 surviving children, and variation among women (i.e., standard deviation) was 3.9 children. The average number of children for men was also 3.6, but the variation among men was 12.1. In other words, the differences in the number of children among men were about three times larger than the differences among women (a ratio of about 3:1, 12.1/3.9). Betzig reports similar ratios for hunter-gatherer, horticultural, and pastoral societies. In all cases, there was more variation in the reproductive success of men than women, but this ranged from a slight difference among the Yomat (Iran, ratio of 1.14) to a large difference among the Kipsigis (Kenya, ratio of 14.5). The !Kung san (Botswana) were right in the middle, with the reproductive variation among men being almost twice that of women.

The sex difference in reproductive outcomes only became larger with the advent of larger-scale societies and empires. In comparison to the !Kung san, reproductive variation among men was eight to forty times larger in humanity's early empires (Betzig, 2012), indicating a substantial increase in the importance of male–male competition and the use of dominance-related strategies during this phase of human history.

Female–Female Competition

As noted in the section on social selection, female–female aggression and female trait elaboration are more common than Darwin (1871) realized. Female–female competition centers around access to resources (e.g., food, territory, paternal investment) that improve the viability and quality of their offspring (Clutton-Brock, 2009; Hare & Simmons, 2019; West-Eberhard, 1983). This competition rarely reaches the intensity of that found in males, but it does result in reproductive variance among females (Silk, 1993; Smuts, 1987). In humans, females often compete with co-wives in polygynous marriages over paternal investment; and the historical record provides copious evidence of women competing to ensure that their children were conferred legitimacy and status by fathers (Ogden, 1999).

The dynamics of female–female competition differ from male-male competition in myriad ways. Women rarely engage in deadly or overtly aggressive forms of competition and they do not form large, hierarchical coalitions with complex role differentiation (Benenson & Markovitz, 2014; Junger, 2011, 2016). Women's competition also depends on the marriage structure of their society, with more intense competition in societies that allow polygynous marriages. Women compete with each other in varied ways, from strategies that enhance traits that are appealing to men (e.g., through cosmetics, clothing, or cosmetic surgery) to the use of relationship manipulation and exclusion of rivals and competitors (Graham-Kevan & Archer, 2005; Wagstaff, 2018). In societies with socially imposed monogamy, women's financial contributions to marriage (e.g., dowry) can be another form of female–female competition. In extreme circumstances, women do engage in overt physical aggression, including the killing of competitors (Goetting, 1988). Generally, however, women's preferred methods of violence are lower risk than that of men (e.g., use of poison) (Mann, 1996).

As compared with males, female–female competition is subtler, less risky, and, in many cases, more strategic than male–male competition (Stockley & Campbell, 2013). The reasons for this are straightforward. For males, the potential reproductive benefits from engaging in overtly aggressive and risky behaviors are often quite large. A male who wins a zero-sum competition against other males may gain numerous mates and sire potentially dozens of offspring, whereas the loser often leaves no offspring and may forfeit his life. In most species, females do not gain additional offspring from winning overt aggressive contests with other females and they risk harm to self that adversely affects their ability to raise offspring (Benenson, 2013). Thus, across the lifespan, girls and women use competitive strategies that reduce the risk of overt aggression and physical or verbal retaliation, including camouflaging competition, excluding rivals, and avoiding direct confrontation.

Polygynous Societies

Polygyny is common across human societies and has more than likely represented the modal mating pattern over at least the last four million years of human evolution (Geary, 2021; Henrich et al., 2012; Marlowe, 2000; Murdock, 1981). Within polygynous societies, women compete with other wives of their husbands, as well as their husbands' female kin. As explained in the section on social selection, often this competition revolves around paternal care and investment as well as legitimacy (i.e., does the husband recognize the woman's offspring as his own? (Geary et al., 2014). Generally, polygynous societies are more violent and less wealthy than socially monogamous ones, partially due to lower levels of cooperation and increased levels of violence (Henrich, Boyd, & Richerson, 2012). Similarly, for reasons that are not completely understood, the children of polygynously married women are often less healthy and face greater mortality risk than monogamously married women (Josephson, 2002; Lawson & Gibson, 2018; Strassmann, 1997; Strassmann & Gillespie, 2002). Nevertheless, in certain situations, children are better off with mothers married to wealthy polygynous men than poor monogamous men (Lawson et al., 2015).

The ethnographic record of polygynous societies demonstrates that intense competition and relational aggression occurs in hunter-gatherer, agricultural, horticultural, and other traditional societies (Burbank, 1987; Jankowiak, 2008; Jankowiak et al., 2005). These ethnographic surveys demonstrated that female aggression is most commonly targeted against other women, specifically those who represent threats to a woman's relationship with her husband (e.g., co-wives and sexual rivals). Among co-wives, the most common instigators of arguments and relational aggression are the introduction of a new co-wife, especially a younger one, into the family and unequal treatment by the husband. When co-wives are introduced into a family, this generally results in a substantial reduction in the resources that each of the other co-wives will receive from the husband. Further, each co-wife may produce multiple children with the husband, which additionally depletes his resources and increases competition among co-wives for these resources (Burbank, 1987).

As noted, children of polygynously married women are at greater risk for mortality than children of monogamously married women. There are many potential explanations, including decreased paternal investment and increased co-wife competition. Indeed, rumors of co-wives poisoning each other's children are common in the ethnographic and historical records (Strassman, 1997). Murdering the children of co-wives has numerous evolutionary benefits. First, it increases the immediate resources available to their own children. Second, it potentially increases paternal investment by reducing the number of children the husband needs to spend his time with. And, third, it reduces the number of heirs to the husbands' resources, including land, title, and animals. Such competition was particularly acute among noble women in aristocratic societies where sons gained tremendous wealth and resources from fathers, but only if they were recognized as legitimate

(Ogden, 1999). In these societies, women sometimes murdered their husbands before he had additional children with another woman (Herrin, 2004). Famously, Olympias, the mother of Alexander the Great, was suspected of killing her husband, Philip II, before his son with a new wife was old enough to inherit the throne (Cartledge, 2004; Plutarch 2004).

Developed Nations

In developed nations, where monogamous marriage is socially imposed, there may be less intense intrasexual competition, but women still engage in relational aggression and compete over mates and resources. As noted, women and girls engage in less overt and physical aggression than do men and boys, but they manipulate relationships and spread rumors and gossip more than do boys and men (Archer & Coyne, 2005; Card et al., 2008; Björkqvist et al., 1994; Feshbach, 1969; Grotpeter & Crick, 1996; Rose & Rudolph, 2006). Girls' and women's gossip typically focuses on same-sex friends, same-sex foes, or potential romantic partners (McAndrew, 2014). Gossip serves many functions and aids in the formation and consolidation of friendships that provide social and emotional support (Ellwardt et al., 2012). However, gossip is also a component of a broader strategy of relational aggression that is aimed at damaging someone's relationships or social status (Underwood, 2003). Relational aggression is effective because humans are a highly social species and depend upon cooperative relationships to obtain resources including childcare. In small-scale societies, the loss of valued social relationships and the esteem of the larger community would have potentially devasting consequences (Boehm, 2012).

Relational aggression is often subtle, sophisticated, and requires advanced theory of mind skills (i.e., the ability to infer the thoughts and feelings of others), as well as an acute understanding of social dynamics. Behaviors that fall under the definition of relational aggression include withholding positive information about competitors and strategically deploying negative information against rivals. For example, Jenny might inform a popular friend of hers that Jill "hooked up" with a boy at a party, knowing that Jill is friends with Sally and Tiffany who, in turn, hang out with Josh, a high-status boy that Jenny wishes to date. This example makes clear that such competition is quite cognitively demanding and sophisticated. This relational aggression is also quite indirect, covert, and possesses low risk of retaliation: Jenny can always deny that she spread the malicious gossip, which is aided by the circuitous route it leads from her popular friend to Josh. In most cases, the gossip deployed via relational aggression undermines the mate value of same-sex competitors (Reynold et al., 2018) and may lead to the exclusion of these competitors from social groups (Benenson, 2013, Benenson & Markovitz, 2014). Such gossip can also enhance one's own status or solidify existing friendships (McAndrew et al., 2007).

Developmentally, relational aggression emerges during the preschool years, but because of the cognitive and affective demands, it does not become prominent until adolescence where it is most often focused on competition over romantic relationships (Bond et al., 2001; Crick et al., 1997; Smith et al., 2010). As adolescents gain experience in complex social networks, they become increasingly skilled at tactics of relational aggression, especially in creating source confusion for gossip and plausible deniability for derogatory phrases and comments (e.g., "I'm simply worried about Jill because she's sleeping with so many men.").

It is important to note that both sexes use relational aggression as a form of competition against competitors, with men often derogating the social and cultural success of competitors (Buss & Dedden, 1990; Wyckoff et al., 2019). Men also use relational aggression to advance within a coalitional hierarchy by questioning the contributions of other males to the group's success (Winegard et al., 2014). For example, a man might spread malicious gossip about the work ethic of another man within a competitive technology company. However, girls' and women's relational aggression tends to be especially pernicious and is more psychologically damaging to girls and women than to boys and men. Partially, this is because male relational aggression is less effectual because it often has to be supported by observable deficits in the target of the aggression. The contributions of LeBron James to the overall success of the Los Angeles Lakers basketball team are manifest to all members of the group and thus any suggestion that he is a laggard will fall on deaf ears.

The social relationships and reputation that are the target of girls' and women's relational aggression are more difficult to track and thus carry more weight than does relational aggression among boys and men. Moreover, the heightened sensitivity of girls and women to relational aggression results from their revealing more personal and potentially more damaging information to close friends than do boys. These relationships often dissipate, leaving their former friend with considerable personally and socially harmful information that can be used in the context of relational aggression. Women are also more dependent upon a small number of close dyadic relationships for emotional and social support. Thus, anything that threatens the relatively (compared to males) high interpersonal intimacy among girls and women also has the cost of placing them at greater risk of social manipulation, gossip, and other indirect forms of aggression that threaten such relationships (Benenson & Christakos, 2003; Murray-Close et al., 2007).

Many studies, both experimental and observational, indicate that girls and women who are relatively attractive and appear sexually available (e.g., dress in provocative outfits) are particularly likely to be the victims of relational aggression (Leenaars et al., 2008; Reynolds et al., 2018). In one relevant experiment, Vaillancourt and Sharma (2011) found that female college students were likely to derogate attractive potential rivals, but only when the rival was dressed in a "sexy" and revealing outfit. Participants also reported that they would not want to be friends with the sexy-thin rival nor would they want the rival to spend time with their romantic partners. This supports the basic predictions of sexual selection theory, that is, women most often compete on the basis of physical attractiveness and associated traits that help them find high-status mates and secure paternal investment for their children. Girls and women who are more popular with their peers are more likely to be targets of relational aggression, but they are also more likely to use aggressive tactics to achieve social visibility and influence (Vaillancourt, 2013).

Although girls and women usually attempt to disguise female–female competition, it is not always successful. In some instances, a perspicacious victim can discover the source of gossip or innuendo, often through the possession of a group of information-ally connected allies. For example, if Jenny has well-connected sources, she could trace a particularly salacious piece of gossip through a social network and discover the origination point. When this occurs, such relational aggression can escalate to physical violence, especially in contexts where there are few men of high mate value (Campbell, 1995, 1999). In many of these contexts, including low-income neighborhoods in developed nations, being called a "slut" or "whore" is sufficient to prompt physical aggression. In addition to the disparities in male wealth that exist in these environments, men also possess relatively high mortality and incarceration rates which further exacerbates the competition among women (Campbell, 2013).

Competition in WEIRD Societies

Since the industrial revolution (circa 1760–1840), Western societies have experienced a transformation that is unparalleled in human history (Stearns, 2013). In a mere 260 years, the per capita GDP in Western societies has increased from roughly $1000 to $22,000, an incredible explosion in living standards that has revolutionized daily life (Maddison, 2007). This revolution is also associated with dramatic changes in the modes of production, social relations, culture, psychology, and, of course, male and female competition (Winegard et al., 2014). These changes have been especially important in altering the manifestation of male–male competition and, specifically, the levels of physical aggression in Western societies. Because men are responsible for over 95 percent (well over 98 percent if we include warfare) of violent deaths, the dramatic decrease in physical violence among men is one of the more beneficial aspects of modernization (Pinker, 2018).

Decline of Violence

In what follows, we describe the ways in which male–male competition in Western, Educated, Industrialized, Rich and Democratic societies (WEIRD) has changed from the often dominance-based physical aggression of earlier societies to a prestige-based form of competition based upon economic and cultural competition (Henrich, 2020; Maner, 2017). Key to understanding this change is the notion of coalitional value. As we noted, men compete with each other to gain status within the contexts of coalitions that compete with rival coalitions (Winegard et al., 2020). Within the context of large, complicated, and specialized coalitions, those males who add marginal value to the group will be rewarded with status and, concomitantly, resources that make them attractive to women.

As a result, men's level of cooperation and mode of competition is facultatively expressed; that is, contingent upon the values and competitive environments of their respective coalitions. Throughout the vast majority of human history, men's coalitions were formed and maintained because of the real possibility of violent coalitionary warfare (Keeley, 1996; Turchin, 2007). In such milieus, the men who added the most value to their coalitions were usually aggressive, tough, physically formidable, and internalized the values associated with honor cultures such as loyalty, intolerance of insults, and protection of group and family (Cohen & Nisbett, 1994; Mosquera et al., 2002). As illustrated below, the shift in the mode of men's competition closely corresponds with the reduction of between-group warfare in Western societies and the rise of a post-industrial economy.

In many traditional societies, the male death rate due to warfare exceeds 25 percent and in a few ethnographic records it exceeds 50 percent (Keeley, 1996). It is obviously not possible to provide an accurate estimate of male death rates in prehistory related to male-on-male violence, however, the available ethnographic and population genetic data suggest that such violence was extremely common and that males faced a near constant risk of suffering at the hands of other males (Walker & Bailey, 2013; Zeng et al., 2018). The ethnographic record and historical data also suggest that within-group homicide was quite common in traditional societies and remained elevated in the Western world through the middle ages, after which rates decline slowly from roughly 30 per 100,000 to 1–3 per 100,000 (Eisner, 2001, 2014; Wrangham et al., 2006).

Pinker (2012; see also Daly & Wilson, 1988) has documented the dramatic declines in violent deaths across history and has postulated a variety of contributing factors. First, the rise of strong states with a monopoly on the legitimate use of violence suppressed smaller-scale coalitional warfare. Second, the rise of commerce and trade increased nonzero-sum interactions and favored peaceable relations between rival groups (Wright, 2001). Third, the rise of democracy better allowed competing interest groups to solve their political differences without intergroup violence. And, fourth, the rise of cosmopolitanism and the application of reason to human relations increased elite disgust with warfare and led to the creation of institutions and social arrangements that discouraged violence and warfare (Inglehart et al., 2015).

Dominance, Prestige, and Competition

Whatever mix of factors contributed to the decline of violence, it is clear that both homicides and warfare have abated in WEIRD societies and changed the ways in which men compete. Broadly, there has been a shift away from dominance-based (e.g., physical violence) strategies to resolve conflicts of interest and achieve status toward prestige-based strategies (Henrich & Gil-White, 2001). As noted, dominance is achieved and maintained by coercion or the threat of physical violence in mutually agnostic encounters (Mazur, 2005; Rowell, 1966, 1974). Prestige is conceptualized as a voluntary relation of subordination where the subordinate individual esteems and desires to emulate the traits of the prestigious individual (Cheng et al., 2013; Henrich & Gil-White, 2001). If an individual submitted to Genghis Kahn because he feared that not doing so would lead to physical punishment or death, we would say that the Great Kahn possessed dominance-based status. If, however, a person freely submitted to the leadership of Jeff Bezos (CEO and founder of Amazon) because they admired his brilliance, work ethic, and ability to successfully run a modern corporate institution, we would call this prestige-based status.

Throughout history, men's relationships have consisted of mixtures of both dominance and prestige, and these forms of status are often indistinguishably mixed. The Emperor Hadrian, to take one example, inspired many high-status Roman men who emulated his military leadership style and love of art; however, he also evoked fear and awe among these same men as he wielded the full control of the Roman state. It is not possible to determine how much his status was based on prestige and how much was founded upon dominance. Even so, a clear secular pattern is that men's relationships and competition have increasingly taken the form of nonviolent struggles for prestige. While Hadrian possessed and used the awesome coercive power of the Roman State, Jeff Bezos possesses dramatically reduced power to physically bully subordinates; in fact, federal laws prohibit the use of physical intimidation in the workplace, even if Bezos was inclined to do so. Instead, Bezos inspires Amazon workers through his positive vision and example (Stone, 2014).

As noted, one of the most dramatic trends in Western societies is the decline in *between-group* violence and warfare. Historically, rival coalitions, even those with prestige-based within-group status relations, competed with each other via dominance-based status (Gat, 2015; Turchin, 2007). This competition favored groups that were economically productive and possessed a strong warrior-class or military and evidenced high levels of within-group cooperation. Coalitions, villages, fiefdoms, or states that were unable to protect themselves from neighboring rivals faced a very real existential threat. Men in these groups needed to possess traits such as bravery, aggressiveness, and a willingness to take risks, as well as the ability to subjugate their own immediate self-interests to cooperate within their coalition. Even when human social organizations became large and specialized, a relatively large percentage of men were still required to participate in the military. For example, in 1950, 28 percent of men in the United States were Second World War veterans (United States Census Bureau, 2013). It is only in the last fifty or so years that group-based dominance contests (at the level of the nation state) declined enough in WEIRD societies that competition among men has moved dramatically toward nonviolent, prestige-conferring strategies, often based upon cultural contributions (e.g., journalists, writers, academics, artists), economic productivity (e.g., accountants, CEOs, entrepreneurs), or political power (Goldstein, 2011). Men who are able to gain resources through these routes are better able to attract mates and invest in offspring than men who still compete via physical aggression (Geary, 2021).

The rise of prestige-based competition corresponds with broader cultural changes that have taken place in WEIRD societies, such as increasing individualism and a loss of respect for traditional values (Greenfield, 2016). Inglehart (2018) and Turchin (2007) theorize that as people's survival becomes less precarious, threats from other groups decline, and societal affluence increases, many norms and values shift away from survival-based concerns and loyalty to the ingroup toward concerns with self-expression and autonomy. Under conditions of scarcity and high levels of existential insecurity, an emphasis is placed on group solidarity and authoritarian leaders while traditional, hierarchical values are embraced. When resources become plentiful and individuals become more secure due to reductions in within and between-group violence, they begin to encourage diversity, openness to change, individual autonomy, and tolerance of diverse groups. As culture becomes more individualistic and less violent, traditional notions of masculinity and traditional forms of male competition are devalued (Gilmore, 1990). Instead, alternative avenues of competition and status-seeking are opened that favor empathy, creativity, tolerance, and the intellect (Feist, 1998; Jamison, 1989; Miller, 2001).

Importantly, these recently evolved norms of masculinity are objectively valuable to modern coalitions and institutions that compete on the basis of cultural influence (e.g., *The New York Times*, Fox News, academic institutions) and economic productivity (e.g., Wall Street firms, Big Technology companies) where intelligence, openness to experience, and acute understanding of other people's motivations lead to institutional and group level success (Deary et al., 2007; Furnham et al., 2005; Gottfredson, 1997). Bill Gates, as one example, possesses none of the traits associated with traditional masculinity, but his intellectual prowess, self-discipline, and conscientiousness allowed him to build one of the largest corporations on the planet. Despite engaging in no known physical aggression, Gates's competitive ability allowed him to generate a private fortune worth an estimated $114 billion. On the other hand, the domains where traditional masculinity allows for effective competition are rapidly disappearing in WEIRD societies, leading to a crisis in masculinity and, at least partially, an epidemic of opioid overdoses and deaths of despair (Case & Deaton, 2020).

This competition in WEIRD societies is increasingly dependent on the acquisition of evolutionary-novel academic skills, such as mathematics, and overall educational attainment (e.g., a college degree). This is one reason schooling expanded in WEIRD societies and has further expanded over the past century from universal elementary to universal secondary education (Geary, 2007). The attainment of these prestige-based competencies and the associated gains in status further shift selection pressures from favoring traits associated with physical dominance to the cognitive abilities and academic motivations that contribute to achievement in school.

This shift away from traditional or "hegemonic" masculinity toward inclusive forms of masculinity based on evolutionary-novel academic skills is also associated with the rise of victimhood culture (Anderson & McCormack, 2018; Friedersdorf, 2015). According to Campbell and Manning (2014), a victimhood culture engenders competitive victimhood and incentivizes the publicization of slight interpersonal violations, such as microaggressions. Victimhood cultures generally view domination as a form of deviation or oppression that is necessary to punish severely through ostracism and public shame. A superficial approach to victimhood cultures is that they are almost completely bereft of male–male competition. However, as Winegard and Winegard (2018) note, the "wokeism" that is emerging in many institutions in WEIRD societies (e.g., academia, the media, Big Tech) fosters intense status competition where educated elite men signal their solidarity and sympathy with victim groups (e.g., people of color, LGBTQ, women) using arcane language and esoteric social justice narratives. In victimhood cultures, men who are educated and able to articulate woke doctrine gain status at the expense of relatively uneducated men or men who are perceived to be insensitive, boorish, or "unwoke."

The amazing transformation of men's competition, from exploiting the weak and conquering and vanquishing rival coalitions, to competitive signaling over victimhood status and solidarity with those perceived to be marginalized, is quite remarkable. These verbal and moral struggles for status are highly visible and have influence in some spheres in WEIRD societies, but reflect only one type of niche within these societies. More traditional forms of status-seeking are evident in sporting contests, although with rules to reduce physical aggression, and of course, all large WEIRD societies maintain a standing military. Although less visible and subject to legal disruption, more traditional forms of physical violence to resolve conflicts of interest and improve status are still found in some niches within WEIRD societies (King & O'Riordan, 2019; Wilson & Daly, 1985). Even so, the overall pattern demonstrates that while Darwin's theories of natural and sexual selection place limits on human behavior, culture and society powerfully shape our species in endless and fascinating ways.

Conclusion

In this overview, we have noted the importance of Darwin's (1859, 1871) theories of natural and sexual selection and West-Eberhard's (1979, 1983) theory of social selection in understanding the evolution of human competition. This competition is ubiquitous and occurs because resources, including mates, are limited. As we've documented, human competition manifests in myriad ways depending upon environmental factors including marriage systems, resources, institutions, and culture. Throughout our evolutionary history, male–male competition was quite often deadly, with a large percentage of males meeting their fate at the hands of other males (Pinker, 2012). In the last sixty years, violent forms of male competition in WEIRD societies have been greatly suppressed, leading to unprecedented peace and prosperity (Henrich, 2020); this is part of a larger-scale centuries-long decline in violence that was interrupted by the two World Wars (Daly & Wilson, 1988; Eisner, 2003). However, men still compete intensely with each other for control of important social and cultural resources such as high-status occupations, money, and a reputation for virtue. The men who make it to the top of modern status hierarchies—Jeff Bezos, Bill Gates, Barack Obama—possess traits such as intelligence, conscientiousness, ambition, empathy, and self-discipline that allow them to add significant value to their respective coalitions.

Women's competition, because it is less visible and salient, has historically been ignored or minimized by scholars and social commentators, including Darwin (1871) who failed to appreciate the significance of female–female competition. As we have noted, female–female competition can be intense and, in extreme cases, leads to overt physical aggression (Campbell, 1995). However, girls and women tend to mask their competition, and use indirect forms of aggression such as gossip, more than men do. In recent years, the aggression of adolescent females has gained widespread attention, perhaps due to the rise of social media and the decline of hegemonic styles of masculinity in middle and high school (Archer & Coyne, 2005; Simmons, 2011). This increased attention has led to insights into the competitive strategies of girls and women, and it has demonstrated unequivocally that females are not bereft of competition (Geary, 2021).

It is, of course, impossible to prognosticate, but we believe that the trend away from more explicit forms of competition, including physical aggression, will continue. There are strong cultural trends toward self-expression values and noncoercion that are unlikely to reverse in the near future (Inglehart, 2018). These trends are historically unique and are to be cherished. That said, human competition is not going anywhere. The desire to gain status and to defeat or outcompete rivals is a core feature of human nature. Rather than lament that humans can be deeply destructive, we are better served using the Darwinian lens to understand how and why competition manifests as it does and creating salubrious outlets for this behavior.

References

Alexander, R. D. (1989). Evolution of the human psyche. In P. Mellars & C. Stringer (Eds.), *The human revolution: Behavioural and biological perspectives on the origins of modern humans* (pp. 455–513). Princeton University Press.

Anderson, C., Hildreth, J. A. D., & Howland, L. (2015). Is the desire for status a fundamental human motive? A review of the empirical literature. *Psychological Bulletin, 141*, 574–601.

Anderson, M. 1994. *Sexual selection.* Princeton University Press.

Anderson, E., & McCormack, M. (2018). Inclusive masculinity theory: Overview, reflection and refinement. *Journal of Gender Studies, 27*, 547–561.

Archer, J. (2009). Does sexual selection explain human sex differences in aggression? *Behavioral and Brain Sciences, 32*, 249–311.

Archer, J., & Coyne, S. M. (2005). An integrated review of indirect, relational, and social aggression. *Personality and Social Psychology Review, 9*, 212–230.

Benenson, J. F. (2013). The development of human female competition: allies and adversaries. *Philosophical Transactions of the Royal Society B: Biological Sciences, 368*, 1–11.

Benenson, J. F., & Christakos, A. (2003). The greater fragility of females' versus males' closest same-sex friendships. *Child Development, 74*, 1123–1129.

Benenson, J. F., & Markovitz, H. (2014). *Warriors and worries: The survival of the sexes.* Oxford University Press.

Betzig, L. L. (1986). *Despotism and differential reproduction: A Darwinian view of history.* Aldine Publishing Company.

Betzig, L. (1993). Sex, succession, and stratification in the first six civilizations: How powerful men reproduced, passed power on to their sons, and used power to defend their wealth, women, and children. In L. Ellis (Ed.), *Social stratification and socioeconomic inequality: A comparative biosocial analysis* (pp. 37–74). Praeger.

Betzig, L. (2012). Means, variances, and ranges in reproductive success: Comparative evidence. *Evolution and Human Behavior, 33*, 309–317.

Björkqvist, K., Österman, K., & Lagerspetz, K. M. (1994). Sex differences in covert aggression among adults. *Aggressive Behavior, 20*, 27–33.

Boehm, C. (2012, May 18). Ancestral hierarchy and conflict. *Science, 336*, 844–847.

Bond, L., Carlin, J. B., Thomas, L., Rubin, K., & Patton, G. (2001). Does bullying cause emotional problems? A prospective study of young teenagers. *British Medical Journal, 323*, 480–484.

Borgerhoff Mulder, M. B., Bowles, S., Hertz, T., Bell, A., Beise, J., Clark, G., & Irons, W. (2009). Intergenerational wealth transmission and the dynamics of inequality in small-scale societies. *Science, 326*, 682–688.

Burbank, V. K. (1987). Female aggression in cross-cultural perspective. *Behavior Science Research, 21*, 70–100.

Buss, D. M., & Dedden, L. A. (1990). Derogation of competitors. *Journal of Social and Personal Relationships, 7*, 395–422.

Campbell, A. (1995). A few good men: Evolutionary psychology and female adolescent aggression. *Ethology & Sociobiology, 16*, 99–123.

Campbell, A. (1999). Staying alive: Evolution, culture, and women's intrasexual aggression. *Behavioral and Brain Sciences, 22*, 203–214.

Campbell, A. (2013). The evolutionary psychology of women's aggression. *Philosophical Transactions of the Royal Society B: Biological Sciences, 368*, 1–11.

Campbell, B., & Manning, J. (2014). Microaggression and moral cultures. *Comparative sociology, 13*, 692–726.

Card, N. A., Stucky, B. D., Sawalani, G. M., & Little, T. D. (2008). Direct and indirect aggression during childhood and adolescence: A meta-analytic review of gender differences, intercorrelations, and relations to maladjustment. *Child Development, 79*, 1185–1229.

Cartledge, P. (2004). *Alexander the Great*. Vintage.

Case, A., & Deaton, A. (2020). *Deaths of despair and the future of capitalism*. Princeton University Press.

Chagnon, N. A. (1979). Is reproductive success equal in egalitarian societies. In N. A. Chagnon and W. Irons (Eds.), *Evolutionary biology and human social behavior: An anthropological perspective* (pp. 374–401). Duxbury Press.

Chagnon, N. A. (1988, February 26). Life histories, blood revenge, and warfare in a tribal population. *Science, 239*, 985–992.

Chagnon, N. A. (1997). *Yanomamö* (5th ed.). Harcourt.

Chagnon, N. A. (2013). *Noble savages: My life among two dangerous tribes—the Yanomamö and the anthropologists*. Simon and Schuster.

Cheng, J. T., Tracy, J. L., Foulsham, T., Kingstone, A., & Henrich, J. (2013). Two ways to the top: Evidence that dominance and prestige are distinct yet viable avenues to social rank and influence. *Journal of Personality and Social Psychology, 104*, 103–125.

Clutton-Brock, T. H. (1991). *The evolution of parental care*. Princeton University Press.

Clutton-Brock, T. (2009). Sexual selection in females. *Animal Behavior, 77*, 3–11.

Clutton-Brock, T. H., & Pemberton, J. M. (Eds.). (2004). *Soay sheep: Dynamics and selection in an island population*. Cambridge University Press.

Cohen, D., & Nisbett, R. E. (1994). Self-protection and the culture of honor: Explaining southern violence. *Personality and Social Psychology Bulletin, 20*, 551–567.

Crick, N. R., Casas, J. F., & Mosher, M. (1997). Relational and overt aggression in preschool. *Developmental Psychology, 33*, 579–588.

Currie, T. E., Turchin, P., Turner, E., & Gavrilets, S. (2020). Duration of agriculture and distance from the steppe predict the evolution of large-scale human societies in Afro-Eurasia. *Humanities and Social Sciences Communications, 7*, 34.

Daly, M. (2016). *Killing the competition: Economic inequality and homicide*. Transaction Publishers.

Daly, M., & Wilson, M. (1988). *Homicide*. Aldine de Gruyter.

Darwin, C. (1859). *On the origin of species by means of natural selection*. John Murray.

Darwin C. (1871). *The descent of man, and selection in relation to sex*. John Murray

Deary, I. J., Strand, S., Smith, P., & Fernandes, C. (2007). Intelligence and educational achievement. *Intelligence, 35*, 13–21.

de Waal, F. B. M. (2000). Primates: A natural heritage of conflict resolution. *Science, 289*, 586–590.

Eisner, M. (2001). Modernization, self-control and lethal violence. The long-term dynamics of European homicide rates in theoretical perspective. *British Journal of Criminology*, *41*, 618–638.

Eisner, M. (2003). Long-term historical trends in violent crime. *Crime and Justice*, *30*, 83–142.

Eisner, M. (2014). From swords to words: Does macro-level change in self-control predict long-term variation in levels of homicide? *Crime and Justice*, *43*, 65–134.

Ellwardt, L., Steglich, C., & Wittek, R. (2012). The co-evolution of gossip and friendship in workplace social networks. *Social Networks*, *34*, 623–633.

Ember, C. R. (1978). Myths about hunter-gatherers. *Ethnology*, *17*, 439–448.

Ember, C. R., & Ember, M. (1994). War, socialization, and interpersonal violence: A cross-cultural study. *Journal of Conflict Resolution*, *38*, 620–646.

Feist, G. J. (1998). A meta-analysis of personality in scientific and artistic creativity. *Personality and Social Psychology Review*, *2*, 290–309.

Feldblum, J. T., Manfredi, S., Gilby, I. C., & Pusey, A. E. (2018). The timing and causes of a unique chimpanzee community fission preceding Gombe's "Four-Year War". *American Journal of Physical Anthropology*, *166*, 730–744.

Feshbach, N. D. (1969). Sex differences in children's modes of aggressive responses toward outsiders. *Merrill-Palmer Quarterly*, *15*, 249–258.

Flinn, M. V., Geary, D. C., & Ward, C. V. (2005). Ecological dominance, social competition, and coalitionary arms races: Why humans evolved extraordinary intelligence. *Evolution and Human Behavior*, *26*, 10–46.

Friedersdorf, C. (September 11, 2015). The rise of victimhood culture. *The Atlantic*. https://www.theatlantic.com/politics/archive/2015/09/the-rise-of-victimhood-culture/404794/

Furnham, A., Zhang, J., & Chamorro-Premuzic, T. (2005). The relationship between psychometric and self-estimated intelligence, creativity, personality and academic achievement. *Imagination, Cognition and Personality*, *25*, 119–145.

Gat, A. (2006). *War in human civilization*. Oxford University Press.

Gat, A. (2015). Proving communal warfare among hunter-gatherers: The quasi-rousseauan error. *Evolutionary Anthropology: Issues, News, and Reviews*, *24*, 111–126.

Gat, A. (2019). Is war in our nature? *Human Nature*, *30*, 149–154.

Geary, D. C. (2005). *The origin of mind: Evolution of brain, cognition, and general intelligence*. American Psychological Association.

Geary, D. C. (2007). Educating the evolved mind: Conceptual foundations for an evolutionary educational psychology. In J. S. Carlson & J. R. Levin (Eds.), *Educating the evolved mind* (pp. 1–99, 177–202, Vol. 2, Psychological perspectives on contemporary educational issues). Information Age.

Geary, D. C. (2015). *Evolution of vulnerability: Implications for sex differences in health and development*. Elsevier Academic Press.

Geary, D. C. (2021). *Male, female* (3rd ed.). American Psychological Association.

Geary, D. C., Winegard, B., & Winegard, B. (2014). Reflections on the evolution of human sex differences: Social selection and the evolution of competition among women. In V. A. Weekes-Shackelford & T. K. Shackelford (Eds.), *Evolutionary perspectives on human sexual psychology and behavior* (pp. 395–414). Springer.

Gilmore, D. D. (1990). *Manhood in the making*. Yale University Press.

Goetting, A. (1988). When females kill one another: The exceptional case. *Criminal Justice and Behavior*, *15*, 179–189.

Goldstein, J. S. (2011). *Winning the war on war: The decline of armed conflict worldwide*. Penguin.

Goodall, J. (1986). *The chimpanzees of Gombe: Patterns of behavior*. The Belknap Press.

Gottfredson, L. S. (1997). Why g matters: The complexity of everyday life. *Intelligence*, *24*, 79–132.

Graham-Kevan, N., & Archer, J. (2005). Investigating three explanations of women's relationship aggression. *Psychology of Women Quarterly*, *29*, 270–277.

Greenfield, P. M. (2016). Social change, cultural evolution, and human development. *Current Opinion in Psychology*, *8*, 84–92.

Grotpeter, J. K., & Crick, N. R. (1996). Relational aggression, overt aggression, and friendship. *Child Development*, *67*, 2328–2338.

Grueter, C. C., Chapais, B., & Zinner, D. (2012). Evolution of multilevel social systems in nonhuman primates and humans. *International Journal of Primatology*, *33*, 1002–1037.

Hamilton, W. D., & Zuk, M. (1982, October 22). Heritable true fitness and bright birds: A role for parasites? *Science, 218,* 384–387.

Hare, R. M., & Simmons, L. W. (2019). Sexual selection and its evolutionary consequences in female animals. *Biological Reviews, 94,* 929–956.

Henrich, J. (2020). *The WEIRDest people in the world: How the West became psychologically peculiar and particularly prosperous.* Farrar, Straus and Giroux.

Henrich, J., Boyd, R., & Richerson, P. J. (2012). The puzzle of monogamous marriage. *Philosophical Transactions of the Royal Society B: Biological Sciences, 367,* 657–669.

Henrich, J., & Gil-White, F. J. (2001). The evolution of prestige: Freely conferred deference as a mechanism for enhancing the benefits of cultural transmission. *Evolution and Human Behavior, 22,* 165–196.

Herrin, J. (2004). *Women in purple: Rulers of medieval Byzantium.* Princeton University Press.

Hill, G. E. (2014). Cellular respiration: The nexus of stress, condition, and ornamentation. *Integrative and Comparative Biology, 54,* 645–657.

Hirschfeld, K. (2015). *Gangster states: Organized crime, kleptocracy, and political collapse.* Macmillan.

Hobbes, T. (1651). *Leviathan, or the matter, forme, & power of a common-wealth ecclesiastical and civill.* Andrew Crooke.

Hopcroft, R. L. (2006). Sex, status, and reproductive success in the contemporary United States. *Evolution and Human Behavior, 27,* 104–120.

Inglehart, R. F. (2018). *Cultural evolution: People's motivations are changing, and reshaping the world.* Cambridge University Press.

Inglehart, R. F., Puranen, B., & Welzel, C. (2015). Declining willingness to fight for one's country: The individual-level basis of the long peace. *Journal of Peace Research, 52,* 418–434.

Irons, W. (1979). Political stratification among pastoral nomads. In L'Equipe Ecologie et Anthropologie des Societes Pastorales (Eds.), *Pastoral production and society* (pp. 361–374). Cambridge University Press.

Jaffe, K., Urribarri, D., Chacon, G. C., Diaz, G., Torres, A., & Herzog, G. (1993). Sex-linked strategies of human reproductive behavior. *Social Biology, 40,* 61–73.

Jamison, K. R. (1989). Mood disorders and patterns of creativity in British writers and artists. *Psychiatry: Interpersonal and Biological Processes, 52,* 125–134.

Janicke, T., Häderer, I. K., Lajeunesse, M. J., & Anthes, N. (2016). Darwinian sex roles confirmed across the animal kingdom. *Science Advances, 2,* e1500983.

Jankowiak, W. (2008). Cowives, husband, and the Mormon polygynous family. *Ethnology, 47,* 163–180.

Jankowiak, W., Sudakov, M., & Wilreker, B. C. (2005). Cowife conflict and cooperation. *Ethnology, 44,* 81–98.

Jones, A. G., & Ratterman, N. L. (2009). Mate choice and sexual selection: What have we learned since Darwin? *Proceedings of the National Academy of Sciences, 106,* 10001–10008.

Josephson, S. C. (2002). Does polygyny reduce fertility? *American Journal of Human Biology, 14,* 222–232.

Junger, S. (2011). *War.* Hachette.

Junger, S. (2016). *Tribe: On homecoming and belonging.* Hachette.

Keeley, L. H. (1996). *War before civilization: The myth of the peaceful savage.* Oxford University Press.

King, R., & O'Riordan, C. (2019). Near the knuckle: How evolutionary logic helps explain Irish Traveller bare-knuckle contests. *Human Nature, 30,* 272–298.

Kissel, M., & Kim, N. C. (2019). The emergence of human warfare: Current perspectives *American Journal of Physical Anthropology, 168,* 141–163.

Kotiaho, J. S., & Puurtinen, M. (2007). Mate choice for indirect genetic benefits: scrutiny of the current paradigm. *Functional Ecology, 21,* 638–644.

Kuijper, B., Pen, I., & Weissing, F. J. (2012). A guide to sexual selection theory. *Annual Review of Ecology, Evolution, and Systematics, 43,* 287–311.

Lawson, D. W., & Gibson, M. A. (2018). Polygynous marriage and child health in sub-Saharan Africa: What is the evidence for harm? *Demographic Research, 39,* 177–208.

Lawson, D. W., James, S., Ngadaya, E., Ngowi, B., Mfinanga, S. G., & Borgerhoff Mulder, M. (2015). No evidence that polygynous marriage is a harmful cultural practice in northern Tanzania. *Proceedings of the National Academy of Sciences of the United States of America, 112,* 13827–13832.

Leenaars, L. S., Dane, A. V., & Marini, Z. A. (2008). Evolutionary perspective on indirect victimization in adolescence: The role of attractiveness, dating and sexual behavior. *Aggressive Behavior, 34,* 404–415.

Loyau, A., Jalme, M. S., & Sorci, G. (2005). Intra-and intersexual selection for multiple traits in the peacock (*Pavo cristatus*). *Ethology, 111,* 810–820.

Maddison, A. (2007). *Contours of the world economy I-2030 AD: Essays in macro-economic history*. Oxford University Press.

Maner, J. K. (2017). Dominance and prestige: A tale of two hierarchies. *Current Directions in Psychological Science, 26*, 526–531.

Mann, C. R. (1996). *When women kill*. SUNY Press.

Mann, M. (2012). *The sources of social power: A history of power from the beginning to AD 1760* (2nd ed.). Cambridge University Press.

Marlowe, F. (2000). Paternal investment and the human mating system. *Behavioural processes, 51*, 45–61.

Marmot, M. (2004). Status syndrome. *Significance, 1*, 150–154.

Mayr, E. (1977). Darwin and natural selection: how Darwin may have discovered his highly unconventional theory. *American Scientist, 65*, 321–327.

Mazur, A. (2005). *The biosociology of dominance and deference*. Rowman & Littlefield.

McAndrew, F. T. (2014). The "sword of a woman": Gossip and female aggression. *Aggression and Violent Behavior, 19*, 196–199.

McAndrew, F. T., Bell, E. K., & Garcia, C. M. (2007). Who do we tell and whom do we tell on? Gossip as a strategy for status enhancement. *Journal of Applied Social Psychology, 37*, 1562–1577.

McDonald, M. M., Navarrete, C. D., & Van Vugt, M. (2012). Evolution and the psychology of intergroup conflict: The male warrior hypothesis. *Philosophical Transactions of the Royal Society B: Biological Sciences, 367*, 670–679.

McMenamin, D. (July 27, 2016). When LeBron swooped in and changed the course of Cavs' history. *Sports Illustrated*. https://www.espn.com/nba/playoffs/2016/story/_/id/16544563/nba-finals-2016-oral-history-lebron-chasedown-block

Miller, G. F. (2001). *The mating mind: How sexual choice shaped the evolution of human nature*. Anchor.

Mitani, J. C. (2009). Cooperation and competition in chimpanzees: current understanding and future challenges. *Evolutionary Anthropology: Issues, News, and Reviews: Issues, News, and Reviews, 18*, 215–227.

Mitani, J. C., Watts, D. P., & Amsler, S. J. (2010). Lethal intergroup aggression leads to territorial expansion in wild chimpanzees. *Current Biology, 20*, R507–R508.

Mosquera, P. M. R., Manstead, A. S., & Fischer, A. H. (2002). Honor in the Mediterranean and northern Europe. *Journal of Cross-Cultural Psychology, 33*, 16–36.

Murdock, G. P. (1981). *Atlas of world cultures*. University of Pittsburgh Press.

Murray-Close, D., Ostrov, J. M., & Crick, N. R. (2007). A short-term longitudinal study of growth of relational aggression during middle childhood: Associations with gender, friendship intimacy, and internalizing problems. *Development and Psychopathology, 19*, 187–203.

Nowak, M. (2012). *Super cooperators: Altruism, evolution, and why we need each other to succeed*. Free Press.

Ogden, D. (1999). *Polygamy, prostitutes and death: The Hellenistic dynasties*. Duckworth.

Packer, C., Gilbert, D. A., Pusey, A. E., & O'Brieni, S. J. (1991, June 13). A molecular genetic analysis of kinship and cooperation in African lions. *Nature, 351*, 562.

Pinker, S. (2012). *The better angels of our nature: Why violence has declined*. Penguin.

Pinker, S. (2018). *Enlightenment now: The case for reason, science, humanism, and progress*. Penguin.

Plutarch. (2004). *The life of Alexander the Great* (J. Dryden, Trans.). Modern Library.

Preston, B. T., Stevenson, I. R., Pemberton, J. M., Coltman, D. W., & Wilson, K. (2003). Overt and covert competition in a promiscuous mammal: the importance of weaponry and testes size to male reproductive success. *Proceedings of the Royal Society of London. Series B: Biological Sciences, 270*, 633–640.

Raffield, B., Price, N., & Collard, M. (2017). Male-biased operational sex ratios and the Viking phenomenon: an evolutionary anthropological perspective on Late Iron Age Scandinavian raiding. *Evolution and Human Behavior, 38*, 315–324.

Reynolds, T., Baumeister, R. F., & Maner, J. K. (2018). Competitive reputation manipulation: Women strategically transmit social information about romantic rivals. *Journal of Experimental Social Psychology, 78*, 195–209.

Rico-Guevara, A., & Hurme, K. J. (2019). Intrasexually selected weapons. *Biological Reviews, 94*, 60–101.

Robinson, M. R., & Kruuk, L. E. (2007). Function of weaponry in females: the use of horns in intrasexual competition for resources in female Soay sheep. *Biology Letters, 3*, 651–654.

Rose, A. J., & Rudolph, K. D. (2006). A review of sex differences in peer relationship processes: Potential trade-offs for the emotional and behavioral development of girls and boys. *Psychological Bulletin, 132*, 98–131.

Rowell, T. E. (1966). Hierarchy in the organization of a captive baboon group. *Animal Behaviour, 14*, 430–443.

Rowell, T. E. (1974). The concept of social dominance. *Behavioral Biology, 11*, 131–154.

Salzano, F. M., Neel, J. V., & Maybury-Lewis, D. (1967). I. Demographic data on two additional villages: Genetic structure of the tribe. *American Journal of Human Genetics, 19*, 463–489.

Scheidel, W. (2017). *The great leveler: Violence and the history of inequality from the stone age to the twenty-first century*. Princeton, NJ: Princeton University Press.

Shenk, M. K., Borgerhoff Mulder, M., Beise, J., Clark, G., Irons, W., Leonetti, D., Low, B. S., Bowles, S., Hertz, T., Bell, A., & Piraino, P. (2010). Intergenerational wealth transmission among agriculturalists: foundations of agrarian inequality. *Current Anthropology, 51*, 65–83.

Silk, J. B. (1993). The evolution of social conflict among female primates. In W. A. Mason & S. P. Mendoza (Eds.), *Primate social conflict* (pp. 49–83). State University of New York Press.

Simmons, R. (2011). *Odd girl out: The hidden culture of aggression in girls*. First Mariner Books.

Slagsvold, T. (1986). Nest site settlement by the pied flycatcher: does the female choose her mate for the quality of his house or himself? *Ornis Scandinavica, 17*, 210–220.

Smith, R. L., Rose, A. J., & Schwartz-Mette, R. A. (2010). Relational and overt aggression in childhood and adolescence: Clarifying mean-level gender differences and associations with peer acceptance. *Social Development, 19*, 243–269.

Smuts, B. B. (1987). Gender, aggression, and influence. In B. B. Smuts, D. L. Cheney, R. M. Seyfarth, R. W. Wrangham, & T. T. Struhsaker (Eds.), *Primate societies* (pp. 400–412). The University of Chicago Press.

Soler, J. J., Cuervo, J. J., Møller, A. P., & De Lope, F. (1998). Nest building is a sexually selected behaviour in the barn swallow. *Animal Behavior, 56*, 1435–1442.

Stearns, P. N. (2013). *The industrial revolution in world history* (4th ed.). Westview Press.

Stockley, P., & Bro-Jørgensen, J. (2011). Female competition and its evolutionary consequences in mammals. *Biological Reviews, 86*, 341–366.

Stockley, P., & Campbell, A. (2013). Female competition and aggression: interdisciplinary perspectives. *Philosophical Transactions of the Royal Society B: Biological Sciences, 368*, 1–11.

Stone, B. (2014). *The everything store: Jeff Bezos and the age of Amazon*. Little, Brown and Company.

Strassmann, B. I. (1997). Polygyny as a risk factor for child mortality among the Dogon. *Current Anthropology, 38*, 688–695.

Strassmann, B. I., & Gillespie, B. (2002). Life-history theory, fertility and reproductive success in humans. *Proceedings of the Royal Society B: Biological Sciences, 269*, 553–562.

Tanner, J. M. (1990). *Foetus into man: Physical growth from conception to maturity*. Harvard University Press.

Tobias, J. A., Montgomerie, R., & Lyon, B. E. (2012). The evolution of female ornaments and weaponry: Social selection, sexual selection and ecological competition. *Philosophical Transactions of the Royal Society B: Biological Sciences, 367*, 2274–2293.

Trivers, R. L. (1972). Parental investment and sexual selection. In B. Campbell (Ed.), *Sexual selection and the descent of man 1871–1971* (pp. 136–179). Aldine Publishing.

Turchin, P. (2007). *War and peace and war: The rise and fall of empires*. Plume.

Turchin, P., Currie, T. E., Turner, E. A., & Gavrilets, S. (2013). War, space, and the evolution of Old World complex societies. *Proceedings of the National Academy of Sciences, 110*, 16384–16389.

Underwood, M. K. (2003). *Social aggression among girls*. The Guilford Press.

United States Census Bureau. (2013). *World War II: 70 years on*. https://www.census.gov/history/pdf/ww2info graphic.pdf

Vaillancourt, T., & Sharma, A. (2011). Intolerance of sexy peers: Intrasexual competition among women. *Aggressive Behavior, 37*, 569–577.

Vaillancourt, T. (2013). Do human females use indirect aggression as an intrasexual competition strategy? *Philosophical Transactions of the Royal Society B: Biological Sciences, 368*, 1–7.

von Schantz, T., Bensch, S. B., Grahn, M., Hasselquist, D., & Wittzell, H. (1999). Good genes, oxidative stress and condition-dependent sexual signals. *Proceedings of the Royal Society of London B: Biological Sciences, 266*, 1–12.

Wagstaff, D. L. (2018). Comparing mating motivations, social processes, and personality as predictors of women's cosmetics use. *Evolutionary Behavioral Sciences, 12*, 367–380.

Walker, R. S., & Bailey, D. H. (2013). Body counts in lowland South American violence. *Evolution and Human Behavior, 34*, 29–34.

West-Eberhard, M. J. (1979). Sexual selection, social competition, and evolution. *Proceedings of the American Philosophical Society, 123*, 222–234.

West-Eberhard, M. J. (1983). Sexual selection, social competition, and speciation. *The Quarterly Review of Biology, 58*, 155–183.

White, D. R., & Burton, M. L. (1988). Causes of polygyny: Ecology, economy, kinship, and warfare. *American Anthropologist, 90*, 871–887.

Williams, G. C. (1966). *Adaptation and natural selection: A critique of some current evolutionary thought.* Princeton University Press.

Wilson, M., & Daly, M. (1985). Competitiveness, risk taking, and violence: The young male syndrome. *Ethology and Sociobiology, 6*, 59–73.

Winegard, B., Kirsch, A., Vonasch, A., Winegard, B., & Geary, D. C. (2020). Coalitional Value Theory: an Evolutionary Approach to Understanding Culture. *Evolutionary Psychological Science.* https://doi.org/10.1007/s40806-020-00235-z

Winegard, B., Reynolds, T., Baumeister, R. F., & Plant, E. A. (2016). The coalitional value theory of antigay bias. *Evolutionary Behavioral Sciences, 10*, 245–269.

Winegard, B., & Winegard, B. (2018, September 21). The preachers of the great awokening. *Quillette.* https://quillette.com/2018/09/21/the-preachers-of-the-great-awokening/

Winegard, B., Winegard, B., & Geary, D. C. (2014). Eastwood's brawn and Einstein's brain: An evolutionary account of dominance, prestige, and precarious manhood. *Review of General Psychology, 18*, 34–48.

Wrangham, R. W. (1999). Evolution of coalitionary killing. *Yearbook of Physical Anthropology, 42*, 1–30.

Wrangham, R. W., Wilson, M. L., & Muller, M. N. (2006). Comparative rates of violence in chimpanzees and humans. *Primates, 47*, 14–26.

Wright, R. (2001). *Nonzero: The logic of human destiny.* Vintage.

Wyckoff, J. P., Asao, K., & Buss, D. M. (2019). Gossip as an intrasexual competition strategy: Predicting information sharing from potential mate versus competitor mating strategies. *Evolution and Human Behavior, 40*, 96–104.

Zahavi, A. (1975). Mate selection: A selection for a handicap. *Journal of Theoretical Biology, 53*, 205–214.

Zeng, T. C., Aw, A. J., & Feldman, M. W. (2018). Cultural hitchhiking and competition between patrilineal kin groups explain the post-Neolithic Y-chromosome bottleneck. *Nature Communications, 9*, 2077.

Motivational and Emotional Approaches

Competitive Arousal: Sources, Effects, and Implications

Gillian Ku *and* Marc T. P. Adam

Abstract

Competition and competitive contexts inherently contain elements that generate arousal (sympathetic activation of the autonomic system). In addition to the arousal experienced from competing against another person(s), other elements in competitive contexts, such as time pressure, audience effects, competing for scarce and/or valued items, etc., can create arousal. This chapter elaborates on how competition and competitive contexts can generate arousal, which then affects decision making. Simultaneously, the authors discuss how arousal that is independent of the competitive context can have similar decision-making effects. On one hand, arousal can facilitate and improve decision making. On the other hand, it can impair sound and rational decision making. This chapter gives an overview of the concept of competitive arousal by providing a review of what is known about the nature of competitive arousal, the factors that influence its emergence, moderators, and its effects on decision making. The authors conclude with several open questions as well as a general discussion of the theoretical and practical implications of competitive arousal in different decision making contexts.

Key Words: arousal, auctions, competitions, adrenaline, decision making

Introduction

When we think of professional athletes and the competitions in which they engage, we are often reminded of the adrenaline rush they experience. For instance, track and field athlete, Libbie Hickman, who participated in the 2000 Olympics was quoted as saying, "Passing competitors always gives you a lift. It probably has a physical effect, too, because you get a surge of adrenaline" (Will-Weber, 2002). However, such adrenaline rushes also occur in other types of competitive interactions that are unrelated to sports, such as auctions, negotiations, mergers and acquisitions, and the competition between job candidates for a position or between office colleagues for a coveted promotion. As such, an adrenaline rush, or more precisely, arousal (i.e., sympathetic activation of the autonomic nervous system; Schachter & Singer, 1962) is part and parcel of competition.

Interestingly, this arousal has been differentially experienced as beneficial and detrimental. On one hand, Karch Kiraly (who was famously voted as the greatest volleyball player of all time by the International Olympic Committee) reported, "I have adrenaline going and then focus on what I have to do and do it well. I know we'll have a good chance to win the match that way" (Staph, 2005). On the other hand, Murnighan (2002) discussed how arousal can result in overbidding, noting "Long-held folk wisdom on auctions suggests that people occasionally get caught up in auction fever; that is, their adrenaline starts to rush, their emotions block their ability to think clearly, and they end up bidding much more than they ever envisioned" (Murnighan, 2002, p. 63). Consistent with this latter, impairment view of arousal, Ku et al. (2005) proposed a "competitive arousal model" to understand how arousal can result in overbidding and auction fever. According to the authors, "the competitive arousal model posits that numerous factors can increase arousal and that arousal can impair calm, careful decision-making" (p. 92).

The current chapter builds on Ku et al.'s (2005) competitive arousal model to provide a more comprehensive and integrative framework that captures the sources, moderators, and effects of arousal in competitive interactions (see Figure 8.1). By critically reviewing and synthesizing research in social psychology, management, economics, information systems, and sports psychology, we seek to better understand (1) the sources of arousal when humans engage in competition as well as (2) when and how arousal can improve or impede performance and decision making in competitive contexts. Based on our review, we offer a revised definition of competitive arousal, discuss theoretical and practical implications, and suggest avenues for future research.

We build on the structure of the conceptual framework as a roadmap for the remainder of this chapter. Focusing on the center part of the framework, the chapter first starts by defining competitive arousal and differentiating it from other emotion-related constructs. Second, we elaborate on the current body of knowledge on the sources of arousal, paying particular attention to arousal that occurs within the competitive context as well as arousal

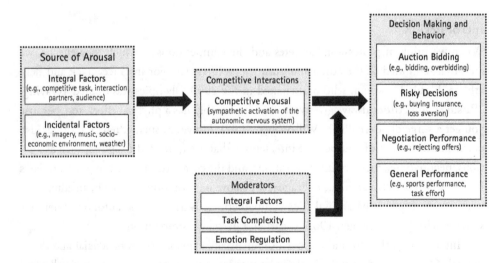

Figure 8.1 Conceptual Framework of Sources, Moderators, and Effects of Competitive Arousal

that occurs outside the competitive context. Third, we consider competitive arousal's disparate effects on decision making and behavior. Fourth, we summarize the relatively more limited literature on factors that moderate competitive arousal's effects. Finally, we conclude with a general discussion of competitive arousal, future research opportunities in this area, and implications for practice.

Arousal and Related Constructs

To better understand the nature of human emotions, researchers (e.g., Holbrook & Batra, 1987; Mano, 1991; Russell, 1980) have theoretically argued and empirically demonstrated that emotions can be described along two dimensions—valence and arousal. Whereas valence represents how pleasant or unpleasant emotion is (e.g., happy vs. sad), arousal represents the level of activation. For instance, although both contentment and excitement are pleasant emotions, contentment is low in arousal/activation and excitement is high in arousal/activation. Whereas considerable research has examined the effects of positive and negative affect (e.g., Forgas, 1989; Schwarz, 2000) on decision making and negotiations, with more recent work targeting the effects of specific emotions (Keltner et al., 1993; Lerner & Keltner, 2000), the current review focuses on the arousal dimension of emotions.

Formally, arousal is the sympathetic activation of the autonomic nervous system (Schachter & Singer, 1962). The autonomic nervous system regulates bodily functions including heart rate, digestion, and respiratory rate. It can be partitioned roughly into the sympathetic and the parasympathetic nervous system, both of which typically function in opposition to each other (Cacioppo et al., 2007). The sympathetic branch activates the organism for "fight or flight," and the parasympathetic branch promotes digestion and recreation. Physiologically, this fight or flight is experienced in numerous ways, including increased heart rate, pupil dilation, and skin conductance (e.g., Bradley et al., 2008; Teubner et al., 2015). Anecdotally, arousal is the adrenaline rush that the quotes mentioned in the introduction section discuss.

Given our interest in competitive interactions, we define *competitive arousal* as the *integrally and/or incidentally induced arousal humans experience before, during, or after engaging in competitive interactions*. In comparison to previous conceptualizations of competitive arousal (e.g., Ku et al., 2005), several points are noteworthy about our definition. First, as already mentioned, competitive interactions can include a myriad of activities, ranging from sports to auction bidding to competing for jobs. What is common to all of these activities is that they involve interactions with other individuals where interests are diverging (e.g., winning a race or auction). Second, complementary to a host of existing research that theorizes based on the concept of competitive arousal but then focuses on specific emotions (e.g., fear, excitement), our definition directly addresses the arousal dimension of affect. Third, it is important to realize that our definition encompasses arousal that may be experienced in anticipation of competition, during competition, and after competition. Finally, and as will become a focal point in the next section, competitive arousal may stem from within the competitive context or from outside. We return to our updated definition of competitive arousal in the general discussion.

Source of Competitive Arousal

Competitive arousal can stem from many sources. Broadly, we can distinguish between integral and incidental sources of arousal. Integral sources are those that are inherently linked to the competitive context, such as the nature of the competitive task, the interaction with competitors, and the presence of an audience that observes the competition. In contrast, incidental sources are not directly related to the competitive context. Examples include exposure to affective imagery and sounds (Bradley et al., 2008), consumption of caffeinated beverages (Barry et al., 2005), or the presence of attractive individuals (Dutton & Aron, 1974) during or immediately before the competitive event.

Although incidentally induced arousal may have "nothing" to do with the competitive interaction, a number of findings have suggested that incidentally induced emotions can have effects that are consistent with those of integrally induced emotions (e.g., Pham, 2007; Rick & Loewenstein, 2008; Vohs et al., 2007). For instance, integrally and incidentally manipulated arousal similarly affected negotiators—arousal benefited negotiators when they had a positive attitude towards negotiations but harmed negotiators when they had a negative attitude (Brown & Curhan, 2013). Similarly, rivalry and time pressure (which are integral to an auction) can increase arousal and bidding (Adam et al., 2015; Ku et al., 2005; Malhotra, 2010), but incidentally induced arousal from energetic music and arousing images can have similar effects (Adam et al., 2019). As such, in understanding the sources of competitive arousal, it is important to consider both integral and incidental sources.

Below, to provide clarity, we review separately the empirical research on integral and incidental sources of arousal in competitive contexts (see Table 8.1). However, it is important to understand that in practice, these sources are often intertwined. For instance, an individual may experience arousal that is incidentally induced from having a double espresso prior to bidding in a housing auction. The arousal from the espresso may fuel an initial bid, but when outbid by a rival, the incidentally induced arousal from the espresso may combine with the integrally induced arousal from rivalry to further affect decision making. Similarly, we can often observe professional athletes purposefully listening to music before their competition starts: Boxers walk to the ring listening to their personal anthems, soccer players and sprinters are seen with earphones as they walk to the pitch or the starting line. Thus, arousal instigated by factors integral to the competitive context (e.g., rivalry, time pressure) cannot be seen in isolation from the incidental factors in the general socioeconomic environment.

Two final points should be made with regards to our review of the sources of competitive arousal. First, although our review focuses on competitive arousal, to be thorough and to provide context and background, we also discuss some research on arousal outside of the competitive context. Additionally, as mentioned when we defined competitive arousal, the current state of research often investigates specific emotions (e.g., fear, excitement)

Table 8.1 Integral and Incidental Factors as Sources of Competitive Arousal with Citation	
Factor	Source of arousal and article

Characteristics of the competitive task	• Prize or stakes (Astor, Adam, Jerčić, et al., 2013; Delgado et al., 2008; Teubner et al., 2015)
	  • Value uncertainty (Ehrhart et al., 2015)
	  • Uniqueness and scarcity (Ku et al., 2005; Nichols, 2012)
	• Winning vs. losing (Adam et al., 2015; Adam et al., 2013; Astor, Adam, Jerčić, et al., 2013; Ding et al., 2005; Teubner et al., 2015; van den Bos, Talwar, et al., 2013)
	  • Fairness (Sanfey et al., 2003; van't Wout et al., 2006)
	• Sunk costs (Hafenbrädl & Woike, 2018; Ku et al., 2005)
	  • Pseudo-losses (Ehrhart et al., 2015)
	  • Automatic or active bidding (Ehrhart et al., 2015)
	• Time pressure (Adam et al., 2015; Adam et al., 2013; Adam et al., 2018; El Haji et al., 2019; Ku et al., 2005; Malhotra, 2010)

Characteristics of interaction partners	• Co-action or competing (Delgado et al., 2008; Engelmann et al., 2016; Li et al., 2013; Nichols, 2012; Yu et al., 2014)
	• Human/computer counterparts (Adam et al., 2015; Adam et al., 2018; Häubl & Popkowski Leszczyc, 2019; Rilling et al., 2008; Sanfey et al., 2003; Teubner et al., 2015; van't Wout et al., 2006; van den Bos et al., 2008)[3]
	  • Rivalry (Nichols, 2012; Pazzaglia et al., 2012; To et al., 2018; van den Bos, Golka, et al., 2013)
	  • Identifiability of counterpart (Adam et al., 2015; Haran & Ritov, 2014; Ku et al., 2005; van den Bos, Golka, et al., 2013)
	  • Trash talking (Malhotra, 2010; Yip et al., 2018)
	• Number of counterparts (Häubl & Popkowski Leszczyc, 2019; Ku et al., 2005; Malhotra, 2010)

Audience of the competition	• Presence of an audience (Ku et al., 2005; Murray & Raedeke, 2008)
Incidental factors outside the competition	• Competition-based bonus/chance-based bonus (Adam et al., 2019) • Music (Adam et al., 2019) • Time pressure (Adam et al., 2019) • Images (Adam et al., 2016; Adam et al., 2019) • Cognitive dissonance (Adam et al., 2019) • Witnessing competition (Raghabendra et al., 2018)

instead of directly focusing on the arousal dimension of affect when theoretically discussing or empirically operationalizing competitive arousal. Again, to be thorough, we include this research in our review. Second, measuring arousal is not a trivial task and researchers have relied on a variety of means including self-report and physiological measures such as heart rate, skin conductance, and brain activity. In our review, we attempt to be both comprehensive and discerning. Thus, if an article speaks conceptually of competitive arousal but does not actually measure it, we have chosen to include it. However, as relevant, we additionally provide information on whether and how competitive arousal has been measured. Table 8.2 provides a summary of this information.

Table 8.2 Key Competitive Arousal Articles Listed Chronologically

Article	Context	Measurement of Competitive Arousal
(Rauch et al., 1999)	Autobiographical scripts	PET scan
(Murnighan, 2002)	Auctions (dollar)	Anecdotal, interviews
(Sanfey et al., 2003)	Bargaining (ultimatum game)	fMRI (insula)
(Ding et al., 2005)	Auctions (reverse auctions)	Self-report
(Ku et al., 2005)	Auctions (charity)	Self-report
(van't Wout et al., 2006)	Bargaining (ultimatum game)	SC
(Delgado et al., 2008)	Auctions (first-price sealed bid)	fMRI
(Murray & Raedeke, 2008)	Golf	HR, self-report
(Rilling et al., 2008)	Bargaining (ultimatum game)	fMRI (posterior cingulate, hypothalamus)
(van den Bos et al., 2008)	Auctions	None
(Malhotra, 2010)	Auctions (charity)	None
(Wolframm & Micklewright, 2010)	Equestrian sports	Self-report
(Nichols, 2012)	Consumer behavior	Self-report
(Pazzaglia et al., 2012)	English Premier League	Archival data
(Adam et al., 2013)	Auctions (Dutch)	HR, SC, self-report
(Astor, Adam, Jerčić, et al., 2013)	Auctions (first-price sealed-bid)	HR, SC
(Li et al., 2013)	Insight problem solving	EEG, self-report
(van den Bos, Golka, et al., 2013)	Auctions (multi-player sealed bid)	Testosterone, cortisol, self-report
(van den Bos, Talwar, et al., 2013)	Auctions (first-price sealed bid)	fMRI, self-report
(Haran & Ritov, 2014)	Effort-based and accuracy task and auction (first-price sealed bid)	None
(Yu et al., 2014)	Group buying	None
(Adam et al., 2015)	Auctions (ascending clock)	HR, SC, self-report
(Ehrhart et al., 2015)	Auctions (second-price sealed-bid, ascending clock)	None
(Teubner et al., 2015)	Auctions (first-price sealed-bid)	HR, SC
(Adam et al., 2016)	Auctions (first-price sealed-bid)	HR, SC, self-report
(Engelmann et al., 2016)	Resource acquisition task	None
(Adam et al., 2018)	Bargaining (Rubinstein game)	HR, SC
(Hafenbrädl & Woike, 2018)	Auctions (dollar and first-price)	None
(Raghabendra et al., 2018)	Pay what you want entrance fee and effort-based task	None

Table 8.2 *Continued*		
Article	Context	Measurement of Competitive Arousal
(To et al., 2018)	NFL and Columbia card task	HR, SC
(Yip et al., 2018)	Effort-based task and creativity task	None
(Adam et al., 2019)	Auctions (first-price sealed-bid)	HR, self-report
(El Haji et al., 2019)	Auctions (second-price sealed bid)	None
(Häubl & Popkowski Leszczyc, 2019)	Auctions (open ascending)	Self-report

Note: HR = heart rate, SC = skin conductance.

Integral Factors Related to the Competitive Task

Many aspects of competitive tasks inherently generate competitive arousal. For instance, fundamental to many competitions is a prize or stakes. Perhaps unsurprisingly, higher valuations and higher nominal payoffs in auctions generate greater physiological arousal in terms of skin conductance and heart rate (Astor, Adam, Jähnig, et al., 2013; Teubner et al., 2015), with these effects more pronounced when there is uncertainty around valuations (Ehrhart et al., 2015). Similarly, bidding for money generates more pronounced neural activation than bidding for points (Delgado et al., 2008). Thus, more valuable prizes and higher stakes are more competitively arousing. However, acknowledging that the value of a prize can depend on non-monetary factors, researchers have argued that more unique items are associated with scarcity, which can then increase competitive arousal (Ku et al., 2005; Nichols, 2012).

Another fundamental characteristic of competitive tasks is that they involve winning and losing, which can also affect competitive arousal. For instance, winning and losing per se generate affective responses as seen in self-reported and fMRI measures (van den Bos, Talwar, et al., 2013). Through skin conductance, heart rate, and self-reported measures, Adam and colleagues (Adam et al., 2015; Astor, Adam, Jerčić, et al., 2013; Teubner et al., 2015) have found that winning in different types of auctions (sealed-bid and ascending auctions) causes greater physiological arousal than losing the auction. Interestingly, the reverse is true in descending auctions: Adam et al. (2013) found greater physiological arousal (in terms of skin conductance) when participants experienced losses rather than wins. These differential effects of winning and losing on competitive arousal can be understood by considering the auction mechanisms and bidder experience involved. In particular, in ascending auctions where multiple bidders participate and push up the price until there is one winning bidder left, bidders control when they stop bidding and drop out of an auction, which means that losing does not come with any surprise whereas winning has an element of (pleasant) surprise. In contrast, in descending auctions, bidders make a single bid to win and end the auction, meaning that winning comes with little surprise whereas losing can be (unpleasantly) surprising (Adam et al., 2015). Thus, winning and losing can affect individuals' competitive arousal, although the auction mechanism needs to be taken into account.

Researchers have further explored these ideas of winning and losing. For instance, winning and losing in earlier rounds of bidding can also affect (self-reported) excitement and frustration, which can then impact *subsequent* rounds of bidding (Ding et al., 2005). Finally, the experience of winning and losing in competitive contexts will often be accompanied by fairness and unfairness judgments. Unsurprisingly, perceived *unfairness* is associated with greater emotional reactions and physiological arousal than perceived *fairness*. For instance, in the context of ultimatum games, unfair proposals generate more anterior insula activity (an area of the brain that has been consistently found to be involved in the evaluation and representation of negative emotional states) and skin conductance than fair proposals (Sanfey et al., 2003; van't Wout et al., 2006).

Another extension of these ideas of winning and losing pertains to the experience of pseudo-losses. Ehrhart et al. (2015) found that being the high bidder and losing that position can also affect bidding, in theory because bidders are forming attachments to the auctioned item and then "losing" the item when they are outbid. Interestingly, these effects were particularly pronounced if bidders achieved their high bidder position based on their own bidding action rather than achieving the high bidder position through a lottery draw (Ehrhart et al., 2015). Relatedly, bidders accrue sunk costs when bidding in auctions. For instance, bidding in an auction can take time and energy (to research the item, to attend the auction, etc.). When outbid, bidders may escalate their commitments to these sunk costs by bidding higher (Ku et al., 2005) because they hope to justify and rationalize their time and energy spent (Staw, 1976). Some research argued and found through self-report measures that sunk costs are competitively arousing (Hafenbrädl & Woike, 2018; Ku et al., 2005). Thus, even though self-justification has been found to be a primary driver of escalation of commitment (Staw & Ross, 1989), this tantalizing finding suggests a different mechanism (i.e., competitive arousal) by which sunk costs can impact decision making.

Finally, much research has focused on how competitive tasks involve time pressure, which can then increase competitive arousal. Time pressure has been operationalized in numerous ways, all of which fundamentally revolve around limiting individuals' time to make decisions. For instance, time pressure has often been studied in auctions which inherently involve making quick decisions. To examine the effects of time pressure in auctions, some experimenters manipulated the amount of time participants had to make their bid decisions (El Haji et al., 2019). Similarly, studies examined bid decisions either earlier in an auction where there is less time pressure or later in the auction where there is more time pressure (Ku et al., 2005; Malhotra, 2010). Finally, time pressure has also been examined in terms of the speed by which bids increase in ascending auctions (Adam et al., 2015) or decrease in descending auctions (Adam, Teubner, et al., 2018). Outside of the auction context, Adam et al. (2018) also examined how changing the discount factor in negotiations where the size of the pie shrank in smaller or larger increments affected competitive arousal. Whereas some of this research has not measured competitive arousal (El Haji et al., 2019; Ku et al., 2005; Malhotra, 2010) but has instead relied on research in non-competitive domains to clarify the link between time pressure and arousal (Cates et al., 1996; Maule et al., 2000), some studies have established that time pressure in competitive tasks increases competitive arousal (Adam et al., 2013, 2015, 2018). For instance, Adam and colleagues (Adam et al., 2015; Adam et al., 2013; Adam et al., 2018) found that time pressure increased self-reports of arousal, as well as physiological measures of heart rate and skin conductance.

Integral Factors Related to Interaction Partners

Competitive tasks inherently involve some form of interaction with one or more counterparts, and certain characteristics of these interaction partners can increase competitive arousal. For instance, psychologists have long recognized that co-actors can increase one's physiological arousal (Zajonc, 1965, 1968). Building on this research, a number of studies in different competitive contexts found that engaging in a task with a counterpart, i.e., competing against someone, increases competitive arousal (e.g., Engelmann et al., 2016; Li et al., 2013; Nichols, 2012; Yu et al., 2014). Similarly, although winning and losing generate affective responses as seen in self-reported and fMRI measures (van den Bos, Talwar, et al., 2013), these responses relate to the inherent *social* nature of the competitive context. In a particularly compelling demonstration, Delgado et al. (2008) found that losing an auction to a counterpart induced activation in brain regions associated with actual monetary losses. This is striking because (1) losing an auction did not incur an actual monetary loss and (2) these brain activation patterns were not observed when losing in an equivalent lottery setting where no social interaction was involved.

The importance of social interaction in generating competitive arousal can also be seen in studies that have manipulated competitive interactions with either a human counterpart or a computer agent. Akin to Delgado et al.'s finding (2008), participants experienced greater physiological arousal in terms of increased heart rate and skin conductance when bidding and bargaining against a human counterpart than with a computer agent (Adam et al., 2015, 2018; Teubner et al., 2015). Similarly, when playing an ultimatum game, there was greater anterior insula activation (an area of the brain related to emotions) when responding to unfair offers from human than from computer counterparts (Rilling et al., 2008; Sanfey et al., 2003). Again, in the context of ultimatum games, participants exhibited greater skin conductance in response to unfair offers than to fair offers, but only when their counterparts were human (van't Wout et al., 2006). Thus, not only is co-action and competing important in creating competitive arousal, competing with an actual human may be necessary, without which competitive arousal and its downstream consequences may fail to materialize (Häubl & Popkowski Leszczyc, 2019; van't Wout et al., 2006; van den Bos et al., 2008).

In addition to the human agency of counterparts, their actions and/or appearance can also be an important driver of competitive arousal.[1] For instance, the evenness of the match, and the repeated nature of interactions have been shown to increase rivalry which, in turn, heightens competitive arousal as measured by heart rate and skin conductance (Nichols, 2012; To et al., 2018; see also van den Bos, Golka, et al., 2013). Interestingly, soccer players who were transferred in the English Premier League may have experienced competitive arousal (although it should be noted that the authors specifically measured anger and pressure for having to prove their loyalty) when they were in head-to-head competition with their old donor teams (Pazzaglia et al., 2012).

Additional research suggests the role of identifiability in stimulating competitive arousal. For instance, Haran and Ritov (2014) argued that rivalry (and therefore presumably competitive arousal) increased when the counterpart was identifiable, even when that identification was minimal (e.g., randomly determined four-digit ID numbers). Similarly, competitive arousal is likely to be higher when photographs make the parties involved clear (van den Bos, Golka, et al., 2013) or when bidding in live vs. internet auctions, where the former allows greater visibility and identification of competitors (Ku et al., 2005). Also, when participants bid against others with bidder avatars and nicknames, they reported more arousal than did participants who bid against others with no further identifying information (Adam et al., 2015).

Another interesting means by which a competitive relationship can be intensified is through trash-talking or making "boastful comments about the self or insulting comments about an opponent that are delivered by a competitor typically before or during a competition" (Yip et al., 2018, p. 126). Yip et al. (2018) and Malhotra (2010) argued that trash-talking can increase competitive arousal by increasing individuals' focus on winning and ensuring that their counterparts lose.

A final and fundamental characteristic of interaction partners is the number of parties involved (Garcia & Tor, 2009). Consistent with our discussion about the intensity of the relationship, fewer rather than more counterparts actually increases competitive arousal. For instance, Ku et al. (2005) found that participants reported greater arousal (in terms of excitement and anxiety) when bidding against few rather than more bidders. Similar effects have been reported in auctions in the field (Ku et al., 2005; Malhotra, 2010) and in controlled experiments (Häubl & Popkowski Leszczyc, 2019), but no studies have measured the influence of the number of interaction partners on competitive arousal physiologically, which is surprising given this fundamental aspect of competition.

Integral Factors Related to the Audience of the Competition

In addition to examining how characteristics of the competitive task and interaction partners affect competitive arousal, psychologists have long acknowledged that the presence of an audience can create arousal (Guerin, 1986; Zajonc, 1965; Zajonc & Sales, 1966). In the competitive context, Murray and Raedeke (2008) found that participants engaging in a golf putting competition experienced elevated heart rates and reported greater arousal (in terms of anxiety) when there was an audience present. Additionally, although live auctions create greater identifiability compared to internet auctions, live auctions also create audience effects, which Ku et al. (2005) argued would increase competitive arousal.

Incidental Factors Related to Stimuli Outside the Competition

Whereas the majority of research has examined how elements integral to competitive contexts can generate competitive arousal, emerging research has considered how incidental factors can generate arousal, which can then have similar effects to integrally induced competitive arousal. Thus, elements outside of a competitive context can be arousing, but only when brought into the competitive context does this arousal become *competitive* arousal. For instance, Adam and colleagues manipulated arousal in a pre-auction task that either involved a competition-based bonus, fast-paced music, and time pressure or a chance-based bonus, calming music, and low time pressure. The incidental manipulation of competitive arousal increased physiological arousal, which then affected bidding (Adam et al., 2019). Similarly, theorizing about arousal in general rather than competitive arousal specifically, Brown and Curhan (2013) examined how physical exercise (using a treadmill) increased heart rates which then affected a subsequent negotiation.

Competitive arousal has also been created incidentally through presenting participants with different images (Adam et al., 2016; Adam et al., 2019) and has even been created through cognitive dissonance (Adam et al., 2019). Thus, when participants willingly wrote a counter-attitudinal essay, they experienced arousal which then affected auction bidding (Adam et al., 2019). Importantly, the effects of incidentally induced competitive arousal have been measured physiologically through heart rate and skin conductance measures (Adam et al., 2016, 2019). Finally, although we know that audiences can create competitive arousal in competitors (Murray & Raedeke, 2008), research has also found that non-competitors who witness competitions (e.g., audiences) may also experience competitive arousal (as measured by social comparison and rivalry motivations; Raghabendra et al., 2018).

In summary, as can be seen in our examination of the current research, much research has examined how characteristics of the competitive tasks inherently generate competitive arousal. Similarly, a lot of research has focused on how characteristics of interaction partners increases competitive arousal. Interestingly, because rivalry can increase competitive arousal (Ku, 2008; To et al., 2018), researchers have also examined in-depth how intensifying the relationship among interaction partners can increase competitive arousal. Finally, some research has considered how audience effects can impact competitive arousal.

In contrast to focusing on these integral sources of competitive arousal, more recent research has considered how incidentally induced arousal can combine with a competitive context to create competitive arousal. The study of incidentally created competitive arousal is noteworthy on several dimensions. First, it opens up a multitude of avenues for researchers and practitioners to increase competitive arousal. Thus, anything ranging from a double espresso (Barry et al., 2005) to exercise (Brown & Curhan, 2013) to hearing violent stories (White et al., 1981) before a competitive event could potentially increase competitive arousal. Second, by showing that incidentally induced arousal affected subsequent auction bidding, Adam et al. (2019) were able to present the first causal evidence that auction fever exists. Prior to their research, evidence of auction fever relied on an examination of the effects of integrally induced competitive arousal on bidding and it was thus impossible to disentangle whether arousal (from rivalry for example) affected bids or whether bids affected arousal.

Effects on Decision Making and Behavior

Research has explored the effects of arousal across a range of tasks and domains (for reviews, see Peters et al., 2006; Rick & Loewenstein, 2008). On one hand, arousal is an essential guide for human decision making (Bechara & Damasio, 2005; Bechara et al. 1997). Consistent with the somatic marker hypothesis, experiencing arousal directs our attention and provides focus, allowing individuals to make advantageous choices even before they cognitively realize the best strategy (Bechara & Damasio, 2005). Similarly, arousal in response to monetary losses is critical for making financially beneficial decisions (Bechara & Damasio, 2005). Finally, research on social facilitation has demonstrated that arousal can improve task performance when the task is easy, well-learned, or when individuals are experts (Brown & Curhan, 2013; Zajonc, 1965).

On the other hand, arousal can impair decision making and performance by narrowing attentional capacity, limiting information processing, and reducing cognitive flexibility, which can then impede thorough decision making (Easterbrook, 1959; Lewinsohn & Mano, 1993; Loewenstein, 1996; Mano, 1992; Staw et al., 1981). For instance, compared to low arousal, high arousal is linked to increased risk taking (Mano, 1991) and greater loss aversion (Sokol-Hessner et al., 2008). The impairing effects of arousal are particularly likely when tasks are difficult, novel, or when individuals are novices (Zajonc, 1965).

A final manner in which arousal can affect decision making and performance is through an attributional process (Schachter & Singer, 1962). When people experience physiological arousal, they need to make sense of it and attribute it to their environmental stimuli. In their classic study, Schachter and Singer (1962) found that participants experienced physiological arousal (induced through an epinephrine injection) differentially depending on whether they interacted with a confederate in a fun, joyful manner or with a confederate who became increasingly irritated and annoyed. In the former case, participants reported higher levels of happiness and lower levels of anger. However, when interacting with the angry confederate, participants tended to match their behavior to the angry confederate. Interestingly, arousal can also be attributed to *non-causal* stimuli. For instance, arousal from crossing a shaky bridge can be attributed to romantic interest in an experimenter (Dutton & Aron, 1974).

Next, we review the effects of competitive arousal in different domains: auctions, risky decisions, negotiation performance, and general performance, while discussing the general mechanisms for these effects.

Auction Bidding

Because much research has examined competitive arousal in auction bidding contexts, a common effect has surrounded bidding and overbidding. Across a variety of different auction types (e.g., first- or second-price, sealed bid or open bid, online or live, common value or independent private value, single-pay or all-pay),[2] abundant research has demonstrated competitive arousal increases bidding and willingness to pay in auctions (Adam et al., 2015; Adam et al., 2019; Ehrhart et al., 2015; Hafenbrädl & Woike, 2018; Haran & Ritov, 2014; Häubl & Popkowski Leszczyc, 2019; Ku et al., 2005; Malhotra, 2010; Murnighan, 2002; van den Bos, Golka, et al., 2013). These findings have been demonstrated with integrally and incidentally induced competitive arousal, with different physiological measures of competitive arousal (e.g., Astor, Adam, Jerčić, et al., 2013; Delgado et al., 2008; van den Bos, Golka, et al., 2013), as well as in controlled laboratory experiments and field settings (Ku et al., 2005; Malhotra, 2010). As a result of the effects on bidding, competitive arousal has also been shown to increase overbidding, where overbidding has been operationalized as bidding past the value of the prize or pre-set limits (Adam et al., 2015; Adam et al., 2019; Delgado et al., 2008; Hafenbrädl & Woike, 2018; Ku et al., 2005; Murnighan, 2002; van den Bos, Golka, et al., 2013).

To explain why competitive arousal increases bidding and overbidding, researchers have typically relied on arousal's impairment effects, where competitive arousal narrows attentional capacity, reduces cognitive deliberation, limits information processing, and reduces cognitive flexibility (Easterbrook, 1959; Lewinsohn & Mano, 1993; Loewenstein, 1996; Mano, 1992; Staw et al., 1981) as well as increases risk taking (see below and also Adam et al., 2016; Adam et al., 2015; Ku et al., 2005). Additionally, researchers also point towards an increased focus on winning (Adam et al., 2015; Hafenbrädl & Woike, 2018; Häubl & Popkowski Leszczyc, 2019; Malhotra, 2010; van den Bos, Golka, et al., 2013) and not losing (Adam et al., 2015; Delgado et al., 2008; Haran & Ritov, 2014; van den Bos, Golka, et al., 2013) as reasons for why individuals bid more and overbid. Finally, competitive arousal could also increase bidding and overbidding because it is attributed to interest in the auction item (Adam et al., 2019).

Risky Decisions

Although competitive arousal increases bidding and overbidding, this is not always the case. Indeed, competitive arousal can also lower bids (Adam et al., 2016; Adam et al., 2013; El Haji et al., 2019; Teubner et al., 2015). Although initially surprising, these findings can be reconciled by understanding that competitive arousal increases risk-taking. When risk-taking combines with different auction types and different characteristics of the item, competitive arousal can result in higher or lower bids. For instance, Adam et al. (2013) examined the role of competitive arousal in descending auctions where bidders make a single bid to win the auction. Because competitive arousal increases risk-taking, this translates to placing *lower* bids in descending auctions (but higher bids in ascending auctions). Similarly, when bidders are certain about the value of the item (as in the case of an independent private value auction), lower bids in first-price sealed bid auctions are associated with higher risk taking (Adam et al., 2016). Correspondingly, Teubner et al. (2015) observed that high competitive arousal levels (as measured by heart rates) were associated with lower bids in first-price sealed-bid auctions. These findings highlight the importance of the auction type and the effects of competitive arousal on risk-taking.

Competitive arousal is also linked to risk taking in other contexts (To et al., 2018; Yip et al., 2018). For instance, NFL teams are more likely to take risks (in terms of making two-point attempts and going for a fourth down) when competing against rivals because rivalry increases competitive arousal (To et al., 2018). Interestingly, some research has also shown that competitive arousal can increase unethical behavior in terms of cheating, which can be seen as a form of risky behavior. In particular, because trash-talking is related to competitive arousal and rivalry, participants who were targets of trash-talking were more likely than control participants to inflate their performance on an anagram task (Yip et al., 2018). It is noteworthy that these findings are consistent with research that has found that arousal outside a competitive domain increases risk-taking in terms of paying less for insurance to protect against potential losses but paying more for lotteries for gains, in line with theorizing that arousal impairs decision making by restricting attentional capacity (Mano, 1994).

Negotiation Performance

Some research has also examined the effects of competitive arousal in negotiations and bargaining (Adam et al., 2018; Rilling et al., 2008; Sanfey et al., 2003; van't Wout et al., 2006; Yip et al., 2018; Yu et al., 2014). For instance, competitive arousal is associated with greater likelihood of rejecting unfair offers in ultimatum games (Sanfey et al., 2003; van't Wout et al., 2006) and Rubinstein games (Adam et al., 2018). In Rubinstein games, the size of the pie shrinks from round to round if the responder rejects the proposer's offer. As a result, competitive arousal results in unnecessarily prolonged negotiations (i.e., additional rounds of bargaining) and economically inefficient outcomes where the final size of the pie is reduced (Adam et al., 2018). Similar inefficiencies in terms of reduced pie size have been found when interaction partners engage in trash talking (Yip et al., 2018). Finally, Brown and Curhan (2013) found that incidentally induced arousal could both increase and decrease subjective and objective value in a negotiation: When participants had *positive* prior attitudes about negotiations, high arousal resulted in greater subjective and objective outcomes than did low arousal. In contrast, when participants had *negative* prior attitudes about negotiations, high arousal resulted in lower subjective and objective outcomes than did low arousal (Brown & Curhan, 2013).

The psychological mechanisms involved in how competitive arousal affects decision making in negotiations and bargaining are not completely clear. For instance, a focus on winning and not losing may drive some the effects above. However, it may also be the case that competitive arousal impairs thorough decision making because people behave impulsively, for instance, when receiving unfair offers from human counterparts. Finally, Brown and Curhan's (2013) findings that incidentally induced arousal can both improve and impair negotiation outcomes are consistent with prior research on how arousal can increase one's dominant response (Zajonc, 1965). It is also noteworthy that the authors suggested an attributional logic to their findings: participants would construe their arousal as negative or positive affect depending on their prior negotiation attitudes, and that this affect would drive subjective and objective outcomes (Brown & Curhan, 2013).

General Performance

Competitive arousal has been shown to improve performance on a variety of tasks including reward retrieval, effort-based performance, estimation tasks, showjumping, as well as individual and team performance in football (Engelmann et al., 2016; Haran & Ritov, 2014; Li et al., 2013; Pazzaglia et al., 2012; Wolframm & Micklewright, 2010; Yip et al., 2018; Yu et al., 2014). For instance, participants (children and chimpanzees) acquired more resources when competing with another individual than when the other individual was present but not directly observable (Engelmann et al., 2016). Similarly, trash-talking increased perceived rivalry and desire to see one's opponent do poorly, which then increased effort-based performance (Yip et al., 2018).

In contrast, other studies have found that competitive arousal impedes task performance in terms of golf putting, dressage, and creativity (Murray & Raedeke, 2008; Wolframm & Micklewright, 2010; Yip et al., 2018). For instance, competitive arousal from an audience (as measured by changes in heart rate and self-reported measures of anxiety) decreased performance in a golf putting task that involved novices (Murray & Raedeke, 2008). Similarly, competitive arousal had a debilitating effect on dressage performance (Wolframm & Micklewright, 2010).

These opposing effects that competitive arousal can have on general performance, both improving and impeding performance, can be reconciled by Zajonc's (1965) work on social facilitation, where arousal improves performance on well-learned tasks but impairs performance on novel tasks. Put differently, arousal and competitive arousal should increase the dominant response. Thus, if a task is easy to perform or if you're an expert, competitive arousal should improve performance. However, if a task is complicated or you're a novice, competitive arousal should impair performance.

Overall, competitive arousal has been found to have consistent effects on auction bidding and risky decisions. Despite robust findings that competitive arousal increases bidding and overbidding, its effects are generally poorly understood and forecasted ahead of time by decision makers (Adam et al., 2019; Hafenbrädl & Woike, 2018), making it ever more critical that competitive arousal research be translated into advice for practitioners. Additional but more limited research has examined competitive arousal's effects on negotiation and bargaining as well as unethical behavior, suggesting potential avenues for future research.

Moderating Influences

A final, but more limited area of research considers how factors can moderate competitive arousal's effects.

Integral Factors

Returning to our discussion on integral factors that generate competitive arousal, competitive arousal's effects seem to be reduced or mitigated if interaction partners are computers rather than human beings. Hence, interacting with a human counterpart does not only yield higher arousal than interacting with a computer, it also strengthens the link between arousal and behavior. For instance, the link between competitive arousal and bidding is stronger if individuals compete with human bidders rather than computer agents (Adam et al., 2015; Teubner et al., 2015). Similar results have been found with negotiations and bargaining games where the relationship between competitive arousal and offer rejection was greater with human counterparts than with computer agents (Adam et al., 2018; Rilling et al., 2008; Sanfey et al., 2003; van't Wout et al., 2006). Additionally, researchers found that the winner's curse was driven by bidding against other humans but not computers (van den Bos et al., 2008). Also as discussed, competitive arousal's effects depend on the structure of the competitive interaction. For instance, competitive arousal has been linked to higher prices in ascending clock auctions (Adam et al., 2015), but to lower prices in descending clock (Dutch) auctions (Adam et al., 2013).

Task Complexity

Other research has followed in the tradition of Zajonc's (1965) social facilitation to show that competitive arousal can both improve and harm performance, depending on the task. For instance, dressage performance was impaired by competitive arousal whereas showjumping was helped by competitive arousal (Wolframm & Micklewright, 2010). The authors reasoned that dressage is more complicated and intellectually taxing than showjumping, which resulted in competitive arousal impairing performance in the former but improving performance in the latter (Wolframm & Micklewright, 2010).

Emotion Regulation

A final cluster of research considers how individuals can learn not to be adversely affected by competitive arousal. For instance, Adam et al. (2016) found that emotional regulation strategies can impact competitive arousal's effects on bidding. In particular, when participants attempted to suppress their emotions in response to seeing affective images, their bidding was more affected. Finally, when individuals have direct experience in a similar competitive situation or learn about a competitive situation's effects on others' decisions, their subsequent performance improved (Hafenbrädl & Woike, 2018). In general, regulating one's reactions to competitive arousal may be difficult because individuals do not accurately forecast its effects ahead of time (Adam et al., 2019; Hafenbrädl & Woike, 2018).

Knowledge Gaps and Directions for Future Research

Our review has immediately highlighted four main areas of potential research. First, much of the research on competitive arousal has been conducted in auctions and focused on the outcomes of bidding and overbidding. Although this is theoretically important and practically valuable given the ubiquity of auctions, future research should consider how competitive arousal has implications in other *domains of competitive interactions*. For instance, although researchers have examined how competitive arousal can impact negotiations and bargaining, the quantity of research in this domain is surprisingly limited and fails to consider sufficient types of negotiations (e.g., distributive, integrative, disputes) and sufficient types of negotiation outcomes (e.g., size of pie claimed, total size of the pie, negotiator satisfaction, impasse rates, etc.). Just as auctions are ubiquitous, so too are negotiations. However, beyond auctions and negotiations, competitions abound, whether in sports or organizations, and future research should consider how competitive arousal plays out in these contexts. As a more speculative example, competitive arousal may even be at play when romantic partners compete for the attention of an individual.

Second, much research has examined the antecedents of competitive arousal. As such, it would be extremely interesting to understand competitive arousal's *full range of effects* on human decision making and behavior. For example, even within the auction context, the primary effects studies are bidding and overbidding, but other interesting behavioral outcomes are relevant (e.g., collusion). Similarly, thinking about competitive arousal's effects outside the auction arena would be valuable and we have already noted that it would be interesting to consider competitive arousal's effects on unethical behavior. Additionally, it would be important to understand more instances in which competitive arousal may improve performance. One potential area where competitive arousal may help performance is increasing motivation to learn and improve (although interestingly, competitive arousal may impede actual learning and improvement (Zajonc, 1965)). More generally and consistent with our model's move away from focusing on just the detrimental effects of competitive arousal, it would be interesting for research to examine how competitive arousal can be harnessed.

Third, as noted earlier, researchers have discussed different mechanisms such as competitive arousal, perceptions of rivalry, and competitive intensity (see footnote 1). As researchers pursue further work on competitive arousal, the *interrelationships* among these different but related constructs need to be disentangled to provide theoretical clarity and parsimony. For instance, we discussed how escalation of commitment (Staw, 1976) is primarily driven by justification needs—when someone receives negative feedback about an investment decision, they often invest further to justify and rationalize their sunk costs. However, we reviewed findings (Hafenbrädl & Woike, 2018; Ku et al., 2005) that sunk costs might be arousing, suggesting a need to better understand escalation of commitment's mechanisms and when each of these mechanisms is at play in competitive contexts. Additionally, research may want to consider how competitive arousal is related to yet other constructs. For example, choking or "performing more poorly than expected given one's skill" (Beilock & Carr, 2001) may be related to or driven in part by competitive arousal.

Fourth, more research needs to think about the *moderators of competitive arousal*. Conceptually, we can think of moderators that will increase the amount of competitive arousal that is created. For instance, how do rivalry and time pressure combine to create competitive arousal? Are there factors that combine in an interactive (rather than additive) fashion to increase arousal? Anecdotally, the combination of social competition and scarcity may be particularly potent as evidenced by Black Friday sales. Alternatively, and consistent with the notion of harnessing competitive arousal, we can think of moderators that will moderate competitive arousal's effects. For instance, what are the psychological and structural variables that will cause competitive arousal to impede vs. improve performance? Some research has found that competitive arousal's detrimental effects are mitigated or reduced when interacting with computer agents (Adam et al., 2015; Adam et al., 2018; Rilling et al., 2008; Sanfey et al., 2003; Teubner et al., 2015; van't Wout et al., 2006; van den Bos et al., 2008), but are there other structural elements? Research on how individuals can learn not to be adversely affected by competitive arousal may be particularly relevant and interesting in this regard.

Perhaps most theoretically striking in our review is that the current research on competitive arousal borrows heavily on prior research on arousal. Thus, competitive arousal theorizing has relied heavily on findings that arousal can increase risk taking, reduce careful deliberation, and increase one's dominant response. Interestingly, one classic arousal finding that has not been examined is the *Yerkes Dodson law* (Yerkes & Dodson, 1908), where physiological arousal improves performance, but only up to a point, after which arousal becomes "too high" and impedes performance. Because research has seldom varied the amount of competitive arousal experienced, this remains an area to apply previously known arousal findings to the competitive context.

Although building on prior arousal research to theorize its role in competitive contexts is logical and valuable, a large unanswered question is whether there is *something unique about competitive arousal* that adds to our understanding of arousal more generally. Put differently, what is so special about arousal in a competitive context? For instance, if competitive arousal changes perceptions in a way that arousal does not, one could hypothesize that competitive arousal would lead individuals to view ambiguously competitive situations in a more competitive light, that is, competitive arousal could beget a competitive mindset that has further knock-on effects on cognition, perception, and motivation. Another means of understanding the unique contributions of competitive arousal may involve realizing that arousal primarily affects and interacts with cognition and secondarily with motivation. In contrast, because an interpersonal context is part and parcel of competitive arousal, competitive arousal may have effects on motivation (e.g., winning, not losing, learning) that may not be as apparent with arousal. In our view, research that can better identify the unique contributions of competitive arousal (over more general arousal) would be extremely theoretically interesting.

Stepping yet further back, we are left with a question of *why competitive arousal exists*. Consistent with views that arousal has an evolutionary and functional basis (Bechara & Damasio, 2005; Bechara et al., 1997), it may be the case that competitive arousal better allows individuals to compete for scarce resources and, hence, promote survival. Competitive arousal can clarify interest in items, focus attention, and generate action to acquire the resources. Conceptually, these benefits would accrue when competitive arousal is not too high (Yerkes & Dodson, 1908) and when tasks are well-learned or easy. The benefits of competitive arousal are probably best seen in professional athletes who harness competitive arousal in their sports. Where competitive arousal would fail is when interdependencies actually involve cooperation (Yip et al., 2018), when levels of competitive arousal become overwhelming, and when tasks are new or difficult.

General Discussion

Clarifying and Redefining Competitive Arousal

Based on our review, we first return to the definition of competitive arousal because a precise definition will aid in future research. We previously defined *competitive arousal as the integrally and/or incidentally induced arousal humans experience before, during, or after engaging in competitive interactions*. In comparison to other definitions, our definition provides clarity on what competitive arousal is and what it is not, as well as where it is applicable.

First, although competitive arousal was first conceived in auction bidding to explain auction fever (Ku et al., 2005), we clarify that competitive arousal is actually applicable to a host of competitive contexts, be it auctions, negotiations, sports, or competitions for jobs and promotions. As mentioned, what is common in these competitive contexts is that they involve interactions with other individuals who have diverging interests. Decoupling the concept of competitive arousal from the setting of auction bidding enables researchers to better understand underlying psychological mechanisms, to integrate findings from a wider body of literature (e.g., sports psychology, management), and then to apply these to a large set of contexts.

Second, our review and revised definition highlight that competitive arousal is focused on understanding the effects of the arousal dimension of affect (and not the quality of specific emotions) on decision making and performance in competitive contexts. Highlighting the focus on arousal is important since existing research that has used competitive arousal as a theoretical tool has often focused on specific emotions, resulting in lack of clarity about antecedents, effects, and moderators of competitive arousal. For instance, in Ku et al.'s (2005) seminal paper, the authors measured competitive arousal with self-reported anxiety and excitement. Although findings were consistent with the authors' hypothesis on the role of rivalry and sunk costs, anxiety is a negatively valenced emotion and excitement is a positively valenced emotion, creating imprecision and ambiguity around their findings. Thus, although the study of valence and specific emotions is important to understand human behavior in competitive contexts, competitive arousal research should primarily focus on the arousal dimension of affect.

Third, and associated with the theoretical focus on arousal, our refined definition of competitive arousal signifies a need for empirical operationalizations to hone in on measuring (or manipulating) arousal. Unfortunately, this is not an easy task. First and foremost, the experience of emotion is fundamentally complex, involving both arousal and valence, making it difficult to isolate the effects of arousal. Additionally, although physiological measures such as heart rate and skin conductance target physiological arousal, such measures are not easy to execute, even in controlled laboratory experiments, let alone in the field. And even though these physiological measures may precisely capture participant's arousal, they provide only limited insight into valence (Astor, Adam, Jerčić, et al., 2013), making it difficult to understand the full picture of a participant's emotions without complementarily assessing the valence dimension with other methods (e.g., self-report).

Fourth, as highlighted by some of the reviewed papers, competitive arousal can arise before, during, and after a competition. For instance, pre-competition arousal can have effects on performance (Wolframm & Micklewright, 2010) and post-auction winning and losing can generate physiological arousal (Adam et al., 2015; Astor, Adam, Jerčić, et al., 2013; Teubner et al., 2015). Importantly, the emotional (excitement and frustration) consequences of winning and losing in earlier rounds of bidding can then affect *subsequent* rounds of bidding (Ding et al., 2005). Thus, by highlighting that competitive arousal can occur before, during, and after the competitive interaction, our framework opens up a new domain for the temporal study of competitive arousal over time. For instance, there is little research into how the anticipation of an upcoming competitive interaction (e.g., a housing auction) may affect other decision making contexts (e.g., risky driving). Similarly, further examination of individuals' inabilities to accurately forecast the effects of competitive arousal (Adam et al., 2019) becomes important, as does an understanding of how competitive arousal can cascade from one competitive interaction to another (e.g., negotiating a contract before attending an auction).

Finally, and perhaps most different from earlier definitions of competitive arousal, our definition includes incidentally induced competitive arousal in which arousal is not directly related to the competitive context. By appreciating that incidentally and integrally induced emotions have similar and consistent effects (e.g., Pham, 2007; Rick & Loewenstein, 2008; Vohs et al., 2007), our revised definition highlights that there are many sources of arousal that can potentially impact competitive interactions, even though they may initially seem to have "nothing" to do with the competitive context. Thus, the coffee one drinks, the music one listens to, and the posters one sees on route to a competition may start off as arousal but when introduced into a competitive context, can become competitive arousal (Adam et al., 2019). Overall, we hope our revised definition brings clarity to researchers while also generating new research ideas.

Competitive Arousal Framework

Building on this revised definition, we also attempted to provide a more comprehensive and integrative framework of competitive arousal that synthesizes the existing findings of the extant literature. As previously discussed, according to Ku et al. (2005), "the competitive arousal model posits that numerous factors can increase arousal and that arousal can impair calm, careful decision-making" (p. 92). Absent in this model is a proper understanding of the antecedents, consequences, and moderators of competitive arousal, which we present in our framework (see Figure 8.1). First, as discussed in our revised definition of competitive arousal, a more comprehensive and thorough understanding of the sources of competitive arousal is necessary. In this vein, our integrative framework may serve as a shared frame of reference to identify the integral and/or incidental factors of competitive arousal as well as its impact on human decision making and behavior.

Second, Ku et al.'s original model focused on the detrimental effects of competitive arousal. Unfortunately, this does not capture the full array of effects that competitive arousal can have. In fact, competitive arousal can actually *improve* performance in a variety of domains (Engelmann et al., 2016; Haran & Ritov, 2014; Li et al., 2013; Pazzaglia et al., 2012; Yip et al., 2018; Yu et al., 2014). This is consistent with prior research on the effects of arousal where arousal is a necessary component of decision making, focusing individuals' attention to important cues in the environment and without which, individuals actually make disadvantageous decisions (Bechara & Damasio, 2005; Bechara et al., 1997). Similarly, research on arousal has shown that it can improve performance in well-learned or easy tasks or where individuals have expertise (Brown & Curhan, 2013; Zajonc, 1965). At a more subtle level, focusing on competitive arousal's detrimental effects on thorough decision making makes competitive arousal a "bad thing." However, this is overly simplistic. For instance, although competitive arousal can increase bidding and overbidding, whether this is good or bad partly depends on the perspective taken. If, for instance, an auctioneer deliberately increased competitive arousal through energizing music, scarcity, rivalry, etc., and bidders were more likely to bid and overbid, the associated increase in revenues can be seen as advantageous (from the auctioneer's perspective). However, this same bidding and overbidding is arguably detrimental from the bidder's perspective, particularly when bidding reaches a point where prices exceed the value of the item. Additionally, competitive arousal has effects that are neither good nor bad. For instance, competitive arousal can be attributed as interest in an auction item (Adam et al., 2019). Thus, as captured in our framework, an accurate understanding of competitive arousal needs to move away from focusing on the detrimental effects of competitive arousal on decision making to include and appreciate its full range of effects.

Finally, Ku et al.'s competitive arousal model does not focus on understanding moderators of competitive arousal's effects. Interestingly, in our review of the existing literature, this has unfortunately continued to be the case. Indeed, as we discussed in the future research avenues section, examining moderators is clearly needed.

Practical Implications

We believe that our review highlights some advice for practitioners. First and foremost, sources of competitive arousal abound, particularly when we consider that incidentally induced competitive arousal can also affect decision making and performance. As such, practitioners should understand how not to let this competitive arousal negatively impact their decision making and performance. Such interventions may include anything from understanding the effects of competitive arousal (Zajonc, 1965) to attributing competitive arousal to other sources (Savitsky et al., 1998; White et al., 1981; Zanna & Cooper, 1974) to using biofeedback as a warning system of when one is too competitively aroused (Astor, Adam, Jerčić, et al., 2013; Lux et al., 2018). Practitioners may also be interested in understanding how competitive arousal can be beneficial to them. For instance, auctioneers may want to stoke competitive arousal in their bidders so that bidding and overbidding increase. For these auctioneers, it becomes particularly useful that the effects of competitive arousal are not forecasted ahead of time (Adam et al., 2019).

Competitive arousal's practical benefits to sellers and costs to buyers is highlighted in bidding wars for organizations and properties. For instance, in the Australian housing market, realtors discuss the benefits of selling properties through auction, noting that auction fever is more likely to drive up the price of a property "well above its market value" (Ray White, 2018). At the same time, realtors advise potential home owners to be aware of auction fever and not to "lose [one's] head" (LJHooker, 2015).

Conclusion

Competitive interactions are often accompanied by an adrenaline rush or physiological arousal, which can then impact decisions and performance. We have attempted to review the current state of literature on competitive arousal to better understand its antecedents, effects, and moderators. In so doing, we are able to offer a revised definition of competitive arousal along with an integrative framework and identification of knowledge gaps that warrant further research. We hope that this review assists researchers and practitioners in conceptualizing the phenomenon.

Notes

1. It is important to note that research in this area has discussed a range of different mechanisms, including competitive arousal, perceptions of rivalry, and competitive intensity. At this stage, a unified picture describing the interrelationships and boundary conditions of these factors has not been formulated.
2. In first-price auctions, the winner pays what they bid whereas in second-price auctions, the winner pays the second-highest bid. In sealed-bid auctions, individuals make a secret bid whereas open bid auctions involve public bidding. Common value auctions involve items where there is consensus on the value of the item, although this may not be known until the auction is complete. In independent private value auctions, each bidder's valuation is independent of and unaffected by others' valuations. Finally, in single-pay auctions, only the auction winner pays whereas all bidders in all-pay auctions must pay, regardless of whether they win the auction (for a review, see McAfee & McMillan, 1987).
3. Häubl and Popkowski Leszcyc (2019) examined the effects of speed of competitor reactions, finding that speed of competitor reactions increased competitive intensity which then increased a desire to win and willingness to pay in auctions. Although the authors specifically ruled out competitive arousal as a mediating mechanism, their measure of competitive arousal (based on Ku et al., 2005) was a self-report measure of anxiety and excitement, which failed to isolate the arousal component of affect. Thus, we include this very interesting citation in our review while acknowledging that additional research is necessary to properly determine if Häubl and Popkowski Leszcyc's constructs and mechanisms are related to or distinct from competitive arousal.

References

Adam, M. T. P., Astor, P. J., & Krämer, J. (2016). Affective images, emotion regulation and bidding behavior: An experiment on the influence of competition and community emotions in internet auctions. *Journal of Interactive Marketing 35* (1), 56–69.

Adam, M. T. P., Krämer, J., & Müller, M. B. (2015). Auction fever! How time pressure and social competition affect bidders' arousal and bids in retail auctions. *Journal of Retailing 91* (3), 468–485.

Adam, M. T. P., Krämer, J., & Weinhardt, C. (2013). Excitement up! Price down! Measuring emotions in Dutch auctions. *International Journal of Electronic Commerce 17* (2), 7–39.

Adam, M. T. P., Ku, G., & Lux, E. (2019). Auction fever: The unrecognized effects of incidental arousal. *Journal of Experimental Social Psychology 80* (1), 52–58.

Adam, M. T. P., Teubner, T., & Gimpel, H. (2018). No rage against the machine: How computer agents mitigate human emotional responses in electronic negotiations. *Group Decision and Negotiation 27* (4), 543–571.

Astor, P. J., Adam, M. T. P., Jähnig, C., & Seifert, S. (2013). The joy of winning and the frustration of losing: A psychophysiological analysis of emotions in first-price sealed-bid auctions. *Journal of Neuroscience, Psychology, and Economics 6* (1), 14–30.

Astor, P. J., Adam, M. T. P., Jerčić, P., Schaaff, K., & Weinhardt, C. (2013). Integrating biosignals into Information Systems: A NeuroIS tool for improving emotion regulation. *Journal of Management Information Systems 30* (3), 247–278.

Barry, R. J., Rushby, J. A., Wallace, M. J., Clarke, A. R., Johnstone, S. J., & Zlojutro, I. (2005). Caffeine effects on resting-state arousal. *Clinical Neurophysiology 116* (11), 2693–2700.

Bechara, A., & Damasio, A. R. (2005). The somatic marker hypothesis: A neural theory of economic decision. *Games and Economic Behavior 52* (2), 336–372.

Bechara, A., Damasio, H., Tranel, D., & Damasio, A. R. (1997). Deciding advantageously before knowing the advantageous strategy. *Science 275* (5304), 1293–1295.

Beilock, S. L., & Carr, T. H. (2001). On the fragility of skilled performance: What governs choking under pressure? *Journal of Experimental Psychology: General 130* (4), 701–725.

Bradley, M. M., Miccoli, L., Escrig, M. A., & Lang, P. J. (2008). The pupil as a measure of emotional arousal and autonomic activation. *Psychophysiology 45* (4), 602–607.

Brown, A. D., & Curhan, J. R. (2013). The polarizing effect of arousal on negotiation. *Psychological Science 24*, 1928–1935.

Cacioppo, J. T., Tassinary, L. G., & Berntson, G. G. (Eds.). (2007). *Handbook of Psychophysiology* (3rd ed.). Cambridge University Press.

Cates, D. S., Shontz, F. C., Fowler, S., Vavak, C. R., Dell'Oliver, C., & Yoshinobu, L. (1996). The effects of time pressure on social cognitive problem-solving by aggressive and nonaggressive boys. *Child Study Journal 26* (3), 163–191.

Delgado, M. R., Schotter, A., Ozbay, E. Y., & Phelps, E. A. (2008). Understanding overbidding: Using the neural circuitry of reward to design economic auctions. *Science 321* (5897), 1849–1852.

Ding, M., Eliashberg, J., Huber, J., & Saini, R. (2005). Emotional bidders: An analytical and experimental examination of consumers' behavior in a priceline-like reverse auction. *Management Science 51* (3), 352–364.

Dutton, D. G., & Aron, A. P. (1974). Some evidence for heightened sexual attraction under conditions of high anxiety. *Journal of Personality and Social Psychology 30* (4), 510–517.

Easterbrook, J. A. (1959). The effect of emotion on cue utilization and the organization of behavior. *Psychological Review 66* (3), 183–201.

Ehrhart, K.-M., Ott, M., & Abele, S. (2015). Auction fever: Rising revenue in second-price auction formats. *Games and Economic Behavior 92*, 206–227.

El Haji, A., Krawczyk, M., Sylwestrzak, M., & Zawojska, E. (2019). Time pressure and risk taking in auctions: A field experiment. *Journal of Behavioral and Experimental Economics 78*, 68–79.

Engelmann, J. M., Herrmann, E., & Tomasello, M. (2016). The effects of being watched on resource acquisition in chimpanzees and human children. *Animal Cognition 19* (1), 147–151.

Forgas, J. P. (1989). Mood effects on decision making strategies. *Australian Journal of Psychology 41* (2), 197–214.

Garcia, S. M., & Tor, A. (2009). The N-Effect: More competitors, less competition. *Psychological Science 20* (7), 871–877.

Guerin, B. (1986). Mere presence effects in humans: A review. *Journal of Experimental Social Psychology 22*, 38–77.

Hafenbrädl, S., & Woike, J. K. (2018). Competitive escalation and interventions. *Journal of Behavioral Decision Making 31* (5), 695–714.

Haran, U., & Ritov, I. (2014). Know who you're up against: Counterpart identifiability enhances competitive behavior. *Journal of Experimental Social Psychology 54*, 115–121.

Häubl, G., & Popkowski Leszczyc, P. L. L. (2019). Bidding frenzy: Speed of competitor reaction and willingness to pay in auctions. *Journal of Consumer Research 45* (6), 1294–1314.

Holbrook, M. B., & Batra, R. (1987). Assessing the role of emotions as mediators of consumer responses to advertising. *Journal of Consumer Research 14* (3), 404–420.

Keltner, D., Ellsworth, P. C., & Edwards, K. (1993). Beyond simple pessimism: Effect of sadness and anger on social perception. *Journal of Personality and Social Psychology 64* (5), 740–752.

Ku, G. (2008). Learning to de-escalate: The effects of regret in escalation of commitment. *Organizational Behavior and Human Decision Processes 105*, 221–232.

Ku, G., Malhotra, D., & Murnighan, J. K. (2005). Towards a competitive arousal model of decision-making: A study of auction fever in live and internet auctions. *Organizational Behavior and Human Decision Processes 96* (2), 89–103.

Lerner, J. S., & Keltner, D. (2000). Beyond valence: Toward a model of emotion-specific influences on judgment and choice. *Cognition and Emotion 14* (4), 473–493.

Lewinsohn, S., & Mano, H. (1993). Multi-attribute choice and affect: The influence of naturally occurring and manipulated moods on choice processes. *Journal of Behavioral Decision Making 6* (1), 33–51.

Li, Y., Xiao, X., Ma, W., Jiang, J., Qiu, J., & Zhang, Q. (2013). Electrophysiological evidence for emotional valence and competitive arousal effects on insight problem solving. *Brain Research 1538* (61–72).

LJHooker. (2015). Buying at auction guide. https://www.ljhooker.com.au/ebooks/buying-at-auction-guide.

Loewenstein, G. F. (1996). Out of control: Visceral influences on behavior. *Organizational Behavior and Human Decision Processes 65* (3), 272–292.

Lux, E., Adam, M. T. P., Dorner, V., Helming, S., Knierim, M. T., & Weinhardt, C. (2018). Live biofeedback as a user interface design element: A review of the literature. *Communications of the Association for Information Systems 43* (1), 257–296.

Malhotra, D. (2010). The desire to win: The effects of competitive arousal on motivation and behavior. *Organizational Behavior and Human Decision Processes 111* (2), 139–146.

Mano, H. (1991). The structure and intensity of emotional experiences: Method and context convergence. *Multivariate Behavioral Research 38*, 689–703.

Mano, H. (1992). Judgments under distress: Assessing the role of unpleasantness and arousal in judgment formation. *Organizational Behavior and Human Decision Processes 52*, 216–245.

Mano, H. (1994). Risk-taking, framing effects, and affect. *Organizational Behavior and Human Decision Processes 57* (1), 38–58.

Maule, A. J., Hockey, G. R., & Bdzola, L. (2000). Effects of time-pressure on decision-making under uncertainty: Changes in affective states and information processing strategy. *Acta Psychologica 104* (3), 283–301.

McAfee, R. P., & McMillan, J. (1987). Auctions and bidding. *Journal of Economic Literature 25* (2), 699–738.

Murnighan, J. K. (2002). A very extreme case of the dollar auction. *Journal of Management Education 26*, 56–69.

Murray, N. P., & Raedeke, T. D. (2008). Heart rate variability as an indicator of pre-competitive arousal. *International Journal of Sport Psychology 39* (4), 346–355.

Nichols, B. S. (2012). The development, validation, and implications of a measure of consumer competitive arousal (CCAr). *Journal of Economic Psychology 33* (1), 195–205.

Pazzaglia, F., Flynn, S., & Sonpar, K. (2012). Performance implications of knowledge and competitive arousal in times of employee mobility: The immutable law of the ex. *Human Resource Management 51* (5), 687–707.

Peters, E., Västfjäll, D., Gärling, T., & Slovic, P. (2006). Affect and decision making: A "hot" topic. *Journal of Behavioral Decision Making 19* (2), 79–85.

Pham, M. T. (2007). Emotion and rationality: A critical review and interpretation of empirical evidence. *Review of General Psychology 11* (2), 155–178.

Raghabendra, P. K., Kunter, M., & Mak, V. (2018). The influence of a competition on noncompetitors. *Proceedings of the National Academy of Sciences 115* (11), 2716–2721.

Rauch, S. L., Shin, L. M., Dougherty, D. D., Alpert, N. M., Orr, S. P., Lasko, M., . . . Pitman, R. K. (1999). Neural activation during sexual and competitive arousal in healthy men. *Psychiatry Research: Neuroimaging 91* (1), 1–10.

Ray White. (2018). FAQ: What are the benefits of selling through auction?. Retrieved January 16, 2020, from https://www.raywhite.com/blog/advice-and-tips/faq-what-are-the-benefits-of-selling-through-auction/.

Rick, S., & Loewenstein, G. F. (2008). The role of emotion in economic behavior. In M. L. Lewis, J. M. Haviland-Jones, & L. F. Barrett (Eds.), *Handbook of Emotions* (3rd ed.) (pp. 138–156). The Guildford Press.

Rilling, J. K., King-Casas, B., & Sanfey, A. G. (2008). The neurobiology of social decision-making. *Current Opinions in Neurobiology 18* (159–165).

Russell, J. A. (1980). A circumplex model of affect. *Journal of Personality and Social Psychology 39* (6), 1161–1178.

Sanfey, A. G., Rilling, J. K., Aronson, J. A., Nystrom, L. E., & Cohen, J. D. (2003). The neural basis of economic decision-making in the ultimatum game. *Science 300* (5626), 1755–1758.

Savitsky, K., Medvec, V. H., Charlton, A. E., & Gilovich, T. (1998). "What, me worry?": Arousal, misattribution, and the effect of temporal distance on confidence. *Personality and Social Psychology Bulletin 24* (5), 529–536.

Schachter, S., & Singer, J. E. (1962). Cognitive, social, and physiological determinants of emotional state. *Psychological Review 69*, 379–399.

Schwarz, N. (2000). Emotion, cognition, and decision making. *Cognition and Emotion 14* (4), 433–440.

Sokol-Hessner, P., Hsu, M., Curley, N. G., Delgado, M. R., Camerer, C. F., & Phelps, E. A. (2008). Thinking like a trader selectively reduces individuals' loss aversion. *Proceedings of the National Academy of Sciences of the United States of America 106* (13), 5035–5040.

Staph, J. (2005). Interview with Karch Kiraly. *Stack.com.* https://www.stack.com/a/interview-with-karch-kiraly.

Staw, B. M. (1976). Knee-deep in the big muddy: A study of escalating commitment to a chosen course of action. *Organizational Behavior and Human Performance 16*, 27–44.

Staw, B. M., & Ross, J. (1989). Understanding behavior in escalation situations. *Science 246*, 216–220.

Staw, B. M., Sandelands, L. E., & Dutton, J. E. (1981). Threat-rigidity effects in organizational behavior: A multilevel analysis. *Administrative Science Quarterly 26*, 501–524.

Teubner, T., Adam, M. T. P., & Riordan, R. (2015). The impact of computerized agents on immediate emotions, overall arousal and bidding behavior in electronic auctions. *Journal of the Association for Information Systems 16* (10), 838–879.

To, C., Kilduff, G. J., Ordoñez, L., & Schweitzer, M. E. (2018). Going for it on fourth down: Rivalry increases risk taking, physiological arousal, and promotion focus. *Academy of Management Journal 61* (4), 1281–1306.

van't Wout, M., Kahn, R. S., Sanfey, A. G., & Aleman, A. (2006). Affective state and decision-making in the ultimatum game. *Experimental Brain Research 169* (4), 564–568.

van den Bos, W., Golka, P. J. M., Effelsberg, D., & McClure, S. M. (2013). Pyrrhic victories: The need for social status drives costly competitive behavior. *Frontiers in Neuroscience 7*, 1–11.

van den Bos, W., Li, J., Lau, T., Maskin, E., Cohen, J. D., Montague, P. R., & McClure, S. M. (2008). The value of victory: social origins of the winner's curse in common value auctions. *Judgment and Decision Making 3* (7), 483–492.

van den Bos, W., Talwar, A., & McClure, S. M. (2013). Neural correlates of reinforcement learning and social preferences in competitive bidding. *Journal of Neuroscience 33* (5), 2137–2146.

Vohs, K. D. V., Baumeister, R. F., & Loewenstein, G. (Eds.). (2007). *Do Emotions Help or Hurt Decisionmaking?: A Hedgefoxian Perspective*. Russell Sage Foundation.

White, G. L., Fishbein, S., & Rutstein, J. (1981). Passionate love and the misattribution of arousal. *Journal of Personality and Social Psychology 41* (1), 56–62.

Will-Weber, M. (2002). Nothing but the best. *Runner's World*. https://www.runnersworld.com/uk/health/a760 147/nothing-but-the-best.

Wolframm, I. A., & Micklewright, D. (2010). Pre-competitive arousal, perception of equine temperament and riding performance: Do they interact? *Comparative Exercise Physiology 7* (1), 27–36.

Yerkes, R. M., & Dodson, J. D. (1908). The relation of strength of stimulus to rapidity of habit-formation. *Journal of Comparative Neurology and Psychology 18* (5), 459–482.

Yip, J. A., Schweitzer, M. E., & Nurmohamed, S. (2018). Trash-talking: Competitive incivility motivates rivalry, performance, and unethical behavior. *Organizational Behavior and Human Decision Processes 144* (1), 125–144.

Yu, M. Y., Lang, K. R., & Pelaez, A. (2014). Evaluating electronic market designs: The effects of competitive arousal and social facilitation on electronic group buying. Paper presented at the Proceedings of the Hawaii International Conference on System Sciences.

Zajonc, R. B. (1965). Social facilitation. *Science 149*, 269–274.

Zajonc, R. B. (1968). Social facilitation. In D. Cartwright & A. Zander (Eds.), *Group dynamics: Research and theory* (3rd ed.) (pp. 63–73). Harper & Row Publishers.

Zajonc, R. B., & Sales, S. M. (1966). Social facilitation of dominant and subordinate responses. *Journal of Experimental Social Psychology 2*, 160–168.

Zanna, M. P., & Cooper, J. (1974). Dissonance and the pill: An attribution approach to studying the arousal properties of dissonance. *Journal of Personality and Social Psychology 29* (5), 703–709.

Motivational Dynamics Underlying Competition: The Opposing Processes Model of Competition and Performance

Kou Murayama, Andrew J. Elliot, *and* Mickaël Jury

Abstract

The chapter delineates motivational mechanisms underlying how competition affects performance. The authors propose an opposing processes model of competition and performance in which competition positively influences performance via the adoption of performance-approach goals (i.e., trying to do better than others), whereas competition impairs performance via the adoption of performance-avoidance goals (i.e., trying to avoid doing worse than others). In competitions, these positive and negative goal processes often cancel each other out, producing a seemingly weak or non-existent relationship between competition and performance. The authors review empirical evidence for the proposed model, discuss the implications of the model in relation to other theoretical perspectives on competition, and speculate on the possibility that competition can play an instrumental role in sustainable engagement in a task.

Key Words: competition, achievement motivation, achievement goals, approach-avoidance, performance

For better or worse, competition strongly drives people's motivation. When we are put in competition, our mental state changes considerably—competition makes our goals specific and explicit (Locke & Latham, 1990), makes incentive structure salient (Garcia et al., 2013), activates explicit social comparison processes (Mussweiler & Epstude, 2009), and evokes self-evaluative concerns (Butler, 1987; Jury et al., 2015); all of these come together to strongly influence our behavior. Given this powerful motivating function, it is not surprising that people are inclined to implement competition as a way to motivate people to obtain better outcomes (Murayama et al., 2016). In fact, the idea that competition is important and valuable to facilitate productive performance seems the default assumption in many contemporary cultures. In a number of theories in psychology competition has been posited to facilitate people's productivity and performance (Abra, 1993; Locke, 1968; McClelland et al., 1976; Swab & Johnson, 2019; Worrell et al., 2016), and there is empirical evidence supporting this idea (e.g., Okebukola, 1984; Scott & Cherrington,

1974; Shalley & Oldham, 1997; van de Pol et al., 2012). Indeed, one of the first experimental studies in social psychology, in which Norman Triplett (1897) examined children's performance on a fishing reel task, showed that children (at least numerically) performed better when in competition with another child.

However, we can also imagine that competition fails to produce optimal outcomes because competition often causes considerable stress and elicits fearful concerns about failure. There are several extant theories that posit competition is harmful and detrimental to task outcomes (Bonta, 1997; Deutsch, 1949; Kohn, 1986; Ulrich, 2008), and empirical evidence also supports the idea showing that competition can impair task performance (e.g., Butler, 1989; Johnson et al. 1979) or at most have little positive effect (e.g., Hinsz, 2005; Johnson et al., 1985).

Here we face a big question. On one hand, competition is unequivocally motivating. On the other hand, competition sometimes facilitates, sometimes impairs, and sometimes has little effect on performance. These propositions seem contradictory. How then can we accommodate these perspectives? We believe the answer lies in the fact that not all motivation facilitates performance and productivity. Decades of studies on human motivation have revealed that motivation is not a unitary concept, and there are a variety of motivational processes that influence learning, decision making, and performance in different ways (Elliot et al., 2017). Competition is clearly motivating for people and influences the way they perform, but this does not necessarily mean that competition always facilitates performance.

To understand the motivational dynamics underlying competition, we focus on two motivational processes particularly relevant in the context of competition—performance-approach goal and performance-avoidance goal pursuit as studied in the achievement goal literature. In the following, we first review the literature on these goals, and then describe an opposing processes model of competition and performance (Murayama & Elliot, 2012a) that provides a motivational account of the psychological processes underlying competition. We then discuss how this model can accommodate and integrate different theoretical perspectives on competition, followed by a discussion on future agenda items to advance the field.

Performance-Approach and Performance-Avoidance Achievement Goals

An achievement goal is conceptualized as a cognitive representation of a desired end state for people's competence-relevant engagement (Dweck & Leggett, 1988; Elliot, 1999; Nicholls, 1989). In achievement or competence-relevant situations, people adopt a variety of different idiographic goals but studies on achievement motivation have identified a few distinct types of goals that have different consequences for the self-regulation process. The first types of achievement goals identified in the literature were mastery goals (also called learning goals) and performance goals (also called ego goals; Ames, 1992; Dweck, 1986; Nicholls, 1984). A mastery goal may be defined as the goal to gain personal competence, as defined by absolute/intrapersonal standards, which often come with the motivation to achieve personal development and task mastery. On the other hand, a performance goal may be defined as the goal to gain personal competence as defined by normative or comparative standards—i.e., the goal to perform well in comparison to other people. Empirical investigation of achievement goals based on this dichotomous mastery-performance model dominated the literature from the 1980s through the mid-to-late 1990s.

It is easy to imagine that people are likely to adopt performance goals in a competitive situation, evaluating their own competence in terms of how good they are in comparison to other competitors. In fact, putting participants in a competition was a common way to experimentally manipulate performance goals in the early achievement goal literature (e.g., Ames, 1984). Interestingly, however, despite the seemingly close conceptual link between competition and achievement goals, these two literatures did not have the type of close communication or cross-fertilization with each other that one might expect. In fact, achievement goal researchers in this early period focused mainly on mastery goals, which were repeatedly shown to be associated with a host of positive outcomes such as self-efficacy and task enjoyment (Miller et al., 1996; Pintrich & DeGroot, 1990). Nevertheless, the empirical findings on performance goals at the time exhibited an interesting parallel with the empirical findings observed in the literature on competition. Specifically, much like empirical work on competition and downstream outcomes, achievement goal researchers found either positive, negative, or negligible relationships of performance goals with a variety of different outcomes (Elliot, 1999; Elliot & Church, 1997): Some studies showed that performance goals are associated with positive outcomes such as self-efficacy and task performance (e.g., Meece et al., 1988; Pintrich & Garcia, 1991), while others observed detrimental effects of performance goals on these variables (e.g., Graham & Golan, 1991; see also Ames, 1992 for a review). There are also many other studies showing that performance goals are not reliably associated with achievement-relevant outcomes (e.g., Miller et al., 1993; Nolen & Haladyna, 1990).

To address the seemingly contradictory findings, Elliot and colleagues proposed to bifurcate performance goals into two different types (e.g., Elliot & Church, 1997; Elliot & Harackiewicz, 1996): performance-approach goals and performance-avoidance goals. A performance-approach goal may be defined as the goal to achieve high competence in comparison to other people (i.e., "My goal is to do better than others"), whereas a performance-avoidance goal is the goal to avoid incompetence in comparison to other people (i.e., "My goal is to avoid doing worse than others"). This distinction was theoretically grounded in the long-standing distinction between approach and avoidance motivation, which has been proposed and investigated (often using different names) in different forms across a variety of different disciplines (Elliot & Covington, 2001). Examples include psychological need (need for achievement and fear of failure; Atkinson, 1957), goal gradients (approach vs. avoidance gradients; Miller, 1944), attachment styles (secure vs. insecure; Bowlby, 1969), temperaments (behavioral activation vs. behavioral inhibition; Gray, 1987), message framing (positive vs. negative framing; Tversky & Kahneman, 1981), and regulatory focus (promotion focus vs. prevention focus; Higgins, 1997).

Elliot and colleagues argued that the distinction between performance-approach and performance-avoidance goals was important to resolving the apparent inconsistency in empirical findings for performance goals (Elliot, 1999; Elliot & Thrash, 2001). They indicated that performance-approach goals are rooted in appetitive motivation to approach desirable outcomes, and direct us to focus on achieving a high standard of excellence, whereas performance-avoidance goals are rooted in aversive motivation to avoid feared outcomes, and direct our attention to the possibility of losing and its implications. As such, performance-approach goals were posited to be associated with more adaptive outcomes than performance-avoidance goals. Empirical research has supported these ideas. For example, many studies have shown that items assessing performance-approach goals (e.g., "My aim is to perform well relative to other students") are positive predictors of task performance (e.g., exam performance), whereas items assessing performance-avoidance goals (e.g., "My aim is to avoid doing worse than other students") negatively predict the same performance outcomes (Elliot & Church, 1997; Elliot & Murayama, 2008; Harackiewicz et al., 2002; for meta-analyses see Hulleman et al., 2010; Van Yperen et al., 2014). This is the case despite the fact that measures of these goals share considerable semantic similarity (i.e., only the contextual framing is different; see Tversky & Kahneman, 1981). In short, the bifurcation of performance-approach and performance-avoidance goals considerably clarified the relationship between achievement goals and achievement-relevant outcomes.

The Opposing Processes Model of Competition and Performance

The distinction between performance-approach goals and performance-avoidance goals provides theoretical insight into the motivational dynamics underlying competition. More specifically, the inconsistent findings on the relationship between competition and performance can be seen as a result of the divergent, opposing effects of performance-approach goals and performance-avoidance goals on downstream outcomes in competition contexts. Murayama and Elliot (2012a) devised a conceptual model of these competition and achievement goal processes that they labeled the opposing processes model of competition and performance (see Figure 9.1).

The starting point of the model is competition, be it trait competitiveness, perceived environmental competitiveness, or structural competition. People's perceived environmental competitiveness is the most proximal predictor of the two performance-based goals in the model. Note that perceived environmental competitiveness is not merely the reflection of the objective reward structure in the situation. When people are put in a competitive reward structure (which we often call "structural competition," i.e., outcomes are evaluated in comparison to another competitor or competitors, not an absolute

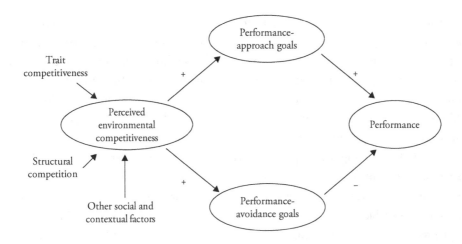

Figure 9.1 A schematic picture of the opposing processes model of competition and performance. Competition is only weakly related to performance, but this is due to the positive indirect effect of performance-approach goals and the negative indirect effect of performance-avoidance goals.

criterion), they are likely to perceive the situation as competitive. However, the extent to which people perceive the presence of competitiveness depends on other situational and social cues (e.g., how the competition is framed, the nature of the task, one's relationship with competitors, etc.) and people's personality traits. The most relevant personality trait in this context is trait competitiveness, which represents a dispositional and stable preference to compete with others in achievement situations (Spence & Helmreich, 1983). Research has suggested that those with high trait competitiveness tend to perceive others and environments as more competitive (Aksoy & Weesie, 2012; Fletcher & Nusbaum, 2010; Schrock et al., 2016). For example, Elliot, Jury, and Murayama (2018) showed that trait competitiveness is a positive predictor of perceived environmental competitiveness, both in academic and job contexts, a phenomenon they labelled "competitiveness projection."

Once people (subjectively) recognize that they are in a competitive environment, social comparison process becomes salient, and they come to evaluate their own competence based on a normative standard. This use of an evaluative standard of competence leads them to adopt performance goals, more specifically, performance-approach and performance-avoidance goals. Importantly, these two goals have opposite consequences as noted earlier—performance-approach goals tend to facilitate task performance, whereas performance-avoidance goals tend to impair performance. These facilitating and debilitating goal processes are often of comparable magnitude and, as a consequence, the effects of the two performance-based goals commonly cancel each other out, producing an overall weak or non-existent relationship between competition and performance. Conceptually, this means that competition puts people in a type of motivational conflict regarding approach and avoidance goals. On the upside, competition strengthens people's appetitive strivings for desirable outcomes through performance-approach goals, increasing the likelihood of obtaining optimal outcomes. On the downside, however, competition increases people's performance anxiety and concerns about failure through performance-avoidance goals, preventing people from achieving optimal performance. The idea of approach-avoidance conflict has a long history in the literature on achievement motivation (e.g., Atkinson, 1957; Lewin et al., 1944) and competition can be considered a natural setting that strongly elicits such motivational conflicts.

Statistically speaking, the opposing processes model posits a version of inconsistent mediation that explains the link between competition and performance. Inconsistent mediation occurs when there is a weak (often non-significant) relationship between the independent variable and the dependent variable, which can be explained by indirect and direct effects that have different signs (MacKinnon et al. 2000; Shrout & Bolger, 2002). In the proposed model (Figure 9.1), there is a positive indirect effect through performance-approach goals and a negative indirect effect through performance-avoidance goals, both of which combine to produce a relatively weak or negligible total effect between competition and performance. One important implication of this inconsistent mediation is that a weak overall relationship (i.e., weak total effect) signals the possibility of conflicting motivational processes rather than the absence of any interesting relationship. From a traditional perspective of research practice, researchers are likely to be discouraged when observing a non-significant effect or inconclusive findings, and we can easily imagine that this has been the case for many researchers who have examined the link between competition and performance in the past. The opposing processes model dramatically changes this traditional way of thinking. Indeed, a weak/negligible overall relationship is the key to deeply understanding the motivational dynamics underlying the relationship between competitive and performance.

Empirical Support

The opposing processes model of competition and performance is based on a few presuppositions. First, when performance-approach and performance-avoidance goals are not included in statistical modelling, competition and performance are at most only weakly related, due to the mutual cancelling effects of these two (hidden) motivational variables. Second, competition enhances *both* performance-approach and performance-avoidance goals. Third, performance-approach goals positively predict performance, whereas performance-avoidance goals negatively predict performance.

To test the first presupposition, Murayama and Elliot (2012a) conducted a meta-analysis that examined the relationship between competition and performance in the extant literature. The meta-analysis distinguished between three different types of studies: (1) studies that assessed trait competitiveness as an individual difference, (2) studies that assessed perceived environmental competitiveness, and (3) studies that manipulated competition (i.e., "structural competition") in an experimental setting. The results were sobering (at least for theorists in either the pro-competition or anti-competition camps), but consistent with the opposing processes model. Specifically, the correlation coefficient between trait competitiveness and performance (65 studies, total N = 14,721) was very small, r =.05, 95% CI [0.02, 0.08]; the correlation between perceived environmental competitiveness and performance (33 studies, total N = 11,439) was negligible, r = −.01, 95% CI [−0.06, 0.04]; the effects of structural competition on performance was also negligible, Hedge's g = 0.04, 95% CI [−0.08, 0.16]. In addition, we combined these three types of effect sizes and the integrated effect size was again negligible, r = .03, 95% CI [−0.00, 0.06]. Therefore, we can conclude that the overall relationship between competition and performance is weak-to-non-existent, leaving open the possibility that it is mediated by divergent, conflicting psychological processes.

Murayama and Elliot (2012a) also conducted a further meta-analysis to test the second and the third presuppositions. More specifically they collected previous studies that assessed at least two of the following key variables in the model: competition, performance-approach goals, performance-avoidance goals, and task performance. For the relationship between competition and performance, they had already conducted a meta-analysis to obtain the correlation. In the same fashion, they meta-analyzed the correlations of all pairs of variables and created a "meta-correlation matrix" of these four variables of interest. This meta-correlation matrix provided strong support for the opposing processes model. Specifically, competition was strongly correlated with performance-approach goals, r = .41, 95% CI [.36, .46] and performance-avoidance goals, r = .30, 95% CI [.25, .35], suggesting that competition is likely co-activate both of these goals (although it is important to acknowledge that the relationships are correlational). Performance-approach goals positively predicted task performance, r = .10, 95% CI [.08, .12], whereas performance-avoidance goals were a negative predictor, r = −.12, 95% CI [−.14, −.10]. To provide a more complete test of the full model, they also conducted meta-analytic structural equation modelling with the obtained meta-correlation matrix (Cheung & Chan, 2005). The results were consistent with those observed in the meta-correlation matrix—while competition was positively associated with performance-approach and performance-avoidance goals, standardized b = 0.41 and .29, p < .01, respectively, performance was positively predicted by performance-approach goals, standardized b = 0.15, p < .01 and negatively predicted by performance-avoidance goals, standardized b = −0.17, p < .01. Importantly, the model showed a good fit to the data, χ^2 (1) = 1.03, p = .31, suggesting that the weak/non-existent relationship between competition and performance is well explained by the inconsistent mediation effects of performance-approach and performance-avoidance goals.

To further test the proposed model, Murayama and Elliot (2012a) also conducted two new prospective survey studies in a university psychology class (focusing on trait competitiveness and perceived environmental competitiveness) and a new lab experiment. Each of these new studies also provided strong support for the opposing processes model. For example, in one survey study, students' trait competitiveness positively and significantly predicted the adoption of performance-approach and performance-avoidance goals for the class (assessed three weeks later), which in turn predicted exam performance at the end of the class (in opposite directions)—performance-approach goals positively predicted exam performance, whereas performance-avoidance goals negatively predicted it (for a replication of these indirect effects, see Elliot et al., 2018). Finally, in a lab experiment, participants worked in pairs on an anagram task. Half of the participants were instructed that they would do the task in competition with the other participant (competition group), whereas the other half of the participants were simply informed that they would do the task individually (control group). Participants in the competition group showed higher performance-approach goals and performance-avoidance goals in comparison to those in the control group, suggesting that competition made participants adopt performance-approach and performance-avoidance goals at the same time. Importantly, the competition manipulation did not have a statistically significant effect on performance, but performance-approach and performance-avoidance goals predicted task performance in opposite directions (i.e., performance-approach goals was a positive predictor, whereas performance-avoidance goals were a negative predictor), supporting the opposing processes model.

Subsequent research has put the opposing processes model to test in other ways. For example, Hangen et al. (2016) showed that the model can be extended from performance-based goals to challenge and threat physiology, and from performance outcomes to risk-taking outcomes. Sommet et al. (2019) demonstrated that the model can be applied to the issue of income inequality in real-world economic environments; specifically, local income inequality positively predicted perceptions of local competitiveness which, in turn, positively predicted economic performance-approach and performance-avoidance goals. Elliot, Weissman et al. (2021) documented that initial social comparison information about an opponent (whether one is competing against a strong or weak opponent), and associated performance expectancies, are important variables predicting performance-approach (but, contrary to predictions, not performance-avoidance) goal pursuit in competition contexts; specifically, downward comparison predicted positive performance expectancies which, in turn, positively predicted performance-approach goals. These studies illustrate the broad applicability and potential generativity of the opposing processes model.

Theories of Competition through the Lens of the Opposing Processes Model of Competition and Performance

We are not the first theorists to contend that competition has both positive and negative effects. Close scrutiny of past theorizing on competition and related phenomena reveals a number of nuanced perspectives on how competition could have positive or negative influences on task performance, identifying a number of critical factors that could make competition adaptive or maladaptive. Importantly, our proposed model on

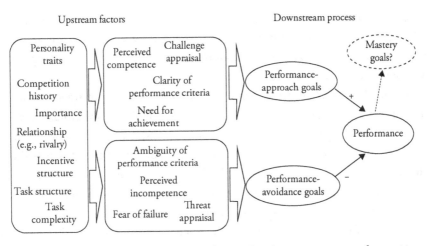

Upstream factors

Downstream process

Figure 9.2 Performance-approach and performance-avoidance goals as downstream processes of competition –> performance relations.

competition is not meant to compete with these theoretical perspectives—rather, most of the proposed factors can be seen as affecting the competition–performance relationship by selectively influencing the adoption of performance-approach goals or performance-avoidance goals. That is, the existing theories on competition and related phenomena mostly focus on upstream factors operative in competitive situations, that we think eventuate in the adoption of performance-approach and performance-avoidance goals downstream (see Figure 9.2). In this respect, the proposed model and the existing theories of competition may be seen as complementary, providing a more comprehensive picture of the competition–performance relationship as a whole. To illustrate, we will overview some existing theoretical perspectives on competition and related phenomena, and explain how they are related to the proposed opposing processes model.

Social Interdependence Theory

Social independence theory (Deutsch, 1949; Johnson & Johnson, 1989) addresses how the structure of relations among individuals influences outcomes. The interdependence structure includes cooperative (positive interdependence), competitive (negative interdependence), and individualistic (no interdependence) relations. The theory primarily emphasizes the positive effects of cooperative situations on a number of psychological and performance outcomes (for meta-analyses, see Johnson et al., 2014; Johnson et al., 1981; Roseth et al., 2008). Competitive situations, on the other hand, are basically viewed as maladaptive because they create negative interpersonal emotions which are presumed to hamper task performance and learning processes (Johnson & Johnson, 1989). At the same time, researchers in this area (Johnson & Johnson, 1975/1999, 1978; Stanne et al., 1999) have also noted the possibility that competition can be appropriate and productive ("constructive competition"). The conditions for constructive competition include: (1) when winning is relatively unimportant; (2) when all participants have a reasonable chance of winning; (3) when the rules, procedures, and criteria for winning are clear and specific; and (4) when participants are able to monitor each other's progress and engage in social comparison (Johnson et al., 2012).

Importantly, several of the conditions described above create situations in which performance-approach goals are likely to emerge and performance-avoidance goals are likely to be less prominent; as such, our model can explain why these conditions are likely to produce adaptive outcomes in competition. For example, high-stakes situations heighten perceived performance pressure, likely producing distracting concerns and worries about one's competence. These concerns and worries are the source of the adoption of performance-avoidance goals (Brodish & Devine, 2009; Jury et al., 2019; see also Crouzevialle & Butera, 2017 for an alternative perspective). On the other hand, situations designed to downplay the importance of winning would likely facilitate the adoption of performance-approach goals; thus such situations would bring adaptive outcomes. In addition, ensuring that everyone can win is likely to increase the perceived competence of participants. Because perceived competence is a critical source of the adoption of performance-approach goals (Kumar & Jagacinski, 2011; Senko & Harackiewicz, 2005), such situations are likely to result in improved performance. Finally, because past work has shown that ambiguity regarding one's level of performance makes performance-approach goals less effective (Darnon et al., 2007), providing clear and specific performance criteria should facilitate the adoption of performance-approach goals over performance-avoidance goals. Therefore, clear and specific performance criteria are likely to produce enhanced task performance. Overall, these observations suggest that performance-approach and performance-avoidance goals can be proximal mediators through which constructive competition can produce positive outcomes (Murayama & Elliot, 2012b).

Social Facilitation and Inhibition

Since the seminal work by Triplett (1897), social psychologists have shown that the mere presence of others can facilitate task performance, a phenomenon called social facilitation (Aiello & Douthitt, 2001; Guerin, 1993). Interestingly, this line of research has also shown that the presence of others can impair task performance under certain conditions, which is called social inhibition. Although this literature does not directly focus on competition, it is reasonable to assume that the mere presence of others triggers social comparison processes, which is the basis of psychological mechanisms underlying competition (Garcia et al., 2013). Importantly, from the standpoint of the opposing processes model, we can hypothesize that social facilitation occurs when performance-approach goals are dominant, whereas social inhibition occurs when performance-avoidance goals are dominant. In fact, previous studies have identified moderators of the social facilitation effect, and these factors seem to fit well with the opposing processes model of competition and performance. For example, one crucial moderator that has been identified is task complexity. Specifically, the social facilitation effect is observed when the task is simple, whereas task performance is impaired when the task is complex (Bond & Titus, 1983). Simple tasks have clear performance criteria, which is likely to enhance the adoption of performance-approach goals, as discussed above. In addition, for simple tasks, the development of task skill is a more visible and readily perceived process, and people may be able to develop a stronger sense of competence accordingly relative to complex tasks; this too is a critical predictor of performance-approach goals.

Another moderator that has been identified in the literature is personality traits. Specifically, in a meta-analysis Uziel (2007) found that those who have a so-called "positive orientation" personality trait, which includes extraversion and high self-esteem, tend to show the social facilitation effect. On the other hand, those who have a "negative orientation" personality trait, which includes trait anxiety and low self-esteem, tend to show the social inhibition effect. These effects were statistically independent of the effects of task complexity. Previous studies in the achievement goal literature showed that such positive and negative orientation personality traits are related to performance-approach and performance-avoidance goals, respectively (Elliot & Thrash, 2002). As such, the moderation by positive/negative personality traits can be easily interpreted in accord with the opposing processes model: Those who possess positive orientation personality traits tend to adopt performance-approach goals in the presence of others, which produces a social facilitation effect, while those who have negative orientation personality traits tend to adopt performance-avoidance goals in the presence of others, resulting in a social inhibition effect.

Challenge and Threat

Competitive contexts elicit two different types of stress responses—challenge and threat. According to the biopsychosocial model of challenge and threat (Blascovich & Mendes, 2000), an achievement situation such as competition prompts people to evaluate resource availability and task demands. When people appraise resources as abundant and task demands as low, a state of challenge arises, which is associated with activation of the sympathetic-adrenomedullary (SAM) axis. When people appraise resources as scarce and task demand as high, a state of threat arises, which is associated with activation of the SAM and hypothalamic-pituitary-adrenal axes (Seery, 2013). Critically, challenge tends to be associated with better performance than threat (e.g., Chalabaev et al., 2009; Turner et al., 2012).

Although the research on challenge and threat is not primarily proposed to address competition settings, it provides insight into when competition is adaptive and when it is not. More specifically, the model indicates that competitive situations can either facilitate or impair task performance, depending on whether the situation evokes challenge or threat. As alluded to earlier, Hangen et al. (2016) have shown that in a competitive context individuals differ in their profile of physiological responses to the situation;

some exhibit a challenge-related pattern (e.g., elevated cardiac output), whereas others exhibit a threat-related pattern (e.g., decreased cardiac output). They further showed that participants with a challenge pattern of physiological reactivity engaged in more risk-seeking behavior than those who showed a threat pattern of reactivity. From the perspective of the opposing processes model of competition and performance, challenge and threat can be considered as closely tied to the adoption of performance-approach and performance-avoidance goals, respectively. Performance-approach goals and performance-avoidance goals may be a mediator of the relationship between challenge/threat appraisals and task performance (see McGregor & Elliot, 2002), and/or challenge/threat appraisals may mediate the relationship between the two performance goals and performance (see Chalabaev et al., 2009); that is, the links between these goal and appraisal constructs may be reciprocal in nature. Further integration of these goal and appraisal literatures seems destined to shed further light on the role of appetitive and aversive processes in competition contexts.

Rivalry

Research on rivalry (see Converse, Reinhard, & Austin, this volume) has found that the presence of a rival (i.e., an opponent with similar ability against whom the focal person has a long history of competing) results in enhanced motivation and performance (Kilduff, 2014; Pike et al., 2018). This effect of rivalry should be primarily driven by the relationship history with the rival, but at the same time it is possible that the presence of a rival could facilitate the adoption of performance-approach goals that enhance performance. For example, having a rival should increase the clarity of one's goals (i.e., clearer performance criteria), which is a factor that is related to the adoption of performance-approach goals (Darnon et al., 2007). In addition, because rivals are likely to perform at a similar level as the focal person, rivalry brings moderate (optimal) challenge which should facilitate achievement motivation in general (McClelland et al., 1976) and performance-approach goals in particular (Elliot & Murayama, 2008). In fact, a recent study has shown that rivalry is positively related to the adoption of performance-approach goals (Kilduff et al., 2016).

Choking Under Pressure

When placed in a high-stakes situation, people often feel considerable anxiety and pressure that interferes with optimal performance. Baumeister and Showers (1986) described such a phenomenon as "choking under pressure," and argued that competition is one of the prominent situations that causes choking. Since their seminal paper, a number of studies have examined the psychological mechanisms operative in choking under pressure (e.g., Beilock & Carr, 2001; Gimmig et al., 2006; Gucciardi & Dimmock, 2008).

Importantly, Baumeister and Showers (1986) noted that people are more likely to suffer from choking when (1) the task is complex, (2) people's perceived competence is low, and (3) people possess anxiety-related personality traits. As can be readily seen, these are the exact factors that we have already discussed as promoting the adoption of performance-avoidance goals as opposed to performance-approach goals. Thus, we think it likely that choking under pressure impairs task performance through the adoption of performance-avoidance goals (but see also Smeding, Darnon, & Van Yperen, 2015). In fact, previous research has found that reappraisal in competitive contexts reduces threat responses (which are closely related to performance-avoidance goals, as discussed above) and prevents choking under pressure (Lee et al., 2015).

Further Ahead: Competition as the Basis for Autonomous Engagement?

As shown in the previous literature review, we believe that the proposed opposing processes model can be straightforwardly integrated with other existing theories focusing on how competition influences performance. The different theoretical perspectives may be seen as complementary parts of a more complete and full model—performance-approach and performance-avoidance goals may primarily be seen as downstream mediators that pull together a number of factors identified as important in the literature (see Figure 9.2). At the same time, however, there is other literature indicating the possibility that competition influences performance through a slightly different route than performance-based goals.

This possibility is especially noticeable in the literature on trait competitiveness. As indicated earlier, trait competitiveness represents one's enduring preference for competitive situations. Traditional theoretical perspectives on trait competitiveness consider it a unidimensional construct (e.g., Spence & Helmreich, 1983) and we followed that convention when introducing the opposing processes model. However, several theorists have proposed different subtypes of trait competitiveness. Among them, Ryckman et al. (1997) drew a distinction between *hypercompetitive attitude* and *personal-development competitive attitude*. Hypercompetitive attitude refers to a strong urge to engage in competition in order to win (or to avoid losing) at any cost as a means of maintaining feelings of self-worth. On the other hand, personal-development competitive attitude refers to a person's tendency to focus on using the competitive experience to facilitate personal growth and development, instead of winning the competition (Ryckman et al., 1997). Hypercompetitiveness is similar to traditional trait competitiveness (in fact, the meta-analysis we discussed earlier coded hypercompetitiveness as trait competitiveness), but the personal-development competitive attitude has the remarkable characteristic that it focuses on intrapersonal development rather than interpersonal comparison. Previous studies have shown that personal-development competitive attitude is positively related to positive psychological functioning (Ryckman et al., 1996). Orosz et al. (2018) developed a multidimensional scale of competition that included a highly similar construct (namely "self-developmental competitive orientation").

This focus on personal growth has also been attended to in the literature on envy (see Montal-Rosenberg & Moran, this volume). Envy is an affective state that occurs in response to upward comparison (i.e., social comparison with superior others). Upward comparison signals relative inferiority and incompetence, which is likely to prompt people to adopt performance-avoidance goals. In line with this idea, research on envy typically shows that envy is related to negative consequences (Vecchio, 2000). However, recent studies have distinguished two different types of envy that can emerge in a competitive context—malicious envy and benign envy (van de Ven, 2016). Malicious envy is what traditional research on envy has focused on; it elicits negative behavior and results in maladaptive consequences. On the other hand, benign envy is defined as envy that leads to motivation for self-improvement and development, and empirical work has shown that benign envy is associated with positive performance outcomes (e.g., van de Ven et al., 2011). This work on benign envy suggests that people can focus on self-development and growth even in competitive situations.

These lines of work suggest the interesting possibility that people may adopt mastery goals as well as performance-approach and performance-avoidance goals in competitive contexts. As indicated earlier, a mastery goal is a goal by which people evaluate their competence against an intraindividual or task-based standard, which is typically associated with the motivation for personal development and task mastery. As such, traditional work on achievement goals has assumed that mastery goals have little or nothing to do with competitive situations. However, this view has been challenged by several researchers. For example, Butler (1989; 1992) showed that people often use normative standards for the purpose of self-improvement in contexts where mastery goals are encouraged. Régner et al., (2007) showed that mastery goals, as well as performance-approach and performance-avoidance goals, are positively related to social comparison orientation in high-school students (see also Bounoua et al., 2012). In the same vein, Darnon and colleagues (2010) showed that mastery goals are positively related to social comparison orientation in the same contexts that elicits performance-approach goals. Finally, Jury et al. (2015) demonstrated that in competitive contexts in which both social comparison and temporal comparison are salient, individuals can either endorse mastery goals or performance-based goals. These observations are consistent with the literature on social comparison arguing that social comparison information is useful for self-assessment and self-improvement (Festinger et al., 1950; Taylor & Lobel, 1989).

We still believe that the adoption of performance-approach and/or performance-avoidance goals is the default reaction of people when they are placed in a competitive context, but it is possible that some people adopt mastery goals to overcome the motivational conflict between performance-approach and performance-avoidance goals. This possibility provides a new look at the motivational process underlying competition (see Ryan & Reeve, this volume). Mastery goals are typically only weakly (but positively) related to task performance but are strongly associated with a host of positive psychological experiences such as enjoyment and intrinsic motivation (e.g., Elliot & Church, 1997; Pekrun et al., 2009; for a meta-analysis, see Hulleman et al., 2010). Such positive subjective experiences are the source of long-term engagement and task interest (Deci & Ryan, 1985; Renninger & Hidi, 2016). As such, the adoption of mastery goals during competition may support long-term engagement in the task.

Typically, competitive engagement is short-lived. This is because the rewarding outcome is no longer available once the competition is over: When the winner is announced, unless there is a next game, there is no longer an obvious incentive to continue to engage with the task or activity. However, mastery goals that are adopted during a competition may provide a basis for long-term engagement in a task that lasts beyond the competitive context; mastery goals can create an internal performance criterion against which people continue to strive without any explicit normative outcome or feedback. A similar idea is also suggested by the reward-learning framework of knowledge acquisition (Murayama, 2019; Murayama et al., 2019). According to this framework, regardless of the type of motivation or goals, people's engagement is supported by a common reward-learning process. Importantly, people have the capacity to generate internal rewards (e.g., a feeling of enjoyment) to sustain task engagement without any extrinsic incentives, but incentives or motivation plays an instrumental role for this autonomous process to be "started-up." Competition can be one such instrumental factor, and from this perspective, we can delineate a potential developmental trajectory for motivation in competitive situations. Specifically, competition strongly motivates people to acquire a competitive incentive via the adoption of performance-approach and performance-avoidance goals. When performance-approach goals become dominant (due to the factors we identified earlier), people are more likely to obtain successful outcomes, through which they develop the feeling of competence (initially defined in normative terms). Such a feeling of competence forms the basis of the internal generation of rewards for self-improvement and task mastery, which facilitate the adoption of mastery goals. The resultant internal self-rewarding process then supports continuing engagement in the task. In other words, even if one is initially forced to participate in a competitive situation, it is possible that the person develops their own interest and autonomous engagement over time through successful outcomes. This is still an underexamined topic which is worthy of more research attention.

Final Thoughts

One striking observation from our conceptual and empirical overview is that, despite the enormous number of studies examining the competition–performance relationship, the majority of research has not paid attention to the psychological process underlying the effect. In many studies, researchers have simply examined the relationship between competition (assessed or manipulated) and performance, and simply described the relationship without providing detailed empirical evidence of why such relations were observed. This is unfortunate; as noted earlier, the lack of a process perspective makes interpretation of the null effect very difficult, and researchers may even abandon exploration of such relationships despite the fact that the null results may be a consequence of interesting motivational dynamics. Even if researchers find some effects of competition, either positive or negative, without knowing the psychological process, it would be difficult for them to explain why the obtained results were different from other, earlier studies. In the meta-analysis that we conducted (Murayama & Elliot, 2012a), although the overall effect of competition on performance was very small (to non-existent), the observed effect sizes varied substantially between studies, indicating that there are some cases when competition was positively related to task performance and other cases when it was negatively related. We believe that the relative dominance of performance-approach and performance-avoidance goals in a situation can explain the heterogeneity of effect size, but we were unable to test this hypothesis because few of these studies measured/manipulated any process-related variables. Future research should examine the competition-performance relationship in a more fine-grained manner, focusing more on psychological processes than outcomes.

Another noteworthy observation from the existing literature is that, in experimental studies in particular, competition has been mainly studied with regard to short, one-off tasks, and the long-term implications of competitive situations have not been well-studied. As we suggested toward the end of our chapter, to understand the function of competition in everyday, real life settings, it is essential to shed more light on the longer-term developmental trajectories of competitive motivation. That is, to better understand the competitive motivation of professional tennis players, for example, we need to scrutinize their personal histories of competition with other players. Our proposed model is useful in understanding the short-term dynamics of the competition–performance relationship, but future studies would do well to take a longitudinal and developmental perspective in order to examine the generalizability of the proposed model and, possibly, to extend it beyond its current form.

References

Abra, J. C. (1993). Competition: Creativity's vilified motive. *Genetic, Social, and General Psychology Monographs, 119*(3), 289–342.

Aiello, J. R., & Douthitt, E. A. (2001). Social facilitation from Triplett to electronic performance monitoring. *Group Dynamics: Theory, Research, and Practice, 5*(3), 163–180. https://doi.org/10.1037/1089-2699.5.3.163

Aksoy, O., & Weesie, J. (2012). Beliefs about the social orientations of others: A parametric test of the triangle, false consensus, and cone hypotheses. *Journal of Experimental Social Psychology, 48*(1), 45–54. https://doi.org/10.1016/j.jesp.2011.07.009

Ames, C. (1984). Achievement attributions and self-instructions under competitive and individualistic goal structures. *Journal of Educational Psychology, 76*(3), 478–487. https://doi.org/10.1037/0022-0663.76.3.478

Ames, C. (1992). Classrooms: Goals, structures, and student motivation. *Journal of Educational Psychology, 84*, 261–271. https://doi.org/10.1037/0022-0663.84.3.261

Atkinson, J. W. (1957). Motivational determinants of risk-taking behavior. *Psychological Review, 64*, 359–372. https://doi.org/10.1037/h0043445

Baumeister, R. F., & Showers, C. J. (1986). A review of paradoxical performance effects: Choking under pressure in sports and mental tests. *European Journal of Social Psychology, 16*(4), 361–383. https://doi.org/10.1002/ejsp.2420160405

Beilock, S. L., & Carr, T. H. (2001). On the fragility of skilled performance: What governs choking under pressure? *Journal of Experimental Psychology: General, 130*(4), 701–725. https://doi.org/10.1037/0096-3445.130.4.701

Blascovich, J., & Mendes, W. B. (2000). Challenge and threat appraisals: The role of affective cues. In J. P. Forgas (Ed.), *Feeling and thinking: The role of affect in social cognition* (pp. 59–82). Cambridge University Press.

Bond, C. F., & Titus, L. J. (1983). Social facilitation: A meta-analysis of 241 studies. *Psychological Bulletin, 94*(2), 265–292. https://doi.org/10.1037/0033-2909.94.2.265

Bonta, B. D. (1997). Cooperation and competition in peaceful societies. *Psychological Bulletin, 121*(2), 299–320. https://doi.org/10.1037/0033-2909.121.2.299

Bounoua, L., Cury, F., Regner, I., Huguet, P., Barron, K. E., & Elliot, A. J. (2012). Motivated use of information about others: Linking the 2 × 2 achievement goal model to social comparison propensities and processes. *British Journal of Social Psychology, 51*(4), 626–641. https://doi.org/10.1111/j.2044-8309.2011.02027.x

Bowlby, J. (1969). *Attachment.* Basic Books.

Brodish, A. B., & Devine, P. G. (2009). The role of performance-avoidance goals and worry in mediating the relationship between stereotype threat and performance. *Journal of Experimental Social Psychology, 45*(1), 180–185. https://doi.org/10.1016/j.jesp.2008.08.005

Butler, R. (1987). Task-involving and ego-involving properties of evaluation: Effects of different feedback conditions on motivational perceptions, interest, and performance. *Journal of Educational Psychology, 79*, 474–482. https://doi.org/10.1037/0022-0663.79.4.474

Butler, R. (1989). Mastery versus ability appraisal: A developmental study of children's observations of peer work. *Child Development, 60*(6), 1350–1361. https://doi.org/10.2307/1130926

Butler, R. (1992). What young people want to know when: Effects of mastery and ability goals on interest in different kinds of social comparisons. *Journal of Personality and Social Psychology, 62*, 934–943. https://doi.org/10.1037/0022-3514.62.6.934

Chalabaev, A., Major, B., Cury, F., & Sarrazin, P. (2009). Physiological markers of challenge and threat mediate the effects of performance-based goals on performance. *Journal of Experimental Social Psychology, 45*(4), 991–994. https://doi.org/10.1016/j.jesp.2009.04.009

Cheung, W. L., & Chan, W. (2005). Meta-analytic structural equation modeling: A two-stage approach. *Psychological Methods, 10*, 40–64. https://doi.org/10.1037/1082-989X.10.1.40

Crouzevialle, M., & Butera, F. (2017). Performance goals and task performance: Integrative considerations on the distraction hypothesis. *European Psychologist, 22*(2), 73–82. https://doi.org/10.1027/1016-9040/a000281

Darnon, C., Dompnier, B., Gillieron, O., & Butera, F. (2010). The interplay of mastery and performance goals in social comparison: A multiple-goal perspective. *Journal of Educational Psychology, 102*(1), 212–222. https://doi.org/10.1037/a0018161

Darnon, C., Harackiewicz, J. M., Butera, F., Mugny, G., & Quiamzade, A. (2007). Performance-approach and performance avoidance goals: When uncertainty makes a difference. *Personality and Social Psychology Bulletin, 33*(6), 813–827. https://doi.org/10.1177/0146167207301022

Deci, E. L., & Ryan, R. M. (1985). *Intrinsic motivation and self-determination in human behavior.* Plenum.

Deutsch, M. (1949). A theory of cooperation and competition. *Human Relations, 2*, 129–152. https://doi.org/10.1177/001872674900200204

Dweck, C. S. (1986). Motivational process affects learning. *American Psychologist, 41*, 1010–1018. https://doi.org/10.1037/0003-066X.41.10.1040

Dweck, C. S., & Leggett, E. L. (1988). A social-cognitive approach to motivation and personality. *Psychological Review, 95*, 256–273. https://doi.org/10.1037/0033-295X.95.2.256

Elliot, A. J. (1999). Approach and avoidance motivation and achievement goals. *Educational Psychologist, 34*, 169–189. https://doi.org/10.1207/s15326985ep3403_3

Elliot, A. J., & Church, M. A. (1997). A hierarchical model of approach and avoidance achievement motivation. *Journal of Personality and Social Psychology, 72*, 218–232.

Elliot, A. J., & Covington, M. V. (2001). Approach and avoidance motivation. *Educational Psychology Review, 13*, 73–92. https://doi.org/10.1023/A:1009009018235

Elliot, A. J., Dweck, C. S., & Yeager, D. S. (Eds.). (2017). *Handbook of competence and motivation* (2nd ed). Guilford Press.

Elliot, A. J., & Harackiewicz, J. M. (1996). Approach and avoidance achievement goals and intrinsic motivation: A mediational analysis. *Journal of Personality and Social Psychology, 70*, 461–475. https://doi.org/10.1037/0022-3514.70.3.461

Elliot, A. J., Jury, M., & Murayama, K. (2018). Trait and perceived environmental competitiveness in achievement situations. *Journal of Personality, 86*(3), 353–367. https://doi.org/10.1111/jopy.12320

Elliot, A. J., & Murayama, K. (2008). On the measurement of achievement goals: Critique, illustration, and application. *Journal of Educational Psychology, 100*(3), 613–628. https://doi.org/10.1037/0022-0663.100.3.613

Elliot, A. J., & Thrash, T. M. (2001). Achievement goals and the hierarchical model of achievement motivation. *Educational Psychology Review, 13*, 139–156. https://doi.org/10.1023/A:1009057102306

Elliot, A. J., & Thrash, T. M. (2002). Approach-avoidance motivation in personality: Approach and avoidance temperaments and goals. *Journal of Personality and Social Psychology, 82*, 804–818. https://doi.org/10.1037/0022-3514.82.5.804

Elliot, A. J., Weissman, D., Hangen, E., & Thorstenson, C. A. (2021). Social comparison information, performance expectancy, and performance goal adoption. *Motivation Science, 7*, 56–67.

Festinger, L., Schacter, S., & Back, K. W. (1950). *Social pressures in informal groups: A study of human factors in housing.* Harper.

Fletcher, T. D., & Nusbaum, D. N. (2010). Development of the competitive work environment scale: A multidimensional climate construct. *Educational and Psychological Measurement, 70*(1), 105–124. https://doi.org/10.1177/0013164409344492

Garcia, S. M., Tor, A., & Schiff, T. M. (2013). The psychology of competition: A social comparison perspective. *Perspectives on Psychological Science, 8*(6), 634–650. https://doi.org/10.1177/1745691613504114

Gimmig, D., Huguet, P., Caverni, J.-P., & Cury, F. (2006). Choking under pressure and working memory capacity: When performance pressure reduces fluid intelligence. *Psychonomic Bulletin & Review, 13*(6), 1005–1010. https://doi.org/10.3758/BF03213916

Graham, S., & Golan, S. (1991). Motivational influences on cognition: Task involvement, ego involvement, and depth of information processing. *Journal of Educational Psychology, 83*(2), 187–194. https://doi.org/10.1037/0022-0663.83.2.187

Gray, J. A. (1987). *The psychology of fear and stress* (2nd ed.). Cambridge University Press.

Gucciardi, D. F., & Dimmock, J. A. (2008). Choking under pressure in sensorimotor skills: Conscious processing or depleted attentional resources? *Psychology of Sport and Exercise, 9*(1), 45–59. https://doi.org/10.1016/j.psychsport.2006.10.007

Guerin, B. (1993). *Social facilitation.* Editions de la Maison des Sciences de l'Homme.

Hangen, E. J., Elliot, A. J., & Jamieson, J. P. (2016). The opposing processes model of competition: Elucidating the effects of competition on risk-taking. *Motivation Science, 2*(3), 157–170. https://doi.org/10.1037/mot0000038

Harackiewicz, J. M., Barron, K. E., Pintrich, P. R., Elliot, A. J., & Thrash, T. M. (2002). Revision of achievement goal theory: Necessary and illuminating. *Journal of Educational Psychology, 94*, 638–645. https://doi.org/10.1037/0022-0663.94.3.638

Higgins, E. T. (1997). Beyond pleasure and pain. *American Psychologist, 52*, 1280–1300. https://doi.org/0.1037/0003-066X.52.12.1280

Hinsz, V. B. (2005). The influences of social aspects of competition in goal-setting situations. *Current Psychology, 24*(4), 258–273. https://doi.org/10.1007/s12144-005-1027-4

Hulleman, C. S., Schrager, S. M., Bodmann, S. M., & Harackiewicz, J. M. (2010). A meta-analytic review of achievement goal measures: Different labels for the same constructs or different constructs with similar labels? *Psychological Bulletin, 136*, 422–449. https://doi.org/10.1037/a0018947

Johnson, D. W., & Johnson, R. T. (1975/1999). *Learning together and alone: Cooperative, competitive, and individualistic learning* (5th ed.). Allyn & Bacon.

Johnson, D. W., & Johnson, R. T. (1978). Cooperative, competitive, and individualistic learning. *Journal of Research & Development in Education, 12*(1), 3–15.

Johnson, D. W., & Johnson, R. T. (1989). *Cooperation and competition: Theory and research.* Interaction Book Company.

Johnson, D. W., Johnson, R. T., & Roseth, C. J. (2012). Competition and performance: More facts, more understanding? Comment on Murayama and Elliot (2012). *Psychological Bulletin, 138*(6), 1071–1078. https://doi.org/10.1037/a0029454

Johnson, D. W., Johnson, R. T., Roseth, C., & Shin, T. S. (2014). The relationship between motivation and achievement in interdependent situations. *Journal of Applied Social Psychology, 44*(9), 622–633. https://doi.org/10.1111/jasp.12280

Johnson, D. W., Johnson, R. T., & Skon, L. (1979). Student achievement on different types of tasks under cooperative, competitive, and individualistic conditions. *Contemporary Educational Psychology, 4*(2), 99–106. https://doi.org/10.1016/0361-476X(79)90063-8

Johnson, D. W., Maruyama, G., Johnson, R., Nelson, D., & Skon, L. (1981). Effects of cooperative, competitive, and individualistic goal structures on achievement: A meta-analysis. *Psychological Bulletin, 89,* 47–62. https://doi.org/10.1037/0033-2909.89.1.47

Johnson, R. T., Johnson, D. W., & Stanne, M. B. (1985). Effects of cooperative, competitive, and individualistic goal structures on computer-assisted instruction. *Journal of Educational Psychology, 77*(6), 668–677. https://doi.org/10.1037/0022-0663.77.6.668

Jury, M., Quiamzade, A., Darnon, C., & Mugny, G. (2019). Higher and lower status individuals' performance goals: The role of hierarchy stability. *Motivation Science, 5*(1), 52–65. https://doi.org/10.1037/mot0000105

Jury, M., Smeding, A., & Darnon, C. (2015). Competing with oneself or with others: Achievement goal endorsement in amateur golf competition. *International Journal of Sport Psychology, 46,* 258–273. https://doi.org/10.7352/IJSP2015.46.258.

Kilduff, G. J. (2014). Driven to win: Rivalry, motivation, and performance. *Social Psychological and Personality Science, 5*(8), 944–952. https://doi.org/10.1177/1948550614539770

Kilduff, G. J., Galinsky, A. D., Gallo, E., & Reade, J. J. (2016). Whatever it takes to win: Rivalry increases unethical behavior. *Academy of Management Journal, 59*(5), 1508–1534. https://doi.org/10.5465/amj.2014.0545

Kohn, A. (1986). *No contest: The case against competition.* Houghton, Mifflin and Company.

Kumar, S., & Jagacinski, C. M. (2011). Confronting task difficulty in ego involvement: Change in performance goals. *Journal of Educational Psychology, 103*(3), 664–682. https://doi.org/10.1037/a0023336

Lee, J. M., Samuel, J. V., Mark, R. W., & Paul, F. (2015). Reappraising threat: How to optimize performance under pressure. *Journal of Sport and Exercise Psychology, 37*(3), 339–343. https://doi.org/10.1123/jsep.2014-0186

Lewin, K., Dembo, T., Festinger, L., & Sears, P. S. (1944). Level of aspiration. In J. M. Hunt (Ed.), *Personality and the behavior disorders* (pp. 333–378). Oxford: Ronald Press.

Locke, E. A. (1968). Toward a theory of task motivation and incentives. *Organizational Behavior & Human Performance, 3*(2), 157–189. https://doi.org/10.1016/0030-5073(68)90004-4

Locke, E. A., & Latham, G. P. (1990). *A theory of goal setting & task performance.* Prentice-Hall, Inc.

MacKinnon, D. P., Krull, J. L., & Lockwood, C. M. (2000). Equivalence of the mediation, confounding and suppression effect. *Prevention Science, 1*(4), 173–181. https://doi.org/10.1023/a:1026595011371

McClelland, D. C., Atkinson, J. W., Clark, R. A., & Lowell, E. L. (1976). *The achievement motive.* Irvington.

McGregor, H. A., & Elliot, A. J. (2002). Achievement goals as predictors of achievement-relevant processes prior to task engagement. *Journal of Educational Psychology, 94,* 381–395. https://doi.org/10.1037/0022-0663.94.2.381

Meece, J. L., Blumenfeld, P. C., & Hoyle, R. H. (1988). Student's goal orientations and cognitive engagement in classroom activities. *Journal of Educational Psychology, 80,* 514–523.

Miller, N. (1944). Experimental studies of conflict. In J. Hunt (Ed.), *Personality and the behavioral disorders* (pp. 431–465). Ronald Press.

Miller, R. B., Behrens, J. T., Greene, B. A., & Newman, D. (1993). Goals and perceived ability: Impact on student valuing, self-regulation, and persistence. *Contemporary Educational Psychology, 18,* 2–14. https://doi.org/10.1006/ceps.1993.1002

Miller, R. B., Greene, A., Montalvo, G. P., Ravindran, B., & Nicholls, J. D. (1996). Engaging in academic work: The role of learning goals, future consequences, pleasing others, and perceived ability. *Contemporary Educational Psychology, 21,* 388–422. https://doi.org/10.1006/ceps.1996.0028

Murayama, K. (2019). A reward-learning framework of autonomous knowledge acquisition: An integrated account of curiosity, interest, and intrinsic-extrinsic rewards. https://osf.io/zey4k/

Murayama, K., & Elliot, A. J. (2012a). The competition–performance relation: A meta-analytic review and test of the opposing processes model of competition and performance. *Psychological Bulletin, 138*(6), 1035–1070. https://doi.org/10.1037/a0028324

Murayama, K., & Elliot, A. J. (2012b). Further clarifying the competition–performance relation: Reply to D. W. Johnson et al. (2012). *Psychological Bulletin, 138*(6), 1079–1084. https://doi.org/10.1037/a0029606

Murayama, K., Fitzgibbon, L., & Sakaki, M. (2019). Process account of curiosity and interest: A reward learning framework of knowledge acquisition. *Educational Psychological Review, 31,* 875–895. https://doi.org/10.1007/s10648-019-09499-9

Murayama, K., Kitagami, S., Tanaka, A., & Raw, J. A. L. (2016). People's naiveté about how extrinsic rewards influence intrinsic motivation. *Motivation Science, 2*(3), 138–142. https://doi.org/10.1037/mot0000040

Mussweiler, T., & Epstude, K. (2009). Relatively fast! Efficiency advantages of comparative thinking. *Journal of Experimental Psychology: General, 138*(1), 1–21. https://doi.org/10.1037/a0014374

Nicholls, J. G. (1984). Achievement motivation: Conceptions of ability, subjective experience, task choice, and performance. *Psychological Review, 91*, 328–346. https://doi.org/10.1037/0033-295X.91.3.328

Nicholls, J. G. (1989). *The competitive ethos and democratic education.* Harvard University Press.

Nolen, S. B., & Haladyna, T. M. (1990). Motivation and studying in high school science. *Journal of Research in Science Teaching, 27*(2), 115–126. https://doi.org/10.1002/tea.3660270204

Okebukola, P. A. (1984). In search of a more effective interaction pattern in biology laboratories. *Journal of Biological Education, 18*(4), 305–308. https://doi.org/10.1080/00219266.1984.9654661

Orosz, G., Tóth-Király, I., Büki, N., Ivaskevics, K., Bőthe, B., & Fülöp, M. (2018). The four faces of competition: The development of the multidimensional competitive orientation inventory. *Frontiers in Psychology, 9*(779). https://doi.org/10.3389/fpsyg.2018.00779

Pekrun, R., Elliot, A. J., & Maier, M. A. (2009). Achievement goals and achievement emotions: Testing a model of their joint relations with academic performance. *Journal of Educational Psychology, 101*(1), 115–135. https://doi.org/10.1037/a0013383

Pike, B. E., Kilduff, G. J., & Galinsky, A. D. (2018). The long shadow of rivalry: Rivalry motivates performance today and tomorrow. *Psychological Science, 29*(5), 804–813. https://doi.org/10.1177/0956797617744796

Pintrich, P. R., & DeGroot, E. V. (1990). Motivational and self-regulated learning components of classroom academic performance. *Journal of Educational Psychology, 82*, 33–40. https://doi.org/10.1037/0022-0663.82.1.33

Pintrich, P. R., & Garcia, T. (1991). Student goal orientation and self-regulation in the college classroom. In M. L. Maehr & P. R. Pintrich (Eds.), *Advances in motivation and achievement* (Vol. 7, pp. 371–402). Greenwich, CT: JAI Press.

Régner, I., Escribe, C., & Dupeyrat, C. (2007). Evidence of social comparison in mastery goals in natural academic settings. *Journal of Educational Psychology, 99*(3), 575–583. https://doi.org/10.1037/0022-0663.99.3.575

Renninger, K. A., & Hidi, S. (2016). *The power of interest for motivation and engagement.* Routledge.

Roseth, C. J., Johnson, D. W., & Johnson, R. T. (2008). Promoting early adolescents' achievement and peer relationships: The effects of cooperative, competitive, and individualistic goal structures. *Psychological Bulletin, 134*(2), 223–246. https://doi.org/10.1037/0033-2909.134.2.223

Ryckman, R. M., Hammer, M., Kaczor, L. M., & Gold, J. A. (1996). Construction of a personal development competitive attitude scale. *Journal of Personality Assessment, 66*(2), 374–385. https://doi.org/10.1207/s15327752jpa6602_15

Ryckman, R. M., Libby, C. R., van den Borne, B., Gold, J. A., & Lindner, M. A. (1997). Values of hypercompetitive and personal development competitive individuals. *Journal of Personality Assessment, 69*(2), 271–283. https://doi.org/10.1207/s15327752jpa6902_2

Schrock, W. A., Hughes, D. E., Fu, F. Q., Richards, K. A., & Jones, E. (2016). Better together: Trait competitiveness and competitive psychological climate as antecedents of salesperson organizational commitment and sales performance. *Marketing Letters, 27*(2), 351–360. https://doi.org/10.1007/s11002-014-9329-7

Scott, W. E., & Cherrington, D. J. (1974). Effects of competitive, cooperative, and individualistic reinforcement contingencies. *Journal of Personality and Social Psychology, 30*(6), 748–758. https://doi.org/10.1037/h0037534

Seery, M. D. (2013). The biopsychosocial model of challenge and threat: Using the heart to measure the mind. *Social and Personality Psychology Compass, 7*(9), 637–653. https://doi.org/10.1111/spc3.12052

Senko, C., & Harackiewicz, J. M. (2005). Regulation of achievement goals: The role of competence feedback. *Journal of Educational Psychology, 97*, 320–336. https://doi.org/10.1037/0022-0663.97.3.320

Shalley, C. E., & Oldham, G. R. (1997). Competition and creative performance: Effects of competitor presence and visibility. *Creativity Research Journal, 10*(4), 337–345. https://doi.org/10.1207/s15326934crj1004_5

Shrout, P. E., & Bolger, N. (2002). Mediation in experimental and nonexperimental studies: New procedures and recommendations. *Psychological Methods, 7*(4), 422–445. https://doi.org/10.1037/1082-989x.7.4.422

Smeding, A., Darnon, C., & Van Yperen, N. W. (2015). Why do high working memory individuals choke? An examination of choking under pressure effects in math from a self-improvement perspective. *Learning and Individual Differences, 37*, 176–182. https://doi.org/10.1016/j.lindif.2014.11.005

Sommet, N., Elliot, A. J., Jamieson, J., & Butera, F. (2019). Income inequality, perceived competitiveness, and approach-avoidance motivation. *Journal of Personality, 87*, 767–784. https://doi.org/10.1111/jopy.12432

Spence, J. T., & Helmreich, R. L. (1983). Achievement-related motives and behavior. In J. T. Spence (Ed.), *Achievement and achievement motives: Psychological and sociological approaches* (pp. 10–74). Freeman.

Stanne, M. B., Johnson, D. W., & Johnson, R. T. (1999). Does competition enhance or inhibit motor performance: A meta-analysis. *Psychological Bulletin, 125*, 133–154. https://doi.org/10.1037/0033-2909.125.1.133

Swab, R. G., & Johnson, P. D. (2019). Steel sharpens steel: A review of multilevel competition and competitiveness in organizations. *Journal of Organizational Behavior, 40*(2), 147–165. https://doi.org/10.1002/job.2340

Taylor, S. E., & Lobel, M. (1989). Social comparison activity under threat: Downward evaluation and upward contacts. *Psychological Review, 96*, 569–575.

Triplett, N. (1897). The dynamogenic factors in pacemaking and competition. *American Journal of Psychology, 9*, 507–533. https://doi.org/10.2307/1412188

Turner, M. J., Jones, M. V., Sheffield, D., & Cross, S. L. (2012). Cardiovascular indices of challenge and threat states predict competitive performance. *International Journal of Psychophysiology, 86*(1), 48–57. https://doi.org/10.1016/j.ijpsycho.2012.08.004

Tversky, A., & Kahneman, D. (1981). The framing of decisions and the psychology of choice. *Science, 211*, 453–458. https://doi.org/10.1126/science.7455683

Ulrich, P. (2008). *Integrative economic ethics: Foundations of a civilized market economy.* Cambridge University Press.

Uziel, L. (2007). Individual differences in the social facilitation effect: A review and meta-analysis. *Journal of Research in Personality, 41*(3), 579–601. https://doi.org/10.1016/j.jrp.2006.06.008

van de Pol, P. K., Kavussanu, M., & Ring, C. (2012). Goal orientations, perceived motivational climate, and motivational outcomes in football: A comparison between training and competition contexts. *Psychology of Sport and Exercise, 13*(4), 491–499. https://doi.org/10.1016/j.psychsport.2011.12.002

van de Ven, N. (2016). Envy and its consequences: Why it is useful to distinguish between benign and malicious envy. *Social and Personality Psychology Compass, 10*(6), 337–349. https://doi.org/10.1111/spc3.12253

van de Ven, N., Zeelenberg, M., & Pieters, R. (2011). Why envy outperforms admiration. *Personality and Social Psychology Bulletin, 37*(6), 784–795. https://doi.org/10.1177/0146167211400421

Van Yperen, N. W., Blaga, M., & Postmes, T. (2014). A meta-analysis of self-reported achievement goals and nonself-report performance across three achievement domains (work, sports, and education). *PLoS One, 9*(4), e93594. https://doi.org/10.1371/journal.pone.0093594

Vecchio, R. P. (2000). Negative emotion in the workplace: Employee jealousy and envy. *International Journal of Stress Management, 7*(3), 161–179. https://doi.org/10.1023/A:1009592430712

Worrell, F. C., Knotek, S. E., Plucker, J. A., Portenga, S., Simonton, D. K., Olszewski-Kubilius, P., Schultz, S. R., & Subotnik, R. F. (2016). Competition's role in developing psychological strength and outstanding performance. *Review of General Psychology, 20*(3), 259–271. https://doi.org/10.1037/gpr0000079

Competition and Goal Pursuit: A Temporally Dynamic Model

Szu-chi Huang *and* Stephanie Lin

Abstract

Competition is prevalent in goal pursuit. These goals may explicitly include outperforming others in a competition, or they can be implicit, such that people internally compare and compete with peers during the pursuit of their own individual goals. In this chapter, we examine competitions from the perspective of goal pursuit theories and answer the critical question of *when* each driver of motivation should exert the most impact in explicit and implicit competitions. We present a *temporally dynamic goal pursuit model* that explains how people's motivation and effort exertion evolve over the course of explicit competition, as well as how, and when, people may implicitly compete and even sabotage others who are pursuing an individual goal alongside them.

Key Words: temporally dynamic goal pursuit model, implicit competition, explicit competition, outperform, driver of motivation

Introduction

Competition is prevalent in goal pursuit. These goals may explicitly include outperforming others, or goals to win a competition. For instance, students have goals to win academic awards, athletes have goals to win championships, businesses and organizations have goals to gain market share, and political candidates have goals to attain leadership positions and global influence. Even when winning or outperforming others is not the explicit goal, individuals may implicitly compete with others around them during the pursuit of their goals. Students may implicitly compete with their peers for the highest standardized testing score, and participants of a weight loss program may internally compete with their groupmates on the amount of weight lost. For both explicit and implicit competitions, the goals that individuals adopt guide their effort, affect their planning, and determine their perceptions, thoughts, emotions, and actions. In this chapter, we examine competitions from the perspective of goal pursuit theories, and discuss a *temporally dynamic goal pursuit model* that explains how people's motivation and effort exertion both evolve over the course of a competition, as well as how people may compete with and even sabotage each other when pursuing an individual goal alongside others.

Prior literature in the domain of goal pursuit has identified a rich set of variables that affect people's motivation to achieve a goal, including the goal's value, expectancy of attaining the goal, and discrepancy feedback. Below, we briefly discuss each of these variables and apply these constructs to the development of our temporally dynamic goal pursuit model. Then, we examine how some of these variables can exert a dynamic impact on motivation in (1) explicit competitions and (2) implicit competitions. Finally, we discuss how other streams of research interact with our temporally dynamic model of goal pursuit in competitive contexts.

Motivation in Goal Pursuit

A goal is defined as a desired end state. There are two main types of goals (Elliot et al., 2005; Harackiewicz et al., 1998). First, mastery goals correspond to the desire to progress and improve one's own abilities. Second, performance goals correspond to the desire to outperform others (performance-approach goals) or to not be outperformed by others (performance-avoidance goals). In this chapter, we focus on performance goals, specifically approach goals in explicit and implicit competitions. In explicit competitions, the desired end state represents a level of performance proficiency higher than other opponents; in implicit competitions, the desired end state represents a specific level of performance proficiency that one wishes to attain within a specified time period (Latham & Locke, 2006). As human beings, we envision these desired end states and continue to strive toward them, often until our experienced states sufficiently approximate these desired states (Gollwitzer & Moskowitz, 1996).

Goal pursuit theories have outlined countless constructs that all affect motivation in the pursuit of these desired end states. Here, we focus our review on classic goal-setting theory (Locke & Latham, 1984, 1990) and a few central constructs that are determinants of commitment in goal pursuit—value, expectancy, and discrepancy feedback. Specifically, we begin by briefly reviewing three key tenants that have been examined extensively in the goal-setting literature (Locke & Latham, 1990, 2002): (1) specific and challenging goals lead to higher task performance, (2) commitment to these goals is determined by a combination of value of the goal and expectancy of goal attainment, and (3) effort exertion to these goals is affected by the feedback about one's discrepancy from the goal.

Tenet 1. Specific and Challenging Goals Lead to Higher Task Performance

The classic goal-setting theory proposes that a specific and challenging goal leads to higher task performance than a vague goal, such as a goal to simply "do your best," or a specific and easy goal (Locke & Latham, 1990). This assertion has been supported in over 500 empirical studies (e.g., Huber & Neale, 1987; Latham et al., 2002; Locke & Latham, 2002). For instance, in classic field studies involving real organizations, those given quotas tend to perform better than those with goals to do their best (Latham & Locke, 1975; Yukl & Latham, 1978). The setting of a specific, challenging goal can come from oneself as well as by adopting a standard assigned by others (Oettingen et al., 2004). Both types can increase task performance.

Importantly, this assertion has been shown to be moderated by various goal-related variables, such as one's self-perceived ability and task difficulty, the value or valence of the goal, and the feedback one receives, among others (Locke & Latham, 1990). We review moderators relevant to our current model in tenets 2 and 3.

Tenet 2. Commitment to a Specific and Challenging Goal Occurs as a Function of Value of the Goal and Expectancy of Attainment

Value and expectancy work together to motivate individuals to stay committed to their specific, challenging goals (Gollwitzer & Oettingen, 2012; Latham & Locke, 2006; Locke & Latham, 1990; Locke et al., 1988). High but achievable goals consistently lead to greater effort, focus, and persistence than moderate or easy goals across a wide range of participants, including loggers, engineers, scientists, entrepreneurs, professors, and students. This positive relationship between value, expectancy, and the resulting commitment has been thoroughly theorized in models that depict goal pursuit processes (e.g., Atkinson, 1957; Vroom, 1964). While valence (or value) is often identified as a key determinant of one's ongoing commitment to a goal (Dossett et al., 1979; Mento et al., 1980; Oldham, 1975), the expected probability of obtaining the goal is also consistently shown to positively relate to individuals' commitment during goal pursuit (Dachler & Mobley, 1973; Kolb & Boyatzis, 1970; Locke et al., 1984).

The impact of value and expectancy on commitment can further be found in the literature on desirability and feasibility. Gollwitzer and Moskowitz (1996), for instance, argued that goal-directed behaviors are initiated based on the desirability and feasibility of the goal, in relation to the desirability and feasibility of other competing goals. That is, while one can potentially set different weight loss goals (e.g., to lose 5 pounds, 10 pounds, or 30 pounds), the goal that provides both high desirability and high feasibility (e.g., 10 pounds of weight loss in two months) leads to the highest level of commitment. Oettingen et al. (2004) similarly argued that perceived feasibility and desirability affect not only goal selection but also the intensity of subsequent goal strivings, such that the higher the feasibility and desirability beliefs, the more intensely people work toward a goal. In contrast, people give up on goals that turn out to be much harder to achieve than originally anticipated (i.e., when feasibility beliefs need to be corrected downward) or much less attractive than originally thought (i.e., when desirability beliefs are corrected downward).

In this chapter, we highlight the role of expectancy. The expectancy belief includes the belief that a goal-directed action will lead to the desired outcome (i.e., outcome expectation, Bandura, 1994; Wood & Bandura, 1989; instrumentality belief, Vroom, 1964), the perceived likelihood of attaining the desired outcome (Oettingen, 1996), and beliefs about self-efficacy (Oettingen et al., 2004; Wood & Bandura, 1989). When faced with difficulties in goal pursuit, people who have low expectancy beliefs tend to relax their efforts and abort their attempts prematurely; in contrast, those who have high expectancy beliefs exert greater effort to overcome the challenge to reach the goal (Bandura & Cervone, 1983; Jacobs et al., 1984; Weinberg et al., 1979).

Similarly, self-efficacy—or the belief that one has the capabilities to mobilize the motivational resources, cognitive resources, and courses of action needed to reach a desirable outcome (Bandura, 1986, 1988)—may fluctuate based on one's experience and the perceived difficulty of the performance standard or the goal. While prior successes strengthen efficacy beliefs, experiences of failure weaken it. The perceived difficulty of the goal further affects self-efficacy beliefs; while persisting through a challenging task can meaningfully bolster one's self-efficacy, an easy success does not similarly strengthen this belief (Wood & Bandura, 1989). As expectancy beliefs are rooted in one's continuous assessments of one's own abilities, as well as the likelihood of attaining the goal, it is directly linked to the feedback one receives.

Tenet 3. Discrepancy Feedback from Goal Attainment Affects Effort Exertion to Specific and Challenging Goals

Recognizing a discrepancy between one's current goal progress and the end goal is important for both goal setting and goal pursuit. Goal setting is first and foremost a discrepancy-creating process in that setting a goal creates constructive discontent with our present performance or self-image (Latham & Locke, 2006). As such, a goal stimulates effort towards its attainment only when people recognize an important discrepancy between their status quo and the set goal (Bandura & Cervone, 1983). Bandura (1989, 1991) therefore proposes that giving frequent feedback on discrepancy constitutes a powerful measure to stimulate continuous goal-directed efforts.

In fact, many theories of motivation and self-regulation are founded on a negative feedback control model (Carver & Scheier, 2002; Lord & Hanges, 1987; Spates & Kanfer, 1977), which underscores a discrepancy reduction mechanism as the motivator and regulator of human actions. Perceived discrepancy between performance and an internal (or external) standard triggers actions to reduce the incongruity; if the performance matches the standard, no action will be taken. Human motivation in the pursuit of approach goals thus relies on both a discrepancy production process of goal setting and a discrepancy reduction process that exerts effort to bring one closer to the goal standard.

According to Locke et al. (1981), because commitment implies the exertion of effort *over time* toward the accomplishment of a goal, it should fluctuate depending on the real-time feedback one receives, and thus be adjusted accordingly. Continuing to commit to, and exert effort in, the pursuit of a goal where the discrepancy has become too large would induce unnecessary costs on goal pursuers (Campion & Lord, 1982); hence, it is logical that one would carefully monitor progress and performance, and adjust the level of effort exertion based on the feedback one receives.

So far, we have briefly reviewed classic goal setting theory and findings that underscore the important roles that goal setting, goal value, attainment expectancy, and discrepancy feedback play, respectively, during a goal pursuit process. Next, we apply these theories to answer the critical question of *when* each of these variables should exert the most impact on people's motivation over the course of goal pursuit. This is an especially relevant question for understanding how motivation evolves during explicit and implicit competitions because all these variables can change rapidly from one moment to another over the course of a competition based on the opponent's perceptions and behaviors.

Introducing a Temporally Dynamic Goal Pursuit Model

We present the *temporally dynamic goal pursuit model* developed by Huang and colleagues (Huang & Zhang, 2011, 2013; Huang et al., 2019; Huang et al., 2012; Koo & Fishbach, 2008; Louro et al., 2007), which suggests that the early stage of goal pursuit can be drastically different from the late stage, and identify the unique driving forces in each stage. In contrast to prior temporal models that theorize the entire process from pre-planning to post-completion (Gollwitzer & Moskowitz, 1996), our temporal model focuses specifically on the "action phase" of the goal; that is, between the initiation and completion of goal-directed actions. For instance, in the goal of solving a puzzle, the action phase includes the progression from the start of placing the first piece to the end of the completion of the puzzle. For longer-term goals like academic goals or weight loss goals, making progress from the beginning to the end can take several years, or even decades. Importantly, we propose that the impact of goal-related variables discussed earlier—such as the goal's expectancy and the feedback on discrepancy—on people's motivation should naturally fluctuate during this action phase. That is, while some variables may greatly affect motivation during the early stage of goal pursuit, a different set of variables may dominate as one enters the late stage of the pursuit and is approaching the end point. As a result, the variables that drive motivation and effort in the beginning may not effectively carry one past the finish line.

As discussed in tenet 2, a person's commitment to a goal is largely determined by his or her expectation of eventually attaining it. A critical question that our temporally dynamic model attempts to answer is: When does the goal's attainability matter the most during the course of goal pursuit? We propose that the goal's attainability (i.e., expectancy belief) should dominate when one is in the early stage of goal pursuit and has accumulated little to no progress. This is because during the early stage of goal pursuit, there is high uncertainty regarding how the rest of the process would unfold and whether one has what it takes to actually attain the goal. Accordingly, discrepancy feedback (i.e., tenet 3) that helps to assure the goal's attainability early on should solicit high motivation; in contrast, early discrepancy feedback that casts doubt on a goal's attainability would be especially demotivating.

To test this possibility, we (Huang & Zhang, 2011) teamed up with Relief Nursery—a nationally recognized nonprofit organization dedicated to preventing child abuse—to solicit volunteers for the organization. We distributed campaign letters on campus and asked students and staff members to sign up as volunteers; our goal was to recruit 1,200 volunteer hours for the organization. One version of the letter indicated that we were 800 hours away from reaching the campaign goal of 1,200 volunteer hours (early stage condition), whereas another version of the letter indicated that we were 200 hours away from reaching the goal (late stage condition). Additionally, some participants were then told that sign-ups had been fast (10 committed hours per day), whereas other participants were told that sign-ups had been slow (10 committed hours per week).

According to our temporally dynamic goal pursuit model, in the early stage condition, participants should have felt high uncertainty regarding whether we could reach the campaign goal or not. Thus, they should have been motivated by high expectancy of goal attainment. Indeed, highlighting that the sign-up rate in the past few weeks had been fast led to a higher belief of the goal's attainability, resulting in greater motivation to contribute to the campaign; the participants approached were willing to sign up for 10.36 hours on average when receiving this letter. In contrast, highlighting a low sign-up rate was demotivating in this early stage; the subjects approached were willing to sign up for only 5.13 hours on average when receiving this letter (see Figure 10.1).

Importantly, this pattern reversed for the late stage condition. According to our temporally dynamic goal pursuit model, once sufficient progress is made, people become relatively confident that the goal is attainable and thus are quite committed to the pursuit (Koo & Fishbach, 2008; Wood & Bandura, 1989). With this certainty in mind (i.e., a

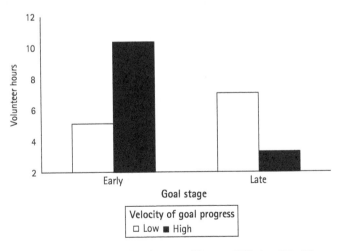

Figure 10.1 Volunteer Hours as a Function of Goal Stage and Perceived Velocity of Goal Progress (Huang & Zhang, 2011).

belief that "I/We can get there"), our temporally dynamic goal pursuit model theorizes that people shift their focus to the next question: *When* will I get there? That is, people begin to question instead whether they are reducing *the remaining discrepancy* at an acceptable speed and thus exert effort to ensure that they are efficiently closing the remaining gap to reach the goal. Therefore, at this late stage of goal pursuit, highlighting that the sign-up rate in the past few weeks had been fast conversely led to low motivation and few sign-ups—participants were willing to sign up for only 3.32 hours on average—because it suggested that no more effort was needed to reduce the remaining discrepancy. In contrast, a low sign-up rate of only 10 committed hours per week was able to motivate the approached participants to sign up for more hours (7.06 hours on average) during this late stage, such that the remaining discrepancy could be closed as soon as possible.

We have captured this temporal shift from questioning the goal's attainability to focusing on closing the remaining discrepancy across a variety of goal pursuit contexts and through different motivated behaviors, such as prosocial and donation campaigns, in-lab math and cognition tasks, and loyalty programs in collaboration with companies (Huang & Zhang, 2011, 2013).

Similarly, we also explore how individuals and organizations can better structure their goals based on this temporally dynamic model; we found that dividing a big goal into smaller sub-goals helps to increase the perception of attainability and thus motivate effort early on; however, it is important to switch to focus on the big, overall goal as one enters the late stage of the pursuit so that the ultimate value of the end goal is highlighted and the last-mile effort can be better motivated to close the remaining discrepancy (Huang et al., 2017b).

In other work, we find that people dynamically change their construal of goal progress, such that goal pursuers tend to exaggerate progress early on to ensure the perception of attainability, but once they enter the late stage and are approaching the endpoint, they conversely downplay their progress in order to motivate greater effort to close the discrepancy (Huang et al., 2012). Furthermore, consistent with the classic goal theories outlined above, our temporally dynamic model should apply only when the value of achieving the goal is high (tenet 2); that is, people should be motivated by expectancy in the early (vs. late) stage of goal pursuit for goals they deem to be important. We found that, indeed, the exaggeration of early progress and the downplaying of later progress only occurred for goals that had high value to participants.

What can we gain by examining competitions through this lens of goal pursuit? We believe that this approach sheds light on two unique processes (see Figure 10.2). First, we can draw upon the temporally dynamic goal pursuit model to understand how people's motivation evolves during competitions, as well as how various goal-related factors—such as the expectancy of goal attainment and discrepancy feedback—dynamically affect effort exertion during competitions. Similar to how individuals are motivated by faster progress (Huang & Zhang, 2011) and achievement feedback (e.g., of subgoals, Huang et al.,

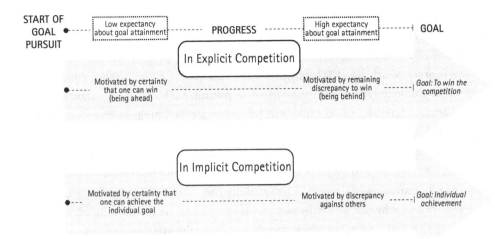

Figure 10.2 A Temporally Dynamic Model for Competitive Goal Pursuit.

2017b) in the early stage of goal pursuit, we suggest that individuals are motivated by feedback that they are ahead of their opponents in the early stage of explicit competitive goals. However, just as individuals begin focusing on reducing discrepancy towards the end goal in the late stage of goal pursuit (Huang & Zhang, 2011; Huang et al., 2017b), we suggest they are motivated by being behind of their opponents in the late stage of competitive goals. Part I elaborates on this theorizing and discusses relevant evidence. Second, this approach allows us to explore how and when individual (i.e., non-zero-sum) goal pursuits may turn into implicitly competitive goal pursuits. Just as people may exaggerate progress in the early stage to ensure attainability and downplay it in the late stage to create motivating discrepancy (Huang et al., 2012), we suggest that people focus on progressing towards their individual goals in the early stage, and focus on additional discrepancies between themselves and other people pursuing similar goals to further motivate themselves in the late stage. Part II discusses this aspect of our model and present related empirical evidence.

Part I: Temporally Dynamic Model for Explicit Competitions

Just like individual goal pursuits, competitions involve the setting of the competitive goal, and are affected by the perceived value of winning, expectancy beliefs, and discrepancy feedback during the competition. Below, we first review how explicit competitions constitute a goal, and how they may differ from traditional individual goals. We then review how our three tenets are affected by, and how they affect, motivation in explicit competitions. Finally, we apply our temporally dynamic model of goal pursuit to explicit competitions to introduce novel predictions as to how motivation evolves during the course of these competitions.

The Goal in Explicit Competitions

Unlike the pursuit of an individual goal, in which one's success depends solely on the amount of effort one is willing to invest and the amount of progress one is able to accumulate (Carver & Scheier, 2002; Higgins, 1987; Locke & Latham, 2006), competition constitutes a unique type of *interdependent* goal pursuit, such that a contestant's success in competition depends not only on his or her own effort and progress, but also on other opponents' effort and progress.

Take weight loss for example. For an individual weight loss goal (e.g., to lose 10 pounds), one is concerned only about one's current weight and one's ideal weight. In this context, the attainment of the weight loss goal depends only on how much one is willing to adhere to a healthy diet and daily exercise. If weight loss becomes a competition, such as the popular reality television show *The Biggest Loser*, the attainment of the goal is no longer contingent upon the progress one makes towards one's own ideal weight; it now depends on the amount of weight one loses compared to other contestants. That is, a contestant can "win" the weight loss competition by losing merely two pounds of weight, as long as the other contestants lose less weight or even gain weight by the end of the contest.

When one enters a competition, one's desired end state is to win. Because of the interpersonal and interdependent nature of competitions, this desired end state is inevitably shared among other contestants who enter the same competition. As a result, the attainment of this desired end state is *negatively correlated* among all the contestants in the competition (Deutsch, 1949). When one contestant successfully attains this desired end state (i.e., wins the prize, award, or championship), the other contestants are no longer able to achieve the same desired end state in this competition. Because people's success or failure is explicitly judged against others' performance in a competition (Locke, 1968), competitive goal pursuits result in unique behaviors and interactions that reduce others' chances of attaining their goal of winning. For instance, in competitions, people work toward their own goal at the expense of others, withholding information and ideas and maybe even being tempted to obstruct the goal progress of others (Deutsch, 1949; Johnson et al., 1981; Stanne et al., 1999).

How Competition Affects and Is Affected by Goal Variables

GOAL SETTING IN COMPETITION

Competition constitutes a unique form of goal setting in that the performance of other people often serves as the specific goal standard for which to strive. Accordingly, competition can influence how people set their goals and how they derive motivation from it in multiple ways (Locke & Latham, 1984). In addition to envisioning an overall goal of winning, one may also set specific goals, such as a specific performance level, that would help them defeat the opponents.

Competitive contexts tend to inspire people to set higher goals than they otherwise would. In organizational contexts, for instance, competition with other firms can lead to the need to create more innovative products to outperform industry standards set by others (Locke, 1968). Single-shot competitions also can lead to higher goal-setting. For instance, in one study, competition was manipulated by either informing participants that their performance on an idea-generation task would be evaluated against others' performance or not. Those who were given a competitive goal set higher individual goals for themselves than those who were told they were not going to be evaluated against others (Hinsz, 2005).

VALUE OF WINNING

Competition can affect the value of winning by introducing extrinsic motivation, as well as by affecting one's own intrinsic motivation. Whereas the desire to simply improve one's running skills and achieve a fast time is an internal motivator, the desire to win a race can be thought of as an external motivator. Adding this external motivation can indeed increase the value of the goal. For instance, in a study on children, Tseng (1969) showed that providing rewards for winners in competitions effectively increased their perceived value of winning, as well as the tension and frustration when they failed to win. This effect of extrinsic rewards heightening the perception of value and exacerbating the frustration for failing further spilled over into subsequent competitions as well.

However, adding competition to a goal can also affect the value of the goal that is derived from one's intrinsic motivation to do well. The value of achieving a goal is higher when that goal is in line with people's intrinsic needs, attitudes, and self-concepts (Gollwitzer & Oettingen, 2012). Adding competition can shift the main goal from achieving something relevant to one's own needs and self-concepts (e.g., gaining a skill that will increase one's self-evaluation) to a goal that is less self-relevant—winning. As classic motivation research suggests, extrinsic motivation (such as tangible rewards) can provide overjustification, or "crowding out," of intrinsic motivation (Lepper et al., 1973). In this manner, competition can result in lower intrinsic motivation, compared to not setting a competitive goal at all (Reeve & Deci, 1996). Introducing more intrinsic rewards in the context of a competition can potentially combat the negative effects of competition on performance. For instance, Vansteenkiste et al. (2014) found that when volleyball players adopted a goal that focused them on mastering the task (an intrinsic reason for winning) and doing as well as they possibly could, they enjoyed the competition more, were more helpful towards their teammates, and were more satisfied with their performance at the end. Notably, for certain individuals, competitions can actually increase intrinsic motivation by increasing these individuals' perceived level of challenge, positive affect, competence, and eagerness to win (Epstein & Harackiewicz, 1992; Tauer & Harackiewicz, 1999), such as those high in achievement motivation (Epstein & Harackiewicz, 1992; Tauer & Harackiewicz, 1999), trait competitiveness (Brown & Peterson, 1994; Spence & Helmreich, 1983), and/or who are "Type A" (Friedman & Ulmer, 1984).

EXPECTANCY BELIEFS

Just as expectancy in goal pursuit can influence commitment, expectancy that one can win also largely affects one's motivation in competitions. When a contestant realizes that he or she is too far behind and no matter how hard he or she tries, winning is not probable, it would make sense for this contestant to reduce commitment, reserving effort and resources instead of investing more into this competition. In an early experiment with children, for instance, members of a group that was defeated on the first of four days of competition never overcame their initial failure and ended up attaining inferior scores for the entire duration of the competition because their perceived chance of winning had plummeted early on (Hurlock, 1927). More recently, a correlational study using Chinese managers and employees revealed that competition can be demotivating when winning was perceived to be highly improbable (Tjosvold et al., 2003). Thus, as perceived value and expectancy work together to motivate individuals in goal pursuit broadly, a high perceived value of winning and the belief that one can indeed win contribute to a contestant's commitment and effort exertion during a competition.

Increasing efficacy beliefs in competition can help increase expectancy and thus increase motivation. For instance, it has been shown in competitive contexts that being overtaken by one's competition is demotivating because it decreases the belief of self-efficacy, making people more critical of their performance and further reducing their abilities to think analytically. In contrast, overtaking one's competition is motivating because it increases perceived self-efficacy and subsequently induces positive self-evaluations and improves people's abilities to select efficient strategies for the task (Bandura & Jourden, 1991). Thus, competition is more than an antecedent that contributes to the expectancy of goal attainment (Hollenbeck & Klein, 1987); the feedback that people receive during a competition—ahead or behind, and by how much—further affects their real-time expectancy assessments, which alter their effort exertion in the competition.

DISCREPANCY FEEDBACK

While discrepancy from the goal may be self-evident and clear in individual goal pursuits (e.g., a 10-pound weight loss goal delineates a clear and fixed discrepancy of 10 pounds), the discrepancy that drives motivation in competitions is more dynamic and less straightforward. Whereas the goal of success or winning is specific, the performance level required to achieve that goal remains unclear (Mulvey & Ribbens, 1999). When performance is sequential, the performance of previous competitors may become the goal of subsequent competitors (Locke et al., 1981); however, future competitors can perform at a higher level and thus the performance level needed to win is still unspecified. When performance is simultaneous between a contestant and an opponent, the performance level needed to win varies as the competition continues and is not explicit until the competition is completed. Thus, although people can observe where they are relative to their competitors, they can only indirectly infer expectancy (i.e., likelihood of winning) and discrepancy (i.e., the amount of effort required to achieve the goal of winning) from that feedback. Hence, while in individual goal pursuits a specific performance standard is constant and thus the discrepancy between one's current performance and the end goal is transparent, in competitions, the minimum performance required to win varies dynamically until the final performance of all contestants is revealed.

How do these variables, together, affect people's motivation during explicit competitions? We posit that to fully capture the effect of explicit competitions on motivation and performance, one needs to consider the *temporal dynamics* over the course of a competition; that is, how goal-related variables fluctuate based on the stage of competition one is in. While a person may feel highly uncertain about his or her chance of winning early in a competition, these feelings may decrease as one approaches the late stage of a competition.

Temporal Dynamics over the Course of an Explicit Competition

To take into account the dynamic and changing nature of explicit competitions, we expand the temporally dynamic goal pursuit model from an individual context to a competitive one (Huang et al., 2017a). For an individual goal pursuit, the attainment of the goal depends solely on one's personal performance against the endpoint; hence, the probability of goal attainment can be easily derived by comparing one's current progress to their desired end-state—an end-state that remains fixed and static throughout the pursuit. In contrast, in a competition, goal success is *interdependent*: achieving the goal to win depends on whether the contestant outperforms an opponent by the end of the competition or not (Deutsch, 1962; Johnson & Johnson, 1974; Kelley & Thibaut, 1954). Because goal success is interdependent, one's distance to "the goal" remains dynamic and can change at any moment over the course of a competition; as a result, contestants' *temporary standing*—currently being ahead of (vs. behind) the opponent—conveys critical information that determines their motivation. Importantly, we argue that contestants' temporary standing signals *both* the expectancy of winning (i.e., the key motivator during the early stage of goal pursuit), as well as the estimated amount of effort required to close the remaining discrepancy to win (i.e., the key motivator during the late stage of goal pursuit).

Recall that our model predicts that in individual goal pursuit, due to uncertainty about whether one can attain the goal that is salient at the beginning of the pursuit, high expectancy of attainment drives individuals' motivation during this early stage. This remains true in explicit competitions. At the onset of a competition, especially one that involves an element of novelty (e.g., a new opponent, a new field or court, a new technique or play), uncertainty about one's ability to achieve the goal to win is high. Contestants may have little information about their opponent's abilities and potentially even their own, which makes their chance of winning unclear. As in individual goal pursuit, assurance that one has a high chance of reaching one's goal (in this case, to win the competition) should therefore be motivating at this time. Accordingly, learning that one is currently ahead of the opponent should make winning seem more attainable, and thus should increase contestants' motivation in the early stage.

In Huang et al. (2017a), we had participants compete in a "Geography Bee" contest in which they ostensibly competed against another student to identify states and provinces; the winner would earn a chance to receive a monetary prize. During the five-round contest, we found that when contestants just completed two rounds of Geography Bee and thus were in the early stage of the contest, knowing that they were currently ahead of their opponent motivated greater effort than when they were behind their opponent. Specifically, participants were told their next task would be to identify provinces in China, and were given the chance to study a map of China that would help them perform well on the next task. Those who were ahead of their partners in this early stage spent more time studying the map than those who were behind their partners (see Figure 10.3). This increase in competitive effort also led to better actual performance in the next round.

We further gained insight into the psychological process that led to this greater effort in the early stage. We informed half of the participants that their likelihood of winning actually would *not* depend on whether they were ahead or behind at this early stage. This disrupted the positive signal about the attainability of their goal to win that participants usually gain from the feedback that they were ahead of their competitor. In this uncertain expectancy condition, participants' effort and performance did not differ just because they were currently ahead (or behind). This comported with our theory that being ahead (vs. behind) leads to greater motivation and performance in the early stage of competitions by increasing contestants' perceived attainability of winning.

As one progresses from the early to the late stage of goal pursuit, our model and earlier work suggests that people shift their focus from whether they can attain their goal to

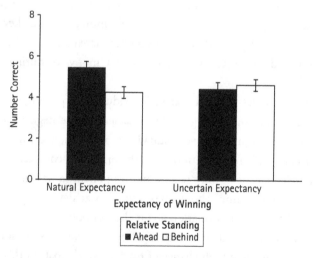

Figure 10.3 Motivation (Number Correct in Next Round) as a Function of Relative Standing and Expectancy of Winning at Early Stage of Competition (Huang et al., 2017a, Study 3a).

when that goal will be achieved (Huang & Zhang, 2011). Thus, this temporally dynamic model suggests that when one approaches the end of a competition, the overall attainability of the win becomes less of a concern. Instead, at this point, contestants shift from assessing their chance of winning to focusing on what still needs to be done in order to win. Motivation in this stage thus depends on the estimated amount of effort required to reduce the remaining discrepancy towards winning.

This shift in focus makes being ahead of one's opponent counterproductive in the late stage of a competition. When contestants' main focus is on how much additional effort is required in order to win, being ahead can lead contestants to relax and reduce their efforts prematurely—premature because in competitions, the goal standard remains dynamic and relative. Even if a contestant is in the lead, so long as there is time remaining in the competition and the size of the discrepancy is not overly large, the final outcome could still change, and additional effort is warranted to secure the win.

Through another five-round Geography Bee contest, we found that when contestants had completed four rounds of Geography Bee and thus were in the late (but not final) stage of the contest, knowing that they were currently ahead of (vs. behind) their opponent led to worse performance in the last round (see Figure 10.4). We also included another condition in which we informed half of the participants that the competition was not over yet and that they would still need more points to win regardless of their current standing relative to their competitor. This thus disrupted the positive signal about the remaining discrepancy to winning that they would usually gain from feedback that they were ahead of their competitor. In this condition, participants put in high effort even when they were ahead of their competitor, suggesting that being ahead (vs. behind) led to worse performance in the late stage of a competition by reducing the perceived amount of effort needed to win.

Thus, extending the temporally dynamic goal pursuit model from an individual context to a competitive context allows us to underscore a unique component that only exists in competitions—temporary standing against the opponent—and identify its dynamic impact on motivation and performance over the course of a competition. As it turns out, being ahead does not uniformly motivate greater effort exertion during a competition—it depends on *when* this information is provided.

Based on these insights, we launched a field experiment across two campuses of a public university in China (totaling 2,543 undergraduate students; Huang et al., 2017a). We hosted a six-day used-book donation competition between these two campuses, with a promise to match the donations with an additional $500 for the winning campus. At the end of the fourth day of the donation competition (i.e., the late stage of the competition), we emailed all contestants a report on their current status; the students from the winning (vs. losing) campus learned that their campus was currently ahead (vs. behind) in the race. We recorded how many students signed up to donate (i.e., the participation rate) as well as how many books they actually donated after receiving the information on their campus'

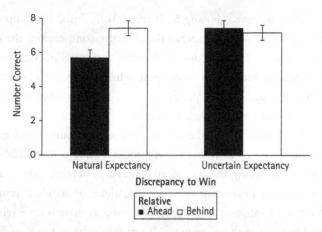

Figure 10.4 Motivation (Number Correct in Next Round) as a Function of Relative Standing and Discrepancy to Win at Late Stage of Competition (Huang et al., 2017a, Study 3b).

temporary standing, and found that, consistent with lab studies' results, students from the leading campus donated significantly fewer books during the last two days of the competition than those from the losing campus.

In an effort to increase the total donation amount and avoid any premature relaxation/disengagement, for half of the students at both campuses, we introduced an intervention that provided them with an additional piece of information—that the signups at their campus were still *10 percent lower than their best year*. Having this additional information about past (and better) performance effectively attenuated the demotivating effect of being ahead as it provided another meaningful, negative performance discrepancy for these students to strive for. Put together, the intervention effectively increased donations by motivating 160 students to donate another 387 books (see Figure 10.5).

So far, we have drawn upon the goal pursuit literature to examine how people's motivation dynamically evolves during competitions. We further identified how specific goal-related factors—a goal's expectancy and remaining discrepancy—can drive motivation and performance during different stages of a competition. We will now explore the second process: How and when individual goal pursuits can turn into implicit competitions, and the unique temporal dynamics that emerge when people compete during the pursuit of their shared, individual goals.

Part II: Temporally Dynamic Model for Implicit Competitions

Thus far, we have examined explicit competitions when the goal is to win. However, often, people are not explicitly competing with each other, and outperforming others is not the goal they set for themselves. Instead, they pursue individual goals in parallel with others. For instance, we may train for a marathon with a time goal of four hours alongside a friend, study for the SATs with an individual score goal of 1400 with a classmate, or

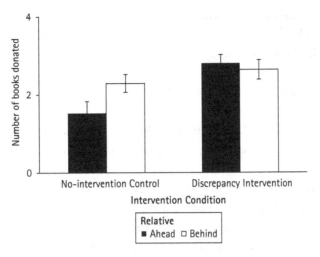

Figure 10.5 Number of Books Donated as a Function of Relative Standing and Discrepancy Intervention (Huang et al., 2017a, Study 5).

engage in a weight loss goal of losing 10 pounds with others in a support group. Unlike explicitly competitive contexts, the ability to achieve one's individual goal does *not* depend on anyone else's performance—the goal pursuer and his or her partners can reach their own individual goals separately and successfully. How, and when, do people become competitive in these individual goal pursuits?

Shifting Goals in Individual Goal Pursuit

It is clear that people naturally compare themselves to others even when not in explicit competitions (see Garcia & Tor, this volume; Festinger, 1954). Indeed, faring well is often only meaningful to the extent that one is faring better than others; outperforming others thus often leads to more positive affect and positive self-evaluative consequences than simply doing well (Klein, 1997). Furthermore, people tend to rely more on social comparison information than focusing on improving relative to past performance—even those who explicitly claim to have mastery goals (i.e., goals to achieve some objective standard; Van Yperen & Leander, 2014). Thus, feelings of competition can naturally arise even when people's objective success in goal attainment (e.g., losing 10 pounds or getting a 1400 on the SATs) does not depend on others' failure in attaining similar individual goals.

Thus, in parallel goal pursuits, when people pursue an individual goal alongside others, they may shift their goal target between focusing on their own individual goal and focusing on a competitive goal to outperform others around them. In this section, we first review goal variables that prompt feelings of competition, which can lead people to place relatively more importance on outperforming others than on their own objective performance standard. We then discuss the application of the temporally dynamic model of goal pursuit to the shift between individual and competitive goals in implicit competitions. We also discuss consequences of these competitive feelings for one's own goal attainment. Finally, we discuss how certain situations (i.e., rank order) can even shift to become explicitly competitive.

How Goal Variables Affect Implicit Competition

GOAL SETTING

Just as competition can lead people to set higher goals, goal setting can also lead people to become more competitive. Indeed, after goal setting occurs, people seem to naturally compete, even when the goal is not zero-sum (i.e., everyone can attain the goal), and there is no tangible reward for "winning" over others (Locke & Latham, 1984; Mitchell & Silver, 1990). Although goal setting can help improve performance, focus on specific goals can foster competition and decrease helping behavior (Wright et al., 1993), particularly if the goals are difficult and the value of goal attainment is high.

VALUE AND EXPECTANCY OF THE GOAL

Earlier, we discussed that the introduction of competition can interfere with one's intrinsic motivation by acting as extrinsic motivation. Interestingly, in the context of implicit competition, the *more* intrinsically valuable a goal is, the more people turn their goal pursuit into a pseudo competition against others.

For instance, research on social comparison has shown that people feel a greater need to outperform close others when the domain is highly self-relevant—or valuable—to them (Garcia et al., 2013; Tesser, 1988). As people are more committed to goals that have high value to them, they should be particularly sensitive to trying to assess their competence and performance level on these goals. One natural way to assess one's competence is by comparing oneself to others (Festinger, 1954; Hoffman et al., 2016). Outperforming others thus serves as a strong signal that one has high self-efficacy in these domains. Indeed, in prior research, those who do poorly in a domain that is relevant to their identity (e.g., intelligence) sabotage others' performance more (Tesser, 1988). Notably, in those identity-relevant domains, they sabotage others who are the most threatening to them, for instance, close and similar others (Tesser & Campbell, 1982; Tesser & Smith, 1980). These social targets are people's most salient comparison, and thus, outperforming them is more affirming of their competence and efficacy beliefs.

DISCREPANCY FEEDBACK

As mentioned earlier, feedback about one's discrepancy from an end-goal is an important motivator in goal pursuit. However, when one pursues an individual goal parallel to others, one may have two goal targets: the explicit goal to reach one's final endpoint, and an implicit goal to outperform others. Although one can receive feedback about one's goal progress relative to the individual endpoint, one can also receive feedback relative to another relevant, social standard: one's discrepancy from fellow goal pursuers (Locke,

1968). The mere existence of others can highlight this implicit competitive goal (to reduce the discrepancy between oneself and one's pseudo-competitor). For instance, a runner may have a personal goal to run a mile in eight minutes, but seeing another individual on track to finish in seven minutes and 45 seconds may push her to try to reduce the discrepancy between her eight minute finish and this pseudo-competitor's finishing time.

This is especially true if given clear feedback about one's discrepancy from others, even if the situation is not explicitly competitive. In a managerial context, managers who were provided feedback about others' performance became more competition-oriented (Armstrong & Collopy, 1996). This also occurs in an individual context. In one study, Oettingen et al. (2004) asked participants to perform a speed-accuracy trade-off task on the computer, while having access to another participant's (bogus) performance information at the bottom of the screen. The authors further assigned participants either a goal to "be fast but accurate" or a goal to "be as accurate as possible." When participants were confronted with a comparatively faster pseudo opponent, those who had a goal to be fast and accurate experienced a performance discrepancy on speed whereas those who had an accuracy goal did not. As a result, the feedback induced competitive behaviors only among the former group of participants, increasing their speed (to reduce the speed discrepancy against their pseudo opponent) while reducing their accuracy in the task. In this case, social comparison information induced competition that actually derailed people from their goal (i.e., to be both fast and accurate).

Temporal Dynamics over the Course of an Implicit Competition

As the temporally dynamic goal pursuit model suggests, the driving role of expectancy changes over the course of goal pursuit. While at the beginning of the pursuit, people have low expectancy about the goal's attainment, this expectancy belief naturally increases as they make progress toward the goal (Huang & Zhang, 2011). When expectancy is high, uncertainty about whether one can reach one's individual goal is alleviated, making people focus more on reducing the remaining discrepancy. In the context of explicit competitions, this suggests that knowing one is likely to win at the late stage of a competition can derail effort, whereas being behind one's competitor drives greater effort at this stage. What predictions does this temporal model make regarding one's perceptions of (implicit) competition in shared individual goal pursuits?

We posit that at the beginning of an individual goal pursuit, people are mostly focused on assessing the expectancy that they will be able to attain their goal. For instance, those who have just started on a journey to lose 10 pounds will be motivated to reduce their uncertainty to achieve that goal. During this time, they may even turn to those pursuing their goals in parallel for help and support (Huang et al., 2015). However, towards the end of an individual pursuit, as people feel more certain that they can reach their goal, we propose that people shift their focus from their individual endpoints to outperforming others who are striving for similar goals. That is, as their explicit goal becomes clearly achievable, their natural competitive edge emerges to set a new goal: to achieve their goal faster (e.g., losing 10 pounds before anyone else) or better (e.g., losing 12 pounds when others only lost 10) than others. This can lead to a variety of effects, including (1) tapering off of cooperation and distancing, (2) enhanced vigilance of social comparison, and (3) direct sabotage behavior.

TAPERING OFF OF COOPERATION

When people begin their goal pursuits alongside others and experience high uncertainty, their primary concern is to decrease this uncertainty and ensure the expectancy of goal attainment. Thus, their mentality towards other people pursuing the same individual goal tends to be that they are "in it together," which manifests itself in their interpersonal communication. For instance, real-world data (Huang et al., 2015) has shown that Weight Watchers participants begin their weight loss journey feeling close and cooperative with others and indicate thoughts of companionship. They feel inspired by others, share tips and tricks with each other (e.g., sharing recipes, snacks with low calorie "point" values), and commiserate when they face setbacks. However, as they approach their goal weights, their cooperative nature recedes. They stop regularly attending meetings, and report feelings of distancing and reluctance to share information with others.

Echoing the findings that people feel most competitive with relevant social comparison targets (Tesser & Campbell, 1982), the temporal shift towards competitive feelings is especially apparent with relevant social comparison targets. In one experiment (Huang et al., 2015), participants volunteered for a walking program with a goal to reach 100,000 steps at the end of the week. They were partnered with an [ostensible] partner who was pursuing the goal for the same reason (more relevant social comparison target), or for a different reason (less relevant social comparison target). They were then given opportunities to share tips and tricks with their partners at various times during the goal pursuit. Those whose partners were less relevant social comparison targets communicated with their partners throughout the week. Those whose partners were more relevant social comparison targets started out sharing as much with their partners as those with the less relevant partners. However, by the end of the week, they were reluctant to share such information, therefore displaying a decrease in cooperation.

VIGILANCE OF OTHERS

Although people become less cooperative and less helpful with others as they progress in their goal pursuit, this does not necessarily mean they no longer deem those goal pursuers relevant. Indeed, other research has shown that, as people approach the end of a goal, they become more vigilant of others pursuing that goal (Huang, 2018).

In Huang (study 1, 2018), participants played 10 rounds of a Nintendo Wii bowling game. At any time, they could turn towards a laptop monitor that would display how a participant, ostensibly in the other room, was doing. Towards the beginning, participants showed interest in the other participants' performance; as this is the time when people exhibit cooperative feelings (Huang et al., 2015) and experience high uncertainty of goal attainment (Huang et al., 2019), this vigilance was unlikely to result from competitive feelings. Instead, they may have been using these social others as an informative benchmark (Festinger, 1954; Suls et al., 2002) to alleviate uncertainty and to recruit social resources when needed.

However, towards the middle of the game, participants paid attention less to what others were doing around them. This is explained by a lull in motivation that takes place in the middle of goal pursuit (Bonezzi et al., 2011; Huang, 2018). Importantly, when the end of the game is back in sight, they again became vigilant of others' performance. Unlike the beginning of goal pursuit, though, when vigilance to social information is likely driven by informational and cooperative value, this vigilance was likely caused by a competitive desire to outperform the other participants as they neared their own end goals. This same effect was found in eye-tracking fixations, and also in behavioral choice outcomes (i.e., choosing to view a partner's performance or not during a week-long walking challenge). This suggests that, when entering the late stage of one's individual goal, goal pursuers begin viewing others who are pursuing the same goal as competitors, resulting in higher vigilance driven by the desire to not only achieve their goal, but also to outperform others.

SABOTAGE BEHAVIOR

More direct evidence that people begin to view goal pursuit as competition as they enter the late stage of the pursuit is the fact that they begin engaging in active sabotage of their pseudo opponents. In one study (Huang et al., 2019), for instance, participants played rounds of a word game (creating as many words out of a word string as possible) towards a 100-point goal that would result in a monetary bonus if achieved. Importantly, it was emphasized that *all* participants could win this bonus if they reached 100 points; thus, their success did not depend on anyone else's performance. They were assigned a partner, but to ensure that participants did not think there was an explicit competitive goal, they were told that some pairs were assigned to complete the tasks together, and some separately—they happened to be in the "separate" condition. After one, two, three, or four rounds of the game, participants were given performance feedback (gained 22, 42, 62, or 82 points) and the performance of their partner, who achieved similar progress. They were then given a chance to choose three words, one of which the other participant would be given as the word string in their last round. A linear pattern emerged such that the further along participants were in their own goal pursuit, the harder the word strings they selected for their partners.

Furthermore, we found that sabotage behavior was driven by an increase in the expectancy of goal attainment when near the goal. In another set of studies (Huang et al., 2019), we manipulated whether participants had made low (23 points) or high (73 points)

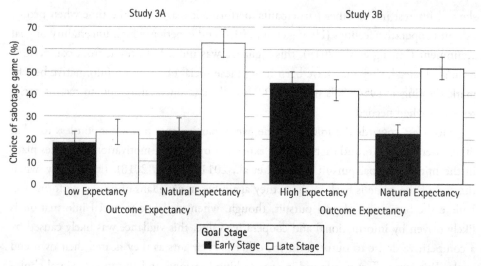

Figure 10.6 Sabotage of Other Participant as a Function of Goal Stage and Expectancy (Huang et al., 2019, Studies 3A and 3B).

progress towards a 100-point goal. In a "natural expectancy" condition, participants were not given any additional feedback. In these conditions, we replicated our earlier findings that those in the late stage condition chose to sabotage their partners more than those in the early stage condition. However, we ran two studies containing an additional condition: in one study (Study 3A, see Figure 10.6), half the participants were additionally told that, regardless of their goal progress, goal attainment was uncertain (i.e., all participants had only a 20–25 percent chance of reaching 100 points); in the other study (Study 3B, see Figure 10.6), half the participants were told that, regardless of their goal progress, goal attainment was certain (i.e., all participants had a 70–75 percent chance of reaching 100 points). When goal attainment was made uncertain, participants did not sabotage more in the late stage of goal pursuit than when they were in the early stage of goal pursuit. The high uncertainty led participants who would ordinarily shift towards a competitive mindset to remain focused on making objective progress towards their individual goal to ensure its attainment. In contrast, when goal attainment was made certain, participants sabotaged in the early stage of the pursuit as much as they did in the late stage; the high expectancy of goal attainment allowed them to shift to a competitive mindset earlier on, focusing on bringing their competitor down to get ahead. These findings underscore the driving role of expectancy in our temporally dynamic model of goal pursuit and the effects of early versus late stage on competitive sabotage behavior.

Consequences of Competition on Individual Goal Pursuit

Although implicit competition in parallel goal pursuit can be a motivating force, it can also be counterproductive. First, recent research has shown that seeing other people reach the goal before they get a chance to overtake them can demotivate people, even if they still have a chance to reach the same goal and the same objective outcome for themselves (Chan & Briers, 2018). Although being outperformed by another person pursuing the same goal can be motivating (relative to when one has no social comparison information), this is not the case when the person has crossed the finish line and achieved the goal (and thus is no longer "beatable").

The above effect may not occur if people are able to successfully sabotage others and keep them from reaching the goal before they do. However, even sabotaging others can be counterproductive. Sabotage behaviors can distract people from their objective goal targets. For instance, focusing too much on outperforming others can lead people to place more importance on relative progress over objective progress, which may in turn lead them to fare objectively worse on their own individual goals. In a marketing context, those who were given information about competitors' performance (which, as stated above, increases competitive orientation) were more likely to choose pricing strategies that would lead them to a better relative five-year profit compared to their competitors (e.g., –$100 million for their competitor and +$40 million for themselves) than a higher objective five-year profit with a lower relative profit compared to their competitors (e.g., +$40 million for their competitor and +$80 million for themselves; Armstrong & Collopy, 1996).

We have also seen this pattern in our own work on temporal dynamics of shared goal pursuit (Huang et al., 2019). We gave participants the goal of achieving 100 points in order to win a gift card; any participant who gained 100 points would receive this gift card, and thus, the goal was individual (i.e., non-zero-sum). We manipulated whether participants were close to the goal (reaching 85 points, thereby feeling relatively certain of their goal attainment, increasing focus on competition) or still far from their goal (reaching only 35 points, thereby feeling relatively uncertain of their goal attainment, increasing focus on reaching their own goal). At this point, we gave participants a choice that either gave them a relative advantage compared to another participant (–2.5 points for their competitor and +2.5 points for themselves) or that gave them a higher objective progress, but a relative disadvantage compared to the other participant (an expected outcome of +12.5 for their competitor and +7.5 for themselves). Those feeling competitive (due to being closer to their individual end goal) ironically were more likely to focus on achieving a relative advantage (choosing the game that would harm the other participant while only helping themselves slightly) than a game that would advance them to their end goal faster for the gift card while putting them at a disadvantage relative to the other participant (Huang et al., 2019).

Even outside of redirecting one's attention and resource allocation towards competition, our research shows that sabotaging others can directly lower motivation (Huang et al., 2019). For instance, after being given the chance to sabotage, participants were also given the opportunity to individually pursue their own goal again (e.g., to work on a word scramble task in which gaining 100 points leads to winning a gift card—a gift card that can be won by any number of participants who reach the individual goal of 100 points).

At that point, participants had the chance to pursue their goal without simultaneously being given the chance to sabotage others or take on strategies that would hinder others. We found that participants who sabotaged earlier lost motivation and spent less time on the final task. This was due to the fact that the effort put into sabotaging the other participant created a positive discrepancy between themselves and others, leading them to believe they could relax their strivings. We found this to be the case when both sabotage behaviors were chosen and manipulated. For instance, those who were nudged to sabotage via a default manipulation (i.e., harder questions being pre-selected for the other participants) showed less motivation on their own future tasks as well.

However, sabotage may not always lead to demotivation; this should mainly be the case when sabotaging successfully gives one a positive discrepancy over others (Huang et al., 2019). Indeed, we found that, when the sabotage effort (i.e., choosing difficult word strings for the participant) did not end up affecting the other participant (i.e., the words were not sent in the end, but stored in a database), participants remained motivated. This suggests that sabotage may lead to other motivational effects depending on the resulting distance between the participant and others involved in goal pursuit. For instance, in an unpublished study (Huang & Lin, 2022), we found that sabotaging others who were much further ahead led participants to become even more motivated because sabotage in this case did not move them ahead of the other participant, but instead decreased the discrepancy between themselves and the more successful participant. This may actually enhance competitive feelings and increase motivation for participants to ultimately overtake this participant.

Future Directions

In this chapter, we have reviewed goal-related constructs (goal setting, expectancy, value, and discrepancy feedback) with relation to explicit and implicit competitions and presented our temporally dynamic model of goal pursuit. Our work broadens the understanding of competitions from a goal pursuit lens in that it suggests that (1) different types of feedback and different levels of temporary standing are motivating at different stages of an explicitly competitive goal, and that (2) implicit competition can emerge during the pursuit of individual goals depending on the stage of the pursuit one is in. To develop this framework, we constrained ourselves to contexts with only one explicit goal (one competitive goal to win, or one individual goal, e.g., to lose weight). Our empirical contexts also usually only included one other competitor (always a stranger), whereas in reality, we often compete with larger groups and people we know better.

In repeated competition, for instance, people may develop rivalries (Converse & Reinhard, 2016; see also Converse, Reinhard, & Austin, this volume). These are established competitive relationships that emerge over time. These rivalries may increase the intrinsic motivation to win a competition, leading people to perceive more value (i.e., psychological satisfaction) from outperforming a rival than an anonymous competitor.

Also, in repeated competitions (e.g., racing against the same rival repeatedly at different track meets), people may have more understanding of their own abilities and likelihood of outperforming a rival, even at the beginning of competition. Thus, being behind their competitor may not lead to the same demotivation in the early stage of the race, compared to those competing against another person for the first time, or competing in a novel task for the first time.

Furthermore, people develop relationships with their rivals and competitors. For instance, people compete with fellow employees at the same organization for financial rewards and promotions. They may even consult each other throughout an explicit competition. In these situations, competition can be constructive and can strengthen such relationships, as people may feel more comfortable sharing resources with competitors with whom they have an outside relationship (Tjosvold et al., 2003). At the same time, socially close others are more relevant comparison targets (Tesser, 1988), thereby increasing the psychological value in outperforming them (e.g., making us feel more competent). Thus, being socially close to others may moderate the temporally dynamic effects discussed so far, such that at the beginning of a shared pursuit, we may be particularly close to those others, offering and asking for more help. For instance, at the beginning of a weight loss goal, people may be more cooperative with friends than strangers, sharing diet and exercise tips. However, towards the end of the goal, when a competitive mindset dominates, people may become particularly committed to outperforming their friends, who constitute their most relevant comparison targets (e.g., Tesser, 1988).

Adding in an element of complication, though, is the fact that sabotaging friends should be morally more repugnant than sabotaging strangers. Thus, it is possible that the competitive spirit in the late stage of goal pursuit would manifest in ways outside of direct sabotage, such as distancing or working particularly hard at one's own goal, rather than blatantly harming the other person's goal pursuit. Indeed, in other research, we (Lin et al., 2014) found that people will sabotage their close friends, but only to the extent that it is morally justifiable to do so—for instance, if they can convince themselves that their sabotage act (e.g., hiding a topic from a friend that may show up on a test) as unlikely to actually harm their friend (the topic is not likely to show up on the test; Lin et al., 2014).

It is also important to note that there are situations that land between explicit competitions and individual goal pursuits. For instance, a restaurant that is ranked #68 out of 100 may have a general individual goal to do well, but may not have an explicit goal to outperform its immediate competitors. Moving up from #68 to #67 may not be a high-value goal for the restaurant. They may instead focus simply on mastery goals, such as trying to perfect their cuisine in order to attract new customers, without explicitly feeling the need to compete with others.

In these cases, a shift between trying to do one's best and trying to outperform others seems to occur when one is closer to a meaningful standard, such as making a "Top 10" list. We consider this a unique type of shift from implicit to explicit competition because being close to the tangible standard turns an originally non-zero-sum situation into an explicitly zero-sum game; only a certain number of people can be in the top 10, and therefore one must outperform others to be placed in that top 10. Even when one has a clearly individual mastery goal, researchers have found that getting closer to a meaningful standard (e.g., top 10) increases the salience of social comparison (Garcia & Tor, 2007). This enhanced social comparison leads to competitive behavior, such as sabotaging others (Poortvliet, 2013). In an organizational context (e.g., a restaurant trying to reach a "Top 10" in Yelp reviews), this increase in competitive behavior can lead companies to try to differentiate themselves from their competition, thereby taking more innovative risks (Vashevko, 2019).

People are also averse to being in last place, which constitutes another meaningful standard (Kuziemko et al., 2014; Vriend et al., 2016). This last-place aversion can lead to making riskier decisions (e.g., choosing riskier gambles) to move out of last place than one would make when at other ranks. Furthermore, when close to last place (i.e., second-to-last), people actively sabotage the person currently in last place (e.g., by helping the person above them in rank rather than below them in rank) in order to keep the person in last place from moving ahead of them.

Hence, in a rank-order context, originally non-competitive situations begin to mimic explicit competitions, as being close to certain standards creates a zero-sum context in which one's success depends on others' relative worse performance. Thus, the shift from mastery goals to explicit competitive goals when nearing relevant standards mirrors the shift from individual to competitive goals when nearing the attainment of one's goals. This may reflect a similar psychological process whereby the goal attainment itself is a relevant standard, and nearing that standard makes salient that one person can reach that standard before others do. We encourage future research to examine how temporal dynamics relate to and play a role in different competitive contexts, including group and repeated competitions (with strangers, rivals, and close others), and in rank-order contexts.

As mentioned in the very beginning, this chapter focuses on performance goals—specifically approach goals—in competitions (Elliot et al., 2005; Harackiewicz et al., 1998; Pintrich & Schunk, 2002). In these situations, one's goal is to reach a performance level that outperforms others. However, we believe that the temporally dynamic model of goal pursuit can be applicable to performance-avoidance goals as well. In the pursuit of avoidance goals, the performance standard is represented by a dynamic threshold that prevents one from being outperformed by others. In the early stage of such pursuits, the attainability of the goal may not be clear as one knows little about the opponent's abilities and the context; hence, knowing that one is currently *not* falling behind can ensure the attainability of this avoidance goal and thus sustains motivation. In the late stage of the competition, attainability will become less of a concern and the competitor should in turn focus on discrepancy (to ensure that there is none); accordingly, knowing that one may fall behind (e.g., learning that the opponent has recently acquired a new tool) or realizing that one is slightly behind would drive greater effort.

The pursuit of individual goals can constitute avoidance goal pursuit as well. For instance, one can strive to avoid gaining weight. Can these individual pursuits turn into competitions? We believe so. When striving to maintain weight, one may similarly use peers as benchmarks and strive to avoid appearing unable to maintain weight (or falling behind on the weight-maintenance goal compared to these peers). As time goes by and one feels more certain that this goal is indeed attainable, such as when one has successfully maintained weight for six months, this person can again view the individual goal as a competition. When one conducts a goal-inconsistent act (e.g., having a big Thanksgiving dinner), one may similarly try to pull others down as a way to avoid falling behind in this pseudo weight-maintenance competition, as suggested by recent research (Lin et al., 2020). We encourage future research to explore these rich possibilities when the pursuit of an avoidance individual goal leads to competitive behaviors.

Concluding Remarks

Integrating goal pursuit theory and constructs can be helpful in predicting and understanding when competition will lead to stronger commitment and greater effort exertion. Our temporally dynamic goal pursuit model specifically suggests that having a competitive advantage can be particularly motivating in the early stage of goal pursuit whereas being slightly behind the competition in the late stage is particularly motivating. The impact of goal variables thus changes dynamically depending on one's current progress. Furthermore, in individual goal pursuit, when one pursues a goal in parallel to others, people are more likely to cooperate when they begin their goal pursuit process and to shift their focus to a competitive goal (i.e., outperforming other goal pursuers) in the late stage of their pursuit. Such shift can lead to detrimental effects not only on the pseudo competitors but also oneself.

References

Armstrong, J. S., & Collopy, F. (1996). Competitor orientation: Effects of objectives and information on managerial decisions and profitability. *Journal of Marketing Research 33*, 188–199.

Atkinson, J. W. (1957). Motivational determinants of risk-taking behavior. *Psychological Review 64*, 359–372.

Bandura, A. (1986). The explanatory and predictive scope of self-efficacy theory. *Journal of Social and Clinical Psychology 4*, 359–373.

Bandura, A. (1988). Self-regulation of motivation and action through goal systems. In V. Hamilton, G. H. Bower, & N. H. Frijda (Eds.), *Cognitive perspectives on emotion and motivation* (4th ed., vol. 108, pp. 37–61). Springer.

Bandura, A. (1989). Social cognitive theory. In R. Vasta (Ed.), *Annals of child development, Vol 6. Six theories of child development* (vol. 6, pp. 1–60). JAI Press.

Bandura, A. (1991). Social cognitive theory of self-regulation. *Organizational Behavior and Human Decision Processes 50*, 248–287.

Bandura, A. (1994). *Self-Efficacy* (vol. 4, pp. 71–81). John Wiley & Sons, Inc.

Bandura, A., & Cervone, D. (1983). Self-evaluative and self-efficacy mechanisms governing the motivational effects of goal systems. *Journal of Personality and Social Psychology 45*, 1017–1028.

Bandura, A., & Jourden, F. J. (1991). Self-regulatory mechanisms governing the impact of social comparison on complex decision making. *Journal of Personality and Social Psychology 60*, 941–951.

Bonezzi, A., Brendl, C. M., & De Angelis, M. (2011). Stuck in the middle. *Psychological Science 22*, 607–612.

Brown, S. P., & Peterson, R. A. (1994). The effect of effort on sales performance and job satisfaction. *Journal of Marketing 58*, 70–80.

Campion, M. A., & Lord, R. G. (1982). A control systems conceptualization of the goal-setting and changing process. *Behavior Therapy 30*, 265–287.

Carver, C. S., & Scheier, M. F. (2002). Control processes and self-organization as complementary principles underlying behavior. *Personality and Social Psychology Review 6*, 304–315.

Chan, E., & Briers, B. (2018). It's the end of the competition: When social comparison is not always motivating for goal achievement. *Journal of Consumer Research 46*, 351–370.

Converse, B. A., & Reinhard, D. A. (2016). On rivalry and goal pursuit: Shared competitive history, legacy concerns, and strategy selection. *Journal of Personality and Social Psychology 110*, 191–213.

Dachler, H. P., & Mobley, W. H. (1973). Construct validation of an instrumentality-expectancy-task-goal model of work motivation: Some theoretical boundary conditions. *Journal of Applied Psychology 58*, 397–418.

Deutsch, M. (1949). A theory of co-operation and competition. *Human Relations 2*, 129–152.

Deutsch, M. (1962). Cooperation and trust: Some theoretical notes. In M. R. Jones (Ed.), *Nebraska Symposium on Motivation* (pp. 275–320). University of Nebraska Press.

Dossett, D. L., Latham, G. P., & Mitchell, T. R. (1979). Effects of assigned versus participatively set goals, knowledge of results, and individual differences on employee behavior when goal difficulty is held constant. *Journal of Applied Psychology 64*, 291–298.

Elliot, A. J., Shell, M. M., Henry, K. B., & Maier, M. A. (2005). Achievement goals, performance contingencies, and performance attainment: An experimental test. *Journal of Educational Psychology 97*, 630–640.

Epstein, J. A., & Harackiewicz, J. M. (1992). Winning is not enough: The effects of competition and achievement orientation on intrinsic interest. *Personality and Social Psychology Bulletin 18*, 128–138.

Festinger, L. (1954). A theory of social comparison processes. *Human Relations 7*, 117–140.

Friedman, M., & Ulmer, D. (1984). *Treating type A behavior—and your heart*. Random House Incorporated.

Garcia, S. M., & Tor, A. (2007). Rankings, standards, and competition: Task vs. scale comparisons. *Organizational Behavior and Human Decision Processes 102*, 95–108.

Garcia, S. M., Tor, A., & Schiff, T. M. (2013). The psychology of competition: A social comparison perspective. *Perspectives on Psychological Science 8*, 634–650.

Gollwitzer, P. M., & Moskowitz, G. B. (1996). Goal effects on action and cognition. In E. T. Higgins (Ed.), *Social psychology handbook of basic principles* (pp. 361–399). Guilford.

Gollwitzer, P. M., & Oettingen, G. (2012). *Goal Pursuit* (pp. 1–26). Oxford University Press.

Harackiewicz, J. M., Barron, K. E., & Elliot, A. J. (1998). Rethinking achievement goals: When are they adaptive for college students and why? *Educational Psychologist 33*, 1–21.

Higgins, E. T. (1987). Self-discrepancy: A theory relating self and affect. *Psychological Review 94*, 319–340.

Hinsz, V. B. (2005). The influences of social aspects of competition in goal-setting situations. *Current Psychology 24*, 258–273.

Hoffman, P. J., Festinger, L., & Lawrence, D. H. (2016). Tendencies toward Group Comparability in Competitive Bargaining. *Human Relations 7*, 141–159.

Hollenbeck, J. R., & Klein, H. J. (1987). Goal commitment and the goal-setting process: Problems, prospects, and proposals for future research. *Journal of Applied Psychology 72*, 212.

Huang, S.-C. (2018). Social information avoidance: When, why, and how it is costly in goal pursuit. *Journal of Marketing Research 55*, 382–395.

Huang, S.-C., & Lin, S. C. (2022). Discrepancy from goal pursuit partners moderates effects of sabotage on motivation. Unpublished data.

Huang, S.-C., & Zhang, Y. (2011). Motivational consequences of perceived velocity in consumer goal pursuit. *Journal of Marketing Research 48*, 1045–1056.

Huang, S.-C., & Zhang, Y. (2013). All roads lead to Rome: The impact of multiple attainment means on motivation. *Journal of Personality and Social Psychology 104*, 236–248.

Huang, S.-C., Broniarczyk, S. M., Zhang, Y., & Beruchashvili, M. (2015). From close to distant: The dynamics of interpersonal relationships in shared goal pursuit. *Journal of Consumer Research 41*, 1252–1266.

Huang, S.-C., Etkin, J., & Jin, L. (2017a). How winning changes motivation in multiphase competitions. *Journal of Personality and Social Psychology 112*, 813–837.

Huang, S.-C., Jin, L., & Zhang, Y. (2017b). Step by step: Sub-goals as a source of motivation. *Organizational Behavior and Human Decision Processes 141*, 1–15.

Huang, S.-C., Lin, S. C., & Zhang, Y. (2019). When individual goal pursuit turns competitive: How we sabotage and coast. *Journal of Personality and Social Psychology 117*, 605–620.

Huang, S.-C., Zhang, Y., & Broniarczyk, S. M. (2012). So near and yet so far: The mental representation of goal progress. *Journal of Personality and Social Psychology 103*, 225–241.

Huber, V. L., & Neale, M. A. (1987). Effects of self- and competitor goals on performance in an interdependent bargaining task. *Journal of Applied Psychology 72*, 197–203.

Hurlock, E. B. (1927). The use of group rivalry as an incentive. *The Journal of Abnormal and Social Psychology 22*, 278–290.

Jacobs, B., Prentice-Dunn, S., & Rogers, R. W. (1984). Understanding persistence: An interface of control theory and self-efficacy theory. *Basic and Applied Social Psychology 5*, 333–347.

Johnson, D. W., & Johnson, R. T. (1974). Instructional goal structure: Cooperative, competitive, or individualistic. *Review of Educational Research 44*, 213–240.

Johnson, D. W., Maruyama, G., Johnson, R., Nelson, D., & Skon, L. (1981). Effects of cooperative, competitive, and individualistic goal structures on achievement: A meta-analysis. *Psychological Bulletin 89*, 47–62.

Kelley, H. H., & Thibaut, J. W. (1954). Experimental studies of group problem solving and process. In G. Lindzey (Ed.), *Handbook of social psychology* (Vol. 2, pp. 735–785). Addison-Wesley Publishing Co.

Klein, W. M. (1997). Objective standards are not enough: Affective, self-evaluative, and behavioral responses to social comparison information. *Journal of Personality and Social Psychology 72*, 763–774.

Kolb, D. A., & Boyatzis, R. E. (1970). Goal-setting and self-directed behavior change. *Human Relations 23*, 439–457.

Koo, M., & Fishbach, A. (2008). Dynamics of self-regulation: How (un)accomplished goal actions affect motivation. *Journal of Personality and Social Psychology 94*, 183–195.

Kuziemko, I., Buell, R. W., Reich, T., & Norton, M. I. (2014). "Last-place aversion": Evidence and redistributive implications. *The Quarterly Journal of Economics 129*, 105–149.

Latham, G. P., & Locke, E. A. (1975). Increasing productivity and decreasing time limits: A field replication of Parkinson's law. *Journal of Applied Psychology 60*, 524–526.

Latham, G. P., & Locke, E. A. (2006). Enhancing the benefits and overcoming the pitfalls of goal setting. *Organizational Dynamics 35*, 332–340.

Latham, G. P., Locke, E. A., & Fassina, N. E. (2002). The high performance cycle: Standing the test of time. In S. Sonnentag (Ed.), *Psychological management of individual performance* (pp. 201–228). John Wiley & Sons, Ltd.

Lepper, M. R., Greene, D., & Nisbett, R. E. (1973). Undermining children's intrinsic interest with extrinsic reward: A test of the "overjustification" hypothesis. *Journal of Personality and Social Psychology 28*, 129–137.

Lin, S. C., Wheeler, S. C., & Huang, S.-C. (2014). Have your cake and make her eat it too: Sabotaging others while maintaining moral self-integrity. In J. Cotte & S. Wood (Eds.), *NA - Advances in consumer research volume* (Vol. 42, pp. 580–581). Presented at the Annual Meeting of The Association for Consumer Research, Baltimore, MD.

Lin, S. C., Wheeler, S. C., & Xue, S. (2020). Have your cake and make her eat it too: Influencing one's social influence to justify indulgence. In J. J. Argo, T. M. Lowrey, & H. J. Schau (Eds.), *NA - Advances in consumer research volume* (Vol. 48, pp. 1124–1128). Presented at the Association for Consumer Research, Virtual.

Locke, E. A. (1968). Toward a theory of task motivation and incentives. *Organizational Behavior and Human Performance 3*, 157–189.

Locke, E. A., & Latham, G. P. (1984). Goal setting: A motivational technique that works! *Organizational Dynamics 8*, 68–80.

Locke, E. A., & Latham, G. P. (1990). *A theory of goal setting & task performance*. Prentice-Hall, Inc.

Locke, E. A., & Latham, G. P. (2002). Building a practically useful theory of goal setting and task motivation: A 35-year odyssey. *American Psychologist 57*, 705–717.

Locke, E. A., & Latham, G. P. (2006). New directions in goal-setting theory. *Current Directions in Psychological Science 15*, 265–268.

Locke, E. A., Frederick, E., Lee, C., & Bobko, P. (1984). Effect of self-efficacy, goals, and task strategies on task performance. *Journal of Applied Psychology 69*, 241–251.

Locke, E. A., Latham, G. P., & Erez, M. (1988). The determinants of goal commitment. *Academy of Management Review 13*, 23–39.

Locke, E. A., Shaw, K. N., Saari, L. M., & Latham, G. P. (1981). Goal setting and task performance: 1969–1980. *Psychological Bulletin 90*, 125–152.

Lord, R. G., & Hanges, P. J. (1987). A control system model of organizational motivation: Theoretical development and applied implications. *Behavioral Science 32*, 161–178.

Louro, M. J., Pieters, R., & Zeelenberg, M. (2007). Dynamics of multiple-goal pursuit. *Journal of Personality and Social Psychology 93*, 174–193.

Mento, A. J., Cartledge, N. D., & Locke, E. A. (1980). Maryland vs Michigan vs Minnesota: Another look at the relationship of expectancy and goal difficulty to task performance. *Behavior Therapy 25*, 419–440.

Mitchell, T. R., & Silver, W. S. (1990). Individual and group goals when workers are interdependent: Effects on task strategies and performance. *Journal of Applied Psychology 75*, 185–193.

Mulvey, P. W., & Ribbens, B. (1999). The effects of intergroup competition and assigned group goals on group efficacy and group effectiveness. *Human Relations 30*, 651–677.

Oettingen, G. (1996). Positive fantasy and motivation. In P. M. Gollwitzer & J. A. Bargh (Eds.), *The psychology of action: Linking cognition and motivation to behavior* (pp. 236–259). The Guilford Press.

Oettingen, G., Bulgarella, C., Henderson, M., & Gollwitzer, P. M. (2004). The self-regulation of goal pursuit. In R. A. Wright, J. Greenberg, & S. S. Brehm (Eds.), *Motivational analysis of social behavior Building on Jack Brehms contributions to psychology* (pp. 225–244). Lawrence Erlbaum Associates Publishers.

Oldham, G. R. (1975). The impact of supervisory characteristics on goal acceptance. *Academy of Management Journal 18*, 461–475.

Pintrich, P. R., & Schunk, D. H. (2002). *Motivation in education: Theory, research, and applications.* Prentice Hall.

Poortvliet, P. M. (2013). Harming others' task-related efforts. *Social Psychology 44*, 373–379.

Reeve, J., & Deci, E. L. (1996). Elements of the competitive situation that affect intrinsic motivation. *Personality and Social Psychology Bulletin 22*, 24–33.

Spates, C. R., & Kanfer, F. H. (1977). Self-monitoring, self-evaluation, and self-reinforcement in children's learning: A test of a multistage self-regulation model. *Behavior Therapy 8*, 9–16.

Spence, J. A., & Helmreich, R. L. (1983). Achievement related motives and behavior. In J. T. Spence (Ed.), *Achievement and achievement motives* (pp. 143–168). Freeman.

Stanne, M. B., Johnson, D. W., & Johnson, R. T. (1999). Does competition enhance or inhibit motor performance: A meta-analysis. *Psychological Bulletin 125*, 133–154.

Suls, J. E., Martin, R., & Wheeler, L. (2002). Social comparison: Why, with whom, and with what effect? *Current Directions in Psychological Science 11*, 159–163.

Tauer, J. M., & Harackiewicz, J. M. (1999). Winning isn't everything: Competition, achievement orientation, and intrinsic motivation. *Journal of Experimental Social Psychology 35*, 209–238.

Tesser, A. (1988). Toward a self-evaluation maintenance model of social behavior. *Advances in Experimental Social Psychology 21*, 181–228.

Tesser, A., & Campbell, J. D. (1982). Self-evaluation maintenance and the perception of friends and strangers. *Journal of Personality 50*, 261–279.

Tesser, A., & Smith, J. (1980). Some effects of task relevance and friendship on helping: You don't always help the one you like, *Journal of Experimental Social Psychology 16*, 582–590.

Tjosvold, D., Johnson, D. W., Johnson, R. T., & Sun, H. (2003). Can interpersonal competition be constructive within organizations? *The Journal of Psychology 137*, 63–84.

Tseng, S. (1969). *An experimental study of the effect of three types of distribution of reward upon work efficiency and group dynamics.* Columbia University Press.

Van Yperen, N. W., & Leander, N. P. (2014). The overpowering effect of social comparison information. *Personality and Social Psychology Bulletin 40*, 676–688.

Vansteenkiste, M., Mouratidis, A., van Riet, T., & Lens, W. (2014). Examining correlates of game-to-game variation in volleyball players' achievement goal pursuit and underlying autonomous and controlling reasons. *Journal of Sport and Exercise Psychology 36*, 131–145.

Vashevko, A. (2019). Does the middle conform or compete? Quality thresholds predict the locus of innovation. *Organization Science 30*, 88–108.

Vriend, T., Jordan, J., & Janssen, O. (2016). Reaching the top and avoiding the bottom: How ranking motivates unethical intentions and behavior. *Organizational Behavior and Human Decision Processes 137*, 142–155.

Vroom, V. H. (1964). *Work and motivation.* Krieger Publishing Company.

Weinberg, R., Gould, D., & Jackson, A. (1979). Expectations and performance: An empirical test of Bandura's self-efficacy theory. *Journal of Sport Psychology 1*, 320–331.

Wood, R., & Bandura, A. (1989). Social cognitive theory of organizational management. *Academy of Management Review 14*, 361–384.

Wright, P. M., George, J. M., Farnsworth, S. R., & McMahan, G. C. (1993). Productivity and extra-role behavior: The effects of goals and incentives on spontaneous helping. *Journal of Applied Psychology 78*, 374–381.

Yukl, G. A., & Latham, G. P. (1978). Interrelationships among employee participation, individual differences, goal difficulty, goal acceptance, goal instrumentality, and performance. *Personnel Psychology 31*, 305–323.

Intrinsic Motivation, Psychological Needs, and Competition: A Self-Determination Theory Analysis

Richard M. Ryan *and* Johnmarshall Reeve

Abstract

Competition is an apt place to experience intrinsic motivation, as competitive settings are often rich with optimal challenges and immediate, effectance-relevant feedback. Yet competition can also undermine intrinsic motivation and sustained engagement by introducing controlling pressures and negative feedback. To explain the contrasting effects of competitive settings on intrinsic motivation, this chapter presents a self-determination theory analysis. According to the theory, when elements of competitive settings are experienced as controlling or pressuring, they undermine competitors' autonomy, decreasing intrinsic motivation. However, when these elements are perceived as both non-controlling and competence-informing, they can satisfy both autonomy and competence needs, enhancing intrinsic motivation. Unpacking these motivational crosscurrents, the authors identify the motivational implications of different elements of competition, including competitive set, pressure to win, feedback and competitive outcomes, challenge, leaders' motivating styles, team interpersonal climate, and intrapersonal events such as ego-involvement. The authors also examine both positive and negative effects of competition on the need for relatedness. The chapter concludes by discussing how conditions that foster the need-satisfying aspects of competition not only enhance intrinsic motivation but also help prevent the emergence of competition's darker sides, such as cheating, doping, objectifying opponents, aggression, and poor sportspersonship.

Key Words: intrinsic motivation, controlling pressures, negative feedback, self-determination theory, autonomy

Intrinsic Motivation, Psychological Needs, and Competition: A Self-Determination Theory Analysis

Competition is a complex social event that presents different faces. Competition can offer participants its inspiring positive face, including a sense of challenge and excitement, standards of excellence, and opportunities for expressing skills and talents. But competitive settings can have a less attractive, demotivating face, involving experiences of pressure, social comparison, ego-involvement, and threat of public failure. Reflecting this complexity are the mixed empirical findings regarding the effects of competition on competitors' motivational and well-being outcomes, with studies showing both positive (Reeve & Deci, 1996; Tauer & Harackiewicz, 1999) and negative (Adachi & Willoughby, 2011; Deci et al., 1981) effects. Misunderstandings concerning when and why competition creates these positive or negative effects shows up in applied settings when leaders introduce competition to "motivate" people, with effects that sometimes increase engagement and effort (e.g., Frederick-Recascino & Schuster-Smith, 2003; Studer et al., 2016) and at other times foster disengagement and produce collateral damage (e.g., Hanus & Fox, 2015).

To understand competition's motivational crosscurrents in this chapter we apply *self-determination theory* (SDT; Ryan & Deci, 2017), with a special emphasis on one of its longstanding "mini-theories," *cognitive evaluation theory* (CET; Deci & Ryan, 1980). CET was the first of SDT's six core mini-theories and is specifically focused on elements in social environments and within individuals that enhance or undermine *intrinsic motivation*. Intrinsic motivation is the motivation to engage an activity out of interest and enjoyment. Intrinsic motivation energizes behaviors across the lifespan, from the active exploration of infants, to "Bingo" night attendance in retirement communities. In SDT, intrinsic motivation is understood to play an important role in psychological growth and development, both as a source of interest-based learning, and in the building of competencies and identities (Ryan & Deci, 2017).

Competition can be broadly defined to encompass nearly all events where social comparison is involved (e.g., Garcia, Tor, & Schiff, 2013). However, for present purposes we focus on *competitive situations* in which people are working to outperform opponents on some mental or physical task. Competitive situations would appear to be natural places to express intrinsic motivation, and indeed they are. For example, studies identify intrinsic motivation as the driving force behind youth and amateur sport participation (Baily, Cope, & Pearce, 2013; Weiss et al., 2012). Similarly, those entering music performance competitions and careers are robustly driven by intrinsic motivation (Evans & Ryan, in press). Research on motivational design in video games also suggests that competitive situations provide many opportunities to experience intrinsic motivation (Rigby & Ryan, 2011).

Yet, competitive settings can directly frustrate basic psychological needs and demotivate participants. Indeed, CET may be best known in this area for early demonstrations that competitive settings involving a pressure to win can decrease intrinsic motivation and enjoyment relative to non-competitive engagement in the same activity (e.g., Deci et al., 1981). As "gatekeepers" to awards and opportunities, competitions are also often experienced as "gate closers" by many, if not most, participants. A "loser" at the science fair who was really motivated for the prize may subsequently decide science is not for him. The child who feels sidelined by her coach and thus incompetent may not want to sign up again for soccer. Even for skillful competitors, pressures from others, and on oneself, to perform can crowd out enjoyment and interest.

It is precisely because competition can produce such varied outcomes, sometimes enhancing and sometimes impairing intrinsic motivation, that it has been of longstanding interest within the CET literature. In what follows we review CET and use this framework to highlight how processes associated with needs for autonomy and competence can produce both positive and negative outcomes in competitive settings. We also examine how competitive settings can affect another focus of SDT, namely people's need for relatedness and the quality of their connections with others. We end by discussing motivationally constructive experiences, and their role in preventing many of the "darker" outcomes seen in competitive settings.

Cognitive Evaluation Theory

Cognitive evaluation theory (CET) is one of six mini-theories within the larger framework of self-determination theory (SDT; Ryan & Deci, 2019). CET was created to explain how motivationally relevant external events such as rewards, praise, evaluations, deadlines, and competitions can sometimes enhance but other times undermine a person's intrinsic motivation (Deci & Ryan, 1980).

CET is rooted in two key assumptions. First, it assumes that everyone, to the extent they have health and vitality, possesses propensities to be intrinsically motivated; that is, to take interest in activities and engage one's skills and capacities. Intrinsic motivation reflects the inherent human desire to seek out novelty and challenge, explore, investigate, learn, and stretch and extend one's abilities (Ryan & Deci, 2017). It is this inherent tendency to want to stretch and express capacities that SDT uses to account for our active human natures, including the broad and pan-cultural appeal of competitive games and sports that people do for "fun." In fact, research shows that the primary reasons people engage in competitive sports (Frederick & Ryan, 1995) and games (Rigby & Ryan, 2011) is because they find them inherently enjoyable and intrinsically motivating. In fact, intrinsic motivation far more robustly explains motivation for such competitive activities than factors such as seeking rewards, trophies, or other extrinsic motivators.

Yet, for intrinsic motivation to be maintained, a second CET assumption is that certain types of experiences are required—namely the satisfaction of basic psychological needs for autonomy, competence, and relatedness (Ryan & Deci, 2017). *Autonomy* is the psychological need to experience volition and personal ownership during one's behavior. Its hallmarks are feelings of willingness and self-endorsement. Its opposite, heteronomy is a sense of being controlled by forces outside the self. *Competence* is the psychological need for experiences of mastery and growth. Its hallmarks are feelings of effectance and a sense of making progress. Finally, *relatedness* is the psychological need for acceptance and belonging in social relationships. Its hallmarks are feelings of social connection, acceptance, and inclusion. SDT suggests that satisfaction of these three needs enhances intrinsic motivation, whereas their frustration diminishes it. When competitive activities are structured in ways that allow satisfaction of these needs, they enhance intrinsic motivation and sustained persistence. Still, competitive structures can thwart need satisfactions and drive participants away from the activity or domain.

SDT, and CET in particular, suggests that elements within social environments (e.g., classrooms, organizations, sport teams) and relationships (e.g., coach-athlete, peer to peer) can be need supportive or need thwarting. When social contexts or motivators pressure participants to behave in a prescribed way, pressure participants to meet externally imposed standards, or offer contingent rewards to control their behavior, they tend to especially thwart the need for autonomy—and hence to undermine intrinsic motivation. On the other hand, when events or persons encourage choice and volition, communicate effectance, and convey inclusion, they tend to be need-supportive—and hence to enhance intrinsic motivation. Stated more succinctly, CET's two assumptions are that: (1) people are inherently prone to be intrinsically motivated; and (2) people possess a set of three basic psychological needs that, when supported, tend to enhance intrinsic motivation, but, when thwarted, undermine intrinsic motivation. Grounded in these assumptions, CET can be stated in a set of five propositions, yielding empirically confirmable hypotheses. Below we present paraphrased versions of each proposition along with illustrative evidence (for the formally stated versions see Ryan & Deci, 2017).

By using CET, the effect of an external event will have on the person's intrinsic motivation can be predicted in advance. Essentially, CET predicts that relatively controlling events frustrate autonomy and undermine intrinsic motivation, relatively informational events satisfy competence needs and promote intrinsic motivation, and relatively amotivating events (those that frustrate both autonomy and competence), undermine intrinsic motivation. The hypothesis-driven, predictive power of CET to explain the ups and downs of intrinsic motivation has been demonstrated across a wide range of external events: rewards (Deci et al., 1999), rules/limits (Koestner et al., 1984), choices (Patall et al., 2008), praise (Henderlong & Lepper, 2002), positive feedback (Ryan, 1982), negative feedback (Carpentier & Mageau, 2013), corrective feedback (Mouratidis et al., 2010), verbal communications (Curran et al., 2013), performance goals (Vansteenkiste et al., 2004), assessment criteria (Haerens et al., 2018), and behavior change requests (Vansteenkiste et al., 2018) among others. In each of these areas research shows that there can be contrasting effects on intrinsic motivation as a function of (mediated by) how elements in the situation impact basic psychological needs. CET's basic premises concerning the role of autonomy and competence in intrinsic motivation has also had support from a variety of methods, including behavioral experiments (e.g., Deci et al., 1999), field studies (e.g., Bartholomew et al., 2011; White & Sheldon, 2014), and studies of neuropsychological foundations (Di Domenico & Ryan, 2017; Lee & Reeve, 2017, 2020; Reeve & Lee, 2019).

CET Applied to Competition

Many experimental investigations have been conducted with the explicit purpose of using CET to examine the positive and negative sides of competitive situations (Abuhamdeh et al., 2015; Deci et al., 1981; Epstein & Harackiewicz, 1992; McAuley & Tammen, 1989; Reeve et al., 1986; Reeve & Deci, 1996; Reeve et al., 1985, 1987; Standage et al., 2005; Tauer & Harackiewicz, 1999; Vallerand et al., 1986a, 1986b; Vallerand & Reid, 1984; Vansteenkiste & Deci, 2003). Typically, experimental studies in this area have employed a methodology in which two unfamiliar participants engage in an activity (e.g., a puzzle, shooting basketball free throws) as the experimenter manipulates different elements of the competition situation, including (1) the competitive set, (2) pressure to win, (3) the supervisor's motivating style, (4) feedback and competitive outcome, and (5) the interpersonal climate, among other elements. Experimental conditions are then contrasted in terms of people's subsequent *free choice behavior*, or their volitional persistence when not under external pressure or inducement. This behavioral persistence measure is the gold standard for assessments of intrinsic motivation, although subjective reports of interest/ enjoyment are also sometimes examined as an additional indicator of intrinsic motivation (Ryan et al., 2019).

Competitive settings can facilitate or undermine intrinsic motivation in various ways. First, supporting competence satisfactions, competitive settings are rich with effectance-relevant feedback, both momentary and cumulative. At the momentary level within competitions, people are often exercising their fullest capacities. Matching wits and/or physical skills with others invariably involves challenges and micro-challenges that provide a steady stream of positive and negative effectance feedback. This is an incredible "informational fuel" for the fires of intrinsic motivation. At a more cumulative level, victories in games, moving up in the rankings, making playoffs, earning scholarships and prizes, and winning championships are competitive structures providing more summative feedback of mastery and success. Thus, competitive settings can offer multi-layered opportunities for competence satisfactions. Conversely, competitive contexts often also involve plenty of critique and negative competence feedback, negative social comparisons, and at the summative level, experiences of losing, often in very public ways. When such sources of evaluative feedback (especially negative evaluative feedback) are pervasive, they can diminish intrinsic motivation, and spawn amotivation.

People autonomously gravitate to activities where they can experience such rich sources of competence feedback and opportunities for self-expression, from the world of video games to martial arts, and from soccer to spelling bees (Ryan & Rigby, 2020). Yet competition can also often involve controlling pressures that interrupt feelings of volition and interest. Sometimes the pressure is from others (coaches, parents, managers), sometimes from the self (e.g., ego-involvement, contingent self-esteem, perfectionism). These varied types of pressures to win can diminish autonomy, decrease motivation, and harm well-being, thus pointing to the "dark side" of competitive engagements. Moreover, because competitions can involve "high stakes" involving the distribution of rewards or resources, they can sometimes create a narrow focus for motivation, and lead to "any means to the end" strategies that can include objectifying opponents and compromising ethics. We now consider a few of these variations and outcomes as we review each of CET's formal propositions and evidence from competition-related research regarding each.

CET Proposition 1

External events vary in how supportive of autonomy or controlling they are. The more controlling the event is (or is perceived to be), the more likely it is to frustrate autonomy, undermine intrinsic motivation, and promote external regulation. The more non-controlling and autonomy supportive the event is, the more likely it is to maintain intrinsic motivation.

Proposition 1 reflects the idea that a person cannot be intrinsically motivated without a sense of volition and willingness for what they are doing—they need autonomy. But autonomy is a contextually sensitive variable, readily affected by the relative salience of various elements in one's environment (Ryan & Deci, 2017).

COMPETITIVE SET AND PRESSURE TO WIN

In some experiments competitive set is introduced with the instruction to "beat the other person." "Beat the other" can involve direct competition (face-to-face), indirect competition (non-face-to-face), zero-sum competition (one winner, one loser), or a tournament structure (one winner, many losers). In experimental contexts the introduction of such "win-focused" instructional sets tends to be experienced as moderately controlling in that it orients the person toward trying to obtain the outcome/reward of winning rather than on enjoying one's engagement in the task per se, undermining intrinsic motivation measured behaviorally (Deci et al., 1981).

But the extent to which "winning is the goal" for participants can vary. Pressure to win can be more strongly induced with instructions such as: "It doesn't matter whether you figure out how the puzzle works. The only thing that matters is which of you wins the competition" (Reeve & Deci, 1996, p. 27). Using this induction, Reeve and Deci found that it led to lower intrinsic motivation than both a comparative competition condition without the exclusive emphasis on winning, and a no competition comparison. The negative results for the "pressure to win" condition were associated with (i.e., mediated by) diminished reports of self-determination or autonomy. What such pressures appear to do is to redirect the competitor's attention and goal-striving away from engaging something interesting or from having fun to the goal of "Just Win, Baby" (the infamous mantra of Al Davis, ex-owner of an American football team). When the pressure to win is made particularly salient, even clear winners in competition can show lower intrinsic motivation (Reeve & Deci, 1996).

COMPETITIVELY CONTINGENT REWARDS

This re-orientation is often made more salient by the introduction of competitively contingent rewards in which winning brings tangible (e.g., money, career advancement) or symbolic (e.g., trophies, status) rewards. A competitively contingent reward is the receipt of a reward specifically for beating an opponent. Across experimental studies, competitively contingent rewards have been meta-analytically shown to undermine intrinsic motivation, even for winners, relative to no-reward controls who also win (Deci et al., 1999). However, the research in this area is relatively limited, especially given the complexity and variations in how competition-contingent rewards are used in real-world settings.

Vansteenkiste and Deci (2003) investigated the effects of competitively contingent rewards in a unique format where losers could get positive feedback and contingent rewards for hitting pre-established standards. This stands in contrast to many competitive situations where "winner takes all." They showed that competition losers who nonetheless received positive information about their performance (i.e., that their performance exceeded a pre-established standard) experienced all of the following: high perceived competence, high self-reported interest, and, high free-choice persistence—indeed, outcomes similar to those of competitive winners. In a separate condition, losers who received an external reward for meeting the performance standard showed high perceived competence and self-reported interest but, on a behavioral measure, low free-choice persistence. The researchers concluded that the effects of competition on intrinsic motivation are far more favorable when the focus is on performing well relative to a task-based standard rather than on trying to win or trying to win a contingent reward.

It's important to note that the undermining effect of rewards specified in CET is specific to people's *intrinsic motivation*—that is their enjoyment of the activity per se. SDT argues that reward contingencies can extrinsically motivate efforts, although their use as a central external motivator often has additional, and predictable, negative side effects. An interesting example of such effects in competitive contexts was observed by White and Sheldon (2014). Using performance statistics and pay data from professional baseball and basketball players, they investigated how the potential to gain external incentives in a "contract year" (CY)—a year when players are competing for salary advantages—affects their immediate and subsequent performance. Using CET among other perspectives, they predicted and found a boost in some scoring statistics during the CY (relative to the pre-CY), although there was no difference in non-scoring statistics unlikely to be advantageous. As expected in the industry, enhanced CY scoring performance predicted salary raises in both sports. However, White and Sheldon also predicted and found an undermining effect on a number of statistical indicators of performance in the post-CY, relative to both the CY and the pre-CY baseline, a pattern suggestive of the undermining effect predicted by CET. We note, however, that in this study the "mediating" motivational variables were not specifically measured, which would help confirm this interpretation.

In competitive settings, systems of reward and recognition can clearly both mobilize as well as undermine participants' engagement and efforts, largely as a function of issues of autonomy and one's perceived locus of causality. But to fully understand the varied impacts of competitive rewards, and especially their positive sides, we must turn next to another salient issue in competitive settings, the need for competence, which is the focus of CET's second proposition.

CET Proposition 2

External events vary in how informational they are. Informational events are those that communicate or aid one's sense of effectance. The more informational the event is, the more likely it is to satisfy competence needs and enhance intrinsic motivation. The more the event communicates ineffectance, the more likely it is to frustrate a sense of competence, undermine intrinsic motivation, and promote amotivation.

Whereas the competitive set and pressure to win relate mostly to the need for autonomy (CET Proposition 1), feedback, performance expectancies, and the competitive outcome relate mostly to the need for competence (Proposition 2). Specifically, SDT sees intrinsic motivation as entailing the active desire to assimilate and express skills and knowledge. The nutriment for this active desire lies in opportunities for growth and learning in which one is able to acquire and exercise skills while receiving positive and "effectance-relevant" (White, 1959) feedback. Oppositely, CET predicts that no feedback or pervasive negative feedback undermines intrinsic motivation and persistence.

A large body of data has supported this general CET proposition, showing that negative feedback or an absence of feedback diminishes intrinsic motivation through lowered competence satisfaction, and that positive or constructive feedback, if non-controlling and effectiveness-focused, enhances intrinsic motivation (e.g., see meta-analysis by Fong et al., 2019). Because competitive settings are usually rich with feedback, they can strongly satisfy needs for competence, and in doing so enhance intrinsic motivation. Yet the very nature of competition entails that some competitors will also be given negative feedback, which can undermine motivation and lead to disengagement from the activity.

FEEDBACK AND COMPETITIVE OUTCOME

Competitive settings offer one obvious source of positive and negative feedback—namely winning and losing. Expectably, these typically have positive and negative effects on intrinsic motivation measured both behaviorally and subjectively (e.g., Reeve & Deci, 1996; Weinberg & Ragan, 1979). Winning brings immediate, objective, ability-diagnostic, and social-comparison-based competence-affirming feedback that enhances intrinsic motivation while losing brings incompetence-affirming feedback that undermines intrinsic motivation (Reeve et al., 1985; Vallerand et al., 1986a; Vallerand & Reid, 1984).

Competitive outcome affects intrinsic motivation because it communicates competence vs. incompetence. But competitors often have access to pre-competition competence-related information, and this pre-performance message of competence has a similar effect on intrinsic motivation as does the post-performance outcome (Epstein & Harackiewicz, 1992; Reeve et al., 1987). When competitors expect to do well (because of successful past performances or because they are about to compete against an inferior opponent), they tend to report high perceived competence, which contributes to their interest in the activity; and when competitors expect to do poorly (because of unsuccessful past performances or because they are about to compete against a superior opponent), they tend to report low perceived competence, which undermines their interest in the activity (Elliot et al., 2021).

Both of these effects on intrinsic motivation—the competitive outcome and the competitor's pre-performance expectancies—are mediated via perceived competence (Reeve & Deci, 1996). That is, competitive outcome affects perceived competence and it is perceived competence, rather than the competitive outcome per se, that explains the ups and downs of intrinsic motivation in competition. Because that is the case, it is possible to lose a competition yet still experience high levels of perceived competence and, hence, intrinsic motivation, as shown in the Vansteenkiste and Deci (2003) experiment described earlier in which competitors who performed up to standards but still lost the competition showed a motivational profile that was interchangeable with competitive winners. This result makes two things clear about competitive outcomes: (1) competitive outcomes includes both objective winning and losing, but it also includes both subjective winning and losing (McAuley & Tammen, 1989); and, (2) it is perceived competence (rather than the objective competitive outcome per se) that explains variations in intrinsic motivation.

CHALLENGE

It is not uncommon to hear competitors explain their competitive enthusiasm by expressing, "I love a challenge." The suggestion is that part of the appeal of competition is the offering of a challenge that affords one the opportunity to express and test one's skills. But, curiously, it is not the competitive set per se that creates the psychological experience of perceived challenge. In one study that looked at the moment right before task engagement began, competitors reported no more perceived challenge than did non-competitors (Reeve & Deci, 1996). The experience of perceived challenge only arose after performance and incoming diagnostic feedback began. It was getting results and then trying to lift one's performance up to produce favorable results that created the experience of perceived challenge. Thus, it is not competition per se that creates perceived challenge; instead, competition creates an opportunity to experience optimal challenges, and to receive immediate, objective information about how well one is doing.

Unlike other elements of competition discussed thus far, challenge has been primarily studied as a dependent measure (Reeve & Deci, 1996) or as an individual difference characteristic in terms of a tendency to make challenge (rather than threat) appraisals during competition (Jones et al., 2009). Empirical investigations that experimentally manipulate a sense of challenge as an independent variable in a competitive setting are rare. Fang et al. (2018) presented one experimental paradigm to manipulate challenge in which an experimental group was faced with a highly difficult "competence frustrating" task in the first session while those in a control group had a more optimally challenging or medium difficulty task. In a second session, both groups were given a medium difficult task. Experimental group participants evidenced an enlarged feedback-related negativity (FRN) loss–win difference wave (d-FRN) compared to those in the control group, indicating that these competence-frustrated participants had enhanced motivation to gain positive competence input on the subsequent task. This points to the dynamic nature of the need for competence, as this pattern suggested a compensatory increase in effort to redress an experience of ineffectance. Nonetheless, the preponderance of evidence suggests that negative feedback and over-challenge typically result in withdrawal of effort and amotivation over time (Hom & Maxwell, 1983).

In the view of SDT, what makes a competitive challenge "optimal" and thus apt to enhance intrinsic motivation, is that opponents are matched such that each can experience positive feedback within play. This ensures, over time, sufficient positive feedback to maintain engagement. Well-designed competitive game environments often build this in, with players matched primarily against others at a comparable level, and procedures for "leveling up" and challenge regulation (Rigby & Ryan, 2011). Persistent incomparable matches become fun for neither competitor, as they provide little by way of "effectance relevant" feedback.

In fact, perceiving competitive situations as optimally challenging, rather than threatening, matters to positive experience, and likely persistence over time. For example, Moore et al. (2012) manipulated challenge and threat appraisals in competitive situations. Challenge appraisals encourage competitors to focus on the task and on performing effectively, while threat appraisals encourage competitors to focus on possible mistakes and being evaluated negatively in front of an audience of others. Experimentally-induced challenge appraisals led competitors to focus more on the task ("attentional focus"), to perform better, and to experience more adaptive emotional and physiological states, whereas experimentally-induced threat appraisals led competitors to focus more on external evaluation, perform worse, and experience more maladaptive emotional and physiological states (Moore et al., 2013).

In sum, competitive settings provide myriad opportunities for feedback, both direct and immediate in the activity, and indirect from coaches, audiences, and involved others. CET proposition 2 suggests that to the extent such feedback enhances feelings of growth and competence, intrinsic motivation is enhanced. This happens most robustly in environments with positive, constructive feedback embedded within optimal challenges.

CET Proposition 3

External events have three aspects—a controlling aspect, an informational aspect, and an amotivating aspect. The relative salience of these three aspects determines the "functional significance" of the event, or how that event will affect the person's intrinsic motivation.

Events salient as informational enhance intrinsic motivation, those salient as controlling or as conveying incompetence undermine it.

Proposition 3 highlights the psychological nature of events—and that how people construe a situation determines their subsequent motivation and behavior. In particular, people are sensitive to both autonomy and competence affordances and frustrations, and situations will vary in terms of what is most salient. Thus, fundamental to proposition 3 is the idea that psychological experiences associated with autonomy and competence *mediate* between events and intrinsic motivation-relevant outcomes.

As an illustration, consider Peng et al.'s (2012) experiment in an exergame context in which they looked at features in the game design expected to support autonomy (e.g., avatar customization options, choice in character crafting) and competence (e.g., dynamic challenge regulator, points for "heroism"). They performed a 2 (autonomy-supportive game features on or off) by 2 (competence-supportive game features on or off) and showed in accord with CET that activating autonomy features enhanced intrinsic motivation, a result mediated by increased autonomy satisfaction; activating competence features also enhanced intrinsic motivation, a result mediated by increased competence satisfaction.

Proposition 3 identifies that the effect of events on intrinsic motivation depends on the relative salience of controlling and informational elements in a situation. This proposition can be applied to both micro and macro elements in competitions. For instance, a reward for winning and no rewards for any other competitors conveys a different functional significance than distributed rewards (Vansteenkiste & Deci, 2003). Similarly, how scores are posted and evaluated will have impact on competence and autonomy (e.g., headlines, rankings, leaderboards, private communication; Hanus & Fox, 2015). But beyond such a feature-to-feature approach, a big factor that makes any activity feel more controlled or more autonomous is the relational climate in which it occurs. This leads us to CET's next proposition.

CET Proposition 4

Interpersonal contexts vary with regards to how controlling, autonomy supportive, or amotivating they are. Autonomy-supportive interpersonal contexts enhance basic psychological need satisfactions and intrinsic motivation. Controlling and amotivating social contexts frustrate people's basic psychological needs and undermine intrinsic motivation.

The motivating style and the interpersonal climate established by one's managers, coaches or leaders or, in team units, by one's teammates, can often tip competitive settings toward being experienced as informational, controlling, or amotivating.

LEADER'S MOTIVATING STYLE

Sometimes competitors go at it alone, but more often than not competitors work with a coach, manager, mentor, teacher, or parent. Such leaders often play a motivational role, encouraging the competitor to put forth effort, such as during training, practice, and competition. As they do so, they display a particular motivating style, which can be characterized as autonomy-supportive and informational or controlling and need thwarting (Bartholomew et al., 2010; Curran et al., 2014; Mageau & Vallerand, 2003). Attesting to the importance of such styles, Cumming et al. (2007) found that much more central to youth athletes' evaluations of coaches than their winning percentage was the degree to which they were autonomy supportive and did not foster ego-involvement.

Autonomy-supportive leaders (be they mentors, coaches or parents) tend to adopt an interpersonal tone of understanding that leads to needs-supportive behaviors such as perspective taking, affording choices and opportunities to pursue interests, providing meaningful rationales for demands, and acknowledging and accepting negative feelings (Mageau & Vallerand, 2003; Reeve & Cheon, 2021). This interpersonal tone and collection of autonomy-supportive behaviors create opportunities for social interactions and an interpersonal relationship that allows competitors to experience need satisfaction and intrinsic motivation. Controlling leaders, on the other hand, tend to adopt an interpersonal tone of pressure in which the leader takes charge in day-to-day interactions, prescribes what the competitor should think, feel, and do, and applies pressure to align the competitor with the leader's goals (Bartholomew et al., 2010). This interpersonal tone and "my way or the highway" relationship style frustrates competitors' psychological needs and undermines intrinsic motivation (Bartholomew et al., 2011, 2018; Ntoumanis, 2012).

An interesting question to ask is: Why would a leader (coach) be controlling? A controlling motivating style is typically the product of pressures from above, pressures from below, and pressures from within (Pelletier et al., 2002; Reeve, 2009). For instance, leaders, such as sport coaches, take on a double accountability burden of being held responsible for their athletes' behavior and win–loss outcomes. This accountability can lead the coach to push and pressure athletes toward specific behaviors and outcomes. Being controlling can also be culturally valued. In such a cultural context, controlling supervisory behaviors can be taken as valued indicators of coaching competence.

Alternatively, a second question to ask is: Why would a leader be autonomy-supportive? The answer here is because an autonomy-supportive motivating style promotes adaptive motivation and functioning. It yields a wealth of benefits—for the supervisor (e.g., job satisfaction, teaching efficacy), for the supervised (e.g., need satisfaction, intrinsic motivation), and for the larger interpersonal climate (more supportive, less conflictual) (Reeve & Cheon, 2021).

Having discussed how leaders, coaches, and important others can affect the experience of competition and thus intrinsic motivation, we now turn to the inner side of these dynamics—how self-motivating styles can be either informational, self-controlling, or amotivating, impacting intrinsic motivation.

CET Proposition 5

Intrapersonal events vary in how internally informational, internally controlling, or internally amotivating they are. Internally informational events enhance intrinsic motivation by facilitating autonomy and competence, whereas internally controlling events undermine intrinsic motivation by frustrating autonomy; and internally amotivating events undermine intrinsic motivation by frustrating competence.

Like external events (i.e., competition; Standage et al., 2005) and interpersonal contexts (i.e., peer climate; Ntoumanis & Vazou, 2005), intrapersonal events can also be experienced as informational and task-involving or as controlling and ego-involving (Ryan, 1982). Intrapersonal events are "self-administered" events, such as the inner praise, self-talk, and self-criticism competitors enact. This means that people can bring all the external-environmental elements of the competitive situation into themselves, and further, these intrapersonal events have motivational effects that mimic those of their corresponding external events. CET's fifth and final proposition thus stipulates that intrapersonal events can be needs-supportive, informational, and facilitating of intrinsic motivation, just as they alternatively can be needs-frustrating, controlling, and undermining of intrinsic motivation (Ryan & Deci, 2017).

EGO-INVOLVEMENT AS AN "INTERNALLY CONTROLLING" STATE

Competitive pressures and performance goals sometimes bend a competitor's task-involvement into *ego-involvement*, defined as motivation driven by self-esteem concerns (Ryan, 1982). Ego-involvement is especially evident whenever a competitor has internalized external contingencies such that they now define their own worth in terms of competitive success. Ego-involvement occurs as the competitor compares himself or herself with others in an evaluative sense in which a positive view of the self becomes contingent upon beating or out-performing others. In this sense, ego-involvement is a self-administered event that parallels the socially administered pressure to win, as both are controlling and pressuring experiences, though one emerges intrapersonally while the other emerges interpersonally.

When it occurs, ego-involvement tends to thwart psychological need satisfaction (especially autonomy and relatedness) and undermine intrinsic motivation and well-being. For example, Standage et al. (2005) investigated both ego-involving and task-involving conditions for participants either competing, cooperating, or individually engaged in a physical co-ordination task. They found that participants in the task-involving conditions and those who worked in cooperation reported greater levels of need satisfaction and well-being, whereas those in the ego-involving conditions, individual or competitive, showed higher levels of negative affect. Although as expected from proposition 2, winning resulted in higher levels of need satisfaction and positive affect, and losing in higher negative affect; further, losing individually in an ego-involving condition led to the highest levels of negative affect and lower need satisfaction.

Self-talk includes all those overt and covert verbalizations one addresses to the self (e.g., inner speech, internal dialogue, verbal rehearsal); it represents an intrapersonal event that can be internally informational (e.g., self-encouraging), internally controlling (self-pressuring, self-attacking), or internally amotivating (self-blaming, self-neglecting). As long ago highlighted by Gallaway (1997), competitors in varied sports are affected by the "inner game" in which they coach themselves, either harshly or supportively.

Oliver et al. (2010) studied such self-talk in a student population focused on an examination. They found examples of informational self-talk, such as students' highlighting opportunities for choice and self-initiative, reviewing meaningful rationales for working, and giving oneself positive feedback. Controlling, pressuring, and critical self-talk was more intrusive and pressuring. They found that informational self-talk enhanced positive affect, whereas controlling self-talk exacerbated anxiety and stress, especially when performance was relatively poor. A principle finding was that it was not the content of the self-talk that was particularly predictive of outcomes such as adaptive vs. maladaptive coping but it was, instead, the functional significance of that self-talk to the person. More recently, Amado et al. (2019) showed that informational self-talk during competitions for both volleyball and basketball players was associated with greater autonomy and competence satisfactions and better concentration during the competitive events.

The Effects of Competition on Relatedness

Because CET is focused on intrinsic motivation, which can be relevant to both solo and interactive tasks, its focus is primarily on how events impact competence and autonomy satisfaction. However, competition is inherently an interpersonal activity, even if opponents are strangers or anonymous. In competition there are both people with you, and against you. Thus, as with its complex nature with respect to motivation, competition has a varied impact on the third basic psychological need in SDT—the need for *relatedness*. SDT argues that relatedness, as a basic need, is fundamental to wellness. It is also something that is determined by how others treat one, including whether they objectify the person, or respect them as an autonomous agent (Ryan & Deci, 2017).

Typically, one thinks of competition as dividing people via the idea of conflict. Moreover, because the goal of experimental studies of competition is isolating the effects of competition per se, participants are usually strangers with no prior relationship (Kilduff et al., 2010). Findings in such settings indicate that, in comparison to non-competitive and cooperative situations, competition generally results in lower interpersonal attraction between participants (e.g., see Stanne et al., 1999). However, in contrast to laboratory settings, in many competitive settings within real-world organizations such as sport leagues, game clubs, businesses, and classrooms, participants are embedded in ongoing relationships that can be enhanced or harmed by elements of competition, especially those related to teamwork, controlling pressures, and autonomy-support.

COMPETITION BETWEEN (AND COOPERATION WITHIN) GROUPS/TEAMS

Although competition between individuals may, under certain conditions, rupture relationships, teaming up with others to compete can do the opposite—it can build relatedness. In fact, one of the most often reported positive experiences associated with competition is that of camaraderie. Team competitions introduce teammates, and with teammates come the prospect for intragroup cooperation, even during intergroup competition (Tauer & Harackiewicz, 2004). Teammates give competitors opportunities for collaboration, interpersonal support, and working together, ways of interacting that enable need satisfaction experiences, including not only relatedness satisfaction but also autonomy and competence satisfaction (Standage et al., 2005). These peer-to-peer (teammate) interactions and relationships, over time, give rise to a prevailing interpersonal climate.

Demonstrating the power of team collaboration, Adachi et al. (2016) examined whether playing violent video games together with an outgroup member can improve intergroup attitudes. In an initial experiment they had Canadians play a violent video game (*Call of Duty: Black Ops*) against zombies, either independently (i.e., at the same time but solo) or as a team with either a fellow Canadian or, alternatively, with a (supposed) University of Buffalo participant. As expected, cooperative team play significantly improved pro-outgroup participant attitudes and behavior, effects explained by heightened feelings of being psychologically connected and on the same side. In a second experiment similar effects were found whether teaming up for violent or nonviolent video gaming. Playing together as a team, even for these short intervals, led to a reduction in prejudice toward both University of Buffalo students and Americans more generally from pre-game to post-game. Such research shows that working together toward a common competitive goal can increase cohesion and relatedness, even among groups comprised of out-group members (see also Adachi et al., 2014).

However, whether teammates support each other varies, and a team or work groups' climate is often strongly influenced by the general coaching or leadership climate (proposition 4). This was nicely illustrated in a study from Hodge and Lonsdale (2011). Studying competitive players from a variety of sports, they reported that autonomy-supportive coaching styles predicted teammates' prosocial behavior toward teammates, an association that was mediated by autonomous motivation. More controlled motivation was, in contrast, associated with higher antisocial behavior toward teammates, as well as toward opponents, an effect mediated by moral disengagement (Bandura, 2002).

COMPETITION WITHIN GROUPS

Although between-group competitions can clearly occasion greater within-group cohesion and acceptance, competition *within* organizations or groups sometimes can do the opposite. The interpersonal climate that emerges among teammates or colleagues sometimes encourages strivings for improvement, task mastery, interpersonal inclusion, relational support, and working together (a relationship-supportive, task-involving interpersonal climate). Yet on some teams, and especially within organizations or teams where leaders make rewards or status contingent on competitive outcomes between team members, the interpersonal climate can be one of social comparison, social dominance struggles, normative ability hierarchies, interpersonal conflicts, and ego-involvement (Ntoumanis & Vazou, 2005). Task-involving interpersonal climates tend to be informational and thus enhance need satisfaction and intrinsic motivation, while ego-involving interpersonal climates tend to be controlling and thus promote need frustration that undermines intrinsic motivation (Hodge & Gucciardi, 2015).

Anderson et al. (2007) interviewed mid-career scientists about the influence of competition on their professional peer relationships and scientific work. Findings suggested that competitions related to the distribution of resources and prizes were perceived as leading to less openness and sharing of information and methods, decreased ability for others to use one's work, distortions in the peer-review process, harm to personal relationships, and sometimes questionable research practices.

Clearly, although competition mobilizes people toward an end, it also can pit people against each other in ways that can damage teamwork and other organizational goals. Again, this points out the dual nature of competitive settings which can be a positive or negative influence on relatedness, as a function of one's motives and goals.

Competition's Bright and Dark Sides

The basic premise of CET is that external events, interpersonal contexts, and intrapersonal events can be experienced as informational and thus supportive of psychological needs and intrinsic motivation, or as controlling and thus undermining of psychological needs and intrinsic motivation. Given this core premise, it follows that it is possible to present the competitive experience in an informational, needs-supportive, and intrinsic motivation-friendly way, or oppositely in ways that are more controlling or amotivating. As shown in Figure 11.1, CET argues that by decreasing the salience of competition's controlling, pressuring, and needs-frustrating elements and increasing the salience of its informational and needs-satisfying elements, competitors' intrinsic motivation and positive experiences can be enhanced.

Competition is not inherently controlling. Instead, all the elements displayed in Figure 11.1 that flow from an initial competitive set are variables, each of which can be presented in either an informational or a controlling way. The interpersonal climate, influenced by leadership, can be autonomy-supportive or controlling, performance goals can feel controlling or informational, feedback can communicate effectance or ineffectance, rewards can be offered in controlling or competence-affirming ways, and engagement can be task-involved or ego-involved.

One primary tipping point that determines whether the competitive set tilts toward a controlling or an informational orientation is the leader's motivating style. Although we discussed this issue under CET proposition 4, we highlight this particular tipping point again because motivating style has been shown to affect all the elements of competition displayed in Figure 11.1 (Reeve & Cheon, 2021). Guided by SDT, formal autonomy-supportive interventions have been developed and implemented. What all of these experimentally-based interventions have shown is that (1) leaders (e.g., coaches, mentors, teachers) can learn how to be more autonomy supportive and less controlling and, when they do, (2) those they supervise (e.g., athletes, students) benefit in important ways, including greater engagement, more need satisfaction, and enhanced intrinsic motivation (Reeve & Cheon, 2014, 2021).

As one case in point, consider the experimentally-based intervention study in which a group of SDT theorists were invited to work with a national team of athletes who were preparing for the Paralympic games (Cheon, Reeve, Lee, & Lee, 2015). We highlight this intervention study because this particular competitive situation, prior to the intervention, featured all the "Controlling Elements" entries in Figure 11.1, but none of the "Informational Elements" entries, largely because the pressure to win was so exaggerated. Thirty-three professional coaches from ten different Olympic sports (e.g., swimming, archery) were randomly assigned into either an autonomy-supportive intervention experimental condition or a no-intervention control condition. In the control group, athletes

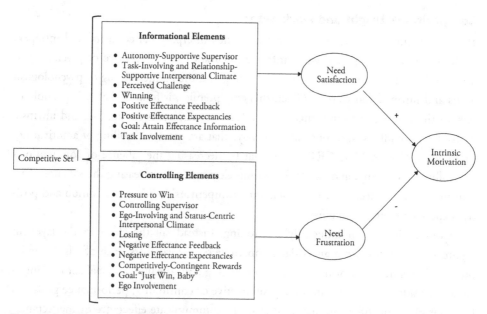

Figure 11.1 The competitive set introduces a variety of informational elements that support need satisfaction and intrinsic motivation, as well as a variety of controlling elements that promote need frustration and undermine intrinsic motivation.

and coaches experienced dramatic longitudinal declines in a multitude of measures of motivation, engagement, and functioning during the two months of intense training leading up to the Games. In the intervention group, however, none of the measures of motivation (including need satisfaction and need frustration), engagement, and functioning deteriorated but were, instead, maintained. One interesting finding was that coaches who learned how to be more autonomy supportive showed a strong increase in their job satisfaction during the otherwise intensely pressuring training months. Interestingly, athletes of the intervention-enabled autonomy-supportive coaches not only had more positive experiences, but won significantly more Olympic medals than did the athletes of coaches who relied on their "practice as usual" (i.e., controlling) motivating style. This shows how a competitive setting can be *both* performance supportive and psychological need supportive.

Competition's Dark Side

Controlling and need thwarting elements can bring out the dark side of competition, with effects that go well beyond diminished intrinsic motivation. "Dark side" is a strong term, but it highlights that, when competition is made to feature highly controlling elements, it can, via pressures and need frustrations, foster problematic attitudes and behaviors such as an acceptance of cheating, doping, poor sportspersonship, and objectifying opponents.

ACCEPTANCE OF CHEATING

Acceptance of cheating is an antisocial attitude that refers to endorsement of rule violations and unfair play (Lee et al., 2007). Acceptance of cheating is considered to be antisocial because it inflicts volitional harm on others, as its purpose is to achieve an illegitimate advantage or gain at the expense of one's competitors. In a sports context, it is strongly associated with antisocial behaviors and poor sportspersonship (Ntoumanis et al., 2012).

Competition does not cause acceptance of cheating, but competitive settings can introduce elements that may do so. Intense controlling coaching—the kind that manifests in yelling, shaming, and intimidating, which itself is often a product of the pressure to win, produces psychological need frustrations in competitors. This experience of need frustration (along with the negative emotions it triggers, such as anger) has been shown to be a direct antecedent of acceptance of cheating (Cheon et al., 2018). Yet when competitors are randomly assigned to autonomy-supportive supervision, they experience gains in basic psychological need satisfactions, as well as declines in need frustrations, and because of these benefits, lower acceptance of cheating (Cheon et al., 2018).

DOPING

Doping refers to the use of illegal performance-enhancing drugs and methods to improve performance. Doping is considered to represent maladaptive functioning because it violates the rules of competition, violates the spirit of sport, and can lead to health risks. Like cheating, competition does not cause a propensity to engage in doping, but it may introduce elements that do so. Ego-involved athletes who compete with controlled motivations (external regulation, introjected regulation) and who are surrounded by teammates who dope are more inclined to engage in doping behavior, while task-involved athletes are less inclined to do so (Ntoumanis et al., 2014). Donahue et al. (2006) reported that the more intrinsically motivated athletes were, the more they expressed more sportsperson-like attitudes and less likely they were to use performance-enhancing drugs. Similar findings were derived from a sample of Olympic-level athletes (Barkoukis et al., 2011), and Hodge et al. (2013), in contrast, found that it was coaches' controlling behaviors that predicted risk to such drug use.

Training coaches how to be more autonomy supportive in their communication with athletes can decrease athletes' doping intentions and attitudes, effects that occur partly because training in autonomy-supportive techniques enhances coaches' confidence to create and sustain an anti-doping, morally engaged, team culture (Ntoumanis et al., 2014; Ntoumanis & Standage, 2009).

POST-COMPETITION AGGRESSION

A common phenomenon observable by anyone surrounding competitive settings is post-competition aggression. One place this has been studied is in video games, where competition is a common feature (Rigby & Ryan, 2011). Przybylski et al. (2014) demonstrated how elements in games that frustrated feelings of competence predicted post-game indicators of aggression, a result found across violent and non-violent contents. Further looking at post-game aggression in an experimental setting, Adachi and Willoughby (2011) compared the effects competitive and non-competitive games, crossed with violent and non-violent game contents. They similarly reported that whereas violent game contents did not raise aggressive behavior compared with nonviolent contents, more competitive games produced greater levels of aggressive behavior compared to less competitive ones. They concluded that competition, rather than violence, may be the video game characteristic that has the larger influence on aggressive behavior.

Subsequently, Addachi and Willougby (2013), using longitudinal methods, investigated the longer-term relations between video game competition and aggression. They reasoned that if the associations between video games and aggression is due to competitive elements rather than violent contents, then other competitive activities such as competitive gambling should also predict aggression. They thus tested what they called a "socialization" hypothesis, that competitive video game play and competitive gambling lead to more aggression over time, against a "selection" hypothesis that aggressive people are prone to more competitive game play and competitive gambling over time. To test this, they surveyed adolescents over grades nine through twelve about their aggressive behaviors, video game use, and gambling. Results from longitudinal modeling suggested that greater competitive game play and competitive gambling predicted higher levels of aggression over time, supporting the socialization hypothesis. That is, competitive settings may generally foster post-event aggression, perhaps via the ego-involvement they can engender and the competence frustrations that can inevitably occur.

COMPETITIVE ETHICS AND POOR SPORTSPERSONSHIP

The topic of competition and its varied motivations brings up a closely related topic concerning what might be considered, if not the ethics of competition, perhaps its code of honor—namely being a good "sport" or competitor. Interesting, particularly from an SDT perspective, what makes a good competitor is someone who is focused on the informational aspects of competition rather than the controlled, ego-involved, sides of competition. Good competitors do not gloat in victory or discount opponents in a loss. They acknowledge good play, and the outcome is not (contrary to the classic Lombardi adage) the "only" thing or even the most important thing (e.g., good sportspersons would not cheat to win).

Exemplifying this within SDT research was a study by Vansteenkiste et al. (2010), in which they looked at the extrinsic versus intrinsic goal orientations of football (soccer) competitors in relation to objectifying opponents. These researchers found that game-to-game variation in the degree to which coaches' talk and behavior pre-game was need thwarting (e.g., controlling, pressuring, critical) related positively to variation in players' adoption of an objectifying stance, which, in turn, related to anti-social behavior oriented toward opponents, the referees, and even teammates. Supplementary analyses indicated that these effects also obtained for an objective marker of moral functioning (i.e., number of yellow cards) and further that players' level of competition-contingent pay related to their anti-social behavior via an objectifying stance. In short, competition can be intrinsically motivating especially when people are good sports, such that skills get fairly tested. But controlling conditions and rewards can often conduce to bad sport behavior.

It appears that the very conditions that are associated with need support and intrinsic motivation among competitors are the same ones associated with better competitive behaviors. In fact, studies showed that need satisfaction predicts more autonomous motivation in competitive athletes, and autonomous motivation in turn predicted more moral sport-related conduct and attitudes (Mallia et al., 2019; Ntoumanis & Standage, 2009). Bottom line: In focusing on being a "good sport" or "good competitor," coaches and mentors are also focusing on intrinsic motivation—because they will be emphasizing the inherently satisfying aspects of competition and mastery, and deemphasizing the controlling and ego involving elements. In doing so, they are also furthering all competitors' (including opponents') well-being and positive experience.

Conclusion

Competitive settings offer features that, depending on their relative salience, can positively or negatively influence the subsequent motivation, performance, and wellness of competitors. These ups and downs associated with competition are addressed by cognitive evaluation theory, a mini-theory within the larger framework of SDT, which suggests that how various elements common to competitive settings impact motivation and wellness via their effects on competitors' basic psychological needs for competence, autonomy, and relatedness. Informational, autonomy- and competence-supportive, conditions increase intrinsic motivation, whereas controlling, need-frustrating conditions decrease intrinsic motivation and contribute to amotivation and negative experience.

CET thus provides a framework that can be readily applied. Practitioners from sport coaches to classroom teachers, and from video-games designers to human resource experts can create competitive settings that are relatively high in their informational salience and basic psychological need-satisfactions, and relatively low on perceptions of external control, self-esteem pressures, and exclusion, thereby minimizing need-frustrations. When this occurs not only will competitors have more positive experiences and well-being; they are also more likely to persist in the competitive activity over time.

Although we focused on competition using the lens of CET, it is also the case that other mini-theories within SDT are highly relevant. For example, studies show that theories about intrinsic and extrinsic aspirations ("goal content theory"), individual differences ("causality orientation theory"), internalization ("organismic integration theory"), well-being and vitality ("basic psychological needs theory"), and relationships ("relationship motivation theory") all bear on competitive settings. Future research and reviews can focus on these important applications of the theory. We also note that many of the experimental studies in this area focus on pure competition between strangers, and often on winners, and more research on the nuanced presentations and social complexities of real-world competitive settings for both winners and losers, and non-strangers, are needed. Nonetheless, the research to date stemming from CET tells an important story. People can enjoy and be inspired by competition, and they can be demoralized and discouraged by it. Therefore, critical to designing competitive settings is an emphasis on elements that can support participants' experiences of autonomy, competence, and relatedness.

References

Abuhamdeh, S., Csikszentmihalyi, M., & Jalal, B. (2015). Enjoying the possibility of defeat: Outcome uncertainty, suspense, and intrinsic motivation. *Motivation and Emotion, 39*(1), 1–10.

Adachi, P. J., Hodson, G., Willoughby, T., Blank, C., & Ha, A. (2016). From outgroups to allied forces: Effect of intergroup cooperation in violent and nonviolent video games on boosting favorable outgroup attitudes. *Journal of Experimental Psychology: General, 145*(3), 259.

Adachi, P. J. C., Hodson, G., Willoughby, T., & Zanette, S. (2014). Brothers and sisters in arms: Intergroup cooperation in a violent shooter game can reduce intergroup bias. *Psychology of Violence, 5*(4), 455–462.

Adachi, P. J. C., & Willoughby, T. (2011). The effect of video game competition and violence on aggressive behavior: Which characteristic has the greatest influence? *Psychology of Violence, 1,* 259–274.

Adachi, P. J. C., & Willoughby, T. (2013). Demolishing the competition: The longitudinal link between competitive video games, competitive gambling, and aggression. *Journal of Youth and Adolescence, 42,* 1090–1104.

Amado, D., Maestre, M., Montero-Carretero, C., Sánchez-Miguel, P. A., & Cervelló, E. (2019). Associations between self-determined motivation, team potency, and self-talk in team sports. *Journal of Human Kinetics, 70*(1), 245–259.

Anderson, M. S., Ronning, E. A., De Vries, R., & Martinson, B. C. (2007). The perverse effects of competition on scientists' work and relationships. *Science and Engineering Ethics, 13*(4), 437–461.

Baily, R., Cope, E. J., & Pearce, G. (2013). Why do children take part in, and remain involved in sport? A literature review and discussion of implications for sports coaches *International Journal of Coaching Science, 7*(1), 56–75.

Bandura, A. (2002). Selective moral disengagement in the exercise of moral agency. *Journal of Moral Education, 31*, 101–119.

Barkoukis, V., Lazuras, L., Tsorbatzoudis, H., & Rodafinos, A. (2011). Motivational and sportspersonship profiles of elite athletes in relation to doping behavior. *Psychology of Sport and Exercise, 12*(3), 205–212.

Bartholomew, K. J., Ntoumanis, N., Mouratidis, A., Katartzi, E., Thøgersen-Ntoumani, C., & Vlachopoulos, S. (2018). Beware of your teaching style: A school-year long investigation of controlling teaching and student motivational experiences. *Learning and Instruction, 53*, 50–63.

Bartholomew, K. J., Ntoumanis, N., Ryan, R. M., & Thøgersen-Ntoumani, C. (2011). Psychological need thwarting in the sport context: Assessing the darker side of athletic experience. *Journal of Sport and Exercise Psychology, 33*, 75–102.

Bartholomew, K. J., Ntoumanis, N., & Thøgersen-Ntoumani, C. (2010). The controlling interpersonal style in a coaching context: development and initial validation of a psychometric scale. *Journal of Sport & Exercise Psychology, 32*, 193–216.

Carpentier, J., & Mageau, G. A. (2013). When change-oriented feedback enhances motivation, well-being, and performance: A look at autonomy-supportive feedback in sport. *Psychology of Sport and Exercise, 14*, 423–435.

Cheon, S. H., Reeve, J., Lee, J., & Lee, Y. (2015). Giving and receiving autonomy support in a high-stakes sport context: A field-based experiment during the 2012 London Paralympic Games. *Psychology of Sport and Exercise, 19*, 59–69.

Cheon, S. H., Reeve, J., & Ntoumanis, N. (2018). A needs-supportive intervention to help PE teachers enhance students' prosocial behavior and diminish antisocial behavior. *Psychology of Sport and Exercise, 35*, 74–88.

Cumming, S. P., Smoll, F. L., Smith, R. E., & Grossbard, J. R. (2007). Is winning everything? The relative contributions of motivational climate and won–lost percentage in youth sports. *Journal of Applied Sport Psychology, 19*(3), 322–336.

Curran, T., Hill, A. P., Hall, H. K., & Jowett, G. E. (2014). Perceived coach behaviors and athletes' engagement and disaffection in youth sport: The mediating role of the psychological needs. *International Journal of Sport Psychology, 45*, 559–580.

Curran, T., Hill, A., & Niemiec, C. (2013). A conditional process model of children's behavioral engagement and behavioral disaffection in sport based on self-determination theory. *Journal of Sport & Exercise Psychology, 35*, 30–43.

Deci, E. L., Betley, G., Kahle, J., Abrams, L., & Porac, J. (1981). When trying to win: Competition and intrinsic motivation. *Personality and Social Psychology Bulletin, 7*, 79–83.

Deci, E. L., Koestner, R., & Ryan, R. M. (1999). A meta-analytic review of experiments examining the effects of extrinsic rewards on intrinsic motivation. *Psychological Bulletin, 126*(6), 627–668.

Deci, E. L., & Ryan, R. M. (1980). The empirical exploration of intrinsic motivational processes. In L. Berkowitz (Ed.), *Advances in experimental social psychology* (pp. 39–80). Academic Press.

Di Domenico, S., & Ryan, R. M. (2017). The emerging neuroscience of intrinsic motivation: A new frontier in self-determination research. *Frontiers in Human Neuroscience, 11*, 145.

Donahue, E. G., Miquelon, P., Valois, P., Goulet, C., Buist, A., & Vallerand, R. J. (2006). A motivational model of performance-enhancing substance use in elite athletes. *Journal of Sport and Exercise Psychology, 28*(4), 511–520.

Elliot, A. J., Weissman, D., Hangen, E., & Thorstenson, C. A. (2021). Social comparison information, performance expectancy, and performance goal adoption. *Motivation Science, 7*(1), 56–67.

Epstein, J. A., & Harackiewicz, J. M. (1992). Winning is not enough: The effects of competition and achievement orientation on intrinsic interest. *Personality and Social Psychology Bulletin, 18*, 128–138.

Evans, P., & Ryan, R. M. (In press). Intrinsic and extrinsic motivations in music. In G. McPherson (Ed.), *The Oxford handbook of music performance* (Vol. 1). Oxford University Press.

Fang, H., He, B., Fu, H., Zhang, H., Mo, Z., & Meng, L. (2018). A surprising source of self-motivation: Prior competence frustration strengthens one's motivation to win in another competence-supportive activity. *Frontiers in Human Neuroscience, 12*, 314.

Fong, C. J., Patall, E. A., Vasquez, A. C., & Stautberg, S. (2019). A meta-analysis of negative feedback on intrinsic motivation. *Educational Psychology Review*, *31*, 121–162.

Frederick, C. M., & Ryan, R. M. (1995). Self-determination in sport: A review using cognitive evaluation theory. *International Journal of Sport Psychology*, *26*, 5–23.

Frederick-Recascino, C. M., & Schuster-Smith, H. (2003). Competition and intrinsic motivation in physical activity: A comparison of two groups. *Journal of Sport Behavior*, *26*(3), 240–254.

Gallaway, T. (1997). *Inner tennis*. Random House.

Garcia, S. M., Tor, A., & Schiff, T. M. (2013). The psychology of competition: A social comparison perspective. *Perspectives on Psychological Science*, *8*(6), 634–650.

Hanus, M. D., & Fox, J. (2015). Assessing the effects of gamification in the classroom: A longitudinal study on intrinsic motivation, social comparison, satisfaction, effort, and academic performance. *Computers & Education*, *80*, 152–161.

Haerens, L., Krijgsman, C., Mouratidis, A., Borghouts, L., Cardon, G., & Aelterman, N. (2018). How does knowledge about the criteria for an upcoming test relate to adolescents' situational motivation in physical education? A self-determination theory perspective. *European Physical Education Review*, *20*(11), 1–19.

Henderlong, J., & Lepper, M. R. (2002). The effects of praise on children's intrinsic motivation: A review and synthesis. *Psychological Bulletin*, *128*(5), 774–795.

Hodge, K., & Gucciardi, D. F. (2015). Antisocial and prosocial behavior in sport: the role of motivational climate, basic psychological needs, and moral disengagement. *Journal of Sport & Exercise Psychology*, *37*, 257–273.

Hodge, K., Hargreaves, E. A., Gerrard, D., & Lonsdale, C. (2013). Psychological mechanisms underlying doping attitudes in sport: Motivation and moral disengagement. *Journal of Sport and Exercise Psychology*, *35*(4), 419–432.

Hodge, K., & Lonsdale, C. (2011). Prosocial and antisocial behavior in sport: The role of coaching style, autonomous vs. controlled motivation, and moral disengagement. *Journal of Sport and Exercise Psychology*, *33*(4), 527–547.

Hom, Jr., H. L., & Maxwell, F. R. (1983). The impact of task difficulty expectations on intrinsic motivation. *Motivation and Emotion*, *7*, 19–24.

Jones, M., Meijen, C., McCarthy, P. J., & Sheffield, D. (2009). A theory of challenge and threat states in athletes. *International Review of Sport and Exercise Psychology*, *2*(2), 161–180.

Kilduff, G. J., Elfenbein, H. A., & Staw, B. M. (2010). The psychology of rivalry: A relationally dependent analysis of competition. *Academy of Management Journal*, *53*, 943–969.

Koestner, R., Ryan, R. M., Bernieri, F., & Holt, K (1984). Setting limits on children's behavior: The differential effects of controlling versus informational styles on children's intrinsic motivation and creativity. *Journal of Personality*, *54*, 233–248.

Lee, M. J., Whitehead, J., & Ntoumanis, N. (2007). Development of the Attitudes to Moral Decision-making in Youth Sport Questionnaire (AMDYSQ). *Psychology of Sport and Exercise*, *8*, 369–392.

Lee, W., & Reeve, J. (2017). Identifying the neural substrates of intrinsic motivation during task performance. *Cognitive, Affective, and Behavioral Neuroscience*, *17*, 939–953.

Lee, W., & Reeve, J. (2020). Remembering pleasure and personal meaning from episodes of intrinsic motivation: An fMRI study. *Motivation and Emotion*, *44*, 810–818.

McAuley, E., & Tammen, V. V. (1989). The effects of subjective and objective competitive outcomes on intrinsic motivation. *Journal of Sport and Exercise Psychology*, *11*, 84–93.

Mageau, G. A., & Vallerand, R. J. (2003). The coach–athlete relationship: A motivational model. *Journal of Sports Sciences*, *21*, 883–904.

Mallia, L., Lucidi, F., Zelli, A., Chirico, A., & Hagger, M. S. (2019). Predicting moral attitudes and antisocial behavior in young team sport athletes: A self-determination theory perspective. *Journal of Applied Social Psychology*, *49*(4), 249–263.

Moore, L. J., Vine, S. J., Wilson, M. R., & Freeman, P. (2012). The effect of challenge and threat states on performance: An examination of potential mechanisms. *Psychophysiology*, *49*(10), 1417–1425.

Moore, L. J., Wilson, M. R., Vine, S. J., Coussens, A. H., & Freeman, P. (2013). Champ or chump?: Challenge and threat states during pressurized competition. *Journal of Sport & Exercise Psychology*, *35*(6), 551–562.

Mouratidis, A., Lens, W., & Vansteenkiste, M. (2010). How you provide corrective feedback makes a difference: The motivating role of communicating in an autonomy-supportive way. *Journal of Sport and Exercise Psychology*, *32*, 619–637.

Ntoumanis, N. (2012). A self-determination theory perspective on motivation in sport and physical education: Current trends and possible future directions. In G. C. Roberts & D. C. Treasure (Eds.), *Advances in motivation in sport and exercise* (pp. 91–128). Human Kinetics.

Ntoumanis, N., Ng, J. Y. Y., Barkoukis, V., & Backhouse, S. (2014). Personal and psychosocial predictors of doping use in physical activity settings: A meta-analysis. *Sports Medicine, 44*, 1603–1624.

Ntoumanis, N., & Standage, M. (2009). Morality in sport: A self-determination theory perspective. *Journal of Applied Sport Psychology, 21*, 365–380.

Ntoumanis, N., Taylor, I. M., & Thøgersen-Ntoumani, C. (2012). A longitudinal examination of coach and peer motivational climates in youth sport: Implications for moral attitudes, well-being, and behavioral investment. *Developmental Psychology, 48*, 213–223.

Ntoumanis, N., & Vazou, S. (2005). Peer motivational climate in youth sport: Measurement development and validation. *Journal of Sport and Exercise Psychology, 27*, 432–455.

Oliver, E. J., Markland, D., & Hardy, J. (2010). Interpretation of self-talk and post-lecture affective states of higher education students: A self-determination theory perspective. *British Journal of Educational Psychology, 80*, 307–323.

Patall, E. A., Cooper, H., & Robinson, J. C. (2008). The effects of choice on intrinsic motivation and related outcomes: A meta-analysis of research findings. *Psychological Bulletin, 134*(2), 270–300.

Pelletier, L. G., Séguin-Lévesque, C., & Legault, L. (2002). Pressure from above and pressure from below as determinants of teachers' motivation and teaching behaviors. *Journal of Educational Psychology, 94*(1), 186–196.

Peng, W., Lin, J.-H., Pfeiffer, K. A., & Winn, B. (2012). Need satisfaction supportive game features as motivational determinants: An experimental study of a self-determination-theory-guided exer-game. *Media Psychology, 15*(2), 175–196.

Przybylski, A. K., Deci, E. L., Rigby, C. S., & Ryan, R. M. (2014). Competence-impeding electronic games and players' aggressive feelings, thoughts, and behaviors. *Journal of Personality and Social Psychology, 106*(3), 441–457.

Reeve, J. (2009). Why teachers adopt a controlling motivating style toward students and how they can become more autonomy supportive. *Educational Psychologist, 44*, 159–178.

Reeve, J., & Cheon, S. H. (2014). An intervention-based program of research on teachers' motivating styles. In S. Karabenick & T. Urdan (Eds.) *Advances in motivation and achievement: Motivational interventions* (Vol. 18, pp. 293–339). Emerald Group Publishing.

Reeve, J., & Cheon, S. H. (2021). Autonomy-supportive teaching: Its malleability, benefits, and potential to improve educational practice. *Educational Psychologist, 56*(1), 54–77.

Reeve, J., Cole, S. G., & Olson, B. C. (1986). The Zeigarnik effect and intrinsic motivation: Are they the same? *Motivation and Emotion, 10*, 231–243.

Reeve, J., & Deci, E. L. (1996). Elements of the competitive situation that affect intrinsic motivation. *Personality and Social Psychology Bulletin, 22*, 24–33.

Reeve, J., & Lee, W. (2019). A neuroscience perspective on basic psychological needs. *Journal of Personality, 87*(1), 102–114.

Reeve, J., Olson, B. C., & Cole, S. G. (1985). Motivation and performance: Two consequences of winning and losing in competition. *Motivation and Emotion, 9*, 291–298.

Reeve, J., Olson, B. C., & Cole, S. G. (1987). Intrinsic motivation in competition: The intervening role of four individual differences following objective competence information. *Journal of Research in Personality, 21*, 148–170.

Rigby, C. S., & Ryan, R. M. (2011). *Glued to Games: The attractions, promise and perils of video games and virtual worlds*. Praeger.

Ryan, R. M. (1982). Control and information in the intrapersonal sphere: An extension of cognitive evaluation theory. *Journal of Personality and Social Psychology, 43*, 450–461.

Ryan, R. M., & Deci, E. L. (2017). *Self-determination theory: Basic psychological needs in motivation, development, and wellness*. Guilford Press.

Ryan, R. M., & Deci, E. L. (2019). Brick by brick: The origins, development, and future of self-determination theory. In A. J. Elliot (Ed.), *Advances in Motivation Science, Vol. 6* (pp. 111–156). Elsevier Inc. https://doi.org/10.1016/bs.adms.2019.01.001

Ryan, R. M., & Rigby, C. S. (2020). Motivational foundations of game-based learning. In J. L. Plass, R. E. Mayer, & B. D. Homer (Eds.), *Handbook of Game-based Learning*. MIT Press.

Ryan, R. M., Ryan, W. S., & Di Domenico, S. I. (2019). Effects of rewards on self-determination and intrinsic motivation: Revisiting Deci (1971). In P. J. Corr (Ed.), *Revisiting the Classic Studies: Personality and Individual Differences*. London, UK: Sage.

Standage, M., Duda, J., & Pensgaard, A. M. (2005). The effect of competitive outcome and task-involving, ego-involving, and cooperative structures on the psychological well-being of individuals engaged in a co-ordination task: A self-determination approach. *Motivation and Emotion, 29*(1), 41–68.

Stanne, M. B., Johnson, D. W., & Johnson, R. T. (1999). Does competition enhance or inhibit motor performance: A meta-analysis. *Psychological Bulletin, 125*(1), 133–154.

Studer, B., Van Dijk, H., Handermann, R., & Knecht, S. (2016). Increasing self-directed training in neurore-habilitation patients through competition. *Progress in Brain Research, 229*, 367–388.

Tauer, J. M., & Harackiewicz, J. M. (1999). Winning isn't everything: Competition, achievement motivation, and intrinsic motivation. *Journal of Experimental Social Psychology, 35*, 209–238.

Tauer, J. M., & Harackiewicz, J. M. (2004). The effects of cooperation and competition on intrinsic motivation and performance. *Journal of Personality and Social Psychology, 81*(6), 849–861.

Vallerand, R. J., Gauvin, L. I., & Halliwell, W. R. (1986a). Effects of zero-sum competition on children's intrinsic motivation and perceived competence. *The Journal of Social Psychology, 126*(4), 465–472.

Vallerand, R. J., Gauvin, L. I., & Halliwell, W. R. (1986b). Negative effects of competition on children's intrinsic motivation. *The Journal of Social Psychology, 126*(5), 649–656.

Vallerand, R. J., & Reid, G. (1984). On the causal effects of perceived competence on intrinsic motivation: A test of cognitive evaluation theory. *Journal of Sport Psychology, 6*(1), 94–102.

Vansteenkiste, M., Aelterman, N., De Muynck, G.-J., Haerens, L., Patall, E., & Reeve, J. (2018). Fostering personal meaning and self-relevance: A self-determination theory perspective on internalization. *Journal of Experimental Education, 86*, 30–49.

Vansteenkiste, M., & Deci, E. L. (2003). Competitively contingent rewards and intrinsic motivation: Can losers remain motivated? *Motivation and Emotion, 27*(4), 273–299.

Vansteenkiste, M., Mouratidis, A., & Lens, W. (2010). Detaching reasons from aims: Fair play and well-being in soccer as a function of pursuing performance-approach goals for autonomous or controlling reasons. *Journal of Sport and Exercise Psychology, 32*(2), 217–242.

Vansteenkiste, M., Simons, J., Soenens, B., & Lens, W. (2004). How to become a persevering exerciser? The importance of providing a clear, future intrinsic goal in an autonomy-supportive manner. *Journal of Sport & Exercise Psychology, 26*, 232–249.

Weinberg, R. S., & Ragan, J. (1979). Effects of competition, success/failure, and sex on intrinsic motivation. *Research Quarterly. American Alliance for Health, Physical Education, Recreation and Dance, 50*(3), 503–510.

Weiss, M. R., Amorose, A. J., & Kipp, L. E. (2012). Youth motivation and participation in sport and physical activity. In R. M. Ryan (Ed.), *The Oxford handbook of human motivation* (pp. 520–553). Oxford University Press.

White, R. W. (1959). Motivation reconsidered: The concept of competence. *Psychological Review, 66*(5), 297–333.

White, M. H., & Sheldon, K. M. (2014). The contract year syndrome in the NBA and MLB: A classic under-mining pattern. *Motivation and Emotion, 38*(2), 196–205.

Envy: A Prevalent Emotion in Competitive Settings

Ronit Montal-Rosenberg *and* Simone Moran

Abstract

Envy is a prevalent emotional response to comparisons individuals make with superior others. In this article, the authors review the psychological literature on envy and discuss the relevance of envy to competitive contexts, positing a bidirectional relationship between envy and competition. The authors begin by presenting the various conceptualizations of envy, emphasizing the widely accepted notion that envy can entail distinct consequences—pulling down the envied target (i.e., malicious or destructive consequences) versus self-improvement (i.e., benign or constructive consequences). In the remaining parts of the article, the authors provide an elaborate discussion of the malicious (destructive) and benign (constructive) consequences of envy in terms of cognitions, intentions, behaviors, and wellbeing. The authors proceed by discussing the determinants of these types of envy consequences, categorized into factors related to the situation, factors related to the superior envied target, and characteristics of the envious individual. Finally, the authors discuss interventions that may reduce the destructive consequences of envy among competitors.

Key Words: envy, competition, emotional response, self-improvement, intention, wellbeing, malicious consequences, benign consequences, social comparison

Envy is a prevalent, unpleasant emotional response to unfavorable social comparisons; that is, comparisons people make with others whom they perceive as superior to themselves. As such, envy is highly relevant in the context of competition. Envy has been identified as a universal, deep-seated, and powerful emotion, and as essential for understanding human experience (Aristotle, 1991; Bacon, 1890; Foster et al., 1972; Heider, 1958; Klein, 1957; Schoeck, 1969; Smith et al., 1999). It is common across cultures (Foster et al., 1972; Schoeck, 1969; Teitelbaum, 1976; Walcot, 1978), and has been demonstrated to impact a variety of domains, such as consumer behavior (Belk, 2011), organizational behavior (Duffy et al., 2012; Mouly & Sankaran, 2002; Vecchio, 1995, 2000), morality (Parks et al., 2002), and the development of stereotypes (Cuddy et al., 2007; Fiske, 2010), etc. In addition to being conceptualized as a dispositional trait (Gold, 1996; Smith et al., 1999), envy is defined as a situationally driven emotion—namely, as a state that occurs "when a person lacks another's superior quality, achievement, or possession, and either desires it or wishes that the other lacked it" (Parrott & Smith, 1993, p. 906).

Although envy, the focus of the current chapter, is often confused with jealousy, the literature distinguishes between the two (e.g., Andiappan & Dufour, 2020; Parrott & Smith, 1993; Smith et al., 1988). Jealousy pertains to a specific case of envy, whereby the superior *thing* that one desires or wishes the other lacked, is a significant relationship with another person (Hupka, 1991; Rorty, 1988). To put it differently, when we view the social comparison target as superior to ourselves, envy arises. When the superiority of the comparison target is related to the fact that the target threatens a relationship which we desire with a third party, jealousy arises (Andiappan & Dufour, 2020). Accordingly, envy typically involves *two* people (or two entities) and occurs when one lacks *something* enjoyed by another, whereas jealousy typically involves *three* people and occurs when one fears losing *someone* to another person.

Varying Conceptualizations of Envy

Envy was initially conceptualized as a uniform and hostile emotion with malicious interpersonal outcomes (e.g., Smith & Kim, 2007). From an evolutionary perspective, however, envy can also serve as a motivator for self-improvement. Specifically, envy is an emotion that alerts individuals to the benefits that rivals are enjoying, and thus can serve as a motivator for individuals to acquire those same benefits for themselves (Hill & Buss, 2006). Indeed, recent conceptualizations acknowledge the duality of envy, and posit that envy entails not only destructive but also constructive aspects. Specifically, it is currently recognized that envy can manifest in a desire to reduce the unfavorable gap by means of degrading the advantageous envied competitor (i.e., destructive or malicious motivations) or by attempting to improve ones' own position (i.e., constructive or benign motivations) (Duffy et al., 2012; Montal-Rosenberg & Moran, 2020; Van de Ven et al., 2009). However, there is some disagreement about the extent to which these two aspects represent two distinct emotions: malicious envy and benign envy (i.e., Dual Envy Theory), or merely varying consequences of the same emotion (i.e., Pain of Envy Theory).

According to the Dual Envy Theory (e.g., Van de Ven et al., 2009; Van de Ven et al., 2015), envy emanates in two distinct forms—malicious and benign—that vary not only in consequences but also in feelings and thoughts. Malicious envy is threat-oriented and entails hostile feelings, thoughts, and action tendencies aimed at harming the envied other. Benign envy is challenge-oriented and entails feelings, thoughts, and action tendencies aimed at self-improvement.

According to the Pain of Envy Theory, envy is a uniform emotion driven by pain (following an upward social comparison), which then leads to varying consequences in terms of action tendencies (Cohen-Charash & Larson, 2016, 2017; Cohen-Charash, 2009; Lange et al., 2018; Tai et al., 2012). Contrary to Dual Envy Theory, the benign and malicious envy aspects are merely deemed to represent different emergent consequences—constructive versus destructive—of a unified pain-driven emotion.

Importantly, whether viewing envy as a unified general pain-driven emotion with benign (constructive) and malicious (destructive) consequences, or as two separate emotions, there is agreement that envy can lead to diverse consequences—pulling down the envied target (i.e., malicious or destructive consequences) versus self-improvement (i.e., benign or constructive consequences)—that should be distinguished.

Envy and Competition

Competition is a potential catalyst of social comparisons (Duffy & Shaw, 2000). It typically involves allocating scarce resources and unequal outcomes—namely, differential rankings, winners, and losers—and thus leads people to compare themselves with others in order to assess their relative standing. Correspondingly, envy, which, as noted above, is a prevalent emotional response to upward social comparisons, is very common in competitive settings. In fact, Smith and Kim (2007) suggest that envy is the strongest, most prevalent emotional consequence of perceiving superior competitors (Smith & Kim, 2007). Supporting this notion, competitive feelings accompanying competitive situations have been shown to be positively related to feelings of envy (Ben-Ze'ev, 1990). Competing and losing in a competition was found to lead to feelings of envy toward the winner, or the superior contestant (Ben-Ze'ev, 1992; Kohn, 1992). In the organizational context, competitive reward structures (i.e., pay-for-performance) and competition over differential rewards (e.g., promotions, grants, valued assignments, or office space) have been posited to induce envy (Duffy & Shaw, 2000; Tesser, 1988; Vecchio, 2000).

Consistent with the literature on intensifiers of social comparisons (Festinger, 1954; Goethals & Darley, 1977; Hoffman et al., 1954; Suls & Wheeler, 2000; Tesser, 1988), envy is particularly likely to be evoked towards upward social comparison targets who are similar to the self (Goethals & Darley, 1977; Kilduff et al., 2010; Parrott, 1991; Salovey & Rodin, 1984; Salovey & Rothman, 1991; Schaubroeck & Lam, 2004; Tesser, 1991), and when the upward social comparison dimension is highly self-relevant (Hoffman et al., 1954; Salovey & Rodin, 1991; Silver & Sabini, 1978; Tesser, 1991). To that end, envy is likely to evolve among competitors, who likely share the goal of succeeding in the competition. Moreover, feelings of envy are likely to intensify as a function of the degree of similarity between the competitors (e.g., among people who work in the same department or organization, academics within the same discipline, contestants who compete in the same sports league), as well as the extent to which the competition is over resources, achievements, or rewards that competitors view as significant (e.g., valued promotions at the workplace, esteemed academic grants, cherished sports medals and awards).

In addition to being a consequence of competition, social comparisons are also an important cause of competitive behavior (Festinger, 1954; Garcia et al., 2013; Hoffman et al., 1954; Seta, 1982; Tesser, 1988). Correspondingly, envying superior others can impact

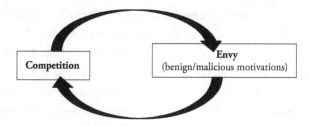

Figure 12.1 The bidirectional relationship between competition and envy. Competition frequently triggers envy towards the winner/superior contestant. Envy and its consequent motivations can in turn impact the desire to compete, as well as the type of competitive tactics that are employed, in an attempt to lessen or reverse the unfavorable gap.

the desire to compete, and the strategies that are employed in an attempt to lessen or reverse the unfavorable gap (Bers & Rodin, 1984).

As depicted in Figure 12.1, we propose that the link between envy and competition is bidirectional. Competition frequently triggers envy towards superior contestants, and envy, in turn, impacts the desire to compete as well as the competitive tactics that individuals employ in order to lessen or reverse the unfavorable gap. As we further discuss in this chapter, factors related to the competition (e.g., appraisals of the winners' deservingness and perceived control over outcomes), to the superior competitors (e.g., their perceived warmth, the extent to which they encounter failures, the type of pride they express), and to the under-performing competitors (e.g., their proneness to experience envy and its benign and malicious types), influence the emergence of envy and the type of consequent motivations (i.e., benign or constructive vs. malicious or destructive) that arise towards superior competitors. In turn, envy and the type of consequent motivations that it triggers influence the way people react to the competition and to their competitors. When benign or constructive envy motivations are aroused, people primarily attempt to improve their own position, whereas when malicious or destructive envy motivations are aroused, people primarily attempt to harm their competitors' positions.

Next, we review the literature pertaining to the varying malicious (destructive) and benign (constructive) consequences of envy in terms of cognitions, intentions, behaviors, and wellbeing. This is followed by discussing the literature on factors that are proposed to determine which type of envy consequences emerge—benign (constructive) versus malicious (destructive).

Consequences of Envy

Cognitive Consequences

Research investigating the effects of envy on cognition suggests that envy towards advantaged others leads to greater attention to and better recall of information about the advantaged targets (Hill et al., 2011). Envious (vs. control) participants invested more time in reading fictitious interviews with upward comparison targets and afterward, had better memory about this information.

Recent research differentiating between benign and malicious forms of envy (Crusius & Lange, 2014) suggests that the specific attentional focus of envious individuals varies as follows: (a) people who experience malicious envy, but not those who experience benign envy, focus more on the *envied person* than on the envied person's advantage; and (b) people who experience benign (compared to malicious) envy focus more on the *means* to improve their achievements. Specifically, in their experiments (Crusius & Lange, 2014), participants first recalled episodes that evoked either benign or malicious envy. They then completed a variant of the dot probe task, which is widely used to measure the deployment of attention (e.g., Bar-Haim et al., 2007). In this paradigm, participants are required to detect whether a dot appears on the right or left side of a computer screen. Importantly, before the dot appears, a pair of cues is displayed at the potential locations of the dot. If participants shift their attention to one of the two cues, they should react faster to a dot that subsequently appears at the location that is congruent rather than incongruent with the location of the attention capturing cue. In Cruise and Lange's (2014) work, these dot-preceding cues were manipulated to be the envied person's name, the envied object (e.g., an academic achievement), or means to achieve the envied outcome (e.g., books, slides, library in the case of recalling an academic-achievement related episode). Following recollection of malicious-envy (rather than benign-envy) episodes, dot detection was faster when the dot location was congruent with the envied person cue than when its location was congruent with the envied object cue. In contrast, after recalling benign-envy (rather than malicious-envy) episodes, trials in which the dot appeared at a location that was congruent with means to achieve the envied outcome cue led to faster detection times than trials in which the dot appeared at locations congruent with the envied person cue. Thus, participants who were maliciously envious of another person's academic achievement shifted their attention toward the person they envied. In contrast, participants who were benignly envious of another person's academic achievement, shifted their attention toward stimuli that represented objects conducive to improving academic performance.

As for perceptions, work highlighting malicious cognitions associated with envy implies that perceptual derogation and devaluation, such as dwelling on imagined or real weaknesses of the envied target, is one of the strategies used to cope with the unpleasant feelings of envy (Vecchio, 1995). In contrast, work on benign-envy cognitions refers to perceiving the superior others in a positive light, and typically liking and admiring them (Van de Ven et al., 2009).

Intentional and Behavioral Consequences
A vast amount of the envy literature documents the malicious intentions and behaviors associated with envy. Malicious envy is frequently argued to be a "call for action" to engage in interpersonal harm doing, particularly actions that "reduce or, better yet, fully remove the envied person's advantage" (Smith & Kim, 2007, p. 53). Social undermining behaviors, such as belittling, gossiping, withholding information, giving "the silent treatment",

and so on, have been documented as forms of aggression towards envied targets (Braun et al., 2018; Duffy et al., 2012; Salmivalli, 2001).

Specifically, envious individuals have been found to belittle the envied target (Salovey & Rodin, 1984; Vecchio, 1995). Salovey and Rodin (1984) found that participants were more likely to disparage an outperformer and less likely to desire his or her friendship. Vecchio (1995) suggests that envious individuals tend to denigrate envied targets by causing them to behave in a humiliating or antisocial manner, as well as by means of backstabbing and spreading gossip, misinformation, and disinformation.

Numerous studies have also linked malicious envy motivations to schadenfreude, which is taking pleasure at the misfortunes of others (e.g., Cikara & Fiske, 2012; Krizan & Johar, 2012; Smith et al., 1996; van de Ven et al., 2015; Van Dijk et al., 2006). This line of research implies that malicious envy is often associated with feeling amused and pleased by outperformers' misfortunes.

Malicious consequences of envy have additionally been found with regard to dishonest behaviors. Moran and Schweitzer (2008), for example, found envy to increase egoistic dishonesty. Namely, individuals who negotiated with superior, envied (versus neutral) counterparts were more likely to engage in deceptive negotiation tactics. Gino and Pierce (2009) found envy to reduce altruistic dishonesty aimed at helping others. Specifically, in their study, undergraduates who were envious of their partners were less likely to overstate their partners' grades.

Research in the organizational context has shown that malicious envy leads to social undermining of envied co-workers (Duffy et al., 2012), and recent work has documented similar effects when the maliciously envied person is one's supervisor. Specifically, employees' malicious envy towards their supervisors was positively related to engaging in counterproductive work behaviors, such as interfering with the supervisor's performance (Braun et al., 2018).

Because the expression of envy-driven hostility is socially unacceptable, peoples' malicious motivations towards envied others are often manifested by covert, rather than overt, means. These include behaviors such as not looking at the envied person and otherwise avoiding him or her (Crusius & Lange, 2014; Yoshimura, 2010), a reduced tendency to form close relationships with envied individuals (Salovey & Rodin, 1984), and a general reluctance to avoid using social network sites that typically portray others' self-enhancing presentations (Wenninger et al., 2019). In work-related contexts, covert reactions are often manifested in absenteeism (Duffy & Shaw, 2000), turnover intentions (Vecchio, 2005), the tendency to quit (Cohen-Charash, 2009), and decreased voluntary organizational citizenship behaviors (Kim et al., 2010).

Another relatively implicit manifestation of malicious envy is covert victimization (e.g., Jensen et al., 2014; Kim & Glomb, 2014). Covert victimization includes behaviors that harm a target where the offender's actions are disguised and subtle in nature, such as withholding job-related information or giving someone the "silent treatment" (Baron et al., 1999; Kaukiainen et al., 2001). Consistently, it was found that high (vs. low) performers tended to experience more covert forms of victimization from peers (Jensen et al., 2014) and that they were more likely to be targets of victimization (Kim & Glomb, 2014).

In recent research, Montal-Rosenberg and Moran (2020) explored and demonstrated another implicit and covert means of undermining envied targets—namely, helping them in a way that retains their future dependence, rather than in a way that increases their autonomy. Specifically, they found that malicious motivations towards envied peers reduced peoples' willingness to provide these peers with help, particularly with autonomous help; that is, help that entails providing tools and thereby enables the help recipient to independently solve similar problems in the future. An additional study focusing on envy and help-seeking behaviors (Montal-Rosenberg & Moran, 2019) demonstrated that people are also less likely to seek help, particularly autonomous help from superior peers who instigate malicious envy motivations. Their results further imply that this reluctance to seek autonomous help from envied peers is, at least to some extent, driven by the desire to avoid increasing the envied peers' feelings of empowerment and competence.

The literature pertaining to the benign and constructive intentional and behavioral consequences of envy is less extensive. In general, the experience of benign envy leads to action tendencies directed at moving-up to the superior person's position. One of the first studies demonstrating that unfavorable envy-evoking outcomes can, under some circumstances, have constructive consequences, was an organizational context field study conducted by Schaubroeck and Lam (2004). Their results suggest that promotion rejectees sometimes respond to the unfavorable envy-evoking outcome by increasing their job performance, and that this constructive response is more likely among those who believe that they too have a chance to be promoted in the future.

Researchers who distinguish between benign and malicious envy have documented varying constructive consequences of benign envy across a variety of contexts. For example, Van de Ven et al. (2011b) found that benignly envious individuals invested more time working on tasks, performed better, and planned to study more. Lange and Crusius (2015a) demonstrated that benign envy leads to setting higher goals and consequently to faster race running. Similarly, Sterling et al. (2016) found a positive relation between benign envy and increased work effort.

Interestingly, recent work by Salerno et al. (2019) suggests that malicious envy can also sometimes motivate self-improvement, provided the opportunities to do so occur outside the envy-eliciting domain. According to this notion, both types of envy instigate self-improvement goal pursuit, but the type of goal pursuit differs. Namely, Salerno et al. (2019) refer to the distinction between two types of goal pursuit. Process-focused goal pursuit highlights the activities people perform on their way to attaining a goal. Conversely, outcome-focused goal pursuit highlights the benefits that people acquire upon attaining a goal, independent of the activities performed to get there (Touré-Tillery & Fishbach, 2014). To illustrate, consider an individual with a self-improvement goal of losing weight.

A weight loss program highlighting the successful outcomes (such as expected weight loss or before/after waist size) should appeal to people with outcome-focused goals. A weight loss program highlighting the program activities leading to weight loss (such as calorie reductions and exercising) should appeal to people with process-focused goals. Salerno et al. (2019) argue that benign envy, which typically instigates a belief that rewards are effort dependent, motivates the pursuit of process-focused goals. Malicious envy, in contrast, which typically instigates a belief that rewards are not dependent on effort, motivates pursuing outcome-focused goals. In line with this argument, they found that a benign envy induction increased participants' motivation when performing a task that was framed as effective for improving the type of thinking necessary for reaching academic goals (i.e., a process goal frame). A malicious envy induction, on the other hand, increased participants' motivation when the same task was framed as effective for attaining academic goals (i.e., an outcome goal frame).

Additional research by Van de Ven et al. (2009) on benign envy suggests that people who experience benign envy generally tend to compliment those they envy, and seek to develop closer relationships with them. Other work by Van de Ven et al. (2011a) suggests that benign envy can increase envious individuals' readiness to pay a premium for desirable products that are owned by the target they envy. Specifically, in one of their experiments, after being faced with a confederate who possesses a desirable iPhone, participants were willing to pay a premium to buy a similar iPhone in the condition that induced benign envy, but not in the condition that induced malicious envy.

Wellbeing Consequences

Benign and malicious forms of envy have been suggested to have differing implications for envious individuals' wellbeing as well. Specifically, it was found that dispositional benign envy was positively associated with subjective happiness and life satisfaction. In contrast, dispositional malicious envy was negatively associated with subjective happiness and life satisfaction (Briki, 2019). This difference is proposed to be accounted for by corresponding individual differences in self-control (i.e., the ability to stimulate goal-directed means and override goal-disruptive impulses). According to this account, individuals who are more prone to experience malicious (rather than benign) envy are characterized by relatively lower trait self-control, which in turn, leads to lower happiness and life satisfaction.

Determinants of Envy Consequences

What determines whether envy will produce the above described benign (constructive) or malicious (destructive) consequences? Below we present the key determinants that have been offered in the literature, divided into three categories: (a) factors related to the situation, (b) factors related to the envied target, and (c) characteristics of the envious individual.

Situational Factors

One of the core situational appraisals that have been identified to underlie the development of benign versus malicious consequences of envy is perceived deservedness of the advantage (Van de Ven et al., 2012); that is, the extent to which the envied person's advantage is perceived as deserved. A student who is perceived as getting a good grade and winning a competitive scholarship due to studying hard is perceived to deserve it, while a student who is perceived as getting a good grade and winning the scholarship by cheating, or due to good luck or family ties, is perceived to be undeserving. Envy-eliciting situations in which the other is undeservedly better off evoke malicious envy, while situations in which the other is deservedly better off are more likely to evoke benign envy. In a recent experiment, Montal-Rosenberg and Moran (2020) demonstrated the effect of (un)deservingness on the consequences of envy in a work-related competition context. Specifically, participants were confronted with a scenario in which they competed for a promotion, and then learned that the promotion was granted to their teammate, who was either the CEO's nephew (i.e., low deservingness condition) or a highly devoted and hard worker (i.e., high deservingness condition). Results confirmed that losing the competition to the CEO's nephew, but not to the devoted hard worker, triggered malicious envy motivations and reduced the willingness to provide the promoted peer with help.

A second somewhat related situational appraisal is perceived control over the situation, which refers to the extent to which the envious person believes he/she has the ability to change the situation (Van de Ven et al., 2012). For example, a person will experience relatively low control over a situation when the desired object is very hard to achieve (Lange & Crusius, 2015a). Notably, (un)deservedness and perceived control are not completely independent. Undeserved situations by definition constitute an inconsistency between what someone invests in a situation and what they get out of it, and thus decrease the perceived control over the situation (Feather, 1999). However, perceiving an advantage as deserved does not necessarily imply that it is also controllable. In line with this point, Van de Ven et al. (2012) found that when the advantage of the upward social comparison target was perceived as deserved, higher perceived control over obtaining the desired object intensified the benign envy that was evoked.

Envy Target Characteristics

Perceived characteristics of the superior target have also been found to determine envy and the type of consequences it instigates. Fiske et al.'s (2007) framework suggests that one of these characteristics is the superior target's perceived warmth. Indeed, social judgments are powerfully influenced by assessments of competence and warmth (Fiske et al., 1999; Fiske et al., 2002; White, 1980; Wojciszke, 1994). The Stereotype Content Model (SCM; Fiske et al., 2002) describes how perceptions of warmth and competence shape emotions, and Cuddy et al. (2007) extended this model to develop the Behaviors from Intergroup Affect and Stereotypes (BIAS) map. According to the BIAS map, competent (or superior) others who are judged to be cold trigger envy and elicit other-harming intentions, yet competent or superior others who are judged to be warm elicit admiration, and evoke other-facilitating intentions. In congruence with this notion, research by Moran et al. (2009) empirically demonstrated that high performers can curtail the extent to which they trigger malicious envy motivations and behaviors. High performers who conveyed "warmth information" (e.g., shared information about their close relationships with family, friends, and pets) induced less malicious envy motivations, intentions, and actual harming behaviors than high performers who did not convey information cuing warmth.

A related envied target factor recently found to reduce malicious envy is revealing failures (Brooks et al., 2019). In particular, by revealing both successes and failures encountered on the path to success (compared to revealing only successes), targets of envy decreased observers' malicious envy towards them.

Expressing authentic pride (success attributed to effort) versus hubristic pride (success attributed to talent) was also found to modulate malicious and benign intentions and behaviors toward superior envied targets. After excelling in an exam or winning a sports competition, the student or winner might be proud because of the effort that he or she invested in studying or training (authentic pride) or due to his or her personal abilities (hubristic pride). It was found that pride displays often co-occur with envy and substantially increase its intensity. Displaying authentic pride was found to cause a likable impression. It instigated benign envy, and correspondingly evoked constructive behaviors directed at self-improvement. Displaying hubristic pride, on the other hand, caused a less likable impression. It instigated malicious envy and correspondingly evoked destructive behaviors aimed at damaging the status of the proud other (Lange & Crusius, 2015b). Similarly, in a field experiment at an entrepreneurial pitch competition, Brooks et al. (2019) provided evidence of a correlation between the type of pride (i.e., perceived authentic versus hubristic pride) of successful entrepreneurs and the extent to which these entrepreneurs elicit benign envy and malicious envy in their observers.

An additional envied target characteristic that has been suggested to modify the type of envy consequences that evolve is narcissism. Narcissism is characterized as holding highly inflated, unrealistically positive, grandiose views of oneself (Campbell et al., 2011; Gebauer et al., 2012). Superior targets' trait narcissism was found to facilitate the evolvement of malicious rather than benign envy consequences. Specifically, in their recent work exploring workplace envy towards supervisors, Braun et al. (2018) found that supervisors' trait narcissism negatively predicted employees' benign envy towards their supervisors and positively predicted employees' malicious envy motivations and corresponding intentions to engage in supervisor targeted counterproductive work behaviors.

Characteristics of the Envious Individual

Envy is not conceptualized solely as situational. Rather, people differ in their chronic proneness to experience envy (Smith et al., 1999). Thus, some people experience envy more often than others do. People who are prone to envy tend to over-persist in comparing their own state with that of others (Smith et al., 1999) and frequently experience episodic envy following upward social comparisons (Smith et al., 1996). In line with the initial conceptualization of envy as a unitary construct with malicious consequences, dispositional envy was originally conceptualized as involving the following two affective components: feelings of inferiority and feelings of ill will. Previous studies have demonstrated mainly the negative consequences of being prone to this envy construct. For example, proneness to envy (measured by the enviousness scale; Gold, 1996), was positively associated with inferiority feelings, trait anger, irritability, and also depression, anxiety, phobic anxiety, somatization, and obsessive compulsiveness. Consistently, dispositional envy (measured by the dispositional envy scale [DES]; Smith et al., 1999) was negatively associated with life satisfaction, vitality, and happiness, indicating that envy-prone individuals are more likely to have low feelings of aliveness and energy and to express unhappiness with their lives (Milfont & Gouveia, 2009).

In the context of interpersonal relationships and behaviors, dispositional envy has been found to be negatively related to prosocial tendencies (Yu et al., 2018), and cooperating behavior (Parks et al., 2002), and positively related to schadenfreude (Krizan & Johar, 2012), as well as to counterproductive work behaviors, such as political deviance, aggression, and other harmful behaviors toward employees and organizations (Cohen-Charash & Mueller, 2007; Kim et al., 2013). Dispositional envy has also been found to be positively related to unfairness beliefs, and these beliefs have been suggested to play a role in the consequent decreased pro-social tendencies (De Clercq et al., 2018).

Recently, corresponding with the development of the dual conceptualization of envy, Lange and Crusius (2015a) suggested that people also differ in their propensity to experience the different types of envy; that is, in their dispositional benign and malicious envy propensities. Using the recently developed Benign and Malicious Envy Scale (BeMaS), they examined the relationship between dispositional malicious envy and dispositional benign envy in the context of competition. Their results suggest that dispositional benign envy is positively associated with hope for success whereas dispositional malicious envy is positively associated with fear of failure (Lange & Crusius, 2015a; Lange et al., 2016). Corresponding to these links, dispositional benign envy predicted higher goal setting and consequent faster race performance of marathon runners. In contrast, dispositional malicious envy predicted race goal disengagement (Lange & Crusius, 2015a). Using the same scale, it was recently found that individuals' chronic tendency to experience malicious envy is negatively related to their willingness to provide their superior peers with help, especially autonomous help (Montal-Rosenberg & Moran, 2020).

Peoples' dispositional benign and malicious envy tendencies have also been found to be related to their trait narcissism. Narcissism is proposed to have two facets, namely narcissistic admiration and narcissistic rivalry. These two facets of narcissism determine the way in which narcissists pursue their goal of maintaining a grandiose self. The behavioral pattern of narcissistic admiration is assumed to be driven by hope for greatness and success, causing a self-regulatory strategy of assertive self-enhancement. The behavioral pattern of narcissistic rivalry, in contrast, is assumed to be driven by fear of failure, prompting a self-regulatory strategy of antagonistic self-protection. Consistent with this notion, hope for success, which is related to narcissistic admiration, was found to be associated with benign envy, whereas fear of failure, which is related to narcissistic rivalry was found to be associated with malicious envy (Lange et al., 2016).

Last, another documented antecedent of benign and malicious envy is self-esteem, particularly high explicit self-esteem type. Explicit self-esteem has been differentiated in terms of two types: discrepant versus congruent high explicit self-esteem (Smallets et al., 2016). In both of these types of high explicit self-esteem (H-ESE), the explicit self-esteem, which is the conscious self-view, is high. However, the implicit self-esteem, which is the non-conscious self-view, differs. While in congruent H-ESE the conscious self-view is also high, in discrepant H-ESE, the nonconscious self-view is low. Previous work proposes that the self-worth of individuals with discrepant H-ESE, albeit being positive, is fragile and vulnerable, and thus requires validation by means such as feeling superior to others (Kernis et al., 2008). In contrast, congruent H-ESE reflects secure, deep-seated self-worth without a need to compete with others. Following this logic, Smallets et al. (2016) predicted and demonstrated that people with discrepant H-ESE tend to view successful others as threats and respond to them in ways consistent with malicious envy. In contrast, people with congruent H-ESE see successful others as guides for self-improvement. Indeed, in their empirical work, they found support for this notion. When encountered with upward social comparison targets, discrepant H-ESE participants exhibited malicious envy. They responded by rating these targets negatively across a variety of attributes and as deserving to fail. Congruent H-ESE participants, on the other hand, exhibited benign envy. They responded by persisting longer at a difficult task.

Potential Interventions and Concluding Remarks

We conclude this chapter by discussing potential interventions that may minimize the destructive or malicious consequences of envy and enhance the constructive or benign ones. First, given that perceived deservingness and sense of control or ability to change the situation are key factors in determining the evolvement of benign versus malicious envy (Van de Ven et al., 2012), interventions fostering distributive justice, exemplifying the use of ethical standards, or endorsing an ethical organizational culture may reduce manifestations of malicious envy and increase the arousal of benign envy (see also Floyd et al., 2016).

Relatedly, employing transparent, objective, and accepted criteria for differential evaluations or unequal resource allocations is also likely to increase the probability that envy will result in benign rather than malicious consequences. Thus, while previous work in the organizational literature has documented a positive relation between *outcome* pay transparency and counterproductive workplace behaviors (Belogolovsky & Bamberger, 2014; SimanTov-Nachlieli & Bamberger, 2020), based on the envy literature reviewed here, we posit that *process* pay transparency may moderate this negative relation by altering the type of envy motivations triggered when encountering highly paid peers. Moreover, interventions that promote the adoption of beliefs in a procedurally just world; that is, augment peoples' beliefs that they are generally subjected to fair processes, or interventions promoting people's general sense of control over the situation, may also be effective in enhancing benign rather than malicious envy outcomes.

As noted above, perceived control over the situation refers to the extent to which the envious person believes he or she has the ability to change the situation (Van de Ven et al., 2012). Corresponding with this idea, it seems reasonable to predict that the extent to which people hold an incremental implicit theory, according to which people's abilities are malleable and controllable, rather than an entity theory, according to which abilities are fixed and uncontrollable (Dweck, 1986), will also determine the extent to which they experience malicious or benign envy following upward social comparison. Thus, interventions that induce the adoption of incremental implicit theories can potentially motivate people who encounter successful others to level the unfavorable gap by means of self-improvement (i.e., benign envy), rather than by attempting to harm the superior others (i.e., malicious envy).

A different route to moderating the destructive versus constructive effects of malicious and benign envy motivations may be to vary the costs and benefits associated with enacting them. Factors that increase the costs of engaging in malicious other-harming behaviors and/or that augment the benefits of being benevolent and cooperating may shift envy manifestations away from their malicious forms and towards their benign ones. An example of one such factor is task interdependence (i.e., the extent to which the social comparison occurs among individuals who are dependent on one another to complete a task). In high interdependent environments, benevolent behaviors are highly valued and malevolent ones are often penalized (e.g., Anderson & Williams, 1996; Grant & Patil, 2012; Warburton & Terry, 2000). Indeed, in their recent work on envy in teams, Montal-Rosenberg and Moran (2020) report preliminary results suggesting that the malicious consequences of teammate envy may be moderated in high-task-interdependent environments. Supporting this general notion of interdependence, in collectivistic (vs. individualistic) cultures, people tend to focus more on group goals (e.g., completing the task) than on individual goals (e.g., getting personal rewards; Gudykunst et al., 1992) which are naturally more salient when team interdependence is high. Thus, the superior achievements of an in-group member in these cultures are more likely to be perceived as a group achievement than as an individual achievement (Brewer & Weber, 1994; Oyserman & Lee, 2008). Accordingly, an envious person in interdependent groups/teams can bask in the glow of the envied target's glory if the envied target is an in-group member.

Last, another way to possibly moderate malicious envy consequences may be self-regulation. Because expressing malicious envy violates social norms (Foster et al., 1972; Heider, 1958; Silver & Sabini, 1978), and is also painful (Takahashi et al., 2009) and threatening to individuals' positive self-views (Tesser, 1988), people are likely to be motivated to counteract and control their malicious envy reactions. Indeed, Smith and Kim (2007) suggest that people often deny envy and suppress overt malicious envy intentions. Supporting this view, neuroimaging studies have found activation of brain areas related to emotional control when people are confronted with superior others (Joseph et al., 2008). Furthermore, numerous languages contain envy-related words that depict a positive, rather than negative, emotional experience. For example, the term *firgun* in Hebrew, refers to "happiness at another's success" (Cohen-Charash et al., 2008), and the term *mudita* in Pali, a language used in India by Buddhists, refers to "rejoicing in the good fortune of others" (Menon & Thompson, 2010).

While people may often be motivated to self-regulate their envy and transform it from a negative experience with destructive consequences into a more positive and constructive experience, there is need to further assess mechanisms for doing so. One potential mechanism may be to engage in emotion regulation. Gross (1998, 2001), describes five specific emotion regulation strategies that operate either before an emotional experience (i.e., antecedent-focused strategies) or after an emotional experience (i.e., response-focused strategies). Cognitive reappraisal, for example, is an antecedent-focused strategy. Specifically, it is a form of cognitive change that involves construing an emotion eliciting episode in a way that changes its emotional impact. To illustrate, an individual may cognitively reframe the envy episode (e.g., losing in a competition to a competitor) such that the envied person is perceived as deserving the competitive advantage, and by doing so transforms the envy eliciting experience into one that manifests in a benign rather than malicious form. Indeed, it was found that cognitive reappraisal can be effective for curtailing negative emotions and transforming them to positive ones (Gross, 2002). Expressive suppression, in contrast, is a response-focused strategy that involves inhibiting the emotion expressive behavior. For example, maliciously envious individuals may "bite their tongue," try to appear indifferent, and avoid showing that they are feeling upset and hostile. A vast amount of empirical evidence (e.g., Gross, 2001, 2002; Gross & John, 2003; John & Gross, 2004) suggests that reappraisal is generally a more effective emotion regulation strategy than suppression. Suppression, which often results in a dissonance between what one feels and what one expresses, has correspondingly been found to entail greater physiological, cognitive, and interpersonal costs than cognitive reappraisal.

To conclude, in this chapter, we have proposed that competition often activates envy towards the winner/superior contestant, and envy in turn influences the desire to compete, as well as the type of competitive strategies that are employed. As we have discussed, the desire to level the unfavorable gap relative to envy eliciting targets can evoke strategies that are directed toward pulling down the envied competitor (i.e., destructive or malicious envy consequences), or strategies directed toward self-improvement (i.e., constructive or benign envy consequences). Throughout this chapter we have presented findings regarding varying malicious (destructive) and benign (constructive) consequences of envy in terms of cognitions, action tendencies, and wellbeing. We have also discussed numerous situational factors, as well as individual differences, that can shape the type of envy consequences that emerge. Finally, we have concluded by suggesting interventions to transform the emergence of envy that often arises among competitors to be benign and constructive rather than malicious and destructive.

References

Anderson, S. E., & Williams, L. J. (1996). Interpersonal, job, and individual factors related to helping processes at work. *Journal of Applied Psychology, 81*(3), 282.

Andiappan, M., & Dufour, L. (2020). Jealousy at work: A tripartite model. *Academy of Management Review, 45*(1), 205–229.

Aristotle, O. R. (1991). *Trans. George A. Kennedy*. Oxford University Press.

Bacon, F. (1890). *The essays or counsels, civil and moral, of Francis Bacon*. Clarendon Press.

Bar-Haim, Y., Lamy, D., Pergamin, L., Bakermans-Kranenburg, M. J., & Van Ijzendoorn, M. H. (2007). Threat-related attentional bias in anxious and nonanxious individuals: a meta-analytic study. *Psychological Bulletin, 133*(1), 1.

Baron, R. A., Neuman, J. H., & Geddes, D. (1999). Social and personal determinants of workplace aggression: Evidence for the impact of perceived injustice and the Type A behavior pattern. *Aggressive Behavior: Official Journal of the International Society for Research on Aggression, 25*(4), 281–296.

Belk, R. (2011). Benign envy. *AMS Review, 1*(3–4), 117–134.

Belogolovsky, E., & Bamberger, P. A. (2014). Signaling in secret: Pay for performance and the incentive and sorting effects of pay secrecy. *Academy of Management Journal, 57*(6), 1706–1733.

Ben-Ze'ev, A. (1990). Envy and jealousy. *Canadian Journal of Philosophy, 20*(4), 487–516.

Ben-Ze'ev, A. (1992). Envy and inequality. *The Journal of Philosophy, 89*(11), 551–581.

Bers, S. A., & Rodin, J. (1984). Social-comparison jealousy: A developmental and motivational study. *Journal of Personality and Social Psychology, 47*(4), 766.

Braun, S., Aydin, N., Frey, D., & Peus, C. (2018). Leader narcissism predicts malicious envy and supervisor-targeted counterproductive work behavior: Evidence from field and experimental research. *Journal of Business Ethics, 151*(3), 725–741.

Brewer, M. B., & Weber, J. G. (1994). Self-evaluation effects of interpersonal versus intergroup social comparison. *Journal of Personality and Social Psychology, 66*(2), 268.

Briki, W. (2019). Harmed trait self-control: Why do people with a higher dispositional malicious envy experience lower subjective wellbeing? A cross-sectional study. *Journal of Happiness Studies, 20*(2), 523–540.

Brooks, A. W., Huang, K., Abi-Esber, N., Buell, R. W., Huang, L., & Hall, B. (2019). Mitigating malicious envy: Why successful individuals should reveal their failures. *Journal of Experimental Psychology: General, 148*(4), 667.

Campbell, W. K., Hoffman, B. J., Campbell, S. M., & Marchisio, G. (2011). Narcissism in organizational contexts. *Human Resource Management Review, 21*(4), 268–284.

Cikara, M., & Fiske, S. T. (2012). Stereotypes and schadenfreude: Affective and physiological markers of pleasure at outgroup misfortunes. *Social Psychological and Personality Science, 3*(1), 63–71.

Cohen-Charash, Y. (2009). Episodic envy. *Journal of Applied Social Psychology, 39*(9), 2128–2173.

Cohen-Charash, Y, Erez, M., & Scherbaum, C. A. (2008). Firgun—Being happy for another person's good fortune. Annual Meeting of the Society for Industrial and Organizational Psychology, San Francisco.

Cohen-Charash, Yochi, & Larson, E. C. (2016). What is the nature of envy. In R. H. Smith et al. (Eds.), *Envy at Work and in Organizations* (pp. 1–37). Oxford University Press.

Cohen-Charash, Yochi, & Larson, E. C. (2017). An emotion divided: Studying envy is better than studying "benign" and "malicious" envy. *Current Directions in Psychological Science, 26*(2), 174–183.

Cohen-Charash, Yochi, & Mueller, J. S. (2007). Does perceived unfairness exacerbate or mitigate interpersonal counterproductive work behaviors related to envy? *Journal of Applied Psychology, 92*(3), 666.

Crusius, J., & Lange, J. (2014). What catches the envious eye? Attentional biases within malicious and benign envy. *Journal of Experimental Social Psychology, 55*, 1–11.

Cuddy, A. J. C., Fiske, S. T., & Glick, P. (2007). The BIAS map: behaviors from intergroup affect and stereotypes. *Journal of Personality and Social Psychology, 92*(4), 631.

De Clercq, D., Haq, I. U., & Azeem, M. U. (2018). The roles of informational unfairness and political climate in the relationship between dispositional envy and job performance in Pakistani organizations. *Journal of Business Research, 82*, 117–126.

Duffy, M. K., Scott, K. L., Shaw, J. D., Tepper, B. J., & Aquino, K. (2012). A social context model of envy and social undermining. *Academy of Management Journal, 55*(3), 643–666.

Duffy, M. K., & Shaw, J. D. (2000). The Salieri syndrome: Consequences of envy in groups. *Small Group Research, 31*(1), 3–23.

Dweck, C. S. (1986). Motivational processes affecting learning. *American Psychologist, 41*(10), 1040.

Feather, N. T. (1999). Judgments of deservingness: Studies in the psychology of justice and achievement. *Personality and Social Psychology Review, 3*(2), 86–107.

Festinger, L. (1954). A theory of social comparison processes. *Human Relations, 7*(2), 117–140.

Fiske, S. T. (2010). Envy up, scorn down: How comparison divides us. *American Psychologist, 65*(8), 698.

Fiske, S. T., Cuddy, A. J. C., & Glick, P. (2007). Universal dimensions of social cognition: Warmth and competence. *Trends in Cognitive Sciences, 11*(2), 77–83.

Fiske, S. T., Cuddy, A. J. C., Glick, P., & Xu, J. (2002). A model of (often mixed) stereotype content: competence and warmth respectively follow from perceived status and competition. *Journal of Personality and Social Psychology, 82*(6), 878.

Fiske, S. T., Xu, J., Cuddy, A. C., & Glick, P. (1999). (Dis) respecting versus (dis) liking: Status and interdependence predict ambivalent stereotypes of competence and warmth. *Journal of Social Issues, 55*(3), 473–489.

Floyd, T. M., Hoogland, C. E., & Smith, R. H. (2016). The role of leaders in managing envy and its consequences for competition in organizations. In *Leadership lessons from compelling contexts* (pp. 129–156). Emerald Group Publishing Limited.

Foster, G. M., Apthorpe, R. J., Bernard, H. R., Bock, B., Brogger, J., Brown, J. K., Cappannari, S. C., Cuisenier, J., D'Andrade, R. G., & Faris, J. (1972). The anatomy of envy: A study in symbolic behavior [and comments and reply]. *Current Anthropology, 13*(2), 165–202.

Garcia, S. M., Tor, A., & Schiff, T. M. (2013). The psychology of competition: A social comparison perspective. *Perspectives on Psychological Science, 8*(6), 634–650.

Gebauer, J. E., Sedikides, C., Verplanken, B., & Maio, G. R. (2012). Communal narcissism. *Journal of Personality and Social Psychology, 103*(5), 854.

Gino, F., & Pierce, L. (2009). Dishonesty in the name of equity. *Psychological Science, 20*(9), 1153–1160.

Goethals, G. R., & Darley, J. M. (1977). Social comparison theory: An attributional approach. In J. M. Suls & R. L. Miller (Eds.), *Social Comparison Processes: Theoretical and Empirical Perspectives* (pp. 259–278). Halsted/Wiley.

Gold, B. T. (1996). Enviousness and its relationship to maladjustment and psychopathology. *Personality and Individual Differences, 21*(3), 311–321.

Grant, A. M., & Patil, S. V. (2012). Challenging the norm of self-interest: Minority influence and transitions to helping norms in work units. *Academy of Management Review, 37*(4), 547–568.

Gross, J. J. (1998). The emerging field of emotion regulation: An integrative review. *Review of General Psychology, 2*(3), 271–299.

Gross, J. J. (2001). Emotion regulation in adulthood: Timing is everything. *Current Directions in Psychological Science, 10*(6), 214–219.

Gross, J. J. (2002). Emotion regulation: Affective, cognitive, and social consequences. *Psychophysiology, 39*(3), 281–291.

Gross, J. J., & John, O. P. (2003). Individual differences in two emotion regulation processes: implications for affect, relationships, and well-being. *Journal of Personality and Social Psychology, 85*(2), 348.

Gudykunst, W. B., Gao, G. E., Schmidt, K. L., Nishida, T., Bond, M. H., Leung, K., Wang, G., & Barraclough, R. A. (1992). The influence of individualism collectivism, self-monitoring, and predicted-outcome value on communication in ingroup and outgroup relationships. *Journal of Cross-Cultural Psychology, 23*(2), 196–213.

Heider, F. (1958). *The psychology of interpersonal relations Hillsdale*. LEA.

Hill, S. E., & Buss, D. M. (2006). Envy and positional bias in the evolutionary psychology of management. *Managerial and Decision Economics*, *27*(2-3), 131–143.

Hill, S. E., DelPriore, D. J., & Vaughan, P. W. (2011). The cognitive consequences of envy: Attention, memory, and self-regulatory depletion. *Journal of Personality and Social Psychology*, *101*(4), 653.

Hoffman, P. J., Festinger, L., & Lawrence, D. H. (1954). Tendencies toward group comparability in competitive bargaining. *Human Relations*, *7*(2), 141–159.

Hupka, R. B. (1991). The motive for the arousal of romantic jealousy: Its cultural origin. In P. Salovey (Ed.), *The psychology of jealousy and envy* (p. 252–270). Guilford Press.

Jensen, J. M., Patel, P. C., & Raver, J. L. (2014). Is it better to be average? High and low performance as predictors of employee victimization. *Journal of Applied Psychology*, *99*(2), 296.

John, O. P., & Gross, J. J. (2004). Healthy and unhealthy emotion regulation: Personality processes, individual differences, and life span development. *Journal of Personality*, *72*(6), 1301–1334.

Joseph, J. E., Powell, C. A. J., Johnson, N. F., & Kedia, G. (2008). The functional neuroanatomy of envy. In R. Smith (Ed.), *Envy: Theory and Research* (pp. 245–263). Oxford University Press.

Kaukiainen, A., Salmivalli, C., Björkqvist, K., Österman, K., Lahtinen, A., Kostamo, A., & Lagerspetz, K. (2001). Overt and covert aggression in work settings in relation to the subjective well-being of employees. *Aggressive Behavior: Official Journal of the International Society for Research on Aggression*, *27*(5), 360–371.

Kernis, M. H., Lakey, C. E., & Heppner, W. L. (2008). Secure versus fragile high self-esteem as a predictor of verbal defensiveness: Converging findings across three different markers. *Journal of Personality*, *76*(3), 477–512.

Kilduff, G. J., Elfenbein, H. A., & Staw, B. M. (2010). The psychology of rivalry: A relationally dependent analysis of competition. *Academy of Management Journal*, *53*(5), 943–969.

Kim, E., & Glomb, T. M. (2014). Victimization of high performers: The roles of envy and work group identification. *Journal of Applied Psychology*, *99*(4), 619.

Kim, S. K., Jung, D.-I., & Lee, J. S. (2013). Service employees' deviant behaviors and leader–member exchange in contexts of dispositional envy and dispositional jealousy. *Service Business*, *7*(4), 583–602.

Kim, S., O'Neill, J. W., & Cho, H.-M. (2010). When does an employee not help coworkers? The effect of leader–member exchange on employee envy and organizational citizenship behavior. *International Journal of Hospitality Management*, *29*(3), 530–537.

Klein, P. L. (1957). An evaluation of cervical traction on the maxilla and the upper first permanent molar. *The Angle Orthodontist*, *27*(1), 61–68.

Kohn, A. (1992). *No contest: The case against competition*. Houghton Mifflin Harcourt.

Krizan, Z., & Johar, O. (2012). Envy divides the two faces of narcissism. *Journal of Personality*, *80*(5), 1415–1451.

Lange, J., & Crusius, J. (2015a). Dispositional envy revisited: Unraveling the motivational dynamics of benign and malicious envy. *Personality and Social Psychology Bulletin*, *41*(2), 284–294.

Lange, J., & Crusius, J. (2015b). The tango of two deadly sins: The social-functional relation of envy and pride. *Journal of Personality and Social Psychology*, *109*(3), 453.

Lange, J., Crusius, J., & Hagemeyer, B. (2016). The evil queen's dilemma: Linking narcissistic admiration and rivalry to benign and malicious envy. *European Journal of Personality*, *30*(2), 168–188.

Lange, J., Weidman, A. C., & Crusius, J. (2018). The painful duality of envy: Evidence for an integrative theory and a meta-analysis on the relation of envy and schadenfreude. *Journal of Personality and Social Psychology*, *114*(4), 572.

Menon, T., & Thompson, L. (2010). Envy at work. *Harvard Business Review*, *88*(4), 74–79.

Milfont, T. L., & Gouveia, V. V. (2009). A capital sin: Dispositional envy and its relations to wellbeing. *Interamerican Journal of Psychology*, *43*(3), 547–551.

Montal-Rosenberg, R., & Moran, S. (2019). Seeking less efficient help: Effects of envy on help seeking in teams. The 27th Subjective Probability, Utility, and Decision Making Conference (SPUDM).

Montal-Rosenberg, R., & Moran, S. (2020). Envy and help giving. *Journal of Personality and Social Psychology*. Advanced online publication. https://doi.org/10.1037/pspi0000340

Moran, S., & Schweitzer, M. E. (2008). When better is worse: Envy and the use of deception. *Negotiation and Conflict Management Research*, *1*(1), 3–29.

Moran, S., Schweitzer, M. E., & Miller, M. (2009). How competence curtails cooperation: Envy, warmth and schadenfreude. Annual Meeting of the Academy of Management, Chicago, IL.

Mouly, V. S., & Sankaran, J. K. (2002). The enactment of envy within organizations: Insights from a New Zealand academic department. *The Journal of Applied Behavioral Science, 38*(1), 36–56.

Oyserman, D., & Lee, S. W. S. (2008). Does culture influence what and how we think? Effects of priming individualism and collectivism. *Psychological Bulletin, 134*(2), 311.

Parks, C. D., Rumble, A. C., & Posey, D. C. (2002). The effects of envy on reciprocation in a social dilemma. *Personality and Social Psychology Bulletin, 28*(4), 509–520.

Parrott, W. G. (1991). Experiences of envy and jealousy. *The Psychology of Jealousy and Envy, 1991*, 3–30.

Parrott, W. G., & Smith, R. H. (1993). Distinguishing the experiences of envy and jealousy. *Journal of Personality and Social Psychology, 64*(6), 906.

Rorty, A. O. (1988). *Mind in action: Essays in the philosophy of mind*. Beacon Press.

Salerno, A., Laran, J., & Janiszewski, C. (2019). The bad can be good: When benign and malicious envy motivate goal pursuit. *Journal of Consumer Research, 46*(2), 388–405.

Salmivalli, C. (2001). Feeling good about oneself, being bad to others? Remarks on self-esteem, hostility, and aggressive behavior. *Aggression and Violent Behavior, 6*(4), 375–393.

Salovey, P., & Rodin, J. (1984). Some antecedents and consequences of social-comparison jealousy. *Journal of Personality and Social Psychology, 47*(4), 780.

Salovey, P., & Rodin, J. (1991). Provoking jealousy and envy: Domain relevance and self-esteem threat. *Journal of Social and Clinical Psychology, 10*(4), 395–413.

Salovey, P., & Rothman, A. J. (1991). Envy and jealousy: Self and society. In P. Salovey (Ed.), *The psychology of jealousy and envy* (p. 271–286). Guilford Press.

Schaubroeck, J., & Lam, S. S. K. (2004). Comparing lots before and after: Promotion rejectees' invidious reactions to promotees. *Organizational Behavior and Human Decision Processes, 94*(1), 33–47.

Schoeck, H. (1969). *Envy*. Liberty Press.

Seta, J. J. (1982). The impact of comparison processes on coactors' task performance. *Journal of Personality and Social Psychology, 42*(2), 281.

Silver, M., & Sabini, J. (1978). The perception of envy. *Social Psychology, 41*(2), 105–117.

SimanTov-Nachlieli, I., & Bamberger, P. (2020). Pay communication, justice, and affect: The asymmetric effects of process and outcome pay transparency on counterproductive workplace behavior. *Journal of Applied Psychology, 106*(2), 230–249.

Smallets, S., Streamer, L., Kondrak, C. L., & Seery, M. D. (2016). Bringing you down versus bringing me up: Discrepant versus congruent high explicit self-esteem differentially predict malicious and benign envy. *Personality and Individual Differences, 94*, 173–179.

Smith, R. H., & Kim, S. H. (2007). Comprehending envy. *Psychological Bulletin, 133*(1), 46.

Smith, R. H., Kim, S. H., & Parrott, W. G. (1988). Envy and jealousy: Semantic problems and experiential distinctions. *Personality and Social Psychology Bulletin, 14*(2), 401–409.

Smith, R. H., Parrott, W. G., Diener, E. F., Hoyle, R. H., & Kim, S. H. (1999). Dispositional envy. *Personality and Social Psychology Bulletin, 25*(8), 1007–1020.

Smith, R. H., Turner, T. J., Garonzik, R., Leach, C. W., Urch-Druskat, V., & Weston, C. M. (1996). Envy and schadenfreude. *Personality and Social Psychology Bulletin, 22*(2), 158–168.

Sterling, C. M., van de Ven, N., & Smith, R. H. (2016). The two faces of envy: Studying benign and malicious envy in the workplace. In *Envy at work and in organizations: Research, theory, and applications* (pp. 57–84). Oxford University Press.

Suls, J., & Wheeler, L. (2000). A selective history of classic and neo-social comparison theory. In *Handbook of social comparison* (pp. 3–19). Springer.

Tai, K., Narayanan, J., & McAllister, D. J. (2012). Envy as pain: Rethinking the nature of envy and its implications for employees and organizations. *Academy of Management Review, 37*(1), 107–129.

Takahashi, H., Kato, M., Matsuura, M., Mobbs, D., Suhara, T., & Okubo, Y. (2009). When your gain is my pain and your pain is my gain: neural correlates of envy and schadenfreude. *Science, 323*(5916), 937–939.

Teitelbaum, J. (1976). The leer and the loom—social controls on handloom weavers. In C. Mahoney (Ed.), *The evil eye* (pp. 63–75). Columbia University Press.

Tesser, A. (1988). Toward a self-evaluation maintenance model of social behavior. In L. Berkowitz (Ed.), *Advances in experimental social psychology* (Vol. 21, pp. 181–227). Academic Press.

Tesser, Abraham. (1991). Emotion in social comparison and reflection processes. In J. Suls & T. A. Wills (Eds.), *Social comparison: Contemporary theory and research* (p. 115–145). Lawrence Erlbaum Associates, Inc.

Touré-Tillery, M., & Fishbach, A. (2014). How to measure motivation: A guide for the experimental social psychologist. *Social and Personality Psychology Compass, 8*(7), 328–341.

van de Ven, N., Hoogland, C. E., Smith, R. H., Van Dijk, W. W., Breugelmans, S. M., & Zeelenberg, M. (2015). When envy leads to schadenfreude. *Cognition and Emotion, 29*(6), 1007–1025.

Van de Ven, N., Zeelenberg, M., & Pieters, R. (2009). Leveling up and down: the experiences of benign and malicious envy. *Emotion, 9*(3), 419.

Van de Ven, N., Zeelenberg, M., & Pieters, R. (2011a). The envy premium in product evaluation. *Journal of Consumer Research, 37*(6), 984–998.

Van de Ven, N., Zeelenberg, M., & Pieters, R. (2011b). Why envy outperforms admiration. *Personality and Social Psychology Bulletin, 37*(6), 784–795.

Van de Ven, N., Zeelenberg, M., & Pieters, R. (2012). Appraisal patterns of envy and related emotions. *Motivation and Emotion, 36*(2), 195–204.

Van Dijk, W. W., Ouwerkerk, J. W., Goslinga, S., Nieweg, M., & Gallucci, M. (2006). When people fall from grace: Reconsidering the role of envy in schadenfreude. *Emotion, 6*(1), 156.

Vecchio, R. (1995). *It's not easy being green: Jealousy and envy in the workplace. Research in personnel and human resources management.* JAI Press.

Vecchio, R. P. (2000). Negative emotion in the workplace: Employee jealousy and envy. *International Journal of Stress Management, 7*(3), 161–179.

Vecchio, Robert. (2005). Explorations in employee envy: Feeling envious and feeling envied. *Cognition & Emotion, 19*(1), 69–81.

Walcot, P. (1978). *Envy and the Greeks: A study of human behaviour.* Aris & Phillips.

Warburton, J., & Terry, D. J. (2000). Volunteer decision making by older people: A test of a revised theory of planned behavior. *Basic and Applied Social Psychology, 22*(3), 245–257.

Wenninger, H., Cheung, C. M. K., & Krasnova, H. (2019). College-aged users behavioral strategies to reduce envy on social networking sites: A cross-cultural investigation. *Computers in Human Behavior, 97*, 10–23.

White, G. M. (1980). Conceptual universale in interpersonal language. *American Anthropologist, 82*(4), 759–781.

Wojciszke, B. (1994). Multiple meanings of behavior: Construing actions in terms of competence or morality. *Journal of Personality and Social Psychology, 67*(2), 222.

Yoshimura, C. G. (2010). The experience and communication of envy among siblings, siblings-in-law, and spouses. *Journal of Social and Personal Relationships, 27*(8), 1075–1088.

Yu, Z., Hao, J., & Shi, B. (2018). Dispositional envy inhibits prosocial behavior in adolescents with high self-esteem. *Personality and Individual Differences, 122*, 127–133.

PART IV

Cognitive and Decision-Making Approaches

Judgmental Biases in the Perception of Competitive Advantage: On Choosing the Right Race to Run

David Dunning

Abstract

Competing successfully often means choosing the right competitions to enter, preparing for them adequately, and knowing when to quit. Many psychological phenomena, however, lead people to misjudge how their skills, talents, and prospects compare to peers they are competing against. Typically, these psychological tendencies lead people to a sense of illusory superiority, in which people overestimate their chances in competition. Example phenomena include relying on self-flattering conceptions of skill, focusing on optimistic scenarios while neglecting pessimistic ones, emphasizing one's intentions and agency in producing outcomes while neglecting the impact of external forces, failing to have the competence to fully recognize competence in others, and quizzically not considering the skills of others when making decisions about whether to compete with them. Some specific circumstances, however, lead to underestimation of self. Those with negative self-views may discount their performances unduly. Top performers may not know how distinctive their skills are. In short, mistaken or biased views of the self may lead people to make decisions about competition that undermine their potential success in them.

Key Words: competition, self-assessment, social comparison, illusory superiority, market entry, self-agency, errors and biases

According to the classic joke, a bear surprises two hikers in the woods. One immediately starts running, to which the other hiker exclaims, "Why run? You'll never outrun the bear." Answers the runner, "I don't have to outrun the bear, I just have to outrun you."

The joke points to one basic fact about human affairs. Successes and failures often depend not on absolute level of skill, but how one's skill compares to the skill level of others. A runner wins an Olympic gold medal not by beating a certain time limit, but by being the first among many to cross the finish line no matter how long it takes. As economists term it, rewards in life are often *positional* (Schneider, 2007). The utility people derive from their efforts depends not on how much of some good or status they have in an absolute sense. Instead, it derives from what position that good or status places the individual in relation to other people.

Thus, if the ancient Greeks were right in their advice for people to "know thyself," evaluating one's position accurately relative to others seems quite key. Negotiating life successfully often requires having accurate perceptions where one stands relative to other people; indeed, knowing one's position often is a prerequisite for effectively improving upon it.

Accurate self-assessment of one's position along skill and expertise dimensions is particularly crucial for knowing which competitions to enter and which to leave. Knowing the position of one's skills allows the individual to take proper advantage of those skills. Knowing one's shortcomings aids a person to make wise decisions about where to aim efforts at self-improvement, or when to give up and move along to some other endeavor.

This chapter focuses on recent decades of psychological work examining how accurately people evaluate their position, focusing on how those assessment influence people's outcomes in competition. The work suggests that people display systematic imperfections in their evaluations, often overrating their skill, expertise, and position. The chapter also describes the underlying psychological dynamics that produce these mistaken ideas of a person's readiness to compete.

Illusory Superiority

This chapter begins with a simple overall observation repeatedly affirmed by decades of empirical study. When it comes to self-perception of position, people display a pervasive propensity to overrate themselves, believing that they possess a level of competence, character, and status that is far too positive to be realistic (Dunning et al., 2004). In the most common demonstration of this effect, researchers show that people on average tend to rate themselves as anything but average. They typically tend to rate themselves superior to most others, a mathematically impossible result because it is impossible for the average person's skills to be above average (Alicke & Govorun, 2005; Weinstein, 1980).

In a phrase, people suffer from *illusory superiority*. They see themselves as more moral, intelligent, invulnerable to illness, and better drivers than their peers (for reviews, see Alicke & Govorun, 2005; Dunning et al., 2004). In one telling example, a full 32 percent of the engineers in one Silicon Valley firm thought their skills placed them in the top five percent among colleagues in their firm. In a second firm, the figure was 42 percent (Zenger, 1992). Business executives think their company is more likely to succeed than the average firm in their business sector (Cooper et al., 1988; Larwood & Whittaker, 1977). A full 94 percent of college professors claim they do above average work (Cross, 1977).

This phenomenon extends even down to competitive situations. Chess and poker players forecast they will place much higher in tournaments than they actually do (Park & Santos-Pinto, 2010). Lawyers discussing an upcoming case express high confidence that they will meet the minimum goal they have set for their client. At median in one study, they stated they had a 70 percent chance of meeting that goal, but actually met it only 56 percent of the time (Goodman-Delahunty et al., 2010; see also Loftus & Wagenaar, 1988).

The relevance of this illusory superiority for competitive outcomes is best illustrated by an experiment focusing on the decision to enter a competition (Camerer & Lovallo, 1999). Groups of students were brought into the laboratory and were told that they had a choice about whether to enter a game involving a competition for financial rewards. Those who stayed out would receive some set amount of money, but those who entered the competition could win much more. Of course, there was also a risk that they could lose money as well.

In their rules, the experimenters first explained that all participants would be ranked from top to bottom, but participants would not be told their rank. Then, the experimenters stated that all participants would then have to decide whether to enter a competition based on those ranks. The experimenters would announce the maximum number of entrants guaranteed money if they entered the competition. All top-ranking entrants would earn money if the number of people choosing to enter stayed at or below the announced number. However, if too many people entered, those with lower rank beyond the set number would instead lose money. The key, thus, to make wise decisions about whether to enter was reaching accurate guesses of one's rank among all the entrants.

In some rounds of this game, group members were told that rank was determined solely by a random number generator. Under these conditions, the number of group members entering the competition roughly matched the optimal number for all to win, replicating past research on this situation (Kahneman, 1988; Rapoport, 1995). On average, the group as a whole gained $16.87 over what they would have earned if no one entered the competition.

The picture changed, however, when rank was based on skill rather than luck. Participants were told that rank would be based on performance on a quiz, sometimes involving general knowledge and sometimes sports. Under these instructions, too many group members generally entered the competition. Many lost money. The average group profit, relative to no one entering the competition, was negative: -$1.56. The researchers showed, with further data, that the reason too many participants entered these skill-based competitions was because their guesses on their rank consistently exceeded the rank they actually attained. In short, illusory superiority caused too many participants to enter competitions, to the detriment of those less skilled.

This experimental result echoes real-world patterns. Would-be entrepreneurs tend to start companies in new markets at a rate that greatly exceeds the market's ability to bear new entrants. As a consequence, a large number of start-ups fail within a few years (Dunne et al., 1988; Mata & Portugal, 1994; Tor, 2002; Wagner, 1994). In a survey of over 11,000 manufacturing firms that started, for example, in 1976, over 20 percent had closed within two years, over half within six years, with only 35 percent still surviving 10 years later (Audretsch, 1991).

Mechanisms Underlying Illusory Superiority

Over years of empirical study, researchers have identified many psychological mechanisms that conspire to make people overestimate themselves. These mechanisms can be placed into two general categories. The first category is motivational in nature, a function of the drive people hold to maintain a sense of positive self-esteem and place in the world (for a review, see Kunda, 1990). Their preferences drive their predictions, in that people are biased toward believing that events they want to happen are more likely to occur than events they disfavor—even when the objective probabilities between positive and negative are equal (Cohen & Wallsten, 1992; Irwin, 1953). People overbelieve their preferred candidates will win elections (Granberg & Bent, 1983; Krizan et al., 2010) and that their favorite sports team will win the next game (Babad & Katz, 1991; Massey et al., 2011). Not surprisingly, the degree of illusory superiority that people display depends on the desirability of the skill or event in question (Alicke, 1985; Weinstein, 1980).

The second class of expectations require no motivation but instead rests on cognitive or informational factors. This class involves either analytical mistakes people make in their judgments about or deficits in the information people have available to them at the time they reach their conclusions. Psychological research has catalogued a litany of such errors or informational deficits (Gilovich et al., 2002). As such, it is not a surprise that some items in this catalog would mislead people's beliefs about their chances of competitive success.

Motivational Mechanisms

Let us consider each category in turn, beginning with mechanisms that arise out of the motivation to maintain a favorable self-view.

SELF-FLATTERING DEFINITIONS OF SKILL

One primary source of illusory superiority are the attributes people emphasize in their definitions for social traits and categories. Many intellectual, professional, and social tasks are complex and multi-dimensional. The exact aptitudes and attributes that support that skill are open to debate. For example, what exact attributes are necessary to be an effective leader? Is an effective leader a "people-person," who nurtures and maintains the morale and self-esteem of team members, inspiring them to achieve? Or is an effective leader a taskmaster, pushing people to work harder and longer while not being distracted by their morale and well-being? In academics, does a good student work hard to know every single detail of class material, or does a successful student just find one creative argument to impress the instructor?

When tasks are complex, people tend to adopt definitions that are egocentric and self-flattering. They tend to emphasize the skills and attributes they already have. The nurturant individual defines leadership in a people-oriented way; a task-oriented person emphasizes task skills over people skills in their definition of leadership (Dunning et al., 1989; Dunning et al., 1991; Santos-Pinto & Sobel, 2005). Work shows people fail to produce biased and overinflated self-ratings when the characteristic in question is narrow and well-defined (e.g., *athletic, punctual, sarcastic*). However, when the characteristic is multi-dimensional (e.g., *sophisticated, talented, idealistic*), people show ample levels of illusory superiority. In short, people see themselves as superior because they literally define their terms in such a way to ensure it.

It could be argued that these egocentric definitions are, in a sense, rational. Under their personal definition, they are truly above average. Thus, when so many people claim to be superior, they are all right because they are making claims under the specific self-centric definitions they use (Santos-Pinto & Sobel, 2005). Moreover, people develop their self-based definitions on their life history of success. A mathematically-oriented student achieves academic success through math; a verbally-oriented student succeeds through the use of words. Thus, as each contemplates what it means to be a good student or an intelligent person, their reading of the evidence they have gained through their personal life experience suggests they have the central skills necessary to achieve. Their self-serving definition of success can arise from an honest reading of the small and constrained corner of evidence that each person has (Story & Dunning, 1998).

This analysis, however, breaks down in the context of competition. People not only use their egocentric definitions when judging themselves. They also impose their definitions onto other people, judging other people based on how well those others match their self-serving criteria (Dunning et al., 1991). They act as though their definition is not their definition, but *the* definition, the one that really matters. This practice can only lead people to overestimate how well they will succeed in any competition.

However, direct empirical evidence also suggests that self-serving definitions are produced out of the motivation to maintain self-esteem. When a person's self-esteem is called into question, they tend to develop more egocentric and self-flattering definitions of success on the spot. For example, after failing at an intellectual task relevant to getting into graduate school, people reclaim their self-esteem by concluding that their personal attributes are more crucial for success in marriage (Dunning et al., 1995).

OVERWEIGHTING THE OPTIMISTIC

Despite knowing their pasts are filled with both good and bad, people tend to view the future as holding only bright and positive events. If asked to report positive and negative events from their past, participants do so at equivalent speed. However, if asked to forecast positive and negative events that may happen in their future, participants take much longer to report potential negative events than they do positive ones (Newby-Clark & Ross, 2003). In short, despite the knowledge that their histories are mixed with joy and sorrow, they see the future as containing much more of the former than the latter. It is more difficult and takes longer to imagine aversive future events.

People also give too much weight to optimistic scenarios when forecasting the future over more realistic or pessimistic ones. As an example, college students were asked to predict how quickly they would finish a major academic project. They were also asked to give best- and worst-case scenarios for finishing that project. The original prediction they gave fell much closer to their best-case scenario than to their worst case, and expressly generating a pessimistic scenario did not cause people to become more negative in their predictions. However, generating a pessimistic scenario for another person did (Newby-Clark et al., 2000).

The same pattern arose when people were explicitly asked to compare their futures to others. In one example, participants across several studies were asked to focus on health risk factors they had but that other people tended not to have. This intervention did nothing to make participants more cautious in their ratings of their health risks. However, asking them to focus on others with high health risks caused participants to express more illusory superiority on their future health (Weinstein & Klein, 1995).

Moreover, when hearing positive news, people tend to update their self-impressions much more than when hearing negative news—a finding that more directly implicates motivational factors in the emphasis on the optimistic. In one example, college students were brought into a group and had their intelligence and physical attractiveness assessed (Eil & Rao, 2011). They were then told they were going to experience a series of comparisons with other people in the group. In each of those comparisons, some other group member would be chosen at random and the participant (privately) would be told whether they rated higher or lower than that other person along the critical dimension. Their task, after each comparison, was to revise how well or poorly they ranked among the group.

In this task, participants tended to play favorites with the news. Their reaction to good and bad news was asymmetric. Participants tended to revise upward, and appropriately, when told they compared favorably to the other individual. However, they resisted revising their rank down when the comparison was a negative one (Eil & Rao, 2011). Other work reveals a similar activity. Told good news that people in general experience some good event, like earning more than a million dollars in their lifetime, and people revise their estimates of their own personal chances in an optimistic direction. However, if told that people in general are likely to confront some bad event in the future, like contracting cancer, and their personal estimates fail to move all that much (Garrett & Sharot, 2014).

OVERWEIGHTING INTENTIONS

People also give an inordinate amount of weight to their intentions when forecasting their future, but do not do so for other people. In doing so, they seem to think of themselves as a somewhat different species from other people, including those against whom they might be competing.

That is, in explaining and forecasting their own behavior and outcomes, people emphasize their personal agency more than they do for others. People think of themselves as having more free will than other people do (Pronin & Kugler, 2010). More than they do for other people, they emphasize the person they have a potential to become rather than the more flawed one they are in the present (Williams et al., 2012). They also give more emphasis to their own aspirations than they do for others when predicting future outcomes (Helzer & Dunning, 2012), and believe their behavior comes more from the force of their own character rather than being forced from external situational influences (Balcetis & Dunning, 2008, 2013; Epley & Dunning, 2000). They also rest predictions about their future achievements primarily on the plans they construct rather than on barriers and obstacles that may foil them (Buehler et al., 1994).

In part, this emphasis for the self on agency and intention comes from the motivation to believe that one is in control. Being in control is desirable (Burger & Cooper, 1979), and lets people believe that their fates will be positive ones (McKenna, 1993; Weinstein, 1980). However, this emphasis is not totally a product of motivation. People have good reason to focusing on the question of what they can control. People spend their lives trying to achieve pleasurable outcomes while avoiding aversive ones, and this constant everyday struggle leads them to focus on their personal agency more than they do for other people. Their ability to control events is a central issue in their lives, and beliefs about their control over events importantly informs the decisions they make. In contrast, the agency of other people does not matter as much as it does for the self. Instead, the major question people monitor about others is whether those other people are moral, communal, and trustworthy—that is, will those other people treat them well (Abele & Wojciszke, 2014).

This overweighting of agency and intention for the self relative to others, however, leads people toward bias: an over-optimism in projecting how well they will do relative to peers. People display more illusory superiority along characteristics they view as controllable, such as *resourceful* and *disciplined*, than they do for those seen as uncontrollable, such as *intelligent* and *creative* (Alicke, 1985). People's predictions of how much money they will spend over the next month largely rest on their intentions to rein in their spending. Their actual spending, however, tends not to cohere with those intentions at all (Koehler & Poon, 2006).

In a specific example of the biases resulting from overweighting intentions for the self but not for others, Helzer and Dunning (2012) asked college students to predict how well they would do in an upcoming college exam, comparing the weight given to two pieces of information. The first piece was how well the student had done on a previous exam in the class. The second was the exam score the student aspired to achieve in the upcoming exam. Students were also given the same information about a peer and asked to predict that peer's upcoming exam score as well. When predicting the peer, participants gave greater weight to the peer's past performance rather than that student's aspiration. However, for the self, students weighted aspiration more than past behavior. This differential weighting led students to make more unduly optimistic predictions about their own upcoming exam score relative to what they predicted for their peer's score.

This tendency to overweight agency for the self was also revealed when students engaged in two prediction games involving a chance to win money. In the first game, they chose pieces of information to help them predict the upcoming exam score that a peer would attain. Participants overwhelmingly chose to find out about their peer's score on a previous exam over the score being targeted by that peer for the upcoming exam. However, in the second game, the tables were turned, with some peer having to predict the upcoming score of the participant. In this case, participants gave that peer information about their past score and their aspiration level for the next exam at equal rates (Helzer & Dunning, 2012). In short, in predicting others, past behavior mattered. For the self, aspirations mattered just as much.

Cognitive Mechanisms

The second class of mechanisms are more purely cognitive in nature, focusing on how people habitually neglect relevant information in their social comparisons or simply have fail to have that information available to them.

REFERENCE GROUP NEGLECT

People misjudge their position relative to others because they paradoxically neglect to do make any comparison when making comparative judgments. Instead, they give great weight, sometimes exclusive weight, to their own strengths and weaknesses while largely ignoring the strengths and weaknesses that others may have. In short, they make no comparison even though the question in play is comparative, a phenomenon known as *reference group neglect* (Camerer & Lovallo, 1999; Kruger, 1999).

For example, in studies of entering competitions, researchers find that participants base their decisions about whether to enter almost entirely on confidence in their own skill while giving little or any consideration about the skills among people they will compete against. That is, it is only confidence in one's own skill that matters, not how that skill compares to that of others (Bolger et al., 2008). Further, after taking a competition focused on easy questions (e.g., Who was the first President of the United States?), too many people choose to enter a competition. People apparently neglect the fact that the questions will also be easy for everyone else in the competition. When the questions are difficult (e.g., Who was voted *Time* magazine's Man of the Year in 1938), too few enter the competition, again ignoring the fact that the questions will be hard for everyone (Moore & Cain, 2007).

This neglect of the other people in comparative judgments leads people to overestimate their chances to succeed in certain situations and to underestimate it in others. When the task is easy, people are confident they can succeed. For example, college students think of themselves as particularly knowledgeable on simple and familiar topics, such as pop music and television sitcoms. These rosy self-assessments lead them to overestimate the chances they will win a trivia contest on those topics against a peer, not recognizing that these topics are equally easy for everyone else. When topics are difficult, however, people show the opposite bias, acting as though they are the only one who will experience the difficulty. On esoteric and challenging topics, such as 19th-century French painting and Baroque music, college students tend to think they are likely to lose a trivia contest against any peer—neglecting that these topics are equally demanding for anyone they might compete against (Kruger, 1999).

In perhaps the starkest demonstration that people neglect other people in decisions to enter competitions, Huberman and Rubinstein (2001) presented students with two different competitions to enter, where the most successful entrant would win $200. Both competitions involved pure chance, and students would be competing against all those who also chose that competition. In one, participants had to guess the outcomes of 20 different coin flips. In the second, participants had to predict the outcome of 20 different rolls of a die. A full 74 percent choose to guess the coin flips, presumably because that was an easier event to predict (involving only the two outcomes of heads or tails) than predicting a die (which involved six different outcomes).

However, this decision was irrational, in that 86 percent correctly thought that most other people would also choose to compete on the coin flip. Thus, they were choosing to enter the competition that would contain the most competitors, significantly lowering their chance to win. The competition that would have the lowest number of competitors, thus presenting the greatest chance to win, was the competition involving die rolls. Nonetheless, a full 66 percent of participants chose the die roll even though they explicitly knew it would be the competition with the greatest number of competitors (Huberman & Rubinstein, 2001).

This neglect of others in decisions to compete also extends to the real world. Business owners who start their own company describe their decisions as centered almost exclusively on their own ability as well as internal characteristics of the firm they were considering founding. External factors, such as the prevailing economic climate and potential competition are largely neglected (Moore et al., 2007).

This overall easy-difficult pattern is echoed in data collected by Dun & Bradstreet on business starts. People start businesses more frequently in industries rated by MBA students as something they already understand and that are simple to succeed in (e.g., food or liquor stores) than they do in industries that MBA students perceived as more difficult (e.g., forestry or agricultural services) (Cain et al., 2015).

Further, people in competitions tend to think that changing conditions influence them much more than they do anyone else, not recognizing how those changes affect everyone equally. In a class in which the instructor graded on a curve, students expressed much delight when that instructor added 10 points to everybody's score, neglecting the fact that adding same amount to everyone's score left their grades unchanged. In a poker game, the introduction of wild cards led players to bet more on their hands. Of course, their chance of being dealt a good hand had been raised, but players did not seem to recognize that wild cards helped the hands of their competitors just as much. In reality, their chance of winning was largely unchanged (Windschitl et al., 2003).

People are all flawed intellects. They all have gaps in their knowledge and corrupt their expertise with many mistaken ideas (Dunning, 2015). These deficits can lead people to reach overly optimistic conclusions about their chances of winning in competitions.

These mistaken assessments arise because people's intellectual and social flaws are frequently invisible to them. Lacking expertise, they lack the knowledge necessary to recognize just how much expertise they lack. Work on the *Dunning-Kruger effect* (Dunning, 2011; Ehrlinger et al., 2008; Kruger & Dunning, 1999) shows just how dramatically people fail to recognize the depths of their incompetence and ignorance. In one demonstration of this phenomenon, among students taking an exam in a psychology class, those who scored in the bottom 25 percent of students (and thus earning Ds and Fs for their performance) thought they outperformed a majority of their peers (Dunning et al., 2003). To be sure, they were not as positive about their performance as were top performing peers, but their confidence was not that far behind.

Just how invisible are people's flaws and mistakes? Research from medical education shows the most telling evidence. Interns at a teaching hospital, after being paced through some common medical procedures, all agreed that they knew venipuncture well enough to teach the procedure to others. Only 10 percent of their instructors, after viewing the interns attempt the procedure, agreed (Barnsley et al., 2004). First-year nursing students dressing wounds caught only 15 percent of the mistakes they made handling swabs and 24 percent of the errors they made handling cleaning solutions (Watts et al., 2009). Of first-year medical students completing a cardio-pulmonary resuscitation (CPR) exercise, only three of 95 felt they had failed. Expert examiners failed a much larger figure of 36 (Vnuk et al., 2006).

Recent evidence also suggests that people have a much more difficult time spotting their own errors relative to errors made by others. College students, in one recent study, took a quiz on logical reasoning, indicating for each answer the chance that they were correct, from zero to 100 percent. They then reviewed the answers of three other randomly selected peers, again rating the likelihood that each answer was right.

When it came to judging peers, participants were quite good at distinguishing right from wrong answers. When peers reached accurate answers, participants rated those answers as having a 74 percent chance of being right. Participants rated the wrong answers as having only a 40 percent chance of being right—a clear distinction of 34 percent. However, for their own answers, participants did not differentiate as well between right and wrong answers. They were 76 percent confident in their right answers and a full 62 percent confident in their errors—a discrepancy of only 14 percent. Interestingly, top-performing participants showed this bias the most. They more accurately spotted and downrated the errors of their peers. However, when it came to their own errors, they were just as confident as their more poorly performing counterparts (Dunning, 2020).

Two notes should be made about this result. First, the invisibility of one's own errors, relative to those of others is largely inevitable. People always choose the answer, option, or strategy that they think is the best. That is true of their right answer, but it also includes their errors (Capen et al., 1971; Dunning, 2019). The choices of other people, however, do not have this characteristic. There is no choice bias to contaminate ratings of confidence. That is, the errors other people make are not the choices people themselves would make, and so they are better positioned to identify those choices as flawed.

Second, this asymmetry in spotting the errors of others versus the self may come into play during competitions. People may overrate their themselves in competitive situations because their errors are relatively invisible to them, whereas the errors of others are more obvious. Indeed, in the logic quiz study described above, participants were asked whether they felt they had outperformed, tied, or underperformed each peer whose answers they rated. Participants reported perceptions that were overly optimistic. They judged that they had outperformed each peer roughly 48 percent of the time, but the true rate was significantly lower at 38 percent (Dunning, 2020).

Further, not seeing flaws in performance is exacerbated when the errors involve those of omission rather than commission. More specifically, people may have awareness of errors they actively make, but have little to no sense of when the error involves missing something. College students asked to solve puzzles involving the word-search game Boggle have very little awareness of just how many words they fail to see. In one instance, students on average found roughly 24 words and felt they had missed 18 other words. In reality, they had missed roughly 154 words that were present and discoverable in the Boggle puzzle. Being alerted to the true number of words they had missed caused them to be more cautious in an upcoming competition against another student. In that study, participants could bet up to $2 on whether they had found more Boggle words than a randomly-selected student. Those on average not shown their errors of omission bet $1.13. Those shown all the words they had missed bet only $.88, nearly a 25 percent reduction (Caputo & Dunning, 2005).

Another consequence of flawed intellects involves evaluating the skill of others. People may be generally accurate in spotting when other people make errors, but they tend to have great difficulty in identifying top performers whose competence far exceeds their own. In short, people often fail to have the expertise necessary to spot the true experts among them (Dunning, 2015). Chess players asked to rate the skill of other players, after seeing their performance on a quiz testing skill at responding to tricky game situations, misjudge the performance of top players more than they do those at the bottom. When judging a bad chess play who chose the wrong move in 12 out of 12 different situations, chess players overestimated the performance somewhat, thinking the player chose on average 2.4 correct moves. However, when judging someone who chose the optimal move in every single case, chess players judged only 7.5 (only 63 percent) of the moves to be correct (Dunning & Cone, 2020).

The same pattern arises in judgments in history, financial literacy, global literacy, and gambles in blackjack. People grossly underestimate peers who show top-shelf competence but are much more accurate in spotting bottom-level performance. Asthma sufferers, for example, identify the person (out of a group of four) giving perfect advice on how to use an inhaler only 26 percent of the time, although they can spot the person giving the worst advice 44 percent of the time. They spot the person in a group of four placing seven historical events in their proper order only 47 percent of the time, although they can spot the person doing the worst job 70 percent of the time (Dunning & Cone, 2020).

Exceptions

Although the main finding over decades of research is that people tend to overestimate themselves and the position of their skills relative to others (Dunning et al., 2004), it is important to consider those circumstances in which the tendency either evaporates or even reverses.

A Methodological Note

First, looking over the research, one has to consider the possibility that findings of illusory superiority and overconfidence may be overstated. This issue does not apply to experimental findings in the lab where people are randomly assigned to studies or the conditions within them, but it may apply to field studies in which people can assign themselves to be observed. Consider the finding that would-be entrepreneurs tend to enter new markets too much, with many then facing quick failure (Dunne et al., 1988; Mata & Portugal, 1994; Wagner, 1994). These findings do reveal overconfidence, since new business entry often exceeds market capacity, but they may also overstate overconfidence in business people in general.

That overstatement arises because of the methodological problem of *survivorship bias* (Elton et al., 1996; Hernán et al, 2004). The bias refers to not being mindful of who exactly selects themselves to become visible and thus included in a dataset. In the case of excess entry into business, overconfident people are more likely to start a business and thus are more likely to make themselves visible in the data. All those who potentially underestimate themselves never start a business, remain invisible, and thus never make it to the dataset. As a consequence, findings of overconfidence among entrepreneurs may overstate overconfidence within the general population of business people.

Experimental evidence supports this relevance of this issue. In entry experiments done in the laboratory, people who know the topic of the competition, such as expertise in trivia or sports, before they decide to volunteer for the experiment show much more overconfidence than those who find out the topic only after they volunteer (Camerer & Lovallo, 1999). Presumably, knowing the topic beforehand allows the most confident to sign-up and those least confident to move to some other experiment, thus exacerbating the overconfidence found by researchers.

In addition, important circumstances that place bounds on illusory superiority also exist.

THE OBJECT OF COMPARISON

The degree of illusory correlation a person expresses may depend on whom, or what, they compare themselves to. When the comparison involves rating the self against a general, abstract, or vague referent—such as people in general or the average peer—people display ample level of illusory superiority. However, if the comparison is to a specific person, things change. Students, for example, asked to compare themselves to a specific other person in the room still show illusory superiority, but the magnitude of the bias is greatly reduced. Personal contact with the other person further diminishes the effect (Alicke et al., 1995).

Culture

Illusory superiority also differs across cultures. Overrating the self seems to be more of a Western phenomenon, found in North American and Western Europe—that is, cultures that emphasize individualism—than anywhere else. By contrast, in cultures that emphasize collectivism, like those in Asia, people do not tend to rate themselves as superior to their peers (Heine & Hamamura, 2007; Heine & Lehman, 1997; Heine et al., 1999).

This cultural difference may arise, in part, because Eastern cultures have a different conception of agency than do Western cultures. Recall the argument made above that people exhibit illusory correlation because they emphasize agency and intention more in self-forecasting than in forecasting other people. In doing so, they focus on their plans, aspirations, free will, and potential (Balcetis & Dunning, 2008; Helzer & Dunning, 2012; Pronin & Kugler, 2010; Williams et al., 2012).

This vision of agency, a characteristic of individualist cultures, has been described as *disjoint*, in that people construe themselves as imposing their will on the external environment and other people (Savani et al., 2008; Savani et al., 2010). This view of agency is not a characteristic of more collective cultures, like those of Japan and Asia. There, the tendency is toward *conjoint agency*, emphasizing instead how people can shape their behavior to fit the environment and social roles. One does not impose. Rather, one adapts (Savani et al., 2008; Savani et al., 2010). It is likely that this different view of moving in the world leads to more humble views about how one compares to others.

Where Illusory Superiority Might Reverse

NEGATIVE SELF-VIEWS

A large part of illusory superiority in specific situations and competitions also comes from pre-conceived notions people carry about their skills and expertise. A student's belief about how well they have performed on a college exam may depend as much, if not more, on how they perceived their skill walking into the exam room more than on their actual performance on the exam itself (Atir et al., 2015; Bradley, 1981; Critcher & Dunning, 2009; Ehrlinger & Dunning, 2003). Boost a person's overall self-view on their knowledge of geography and they think they have performed much better on a geography quiz, relative to how they think they have performed after their self-view is undermined instead (Ehrlinger & Dunning, Study 3). Indeed, boost their self-view that they know geography and they claim at a greater rate to have knowledge of cities that they cannot possibly know because those cities do not exist (Atir et al., 2015).

Much of the time, people hold positive self-views and these pre-existing self-views bias them toward thinking they are doing well. However, at times, people hold overly negative views, and this can cause them to underestimate themselves. In a telling example, consider the common finding that girls, starting in their teen years, begin to disproportionately exit the path toward careers in STEM (science, technology, engineering, and math) relative to boys (National Science Foundation, 2000).

Could this greater exit for female relative to male students arise because of negative pre-conceived notions about their scientific talent? In one laboratory study, female college students given a pop quiz on science claimed they had performed much worse than male students claimed, although the two groups did not differ in their objective performance. These different perceptions bore no relation to actual performance, but instead were tightly connected to how students rated their scientific talent in general at the beginning of the laboratory session before the quiz began. Moreover, women more often than men rejected taking part in a science game show competition to take place later in the semester—and this difference was predicted primarily by self-perceptions rather than by the reality of quiz performance. Actual performance, in fact, did not predict at all the resistance to taking part in the game show (Ehrlinger & Dunning, 2003, Study 4).

THE PLIGHT OF TOP PERFORMERS

Underestimation of self is also likely also a characteristic of top-performers. They often fail to recognize how special or exclusive their skills and knowledge are relative to their peers because they make an error in social judgment. In classic studies of the Dunning-Kruger effect, for example, those in the top 25 percent of performers consistently underestimate the percentile their performance falls in. They do not know just how distinctive their expertise is relative to their peers. As such, if there is an error of people lacking expertise overestimating themselves in competition, there is a complementary error among true experts in that they that they underestimate their potential success.

Top performers underestimate their rank among others because what they know seems obvious to them, so they overestimate how much other people know as well. They believe that the tasks that come easy to them must also come easy to other people (Ehrlinger et al., 2008). In short, they suffer a *curse of knowledge*, thinking other people share the same level of expertise as they have themselves (Camerer et al., 1989; Nickerson et al., 1987). Correcting those misperceptions of shared expertise goes a long way toward curing top performers of their overly modest self-ratings. Showing students, for example, who have excellent grammar skills the writing choices of their peers prompts them to recognize just how distinctive their expertise really is. After seeing a representative sample of other college students grappling with a grammar quiz causes skilled students to rate themselves more highly. This result emerges even though students with poor grammar skills fail to change their self-rated ability after seeing the choices of others (Kruger & Dunning, 1999, Study 3).

Concluding Remarks

At times, competitions are thrust upon individuals, such as in the bear and hiker joke that begins this chapter. At other times, people have a choice about which competitions they enter, persist in, or potentially leave.

Success and happiness in life often means choosing the right competitions and navigating them well, while avoiding those not worth the effort and disappointment. A number of psychological dynamics, however, impede people's accuracy in gauging which competitions to enter, how much they need to prepare, and how much success they will attain. For the most part, these dynamics lead people to overestimate their chances: People define skills in ways that are self-flattering. They lean on optimistic scenarios over pessimistic ones in their predictions and plans. They overweight their agency when forecasting their futures relative to any forecasts about others. They fail to evaluate skill and expertise correctly, spotting error among others more accurately than they do for themselves, while failing fully to recognize expertise in others exceeding their own. All the while, they make comparative decisions after not weighing both sides of the comparative ledger, basing their decisions to enter competitions on their own attributes and knowledge while failing to give proper weight to the attributes and knowledge of others. There are times, however, that the bias toward overestimation recedes or reverses.

Luckily, life does not confront people with choices as stark and consequential as whether to run from a bear in the woods, but it does present people with decisions about competitions that are no less important once added together across a lifetime. Life can be a walk in the woods, just as long as one chooses the right path to race others on.

References

Abele, A. E., & Wojciszke, B. (2014). Communal and agentic content in social cognition: A dual perspective model. In M. P. Zanna & J. M. Olson (Eds.), *Advances in experimental social psychology* (vol. 50, pp. 195–225). Academic Press.

Alicke, M. D. (1985). Global self-evaluation as determined by the desirability and controllability of trait adjectives. *Journal of Personality and Social Psychology 49* (6), 1621–1630.

Alicke, M. D., & Govorun, O. (2005). The better-than-average effect. In M. D. Alicke, D. A. Dunning, & J. I. Krueger (Eds.), *The self in social judgment* (pp. 85–106). Psychology Press.

Alicke, M. D., Klotz, M. L., Breitenbecher, D. L., Yurak, T. J., & Vredenburg, D. S. (1995). Personal contact, individuation and the better than average effect. *Journal of Personality and Social Psychology 68* (5), 804–825.

Atir, S., Rosenzweig, E., & Dunning, D. (2015). When knowledge knows no bounds: Self-perceived expertise predicts claims of impossible knowledge. *Psychological Science 26* (8), 1295–1303.

Auderetsch, D. B. (1991). New-firm survival and the technological regime. *The Review of Economics and Statistics 73* (3), 441–450.

Babad, E., & Katz, Y. (1991). Wishful thinking—against all odds. *Journal of Applied Social Psychology 21* (23), 1921–1938.

Balcetis, E., & Dunning, D. (2008). A mile in moccasins: How situational experience reduces dispositionism in social judgment. *Personality and Social Psychology Bulletin 34* (1), 102–114.

Balcetis, E., & Dunning, D. (2013). Considering the situation: Why people are better social psychologists than self-psychologists. *Self and Identity 12* (1), 1–15.

Barnsley, L., Lyon, P., Ralson, S., Hibbert, E., Cunningham, I., Gordon, F., & Field, M. J. (2004). Clinical skills in junior medical officers: A comparison of self-reported confidence and observed competence. *Medical Education 38* (4), 358–367.

Bolger, F., Pulford, B. D., & Colman, A. D. (2008). Market entry decisions: Effects of absolute and relative confidence. *Experimental Psychology 55* (2), 495–515.

Bradley, M. J. (1981). Overconfidence in ignorant experts. *Bulletin of the Psychonomic Society 17* (2), 82–84.

Buehler, R., Griffin, D., & Ross, M. (1994). Exploring the "planning fallacy": Why people underestimate their task completion times. *Journal of Personality and Social Psychology 67* (3), 366–381.

Burger, J. M., & Cooper, H. M. (1979). The desirability of control. *Motivation and Emotion 3* (4), 381–393.

Cain, D. M., Moore, D. A., & Haran, U. (2015). Making sense of overconfidence in market entry. *Strategic Management Journal 36* (1), 1–18.

Camerer, C., & Lovallo, D. (1999). Overconfidence and excess entry: An experimental approach. *The American Economic Review 89* (1), 306–318.

Camerer, C., Loewenstein, G., & Weber, M. (1989). The curse of knowledge in economic settings: An experimental analysis. *Journal of Political Economy 97* (5), 1232–1254.

Capen, E. C., Clapp, R. V., & Campbell, W. M. (1971). Competitive bidding in high-risk situations. *Journal of Petroleum Technology 23* (6), 641–653.

Caputo, D. D., & Dunning, D. (2005). What you don't know: The role played by errors of omission in imperfect self-assessments. *Journal of Experimental Social Psychology 41* (5), 488–505.

Cohen, B. L., & Wallsten, T. S. (1992). The effect of constant outcome value on judgments and decision making given linguistic probabilities. *Journal of Behavioral Decision Making 5* (1), 53–72.

Cooper, A. C., Woo, C. Y., & Dunkelberg, W. C. (1988). Entrepeneurs' perceivedchances for success. *Journal of Business Venturing 3* (2), 97–108.

Critcher, C. R., & Dunning, D. (2009). How chronic self-views influence (and mislead) self-evaluations of performance: Self-views shape bottom-up experiences with the task. *Journal of Personality and Social Psychology 97* (6), 931–945.

Cross, P. (1977). Not can but *will* college teaching be improved? *New Directions for Higher Education 17*, 1–15.

Dunne, T., Roberts, M. J., & Samuleson, L. (1988). Patterns of firm entry and exit in U.S. manufacturing industries. *Rand Journal of Economics 19* (4), 495–515.

Dunning, D. (2011). The Dunning-Kruger effect: On being ignorant of one's own ignorance. In J. Olson & M. P. Zanna (Eds.), *Advances in experimental social psychology* (vol. 44, pp. 247–296). Elsevier.

Dunning, D. (2015). On identifying human capital: Flawed knowledge leads to faulty judgments of expertise by individuals and groups. In S. Thye & E. Lawler (Eds.), *Advances in Group Processes* (vol. 32, pp. 149–176). Emerald.

Dunning, D. (2019). The best option illusion in self and social assessment. *Self & Identity 18* (4), 349–362.

Dunning, D. (2020). *Our errors are invisible to us relative to those of others*. Unpublished manuscript, University of Michigan.

Dunning, D., & Cone, J. (2020). *The Cassandra quandary: On difficulties of identifying expertise among people who outperform the self*. Unpublished manuscript, University of Michigan.

Dunning, D., Heath, C., & Suls, J. (2004). Flawed self-assessment: Implications for health, education, and the workplace. *Psychological Science in the Public Interest 5* (3), 71–106.

Dunning, D., Johnson, K., Ehrlinger, J., & Kruger, J. (2003). Why people fail to recognize their own incompetence. *Current Directions in Psychological Science 12* (3), 83–86.

Dunning, D., Leuenberger, A., & Sherman, D. A. (1995). A new look at motivated inference: Are self-serving theories of success a product of motivational forces? *Journal of Personality and Social Psychology 69* (1), 58–68.

Dunning, D., Meyerowitz, J. A., & Holzberg, A. D. (1989). Ambiguity and self-evaluation: The role of idiosyncratic trait definitions in self-serving assessments of ability. *Journal of Personality and Social Psychology 57* (6), 1082–1090.

Dunning, D., Perie, M., & Story, A. L. (1991). Self-serving prototypes of social categories. *Journal of Personality and Social Psychology 61* (6), 957–968.

Ehrlinger, J., & Dunning, D. (2003). How chronic self-views influence (and potentially mislead) estimates of performance. *Journal of Personality and Social Psychology 84* (1), 5–17.

Ehrlinger, J., Johnson, K., Banner, M., Dunning, D., & Kruger, J. (2008). Why the unskilled are unaware? Further explorations of (lack of) self-insight among the incompetent. *Organizational Behavior and Human Decision Processes 105* (1), 98–121.

Eil, D., & Rao, J. M. (2011). The good news-bad news effect: Asymmetric processing of objective information about yourself. *American Economic Journal: Microeconomics 3* (2), 114–138.

Elton, E. J., Gruber, M. J., & Blake, C. J. (1996). Survivorship bias and mutual fund performance. *The Review of Financial Studies 9* (4), 1097–1120.

Epley, N., & Dunning, D. (2000). Feeling "holier than thou": Are self-serving assessments produced by errors in self or social prediction? *Journal of Personality and Social Psychology 79* (6), 861–875.

Garrett, N., & Sharot, T. (2014). How robust is the optimistic update bias for estimating self-risk and population base rates. *PLos ONE 9*, e98848.

Gilovich, T., Griffin, D., & Kahneman, D. (Eds.). (2002). *Heuristics and biases: The psychology of intuitive judgment*. Cambridge University Press.

Goodman-Delahunty, J., Granhag, P. A., Hartwig, M., & Loftus, E. F. (2010). Insightful or wishful: Lawyers' ability to predict case outcomes. *Psychology, Public Policy, and Law 16* (2), 133–157.

Granberg, D., & Brent, E. (1983). When prophecy bends: The preference–expectation link in U.S. presidential elections, 1952–1980. *Journal of Personality and Social Psychology 45* (3), 477–491.

Heine, S. J., & Hamamura, T. (2007). In search of East Asian self-enhancement. *Personality and Social Psychology Review 11* (1), 4–27.

Heine, S. J., & Lehman, D. R. (1997). The cultural construction of self-enhancement: An examination of group-serving biases. *Journal of Personality and Social Psychology 72* (6), 1268–1283.

Heine, S. J., Lehman, D. R., Markus, H. R., & Kitayama, S. (1999). Is there a universal need for positive self-regard? *Psychological Review 106* (4), 766–794.

Helzer, E. G., & Dunning, D. (2012). Why and when peer prediction is superior to self-prediction: The weight given to future aspiration versus past achievement. *Journal of Personality and Social Psychology 103* (1), 38–53.

Hernán, M. A., Hernández-Días, S., & Robins, J. M. (2004). A structural approach to selection bias. *Epidemiology 15* (5), 615–625.

Huberman, G., & Rubinstein, A. (2001). Correct belief, wrong action and a puzzling gender difference (March 25, 2001). Unpublished manuscript. Available at SSRN: https://ssrn.com/abstract=264293.

Irwin, F. W. (1953). Stated expectations as functions of probability and desirability of outcomes. *Journal of Personality 21* (3), 329–335

Kahneman, D. (1988). Experimental economics: A psychological perspective. In R. Tietz, W. Albers, & R. Selten (Eds.), *Bounded rational behavior in experimental games and markets* (pp. 11–18). Springer-Verlag.

Koehler, D. J., & Poon, C. S. K. (2006). Self-predictions overweight strength of current intentions. *Journal of Experimental Social Psychology 42* (4), 517–524.

Krizan, Z., Miller, J. C., & Johar, O. (2010). Wishful thinking in the 2008 U.S. presidential election. *Psychological Science 21* (1), 140–146.

Kruger, J. (1999). Lake Wobegon be gone! The "below-average effect" and the egocentric nature of comparative ability judgments. *Journal of Personality and Social Psychology 77* (2), 221–232.

Kruger, J. M., & Dunning, D. (1999). Unskilled and unaware of it: How difficulties in recognizing one's own incompetence lead to inflated self-assessments. *Journal of Personality and Social Psychology 77* (6), 1121–1134.

Kunda, Z. (1990). The case for motivated reasoning. *Psychological Bulletin 108* (3), 480–498.

Larwood, L., & Whittaker, W. (1977). Managerial myopia: Self-serving biases in organizational planning. *Journal of Applied Psychology 62* (2), 194–198.

Loftus, E. F., & Wagenaar, W. A. (1988). Lawyers' predictions of success. *Jurimetrics Journal 28* (4), 437–453.

Massey, C., Simmons, J. P., & Armor, D. A. (2011). Hope over experience: Desirability and the persistence of optimism. *Psychological Science 22* (2), 274–281.

Mata, J., & Portugal, P. (1994). Life duration of new firms. *Journal of Industrial Economics 42* (3), 227–245.

McKenna, F. P. (1993). It won't happen to me: Unrealistic optimism or illusion of control? *British Journal of Psychology 84* (1), 39–50.

Moore, D. A., & Cain, D. M. (2007). Overconfidence and underconfidence: When and why people underestimate (and overestimate) the competition. *Organization Behavior and Human Decision Processes 103* (2), 197–213.

Moore, D. A., Oesch, J. M., & Zietsma, C. (2007) What competition? Myopic self-focus in market-entry decisions. *Organization Science 18* (3), 440–454.

National Science Foundation. (2000). *Women, minorities, and persons with disabilities in science and engineering.* National Science Foundation.

Newby-Clark, I. R., & Ross, M. (2003). Conceiving the past and future. *Personality and Social Psychology Bulletin 29* (7), 807–818.

Newby-Clark, I. R., Ross, M., Buehler, R., Koehler, D. J., & Griffin, D. (2000). People focus on optimistic and disregard pessimistic scenarios while predicting their task completion times. *Journal of Experimental Psychology: Applied 6* (3), 171–182.

Nickerson, R. S., Baddeley, A., & Freeman, B. (1987). Are people's estimates of what other people know influenced by what they themselves know? *Acta Psychologica 64* (3), 245–259.

Park, Y. J., & Santos-Pinto, L. (2010). Overconfidence in tournaments: Evidence from the field. *Theory and Decision 69* (1), 143–166.

Pronin, E., & Kugler, M. B. (2010). People believe they have more free will than others. *PNAS Proceedings of the National Academy of Sciences of the United States of America 107* (52), 22469–22474.

Rapoport, A. (1995). Individual strategies in a market-entry game. *Group Decision and Negotiation 4*, 117–133.

Santos-Pinto, L., & Sobel, J. (2005). A model of positive self-image in subjective assessment. *American Economic Review 95* (5), 1386–1402.

Savani, K., Markus, H. R., & Conner, A. L. (2008). Let your preference by your guide? Preferences and choices are more tightly linked for North Americans and for Indians. *Journal of Personality and Social Psychology 95* (4), 861–876.

Savani, K., Markus, H. R., Naidu, N. V. R., Kumar, S., & Berlia, V. (2010). What counts as a choice? U. S. Americans are more likely than Indians to construe actions as choices. *Psychological Science 21* (3), 391–398.

Schneider, M. (2007). The nature, history and significance of the concept of positional goods. *History of Economics Review 45* (1), 60–81.

Story, A. L., & Dunning, D. (1998). The more rational side of self-serving prototypes: The effects of success and failure performance feedback. *Journal of Experimental Social Psychology 34* (6), 513–529.

Tor, A. (2002). The fable of entry: Bounded rationality, market discipline, and legal policy. *Michigan Law Review 101* (2), 482–568.

Vnuk, A., Owen, H., & Plummer, J. (2006). Assessing proficiency in adult basic life support: Student and expert assessment and the impact of video recording. *Medical Teacher 28* (5), 429–434.

Wagner, J. (1994). The post-entry performance of new small firms in German manufacturing industries. *Journal of Industrial Economics 42* (2), 141–154.

Watts, W. E., Rush, K., & Wright, M. (2009). Evaluating first-year nursing students' ability to self-assess psychomotor skills using video. *Nursing Education Perspectives 30* (4), 214–219.

Weinstein, N. D. (1980). Unrealistic optimism about future life events. *Journal of Personality and Social Psychology 39* (5), 806–820.

Weinstein, N. D., & Klein, W. M. (1995). Resistance of personal risk perceptions to debiasing interventions. *Health Psychology 14* (2), 132–140.

Williams, E., Gilovich, T., & Dunning, D. (2012). Being all that you can be: How potential performances influence assessments of self and others. *Personality and Social Psychology Bulletin 38* (2), 143–154.

Windschitl, P. D., Kruger, J., & Simms, E. N. (2003). The influence of egocentrism and focalism on people's optimism in competitions: When what affects us equally affects me More. *Journal of Personality and Social Psychology 85* (3), 389–408.

Zenger, T. R. (1992). Why do employers only reward extreme performance? Examining the relationships among performance, pay, and turnover. *Administrative Science Quarterly 37* (2), 198–219.

CHAPTER 4

Social Dilemmas: From Competition to Cooperation

Poonam Arora, Tamar Kugler, *and* Francesca Giardini

Abstract

Social dilemmas are interdependent decisions where the outcomes depend upon choices made by every decision maker. Importantly, the incentive structure sets up a dominant strategy of non-cooperation such that everyone ends up worse off than if all had cooperated, but each individual is better off not cooperating regardless of what others do. Thus, social dilemmas are mixed-motive situations that require a choice between short-term individual gain and long-term collective gain. Social dilemma researchers have adopted a variety of approaches to studying cooperation ranging from considering it as a constructed context-dependent choice that is affected by incentives and economic nudges, group affiliation, norms, and social nudges, while others investigate individual differences and personal perceptions of value. This chapter organizes current topical knowledge through the lens of the Theory of Planned Behavior (TPB), where cooperation is the expressed behavior when an intent to cooperate emerges (consciously or sub-consciously) from a positive attitude towards the act of cooperating, from a dominant cooperative norm, or the interaction of attitude and norms, and is supported by the perception that one has the freedom to cooperate (behave cooperatively). The chapter provides a broad review of the field to understand mechanisms that both increase likelihood of cooperative behavior and those that result in cooperative breakdowns, as well as possible solutions to further effective cooperation.

Key Words: social dilemmas, cooperation, Theory of Planned Behavior (TPB), motivation to cooperate, attitude towards cooperation, cooperative norms

Social Dilemmas: From Competition to Cooperation

Interdependent social dilemmas surround us. Broadly defined, these are "situations in which short-term self-interest is at odds with longer-term collective interests" (van Lange et al., 2013). Deciding whether to make a donation to a public radio station, consume single-use plastic products, put effort into a team project, choose to water one's lawn during a dry summer versus conserve water, or enter a clinical trial for a drug are all examples of social dilemmas encountered in our day-to-day lives.

Such dilemmas involve interdependent decisions where the outcomes for all decision makers depend upon choices made by every decision maker. Importantly, the incentive structure is designed such that if each individual follows the dominant strategy of non-cooperation, everyone will end up worse off than if all had cooperated (Dawes, 1980), but each individual is better off not cooperating regardless of what others do. Thus, social dilemmas are essentially mixed-motive situations that require a choice between short-term individual gain, or the competitive option, and long-term collective gain, or the cooperative option. In most social dilemmas a small number of people consistently (and maybe irrationally) choose the non-dominant option to cooperate. This highlights the main questions with which social dilemma researchers grapple: Why and when do participants in a social dilemma cooperate?

Building on Rational Choice Theory, social dilemmas research has focused on why people cooperate when it is apparently irrational and nonbeneficial (Camerer, 2003), and what the circumstances and conditions are that lead people to choose cooperation over competition. The inherent assumption here is that because individuals are utility maximizers, there would be no strictly rational reason to cooperate and attain the resulting lower outcomes. And yet, cooperation is readily observed in both artificial, laboratory-based dilemmas and in real-world dilemmas (see Dawes & Messick, 2000 for a complete review). Natural resource use, collective living arrangements, and effective institutions across the globe show that cooperation can be achieved regardless of the prediction of rational choice theory (Ostrom, 1990).

Social dilemma researchers have adopted a variety of approaches to studying cooperation. Some treated it as a constructed context-dependent choice that is affected by incentives and economic nudges, group affiliation, norms, and social nudges, while others investigated individual differences and personal perceptions of value. A central underlying assumption across all approaches is that cooperation is a positive and desirable outcome. Indeed, many researchers ask not only when people cooperate, but also how people can be nudged through, say, choice architecture, to increase their levels of cooperation. While this is commonly the case, it is worth noting that there are settings where individual rationality can be more beneficial, even at the collective level. For example, when social dilemmas are embedded within an intergroup conflict, mobilizing collective action and cooperation within one's in-group escalates conflict with the out-group and increases costs across all groups (Bornstein, 1992, 2003; Kugler & Bornstein, 2013).

The social dilemmas field differentiates between two person dilemmas (e.g., Prisoner's Dilemmas, Chicken Dilemmas, and Stag Hunt or Assurance dilemmas—see Halevy et al., 2012, for a review of game structures), and more complex multi-person dilemmas (e.g., public goods dilemmas, common pool resource dilemmas, and volunteer dilemmas), as well as between dilemmas where the strategy space is binary (i.e., participants choose between cooperating and defecting) and dilemmas where cooperation is a spectrum, and individuals choose their level of desired cooperative behavior. There are, however, considerable commonalities in the mental representations of all dilemmas that can be fundamentally expressed as four basic two-person payoff structures (Halevy et al., 2012). These four games collectively encapsulate many of the psychological processes that influence choice in dilemmas and their behavioral and social consequences. Another element of choice in dilemmas is whether decision-makers make their choice simultaneously with other decision-makers or sequentially, where the order can matter. We focus here on individual choices in simultaneous settings, though we highlight significant aspects of sequential dilemmas when relevant.

Over the last half-century, one productive line of research has considered the tendency to cooperate as an individual difference. Social Value Orientations (SVOs, e.g., Balliet et al., 2009; Messick & McClintock, 1968; van Lange et al., 1997), differences in risk attitudes and preferences (Holt & Laury, 2002; Raub & Snijders, 1997), and responses to emotions (e.g., Kugler et al., 2012; also see later in this chapter) are all examples of individual difference variables that affect the choice to cooperate. In the same vein, research considering personality traits finds that agreeableness among the Big-5 personality traits is a predictor of cooperative behavior (Volk et al., 2011).

A second research approach has considered situational motivations for cooperation, such as the structure of the game (Bornstein, 2004; Messick, 1999), the setting surrounding the game and the related social mechanisms (Brewer & Schneider, 1990; van Lange, 2000) or interactions between situation and individual (Arora et al., 2016; Kugler & Bornstein, 2013). A third approach focused on those who were most impacted by the interdependent choice—who they were (Arora & Tedeschi, 2019; Brewer, 1999), what they were likely to do (Arora et al., 2012, 2016), and, whether they could control what they were likely to do or influence what others might do (Croson, 2000; Kelley & Thibaut, 1978).

Theory of Planned Behavior: Our Theoretical Framework

The purpose of this review is not to summarize everything known about social dilemmas—that would take a few books—and several excellent reviews of this field already exist (Milinski, 2019; van Lange et al., 2013; Weber et al., 2004). Instead, we organize current topical knowledge through the lens of the Theory of Planned Behavior (Ajzen, 1985, 1987). The Theory of Planned Behavior (TPB or the theory), as adapted for social dilemmas and illustrated in Figure 14.1, posits that behavior results from attitudes (derived from beliefs and an evaluation of their outcomes) that interact with subjective norms (derived from normative beliefs and the motivation to comply with them) and together give rise to a behavioral intention that then translates into behavior. The original theory places perceived control as a precursor to the intention itself. In our adapted framework, we place the perceptions and actual beliefs about control over the action as well as perceived power as moderators that impact the translation of intention into behavior. This also allows us to consider separately individual control over actions, and beliefs regarding the control of others over their own actions.

Put simply, cooperation is the expressed behavior when an intent to cooperate emerges (consciously or sub-consciously) from a positive attitude towards the act of cooperating,

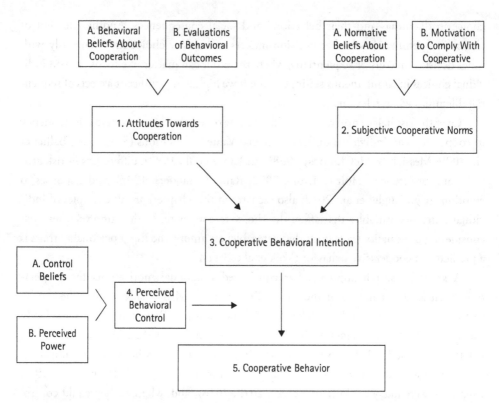

Figure 14.1 An adapted framework of combined theories of reasoned action and planned behavior for application to social dilemmas (based on Ajzen, 1991; Fishbein, 1979).

from a dominant cooperative norm, or the combination of attitude and norms, and is supported by the perception that decision-makers in the dilemma participants have the freedom to cooperate (behave cooperatively). Consider the choice to wear a mask in public as a preventative measure during a pandemic. According to the TPB, a decision maker may choose to wear a mask due to a positive attitude towards wearing masks, a willingness to follow a norm of wearing masks, or a combination of attitudes and norms, which lead to an intention and eventually to the behavior of wearing a mask. Of course, things can go wrong along the way. An individual propensity leading to a positive attitude towards wearing a mask may interact with a norm that ridicules mask wearing, or widespread beliefs that masks are not effective. An intention to wear a mask may not translate into mask wearing when there is a mask shortage (moderating effect of control). We discuss examples of cooperation breakdowns and mechanisms attempting to solve them later in this chapter.

Although the interdependency of outcomes in social dilemmas complicates this reasoned and process-oriented approach, our chosen theoretical lens provides an integrated view of current research while also highlighting areas for future work. Existing theoretical approaches to social dilemmas have focused primarily on sources underlying the motivation to cooperate in psychology, contextual and structural features that might facilitate cooperation in sociology, or the payoffs and associated incentives in economics. The importance of these aspects is hard to deny, but equally important is to determine the building blocks of the decision-making process and how they are connected. By discussing current work on social dilemmas in terms of attitudes, norms, and perceived control we intend to demonstrate why an integrated approach is needed, and how this can benefit the field. Centrally, by going beyond single individual and contextual variables of influence, TPB allows for an interpretation of process by which an individual arrives at the choice to cooperate. Moreover, it identifies underlying assumptions and gaps that ought to be addressed before social dilemma researchers can offer effective prescriptive advice to policy makers.

Despite the fact that TPB is considered to be a general and parsimonious model that can predict a large range of motivated behaviors (see Armitage & Conner, 2001, for a meta-analytic review), there has been no shortage of criticism towards TPB. For example, Sniehotta et al. (2014) raise concerns both about the validity and the utility of the theory and question the mediated processes that constitute TPB. Our interest in TPB is more as an organizing framework for the existing research on social dilemmas and less as a model in need of testing, limiting the threats of this criticism.

Towards this goal, the next sections of this chapter organize our knowledge of social dilemmas within the building blocks of TPB as laid out in Figure 14.1. For each numbered box in the figure, we review relevant antecedents (labeled A and B) and explain how they combine into attitude, norms, or perceived control and power. We then discuss how these building blocks lead to the construction of behavioral intent and expressed cooperative behavior.

Attitudes Towards Cooperation

Attitudes towards cooperation (Box 1 in Figure 14.1) are composed of behavioral beliefs about cooperation (Box 1A) as well as subjective values associated with the outcomes of cooperative behavior (Box 1B). Generally, positive attitude results from some combination of positive subjective beliefs towards cooperation and the associated outcomes of such behaviors.

ATTITUDE TOWARDS COOPERATION: BEHAVIORAL BELIEFS ABOUT COOPERATION

These are beliefs about cooperation that are associated with a specific outcome that holds a certain subjective value for an individual. In the next sections we discuss how such beliefs may be formed, and whether they are associated with a positive or negative outcome.

Individually Motivated Behavioral Beliefs about Cooperation

The TPB framework begins by considering how a decision maker's underlying cognitive and affective beliefs about being cooperative in a dilemma impact the resulting attitude towards cooperation. These beliefs arise from multiple sources, including the pursuit of desirable outcomes and avoidance of undesirable ones. Arguably, selfish actors, when faced with two choices, will hold a positive view of the choice that results in the more desirable outcome for themselves. In a social dilemma, non-cooperation typically results in better outcomes in terms of the resources at stake. However, a decision maker may have a positive view of the act of cooperation itself (rather than the outcome associated with it). Attitudes towards cooperation can therefore arise from a strong personal conviction or an innately held belief. For example, consistent or unconditional cooperators hold a sufficiently positive view of cooperation regardless of their final outcome or the behavior of others (Elster, 1985; Weber & Murnighan, 2008), akin to the environmentalist who decides to not fly for work or vacation, even at the cost of giving up highly desirable outcomes. Similarly, a group member who chooses to do more than their fair share to ensure a successful team project even when others free ride, may derive value from that cooperative action, suggesting a positive attitude towards cooperation.

Researchers have approached this innate difference in the value ascribed to cooperation, or the relative importance of outcomes obtained by interdependent others versus one's own outcomes as an individual difference in one's social value orientation (SVO). Cooperative behaviors demonstrated across a variety of social contexts can be accounted for by SVOs (Messick & McClintock, 1968; Murphy et al., 2011; van Lange et al., 1997). SVO also predicts cooperative behavior in social dilemmas (e.g., Balliet et al., 2009). The orientations captured by the SVO measure are altruistic, cooperative, individualistic, and competitive (altruistic and cooperative orientations are often labeled together as prosocial orientations, while individualistic and competitive orientations are considered proself orientations (Forsyth, 2006; Messick & McClintock, 1968; McClintock & Allison, 1989; van Lange, 1999). These four orientations manifest themselves when decision makers strive to: (i) maximize their own payoff (individualistic), (ii) maximize the difference (to their benefit) between their payoff and another's payoff (competitive), (iii) maximize combined payoffs or minimize the difference between their payoff and another's payoff (cooperative), (iv) maximize another's payoff at the cost of their own payoff (altruistic).

Beyond a basic propensity to cooperate themselves, prosocial individuals are also more likely to reciprocate another's anticipated or actual level of cooperation (van Lange, 1999). As they are generally more socially oriented, they are also more likely to give significantly more of their time to a cause and to help others than proselfs (McClintock & Allison, 1989). Proselfs, however, do not necessarily endorse free riding or being selfish. They simply see cooperation as too costly. Motivated by self-interest, they perceive situational constraints, such as being taken advantage of, as being sufficient to prevent them from cooperation. For them, cooperation is an unnecessary risk (Attari et al., 2014).

Affective reactions are some other building blocks that shape attitudes towards cooperation. The literature on emotions in social dilemmas differentiates between experienced emotions and expressed emotions within this context. The affect-as-information theory (Schwartz & Clore, 1988, 2003; Chanes et al., 2018), which is a model of evaluative processing, suggests that experienced emotions act as an embodied source of information (Storbeck & Clore, 2008) and provide guidance regarding decision alternatives. In this case, different affective reactions to the possibility of cooperating (or not cooperating) inform the individual whether this behavior is desirable. Similarly, the Appraisal Tendency Framework (ATF; Lerner & Keltner, 2000, 2001) stipulates that experienced emotions lead to changes in cognitive appraisals (which are really no different than attitudes) and, in turn, inform behavioral decisions (see Lerner et al., 2015 for a review). For example, experienced emotions affect levels of trust (Dunn & Schweitzer, 2005; Kugler et al., 2020): anger and disgust decrease trust, while happiness increases it. Discrete emotions also shape risk attitudes (Keltner et al., 1993). Kugler, Connolly and Ordonez (2012) demonstrate that incidental anger and fear change cooperation levels in a Stag Hunt game. Guilt increases cooperation in social dilemmas (Ketelaar & Au, 2003), and empathic feelings towards a partner also increase cooperation (Rumble et al., 2010).

Expressed emotions (for example, through facial expressions) act as signals of intentions, and help establish cooperation tendencies. Wubben (2010) demonstrates that anger signals lower cooperation tendencies than guilt, which can promote successful coordination in dilemmas. Stouten and de Cremer (2010) show that expressed emotions moderated the effect of communication on cooperation: when participants in a dilemma expressed happiness, they were perceived as honest, increasing the effectiveness of communication on cooperation, while anger had the opposite effect. de Melo and Terada (2020) show that expressed emotions increased or decreased cooperation in Prisoner's Dilemmas.

Socially Motivated Behavioral Beliefs about Cooperation

Attitudes can also emerge from individual perceptions of context-appropriate behavior or be inferred from actions taken in the past. Some individuals choose to cooperate when cooperation is seen as the appropriate response to the context (Arora et al., 2012; 2004). Essentially, they seek to answer the question "What does a person like me do in a situation like this?" (Logic of Appropriateness, March & Olsen, 2004). Cooperation thus emerges from who is the me (identity of the person) in this situation (context) and what is the appropriate action (norm or rule). The response to the question of who is the "me" in the situation can result in multiple attitudes towards cooperation that can even be contradictory.

The topic of identity vis-à-vis others who benefit from cooperation is well-researched: in-group members, or those who can be thought of as "us" versus "them," benefit from a more positive attitude towards cooperation (Balliet et al., 2014). This is, in part, because identifying with like or valued others transforms the underlying attitude towards cooperation while also projecting one's own willingness to cooperate on other in-group members (Brewer, 2008). Studies that systematically manipulated group identification found that as the level of identification increased, so did the level of cooperation and the trust in other group members. Notably, higher levels of cooperation were also accompanied by an increased accessibility of other-related concepts as measured by an implicit word completion task (Arora et al., 2012). Participants were asked to complete words to test for the accessibility of social constructs. For example, the following incomplete word SHA_E could be finished as a word with a social meaning (SHARE) or in several less social ways (e.g., SHAKE or SHAPE). Words used were controlled for their natural frequency in the English language. Such patterns of results were observed independent of whether the cooperative choice was to take place immediately in the present, or in the future.

Consistent with the goal-transformation hypothesis, identification with the in-group makes collective or social goals salient, transforming individual motives into collective ones. There is an expectation that others in the group will also engage in behavior that achieves collective goals (Kramer & Wei, 1999). Evidence of cooperation with the in-group has been accumulating for half a century (Brewer, 1979; Tajfel et al., 1971; Tajfel & Turner, 1978), exists even in minimal group settings (Arora, Logg & Larrick, 2016; Tajfel, 1970), and is especially notable when the in-group is contrasted with an out-group (Bornstein, 1992; Bornstein & Ben Yossef, 1994; Halevy et al., 2008). The theoretical underpinnings of in-group bias emerge from Social Identity Theory (Tajfel & Turner, 1986), which claims that in addition to a personal identity, individuals possess a social identity derived from their group memberships. Cooperation with their in-groups serves to maintain a positive social identity vis-à-vis the out-group. Bounded Reciprocity Theory (Kiyonari & Yamagishi, 2004; Yamagishi et al., 1999; Yamagishi & Mifune, 2009) provides a complementary theoretical framework, positing that from an evolutionary perspective, groups are essential to survival and operate through a generalized exchange network where group members must retain a reputation as cooperators to benefit from in-group cooperative exchanges, or reciprocity.

Surprisingly, although proselfs generally associate a higher cost with cooperation, strong identification with in-group can actually result in them cooperating more with that in-group, relative to prosocials (de Cremer & van Dijk, 2002), mainly because identification transforms which goals and payoffs they seek to maximize. Greater group identification results in a greater focus on payoffs for the group and the group's goals, decreasing the emphasis on individual payoffs. Feedback about cooperation by the group as a whole, however, attenuates this effect of individual differences in SVO. Specifically, when overall group cooperation rates are low (i.e., there is group failure), cooperation rates increase if group identity is salient, but decrease if personal identity is salient, regardless of a person's SVO. When group cooperation rates are high, there are no differences between saliency of group and personal identity (de Cremer & van Dijk)—everyone cooperates because everyone else is cooperating.

Cooperation in a social dilemma is a result of a choice constructed within the constraints of the decision setting (Slovic, 1995). Social and group contexts, as well as individual preferences, are constraints that influence this choice, in part by changing how outcomes are framed and evaluated (Weber et al., 2004). There is a weighing of the costs and benefits of cooperation to decide whether the outcomes are a net positive for oneself, and given the interdependence, for others such that a positive evaluation of the outcomes results in greater likelihood of cooperation. What is surprising is that cooperation can occur even when the monetary and tangible payoffs are higher for defection. Kelley and Thibaut (1978) suggested that payoffs are transformed, often automatically or subconsciously, to account for intangible positives afforded by the choice, such as positive self-image, a feeling of belongingness, and social approval from an in-group. Thus, cooperation is essentially a positive constructed choice that results when transformations of payoffs end in a positive evaluation of total outcomes (tangible and intangible).

Arora et al. (2012) illustrate these kinds of transformations empirically: consider Table 14.1, which shows the theoretical tangible and intangible outcomes for cooperation (C) and defection (D) in a symmetrical four-player game with both experimenter-imposed rank-ordered tangible payoffs and context dependent payoffs that may encourage cooperation. The number of cooperative choices made by the members of the group is shown in the first column; resulting tangible payoffs to cooperators and to defectors are shown in the next two columns, ranked from 8 (high) to 1 (low). Thus, if all four cooperate, the outcome is 7, the second highest; but each of the four has a financial incentive to defect (and get 8 rather than 7, at the expense of the three remaining cooperators, who would each get 5). The payoff structure is similar when fewer group members cooperate: cooperators always have an incentive to defect. The Nash equilibrium (taking into account only strict financial outcomes) dictates that no group members cooperate, and therefore each member will receive the associated payoff of 2, the second lowest. However, this model allows for an implicit reward for full cooperation by all group members (e.g., a good team feeling associated with full cooperation). If this reward (indicated by $+ c_4$ in Table 14.1) is sufficiently big, the combination of the tangible outcome 7 and intangible outcome $+ c_4$ may be greater than tangible outcome 8 (the highest payoff). Given this total outcome, when all cooperate, nobody has an incentive to defect. The model also allows for the possibility of sanctions (indicated in the last column of Table 14.1). These sanctions intangibly reduce the value of defection. The transformed tangible and intangible outcomes together can give rise to an equilibrium in which all cooperate.

One of the appealing features of this model is that the tangible and intangible outcomes need not be the same for all players. In particular, $+c_4$ and $-d_3$ might be smaller for a defector than for a cooperator, explaining why behavior varies across different people. There could, nonetheless, be sufficient intrinsic rewards for cooperation $(+c_3)$ for each of the other three people to produce an equilibrium where three group members cooperate,

Table 14.1. Financial and Social Outcomes for Cooperation (C) and Defection (D) in a Symmetrical Four-Player Game (Adapted from Arora et al., 2012).

Number of players choosing C	Financial reward for choosing		Context-based motivation for choosing C	
	C	D	Gain intrinsic reward	Avoid social sanction
4	7	-	$+c_4$	–
3	5	8	$+c_3$	$-d_3$
2	3	6	?	$-d_2$
1	1	4		?
0	-	2		

and one defects. Regardless, as fewer participants cooperate, intangible positives weaken, and thus defection by all participants remains an equilibrium: when all defect, nobody has an incentive to cooperate. This example illustrates how the evaluation process of the behavioral outcomes (encapsuled in the internal transformation of payoff as originally suggested by Kelley & Thibaut, 1978) could account for cooperative behavior.

Attitudes towards cooperation can become more positive when others cooperate (or when one thinks they are likely to cooperate). In the same way, they may turn more negative when others defect (or one expects others to defect). The literature of conditional cooperators (Fischbacher & Gachter, 2006; Fischbacher et al., 2001; Keser & van Winden, 2000) posits a mixture of types that vary in their attitude to cooperation. About 50 percent of the individuals are conditional cooperators and match their contributions to those of others in their group. The next 25 percent are unconditional cooperators, and cooperate regardless of what others do, while 25 percent are consistent free riders (Fischbacher & Gachter, 2010). The existence of different types of dilemma participants provides a simple explanation to the well-known finding of decreasing levels of cooperation over time in repeated social dilemmas (e.g., Andreoni, 1988; Ledyard, 1994)—conditional cooperators negatively revise their attitude towards cooperation after interacting with free riders. It is interesting to note that the prevalence of conditional cooperation varies across cultures. Comparing behavior across locations in Austria, Japan, and the U.S., Kocher and collogues (2008) found that both the relative frequency of conditional cooperators and the extent of conditional cooperation is significantly higher among U.S. participants than elsewhere.

Attitudes towards cooperation, therefore, include an evaluation of the likelihood of others taking advantage of one's cooperation. Although cooperation can be highly valued, being taken advantage of is aversive, so one is only likely to cooperate if the probability of or value assigned to being taken advantage of is low. Indeed, Attari et al. (2014) found that the stronger one's belief that others are likely to free-ride or treat the cooperator like a sucker who should have known better, the lower the likelihood of cooperation.

Subjective Cooperative Norms

Subjective norms about cooperation (Box 2 in Figure 14.1) emerge from a comprehensive set of beliefs regarding cooperative tendencies (Box A) and expectations of relevant or important others (Box B). These beliefs interact with the decision maker's motivation to exhibit the prescribed behavior. The two components collectively yield subjective cooperative norms.

SUBJECTIVE COOPERATIVE NORMS: NORMATIVE BELIEFS ABOUT COOPERATION

Norms are powerful determinants of individual behavior (Asch, 1956). Individuals follow them because they tend to satisfy the identity-based reasons people join groups (White et al., 2009). Additionally, they efficiently and effectively coordinate behavior in groups (Weber et al., 2004). Finally, they offer information about what a social referent might expect the decision maker to do in certain situations, and because non-compliance with certain norms can lead to social punishment, including ostracism (Kurzban & Leary, 2001; Williams, 2007), they also inform the limits of acceptable behavior.

In social dilemmas, social normative beliefs (Box 2A) constitute a central explanation for why people cooperate (Biel & Thogersen, 2007; Coleman, 1990; Kerr, 1995; Ostrom, 1998; Pillutla & Chen, 1999). Homeowners cooperate to reduce energy consumption to follow a neighborhood norm (Schultz et al., 2007), and hotel guests reuse towels to match a norm established by unknown but similar others (Goldstein et al., 2007). A common sight in many affluent suburban public schools throughout America are parents who volunteer their time and effort to raise funds for school activities even when their kids may not directly benefit because supporting the school is the communal norm. In fact, the power of group norms can be such that individuals publicly conform to them even as they privately disagree with them, especially if conformity ensures group membership (Deutsch & Gerard, 1955; Noelle-Neumann, 1974). Arguably, congressional representatives who vote along party lines even when they do not personally fully agree with the nature of their vote, do so as a gesture of public conformity to maintain their standing in the party.

In general, the observed or descriptive norm is the same as the expected or injunctive group norm (Cialdini & Goldstein, 2004), and is therefore reflective of group values. However, the injunctive or expected norm for a group, which may be derived from the group's identity and value statement, might not be what its members actually practice (Cialdini et al., 1990), much like the saying "do as I say, not as I do". When injunctive norms differ from descriptive norms, it is unclear what an individual group member should do under such circumstances. There are several reasons to believe that, when presented with conflicting norms, descriptive norms exert a heavier pull. Observing how others actually behave produces both informational and normative influence (Deutsch & Gerard, 1955): it provides information about what is normal or smart in this circumstance, and it creates additional pressure to fit in. Conforming to observed behavior is also attractive for reasons of fairness. When members of a group are defectors, independent of the group's stated value of cooperation, any single individual will receive an equal outcome by also defecting but will receive a worse overall outcome by cooperating. People are highly motivated to avoid unfavorable inequality (Loewenstein et al., 1989). Thus, when a descriptive norm of defection is pitted against an injunctive norm of cooperation, many factors push toward matching the descriptive norm, including self-interest, informational and normative influence, and fairness considerations. Not surprisingly, this influence of descriptive norms is heightened when identification with a group is high (Terry & Hogg, 1996).

However, despite overwhelming evidence of individual compliance with descriptive norms, Williams and Karau (1991) found that when an individual values an outcome, such as a high-quality project report that is not supported by a social loafing norm, the individual is likely to ignore the norm and perform to ensure the desired outcome is achieved. Arora et al. (2016) found that group members were even willing to overcompensate at a personal cost to make up for defectors to ensure a meaningful outcome was achieved. These individuals are willing to be "suckered," at least in the short run (Kerr, 1983). Additionally, Yamagishi (1988) found that Japanese participants surrounded by loafing group members would rather exit the situation than accept the pressure to loaf. Here, group members choose to walk away from the group rather than follow a non-valued descriptive norm.

SUBJECTIVE COOPERATIVE NORMS: MOTIVATION TO COMPLY WITH COOPERATIVE NORMS

According to Goal Framing Theory (Lindenberg, 1998) norm-guided behavior stems from a combination of external cues and internal motivations that activate different goals and behaviors, or norm-relevant behavior is expressed when there is a motivation to comply with the underlying norm (Box 2B). Prosocial actions result from the combination of cognitive-motivational processes that creates core motivations (i.e., frames). When faced with a social dilemma, individuals act on the basis of the most salient frame. The resolution of social dilemmas depends on stable norm-guided behavior supported by an active normative goal-frame whereas the other two overarching goals are in the background, with a weaker influence on these processes (Lindenberg & Steg, 2007). There are three different master frames that represent core motivations: a *normative* frame (which is based on the goal "to act appropriately"), a *gain* frame (with the goal "to increase one's resources"), and a *hedonic* frame (with the goal "to feel better"). The normative frame is the less stable and needs more social support for its stability than the other frames. Prosocial behavior in a gain frame is very sensitive to the influence of its relative costs compared to the costs of other alternatives leading to gain. In a hedonic frame, the occurrence of a prosocial behavior can react mostly to changes in moods and to the emotional tone of the situation. Norm compliance thus depends on the choice of the main frame (i.e., the one in the foreground), which is influenced by situational aspects (social, institutional, and cultural factors) and by individual characteristics, such as personality traits and skills.

We return here to the discussion of conditional cooperators, who may choose to cooperate because they follow the norm established by unconditional cooperators (Andreoni, 1995). It has been argued that such unconditional cooperators who act from duty, from kindness, or for the satisfaction derived from the act of cooperation, are essential as they pave the way for others to also cooperate. Together, these unconditional and conditional cooperators help raise the level of cooperation sufficiently to discourage free riding for fear of social shame, making cooperation a sticky norm (Tadelis, 2011).

External Motivation (Formal and Informal)

Beyond internal attitudes, motivation to comply with social pressure can be increased through formal punishment and sanctions, as well as through informal or socially imposed evaluations of cooperation (Yamagishi, 1986). Punishment and reputation are by far the most common solutions to cooperation dilemmas, both in the field and in the lab, and they work by changing the perceived payoff matrix, thus making cooperation more attractive than defection. Punishment has been widely recognized as an effective solution to the problem of free riding (Chaudhuri, 2011), because it makes defection costly and therefore less attractive (Hardin, 1968). Returning to Table 14.1, punishment increases the cost of defection by changing the values of (D). A large body of experimental evidence shows that individuals are willing to punish noncooperators, and a meta-analysis involving 187 studies reveals that punishments and rewards have an equivalent positive effect on cooperation (Balliet et al., 2011), and incentives were more effective when they were costly to administer and when participants continued to interact in the same group.

Not only are people willing to sanction their peers at a cost to themselves, but their threat is credible enough to raise cooperation to high levels, as many economic experiments with real monetary incentives demonstrate (Fehr & Gachter, 2000, 2002). This has been interpreted by economists as an indication of a preference for "strong reciprocity" which would make cooperation possible even when the potential punishers are not themselves the victims (Fehr & Fischbacher, 2004), and in one-shot games (Gachter & Herrmann, 2009; Walker & Halloran, 2004). In the latter situation there is no expectation of future interactions; therefore, it is not possible to benefit from the behavioral change the punishment is supposed to induce, nor is there benefit from reputation. It is worth noting that the effectiveness of punishment in enforcing cooperation has been criticized by many for multiple reasons (Guala, 2012; Raihani & Bshary, 2019). First, the option of costly punishment does not increase the average payoff of the group and its costs offset the expected benefits on cooperation (Dreber et al., 2008). Second, punishment can escalate conflict and when counter-punishment is possible, the possibility of revenge weakens cooperators' willingness to punish free riders and leads to the breakdown of cooperation (Giardini et al., 2014; Nikiforakis, 2008). Third, peer-punishment as defined in economic experiments, in which participants can freely choose to invest part of their money to reduce the payoffs of free-riders, is rarely observed in human societies. Ethnographic evidence shows that punishment is often distributed and is not very costly (Boehm, 1987; Ellickson, 1991), with ridicule, gossip and ostracism being the most common forms of punishment in small-scale societies (Guala, 2012). In addition, low-cost, informal punishment is often accompanied by centralized sanctioning systems characterized by formal authority and enforcement. Finally, modeling work shows that punishment does not make cooperation evolutionarily stable, and the most efficient strategy for indirect reciprocity is to withhold help for defectors rather than to punish them (Ohtsuki & Iwasa, 2006). By using an agent-based simulation, Giardini and colleagues (2014) investigated the evolutionary stability of cooperation under two different regimes: punishment and reputation. Their results show that punishment is effective only if it is not costly, whereas when agents refused to interact with defectors because of their reputations, cooperation rates increased and were stable.

When re-encounters are likely and individuals can exchange information about absent others, reputation becomes a powerful tool for enforcing cooperation. Reputation, broadly defined as a set of evaluations that are generally held about the qualities of someone, can be used to decide in advance which strategy to play (Axelrod, 1984), but can also work as a positive incentive for cooperation. Theories of indirect reciprocity explain large scale human cooperation in terms of conditional helping by individuals who want to uphold a reputation and then be included in future cooperation (Alexander, 1987; Nowak & Sigmund, 1998; Panchanathan & Boyd, 2004). In a "market for cooperators" (Hammerstein & Noe, 2016) or when partner choice is available (Barclay & Willer, 2007), building a reputation for generosity is a long-term investment because competition for the most altruistic partners leads to the exclusion of non-altruists (Roberts, 1998). A good reputation pays off by attracting help from others, even from strangers or members from another group, if the recipient's reputation is known (Milinski, 2019).

The importance of reputation has been widely demonstrated in laboratory experiments as well, where participants are more generous when there are opportunities to build reputation (Beersma & Van Kleef, 2011; Piazza & Bering, 2008; Sommerfeld et al., 2008; Sommerfeld et al., 2007). Moreover, subtle, and implicit reputational cues, such as a pair of looking eyes displayed in the background, are effective in modifying behavior in different experimental settings as well as in naturalistic contexts (Bateson et al., 2006; Burnham & Hare, 2007; Haley & Fessler, 2005). A recent meta-analysis of 15 experiments involving 2035 participants shows that photographs or stylized images of eyes reduced antisocial behavior by 35 percent (Dear et al., 2019). This sensitivity to subtle cues that one's reputation is at stake could be related to impression management (Baumeister, 1982; Goffman, 1978, p. 56), which is expected to increase subjective well-being in three different ways: by maximizing one's benefits in social life, by maintaining self-esteem, and by creating an identity (Leary & Kowalski, 1990).

Visibility is as effective in promoting cooperation as gossip. The informal exchange of evaluative information about an absent third party (Emler, 2019) works as a way of disciplining minor norm violations in groups, from cattle ranchers (Ellickson, 1991) to rowing teams (Kniffin & Wilson, 2010), while in organizational settings it has been related to positive outcomes like bonding with colleagues, but also to entertainment and information seeking (Rosnow & Fine, 1976). Evidence from different kinds of small, close-knit communities (Boehm, 2012; Greif, 1989), but also from larger groups and organizations (Ellwardt et al., 2012; Kniffin & Wilson, 2005; Wittek & Wielers, 1998) consistently shows that reputation is transmitted through gossip, which is a powerful and efficient tool for social control (Giardini & Wittek, 2019). Concerns about being identified and gossiped about play an important role in promoting social behavior. The threat of gossip may have encouraged the evolution of altruistic behavior or even society (Dunbar, 2004) by activating reputational concerns (Piazza & Bering, 2008).

The concern for status can also play a role in eliciting cooperation. If individuals highly value their status within a group, they are more likely to participate in *visible* acts that have a positive impact on their visibility. For example, Griskevicius et al. (2010) identified a concern for status by studying participants' green product purchasing habits. The participants had a greater propensity to purchase green products when shopping in public, but not when shopping in private. There was also an increased willingness to purchase the green products when these were more expensive than their non-green alternatives, amplifying the idea that reputation affects cooperative behaviors. Non-profit organizations are highly aware of the influence of such social impressions and use this pressure to their advantage by providing their supporters and benefactors with visible bands and badges so they can show off their good deeds and self-sacrifice (e.g., "I donated blood," "I voted," and "I got vaccinated" stickers and wristbands, etc.). If the individual values the outcome of the deed, then they likely belong to groups that value the same outcome. By displaying this badge, the good doer is showing that they are contributing toward the collective values of the group, indicating that the individual is a highly contributing group member. However, sometimes belonging to a group becomes important enough that an individual is willing to cooperate regardless of the potential to boost social impressions. This external motivation can translate into an internal change in attitudes (essentially reversing the causality in the model). When the external manifestation becomes important enough to determine action regardless of its visibility, it then becomes an internal source of motivation.

Internal Motivation

Cooperation can be internally motivated, including by one's sense of self and moral identity. It is interesting to consider group identity here because greater identification with an in-group increases observed cooperative behavior (Brewer & Kramer, 1986; Caporael et al., 1989; de Cremer & van Vugt, 1999; Kramer & Brewer, 1984). This could be because affiliating with a group raises the relative importance of group outcomes (Brewer, 1999) and goals (Krantz et al., 2008), thus impacting attitudes as discussed above, or, because a stronger group identity increases the salience of group norms (Jetten et al., 1997). Under such conditions, choices are made to support and fulfill multiple context-dependent goals (Krantz & Kunreuther, 2007), including following group norms. Group norms associated with group affiliation have been shown to mediate cooperation towards an in-group (Jackson, 2008).

The strength of the group norms is influential in determining the behavior, and subsequent cooperation, of members. Thus, the presence of a strong cooperative group norm essentially signals that the likelihood of exploitation by current group members of cooperative behavior is less likely. An additional benefit experienced of following the norm is greater acceptance by the group. In contrast, there can also be the incurrence of a significant cost when strong group norms are violated, such as the threat of being ostracized and excluded. Although smaller groups may not completely ostracize and exclude non-cooperative members, there is still a risk of social marginalization and the possibility of becoming less involved in important decisions (van Lange et al., 2013). If a member identifies strongly with the group, this can put their need to belong in jeopardy (Williams, 2007). With the hefty loss associated with violating group norms, pressure to publicly conform and adhere to the norms intensifies, thus further confirming that the likelihood of cooperation within a group increases when ostracism and social exclusion is possible (van Lange et al., 2013).

Subjective norms towards cooperation arise from the combination of normative beliefs and the individual motivation to comply with those beliefs. The presence of a cooperative norm, although necessary, is not sufficient if the decision maker does not have a reason to exert the effort to comply with said norm. Thus, the choice emerges from weighting the tangible and intangible benefits of following a cooperative norm (+c values in Table 14.1) against the tangible and intangible costs of not following the norm (-d values in Table 14.1). Not surprisingly, the intangible aspects of such a choice (reputation, ostracism by a desired group) often exert far greater influence than the economic tangible outcomes in the choice to cooperate.

Behavioral Intention: To Cooperate or Not to Cooperate

Attitudes frequently do not result in a congruent action (see Kraus, 1995 for a meta-analytic review) suggesting the need for an additional step in the decision process. Within TPB this step is the creation of behavioral intentions (Box 3 in Figure 14.1) that result from the total sum of one's attitudes (Box 1; behavioral beliefs and evaluation of outcomes associated with those beliefs) and subjective norms (Box 2; social norms and the motivation to comply with them). These intentions are the prerequisite for expressed behavior; however, intentions do not automatically translate into behavior, as the link between intention and action can be moderated by perceptions of one's control over one's actions, power of others over one's actions, trust in the structure of the decision, and the role of institutions in the cooperative enterprise. Without an intention to act, the likelihood of action is very low.

As mentioned above, trust plays a critical role both in creating the intention to cooperate as well as translating this intention into action. Trust has been conceptualized both as an individual pre-disposition and an attitude shaped by situational factors (Stouten et al., 2006). Traditionally considered a facilitator of cooperation and social exchange (Cook & Cooper, 2003), trust has been documented as one of the most important ingredients for enhancing cooperation (Dawes, 1980; van Lange et al., 2017). When trust is high, individuals are less worried about being exploited (Yamagishi & Sato, 1986) and expect higher levels of reciprocity (Parks & Hulbert, 1995). Therefore, high levels of trust are traditionally associated with cooperative behavior in dilemmas (Dawes, 1980; de Cremer & Van Vugt, 1999; Kramer et al., 1996), although de Cremer et al. (2001) show that low trustors increase their contribution levels to match high trustors when individual accountability is high, highlighting the role that trust plays in forming expectations regarding others, rather than direct attitudes towards cooperation. Trust also moderates the effects of communication (and cheap talk) between opponents in social dilemmas, such that high trustors increase cooperative behavior following cooperative messages from a counterpart, but low trustors do not (Parks et al., 1996). While many researchers consider generalized trust as a trait or predisposition (Hayashi et al., 1999; Yamagishi & Yamagishi, 1994), situational factors also affect levels of trust. Trust can even interact with aspects of a social dilemma in unexpected ways. For example, Mulder et al. (2006) demonstrate that the existence of sanction systems, which are meant to increase cooperative behavior, can act to reduce trust in others' reciprocal intentions by providing an external motive for contributing (e.g., to avoid punishment), and therefore undermine cooperation.

The influences on the choice to cooperate discussed thus far can be thought of as factors that collectively and interactively result in an intention to cooperate. Notably, their impact on a one-time choice to cooperate is likely to be different than cooperation sustained over time. Ongoing cooperation can take the form of a single choice that is repeated multiple times, as in a pre-commitment to cooperate that has then to be sustained, or repeated choices that are effectively made anew each time cooperation is required, and are therefore able to include new information. We note here that intangible costs and benefits from gossip, reputation effects, and the potential for reciprocity by others to one's cooperative act, can, and do, exert considerable influence on repeated choices, especially when these choices allow for the incorporation of feedback and new information in recreating the intention to cooperate. A repeated choice allows for Table 14.1 to be updated to reflect the true costs and benefits being realized, and whether or not the decision maker's trust in others was justified.

From Intention to Behavior: Cooperation as a Constructed Choice

Figure 14.1 describes how the translation of an intention (Box 3) into behavior (Box 5) is impacted by the actor's perceived behavioral control over the action (Box 4) such that when there is a lack of control (real or perceived), the likelihood of behavior based on an intention decreases. Thus, Boxes 4 and 5 in Figure 14.1 are inexorably intertwined and we address them together in this section. In case of social dilemmas there can be interdependence even in the perceived control (Box 4A) and power over actions (Box 4B). Thus, beyond control over one's own choice, there is a perception of the control others have over their choice, and any control one may have over choices made by the other(s) in the dilemma.

Consider the vast literature on justice and fairness that indicates perceptions of fairness violation are reduced when agency and accountability are not present (Folger & Cropanzano, 2001; Gilliland et al., 2001). This addresses the perception of the control others have over their choice and findings showing that defectors may not be punished for their non-cooperation if they are perceived not to have had control over their negative behavior. Studies about the moral wiggle room (Dana et al., 2007) around taking responsibility for one's action further illustrate that when decision makers can manage the social context such that their non-cooperation is unlikely to impact their social standing or reputation, they are more likely to defect or show non-cooperation. Similar "strategic ignorance" experiments by Larson and Capra (2009), Matthey and Regner (2011), Feiler (2014), van der Weele (2014), and Grossman (2014) find that when participants can choose to not be informed about the consequences of their choice on others, they tend to use that option and make non-cooperative choices. Furthermore, Fershtman and Gneezy (2001), Hamman et al. (2010), Bartling and Fischbacher (2012), Coffman (2011), and Oexl and Grossman (2013) find that in a dictator game, if participants can delegate responsibility for their action to someone else, they are more likely to behave selfishly. Giving is substantially motivated by the existence of a transparent relationship between the giver and the recipient. If situational excuses for selfish behavior exist, people seem to make use of that "moral wiggle room" and giving tends to be smaller (Andreoni & Bernheim, 2009; Dana et al., 2007).

Control over others' choices, which has been defined as power over others (Raven, 1993, 2008), is less well-understood in the context of social dilemmas. Molho et al. (2019) studied the impact of power in social dilemmas by examining the differences in cooperation by those in high versus low power positions, finding no effect of power. Although this was a study about the impact of having power on cooperation, it did not explore the role of power on the choices of others but on one's own choice to cooperate. Clearly, the role of power on other's choices is an area ripe for future research. Studies about status, which can be thought of as a subtle expression of social power, have examined its impact on the choices of others. Arora and Tedeschi (2019) find that participants in positions of low status are more likely to make choices that ensure higher gains for participants in positions of higher status, even when it means they themselves obtain lower outcomes. Additional research is needed if we are to better and more fully understand how the perception of control over choices by self and others influences the translation of a cooperative intent into a cooperative action.

Taken together, the research on moral wiggle room, control over actions, power, and status suggest that the gap between intent and action is a vital step that has perhaps not been well explored in social dilemma research. Especially given the interdependent nature of dilemmas, and as detailed throughout this chapter, the creation of an intention must necessarily include the impact (tangible and intangible) of one's action on others, and consequently, others' possible responses to one's action. In this sense, moral wiggle room appears to reduce the cost of defection and its consequences. In contrast, status appears to raise the cost of defection for those at lower status. Understanding how control over one's actions and power over the action of others remain areas to be addressed by future research.

Conclusion

The nearly half-century of research on social dilemmas has provided considerable insights into why and when decision makers choose to cooperate and maximize collective benefits over rational selfish outcomes. In this chapter we use a structured approach that examines the decision process resulting in cooperative behavior, rather than limiting the behavior to an observed outcome. Unpacking the process allows for an exploration of the antecedents of cooperation, and the influences upon it, even as it identifies gaps in our current knowledge. Cooperation, so far considered mostly as a single observed outcome, is a complex behavior amalgamated from many building blocks and variables. This chapter considers each building block and the possible interactions among them. Little is known about these interactions, and yet, any prescriptions about cooperative behavior can only be possible once such interactions are better understood.

Social dilemmas are ubiquitous and exist at the center of most societal issues, including the wicked problems of our time, such as climate change (Boyd et al., 2018). What we have learned about cooperation has the capacity to inform solutions and policies for such critical issues. However, despite the existing large body of knowledge, there are still some issues that cannot be described (or even well-defined) when focusing on cooperation only as an outcome. A process view also suggests avenues for future research by pointing at a set of elements that have been so far disregarded. A non-exhaustive list would consist of repeated games in large groups, variables that impact the translation of intent to action, structural hierarchies, power and status influences, freedom of choice, and expectations of others' actions. In addition, contextualizing the choices and providing thick descriptions of the cultural and institutional settings in which social dilemmas are embedded are vital elements that remain to be examined.

Cooperation in social dilemmas is, perhaps, a paradox. From the outset, it is viewed as the less desirable outcome and when coupled with the belief that others are self-interested, can help explain why there is frequently insufficient cooperation. At the same time, the building blocks of cooperative behavior are essential to our social functioning. These blocks, when situated appropriately within their social context, serve to lower the costs of cooperation, and create the basis by which society can thrive. We suggest that a part of the desire to cooperate arises from within the individual, such as one's attitudes and personal orientations, while the rest is derived from social interactions, whether with unknown others or with those within ones' close social networks. Together, these motivate cooperation, which is not only adaptive for individuals, but also an essential glue that holds together our social structures.

All authors contributed equally to this article.

References

Ajzen, I. (1985). From intentions to actions: A theory of planned behavior. In J. Kuhl & J. Beckmann (Eds.), *Action control* (pp. 11–39). Springer.

Ajzen, I. (1987). Attitudes, traits, and actions: Dispositional prediction of behavior in personality and social psychology. *Advances in Experimental Social Psychology, 20*, 1–63.

Ajzen, I. (1991). The theory of planned behavior. *Organizational Behavior and Human Decision Processes, 50*(2), 179–211.

Alexander, R. D. (1987). *The biology of moral systems.* Transaction Publishers.

Andreoni, J. (1988). Why free ride?: Strategies and learning in public goods experiments. *Journal of Public Economics, 37*(3), 291–304.

Andreoni, J. (1995). Cooperation in public-goods experiments: kindness or confusion? *The American Economic Review, 85*(4), 891–904.

Andreoni, J., & Bernheim, B. D. (2009). Social image and the 50–50 norm: A theoretical and experimental analysis of audience effects. *Econometrica, 77*(5), 1607–1636.

Armitage, C. J., & Conner, M. (2001). Efficacy of the theory of planned behaviour: A meta-analytic review. *British Journal of Social Psychology, 40*(4), 471–499.

Arora, P., & Tedeschi, G. A. (2019). The dark side of competition: Modeling status games. *Managerial and Decision Economics, 40*(7), 761–771.

Arora, P., Logg, J., & Larrick, R. (2016). Acting for the greater good: Identification with group determines choices in sequential contribution dilemmas. *Journal of Behavioral Decision Making, 29*(5), 499–510.

Arora, P., Peterson, N. D., Krantz, D. H., Hardisty, D. J., & Reddy, K. S. (2012). To cooperate or not to cooperate: Using new methodologies and frameworks to understand how affiliation influences cooperation in the present and future. *Journal of Economic Psychology, 33*(4), 842–853.

Asch, S. E. (1956). Studies of independence and conformity: I. A minority of one against a unanimous majority. *Psychological Monographs: General and Applied, 70*(9), 1.

Attari, S. Z., Krantz, D. H., & Weber, E. U. (2014). Reasons for cooperation and defection in real-world social dilemmas. *Judgment & Decision Making, 9*(6), 316–334.

Axelrod, R. (1984). *The evolution of cooperation.* Basic Books.

Balliet, D., Mulder, L. B., & van Lange, P. A. (2011). Reward, punishment, and cooperation: A meta-analysis. *Psychological Bulletin, 137*(4), 594.

Balliet, D., Parks, C., & Joireman, J. (2009). Social value orientation and cooperation in social dilemmas: A meta-analysis. *Group Processes & Intergroup Relations, 12*(4), 533–547.

Balliet, D., Wu, J., & De Dreu, C. K. (2014). Ingroup favoritism in cooperation: A meta-analysis. *Psychological Bulletin, 140*(6), 1556.

Barclay, P., & Willer, R. (2007). Partner choice creates competitive altruism in humans. *Proceedings of the Royal Society B: Biological Sciences, 274*(1610), 749–753.

Bartling, B., & Fischbacher, U. (2012). Shifting the blame: On delegation and responsibility. *The Review of Economic Studies, 79*(1), 67–87.

Bateson, M., Nettle, D., & Roberts, G. (2006). Cues of being watched enhance cooperation in a real-world setting. *Biology Letters, 2*(3), 412–414.

Baumeister, R. F. (1982). A self-presentational view of social phenomena. *Psychological Bulletin, 91*(1), 3.

Beersma, B., & Van Kleef, G. A. (2011). How the grapevine keeps you in line: Gossip increases contributions to the group. *Social Psychological and Personality Science*, 2(6), 642–649.

Biel, A., & Thøgersen, J. (2007). Activation of social norms in social dilemmas: A review of the evidence and reflections on the implications for environmental behaviour. *Journal of Economic Psychology*, 28(1), 93–112.

Boehm, C. (1987). *Blood revenge: The enactment and management of conflict in Montenegro and other tribal societies*. University of Pennsylvania Press.

Boehm, C. (2012). Gossip and reputation in small-scale societies. In F. Giardini & R. Wittek (Eds.), *The Oxford handbook of gossip and reputation* (pp. 253–274). Oxford University Press.

Bornstein, G. (1992). The free-rider problem in intergroup conflicts over step-level and continuous public goods. *Journal of Personality and Social Psychology*, 62(4), 597.

Bornstein, G. (2003). Intergroup conflict: Individual, group, and collective interests. *Personality and Social Psychology Review*, 7(2), 129–145.

Bornstein, G. (2004). Cooperation in intergroup social dilemmas. In R. Suleiman, D. V. Budescu, I. Fischer, & D. M. Messick (Eds.), Contemporary psychological research on social dilemmas (pp. 227–247). Cambridge University Press.

Bornstein, G., & Ben-Yossef, M. (1994). Cooperation in intergroup and single-group social dilemmas. *Journal of Experimental Social Psychology*, 30(1), 52–67.

Boyd, R., Richerson, P. J., Meinzen-Dick, R., De Moor, T., Jackson, M. O., Gjerde, K. M., Harden-Davis, H., Frischman, B. M., Madison, M. J., Strandsburg, K. J., McLean, A. R., & Dye, C. (2018). Tragedy revisited. *Science*, 362(6420), 1236–1241.

Brewer, M. B. (1979). In-group bias in the minimal intergroup situation: A cognitive-motivational analysis. *Psychological Bulletin*, 86(2), 307.

Brewer, M. B. (1999). The psychology of prejudice: Ingroup love and outgroup hate? *Journal of social issues*, 55(3), 429–444.

Brewer, M. B. (2008). Depersonalized trust and ingroup cooperation. In J. I. Krueger (Ed.), *Rationality and social responsibility: Essays in honor of Robyn Mason Dawes* (pp. 215–232). Psychology Press.

Brewer, M. B., & Kramer, R. M. (1986). Choice behavior in social dilemmas: Effects of social identity, group size, and decision framing. *Journal of Personality and Social Psychology*, 50(3), 543.

Brewer, M. B., & Schneider, S. (1990). Social identity and social dilemmas: A double-edged sword. In D. Abrams & M. A. Hogg (Eds.), Social identity theory: Constructive and critical advances (pp. 169–184). Harvester Wheatsheaf.

Burnham, T. C., & Hare, B. (2007). Engineering human cooperation. *Human Nature*, 18(2), 88–108.

Camerer, C. F. (2003). *Behavioral game theory: Experiments in strategic interaction*. Russell Sage Foundation.

Caporael, L. R., Dawes, R. M., Orbell, J. M., & Van de Kragt, A. J. (1989). Selfishness examined: Cooperation in the absence of egoistic incentives. *Behavioral and Brain Sciences*, 12(4), 683–699.

Chanes, L., Wormwood, J. B., Betz, N., & Barrett, L. F. (2018). Facial expression predictions as drivers of social perception. *Journal of Personality and Social Psychology*, 114(3), 380.

Chaudhuri, A. (2011). Sustaining cooperation in laboratory public goods experiments: A selective survey of the literature. *Experimental Economics*, 14(1), 47–83.

Cialdini, R. B., & Goldstein, N. J. (2004). Social influence: Compliance and conformity. *Annual Review of Psychology*, 55, 591–621.

Cialdini, R. B., Reno, R. R., & Kallgren, C. A. (1990). A focus theory of normative conduct: Recycling the concept of norms to reduce littering in public places. *Journal of Personality and Social Psychology*, 58(6), 1015.

Coffman, L. C. (2011). Intermediation reduces punishment (and reward). *American Economic Journal: Microeconomics*, 3(4), 77–106.

Coleman, J. S. (1990). Commentary: Social institutions and social theory. *American Sociological Review*, 55(3), 333–339.

Cook, K. S., & Cooper, R. M. (2003). Experimental studies of cooperation, trust, and social exchange. In E. Ostrom & J. Walker (Eds.), *Trust and reciprocity: Interdisciplinary lessons from experimental research* (pp. 209–244). Russell Sage Foundation.

Croson, R. T. (2000). Thinking like a game theorist: Factors affecting the frequency of equilibrium play. *Journal of Economic Behavior & Organization*, 41(3), 299–314.

Dana, J., Weber, R. A., & Kuang, J. X. (2007). Exploiting moral wiggle room: Experiments demonstrating an illusory preference for fairness. *Economic Theory*, 33(1), 67–80.

Dawes, R. M. (1980). Social dilemmas. *Annual Review of Psychology*, 31(1), 169–193.

Dawes, R. M., & Messick, D. M. (2000). Social dilemmas. *International Journal of Psychology*, *35*(2), 111–116.

De Cremer, D., & Van Dijk, E. (2002). Reactions to group success and failure as a function of identification level: A test of the goal-transformation hypothesis in social dilemmas. *Journal of Experimental Social Psychology*, *38*(5), 435–442.

De Cremer, D., & Van Vugt, M. (1999). Social identification effects in social dilemmas: A transformation of motives. *European Journal of Social Psychology*, *29*(7), 871–893.

De Cremer, D., Snyder, M., & Dewitte, S. (2001). "The less I trust, the less I contribute (or not)?" The effects of trust, accountability and self-monitoring in social dilemmas. *European Journal of Social Psychology*, *31*(1), 93–107.

de Melo, C. M., & Terada, K. (2020). The interplay of emotion expressions and strategy in promoting cooperation in the iterated prisoner's dilemma. *Scientific Reports*, *10*(1), 1–8.

Dear, K., Dutton, K., & Fox, E. (2019). Do "watching eyes" influence antisocial behavior? A systematic review & meta-analysis. *Evolution and Human Behavior*, *40*(3), 269–280.

Deutsch, M., & Gerard, H. B. (1955). A study of normative and informational social influences upon individual judgment. *The Journal of Abnormal and Social Psychology*, *51*(3), 629.

Dreber, A., Rand, D. G., Fudenberg, D., & Nowak, M. A. (2008). Winners don't punish. *Nature*, *452*(7185), 348–351.

Dunbar, R. I. (2004). Gossip in evolutionary perspective. *Review of General Psychology*, *8*(2), 100–110.

Dunn, J. R., & Schweitzer, M. E. (2005). Feeling and believing: The influence of emotion on trust. *Journal of Personality and Social Psychology*, *88*(5), 736.

Ellickson, R. C. (1991). *Order without law*. Harvard University Press.

Ellwardt, L., Steglich, C., & Wittek, R. (2012). The co-evolution of gossip and friendship in workplace social networks. *Social Networks*, *34*(4), 623–633.

Elster, J. (1985). Rationality, morality, and collective action. *Ethics*, *96*(1), 136–155.

Emler, N. (2019). Human sociality and psychological foundations. In F. Giardini & R. P. M. Wittek (Eds.), *The Oxford handbook of gossip and reputation* (p. 47–68). Oxford University Press.

Fehr, E., & Fischbacher, U. (2004). Third-party punishment and social norms. *Evolution and human behavior*, *25*(2), 63–87.

Fehr, E., & Gachter, S. (2000). Cooperation and punishment in public goods experiments. *American Economic Review*, *90*(4), 980–994.

Fehr, E., & Gächter, S. (2002). Altruistic punishment in humans. *Nature*, *415*(6868), 137–140.

Feiler, L. (2014). Testing models of information avoidance with binary choice dictator games. *Journal of Economic Psychology*, *45*, 253–267.

Fershtman, C., & Gneezy, U. (2001). Strategic delegation: An experiment. *RAND Journal of Economics*, Vol. 32, No. 2, Summer 2001, 352–368.

Fischbacher, U., & Gächter, S. (2006). Heterogeneous social preferences and the dynamics of free riding in public goods. IZA Discussion Papers, No. 2011.

Fischbacher, U., & Gachter, S. (2010). Social preferences, beliefs, and the dynamics of free riding in public goods experiments. *American economic review*, *100*(1), 541–56.

Fischbacher, U., Gächter, S., & Fehr, E. (2001). Are people conditionally cooperative? Evidence from a public goods experiment. *Economics letters*, *71*(3), 397–404.

Fishbein, M. (1979). A theory of reasoned action: Some applications and implications.

Folger, R., & Cropanzano, R. (2001). Fairness theory: Justice as accountability. *Advances in organizational justice*, *1*(1-55), 12.

Forsyth, D. R. (2006). *Group dynamics*. Thomson.

Gächter, S., & Herrmann, B. (2009). Reciprocity, culture and human cooperation: Previous insights and a new cross-cultural experiment. *Philosophical Transactions of the Royal Society B: Biological Sciences*, *364*(1518), 791–806.

Giardini, F., & Wittek, R. (2019). Gossip, reputation, and sustainable cooperation: Sociological foundations. In F. Giardini & R. Wittek (Eds.), *The Oxford handbook of gossip and reputation* (pp. 23–46). Oxford University Press.

Giardini, F., Paolucci, M., Villatoro, D., & Conte, R. (2014). Punishment and gossip: Sustaining cooperation in a public goods game. In B. Kamiński & G. Koloch (Eds.), *Advances in social simulation* (pp. 107–118). Springer.

Gilliland, S. W., Groth, M., Baker IV, R. C., Dew, A. E., Polly, L. M., & Langdon, J. C. (2001). Improving applicants' reactions to rejection letters: An application of fairness theory. *Personnel Psychology*, *54*(3), 669–703.

Goffman, E. (1978). *The presentation of self in everyday life*. Harmondsworth.

Goldstein, N., Cialdini, R., & Griskevicius, V. (2007). A room with a viewpoint: Using normative appeals to motivate energy conservation in a hotel setting. In G. Fitzsimons, V. Morwitz, & M. N. Duluth (Eds.), *Association for consumer research, v ol. 34* (pp. 47–48). ACR North American Advances.

Greif, A. (1989). Reputation and coalitions in medieval trade: Evidence from the geniza documents. *Journal of Economic History*, *49*(4), 857–882.

Griskevicius, V., Tybur, J. M., & Van den Bergh, B. (2010). Going green to be seen: Status, reputation, and conspicuous conservation. *Journal of Personality and Social Psychology*, *98*(3), 392.

Grossman, Z. (2014). Strategic ignorance and the robustness of social preferences. *Management Science*, *60*(11), 2659–2665.

Guala, F. (2012). Reciprocity: Weak or strong? What punishment experiments do (and do not) demonstrate. *Behavioral and Brain Sciences*, *35*(1), 1–15. https://doi.org/10.1017/S0140525X11000069.

Halevy, N., Bornstein, G., & Sagiv, L. (2008). "In-group love" and "out-group hate" as motives for individual participation in intergroup conflict: A new game paradigm. *Psychological Science*, *19*(4), 405–411.

Halevy, N., Chou, E. Y., & Murnighan, J. K. (2012). Mind games: The mental representation of conflict. *Journal of Personality and Social Psychology*, *102*(1), 132.

Haley, K. J., & Fessler, D. M. (2005). Nobody's watching?: Subtle cues affect generosity in an anonymous economic game. *Evolution and Human Behavior*, *26*(3), 245–256.

Hamman, J. R., Loewenstein, G., & Weber, R. A. (2010). Self-interest through delegation: An additional rationale for the principal-agent relationship. *American Economic Review*, *100*(4), 1826–1846.

Hammerstein, P., & Noë, R. (2016). Biological trade and markets. *Philosophical Transactions of the Royal Society B: Biological Sciences*, *371*(1687), 20150101.

Hardin, G. (1968). *The tragedy of the commons*. Science.

Hayashi, N., Ostrom, E., Walker, J., & Yamagishi, T. (1999). Reciprocity, trust, and the sense of control: A cross-societal study. *Rationality and Society*, *11*(1), 27–46.

Holt, C. A., & Laury, S. K. (2002). Risk aversion and incentive effects. *American Economic Review*, *92*(5), 1644–1655.

Jackson, J. W. (2008). Reactions to social dilemmas as a function of group identity, rational calculations, and social context. *Small Group Research*, *39*(6), 673–705.

Jetten, J., Spears, R., & Manstead, A. S. (1997). Strength of identification and intergroup differentiation: The influence of group norms. *European Journal of Social Psychology*, *27*(5), 603–609.

Kelley, H. H., & Thibaut, J. W. (1978). *Interpersonal relations: A theory of interdependence*. Wiley.

Keltner, D., Ellsworth, P. C., & Edwards, K. (1993). Beyond simple pessimism: Effects of sadness and anger on social perception. *Journal of Personality and Social Psychology*, *64*(5), 740.

Kerr, N. (1995). Norms in social dilemmas. In D. Schroeder (Ed.), *Social dilemmas: Perspectives on individuals and groups*. Praeger, 31–48.

Kerr, N. L. (1983). Motivation losses in small groups: A social dilemma analysis. *Journal of Personality and Social Psychology*, *45*(4), 819.

Keser, C., & Van Winden, F. (2000). Conditional cooperation and voluntary contributions to public goods. *Scandinavian Journal of Economics*, *102*(1), 23–39.

Ketelaar, T., & Tung Au, W. (2003). The effects of feelings of guilt on the behaviour of uncooperative individuals in repeated social bargaining games: An affect-as-information interpretation of the role of emotion in social interaction. *Cognition and Emotion*, *17*(3), 429–453.

Kiyonari, T., & Yamagishi, T. (2004). Ingroup cooperation and the social exchange heuristic. In R. Suleiman, D. V. Budescu, I. Fischer, & D. M. Messick (Eds.), Contemporary psychological research on social dilemmas (pp. 269–286). Cambridge University Press.

Kniffin, K. M., & Sloan Wilson, D. (2010). Evolutionary perspectives on workplace gossip: Why and how gossip can serve groups. *Group & Organization Management*, *35*(2), 150–176.

Kniffin, K. M., & Wilson, D. S. (2005). Utilities of gossip across organizational levels. *Human Nature*, *16*(3), 278–292.

Kocher, M. G., Cherry, T., Kroll, S., Netzer, R. J., & Sutter, M. (2008). Conditional cooperation on three continents. *Economics Letters*, *101*(3), 175–178.

Kramer, R. M., & Brewer, M. B. (1984). Effects of group identity on resource use in a simulated commons dilemma. *Journal of Personality and Social Psychology*, *46*(5), 1044.

Kramer, R. M., & Wei, J. (1999). Social uncertainty and the problem of trust in social groups: The social self in doubt. In T. R. Tyler, R. M. Kramer, & O. P. John (Eds.), *The psychology of the social self* (pp. 145–168). Lawrence Erlbaum Associates Publishers.

Kramer, R. M., Brewer, M. B., & Hanna, B. A. (1996). Collective trust and collective action: The decision to trust as a social decision. In R. M. Kramer & T. R. Tyler (Eds.), *Trust in organizations: Frontiers of theory and research* (pp. 357–389). Sage Publication, Inc.

Krantz, D. H., & Kunreuther, H. C. (2007). Goals and plans in decision making. *Judgment and Decision Making*, *2*(3), 137–168.

Krantz, D. H., Peterson, N., Arora, P., Milch, K., & Orlove, B. (2008). Individual values and social goals in environmental decision making. In T. Kugler, J. C. Smith, T. Connolly, & Y. J. Son (Eds.), *Decision modeling and behavior in complex and uncertain environments* (pp. 165–198). Springer.

Kraus, S. J. (1995). Attitudes and the prediction of behavior: A meta-analysis of the empirical literature. *Personality and Social Psychology Bulletin*, *21*(1), 58–75.

Kugler, T., & Bornstein, G. (2013). Social dilemmas between individuals and groups. *Organizational Behavior and Human Decision Processes*, *120*(2), 191–205.

Kugler, T., Connolly, T., & Ordóñez, L. D. (2012). Emotion, decision, and risk: Betting on gambles versus betting on people. *Journal of Behavioral Decision Making*, *25*(2), 123–134.

Kugler, T., Ye, B., Motro, D., & Noussair, C. N. (2020). On trust and disgust: Evidence from face reading and virtual reality. *Social Psychological and Personality Science*, *11*(3), 317–325.

Kurzban, R., & Leary, M. R. (2001). Evolutionary origins of stigmatization: The functions of social exclusion. *Psychological Bulletin*, *127*(2), 187.

Larson, T., & Capra, C. M. (2009). Exploiting moral wiggle room: Illusory preference for fairness? A comment. *Judgment and Decision Making*, *4*(6), 467.

Leary, M. R., & Kowalski, R. M. (1990). Impression management: A literature review and two-component model. *Psychological Bulletin*, *107*(1), 34.

Ledyard, J. O. (1994). Public goods: A survey of experimental research. (No. 9405003). EconWPA.

Lerner, J. S., & Keltner, D. (2000). Beyond valence: Toward a model of emotion-specific influences on judgement and choice. *Cognition & Emotion*, *14*(4), 473–493.

Lerner, J. S., & Keltner, D. (2001). Fear, anger, and risk. *Journal of Personality and Social Psychology*, *81*(1), 146.

Lerner, J. S., Li, Y., Valdesolo, P., & Kassam, K. (2015). Emotion and decision making. *Annual Review of Psychology*, *66*(1), 799–823.

Lindenberg, S. (1998). The microfoundations of solidarity: A framing approach. In P. Doreian, T.J. Fararo (Eds.), The problem of solidarity (61–90). Routledge

Lindenberg, S., & Steg, L. (2007). Normative, gain and hedonic goal frames guiding environmental behavior. *Journal of Social Issues*, *63*(1), 117–137.

Loewenstein, G. F., Thompson, L., & Bazerman, M. H. (1989). Social utility and decision making in interpersonal contexts. *Journal of Personality and Social Psychology*, *57*(3), 426.

March, J. G., & Olsen, J. P. (2004). The logic of appropriateness. In R. E. Goodin (Ed.), *The Oxford handbook of political science*, 478–497.

Matthey, A., & Regner, T. (2011). Do I really want to know? A cognitive dissonance-based explanation of other-regarding behavior. *Games*, *2*(1), 114–135.

McClintock, C. G., & Allison, S. T. (1989). Social value orientation and helping behavior 1. *Journal of Applied Social Psychology*, *19*(4), 353–362.

Messick, D. M. (1999). Alternative logics for decision making in social settings. *Journal of Economic Behavior & Organization*, *39*(1), 11–28.

Messick, D. M., & McClintock, C. G. (1968). Motivational bases of choice in experimental games. *Journal of Experimental Social Psychology*, *4*(1), 1–25.

Milinski, M. (2019). Gossip and reputation in social dilemmas. In F. Giardini & R. Wittek (Eds.), *The Oxford handbook of gossip and reputation* (p. 193–213). Oxford University Press.

Molho, C., Balliet, D., & Wu, J. (2019). Hierarchy, power, and strategies to promote cooperation in social dilemmas. *Games*, *10*(1), 12.

Mulder, L. B., Van Dijk, E., De Cremer, D., & Wilke, H. A. (2006). Undermining trust and cooperation: The paradox of sanctioning systems in social dilemmas. *Journal of Experimental Social Psychology*, *42*(2), 147–162.

Murphy, R. O., Ackermann, K. A., & Handgraaf, M. (2011). Measuring social value orientation. *Judgment and Decision Making*, *6*(8), 771–781.

Nikiforakis, N. (2008). Punishment and counter-punishment in public good games: Can we really govern ourselves? *Journal of Public Economics*, *92*(1–2), 91–112.

Noelle-Neumann, E. (1974). The spiral of silence a theory of public opinion. *Journal of Communication*, *24*(2), 43–51.

Nowak, M. A., & Sigmund, K. (1998). Evolution of indirect reciprocity by image scoring. *Nature*, *393*(6685), 573–577.

Oexl, R., & Grossman, Z. J. (2013). Shifting the blame to a powerless intermediary. *Experimental Economics*, *16*(3), 306–312.

Ohtsuki, H., & Iwasa, Y. (2006). The leading eight: Social norms that can maintain cooperation by indirect reciprocity. *Journal of Theoretical Biology*, *239*(4), 435–444.

Ostrom, E. (1998). A behavioral approach to the rational choice theory of collective action: Presidential address, American Political Science Association, 1997. *American Political Science Review*, *92*(1), 1–22.

Ostrom, E. (1990). *Governing the commons: The evolution of institutions for collective action*. Cambridge University Press.

Panchanathan, K., & Boyd, R. (2004). Indirect reciprocity can stabilize cooperation without the second-order free rider problem. *Nature*, *432*(7016), 499–502.

Parks, C. D., & Hulbert, L. G. (1995). High and low trusters' responses to fear in a payoff matrix. *Journal of Conflict Resolution*, *39*(4), 718–730.

Parks, C. D., Henager, R. F., & Scamahorn, S. D. (1996). Trust and reactions to messages of intent in social dilemmas. *Journal of Conflict Resolution*, *40*(1), 134–151.

Piazza, J., & Bering, J. M. (2008). Concerns about reputation via gossip promote generous allocations in an economic game. *Evolution and Human Behavior*, *29*(3), 172–178.

Pillutla, M. M., & Chen, X. P. (1999). Social norms and cooperation in social dilemmas: The effects of context and feedback. *Organizational Behavior and Human Decision Processes*, *78*(2), 81–103.

Raihani, N. J., & Bshary, R. (2019). Punishment: One tool, many uses. *Evolutionary Human Sciences*, 1(e12), 1–26.

Raub, W., & Snijders, C. (1997). Gains, losses, and cooperation in social dilemmas and collective action: The effects of risk preferences, *Journal of Mathematical Sociology*, *22*(3), 263–302.

Raven, B. H. (1993). The bases of power: Origins and recent developments. *Journal of Social Issues*, *49*(4), 227–251.

Raven, B. H. (2008). The bases of power and the power/interaction model of interpersonal influence. *Analyses of Social Issues and Public Policy*, *8*(1), 1–22.

Roberts G. (1998). Competitive altruism: From reciprocity to the handicap principle. *Proceedings of the Royal Society B: Biological Sciences*, *265*(1394), 427–431.

Rosnow, R. L., & Fine, G. A. (1976). *Rumor and gossip: The social psychology of hearsay*. Elsevier.

Rumble, A. C., van Lange, P. A., & Parks, C. D. (2010). The benefits of empathy: When empathy may sustain cooperation in social dilemmas. *European Journal of Social Psychology*, *40*(5), 856–866.

Schultz, P. W., Nolan, J. M., Cialdini, R. B., Goldstein, N. J., & Griskevicius, V. (2007). The constructive, destructive, and reconstructive power of social norms. *Psychological Science*, *18*(5), 429–434.

Schwarz, N., & Clore, G. L., (1988). How do I feel about it? Informative functions of affective states. *Affect, Cognition and Social Behavior*, *1*, 44–62.

Schwarz, N., & Clore, G. L. (2003). Mood as information: 20 years later. *Psychological Inquiry*, *14*(3–4), 296–303.

Slovic, P. (1995). The construction of preference. *American Psychologist*, *50*(5), 364.

Sniehotta, F. F., Presseau, J., & Araújo-Soares, V. (2014). Time to retire the theory of planned behaviour. *Health Psychology Review*, *8*(1), 1–7.

Sommerfeld, R. D., Krambeck, H. J., & Milinski, M. (2008). Multiple gossip statements and their effect on reputation and trustworthiness. *Proceedings of the Royal Society B: Biological Sciences*, *275*(1650), 2529–2536.

Sommerfeld, R. D., Krambeck, H.-J., Semmann, D., & Milinski, M. (2007). Gossip as an alternative for direct observation in games of indirect reciprocity. *Proceedings of the National Academy of Sciences, 104*(44), 17435–17440.

Storbeck, J., & Clore, G. L. (2008). Affective arousal as information: How affective arousal influences judgments, learning, and memory. *Social and Personality Psychology Compass, 2*(5), 1824–1843.

Stouten, J., & De Cremer, D. (2010). "Seeing is believing": The effects of facial expressions of emotion and verbal communication in social dilemmas. *Journal of Behavioral Decision Making, 23*(3), 271–287.

Stouten, J., De Cremer, D., & Van Dijk, E. (2006). Violating equality in social dilemmas: Emotional and retributive reactions as a function of trust, attribution, and honesty. *Personality and Social Psychology Bulletin, 32*(7), 894–906.

Tadelis, S. (2011). The power of shame and the rationality of trust. *Haas School of Business working paper, 3*(2).

Tajfel, H. (1970). Experiments in intergroup discrimination. *Scientific American, 223*(5), 96–103.

Tajfel, H., & Turner, J. C. (1978). Intergroup behavior. In C. Tajfel & H. Fraser (Eds.), *Introducing social psychology* (pp. 401–466). Penguin Books.

Tajfel, H., & Turner, J. C. (1986). The social identity theory of intergroup behavior. In S. Worchel & W. G. Austin (Eds.), *Psychology of intergroup relations* (pp. 33–47). Nelson-Hall.

Tajfel, H., Billig, M. G., Bundy, R. P., & Flament, C. (1971). Social categorization and intergroup behaviour. *European Journal of Social Psychology, 1*(2), 149–178.

Terry, D. J., & Hogg, M. A. (1996). Group norms and the attitude-behavior relationship: A role for group identification. *Personality and Social Psychology Bulletin, 22*(8), 776–793.

Van der Weele, J. J. (2014). Inconvenient truths: Determinants of strategic ignorance in moral dilemmas. *Available at SSRN 2247288.*

van Lange, P. A. (1999). The pursuit of joint outcomes and equality in outcomes: An integrative model of social value orientation. *Journal of Personality and Social Psychology, 77*(2), 337.

van Lange, P. A. (2000). Beyond self-interest: A set of propositions relevant to interpersonal orientations. *European Review of Social Psychology, 11*(1), 297–331.

van Lange, P. A., De Bruin, E., Otten, W., & Joireman, J. A. (1997). Development of prosocial, individualistic, and competitive orientations: Theory and preliminary evidence. *Journal of Personality and Social Psychology, 73*(4), 733.

van Lange, P. A., Joireman, J., Parks, C. D., & Van Dijk, E. (2013). The psychology of social dilemmas: A review. *Organizational Behavior and Human Decision Processes, 120*(2), 125–141.

van Lange, P. A., Rockenbach, B., & Yamagishi, T. (Eds.). (2017). *Trust in social dilemmas.* Oxford University Press.

Volk, S., Thöni, C., & Ruigrok, W. (2011). Personality, personal values and cooperation preferences in public goods games: A longitudinal study. *Personality and Individual Differences, 50*(6), 810–815.

Walker, J. M., & Halloran, M. A. (2004). Rewards and sanctions and the provision of public goods in one-shot settings. *Experimental Economics, 7*(3), 235–247.

Weber, J. M., & Murnighan, J. K. (2008). Suckers or saviors? Consistent contributors in social dilemmas. *Journal of Personality and Social Psychology, 95*(6), 1340.

Weber, J. M., Kopelman, S., & Messick, D. M. (2004). A conceptual review of decision making in social dilemmas: Applying a logic of appropriateness. *Personality and Social Psychology Review, 8*(3), 281–307.

White, K. M., Smith, J. R., Terry, D. J., Greenslade, J. H., & McKimmie, B. M. (2009). Social influence in the theory of planned behaviour: The role of descriptive, injunctive, and in-group norms. *British Journal of Social Psychology, 48*(1), 135–158.

Williams, K. D. (2007). Ostracism. *Annual Review of Psychology, 58*, 425–452.

Williams, K. D., & Karau, S. J. (1991). Social loafing and social compensation: The effects of expectations of co-worker performance. *Journal of Personality and Social Psychology, 61*(4), 570.

Wittek, R., & Wielers, R. (1998). Gossip in organizations. *Computational & Mathematical Organization Theory, 4*(2), 189–204.

Wubben, M. (2010). *Social functions of emotions in social dilemmas.* (No. EPS-2010-187-ORG). Erasmus University Rotterdam.

Yamagishi, T. (1986). The provision of a sanctioning system as a public good. *Journal of Personality and Social Psychology, 51*(1), 110.

Yamagishi, T. (1988). Exit from the group as an individualistic solution to the free rider problem in the United States and Japan. *Journal of Experimental Social Psychology, 24*(6), 530–542.

Yamagishi, T., & Mifune, N. (2009). Social exchange and solidarity: In-group love or out-group hate? *Evolution and Human Behavior, 30*(4), 229–237.

Yamagishi, T., & Sato, K. (1986). Motivational bases of the public goods problem. *Journal of Personality and Social Psychology, 50*(1), 67–73.

Yamagishi, T., Kikuchi, M., & Kosugi, M. (1999). Trust, gullibility, and social intelligence. *Asian Journal of Social Psychology, 2*(1), 145–161.

Yamagishi, T., & Yamagishi, M. (1994). Trust and commitment in the United States and Japan. *Motivation and Emotion, 18*(2), 129–166.

Self-Evaluation in Competition Pools

Mark D. Alicke, Yiyue Zhang, Nicole B. Stephenson, *and* Ethan Zell

Abstract

This chapter provides an overview of theory and research on competition pools, namely, salient groups in which social comparisons occur routinely and exert a significant impact on self-evaluations. The authors conceptualize competition pools broadly to include competitions among friends, family, coworkers, teammates, and classmates. After a brief overview of social comparison theory, the authors describe the impact of social comparisons that arise in competition pools. Further, the authors note that effects of social comparisons often occur alongside effects of intrapersonal or temporal comparisons. Next, the authors discuss research on how people evaluate referents who outperform them in competition pools. This research, including work on the genius effect and referent status neglect, suggests that people selectively consider the skill level of the referent in order to maintain a positive self-image. The authors then turn to the distinction between local versus global competition pools. Informed by research on the big-fish-little-pond effect and local dominance, the authors argue that social comparisons are most impactful when made locally, among a few immediate others, as opposed to globally, with larger groups. Finally, the chapter concludes by highlighting broader implications of research on competition pools for social comparison theory as well as directions for future research.

Key Words: competition, self-evaluation, social comparison, temporal comparison, big-fish-little-pond effect, local dominance

Introduction

Since its inception over 60 years ago (Festinger, 1954), *social comparison theory* has inspired hundreds of empirical studies, even if the "theory" is more an amorphous group of suggestions than a coherent, internally consistent model. Festinger's foundational assumption was that self-knowledge is constructed from information acquired in comparisons with other people. If the link between social comparison and self-knowledge seems obvious in hindsight, it is due in no small measure to Festinger's formulation, which cemented social comparison as one of the core issues in social psychology.

Social comparisons are pervasive—they occur among people who know each other well (e.g., close friends, siblings, intimate relationship partners) as well as strangers. The fact that social comparisons occur both above and below conscious awareness greatly extends their range (Chatard et al., 2017; Mussweiler et al., 2004). The automatic nature of comparisons makes it nearly impossible to avoid them. One study showed that participants continued to compare their own task performance to another's even when they realized that the other person had a significant advantage or disadvantage (Gilbert et al., 1995). Additionally, diary research has shown that, on average, people make two social comparisons per day (Wheeler & Miyake, 1992), and those refer only to the ones that they made consciously and can recall.

In this chapter, we examine *competition pools*, namely, salient groups in which social comparisons occur routinely and exert a significant impact on self-evaluations. We conceptualize competition pools broadly to include competitions among friends, family, coworkers, teammates, and classmates. They can be formal (e.g., athletes competing in the Olympics, students competing on a standardized test), informal (e.g., people comparing their vacation to the vacations of others on social media), or constructed on the spot (e.g., people comparing their social skills to friends at a dinner party or their car to others in a lot). First, we begin by describing key aspects of Festinger's (1954) social comparison theory and how it anticipated later research on competition pools. Next, we describe contemporary research on comparison processes in competition pools, the importance of referent characteristics in competition pools, and the relative effects of local versus global competition pools. Lastly, we summarize core findings on the impact of competition pools and highlight gaps in need of future research.

Social Comparison Theory

Because social comparison research has ramified in so many directions, and given that Festinger's original propositions have been qualified in so many ways, it seems best to refer to social comparison as a field of research rather than as a theory. Perhaps the biggest change in this field from Festinger's original conception concerns the nature of the comparison referent (i.e., the competitor or person with whom people compare themselves). Festinger focused on concrete comparisons with competitors whose abilities varied in relation to the comparison subject's. However, one of the largest social comparison literatures involves comparisons with a hypothetical, average peer (Alicke & Govorun, 2005; Zell et al., 2020). In addition, people compare with imagined possible or future selves (Markus & Nurius, 1986; Pronin et al., 2008), and with past selves that may also be largely constructed (Wilson & Ross, 2001, 2003).

Although the early history of social comparison research focused on the comparison targets that people preferred, investigators have since recognized that most social comparisons are inadvertent rather than orchestrated (Alicke et al., 2012). As a result, the emphasis in the field has shifted from assessing social comparison antecedents to investigating its consequences. Thus, social comparison research now encompasses a sizable literature that extends into areas that Festinger couldn't have envisioned (for a recent review of the field, see Suls et al., 2020).

Despite its grand scope, most social comparison research has been inspired by its fundamental premises. Festinger began with the assumption that social comparisons were required when physical standards were unavailable. As we have noted elsewhere (Alicke et al., 2013), this tenet was misleading. Physical standards are limited to providing feedback about one's abilities vis-à-vis the environment. This type of self versus environment comparison is useful, for example, for estimating one's ability to jump across a ditch: Accurate estimations avoid ruined shoes or worse. We refer to such assessments as instrumental self-analysis.

People who live in social groups, however, compete for social and material resources, sometimes immediately, but always, potentially. Simply knowing one's capabilities in relation to the environment is insufficient in competition pools, where it is imperative to assess one's characteristics relative to others. Further, many summaries of behavioral tendencies, abilities, emotional responses, and preferences make sense only with reference to others. Rudeness, for example, is an irrelevant trait on a deserted island. Further, even traits that could be assessed on a purely temporal basis, including mental and physical skills, accrue new meaning in competition pools. We refer to the development of such self-knowledge as social self-analysis. For people who live in social groups, virtually all trait self-ascriptions entail social self-analysis, even if the comparisons they are based on are imagined or constructed rather than direct. In this regard, competition is at least implicit in all social self-analysis.

A second source of conceptual confusion in the extant social comparison literature concerns the distinction between social and temporal comparison. These are not, as they have been treated, two isolated comparison dimensions. Rather, most comparisons are assessed with reference to both dimensions (Zell & Strickhouser, 2020). A person on a diet, for example, is likely to assess both his temporal progress—whether he is losing weight compared to where he started—and his social standing—how his weight compares to others.

A more accurate way to categorize comparisons, therefore, is to distinguish between interpersonal and intrapersonal comparisons (corresponding to the traditional social versus temporal comparison distinction), and among contemporaneous, past, and future comparisons. This scheme yields six different comparison types (Alicke et al., 2013). An interpersonal contemporaneous comparison corresponds to the prototypic social comparison in which Albert races his older sister, Cordelia, to see who is faster. An interpersonal past comparison occurs when Albert learns that Cordelia ran much faster than him when she was his age. An interpersonal future comparison involves Albert imagining whether he will run as fast as Cordelia when he is her age. Intrapersonal comparisons involve comparisons with one's own past, present, and future selves. Thus, Albert might compare his skills at football and baseball (intrapersonal, contemporaneous; Strickhouser & Zell, 2015), his present football skill to his skill at a former time (intrapersonal, past), and his present skill to his anticipated future level (intrapersonal, future). Below, we describe research that directly tests the self-evaluative effects of intrapersonal and interpersonal comparisons.

Comparison Processes in Competition Pools

Having briefly introduced key aspects of social comparison theory, we now turn to its implications for competition pools. We argue that social comparison theory can be used to understand the self-evaluative effects of competition pools, and in particular, the intrapersonal and interpersonal comparisons that arise within them.

Social Comparison and Competition

Perhaps the most defining feature of competition is the desire to outperform one or more other individuals. Festinger (1954) assumed that a competitive drive, the "unidirectional drive upward," was a primary social comparison motive, although subsequent research has questioned this assumption (Gerber et al., 2018; Taylor et al., 1983). Even more fundamental than comparison direction (i.e., upward, downward, or lateral) is the ultimate purpose for which comparisons occur, namely self-assessment.

Although the preponderance of social comparison theory and research has focused on self-assessment, and especially on ability assessment, social comparisons actually serve numerous functions. One function is to facilitate coordination with a group. For example, people might want to compare their own knowledge, abilities, and values with a group's to assess whether they fit with the group's goals and orientations. Social comparison is also useful in developing skills. A vocalist could, for example, learn something about dynamics or phrasing by listening to another singer. People also compare with others to learn standards of social and moral behavior (e.g., informational social influence, Deutsch & Gerard, 1955).

Social comparisons are not, therefore, necessarily competitive. Nevertheless, competition is at least indirectly implied in many social comparisons that inform personal identity. As Festinger (1954) assumed, humans are motivated to know where their abilities and characteristics stand relative to others, to improve their own performance, and to minimize the distance between their own and others' performance levels.

Social versus Temporal Comparisons

Although the impact of social comparisons depends on the nature of the target and the importance of the comparison dimension, social comparisons are influential even when they are made with complete strangers (Zell & Alicke, 2010), especially on ability dimensions (Alicke et al., 2013). Festinger's (1954) "unidirectional drive upwards" assumed a competitive drive to match or exceed superior performers, and subsequent research (Collins, 2000) has shown that upward comparisons do at least sometimes lead to upward assimilation; that is, to a tendency to move one's own skill in the direction of the outperformer's. Research has shown that such upward comparisons encourage competitive behavior (Tesser, 1988), which can include attempts to impede the outperformer. A classic example is a study by Hoffman et al. (1954). When one participant in a group of three began outperforming the other two by a significant margin, the other two participants attempted to prevent the high performer from gaining additional points. In this way, the performance difference was reduced.

In another study, which pitted temporal against social comparison, participants learned that they were getting better or worse at a task, and that their performance was better or worse than average (Zell & Alicke, 2009a). Compared to observers, who based their evaluations of participants solely on their social comparison status, participants evaluated themselves with reference to both types of information: more favorably when they were improving, and more favorably when they were better than average. Further, when the performance feedback actors received suggested that they were getting worse, their self-evaluation ratings were approximately equal to that of the observers. However, when their fortunes improved, participants used this temporal information as a basis for evaluating themselves more favorably than observers.

These findings suggest that individuals use both social and temporal comparison information to evaluate themselves, but rely primarily on social comparison information to evaluate others. To take a concrete example, a person who is dieting may evaluate his progress both in terms of whether he is losing weight, and with regard to whether he weighs more or less than his peers. It seems natural that people's own temporal experience would be more salient to them than to observers, which may account for observers' relying only on social comparison data.

The greater reliance on temporal information may also affect self-assessments in competition pools. A younger sibling who is catching up in ability to an older one may be buoyed by this progress, for example, whereas the older sibling is satisfied by remaining in the driver's seat, for the time being. This topic, which to our knowledge has not yet been investigated, is a natural line for further investigation, involving self-assessments between superior and inferior performers whose relative abilities are widening or diminishing.

Referents in the Competition Pool

In addition to influencing self-assessment, competition pools also affect judgments of the comparison referent. Here, we first discuss research on how people evaluate referents who outperform them in competition pools. Then, we describe research suggesting that people selectively consider the skill level of the referent in order to maintain a positive self-image.

The Genius Effect

Despite the many excuses and self-serving mechanisms that people have at their disposal to deflect the negative implications of reproachful behavior or inferior performance, objective circumstances are sometimes too obvious to be denied. A tennis enthusiast who loses 10 times in a row to his roommate eventually must acknowledge his roommate's superior skills to avoid appearing ludicrous. In such circumstances, people have recourse to what we have called the "genius effect" (Alicke et al., 1997), which entails exaggerating the outperformer's ability. By exaggerating the outperformer's ability, people can maintain a relatively favorable position for themselves on the performance dimension. That is, assuming a constant distance between the outperformer and self, a high status for the outperformer maintains a relative high status for oneself.

In one study, participants were presented with a series of incomplete figures and asked to supply the missing segment. Items had been pretested so that the average participant could answer three of 10 items correctly. Participants completed this task in the same room with a confederate, and participants and confederates were instructed to grade each other's tests. The participant and confederate then exchanged tests so they could see each other's scores. Observers were given a copy of the test, and watched these proceedings from behind a one-way mirror. The main response measure was participants' and observers' ratings of the participant's and confederate's perceptual intelligence.

Results indicated that whereas participants and observers did not differ in their ratings of the participant's perceptual intelligence, participants rated the confederate's ability higher than did observers. This finding was replicated in a second study in which responses were private, to diminish impression-management concerns. In a third study, similar findings were obtained in conditions in which the participant outperformed the confederate. Thus, not only are people motivated to view outperformers as people of superior talent, they also elevate the ability of inferior performers to burnish the significance of their own task performance (Alicke et al., 1997).

The main implications of the genius effect for competition pools involve the kinds of comparison situations people are willing to enter, and their consequences. One possibility is that individuals will be less reluctant to enter competitions in which the outperformer is a "genius" because they will see the consequences of being outperformed as essentially irrelevant to their perceived status on the performance dimensions (Lockwood & Kunda, 1997). In fact, one might feel as though there is nothing to lose, and much to gain, in such competitions. Suppose an avid club tennis player had the opportunity to play a practice set with Roger Federer. If the club player managed to win one game by hitting a few lucky serves, the fact that he didn't get another point in the remaining 10 games might be viewed as a mighty victory. Thus, people may be eager to enter into certain competitions that they are sure to lose, and may actually benefit from the loss.

Selective use of Referent Status

The status of a competitor can also be used in a self-serving way in some social comparison contexts. For example, in research on *referent status neglect* (Zell et al., 2015), participants completed a lie detection test and received feedback indicating that they ranked better or worse than the previous participant (social comparison) and that the previous participant ranked above average or below average in comparison to a few hundred test-takers (referent status). Participants who learned that they had outperformed a competitor evaluated themselves positively regardless of whether their competitor was noted to be above or below average. On the other hand, when participants lost to the competitor, they rated themselves more favorably when their competitor was above average. These data suggest that people selectively highlight referent status information when it has favorable implications for the self.

Although Festinger originally focused on direct, explicit comparisons, implicit or vicarious comparisons vastly outnumber live, direct ones. Besides the implicit comparisons that occur when people unconsciously gauge their characteristics and skills with reference to family members, friends, and associates, the less direct comparisons that occur via mass media and social media provide a huge data base for competition pools (Verduyn et al., 2020). Although social comparison theorists originally thought that comparisons tended to be made with others who were similar on the comparison dimension (Tesser, 2003), it has become clear that comparisons are much more haphazard, and that "inappropriate" comparisons with people who may have had completely different experiences and circumstances are ubiquitous (Verduyn et al., 2020). Such comparisons occur even when they are neither sought nor intended. In some instances, implicit comparisons may be more insidious and impactful than explicit ones because individuals, being caught off-guard, may have less opportunity or incentive to ignore or counterargue them.

One unexplored facet of competition pools is what we call "social comparison transitivity" (Alicke et al., 2013). This refers to the fate of a competitor in subsequent competitions. For example, suppose Person A outperforms Person B, and then Person C outperforms Person B. Logically, this might reduce the perceived value of Person A's victory, especially in comparison to a situation in which Person B outperforms Person C. Many other conditions are possible here, involving combinations of Person A, Person B, and Person C's performance. Predictions can be made from both a transitivity logic standpoint, assuming a perfectly rational comparer, and a self-enhancement perspective, assuming a comparer whose goal is to maximize her self-view on the performance dimension. Based on previous self-enhancement research (Alicke & Sedikides, 2009, 2011), we would expect that comparers would tend to use transitivity information when it is self-serving (e.g., when the person they outperform outperforms someone else), but not when it is deflating (e.g., when the person they outperform is outperformed by another person).

Local and Global Competition Pools

Many studies have assessed the consequences of making upward, downward, or lateral comparisons, referring to a referent who has higher, lower, or equal status to themselves on the performance dimension, with complex results (e.g., Major et al., 1991). When people make such comparisons, regardless of whether they know the comparison referent's status on the judgment dimension in advance, they usually have the opportunity to extrapolate beyond any given competition pool in assessing their own standing. Suppose, for example, that Romeo and Boomer are in the same chemistry class, and Romeo gets an C on the same test on which Boomer receives a A. All Romeo knows is that Boomer is a pretty brainy guy, and so figures that being far behind Boomer is no great shame. But he might wonder, further, just how smart Boomer is. Is he the smartest kid in the class? Where does he stand at the university? Where does the university stand in relation to other universities? And so on.

Because social comparisons tend to be made with convenience samples (i.e., with whomever happens to be around), such as friends, families, and associates, and due to the general tendency to undervalue larger, base-rate data (Klein, 1997), people tend to take comparisons at face value, without considering the larger context. In fact, larger data sources are frequently absent for many of the self-assessments people might wish to make. If Annabelle's roommate, Natasha, is a better cook than her, what does this say about Annabelle, and what does it say about Natasha? Unlike IQ or SAT scores, there is no large population data within which to locate Natasha's skills. And, if there were, would people use them? In fact, research has shown that comparisons to those around us are sometimes more impactful than objective information, such as statistics or population norms (Klein, 1997).

Overreliance on convenience comparisons at the expense of larger samples can lead people to draw unwarranted conclusions about their abilities and characteristics. A person who smokes a pack of cigarettes a day, in a group of two pack-a-day smokers, may harbor the unrealistic, and detrimental, belief that her cigarette smoking is moderate. Conversely, a person who exercises regularly among a group of unusually athletic friends may worry that he is terribly out of shape. Two research traditions are relevant for assessing this issue: the big-fish-little-pond effect and local dominance.

Big-Fish-Little-Pond Effect

The big-fish-little-pond effect (BFLPE) was the first line of research to assess the relative effects of local versus more general competition pools on ability assessment. The original studies on the BFLPE showed that average-ability students reported more favorable academic self-concepts when they attended schools that were less as opposed to more academically selective (Marsh, 1987; Marsh & Hau, 2003). The BFLPE is presumably due to students comparing their academic competency and success with those of their immediate peers, such as their classmates and schoolmates, and using these local competition pools to form their academic self-concepts, at the expense of considering where their school ranks versus others. As a result, students with objectively equal ability tend to have lower academic self-concepts in schools where the average academic performance is high, and relatively higher academic self-concepts in schools in which the average academic performance is low (Marsh & Craven, 1997).

Considerable research supports this interpretation of the BFLPE. For example, Marsh and Hau (2003) measured the self-concepts and objective achievements of more than 100,000 teenagers from 26 countries and found a robust negative effect of school-average achievement on students' academic self-concepts, after controlling for individual student achievement. Further, a longitudinal study demonstrated that the negative effect of school-average achievement on academic self-concept remained after graduation from high school, suggesting that the BFLPE can have long-lasting consequences (Marsh et al., 2007). Lastly, although BFLPE research has focused mostly on academic self-concept ratings, researchers have reported similar findings when examining other outcome measures, such as emotional well-being (Diener & Fujita, 1997; Pekrun et al., 2019).

Research on the BFLPE has found that the disproportionate focus on standing in local competition pools is resistant to a variety of potential moderating factors (Marsh & Seaton, 2015). One study examined the robustness of the BFLPE across 16 student characteristics, including socio-economic status, motivation, self-efficacy, and learning strategies (Seaton et al., 2009). Of these 16 potential moderators, only four were found to significantly moderate the size of the BFLPE. Specifically, the BFLPE was more pronounced for students who were more intelligent, anxious, competitive, and students who used memorization as a learning strategy. Student academic ability, however, was not a significant moderator. In sum, these results support the generalizability of the BFLPE across several student characteristics and suggest that although some student characteristics reduce the size of the BFLPE, such as being less intelligent, anxious, or competitive, they do not eliminate it.

Recent research corroborates the robustness and universality of the BFLPE. Along these lines, the BFLPE obtains in elementary, middle, and high-school students (Marsh et al., 2007, 2015), high and low ability students (Marsh et al., 1995, 2014), and among students in over 65 countries across the world (Marsh et al., 2015, 2019). Moreover, a meta-analysis of the BFLPE literature, including 33 studies and over one million participants from four continents, yielded an overall BFLPE that was medium in size and largely robust to a variety of moderating factors (Fang et al., 2018). A key limitation of many studies on the BFLPE is that they use correlational designs, which prevents causal conclusions about the impact of competition pools on self-evaluations. Nonetheless, experimental studies which randomly assign people to conditions provide causal evidence for the positive impact of being a big fish in a little pond, and negative impact of being a little fish in a big pond, on self-evaluations (Zell & Alicke, 2009b; Zell & Lesick, 2021).

Local Dominance

Classic social comparison research emphasized comparisons between the self and one other individual. As noted, even these competition pools have implications beyond the immediate context, depending on how the comparison target is construed. If someone is outperformed by a superstar, the comparison may be viewed as irrelevant to the individual's self-concept (Lockwood & Kunda, 1997). Conversely, someone who outperforms a superstar receives an enormous boost to their self-image. In most comparisons, though, the meaning is more ambiguous. We may recognize that a superior performer is good, without having a very confident idea of how good she actually is.

We refer to comparisons with an immediate, concrete competition pool as local comparisons, and with larger, more abstract pools as global comparisons (Buckingham & Alicke, 2002; Zell & Alicke, 2010). These terms are relative. For example, in a comparison between two college football players, the local comparison is the traditional Person A compares with Person B competition pool, and the global comparison might be with reference to the whole football team. So, Person A might want to know where he stands with regard to Person B, and where Person B ranks talent-wise on the team as a whole. Or, one might compare their own team to another in their conference (local comparison), with reference to the conference as a whole (global comparison). Or, one could compare their own conference to all conferences in the region (local comparison), and the region to other regions (global comparison), and so on.

The phrase *local dominance* refers to the consistent finding that social comparisons are most impactful when made locally, among a few immediate others, as opposed to globally, with larger groups (Zell & Alicke, 2010, 2020). A prototypical example of the effect is one in which a person learns that she is the highest or lowest performer in a group of five, and that her score falls at the 84th or 32nd percentile of 1,500 other students at the university who have taken the same test (Zell & Alicke, 2009b; Study 4). In assessing their task ability, the findings of these studies show that the effect of the local comparison is larger than that of the global comparison and that it eradicates the effect of the global comparison that typically occurs when this standard is provided alone. These findings are not due to people simply ignoring the larger sample information. In control conditions, in which global information is presented alone, it has a large effect on self-judgments; that is, people who fall into a high percentile evaluate themselves far more favorably than those who fall into a low percentile. It is only when global information is accompanied by local comparison information that its effect is negated; hence the phrase, *local dominance*.

The local dominance effect does not seem limited to familiarity or connection to the local group. Such effects have been obtained in a context in which individuals thought they were competing on the internet with four other students who attended a different university than them. It does not depend on the abstractness of larger, population information, as it has been obtained in a situation in which participants saw their own highlighted scores near the beginning (high percentile) or end (low percentile) of a long printout of all 1,500 scores (Zell & Alicke, 2010). The local dominance effect persists in studies using different performance tasks and feedback manipulations (Alicke et al., 2010; Zell & Alicke, 2013; Zell et al., 2015). Further, local comparisons have a stronger effect on task enjoyment and intrinsic motivation than global comparisons (Zell et al., 2017).

A local dominance study that emphasizes the importance of salient competition pools assessed whether high-ranking members of low-quality groups evaluated themselves more favorably than low-ranking members of high-quality groups, even when the former had a lower objective performance level (Alicke et al., 2010). In this study, 10 participants were split into two groups of five. Students took a test assessing their ability to detect lies, and learned that among the current 10 participants, they ranked fifth or sixth. In the control conditions, half the participants were told that they ranked fifth in the group of 10, and half were told that they ranked sixth. In the experimental conditions, half the participants were told that they ranked fifth overall but worst in their five-person group, whereas the other group was told that they ranked sixth overall but best in their five-person group.

As the local dominance effect predicts, participants evaluated their test performance and overall lie detection ability more favorably when they ranked best in their five-person group but sixth overall than worst in their five-person group but fifth overall (Alicke et al., 2010). In these conditions, therefore, participants' overreliance on local comparison information led them to evaluate themselves more favorably when they ranked sixth than fifth. These findings demonstrate that the local dominance effect perseveres even when good members of bad groups have objectively worse performance than bad members of good groups.

Furthermore, comparisons with the control conditions showed that students evaluated themselves significantly more favorably when they learned that they ranked sixth out of 10 but best in their five-person group as opposed to simply learning that they ranked sixth out of 10. Additionally, students evaluated themselves significantly less favorably when they ranked fifth out of 10 but worst in their five-person group as opposed to just fifth out of 10. The contrasts show that the exact same performance level has very different self-evaluative consequences depending on whether it is linked to a local competition pool or a larger pool (Alicke et al., 2010).

We view the BFLPE as a special case of local dominance. This view is supported in a study by Huguet et al. (2009), in which approximately 2,000 French sixth-graders estimated the perceived rank of their academic abilities relative to other students in their class, and also completed academic self-concept measures. Results indicated that school achievement was negatively associated with academic self-concepts, with academic ability equated. This effect was eliminated, however, after controlling for students' perceived rank in their class, suggesting that perceived academic competence is driven by local competition pools.

The local dominance effect has proven to be one of the most robust social comparison phenomena (Gerber et al., 2018), and can be understood with reference both to the distant past—the social conditions in which humans evolved—and present conditions, the kinds of social groups they typically find themselves in. For most of their history, homo sapiens lived in small groups. Even in modern times, with far greater mobility, people continue to group themselves into family and friendship units. Before the advent of mass media, and large-scale polling, social comparisons were exclusively local. Comparisons within local competition pools, therefore, is endemic to the history of the species.

Developmentally, children compare themselves with their friends, families, and acquaintances, far before they begin to receive standardized test scores, or compare their video game scores to others on the internet. As a result, local comparisons are more habitual, and more emotionally impactful, than those made with disembodied internet targets, or anonymous test score takers.

Although favorable local comparisons can have positive emotional benefits, these beneficial effects are offset by overconfidence when they are extremely discrepant with population norms. In general, we assume that the disproportionate reliance on local competition pools primarily has deleterious outcomes. For example, a high school student who takes the SAT may compare his score to that of his friends, as well as to the general population of all students taking the SAT that year. The local dominance effect suggests that the student's peer group will have a stronger impact on his ability self-assessment than population norms. If his friends happen to be poor test-takers, the student may have an inflated sense of his math and writing abilities because of his strong performance in his local group. Conversely, if a student fares the worst of his friend group, but his friends happen to be excellent standardized test performers, he may have an unjustified negative view of his academic abilities (Zell & Alicke, 2010). Low academic self-concept negatively predicts later academic achievement and aspirations (Marsh & O'Mara, 2008; Nagengast & Marsh, 2012), which suggests that local dominance effects may have long-term negative consequences. Outside the test-taking context, research as also shown that local comparisons dominate health risk assessments, which could lead to an illusion of safety and more risk-taking behavior, or unnecessary health-related anxiety (Zell & Alicke, 2013).

Overreliance on local comparisons may also lead people to enter competitions that they are likely to lose. For example, a card player who consistently takes home the pot on his weekly poker night might become overconfident in his bluffing abilities, with disastrous consequences when he enters a high-stakes poker game with more skilled players. Additionally, fledgling students in prestigious academic programs that involve Science, Technology, Engineering, and Mathematics (STEM) may exit these programs, despite the strong possibility of a prosperous career had they persisted.

Finally, recent research suggests that local dominance effects may extend to extreme competition pools, that is, very high and very low rank groups (Zell & Lesick, 2021). Participants in these studies completed a verbal test and received manipulated feedback indicating that they ranked better than 85 percent of students at a university that ranked better than only 15 percent of universities taking part in the study or better than 15 percent of students at a university that ranked better than 85 percent of universities. Results were consistent with the predicted *huge-fish-tiny-pond effect*, such that participants evaluated themselves much more favorably when they ranked far above average in a far below average school than far below average in a far above average school. These data suggest that high rank in local competition pools is uplifting, even when that pool mostly contains poor performers. Similarly, low rank is demoralizing even when the local competition pool mostly contains outstanding performers.

Although research has examined the impact of local and global competition pools on self-evaluations, relatively few studies have examined the types of competition pools people choose to enter. People prefer to work in companies where they have high status, even if these companies pay less than others (Frank, 1985). Further, although preferences vary by culture, European Americans prefer to have high rank in a low rank school than low rank in a high rank school (Wu et al., 2018). These data suggest that decisions to enter and exit competition pools may be driven in part by perceived rank in these pools.

Summary and Conclusions

Social comparison and competition are intimately related. On the one hand, social comparison serves purposes other than ability assessment, such as learning norms and fitting one's abilities and characteristics to appropriate situations. On the other hand, virtually all competitions entail some type of social comparison. Social comparison influences the types of competition pools people decide to enter, and the outcome of competition provides individuals with information about their relative standing. Even extremely remote, non-personal competition pools, such as assessing one's Twitter following in comparison to others, can be highly competitive and evoke significant emotional reactions (Verduyn et al., 2020).

The prototypical competition is one in which two or more people engage in a task in which their relative performance can be gauged. In many competition pools, however, only one member is emotionally involved in the competition. A younger sibling, for example, may feel very competitive with an older one, and be affected by their relative performance and status, while the older sibling is completely oblivious. In this chapter, we have defined competition pools broadly to include any social comparison in which one or more parties experience self-evaluative consequences as a result of another's status, behavior, or performance outcome. Further, we have described the social comparison processes that emerge in competition pools, the importance of referent characteristics in competition pools, and the critical distinction between local and global competition pools for self-evaluation.

Broader Implications

Whereas the early history of social comparison research focused on selected, explicit comparisons, the later history of research in this field has emphasized haphazard, implicit ones. In this regard, it can be said that people are frequently in competition pools without realizing it, and that the social comparison consequences of such competitions can be significant. In fact, the self-enhancement and self-protection (Alicke & Sedikides, 2009; Sedikides & Alicke, 2019) strategies that people routinely deploy to deflect unwanted self-implications may be annulled when unfavorable comparisons are made unconsciously.

The research areas of social comparison and competition have traditionally been separate ones, with only occasional attempts to connect the two (Garcia et al., 2006, 2013). We have tried to bring them closer together, especially by considering the types of competition pools that people engage in, and the background context in which they occur. Local competition pools, especially those that involve relatively small groups, are likely to be the conditions that stimulate the most competitive motives. Although people are perfectly capable of evaluating themselves with reference to larger population statistics when local information is unavailable, research on the local dominance effect has demonstrated repeatedly that local comparisons are the most impactful, even when the comparison targets have no direct connection to the person making the comparison.

Future Directions

Not only are competition pools unlimited by face-to-face competitive situations, people also engage in imagined competitions, the outcomes of which may influence their current self-assessments. Estimating, for example, that one is improving so rapidly that they will eventually overtake important comparison targets (what we refer to as interpersonal, future comparisons), may suffice to bolster present self-evaluations even in losing competitions. Such imagined comparisons are likely to be primarily self-serving (Kanten & Teigen, 2008; Williams et al., 2012). Thus, future research should examine whether projecting a favorable future ameliorates a more middling present.

People also compete with themselves. Ambitious people spend most of their lives trying to get better at their occupations, their hobbies, and their relationships. In so doing, they may actually downgrade their past capabilities to place their present ones in the most positive light (Wilson & Ross, 2003). Of course, with age, people begin to lose some of these competitions with themselves. An interesting line for future research would be to assess conditions that contrast declining ability with social status. How does a former professional basketball player, who is still more talented than 99 percent of the population, assess her abilities when they have declined significantly from her own high standards? Is this a place in which global comparisons might assuage the impact of declining ability, or does the local comparison (in this case, with oneself) continue to dominate?

Moreover, social comparison theory has rarely considered the consequences of leaving or exiting a competition pool. One possibility is that self-evaluations continue to be impacted by status in a competition pool, even after leaving the pool. Along these lines, student's rank in high school predicts academic self-evaluations several years after graduation (Marsh et al., 2007). In other contexts, however, comparisons with others in a new competition pool overwrites or replaces the impact of a prior competition pool. For example, self-evaluations of academic ability are associated with student's rank in their current class but not their rank in a previous class (von Keyserlingk et al., 2019).

Additional research that clarifies the effects of entering and exiting competition pools, especially during important life transitions, would be informative.

Finally, future research in social comparison could be expanded greatly by considering the personal motives operating in competition pools. Depending on the structure of outcome interdependence (Kelley & Thibaut, 1978), comparers may be relatively open or closed to information about themselves. Further, the meaning of the information obtained may change. For example, self-assessment becomes ambiguous if we believe that someone is ingratiating, that a competitor is not trying hard, or that our own emotional reactions to a situation are far different from that of others. Interestingly, social comparison outcomes can also be skewed when the comparer harbors competitive motives of which the comparison target is unaware. If the comparer believes that he is in a life or death competition, whereas the comparison target believes he is involved in a casual, friendly game, the comparer may wind up with an unjustified boost to his ability self-image. These are a few of the many motives that may operate in competition pools, that await further investigation.

References

Alicke, M. D., & Govorun, O. (2005). The better-than-average effect. In M. D. Alicke, D. A. Dunning, & J. I. Krueger (Eds.), *The self in social judgment* (pp. 85–106). Psychology Press.

Alicke, M. D., Guenther, C. L., & Zell, E. (2012). Social self-analysis: Constructing and maintaining personal identity. In M. R. Leary & J. P. Tangney (Eds.), *Handbook of self and identity* (2nd ed., pp. 291–308). Guilford Press.

Alicke, M. D., LoSchiavo, F. M., Zerbst, J., & Zhang, S. (1997). The person who outperforms me is a genius: Maintaining perceived competence in upward social comparison. *Journal of Personality and Social Psychology 73* (4), 781–789. https://doi.org/10.1037/0022-3514.73.4.781.

Alicke, M. D., & Sedikides, C. (2009). Self-enhancement and self-protection: What they are and what they do. *European Review of Social Psychology 20*, 1–48. https://doi.org/10.1080/10463280802613866.

Alicke, M. D., & Sedikides, C. (Eds.). (2011). *Handbook of self-enhancement and self-protection.* Guilford Press.

Alicke, M. D., Zell, E., & Bloom, D. L. (2010). Mere categorization and the frog-pond effect. *Psychological Science 21* (2), 174–177. https://doi.org/10.1177/0956797609357718.

Alicke, M. D., Zell, E., & Guenther, C. L. (2013). Social self-analysis: Constructing, protecting, and enhancing the self. In J. M. Olson & M. P. Zanna (Eds.), *Advances in experimental social psychology* (Vol. 48, pp. 173–234). Elsevier Academic Press.

Buckingham, J. T., & Alicke, M. D. (2002). The influence of individual versus aggregate social comparison and the presence of others on self-evaluations. *Journal of Personality and Social Psychology 83* (5), 1117–1130. https://doi.org/10.1037/0022-3514.83.5.1117.

Chatard, A., Bocage-Barthélémy, Y., Selimbegović, L., & Guimond, S. (2017). The woman who wasn't there: Converging evidence that subliminal social comparison affects self-evaluation. *Journal of Experimental Social Psychology 73*, 1–13. https://doi.org/10.1016/j.jesp.2017.05.005.

Collins, R. L. (2000). Among the better ones: Upward assimilation in social comparison. In J. Suls & L. Wheeler (Eds.), *Handbook of social comparison: Theory and research* (pp. 159–171). Kluwer Academic Publishers. https://doi.org/10.1007/978-1-4615-4237-79.

Deutsch, M., & Gerard, H. B. (1955). A study of normative and informational social influences upon individual judgment. *Journal of Abnormal and Social Psychology 51* (3), 629–636. https://doi.org/10.1037/h0046408.

Diener, E., & Fujita, F. (1997). Social comparisons and subjective well-being. In B. P. Buunk & F. X. Gibbons (Eds.), *Health, coping, and well-being: Perspectives from social comparison theory* (pp. 329–357). Lawrence Erlbaum Associates Publishers.

Fang, J., Huang, Z., Zhang, M., Huang, F., Li, Z., & Yuan, Q. (2018). The big-fish-little-pond effect on academic self-concept: A meta-analysis. *Frontiers in Psychology 9*, 1–11. https://doi.org/10.3389/fpsyg.2018.01569.

Festinger, L. (1954). A theory of social comparison processes. *Human Relations 7*, 117–140. https://doi.org/10.1177/001872675400700202.

Frank, R. H. (1985). *Choosing the right pond: Human behavior and the quest for status*. Oxford University Press.

Garcia, S. M., Tor, A., & Gonzalez, R. (2006). Ranks and rivals: A theory of competition. *Personality and Social Psychology Bulletin 32* (7), 970–982. https://doi.org/10.1177/0146167206287640.

Garcia, S. M., Tor, A., & Schiff, T. M. (2013). The psychology of competition: A social comparison perspective. *Perspectives on Psychological Science 8* (6), 634–650. https://doi.org/10.1177/1745691613504114.

Gerber, J. P., Wheeler, L., & Suls, J. (2018). A social comparison theory meta-analysis 60+ years on. *Psychological Bulletin 144* (2), 177–197. https://doi.org/10.1037/bul0000127.

Gilbert, D. T., Giesler, R. B., & Morris, K. A. (1995). When comparisons arise. *Journal of Personality and Social Psychology 69* (2), 227–236. https://doi.org/10.1037/0022-3514.69.2.227.

Hoffman, P. J., Festinger, L., & Lawrence, D. H. (1954). Tendencies toward group comparability in competitive bargaining. *Human Relations 7*, 141–159. https://doi.org/10.1177/001872675400700203.

Huguet, P., Dumas, F., Marsh, H., Régner, I., Wheeler, L., Suls, J., Seaton, M., & Nezlek, J. (2009). Clarifying the role of social comparison in the big-fish–little-pond effect (BFLPE): An integrative study. *Journal of Personality and Social Psychology 97* (1), 156–170. https://doi.org/10.1037/a0015558.

Kanten, A. B., & Teigen, K. H. (2008). Better than average and better with time: Relative evaluations of self and others in the past, present, and future. *European Journal of Social Psychology 38* (2), 343–353. https://doi.org/10.1002/ejsp.457.

Kelley, H. H., & Thibaut, J. W. (1978). *Interpersonal relations: A theory of interdependence*. Wiley.

Klein, W. M. (1997). Objective standards are not enough: Affective, self-evaluative, and behavioral responses to social comparison information. *Journal of Personality and Social Psychology 72* (4), 763–774. https://doi.org/10.1037/0022-3514.72.4.763.

Lockwood, P., & Kunda, Z. (1997). Superstars and me: Predicting the impact of role models on the self. *Journal of Personality and Social Psychology 73* (1), 91–103. https://doi.org/10.1037/0022-3514.73.1.91.

Major, B., Testa, M., & Blysma, W. H. (1991). Responses to upward and downward social comparisons: The impact of esteem-relevance and perceived control. In J. Suls & T. A. Wills (Eds.), *Social comparison: Contemporary theory and research* (pp. 237–260). Lawrence Erlbaum Associates.

Markus, H., & Nurius, P. (1986). Possible selves. *American Psychologist 41* (9), 954–969. https://doi.org/10.1037/0003-066X.41.9.954.

Marsh, H. W. (1987). The big-fish-little-pond effect on academic self-concept. *Journal of Educational Psychology 79* (3), 280–295. https://doi.org/10.1037/0022-0663.79.3.280.

Marsh, H. W., Abduljabbar, A. S., Morin, A. J. S., Parker, P., Abdelfattah, F., Nagengast, B., & Abu-Hilal, M. M. (2015). The big-fish-little-pond effect: Generalizability of social comparison processes over two age cohorts from Western, Asian, and Middle Eastern Islamic countries. *Journal of Educational Psychology 107* (1), 258–271. https://doi.org/10.1037/a0037485.

Marsh, H. W., Chessor, D., Craven, R. G., & Roche, L. (1995). The effects of gifted and talented programs on ASC: The big fish strikes again. *American Educational Research Journal 32*(2), 285–319. https://doi.org/10.3102/00028312032002285.

Marsh, H. W., & Craven, R. (1997). Academic self-concept: Beyond the dust bowl. In G. D. Phye (Ed.), *Handbook of classroom assessment: Learning, achievement, and adjustment* (pp. 131–198). Academic Press.

Marsh, H. W., & Hau, K.-T. (2003). Big-fish-little-pond effect on academic self-concept: A cross-cultural (26-country) test of the negative effects of academically selective schools. *American Psychologist 58* (5), 364–376. https://doi.org/10.1037/0003-066X.58.5.364.

Marsh, H. W., Kuyper, H., Morin, A. J. S., Parker, P. D., & Seaton, M. (2014). Big-fish-little-pond social comparison and local dominance effects: Integrating new statistical models, methodology, design, theory and substantive implications. *Learning and Instruction 33*, 50–66. https://doi.org/10.1016/j.learninstruc.2014.04.002.

Marsh, H. W., & O'Mara, A. (2008). Reciprocal effects between academic self-concept, self-esteem, achievement, and attainment over seven adolescent years: Unidimensional and multidimensional perspectives of self-concept. *Personality and Social Psychology Bulletin 34* (4), 542–552. https://doi.org/10.1177/0146167207312313.

Marsh, H. W., Parker, P. D., & Pekrun, R. (2019). Three paradoxical effects on academic self-concept across countries, schools, and students: Frame-of-reference as a unifying theoretical explanation. *European Psychologist 24* (3), 231–242. https://doi.org/10.1027/1016-9040/a000332.

Marsh, H. W., & Seaton, M. (2015). The big-fish-little-pond effect, competence self-perceptions, and relativity: Substantive advances and methodological innovation. In A. Elliot (Ed.), *Advances in motivation science* (Vol. 2, pp. 127–184). Elsevier. https://doi.org/10.1016/bs.adms.2015.05.002.

Marsh, H. W., Trautwein, U., Lüdtke, O., Baumert, J., & Köller, O. (2007). The big-fish-little-pond effect: Persistent negative effects of selective high schools on self-concept after graduation. *American Educational Research Journal 44* (3), 631–669. https://doi.org/10.3102/0002831207306728.

Mussweiler, T., Rüter, K., & Epstude, K. (2004). The man who wasn't there: Subliminal social comparison standards influence self-evaluation. *Journal of Experimental Social Psychology 40* (5), 689–696. https://doi.org/10.1016/j.jesp.2004.01.004.

Nagengast, B., & Marsh, H. W. (2012). Big fish in little ponds aspire more: Mediation and cross-cultural generalizability of school-average ability effects on self-concept and career aspirations in science. *Journal of Educational Psychology 104* (4), 1033–1053. https://doi.org/10.1037/a0027697.

Pekrun, R., Murayama, K., Marsh, H. W., Goetz, T., & Frenzel, A. C. (2019). Happy fish in little ponds: Testing a reference group model of achievement and emotion. *Journal of Personality and Social Psychology 117* (1), 166–185. https://doi.org/10.1037/pspp0000230.

Pronin, E., Olivola, C. Y., & Kennedy, K. A. (2008). Doing unto future selves as you would do unto others: Psychological distance and decision making. *Personality and Social Psychology Bulletin 34* (2), 224–236. https://doi.org/10.1177/0146167207310023.

Seaton, M., Marsh, H. W., & Craven, R. G. (2009). Earning its place as a pan-human theory: Universality of the big-fish-little-pond effect across 41 culturally and economically diverse countries. *Journal of Educational Psychology 101* (2), 403–419. https://doi.org/10.1037/a0013838.

Sedikides, C., & Alicke, M. D. (2019). The five pillars of self-enhancement and self-protection. In R. M. Ryan (Ed.), *The Oxford handbook of human motivation* (2nd ed., pp. 307–319). Oxford University Press.

Strickhouser, J. E., & Zell, E. (2015). Self-evaluative effects of dimensional and social comparison. *Journal of Experimental Social Psychology 59*, 60–66. https://doi.org/10.1016/j.jesp.2015.03.001.

Suls, J., Collins, R. L., & Wheeler, L. (Eds.) (2020). *Social comparison, judgment, and behavior*. Oxford University Press.

Taylor, S. E., Wood, J. V., & Lichtman, R. R. (1983). It could be worse: Selective evaluation as a response to victimization. *Journal of Social Issues 39* (2), 19–40. https://doi.org/10.1111/j.1540-4560.1983.tb00139.x.

Tesser, A. (1988). Toward a self-evaluation maintenance model of social behavior. In L. Berkowitz & L. Berkowitz (Eds.), *Advances in experimental social psychology* (Vol. 21, pp. 181–227). Academic Press.

Tesser, A. (2003). Self-evaluation. In M. R. Leary & J. P. Tangney (Eds.). *Handbook of self and identity* (pp. 275–290). Guilford Press.

Verduyn, P., Gugushvili, N., Massar, K., Täht, K., & Kross, E. (2020). Social comparison on social networking sites. *Current Opinion in Psychology 36*, 32–37. https://doi.org/10.1016/j.copsyc.2020.04.002.

von Keyserlingk, L., Becker, M., & Jansen, M. (2019). Academic self-concept during the transition to upper secondary school. *Contemporary Educational Psychology 56*, 152–160. https://doi.org/10.1016/j.cedpsych.2019.01.001.

Wheeler, L., & Miyake, K. (1992). Social comparison in everyday life. *Journal of Personality and Social Psychology 62* (5), 760–773. https://doi.org/10.1037/0022-3514.62.5.760.

Williams, E. F., Gilovich, T., & Dunning, D. (2012). Being all that you can be: The weighting of potential in assessments of self and others. *Personality and Social Psychology Bulletin 38* (2), 143–154. https://doi-org.libproxy.uncg.edu/10.1177/0146167211421937.

Wilson, A. E., & Ross, M. (2001). From chump to champ: People's appraisals of their earlier and present selves. *Journal of Personality and Social Psychology 80* (4), 572–584. https://doi.org/10.1037/0022-3514.80.4.572.

Wilson, A. E., & Ross, M. (2003). The identity function of autobiographical memory: Time is on our side. *Memory 11* (2), 137–149. https://doi.org/10.1080/741938210.

Wu, K., Garcia, S. M., & Kopelman, S. (2018). Frogs, ponds, and culture: Variations in entry decisions. *Social Psychological and Personality Science 9* (1), 99–106. https://doi.org/10.1177/1948550617706731.

Zell, E., & Alicke, M. D. (2009a). Self-evaluative effects of temporal and social comparison. *Journal of Experimental Social Psychology 45* (1), 223–227. https://doi.org/10.1016/j.jesp.2008.09.007.

Zell, E., & Alicke, M. D. (2009b). Contextual neglect, self-evaluation, and the frog-pond effect. *Journal of Personality and Social Psychology 97* (3), 467–482. https://doi.org/10.1037/a0015453.

Zell, E., & Alicke, M. D. (2010). The local dominance effect in self-evaluation: Evidence and explanations. *Personality and Social Psychology Review 14* (4), 368–384. https://doi.org/10.1177/1088868310366144.

Zell, E., & Alicke, M. D. (2013). Local dominance in health risk perception. *Psychology & Health 28* (4), 469–476. https://doi.org/10.1080/08870446.2012.742529.

Zell, E., & Alicke, M. D. (2020). Effects of local and general comparisons on self-assessment. In J. Suls, R. L. Collins, & L. Wheeler (Eds.), *Social comparison, judgment, and behavior* (pp. 143–177). Oxford University Press.

Zell, E., Alicke, M. D., & Strickhouser, J. E. (2015). Referent status neglect: Winners evaluate themselves favorably even when the competitor is incompetent. *Journal of Experimental Social Psychology 56*, 18–23. https://doi.org/10.1016/j.jesp.2014.08.004.

Zell, E., & Lesick, T. L. (2021). Taking social comparison to the extremes: The huge-fish-tiny-pond effect in self-evaluations. *Social Psychological and Personality Science 12* (6), 1030–1038. https://doi.org/10.1177/1948550620956535.

Zell, E., & Strickhouser, J. E. (2020). Comparisons across dimensions, people, and time: On the primacy of social comparison in self-evaluations. *Social Psychological and Personality Science 11* (6), 791–800. https://doi.org/10.1177/1948550619884564.

Zell, E., Strickhouser, J. E., & Alicke, M. D. (2017). Local dominance effects on self-evaluations and intrinsic motivation. *Self and Identity 16* (5), 629–644. https://doi.org/10.1080/15298868.2017.1295100.

Zell, E., Strickhouser, J. E., Sedikides, C., & Alicke, M. D. (2020). The better-than-average effect in comparative self-evaluation: A comprehensive review and meta-analysis. *Psychological Bulletin 146* (2), 118–149. https://doi.org/10.1037/bul0000218.

CHAPTER

16

On Predicting and Being Predicted: Navigating Life in a Competitive Landscape Full of Mind Readers

Oscar Ybarra, Kimberly Rios, Matthew C. Keller, Nicholas Michalak, Iris Wang, *and* Todd Chan

Abstract

We inhabit a world full of other humans. We will cooperate with some, but most will remain strangers or competitors for resources. These potential cooperators and competitors will try to make predictions about us, as we likewise attempt to predict whether they will cooperate or compete. From the target's perspective, such attempts at being judged and predicted should have different implications, depending on whether the one doing the predicting is a potential cooperator or competitor. Using this as the lens for the present analysis, this chapter organizes the psychological literature into a coherent framework to highlight the causes and consequences associated with predicting any given target and to paint a more complex picture of the target experience, as they decide when they will or will not be predicted. The authors conclude the chapter by offering novel predictions and shedding new light on the implications for various areas of research.

Key Words: social prediction, perceiver versus target, behavioral flexibility, unpredictability, social connections, behavioral science

Primate life, including human life, is mixed-motive in nature, bringing with it opportunities to both cooperate and compete. These two broad approaches to social interaction elicit different types of perceptions and behavior that are aimed at adaptive outcomes. In the present chapter we focus on the behavior of the target in social interaction, the person who is the object of another's prediction attempts.

A fundamental social motive is the need to understand and predict other people's behavior. It might be argued that this tendency actually serves as the engine of behavioral science. This inclination is so ingrained and effortless that people try to predict the "behavior" of moving geometric figures (Heider & Simmel, 1944) and they readily ascribe agency to non-human and non-living objects such as the weather, gods, crops, animals, machines, or luck (e.g., Atran & Norenzayan, 2004; Barrett & Keil, 1996; Epley et al., 2008; Guthrie, 1993; Humphrey, 1976; Shtulman, 2008; Waytz et al., 2010). Attempts to judge others, read minds, and predict behavior are activities in which the majority of us engage, doing so regularly if not constantly. Given this state of affairs, the question that helps structure this chapter is this: with so many people trying to predict our behavior and read our minds, how and under what circumstances do people as targets react to these social prediction attempts?

One possibility is that a person can allow others to predict the self and read one's mind. A keen observer of human behavior suggested that there is a sadness to the human condition stemming from the awareness that others will never really know us or know our experiences (Humphrey, 2007). Other researchers suggest that people seek relationships with others whose perceptions are consistent with one's self-views (e.g., Swann et al., 1992). Another distinct possibility, though, is that people as *targets* are attuned to the potential for cooperation or competition in social interaction and will be selective of when they will want to be judged and predicted.

Social life, almost by definition, requires social coordination, which has implications for how targets behave. Much psychological and related research has focused on this class of circumstances. Self-signaling research from economics, for example, suggests that through their decisions individuals signal their predispositions (Bernheim, 1994). Research on "shared reality" advances the idea that people are motivated to verify their views, including self-beliefs, by sharing them with others (Hardin & Higgins, 1996). However, in addition to the deep human tendency to socially coordinate, under various circumstances individuals should also strive to keep others from clearly judging and predicting them. This latter perspective, we argue, is largely missing from available models of social behavior.

A Model of Social Navigation

To navigate life well, individuals need to establish cooperative and supportive social connections with others but also be able to hold their own during competition with others (Chan et al., 2021). Integral to this dialectic is the necessity to predict others and determine whether they will cooperate or compete. But equally important is determining whether we as targets are to be predicted by others.

Cooperative interactions and social connections are at the core of primate life (Jolly, 1966) and central to the human survival strategy (Barash, 1977; Dunbar, 1998). As Trivers (1971) argued, people are predisposed to want to establish cooperative relations with others, and as other researchers have documented, people have a fundamental need to be socially accepted (Baumeister & Leary, 1995). Because supportive social connections provide people with many instrumental and emotional resources (e.g., Cacioppo & Patrick, 2008; Cohen & Wills, 1985; Ybarra, Burnstein et al., 2008, Ybarra, Chan et al., 2008), the desire and possibility for cooperative social interaction should make people more willing to be judged and predicted in such circumstances. Some of the research mentioned earlier on self-signaling and shared reality is consistent with this proposal. Allowing the self to be judged, verified, and predicted engenders interpersonal transparency, which is critical for social acceptance and coordinating with others. But this does not mean people become completely transparent at the first sign of a potential connection without first establishing trust and negotiating relational expectations (cf. Goffman, 1959; Swann & Bosson, 2008).

However, individuals must also be sensitive to potential limits placed on their ability to direct their lives, which can occur because they inhabit a landscape full of people—most of whom are neither kin nor friend—with little interest or time for cooperating but nevertheless a keen interest in predicting others. Thus, when confronted with circumstances in which competition is likely, an individual should be troubled by others' characterization efforts (e.g., judged to have certain traits, being pigeon-holed into a role, being stereotyped) and attempt to keep from being judged and predicted, as social prediction by potential competitors can translate into losses in competitive games and limits on one's agency.

There may be some exceptions to this proposed pattern, although research is required to document them. For instance, even when cooperation is desired, people may not want to be fully predictable in order to maintain some independence or intrigue in interpersonal settings (Norton et al., 2007). Conversely, individuals may still want to be predictable under competitive circumstances. Being seen as someone who is formidable or as someone who cannot be taken advantage of, for example, could prove effective (cf. Zahavi, 1975). Likewise, those who have power in a given situation may seek to make their intentions perfectly understood.

Despite these cases, we propose that people acting as targets should be more open to being predicted when cooperation is desired, but less so when cooperation is unlikely or not desired. Our analysis focuses on the target of perception and their behavioral flexibility, which we argue is many times determined by the dynamic and mixed-motive nature of navigating a mixed-motive landscape with others.

Overview: Predicting and being Predicted Framework

We all try to predict and characterize those around us. By predict, we mean attempts to judge and mentally pin down what a person is like, what she or he values, is experiencing, or is likely to do given the circumstances. For perceivers typically dealing with an uncertain social environment, almost any feature of a person can serve as a basis for social prediction. This can range from the way a person decorates their house to how they dress and speak, to shopping patterns (marketers assume this), emotional expressions, and inferences about goals and intentions. However, perceivers deploy some information categories more readily than others (i.e., those based on age, gender, and race; Brewer, 1988).

This social cognitive processing by perceivers (e.g., categorizing, drawing inferences) need not always lead to prediction, and perceivers may even be unaware that such processing has taken place. But from the *target's* perspective, being characterized amounts to others' attempts—real or imagined—to judge what one is like, values, is experiencing, or is likely to do, which can create potential disadvantages in certain contexts or place limits on one's behavior.

Our analysis is structured around four parts. First, we briefly review research suggesting that people inhabit a landscape full of mind readers and behavioral predictors. That is, people as perceivers show developmental and culturally universal tendencies to *attempt* to read others' behavior and minds. Further, perceivers expect predictions to be confirmed, and their expectations can constrain others' behavior.

Having described this social landscape from the perceiver's perspective, we then discuss how people as targets attempt to deal with others' social prediction attempts. Compared to the perspective of the perceiver described in the research overview, the target's perspective has received limited attention in the psychological and related literatures.

Next, we highlight the central moderator in our analysis and discuss the conditions under which people are more likely to want to be predicted and when this tendency will reverse. Although people strive at times to keep from being predicted to be flexible and adaptive, their goals and outcomes are many times tied to emotionally or instrumentally supportive social connections. Thus, we posit that the cooperative versus competitive contexts will moderate these effects. Finally, we conclude by considering various implications of the present framework.

The present framework integrates across many areas of research that have been studied independently of one another. Our review is not intended to be exhaustive, but we believe the reviewed research—especially the framework in which we place it—offers various insights about human psychology and social behavior. One contribution is that the integration helps explicate the dynamic between the social perceiver and the target of prediction and thus paints a richer picture of how people actually navigate their social environments. Our integration should also allow investigators to see a variety of existing research in a new light—for example, appreciating the potential common motivational underpinnings among research topics that were not previously apparent and, in some cases, adding if not changing the meaning of extant research findings. The value of the integration will also become apparent in its heuristic potential and ability to generate ideas for future research.

Perils to Target's Options: A Mixed-Motive Landscape Full of Mind Readers

Briefly reviewing the findings in this section and integrating across them will help underscore the competitive nature of the social environment people inhabit and the necessity for people as targets to be sensitive to how others perceive them. More specifically, we delineate here several perils to the target that are engendered by the perceiver. In other words, what we review next are the attributes, tendencies, or practices of the perceiver that can potentially imperil the target's flexibility and agency.

The Incessant Tendency to Predict Others

A considerable amount of research in social psychology has focused on the perceiver's knack for categorizing targets, overweighting dispositional information, and judging others with an eye toward cognitive efficiency (e.g., Brewer, 1988; Fiske & Neuberg, 1990; Gilbert et al., 1988; Jones & Davis, 1965; Macrae et al., 1994; Moran et al., 2014; Oosterhof & Todorov, 2008; Trope, 1986). This focus is understandable given that the competitive landscape in which we live puts a premium on the ability to predict others' behavior, their character, intentions, and the nature of our relationships with them (Adolphs, 2001; Chance & Mead, 1953; Humphrey, 1976). Knowledge or "good enough" guesses of others' mental states or behavioral tendencies is thought to facilitate social coordination and navigation (Asch, 1952; Heider, 1958; Tagiuri, 1958).

Given the central role of social prediction in navigating social life, it is easy to understand why the mental architecture for social prediction appears so early in children and across cultures (Hughes & Ensor, 2007; Vinden, 1999; Wellman et al., 2001). Much research indicates that by about the age of three-and-a-half (other studies suggest earlier ages), children develop a theory of mind or the ability to understand that other people can have beliefs, desires, and other mental representations (e.g., Chandler et al., 1989; Roth & Leslie, 1991; Watson et al., 2001). Research into the behavior reading or the mirror neuron system, which allows perceivers to infer others' goals by simulating their behavior, suggests that this system is present in humans as well (Oberman & Ramachandran, 2007; Rizollati & Craighero, 2004). Thus, people enter this world with formidable tools that can be used to draw inferences about others.

Drawing inferences about others or understanding that they have beliefs and intentions need not imply behavior prediction, as prediction can also occur by applying rules about social situations (Clement et al., 2011). However, many times social inferences do form the basis for behavior prediction. Research in social cognition indicates that people spontaneously draw inferences about others' traits and personalities (e.g., Ham & Vonk, 2003; Uleman et al., 2008; Winter & Uleman, 1984; Ybarra & Stephan, 1996, 1999) and use such inferences to predict targets' behavior (McCarthy & Skowronski, 2011). Such tendencies are amplified when perceivers strive for efficiency in judgment (Newman, 1996) and consider behavior that is likely to occur in the more distant future (Nussbaum et al., 2003). Perceivers also tend to be very confident in their predictions of others, even when their predictions do not warrant such confidence (Dunning et al., 1990; Vallone et al., 1990).

Thus, research in person perception suggests that through mechanisms for attempted mind and behavior reading, or through other tools underlying person perception, the perceiver is prepared to regularly attempt to characterize the behavior of targets, try to read targets' minds, and use inferences to make predictions about targets. Whether or not the perceiver succeeds at predicting is a different issue. However, disconfirmed predictions, when noticed, are disquieting for the perceiver.

Perceivers Do Not Like Inconsistency

One implication of the prevalent tendency for people to characterize and predict is that surprises and inconsistencies are disliked. Different findings support this suggestion. First, a person's inconsistent acts require additional cognitive capacity and energy to process (e.g., Srull, 1981; Stangor & Duan, 1991). Second, many times the perceiver undertakes these cognitive efforts to dispel the inconsistencies (e.g., Hastie, 1984). Finally, people who enact inconsistent behaviors—not just the behaviors themselves—are disliked (Barden et al., 2005; Colvin, 1993; Gergen & Jones, 1963; Hendrick, 1972; Kreps et al., 2017).

Being Constrained by Others' Predictions

One implication of perceivers' attempts at social prediction and their annoyance with others' inconsistency involves behavior confirmation in the form of the self-fulfilling prophecy, in which perceiver behavior toward targets is driven by their pre-conceptions. This can elicit expectancy consistent behavior in the target, and then produce confirmation of the perceivers' pre-conceptions (Chen & Bargh, 1997; Darley & Fazio, 1980; Jussim, 1986). For example, men who believed they were interacting with an attractive woman behaved in a warmer and more outgoing manner toward her, which subsequently led the woman to respond in kind (Snyder et al., 1977; for similar effects with racial stereotypes, see Word et al., 1974).

Behavioral confirmation and the constraining effects that perceiver predictions and characterizations can have to inform us about the goals of the perceiver with an interest in efficient social prediction (Snyder & Haugen, 1994). It also suggests that attempts to predict others can place limitations on targets of prediction. It might be expected, however, that people as targets of prediction would have at their disposal various responses and behaviors for trying to deal with this recurring situation depending on who the perceiver is. We turn to these processes next, although we focus on what we consider to be the understudied tendency in individuals of not wanting to be judged and predicted.

Target's Reactions to Perceiver's Attempts to Predict and Characterize the Self

The previous section discussed the many tendencies and practices perceivers deploy to make sense of and predict those around them—and we have argued that these can potentially imperil the target. Researchers have suggested, though, that targets also have an important role to play in social interaction and perception (e.g., Funder, 1995; Hampson, 1997; Hancock & Ickes, 1996; Kenny et al., 2001; Snodgrass et al., 1998; Swann, 1984). Yet lacking in large part from discussions of social perception is the idea that people as targets, at times, may be ill at ease at being characterized and predicted by others. Here, we examine the target's reactions.

From the target's perspective, being predicted means real or imagined attempts by others to judge the self or forecast one's moves. Further, others' prediction attempts may be inferred simply on the basis that they have taken notice. If cooperation with perceivers is unlikely and no interdependence exists, such real or imagined prediction attempts can give rise to behaviors on the part of targets to try to keep from being predicted.

Not wanting to be predicted can be associated with diverse affective, cognitive, and behavioral experiences such as self-consciousness, limited disclosures, or actively attempting to change others' social predictions. Whether these behaviors succeed in not allowing others to predict the self will depend on features of the perceiver, target, and the situation, but the responses themselves share the common goal—not necessarily conscious—to avoid being judged and predicted to maintain behavioral flexibility.

Reactions to Being Characterized and Predicted

We now turn to various responses the target can experience and enact to avoid being characterized and predicted. First, we discuss targets' over-sensitivity to being noticed and feelings of being scrutinized. Next, we discuss other reactions targets can have and the behaviors they can enact in dealing with would-be mind readers and social predictors. We colloquially refer to these reactions and behaviors as the two lines of defense people as targets can enact to avoid being predicted. The upshot to this part of the chapter is that although others can constrain behavior through their tendency to predict, targets have at their disposal various tools to try to limit such social prediction attempts.

(Over) Sensitivity to Being Noticed

One implication of our model is that because people can run risks from being predicted by others (e.g., limits to behavioral flexibility, resource loss), targets are likely to be sensitive to and uncomfortable with the possibility that others are taking notice and scrutinizing the self. Like the experience of pain, which is aversive but signals an important event to the organism requiring attention, the aversive reactions discussed in this section serve as signals to the individual of potential social costs from others' prediction attempts.

PARANOID COGNITION

Paranoid cognition relates to a person's beliefs that they are being scrutinized (Kramer, 1994) and persecuted (Bebbington et al., 2013). Although not psychopathology, most people in novel and ambiguous social situations are capable of becoming vigilant for social cues and ruminating about them (Fenigstein et al., 1975; Preti & Cella, 2010). Further, situational factors and reactions can transform these cognitions into various emotional states, such as anxiety and discomfort (Mor & Winquist, 2002). Thus, in uncertain social situations, mechanisms are in place to signal to the target that others may be attending to and potentially trying to predict the self. The next two phenomena to be discussed help show more clearly how people from non-clinical populations can express related reactions due to contextual factors.

SPOTLIGHT EFFECT

The "spotlight" effect occurs when people overestimate the degree to which their actions and appearance (observable characteristics) are noticed and evaluated by others (Gilovich et al., 2002; Gilovich et al., 2000). Interestingly, feelings that others are taking special notice and that one is being watched are considered classical indicators of paranoid ideology (e.g., Magaro, 1980; Millon, 1981).

In two studies on the "spotlight" effect, participants were asked to wear a t-shirt with a salient image (Gilovich et al., 2000, Studies 1 & 2). In these studies participants overestimated the number of people (observers) who would actually be able to remember the images on the shirts. Thus, participants felt they stood out and that others were scrutinizing them more than was actually the case.

FEELING TRANSPARENT

Feelings of transparency (e.g., Barr & Kleck, 1995; Vorauer & Ross, 1999) may be slightly different manifestations of the reactions underlying the spotlight effect and paranoid cognition more generally. As described by Gilovich et al. (1998), feelings of transparency are nicely illustrated by the protagonist in Edgar Allen Poe's *The Tell-Tale Heart*, in which he tries to suppress his reaction to the crime he has committed while conversing with police officers. The protagonist is so taken by his anxiety that he feels he and the police can hear the beating heart of his victim buried underneath the floorboards. To feel transparent is for a person to feel that one's thoughts and feelings are leaking out for all to see.

The spotlight and transparency effects are typically explained with regard to the unique perspective people have on their experience, how that anchors judgment, and the greater knowledge they have about themselves (e.g., Gilovich et al., 2000). However, this does not preclude other mechanisms may be at work. In particular, we argue that away from supportive and cooperative others, targets do not want to be predicted in order to maintain their behavioral flexibility and agency. Because targets are many times unsure about others' intentions in socially uncertain situations, readily report that others categorize them (Ellemers & Barreto, 2006), and report that others draw strong, correspondent inferences about them (Epley et al., 2002; van Boven et al., 1999), it follows that targets should be sensitive to others noticing and scrutinizing them, which is what all these phenomena have in common.

First Line of Defense: Strategic Legibility

People's reactions to others' attempts to predict them can extend beyond an unwillingness to be scrutinized, to actual strategies they can deploy in interactions with others. For example, in one suggestive study, Hancock and Ickes (1996) showed that nearly half of the variance in perceiver accuracy scores was accounted for by the behavior of the various targets. In other words, how well the perceiver judged the targets seemed to depend on whether or not the targets allowed themselves to be read (Hancock & Ickes, 1996). The behaviors and responses described in this section thus deal with how legible individuals make themselves to others (also see Snodgrass & Rosenthal, 1985).

Other evidence suggesting that targets can short-circuit prediction attempts comes from research on behavioral confirmation. In one study, researchers ran participants through a typical behavioral confirmation paradigm, in which perceivers were given expectancies about a target, and then they were allowed to interact with the targets (Stukas & Snyder, 2002). These researchers included an additional element in the paradigm; after some time, they made participants aware they had confirmed their partner's expectations. The findings from the subsequent interaction indicated that participants exhibited more expectancy disconfirming behaviors, especially when negatively characterized. Thus, when made aware of others' expectations, participants endeavored to alter those predictions.

We argue that people can at times find the prospect of being predicted by others troubling (cf. Kelly, 2000; but see Swann et al., 1992). As a result, targets often try to take an active role in disconfirming others' expectations upon being made aware of them. However, our analysis holds that even when they are unaware of others' expectations, targets can foil social prediction through other means. A study by Smith et al. (1997) is consistent with this suggestion. These investigators used mock job interviews to examine how different interaction goals on the part of the targets influenced behavioral confirmation effects. The applicants in the different conditions were unaware of the positive or negative expectations held about them. In addition, half of the participants playing the applicant role were instructed to be deferential and accommodating and half to be non-deferential. Here we focus on this latter group. The results indicated that non-deferential participants succeeded in not confirming the interviewers' expectations, even when interviewers persisted in asking questions about the target's presumed behavioral tendencies.

The reviewed findings indicate people can undertake behaviors during interaction that can short-circuit behavioral confirmation. Although in the last study such behaviors followed from experimenter instructions, we believe people will readily enact them on their own. For example, much work on reactance theory has shown that people will enact various responses to maintain a threatened behavior (Brehm, 1966), or at least communicate to others they are autonomous (Baer et al., 1980; Heilman & Toffler, 1976). Thus, through either of these processes people can mobilize efforts to try to loosen the hold of others' predictions attempts. The existence of these varied behaviors makes sense because away from supportive others, targets do not want to be predicted and seek to maintain their behavioral flexibility.

Second Line of Defense: Strategic Disclosure

In the section, we discussed that people as targets have a large role to play when others attempt to predict the self—they can be strategically legible or illegible, so to speak. In this section, we consider one class of behaviors people can express to try to avoid being predicted: managing disclosure. Such behaviors are arguably more socially intelligent than "reacting" and asserting one's autonomy indiscriminately.

Disclosure can encompass a broad class of behaviors dealing with how people manage information about the self. The study of self-disclosure becomes more interesting when considered in contexts where the individual has full freedom to disclose information about the self, for example, in therapy. However, the challenge in obtaining full information from clients has long been recognized; people, even while in therapy, can be less than open (Hook & Andrews, 2005).

For example, one large scale survey showed that 42 percent of patients reported having withheld information from therapists in one of several categories (Weiner & Schuman, 1984). Other processes can be more covert. These include hiding thoughts and feelings that are covered in response to therapist questioning and interventions (Hill et al., 1993; Thompson & Hill, 1991), as well as keeping certain events secret, or even explicitly lying about them (Farber, 2003).

Therapy is supposed to be a place where people can disclose intimate thoughts and unburden themselves (Farber, 2003). So, it is noteworthy that even when people have license and the opportunity to fully disclose, they still keep from doing so. One possible reason is that therapy is a socially uncertain situation in which people are aware of being evaluated by someone who is not a friend or family member. We propose that such tendencies are enacted (many times unconsciously) as people strive to keep from being predicted to select personally relevant courses of action. Indeed, reviews of the literature have shown that successfully getting others to accept one's self-presentations is positively related to positive outcomes in domains such as therapy (Kelly, 2000) and one's career (Baumeister, 1989). We suggest that such success could be related in part to keeping at bay others' attempts to predict the self in ways that limit the pursuit of valued goals.

The previous discussion suggests that targets have available various behaviors for dealing with others' prediction attempts during social interaction, but even before any interaction takes place. Many of these phenomena have traditionally been studied independently. However, we propose that a broader, common motivation is also at play—that targets many times do not want to be predicted. This is why targets are prone to overgeneralize scrutiny, attempt to short-circuit others' prediction attempts, and limit and manipulate disclosures. Our perspective thus provides a way to connect these seemingly distinct phenomena. In the next part of the article, we discuss more fully the conditions under which people want to avoid being predicted and when this tendency will not be expressed.

Moderating Role of Cooperative versus Competitive Contexts

Thus far our discussion aims to construct a dynamic that takes place during social navigation, with people as social predictors wanting to efficiently and economically read and understand the persons they encounter. But because social life can bring people face-to-face with competitors with their own motives and goals, people are likely to avoid being predicted to be able to reduce disadvantage or constraints on their behavior. But because social life is mixed-motive, people should balance their unpredictability with greater predictability when the opportunity for cooperation arises. Thus, the key moderator in this framework is the possibility for cooperation broadly defined, that is, some level of interdependence in the situation.

Other potential situational and individual differences moderators could be brought to bear on our proposals, as we will discuss. But from our perspective, the possibility for developing cooperative relationships and reducing the risk from competitive ones plays a central role. Cooperative and supportive social connections are fundamental to people because they provide various instrumental and emotional benefits. However, being accepted by others necessitates some degree of interpersonal transparency if the cooperative connection is to be created and sustained. Specifically, people entertaining the idea of a cooperative social connection initiate and test a process of identity negotiation, in which the involved parties develop a working consensus of "who is who," what role each is to play (Goffman, 1959; Swann & Bosson, 2008), and determine trust and commitment (Rempel et al., 1985).

One implication of our model is that the desire for cooperative interaction should make people relatively more at ease with allowing others to judge and predict them; this has been a major focus in much psychological research. However, when social interactions or contexts become competitive, targets can express various behaviors aimed at foiling prediction. It is this latter perspective that has been considered to a lesser extent in the psychological literature. Below we review several areas of research in support of this proposal.

Social Connections and the Reduction of Feeling Scrutinized

Earlier we discussed people's reactions to being scrutinized. We argued that such reactions and elevated awareness make sense because they can help targets ready themselves for others' possible predictions. Here we examine research that has assessed the role of interaction goals in people's desire to be seen and scrutinized. Our analysis holds that people will weigh their goal to keep from being predicted against social connection needs. Thus, if positive social connection or cooperation is possible, people should be less troubled with being scrutinized by another person.

In one representative study, participants were led to believe they would interact with a second participant in either a competitive or cooperative interaction (Jellison & Ickes, 1974). In addition, half of the participants were told they would have the chance to get additional information about their opponents/partners before the game through an interview procedure. The other participants were simply told they would be interviewed.

The participants in the interviewee role were seated in front of a one-way mirror where they would be interviewed via a telecom system. Then they were taken around to the other room and shown where the interviewer would be seated, making it apparent they would be seen through the one-way mirror. The dependent variable was whether or not participants wanted the panel to the one-way mirror left open. The findings indicated that regardless of interview condition, participants who expected to cooperate were more likely to leave the panel open and thus allow their interaction partners to see them than participants who expected to compete. Although other factors could potentially explain the findings, they are consistent with our proposal indicating that when people anticipate cooperation, they are more at ease with being noticed and scrutinized by others than when they anticipate a competitive interaction.

Other findings show more directly how cooperative and competitive goals influence people's tendencies to not be predicted. In one study, participants imagined taking part in either a cooperative or competitive interaction (Ybarra et al., 2010, Study 1). Then, following an intervening task, participants were simply asked to draw on a sheet of paper the flight pattern of a moth. This paradigm thus helps separate the interaction goal from the response phase. In addition, the outcome had nothing to do with what might be considered attempts at self-presentation or impression management. The findings indicated that participants who imagined taking part in the cooperative game produced moth flight patterns that were easier to characterize statistically, compared to the patterns drawn by participants in the competition condition. Thus, not too different from a gazelle juking and zigzagging to avoid being chased down by a cheetah, the patterns drawn by the latter group were difficult to pin down, and that behavior had nothing to do with presenting the self in any particular way.

Social Connections and Reductions in Prediction Avoidance

Oftentimes, people are motivated to cooperate, get along, and be accepted by others (Baumeister & Leary, 1995). Our analysis suggests that these cooperative contexts should make people more open to being understood and predicted, but not when social connection is undesired or unlikely because of competition. Several lines of research are consistent with this suggestion.

In one study, Snyder and Haugen (1994) had participants take part in a behavioral confirmation paradigm, but in some cases the target had the goal to cooperate and facilitate the interaction. In another condition participants had a knowledge goal where they tried to obtain detailed information about their partners. Here, we focus on the former condition. Further, the perceivers were given negative or positive expectations about their partners (i.e., the targets). The ratings of uninvolved judges indicated the targets were more likely to confirm the perceivers' expectations when they were trying to get along. Thus, when people have a desire to cooperate, they are less likely to counteract others' attempts to predict them, even when these predictions might be regarded as negative.

Other investigators have produced related findings under conditions in which people are instructed to be deferential (Smith et al., 1997). Job applicants who behaved deferentially and thus were being cooperative were more likely to confirm perceiver expectancies than applicants instructed to be more challenging and less cooperative. People who are thought to be more accommodating and cooperative in their behavioral styles are also more likely to be implicated in behavioral confirmation effects (e.g., Christensen & Rosenthal, 1982; Cooper & Hazelrigg, 1988).

We have discussed one central factor—the cooperative or competitive context—that moderates whether or not people will allow the self to be predicted. To be adaptive, people balance the need for cooperative social connection with the need to maintain flexibility when confronting uncertain, competitive social interactions. When cooperation is deemed possible, people are more inclined to allow the self to be predicted and characterized. This does not mean, however, that targets are completely comfortable with being predicted, or that they will be unguarded, as targets also need to test assumptions of trustworthiness and relationship potential (Berg, 1984; Rempel et al., 1985; Ybarra, 2002).

Becoming more predicable could be seen as foregoing one's ability to choose person-ally relevant courses of action. However, allowing the self to be predicted should foster interpersonal transparency, which is necessary for cooperating and being accepted by oth-ers. Given the many benefits of having supportive social connections (e.g., Cohen & Wills, 1985; Lakey & Orehek, 2011; Thoits, 2011; Ybarra, Burnstein et al., 2008, Ybarra, Chan et al., 2008), interpersonal acceptance and cooperation are prevailing goals for people. But as the review has also highlighted, social life is mixed-motive, which means individuals are likely to come across their fair share of competitors and competitive interactions, so there are many occasions for targets to not have an interest in being judged and predicted.

We have reviewed research in support of three main ideas. First, we argue that people as perceivers have many tools at their disposal to try to predict others and read their minds and intentions. The variety of perceiver tools puts in stark relief the situation of the target of perception. Second, we highlight the target's perspective, which has received minimal attention in the literature—itself a potential reflection of the bias to want to predict oth-ers in social life. Specifically, we argue that targets also have various tools of their own to try to maintain control over and provide direction to their lives. Third, we contextualize the roles of perceiver and target with the proposal that targets are more likely to allow themselves to be predicted when they expect or desire cooperation with others, and that the tendency to not want to be judged and predicted is more likely when competition is expected.

Contributions of Analysis, Implications, and Future Research

The present framework integrates many areas of research. In addition to helping explicate the dynamic between the social perceiver and the target of prediction, and providing a richer picture of people as targets, our analysis highlights commonalities across distinct phenomena and areas of research, allowing them to be seen from new perspectives.

For example, much of the research discussed should be familiar to researchers in social perception. But the sheer variety of tools available to the perceiver, and also the links to theory of mind and its development, help contextualize this broad area of research and highlights the pervasiveness with which people judge and attempt to predict others. This part of the review also helps underscore the landscape people as targets come to inhabit and the need to be sensitive to the cooperative and competitive contours of their interactions with others. The second part of the discussion—with its focus on the target's perspective—allows for commonalities to be drawn across many domains as well. The discussion connects, for example, the concept of paranoid cognition to phenomena such as the spotlight effect and feelings of transparency. Further, the latter two phenomena are usually explained from an intrapersonal perspective (Gilovich et al., 1998, 2000, 2002), but the review informs us about factors external to the person, such as the potential uncertainty if not competitive nature of the social environment (e.g., Zimbardo et al., 1981). We will discuss additional cases to demonstrate the integrative potential and implications of the present analysis. However, it is important to first consider evidence that appears to conflict with our framework and to also consider the generality of our propositions.

Conflicting Evidence: Well-Adjusted Personsa and Self–Other Agreement

The present framework should have implications for research on interpersonal agreement and accuracy. However, at least on the surface, recent research in that tradition appears to conflict with our proposals. Human and Biesanz (2011) examined how targets who differed in degree of psychological adjustment were judged by perceivers. The findings indicated that perceivers, following a round robin interaction procedure, achieved significant levels of self–other agreement in judging how the targets differed from other targets (distinctive accuracy). However, this was more the case for targets considered "well-adjusted" (happy, high self-esteem, have purpose in life) and especially when the traits in question were low in observability. The authors explain the results in terms of well-adjusted targets providing perceivers with more cues/information about the self.

Although the research design used by Human and Biesanz (2011) makes it difficult to tell why well-adjusted targets proved to be more predictable, examining their operationalization of "well-adjusted" suggests an explanation and link to our analysis. First, research has shown that well-adjusted persons tend to be more extraverted and agreeable. Also, good adjustment is associated with having positive and trusting relations with others (Ryff, 1989). Taken together, the nomological network of "well-adjusted" suggests a person who has a history of positive, cooperative, and trusting relations with others and or an interest in having such relationships. Interestingly, our analysis predicts that it is under such conditions—cooperative contexts—that individuals should allow the self to be predicted in order to coordinate and be accepted. On second look, then, the work on the well-adjusted person and interpersonal accuracy appears conceptually consistent with the present analysis, although it would be useful to conduct future research in which both personality and cooperative and competitive interaction goals are studied jointly.

Occasions for Targets to be Unpredictable

We have argued that people alter their predictability depending on the cooperative and competitive nature of the circumstances. Given people's need to belong and to be accepted (Baumeister & Leary, 1995), it might be argued that people would have more occasions for being predictable than not wanting to be characterized by others. We have discussed, though, that people are not indiscriminate in their relationship building. Indeed, such injudiciousness would not be very adaptive, as it takes time to judge that others have the positive qualities their behavior suggests (Ybarra, 2002) and to establish trustworthiness (Rempel et al., 1985).

In addition to relationship formation processes and the limited number of strong relationships people can actually develop (cf. Dunbar, 1998)—meaning social life brings people into contact with many others they do not know—there is ample opportunity for conflict and competition, even with known others. As we have reviewed, under competitive circumstances people do not want to be observed and they display tendencies aimed at not being predicted, and there are many opportunities in life for this. Social life is mixed-motive at its core (e.g., Dunbar, 1998)—it involves competition as well as cooperation.

We earlier reviewed research dealing with individuals in therapy. Our point in reviewing that research is not to focus on people in need of therapy, who could be argued to not be representative of society as a whole, but to show that even when people are in situations that give them license to fully disclose, they will not. This also allows us to consider deception more generally. Decades of studies on lie detection, for example, have shown perceivers are not very good at it (e.g., Leach et al., 2009). Further, as discussed earlier, deception is quite "normal" as people use it frequently in daily life (DePaulo et al., 1996; Trivers, 2011). With deception occurring so widely, it seems that many well-adjusted people are trying to not let others know what they intend to do or to let them predict their behavior.

To further illustrate the integrative and general value of our analysis, we turn to additional cases that test a major tenet of the framework—that people seek to avoid being predicted and characterized. The cases are informative because they emphasize the positivity of the avoided characterizations.

Avoiding Positive Character Predictions

A counter perspective to our proposal is that people do not give much thought to avoiding others' predictions. Instead, people just seek to be judged positively by others (e.g., Jones, 1973). Here we review work to make the case that targets many times do not welcome others hoisting predictions upon them, even when positive in nature.

CHOKING UNDER PRESSURE

In examining the stereotype that men are superior to women in math and computer science, Smith and Johnson (2006) showed that men who did not identify with these domains were more likely to choke under pressure and underperform. Further, they actually performed better when the stereotype had been nullified. Similar findings—studying "model minorities"—have been obtained with Asian Americans who are reminded of their ethnic identity before taking a math test, a domain in which they are stereotyped to perform well (Cheryan & Bodenhausen, 2000).

Research by Keller and Bless (2008) also found that even when targets want to meet others' positive expectations, potential costs loom near due to the apprehension of meeting those standards. In this research participants who had a promotion goal—compared to a prevention goal—were more likely to underperform under positive expectancy conditions. Other research has shown that people readily recall experiences of being categorized by others. Further, compared to recalled negative predictions, positive predictions resulted in lower self-confidence (Ellemers & Barreto, 2006).

In addition to conceptually linking these distinct phenomena, our analysis suggests ways in which the negative consequences of being positively characterized might be moderated. Although we know of no research on the model minority that has taken relational context into account, one prediction would be that in the context of cooperative relationships, such feelings of unease with being positively characterized should diminish.

Inviting Negative Predictions and Characterizations

In addition to people at times not wanting to be positively predicted, we suggest people at times will welcome negative predictions. Work by Swann and colleagues has shown people want their negative self attributes recognized (Swann, 1984). However, other researchers seem less certain such effects are generally obtained (e.g., Baumeister & Scher, 1988).

One of the challenges in distinguishing self-verification processes from people's general goal to self-enhance is that other social aspects of the situation have not been taken into account. Our analysis suggests that self-verification effects are more likely to be obtained when targets view the interaction with the other party as more cooperative and thus are less troubled with being characterized negatively by them. Recent meta-analytic evidence is consistent with this proposal, in that people who anticipate social rejection are less likely to self-verify (Kwang & Swann, 2010).

Future Research

In the preceding sections we considered several implications of our framework, in addition to discussing conflicting evidence that on second look can be taken to be partly consistent with our analysis. However, our theoretical analysis and its coverage across distinct literatures allow for the generation of various hypotheses. For example, a literature exists in social psychology and related disciplines that deals with deception and lying. Is it the case that people's motivation to deceive may be elevated when trying to avoid social prediction? Conversely, will being reminded of a cooperative social interaction make people less deceptive and more transparent even under novel or ambiguous social circumstances?

The concepts of behavioral flexibility and adaptiveness play a large role in our analysis, and they are concepts that make strong contact with the idea of choice, which is relevant to many fields. Research has shown that people prefer to have many alternatives and variety when choosing (e.g., Shin & Ariely, 2004), and there are different explanations for the appeal of choice and variety (e.g., Kahneman & Snell, 1990). The present analysis suggests that, under some circumstances, to maintain behavioral flexibility people seek options. However, what is currently unknown are the various ways in which this can be manifested. For example, could choice behavior, as in selecting among consumer goods, shift as a function of the relational context (cf. Ybarra et al., 2012)?

Research on self-judgment can also be considered within the context of behavioral flexibility. Compared to how people as perceivers judge others, people as targets see themselves as multifaceted and their behavior as variable across situations (Hampson, 1997; Monson et al., 1980; Sande et al., 1988). Choosing a large variety of traits and even traits that are antonyms of each other to describe the self, at some level, is not that different from wanting many alternatives in the things one decides to do. Is it possible to shift people's views of self and make them more or less coherent and predictable by manipulating the nature of the relational context?

Self-judgments of other kinds could also be examined as potential moderators. For example, people who score high on private self-consciousness may rely more on personal values and beliefs to guide behavior (Wheeler et al., 2008). Thus, they might be more predictable because behavior is tightly moored to internal guides or through related outcomes such as tendencies to disclose more. In this respect, research has shown that people high in private self-consciousness, rather than being more isolated from others, report more satisfying relationships in part because they share more information about themselves with others (Franzoi et al., 1985).

Another potentially important moderator that should be considered in future research is power. Some social groups or people in certain roles have a greater say in determining the prevailing practices and norms in organizations or society. Further, members of those groups may experience more control over their lives compared, for example, to individuals of lower socio-economic status or some minority group members (Marmot, 2004). Could differences in power translate into some people being relatively less concerned with or less aware they are being predicted and characterized by others (cf. McGuire et al., 1978)? Are minority group members more likely to run through their minds the notion that others are paying attention and trying to judge and predict them (Abalakina-Paap et al., 1999)? And does the availability of desired cooperative connections help bolster people and their sense of control?

Staying with the theme of intergroup relations, research has shown that people prefer ingroups to outgroups (e.g., Brown, 1991). When members of different social groups interact, are tendencies toward unpredictability likely to be activated in such situations (Rios et al., 2013)? If so, might this also contribute to people liking intergroup encounters less than ingroup encounters? For example, in such situations, some interactants may feel scrutinized and uncomfortable and be seen by their interaction partners as shifty and less likable as well.

From the perceiver's perspective, given the behavioral tools targets appear to have to maintain their behavioral flexibility, what is the purpose of the social prediction mechanisms if they are not always effective? And regarding behavioral science more generally, shouldn't a fuller understanding of human behavior also depends on an appreciation of social interaction dynamics and the perspective of a target interested in behavioral flexibility? Is this partly what makes behavioral science a challenging endeavor—in that our subjects at times do not want to be predicted? These are but some of the possible suggestions for future research; we believe the present framework has much heuristic potential, largely based on an appreciation of both perceiver and target in a mixed-motive social world.

Conclusion

We have argued that people come to inhabit a social world full of behavior and mind readers with their own desires and goals. With so many people attempting to predict the self—many of whom are not kin nor friend—the individual trying to navigate social life effectively is at times capable of avoiding being predicted and characterized to be able to select courses of action that best fit current life demands. However, this tendency should be reversed when cooperative social connections are likely because supportive social connections can provide people with many instrumental and emotional benefits. Gaining such benefits necessitates that the person allows the self to be predicted to foster some degree of interpersonal transparency. We have reviewed many different areas of research in support of this framework, in addition to deriving various implications from the analysis. The picture we have attempted to paint is that of the person with an interest in effective social navigation who is flexible at different levels: flexible when away from supportive social connections and dealing with the uncertainties of competitive contexts; and flexible in reining in the tendency to keep from being predicted in the context of cooperative social connections.

As we mentioned, our review has touched on many different areas of research. We believe this framework is a good place to start to further understand key processes in social and personality psychology and related disciplines that focus on the outcomes of social interaction. It is our hope that through the re-casting of such phenomena within the current theoretical framework and the drawing out of various implications, new views are apparent and other views will emerge as we continue to consider the important role of the target of social perception, who has important goals to pursue flexibly in what is many times an uncertain and competitive social world.

Acknowledgments

We would like to thank Walter Stephan and Dick Nisbett for their comments on an earlier version of this manuscript. We would also like to thank Norbert Schwarz for his helpful feedback.

References

Abalakina-Paap, K., Stephan, W. G., Craig, T., & Gregory, W. L. (1999). Belief in conspiracies. *Political Psychology 20*, 637–647.

Adolphs, R. (2001). The neurobiology of social cognition. *Current Opinion in Neurobiology 11*, 231–239.

Asch, S. E. (1952). *Social psychology*. Prentice-Hall.

Atran, S., & Norenzayan, A. (2004). Religion's evolutionary landscape: Counterintuition, commitment, compassion, communion. *Behavioral and Brain Sciences 27* (6), 713–730.

Baer, R., Hinkle, S., Smith, K., & Fenton, M. (1980). Reactance as a function of actual versus project autonomy. *Journal of Personality and Social Psychology 38*, 416–422.

Barash, D. P. (1977). *Sociobiology and behavior*. Elsevier.

Barden, J., Rucker, D. D., & Petty, R. E. (2005). "Saying one thing and doing another": Examining the impact of event order on hypocrisy judgments of others. *Personality and Social Psychology Bulletin 31* (11), 14631474.

Barr, C. L., & Kleck, R. E. (1995). Self-other perception of the intensity of facial expressions of emotion: Do we know what we show? *Journal of Personality and Social Psychology 68*, 608–618.

Barrett, J. L., & Keil, F. C. (1996). Conceptualizing a nonnatural entity: Anthropomorphism in God concepts. *Cognitive Psychology 31*, 219–247.

Baumeister, R. F. (1989). Motives and costs of self-presentation in organizations. In R. A. Giacalone & P. Rosenfeld (Eds.), *Impression management in the organization* (pp. 57–72). Lawrence Erlbaum Associates.

Baumeister, R. F., & Leary, M. R. (1995). The need to belong: Desire for interpersonal attachments as a fundamental human motivation. *Psychological Bulletin 11*, 497–529.

Baumeister, R. F., & Scher, S. J. (1988). Self-defeating behavior patterns among normal individuals: Review and analysis of common self-destructive tendencies. *Psychological Bulletin 104*, 3–22.

Bebbington, P. E., McBride, O., Steel, C., Kuipers, E., Radovanoviĉ, M., Brugha, T., Jenkins, R., Meltzer, H. I., & Freeman, D. (2013). The structure of paranoia in the general population. *The British Journal of Psychiatry 202* (6), 419–427.

Berg, J. H. (1984). Development of friendship between roommates. *Journal of Personality and Social Psychology 46*, 346–356.

Bernheim, D. B. (1994). A theory of conformity. *Journal of Political Economy* 102, 841–877.

Brehm, J. W. (1966). *A theory of psychological reactance*. Academic Press.

Brewer, M. B. (1988). A dual process model of impression formation. In T. K. Srull, (Ed), *Advances in social cognition* (Vol. 1, pp. 1–36). Lawrence Erlbaum Associates.

Brown, D. E. (1991). *Human universals*. McGraw-Hill.

Cacioppo, J. T., & Patrick, B. (2008). *Loneliness: Human nature and the need for social connection*. New York, NY.

Chan, T., Wang, I., & Ybarra, O. (2021). Leading and managing the workplace: The role of executive functions. *Academy of Management Perspectives 35* (1), 142–164.

Chance, M. R. A., & Mead, A. P. (1953). Social behaviour and primate evolution. *Symposia of the Society of Experimental Biology Evolution 7*, 395–439.

Chandler, M., Fritz, A. S., & Hala, S. (1989). Small-scale deceit: deception as a marker of two-, three-, and four-year-olds' early theories of mind. *Child Development 60*, 1263–1277.

Chen, M., & Bargh, J. A. (1997). Nonconscious behavioral confirmation processes: The self-fulfilling consequences of automatic stereotype activation. *Journal of Experimental Social Psychology 33* (5), 541–560.

Cheryan, S., & Bodenhausen, G. V. (2000). When positive stereotypes threaten intellectual performance: The psychological hazards of "model minority" status. *Psychological Science 11*, 399–402.

Christensen, D., & Rosenthal, R. (1982). Gender and nonverbal decoding skill as determinants of interpersonal effects. *Journal of Personality and Social Psychology 42*, 75–87.

Clement, F., Bernard, S., & Kaufmann, L. (2011). Social cognition is not reducible to theory of mind: When children use deontic rules to predict the behaviour of others. *British Journal of Developmental Psychology 29*, 910–928.

Cohen, S., & Wills, T. A. (1985). Stress, social support, and the buffering hypothesis. *Psychological Bulletin 98*, 310–357.

Colvin, C. R. (1993). "Judgeable" people: Personality, behavior, and competing explanations. *Journal of Personality and Social Psychology 64*, 861–873.

Cooper, H., & Hazelrigg, P. (1988). Personality moderators of interpersonal expectancy effects: An integrative research review. *Journal of Personality and Social Psychology 55*, 937–949.

Darley, J. M., & Fazio, R. (1980). Expectancy confirmation processes arising in the social interaction sequence. *American Psychologist 35*, 867–881.

DePaulo, B. M., Kashy, D. A., Kirkendol, S. E., Wyer, M. M., & Epstein, J. A. (1996). Lying in everyday life. *Journal of Personality and Social Psychology 70*, 979–995.

Dunbar, R. I. M. (1998). The social brain hypothesis. *Evolutionary Anthropology 6*, 178–190.

Dunning, D., Griffin, D. W., Milojkovic, J., & Ross, L. (1990). The overconfidence effect in social prediction. *Journal of Personality and Social Psychology 58*, 568–581.

Ellemers, N., & Barreto, M. (2006). Categorization in everyday life: The effects of positive and negative categorizations on emotions and self-views. *European Journal of Social Psychology 36*, 931–942.

Epley, N., Savitsky, K., & Gilovich, T. (2002). Empathy neglect: Reconciling the spotlight effect and the correspondent bias. *Journal of Personality and Social Psychology 83*, 300–312.

Epley, N., Waytz, A., Akalis, S., & Cacioppo, J. T. (2008). When we need a human: Motivational determinants of anthropomorphism. *Social Cognition 26* (2), 143–155.

Farber, B. A. (2003). Patient self-disclosure: A review of the research. *Journal of Clinical Psychology 59*, 589–600.

Fenigstein, A., Scheier, M. F., & Buss, A. H. (1975). Public and private self-consciousness: Assessment and theory. *Journal of Consulting and Clinical Psychology 43*, 522–527.

Fiske, S. T., & Neuberg, S. L. (1990). A continuum of impression formation, from category-based to individuating processes: Influences of information and motivation on attention and interpretation. In M. P. Zanna (Ed.), *Advances in experimental social psychology* (Vol. 23, 1–74). New York: Academic Press.

Funder, D. C. (1995). On the accuracy of personality judgment: A realistic approach. *Psychological Review 102*, 652–670.

Franzoi, S. L., Davis, M. H., Young, R. D. (1985). The effects of private self-consciousness and perspective taking on satisfaction in close relationships. *Journal of Personality and Social Psychology 48*, 1584–1594.

Gergen, K. J., & Jones, E. E. (1963). Mental illness, predictability, and affective consequences as stimulus factors in person perception. *Journal of Abnormal and Social Psychology 67*, 95–104.

Gilbert, D. T., Pelham, B. W., & Krull, D. S. (1988). On cognitive busyness: When person perceivers meet persons perceived. *Journal of Personality and Social Psychology 54*, 733–740.

Gilovich, T., Kruger, J., & Medvec, V. H. (2002). The spotlight effect revisited: Overestimating the manifest variability of our actions and appearance. *Journal of Experimental Social Psychology 38*, 93–99.

Gilovich, T., Medvec, V. H., & Savitsky, K. (2000). The spotlight effect in social judgment: An egocentric bias in estimates of the salience of one's own actions and appearance. *Journal of Personality and Social Psychology 78*, 211–222.

Gilovich, T., Savitsky, K., & Medvec, V. H. (1998). The illusion of transparency: Biased assessments of others' ability to read one's emotional states. *Journal of Personality and Social Psychology 75*, 332–346.

Goffman, E. (1959). *The presentation of self in everyday life*. Doubleday.

Guthrie, S. (1993). *Faces in the clouds: A new theory of religion*. Oxford University Press.

Ham, J., & Vonk, R. (2003). Smart and easy: Co-occurring activation of spontaneous trait inferences and spontaneous situational inferences. *Journal of Experimental Social Psychology 39* (5), 434–447.

Hampson, S. E. (1997). Determinants of inconsistent personality descriptions: Trait and target effects. *Journal of Personality 65*, 249–290.

Hancock, M., & Ickes, W. (1996). Empathic accuracy: When does the perceiver-target Relationship Make a Difference? *Journal of Social and Personal Relationships 13*, 179–199.

Hardin, C. D., & Higgins, E. T. (1996). Shared reality: How social verification makes the subjective objective. In R. M. Sorrentino & E. T. Higgins (Eds.), *Handbook of motivation and cognition (Vol. 3): The interpersonal context* (pp. 28–84). Guilford Press.

Hastie, R. (1984). Causes and effects of causal attribution. *Journal of Personality and Social Psychology 46*, 44–56.

Heider, F. (1958). *The psychology of interpersonal relations*. Wiley.

Heider, F., & Simmel, M. (1944). An experimental study of apparent behavior. *American Journal of Psychology 57*, 243–259.

Heilman, M., & Toffler, B. (1976). Reacting to reactance: An interpersonal interpretation of the need for freedom. *Journal of Experimental Social Psychology 12*, 519–529.

Hendrick, C. (1972). Effects of salience of stimulus inconsistency on impression formation. *Journal of Personality and Social Psychology 22*, 219–222.

Hill, C. E., Thompson, B., Cogar, M., & Denman, D. (1993). Beneath the surface of long-term therapy: therapist and client reports of their own and each other's covert processes. *Journal of Counseling Psychology 40*, 278–287.

Hook, A., & Andrews, B. (2005). The relationship of non-disclosure in therapy to shame and depression. *British Journal of Clinical Psychology 44* (3), 425–438.

Hughes, C., & Ensor, R. (2007). Executive function and theory of mind: Predictive relations from ages 2 to 4. *Developmental psychology 43* (6), 1447.

Human, L. J., & Biesanz, J. C. (2011). Target adjustment and self-other agreement: Utilizing trait observability to disentangle judgeability and self-knowledge. *Journal of Personality and Social Psychology 101*, 202–216.

Humphrey, N. (1976). The social function of intellect. In P. P. G. Bateson & R. A. Hinde (Eds.), *Growing points in ethology* (pp. 303–317). Cambridge University Press.

Humphrey, N. (2007). The society of selves. *Philosophical Transactions of the Royal Society B 362*, 745–754.

Jellison, J. M., & Ickes, W. J. (1974). The power of the glance: Desire to see and be seen in cooperative and competitive situations. *Journal of Experimental Social Psychology 10*, 444–450.

Jolly, A. (1966). Lemur social behavior and primate intelligence. *Science 153*, 501–506.

Jones, E. E., & Davis, K. E. (1965). From acts to dispositions: The attribution process in person perception. In L. Berkowitz (Ed.), *Advances in Experimental Social Psychology* (Vol. 2, pp. 219–266). Academic Press.

Jones, S. C. (1973). Self- and interpersonal evaluations: Esteem theories versus consistency theories. *Psychological Bulletin 79*, 185–199.

Jussim, L. (1986). Self-fulfilling prophecies: A theoretical and integrative review. *Psychological Review 93*, 429–445.

Kahneman, D., & Snell, J. (1990). Predicting utility. In R. M. Hogarth (Ed.), *Insights in decision making: A tribute to Hillel J. Einhorn* (pp. 295–310). University of Chicago Press.

Keller, J., & Bless, H. (2008). Expectancy effects on cognitive test performance: Regulatory focus as a catalyst. *European Journal of Social Psychology 38*, 187–212.

Kelly, A. E. (2000). Helping construct desirable identities: A self-presentational view of psychotherapy. *Psychological Bulletin 126*, 475–494.

Kenny, D. A., Mohr, C. D., & Levesque, M. J. (2001). A social relations variance partitioning of dyadic behavior. *Psychological Bulletin 127*, 128–141.

Kramer, R. M. (1994). The sinister attribution error: Paranoid cognition and distrust in organizations. *Motivation and Emotion: Special Issue: Trust and distrust: Psychological and social dimensions 18*, 199–230.

Kreps, T. A., Laurin, K., & Merritt, A. C. (2017). Hypocritical flip-flop, or courageous evolution? When leaders change their moral minds. *Journal of Personality and Social Psychology 113* (5), 730.

Kwang, T., & Swann, W. B. (2010). Do people embrace praise even when they feel unworthy? A review of critical tests of self-enhancement versus self-verification. *Personality and Social Psychology Review 14*, 263–280.

Lakey, B., & Orehek, E. (2011). Relational regulation theory: A new approach to explain the link between perceived social support and mental health. *Psychological Review 118* (3), 482.

Leach, A. M., Lindsay, R. C. L., Koehler, R., Beaudry, J. L., Bala, N. C., Lee, K., Talwar, V. (2009). The reliability of lie detection performance. *Law and Human Behavior 33*, 96–109.

Macrae, C. N., Milne, A. B., & Bodenhausen, G. V. (1994). Stereotypes as energy-saving devices: A peek inside the cognitive toolbox. *Journal of Personality and Social Psychology 66*, 37–47.

Magaro, P. A. (1980). *Cognition in schizophrenia and paranoia: The interpretation of cognitive processes*. Erlbaum.

Marmot, M. (2004). *The status syndrome*. Henry Holt and Co.

McCarthy, R. J., & Skowronski, J. J. (2011). What will Phil do next? Spontaneously inferred traits influence predictions of behavior. *Journal of Experimental Social Psychology 47*, 321–332.

McGuire, W. J, McGuire, C. V., Child, P., & Fujioka, T. (1978). Salience of ethnicity in the spontaneous self-concept as a function of one's ethnic distinctiveness in the social environment. *Journal of Personality and Social Psychology 36*, 511–520.

Millon, T. H. (1981). *Disorders of personality*. Wiley.

Monson, T. C., Tanke, E. D., and Lund, J. (1980). Determinants of social perception in a naturalistic setting. *Journal of Research in Personality 14*, 104–120.

Mor, N., & Winquist, J. (2002). Self-focused attention and negative affect: A meta-analysis. *Psychological Bulletin 128*, 638–662.

Moran, J. M., Jolly, E., & Mitchell, J. P. (2014). Spontaneous mentalizing predicts the fundamental attribution error. *Journal of Cognitive Neuroscience 26* (3), 569–576.

Newman, L. S. (1996). Trait impressions as heuristics for predicting future behavior. *Personality and Social Psychology Bulletin 22*, 395–411.

Norton, M. I., Frost, J. H., & Ariely, D. (2007). Less is more: the lure of ambiguity, or why familiarity breeds contempt. *Journal of Personality and Social Psychology 92*, 97–105.

Nussbaum, S., Trope, Y., & Liberman, N. (2003). Creeping dispositionism: The temporal dynamics of behavior prediction. *Journal of Personality and Social Psychology 84*, 485–497.

Oberman, L. M., & Ramachandran, V. S. (2007). The simulating social mind: The role of the mirror neuron system and simulation in the social and communicative deficits of autism spectrum disorders. *Psychological Bulletin 133*, 310–327.

Oosterhof, N. N., & Todorov, A. (2008). The functional basis of face evaluation. *Proceedings of the National Academy of Sciences 105* (32), 11087–11092.

Preti, A., & Cella, M. (2010). Paranoid thinking as a heuristic. *Early Intervention in Psychiatry 4* (3), 263–266.

Rempel, J. K., Holmes, J. G., & Zanna, M. P. (1985). Trust in close relationships. *Journal of Personality and Social Psychology 49*, 95–112.

Rios, K., Ybarra, O., & Sanchez-Burks, J. (2013). Outgroup primes induce unpredictability tendencies under conditions of distrust. *Journal of Experimental Social Psychology 49* (3), 372–377.

Rizollati, G., & Craighero, L. (2004). The mirror-neuron system. *Annual Review of Neuroscience 27*, 169–192.

Roth, D., & Leslie, A. M. (1991). The recognition of attitude conveyed by utterance: A study of preschool and autistic children. *British Journal of Developmental Psychology: Special Issue: Perspectives on the Child's Theory of Mind II 9*, 315–330.

Ryff, C. D. (1989). Happiness is everything, or is it? Explorations of the meaning of psychological well-being. *Journal of Personality and Social Psychology 57*, 1069–1081.

Sande, G. N., Goethals, G. R., & Radloff, C. E. (1988). Perceiving one's own traits and others': The multi-faceted self. *Journal of Personality and Social Psychology 54*, 13–20. Shin, J., & Ariely, D. (2004). Keeping doors open: The effect of unavailability in incentives to keep options viable. *Management Science 50*, 575–586.

Shtulman, A. (2008). Variation in the anthropomorphization of supernatural beings and its implications for cognitive theories of religion. *Journal of Experimental Psychology: Learning, Memory, and Cognition 34* (5), 1123.

Smith, D. M., Neuberg, S. L., Judice, T. N., & Biesanz, J. C. (1997). Target complicity in the confirmation and disconfirmation of erroneous expectations: Immediate and longer term implications. *Journal of Personality and Social Psychology 73*, 974–991.

Smith, J. L., & Johnson, C. S. (2006). A stereotype boost or choking under pressure? Positive gender stereotypes and men who are low in domain identification. *Basic and Applied Social Psychology 28*, 51–63.

Snodgrass, S. E., Hecht, M. A., & Ploutz-Snyder, R. (1998). Interpersonal sensitivity: Expressivity or perceptivity? *Journal of Personality and Social Psychology 74* (1), 238.

Snodgrass, S. E., & Rosenthal, R. (1985). Interpersonal sensitivity and skills in decoding nonverbal channels: The value of face value. *Basic and Applied Social Psychology 6* (3), 243–255.

Snyder, M., & Haugen, J. A. (1994). Why does behavioral confirmation occur? A functional perspective on the role of the perceiver. *Journal of Experimental Social Psychology 30*, 218–246.

Snyder, M., Tanke, E. D., & Berscheid, E. (1977). Social perception and interpersonal behavior: On the self-fulfilling nature of social stereotypes. *Journal of Personality and social Psychology 35* (9), 656.

Srull, T. K. (1981). Person memory: Some tests of associative storage and retrieval models. *Journal of Experimental Psychology: Human Learning and Memory 7*, 440–462.

Stangor, C., & Duan, C. (1991). Effects of multiple task demands upon memory for information about social groups. *Journal of Experimental Social Psychology 27*, 357–378.

Stukas, A. A., & Snyder, M. (2002). Targets' awareness of expectations and behavioral confirmation in ongoing interactions. *Journal of Experimental Social Psychology 38*, 31–40.

Swann, W. B. (1984). Quest for accuracy in person perception: A matter of pragmatics. *Psychological Review 91*, 457–477.

Swann, W. B., & Bosson, J. K. (2008). Identity negotiation: A theory of self and social interaction. In O. John, R. Robins, & L. Pervin (Eds.), *Handbook of personality psychology: Theory and research* (pp. 448–471). Guilford.

Swann, W. B., Wenzlaff, R. M., Krull, D. S., & Pelham, B. W. (1992). Allure of negative feedback: Self-verification strivings among depressed persons. *Journal of Abnormal Psychology 101*, 292–306.

Tagiuri, R. (1958). Introduction. In R. Tagiuri and L. Petrullo (Eds.), *Person perception and interpersonal behavior* (pp. 9–16). Stanford University Press.

Thoits, P. A. (2011). Mechanisms linking social ties and support to physical and mental health. *Journal of Health and Social Behavior 52* (2), 145–161.

Thompson, B., & Hill, C. (1991). Therapist perception of client reactions. *Journal of Counseling and Development 69*, 261–265.

Trivers, R. L. (1971). Evolution of reciprocal altruism. *Quarterly Review of Biology 46* (1), 35–57.

Trivers, R. L. (2011). *The folly of fools: The logic of deceit and deception in human life.* Basic Books.

Trope, Y. (1986). Identification and inferential processes in dispositional attribution. *Psychological Review 93*, 239–257.

Uleman, J. S., Adil Saribay, S., & Gonzalez, C. M. (2008). Spontaneous inferences, implicit impressions, and implicit theories. *Annual Review of Psychology 59*, 329–360.

Vallone, R. P., Griffin, D. W., Lin, S., & Ross, L. (1990). The overconfident prediction of future action and outcomes by self and others. *Journal of Personality and Social Psychology 58*, 582–592.

Van Boven, L., Kamada, A., & Gilovich, T. (1999). The perceiver as perceived: Everyday intuitions about the correspondent bias. *Journal of Personality and Social Psychology 77*, 1188–1199.

Vinden, P. G. (1999). Children's understanding of mind and emotion: A multi-culture study. *Cognition and Emotion 13*, 19–48.

Vorauer, J. D., & Ross, M. (1999). Self-awareness and feeling transparent: Failing to suppress one's self. *Journal of Experimental Social Psychology 35*, 415–440.

Watson, A. C., Painter, K. M., & Bornstein, M. H. (2001). Longitudinal relations between 2-year-olds' language and 4-year-olds' theory of mind. *Journal of Cognition and Development 2* (4), 449–457.

Waytz, A., Cacioppo, J., & Epley, N. (2010). Who sees human? The stability and importance of individual differences in anthropomorphism. *Perspectives on Psychological Science 5* (3), 219–232.

Weiner, M. F., & Schuman, O. W. (1984). What patients don't tell their therapists. *Integrative Psychiatry 2*, 28–32.

Wellman, H. M., Cross, D., & Watson, J. (2001). Meta-analysis of theory of mind development: The truth about false belief. *Child Development 72*, 655–684.

Wheeler, S. C., Morrison, K. R., DeMarree, K. G., & Petty, R. E. (2008). Does self-consciousness increase or decrease priming effects? It depends. *Journal of Experimental Social Psychology 44*, 882–889.

Winter, L., & Uleman, J. S. (1984). When are social judgments made? Evidence for the spontaneousness of trait inferences. *Journal of Personality and Social Psychology 47*, 237–252.

Word, C. O., Zanna, M. P., & Cooper, J. (1974). The nonverbal mediation of self-fulfilling prophecies in interracial interaction. *Journal of Experimental Social Psychology 10*, 109–120.

Ybarra, O. (2002). Naive causal understanding of valenced behaviors and its implications for social information processing. *Psychological Bulletin 128*, 421–441.

Ybarra, O., Burnstein, E., Winkielman, P., Keller, M. C., Manis, M., Chan, E., & Rodriguez, J. (2008). Mental exercising through simple socializing: Social interaction promotes general cognitive functioning. *Personality and Social Psychology Bulletin 34*, 248–259.

Ybarra, O., Chan, E., Park, H., Burnstein, E., Monin, B., & Stanik, C. (2008). Life's recurring challenges and the fundamental dimensions: An integration and its implications for cultural differences and similarities. *European Journal of Social Psychology 38*, 1083–1092.

Ybarra, O., Keller, M. C., Chan, E., Garcia, S. M., Sanchez-Burks, J., Morrison, K. R., & Baron, A. S. (2010). Being unpredictable: Friend or foe matters. *Social Psychological and Personality Science 1* (3), 259–267.

Ybarra, O., Lee, S., & Gonzalez, R. (2012). Supportive social connections attenuate the paradox of choice. *Psychological Science 23*, 1186–1192.

Ybarra, O., & Stephan, W. G. (1996). Misanthropic person memory. *Journal of Personality and Social Psychology 70* (4), 691.

Ybarra, O., & Stephan, W. G. (1999). Attributional orientations and the prediction of behavior: The attribution–prediction bias. *Journal of Personality and Social Psychology 76* (5), 718.

Zahavi, A. 1975. Mate selection: A selection for a handicap. *Journal of Theoretical Biology 53*, 205–214.

Zimbardo, P. G., Andersen, S. M., & Kabat, L. G. (1981). Induced hearing deficit generates experimental paranoia. *Science 212*, 1529–1531.

Competition and Risk-Taking

Sandeep Mishra, Cody Fogg, *and* Jeff Deminchuk

Abstract

How does competition motivate risk-taking? In this chapter, the authors consider and define competition through the lens of evolution by natural selection. The authors then review the *relative state model*, a recently developed, evolutionarily informed, mathematically modeled motivational framework that conceptualizes risk-taking as a product of competitive dis/advantage. The authors describe how an understanding of the two key inputs into competitive dis/advantage—embodied capital and situational/ environmental factors—can shed light on risk-taking in the pursuit of proxies of fitness in three key domains: resources, mates, and status. Finally, the authors offer some informed speculation on the proximate psychology of competitive dis/advantage, focusing on how individual differences in the subjective experience of dis/advantage may influence patterns of risk-taking.

Key Words: risk, competition, relative state, risk-sensitivity, ability, need, embodied capital, individual differences

Natural Selection, Competition, and Motivation

Competition is a fundamental part of life, characterizing any situation involving rivals striving to obtain resources or outcomes that cannot be shared. That is, competition describes the acquisition of resources or outcomes in zero-sum games (or negative-sum games, such as war), where one actor's advantage is another actor's disadvantage (Kilduff et al., 2010). Actors are faced with bounded time and energy to compete against rivals for limited resources, opportunities, and outcomes; these competitive pressures influence incentives, coloring costs and benefits of different courses of action, and these costs and benefits drive motivation. Actors can compete over such tangible resources as money, territory, goods, mates, or market share; actors can also compete over more intangible resources, like status, reputation, recognition, or influence. Tangible resources have finite limits; intangible resources, although theoretically unlimited, typically distill into discrete rankings in social hierarchies that end up zero-sum (e.g., social status). Regardless of the specific currency of competition, competition is a ubiquitous and fundamental motivator.

Motivation is in large part a product of incentive structures. As a result, competition is particularly relevant in the context of understanding risk-taking because it offers a framework of motivation for risk-seeking. Risk-taking describes the behavioral choice of relatively higher variance over lower variance options (Bernoulli, 1954; Daly & Wilson, 2001; Friedman & Savage, 1948; Knight, 1921; Mishra, 2014; Real & Caraco, 1986; Rubin & Paul, 1979; Winterhalder et al., 1999). Typically, risk-taking involves some possibility of downside or loss exposure, but also the potential for upside or gain. In most decision-making environments, especially those characterized by competition, risk is tightly linked with reward (Pleskac et al., 2021).

How do actors make decisions around options involving outcome variance? Canonical theories of risk-taking, especially from economics, have centered on the idea that actors make "rational" choices that maximize *utility* (e.g., Bernoulli, 1954; Friedman & Savage, 1948, 1952; Mishra, 2014; von Neumann & Morgenstern, 1944). In these theories, utility is typically defined as value, happiness, or satisfaction that an actor experiences via consumption of a product or service (Friedman & Savage, 1952; von Neumann & Morgenstern, 1944). To provide an example involving risk, decision-makers should prefer an option that offers a 10 percent chance at $100 (a $10 expected value) over an option that offers a 100 percent chance at $5 (a $5 expected value), because the former option offers greater utility (as measured in the form of monetary currency).

Canonical theories of decision-making under risk that center on the idea of rational decision-makers seeking maximization of utility suffer two fundamental flaws. First, the vague definition of the currency of utility. Gaining $10 has clear utility, as does eating ice cream on a hot day or getting a haircut. However, it is difficult to equate these varied choices into a single, measurable currency (Daly & Wilson, 2001; Mishra, 2014). Second, all human and non-human organisms engage in behavior as a product of motivation. The argument that actors are motivated to maximize expected utility does not offer much specificity of prediction—in what domains are actors motivated to maximize utility, and under what circumstances? More foundationally, how is utility quantified and compared, and what role do individual differences play? These key questions may be best answered by considering motivation from a biological perspective.

Because it represents the foundational engine behind all of life—including the minds that reside within—natural selection is a good starting point for reasoning about motivation. All entities that contain inheritable genetic material and undergo competitively variable reproduction are subject to the forces of natural selection (Hamilton, 1963, 1964). These include all living organisms, as well as such non-living agents as viruses. Natural selection describes the differential survival and reproduction of certain individuals over others because of phenotypic fit to environment (Darwin, 1859). Individuals compete with rivals to maximize biological inclusive fitness, which is the reproductive success of self and kin who share genotypes (Hamilton, 1963, 1964). Fitness is a statistical property oriented around specific genotypes or phenotypes, mathematically quantified as the

SANDEEP MISHRA, CODY FOGG, AND JEFF DEMINCHUK

average contribution to the gene pool of a subsequent generation that is attributable to a specific genotype or phenotype (Hamilton, 1963, 1964). The fundamentally relative nature of biological fitness is crucial to highlight because functional evolutionary pressures provide a logic for translation into psychological mechanisms sensitive to relative outcomes, and therefore, sensitive to competition.

Actors do not make decisions to directly maximize biological inclusive fitness. Inclusive fitness cannot be readily perceived, measured, or operated on during the limited lifespan of an individual; as a result, actors' minds must translate the "program" of fitness maximization into proximate, psychological motivations to seek more tangible, operationalizable, and quantifiable currencies (El Mouden et al., 2012; Mishra, 2014; Symons, 1987). Differential survival and reproduction of actors is driven by the acquisition of *proxies* of fitness, which are "outcomes or currencies that were (or are) statistically associated with biological fitness, but not necessarily directly or linearly" (Mishra et al., 2017, p. 177). Positive proxies of fitness include resources, mates, and status. These currencies are not infinitely available to all actors, and thus actors are engaged in competition. That is, actors are engaged in zero-sum (or negative-sum) games to acquire scarce resources, leading to benefits for some actors over others. As a result, any agents subject to natural selection are also fundamentally subject to, and shaped by, competition over proxies of fitness (El Mouden et al., 2012; Mishra, 2014; Symons, 1987). Even positive-sum phenomena, such as cooperation, have fundamentally self-interested elements that reflect competition (Barclay & Willer, 2007; Roberts, 1998). Individual actors do not cooperate because they are altruistic (incurring costs to self to benefit others). Rather, actors cooperate because it generates self-interested gains, such as reputation and the benefits that come with a good reputation (as well as gains to others who are interdependent; West et al., 2007). Success in competition for proxies of fitness determines which individuals enjoy differential survival and reproductive success. Competition for proxies of fitness, like mates, resources, and status/reputation, can therefore be seen as a primary driver of motivation, and this motivation shapes the costs and benefits of risk-taking as a result.

Dis/advantage and Risk-Taking: The Relative State Model

The relative state model of risk-taking is a framework conceived to explain how actors are motivated to make decisions involving risk under conditions of relative dis/advantage (Barclay et al., 2018; Mishra et al., 2017). The model suggests there are two pathways leading to risk-taking behavior—need-based and ability-based. Need-based risk-taking, characterized by risk-sensitivity theory, describes risk-taking as a consequence of competitive disadvantage (Caraco et al., 1980; Kacelnik & Bateson, 1997; Kacelnik & El Mouden, 2013; Mishra, 2014; Mishra & Lalumière, 2010; Mishra et al., 2014; Stephens, 1981; Stephens & Krebs, 1986). Under such conditions of disadvantage, actors engage in risk-taking because non-risky options are less likely to meet one's needs (with need defined as disparity between one's current and goal/desired states; Mishra & Lalumière, 2010).

For example, someone who steals bread to feed their family because they cannot otherwise afford food is engaged in need-based risk-taking. By contrast, the ability-based pathway suggests that actors engage in risk-taking as an affordance of competitive advantage, where risk-taking leads to higher expected payoffs than non-risky options and signals underlying skills or abilities to third parties. For example, a rich person walking into a casino, gambling an exorbitant amount of money, and walking out without concern for lost money is engaged in ability-based risk-taking. The relative state model suggests that for any given risky decision, actors intuit some sense of the probability of success, the probability of failure, the expected value of success, and the expected value of failure, integrating these subjective assessments into a decision to approach or avoid a risk (Mishra et al., 2017).

The relative state model integrates the seemingly disparate pathways of need- and ability-based risk-taking by suggesting that actors perceive some understanding of *relative state*—the interaction of embodied and situational factors within an environment of competition—and then act on the dis/advantage determined by relative state (Barclay et al., 2018; Mishra et al., 2017). Embodied factors describe inherent physical or psychological capabilities of an actor (Kaplan & Gangestad, 2005; Refaie & Mishra, 2020; von Rueden et al., 2015); situational factors determine how embodied factors manifest compared to others in a specific environment of competition (Mishra et al., 2017). The integration of embodied and situational/environmental factors in the form of relative state essentially represents a barometer measure of one's competitive standing relative to others in a given situation.

A recent mathematical model of relative state bearing on fitness consequences (Barclay et al., 2018) strongly supported the core predictions of the initial verbal relative state model and review of supporting evidence (Mishra et al., 2017). The mathematical model indicated that if relative state dictates competitive disadvantage (vs. advantage), actors should engage in risk-taking when no low-risk options are able to satisfy the actor's need. This finding supports the need-based pathway of the relative state model. Conversely, if relative state dictates competitive advantage (vs. disadvantage), the mathematical model indicated that actors should engage risk-taking when they are likely to succeed in risk-taking, experience greater gains from successful risk-taking, or experience less severe losses from unsuccessful risk-taking, thus enjoying greater expected value from risk-taking (Barclay et al., 2018). This finding supports the ability-based pathway of the relative state model.

Determinants of Relative State and Competitive Dis/advantage

Given the influence of relative state and resultant competitive dis/advantage in predicting patterns of risk-taking, what are the central determinants of relative state? This question can be answered by more carefully considering the two components that determine relative state: (1) *embodied capital*—abilities and traits inherent to an individual that represent the somatic product of gene expression over development; and (2) *situational/*

environmental factors—the characteristics of a specific competitive landscape (e.g., nature of rivals, scarcity/abundance of mates, resources, territory) (Mishra et al., 2017). The interaction of embodied capital and situational/environmental factors determines relative state, and therefore determines the degree to which any actor is at competitive dis/advantage. This interaction is not dissimilar to the interaction of "person" and "environment" made famous by Bandura's social cognitive theory (1986), which highlights the importance of understanding a person's psychological, physical, and intellectual capacities in the context of demands placed on capacities by the social and physical environment (see also Lewin, 1935).

Embodied Capital

Every actor is a product of gene-by-environment interaction manifested over developmental time; embodied capital is therefore the expression of one's genotype into a phenotype via development (Kaplan & Gangestad, 2005; Mishra et al., 2017; von Rueden et al., 2015). This process leads to the appearance of traits and abilities that contribute to relative dis/advantage. Embodied capital is not the only form of "capital" that contributes to competitive dis/advantage. Monetary capital dictates individual differences in wealth (and therefore in various social opportunities); social capital dictates different costs and benefits among those who have greater or fewer cooperative social partners (Adler & Kwon, 2002). Monetary capital is a product of the leverage of one's embodied capital (e.g., hard work, intelligence), lifespan decisions (e.g., savings), and cumulative resource accrual over time (i.e., intergenerational wealth transfer). Social capital can also be an ultimate product of embodied capital. Actors can gain prestige-based social capital by cooperating with others, ultimately leading to the accrual of relational value (Leary, 2005), or dominance-based social capital by depriving others of resources, or controlling the flow of resources (Cheng et al., 2013). For ease of exposition, we consider monetary capital and social capital under the umbrella of embodied capital (Mishra et al., 2017).

All things being equal, it would be best for an actor to maximize such forms of embodied capital as attractiveness, intelligence, physical strength, social ability, and/or any other characteristics that contribute to advantage in competition. However, all actors are necessarily constrained by tradeoffs. *Life history theory* offers a theoretical rationale for understanding the costs and benefits that mediate these tradeoffs. Life history theory posits that the developmental environment forces tradeoffs between key life functions that require investment of resources (Stearns, 1992). All organisms must allocate scarce resources like time, energy, motivation, and effort to essential life functions like growth, reproduction, and parenting. One particularly influential tradeoff is between investing in individual growth (somatic effort) or investing in reproduction (reproductive effort). Emphasizing somatic effort results in slower, but greater growth (e.g., larger adult size) as well as delayed reproduction; in contrast, emphasizing reproductive effort results in accelerated growth (e.g., reaching adult size sooner, earlier puberty) as well as earlier reproduction (Kirkwood & Rose, 1991; Stearns, 1992). The nature of these tradeoffs is in part dictated by the qualities of developmental environments, which have an important influence over gene expression.

Harsh and unpredictable environments are, on average, associated with life history tradeoffs that favor faster development, less investment in growth, shorter time horizons, and greater impulsive and risky behavior (Doom et al., 2016; Ellis et al., 2012; Kirkwood & Rose, 1991; Pepper & Nettle, 2017). Unpredictable environments offer unpredictable rewards, facilitating sensitivity to outcome variance and therefore leading to short-term oriented, risky, and impulsive behavior as an adaptation to environmental stochasticity (Pepper & Nettle, 2017). Similarly, harsh developmental environments are typified by scarcity of resources, exposure aggression and adversity, and greater chance of illness (Brumbach et al., 2009). Although there is considerable debate around the degree to which individual differences within species are characterized by life history tradeoffs, especially humans (Cabeza de Baca et al., 2016; Copping et al., 2014), there is clear evidence that harsh and unpredictable environments have influence on the manifestation of embodied capital (e.g., Neugebauer et al., 1999; reviewed in Anderson, 2007; Harris et al., 2001), including cognition and behavior (reviewed in Pepper & Nettle, 2017).

Surprisingly little evidence has directly examined links between embodied capital and risk-taking, especially high embodied capital and ability-based risk-taking. However, some results are suggestive. Refaie and Mishra (2020) showed that three objectively measured indices of embodied capital—attractiveness, intelligence, and dexterity—were negatively associated with risk-propensity in the form of impulsivity, problem gambling tendencies, and criminal outcomes, and positively associated with investment risk-attitudes (a skill-based risk) and self-control. More evidence supports an association between relatively lower embodied capital and greater need-based risk-taking. Lower physical attractiveness has been associated with greater antisocial risk-taking, including crime (e.g., Bobadilla et al., 2012; Mocan & Tekin, 2010; Rosen & Underwood, 2010). There is also strong evidence that lower cognitive ability is associated with greater risk-taking in the form of antisocial behavior, violence, and crime (e.g., Gibson et al., 2001; de Tribolet-Hardy et al., 2014; McGloin & Pratt, 2003). Taken together, evidence is suggestive that embodied capital and risk-taking, especially antisocial risk-taking, are linked.

Situational/Environmental Factors: Scale and Slope of Competition

Embodied capital must manifest within an environment of competition. What situational and/or environmental factors determine the costs and benefits of the fitness landscape that actors compete in? It is useful to consider two interacting factors: *slope of competition*— inequality of outcomes that describes the degree to which "winners take all" (or not)—and *scale of competition*—the degree to which competition is local or global (Gardner & West, 2004; West et al., 2006). When the slope of competition is steep (vs. shallow)—that is, under conditions of high inequality—competition is also more intensely zero-sum, again leading to those who are competitively advantaged enjoying disproportionate rewards compared to close rivals (Sommet et al., 2018). Similarly, when scale of competition is local (vs. global), competition over proxies of fitness (mates, resources, status) occurs among closer rivals, and is more intensely zero-sum. This is because those who are competitively advantaged in local competition increase their fitness more intensely relative to close rivals (Barker & Barclay, 2016; West et al., 2006).

Slope of competition, characterized by greater inequality in the rewards of competition, has been associated with risk-taking in both observational and experimental studies. Aggregate-level inequality at the neighborhood, state, and national levels has been associated with a wide array of risky behaviors and outcomes, including sexual promiscuity and teen pregnancy (Gold et al., 2002), drug and substance abuse (Room, 2005), and antisocial conduct and crime (Daly et al., 2001; Wilson & Daly, 1997), among others (reviewed in Wilkinson & Pickett, 2007, 2009). Evidence from other levels of analysis further support the link between slope of competition and risk-taking; for example, NASCAR drivers take more risks in races with greater prize spreads (Becker & Huselid, 1992).

Competition manifests in its most zero-sum form and is most intensely amplified when steep slope of competition (high inequality) meets *local* scale of competition (vs. global). This interaction appears to be particularly motivating of risk-taking. Krupp and Cook (2018) found in an experimental game that participants who experienced inequality amplified by local competition engaged in the greatest level of risk-taking. Spadoni and Potters (2018) similarly showed that in tournaments where rewards are determined by performance, conditions with more rivals (eight vs. two)—that is, conditions of amplified local competition—led to greater risk-taking. Intense rivalries, characterized by intense local competition, also motivate greater risk-taking. For example, rival NFL teams are more likely to make risky plays (in the form of fourth-down gambles; To et al., 2018), and rival soccer players are more likely to foul and make dirty plays (Kilduff et al., 2015). Within organizations, ranking feedback leads to the elevation of sabotaging behavior, or false inflation of one's own performance (Charness et al., 2013). Laboratory experiments support these findings. For example, students who believed themselves to be competing against others from a rival university engaged in greater risk-taking (To et al., 2018). Even in simpler experiments, risk-taking also increases in experimental conditions characterized by a steep slope of competition, where there are fewer "winners" of prizes (Tsetlin et al., 2004).

Taken together, evidence suggests that key components of the relative state model—embodied capital, steep slope of competition, and local scale of competition—are linked with greater risk-taking. How do these conditions manifest to influence relative state and competitive dis/advantage more specifically? In the next section, we discuss the applicability of the relative state model to understanding risk-taking in key domains of competition.

Domains of Competition and Risk-Taking

Evidence suggests that general conditions of competition appear to lead to greater risk-taking. Mathematical modeling suggests that tournaments characterized by relative performance creates conditions that incentivize risk-taking and minimize effort (Hvide, 2002). Laboratory evidence similarly supports competitive risk-taking. Participants in competitive tournament scenarios show increased risk-taking as level of competitiveness increases and decreased risk-taking when feedback about opponent performance is removed (removing indicators of standing relative to others; Eriksen & Kvaløy, 2017). In the presence of incentives to compete, people engage in greater risk-taking (Garling et al., 2021). Among males, taking part in a competitive tennis match leads to increased risk-taking in a laboratory setting (Black et al., 2013). Previous studies have also shown that information about other people's performance leads to an increase in risky behaviors, but only in competitive zero-sum settings (Brookins et al., 2016). Non-human evidence also supports the zero-sum association between competition and elevated risk-taking. Among chimps and bonobos, competition leads to increased risk-taking (Rosati & Hare, 2012); even among distal relatives, like salmon, foraging in groups leads to greater risk-taking than foraging along due to more intense local competition over resources (Grand & Dill, 1999).

Competition can be considered in a domain-specific manner, shedding more nuanced light on the competition-risk link. Incentives drive motivation, and motivation drives risk-taking. Incentives are particularly salient in ecologically relevant domains that involve three key proxies of fitness: resources, mates, and status. The relative state model suggests that the domain-specificity of relevant embodied capital should have important implications for the downstream domain-specificity of risk-taking (Mishra et al., 2017). If relative state (and its antecedent embodied capital by situational/environmental interaction) confers competitive dis/advantage in any given domain, resultant risk-taking should be expected in that same domain. To the degree that relative state generalizes across domains, risk-taking would appear domain-general. For example, consider someone who is competitively advantaged, possessing great wealth; such an individual may be more attractive to mates *and* more desirable as a cooperative partner. Such an individual may engage in ability-based risk-taking in resource, mating, and status domains owing to the possession of capital that is of relevance across domains (appearing as domain-general risk-taking). In the following sections, we explore domain-specific applications of relative state and competitive dis/advantage as they bear on competition for three key proxies of fitness: resources, mates, and status.

Resource Competition

Acquisition of physical resources—food, water, shelter, territory—are fundamental to survival and reproduction, and therefore to natural selection and competition. In modern human environments, token economies centered on money allow for the acquisition of basic (and manufactured) resources (as well as services), which in turn confers competitive dis/advantage (Hill & Buss, 2010). Regardless of the specific resource currency, the fact that some actors within a situation or environment are able to hold more resources than others gives rise to inequality—or slope of competition—which drives rivalry. Resource-based competition, through its intensification of slope of competition via inequality motivates both need-based and ability-based risk-taking, as we review below.

Substantial empirical evidence suggests that economic inequality (i.e., steep scale of competition over economic resources) is associated with greater need-based risk-taking at aggregate levels. Such diverse forms of risk-taking as drug abuse, sexual promiscuity, property crime, violent crime, and homicide are associated with greater local inequality (reviewed in Wilkinson & Pickett, 2007, 2009). In fact, income inequality is among the single best predictors of homicide rates, within and between countries (Daly & Wilson, 1988; Elgar & Aitken, 2011; Wilson & Daly, 1997). Consistent with these findings, Payne et al. (2017) showed that in high inequality geographical areas (as quantified by the widely-used Gini coefficient) there are more frequent Google searches indicating interest in relatively high-risk behaviors (e.g., "pay day loans," "win money").

Importantly, inequality appears to be more important than poverty in motivating risk-taking (among other behaviors) (Blanchflower & Oswald, 2004; Daly & Wilson, 1988; Luttmer, 2005). The reason is simple: a population characterized by uniformly high poverty but low inequality has little variance in competitive dis/advantage. It is therefore unsurprising that income inequality (relative dis/advantage) predicts risk-taking and other outcomes far more effectively than does poverty, in that inequality is a far more direct index of one of the fundamental determinants of any competitive landscape: slope of competition.

Experimental evidence supports the importance of relative economic disadvantage and resource inequality in facilitating need-based risk-taking. Wohl et al. (2014) showed that people who are reminded of poor economic prospects engaged in greater gambling, with this effect mediated by belief in the need to take risks to make money. Callan et al. (2008) showed that manipulated personal relative deprivation (a subjective experience of being on the losing end of inequality) led to increased gambling behaviors, with those feeling relatively deprived being preoccupied with fairness and experiencing resentment towards others. More directly related to income inequality, Mishra et al. (2015) showed that among pairs of participants, those straightforwardly induced to be disadvantaged by monetary inequality relative to the other participant engaged in greater financial risk-taking on a behavioral task. Krupp and Cook (2018) showed that inequality—especially amplified local inequality—led to increased competition and risk-taking behavior in an experimental economic game. Risk-taking also demonstrably increases in scenarios where there are fewer prizes (i.e., systems characterized more intensely by "winner takes all"; Tsetlin et al., 2004). Payne et al. (2017) showed that economic inequality facilitated risk-taking particularly strongly in situations of upward comparisons that created a perception of "need" among those disadvantaged by inequality.

There is relatively little direct research on the role that dis/advantage or ability plays on risk-taking in resource competition. However, some evidence suggests that those with a competitive advantage are inclined towards greater risk-taking. Anderson and Galinsky (2006) showed that a sense of power increases optimism in the perceived payoffs of risk-taking, and subsequently leads to increased risk-taking. Finke and Huston (2003) note that investors with a higher net worth typically had higher risk-tolerance compared to others; risk-tolerance was in fact the strongest predictor of wealth for individuals over 65, suggesting the presence of a risk-reward link. When managers of competing financial firms are measured against an outside benchmark, top-performing managers tend to be risk-averse; however, when pitted in head to head competition against rivals, competitively advantaged managers appear to shift to risk-proneness (Taylor, 2003). Refaie and Mishra (2020) showed that intelligence was associated with risk-prone attitudes in the financial domain (e.g., stock purchases) where performance benefits from knowledge, analytical thinking, and measured decision-making. People with greater cognitive skills also appear more risk-prone in the gains domain of a lottery task, as well as in a sequential prisoner's dilemma where participants are playing for monetary rewards (Burks et al., 2009). Recently, Deminchuk (2021) showed that people in a hypothetical poker scenario engaged in elevated risk-taking when provided with a particularly favorable (competitively advantaged) hand. Evidence from modern day hunter-gatherers suggests that hunters who have the greatest ability (as measured by average caloric return per hunt, a risky, high variance endeavor) are also the most frequent hunters, particularly in the poorer hunting seasons (Bliege Bird, et al., 2001). It is worth noting some contradictory evidence, however; Mishra, Barclay, and Lalumière (2014) found that cues of competitive advantage (relative intelligence) did not lead to increased risk-taking (although cues of competitive disadvantage did lead to risk-proneness in the same study). It is likely that domain-specific relevance of embodied capital (or perceived relevance) influences risk-taking, although further research is necessary.

Mate Competition

Competition for mates is a fundamental part of life. Sexual selection is a manifestation of a natural selection that describes (1) how members of a biological sex compete with others of the same sex to gain access to members of the opposite sex (*intrasexual competition*; e.g., male-male competition over females), and (2) how members of a biological sex signal to and select mates of the opposite sex (*intersexual competition*; e.g., male attractiveness to females) (reviewed in Jones & Ratterman, 2009; Puts, 2016). Just as natural selection offers a framework for understanding the contours of competition more generally, sexual selection offers a framework for understanding conditions that facilitate competition in the domain of mate choice. Intersexual competition among conspecifics of the same sex, especially when local, amplifies risk-taking. Similarly, intrasexual competition for access to members of the opposite sex, also especially when local, also amplifies risk-taking.

In most species, males are riskier than females (reviewed in Archer, 2009; Byrnes et al., 1999; Campbell, 2004; Daly & Wilson, 2001; Mishra, 2014). Why is this the case? The theory and evidence reviewed in this chapter indicate that competition over scarce resources leads to amplified risk-taking. From a functional point of view, in most sexually reproducing species, female gametes (eggs) are a scarcer resource than male gametes (sperm). Furthermore, reproductive investment is more intense in females than males, especially in mammals, where females must bear the greater costs of gestation (carrying a fetus to term), lactation (spending limited energetic resources in the care of children), and parental care overall. Consequently, in systems characterized by such parental investment asymmetry, there are always more males than females available for mating, creating further asymmetrical competitive pressures across sex (reviewed in Jones & Ratterman, 2009; Puts, 2016).

Effects of competition are further compounded by the fact that in most species, males have substantially higher reproductive variance than females (Bateman, 1948; Clutton-Brock & Vincent, 1991). A single male can sire countless offspring, but a female is limited by physiological capacity and interbirth timing. These circumstances lead to remarkable examples of inequality in fitness outcomes among males. For example, unique components of the genotype of Genghis Khan—famous for siring countless offspring—can be detected in an estimated 0.5 percent of the male population of the entire world (Zerjal et al., 2003). At a fundamental level, then, one sex is subject to more intense competition than the other. Put another way, in most mating systems, the slope of competition is more intense if you are a male competing over females than the other way around, such that males are far more likely to be childless than are females. This asymmetry creates relative scarcity of females, breeds competition among males, and facilitates incentives for risk-taking among males (Clutton-Brock & Vincent, 1991).

Consistent with competitive pressures derived from sexual selection, evidence for sex differences in risk-taking in humans is very strong. Males compared to females take greater risks in nearly every domain, including crime, violence, and antisocial conduct; drug abuse; risky health behaviors; risky sexual activity; dangerous recreational activities; occupational choices involving hazard, driving, interpersonal aggression; and even everyday activities like jaywalking (see Archer, 2009; Daly & Wilson, 2001; Mishra, 2014 for reviews). Operational sex ratios—the ratio of the number of reproductively available females to males—provide a rough index of the intensity of intrasexual and intersexual competition in any given environment (Archer, 2009; Griskevicius et al., 2012). When there is a male skew in operational sex ratio, on average, males are under greater competitive pressures (i.e., under more intense intrasexual and intersexual competition), and females under less (Archer, 2009; Campbell, 2004; Maner & Ackerman, 2020). In most systems, male-skewed sex ratios are associated with greater partner violence and coercion, lesser financial savings, and greater discounting of the future in favor of immediate mating opportunities (Diamond-Smith & Rudolph, 2018; Griskevicius et al. 2012). An abundance of single males is more broadly associated with an increase in crime, homicide, and general societal upheaval (Archer, 2009; Barber, 2003; Daly & Wilson, 1988).

Although on average males engage in more risk-taking than females across taxa, it is hardly a universal. Competition is simply a product of the pressures that exist within any given system or environment. When males are scarcer, some evidence suggests that females tend to increase risk-taking as a consequence (Campbell, 1995, 2004). In species where males provide the bulk of parental care (e.g., seahorses), risk-taking tends to be higher among females; in these circumstances, females are now under more intense competition for relatively scarcer males (Alonzo, 2011). Across animal taxa, in species with mating systems characterized by greater male parental investment (e.g., seahorses), for example, females are the more competitive sex. Similar effects are seen within species. Campbell (1995) provides evidence that young women are particularly prone to increasing risk-acceptance under conditions of competition over sexual reputation, access to resource-rich young men, and protecting relationships from rival women. This shift in typically observed sex-based risk-taking patterns among humans reflects the more general principle that the contours of competition have a powerful situational influence on behavior (Campbell, 2004). In environments with a female-skewed sex ratio, females tend to be relatively riskier. Women in such environments tend to experience greater intrasexual female conflict, a higher divorce rate, more children born out of wedlock, lower rates of monogamy, and a greater number of partners (Archer, 2009; Campbell, 2004; Maner & Ackerman, 2020). Even male-skewed sex ratios can also lead to competition leading to relatively less risky behavior; Maner and Ackerman (2020) review evidence suggesting that in such situations, some men (typically with high resource holding potential and greater embodied capital) can outcompete others by "settling down" sooner and committing to further parental investment. Still, among those who are relatively disadvantaged and find it difficult to obtain a mate (e.g., those with low socioeconomic status or low embodied capital), the general pattern of competition leading to risk-taking remains.

The nuances reviewed above again highlight a fundamental and consistent implication of competition: scarcity determines competitive pressures, and those under competitive pressures adjust tactics to gain relative advantage over rivals. The general principles highlighted through this chapter thus remain the same in the specific domain of mating: competition over scarce or harder-to-attract partners motivates risk-taking. Local competition amplifies this further, as does a more intense slope of competition. Those who are competitively disadvantaged are under pressure to engage in need-based risk-taking to achieve minimally acceptable outcomes; those who are competitively advantaged engage in ability-based risk-taking because of its higher payoffs.

Status Competition

Status, along with resources and mates, is one of the three key positive proxies of fitness that actors strive to acquire and leverage into survival, reproductive success, and inclusive fitness. All social species across taxa form social hierarchies, leading to stratified rankings of individuals' status among dimensions that facilitate competitive dis/advantage (Magee & Galinsky, 2008). These status hierarchies have profound implications for behavior. How are social hierarchies determined and assessed, and what are the implications of these hierarchies for competition and risk-taking?

A growing theoretical and empirical literature suggests that status in humans can be acquired through one of two fundamental pathways: dominance or prestige (Cheng et al., 2013). *Dominance* describes a strategy for the pursuit of social rank that involves such tactics as intimidation, coercion, imposition, and the general use of fear. *Prestige* conversely describes a strategy where social rank is attained through skills, success, and/or knowledge that indicate useful cultural knowledge (Cheng et al., 2013). Both dominance and prestige confer respect, attention, and deference, although they do so through very different tactics.

Relative state manifests as an interaction between one's embodied capital and situational/environmental factors (scale and slope of competition). As with other domains of competition involving other key positive proxies of fitness (resources, mates; reviewed above), the presence and density of local rivals amplifies competition, as does a steep slope of competition characterizing greater inequality of outcomes. If one is in an environment characterized by particularly intense competition (i.e., steep and local competition), it pays more to invest in more competitive tactics as opposed to more cooperative tactics (Barker & Barclay, 2016). These tendencies are amplified by one's own embodied capital. Traits that are associated with enhanced dominance should be associated with more competitive, zero-sum, antisocial tactics, and traits that are associated with enhanced prestige should be associated with less competitive, more cooperative, asocial, or prosocial tactics.

Asocial forms of risk-taking involve an actor exposing themselves to outcome variance in circumstances that do not explicitly involve other social actors. For example, gambling by oneself at a slot machine is a form of asocial risk-taking involving exposure of one's monetary resources to outcome variance. Asocial forms of risk-taking straightforwardly contribute to status via the acquisition of resources. In humans, income/wealth can be achieved through low-variance means (e.g., get an education, obtain a high paying job), but also through high-variance, risky means (e.g., starting a business, investing in the stock market, gambling). Motivation to engage in risk-taking around asocial financial currencies is particularly amplified in the presence of social status competition, particularly among men. In these circumstances, risk-taking around status represents a form of intersexual competition (as reviewed above). Competitive disadvantage relative to higher-status others facilitates a preference for high risk/high reward options, especially among men (Ermer et al., 2008; Mishra et al., 2014). Consistent with this finding, Chan (2015) showed that men exposed to attractive other men engage in greater financial risk-taking. Hill and Buss (2010) similarly provide evidence that men engage in risk-taking when it offers a possibility of rendering them in a superior position relative to competitors. Another example comes from a study of WWII German fighter pilots (Ager et al., 2017). The German air force employed a points system and publicly praised high achieving fighters. Pilots who saw the names of former squad mates took significantly more risks in the upcoming missions. Among the most skilled pilots, this led to significantly more victories and marginally more defeats; however, among the lesser skilled pilots, they achieved only marginally more victories but were much more likely to die (Ager et al., 2017).

Antisocial risk-taking involves actors exposing themselves to outcome variance leading to harm of others. Property crime, for example, exposes people to outcome variance (ranging from "free" resources to jail time), but involves harm to third parties. Antisocial forms of risk-taking are typically associated with dominance-based status-seeking strategies. Such forms of risk-taking as aggression, violence, delinquency, and crime appear to be particularly sensitive to status competition and exemplify need-based risk-taking. An illustrative example of these systemic motivational pressures is *adolescent-limited delinquency*, which describes a pattern of antisocial risk-taking that is characteristically elevated during the adolescent and early adulthood years (reviewed in Moffitt, 1993, 2003; Moffitt & Caspi, 2001; Moffitt et al., 2002). These years are characterized by particularly intense social competition for proxies of fitness: resources, mates, and status (Daly & Wilson, 1988, 1997, 2001; Mishra, 2014; Mishra & Lalumière, 2008; Wilson & Daly, 1985). Younger people who have had less time to acquire skills, resources, and/or social status are at intense competitive disadvantage compared to older rivals. This developmental period is particularly intense for young males; as reviewed earlier, males tend to be riskier than females because of fundamental asymmetries in "supply and demand" (reviewed above), leading to the persistent situational experience of a steeper slope of competition and more intense local competition. Wilson and Daly (1985) termed the particularly high rates of antisocial conduct and crime during adolescent and early adulthood years among males "young male syndrome."

Life course persistent offending—chronic engagement in antisocial risk-taking behavior and crime over the entire lifespan—also demonstrates the importance of competitive pressures in facilitating risk-taking. Those whose relative state dictates that they are persistently competitively dis/advantaged (e.g., due to developmental harshness, like poverty, abuse, or early injury, often associated with persistently lower embodied capital; Moffit, 2003; Moffitt & Caspi, 2001; Moffitt et al., 2002) engage in greater levels of risk-taking. Persistently competitively dis/advantaged actors may have much more to gain and much less to lose from costly risk-taking, compared to those who have lower-risk options with lesser downside costs (reviewed in Lalumière et al., 2005). Persistent disadvantage is particularly difficult to remedy, and so for such actors, risk-taking tends to be stubbornly high across the lifespan (Mishra, 2014; Mishra & Lalumière, 2008; Moffitt, 2003; Moffitt & Caspi, 2001; Moffitt et al., 2002). The domain-generality of persistent disadvantage also leads to what has been termed the *generality of deviance*, referring to very high within-individual correlations among forms of impulsive, reckless criminal behaviors (Hirschi, 1994; e.g., Mishra, Lalumière et al., 2017).

In contrast to asocial and antisocial forms of risk-taking, prosocial risk-taking involves exposure to outcome variance leading to circumstances that benefit others (e.g., Farthing, 2005). For example, first responders like police officers and firefighters who expose themselves to danger to save others are engaged in prosocial risk-taking. Prosocial forms of risk-taking are typically associated with prestige-based status-seeking strategies. Those who can compete without exposing themselves to the very real downsides of antisocial risk-taking (physical harm, social ostracization) should be expected to engage in forms of risk-taking that provide greater payoffs and signal ability to third parties. For example, among the Meriam peoples, maintenance of social status through food sharing and prosocial generosity is a driving force behind hunting, as skilled hunters can gain social status while unskilled ones may lose it if they are unable to provide guests with meat at social gatherings (Bliege Bird et al., 2001; Smith et al., 2003).

Summary: Competition for Proxies of Fitness

The evidence reviewed above highlights the important influence of competition over three key proxies of fitness in facilitating risk-taking. It is important to emphasize that competition over different proxies of fitness—resources, mates, and status/reputation—are not unrelated. Successful competition in any of the three domains can translate into successful competition in the others. For example, having access to bountiful resources can translate into successful mate competition (through enhanced attractiveness), or successful status competition (through enhanced social standing). An understanding of the incentive structures of any given competition, and the relative state that gives rise to competitive dis/advantage within said competition, can shed light on both need-based and ability-based risk-taking. It is particularly important to consider these incentive structures at "nature's joints"—ecologically valid domains of competition over key proxies of fitness.

Thus far, we have focused on reviewing theory and evidence that reflects a primarily functional/evolutionary level of explanation for competition and risk-taking behavior. A key missing piece of this narrative is how functional, evolutionary considerations "translate" to the proximate, psychological level in humans. Objective realities are often tenuously associated with subjective psychological attitudes, beliefs, and interpretations. How do people experience relative state and dis/advantage in their minds? In the next section, we offer some informed speculation on how functional considerations may translate into the proximate psychology of dis/advantage, motivating risk-taking.

The Proximate Psychology of Dis/advantage and Risk-Taking

Actors do not directly act to maximize biological fitness, instead seeking such proxies of fitness as mates, resources, and status/reputation that have been statistically correlated (although not perfectly) with biological fitness over time. As a result, functional, evolutionary pressures must necessarily manifest at a proximate, psychological level (Scott-Phillips et al., 2011). It therefore follows that when making decisions involving risk, minds should possess proximate psychological mechanisms to assess competitive dis/advantage, and act in a manner sensitive to this assessment. Because fitness is necessarily and fundamentally relative, it accordingly follows that psychological social comparison mechanisms should be particularly attuned to relative comparisons.

Festinger (1954) argued in his seminal social comparison theory that it is impossible to understand one's position in a hierarchy—one's competitive dis/advantage—without engaging in subjective social comparisons to relevant others. That is, one cannot understand one's place in the world without comparison to others, and comparison to others informs perceptions of competitiveness (Liu et al., 2021). Consequently, to fully comprehend the effects of competition on risk-taking at an individual level, we must understand how people subjectively interpret the position of themselves and others within competitive environments (Novakowski & Mishra, 2017; Smith & Huo, 2014).

Substantial theorizing and empirical evidence suggest that thought arises as a consequence of two processes: analytical, controlled, explicit conscious processes; and intuitive, reactive, implicit unconscious processes (reviewed in Kahneman, 2017). Both analytical and intuitive processes have important influence on attitudes, behaviors, and outcomes. Analytical appraisals relevant to social comparison assessments include the frequency of social comparisons, content of comparisons, social targets of comparisons, and criteria used to determine relative positions, among others (Garcia et al., 2013). Intuitive processes inherent in social comparison involve emotions like envy, which describes a negative emotional response as a result of unfavorable social comparison (Smith & Kim, 2007). Any strong psychological candidate for subjective indexing of competitive dis/advantage, then, must include both analytical and intuitive components.

A key individual difference that includes both analytical and intuitive components that has been studied in the context of social comparison is *personal relative deprivation*. In a review and meta-analysis, Smith et al. (2012) posited three fundamental components of personal relative deprivation. First, an individual must make a social comparison. Second, there must be a cognitive appraisal of the disparity between self and others, leading to the perception of being disadvantaged. Third, perceived disparity and resultant disadvantage must be seen as unfair or unjust, leading to an emotional reaction of anger and resentment. Importantly, Smith et al.'s (2012) supporting meta-analysis provided compelling empirical support for the notion that together, the three components of personal relative deprivation—social comparison, perceived unfairness, and a negative emotional reaction—are greater than the sum of their component parts. That is, personal relative deprivation is an emergent property of the interactions between these three factors.

If relative deprivation indexes sentiments around one's competitive dis/advantage, it should be accordingly associated with risk-taking. Consistent with this hypothesis, individual differences in personal relative deprivation have been associated with greater risk-taking attitudes, behaviors, and outcomes, including gambling and criminal conduct, with greater relative deprivation predicting greater risk-propensity (Callan et al., 2008; Callan et al., 2011; Mishra & Carleton, 2017; Mishra & Meadows, 2018; Mishra & Novakowski, 2016). Importantly, in many of these studies, subjective interpretations of competitive dis/advantage, like personal relative deprivation, have been shown to explain key variance in outcomes above and beyond objective measures of social or economic status, highlighting the importance of considering subjective (vs. solely objective) assessments.

Although a small but growing body of research on personal relative deprivation suggests an important link to relevant risk-taking attitudes, behaviors, and outcomes, a key limitation of the concept of relative deprivation is its lack of explicit measurement of perceptions of self. Consideration of self is important in many psychological processes; in the domain of social comparison, consideration of self is definitional; Wood (1996) notes that social comparison processes necessarily involve "thinking about information about one or more people in relation to the self" (p. 521). The influential sociometer hypothesis suggests that self-esteem is a particularly important form of a self-appraisal that serves as a "barometer" measure of one's relational value compared to others (reviewed in Leary, 2005). Inasmuch as relational value is an index of competitive standing, self-appraisal represents an important component of general socioemotional comparison reactions. Competitive dis/advantage must necessarily be assessed compared to rivals within a competitive landscape, and this process requires anchoring on the self.

Some recent research on social comparison reactions has sought to more carefully operationalize and measure socioemotional comparison reactions inclusive of the centrally important self-appraisal component. Mishra et al. (2021) constructed a measure of individual differences in perceived disadvantage inclusive of self-appraisals following best psychometric practices. Across several studies, they showed that this measure, which included a self-evaluation component (self-esteem), alongside subjective assessment of fairness/justice (justice sensitivity) and negative emotions in response to social comparison (envy) offers excellent assessment of the latent construct of *perceived disadvantage*. Like personal relative deprivation, perceived disadvantage is an amalgam of analytical and intuitive components; however, the inclusion of self-appraisal in measurement appears to offer superior statistical fit, suggesting a more natural association of components, with envy (emotional appraisal), poor self-esteem (self-appraisal), and justice sensitivity (fairness appraisal) being the three facets of perceived disadvantage (Mishra et al., 2021).

Research on the quantification and measurement of perceived disadvantage is in its infancy. Still, the concept is a promising psychological representation of competitive dis/advantage. Preliminary results suggest that perceived disadvantage explains incremental variance in psychological outcomes above and beyond other measures of social comparison and socioemotional comparison reactions (Mishra et al., 2021). Given the strong links between subjective competitive dis/advantage and relative state, we expect that perceived disadvantage should be associated with risk-taking consistent with the relative state model. If one considers themselves to be in a good relative state—that is, they perceive themselves to be competitively advantaged—they should engage in ability-based risk-taking in circumstances where such risk-taking has higher payoffs than low-risk alternatives, or if such risk-taking signals underlying skills, quality, or embodied capital to third parties. If one considers themselves to be in a poor relative state—that is, they perceive themselves to be competitively disadvantaged—they should engage in need-based risk-taking in circumstances where risk-taking has a higher payoff than alternative low-risk options. We look forward to more rigorous tests of these hypotheses.

Perceived disadvantage is an encouraging candidate for a general psychological index of how one feels about their own competitive position relative to others. However, this general assessment of one's standing must be set against some goal or desired state (reference point; Kahneman, 1992) to translate into motivation to engage in risk-taking. Evidence and theorizing suggest that actors construct two different types of reference points relevant to risk-taking. *Minimal acceptable thresholds* are roughly analogous to need as it has been defined in the relative state model (and in risk-sensitivity theory, March & Shapira, 1992); these thresholds represent minimally acceptable outcomes that allow an actor to gratify disparity between present state and an essential goal state. By contrast, *aspiration levels* describe desired goal states, above and beyond minimally acceptable goals (Heath et al., 1999). An example from foraging hummingbirds is illustrative in distinguishing these two types of goals. Hummingbirds have extremely high energetic needs and must consequently expose themselves to variable (risky) foraging patches in order to obtain nectar to survive and reproduce. Obtaining enough nectar to survive any given day/night is a minimal acceptable threshold (in this case specifically, a starvation threshold). After these basic needs are met, obtaining surplus nectar can be translated into reproductive effort—an aspiration level (Hurly, 2003). Minimal acceptable thresholds can be seen as roughly analogous to "needs," and aspirational levels analogous to "wants"; wants can shift into needs based on how hierarchical goals are accomplished.

Among humans, consideration of a modified version of Maslow's hierarchy of needs (Maslow, 1943) centered on functional considerations may be useful in shedding light on key goal domains, and therefore, the contexts that facilitate the generation of goal-oriented reference points for risk-taking. Kenrick et al. (2010) suggested that Maslow's hierarchy of needs could be "renovated" to account for an ecologically valid set of lower and higher order needs based on life history theory. They suggested the following revised hierarchy of needs, from basic to advanced, following a rigid developmental pathway: (1) survival; (2) self-protection; (3) affiliation; (4) status, respect, and esteem; (5) mate acquisition; (6) mate retention; and (7) parenting. Importantly, these needs cluster neatly onto proxies of fitness (resources, status, and mates, respectively), which, as reviewed above, represent key domains of competition. These needs also assort into "basic" and "advanced" needs, consistent with Maslow's (1943) original theorizing.

Competitive dis/advantage (and its proximate psychological representation, perceived disadvantage) may manifest in each of the domains Kenrick et al. (2010) highlights, informing reference points and subsequent domain-specific risk-taking. It is possible that need-based risk-taking based on minimal acceptable thresholds may be particularly associated with lower-level needs, and ability-based risk-taking based on aspiration levels would be particularly associated with higher-level needs. For example, one might expect greater need-based risk-taking around survival, and more ability-based risk-taking around status or mate competition. Still, drawing distinctions between "needs" and "wants" is extremely difficult (and sometimes impossible) and is often a matter of subjective perspective. We look forward to further research on the distinctions between "need" and "want" motivations, goal structures, reference points, and risk-taking behavior.

General Summary

Competition is ubiquitous, providing unique driving pressures for risk-taking. The evidence reviewed in this chapter suggests that actors are motivated to seek key positive proxies of fitness: resources, mates, and status. The relative state model of risk-taking provides a framework for understanding how the integration of embodied capital and situational/embodied factors, like slope and scale of competition—determine the costs and benefits of risk-taking for any given actor in any given situation in any given domain. Those who are competitively disadvantaged—possessing relatively lesser embodied capital, and/or competing in environments characterized by a steep slope of competition and local scale of competition—appear to engage in greater need-based risk-taking. For need-based actors, risk-taking offers the opportunity to achieve outcomes that would otherwise be unattainable by lower-risk means. Those who are competitively advantaged—possessing relatively higher embodied capital, and/or competing in environments with relatively lesser slope of competition and more global competition—appear to engage in greater ability-based risk-taking. For ability-based actors, risk-taking offers greater payoffs than non-risky options, and/or signals underlying skills or abilities to third parties. Competitive dis/advantage may be indexed in minds by such proximate psychological mechanisms as perceived disadvantage.

Taken together, the theorizing and evidence reviewed in this chapter suggest strong links between competition and risk-taking. The relative state model, although nascent, offers a framework for examining hypotheses linking motivation and risk-taking, especially in the context of competition. We look forward to more empirical work critically examining its predictions.

References

Adler, P. S., & Kwon, S. (2002). Social capital: Prospects for a new concept. *Academy of Management Review 27*, 17–40.

Ager, P., Bursztyn, L., & Voth, H-J. (2017). *Killer incentives: Status competition and pilot performance during World War II.* No. w22992. National Bureau of Economic Research.

Alonzo, S. H. (2011). Sexual selection favours male parental care, when females can choose. *Proceedings of the Royal Society B 279*, 1784–1790.

Anderson, G. S. (2007). *Biological influences on criminal behavior.* CRC Press.

Anderson, C., & Galinsky, A. D. (2006). Power, optimism, and risk-taking. *European Journal of Social Psychology 36*, 511–536.

Archer, J. (2009). Does sexual selection explain human sex differences in aggression? *Behavioral and Brain Sciences 32*, 249–266.

Bandura, A. (1986). *Social foundations of thought and action: A social cognitive theory.* Prentice-Hall Inc.

Barber, N. (2003). The sex ratio and female marital opportunity as historical predictors of violent crime in England, Scotland, and the United States. *Cross-Cultural Research 37*, 373–392.

Barclay, P., Mishra, S., & Sparks, A. M. (2018). State-dependent risk-taking. *Proceedings of the Royal Society B: Biological Sciences 285*, 20180180.

Barclay, P., & Willer, R. (2007). Partner choice creates competitive altruism in humans. *Proceedings of the Royal Society B: Biological Sciences 1610*, 749–753.

Barker, J. L., & Barclay, P. (2016). Local competition increases people's willingness to harm others. *Evolution and Human Behavior 37*, 315–322.

Bateman, A. J. (1948). Intra-sexual selection in Drosophila. *Heredity 2*, 349–368.

Becker, B. E., & Huselid, M. A. (1992). The incentive effects of tournament compensation systems. *Administrative Science Quarterly 37*, 336–350.

Bernoulli, D. (1954). Exposition of a new theory on the measurement of risk. *Econometrica 22*, 23–36. (Original work published in 1738).

Black, A. C., Hochman, E., & Rosen, M. I. (2013). Acute effects of competitive exercise on risk-taking in a sample of adolescent male athletes. *Journal of Applied Sport Psychology 25*, 175–179.

Blanchflower, D. G., & Oswald, A. J. (2004). Well-being over time in Britain and the USA. *Journal of Public Economics 88*, 1359–1386.

Bliege Bird, R., Smith, E. A., & Bird, D. W. (2001). The hunting handicap: Costly signaling in human foraging societies. *Behavioral Ecology and Sociobiology 50*, 9–19.

Bobadilla, L., Metze, A. V., & Taylor, J. (2012). Physical attractiveness and its relation to unprovoked and reactive aggression. *Journal of Research in Personality 47*, 70–77.

Brookins, P., Brown, J., & Ryvkin, D. (2016). *Peer information and risk-taking under competitive and non-competitive pay schemes.* Working paper No. w22486. National Bureau of Economic Research.

Brumbach, B. H., Figueredo, A. J., & Ellis, B. J. (2009). Effects of harsh and unpredictable environments in adolescence on development of life history strategies. *Human Nature 20*(1), 25–51.

Burks, S. V., Carpenter, J. P., Goette, L., & Rustichini, A. (2009). Cognitive skills affect economic preferences, strategic behavior, and job attainment. *Proceedings of the National Academy of Sciences 106*, 7745–7750.

Byrnes, J. P., Miller, D. C., Schafer, W. D. (1999). Gender differences in risk taking: A meta-analysis. *Psychological Bulletin 125*, 367–383.

Cabeza de Baca, T., Wahl, R. A., Barnett, M. A., Figueredo, A. J., & Ellis, B. J. (2016). Adversity, adaptive calibration, and health: The case of disadvantaged families. *Adaptive Human Behavior and Physiology 2*, 93–115.

Callan, M. J., Ellard, J. H., Shead, N. W., & Hodgins, D. C. (2008). Gambling as a search for justice: Examining the role of personal relative deprivation in gambling urges and gambling behavior. *Personality and Social Psychology Bulletin 34*, 1514–1529.

Callan, M. J., Shead, N. W., & Olson, J. M. (2011). Personal relative deprivation, delay discounting, and gambling. *Journal of Personality and Social Psychology 101*, 955–973.

Campbell, A. (1995). A few good men: Evolutionary psychology and female adolescent aggression. *Ethology and Sociobiology 16*, 99–123.

Campbell, A. (2004). Female competition: Causes, constraints, content, and contexts. *The Journal of Sex Research 41*, 16–26.

Caraco, T., Martindale, S., & Whittam, T. S. (1980). An empirical demonstration of risk-sensitive foraging preferences. *Animal Behaviour 28*(3), 820–830.

Chan, E. Y. (2015). Physically attractive males increase financial risk-taking. *Evolution and Human Behavior 36*, 407–413.

Charness, G., Masclet, D., & Villeval, M. C. (2013). The dark side of competition for status. *Management Science 60*, 38–55.

Cheng, J. T., Tracy, J. L., Foulsham, T., Kingston, A., & Henrich, J. (2013). Two ways to the top: Evidence that dominance and prestige are distinct yet viable avenues to social rank and influence. *Journal of Personality and Social Psychology 104*, 103–125.

Clutton-Brock, T. H., & Vincent, A. C. J. (1991). Sexual selection and potential reproductive rates of males and females. *Nature 351*, 58–60.

Copping, L. T., Cambell, A., & Muncer, S. (2014). Psychometrics and life history strategy: The structure and validity of the High K strategy scale. *Evolutionary Psychology.* https://doi.org/10.1177/14747049140 1200115.

Daly, M., & Wilson, M. (1988). *Homicide.* Aldine Transaction.

Daly, M., & Wilson, M. (1997). Crime and conflict: Homicide in evolutionary psychological perspective. *Crime and Justice 22*, 51–100.

Daly, M., & Wilson, M. (2001). Risk taking, intrasexual competition, and homicide. *Nebraska Symposium on Motivation 47*, 1–36.

Daly, M., Wilson, M., & Vasdev, S. (2001). Income inequality and homicide rates in Canada and the United States. *Canadian Journal of Criminology 43*, 219–236.

Darwin, C. (1859). *On the origin of species.* Routledge.

Deminchuk, J. (2021). An empirical test of the relate state model with Texas Hold 'em poker scenarios.

de Tribolet-Hardy, F., Vohs, K., Mokros, A., & Habermeyer, E. (2014). Psychopathy, intelligence, and impulsivity in German violent offenders. *International Journal of Law and Psychiatry 37*(3), 238–244. http://doi.org/10.1016/j.ijlp.2013.11.018.

Diamond-Smith, N., & Rudolph, K. (2018). The association between uneven sex ratios and violence: Evidence from six Asian countries. *PLOS One 13*(6), e0197516.

Doom, J. R., Vanzomeren-Dohm, A. A., & Simpson, J. A. (2016). Early unpredictability predicts increased adolescent externalizing behaviors and substance use: A life history perspective. *Development and Psychopathology 28*, 1505–1516.

Elgar, F. J., & Aitken, N. (2011). Income inequality, trust and homicide in 33 countries. *European Journal of Public Health 21*, 241–246.

Ellis, B. J., Del Giudice, M., Dishion, T. J., Figueredo, A. J., Gray, P., Griskevicius, V. . . ., Wilson, D. S. (2012). The evolutionary basis of risky adolescent behavior: Implications for science, policy, and practice. *Developmental Psychology 48*, 598–623.

El Mouden, C., Burton-Chellew, M., Gardner, A., & West, S. A. (2012). What do humans maximise? In S. Okasha & K. Binmore (Eds.), *Evolution and rationality* (pp. 23–49). Cambridge University Press.

Eriksen, K. W., & Kvaløy, O. (2017). No guts, no glory: An experiment on excessive risk-taking. *Review of Finance 21*, 1327–1351.

Ermer, E., Cosmides, L., & Tooby, J. (2008). Relative status regulates risky decision-making about resources in men: Evidence for the co-evolution of motivation and cognition. *Evolution and Human Behavior 29*, 106–118.

Farthing, G. W. (2005). Attitudes toward heroic and nonheroic physical risk takers as mates and as friends. *Evolution and Human Behavior 26*, 171–185.

Festinger, L. (1954). A theory of social comparison processes. *Human Relations 7*, 117–140.

Finke, M. S., & Huston, S. J. (2003). The brighter side of financial risk: Financial risk tolerance and wealth. *Journal of Family and Economic Issues 24*, 233–256.

Friedman, M. & Savage, L. J. (1948). The utility analysis of choice involving risk. *Journal of Political Economy 56*, 279–304.

Friedman, M. & Savage, L. J. (1952). The expected utility hypothesis and the measurability of utility. *Journal of Political Economy 60*, 463–374.

Garcia, S. M., Tor, A., & Schiff, T. M. (2013). The psychology of competition: A social comparison perspective. *Perspectives on Psychological Science 8*, 634–650.

Gardner, A., & West, S. A. (2004). Spite and the scale of competition. *Journal of Evolutionary Biology 17*, 1195–1203.

Garling, T., Fang, D., Holmen, M., & Michaelsen, P. (2021). Financial risk-taking related to individual risk preference, social comparison and competition. *Review of Behavioral Finance 13*, 125–140.

Gibson, C., Piquero, A., & Tibbetts, S. (2001). The contribution of family adversity and verbal IQ to criminal behavior. *International Journal of Offender Therapy & Comparative Criminology 45*, 574–592.

Gold, R., Kennedy, B., Connell, F., & Kawachi, I. (2002). Teen births, income inequality, and social capital: Developing an understanding of the causal pathway. *Health & Place 8*, 77–83.

Grand, T. C., & Dill, L. M. (1999). The effect of group size on the foraging behaviour of juvenile coho salmon: Reduction of predation risk or increased competition? *Animal Behaviour 58*, 443–451.

Griskevicius, V., Tybur, J. M., Ackerman, J. M., Delton, A. W., Robertson, T. E., & White, A. E. (2012). The financial consequences of too many men: Sex ratio effects on saving, borrowing, and spending. *Journal of Personality and Social Psychology 102*, 69–80.

Hamilton, W. D. (1963). The evolution of altruistic behavior. *American Naturalist 97*, 354–356.

Hamilton, W. D. (1964). The genetical evolution of social behaviour. *Journal of Theoretical Biology 7*, 1–16.

Harris, G. T., Rice, M. E., & Lalumière, M. L. (2001). Criminal violence: The roles of neurodevelopmental insults, psychopathy, and antisocial parenting. *Criminal Justice and Behavior 28*, 402–426.

Heath, C., Larrick, R. P., & Wu, G. (1999). Goals as reference points. *Cognitive Psychology 38*, 79–109.

Hill, S. E., & Buss, D. M. (2010). Risk and relative social rank: Positional concerns and risky shifts in probabilistic decision-making. *Evolution and Human Behavior 31*, 219–226.

Hirschi, T. (1994). The generality of deviance. In T. Hirschi & M. R. Gottfredson (Eds.), *The generality of deviance* (pp. 1–22). Transaction Publishers.

Hurly, A. T. (2003). The twin threshold model: Risk-intermediate foraging by rufous hummingbirds, *Selasphorus rufus*. *Animal Behaviour 66*, 751–761.

Hvide, H. (2002). Tournament rewards and risk taking. *Journal of Labor Economics 20*, 877–898.

Jones, A. G., & Ratterman, N. L. (2009). Mate choice and sexual selection: What have we learned since Darwin? *Proceedings of the National Academy of Sciences 106*, 10001–10008.

Kacelnik, A., & Bateson, M. (1997). Risk-sensitivity: Crossroads for theories of decision-making. *Trends in Cognitive Sciences 1*, 304–309.

Kacelnik, A., & El Mouden, C. (2013). Triumphs and trials of the risk paradigm. *Animal Behaviour 86*, 1117–1129.

Kahneman, D. (1992). Reference points, anchors, norms, and mixed feelings. *Organizational Behavior and Human Decision Processes 51*, 296–312.

Kahneman, D. (2017). *Thinking, fast and slow*. Farrar, Straus, and Giroux.

Kaplan, H., & Gangestad, S. (2005). Life history theory and evolutionary psychology. In D. M. Buss (Ed.), *The Handbook of Evolutionary Psychology* (pp. 68–95). John Wiley & Sons.

Kenrick, D. T., Griskevicius, V., Neuberg, S. L., & Schaller, M. (2010). Renovating the pyramid of needs: Contemporary extensions built upon ancient foundations. *Perspectives on Psychological Science 5*, 292–314.

Kilduff, G. J., Elfenbein, H. A., & Staw, B. M. (2010). The psychology of rivalry: A relationally dependent analysis of competition. *Academy of Management Journal 53*, 943–969.

Kilduff, G. J., Galinsky, A. D., Gallo, E., & Reade, J. J. (2015). Whatever it takes to win: Rivalry increases unethical behavior. *Academy of Management Journal 59*, 1508–1534.

Kirkwood, T. B., & Rose, M. R. (1991). Evolution of senescence: Late survival sacrificed for reproduction. *Philosophical Transactions of the Royal Society B 332*(1262), 15–24. http://doi.org/10.1098/rstb.1991.0028.

Knight, F. H. (1921). *Risk, uncertainty, and profit*. Hart, Schaffner, and Marx.

Krupp, D. B., & Cook, T. R. (2018). Local competition amplifies the corrosive effects of inequality. *Psychological Science 29*, 824–833.

Lalumière, M. L., Harris, G. T., Quinsey, V. L., & Rice, M. E. (2005). *The causes of rape: Understanding individual differences in male propensity of sexual aggression*. American Psychological Association.

Leary, M. R. (2005). Sociometer theory and the pursuit of relational value: Getting to the root of self-esteem. *European Review of Social Psychology 16*, 75–111.

Lewin, K. (1935). *A dynamic theory of personality*. McGraw-Hill.

Liu, Z., Elliot, A. J., & Li, Y. (2021). Social comparison orientation and trait competitiveness: Their interrelation and utility in predicting overall and domain-specific risk-taking. *Personality and Individual Differences 171*, 110451.

Luttmer, E. F. P. (2005). Neighbors as negatives: Relative earnings and well-being. *The Quarterly Journal of Economics 120*, 963–1002.

Magee, J. C., & Galinsky, A. D. (2008). Social hierarchy: The self-reinforcing nature of power and status. *The Academy of Management Annals 2*, 351–398.

Maner, J. K., & Ackerman, J. M. (2020). Ecological sex ratios and human mating. *Trends in Cognitive Science 24*, 98–100.

March, J. G., & Shapira, Z. (1992). Variable risk preferences and the focus of attention. *Psychological Review 99*, 172–183.

Maslow, A. H. (1943). A theory of human motivation. *Psychological Review 50*, 370–396.

McGloin, J. M., & Pratt, T. C. (2003). Cognitive ability and delinquent behavior among inner-city youth: a life-course analysis of main, mediating, and interaction effects. *International Journal of Offender Therapy & Comparative Criminology 47*, 253–271.

Mishra, S. (2014). Decision-making under risk: Integrating perspective from biology, economics, and psychology. *Personality and Social Psychology Review 18*(3), 280–307.

Mishra, S., Barclay, P., & Lalumière, M. L. (2014). Competitive disadvantage facilitates risk-taking. *Evolution and Human Behavior 35*, 126–132.

Mishra, S., Barclay, P., & Sparks, A. (2017). The relative state model: Integrating need-based and ability-based pathways to risk-taking. *Personality and Social Psychology Review 21*(2), 176–198.

Mishra, S., Beshai, S., Feeney, J., Iskric, A., & Novakowski, D. (2021). *Perceived disadvantage: Individual differences in the appraisal of unfavorable social comparison.* Manuscript under review.

Mishra, S., & Carleton, R. N. (2017). Use of online crowdsourcing platforms for gambling research. *International Gambling Studies 17*, 125–143.

Mishra, S., & Lalumière, M. L. (2008). Risk taking, antisocial behavior, and life histories. In J. Duntley & T. K. Shackelford (Eds.), *Evolutionary forensic psychology: Darwinian foundations of crime and law* (pp. 176–197). New York: Oxford University Press.

Mishra, S., & Lalumière, M. L. (2010). You can't always get what you want: The motivational effect of need on risk-sensitive decision-making. *Journal of Experimental Social Psychology 46*(4), 605–611.

Mishra, S., & Meadows, T. J. S. (2018). Does stress mediate the association between personal relative deprivation and gambling? *Stress and Health 34*, 331–337.

Mishra, S., & Novakowski, D. (2016). Personal relative deprivation and risk: An examination of individual differences in personality, attitudes, and behavioral outcomes. *Personality and Individual Differences 90*, 22–26.

Mishra, S., Son Hing, L. S., & Lalumière, M. L. (2015). Inequality and risk-taking. *Evolutionary Psychology 13*. https://doi.org/10.1177/1474704915596295.

Mocan, N., & Tekin, E. (2010). Ugly criminals. *The Review of Economics and Statistics 92*, 15–30.

Moffitt, T. E. (1993). Adolescence-limited and life-course-persistent antisocial behavior: A developmental taxonomy. *Psychological Bulletin 100*, 674–701.

Moffitt, T. E. (2003). Life-course-persistent and adolescence-limited antisocial behavior: A 10-year research review and a research agenda. In B. B. Lahey, T. E. Moffitt, & A. Caspi (Eds.), *Causes of conduct disorder and juvenile delinquency* (pp. 49–75). Guilford Press.

Moffitt, T. E., & Caspi, A. (2001). Childhood predictors differential life-course persistent and adolescence-limited antisocial pathways among males and females. *Development and Psychopathology 2*, 355–375.

Moffitt, T. E., Caspi, A., Harrington, H., & Milne, B. J. (2002). Males on the life-course-persistent and adolescence-limited antisocial pathways: Follow-up at age 26 years. *Development and Psychopathology 1*, 179–207.

Neugebauer, R., Hoek, H. W., & Susser, E. (1999). Prenatal exposure to wartime famine and development of antisocial personality disorder in early adulthood. *Journal of the American Medical Association 282*, 455–462.

Novakowski, D., & Mishra, S. (2017). Relative state, social comparison reactions, and the behavioral constellation of deprivation. *Behavioral and Brain Sciences 40*, e335.

Payne, B. K., Brown-Iannuzzi, J. L., & Hannay, J. W. (2017). Economic inequality increases risk taking. *Proceedings of the National Academy of Sciences 114*, 4643–4648.

Pepper, G. V., & Nettle, D. (2017). The behavioral constellation of deprivation: Causes and consequences. *Behavioral and Brain Sciences 40*, e314.

Pleskac, T. J., Conrad, L., Leuker, C., & Hertwig, R. (2021). The ecology of competition: A theory of risk-reward environments in adaptive decision-making. *Psychological Review 128*, 315–335.

Puts, D. (2016). Human sexual selection. *Current Opinion in Psychology 7*, 28–32.

Real, L., & Caraco, T. (1986). Risk and foraging in stochastic environments. *Annual Review of Ecology and Systematics, 17*, 371–390.

Refaie, N., & Mishra, S. (2020). Embodied capital and risk-related traits, attitudes, behaviors, and outcomes: An exploratory examination of attractiveness, cognitive ability, and physical ability. *Social Psychological and Personality Science 11*, 949–964.

Roberts, G. (1998). Competitive altruism: From reciprocity to the handicap principle. *Proceedings of the Royal Society B: Biological Sciences 265*, 427–431.

Room, R. (2005). Stigma, social inequality and alcohol and drug use. *Drug and Alcohol Review 24*, 143–155.

Rosati, A. G., & Hare, B. (2012). Decision making across social contexts: Competition increases preferences for risk in chimpanzees and bonobos. *Animal Behaviour 84*, 869–879.

Rosen, L. H., & Underwood, M. K. (2010). Facial attractiveness as a moderator of the association between social and physical aggression and popularity in adolescents. *Journal of School Psychology 48*, 313–333.

Rubin, P. H., & Paul, C. W. (1979). An evolutionary model of taste for risk. *Economic Inquiry 17*, 585–596.

Scott-Phillips, T. C., Dickins, T. E., & West, S. A. (2011). Evolutionary theory and the ultimate-proximate distinction in the human behavioral sciences. *Perspectives on Psychological Science 6*, 38–47.

Smith, E. A., Bliege Bird, R., & Bird, D. W (2003). The benefits of costly signaling: Meriam turtle hunters. *Behavioral Ecology 14*, 116–126.

Smith, R. H., & Kim, S. H. (2007). Comprehending envy. *Psychological Bulletin 133*, 46–64.

Smith, H. J., Pettigrew, T. F., Pippin, G. M., & Bialosiewicz, S. (2012). Relative deprivation: A theoretical and meta-analytic review. *Personality and Social Psychology Review 16*, 203–232.

Smith, H. J, & Huo, Y. J. (2014). Relative deprivation: How subjective experiences of inequality influence social behavior and health. *Policy Insights from the Behavioral and Brain Sciences 1*, 231–238.

Sommet, N., Elliot, A. J., Jamieson, J. P., & Butera, F. (2018). Income inequality, perceived competitiveness, and approach-avoidance motivation. *Journal of Personality 87*, 767–784.

Spadoni, L., & Potters, J. (2018). The effect of competition on risk-taking in contests. *Games 9*, 72.

Stearns, S. C. (1992). *The evolution of life histories*. Oxford University Press.

Stephens, D. W. (1981). The logic of risk-sensitive foraging preferences. *Animal Behavior 29*, 628–629.

Stephens, D. W., & Krebs, J. R. (1986). *Foraging theory*. Princeton University Press.

Symons, D. (1987). If we're all Darwinians, what's the fuss about? In C. Crawford, M. Smith, & D. Krebs (Eds.), *Sociobiology and psychology* (pp. 121–146). Erlbaum.

Taylor, J. (2003). Risk-taking behavior in mutual fund tournaments. *Journal of Economic Behavior & Organization 50*, 373–383.

To, C., Kilduff, G. J., Ordonez, L., & Schweitzer, M. E. (2018). Going for it on fourth down: Rivalry increases risk taking, physiological arousal, and promotion focus. *Academy of Management Journal 61*, 1281–1306.

Tsetlin, I., Gaba, A., & Winkler, R. L. (2004). Strategic choice of variability in multiround contests and contests with handicaps. *Journal of Risk and Uncertainty 29*, 143–158.

von Rueden, C. R., Lukaszewski, A. W., & Gurven, M. (2015). Adaptive personality calibration in a human society: Effects of embodied capital on prosocial traits. *Behavioral Ecology 26*(4), 1071–1082.

von Neumann, J., & Morgenstern, O. (1944). *Theory of games and economic behavior*. Princeton University Press.

West, S. A., Gardner, A., Shuker, D. M., Reynolds, T., Burton-Chellow, M., Sykes, E. M., Guinne, M. A., & Griffin, A. S. (2006). Cooperation and the scale of competition in humans. *Current Biology 16*, 1103–1106.

West, S. A., Griffin, A. S., & Gardner, A. (2007). Evolutionary explanations for cooperation. *Current Biology 17*, R661–R672.

Wilkinson, R., & Pickett, M. (2007). The problems of relative deprivation: Why some societies do better than others. *Social Science & Medicine 65*, 1965–1978.

Wilkinson, R., & Pickett, M. (2009). *The spirit level: Why more equal societies almost always do better*. Penguin.

Wilson, M., & Daly, M. (1985). Competitiveness, risk taking, and violence: The young male syndrome. *Ethology and Sociobiology 6*, 59–73.

Wilson, M., & Daly, M. (1997). Life expectancy, economic inequality, homicide and reproductive timing in Chicago neighbourhoods. *British Medical Journal 314*, 1271–1274.

Winterhalder, B., Lu, F., & Tucker, B. (1999). Risk-sensitive adaptive tactics: Models and evidence from subsistence studies in biology and anthropology. *Journal of Archaelogical Research 7*, 301–347.

Wohl, M. J. A., Branscombe, N. R., & Lister, J. J. (2014). When the going gets tough: Economic threat increases financial risk-taking in games of chance. *Social Psychological & Personality Science 5*, 211–217.

Wood, J. V. (1996). What is social comparison and how should we study it? *Personality and Social Psychology Bulletin 22*, 520–537.

Zerjal, T., Xue, Y., Bertorelle, G., Wells, R. S., Bao, W., Zhu, S., & Tyler-Smith, C. (2003). The genetic legacy of the Mongols. *American Journal of Human Genetics 72*, 717–721.

PART V

Social-Personality and Organizational Approaches

Social Comparison and Competition: General Frameworks, Focused Models, and Emerging Phenomena

Stephen M. Garcia *and* Avishalom Tor

Abstract

Scholarship in psychology and related fields has been paying increasing attention in recent decades to the ways in which social comparison processes facilitate competitive attitudes, feelings, and behavior. As part of this development, we first advanced the Social Comparison Model of Competition (Garcia et al., 2013)—a general framework that accounted for the role of both individual and situational factors in this area—and later followed it with the more comprehensive Social Comparison Cycle of Competition (Garcia, Reese, et al., 2020). At the same time, researchers have also proposed a number of focused models to account for specific competitive relationships (e.g., rivalry), contexts (e.g., coaction), and more. In light of these important developments, this chapter briefly reviews the key takeaways from our general frameworks of social comparison and competition, demonstrates the insights offered by recognizing how more specific models fit into general frameworks, and illustrates the continued utility of these general frameworks for the study of emerging phenomena, such as social networks or sustainability, from the perspective of social comparison and competition.

Key Words: competition, social comparison, competitive motivation, competitive feelings, decision making, behavioral economics

People's efforts to "keep up with the Joneses" offer one common illustration of how social comparison breeds competition while competition facilitates social comparison in turn. This interplay between social comparison and competition emerges throughout social and organizational life with respect to corporate profitability, sports performance, popularity, income, academic grades, standardized test scores, fashion brands, vacation destinations, travel classes, the square footage of one's home, and more.

This chapter provides an overview of developing frameworks of social comparison and competition and demonstrates their contribution to the ongoing development of research in this field. To this end, the first section reviews two general frameworks—namely, the basic Social Comparison Model of Competition (Garcia et al., 2013) and the more recent, dynamic view of the relationship between social comparison and competition (Garcia,

Reese, et al., 2020). The second section shows how these general frameworks also help situate within the broader literature those more focused models that limit themselves to particular forms of competition (e.g., rivalry, Converse, Reinhard, & Austin, this volume; Kilduff et al., 2010) or to specific psychological processes that affect the relationship between social comparison and competition (e.g., evaluation apprehension, Chen et al., 2021). The third section concludes by illustrating how the developing frameworks of social comparison and competition enrich our understanding of emerging competitive phenomena.

Social Comparison and Competition: Setting the Stage

Leon Festinger's (1954) original formulation of social comparison theory posited that people compare themselves to others in the two broad social domains of opinions and abilities to fulfill their basic need for self-evaluation. In the case of abilities, Festinger posited that we not only seek to evaluate where we stand compared to others, but also experience a "unidirectional drive upward," to improve our relative standing on the underlying performance dimension. Linking social comparison to competitive behavior, he theorized that "competitive behavior, action to protect one's superiority . . . are manifestations in the social process of these pressures" (Festinger, 1954, p. 126). According to this account, competitive behaviors are a manifestation of the social comparison process. If we observe, or even merely anticipate, a difference in performance, we behave competitively to minimize, overcome, or preempt such a gap in performance.

Festinger's early account thus emphasized competitive behaviors as a manifestation of social comparison, and studies showed that these behaviors can range from blatant displays of competitiveness like sabotage, unethical behavior, or uncooperativeness (e.g., Coen, 2006; Mussweiler & Strack, 2000), to more subtle expressions, such as an unwillingness to maximize joint gains, an unkind recommendation, a tendency to sit further away from a competitor (e.g., Graf-Vlachy et al., 2012; Lee & Gino, 2016; Pleban & Tesser, 1981), or even seemingly cooperative behavior that cloaks competitive intentions (e.g., Greenberg, 1932; Tesser, 1988).

Furthermore, later research revealed the relationship between social comparison and competition to be richer in two important respects. First,, social comparison is not only an antecedent of competition but can also be its consequence (Garcia, Reese, et al., 2020). Second, the competitive phenomena that variously follow social comparison and precede it also include psychological processes, such as competitive feelings or competitive motivation, that are not always accompanied by explicit behaviors (e.g., Eisenkraft et al., 2017).

It is thus unsurprising that some researchers have gone so far as to assert that "[a]ll competition does involve social comparison" (Johnson et al., 2012, p. 1072). Even if one does not fully endorse this strong claim, it is clear that the lens of social comparison can help explain and organize a great many findings about the psychology of competition.

General Frameworks of Social Comparison and Competition

We review two general frameworks that describe the relationship between social comparison and competition. The first is the basic Social Comparison Model of Competition (Garcia et al., 2013), which accounts for the role of both individual and situational factors in producing social comparison concerns and thus competitive attitudes, feelings, or behaviors. The second and more recent framework (Garcia, Reese, et al., 2020), which we designate the Social Comparison Cycle of Competition, explores the dynamic role of social comparison before, during, and after the competition. Because we already discuss these two frameworks at length elsewhere, this section only outlines them and briefly illustrates their application to demonstrate their contribution to organizing a broad swath of relevant findings and opening new avenues for research.

The Social Comparison Model of Competition

This framework describes how individual factors, as well as situational factors, impact social comparison and competitive behavior. Individual factors are idiosyncratic psychological variables that vary from person to person, whereas situational factors are features of the environment—that is, the social comparison landscape—that exert their effects on similarly situated individuals.

INDIVIDUAL FACTORS

The individual factors of social comparison include both personal and relational factors.

Personal Factors

Personal factors encompass individual differences in personality as well as the personal relevance of a particular comparison dimension. One's level of competitiveness (see Parks, this volume; Harris & Houston, 2010; Newby & Klein, 2014; Reese et al., 2022) and other related traits (Gibbons & Buunk, 1999) are individual differences that impact the proclivity to make social comparisons and thus to exhibit competitive behavior (Elliot et al., 2018; Liu et al., 2021). Personal factors also include people's attitudes to an underlying performance dimension (Tesser, 1988). If tennis is important to a person but golf is not, that person will exhibit greater social comparison concerns and competitiveness when playing the former than when playing the latter.

Relational Factors

Relational factors concern the interaction between the actor and other individuals targeted by social comparison rather than the actor's interaction with the performance dimension. One important relational factor is the similarity between actor and comparison target (Goethals & Darley, 1977; Wheeler et al., 1997), which can be due to their similar abilities (e.g., how well one plays tennis) or related attributes, like being of the same gender, age, ethnicity, or another self-identity. Similar targets increase social comparison concerns and competitiveness on the part of the actor, while dissimilar targets do not (Festinger, 1954). Another relational factor is the relationship closeness between actor and comparison target. For instance, people who are acquainted are more likely to engage in social comparison and competitive behavior than people who do not know each other (Tesser et al., 1984; Zuckerman & Jost, 2001).

Intertemporal Variability

Notably, besides varying across people, individual factors can also vary over time within the same individual (Arigo et al., 2020; Buunk, Dijkstra, & Bosma, 2020; Van der Zee et al., 2000). What one finds a relevant performance dimension today may be less relevant in the future (e.g., I may lose my interest in tennis). Those that are similar to me at present may not be as similar in the future (e.g., because my tennis game improved significantly with years of practice but theirs did not). And even the degree of closeness a person feels towards a comparison target may wax and wane over time (Tesser, 1988).

SITUATIONAL FACTORS

Whereas individual factors vary across (and even within) individuals, situational factors are features of the social or natural environment that reside outside the person. Situational factors moderate social comparison and thus competitive behavior, feelings, and attitudes. Although the list of situational factors identified by the literature continues to grow, there is already substantial evidence for the role of the factors enumerated here.

Proximity to a Standard and Ranking Effects

Social comparison concerns and the resulting competitive behavior increase with the proximity of meaningful comparison standards, such as the #1 ranking position, last place, or some other qualitative threshold (Chen et al., 2012; Garcia, Arora et al., 2020; Garcia et al., 2006; Garcia & Tor, 2007; Poortvliet et al., 2009; Vriend et al., 2016). The effects of proximity to a standard have been theoretically and empirically linked to social comparison concerns (Garcia et al., 2006; Garcia, Arora, et al., 2020).

In one study, for example, participants in the lab were more likely to sabotage another's performance with a blast of sound if both participants were highly ranked (Poortvliet et al., 2009; see also Hamstra & Schreurs, 2018). Likewise, high-ranking teams in Major League Baseball are less likely to trade players with each other than intermediate and lower-ranking teams (Garcia & Tor, 2007). This pattern also obtains for the movement of players under free agency; it is rare to see a free agent move from one highly-ranked team to another but more common to see such moves among intermediately-ranked teams (Garcia, Arora, et al., 2020). Other manifestations of the competitive consequences of proximity to a standard include an increased likelihood of engaging in unethical behavior and a diminished likelihood of protesting unethical practices in organizations (Kennedy

& Anderson, 2017). Furthermore, the effect of rankings appears to be sufficiently strong to make the nonverbal facial expressions of people who are highly ranked—whether in reality or by random assignment in experiments—appear more competitive than the expressions of those who are intermediately ranked (Chen et al., 2012).

Number of Competitors

The number of competitors has long been known to influence the intensity of competition (e.g., Porter, 1980). Although some have argued that the intensity of competition increases as the number of competitors increases (e.g., Porter's Five Forces Model, 1980), other research has generally shown an opposite pattern of the intensity of competition increasing as the number of competitors decreases (Boudreau et al., 2011; Casas-Arce & Martínez-Jerez, 2009; Ehrenberg & Bognanno, 1990). Yet much of the earlier work in this area conflated the number of competitors with the expected value of winning a competition. For example, research shows that competitive arousal is greater when two people are bidding for the same item in an auction than when eight people are doing so (Ku et al., 2005), which is unsurprising because the expected value of winning and the resulting incentive to compete is substantially greater in the former case than in the latter (expected values of .50 and .125, respectively).

Findings on the *N-Effect* (Garcia & Tor, 2009; Tor & Garcia, 2010), however, demonstrate that the intensity of competition increases as the number of competitors decreases, even when controlling for expected value. To illustrate, participants in one experiment were asked to complete an easy quiz as fast as they could without compromising accuracy and that those finishing in the top-performing 10 percent in their competition pool would get a cash prize. They were then randomly assigned to a competition pool of either 10 competitors (small-*N* competition) or 100 competitors (large-*N* competition). Results showed that participants completed the easy quiz significantly faster in the small-*N* competition than in the large-*N* competition, with additional studies finding that social comparison concerns also decrease with *N* and that social comparison mediates the effects of *N* on competitiveness.

In addition to this experimental evidence, studies suggest that merely being among a few versus many competitors can affect one's competitive motivation and performance. A panel analysis of scores from the Scholastic Aptitude Test, a college entrance exam, found that as the number of test-takers at a given testing venue increased, the average scores of the test-takers tended to decrease, even after controlling for various demographic factors (Garcia & Tor, 2009). More recent evidence is beginning to reveal other competitive implications of the *N-Effect*, including how applicants are more likely to fake or misrepresent themselves in employment interviews when among few versus many competing applicants (Ho et al., 2019) and how employee promotion contests can increase employee effort when held at the division level—with fewer competing employees—rather than at the firm level (Fang et al., 2020).

Social Category Fault Lines

Intergroup competition is prevalent (Belavadi & Hogg, this volume); we are all members of many types of groups—from demographic ones (e.g., based on gender, race, religion, or country) through self-selected groups (e.g., college, company, or private association), to arbitrary groups (like handedness or pogo-stick jumping ability)—that the literature collectively denotes "social categories" or "social category groups" (McGarty, 1999). In terms of competition, the social identity literature (Hogg, 2000; Turner et al., 1979) established that competition between groups from different social categories, namely *inter-category* competition (e.g., Americans versus French), tends to involve greater social comparison concerns and increased competitive behavior compared to competition between two groups that share a social category, or *intra-category* competition (e.g., Americans versus Americans).

In one study involving a hotel vacancy dilemma (Garcia et al., 2005; see also Garcia, Bazerman, et al., 2010), the intra-category condition asked University of Michigan (UM) student participants to imagine traveling with two groups of UM students. Option A was to have all the students stay at a one-star motel, and Option B was to have one group of students (including the participant) stay at a three-star hotel and the other group at a better four-star hotel. In the inter-category condition, the scenario was identical except that one of the traveling groups was from UM (including the participant) and the other group from Harvard, and Option B stipulated that UM students would be staying at the three-star hotel and Harvard students at the four-star hotel. Results showed that UM participants were more likely to choose Option B to maximize hotel quality in the intra-category condition than in the inter-category one, suggesting that competitive positional concerns are greater between groups of different social categories than between the same social categories. Moreover, social category lines can exert similar effects on third-party allocators, who have greater difficulty maximizing recipients' joints gains when such maximization advantages members of one social category over those of another group (Garcia, Bazerman, et al., 2010; Garcia & Miller, 2007).

Incentive Structure

Incentive structures concern the way in which competitions and their payoffs are designed. What are the goals of the competition? Is it winner-take-all? Is it based on a tournament? Research in this vein draws heavily on the literature on goals (see Huang & Lin, this volume) as well as on economics research on competition structure (e.g., Besley & Ghatak, 2005; Isaac & James, 2000; Keck & Karelaia, 2012).

In the realm of achievement goals, performance-approach goals (Poortvliet & Darnon, 2010; Poortvliet et al., 2007; Urdan & Mestas, 2006)—whereby people try to outperform one another—amplify social comparison concerns and intensify competition. Studies in this area manipulate performance goals versus mastery goals—namely, when individuals strive for self-improvement. People with performance goals try to outperform one another, including by attempting to stifle or sabotage the performance of another (e.g., Ordóñez et al., 2009; Poorvliet et al., 2009). For example, among low ranking participants, those who were given performance goals exhibited more thwarting behavior, gave less accurate information to their partners, and were more likely to sabotage a working partner (Poortvliet et al., 2012), compared to those participants who were given mastery goals (Poorvliet et al., 2009). Similar incentive structure effects are found for tournaments—in which relative performance determines whether one remains or exits a competition and so social comparison pressures are heightened—compared to piece-rate payment schemes (Niederle & Vesterlund, 2011; Pillutla & Ronson, 2005).

The Social Comparison Cycle of Competition Model

The Social Comparison Cycle of Competition highlights the dynamic relationship between social comparison and competition, in which social comparison can precede competition ("before"), occur while competition is taking place ("during"), or result from competitive outcomes ("after").

SOCIAL COMPARISON BEFORE THE COMPETITION

Whether people compete depends on a variety of social comparison factors, such as their beliefs regarding their chances of success relative to other competitors (see Dunning, this volume; Tor, 2002, 2016) and their social comparison preferences, such as whether they prefer to be a "big frog in a small pond" or a "small frog in a large pond" (Alicke et al., 2010; Wu et al., 2018; Zell & Alicke, 2010). Even when individuals are placed in an unavoidably competitive setting, their pre-competition state of mind may still depend on *motives* or *individual differences* that are associated with social comparison.

Motives

The fundamental need for self-evaluation (Festinger, 1954; Thornton & Arrowood, 1966; Goethals & Darley, 1977; Trope, 1986) and the "unidirectional drive upward" (Festinger, 1954; Hoffman et al., 1954) are two key motives that underly social comparison processes. Both of these motives can precede competition, affecting both individuals' propensity to enter optional competitive situations and their mindset prior to competition even when they cannot avoid facing it.

Individual Differences

A variety of individual differences that are linked to social comparison, including social comparison orientation (Gibbons & Buunk, 1999), performance-approach goals (Darnon et al., 2012; Summers et al., 2003), trait competitiveness (Houston et al., 2002; Reese et al., 2022), and more also affect people's propensity to compete and the degree to which they will compare their prospects of success to those of potential competitors (Wheeler et al., 1997).

Once a competition has begun, social comparison and its consequences take on additional forms. In the course of competition, social comparison concerns are fueled by various individual (personal and relational) and situational factors—captured by the basic Social Comparison Model of Competition described above—that facilitate competitive behaviors, attitudes, and feelings. Thus, to understand social comparison during the competition, just refer to the section "The Social Comparison Model of Competition."

SOCIAL COMPARISON AFTER THE COMPETITION

Social comparison processes also occur after the competition, where individuals can compare their performance and outcomes to others (see Garcia, Reese, et al., 2020). Importantly, these post-competition comparisons fulfill the fundamental need for self-evaluation. While individual differences, such as one's social comparison orientation (Gibbons & Buunk, 1999), affect the extent to which one engages in social comparisons post-competition, at this stage—when competitive outcomes have already occurred—social comparisons take the form of downward versus upward comparison.

Downward Comparisons

Downward comparisons take place when we compare our superior performance to that of someone who has performed worse than we did. It is well established that downward comparisons—even to imaginary targets (Taylor, 1983)—can boost self-esteem (Brown et al., 2007; Gibbons & Gerrard, 1989) and thus increase satisfaction with one's competitive performance. Post-competition downward comparisons can also lead to competitive status-preserving behaviors to thwart others who might surpass us (Derks et al., 2016; Garcia, Song, et al., 2010). Research also finds that winners of competitions, who face downward comparisons to all other competitors, can succumb to feelings of entitlement, lying, and cheating more frequently following their success (Schurr & Ritov, 2016).

Upward Comparison

Upward comparisons, on the other hand, occur when people compare to the someone who has outperformed them. Although they can inspire future improvements in performance (Higgins, 2011; Wood, 1989) and satisfy the basic need for self-evaluation (Festinger, 1954), upward comparisons on self-relevant tasks can lead to dejection and envy (see Montal-Rosenberg & Moran, this volume; Lange & Crusius, 2015), even malicious envy (van de Ven et al., 2015). An upward comparison can also lead individuals to physically distance themselves from the target of that comparison (Pleban & Tesser, 1981) and sometimes even to exit extant relationships (Tesser, 1988) or even prevent us from becoming friends with someone (Garcia et al., 2019).

Nonetheless, losing a competition does not always feel bad, as suggested by work on "the agony of victory and thrill of defeat" (Larsen et al., 2004); a loss that involves better-than-expected performance can feel more positive than negative. Likewise, counter-factual thinking can impact the valence of upward comparisons. A classic study on Olympic medalists (Medvec et al., 1995) found that silver medalists can feel worse than bronze medalists, despite placing higher. The former were more likely to compare their performance to a counterfactual in which they won the gold medal—with a resulting painful upward comparison—whereas the latter were more likely to compare to a counter-factual in which they won no medal at all that produces satisfaction.

Following competitions, people often make decisions about whether to pursue another round of competition. In some situations, re-entry into competition is unavoidable, while at other times people are free to choose whether to do so. In the latter case, the usual social comparison factors, previously discussed, which apply before the competition remain relevant. For example, estimates of one's potential performance vis-à-vis prospective competitors (Schlösser et al., 2013; Tor, 2002; Wheeler et al., 1997) or the level of competition one wishes to experience to fulfill the need for self-evaluation (Festinger, 1954) can inform such re-entry decisions.

Focused Models of Social Comparison and Competition

The general frameworks of social comparison and competition not only help organize and reveal connections among the diverse strands of research in this field, but also help situate more focused models that address particular forms of competition or specific psychological processes that affect the interaction between social comparison and competition. We illustrate the benefits of situating such focused models within the general frameworks discussed previously by considering, in turn, two models of rivalry (Converse, Reinhard, & Austin, this volume; Kilduff et al., 2010) and a recent model of evaluation apprehension and competition (Chen et al., 2021).

Specific Competitive Relationships: Models of Rivalry

Rivalry is a particular competitive relationship—one in which parties with a shared competitive history repeatedly strive to outdo one another (cf. Converse et al., this volume). The familiarity and ubiquity of rivalrous relationships in many social domains, from sports and politics to academia and business, have led researchers to develop models that specifically address rivalry, such as the relational model of rivalry (Kilduff et al., 2010; Kilduff, 2019) and the more recent social-cognitive approach to rivalry (Converse & Reinhard, 2016; Converse et al., this volume).

The relational model posits that competing individuals, groups, or organizations are more likely to perceive themselves as rivals depending on three relational factors. The first factor is similarity (Kilduff et al., 2010), with rivalry between two competitors tending to increase with their similarity in ability, performance, or other characteristics. A second factor is repeated competition (Kilduff et al., 2010), with rivalry increasing together with the number of past competitions in which competitors previously faced each other. A third factor is the historic competitiveness of the match-up between competitors, such that competitors who have a history of highly competitive match-ups are more likely to experience a higher degree of rivalry than when the history of match-ups is not so competitive (Kilduff et al., 2010).

This relational model, which has been employed to understand rivalry between individuals in lab experiments, real sports teams, and organizations (Kilduff et al., 2010; Kilduff, 2019), fits well within the general frameworks of social comparison and competition described earlier. For instance, the factors of similarity and shared history outlined in the relational model of rivalry are also among the relational factors of the Social Comparison Model of Competition (Garcia et al., 2013). Whereas the relational model of rivalry highlights how these factors increase competitiveness between rivals in particular, however, the broader social comparison model accounts for the general effect of similarity and shared history on the competitiveness of parties irrespective of whether they are rivals.

One immediate benefit of recognizing how the relational model of rivalry fits into the more general Social Comparison Model of Competition is that the latter model identifies additional individual and situational factors that may shape the behavior of rivals beyond the effects of those relational factors that form rivalrous relationships. Take the situational factor of *proximity to a standard and ranking effects*: Highly-ranked rivals should experience a greater degree of competitiveness than rivals who are both intermediately ranked (e.g., Garcia et al., 2006). Likewise, the situational factor of *number of competitors* might also apply to rivalry, in which case rivals who are among fewer competitors would experience more intense rivalry than rivals who compete among many competitors (e.g., Garcia & Tor, 2009; Tor & Garcia, 2010).

We can gain an even richer understanding of rivalrous interactions, moreover, by situating them within the broader Social Comparison Cycle of Competition (Garcia, Reese, et al., 2020). The static Social Comparison Model (Garcia et al., 2013) already highlights the potential role of extra-relational factors on the competition between rivals—that is, on what happens *during* rivals' competition. The dynamic Social Comparison Cycle perspective suggests, however, that what happens before and after the competition more generally may also apply to rivalry. Before the competition, for example, individual differences (e.g., trait competitiveness or social comparison orientation) may influence the propensity of individuals not just to enter competitions but also to develop lasting rivalries. In fact, the same individual difference factors may also contribute to the formation of rivalrous relationships by operating after the competition, leading certain competitors to engage more in social comparisons or to repeatedly seek to re-enter competition.

Furthermore, the insights provided by situating more specific models—like those concerning rivalry—within the broader frameworks of social comparison and competition are not limited to enriching the former, but can advance our understanding of competition more generally, as illustrated by Converse et al.'s (this volume) social-cognitive approach to rivalry. The social-cognitive approach offers a rich account of rivalry that includes not only its origin in a shared competitive history and the relational factors already present in the earlier relational theory of rivalry (Kilduff et al., 2010) but also additional personal and situational factors that contribute to the cognitive elaboration that forms the competitive relational schema of rivalry. In other words, this more recent model consciously draws on the individual and situational factors identified by the static Social Comparison Model of Competition (Garcia et al., 2013) to inform its more elaborate account of rivalry.

At the same time, however, the social-cognitive approach sheds light on some of the processes through which social comparison may facilitate competition more generally beyond rivalry—that is, by activating competitive relational schema, albeit perhaps schema that are less rich or enduring than the schema that undergird rivalrous relationships. In a similar vein, Converse et al.'s (this volume) model distinguishes between competitiveness as the immediate, proximal consequence of rivalry and its more distal behavioral effects with respect to goal pursuit, identity maintenance, or moral decision making. Yet, if some non-rivalrous competitive interactions are sufficiently significant to generate competitive schema, we might also expect them to produce some of those distal effects of rivalry, such as by competitors exhibiting heightened motivation and greater risk taking (goal pursuit) or an increased propensity to engage in unethical behavior.

Thus, placing focused models of rivalry within the broader frameworks of social comparison and competition can enrich both sets of approaches and generate novel, testable hypotheses about the psychology of rivalry in particular and of competitive behavior, its antecedents and consequences more generally.

A Specific Competitive Context: Coaction and Evaluation Apprehension

One emerging perspective on the social comparison process is the *Comparing and Being Compared Framework* (Chen et al., 2021). The novelty of this framework is in highlighting the reciprocal role of evaluation apprehension in social comparison-based competitive motivation when competitors simultaneously compete on some performance dimension. During such competitions, competitors engage in "coaction"—that is, they work on the same task at the same time. For example, in race car driving, whether Formula One or NASCAR, drivers on the road compete to finish the race as fast as possible. Likewise, during informal, often long-lasting competitions, such as garnering the most invitations to barbeques or dinner parties, people simultaneously strive to outperform one another on a recognized metric.

Notably, however, while social comparisons among contestants increase competitive motivation, as the familiar broad frameworks suggest, the study of social comparison in co-active settings in particular has generally confounded the process of comparison with the reciprocal experience of "being compared" among the co-actors. In other words, at the same time that Actor 1 may compare herself to Actor 2 and thus experience an increase in competitive motivation, Actor 2 may also look back at Actor 1, thereby placing Actor

1 in the position of simultaneously "being compared" that may also increase Actor 1's competitive behavior.

Disentangling this confound in the social comparison literature, the Comparing and Being Compared Framework (Chen et al., 2021) illustrates how the two processes—of comparing to others and being compared to by others—contribute to competitive motivation and how competitive motivation is greatest when both processes are activated. While the comparing process is already well-studied, this new model shows that simply "being compared" suffices to augment competitive motivation. We know from the evaluation apprehension literature (Bartis et al., 1988; Cottrell et al., 1968; Seta & Seta, 1992), for instance, that placing people under evaluation can increase performance on an easy task. While this literature typically manipulated evaluation apprehension through the presence versus absence of an audience, Chen et al. (2021) show that evaluation apprehension effects also obtain when one is simply the target of another's social comparison. Moreover, this research demonstrates that the two processes (of comparing and being compared to) can trigger each other. That is, those who compare to others experience a subsequent increase in their evaluation apprehension regarding being compared to, while those being compared to experience an increase in the tendency to compare themselves to others.

This new Comparing and Being Compared Model, which disentangles decades of research on coactive competitions and reveals the inherently reciprocal process of being compared, can be further enriched when situated within the broader frameworks of social comparison and competition. Specifically, insofar as perceptions of being compared to parallel those of active comparison by oneself, we may expect the same *individual (personal and relational)* and *situational factors* that have been shown to moderate social comparison concerns and competitive behavior (Garcia et al., 2013) to exert similar effects on the experience of being compared. If this were the case, factors such as being compared in a relevant domain (a personal factor), by high-similarity competitors (a relational factor), or among highly-ranked competitors (a situational factor), to a name but a few examples, would also increase evaluation apprehension and competitiveness. Indeed, if substantiated, the familiar factors of social comparison and competition may prove to apply to evaluation apprehension and the experience of being compared more generally (e.g., Cottrell, 1972; Harkins, 1987).

Once again, therefore, placing the specific Comparing and Being Compared Framework for the competitive context of coaction within the broader models of social comparison and competition enriches our understanding of that more focused framework and reveals important new avenues for further exploration.

Illuminating Emerging Phenomena: Social Networks and Sustainability

Besides helping organize a variety of extant findings and highlighting important research questions in the field, the general frameworks offered by the static Social Comparison Model of Competition and the dynamic Social Comparison Cycle of Competition can also contribute to our understanding of emerging social phenomena that involve social comparison and competition. This section illustrates this potential contribution with respect to the increasingly important phenomena of social networks and sustainability.

Social Networks

Social network platforms, such as Facebook, Twitter, or Instagram, represent a relatively new and increasingly important domain in which social comparisons and competitive behavior affect the lives of billions of daily users worldwide. While social networks replicate some aspects of offline social connections and interactions, the environment they provide renders social comparisons unavoidable, frequent, and wide ranging. The networks expose their users to an enormous range of potential comparison targets to which they can compare themselves on a variety of metrics, from numbers of followers, to "friends," "likes," and more, as well as with respect to the content of the social information these targets share, including personal profiles, pictures, achievements, experiences, and so on (cf. Appel et al., 2020).

It is unsurprising, therefore, that researchers have started to recognize the potential role of social comparison in shaping the use of social networks and, in particular, in variously mediating and moderating its psychological and behavioral consequences (Verduyn et al., 2020). Some findings have even directly linked social comparison to social network use. To illustrate, a recent study showed that individuals who are prone to social comparison are more likely to be affected by the number of Instagram "likes" (Sanchez-Hernandez et al., 2022) and meta-analyses of studies of Facebook use report a significant association between increased levels of social comparison and user depression (e.g., Yoon et al., 2019).

These and similar findings fit well within our general models of social comparison and competition, which help organize the emerging evidence and reveal fruitful venues for further exploration. The basic Social Comparison Model of Competition identifies a variety of factors—both individual (personal and relational) and situational—that are likely to impact social comparison and competitive behavior for social network users. For example, the role of individual differences (a personal individual factor) in this area is revealed by studies showing that intensity of Facebook use and frequency of social comparison on Facebook are both associated with users' social comparison orientation (e.g., Lee, 2014; Rozgonjuk et al., 2019).

While researchers have devoted substantial attention to individual differences factors, the Social Comparison Model of Competition highlights additional venues for exploration. To illustrate, other personal factors, such as the relevance of the dimension (e.g., an activity or personal attribute) which can be gleaned from information provided by the user, may encourage social network users to engage in increased social comparison on the network with its attendant behavioral consequences. Similar effects may also follow the relational factors of social comparison, leading to increasing social comparison and competitiveness in the face of greater perceived similarity or closeness (e.g., being a Facebook friend) to one's social network comparison targets.

Further insights are suggested by the dynamic Social Comparison Cycle of Competition model, which also considers the role of social comparisons before and after—and not only during—the competition. For example, the dynamic model makes clear that some of the factors that shape the intensity of social comparison during the competition also bear on individuals' tendency to enter the competition—which in the present context can be operationalized as joining and using social networking sites—as illustrated by recent evidence that users' tendency to engage in social comparisons of ability predicted their self-reported social network addiction (Kim et al., 2021).

The framework offered by the dynamic Social Comparison Cycle of Competition also helps relate the emerging evidence on the effects of social network use to the broader social comparison literature. After all, the overwhelming majority of social comparison research examines one-time comparisons, and even the more recent work on rivalry discussed earlier concerns a limited series of competitive interactions over time. Social network use, on the other hand, particularly for the frequent and intense users that exhibit the most significant effects, concerns numerous repeated comparisons over time, with far more than a single target. From the perspective of the model, however, users' repeated return to a competitive environment on social networks can be understood as reentry "after the competition," driven by the same factors that lead individuals to engage in competition to begin with.

Sustainability

Sustainability poses profound challenges to our way of living, affecting entire economic, political, and social systems, as well as governmental, corporate, and organizational structures across the world. These concerns include resource-related issues, such as the supply of fresh water on the backdrop of droughts or the search for alternative sources of fuel given the scarcity and damaging effects of fossil fuels, as well as ethics and human rights challenges, such as the need to design systems better to allocate scarce social resources more efficiently or equitably. Models of social comparison can thus shed light on the processes of competition and cooperation in the development and allocation of resources for a sustainable future.

Although only a handful of studies connect sustainability issues to social comparison theory (e.g., Bruchmann et al., 2021; Doran et al., 2017; Grevet et al., 2010), the models discussed earlier can help inform solutions and system designs to achieve sustainability goals. Given the tension between competition and cooperation in many resource dilemmas (see Arora, Kugler, & Giardini, this volume), social comparison models can help predict when resource dilemmas will be more intractable. For instance, resource dilemmas will likely be more difficult to resolve when there are only a few competing stakeholders than when there are many, as competition increases with a decreasing number of competitors, notwithstanding the greater ease of coordination when there are only a few versus many stakeholders (Van Huyck et al., 1990). Other factors such as social category fault lines may also amplify or diminish competition in resource dilemmas. For example, to the extent that members of OPEC see themselves as belonging to the same social category, they will become more likely to cooperate, above and beyond what one would expect from the reciprocal monitoring processes and regular meetings of the cartel that are already in place (cf. Leslie, 2010; Reeves & Stucke, 2011; Tor, 2014).

While these social comparison factors may account for the decision making and behaviors of the level of groups and organizations (Skarlicki & Kulik, 2005), they first and foremost apply to individual behaviors. For example, research shows that simply providing visual social comparison information on where people stand relative to others with respect to sustainable practices has the potential reduce people's carbon footprint (Grevet et al., 2010). And research on the local dominance effect (Zell & Alicke, 2010) suggests that people will be influenced more by social comparisons to their neighbors—that is, to people in their proximity—than to more distant others or to some abstract average (Klein, 2003).

Moreover, regarding current trends toward gamification—namely, the turning of ordinary tasks into games—social comparison information could also have greater impact on individual sustainable behaviors like recycling, water and energy conservation and use, the promotion of plant-based diets, and more (e.g., Douglas & Brauer, 2021; Mulcahy et al., 2021). Specifically, gamification may be more effective in facilitating sustainable behavior when it incorporates some of the familiar factors of social comparison, such as by setting up smaller competition pools, establishing and communicating rankings (e.g., via leaderboards), encouraging comparisons with more commensurate or proximate competitors (Allcott, 2011; Allcott & Kessler, 2019) or instituting ad-hoc rivalries (e.g., marketing department versus finance department).

The social comparison and competition frameworks can also speak to the plethora of fairness concerns that are inherent in sustainability debates and distribution systems. Achieving sustainable practices often requires sacrifices, and society needs to decide whether these sacrifices are to be shared equally by the stakeholders, on the basis of need, equity, or perhaps efficiency. Because social comparison processes are inevitable when processing differences between the "haves" and "have-nots," our framework can offer some insights into when violations of equality, equity, or need are more likely to be greater. For example, because social comparison concerns are greater amongst fewer than many competitors, we expect that violations of equitable allocations will be greater when there are only a few than when there are many allocation recipients. There is also evidence (Garcia, Bazerman, et al., 2010) that it is more difficult to allocate unequal but profit maximizing payoffs than to allocate equal but less profitable when the allocation recipients belong to different social categories (i.e., different countries, universities, jurisdictions) than the same social category (i.e., same country, same university, same jurisdiction). Of course, one implication is that it might become even more difficult maximize efficiencies, say in the allocation of water rights, when distinct sub-social categories are made salient (i.e., cities) than when the broader inclusive social category is made salient (i.e., county). Needless to say, social comparison and competition frameworks offer important insights on the challenges of sustainability and the pathways to sustainability solutions.

Conclusion

Social comparison theory offers an important perspective on the psychology of competition. While Festinger (1954) linked social comparison processes to the manifestation of competition long ago, several models have since been developed to understand the role of social comparison in the production of competitive feelings, competitive motivation, and competitive behavior. One such model, the Social Comparison Model of Competition (Garcia et al. 2013) distinguishes between the individual-level factors, which vary from person to person, and the situational factors, which affect similarly situated individuals, and describes how these factors amplify social comparison concerns and thus competitive feelings, motivation, and behavior. The Social Comparison Cycle of Competition (Garcia, Reese, et al., 2020) describes and charts the role of social comparison processes before, during, and after the competition. We also review models of rivalry, including the relational model of rivalry (Kilduff et al., 2010) and the social-cognitive approach to rivalry (Converse & Reinhard, 2016; Converse et al., this volume), as well as the Comparing and Being Compared Framework of head-to-head competitions (Chen et al., 2021) and describe how they fit within the social comparison framework of competition. As this literature continues to grow, we also offer substantive areas of future growth, particularly in the study of social networks and the contemporary issue of sustainability.

References

Alicke, M. D., Zell, E., & Bloom, D. L. (2010). Mere categorization and the frog-pond effect. *Psychological Science 21*(2), 174–177. https://doi.org/10.1177/0956797609357718.

Allcott, H. (2011). Social norms and energy conservation. *Journal of Public Economics 95*, 1082–1095.

Allcott, H., & Kessler, J. B. (2019). The welfare effects of nudges: A case study of energy use social comparisons. *American Economic Journal: Applied Economics 11*, 236–276.

Appel, M., Marker, C., & Gnambs, T. (2020). Are social media ruining our lives? A review of meta-analytic evidence. *Review of General Psychology 24*(1), 60–74. https://doi.org/10.1177/1089268019880891.

Arigo, D., Mogle, J. A., Brown, M. M., Pasko, K., Travers, L., Sweeder, L., & Smyth, J. M. (2020). Methods to assess social comparison processes within persons in daily life: A scoping review. *Frontiers in Psychology 10*, Article 2909. https://doi.org/10.3389/fpsyg.2019.02909.

Bartis, S., Szymanski, K., & Harkins, S. G. (1988). Evaluation and performance: A two-edged knife. *Personality and Social Psychology Bulletin 14*(2), 242–251. https://doi.org/10.1177/0146167288142003.

Besley, T., & Ghatak, M. (2005). Competition and incentives with motivated agents. *American Economic Review 95*, 616–636.

Boudreau, K., Lacetera, N., & Lakhani, K. R. (2011). Incentives and problem uncertainty in innovation contests: An empirical analysis. *Management Science 57*(5), 843–863.

Brown, D. J., Ferris, D. L., Heller, D., & Keeping, L. M. (2007). Antecedents and consequences of the frequency of upward and downward social comparisons at work. *Organizational Behavior and Human Decision Processes 102*(1), 59–75. https://doi.org/10.1016/j.obhdp.2006.10.003.

Bruchmann, K., Chue, S. M., Dillon, K., Lucas, J. K., Neumann, K., & Parque, C. (2021) Social comparison information influences intentions to reduce single-use plastic water bottle consumption. *Frontiers in Psychology 12*, 612662.

Buunk, A. P., Dijkstra, P. D., & Bosma, H. A. (2020). Changes in social comparison orientation over the life-span. *Journal of Clinical and Developmental Psychology 2*, 1–11.

Casas-Arce, P., & Martínez-Jerez, F. A. (2009). Relative performance compensation, contests, and dynamic incentives. *Management Science 55*(8), 1306–1320.

Chen, P., Garcia, S. M., Chai, V., & Gonzalez, R. (2021) Comparing and being compared: Synergistic effects of social comparison and evaluation apprehension in competitive motivation. *Advances in Group Processes 38*, 143–164.

Chen, P., Myers, C. G., Kopelman, S., & Garcia, S. M. (2012). The hierarchical face: Higher rankings lead to less cooperative looks. *Journal of Applied Psychology 97*(2), 479–486. https://doi.org/10.1037/a0026308.

Coen, C. A. (2006) Seeking the comparative advantage: The dynamics of individual cooperation in single vs. multiple-team environments. *Organizational Behavior and Human Decision Processes 100*, 145–159.

Converse, B. A., & Reinhard, D. A. (2016). On rivalry and goal pursuit: Shared competitive history, legacy concerns, and strategy selection. *Journal of Personality and Social Psychology 110*(2), 191–213.

Cottrell, N. B., Wack, D. L., Sekerak, G. J., & Rittle, R. H. (1968). Social facilitation of dominant responses by the presence of an audience and the mere presence of others. *Journal of Personality and Social Psychology 9*(3), 245–250. https://doi.org/10.1037/h0025902.

Cottrell, N.B. (1972). Social facilitation. In C. McClintock (Ed.), *Experimental social psychology*. Holt, Rinehart, & Winston.

Darnon, C., Dompnier, B., & Poortvliet, M. P. (2012). Achievement goals in educational contexts: A social psychology perspective. *Social and Personality Psychology Compass 6*(10), 760–771. https://doi.org/10.1111/j.1751-9004.2012.00457.

Derks, B., Van Laar, C., & Ellemers, N. (2016). The queen bee phenomenon: Why women leaders distance themselves from junior women. *The Leadership Quarterly 27*(3), 456–469. https://doi.org/10.1016/j.leaqua.2015.12.007.

Doran, R., Hanss, D., & Øgaard, T. (2017). Can social comparison feedback affect indicators of eco-friendly travel choices? Insights from two online experiments. *Sustainability 9*(2):196. https://doi.org/10.3390/su9020196.

Douglas, B. D., & Brauer, M. (2021). Gamification to prevent climate change: A review of games and apps for sustainability. *Current Opinion in Psychology 42*, 89–94.

Ehrenberg, R. G., & Bognanno, M. L. (1990). Do tournaments have incentive effects? *Journal of Political Economy 98*(6), 1307–1324.

Eisenkraft, N., Elfenbein, H. A., & Kopelman, S. (2017). We know who likes us, but not who competes against us: Dyadic meta-accuracy among work colleagues. *Psychological Science 28*, 233–241.

Elliot, A. J., Jury, M., & Murayama, K. (2018). Trait and perceived environmental competitiveness in achievement situations. *Journal of Personality 86*(3), 353–367. doi:10.1111/jopy.12320.

Fang, D., Noe, T., & Strack, P. (2020). Turning up the heat: The discouraging effect of competition in contests. *Journal of Political Economy 128*, 1940–1975. https://doi.org/10.1086/705670.

Festinger, L. (1954). A theory of social comparison processes. *Human Relations 7*(2), 117–140.

Garcia, S. M., Arora, P., Reese, Z. A., & Shain, M. J. (2020) Free agency and organizational rankings: A social comparison perspective on signaling theory. *Journal of Behavioral and Experimental Economics 89*, 101576.

Garcia, S. M., Bazerman, M. H., Kopelman, S., Tor, A., & Miller, D. T. (2010). The price of equality: Suboptimal resource allocations across social categories. *Business Ethics Quarterly 20*, 75–88.

Garcia, S. M., & Miller, D. T. (2007). Social categories and group preference disputes: The aversion to winner-take-all solutions. *Group Processes & Intergroup Relations 10*(4), 581–593.

Garcia, S. M., Reese, Z. A., & Tor, A., (2020). Social comparison before, during, and after the competition. In J. Suls, R. Collins, & L. Wheeler (Eds.), *Social comparison, judgment and behavior* (pp. 105–142). Oxford University Press.

Garcia, S. M., Song, H., & Tesser, A. (2010). Tainted recommendations: The social comparison bias. *Organizational Behavior and Human Decision Processes 113*(2), 97–101.

Garcia, S. M., & Tor, A. (2007). Rankings, standards, and competition: Task vs. scale comparisons. *Organizational Behavior and Human Decision Processes 102*, 95–108.

Garcia, S. M., & Tor, A. (2009). The N-effect: More competitors, less competition. *Psychological Science 20*, 871–877.

Garcia, S. M., Tor, A., Bazerman, M., & Miller, D. T. (2005). Profit maximization versus disadvantageous inequality: The impact of self-categorization. *Journal of Behavioral Decision Making 18*, 187–198.

Garcia, S. M., Tor, A., & Gonzalez, R. (2006). Ranks and rivals: A theory of competition. *Personality and Social Psychology Bulletin 32*(7), 970–982.

Garcia, S. M., Tor, A., & Schiff, T. M. (2013). The psychology of competition: A social comparison perspective. *Perspectives on Psychological Science 8*, 634–650.

Garcia, S. M., Weaver, K., & Chen, P. (2019) The status signals paradox. *Social Psychological and Personality Science 10*, 690–696.

Gibbons, F. X., & Buunk, B. P. (1999). Individual differences in social comparison: development of a scale of social comparison orientation. *Journal of Personality and Social Psychology 76*(1), 129.

Gibbons, F. X., & Gerrard, M. (1989). Effects of upward and downward social comparison on mood states. *Journal of Social and Clinical Psychology 8*(1), 14–31.

Goethals, G., & Darley, J. (1977). Social comparison theory: An attributional approach. In J. M. Suls & R. L. Miller (Eds.), *Social comparison processes: Theoretical and empirical perspectives* (pp. 259–278). Hemisphere/Halsted.

Graf-Vlachy, L., König, E., & Hungenberg, H. (2012). Debiasing competitive irrationality: How managers can be prevented from trading off absolute for relative profit. *European Management Journal 30*, 386–403.

Greenberg, P. J. (1932). Competition in children: An experimental study. The *American Journal of Psychology 44*, 221–248.

Grevet, C., Mankoff, J., & Anderson, S. D. (2010). Design and evaluation of a social visualization aimed at encouraging sustainable behavior. 43rd Hawaii International Conference on System Sciences, pp. 1–8, doi:10.1109/HICSS.2010.135.

Hamstra, M. W., & Schreurs, B. (2018). Room for advancement: The regulatory fit of bottom-rank intermediate feedback. *European Journal of Social Psychology 48*, 890–896.

Harkins, S. G. (1987). Social loafing and social facilitation. *Journal of Experimental Social Psychology 23*(1), 1–18.

Harris, P. B., & Houston, J. M. (2010). *Psychological Reports 106*(3), 870–874.

Higgins, E. T. (2011). *Beyond pleasure and pain: How motivation works*. Oxford University Press.

Ho, J. L., Powell, D. M., Barclay, P., & Gill, H. (2019). The influence of competition on motivation to fake in employment interviews. *Journal of Personnel Psychology 18*(2), 95–105. https://doi.org/10.1027/1866-5888/a000222.

Hoffman, P. J., Festinger, L., & Lawrence, D. H. (1954). Tendencies toward group comparability in competitive bargaining. *Human Relations 7*(2), 141–159.

Hogg, M. A. (2000). Social identity and social comparison. In J. Suls, & L. Wheeler (Eds.), *Handbook of social comparison: Theory and research* (pp. 401–421). Kluwer Academic/Plenum Publishers.

Houston, J. M., Mcintire, S. A., Kinnie, J., & Terry, C. (2002). A factorial analysis of scales measuring competitiveness. *Educational and Psychological Measurement 62*(2), 284–298.

Isaac, R., & James, D. (2000). Just who are you calling risk averse? *Journal of Risk and Uncertainty 20*, 177–187.

Johnson, D. W., Johnson, R. T., & Roseth, C. J. (2012). Competition and performance: More facts, more understanding? Comment on Murayama and Elliot (2012). *Psychological Bulletin 138*(6), 1071–1078. https://doi.org/10.1037/a0029454.

Keck, S., & Karelaia, N. (2012). Does competition foster trust? The role of tournament incentives. *Experimental Economics 15*, 204–228.

Kennedy, J. A., & Anderson, C. (2017). Hierarchical rank and principled dissent: How holding higher rank suppresses objection to unethical practices. *Organizational Behavior and Human Decision Processes 139*, 30–49. https://doi.org/10.1016/j.obhdp.2017.01.002.

Kilduff, G. J. (2019). Interfirm relational rivalry: Implications for competitive strategy. *Academy of Management Review 44*, 775–799.

Kilduff, G. J., Elfenbein, H. A., & Staw, B. M. (2010). The psychology of rivalry: A relationally dependent analysis of competition. *Academy of Management Journal 53*(5), 943–969.

Kim, H., Schlicht, R., Schardt, M., & Florack, A. (2021). The contributions of social comparison to social network site addiction. *PLoS One 16*(10), e0257795.

Klein, W. M. P. (2003). Effects of objective feedback and "single other" or "average other" social comparison feedback on performance judgments and helping behavior. *Personality and Social Psychology Bulletin 29*, 418–429.

Ku, G., Malhotra, D., & Murnighan, J. K. (2005). Towards a competitive arousal model of decision-making: A study of auction fever in live and Internet auctions. *Organizational Behavior and Human Decision Processes* *96*(2), 89–103.

Larsen, J. T., McGraw, A. P., Mellers, B. A., & Cacioppo, J. T. (2004). The agony of victory and thrill of defeat: Mixed emotional reactions to disappointing wins and relieving losses. *Psychological Science 15*, 325–330.

Lange, J., & Crusius, J. (2015). The tango of two deadly sins: The social-functional relation of envy and pride. *Journal of Personality and Social Psychology 109*(3), 453–472. https://doi.org/10.1037/pspi0000026.

Lee, S. Y. (2014). How do people compare themselves with others on social network sites? The case of Facebook. *Computers in Human Behavior 32*, 253–260. https://doi.org/10.1016/j.chb.2013.12.009.

Liu, Z., Elliot, A. J., & Li, Y. (2021). Social comparison orientation and trait competitiveness: Their interrelation and utility in predicting overall and domain-specific risk-taking. *Personality and Individual Differences 171*, 110451.

Lee, J. J., & Gino, F. (2016). Envy and interpersonal corruption: Social comparison processes and unethical behavior in organizations. In R. H. Smith, U. G. O. Merlone, & M. K. Duffy (Eds.), *Envy at work and in organizations* (pp. 347–372). Oxford University Press.

Leslie, C. R. (2010). Rationality analysis in antitrust. *University of Pennsylvania Law Review 158*, 261–353.

McGarty, C. (1999). *Categorization in social psychology.* Sage.

Medvec, V. H., Madey, S. F., & Gilovich, T. (1995). When less is more: Counterfactual thinking and satisfaction among Olympic medalists. *Journal of Personality and Social Psychology 69*(4), 603.

Mulcahy, R. F., McAndrew, R., Russell-Bennett, R., & Iacobucci, D. (2021). "Game on!" Pushing consumer buttons to change sustainable behavior: A gamification field study. *European Journal of Marketing 55*, 2593–2619.

Mussweiler, T., & Strack, F. (2000). Consequences of social comparison. In J. Suls & L. Wheeler (Eds.), *Handbook of social comparison* (pp. 253–271). Springer.

Newby, J. L., & Klein, R. G. (2014). Competitiveness reconceptualized: Psychometric development of competitiveness orientation measure as a unified measure of trait competitiveness. *The Psychological Record, 64*, 879–895.

Niederle, M., & Vesterlund, L. (2011). Gender and competition. *Annual Review of Economics 3*, 601–630.

Ordóñez, L. D., Schweitzer, M. E., Galinsky, A. D., & Bazerman, M. H. (2009). Goals gone wild: The systematic side effects of overprescribing goal setting. *Academy of Management Perspectives 23*(1), 6–16.

Pillutla, M. M., & Ronson, S. (2005, August). Do we prefer coworkers who are better or worse than us? Evidence from the "Weakest Link" game. Paper presented at the meeting of the Academy of Management, Honolulu, HI.

Pleban, R., & Tesser, A. (1981). The effects of relevance and quality of another's performance on interpersonal closeness. *Social Psychology Quarterly 44*(3), 278. https://doi.org/10.2307/3033841.

Poortvliet, P. M., Anseel, F., Janssen, O., Van Yperen, N. W., & Van de Vliert, E. (2012). Perverse effects of other-referenced performance goals in an information exchange context. *Journal of Business Ethics 106*(4), 401–414. https://doi.org/10.1007/s10551-011-1005-8.

Poortvliet, P. M., & Darnon, C. (2010). Toward a more social understanding of achievement goals: The interpersonal effects of mastery and performance goals. *Current Directions in Psychological Science 19*, 324–328.

Poortvliet, P. M., Janssen, O., Van Yperen, N. W., & Van de Vliert, E. (2007). Achievement goals and interpersonal behavior: How mastery and performance goals shape information exchange. *Personality and Social Psychology Bulletin 33*(10), 1435–1447. https://doi.org/10.1177/0146167207305536.

Poortvliet, P. M., Janssen, O., Van Yperen, N. W., & Van de Vliert, E. (2009). Low ranks make the difference: How achievement goals and ranking information affect cooperation intentions. *Journal of Experimental Social Psychology 45*, 1144–1147.

Porter, M. E. (1980). *Competitive strategy: Techniques for analyzing industries and competitors.* Free Press.

Reese, Z. A., Garcia, S. M., & Edelstein, R. S. (2022). More than a game: Trait competitiveness predicts motivation in minimally competitive contexts. *Personality and Individual Differences 185*, 111262.

Reeves, A. P., & Stucke, M. E. (2011). Behavioral antitrust. *Indiana Law Journal 86*, 1527–1586.

Rozgonjuk, D., Ryan, T., Kuljus, J. K., Täht, K., & Scott, G. G. (2019). Social comparison orientation mediates the relationship between neuroticism and passive Facebook use. *Cyberpsychology: Journal of Psychosocial Research in Cyberspace 13*(1), 2. https://doi.org/10.5817/CP2019-1-2.

Sanchez-Hernandez, M. D., Herrera, M. C., & Exposito, F. (2022). Does the number of likes affect adolescents' emotions? The moderating role of social comparison and feedback-seeking on Instagram. *Journal of Psychology 156*, 200–223.

Schlösser, T., Dunning, D., Johnson, K. L., & Kruger, J. (2013). How unaware are the unskilled? Empirical tests of the "signal extraction" counterexplanation for the Dunning-Kruger effect in self-evaluation of performance. *Journal of Economic Psychology 39*, 85–100. http://dx.doi.org/10.1016/j.joep.2013.07.004.

Schurr, A., & Ritov, I. (2016). Winning a competition predicts dishonest behavior. *Proceedings of the National Academy of Sciences 113*(7), 1754–1759. https://doi.org/10.1073/pnas.1515102113.

Seta, C. E., & Seta, J. J. (1992). Observers and participants in an intergroup setting. *Journal of Personality and Social Psychology 63*(4), 629–643.

Skarlicki, D. P., & Kulik, C. T. (2005). Third-party reactions to employee (mis)treatment: A justice perspective. In B. M. Staw & R. M. Kramer (Eds.), *Research in organizational behavior: An annual series of analytical essays and critical reviews* (Vol. 26, pp. 183–229). Elsevier Science/JAI Press.

Summers, J. J., Schallert, D. L., & Muse Ritter, P. (2003). The role of social comparison in students' perceptions of ability: An enriched view of academic motivation in middle school students. *Contemporary Educational Psychology 28*(4), 510–523. https://doi.org/10.1016/S0361-476X(02)00059-0.

Taylor, S. E. (1983). Adjustment to threatening events: A theory of cognitive adaptation. *American Psychologist 38*, 1161–1173.

Tesser, A. (1988). Toward a self-evaluation maintenance model of social behavior. In L. Berkowitz (Ed.), *Advances in experimental social psychology* (Vol. 21, pp. 181–227). Academic Press.

Tesser, A., Campbell, J., & Smith, M. (1984). Friendship choice and performance: Self-evaluation maintenance in children. *Journal of Personality and Social Psychology 46*, 561–574.

Thornton, D. A., & Arrowood, A. J. (1966). Self-evaluation, self-enhancement, and the locus of social comparison. *Journal of Experimental Social Psychology Supplement 1*, 40–48.

Tor, A. (2002). The fable of entry: Bounded rationality, market discipline, and legal policy. *Michigan Law Review 101*, 482–568.

Tor, A. (2014). Understanding behavioral antitrust. *Texas Law Review 92*, 574–667.

Tor, A. (2016). Boundedly rational entrepreneurs and antitrust. *Antitrust Bulletin 61*(4), 520–540.

Tor, A., & Garcia, S. M. (2010). The N-Effect: Beyond probability judgments. *Psychological Science 21*(5), 748–749. https://doi.org/10.1177/0956797610368813.

Trope, Y. (1986). Self-enhancement and self-assessment in achievement behavior. In *Handbook of motivation and cognition: Foundations of social behavior* (pp. 610–639). Guilford Press.

Turner, J. C., Brown, R. J., & Tajfel, H. (1979). Social comparison and group interest in ingroup favoritism. *European Journal of Social Psychology 9*, 187–204.

Urdan, T., & Mestas, M. (2006). The goals behind performance goals. *Journal of Educational Psychology 98*(2), 354–365. https://doi.org/10.1037/0022-0663.98.2.354.

van de Ven, N., Hoogland, C. E., Smith, R. H., van Dijk, W. W., Breugelmans, S. M., & Zeelenberg, M. (2015). When envy leads to schadenfreude. Cognition and Emotion 29(6), 1007–1025. https://doi.org/10.1080/02699931.2014.961903.

Van der Zee, K., Buunk, B., Sanderman, R., Botke, G., & van den Bergh, F. (2000). Social comparison and coping with cancer treatment. *Personality and Individual Differences 28*(1), 17–34. https://doi.org/10.1016/S0191-8869(99)00045-8.

Van Huyck, J. B., Battalio, R. C., & Beil, R. O. (1990). Tacit coordination games, strategic uncertainty, and coordination failure. *American Economic Review 80*(1), 234–248.

Verduyn, P., Gugushvili, N., Massar, K., Täht, K., & Kross, E. (2020). Social comparison on social networking sites. *Current Opinion in Psychology 36*, 32–37. https://doi.org/10.1016/j.copsyc.2020.04.002.

Vriend, T., Jordan, J., & Janssen, O. (2016). Reaching the top and avoiding the bottom: How ranking motivates unethical intentions and behavior. *Organizational Behavior and Human Decision Processes 137*, 142–155. https://doi.org/10.1016/j.obhdp.2016.09.003.

Wheeler, L., Martin, R., & Suls, J. (1997). The proxy model of social comparison for self-evaluation of ability. *Personality and Social Psychology Review 1*, 54–61.

Wood, J. V. (1989). Theory and research concerning social comparisons of personal attributes. *Psychological Bulletin 106*(2), 231–248.

Wu, K., Garcia, S. M., & Kopelman, S. (2018). Frogs, ponds, and culture: Variations in entry decisions. *Social Psychological and Personality Science 9*, 99–106.

Yoon, S., Kleinman, M., Mertz, J., & Brannick, M. (2019). Is social network site usage r related to depression? A meta-analysis of Facebook-depression relations. *Journal of Affective Disorders 248*, 65–72.

Zell, E., & Alicke, M. D. (2010). The local dominance effect in self-evaluation: Evidence and explanations. *Personality and Social Psychology Review 14*, 368–384.

Zuckerman, E. W., & Jost, J. T. (2001). What makes you think you're so popular? Self-evaluation maintenance and the subjective side of the "Friendship Paradox." *Social Psychology Quarterly 64*(3), 207–223. https://doi.org/10.2307/3090112.

Psychology of Rivalry:
A Social-Cognitive Approach to
Competitive Relationships

Benjamin A. Converse, David A. Reinhard, *and* Maura M.K. Austin

Abstract

Many of the most important competitions in business, politics, sports, and day-to-day social life occur not between strangers who happen to have negatively linked goals, but between parties who have a shared history of notable competitions—that is, between rivals. Despite psychology's long and rich history of studying competition, the concerted study of rivalry has only been underway for about a decade. This chapter seeks to organize existing rivalry research and guide future investigations by proposing a causal theory that positions shared competitive history as the origin of rivalry; cognitive elaboration as the driving process in the formation of rivalry; a competitive relational schema as the social-cognitive construct that defines rivalry; an expansive view of competition as the proximal consequence of activating rivalry; and behavioral effects with respect to goal pursuit, identity maintenance, and moral decision-making as distal consequences. The first two sections review the seminal development of a relational approach to rivalry and acknowledge empirical challenges in drawing causal conclusions about rivalry. The next three sections describe the proposed causal model, linking a shared competitive history to behavioral consequences as a result of the competitive relational schema. The final sections discuss open questions and opportunities for the future of rivalry research.

Key Words: rivalry, competition, relationships, schemas, motivation, goal pursuit, decision making

The man arrives at his appointment at the usual time. He settles into the chair that he likes in the corner of the room. The doctor offers a warm smile, "Shall we jump right back to where we left off last week?" The man agrees, "I've been thinking about what you asked, Doc, and I think it's right. I am more competitive with him than I am with anyone else. Even over small things, I just immediately feel like I want to beat him. For some reason, it just matters more because it's him. I guess I use him as some kind of measuring stick. I know where I stand compared to him." The man adjusts his focus from the doctor to the window over the doctor's shoulder and gazes out, "It's hard to explain, but it feels like it's never about just this one thing. I don't want to beat him just because of today, it feels bigger than that." The man continues to look out the window. The doctor pauses to see if the man is going to pick back up but he does not. The doctor looks up from the notepad, "The enduring competitive connection, the inflated sense of importance . . . " The man looks from the window to the doctor and the doctor continues, "I believe you are dealing with a case of rivalry."

Beyond the stakes that will be afforded the winner, beyond even the experience of triumphing in a particular event, some competitions seem to matter more because of *whom* they are against. Indeed, many of the most important competitions in business, politics, sports, and day-to-day social life occur not between strangers who happen to have negatively linked goals, but between parties who have a shared history of notable competitions—that is, between rivals. In contrast to "mere competitions," which are a purely structural arrangement (Deutsch, 1949), rivalry is a subjective, relational construct that exists in an individual's mind as a competitive relational schema and persists beyond any specific competitive episode (Converse & Reinhard, 2016; Kilduff et al., 2010).

Working with rivalry as a social-psychological construct involves an inherent tension. On one hand, rivalry lies at the intersection of relationships, goal pursuit, and competition; three concepts at the heart of social psychology. From a phenomenological perspective, few ideas could be considered more social-psychological. On the other hand, rivalry is not a convenient construct for the standard social-psychological approach. It is a social idea that individuals intuitively understand; but its complexity and subjectivity can tempt an unproductive "know-it-when-you-see-it" approach to theorizing and study. Thus, it is useful to be precise in the conceptualization and empirical documentation of what is essential to rivalry versus merely associated with rivalry.

This chapter responds to these challenges by presenting a model of rivalry whose structure was inspired by an unlikely source, an influential model of hopelessness depression (Abramson et al., 1989). The analogy and the opening dramatization are not meant to imply that rivalry is a clinical disorder—nor to make light of clinical disorders—but to illustrate that, structurally, there is theoretical value in applying a similarly structured model to a different cognitive schema and its consequences. Like rivalry behavior, hopelessness depression is intuitively recognizable, yet complex and subjective; also like rivalry behavior, its proximal sufficient cause is a schema through which affected individuals interpret their social landscape.

We borrow and capitalize on three features of the hopelessness-depression model that are particularly useful for describing rivalry. First, like the original, our model centers on a complex but describable cognitive schema—here, a *competitive relational schema*—that serves as a sufficient cause of the relevant experiences and behaviors of the actor. According to the model, the defining social-cognitive feature of rivalry is a mental model of an enduring competitive connection with a specific competitor. The proximal consequence of forming and then activating this schema is *competitive expansion*, the impression that interactions with (or with respect to) the rival have more and broader implications for the self, which in turn modulates behavior in a variety of ways. Second, our model refers to those behavioral consequences as a profile of symptoms. These symptoms are not unique to rivalry, but rivalry should guarantee them (i.e., rivalry is sufficient but not necessary for the consequences). A competition between rivals (versus non-rivals) should guarantee a heighted sense of competition, for example, but a heightened sense of competition does not guarantee the presence of rivalry because it could also be attributable to high stakes or other conditions that may be present in mere competition. Third, our model identifies more distal "contributory causes" (or moderators) of the symptoms of rivalry. These contributory factors do not guarantee the occurrence of rivalry behavior, but they increase the likelihood of rivalry (i.e., the competitive relational schema) forming and therefore promote the relevant behavioral consequences. Our goal in presenting this social-cognitive model is to help arrange a variety of associated constructs into an articulated and testable causal chain. We will highlight the best available evidence for each causal link in the model; we will also highlight areas where the evidence is weak, indirect, or non-existent.

One conceptual challenge that looms over this area is the varied uses of the term "rival" or "rivalry." Within psychology, some authors have used it as a livelier synonym for the term "competitor"; and others have used it in a more relational sense, but with stronger emphasis on acrimonious feelings and interaction (e.g., Lee, 1985; Yip et al., 2018). Outside of psychology, especially in political science, economics, business, and sports management research, rivalry is often defined from a structural point of view, based on the number or nature of previous interactions (e.g., Chen, 1996; Colaresi et al., 2008; Kilduff, 2019; see also Haran & Bereby-Myer, *this volume*; Porac et al., 1995). Our goal in this chapter is not to provide a comprehensive list of these conceptualizations (see Kilduff, 2019; Kilduff et al., 2010; Tyler & Cobbs, 2017), nor to adjudicate whose definition has rights to the term; but we hope that our emphasis on the competitive relational schema as the definitive construct makes clear which theoretical and empirical work informs the current account and which informs relevant but separate issues.

We divide the chapter into six parts. The first section (*Rivalry in Nature*) describes the seminal research that empirically documented rivalry as an identifiable and systematic relational phenomenon, thereby stimulating a new area of research spanning competition, relationships, and goal pursuit. The second section (*An Empirical Caveat*) briefly acknowledges empirical challenges for the research area and corresponding limitations of the model. The third section (*What Rivalry Is*) identifies the competitive relational schema as the definitive social-cognitive marker of rivalry. The fourth section (*The Formation of Rivalry*) positions the competitive relational schema as a proximal sufficient cause of the symptoms of rivalry and describes how social-comparison concerns modulate actors' reflection on their shared competitive history with a potential rival. The fifth section (*What Rivalry Does*) aims to organize and explain the documented consequences of rivalry and to guide the search for new consequences. The sixth section (*Competitive Relational Dynamics*) identifies some exciting challenges and opportunities for the future of rivalry research. Though it is relegated to the background from here, we note that the structure of the chapter, the design of the model, and many of the organizational terms are imported directly from the influential model of hopelessness depression described by Abramsom et al. (1989). We hope to do justice in applying their level of precision to distinguishing between necessary, sufficient, and contributory causes; here to illuminate implications for competitive relationships.

Rivalry in Nature: Establishing Rivalry as a Psychological Construct

The cornerstone of a psychological approach to rivalry can be found in Kilduff et al.'s (2010; Kilduff, 2014) relational treatment of the topic. Until their work, insight into the nature and consequences of rivalry had to be extrapolated from research that examined isolated components of rivalry, such as the nature and number of previous interactions (Chen, 1996; Johnson et al., 2006; Klein et al., 2006), the expectation of future inter- action (Axelrod, 1984; Heide & Miner, 1992; Murnighan & Roth, 1983; Rand et al., 2009), the degree of similarity (Festinger, 1954; Rijsman, 1974; Seta, 1982; Tesser, 1988), or relative status (Garcia et al., 2006). None of these dimensions on its own captures the richness of rivalry, but it is not obvious how to account for that richness. The relational analysis by Kilduff and colleagues (2010) was the first to empirically document that there was *something* there—some systematic variance in competitive relationships.

To declare some unique rivalrous property between two parties, a researcher must be able to point to some marker of uniquely heightened competitiveness that one party (the "actor") feels for a target. The social relations model (Kenny, 1994; Kenny & La Voie, 1984) allows for precisely this analysis, operationalizing the "unique" component as dyadic variance. It allows researchers to ask, for example, whether Earvin feels uniquely competitive with Larry: To qualify as unique, Earvin's competitive feelings about Larry must be stronger than his competitive feelings about third parties (as opposed to Earvin just being hypercompetitive); *and* Earvin's competitive feelings about Larry must be stron- ger than third parties' feelings about Larry (as opposed to Larry just being the target of everyone's competitiveness).

Employing a round-robin design in the context of NCAA basketball, Kilduff and colleagues (2010) recruited sportswriters from 73 universities with major-conference Division I Men's Basketball programs. The participants therefore had expertise on their own team in relation to other teams throughout the network. Reporters rated the extent to which they (as representatives of their team) viewed each other team as a rival (from *not a rival* to *fierce rival*). Indicative of a uniquely relational effect, approximately half of the variance in rivalry ratings was found to be a dyadic effect, with raters reliably reserv- ing their highest rivalry ratings for certain other teams. The social relations analysis of rivalry thus indicates that there is some *there*. Engaged observers of the respective sports programs could reliably point to specific conference competitors as being stronger rivals than others, beyond measurement error, beyond any personal tendencies to have a more competitive view of others, and beyond any shared tendencies to point to a given target as rivals of everyone.

Furthering the construct validity, this research also supported two critical follow-up hypotheses. First, using archival data, the researchers documented that the so-called rivalry relationships were associated with predictable antecedents. Dyads with stronger rivalries tended to be more similar (operationalized as geographic proximity, historic status, and general university characteristics), to have greater historical parity (operationalized as head-to-head winning percentages), and to have had more exposure to one another (operationalized as the number of past meetings). This shows that rivalry can be detected where it ought to be.

Second, the researchers documented hints of an association between rivalry strength and motivation in head-to-head competitions, operationalized as effort-based defensive performance (so-called "hustle plays" like blocked shots). This latter finding was substantially bolstered in follow-up work that showed an association between rivalry strength and motivation-based performance, controlling for covariates, including tangible stakes, negative feelings, and similarity (Kilduff, 2014). This foundational work therefore showed that people recognize something special in certain competitive matchups and, critically for a psychology of rivalry, that it can be reliably measured and predicted.

The relational approach described rivalry as "a subjective competitive relationship that an actor has with another actor that entails increased psychological stakes of competition for the focal actor, independent of the objective characteristics of the situation" (Kilduff et al., 2010, p. 945). Three critical guiding characteristics are included in this description. First, rivalry is a subjective perception of the target. It resides in the actor's mind, not in any objective feature of the situation (Deutsch, 1949). An actor may be more likely to feel rivalry with a similar target, for example, but similarity does not ensure rivalry. Second, rivalry requires history. Negatively linked goals in a given moment are not sufficient. Third, rivalry increases the importance of a competition beyond its given stakes. Rivalry is in some way about more than *this* competition. The social-cognitive view that followed (Converse & Reinhard, 2016; Kilduff & Galinsky, 2017), and that is elaborated in this chapter, builds directly on these empirical and theoretical foundations.

An Empirical Caveat

Before expanding on the proposed model, we must note that little rivalry research to this point has directly measured or manipulated features of the core construct, the competitive relational schema. Research focused on the formation (or antecedents) of rivalry has tended to operationalize rivalry as self-reported *rivalry strength* instead. Research focused on the consequences (or symptoms) of rivalry has tended to use some form of idiographic or cohort approach where the participants themselves or knowledgeable third parties identify the "rivals" and "non-rivals." Where the operationalizations of rivalry rely primarily on self-reported rivalry strength or self-nominated rival primes, a major concern is that participants may be using definitions of "rivalry" that are different from those of any theoretical perspective. Just as different research traditions have used rivalry in different ways, so might participants apply different definitions. It is also possible that different study materials, methods, and contexts could introduce systematic differences—for example, some studies might tacitly encourage participants to think of enmity than of a more neutral enduring competitive connection. We highlight those studies where researchers used more precise manipulations and measures, and those where they took additional steps to try to identify the precise ingredients of rivalry; but we note that most studies do not provide direct evidence for the role of the competitive relational schema and thus can be considered only suggestive evidence for the specific causal links in the proposed model.

What Rivalry Is: The Competitive Relational Schema

Heightened competition is perhaps the most familiar sign of rivalry. But if we allow that rivalry is not the only cause of heightened competition, then where does that leave us in trying to identify rivalry? Like a doctor trying to make a diagnosis, we should regard heightened competition as a clue. It can signal that rivalry may be at hand, especially if it cannot be explained by more common observables. But only by verifying the existence of a competitive relational schema could we be sure that the symptom is due to a rivalry. Thus, instead of anchoring on *what rivalry does* (e.g., heightened competition), our model anchors on *what rivalry is*. That anchor is the *competitive relational schema*, which, according to the model, is sufficient to cause a sense of competitive expansiveness (including heightened competition) and which arises from a set of more distal contributory causes. This section begins with a discussion of the schema and then work backwards (to the left in Figure 19.1) to examine more distal causes.

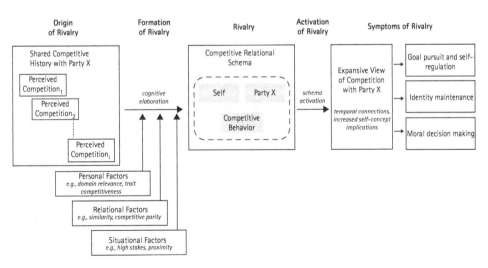

Figure 19.1. Hypothesized causal chain in the social-cognitive approach to rivalry. The competitive relational schema is a working mental model that incorporates representations of the self and the rival competitor with memories, procedural knowledge, goals, plans, and affect that have been relevant to their competitive interactions. It arises from cognitive elaboration of a shared competitive history and manifests as an expansive view of competition.

In our conceptualization, *rivalry, competitive relationship*, and *competitive relational schema* are terms that describe the same idea at different levels of analysis. The schema is the cognitive construct that must be in place for an individual to have the subjective perception of a competitive relationship with another party. In our usage, "rivalry" at a cognitive level *is* the competitive relational schema; and "rivalry" at a social level *is* the competitive relationship. We specify this because, colloquially, "rivalry" is often additionally used to refer to the interaction between rivals (e.g., as shorthand for a competition between rivals) or to associated feelings of competitiveness or enmity within a competition.

A competitive relational schema describes a particular tripartite connection between the three definitional components of a relational schema, a "self-schema" (a mental model guiding how one thinks of the self in the context of the relationship), an "other schema" (a mental model guiding how one thinks of the target in the context of the relationship), and an "interpersonal script" (a mental model guiding how one thinks of the self and other interacting as a unit; Baldwin, 1992). In general, relational schemas are working mental models that incorporate generalizations of the self and other, episodic memories, procedural knowledge, goals, plans, and affect to help people navigate interactions (Bowlby, 1969; Cesario et al., 2006; Higgins, 1987; Horowitz, 1989; Mitchell, 1988; Plaks & Higgins, 2000; Planalp, 1987; Trzebinski, 1985; Schank & Abelson, 1977). Competitive relational schemas generalize from a shared competitive history, and they involve representations of the self and other connected in a chain of competitions (Converse & Reinhard, 2016).

One of our initial rivalry studies, using a comparative cohort design, documented individuals' spontaneous use of the competitive relational schema in interpreting their interactions with a rival versus non-rival competitor (Converse & Reinhard, 2016). Specifically, we examined the free responses of National Football League (NFL) fans who, as part of a priming manipulation designed to activate the schema, had been prompted to describe the nature of their team's interactions with different competitors. The fans had been randomly assigned to one of the two groups, with some asked to discuss interactions with a self-nominated rival and others to discuss interactions with a talented competitor (specifically, the fourth talented competitor that they listed, under the assumption that non-rivals would be less accessible than rivals; Fitzsimons & Shah, 2008; Higgins et al., 1982). In a post-hoc analysis, coders examined the fans' written free-response answers to the question of "why it is important for you to beat the [target team]." Suggesting that participants in the rivalry group had used the competitive relational schema to interpret those interactions, coders found that those participants were more likely to spontaneously refer to specific past meetings or a general shared history as contributing to the importance of current games (see Tyler & Cobbs, 2015, for a descriptive replication of this theme).

Though this cohort design provides an empirical link between the competitive relational schema and what people perceive to be a rivalry relationship, it does not provide evidence for the hypothesized causal role of the schema. Given the centrality of this concept to the model, there is a significant need for corroboration and for continued progress on measuring and manipulating the schema directly. Most of the evidence for the schema concept, as we will discuss in the next section, comes from research on the origins and formation of rivalry. Generally speaking, we infer that the schema is there because it appears where it "ought to" based on principles of cognitive elaboration and social-information processing.

Future studies would also benefit from methods that divorce the manipulation of rivalry from any mention of rivalry, a methodological feature that almost none of the reviewed studies has. One elegant study provides a blueprint for such methods going forward (Kilduff & Galinsky, 2017). In this experiment, researchers artificially created a sense of rivalry—that is, the beginnings of a competitive relational schema—among some participants by running them through a series of repeated, closely contested competitions against a single competitor (rather than a series of less closely contested competitions against a rotating cast of competitors). Though the schema was not assessed directly and can only be inferred, participants in the first condition reported a stronger sense of rivalry in the task. As part of a multi-method approach, manipulations like this one can help to provide causal clarity. Avoiding any mention of "rivals" or "rivalry" in the relevant condition (as well as the control condition) would ensure that the symptoms follow directly from the schematic properties rather than from participants' assumptions or generalizations about how one is expected to behave in a rivalry.

Finally, it is important to note that the schema conceptualization implies that rivalry persists and may have consequences even outside of head-to-head competitions. The competitive relational schema may or may not be active in one's mind at any given moment; but its activation and effects do not require a structurally-defined competition. Training montages in sports movies often depict this idea when they show an athlete gritting his or her way through practice repetitions while thinking of the rival. We do not know of any studies that have documented this effect, but the presumed tripartite connection between actor, competitor, and competition predicts this kind of priming effect. Research has, however, shown that a rival's successful performance against a third-party can motivate the actor to increase his or her own competitive performance (Pike et al., 2018). Because the competitive relational schema may be active outside of competitions with the rival, it may affect the actor's identity vis-à-vis the target as a result of either party's relevant actions, even outside of their competitions with one another, an issue that we return to in the section on consequences.

The Formation of Rivalry: Cognitive Elaboration of Shared Competitive History

How does a person develop a competitive relational schema and, in turn, experience and act on the symptoms of rivalry? An important advantage of the proposed model is that it specifies a sequence of "contributory" events in a causal chain. The origin of the model is one or more perceived competitions with a given target. From there, the model identifies personal, situational, and relational conditions that increase the likelihood of the actor reflecting on and cognitively elaborating the shared competitive history into a relational schema. Thus, none of the contributory conditions is necessary or sufficient for rivalry formation, but each encourages the definitive schema-formation process of cognitive elaboration.

The Origin of Rivalry: Shared Competitive History

As illustrated in Figure 19.1, our hypothesized causal chain begins with perceived competitive interactions. Though these will most often be real and direct competitive interactions—defined from a structural perspective as any time the parties' goals are negatively linked (Deutsch, 1949)—it is theoretically possible that the chain could begin with the mere perception of negatively-linked goals. Whether real or imagined, perceived competition is a necessary but not sufficient distal cause of rivalry. Perceived competition does not guarantee rivalry, but there can be no rivalry without it. What, then, determines whether perceived competition will develop into a competitive relational schema? According to the model, cognitive elaboration is the key mediational link between perceived competition and the presence of a competitive relational schema, and the other contributory causes modulate the likelihood of the cognitive elaboration that makes it happen.

Contributory Causes: Social-Comparison Concerns

In broad terms, the model includes as distal contributory causes any factors that will increase the likelihood of an actor reflecting on past competitive interactions with the target. The more likely the actor is to reflect on a competition with a given competitor, the more likely it is that she or he will form the competitive relational schema that promotes a sense of enduring competitive connection (Hastie et al., 1980; Manis, 1977; Taylor, 1980). The social-cognitive perspective is useful here because it can help to explain and organize the contributory causes that have already been documented (Kilduff et al., 2010; Tyler & Cobbs, 2015), as well as offer predictions about yet undocumented ones.

Anything that increases the actor's concerns with evaluating the self in a given domain or that signals the target's relevance as a good benchmark for doing so would increase social-comparison-driven attention (Festinger, 1954; Goethals, 1986; Suls & Miller, 1977). Social comparison's driving role in competitive behavior is elaborated elsewhere (Garcia et al., 2013; *this volume*). Here, we aim to illustrate how each hypothesized predictor would increase an actor's likelihood of ruminating about the competitor and competitive interactions, thereby increasing his or her likelihood of developing a competitive relational schema. We borrow Garcia and colleagues organization of these conditions into the three sets, personal factors, relational factors, and situational factors (2013; *this volume* —). While their focal goal was to explain competitive behavior at large as the downstream consequence of social comparison, independent of any specific relationship variance, we suggest that their analysis applies equally well to explaining rivalry. The common feature is increased cognitive elaboration.

PERSONAL FACTORS

In the social comparison model of competition, the personal factors are those that can largely be characterized as descriptions of the actor. A prominent personal factor is the relevance of the domain to the actor's identity (Hoffman et al., 1954; Salovey & Rodin, 1984). Actors are unlikely to have high comparison concerns with respect to pursuits that they do not value; they are therefore unlikely to pay much attention to their competitors in such pursuits. People only have rivals in domains that they care about. Other personal factors include individual differences that reflect one's baseline tendency to care about relative standing in the first place, including competitiveness (Houston et al., 2002), belief in a zero-sum game (Różycka-Tran et al., 2015), performance orientation (Poortvliet et al., 2009), and social comparison orientation (Gibbons & Buunk, 1999). There is little research so far that links any of these personal factors to the competitive relational schema or the symptoms of rivalry. In fact, it is common practice to restrict data collection to the high end of each distribution, a practice that reflects the tacit assumption that these dimensions matter but that precludes empirical verification.

A new prediction stemming from this reasoning is that individuals who are in a formative time of their trajectory in some domain would be more likely to reflect on their competitors because they are more likely to be questioning their own status and identity (see also Garcia et al., 2013, on uncertainty in the environment). Thus, for example, academic rivalries may be more likely to form among the untenured than the tenured, athletic rivalries may be more likely to form among rookies than among veterans, and business rivalries may be more likely to form among startups than among established corporations. Relatedly, individuals who are low in self-esteem, whether chronically or temporarily, or who are experiencing times of stress may be more likely to engage in social comparison (Gibbons & Buunk, 1999), meaning that they may be more likely to reflect on competitors in an important domain.

RELATIONAL FACTORS

Not surprisingly, relational factors have received more empirical attention in the rivalry domain, with similarity as the leading example. From both a diagnostic and motivational point of view, similar others are more likely than dissimilar others to prompt social comparison (Festinger, 1954)—they are both more informative as benchmarks and their relative status can be more threatening. As one step toward validating the dyadic competitiveness that they documented through their social relations analysis, Kilduff and colleagues (2010) demonstrated that different operationalizations of similarity (including both trait similarity and performance similarity, or parity) predicted rivalry strength in

NCAA men's basketball. These predictors included teams' relative winning percentage, teams' relative conference title counts, universities' relative academic quality, and universities' relative enrollment.

Relationship closeness is another relational dimension that has been linked to social-comparison concerns and competition in general (Tesser, 1988; Locke, 2007); though it has been largely neglected in rivalry research. Starting with all other things equal, it seems likely that friends who begin to compete are more likely to experience the symptoms of rivalry than are strangers who begin to compete. Put differently, an actor who sees someone as a friend already has a relational schema in place; thus, adding competition as a prominent feature of the dyad's interactions is all that would be needed to cement the competitive relational schema.

SITUATIONAL FACTORS

One of the contributions of the social comparison model of competition is its inclusion of situational factors as additional predictors of social comparison (Garcia et al., 2013; *this volume*). These include settings that involve high stakes; that involve proximity to a meaningful standard (e.g., vying for entry into the "Top 10"; Garcia et al., 2006; Garcia & Tor, 2007); and that include fewer, more identifiable competitors (Garcia & Tor, 2009). Each of these factors has been linked to competitiveness in general but not to rivalry specifically, another opportunity for future rivalry research. Indeed, putting these situational factors together sounds like a potent recipe for rivalry. Imagine, for instance, two members of a small work team within a larger company, who repeatedly bump up against each other in critical promotion windows. It is hard to imagine that they would not become rivals.

Exposure also makes clear predictions about social comparison. From a purely probabilistic perspective, the more that an actor interacts with or hears about a given competitor, the more likely she is to reflect on that competitor. Thus, two employees in the same division are more likely to become rivals than two employees in different divisions simply because they are forced to think about each other more often. This has been well-documented in the sports world with demonstrations that the number of past meetings predicts rivalry strength (Kilduff et al., 2010). Proximity has also been documented as a positive predictor of rivalry (Kilduff et al., 2010), which could reflect mere exposure (closer parties are more likely to interact frequently) and/or similarity (closer parties are more likely to share values, compete over similarly valued resources, etc.; see Tyler & Cobbs, 2015).

Just as identity uncertainty might be a personal factor that increases cognitive elaboration, attributional uncertainty might be a relational factor that increases it. When people encounter uncertainty, they are motivated to reduce that uncertainty (Hogg, 2000; Weary & Edwards, 1996) and they tend to experience stronger reactions to the stimuli that caused the uncertainty (Bar-Anan et al., 2009; Wilson et al., 2005). Thus, for example, a competitor who employs unorthodox strategies may attract more attention from others and evoke stronger reactions, leading to higher likelihood of cognitive elaboration if all other factors are held equal. Incidental uncertainty—for example, uncertainty that is "in the air" during periods of stress or novelty—could have similar effects (Garcia et al., 2013).

SCHEMA FORMATION AND "INSTANT" RIVALRIES

Reasoning about contributory causes can also be valuable in understanding why some rivalries may be formed relatively quickly despite the importance of history. Generally speaking, having had more previous matchups leads to a stronger sense of shared history and, thus, provides more fodder for schema-formation; but sometimes a few remarkable matchups may lead to more reflection than many unremarkable matchups. In sports, for example, teams in the same conference or division may face each other many times per season, but not form a strong rivalry; yet, sometimes a few remarkable games may capture one's imagination and lead to quickly formed, though perhaps less durable, rivalries. Consistent with this idea, rich descriptive research has flagged "defining moments" as a potential predictor of rivalry strength (Tyler & Cobbs, 2015). People tend to reflect extensively on near-misses (Medvec et al., 1995), for example, which means that finishing a close second place for a desired reward may increase one's attention to the winning competitor and promote rivalry. On average, longer histories rather than shorter histories promote rivalry, but a few notable events could theoretically make up for a short history.

What Rivalry Does: Psychosocial Consequences of Rivalry

Many of the documented consequences of rivalry can be grouped into those that affect goal pursuit and those that affect one's identity or self-concept. (In Figure 19.1, we depict those that affect moral decision making as a third category, though our forthcoming discussion illustrates some challenging questions about when and why it follows from a competitive relational schema.) Across the goal-pursuit and identity categories, it seems that the consequences can be explained by a general cognitive *expansion* of the rivalry in one's mind. The interconnections of self, target, and competition-related knowledge and experiences that make up the schema are assumed to facilitate further cognitive connections across time, events, domains, and parties, making events that are associated with the rivalry feel bigger, more interconnected, and more important. We designate expansion as a proximal symptom of the competitive relational schema in our model; and position other documented symptoms more distally, as downstream consequences of expansion.

Expansiveness: More Competition than Meets the Eye

The more that a given event is perceived as having implications for other parts of one's life, the more important it seems, the more strongly it is experienced, and the more likely it should be to spill over into other parts of one's identity (Clore & Reinhard, 2018; Costin & Vignoles, 2020; Linville, 1985, 1987). Thus, as a direct consequence of the competitive relational schema, rivals (versus mere competitors) and rivalry contests (versus mere competitions) should take up more mental real estate; their subjective influence should expand in the actor's mind, and otherwise isolated events involving the self in competition or the target in competition should be interpreted through the relational schema. When this manifests within competitive interactions between rivals, it is well characterized as "heightened competition" (e.g., Kilduff, 2014). Highlighting that it can have implications even outside of interactions with the rival, we refer to it more broadly as *expansion* or *expansiveness*. For instance, without the schema (i.e., without rivalry), a competitor's performance against a third-party means little to the self—it would likely go unnoticed altogether; but with the schema (i.e., with rivalry), the actor would be more likely to consider the competitor's performance with respect to the actor's own status. Similarly, because current competitions are processed with respect to remembered past interactions and expected future interactions—an idea that we have referred to as *embeddedness* in previous work (Converse & Reinhard, 2016)—the consequences of a specific matchup against the rival can feel significantly more important. Rivalry competition, more than mere competition, settles old scores and contributes to one's legacy.

Another cohort study that we conducted linked rivalry to expanded impressions of competition (Converse & Reinhard, 2016, Experiment 1). In this study, a sample of NFL fans randomly prompted to reflect on rivals or non-rivals responded to a brief survey that assessed their impressions of the extent to which the focal teams' games felt "connected to past games between the teams" and "like the newest chapter in a longer narrative"; before then completing a survey that measured the strength of their legacy concerns. Consistent with the proposed model, this study found a stronger sense of expansion among fans in the rivalry condition than among those in the non-rivalry condition: Fans reflecting on rivalry contests felt that current games were more interconnected with the past (i.e., important because of previous matchups) and would have stronger implications in the future (i.e., more impact on one's legacy). This result dovetails with results of another study that documented the increased subjective value of rivalry (Kilduff et al., 2016). In that study, Ohio State fans reported that the "psychological stakes . . . separate of any tangible stakes" would be higher in a contest against their known rival, Michigan, than against closely matched non-rival teams.

Rivalry and Goal Pursuit

If rivalry contests loom larger psychologically, such that participants in those contests value the outcomes more highly, then it follows that participants should exhibit greater motivation. Indeed, a host of field studies and experiments have documented such an effect. In two survey experiments, participants assigned to reflect on rival (vs. non-rival) competitors reported higher motivation in those contests, above and beyond what was attributable to the tangible stakes of the contest (Kilduff, 2014, Studies 1a and 1b). An archival study that cleverly operationalized rivalry based on a summary score of observable antecedents (based on, e.g., demographic similarity, performance parity) found that long-distance runners achieved better times in races that included their rivals (Kilduff, 2014, Study 2). Perhaps reflecting the physiological markers of this enhanced competitive motivation, soccer players about to begin a game against an "extreme" (vs. "moderate") rival exhibited higher testosterone levels (Neave & Wolfson, 2003).

One of the most notable features of rivalry is that it extends beyond the bounds of a head-to-head competition—this carryover appears to include increased motivation. When competitors are involved in a rivalry, each party's performance can motivate the other's performance across contexts that they would not otherwise be invested in. For example, soccer fans will celebrate a rival team's loss to a third-party and report that it reflects well on their focal team even though they were not involved in the defeat (Havard, 2014; Havard & Eddy, 2019). In an archival study of NCAA basketball games, Pike and colleagues (2018) found that a rival team's performance in a matchup with a third-party competitor can generate heightened effort that is sustained across time. Their analysis found that when a college basketball team's rival wins the NCAA championship, they themselves play harder and win more games in the following year regardless of who they are playing.

Looking beyond levels of motivation, research has also documented that rivalry can change *how* people pursue their goals. Many of these regulatory effects can be theoretically traced to the temporal expansion of rivalry. Rivalries orient competitors toward long-term, global, and high-level thinking. Because these construals are associated with a regulatory focus that emphasizes advancement (*promotion concerns*) over security (*prevention concerns*; Förster & Higgins, 2005; Pennington & Roese, 2003), it follows that rivalry should promote an eager rather than cautious style of goal pursuit (Converse & Reinhard, 2016). Supporting this prediction, a series of experiments documented that participants previously invited to reflect on rival (vs. non-rival) competitors subsequently preferred eager as opposed to vigilant goal-pursuit strategies: they were more interested in adding to strengths than minimizing weaknesses, paid more attention to offensive formations than defensive formations, more often opted to jump right into an upcoming task instead of practicing first, and were more inclined to offer gut-feeling answers before checking their work. These results demonstrate that in competitive as well as non-competitive situations, rivalries promote a strategic inclination that reflects eagerness rather than vigilance.

With a rival in mind, competitors are also more likely to take risks because they consider risks in terms of potential gains and are less concerned with the uncertainty (Costello et al., 2019; To et al., 2018). Using an archival analysis on NFL games to compare rival and nonrival matchups, To and colleagues (2018) found that teams are significantly more likely to attempt a two-point conversion instead of the safer one-point field goal choice if they are playing a rival. In three studies, Costello and colleagues (2019) demonstrated that simply thinking about a rival compels people toward riskier choices, even in non-competitive situations. When college students were prompted to think about an upcoming basketball game with a rival as opposed to a non-rival college, they subsequently found "mystery flavor" chips more enticing (Study 1); when participants viewed advertisements about a rivalry game, they were more likely to exchange guaranteed $1 coupons for entry into a riskier lottery option (Study 2); and after reflecting on political rivals, participants became more willing to submit personal information to a stranger to enter into sweepstakes (Study 3).

Rivalry and Identity Maintenance

As an individual's identity becomes increasingly intertwined with the individual's conceptions of a competitor, the motivation to maintain that relational identity should in turn increase. Indeed, people often use their social interactions to "verify and confirm" their own self-conceptions (Swann & Read, 1981). Evidence for increased identity-maintenance concerns in rivalry can be found in a study that modeled sports owners' attempts to actively manage their fans' identities (Berendt & Uhrich, 2018). Across three established rivalry dyads in a German soccer league, researchers tested different methods for reducing fan aggression. Specifically, in the form of newspaper articles or team statements, they manipulated the extent to which rivalry was emphasized or deemphasized. Fans did not respond favorably to being told that their rivalry was unimportant. In one of the studies, the acknowledgment condition included a statement that recognized the tradition and atmosphere of the rivalry, whereas the downplay condition included a statement that said the rivalry game was no more important than other games and instructed fans "not [to] exaggerate the rivalry." Compared to a team statement that made no reference to the teams' rivalry, the acknowledgment condition effectively reduced fans' reported aggression; whereas, compared to the same control, the downplay statement increased fans' aggression. One interpretation of this finding is that actors are motivated to maintain this important relational aspect of their self-concept and social identity (Berendt & Uhrich, 2016; Elsbach & Bhattacharya, 2001). In mere competition, the competitive domain might become integrated into one's identity; in rivalry, the competitive relationship also becomes integrated into one's identity.

Extending this reasoning, it is possible that the expansiveness property of rivalry is implicated in the broader and thornier problem of intractable conflicts (Bar-Tal, 2000, 2007; Coleman, 2014). Research suggests that such conflicts are perpetuated in part because the participants find meaning in them and are motivated to maintain that sense of meaning (e.g., Rovenpor et al., 2019; Northrup, 1989). Future research that merges the social-cognitive perspective with the social-identity perspective may help to illuminate the challenge of seemingly intractable conflict.

Rivalry and Unethical Behavior

One intriguing puzzle for rivalry research is how to account for increased unethical behavior in the context of rivalry. An archival analysis revealed that professional soccer players play dirtier and receive more yellow- and red-card penalties in matchups against rivals (Kilduff et al., 2016, Study 4) and a variety of experiments corroborate and extend this finding. In one experiment (Kilduff & Galinsky, 2017, Experiment 1), undergraduates who had been previously assigned to reflect on interactions with a rival (versus those assigned to reflect on interactions with a non-rival) more strongly endorsed Machiavellian attitudes (e.g., "It is hard to get ahead without cutting corners here and there"; Christie & Geis, 1970). A conceptual replication that cleverly created rivalries in the lab showed the same effect (Experiment 2); and subsequent studies documented real behavioral consequences, with rivalry primes increasing participants' likelihood of cheating and deceiving, both inside and outside of direct competition (Experiments 3 and 4; see also Kilduff et al., 2016).

While the reliability of the behavioral effect appears quite strong given the number and variety of demonstrations, the theoretical path from the competitive relational schema to expansiveness and, in turn, to cheating and poor sportsmanship raises interesting questions. One explanation has focused on the inflated subjective value of rivalry (versus non-rivalry) competitions (Kilduff et al., 2016). The reasoning here includes both an attentional component, which suggests that the inflated importance leads people to focus more on outcomes than on means, and a deliberative component, which suggests that the inflated importance changes the cost-benefit calculation underlying a conscious decision to risk cheating. A slightly different explanation has focused more on shifting identity salience (Kilduff & Galinsky, 2017). The reasoning here is that the relative increase of one's identity as a successful competitor within the context of rivalry crowds out the moral identity that might otherwise protect one from unethical behavior (Aquino & Reed, 2002). With respect to Figure 19.1, this might be better illustrated as following directly from schema activation, such that an increase in the "competitive actor" identity hydraulically decreases the "moral actor" identity.

Each of these pathways to unethical behavior is theoretically coherent in itself, and the identity pathway in particular, has received some initial empirical support (Kilduff & Galinsky, 2017); but they offer a potentially interesting conflict with the finding that rivalry increases legacy concerns (Converse & Reinhard, 2016). Indeed, the more that people expect to remember a choice in the future, and the more they think that an action is diagnostic of who they really are, the more likely they are to show restraint and pursue a virtuous path (Touré-Tillery & Kouchaki, 2020; Touré-Tillery & Fishbach, 2015). From this line of reasoning, then, rivalry should encourage ethical rather than unethical behavior. There are many ways in which these competing explanations might be reconciled—perhaps through the identification of important situational or dispositional moderators—but only additional research can do so. Given the importance of promoting ethical behavior in competitive and individual settings, continued investigation of this phenomenon seems worthwhile.

Linking Distal and Proximal Consequences

Although cohort studies have shown associations between expansiveness and one or more downstream consequences of rivalry, we know of just one study that provides evidence of a causal link between them (Converse & Reinhard, 2016, Experiment 3). This study capitalized on a unique opportunity to hold the competitor target constant and manipulate participants' impressions of expansiveness. It did so by recruiting individuals who were excited but not highly knowledgeable about a particular competitive dyad. Specifically, this experiment took place in the hours leading up to the 2015 FIFA Women's World Cup finals match between the United States and Japan. Conveniently, the two teams had a compelling shared history; and equally convenient, the United States fanbase was well known to have been swept up in World Cup fever without having a lot of background knowledge about the team. This allowed us to randomly assign fans to a control condition or to a condition intended to increase their sense of temporal connection. Participants in the control condition did not receive any additional information about the teams' shared histories and read that players on the team were "block[ing] out everything except this single game." Participants in the expansion condition read about two recent, close, high-stakes games between the two teams; Japan's 2011 defeat of the United States in the previous World Cup final and the United States' subsequent defeat of Japan to win the gold medal in the following year's Olympic Games. Participants in this condition also read (admittedly heavy-handed) commentary about the United States players' desire to "avenge their [previous] loss . . . and prove that their [previous win] was deserved." Participants in the latter condition reported that rivalry was a more important aspect of the focal game than did participants in the control condition; and, moreover, those participants showed a stronger attentional bias for eager rather than cautious strategies, a hypothesized consequence of rivalry.

Aside from this experiment and one other previously reviewed experiment that went a step further back in the causal chain and actually fostered participants' creation of a competitive relational schema in the lab by manipulating their shared history (Kilduff & Galinsky, 2017), most rivalry studies have been unable to hold the target constant. Continuing to identify and develop new methods for directly manipulating antecedents in the causal chain will be of great value in evaluating the current model and in understanding rivalry more generally.

Competitive Relational Dynamics: Opportunities to Expand the Model

The model that we presented in Figure 19.1 and have explicated throughout the chapter is best described as a "snapshot" model. It identifies only the essential causal connections and considers them only in a prospective direction from the original competitions that make up a dyad's competitive history, through a focal actor's reflection on the competitive interactions and formation of a competitive relational schema that constitutes rivalry, and on to the symptoms that follow when the competitive relational schema is active. It does not depict the likely feedback processes that reinforce the rivalry. Moreover, the model is completely situated within one competitive dyad and does not consider how competitive dynamics unfold outside of that dyad.

Our choice to hone the model in this way invites separate opportunities for integration and expansion. First, an expanded model could identify potential feedback loops and auxiliary connections (cf., Garcia et al., 2020). At the broadest level, rivalry is likely to be self-reinforcing. As an actor becomes more invested in the rivalry, her competitions with the rival will encourage even more cognitive elaboration, further reinforcing the schema, and so on. Further, such loops may feedback to both distal and proximal causes in the model. For example, increased rivalry may lead the actor to seek more competitive interactions with the rival (thus increasing the shared history; Johnson, 2012); it may lead actors to increase their sense of domain-importance (thus increasing the personal-factors moderator; Garcia et al., 2020); and it may change activation potential of the schema (thus increasing the variety of contexts in which the rivalry becomes subjectively relevant; Baldwin, 1992).

Second, the model could be integrated with more general models of competitive behavior (e.g., the social comparison model of competition; Garcia et al., 2013) to consider when individuals will have an expansive view of competition independent of the relational path emphasized here. Championship games, for instance, may have many of the ingredients that encourage participants to behave as if they are in a rivalry (e.g., the expectation of remembering this game in the future), even without a rival.

Third, the model might be expanded to consider how rivalries affect individuals' other relationships. The competitive relational schema concept has been applied here to understand how an actor might behave with respect to (if not always in direct interaction with) the specific rival target. Thus, both research and theorizing have focused more on the implications of rivalry for the actor's understanding and evaluation of herself (the self-schema), the rival (the other schema), and of the scripts she develops to guide expectations of her interactions with the rival. Much of the heuristic value of the (broader) relational schema construct, however, is that actors often generalize it to understand other relationships (Baldwin, 1992). This raises an interesting question: Do actors with a strong sense of competitive expansiveness vis-à-vis the rival eventually generalize those expectations to other competitors; or do those actors experience more of a contrast effect, downgrading all other competitions in light of the rivalry? Perhaps ironically, rivalry research—which was founded on the idea that some competitive relationships are distinctive from others (Kilduff et al., 2010)—may be well positioned to ask how rivalry affects the perception of other competitive relationships over time (Andersen & Cole, 1990).

Conclusion

Rivalry can be a slippery construct for psychological science. But this has not stopped researchers from inventing and refining rigorous approaches to its investigation. Only a decade before this chapter was written, the identification of dyadic competitive variance (Kilduff et al., 2010) energized social psychologists and other behavioral scientists to embrace the intrapersonal and interpersonal richness that characterizes rivalry. Now, there are a wide variety of field, archival, and experimental methods available, and in continued development, for studying rivalry rigorously while embracing its complexity. We suggest that the competitive relational schema provides a valuable conceptual anchor for this endeavor, marking a place where relational, social-cognitive, organizational, and behavioral perspectives can pursue cooperative progress toward the understanding of competitive relationships.

References

Abramson, L. Y., Metalsky, G. I., & Allow, L. B. (1989). Hopelessness depression: A theory-based subtype of depression. *Journal of Personality and Social Psychology 96*, 358–372.

Andersen, S. M., & Cole, S. W. (1990). "Do I know you?" The role of significant others in general social perception. *Journal of Personality and Social Psychology 59*, 384–399.

Aquino, K. & Reed, A., II. (2002). The self-importance of moral identity. *Journal of Personality and Social Psychology 83*, 1423.

Axelrod, R. (1984). *The evolution of cooperation*. Basic Books.

Baldwin, M. W. (1992). Relational schemas and the processing of social information. *Psychological Bulletin 112*, 461–484.

Bar-Anan, Y., Wilson, T. D., & Gilbert, D. T. (2009). The feeling of uncertainty intensifies affective reactions. *Emotion 9*, 123–127.

Bar-Tal, D. (2000). *Shared beliefs in a society: Social psychological analysis*. CA: Sage Publications.

Bar-Tal, D. (2007). Sociopsychological foundations of intractable conflicts. *American Behavioral Scientist 50*, 1430–1453.

Coleman, P. T. (2014). Intractable conflict. In P. T. Coleman, M. Deutsch, & E. C. Marcus (Eds.), *The handbook of conflict resolution: Theory and practice, 3rd edn* (pp. 708–744). Jossey-Bass.

Berendt, J., & Uhrich, S. (2016). Enemies with benefits: The dual role of rivalry in shaping sports fans' identity. *European Sport Management Quarterly 16*, 613–634.

Berendt, J., & Uhrich, S. (2018). Rivalry and fan aggression: Why acknowledging conflict reduces tension between rival fans and downplaying makes things worse. *European Sport Management Quarterly 18*, 517–540.

Bowlby, J. (1969). *Attachment and Loss. Volume 1: Attachment*. Hogarth Press.

Cesario, J., Plaks, J. E., & Higgins, E. T. (2006). Automatic social behavior as motivated preparation to interact. *Journal of Personality and Social Psychology 90*, 893–910.

Chen, M. J. (1996). Competitor analysis and interfirm rivalry: Toward a theoretical integration. *Academy of Management Review 21*, 100–134.

Christie, R., & Geis, F. L. (1970) *Machiavellianism*. Academic Press, Incorporated.

Colaresi, M. P., Rasler, K., & Thompson, W. R. (2008). *Strategic rivalries in world politics: Position, space, and conflict escalation*. Cambridge University Press.

Converse, B. A. & Reinhard, D. A. (2016). On rivalry and goal pursuit: Shared competitive history, legacy concerns, and strategy selection. *Journal of Personality and Social Psychology 110*, 191–213.

Costello, P., Walker Reczek, J., & Smith, R. (2019). *Risk and the rivalry mindset: Promotions involving group rivalries increase risky consumption behaviors. ACR North American Advances*.

Costin, V., & Vignoles, V. L. (2020). Meaning is about mattering: Evaluating coherence, purpose, and existential mattering as precursors of meaning in life judgments. *Journal Personality and Social Psychology 118*, 864.

Clore, G. L. & Reinhard, D. A. (2018). Emotional intensity: It's the thought that counts. In R. Davidson, A. Shackman, A. Fox, & R. Lapate (Eds.), *The Nature of Emotion: A volume of short essays addressing fundamental questions in emotion* (pp. 162–164). Oxford University Press.

Deutsch, M. (1949). The effects of cooperation and competition upon group processes. *Human Relations 2*, 199–231.

Elsbach, K. D., & Bhattacharya, C. B. (2001). Defining who you are by what you're not: Organizational dis-identification and the National Rifle Association. *Organization Science 12*, 393–413.

Festinger, L. (1954). A theory of social comparison processes. *Human Relations 7*, 117–140.

Fitzsimons, G. M., & Shah, J. Y. (2008). How goal instrumentality shapes relationship evaluations. *Journal of Personality and Social Psychology 95*, 319–337.

Förster, J., & Tory Higgins, E. (2005). How global versus local perception fits regulatory focus. *Psychological Science 16*, 631–636.

Garcia, S. M., Reese, Z. A., & Tor, A. (2020). Social comparison before, during, and after the competition. In J. Suls, R. L. Collins, & L. Wheeler (Eds.), *Social comparison, judgment, and behavior* (pp. 105–142). Oxford University Press.

Garcia, S. M., & Tor, A. (2007). Rankings, standards, and competition: Task vs. scale comparisons. *Organizational Behavior and Human Decision Processes 102*, 95–108.

Garcia, S. M., & Tor, A. (2009). The N-Effect: More competitors, less competition. *Psychological Science 20*, 871–877.

Garcia, S. M., Tor, A., & Gonzalez, R. D. (2006). Ranks and rivals: A theory of competition. *Personality and Social Psychology Bulletin 32*, 970–982.

Garcia, S. M., Tor, A., & Schiff, T. M. (2013). The psychology of competition: A social comparison perspective. *Perspectives on Psychological Science 8*, 634–650.

Gibbons, F. X., & Buunk, B. P. (1999). Individual differences in social comparison: Development of a scale of social comparison orientation. *Journal of Personality and Social Psychology 76*, 129–142.

Goethals, G. R. (1986). Social comparison theory: Psychology from the lost and found. *Personality and Social Psychology Bulletin, 12*, 261–278.

Hastie, R., Ostrom, T., Ebbesen, E., Wyer, R., Hamilton, D., & Carlston, D. (1980), *Person memory: The cognitive basis of social perception.* Erlbaum.

Havard, C. T. (2014). Glory out of reflected failure: The examination of how rivalry affects sport fans. *Sport Management Review 17*, 243–253.

Havard, C. T., & Eddy, T. (2019). The impact of negative media stories on fan perceptions and behavior toward rival teams. *International Journal of Sports Management 20*, 150–170.

Heide, J. B., & Miner, A. S. (1992). The shadow of the future: Effects of anticipated interaction and frequency of contact on buyer-seller cooperation. *Academy of Management Journal 35*, 265–291.

Higgins, E. T. (1987). Self-discrepancy: A theory relating self and affect. *Psychological Review 94*, 319–340.

Higgins, E. T., King, G. A., & Mavin, G. H. (1982). Individual construct accessibility and subjective impressions and recall. *Journal of Personality and Social Psychology 43*, 35–47.

Hoffman, P., Festinger, L., & Lawrence, D. (1954). Tendencies toward group comparability in competitive bargaining. *Human Relations 7*, 141–159.

Hogg, M. A. (2000). Subjective uncertainty reduction through self-categorization: A motivational theory of social identity processes. *European Review of Social Psychology 11*, 223–255.

Horowitz, M. J. (1989). Relationship schema formulation: Role-relationship models and intrapsychic conflict. *Psychiatry 52*, 260–274.

Houston, I. M., Mcintire, S., Kinnie, I., & Terry, C. (2002). A factor analysis of scales measuring competitiveness. *Educational and Psychological Measurement 62*, 284–298.

Johnson, C. (2012). Behavioral responses to threatening social comparisons: From dastardly deeds to rising above. *Social & Personality Psychology Compass 6*, 515–524.

Johnson, M. D., Hollenbeck, J. R., Humphrey, S. E., Ilgen, D. R., Jundt, D., & Meyer, C. J. (2006). Cutthroat cooperation: Asymmetrical adaptation to changes in team reward structures. *Academy of Management Journal 49*, 103–119.

Kenny, D. A. (1994). *Interpersonal perception: A social relations analysis.* Guilford Press.

Kenny, D. A., & La Voie, L. (1984). The social relations model. In L. Berkowitz (Ed.), *Advances in Experimental Social Psychology*, (pp. 142–182). Academic Press.

Kilduff, G. J. (2014). Driven to win: Rivalry, motivation, and performance. *Social Psychological and Personality Science 5*, 944–952.

Kilduff, G. J. (2019). Interfirm relational rivalry: Implications for competitive strategy. *Academy of Management Review 44*, 775–799.

Kilduff, G. J., Elfenbein, H. A., & Staw, B. M. (2010). The psychology of rivalry: A relationally dependent analysis of competition. *Academy of Management Journal 53*, 943–969.

Kilduff, G. J., & Galinsky, A. D. (2017). The spark that ignites: Mere exposure to rivals increases Machiavellianism and unethical behavior. *Journal of Experimental Social Psychology 69*, 156–162.

Kilduff, G. J., Galinsky, A. D., Gallo, E., & Reade, J. J. (2016). Whatever it takes to win: Rivalry increases unethical behavior. *Academy of Management Journal 59*, 1508–1534.

Klein, J. P., Goertz, G., & Diehl, P. F. (2006). The new rivalry dataset: Procedures and patterns. *Journal of Peace Research 43*, 331–348.

Lee, M. J. (1985). From rivalry to hostility among sports fans. *Quest 37*, 38–49.

Linville, P. W. (1985). Self-complexity and affective extremity: Don't put all of your eggs in one cognitive basket. *Social Cognition 3*, 94–120.

Linville, P. W. (1987). Self-complexity as a cognitive buffer against stress-related illness and depression. *Journal of Personality and Social Psychology 52*, 663–676.

Locke, K. D. (2007). Personalized and generalized comparisons: Causes and consequences of variations in the focus of social comparisons. *Personality and Social Psychology Bulletin 33*, 213–225.

Manis, M. (1977). Cognitive social psychology. *Personality and Social Psychology Bulletin 3*, 550–566.

Medvec, V. H., Madey, S. F., & Gilovich, T. (1995). When less is more: Counterfactual thinking and satisfaction among Olympic medalists. *Journal of Personality and Social Psychology 69*, 603–610.

Murnighan, J. K., & Roth, A. E. (1983). Expecting continued play in prisoner's dilemma games: A test of several models. *Journal of Conflict Resolution 27*, 279–300.

Mitchell, S. A. (1988). *Relational concepts in psychoanalysis.* Harvard University Press.

Neave, N., & Wolfson, S. (2003). Testosterone, territoriality, and the "home advantage". *Physiology & Behavior 78*, 269–275.

Northrup, T. 1989. The dynamic of identity in personal and social conflict. In L. Kriesberg, T. Northrup, & S. Thorson (Eds.), *Intractable conflicts and their transformation* (pp. 55–82). Syracuse University Press.

Pennington, G. L., & Roese, N. J. (2003). Regulatory focus and temporal distance. *Journal of Experimental Social Psychology 39*, 563–576.

Pike, B. E., Kilduff, G. J., & Galinsky, A. D. (2018). The long shadow of rivalry: Rivalry motivates performance today and tomorrow. *Psychological Science 29*, 804–813.

Porac, J. F., Thomas, H., Wilson, F., Paton, D., & Kanfer, A. (1995). Rivalry and the industry model of Scottish knitwear producers. *Administrative Science Quarterly, 2*(2), 203–227.

Rovenpor, D. R., O'Brien, T. C., Roblain, A., De Guissmé, L., Chekroun, P., & Leidner, B. (2019). Intergroup conflict self-perpetuates via meaning: Exposure to intergroup conflict increases meaning and fuels a desire for further conflict. *Journal of Personality and Social Psychology 116*, 119–140. https://doi.org/10.1037/pspp0000169.

Różycka-Tran, J., Boski, P., & Wojciszke, B. (2015). Belief in a zero-sum game as a social axiom: A 37-nation study. *Journal of Cross-Cultural Psychology 46* (4), 525–548.

Schank, R. C., & Abelson, R. P. (1977). *Scripts, plans, goals, and understanding.* Erlbaum.

Salovey, P., & Rodin, J. (1984). Some antecedents and consequences of social-comparison jealousy. *Journal of Personality and Social Psychology 47*, 780–792.

Suls, J. M., & Miller, R. L. (Eds.). (1977). *Social comparison processes: Theoretical and empirical perspectives.* Hemisphere.

Swann, W. B. & Read, S. J. (1981). Self-verification processes: How we sustain our self-conceptions. *Journal of Experimental Social Psychology 17*, 351–372.

Taylor, S. E. (1980). The interface of cognitive and social psychology. In J. Harvey (Ed.), *Cognition, social behavior, and the environment* (pp. 189–211). Erlbaum.

Trzebinski, J. (1985). Action-oriented representations of implicit personality theories. *Journal of Personality and Social Psychology 48*, 1266–1278.

Tyler, B. D., & Cobbs, J. B. (2015). Rival conceptions of rivalry: Why some competitions mean more than others. *European Sport Management Quarterly 15*, 227–248.

Tyler, B. D., & Cobbs, J. B. (2017). All rivals are not equal: Clarifying misrepresentations and discerning three core properties of rivalry. *Journal of Sports Management 31*, 1–14.

Planalp, S. (1987). Interplay between relational knowledge and events. In R. Burnett & P. McGhee (Eds.), *Accounting for relationships: Explanations, representation and knowledge* (pp. 175–191). Methuen Publishing.

Plaks, J. E., & Higgins, E. T. (2000). Pragmatic use of stereotyping in teamwork: Social loafing and compensation as a function of inferred partner-situation fit. *Journal of Personality and Social Psychology 79*, 962–974. http://dx.doi.org/10.1037/0022-3514.79.6.962.

Poortvliet, P. M., Janssen, O., Van Yperen, N. W., & Van de Vliert, E. (2009). Low ranks make the difference: How achievement goals and ranking information affect cooperation intentions. *Journal of Experimental Social Psychology 45*, 1144–1147.

Rand, D. G., Dreber, A., Ellingsen, T., Fudenberg, D., & Nowak, M. A. (2009). Positive interactions promote public cooperation. *Science 325*, 1272–1275. http://dx.doi.org/10.1126/science.1177418.

Rijsman, J. B. (1974). Factors in social comparison of performance influencing actual performance. *European Journal of Social Psychology 4*, 279–311.

Seta, J. J. (1982). The impact of comparison processes on coactors' task performance. *Journal of Personality and Social Psychology 42*, 281–291.

Tesser, A. (1988). Toward a self-evaluation maintenance model of social behavior. In L. Berkowitz (Ed.), *Advances in experimental social psychology: Vol. 21. Social psychological studies of the self: Perspectives and programs* (pp. 181–227). Academic Press. http://dx.doi.org/10.1016/S0065-2601(08)60227-0.

To, C., Kilduff, G. J., Ordóñez, L., & Schweitzer, M. E. (2018). Going for it on fourth down: Rivalry increases risk taking, physiological arousal, and promotion focus. *Academy of Management Journal 61*, 1281–1306.

Touré-Tillery, M., & Fishbach, A. (2015). It was(n't) me: Exercising restraint when choices appear self-diagnostic. *Journal of Personality and Social Psychology 109*, 1117–1131.

Touré-Tillery, M., & Kouchaki, M. (2020). You will not remember this: How memory efficacy influences virtuous behavior. *Journal of Consumer Research 47* (5), 737–754.

Weary, G., & Edwards, J. A. (1996). Causal-uncertainty beliefs and related goal structures. In R. M. Sorrentino & E. T. Higgins (Eds.), *Handbook of motivation and cognition: The interpersonal context* (vol. 3, pp. 148–181). Guilford Press.

Wilson, T. D., Centerbar, D. B., Kermer, D. A., & Gilbert, D. T. (2005). The pleasures of uncertainty: prolonging positive moods in ways people do not anticipate. *Journal of Personality and Social Psychology 88*, 5–21.

Yip, J. A., Schweitzer, M. E., & Nurmohamed, S. (2018). Trash-talking: Competitive incivility motivates rivalry, performance, and unethical behavior. *Organizational Behavior and Human Decision Processes 144*, 125–144.

The Psychology of Status Competitions within Organizations: Navigating Two Competing Motives

Sarah P. Doyle, Sijun Kim, *and* Hee Young Kim

Abstract

Status hierarchies, which represent how individuals stack up based on the amount of influence and respect they have relative to others, develop quickly as group members make judgments and inferences about others' competencies or expected contributions to the group. While quick to emerge, one's place in the hierarchy is not entirely fixed. Because occupying higher status offers a number of rewards and benefits, people vie with others to achieve the higher status positions, and seek to maintain them by engaging in behaviors that have downstream effects on group and individual outcomes. Scholars have directed increasing attention to the unique psychology associated with status seeking to understand the consequences of hierarchical competitions. This emerging body of work highlights the dual concerns (i.e., self-oriented and other-oriented concerns) inherent in the pursuit of status and offers new insights to aid our understanding of status competitions. In this chapter, the authors first review the literature that explores the mixed-motive psychology of status striving, noting the potentially beneficial and destructive behavioral outcomes that status competitions can elicit within workgroups. Next, the authors detail some of the structural, temporal, relational, and individual properties that may exacerbate people's self-interested status concerns. The chapter concludes by discussing some of the organizational implications of this body of work and reviewing potentially rich opportunities for future research on status competitions.

Key Words: status competition, social hierarchy, status striving, status motives, psychology of status, status change

Introduction

It is well-established that hierarchical work environments can foster a highly competitive environment within organizations and work teams. For example, employees at Amazon "race" with their colleagues to fill customer orders, tracking their progress in a virtual gaming system (Bensinger, 2019). At Target, cashiers are provided a "score" and compared based on the time it takes to scan products (Cain, 2018). And in 2015, Microsoft acquired a software ("FantasySalesTeam") that allows their organization to run contests similar to those found in fantasy sports in which managers "draft" teams of sales employees and compete with one another for "bragging rights" (Stutz, 2015). Such efforts are predicated on the idea that our brains are tuned to compare ourselves to others and the inherent desire for status (i.e., to be seen as a valuable contributor to one's organization or work group) can bring about a number of positive behaviors, such as effort, motivation, or performance (Anderson et al., 2015).

Yet, despite these potentially beneficial outcomes, it is not hard to identify examples where the desire for status has resulted in highly counterproductive, and even unethical, behaviors (e.g., creating fake accounts to inflate performance [see the example of Wells Fargo in Morran, 2013]; rigging product software to beat out competition [see Volkswagen's "defeat device" in Hotten, 2015]; incivility, undermining, and workplace harassment to rise in rank [see the example of Uber in Isaac, 2017]). These types of unfortunate examples are so pervasive that—regardless of the organization or industry—people seem to directly associate hierarchical environments with corruption and unethical practices because of the intense competition that can ensue within them (Fath & Kay, 2018). In light of these functional and dysfunctional consequences, an active question among scholars and practitioners is whether a status hierarchy, and the competitions for status that predictably emerge within it, promote benefits or lead to costs to organizational functioning (see Bendersky & Pai, 2018; Blader & Yu, 2017; Mitchell et al., 2020; and Pettit & Marr, 2020 for recent reviews).

In an effort to understand when and why hierarchical competition results in either positive or negative behaviors, scholarly attention has been increasingly paid to the unique psychology associated with status (Blader & Yu, 2017). A wealth of research documents the self-interested and individualistic motives that play a role in the pursuit of status (Flynn & Amanatullah, 2012; Kim et al., 2019; Pettit et al., 2010), as having higher status satisfies people's desire to feel positively distinguished from others (Maslow, 1943). Nevertheless, an individual's ability to obtain status ultimately depends on others' perceptions of them, and therefore, one's pursuit of status also impacts the amount of attention they pay towards others, with implications for various group-serving motivations and behaviors (e.g., Blader & Chen, 2012; Flynn et al., 2006; Hardy & Van Vugt, 2006; Willer, 2009).

In this chapter, we organize extant research which informs us about the complex psychology underlying the pursuit of status, and its impact on status competitions. To do so, we (1) provide a conceptual overview of status and status conferral; (2) unpack the inward (e.g., self-centered) and outward (e.g., group-oriented) psychological processes underlying the pursuit of status, noting the beneficial and destructive behaviors that competitions for status can elicit; and (3) detail the structural, temporal, relational, and individual properties that exacerbate self-interested status concerns (and the dysfunctional behaviors that may result). We conclude by reviewing some of the implications of this work and fruitful areas for future research.

The Pursuit and Conferral of Status in Workgroups

Status is defined as "the prominence, respect, and influence individuals enjoy in the eyes of others" (Anderson et al., 2001, p. 116) and reflects the perceived value of an individual to their workgroup. Broadly speaking, an individual's status reflects the person's perceived usefulness to the completion of the group's goals. Accordingly, status is conferred to those who are seen to possess—and importantly, are also expected to leverage—the valuable skills, competencies, or qualities that could facilitate the group's success (Blau, 1964). Therefore, while status is informed by an individual's competencies or qualities, the process of status conferral is dependent on others' perceptions. That is, expertise or competence alone does not warrant the conferral of status; rather, these qualities must be perceived as relevant to the group's present goals, and the individuals who possess such qualities should demonstrate their willingness to leverage them for the group's collective interests to obtain status. In this way, the process of status conferral within groups is a social exchange, whereby people are granted status in return for their perceived—or expected—contributions.

Within groups, status hierarchies represent how much status each person has relative to one another (Magee & Galinsky, 2008). In essence, they let individuals know where they "stack up" in comparison to others. Our tendency to compare the capabilities and value of others, and to order them from "best" to "worst," is thought to be hard-wired in people and occurs almost instantaneously in work groups (Hoffman et al., 1954). Because of these comparative processes, the experience of status is highly context-dependent and an individual's ability to have higher status depends not only on their own perceived capabilities and value, but also on the perceived capabilities and value of others to whom one is being compared. As a result, while status is operationalized as an individual variable, it is *de facto* a relational property within workgroups (Christie & Barling, 2010). People tend to care more about where they stand relative to others (as compared to the amount of status they have, objectively speaking) (Crosby, 1976; Smith et al., 1994) and consequently, status is frequently experienced as a limited resource whereby the conferral of status to one individual necessitates the withdrawal of status from another (He et al., 2020; Sirola & Pitesa, 2017).

Despite the informal processes and inherent subjectivity that characterize the conferral of status, there is a general level of consensus surrounding the status hierarchies that emerge within groups. From an evolutionary perspective, our ability to assess the expected contributions of others and distinguish among those who may contribute more or less to the group is an adaptive response and should enable the group to perform more effectively (Ellis, 1994). Indeed, much research has documented the coordination benefits associated with social hierarchies (Anderson & Brown, 2010; Tiedens & Fragale, 2003). For example, hierarchies tend to be reliable signals of each group member's relative capabilities (Gruenfeld & Tiedens, 2010) and therefore help to clarify role expectations and the division of labor (Halevy et al., 2011; Sanner & Bunderson, 2018). Therefore, status hierarchy reduces uncertainty and improves the quality of collective decision-making (De Kwaadsteniet & van Dijk, 2010).

However, the potential for smooth coordination among group members, guided by a consensually agreed-upon hierarchy, is often undermined and threatened by people's persistent desire effort to achieve higher status. A recent meta-analysis found that hierarchical differentiation, on average, harmed, rather than helped, team performance (Greer et al., 2018). Status hierarchy is likely to amplify conflict-enabling states within the team as people vie for higher status, and the heightened status conflict is argued to harm the group's ability to perform (Bendersky & Hays, 2012; Pai & Bendersky, 2020). Overall, these results suggest that hierarchies may harm performance when they enable intra-team competition in which group members attempt to jockey with each other for higher status positions.

This intra-team competition that can emerge within social hierarchies is not surprising when one considers the value that is associated with high status. Those who are seen as higher status in the hierarchy are afforded a number of benefits: more opportunities to speak, more influence over group decisions, greater access to scarce resources, and a higher likelihood of receiving monetary rewards (see Anderson et al., 2015 for review). Furthermore, higher status individuals are believed to be evaluated more positively than their lower status counterparts (e.g., intelligence, work ethic, skill; Oldmeadow & Fiske, 2007; Varnum, 2015). Not only does higher status offer a number of extrinsic rewards, but an individual's status is also central to their sense of self as perceptions of social worth satisfy peoples' fundamental desire for a positive self-concept (Anderson & Kilduff, 2009a). Notably, the inherent desire for status is so pervasive that it even appears to transcend various contexts such as cultures, gender, and generations (Anderson et al., 2015).

For individuals who seek to attain higher status, it is fortunate that their status can change in the eyes of others (Bendersky & Shah, 2012, 2013). Whereas certain antecedents, or demographic predictors, of status are relatively more static and hence may be more difficult to change at one's own discretion (e.g., socioeconomic status, race, gender, age, education), an emerging body of research highlights the dynamic nature of social status in workgroups (see Bendersky & Pai, 2018; Pettit & Marr, 2020, for reviews). According to this stream of research, individuals may gain or lose status from one point in time to another. Through repeated interactions, the initial status hierarchy is "re-negotiated" as people reassess the expected value and contributions of each person to the group (Berger et al., 1972; Overbeck et al., 2005). Although people often accept their place in more stable and formalized hierarchical work environments (Berger et al., 1998; Correll & Ridgeway, 2006; Whyte, 1943), they are regularly on the lookout for opportunities to elevate their status in groups with more unstable and mutable status hierarchies (Hays & Bendersky, 2015). Because of the dynamic properties of social status conferral within workgroups, people may alter their behaviors in an attempt to influence the group's perception of them in service of their status (Goffman, 1969; Owens & Sutton, 2001).

In their paper focusing squarely on understanding the behaviors associated with status competitions, Kim et al. (2019) examine the different ways in which people try to maneuver and negotiate their status. These attempts to maneuver for status, also called "status moves" (Goffman, 1969), reflect the strategic actions that people deliberately engage in, "to manipulate the status structure of the group" (Owens & Sutton, 2001, p. 304). As group members make moves and countermoves in an effort to positively affect their status, status competitions emerge (Porath et al., 2008). As detailed in Kim et al. (2019), these status moves can be enacted in different ways. For example, individuals may seek to bolster their status directly (i.e., positive status moves), engaging in efforts that are intended to demonstrate their value to the group (e.g., developing skills or competencies, demonstrating group commitment). Alternatively, recognizing the relative nature of status, individuals might instead try to undermine or diminish the status of another person in the group (i.e., negative status moves) (e.g., withholding resources; denigrating the perceived skills or competencies of another individual) to make themselves look better than the denigrated peer. Accordingly, competitions for status can result in greater motivation or effort, but also in contentious conflict or arguments in which people attempt to show off their superior expertise to that of others whom they aspire to challenge (Gould, 2003).

Regardless of its valence (i.e., positive or negative), status moves are employed with a similar goal in mind: to display an actor's relative value and increase their perceived or expected contributions to the group as compared to those of others. Nevertheless, the ultimate "success" of these status moves in fulfilling this goal—even of positive moves—depends on observers' perceptions and their evaluations of these behaviors. As status is subjectively evaluated (Blau, 1964) and conferred to those individuals who effectively signal their competence or commitment to the group (Correll & Ridgeway, 2006), observers decide whether those signals are accurate and legitimate indicators of an individual's actual competence or commitment (Anderson, Brion, et al., 2012; Anderson & Kilduff, 2009b; Kennedy et al., 2013). For that reason, when observers "see through" the ulterior selfish motives of the actor and perceive that they have performed status moves out of disproportionately selfish motives (e.g., contributions to the group only when there are obvious benefits to the self), even their positive moves may not lead to the conferral of greater status. Therefore, it is unsurprising that people work hard to conceal their status-striving motives due to the stigma associated with such motives (Kim & Pettit, 2015).

Considering the complexity associated with the successful pursuit of status, scholars have identified behaviors that are particularly relevant to status attainment (see Anderson & Kilduff, 2009b, for review). Hardy and Van Vugt (2006) proposed the competitive altruism hypothesis, which argues that people seek to increase their status by displaying generosity and self-sacrificial behaviors (e.g., helping [Flynn et al., 2006]; contributing to a public fund [Willer, 2009]; or engaging in group-directed efforts [Lount et al., 2017]). Because status reflects perceived value to the group (Correll & Ridgeway, 2006), it is easy to see why the successful pursuit of status would be closely linked to behaviors and motivations that appear to put one's self-interests aside, and signal a desire to contribute to the collective.

Yet, if engaging in group-oriented behavior leads to greater status, then why don't people always engage in prosocial behavior and universally act in the best interest of the group to gain status? In other words, why do people often engage in highly self-interested behaviors that can potentially undermine their status in the group, especially given that others can often see through their selfish motives? To address these questions, a growing body of research has directed scholarly attention towards unpacking the mixed psychological motives that operate simultaneously when people compete for status: whereas individuals must demonstrate their competence, commitment, and concern for the group to attain status, they also have a strong desire to put their personal interests ahead of the group's (Raz et al., 2021). Accordingly, the pursuit of status can be likened to a social dilemma where "people weigh their own personal status concerns (i.e., if another person gains or loses status what is the implication for my own status?) against collective interests (i.e., affording status solely based on a person's contribution to collective goals)" (Pettit & Marr, 2020, p. 235).

Psychology of Status Striving: A Social Dilemma

Despite the benefits that accrue to those who are perceived to contribute to the group's collective goals and interests, people who seek to attain status are not always inclined to expend their energy and resources towards such efforts because providing help to others can put one's personal status at risk. Indeed, status is often construed as a zero-sum commodity within groups (i.e., a group member's gain comes at the loss of another) and the incentives to climb the status hierarchy (e.g., access to resources, greater influence) pose a challenge especially in interdependent contexts, where people are expected to help the teammates with whom they are competing for the very same coveted rewards (Campbell et al., 2017). Indeed, in his book *Give and Take* (Grant, 2013), Grant describes three kinds of people in the workplace: takers, givers, and matchers. Whereas takers are those that have very little concern for others and act primarily out of self-interest, givers go out of their way to help others without seeking anything in return. For those seeking to manage their status, both extreme forms of taking and giving may be seen as disadvantageous to one's status (at least, in the short term) because they can undermine one's perceived value to the group: takers may be perceived as overly selfish (Kim & Pettit, 2015) while givers may engage in prosocial behaviors at the expense of their work and career progress (Koopman et al., 2016). As a result, Grant identifies that the majority of people are matchers—navigating the desire to help others whilst protecting ourselves and striving to stay at equilibrium between giving and taking. Through "matching" people can escape the relationship and reputational damage associated with takers, while simultaneously protecting themselves against the exploitation and exhaustion that afflict givers.

The notion that people pursue and vie for status through delicately balancing these self- and other-oriented concerns builds upon early conceptualizations of status conferral as a social negotiation in the sociological literature (Day & Day, 1977; Goffman, 1969; Maines, 1982) and is central to our understanding of the psychology and impact of status competitions. This perspective, frequently described as a "bounded functionalist" account of status, notes that group members are motivated towards the collective success of their group, "yet they are constrained in their ability to do so because of their individual self-interests" (Anderson & Willer, 2014, p. 47). The strength of an individual's concerns surrounding their relationships with others (i.e., relational or other-oriented concerns), their personal status within the group relative to others (i.e., personal or self-oriented concerns), and the relative priority of these concerns can shape the ways people maneuver for status.

Relational and Other-Oriented Status Concerns

Because signaling commitment to the group is associated with higher status, research has dedicated a great deal of attention towards the relational and other-oriented concerns that underlie the pursuit of status in workgroups. Other-concern reflects a heightened awareness of others and their needs (De Dreu & Nauta, 2009). It is frequently defined as a concern for others primarily rooted in a sense of empathy and care for the collective, and has commonly been associated with an increased desire to fulfill the group's goals (Bechtoldt et al., 2010). As a result, other-concern is a psychological state that predicts a number of prosocial behaviors in organizations and can increase an individual's willing-ness to expend personal resources to assist those in need (Grant & Mayer, 2009). Much of the research focusing squarely on the other-oriented concerns that underlie the pursuit of status highlights the beneficial group or organizational consequences associated with the desire for higher status.

There are a number of reasons that help to explain why the desire for status heightens other-concern and other relational concerns. Specifically, research has argued and provided support for motivational, structural, and attentional explanations for this relationship. From a primarily motivational standpoint, the desire to be positively evaluated by others can increase goal commitment and performance (Klein et al., 2020). Further, a sense of duty or an intrinsic desire to contribute to the collective is engendered in certain individuals who already have or are pursuing higher status. Specifically, building upon the social exchange theories of status conferral, scholars have argued that higher status group members may feel a sense of duty to give back to those who have given them status (Berger et al., 1980; Gould, 2002; Henrich & Gil-White, 2001). For instance, Willer (2009) documents that these individuals are willing to give their own personal resources to others (e.g., monetary contributions), even when they have an option to appropriate the resources for themselves. Relatedly, with the expertise they purportedly have, higher status individuals may demonstrate a greater motivation to help others develop their skills so that these individuals can learn and complete their tasks alone in the future (i.e., autonomous help; Nadler, 1997). While teaching others how to do something potentially dilutes one's personal value—because they are no longer the only one who possesses this unique set of expertise—higher status individuals may believe it is their responsibility to give back to those who granted them status and to help those most in need (Cheng et al., 2010).

In tandem with the motivational underpinnings associated with status and other-oriented concerns and behaviors, the structural benefits that accompany status may further solidify the relationship between status and other-concern. Higher-status people often make disproportionate contributions that serve their group's collective interests because they possess the necessary resources and capabilities to do so. A higher level of status is typically accompanied with greater access to organizational resources (Thye, 2000) and, therefore, provides individuals more opportunities to contribute to the group (Nembhard & Edmondson, 2006). These structural benefits, coupled with group-oriented motivation, can help higher status individuals engage in behaviors that are intended to benefit the group even if such actions are potentially costly to the self. For instance, even though voice is inherently risky for the individual speaking up (Carpini et al., 2017; Detert & Edmondson, 2011), higher status may enable people to speak up on behalf of others (Howell et al., 2019; Janssen & Gao, 2015; Kim et al., in press) partly because of the recognition that the voice recipient (e.g., leader) is more likely to consider and enact suggestions that come from the most esteemed individuals (Howell et al., 2015; McClean et al., 2021). The tendency for higher status individuals to speak up can result in a virtuous cycle as those who voice are likely to receive more status for engaging in this risky yet group-oriented behavior (McClean et al., 2018; Weiss & Morrison, 2019).

Finally, there is an attentional basis for the relationship between status and relational concerns. As an individual's status relies on others' perceptions, it orients people's attention outward (Blader & Chen, 2012) and leads them to vigilantly monitor how they are seen in the eyes of others. An outward-orientation enables individuals to take others' perspectives (Blader et al., 2016) and, therefore, can facilitate a variety of other-oriented concerns or behaviors (e.g., treating others fairly; Blader & Chen, 2012). Both the successful maintenance and pursuit of status—especially for those with lower status who still need to "prove" that they are worthy of status—requires individuals to shift their attention outward to effectively understand how to get others' approval and demonstrate their willingness to behave in ways that promote collective interests (Blader & Yu, 2017).

Overall, for individuals who have or desire higher status, other-oriented concerns and behaviors can ensue because it is a vehicle through which they can demonstrate their usefulness and value to the group. Yet, despite the functional social exchange processes associated with status striving, people do not invariantly engage in behaviors that promote the collective good. In fact, they frequently display behaviors that are self-centered and potentially harmful to others. Thus, below we discuss how the desire for status can heighten self-oriented concerns as well and detail the difficulties of navigating these dual motives in the successful pursuit of status.

Personal and Self-Oriented Status Concerns

Much research has also found support for the self-oriented concerns that accompany the pursuit of status in workgroups. Self-concern is conceptualized as a heightened attention on one's own instrumental value, contributions, or competence (De Dreu & Nauta, 2009). We discuss these self-oriented concerns in the context of status competitions in which people are concerned about how their personal competencies are seen in the eyes of others (i.e., how do others view my personal value, contributions, or competence?) and, importantly, where they stand relative to others on these valued dimensions.

Although the demonstration of group-serving behaviors plays a prominent role in the conferral of status, such behaviors consume a great deal of time, energy, and personal resources (Bolino et al., 2018; Gabriel, Koopman, et al., 2018). While expending these resources on others benefits the group, doing so could subsequently undermine one's ability to complete their own work tasks (Koopman et al., 2016), decrease one's performance or perceived competence, and negatively impact their status in the future. Further, helping others could directly increase the performance, competencies, and value of other group members at the cost of one's own (Kakkar et al., 2019; Mueller & Kamdar, 2011). Through helping and sharing valuable knowledge and expertise with others, people risk becoming expendable, threatening the sustainability of their own unique value in the group (Nadler, 2015, 2018). If others can do exactly the same thing as oneself, what does that mean for their personal utility to the group? Thus, what is best for another group member (or the group) may not always be aligned with what is best for oneself. Accordingly, when competing with others for status, people consider not only whether their behaviors will be seen to contribute to the group's goals, but also how their actions might affect their own perceived value relative to that of others.

When self-interested status concerns are particularly salient and overshadow relational concerns, people may employ a number of behaviors in the service of their status, some of which are particularly destructive to others and the success of the group (e.g., social undermining [Reh et al., 2018]; cheating [Pettit et al., 2016]). In most instances, however, status-striving behaviors—even when they are primarily driven by self-interests—are relatively subtle and covert. Because status is conferred based on *perceived* (and not necessarily actual) value to group, people tend to be strategic about their actions and engage in behaviors that are ostensibly group-oriented yet have underlying self-serving motivations below the surface.

Closer inspection into the psychology and motivation underlying such behaviors often elucidates people's tendency to prioritize their self-interests over those of other stakeholders. For example, people may choose *not* to help those most in need, but instead strategically help those in higher status positions, because such individuals might be better able to positively affect their status (Van der Vegt et al., 2006). Helping others who struggle to complete their responsibilities would be beneficial for the achievement of the group's goals (Laughlin & Ellis, 1986), but doing so might also require more effort whilst offering little personal benefits in return. Beyond the extra resources required to help them, there is also the fear that merely interacting with lower status individuals could negatively impact one's status by association (i.e., "status leakage"; Acharya & Pollock, 2013; Podolny, 2010). Thus, people's helping behaviors are often shaped by underlying self-interests, in particular, by their expectations of future returns on their acts of kindness as they are cognizant of the fact that the recipients of help are hardwired to reciprocate the favor (Cialdini, 2001).

Relatedly, research on visibility has highlighted that other seemingly group-oriented behaviors may be shaped by an individual's concerns about their personal status and how their behaviors will be seen by others. For instance, higher status individuals may choose to only put forth effort or display prosocial behavior when others are watching or they can be publicly observed (Griskevicius et al., 2010; Hardy & Van Vugt, 2006; Lount et al., 2019). In the absence of such visibility, individuals might choose to expend effort elsewhere to protect personal time and resources, suggesting that their efforts might not be driven—at least, entirely—by sense of duty or a desire to help the collective.

The experience of status threat plays a particularly significant role in driving the self-interested behaviors that are frequently associated with status competitions. When people feel that their status is being threatened, they may be particularly motivated to maintain or avoid the loss of their status. For instance, to protect oneself from status loss, they may withhold help towards those individuals who are seen as particularly threatening (Doyle et al., 2016). Alternatively, people may help as a way to "put others in their place," or offer unsolicited help in an effort to protect their standing and maintain a superior status position (Shnabel et al., 2016). Through providing help or verbal displays of "support," people may subtly demean the competencies of another (e.g., see "backhanded compliments"; Sezer et al., 2019) and indirectly communicate to others that the target of help is incapable of completing the task independently (Halabi et al., 2011). The type and amount of provided help also matters. As opposed to teaching others how to complete a task independently in the future, status threat motivates people to provide others with the complete solution. While such dependency-oriented assistance may be seen to aid efficiency and help the group complete their tasks in the short term, it also prevents the recipient's ability to develop the solution and necessary expertise on their own (Nadler & Halabi, 2006), which ultimately undermines the group's ability to sustain a high level of performance in the future.

In contrast to effortful and prosocial behaviors (e.g., helping), status competitions also lead people to engage in behaviors that more directly harm others and are clearly in opposition of the group's collective goals. For instance, concerns surrounding one's personal status can result in dominating or antisocial motivations and behaviors (Poortvliet,

2013). People may denigrate others by directly expressing aggressions (Kim et al., 2019), undermine others (Pettit, 2011), or withhold necessary support that others deserve (Garcia et al., 2010). Alternatively, people may cheat to overstate their personal performance and signal unwarranted competence (Pettit et al., 2016; Vriend et al., 2016). In doing so, they may also justify such actions by reasoning that what benefits them (i.e., inflating their performance ratings) should indirectly benefit the group as well (Treviño et al., 2014), even though the alleged benefits could come at the expense of others and jeopardize the group's interests. While these self-centered behaviors are occasionally considered effective pathways to protect and/or attain status (Cheng et al., 2013), high status actors who display such actions may also be at risk of being penalized more harshly (Kakkar et al., 2020). Indeed, people who employ overtly harmful or transgressive behaviors in pursuit of status are often found unsuccessful in achieving their goal (i.e., ascending in the group's hierarchy) (Anderson & Kilduff, 2009b).

Overall, the psychology associated with competing and striving for status is complex. On the one hand, group members are motivated towards the collective success of their group; however, they are also motivated by individual self-interests to protect personal status and obtain higher status than others. In extreme cases where self-interested status concerns completely overtake collective concerns, hierarchies can elicit a highly competitive and conflictual environment and group functioning is likely to break down. As a result, it is important to understand the factors that trigger and exacerbate the unhealthy consequences associated with status competitions.

Drivers of Self-Interested Status Concerns and Behaviors

A key premise of this chapter is that perceptions of hierarchy instability and mutability provide a foundation for the emergence and perpetuation of status competitions (Hays & Bendersky, 2015). Otherwise, why would people compete for status if there was no opportunity and possibility for it to change? Accordingly, the experience of status change, or the mere potential for one's status to change, directly relates to, or at least operates in the background of, much of the work discussed below. From this dynamic perspective of status hierarchy (Bendersky & Pai, 2018), scholars have identified a number of factors that can trigger some of the dysfunctional consequences associated with status competitions. These factors span across multiple levels of analysis—relating to the organizational or structural elements of the hierarchy (i.e., structural properties), individual experiences within dynamic and contested hierarchies over time (i.e., temporal properties), dyadic or relational characteristics (i.e., relational properties), and individual qualities or dispositions (i.e., individual properties).

Structural Properties of Contested Hierarchies

One important structural attribute that can shape the experience and consequences of status competitions is the level of status dispersion, defined as the magnitude of status inequality between group members (Christie & Barling, 2010). Traditionally, status hierarchies were thought to order themselves in a perfectly stepwise function with equidistant and ordinal differences between status rankings: the status difference between the 1st and 2nd ranked status positions is identical to that between the 3rd and 4th ranked status positions. However, status differences are based primarily on *perceptions* of value that are unlikely to be equally distributed across group members. As a result, recent research has increasingly recognized that prior conceptualizations of hierarchy may, at times, oversimplify how hierarchies take shape (Bunderson et al., 2016; Groysberg et al., 2011) and has shed new light on the value associated with considering its structural differences.

Indeed, there are a number of different forms that status hierarchies may take, with important consequences for intra-group experiences and competitive behaviors. For example, in organizations where status is conferred only to the few and rare superstars (while the rest of the organizational employees are relegated to low status positions), there will be large dispersion of status. Large status dispersion—where a small number of people take a disproportionately large proportion of the rewards—can trigger intense competition, incivility, or undermining behavior (Kim & Wiesenfeld, 2017), as those with lower status will want to be included in the exclusively high-status echelon in order to reap the same benefits. On the other extreme are groups and organizations where there are small status differences between the superstars and average employees who form the backbone of the organization (i.e., small status dispersion). In such circumstances, it is possible that group members will be less likely to compete as fiercely for status as the reward differential may not be highly pronounced (Anderson & Brown, 2010). In an effort to reduce the damaging effects of large dispersion, organizers of status contests might choose to distribute slack resources to those lower in the hierarchy, minimizing dispersion ("Mark Effect"; Bothner et al., 2011). While minimizing dispersion is arguably better for equal distribution of organizational resources, continuing to invest more heavily in the elite members of the group and further widening the distribution of rewards ("Matthew effect"; Merton, 1968) may be preferred under certain circumstances (e.g., small tournaments with a small set of superstars and situations in which there are acute advantages from receiving slack resources; Bothner et al., 2011).

Related to variations in status dispersion, people have different mental representations of hierarchical structures (e.g., pyramids, ladders) (Yu et al., 2019). When people view hierarchy as a structure in which people occupy distinct vertical ranks (i.e., ladder), it may prompt the social comparison processes that fuel competitive behaviors (Garcia et al., 2013) and harm social relationships (Reh et al., 2018). This mindset is argued to threaten the collective success of the group because it motivates people to focus on how they will secure or enhance their personal rank (Greer et al., 2017) and facilitates competitive intra-group hierarchical conflict (Van Bunderen et al., 2018). For example, organizations that employ individual performance-rank appraisals, commonly known as "stacked ranking systems" (Mulligan & Bull Schaefer, 2011) are more vulnerable to the destructive effects of status competitions, such as reduced cooperative behaviors (Chambers & Baker, 2020) and increased unethical behavior (John et al., 2014). As these ranks may serve to convey one's instrumentality to the group, people are inclined to vie for higher ranks by placing undue weight on individual performance over cooperative behaviors to signal their value to the group without elevating that of others. Consequently, it will likely intensify self-interested behaviors and increase the salience of the personal status costs associated with helping others, unless the organization takes proactive steps to signal that prosocial contributions are just as important as visible performance ranking information (Chambers & Baker, 2020). If communality is also recognized as a key basis for status conferral (Fragale, 2006), the competitive behaviors associated with status competitions can be minimized.

Whereas the research discussed above documents that highly differentiated structures can heighten competitive behaviors, these potentially detrimental behaviors are particularly pronounced in groups with too many group members who occupy similar—and high—status positions (Swaab et al., 2014). As an example, Groysberg et al. (2011) document the potential downsides of having a group with many high-status members. Despite having a greater level of pooled expertise, groups with multiple high-status members may experience increased conflict and suffer from a lack of coordination as these individuals feel pressure to constantly prove their superiority and expertise in the group.

Related to the composition of team members in a group, it is noteworthy that organizations have the ability to determine, signal, and alter what is valued within the organizational hierarchy. Research on status jolts provide some of the extreme examples of this and demonstrate instances where the qualities or competencies that are valued change suddenly, drastically altering how people are sorted within the status hierarchy. An organization may introduce a new technology (Joshi, 1991), hire a number of high-status newcomers (Prato & Ferraro, 2018), or shift its criteria for hiring or promotions (Spataro, 2012). Neeley and Dumas (2016) examined how people react to a sudden and unsolicited change in their status, caused by a company-wide mandate to adopt English as lingua franca in a global Japanese organization. In the authors' qualitative study, the primary language of communication of the company had been Japanese until the abrupt change in organizational policy—or "jolt"—arrived. After English replaced Japanese as lingua franca, employees who could not quickly adjust to the newly mandated change found themselves facing a possibility of demotion and status loss whereas those who were already fluent in English found themselves with an unexpected status gain. Overall, the actual or perceived structure of the hierarchy is inevitably influenced by organizational policies and norms that signal what is valued in the organization (e.g., competence, communality) and who is deserving of status. As a result, policies, procedures, or structural elements that facilitate this organizational "value signaling" play a prominent role in shaping intragroup status competitions.

Temporal Properties of Contested Hierarchies

Much of the research regarding the temporal properties of contested hierarchies directly examines how people experience their status over time, including the experience of status change or the imminent possibility of status change. Studying those individuals who are experiencing a change in one's own status, scholars have identified a number of characteristics associated with the change (e.g., direction of change, status level before or after change, speed and legitimacy of change) that can amplify personal status concerns and alter how people respond in contested environments.

Some of the first work in this area considered the role of the *direction* of status change (i.e., a loss versus gain in status) over time. In general, and consistent with the basic tenets of prospect theory (Tversky & Kahneman, 1979), the possibility and actual experience of status loss is documented to be more impactful than that of an equivalent status gain (Pettit et al., 2010). The direction of status change over time critically alters how people construe their status position and choose to maneuver for status moving forward. In their research on the experience of status loss, Marr and Thau (2014) argue that individuals experience a great deal of self-threat when they lose status. With a set of field and experimental studies, they demonstrate that the threatening experience associated with status loss can elicit strong psychological reactions, which can negatively impact their performance in the group. Further, people may blame others for their status loss and even engage in retaliatory behaviors against those who have taken away something of value (Thau et al., 2007). Even if the reason for their loss in status is clearly understood, the shame or embarrassment associated with such negative experiences may potentially lead people to deidentify with their group (Belschak & Den Hartog, 2009) and inadvertently decrease the extent to which people behave in ways that would benefit others (Jones & George, 1998). The negative impact associated with status loss is so aversive (Neeley, 2013) that even the mere possibility that one's status could fall can prompt a number of self-interested behaviors. For instance, Pettit et al. (2016) found that people were inclined to cheat (as opposed to put forth more effort) in order to avoid a potential status loss; yet, they chose not to do so in order to achieve an equivalent status gain. Consistent with the endowment effect (Kahneman et al., 1991), this tendency to cheat in an attempt to avoid a loss is driven by the greater value people place upon their status when they anticipate losing something they possess.

While losing status is particularly threatening and is often associated with more destructive or dysfunctional behaviors than gaining status, the psychology associated with the desire to gain status in contested hierarchies is arguably complex. On the one hand, being afforded greater status motivates a number of group-serving behaviors even when they come at a cost to oneself (e.g., Willer, 2009). On the other hand, it is possible that gaining status will lead to heightened self-interest and a decline in generosity towards others. For instance, gaining status can trigger an anticipation of career advancement (Neeley & Dumas, 2016) which may direct an individuals' attention towards how they would achieve even more success and result in a greater focus on opportunities for personal benefits (Carver & White, 1994; Gray, 1990). Further, higher status individuals who feel particularly entitled to their superior position may believe they have already fulfilled their dutiful contributions to the group and, therefore, more readily justify focusing their attention on themselves and refrain from helping others (Hays & Blader, 2017).

In addition to the direction of change over time, an individual's status level (whether it be before or after the change) is another frequently studied factor impacting the behaviors of people in contested hierarchies. Lower-status individuals arguably have less to lose than those higher in the hierarchy, whereas higher-status individuals are more inclined to view their status position as critically important to their sense of self (Brewer & Gardner, 1996). For these reasons, those high in the hierarchy are likely to perceive the experience of losing status to be particularly threatening (Marr & Thau, 2014). In addition to their aversion towards falling from a higher status position, individuals may also experience increased competitive arousal as they move closer to the very top of the hierarchy (Cassidy & Lynn, 1989; Malhotra, 2010) because of the special value that is placed upon the highest status position, or "first" place (Garcia et al., 2010). Individuals closer to the top of the hierarchy are argued to experience an increase in social comparison concerns (Garcia et al., 2006), engage in riskier behaviors (Garcia & Tor, 2007), and display more self-interested expressions (Chiao et al., 2008; Chen et al., 2012; Vandegrift & Holaday, 2012) than those relatively lower in the hierarchy. While a status loss may seem less consequential to those who are already in lower status positions, people place undue disdain on the "last place" and, therefore, seek to avoid it (i.e., "last place aversion"; Kuziemko et al., 2014; Pan et al., 2014). On the other extreme, low status, and last place in particular, is argued to increase a range of negative psychological states (e.g., anxiety, frustration, threat, and evaluation concerns) (Duguid et al., 2012; McGinn & Newman, 2013; Muscatell et al., 2012) that can minimize self-control and prompt questionable, destructive, or unethical behaviors (e.g., Anicich et al., 2016; Pettit et al., 2016; Wohl et al., 2014). Finally, in addition to the heightened competitive arousal associated with the top or bottom ranks, there may be certain points (or critical levels) within the status hierarchy perceived to be especially contested, and thus can elicit self-interested behaviors. Hierarchies often have important thresholds (e.g., top 10, 25, 50, and 100) that provide unique rewards (Isaac & Schindler, 2014; Rozin et al., 2014). Proximity to these thresholds, or a large clustering of individuals around them, can result in destructive behaviors as people vie with others to secure their place above this threshold (Ku et al., 2005).

A third temporal factor impacting behavioral reactions to status competition is the speed or magnitude of one's status change over time. Combined with the direction of change, the speed or magnitude of status change (i.e., an individual's status trajectory) can create the experience of psychological momentum (Briki & Markman, 2018). The experience of momentum moves individuals' attention away from where they are in the present and brings it toward where they could be in the future, a focus that has a profound impact on individual status concerns and competitive behaviors (e.g., Gilovich et al., 1985). For instance, experiencing a series of consecutive wins or losses (e.g., a streak, Murtha, 2013; upward or downward performance spirals, Rees et al., 2013) is argued to drastically alter people's expectations or confidence and induce risk-seeking behaviors (Lehman and Hahn, 2013). For example, the continuity of streaks (and the psychological momentum they elicit) may lead people to mentally project themselves into the future to "preview" an outcome that has yet to transpire (Suddendorf et al., 2009). When streaks cause people to imagine *unexpected* future outcomes (i.e., favorites [underdogs] imaging a future loss [win]), they are more likely to engage in transgressive behavior because of the uncertainty they feel and the intense emotional reactions (i.e., anxiety or excitement) that such uncertainty can elicit (Doyle et al., 2021). Overall, research on momentum highlights the value in considering not only where an actor ranks (i.e., status level), but also (1) how they arrived at that rank (i.e., their past trajectories), and (2) where they are anticipated to be in the future in predicting self-interested behaviors (see Pettit & Marr, 2020, for review on status trajectories).

While the abovementioned stream of research indirectly suggests that people are generally aware of the possibility that their status could change over time, awareness of such possibility does not mean that people necessarily perceive those status changes to be fair. Perceptions of fairness related to status changes are important to understand because the perceived legitimacy of the hierarchy, or their status legitimacy (i.e., "the extent to which one feels that his or her status is equitable"; Hays & Blader, 2017, p. 18), plays an important role in predicting the functional or dysfunctional consequences of status contests. While status hierarchies are generally agreed upon, disagreements over the status ordering do occur (Bendersky & Hays, 2017; Kilduff, Willer, et al., 2016), and people can vary in the extent to which they feel that the hierarchy, or their individual status, fairly represents where people should stand. When people believe that prominent individuals are deserving of their higher status positions, they are more inclined to support and defer to them and will be less likely to challenge their position (Tyler, 1997). In contrast, a perceived illegitimacy can trigger challenging behaviors and amplify status contests or conflicts within the group (Marr et al., 2019). Despite its costs, however, it is worth noting that a perceived lack of legitimacy may have a potential upside: high-status individuals who have yet to feel deserving of their higher status (i.e., experience less status legitimacy) may actually be *more* inclined to help others than those who feel their status is fair and justified (Hays & Blader, 2017). In such circumstances, people are argued to feel less deserving of their higher status and are more inclined to put forth efforts that will reduce the positive inequity (Anderson, Willer, et al., 2012; see also, unearned status gain; Neeley & Dumas, 2016).

Relational Properties of Contested Hierarchies
Not only are people sensitive and attuned to their own status level, change, or trajectory, but they also pay close attention to the relative status and status trajectory of others

(Kakkar et al., 2019; Kupor et al., 2019). This is not surprising given the relative and often interdependent nature of status—one person's gain (loss) in status typically comes at the expense of someone else's loss (gain) in status. Research on observed "status momentum" (Pettit et al., 2013), documents that third-party observations of a rise or fall in status leads to the prediction that these actors will continue the same trajectory (e.g., a rise [fall] followed by further rises [falls]) in the future. Importantly, people project different speeds at which the trajectory will continue: they typically perceive that upward trajectories will be accelerated, and downward trajectories will slow down or halted, due to their belief that the actor cares a great deal about rising or avoiding a fall in rank (Alessandri et al., 2021; Kupor et al., 2019). These findings point to some of the relational properties that can trigger unhealthy status competitions. Because upward trajectories are expected to continue in the future, the upward momentum of others can be very threatening to other group members, especially when they begin to encroach on those group members' position (Kakkar et al., 2019). Even those who consistently demonstrate their contributions to the group (and do nothing personally to warrant a loss in status) can face the possibility of falling in the hierarchy because of the upward momentum of others. In an effort to secure their superior standing, people may resort to withholding support for others or even attempt to directly undermine those who are most likely to surpass them in status (Pettit, 2011).

As with status trajectory, the proximity of two individuals' status (i.e., interpersonal status distance) is an important relational property that can trigger status threat, especially in highly unstable and contested hierarchies. As the status distance between two individuals decreases, status threat is likely to increase (Fragale et al., 2012; Phillips et al., 2009) and inhibit one's willingness to help these individuals (Doyle et al., 2016). It is noteworthy, however, that status proximity between two individuals does not always facilitate status threat. People may actually prefer interacting with others of similar status (i.e., status homophily; Still & Strang, 2009) and, in such circumstances, status proximity may increase cooperative (e.g., interpersonal helping) behaviors. The extent to which people are competitively or collaboratively oriented towards their peers whose status is proximal to theirs may depend, in part, on the nature of their first interaction. If a similarly ranked "status peer" initiates a competitive behavior, this single behavior can prompt a spiral of interpersonal aggression (Kim et al., 2019). In contrast, because collaborative behaviors in contested hierarchies are unexpected, receiving help or support from someone who might otherwise be considered a direct competitor can strengthen trust and increase a desire to work together in the future (Spataro et al., 2014).

Extending the role of the first interaction, the history of past interactions among group members a play an important role in predicting competitive behaviors (Johnson et al., 2006). For instance, people may be less inclined to cooperate with those they are familiar with because they can get access to unique knowledge by collaborating with unfamiliar, rather than, familiar parties (Kistruck et al., 2016). Further, research on rivalry (Kilduff et al., 2010) has documented that perceived rivalry increases one's motivation to outdo these opponents, facilitating the "whatever it takes" mindset associated with an increase in unethical behavior (Kilduff, Galinsky et al., 2016; Ordóñez et al., 2009; To et al., 2018).

Finally, an actor's social standing relative to their competitor in a focal contest (i.e., underdog or favored standing) has important implications for competitive motivations and behaviors (Nurmohamed et al., 2021; Steele & Lovelace, 2021). For instance, those who are expected to win (i.e., favorites) enter a competition with a primary focus on not losing (i.e., prevention focus) and a strong desire to avoid embarrassment (Dai et al., 2018); in contrast, those actors who are expected to lose (i.e., underdogs) enter a competition with a primary focus on winning (i.e., promotion focus) and a strong desire to prove others wrong (Nurmohamed, 2020). Because of the significant impact that regulatory orientation have on effortful, transgressive, or risk-seeking behaviors (Gino & Margolis, 2011; Lount et al., 2017; To et al., 2018), understanding the impact of relative standing on the psychology of status contests is important.

Individual Properties in Contested Hierarchies

In addition to the features detailed in the research above, there are a number of individual properties that affect status striving behaviors, including but certainly not limited to an individual's dispositions, attitudes, and cultural background. Compared to some of the properties we have discussed previously, these individual-level factors, are arguably more difficult for organizations to modify and, therefore, creates challenges for managers who seek to facilitate a beneficial change in behavior. Nevertheless, how a specific individual responds in contested environments—as a product of these individual properties—may depend on the social context. Accordingly, through understanding the relationship between individual attributes and status striving behaviors, scholarly research may help inform organizational attempts to reorganize employee roles or work groups, such that people are placed in an environment where such qualities will result in more functional—and less dysfunctional—consequences.

Ultimately, an individual's ability to effectively manage the impressions of others is key to the management of status. Impression management is frequently described as a dispositional attribute—with some being more skilled and willing to engage in impression management than others (Turnley & Bolino, 2001). Specifically, individuals who are particularly high on self-monitoring (Flynn et al., 2006) are likely to have relatively more success using these status enhancing techniques than those who are lower on self-monitoring. In an effort to manage their status, individuals may employ a number of tactics intended to alter others' perception of them (Leary & Kowalski, 1990; Bolino et al., 2016). For instance, individuals may ingratiate others and engage in self-presentation tactics (e.g., humblebragging [Sezer, Gino, & Norton, 2018]) to manipulate one's likability and value (Anderson, Brion, et al., 2012; Tice, 1992). In addition, individuals may intentionally look busy by working late or during the weekend in order to elevate how others evaluate their commitment to the group (Bellezza et al., Paharia, & Keinan, 2017; Gershuny, 2005). The degree to which these behaviors are ultimately effective, even for those who are particularly skilled at impression management, is likely to be affected by the social context. For instance, while expressing passion may increase the degree to which one is admired, it can also be perceived by others as threatening and subsequently decrease the respect they receive in highly competitive contexts (Jachimowicz et al., 2019).

Finally, individuals vary in the degree to which they are generally concerned about their status (Blader & Chen, 2011) and such status-related concerns have been found to vary across different cultural backgrounds, gender, and personalities (Hays, 2013; Kim et al., 2019). For instance, extraverts tend to care more about their personal status and put more effort towards achieving their status aspirations (Barrick et al., 2002; Landis & Gladstone, 2017; Roberts & Robins, 2000) than introverts. These extraverted individuals may be conferred a higher level of status initially because their apparent confidence positively affects others' expectations for them (Ashton et al., 2002). However, it is not uncommon for these individuals to fall short of these expectations, and lose status over time (Bendersky & Shah, 2013).

Implications for Practice

From a practical perspective, this body of research suggests that overall, organizational attempts to implement practices that encourage extremely competitive "meritocracy," *or* to completely remove status hierarchies in order to curtail status competitions and contests, may be ill-informed. Yet, while numerous organizations have actively sought to foster status competitions, others have made costly decisions to minimize, if not eliminate, hierarchical differences to eradicate the "detrimental" effects of status competitions. For instance, Zappos invested nearly $350 million to minimize status differences (e.g., by removing job titles) between employees because of the status conflicts that can arise in hierarchical environments (McGregor, 2014)—a move that was not uniformly well-received by its employees. In recognition of the psychology associated with the pursuit of status, and the potentially beneficial behaviors that may result from status competitions, organizations with plans to remove hierarchical differences altogether may need to reevaluate their decisions. Indeed, effectively signaling to employees which qualities are considered valuable to the organization (e.g., competence, effort, cooperative behaviors) may prove fruitful. Doing so necessitates greater attention and focus on the delicate balance between the other- and self-oriented concerns underlying status moves and the factors that make self-interested status concerns particularly salient.

At first glance, the behaviors and psychological concerns that benefit the collective appear to be mutually exclusive with those that benefit an individual's personal self-interests. However, it is worth noting that this need not always be the case. In fact, those who are most successful at managing their status within the workplace have the ability to nimbly navigate these dual concerns (Grant, 2013; De Dreu & Nauta, 2009) and are especially prone to identify, and take advantage of, mutually beneficial opportunities where the group's collective interests are aligned with their personal self-interests. In these instances, it might be in the best interest of the group if an individual focuses one's energy on themselves as opposed to helping others. For example, imagine a star faculty member with the opportunity to secure a very prestigious grant. As opposed to asking the star faculty members to spend the majority of their time helping others, it would be wiser to let them focus their energy on their own work. Not only would it bring out more *individual* benefits (e.g., high-quality publications, another prestigious grant), but it could also return *collective* benefits (e.g., positive recognition and boosted status of the department).

How can organizations then help their employees better balance the two motives that are inevitably present as they pursue status in the workplace? As we noted earlier, organizational incentives and accountability systems can be powerful tools to foster a cooperative environment where group-oriented behavior is rewarded—but individual merit and accomplishments are also acknowledged and rewarded with status (Stewart et al., 2012). Sutton and Hargadon's (1996) qualitative study of brainstorming groups in IDEO, a global design company founded in California's Silicon Valley, illustrates one organizational example that has successfully fostered an environment that values behaviors that serve both the collective and one's self-interested concerns, simultaneously. Specifically, as detailed in their research, a top manager described IDEO as a "peer-oriented meritocracy" in which design engineers seek to enhance their status through enhancing their own technical ability and skills, and then using those skills to help others. Not only is this sentiment understood informally, but it is also built into the compensation structure of the organization as many "compensation decisions are based largely on informal reputation among fellow designers and formal peer reviews" (Sutton & Hargadon, 1996, p. 705). Indeed, when employees observe that the "nice" guys who help others (i.e., those who frequently engage in group-oriented behaviors) tend to finish last in their workplace (Hardy & Van Vugt, 2006) whereas those who put their self-interest above others' get ahead, their group-oriented concern is likely to quickly dissipate. This decline in group-oriented motivation may be especially salient when they believe they are "stuck" or "secure" in their lower or higher status position (see status stability appraisal, Neeley & Dumas, 2016). Yet, when organizations completely eliminate the possibility for employees to get appropriate credit and status for their individual efforts and accomplishments in an effort to boost group-oriented behavior, they may inadvertently reduce their work engagement and motivation as individuals may no longer see the instrumental benefits of their efforts (Han et al., 2015). While an in-depth discussion of organizational policies that would foster such an environment is beyond the scope of this chapter, our earlier examples demonstrate that it is necessary to combine multiple, and perhaps counterbalancing, policies lest status hierarchies (e.g., stacked ranking systems, systems with high degrees of status dispersion) lead to behaviors that are harmful to the group. Therefore, it is shrewd for organizations to consider using hybrid reward system in lieu of solely relying on a single—individual or collective—reward system (Pearsall et al., 2010). Indeed, the policies that lead to the optimal balance between group- and self-oriented concerns in the status-driven workplace remain elusive, but the search seems to be a worthwhile endeavor.

Future Research Directions

There are numerous opportunities for future research concerning status competitions. For instance, despite the increasing scholarly attention towards the unique psychology of status and the dual concerns that accompany the pursuit of status, much of the empirical research to date has focused on uncovering the triggers or consequences of *either* other- *or* self-oriented concerns associated with the pursuit of status. Although considering each of the two has contributed to our understanding of the psychology of status and status competitions, future empirical research needs to systematically examine both psychological processes simultaneously. Doing so would help improve our understanding of the multi-layered psychological processes and outcomes of status. Through examining how and when these motives may work in tandem to predict behaviors, scholars will have opportunities to identify dual pathways that are either countervailing or synergistic as well as moderating factors that can maximize or hinder the integrative potential of the group. A potentially useful avenue for future research in this area is taking a person-centered approach (e.g., latent profile analysis; Gabriel, Campbell, et al., 2018). This approach would allow researchers to investigate the factors that predict individual profiles (i.e., configurations) of status striving motivation, the behavioral impact of these profiles, and provide novel information about how their behaviors evolve as individuals navigate status competitions in a variety of social contexts.

Another promising area for future research concerns the cross-level or spillover effects of hierarchical competition. At present, the social hierarchy literature has predominantly focused on the effects of hierarchical differentiation on intra-team competitive dynamics (Greer et al., 2018), limiting our understanding about how these intra-team dynamics shape inter-team outcomes (and vice versa). Prior research on spillover effects in teams has shown that dynamics between team members at one level tend to result in similar dynamics at another level (Halevy, 2008; Keenan & Carnevale, 1989). Specifically, a more competitive relationship between two individual team members often spills over and leads to greater competition within the team (Jehn et al., 2013), and it also promotes competition toward other groups (Sassenberg et al., 2007). Further, greater competition between groups tends to promote greater competition and power struggles within groups (Van Bunderen et al., 2018) and members of high-status groups are documented to be more concerned about their status within their group (Chang et al., 2017). Nevertheless, and in contrast to the findings above, a handful of research suggests that in-group cohesiveness (i.e., cooperativeness) may be strengthened in inter-group competitive contexts (Halevy et al., 2012), suggesting that more research is needed to examine the competitive dynamics in social hierarchies across different levels of analysis to reconcile these divergent perspectives.

People's lay perceptions of status and hierarchy, and its impact on status competitions, provides another avenue for future research. For instance, status is frequently treated as a zero-sum property in groups, in which higher status for one person necessitates lower status for others. Whereas certain hierarchical contexts (e.g., forced distribution; ordinal rankings) or properties of status for which people compete (e.g., influence) do highlight the zero-sum nature of status (e.g., Berger et al., 2013), scholars have begun to explore the possibility that zero-sum perceptions of status vary (e.g., He et al., 2020; Sirola & Pitesa, 2017; Yu & Greer, 2017). While having higher status rank or influence denotes that another actor must necessarily have lower rank or less influence, more status respect and esteem need not always come at the expense of others. When people perceive that status is not zero-sum, they may be more inclined to pursue more relational concerns by seeking (giving) respect from (to) others as opposed to primarily seeking to elevate their status at the expense of the relegated status of others. Understanding lay perceptions of status hierarchy, as well as the factors that can alter their zero-sum perceptions of status (and even lead individuals to view status as "expandable"), is a particularly fruitful area of future research.

Additionally, in this chapter we have reviewed status competitions through incorporating research which informs us upon numerous dimensions of status (e.g., respect, influence, status rank). However, people may place disproportionate importance on a single status dimension over others. For instance, whereas most people aspire for more respect, not all people are documented to prefer higher rank because of the greater expectations and responsibility that accompany it (Anderson, Willer, et al., 2012). Those who seek to evade such expectations often willingly defer to other group members. In light of the many dimensions of status (Mattan et al., 2017), and people's fluctuating preferences, an exciting avenue for future research is disentangling how and why people compete for one status dimension versus another. The notion that multiple status dimensions exist also raises interesting questions with regards to the experience of divergent status indicators (Audia & Brion, 2007) or the management of multiple status identities (Acharya & Pollock, 2020; Fernandes et al., 2021; Han & Pollock, 2020).

Finally, an important attribute that warrants future research attention is an individual's cultural background, which can influence the extent to which people prioritize self-interested status concerns over collective interests (and vice versa). For example, cross-cultural research comparing East Asian and Western cultures suggests that there are notable differences across these cultures with respect to their experiences and behaviors in groups. East Asian (vs. Western) cultures are known for higher (vs. lower) power distance (defined as the extent to which people accept power inequalities as natural, legitimate, and even desirable) (Hofstede, 1980). As a result, power and status are much more tightly coupled in East Asian (vs. Western) cultures where status is typically a natural concomitant of a person's level of power (Kuwabara et al., 2016; To et al., 2020) and people see "power as status" (Pye, 1985, p. 22). Further, East Asian cultures tend to be more collectivistic (vs. individualistic) than Western cultures, suggesting that they may be more likely to sacrifice personal interests for collective interest and group harmony. These two important differences between Eastern and Western cultures suggest that East Asians (vs. Westerners) may be less likely to aggressively pursue personal status gains in groups, more likely to accept the group status hierarchy as legitimate and desirable, and more inclined to perceive the disruptive effects of personal status-striving efforts on group harmony and the achievement of collective goals.

Notably, despite the existence of cross-cultural research on status as noted above (Kuwabara et al., 2016; Pye, 1985; To et al., 2020), much of the current research has studied status competitions in populations of Western cultural backgrounds, and as a result, findings in the status literature have been heavily driven by research with WEIRD populations (Western, Educated, Industrialized, Rich, and Democratic cultures, Henrich et al., 2010) even though only a mere twelve percent of the global population live in these Western industrialized countries. As such, an exciting avenue of future work is examining how the dual competing motives (i.e., self- and other-oriented concerns) play out in understudied cultural clusters (e.g., Middle East, Sub-Saharan Africa) (e.g., House et al., 2002) to expand our understanding of how culture influences people's status motives and pursuits. The above opportunities for future research on status competitions are by no means exhaustive and indeed there are numerous researchable inquiries that have yet to receive scholarly attention.

Conclusion

A dominant question in the status literature considers whether the status hierarchy, and the status competitions that it prompts, benefit, or hurt organizational functioning. In an attempt to answer this question, two seemingly distinct perspectives on status competitions emerged: one that focuses on the conflictual, self-serving, or unethical behaviors that result from status competitions, and another that highlights the group-oriented efforts or motivations that accompany the pursuit of status. In this chapter, we have reviewed a growing body of research which informs us upon the psychology of status competitions. In doing so, we depart from a dichotomous judgment on whether status competitions are entirely good (functional) or bad (dysfunctional) and move towards considering how to effectively manage the mixed-motive psychology underlying the pursuit of status. Through recognizing that both concerns (i.e., self- and other-oriented) may operate simultaneously in contested status hierarchies, we hope future researchers further develop and shed light on the mixed-motive psychology of status competitions.

References

Acharya, A., & Pollock, T. (2013). Shoot for the stars? Predicting the recruitment of prestigious directors at newly public firms. *Academy of Management Journal, 56*, 1396–1419.

Acharya, A. G., & Pollock, T. (2020). Too many peas in a pod? How overlaps in directors' local and global status characteristics influence board turnover in newly public firms. *Academy of Management Journal*. Advance online publication. https://doi.org/10.5465/amj.2017.1144

Alessandri, G., Cortina, J. M., Sheng, Z., & Borgogni, L. (2021). Where you came from and where you are going: The role of performance trajectory in promotion decisions. *Journal of Applied Psychology, 106*, 599–623.

Anderson, C., Brion, S., Moore, D. A., & Kennedy, J. A. (2012). A status-enhancement account of overconfidence. *Journal of Personality and Social Psychology, 103*, 718–735.

Anderson, C., & Brown, C. E. (2010). The functions and dysfunctions of hierarchy. *Research in Organizational Behavior, 30*, 55–89.

Anderson, C., Hildreth, J., & Howland, L. (2015). Is the desire for status a fundamental human motive? A review of the empirical literature. *Psychological Bulletin, 141*, 574–601.

Anderson, C., John, O. P., Keltner, D., & Kring, A. M. (2001). Who attains social status? Effects of personality and physical attractiveness in social groups. *Journal of Personality and Social Psychology, 81*, 116–132.

Anderson, C., & Kilduff, G. J. (2009a). The pursuit of status in social groups. *Current Directions in Psychological Science, 18*, 295–298.

Anderson, C., & Kilduff, G. J. (2009b). Why do dominant personalities attain influence in face-to-face groups? The competence-signaling effects of trait dominance. *Journal of Personality and Social Psychology, 96*, 491–503.

Anderson, C., & Willer, R. (2014). Do status hierarchies benefit groups? A bounded functionalist account of status. In J. T. Cheng, J. L. Tracy, & C. Anderson (Eds.), *The psychology of social status* (pp. 47–70). Springer.

Anderson, C., Willer, R., Kilduff, G., & Brown, C. (2012). The origins of deference: When do people prefer lower status? *Journal of Personality and Social Psychology, 102*, 1077–1088.

Anicich, E., Fast, N., Halevy, N., & Galinsky, A. (2016). When the bases of social hierarchy collide: Power without status drives interpersonal conflict. *Organization Science, 27*, 123–140.

Ashton, M. C., Lee, K., & Paunonen, S. V. (2002). What is the central feature of extraversion? Social attention versus reward sensitivity. *Journal of Personality and Social Psychology, 83*, 245–252.

Audia, P., & Brion, S. (2007). Reluctant to change: Self-enhancing responses to diverging performance measures. *Organizational Behavior and Human Decision Processes, 102*, 255–269.

Barrick, M. R., Stewart, G. L., & Piotrowski, M. (2002). Personality and job performance: Test of the mediating effects of motivation among sales representatives. *Journal of Applied Psychology, 87*, 43–51.

Bechtoldt, M. N., De Dreu, C. K., Nijstad, B. A., & Choi, H. S. (2010). Motivated information processing, social tuning, and group creativity. *Journal of Personality and Social Psychology, 99*, 622–637.

Bellezza, S., Paharia, N., & Keinan, A. (2017). Conspicuous consumption of time: When busyness and lack of leisure time become a status symbol. *Journal of Consumer Research, 44*, 118–138.

Belschak, F. D., & Den Hartog, D. N. (2009). Consequences of positive and negative feedback: The impact on emotions and extra-role behaviors. *Applied Psychology, 58*, 274–303.

Bendersky, C., & Hays, N. (2012). Status conflict in groups. *Organization Science, 23*, 323–340.

Bendersky, C., & Hays, N. (2017). The positive effects of status conflicts in teams where members perceive status hierarchies differently. *Social Psychological and Personality Science, 8*, 124–132.

Bendersky, C., & Pai, J. (2018). Status dynamics. *Annual Review of Organizational Psychology and Organizational Behavior, 5*, 183–199.

Bendersky, C., & Shah, N. P. (2012). The cost of status enhancement: Performance effects of individuals' status mobility in task groups. *Organization Science, 23*, 308–322.

Bendersky, C., & Shah, N. P. (2013). The downfall of extraverts and rise of neurotics: The dynamic process of status allocation in task groups. *Academy of Management Journal, 56*, 387–406.

Berger, J., Cohen, B. P., & Zelditch, M., Jr. (1972). Status characteristics and social interaction. *American Sociological Review, 37*, 241–255.

Berger, J., Harbring, C., & Sliwka, D. (2013). Performance appraisals and the impact of forced distribution—an experimental investigation. *Management Science, 59*, 54–68.

Berger, J., Ridgeway, C. L., Fisek, M. H., & Norman, R. Z. (1998). The legitimation and delegitimation of power and prestige orders. *American Sociological Review, 63*, 379–405.

Berger, J., Rosenholtz, S. J., & Zelditch, M., Jr. (1980). Status organizing processes. *Annual Review of Sociology, 6*, 479–508.

Bensinger, G. (2019, May 19). 'MissionRacer': How Amazon turned the tedium of warehouse work into a game. *Washington Post*. http://www.washingtonpost.com/

Blader, S. L., & Chen, Y. R. (2011). What influences how higher-status people respond to lower-status others? Effects of procedural fairness, outcome favorability, and concerns about status. *Organization Science, 22*, 1040–1060.

Blader, S. L., & Chen, Y. R. (2012). Differentiating the effects of status and power: a justice perspective. *Journal of Personality and Social Psychology, 102*, 994–1014.

Blader, S. L., Shirako, A., & Chen, Y. R. (2016). Looking out from the top: Differential effects of status and power on perspective taking. *Personality and Social Psychology Bulletin, 42*, 723–737.

Blader, S. L., & Yu, S. (2017). Are status and respect different or two sides of the same coin? *Academy of Management Annals, 11*, 800–824.

Blau, P. (1964). *Exchange and power in social life*. Wiley.

Bolino, M. C., Klotz, A. C., Turnley, W. H., Podsakoff, P. M., MacKenzie, S. B., & Podsakoff, N. P. (2018). The unintended consequences of organizational citizenship behaviors for employees, teams, and organizations. In P. M. Podsakoff, S. B. MacKenzie, & N. P. Podsakoff (Eds.), *The Oxford handbook of organizational citizenship behavior* (pp. 185–202). Emerald Publishing.

Bolino, M., Long, D., & Turnley, W. (2016). Impression management in organizations: Critical questions, answers, and areas for future research. *Annual Review of Organizational Psychology and Organizational Behavior, 3*, 377–406.

Bothner, M. S., Podolny, J. M., & Smith, E. B. (2011). Organizing contests for status: The Matthew effect vs. the Mark effect. *Management Science, 57*, 439–457.

Brewer, M. B., & Gardner, W. (1996). Who is this "We"? Levels of collective identity and self representations. *Journal of Personality and Social Psychology, 71*, 83–93.

Briki, W., & Markman, K. D. (2018). Psychological momentum: The phenomenology of goal pursuit. *Social and Personality Psychology Compass, 12*, e12412.

Bunderson, J. S., Van Der Vegt, G. S., Cantimur, Y., & Rink, F. (2016). Different views of hierarchy and why they matter: Hierarchy as inequality or as cascading influence. *Academy of Management Journal, 59*, 1265–1289.

Cain, Á. (2018, April 30). 8 insider facts about shopping at Target that only employees know. *Business Insider*. http://www.businessinsider.com/

Campbell, E. M., Liao, H., Chuang, A., Zhou, J., & Dong, Y. (2017). Hot shots and cool reception? An expanded view of social consequences for high performers. *Journal of Applied Psychology, 102*, 845–866.

Carpini, J. A., Parker, S. K., & Griffin, M. A. (2017). A look back and a leap forward: A review and synthesis of the individual work performance literature. *Academy of Management Annals, 11*, 825–885.

Carver, C. S., & White, T. L. (1994). Behavioral inhibition, behavioral activation, and affective responses to impending reward and punishment: The BIS/BAS scales. *Journal of Personality and Social Psychology, 67*, 319–333.

Cassidy, T., & Lynn, R. (1989). A multifactorial approach to achievement motivation: The development of a comprehensive measure. *Journal of Occupational Psychology, 62*, 301–312.

Chambers, C. R., & Baker, W. E. (2020). Robust systems of cooperation in the presence of rankings: How displaying prosocial contributions can offset the disruptive effects of performance rankings. *Organization Science, 31*, 287–307.

Chen, P., Myers, C. G., Kopelman, S., & Garcia, S. M. (2012). The hierarchical face: Higher rankings lead to less cooperative looks. *Journal of Applied Psychology, 97*, 479–486.

Cheng, J. T., Tracy, J. L., Foulsham, T., Kingstone, A., & Henrich, J. (2013). Two ways to the top: Evidence that dominance and prestige are distinct yet viable avenues to social rank and influence. *Journal of Personality and Social Psychology, 104*, 103–125.

Cheng, J. T., Tracy, J. L., & Henrich, J. (2010). Pride, personality, and the evolutionary foundations of human social status. *Evolution and Human Behavior, 31*, 334–347.

Chiao, J. Y., Iidaka, T., Gordon, H. L., Nogawa, J., Bar, M., Aminoff, E., . . . & Ambady, N. (2008). Cultural specificity in amygdala response to fear faces. *Journal of Cognitive Neuroscience, 20*, 2167–2174.

Christie, A. M., & Barling, J. (2010). Beyond status: Relating status inequality to performance and health in teams. *Journal of Applied Psychology*, *95*, 920–934.

Chang, J. W., Chow, R. M., & Woolley, A. W. (2017). Effects of inter-group status on the pursuit of intra-group status. *Organizational Behavior and Human Decision Processes*, *139*, 1–17.

Cialdini, R. B. (2001). *Influence: Science and practice* (4th ed.). Allyn & Bacon.

Correll, S. J., & Ridgeway, C. L. (2006). Expectation states theory. In J. Delamater (Ed.), *Handbook of social psychology* (pp. 29–51). Springer.

Crosby, F. (1976). A model of egoistical relative deprivation. *Psychological Review*, *83*, 85–113.

Dai, H., Dietvorst, B. J., Tuckfield, B., Milkman, K. L., & Schweitzer, M. E. (2018). Quitting when the going gets tough: A downside of high-performance expectations. *Academy of Management Journal*, *61*, 1667–1691.

Day, R., & Day, J. A. V. (1977). A review of the current state of negotiated order theory: An appreciation and a critique. *Sociological Quarterly*, *18*, 126–142.

De Dreu, C. K., & Nauta, A. (2009). Self-interest and other-orientation in organizational behavior: implications for job performance, prosocial behavior, and personal initiative. *Journal of Applied Psychology*, *94*, 913–926.

De Kwaadsteniet, E. W., & Van Dijk, E. (2010). Social status as a cue for tacit coordination. *Journal of Experimental Social Psychology*, *46*, 515–524.

Detert, J. R., & Edmondson, A. C. (2011). Implicit voice theories: Taken-for-granted rules of self-censorship at work. *Academy of Management Journal*, *54*, 461–488.

Doyle, S. P., Lount, R. B., Jr., Wilk, S. L., & Pettit, N. C. (2016). Helping others most when they are not too close: Status distance as a determinant of interpersonal helping in organizations. *Academy of Management Discoveries*, *2*, 155–174.

Doyle, S. P., Pettit, N. C., Kim, S., To, C., & Lount, R. B. Jr. (2021). Surging underdogs and slumping favorites: How recent streaks and future expectations drive competitive transgressions. *Academy of Management Journal*. Advance online publication. https://doi.org/10.5465/amj.2019.1008

Duguid, M. M., Loyd, D. L., & Tolbert, P. S. (2012). The impact of categorical status, numeric representation, and work group prestige on preference for demographically similar others: A value threat approach. *Organization Science*, *23*, 386–401.

Ellis, L. (1994). *Social stratification and socioeconomic inequality: Vol. 2. Reproductive and interpersonal aspects of dominance and status*. Praeger.

Fath, S., & Kay, A. C. (2018). "If hierarchical, then corrupt": Exploring people's tendency to associate hierarchy with corruption in organizations. *Organizational Behavior and Human Decision Processes*, *149*, 145–164.

Fernandes, C. R., Yu, S., Howell, T. M., Brooks, A. W., Kilduff, G. J., & Pettit, N. C. (2021). What is your status portfolio? Higher status variance across groups increases interpersonal helping but decreases intrapersonal well-being. *Organizational Behavior and Human Decision Processes*, *165*, 56–75.

Flynn, F. J., & Amanatullah, E. T. (2012). Psyched up or psyched out? The influence of coactor status on individual performance. *Organization Science*, *23*, 402–415.

Flynn, F. J., Reagans, R. E., Amanatullah, E. T., & Ames, D. R. (2006). Helping one's way to the top: Self-monitors achieve status by helping others and knowing who helps whom. *Journal of Personality and Social Psychology*, *91*, 1123–1137.

Fragale, A. R. (2006). The power of powerless speech: The effects of speech style and task interdependence on status conferral. *Organizational Behavior and Human Decision Processes*, *101*, 243–261.

Fragale, A. R., Sumanth, J. J., Tiedens, L. Z., & Northcraft, G. B. (2012). Appeasing equals: Lateral deference in organizational communication. *Administrative Science Quarterly*, *57*, 373–406.

Gabriel, A. S., Campbell, J. T., Djurdjevic, E., Johnson, R. E., & Rosen, C. C. (2018). Fuzzy profiles: Comparing and contrasting latent profile analysis and fuzzy set qualitative comparative analysis for person-centered research. *Organizational Research Methods*, *21*, 877–904.

Gabriel, A. S., Koopman, J., Rosen, C. C., & Johnson, R. E. (2018). Helping others or helping oneself? An episodic examination of the behavioral consequences of helping at work. *Personnel Psychology*, *71*, 85–107.

Garcia, S. M., Song, H., & Tesser, A. (2010). Tainted recommendations: The social comparison bias. *Organizational Behavior and Human Decision Processes*, *113*, 97–101.

Garcia, S. M., & Tor, A. (2007). Rankings, standards, and competition: Task vs. scale comparisons. *Organizational Behavior and Human Decision Processes*, *102*, 95–108.

Garcia, S. M., Tor, A., & Gonzalez, R. (2006). Ranks and rivals: A theory of competition. *Personality and Social Psychology Bulletin, 32*, 970–982.

Garcia, S. M., Tor, A., & Schiff, T. M. (2013). The psychology of competition: A social comparison perspective. *Perspectives on Psychological Science, 8*, 634–650.

Gershuny, J. (2005). Busyness as the badge of honor for the new superordinate working class. *Social Research, 72*, 287–314.

Gilovich, T., Vallone, R., & Tversky, A. (1985). The hot hand in basketball: On the misperception of random sequences. *Cognitive Psychology, 17*, 295–314.

Gino, F., & Margolis, J. D. (2011). Bringing ethics into focus: How regulatory focus and risk preferences influence (un) ethical behavior. *Organizational Behavior and Human Decision Processes, 115*, 145–156.

Goffman, E. (1969). *Strategic interaction.* University of Pennsylvania Press.

Gould, R. V. (2002). The origins of status hierarchies: A formal theory and empirical test. *American Journal of Sociology, 107*, 1143–1178.

Gould, R. V. (2003). *Collision of wills: How ambiguity about social rank breeds conflict.* University of Chicago Press.

Grant, A. M. (2013). *Give and take: A revolutionary approach to success.* Penguin Group.

Grant, A. M., & Mayer, D. M. (2009). Good soldiers and good actors: Prosocial and impression management motives as interactive predictors of affiliative citizenship behaviors. *Journal of Applied Psychology, 94*, 900–912.

Gray, J. A. (1990). Brain systems that mediate both emotion and cognition. *Cognition & Emotion, 4*, 269–288.

Greer, L. L., de Jong, B. A., Schouten, M. E., & Dannals, J. E. (2018). Why and when hierarchy impacts team effectiveness: A meta-analytic integration. *Journal of Applied Psychology, 103*, 591–613.

Greer, L. L., Van Bunderen, L., & Yu, S. (2017). The dysfunctions of power in teams: A review and emergent conflict perspective. In A. P. Brief & B. M. Staw (Eds.), *Research in organizational behavior* (Vol. 37, pp. 103–124). Elsevier.

Griskevicius, V., Tybur, J. M., & Van den Bergh, B. (2010). Going green to be seen: Status, reputation, and conspicuous conservation. *Journal of Personality and Social Psychology, 98*, 392–404.

Groysberg, B., Polzer, J. T., & Elfenbein, H. A. (2011). Too many cooks spoil the broth: How high-status individuals decrease group effectiveness. *Organization Science, 22*, 722–737.

Gruenfeld, D. H., & Tiedens, L. Z. (2010). Organizational preferences and their consequences. In S. T. Fiske, D. T. Gilbert, & G. Lindzey (Eds.), *Handbook of social psychology* (5th ed., Vol. 2, pp. 1252–1287). Wiley.

Halevy, N., Chou, E. Y., Cohen, T. R., & Livingston, R. W. (2012). Status conferral in intergroup social dilemmas: Behavioral antecedents and consequences of prestige and dominance. *Journal of Personality and Social Psychology, 102*, 351–368.

Halevy, N., Y. Chou, E., & D. Galinsky, A. (2011). A functional model of hierarchy: Why, how, and when vertical differentiation enhances group performance. *Organizational Psychology Review, 1*, 32–52.

Halabi, S., Nadler, A., & Dovidio, J. F. (2011). Reactions to receiving assumptive help: The moderating effects of group membership and perceived need for help. *Journal of Applied Social Psychology, 41*, 2793–2815.

Halevy, N. 2008. Team negotiation: Social, epistemic, economic, and psychological consequences of subgroup conflict. *Personality and Social Psychology Bulletin, 34*: 1687–1702.

Han, J. H., Bartol, K. M., & Kim, S. (2015). Tightening up the performance–pay linkage: Roles of contingent reward leadership and profit-sharing in the cross-level influence of individual pay-for-performance. *Journal of Applied Psychology, 100*, 417–430.

Han, J. H., & Pollock, T. (2020). The two towers (or somewhere in between): The behavioral consequences of positional inconsistency across status hierarchies. *Academy of Management Journal, 64*, 86–113. https://doi.org/10.5465/amj.2018.1091

Hardy, C. L., & Van Vugt, M. (2006). Nice guys finish first: The competitive altruism hypothesis. *Personality and Social Psychology Bulletin, 32*, 1402–1413.

Hays, N. A. (2013). Fear and loving in social hierarchy: Sex differences in preferences for power versus status. *Journal of Experimental Social Psychology, 49*, 1130–1136.

Hays, N. A., & Bendersky, C. (2015). Not all inequality is created equal: Effects of status versus power hierarchies on competition for upward mobility. *Journal of Personality and Social Psychology, 108*, 867–882.

Hays, N. A., & Blader, S. L. (2017). To give or not to give? Interactive effects of status and legitimacy on generosity. *Journal of Personality and Social Psychology, 112*, 17–38.

He, T., Derfler-Rozin, R., & Pitesa, M. (2020). Financial vulnerability and the reproduction of disadvantage in economic exchanges. *Journal of Applied Psychology, 105*, 80–96.

Henrich, J., & Gil-White, F. J. (2001). The evolution of prestige: Freely conferred deference as a mechanism for enhancing the benefits of cultural transmission. *Evolution and Human Behavior, 22,* 165–196.

Henrich, J., Heine, S. J., & Norenzayan, A. (2010). The weirdest people in the world? *Behavioral and Brain Sciences, 33,* 61–83.

Hoffman, P. J., Festinger, L., & Lawrence, D. H. (1954). Tendencies toward group comparability in competitive bargaining. *Human Relations, 7,* 141–159.

Hofstede, G. H. (1980). *Culture's consequences: International differences in work-related values.* Sage.

House, R. J., Javidan, M., Hanges, P. J., & Dorfman, P. W. (2002). Understanding cultures and implicit leadership theories across the globe: An introduction to project GLOBE. *Journal of World Business, 37,* 3–10.

Hotten R. (2015, December 10). Volkswagen: The scandal explained. *BBC News.* http://www.bbc.com

Howell, T. M., Burris, E. R., Detert, J. R., & Pettit, N. C. (2019). Don't Shoot the Messenger: Manager Reactions to Voice from Advocates. Paper presented at the annual meeting of the Academy of Management, Boston, MA, August 2019.

Howell, T. M., Harrison, D. A., Burris, E. R., & Detert, J. R. (2015). Who gets credit for input? Demographic and structural status cues in voice recognition. *Journal of Applied Psychology, 100,* 1765–1784.

Isaac, M. S., & Schindler, R. M. (2014). The top-ten effect: Consumers' subjective categorization of ranked lists. *Journal of Consumer Research, 40,* 1181–1202.

Isaac, M. (2017, February 22). Inside Uber's aggressive, unrestrained workplace culture. *The New York Times.* http://www.nytimes.com

Jachimowicz, J., To, C., Agasi, S., Côté, S., & Galinsky, A. (2019). The gravitational pull of expressing passion: When and how expressing passion elicits status conferral and support from others. *Organizational Behavior and Human Decision Processes, 153,* 41–62.

Janssen, O., & Gao, L. (2015). Supervisory responsiveness and employee self-perceived status and voice behavior. *Journal of Management, 41,* 1854–1872.

Jehn, K., Rispens, S., Jonsen, K., & Greer, L. (2013). Conflict contagion: A temporal perspective on the development of conflict within teams. *International Journal of Conflict Management, 24,* 352–373.

John, L. K., Loewenstein, G., & Rick, S. I. (2014). Cheating more for less: Upward social comparisons motivate the poorly compensated to cheat. *Organizational Behavior and Human Decision Processes, 123,* 101–109.

Johnson, M. D., Hollenbeck, J. R., Humphrey, S. E., Ilgen, D. R., Jundt, D., & Meyer, C. J. (2006). Cutthroat cooperation: Asymmetrical adaptation to changes in team reward structures. *Academy of Management Journal, 49,* 103–119.

Jones, G. R., & George, J. M. (1998). The experience and evolution of trust: Implications for cooperation and teamwork. *Academy of Management Review, 23,* 531–546.

Joshi, K. (1991). A model of users' perspective on change: The case of information systems technology implementation. *MIS Quarterly, 15,* 229–242.

Kahneman, D., Knetsch, J. L., & Thaler, R. H. (1991). Anomalies: The endowment effect, loss aversion, and status quo bias. *Journal of Economic Perspectives, 5,* 193–206.

Kakkar, H., Sivanathan, N., & Gobel, M. (2020). Fall from grace: The role of dominance and prestige in the punishment of high-status actors. *Academy of Management Journal, 63,* 530–553.

Kakkar, H., Sivanathan, N., & Pettit, N. C. (2019). The impact of dynamic status changes within competitive rank-ordered hierarchies. *Proceedings of the National Academy of Sciences, 116,* 23011–23020.

Keenan, P. A., & Carnevale, P. J. (1989). Positive Effects of Within-Group Cooperation on Between-Group Negotiation 1. *Journal of Applied Social Psychology, 19,* 977–992.

Kennedy, J. A., Anderson, C., & Moore, D. A. (2013). When overconfidence is revealed to others: Testing the status-enhancement theory of overconfidence. *Organizational Behavior and Human Decision Processes, 122,* 266–279.

Kilduff, G. J., Elfenbein, H. A., & Staw, B. M. (2010). The psychology of rivalry: A relationally dependent analysis of competition. *Academy of Management Journal, 53,* 943–969.

Kilduff, G. J., Galinsky, A. D., Gallo, E., & Reade, J. J. (2016). Whatever it takes to win: Rivalry increases unethical behavior. *Academy of Management Journal, 59,* 1508–1534.

Kilduff, G. J., Willer, R., & Anderson, C. (2016). Hierarchy and its discontents: Status disagreement leads to withdrawal of contribution and lower group performance. *Organization Science, 27,* 373–390.

Kim, H. Y., & Pettit, N. C. (2015). Status is a four-letter word: Self versus other differences and concealment of status-striving. *Social Psychological and Personality Science, 6,* 267–275.

Kim, H. Y., Pettit, N. C., & Reitman, L. E. (2019). Status moves: Evaluations and effectiveness of status behaviors. *Group Processes & Intergroup Relations, 22*, 139–159.

Kim, H. Y., & Wiesenfeld, B. M. (2017). Who represents our group? The effects of prototype content on perceived status dispersion and social undermining. *Personality and Social Psychology Bulletin, 43*, 814–827.

Kim, S., McClean, E. J., Doyle, S. P., Podsakoff, N. P., Lin, E., & Woodruff, T. (in press). The positive and negative effects of social status on ratings of voice behavior: A test of opposing structural and psychological pathways. *Journal of Applied Psychology.*

Kistruck, G. M., Lount, R. B., Jr., Smith, B. R., Bergman, B. J., Jr., & Moss, T. W. (2016). Cooperation vs. competition: Alternative goal structures for motivating groups in a resource scarce environment. *Academy of Management Journal, 59*, 1174–1198.

Klein, H. J., Lount Jr, R. B., Park, H. M., & Linford, B. J. (2020). When goals are known: The effects of audience relative status on goal commitment and performance. *Journal of Applied Psychology, 105*(4), 372–389.

Koopman, J., Lanaj, K., & Scott, B. A. (2016). Integrating the bright and dark sides of OCB: A daily investigation of the benefits and costs of helping others. *Academy of Management Journal, 59*, 414–435.

Ku, G., Malhotra, D., & Murnighan, J. K. (2005). Towards a competitive arousal model of decision-making: A study of auction fever in live and Internet auctions. *Organizational Behavior and Human Decision Processes, 96*, 89–103.

Kupor, D., Brucks, M. S., & Huang, S. C. (2019). And the winner is . . . ? Forecasting the outcome of others' competitive efforts. *Journal of Personality and Social Psychology, 117*(3), 500–521.

Kuwabara, K., Yu, S., Lee, A. J., & Galinsky, A. D. (2016). Status decreases dominance in the West but increases dominance in the East. *Psychological Science, 27*, 127–137.

Kuziemko, I., Buell, R. W., Reich, T., & Norton, M. I. (2014). "Last-place aversion": Evidence and redistributive implications. *Quarterly Journal of Economics, 129*, 105–149.

Landis, B., & Gladstone, J. J. (2017). Personality, income, and compensatory consumption: Low-income extraverts spend more on status. *Psychological Science, 28*, 1518–1520.

Laughlin, P. R., & Ellis, A. L. (1986). Demonstrability and social combination processes on mathematical intellective tasks. *Journal of Experimental Social Psychology, 22*, 177–189.

Leary, M. R., & Kowalski, R. M. (1990). Impression management: A literature review and two-component model. *Psychological Bulletin, 107*, 34–47.

Lehman, D. W., & Hahn, J. (2013). Momentum and organizational risk taking: Evidence from the National Football League. *Management Science, 59*, 852–868.

Lount, R. B., Jr., Doyle, S. P., Brion, S., & Pettit, N. C. (2019). Only when others are watching: The contingent efforts of high status group members. *Management Science, 65*, 3382–3397.

Lount, R. B., Jr., Pettit, N. C., & Doyle, S. P. (2017). Motivating underdogs and favorites. *Organizational Behavior and Human Decision Processes, 141*, 82–93.

Magee, J. C., & Galinsky, A. D. (2008). Social hierarchy: The self-reinforcing nature of power and status. *Academy of Management Annals, 2*, 351–398.

Maines, D. R. (1982). In search of mesostructure: Studies in the negotiated order. *Urban Life, 11*, 267–279.

Malhotra, D. (2010). The desire to win: The effects of competitive arousal on motivation and behavior. *Organizational Behavior and Human Decision Processes, 111*, 139–146.

Marr, J. C., Pettit, N., & Thau, S. (2019). After the fall: How perceived self-control protects the legitimacy of higher-ranking employees after status loss. *Organization Science, 30*, 1165–1188.

Marr, J. C., & Thau, S. (2014). Falling from great (and not-so-great) heights: How initial status position influences performance after status loss. *Academy of Management Journal, 57*, 223–248.

Maslow, A. H. (1943). A theory of human motivation. *Psychological Review, 50*, 370–396.

Mattan, B. D., Kubota, J. T., & Cloutier, J. (2017). How social status shapes person perception and evaluation: A social neuroscience perspective. *Perspectives on Psychological Science, 12*, 468–507.

McClean, E. J., Kim, S., & Martinez, T. M. (2021). Which ideas for change are endorsed? How agentic and communal voice affects endorsement differently for men and women. *Academy of Management Journal.* Advance online publication. https://doi.org/10.5465/amj.2019.0492

McClean, E. J., Martin, S. R., Emich, K. J., & Woodruff, C. T. (2018). The social consequences of voice: An examination of voice type and gender on status and subsequent leader emergence. *Academy of Management Journal, 61*, 1869–1891.

McGinn, L. K., & Newman, M. G. (2013). Status update on social anxiety disorder. *International Journal of Cognitive Therapy, 6*, 88–113.

McGregor, J. (2014, January 3). Zappos says goodbye to bosses. *The Washington Post*. http://www.washingtonpost.com

Merton, R. K. (1968). The Matthew effect in science: The reward and communication systems of science are considered. *Science, 159*, 56–63.

Mitchell, R. L., Bae, K. K., Case, C. R., & Hays, N. A. (2020). Drivers of desire for social rank. *Current Opinion in Psychology, 33*, 189–195.

Morran C. (2013, December 23). Wells Fargo employees say threat of being fired leads to bad behavior. *Consumerist*. http://www.consumerist.com

Mueller, J. S., & Kamdar, D. (2011). Why seeking help from teammates is a blessing and a curse: A theory of help seeking and individual creativity in team contexts. *Journal of Applied Psychology, 96*, 263–276.

Mulligan, J. R., & Bull Schaefer, R. A. (2011). A new hope for rank and yank. *Journal of Leadership & Organizational Studies, 18*, 385–396.

Murtha, B. R. (2013). Peaking at the right time: Perceptions, expectations, and effects. *Organizational Behavior and Human Decision Processes, 120*, 62–72.

Muscatell, K. A., Morelli, S. A., Falk, E. B., Way, B. M., Pfeifer, J. H., Galinsky, A. D., . . . & Eisenberger, N. I. (2012). Social status modulates neural activity in the mentalizing network. *Neuroimage, 60*, 1771–1777.

Nadler, A. (1997). Autonomous and dependent help seeking: Personality characteristics and the seeking of help. In B. Sarason, I. Sarason, & R. G. Pierce (Eds.), *Handbook of personality and social support* (pp. 258–302). Plenum Press.

Nadler, A. (2015). The other side of helping: Seeking and receiving help. In D. A. Schroeder, and W. G. Graziano (Eds.), *The Oxford handbook of prosocial behavior* (pp. 307–328). Emerald Publishing.

Nadler, A. (2018). The human essence in helping relations: Belongingness, independence, and status. In M. van Zomeren, & J. F. Dovidio (Eds.), *The Oxford handbook of the human essence* (pp. 123–134). Oxford University Press.

Nadler, A., & Halabi, S. (2006). Intergroup helping as status relations: Effects of status stability, identification, and type of help on receptivity to high-status group's help. *Journal of Personality and Social Psychology, 91*, 97–110.

Neeley, T. B. (2013). Language matters: Status loss and achieved status distinctions in global organizations. *Organization Science, 24*, 476–497.

Neeley, T. B., & Dumas, T. L. (2016). Unearned status gain: Evidence from a global language mandate. *Academy of Management Journal, 59*, 14–43.

Nembhard, I. M., & Edmondson, A. C. (2006). Making it safe: The effects of leader inclusiveness and professional status on psychological safety and improvement efforts in health care teams. *Journal of Organizational Behavior, 27*, 941–966.

Nurmohamed, S. (2020). The underdog effect: When low expectations increase performance. *Academy of Management Journal, 63*, 1106–1133. https://doi.org/10.5465/amj.2017.0181

Nurmohamed, S., Kundro, T. G., & Myers, C. G. (2021). Against the odds: Developing underdog versus favorite narratives to offset prior experiences of discrimination. *Organizational Behavior and Human Decision Processes*. Advance online publication. https://doi.org/10.1016/j.obhdp.2021.04.008

Oldmeadow, J., & Fiske, S. T. (2007). System-justifying ideologies moderate status = competence stereotypes: Roles for belief in a just world and social dominance orientation. *European Journal of Social Psychology, 37*, 1135–1148.

Ordóñez, L. D., Schweitzer, M. E., Galinsky, A. D., & Bazerman, M. H. (2009). On good scholarship, goal setting, and scholars gone wild. *Academy of Management Perspectives, 23*, 82–87.

Overbeck, J., Correll, J., & Park, B. (2005). Internal status sorting in groups: The problem of too many stars. In M. Thomas-Hunt, M. Neale & E. Mannix (Eds.), *Research on managing groups and teams: Status and groups* (Vol. 7, pp. 169–199). Elsevier.

Owens, D. A., & Sutton, R. I. (2001). Status contests in meetings: Negotiating the informal order. In M. E. Turner (Ed.), *Groups at work: Advances in theory and research* (pp. 299–316). Lawrence Erlbaum Associates.

Pai, J., & Bendersky, C. (2020). Team status conflict. *Current Opinion in Psychology, 33*, 38–41.

Pan, C., Pettit, N., Sivanathan, N., & Blader, S. (2014). Low-status aversion: The effect of self-threat on willingness to buy and sell. *Journal of Applied Social Psychology, 44*, 708–716.

Pearsall, M. J., Christian, M. S., & Ellis, A. P. J. (2010). Motivating interdependent teams: Individual rewards, shared rewards, or something in between? *Journal of Applied Psychology, 95*, 183–191.

Pettit, N. C. (2011). *The dark side of status: Status distance and change as determinants of damaging intragroup behavior*. Unpublished doctoral dissertation, Cornell University.

Pettit, N. C., Doyle, S. P., Lount, R. B., Jr., & To, C. (2016). Cheating to get ahead or to avoid falling behind? The effect of potential negative versus positive status change on unethical behavior. *Organizational Behavior and Human Decision Processes, 137*, 172–183.

Pettit, N. C., & Marr, J. C. (2020). A trajectories-based perspective on status dynamics. *Current Opinion in Psychology, 33*, 233–237.

Pettit, N. C., Sivanathan, N., Gladstone, E., & Marr, J. C. (2013). Rising stars and sinking ships: Consequences of status momentum. *Psychological Science, 24*, 1579–1584.

Pettit, N. C., Yong, K., & Spataro, S. E. (2010). Holding your place: Reactions to the prospect of status gains and losses. *Journal of Experimental Social Psychology, 46*, 396–401.

Phillips, K. W., Rothbard, N. P., & Dumas, T. L. (2009). To disclose or not to disclose? Status distance and self-disclosure in diverse environments. *Academy of Management Review, 34*, 710–732.

Podolny, J. M. (2010). *Status signals: A sociological study of market competition.* Princeton University Press.

Poortvliet, P. M. (2013). Harming others' task-related efforts: The distinct competitive effects of ranking information on performance and mastery goal individuals. *Social Psychology, 44*, 373–379.

Porath, C. L., Overbeck, J., & Pearson, C. (2008). Picking up the gauntlet: How individuals respond to status challenges. *Journal of Applied Social Psychology, 38*, 1945–1980.

Prato, M., & Ferraro, F. (2018). Starstruck: How hiring high-status employees affects incumbents' performance. *Organization Science, 29*, 755–774.

Pye, L. W. (1985). *Asian power and politics: The cultural dimensions of authority.* Belknap Press.

Raz, K., Behfar, K. J., Cowen, A. P., & Thomas-Hunt, M. (2021). In pursuit of status: disentangling status-seeking goals, motives, and behavior. *Academy of Management Discoveries, 7*, 266–293.

Rees, T., Salvatore, J., Coffee, P., Haslam, S. A., Sargent, A., & Dobson, T. (2013). Reversing downward performance spirals. *Journal of Experimental Social Psychology, 49*, 400–403.

Reh, S., Tröster, C., & Van Quaquebeke, N. (2018). Keeping (future) rivals down: Temporal social comparison predicts coworker social undermining via future status threat and envy. *Journal of Applied Psychology, 103*, 399–415.

Roberts, B., & Robins, R. (2000). Broad dispositions, broad aspirations: The intersection of personality traits and major life goals. *Personality and Social Psychology Bulletin, 26*, 1284–1296.

Rozin, P., Scott, S. E., Zickgraf, H. F., Ahn, F., & Jiang, H. (2014). Asymmetrical social Mach bands: Exaggeration of social identities on the more esteemed side of group borders. *Psychological Science, 25*, 1955–1959.

Sassenberg, K., Moskowitz, G. B., Jacoby, J., & Hansen, N. (2007). The carry-over effect of competition: The impact of competition on prejudice towards uninvolved outgroups. *Journal of Experimental Social Psychology, 43*, 529–538.

Sanner, B., & Bunderson, J. S. (2018). The truth about hierarchy. *MIT Sloan Management Review, 59*, 49–52.

Sezer, O., Gino, F., & Norton, M. I. (2018). Humblebragging: A distinct—and ineffective—self-presentation strategy. *Journal of Personality and Social Psychology, 114*, 52–74.

Sezer, O., Prinsloo, E., and Brooks, A., & Norton, M. I., (2019, August 20) *Backhanded compliments: How negative comparisons undermine flattery.* Unpublished manuscript. https://ssrn.com/abstract=3439774

Shnabel, N., Bar-Anan, Y., Kende, A., Bareket, O., & Lazar, Y. (2016). Help to perpetuate traditional gender roles: Benevolent sexism increases engagement in dependency-oriented cross-gender helping. *Journal of Personality and Social Psychology, 110*, 55–75.

Sirola, N., & Pitesa, M. (2017). Economic downturns undermine workplace helping by promoting a zero-sum construal of success. *Academy of Management Journal, 60*, 1339–1359.

Smith, R. H., Parrott, W. G., Ozer, D., & Moniz, A. (1994). Subjective injustice and inferiority as predictors of hostile and depressive feelings in envy. *Personality and Social Psychology Bulletin, 20*, 705–711.

Spataro, S. E. (2012). Not all differences are the same: Variation in the status value of demographic characteristics within and across organizations. *Journal of Business Diversity, 12*, 67–80.

Spataro, S. E., Pettit, N., Sauer, S., & Lount, R. B., Jr. (2014). Interactions among same-status peers: Effects of behavioral style and status level. *Small Group Research, 45*, 314–336.

Steele, L. M., & Lovelace, J. B. (2021). Organizational underdog narratives: The cultivation and consequences of a collective underdog identity. *Academy of Management Review.* Advance online publication. https://doi.org/10.5465/amr.2019.0336

Stewart, G. L., Courtright, S. H., & Barrick, M. R. (2012). Peer-based control in self-managing teams: Linking rational and normative influence with individual and group performance. *Journal of Applied Psychology, 97*, 435–447.

Still, M. C., & Strang, D. (2009). Who does an elite organization emulate? *Administrative Science Quarterly*, *54*, 58–89.

Stutz, B. (2015). Microsoft acquires FantasySalesTeam, an innovative sales gamification platform, to help organizations increase productivity. *Microsoft Blog*. http://www.microsoft.com/

Suddendorf, T., Addis, D. R., & Corballis, M. C. 2009. Mental time travel and the shaping of the human mind. *Philosophical Transactions of the Royal Society B: Biological Sciences*, *364*, 1317–1324.

Sutton, R. I., & Hargadon, A. (1996). Brainstorming groups in context: Effectiveness in a product design firm. *Administrative Science Quarterly*, *41*(4), 685–718.

Swaab, R. I., Schaerer, M., Anicich, E. M., Ronay, R., & Galinsky, A. D. (2014). The too-much-talent effect: Team interdependence determines when more talent is too much or not enough. *Psychological Science*, *25*, 1581–1591.

Thau, S., Aquino, K., & Poortvliet, P. M. (2007). Self-defeating behaviors in organizations: The relationship between thwarted belonging and interpersonal work behaviors. *Journal of Applied Psychology*, *92*, 840–847.

Thye, S. R. (2000). A status value theory of power in exchange relations. *American Sociological Review*, *65*, 407–432.

Tice, D. M. (1992). Self-concept change and self-presentation: The looking glass self is also a magnifying glass. *Journal of Personality and Social Psychology*, *63*, 435–451.

Tiedens, L., & Fragale, A. (2003). Power moves: Complementarity in dominant and submissive nonverbal behavior. *Journal of Personality and Social Psychology*, *84*, 558–568.

To, C., Kilduff, G. J., Ordóñez, L., & Schweitzer, M. E. (2018). Going for it on fourth down: Rivalry increases risk taking, physiological arousal, and promotion focus. *Academy of Management Journal*, *61*, 1281–1306.

To, C., Leslie, L. M., Torelli, C. J., & Stoner, J. L. (2020). Culture and social hierarchy: Collectivism as a driver of the relationship between power and status. *Organizational Behavior and Human Decision Processes*, *157*, 159–176.

Treviño, L. K., Den Nieuwenboer, N. A., & Kish-Gephart, J. J. (2014). (Un)ethical behavior in organizations. *Annual Review of Psychology*, *65*, 635–660.

Turnley, W. H., & Bolino, M. C. (2001). Achieving desired images while avoiding undesired images: Exploring the role of self-monitoring in impression management. *Journal of Applied Psychology*, *86*, 351–360.

Tversky, A., & Kahneman, D. (1979). Prospect theory: An analysis of decision under risk. *Econometrica*, *47*, 263–291.

Tyler, T. R. (1997). The psychology of legitimacy: A relational perspective on voluntary deference to authorities. *Personality and Social Psychology Review*, *1*, 323–345.

Van Bunderen, L., Greer, L. L., & Van Knippenberg, D. (2018). When interteam conflict spirals into intrateam power struggles: The pivotal role of team power structures. *Academy of Management Journal*, *61*, 1100–1130.

Vandegrift, D., & Holaday, B. (2012). Competitive behavior: Tests of the N-effect and proximity to a standard. *Journal of Neuroscience, Psychology, and Economics*, *5*, 182–192.

Van der Vegt, G. S., Bunderson, J. S., & Oosterhof, A. (2006). Expertness diversity and interpersonal helping in teams: Why those who need the most help end up getting the least. *Academy of Management Journal*, *49*, 877–893.

Varnum, M. (2015). Higher in status, (even)better-than-average. *Frontiers in Psychology*, *6*, 496.

Vriend, T., Jordan, J., & Janssen, O. (2016). Reaching the top and avoiding the bottom: How ranking motivates unethical intentions and behavior. *Organizational Behavior and Human Decision Processes*, *137*, 142–155.

Weiss, M., & Morrison, E. W. (2019). Speaking up and moving up: How voice can enhance employees' social status. *Journal of Organizational Behavior*, *40*, 5–19.

Whyte, W. F. (1943). Social organization in the slums. *American Sociological Review*, *8*, 34–39.

Willer, R. (2009). Groups reward individual sacrifice: The status solution to the collective action problem. *American Sociological Review*, *74*, 23–43.

Wohl, M. J., Branscombe, N. R., & Lister, J. J. (2014). When the going gets tough: Economic threat increases financial risk taking in games of chance. *Social Psychological and Personality Science*, *5*, 211–217.

Yu, S. & Greer, L. L., (2017). Does scarcity divide or unite groups? The pivotal role of intra-group diversity. Paper Presented at *the 30th Annual Conference of the International Association of Conflict Management*, Berlin, Germany.

Yu, S., Greer, L. L., Halevy, N., & Van Bunderen, L. (2019). On ladders and pyramids: Hierarchy's shape determines relationships and performance in groups. *Personality and Social Psychology Bulletin*, *45*, 1717–1733.

Social Identity and Intergroup Competition

Sucharita Belavadi *and* Michael A. Hogg

Abstract

This chapter adopts a social identity approach to explain the nature of competition between groups. The role of the self is central in social identity theory. The ways in which the drive to attain a positive sense of self through identification with groups motivates competitive intergroup behavior forms the core of this chapter. The chapter begins with a brief discussion of realistic conflict theory and discusses the role of independent versus interdependent goals between groups in driving competitive versus cooperative intergroup behavior. Social identity theory is then invoked in the remainder of the chapter to discuss how competition between groups is sparked by the need for a clear, distinctive, and positive identity among group members through competition over status with the outgroup. The ways in which intergroup competition is viewed as adaptive by groups in crystalizing group boundaries and negotiating intergroup status and prestige is highlighted. A clearly defined social identity is also essential to group members in the management of self-uncertainty—a primary motive for social identification. The chapter ends with a discussion of contexts in which group members' self-uncertainty is provoked and heightened such that they seek groups with rigidly defined ideologies wherein competitive relations spiral into radical, even violent behavior toward the outgroup and support for ingroup leaders who are authoritarian.

Key Words: social identity, competition, intergroup conflict, self-categorization, social categorization, competitive motivation, self-uncertainty, competitive behavior

Social Identity and Intergroup Competition

Competition is a pervasive aspect of life, as is the need to be better than others. Competition with others and a tussle over status is one way in which we can seek to prevail over others and be better than them. This dynamic can be interpersonal—me versus you. But in many, perhaps most, contexts it is actually intergroup—us versus them, or me as a member of my group versus you as a member of your group. By seeking a more positive outcome than one's competitors, for instance, by supporting and identifying with a victorious sports team or feeling triumphant over the victory of a political party we endorse, we can feel good about ourselves by attaching our self-concepts to something bigger than ourselves—a social identity or group membership. Intergroup competition can be healthy and productive, manifesting as rivalry, for instance in the case of many team sports. But, intergroup competition can also readily transform into destructive conflict and violence (e.g., between nations or political ideologies). Not surprisingly there is an enormous amount of social psychological research on intergroup relations and intergroup conflict (see Tropp, 2012; Yzerbyt & Demoulin, 2010).

The study of intergroup competition requires the existence of groups and therefore an understanding of what, social psychologically speaking, a group is. There are almost as many social psychological definitions of a group as people who study groups; however, one particular perspective that has gained traction over the past forty years is that provided by social identity theory (e.g., Hogg, 2018b; Hogg, Abrams, & Brewer, 2017)—a group is a collection of individuals (present in the same place and time, or distributed across space and/or time) who describe and evaluate themselves in terms of a shared set of identity-defining attributes (perceptions, beliefs, attitudes, feelings, and behaviors). It is this broad definition that is the main framing of our chapter.

Intergroup behavior tends to be competitive due to the operation of social comparison process. Social comparison processes help individuals delineate the boundaries of whom to compete with and whom to seek as guides for behavior (Festinger, 1954; also see Hogg & Gaffney, 2014). We rely on those similar to us as guides—to gain appropriate normative guidance in a given context. In other words, we look to those with whom we share common group memberships and social identities as we are bound by common normative standards with such individuals. We also compare ourselves to dissimilar others with the aim of maintaining distinctiveness and separateness from them and prevailing over them to gain a positive sense of self—that is, we wish to be distinct from and better than outgroup members. In this way, competing with outgroup members serves the purpose of helping us seek a positive identity and higher status, while ingroup members serve as behavioral and cognitive guides.

In this chapter, our primary goal is to discuss the ways in which intergroup divisions and identification with social categories and groups engender intergroup competition over status. We take a social identity approach to explore how a sense of identification with similar others shapes social identities and frames intergroup comparisons with dissimilar others, producing competitive behaviors. According to *social identity theory* (Tajfel & Turner, 1986; Turner et al., 1987; also see Abrams & Hogg, 2010; Hogg, 2016, 2018b; Hogg & Abrams, 1988), we derive a sense of self from our group memberships. By categorizing ourselves as members of a group and acquiring a social identity, we seek a positive sense of self through comparisons across intergroup lines, such that the aim is for *us* to be better than *them*. Thus, competition over status as a means of framing a clear, positive, and distinctive sense of self is at the core of social identity theory.

Before we begin discussing social identity theory and the processes through which it explains intergroup competition and its implications, we begin by reviewing another highly influential social psychological theory that has competition between groups as the central focus in its explication of intergroup hostility—*realistic conflict theory* (also known as *realistic group conflict theory*; Sherif, 1966; Sherif et al., 1961). Realistic conflict theory occupies an important place in the genesis of social identity theory, as it prompted Tajfel and his associates to ask whether intergroup competition was actually *intrinsic* to the mere existence of groups (e.g., Tajfel et al., 1971). This was the platform for re-conceptualizing intergroup relations as an expression of self and identity processes (Tajfel & Turner, 1986), social categorization (Tajfel, 1969), and social comparisons oriented towards differentiation rather than assimilation (Turner, 1975).

Following a discussion of realistic conflict theory, we discuss how social identity theory and self-categorization processes explain competition between groups as a means for group members to gain a positive view of the self. Next, we discuss another primary motive for identification with groups—the need to manage uncertainty about the self. This discussion focuses on the ways in which the need for a distinctive identity that aids in the management of self-uncertainty can spark competitive relations and even extremely polarized intergroup relations. Relying on the processes outlined by *uncertainty-identity theory* (Hogg, 2012, in press), we end the chapter by discussing the conditions under which competition between groups can escalate to conflict and even violent interactions between group members. In this discussion we will pay special attention to the development of zero-sum relations between groups, such that competing groups view resources and status as either/or in nature—that is, if they have more, we have none. Such a view of intergroup relations can have detrimental effects for relations between two groups, as we shall discuss.

Realistic Conflict Theory and the Battle for Scarce Resources

Competition between groups and the role it plays in shaping intergroup hostility and negative views of other group members is at the heart of realistic conflict theory (RCT) (Sherif, 1958, 1966). The type of *goals* that groups strive toward plays a central role in shaping whether relations between the groups are competitive or cooperative. When groups have *competing* or conflicting goals, such that gains for one group mean that the other group has to forgo an advantage, relations between groups become hostile and ingroup norms shape perceptions of outgroup members in uniformly negative terms. Such hostility toward the outgroup shapes identification with one's ingroup and greater cohesion and coordination among ingroup members. It is as though competitive relations with the outgroup over scarce resources brings ingroup members closer together in the pursuit of a common goal.

While competing goals engender hostility between groups, one of the central foci of RCT is also to explicate the conditions under which groups develop cooperative relations. Working toward superordinate goals that require mutually concerted efforts by members of both groups towards the achievement of a valuable common goal should bring about intergroup harmony and cooperation between groups. Where groups have valued goals that can only be achieved with the help of an outgroup, cooperation can thrive, and the fact that each group helps the other group to satisfy its goals improves intergroup sentiments—the cooperation between Britain, America, and the Soviet Union to defeat Germany during the Second World War is a good example; particularly in so far as any improvement in intergroup sentiment between Britain and America on the one hand and the Soviet Union on the other instantly evaporated once Germany had been defeated and the *raison d'être* for the cooperation no longer existed.

Sherif and colleagues tested the central tenets of RCT in their seminal Robbers Cave field experiment (Sherif et al., 1961). The experiment was conducted in the summer of 1954 with twenty-four eleven- and twelve-year old boys who had similar religious and socioeconomic backgrounds but did not know one another and were attending a summer camp at Robbers Cave state park in Oklahoma.

At first, regular friendships were allowed to develop naturally among the boys. Following this phase, the boys were split into two groups of twelve each, such that some boys found their friendships split; some of their friends were now members of the outgroup. Thus, one of the goals of the experiment was to test whether the boys would prioritize ingroup loyalty over their initial friendships within the context of experimentally created competitive relations between the two groups. Within the two groups, the boys were made to strive toward common goals, which they cooperated toward as hierarchical structures developed within each group, with some boys emerging as leaders. One of the key findings of the experiment was that when the boys were made to compete over scarce resources or a reward coveted by both groups (e.g., winning intergroup competitions such as a tug-of-war), intergroup hostility, name-calling, and even violence against the outgroup was observed. Meanwhile, within the group there was elevated ingroup cohesion and solidarity. Thus, as predicted by Sherif and his associates, ingroup loyalty prevailed over initially formed individual friendships when competitive relations between the two groups existed.

Sherif and colleagues found that one way to remedy the intergroup hostility that had developed between the boys was to repeatedly introduce superordinate goals—end results that were valuable to both groups and required the concerted and cooperative effort of both groups of boys. For example, on a camp-out, the food truck bringing provisions became stalled and the boys had to work together to restart it. In fact, this is one of the premises of RCT that the resolution of hostility between competing groups requires continuous and repeated acts of coordination toward a common, superordinate goal by the two conflicting groups.

Thus, the type of goals that groups strive for shape the nature of the relationship between the groups, according to RCT. This relationship could be cooperative when goals are linked and require interdependence. The relationship could also be negative, such that goals are mutually exclusive—a zero-sum relationship exists, wherein the goal can be attained either by *us* or by *them*; if they attain the goal, we will be unable to attain it. The latter scenario should engender competitive relations between groups, as shown by Sherif and colleagues.

The essence of RCT, that intergroup goal relations (mutually exclusive zero-sum goals versus superordinate shared goals) promote intergroup competition and hostile intergroup attitudes and behavior versus intergroup cooperation and favorable intergroup attitudes and behavior, has been widely empirically supported (e.g., Blake & Mouton, 1961; Brewer & Campbell, 1976; Fisher, 1990).

Social Identity Theory and Intergroup Competitive Relations

Sherif's analysis of the social psychology of intergroup cooperation and competition was, at the time, a refreshing departure from a zeitgeist in which prejudice, discrimination, and intergroup conflict tended to be explained in terms of individual differences (e.g., Rokeach, 1948) or people's enduring personality attributes (e.g., Adorno et al., 1950). These, and other, individual difference and personality approaches had limitations (see Billig, 1976) that Sherif's social context orientation overcame. His group-based rather than individual- or personality-level explanation formed an important springboard for the early development of social identity theory (Tajfel & Turner, 1986; for overviews see Abrams & Hogg, 2010; Hogg, 2016, 2018b; Hogg & Abrams, 1988; Hogg et al., 2017).

Minimal Categorization Effect

Social identity theory went a step beyond RCT—it proposed that competitive goals might neither be sufficient nor necessary for competitive intergroup behavior. Intergroup competition might be a far more fundamental part of the human condition. All that might be needed is for a person to be categorized as a member of a self-inclusive category. Tajfel and his colleagues set out to test this novel and provocative idea (Tajfel, 1970; Tajfel et al., 1971). To do this they devised an ingenious experimental paradigm, the *minimal group paradigm*.

The main thrust of the minimal group studies is that categorization into even the most minimally defined groups, created in the laboratory, drives people to favor their own group with the aim of prevailing over the outgroup and doing better than them. In the basic minimal group experiments, participants were randomly assigned into categories that were determined by minimal criteria such as a supposed preference for one of two types of paintings (e.g., Klee vs. Kandinsky) or ostensibly on the basis of a personality trait or some such similar criterion that was determined in the laboratory. Once categorized, participants were asked to perform tasks such as allocating money or points between anonymous members of their own group of the other group. When participants were thus categorized, they allocated more rewards to their own group members than to other group members, and they did this in such a way as to maximize the difference between ingroup and outgroup. It was considered quite astounding at the time that mere categorization into a category that was formed a few minutes ago in a laboratory setting, wherein individuals did not personally know their own group members or the other group's members, produced a competitive and discriminatory orientation between groups.

Subsequent minimal group studies, many of them simply categorizing participants as X- or Y-group members on the basis of no criterion whatsoever, have replicated this finding hundreds of times (for a meta-analytic overview see Mullen et al., 1992). The minimal group categorization effect has also been found to occur automatically (Otten & Wentura, 1999). It has also been shown that the effect is more readily obtained if anonymous participants are socially present (Kerr et al., 2018), and that categorization typically leads to ingroup favoritism (we are better than them); however, when the group feels under threat, the emphasis shifts to outgroup discrimination (they are worse than us) (Mummendey & Otten, 1998).

Collective Self and Social Identity

Social categorization has this powerful effect because the self is involved—even, under some circumstances, in transitory and minimally defined groups. A key premise of social identity theory is that the self-concept is compartmentalized into relatively discrete idiosyncratic or shared social selves and identities that define who we are. Of particular interest are social identities that are associated with social categories—such identities embody the shared attributes (perceptions, feelings, beliefs, attitudes, and behaviors) that define, prescribe, and evaluate a social category. If one belongs to such a category, the identity is internalized as part of who one is.

When we identify with a social category or a group, our sense of self is attached to this group membership when it is cognitively salient in our minds. People can be members of and identify with many different groups and social categories; however, not all these memberships and identities are psychological salient in our minds at all times. When we think of ourselves as a member of a specific group and feel an emotional attachment to this group, our thoughts, feelings, and behavior are shaped by the shared identity defining normative attributes of the group.

Self-Enhancement and Positive Distinctiveness

Human beings have a very strong drive to feel good about themselves. Self-enhancement and the pursuit of self-esteem are very significant motivators of behavior (e.g., Greenberg et al., 1997; Sedikides & Strube, 1997). Where self is defined in terms of social identity this motivation manifests as the pursuit of positive intergroup distinctiveness. In this context, who *we* are is always shaped and understood in relation to who *they* are. Thus, constructing a positive sense of self entails viewing oneself, one's group members and one's group as a whole as better than the outgroup and its members—*they* are seen as distinct from *us*, different from *us*, and not as good as *us*. Social identity dynamics and phenomena are shaped and steered by the self-enhancement motive (Abrams & Hogg, 1988; Rubin & Hewstone, 1998; Tajfel & Turner, 1986).

In intergroup settings, categorization of individuals into *us* versus *them* categories is enough to spark the need to prevail over the other and be better than them. Of course, in a minimal group study created in a laboratory both groups are new and fairly equal in status and prestige. In the real world, social categories and groups almost always differ, often profoundly, in social status—how they are evaluated and viewed by society. There is intergroup competition over status and prestige—a competition to promote or protect the ingroup's relative status. The nature of the competition and the specific actions taken to secure status depend on an array of factors relating to the perceived nature of the status relations between the groups, the available resources, and the realistic probability of success of courses of action. The payoff, however, is significant, especially if one's group membership and identity is central to one's sense of self, as it affects feelings of self-esteem and self-worth.

Subjective Belief Structures

Self-enhancement-driven intergroup competition over status and prestige can take many different forms, configured by an overarching dynamic where higher status groups strive to maintain their status and prestige relative to a lower status outgroup, and lower status groups struggle to remedy their status disadvantage. The former typically have access to material and media resources that allow them to minimize or conceal the reality of status inequality, or they can simply resort to violent repression to enforce such inequality. The latter can attempt to improve its status position by directly confronting the higher status group, but this can come at a high cost. What lower status groups do rests on their beliefs about the nature of intergroup status relations.

Intergroup behavior is steered by *subjective belief structures*, which are based on the nature of *status* relations between groups (e.g., Tajfel & Turner, 1986; see Ellemers, 1993; Hogg, 2016; Hogg & Abrams, 1988). More specifically, these status relations are framed by the extent to which the relations between the groups are believed to be (a) *stable*—will these relations persist or could status relations be overturned? (b) *legitimate*—are the status relations legitimate and justified? (c) *permeable*—can members of the low status group move into and gain acceptance by the higher status group? and (d) do *cognitive alternatives* exist—can people envisage an attainable alternative status quo?

Different combinations of these beliefs feed into different intergroup behaviors. A *social mobility* belief structure, for instance, exists when low status group members believe intergroup boundaries are permeable and it is therefore easy as an individual to simply pass into and secure a new identity as a member of the higher status outgroup. Permeability is typically a fiction that serves the dominant group well. It fragments the subordinate status group into individuals, and disarms the potential that they may rise up en masse to contest the status quo.

When people realize that permeability between groups is in fact low and movement is restricted, a *social change* belief structure exists. If people also believe that status relations are largely stable and legitimate, such that low status group members are accepting of their lower status, *social creativity* strategies are likely to be employed. These might include avoiding comparisons with the higher status group, and instead making ingroup-favoring lateral or downward comparisons with other lower status groups. Another strategy is to redefine the value of ingroup identity and its associated attributes. This can be done by focusing on different, ingroup-favoring, dimensions of comparison. For example, a lower status group could promote the view that while *they* (the higher status group) might be *competent*, we are *warm*; which would compensate for lacking status in one domain by focusing on a domain in which they believe they are superior (e.g., Fiske et al., 2002; Yzerbyt et al., 2005).

Finally, when a social change belief structure is associated with recognition that the status quo is neither legitimate nor stable, and that there is a realistic pathway to an achievable new social order (cognitive alternatives exists) then *social competition* strategies are adopted. These can range from peaceful intergroup competition (e.g., a democratic parliamentary system) to violent revolutionary conflict.

Thus, relations between groups and the context in which they exist with respect to status differences plays a significant role in the nature of the competition between groups, and in the form taken by intergroup behaviors. In the next section, we delve deeper into the cognitive aspects of group identification and the ways in which identification with groups helps us manage uncertainty about the self and the implications such an experience of uncertainty has for relations with the outgroup.

Self-Categorization and Intergroup Relations

We have discussed the ways in which identification with a group and the implication of the self in group memberships can shape competitive relations between groups. In this section, we elaborate on the processes of self-categorization and the means through which we represent our social identities cognitively, such that we begin to share a world-view with our group members. Self-categorization theory (Turner et al., 1987), explains the socio-cognitive processes through which categorization into groups—of both us and them—shapes the development of *shared realities* (e.g., Hogg & Rinella, 2018) for group members and a clear sense of *us* as distinctive from *them*.

When we identify with a group, the groups' social identity becomes psychologically salient in our minds. Our thoughts, feelings, behaviors, and outlook toward the world are shaped by the norms that characterize that specific identity that we share with others categorized as members of that group. We begin to see these others through the lens of group membership and through the lens of a shared identity—we *depersonalize* them. That is, no longer are they viewed as idiosyncratic individuals, but as members of the group. While we depersonalize those categorized as ingroup members, we also categorize and view outgroup members in a similar manner. They are viewed solely in terms of their group memberships and as distinctive and different from *us*.

We represent our group memberships in our minds as *prototypes*—a fuzzy set that captures and represents the attributes of the group and what it stands for by minimizing ingroup differences and maximizing intergroup differences. When group members share a representation of a clear prototype, they also share a consensual view of reality—of what it means to be a group member and the world around them. Thus, clear ingroup prototypes serve the function of creating a well-defined identity with accentuated ingroup similarities, while clearly delineating a distinct outgroup that is different from the ingroup and its norms. A distinctive ingroup identity is therefore always shaped in relation to the outgroup—*we* are what *they* are not.

The formation of such distinctive identities has implications for how the sense of self comes to be framed within groups. Because our sense of self is derived from our group memberships, distinctive and clearly defined identities are especially functional in helping group members manage uncertainty about the self. By assigning attributes of the group to the self, we manage uncertainty about who we are and the world around us.

Uncertainty Reduction and Intergroup Distinctiveness

Let us now elaborate on this process of uncertainty reduction and the ways in which ingroup distinctiveness helps us manage uncertainty about the self. To do this we draw on uncertainty-identity theory (e.g., Hogg, 2007, 2012, 2015, 2018a, in press). Given that distinctiveness from the outgroup shapes clear identities, relations with the outgroup are implicated in the uncertainty reduction motive.

One of the primary drives for why we join and identify with groups is to obtain a framework with which to shape our sense of self. By identifying with groups, we can manage uncertainty about who we are and where we stand in the world—this is the basic premise of uncertainty-identity theory. Self-uncertainty reduction, in addition to the need to derive a positive sense of self from group memberships, form perhaps the two most basic motivations for the need to belong to groups and categorize ourselves and others into groups.

When we identify with groups, we internalize the group's identity and assign the attributes of the group to ourselves to define who we are. The identity and norms of the group, acquired through a process of identity-contingent social influence and sense-making (e.g., Abrams & Hogg, 1990; Hogg, 2018a, 2020a), become our internalized personal guidelines, that we share with fellow ingroup members. They prescribe our thoughts, feelings, and behaviors.

Clear, simple, and consensual ingroup prototypes that define a tight-knit shared reality for ingroup members while spelling out distinctiveness from an outgroup are especially useful in helping individuals manage uncertainty about the self (e.g., Hogg et al., 2007; Sherman et al., 2009). By identifying with a group that is characterized by a well-defined prototype, one can manage uncertainty about the self efficiently, as it provides an unambiguous framework with which to define self.

Through communication-based social comparison processes typically orchestrated by group leadership (e.g., Hogg, 2018a, 2020a), group members can learn how similar others—ingroup members—think and behave, and how competitive intergroup relations and distinctiveness are expressed and managed. Blurred intergroup boundaries and fuzzy ingroup prototypes and identities can pose a particular threat that raises identity uncertainty, which in turn generates self-uncertainty that can motivate identity consolidation and enhanced intergroup distinctiveness, or can lead to disidentification as an individual (group fragmentation and dissolution) or as a subgroup (schism) (e.g., Wagoner et al., 2017; Wagoner & Hogg, 2016; see Hogg, 2020b).

Thus, competitive intergroup relations can be seen as adaptive by groups. It helps them crystallize group boundaries, and helps group members negotiate the identity they share while understanding how this identity comes to be defined within the context of tussle over status and prestige with the outgroup. Groups might thus seek somewhat competitive relations with the outgroup to help understand more clearly where they stand in relation to others and to define a clear identity for themselves.

While groups might view competitive relations as adaptive for understanding and clarifying their place in the world, there are contexts in which such competition between groups might take a serious downturn, spiraling into problems of entrenched, negative relations between the groups, at times resulting in violence and extreme hatred. The struggle over status and prestige in such contexts truly comes to a head such that each group views acts of the other side as threatening the position of their own ingroup. Wars, riots, gang wars, and other such forms of intergroup conflict can be the result of such extreme competitive relations. In such cases, uncertainty about identity-related concerns plays a crucial role, as groups seek to preserve their identities in the face of threats to distinctiveness and status and potential ingroup annihilation.

The Dark Side of Competition: Intergroup Violence and Hatred

So far, we have discussed intergroup processes that explain competition over status, prestige, and the need for a clear identity that is distinctive. Such a tussle over status does not necessarily have negative implications for intergroup relations. Rather it constitutes a struggle for a well-defined, positive identity that is achieved through efforts to be better than a distinctive other. Healthy rivalry and competition between sporting teams would constitute an example of such a tussle over status. As research shows, identification with sports teams means that one derives a positive identity through the victories and triumphs of the team that one identifies with and supports—a phenomenon termed as Basking in Reflected Glory or BIRGing (Cialdini et al., 1976). In such instances, competition with an opposing sports team and its fans helps supporters feel good about themselves by reveling in their team's triumphs.

However, as is all too common, such intergroup contests are not always restricted to the realm of healthy rivalries—competition can escalate into riots, violent outbursts, and destruction of property. These events are often characterized in the media as irrational outbursts by an unruly and impulsive mob—people who are deindividuated and have regressed to a primitive unsocialized state of nature (e.g., Zimbardo, 1970). Social identity theory offers a very different analysis, in which such behaviors are seen as social identity-regulated intergroup behaviors (e.g., Reicher, 1984, 2001). The apparent volatility is because the setting of crowd events is often unusual and people are urgently searching for guidance about what behaviors appropriately embody and express their shared social identity—who should they turn to for guidance, what behaviors are identity-consistent, and what behaviors are not?

In this section, we examine the broader issue of the conditions under which escalation from competitive behavior to radical intergroup behavior takes place. As we discuss, self- and identity-uncertainty play a central role in motivating radical intergroup behavior, as groups seek solace in extremes while they strive to manage uncertainty about epistemic concerns, especially the self. We begin by discussing the role that identity-uncertainty plays in explaining radical intergroup behavior that is dominated by hatred toward the outgroup and its members.

Intergroup Threat, Uncertainty, and Extremism

When people feel uncertain about their sense of self, groups that are unambiguously defined and clearly demarcated from the outgroup, that is, groups that have a distinctive prototype that defines clearly how ingroup members are highly similar and simultaneously distinct from the outgroup, are especially attractive and efficient in helping individuals manage heightened uncertainty (e.g., Hogg et al., 2007; Sherman et al., 2009).

This process of tying one's sense of self to tight-knit, rigid, and closed-off groups under heightened identity-uncertainty can result in extreme intergroup behaviors such as zealotry, intolerance toward outgroup members and ingroup dissenters, xenophobia and skepticism toward outsiders and immigrants, support for totalitarian groups and leaders, and radicalization that encourages violent behaviors toward the outgroup (e.g., Hogg, 2014, 2020b). Many contexts are pervaded with ambiguity that elevates uncertainty among group members; for instance, groups undergoing social and economic upheaval, crises, wars, conflict, pandemics, and even individual circumstances such as divorce and unemployment. In such circumstances, extremely heightened self-uncertainty is likely to drive individuals toward clear answers about their place in the world and future, which are provided by clear-cut social identities that eschew any form of disagreement, dissent, and ambiguity within the group.

Not only is substantial uniformity encouraged within such groups, but such groups also seek to frame distinctive identities by highlighting existential threats to the ingroup through demonization of specific outgroups (e.g., Hogg, 2005; Reicher et al., 2005) and the development and promulgation of conspiracy theories (Douglas et al., 2017). For instance, group members might close in on a shared, rigid reality by viewing outsiders such as immigrants and foreigners with deep suspicion and skepticism— essentially as intentionally plotting the ingroup's demise. This overarching notion of an enemy plotting the demise of one's group and identity is a central thread in populist ideologies (e.g., Bakker et al., 2016).

The underlying processes through which narratives of xenophobia and negative perceptions of immigrants develop have been discussed by Esses et al. (2013). They examine the ways in which media messages about immigrants portrayed as "enemies at the gate" and carriers of disease are related to the dehumanization of immigrants that frames contempt and negative attitudes toward the immigrants. Such narratives of a group of people portrayed as dangerous invaders aiming to contaminate one's land and people will inevitably create uncertainty about the survival and future of one's identity. Given that heightened uncertainty drives people to seek ethnocentric, rigid ideologies that promote hatred toward the outgroup as justified for the safety of one's people, it does not bode well for the treatment of immigrants and refugees and for intergroup relations in general.

Heightened uncertainty motivates people toward a group-centric focus, driving them to seek greater ingroup differentiation in the quest for a distinctive identity (Kruglanski et al., 2006). This need for intergroup differentiation is exaggerated when heightened uncertainty is accompanied by status-related intergroup comparisons and competition. Federico et al. (2013) found that intergroup differentiation was greater when individuals had a higher need for closure—an individual-based discomfort with uncertainty. People made more ingroup favoring ratings when they perceived greater status differences between their racial ingroup and the outgroup. That is, they exaggerated the perceived higher status of their ingroup when they experienced greater uncertainty.

The drive toward group-centrism under heightened uncertainty is especially pronounced in contexts where groups perceive a threat to their ingroup status and standing from the outgroup. When such perceived threats exist in the context of historically competitive and troubled relations between the two groups, intergroup hostility and partisan polarization can go to great extremes. In such conditions the appeal of an identity that spells out clearly how *we* are distinct from and better than *them* might promote individuals to seek radical and even violent solutions to protect the ingroup.

Where a group that has historically benefitted from well-established and secure higher status perceives a threat to their status from a rival outgroup it can react extremely— driving its members to seek rigid narratives that hail ingroup greatness as immutable and unchangeable. In two studies conducted in the context of historically contentious Hindu–Muslim relations in India, Belavadi and Hogg (2021) found that when higher status Hindus perceived a rise in outgroup Muslim status and influence, they reported feeling greater identity-uncertainty about the future of their ingroup and its practices. Heightened identity-uncertainty drove them to prefer a narrative that called attention to the victimization and suffering of their ingroup and the need to preserve the ingroup (compared to those who experienced low uncertainty). Given that Hindus numerically outnumber Muslims in India (for every Muslim there are approximately six Hindus), the need for heightened uncertainty and ingroup preservation is rooted in a subjective concern for the future of the ingroup and its practices.

Gaining and protecting a positive sense of self through identification with groups is one of the most basic motives associated with group identification. A perceived affront or threat to the status and prestige of one's group should cause group members to become concerned about their group's standing, and thus contribute to a polarized and factionalized intergroup terrain that is characterized by extremely divisive and rigid identities. Heightened uncertainty and threats to distinctiveness can thus drive group members to gravitate toward closed-off and rigid identities. Research shows that when subgroup members experience uncertainty and dissensus about what the group stands for at the superordinate level, they are more likely to seek autonomy and separateness from the overarching identity, especially when they view themselves as entitative and as having low voice in the larger identity (Wagoner & Hogg, 2016). Thus, heightened uncertainty in the context of real or perceived threat from an outgroup can cause the splintering of groups into smaller, rigidly shaped identities that are bound by a clear purpose, while creating deep intergroup rifts.

In the next section, we explore another aspect of extreme intergroup competitiveness by discussing ingroup narratives that are born of rigid intergroup divisions and encourage competition over suffering and victimhood as a means to justify hatred and violence toward the outgroup.

Collective and Competitive Victimhood

When groups are engaged in conflict and the lines between groups are starkly drawn, a narrative can develop within each group regarding the immense suffering endured by its members, and this alleged experience of suffering becomes a core and central aspect of the group's identity. This tendency of groups to adopt an identity of victimhood has been termed *collective victimhood* (Bar-Tal et al., 2009; Noor et al., 2017). Within such groups, the outgroup and its members are held accountable for the suffering of the ingroup, while one's own harmful actions against the outgroup are seen as justified and legitimate. On each side of the conflict, identities become entrenched and polarized, such that the ingroup and its members are seen as just and as enduring suffering at the hands of an evil, unjust outgroup. Groups, thus, compete over the experience of collective victimhood and they engage in intergroup *competitive victimhood* (Noor et al., 2008; Noor et al., 2012; Sullivan et al., 2012), such that each group in the conflict claims that its suffering and pain is greater than that of the outgroup and its members.

At first, it appears counterintuitive that groups should compete over a position of victimhood—a position of weakness and diminished agency. However, such a claim of victimhood serves its purpose for groups both high and low in status, such that collective victimhood within groups helps group members gain sympathy and resources from third parties. Claims of collective victimhood also help groups seek legitimization of harmful and violent acts from neutral parties when group members claim to be the sole victims in a conflict with an outgroup (Belavadi & Hogg, 2018). Thus, appearing to be the sole victim in the context of conflict with another group might help groups gain a competitive edge over their rival, as third parties invariably favor the underdog in a competitive context (e.g., see Vandello et al., 2007; Vandello et al., 2011).

Narratives of ingroup collective victimhood that develop within the context of drawn out conflicts are often sustained within groups across generations of group members. They become a defining attribute of the group's social identity in which intergroup relations are characterized as zero-sum, such that if we are victims we can never be perpetrators, while the outgroup is painted in broad strokes as the undeniable demon. Intergroup relations are framed by suspicion and hatred toward the outgroup, as narratives that dehumanize and demonize outgroup members become the norm. Group lines become firmly drawn and it becomes an almost impossible challenge to change perceptions.

The identity-defining narrative of victimhood can very effectively be sustained by mass media and influential ingroup members such as leaders. These sources repeatedly recall instances of past victimization and thus keep alive in collective memory the harm that has been perpetrated against the group and its cherished identity. And of course, although this does little to improve intergroup relations, it can very effectively enhance ingroup entitativity and cohesiveness. It also provides an "echo-chamber" that satisfies the human need, particularly under uncertainty, to confirm and validate one's own world view and identity, which is particularly easy to do online (e.g., Barberá et al., 2015; Colleoni et al., 2014; Peters et al., 2010).

Belavadi and Hogg (2021) found that when high-status group members endorsed an ingroup victimhood speech by a leader in the context of a perceived threat from a lower status outgroup, they were more likely to essentialize ingroup greatness and glory as immutable and unchangeable, thus, adopting a rigid and exalted view of their ingroup. Narratives of victimhood can thus enable group members to come together in times of a perceived crisis and threat to the group while exaggerating intergroup divisions between groups and hampering already troubled intergroup relations.

Ingroup Leaders and Intergroup Competition

Influential ingroup sources such as leaders can play a vital role in espousing and encouraging ingroup narratives that increase and solidify intergroup divisions while helping enhance support for their leadership. Generally speaking, people look to their leaders to define their group's social identity and resolve uncertainty about what the group stands for, and about their own place within the group (Hogg, 2018a, 2020a).

However, leaders, at times, can play up uncertainty among their followers in a quest to build an entitative and distinctive social identity (e.g., Hogg, 2005). Leaders, especially prototypical leaders, are highly influential ingroup members and play a central role in shaping ingroup normative standards, and thus, can sway group members toward uncertainty with the language and rhetoric they use. According to the social identity theory of leadership (Hogg & Van Knippenberg, 2003; Hogg et al., 2012a), leaders that embody the ingroup prototype signify to group members what the group represents as they emphasize ingroup similarities and intergroup differences. Thus, leader influence flows from the position they occupy within the group as prototypical ingroup representatives that embody the group's core attributes.

Given this influential position within the group, leaders can choose to spark identity-uncertainty among group members, for instance, by identifying threats to the ingroup's safety and future, and by alerting members to harm emanating from outgroups and their members. According to social identity framing theory (Seyranian, 2012, 2014; Seyranian & Bligh, 2008), leaders use rhetoric to *unfreeze* and shift conceptions about the group and what the group stands for in order to move followers in a new direction and create a transformed social identity. Leaders rely on provoking uncertainty among followers by breaking frames and presenting new and alternative solutions to frame a new identity.

In a study exploring the impact of leader rhetoric aimed to provoke uncertainty, Hohman et al. (2010) found that when American Democratic Party supporters felt uncertain following a speech they read by George W. Bush, they showed lowered national identification and enhanced identification with the Democrats. The Republicans, who already showed high national identification did not show further increase in identification following exposure to the speech. Thus, the experience of heightened uncertainty provoked by leader rhetoric can drive people to seek distinctive and divisive factions within a larger superordinate identity.

Leaders, thus, in their role as *entrepreneurs of identity* (Reicher & Hopkins, 2003), can wreak havoc for harmonious intergroup relations. Especially when group members experience heightened identity-related self-uncertainty, and the thirst for guidance and leadership can drive them to prefer authoritarian leaders (Rast et al., 2013; also see Kakkar & Sivanathan, 2017) and leaders who deliver an extreme and polarized vision of the group's identity (Gaffney et al., 2014). Clear, simple, and unambiguous messages conveyed by authoritarian leaders, who are typically intolerant of dissent, are especially attractive to uncertain group members.

Of course, while leaders can act as agents of intergroup division, they can also play a role in healing deep intergroup rifts as they hold an influential role within the group. When intergroup divisions exist between distinctively defined subgroups within a larger social identity, it becomes a challenge for leaders to act as "intergroup leaders" to heal these rifts and provide effective leadership while encouraging cooperation between the subgroups. The challenge for leaders here is to not provoke subgroup identity and distinctiveness threat by emphasizing the need to embrace a collective identity that subsumes the subgroups (e.g., see Hornsey & Hogg, 2000). Challenging the distinctiveness of subgroup identities may create greater rifts between subgroups.

It appears that when subgroups face threats to their distinctiveness from other subgroups, leaders who encourage the development of an intergroup relational identity are more effective than leaders who encourage a collective identity (Hogg et al., 2012b; Rast et al., 2018). A relational intergroup identity, unlike a collective identity, does not dissolve subgroup identities to form a collective whole, rather it encourages subgroup distinctiveness to stay intact while encouraging cooperation that serves the larger whole. Thus, a cooperative strategy between distinct subgroups is emphasized. Added to these processes, is the importance of sustaining identity distinctiveness in order to maintain harmonious intergroup relations. An important finding from this research is that when subgroup identity threat is low, a leader who encourages a collective identity that subsumes subgroups within a larger social identity is actually preferred. Thus, leadership effectiveness differs based on the specific relations between the subgroups they are leading.

As the discussion in this section shows, competitive intergroup relations in contexts of threat and deep intergroup divisions can spiral into harmful intergroup behaviors endangering groups on both sides of the divide. Narratives that shape such divisions are typically difficult to overturn, thereby repairing entrenched intergroup relations becomes a challenging task. As such, narratives that solidify intergroup divisions and remind of outgroup threats are handed down through generations and commemorated through monuments, national holidays, and other group symbols, the task of encouraging cooperation between groups is generally a difficult one, especially for leaders who may seek to encourage greater intergroup harmony.

Conclusion

In this chapter, we have taken a social identity approach to discuss how individuals within groups compete over status and prestige. Intergroup competition over status can take several forms depending on contextual variations, as discussed. The self-concept forms the central focus in social identity theory, and it is the need to elevate the self and feel better about oneself that motivates individuals to identify with groups and subsequently compete with dissimilar others with the goal of being better than them. The focus of realistic conflict theory, reviewed briefly above, is slightly different when compared to social identity theory—the central motive for competition and intergroup hostility, according to RCT, is competing goals. Conflicting goals motivate groups to compete over a valuable outcome, and this leads to competition and intergroup hostility; on the other hand, interdependence of intergroup efforts toward the achievement of a mutually valuable outcome produces cooperation. Social identity theory differs from RCT in an important respect, as it states that rather than goals, the mere categorization of individuals into *us* versus *them* categories is sufficient to produce intergroup competitive behavior—as demonstrated by studies within the minimal group paradigm.

In addition to feeling good about the self, we discuss the uncertainty reduction motive that also explains why people seek group memberships. According to uncertainty-identity theory, by attaching one's self to a group and internalizing its identity, one can manage uncertainty about the self. Groups that have clearly delineated boundaries that make them distinct from an outgroup are especially efficient in helping individuals manage uncertainty about the self, as clear ingroup attributes that reduce uncertainty can be assigned to the self. Thus, identifying with groups helps group members seek normative guides—ingroup members—and competitive targets—dissimilar others. Of course, competitive relations between groups are rarely dangerous for intergroup relations and may even be seen as adaptive by groups in seeking a distinctive identity. Intergroup relations become troubled when competitive relations spiral into binary perceptions of the ingroup and the outgroup, such that intergroup narratives are characterized by hate and zealotry. Such conditions are likely in contexts of perceived threat to the ingroup and when group members seek polarized and rigid ideologies as remedies for heightened uncertainty.

As our discussion indicates, intergroup competition, which oftentimes can be healthy and driven by a need to seek clear, positive, and distinctive identities, can escalate into violent, hatred-driven relations between groups. Contexts, such as long-drawn intergroup conflict, wherein group members have increasingly polarized, one-sided negative views about the outgroup, are especially vulnerable to escalation of competition into conflict and violent acts against outgroup members. In such contexts, perceived threat to the status of one's group and uncertainty regarding the future of one's group and its members may drive group members to seek extreme steps to protect group boundaries and preserve social identities.

References

Abrams, D., & Hogg, M. A. (1988). Comments on the motivational status of self-esteem in social identity and intergroup discrimination. *European Journal of Social Psychology, 18*, 317–334.

Abrams, D., & Hogg, M. A. (1990). Social identification, self-categorization and social influence. *European Review of Social Psychology, 1*, 195–228.

Abrams, D., & Hogg, M. A. (2010). Social identity and self-categorization. In J. F. Dovidio, M. Hewstone, P. Glick, & V. M. Esses (Eds.), *The Sage handbook of prejudice, stereotyping and discrimination* (pp. 179–193). Sage.

Adorno, T. W., Frenkel-Brunswik, E., Levinson, D. J., & Sanford, R. M. (1950). *The authoritarian personality.* Harper.

Bakker, B. N., Rooduijn, M., & Schumacher, G. (2016). The psychological roots of populist voting: Evidence from the United States, the Netherlands and Germany. *European Journal of Political Research, 55*(2), 302–320.

Barberá, P., Jost, J. T., Nagler, J., Tucker, J. A., & Bonneau, R. (2015). Tweeting from left to right: Is online political communication more than an echo chamber? *Psychological Science, 26*, 1531–1542.

Bar-Tal, D., Chernyak-Hai, L., Schori, N., & Gundar, A. (2009). A sense of self-perceived collective victimhood in intractable conflicts. *International Review of the Red Cross, 91*, 229–258.

Belavadi, S., & Hogg, M. A. (2018). We are victims! How observers evaluate a group's claims of collective victimhood. *Journal of Applied Social Psychology, 48*, 651–660.

Belavadi, S., & Hogg, M. A. (2021). Who will we be? Uncertainty about the ingroup's future and preference for different types of leader rhetoric. Manuscript submitted for publication, Claremont Graduate University.

Billig, M. (1976). *Social psychology and intergroup relations.* Academic Press.

Blake, R. R., & Mouton, J. S. (1961). Reactions to intergroup competition under win/lose conditions. *Management Science, 7*, 420–435.

Brewer, M. B., & Campbell, D. T. (1976). *Ethnocentrism and intergroup attitudes: East African evidence.* Halsted-Press.

Cialdini, R. B., Borden, R. J., Thorne, A., Walker, M. R., Freeman, S., & Sloan, L. R. (1976). Basking in reflected glory: Three (football) field studies. *Journal of Personality and Social Psychology, 34,* 366.

Colleoni, E., Rozza, A., & Arvidsson, A. (2014). Echo chamber or public sphere? Predicting political orientation and measuring political homophily in Twitter using big data. *Journal of Communication, 64,* 317–332.

Douglas, K. M., Sutton, R. M., & Cichoka, A. (2017). The psychology of conspiracy theories. *Current Directions in Psychological Science, 26,* 538–542.

Ellemers, N. (1993). The influence of socio-structural variables on identity management strategies. *European Review of Social Psychology, 4,* 27–57.

Esses, V. M., Medianu, S., & Lawson, A. S. (2013). Uncertainty, threat, and the role of the media in promoting the dehumanization of immigrants and refugees. *Journal of Social Issues, 69,* 518–536.

Federico, C. M., Hunt, C. V., & Fisher, E. L. (2013). Uncertainty and status-based asymmetries in the distinction between the "good" us and the "bad" them: Evidence that group status strengthens the relationship between the need for cognitive closure and extremity in intergroup differentiation. *Journal of Social Issues, 69,* 473–494.

Festinger, L. (1954). A theory of social comparison processes. *Human Relations, 7,* 117–140.

Fiske, S. T., Cuddy, A., Glick, P., & Xu, J. (2002). A model of (often mixed) stereotype content: Competence and warmth respectively follow from perceived status and competition. *Journal of Personality and Social Psychology, 82,* 878–902.

Fisher, R. J. (1990). *The social psychology of intergroup and international conflict resolution.* Springer.

Gaffney, A. M., Rast, D. E. III, Hackett, J. D., & Hogg, M. A. (2014). Further to the right: Uncertainty, political polarization and the American "Tea Party" movement. *Social Influence, 9,* 272–288.

Greenberg, J., Solomon, S., & Pyszczynski, T. (1997). Terror management theory of self-esteem and cultural worldviews: Empirical assessments and conceptual refinements. *Advances in Experimental Social Psychology, 29,* 61–139.

Hogg, M. A. (2005). Social identity and misuse of power: The dark side of leadership. *Brooklyn Law Review, 70,* 1239–1257.

Hogg, M. A. (2007). Uncertainty–identity theory. *Advances in Experimental Social Psychology, 39,* 69–126.

Hogg, M. A. (2012). Uncertainty-identity theory. In P. A. M. Van Lange, A. W. Kruglanski, & E. T. Higgins (Eds.), *Handbook of theories of social psychology* (pp. 62–80). Sage.

Hogg, M. A. (2014). From uncertainty to extremism: Social categorization and identity processes. *Current Directions in Psychological Science, 23,* 338–342.

Hogg, M. A. (2015). To belong or not to belong: Some self-conceptual and behavioral consequences of identity uncertainty. *Revista de Psicología Social / International Journal of Social Psychology, 30,* 586–613.

Hogg, M. A. (2016). Social identity theory. In S. McKeown, R. Haji, & N. Ferguson (Eds.), *Understanding peace and conflict through social identity theory: Contemporary global perspectives* (pp. 3–17). Springer.

Hogg, M. A. (2018a). Self-uncertainty, leadership preference, and communication of social identity. *Atlantic Journal of Communication, 26,* 111–121.

Hogg, M. A. (2018b). Social identity theory. In P. J. Burke (Ed.), *Contemporary social psychological theories* (2nd ed.) (pp. 112–138). Stanford University Press.

Hogg, M. A. (2020a). Learning who we are from our leaders: How leaders shape group and organizational norms and identities. In L. Argote & J. M. Levine (Eds.), *The Oxford handbook of group and organizational learning* (pp. 587–602). Oxford University Press.

Hogg, M. A. (2020b). Uncertain self in a changing world: A foundation for radicalization, populism and autocratic leadership. *European Review of Social Psychology.* Advance online publication.

Hogg, M. A. (in press). Self-uncertainty and group identification: Consequences for social identity, group behavior, intergroup relations, and society. *Advances in Experimental Social Psychology, 64.*

Hogg M. A., & Abrams, D. (1988). *Social identifications: A social psychology of intergroup relations and group processes.* Routledge.

Hogg, M. A., Abrams, D., & Brewer, M. B. (2017). Social identity: The role of self in group processes and intergroup relations. *Group Processes and Intergroup Relations, 20,* 570–581.

Hogg, M. A., & Gaffney, A. (2014). Prototype-based social comparisons within groups: Constructing social identity to reduce self-uncertainty. In Z. Križan & F. X. Gibbons (Eds.), *Communal functions of social comparison* (pp. 145–174). Cambridge University Press.

Hogg, M. A., & Rinella, M. J. (2018). Social identities and shared realities. *Current Opinion in Psychology*, *23*, 6–10.

Hogg, M. A., & Van Knippenberg, D. (2003). Social identity and leadership processes in groups. *Advances in Experimental Social Psychology*, *35*, 1–52.

Hogg, M. A., Van Knippenberg, D., & Rast, D. E. III. (2012a). The social identity theory of leadership: Theoretical origins, research findings, and conceptual developments. *European Review of Social Psychology*, *23*, 258–304.

Hogg, M. A., Van Knippenberg, D., & Rast, D. E. III. (2012b). Intergroup leadership in organizations: Leading across group and intergroup boundaries. *Academy of Management Review*, *37*, 232–255.

Hogg, M. A., Sherman, D. K., Dierselhuis, J., Maitner, A. T., & Moffitt, G. (2007). Uncertainty, entitativity, and group identification. *Journal of Experimental Social Psychology*, *43*, 135–142.

Hohman, Z. P., Hogg, M. A., & Bligh, M. C. (2010). Identity and intergroup leadership: Asymmetrical political and national identification in response to uncertainty. *Self and Identity*, *9*, 113–128.

Hornsey, M. J., & Hogg, M. A. (2000). Subgroup relations: A comparison of mutual intergroup differentiation and common ingroup identity models of prejudice reduction. *Personality and Social Psychology Bulletin*, *26*, 242–256.

Kakkar, H., & Sivanathan, N. (2017). When the appeal of a dominant leader is greater than a prestige leader. *Proceedings of the National Academy of Sciences*, *114*, 6734–6739.

Kerr, N. L., Ao, X., Hogg, M. A., & Zhang, J. (2018). Addressing replicability concerns via adversarial collaboration: Discovering hidden moderators of the minimal intergroup discrimination effect. *Journal of Experimental Social Psychology*, *78*, 66–76.

Kruglanski, A. W., Pierro, A., Mannetti, L., & De Grada, E. (2006). Groups as epistemic providers: need for closure and the unfolding of group-centrism. *Psychological Review*, *113*, 84.

Mullen, B., Brown, R., & Smith, C. (1992). Ingroup bias as a function of salience, relevance, and status: An integration. *European Journal of Social Psychology*, *22*, 103–122.

Mummendey, A., & Otten, S. (1998). Positive–negative asymmetry in social discrimination. *European Review of Social Psychology*, *19*, 107–143.

Noor, M., Brown, J. R., & Prentice, G. (2008). Precursors and mediators of intergroup reconciliation in Northern Ireland: A new model. *British Journal of Social Psychology*, *47*, 481–495.

Noor, M., Shnabel, N., Halabi, S., & Nadler, A. (2012). When suffering begets suffering the psychology of competitive victimhood between adversarial groups in violent conflicts. *Personality and Social Psychology Review*, *16*, 351–374.

Noor, M., Vollhardt, J. R., Mari, S., & Nadler A. (2017). The social psychology of collective victimhood. *European Journal of Social Psychology*, *47*, 121–134.

Otten, S., & Wentura, D. (1999). About the impact of automaticity in the minimal group paradigm: Evidence from affective priming tasks. *European Journal of Social Psychology*, *29*, 1049–1071.

Peters, K., Morton, T. A., & Haslam, S. A. (2010). Communication silos and social identity complexity in organizations. In H. Giles, S. A. Reid, & J. Harwood (Eds.), *Dynamics of intergroup communication* (pp. 221–234). Peter Lang.

Rast, D. E. III, Hogg, M.A., Giessner, S. R. (2013). Self-uncertainty and support for autocratic leadership. *Self and Identity*, *12*, 635–649.

Rast III, D. E., Hogg, M. A., & Van Knippenberg, D. (2018). Intergroup leadership across distinct subgroups and identities. *Personality and Social Psychology Bulletin*, *44*, 1090–1103.

Reicher, S. D. (1984). The St Pauls' riot: An explanation of the limits of crowd action in terms of a social identity model. *European Journal of Social Psychology*, *14*, 1–21.

Reicher, S. (2001). The psychology of crowd dynamics. In M. A. Hogg & R. S. Tindale (Eds.), *Blackwell handbook of social psychology: Group processes* (pp. 182–208). Blackwell.

Reicher, S., & Hopkins, N. (2003). On the science of the art of leadership. In D. Van Knippenberg & M. A. Hogg (Eds.), *Leadership and power: Identity processes in groups and organizations* (pp. 197–209). Sage.

Reicher, S., Hopkins, N., Levine, M., & Rath, R. (2005). Entrepreneurs of hate and entrepreneurs of solidarity: Social identity as a basis for mass communication. *International Review of the Red Cross*, *87*, 621–637.

Rokeach, M. (1948). Generalized mental rigidity as a factor in ethnocentrism. *Journal of Abnormal and Social Psychology*, *43*, 259–278.

Rubin, M., & Hewstone, M. (1998). Social identity theory's self-esteem hypothesis: A review and some suggestions for clarification. *Personality and Social Psychology Review*, *2*, 40–62.

Sedikides, C., & Strube, M. (1997). Self-evaluation: To thine own self be good, to thine own self be sure, to thine own self be true, and to thine own self be better. *Advances in Experimental Social Psychology, 29*, 209–296.

Seyranian, V. (2012). Constructing extremism: Uncertainty provocation and reduction by leaders. In M. A. Hogg, & D. L. Blaylock (Eds.), *Extremism and the psychology of uncertainty* (pp. 19–35). Wiley-Blackwell.

Seyranian, V. (2014). Social identity framing communication strategies for mobilizing social change. *The Leadership Quarterly, 25*, 468–486.

Seyranian, V., & Bligh, M. C. (2008). Presidential charismatic leadership: Exploring the rhetoric of social change. *The Leadership Quarterly, 19*, 54–76.

Sherif, M. (1958). Superordinate goals in the reduction of intergroup conflicts. *American Journal of Sociology, 63*, 349–356.

Sherif, M. (1966). *Group conflict and cooperation: Their social psychology*. Routledge & Kegan Paul.

Sherif, M., Harvey, O. J., White, B. J., Hood, W. R., & Sherif, C. W. (1961). *Intergroup cooperation and competition: The Robbers Cave experiment*. University Book Exchange.

Sherman, D. K., Hogg, M. A., & Maitner, A. T. (2009). Perceived polarization: Reconciling ingroup and intergroup perceptions under uncertainty. *Group Processes and Intergroup Relations, 12*, 95–109.

Sullivan, D., Landau, M. J., Branscombe, N. R., & Rothschild, Z. K. (2012). Competitive victimhood as a response to accusations of ingroup harm doing. *Journal of Personality and Social Psychology, 102*, 778–795.

Tajfel, H. (1969). Cognitive aspects of prejudice. *Journal of Social Issues, 25*, 79–97.

Tajfel, H. (1970). Experiments in intergroup discrimination. *Scientific American, 223*, 96–102.

Tajfel, H., & Turner, J. C. (1986). The social identity theory of intergroup behaviour. In S. Worchel & W. G. Austin (Eds.), *Psychology of intergroup relations* (2nd ed., pp. 7–24). Nelson-Hall.

Tajfel, H., Billig, M., Bundy, R. P., & Flament, C. (1971). Social categorization and intergroup behaviour. *European Journal of Social Psychology, 1*, 149–177.

Tropp, L. R. (Ed.) (2012). *The Oxford handbook of intergroup conflict*. Oxford University Press.

Turner, J. C. (1975). Social comparison and social identity: Some prospects for intergroup behaviour. *European Journal of Social Psychology, 5*, 5–34.

Turner, J. C., Hogg, M. A., Oakes, P. J., Reicher, S. D., & Wetherell, M. S. (1987). *Rediscovering the social group: A self-categorization theory*. Blackwell.

Vandello, J. A., Goldschmied, N. P., & Richards, D. A. (2007). The appeal of the underdog. *Personality and Social Psychology Bulletin, 33*, 1603–1616.

Vandello, J. A., Michniewicz, K. S., & Goldschmied, N. (2011). Moral judgments of the powerless and powerful in violent intergroup conflicts. *Journal of Experimental Social Psychology, 47*, 1173–1178.

Wagoner, J. A., Belavadi, S., & Jung, J. (2017). Social identity uncertainty: Conceptualization, measurement, and construct validity. *Self and Identity, 16*, 505–530.

Wagoner, J. A., & Hogg, M. A. (2016). Normative dissensus, identity-uncertainty, and subgroup autonomy. *Group Dynamics: Theory, Research, and Practice, 20*, 310–322.

Yzerbyt, V., & Demoulin, S. (2010). Intergroup relations. In S. T. Fiske, D. T. Gilbert, & G. Lindzey (Eds.), *Handbook of social psychology* (5th ed., Vol. 2, pp. 1024–183). Wiley.

Yzerbyt, V., Provost, V., & Corneille, O. (2005). Not competent but warm. . . really? Compensatory stereotypes in the French-speaking world. *Group Processes and Intergroup Relations, 8*, 291–308.

Zimbardo, P. G. (1970). The human choice: Individuation, reason, and order versus deindividuation, impulse, and chaos. In W. J. Arnold & D. Levine (Eds.), *Nebraska symposium on motivation 1969* (Vol. 17, pp. 237–307). University of Nebraska Press.

Benefits and Drawbacks of Trait Competitiveness

Craig D. Parks

Abstract

While evolutionary theory predicts that everyone has some degree of competitive inclination, there is ample evidence that, all else being equal, some people are just simply more highly competitive than others. High competitiveness is colloquially seen as a valuable trait for tasks such as sales, athletic performance, and entrepreneurship, as is low competitiveness for situations which require, or will benefit from, interpersonal or intergroup collaboration. However, the research on trait competitiveness suggests a more complex relationship between one's level of the trait and actual performance than is often assumed. This chapter will review this research, along with the challenges associated with the measurement of competitiveness, the development of competitiveness in children, and cultural differences in trait competitiveness. The chapter will also examine the contribution of competitive inflexibility to a variety of social challenges.

Key Words: competitiveness, trait, personality, self-knowledge, accomplishment, productivity, group performance

Benefits and Drawbacks of Trait Competitiveness

Competitiveness is a quality that threads through lay discussion of many forms of social interaction. Elite athletes are often claimed to possess extremely competitive personalities, and struggling teams are criticized for lacking a killer instinct (best illustrated by baseball manager Leo Durocher's 1946 statement "The nice guys are in seventh place," the basis for the aphorism "Nice guys finish last"). Successful CEOs are lauded for it; the rise and dominance of Uber, for example, is often attributed to co-founder Travis Kalanick's relentless competitiveness (e.g., Isaac, 2017). It is a component of the stereotype of attorneys (a perception which may be accurate; see Riech, 2014). Competitiveness is anecdotally connected to perseverance, confidence, and personal development, although also to arrogance, inflexibility, and micro-management. It is held up as a prime culprit in the failure of close relationships and is beginning to appear in writings about the motivators of helicopter parenting and snowplow parenting. It is discussed as a factor in the decline in many countries of participation in social good works and willingness to support charitable endeavors. It has been debated as a key (positive or negative) contributor to health and to academic achievement.

Clearly, then, the notion of *trait competitiveness* has intuitive appeal. And indeed, ideas about competitiveness as a personal quality can be traced at least to Aesop and his tale of a competition among birds to determine who will be king: A wren so strongly wants to win that it devises a way to technically fly higher than any other bird.[1] This appeal is not surprising. Competition is universally experienced and is an easy concept to understand. Research suggests that a child can grasp the logic of competition by five years of age (Schmidt et al., 2016). Cultures and societies throughout history have placed great emphasis on competition as a tool for fostering collective identity, establishing societal rank, preserving honor, and sublimating internal political tensions (Fisher & van Wees, 2011). In fact, there is evidence that ancient athletes engaged in doping to gain competitive advantage by ingesting things like animal testicles (for testosterone), honey (for carbohydrates), opium (to lessen pain), hallucinogenic fungi (to enhance focus), and wild licorice (for caffeine) (Papagelopoulos et al., 2004). Given this longstanding primacy of competition in daily social life, it is no wonder that people would speculate on the existence of a competition trait. Models of cooperative/competitive choice assign a central role to personality traits and individual differences (Parks et al., 2013), so the notion of a competitiveness trait is plausible.

In this chapter we will review the research on trait competitiveness. We will see that empirical inquiry has not been nearly as deep as one might expect given the sustained interest in the concept. We will also see that, while trait competitiveness does apparently influence a host of behaviors, that influence is more intricate than it might be expected.

The Structure of Trait Competitiveness

The trait perspective defines competitiveness as a desire to win and more generally better others, and enjoyment of the process of trying to win (Spence & Helmreich, 1983). The existence of a competitiveness trait makes sense from an evolutionary perspective. Successful competition for a mate increases the likelihood of gene propagation, and as such, competitive traits would be selected for (Buss, 1988). However, competition against related individuals is counterproductive, so the ability to suppress competitive traits when in a group of kin is also advantageous (Frank, 2003). At the intergroup level, groups that contain competitively oriented members are likely to be successful at outgaining other groups in the pursuit of resources (McDonald et al., 2012).

Competitiveness has been incorporated into many models of personality and individual differences. Horney (1937) described the "hypercompetitive" personality as one which treats all competitions as life-or-death, regardless of the objective value of the outcome at stake; enters a competition expecting not to do well; is incapable of feeling compassion or support for the opponent; and never experiences satisfaction with the competition regardless of the result. Leary and Coffey's (1955) interpersonal diagnosis approach to personality assessment has competitiveness as one of its interaction styles and distinguishes between adjustive competitiveness (manifested, for example, as assertiveness) and maladjustive competitiveness (e.g., exploitation). White (1937) argued that competitiveness is an inverse manifestation of an anxiety trait, with high-anxious people being noncompetitive and low-anxious people being competitive. Competitiveness is a key component of the Type A behavior pattern (Friedman & Rosenman, 1959) and of achievement motivation (Spence et al., 1987). Related to this is research on *social value orientation* (SVO) or a predisposition to favor a particular pattern of outcomes in an interpersonal situation. This work has documented a competitive social value orientation, under which the person generally prefers to outgain all other participants in the interaction, even if personal payoff is less than it could have been (Van Lange, 1999).

There is thus good evidence for competitiveness as a bona fide trait. This raises the questions of how competitiveness develops and why people are differentially competitive. While the research is fairly straightforward regarding the development of competitive tendencies, there is considerable debate surrounding how to explain its differing rate of expression.

Development of Trait Competitiveness

Development of a competitive trait is influenced by both personal experiences and the dynamics of the culture in which one exists. Personally, instillation of competitiveness is impacted by a number of early life experiences: insecure attachment to primary caregivers (Van Lange et al., 1997), successful application of other-ignoring (Ryckman et al., 1997) or manipulative behaviors (Charlesworth, 1996), fear of disappointing others (Choi et al., 2014), and the receipt of (positive or negative) attention as a result of outgaining others (Udvari & Schneider, 2000). Growing up with many siblings (Van Lange et al., 1997), being part of a family of high socioeconomic status (Almås et al., 2016), and having family elders with a strong sense of ethnic identity (Knight et al., 1993) all also contribute to the development of competitive tendencies. At the societal level, a competitive trait tends to be more prevalent in cultures that struggle with resource scarcity (Green et al., 2005) or ecological constraints (Leibbrandt et al., 2013) and are economically underdeveloped (Basabe & Ros, 2005). Societal values also play a role. Societies that emphasize self-enhancement and place value on demonstrated mastery of skills tend to have competition as a prominent feature (Kasser et al., 2007). Cultures that value religiosity tend to emphasize competitiveness, possibly because the different faiths are trying to win adherents within a fixed number of society members and so view all social interactions as competitive (Hunsberger & Jackson, 2005), possibly because of a general expectancy that a third party will always intervene in and resolve a conflict, so there is no need to learn how to seek common ground (Bond et al., 2004).[2] As noted previously, these influences take root early in the life span (Schmidt et al., 2016).

Measurement of Competitiveness

Assessment of trait competitiveness was originally indirect. Researchers would generally use a competition-referencing subscale of an instrument that measured some form of motivation (e.g., the Work and Family Orientation Questionnaire [Helmreich & Spence, 1978]; the Sports Orientation Questionnaire [Gill & Deeter, 1988]; the Jenkins Activity Survey [Jenkins et al., 1979]) on the assumption that the subscale was tapping a stable trait. Attempts to directly measure competitiveness began in earnest in the 1990s with the Hypercompetitive Attitude Scale (Ryckman et al., 1990), Competitiveness Index (Houston et al., 1992; Smither & Houston, 1992), and Personal Development Competitive Attitude Scale (PDCAS) (Ryckman et al., 1996). Each has good psychometric properties. A comparison of the three scales along with multiple indirect measures (Houston et al., 2002) revealed a mean Fisher-z transformed absolute correlation of 0.37 between scales, with a range running from 0.01 to 0.75. Houston et al.'s (2002) conclusion was that "competitiveness" was being conceived of in a variety of ways. In an attempt to bring some regularity to the concept, they proposed distinguishing between competitiveness that is motivated by a drive for superiority (referred to by the authors as Self-Aggrandizement) and that which is motivated by a belief in the benefits of competition (Interpersonal Success). Subsequent work has not gone in this direction, however. A recent review by Swab and Johnson (2019) identified a wider range of definitions of competitiveness, with it being variously conceived of as a system of beliefs about the world, an overarching focus on winning, a philosophy of interpersonal relations, or a priming-susceptible mindset. They additionally reported the emergence of a person-by-situation framework under which competitiveness is a function of environmental factors and individual perceptual biases (e.g., Brown et al., 1998; Murayama & Elliot, 2012).

All these scales are based on the notion that competitiveness is best assessed through belief elicitation. Respondents are instructed to indicate degree of agreement with a series of belief statements ("I want to be the winner every time I play a game," "I feel happy whenever I do better than others on a task," etc.) and presence/strength of the trait is inferred from some type of aggregate score. A different approach to the assessment of competitiveness is the decomposed games approach. This approach assumes that expression of the trait will occur behaviorally by virtue of making consistent, predictable choices across a series of similar tasks. For example, consider a situation in which a person must choose from among three different allocations of resources between self and an unknown other:

10 to Self, 10 to Other
12 to Self, 6 to Other
8 to Self, 1 to Other

The decomposed games approach predicts that a competitive person will favor the last option, because even though own outcome is the smallest available, the option produces the greatest gain relative to Other.[3] Presence of the competitive trait is determined by presenting a number of similar choice situations and observing how often the relative-gain choice is selected, with the typical requirement being that it must be selected at least 75 percent of the time to ascribe competitiveness to the person.

The decomposed games approach has good empirical support (Balliet et al., 2009; Murphy & Ackermann, 2014). A potential limitation is that it is a classification technique only and assumes that all competitive individuals possess the same degree of competitiveness; further, a person whose choice consistency falls below the cutoff is considered unclassifiable. To address this, a continuous analogue of the decomposed game was developed by Murphy and colleagues (Murphy et al., 2011). Their method produces gradations in the assignment of competitiveness to individuals and allows for a degree of competitiveness to be ascribed to all persons. Note also that Murphy et al.'s (2011) method allows for detection of hypercompetitive individuals, which the simple decomposed game cannot do. However, to date there has been no attempt to compare the decomposed games approach to any of the belief-based assessment tools.

Relationship of Competitiveness to Other Traits

Researchers have investigated to what extent competitiveness co-occurs with other personality traits, although given the long history of interest in trait competitiveness, this work has been surprisingly irregular. Perhaps the best known is the notion of a "coronary-disease-prone personality" that has chronic competitiveness at its core. First speculated on over one hundred years ago (Chesney et al., 1981), the idea was formalized by Friedman and Rosenman (1959) as the Type A personality. Despite the centrality of competitiveness as a presumed contributor to Type A, direct tests of trait competitiveness among those classified as Type A are rare and equivocal. In a study of children, Matthews and Angulo (1980) found competitiveness to distinguish Type A and B individuals only when a female teacher was present. Veldjuijzen van Zanten and colleagues (2002) saw no connection between trait competitiveness and the pattern of cardiovascular arousal that is characteristic of Type A individuals. Bartkus and colleagues (1989) showed that Type A was predictive of competitive behavior in salespeople only if work effort was left uncontrolled in the model. In fact, a scan of the literature on Type A suggests that theorists have largely taken as a given that Type A individuals possess high levels of trait competitiveness, considering how frequently authors simply describe the Type A person as "highly competitive" and then move on. There is a clear need for more and systematic research into whether the two traits are in fact related.

There has been interest in possible connections between trait competitiveness and the traits that comprise the five-factor model of personality: Agreeableness, Openness to Experience, Extraversion, Neuroticism, and Conscientiousness. This work has largely returned inconsistent findings, although the variety of conceptions of competitiveness has clearly been a confounding factor. In general, Agreeableness and Extraversion both seem to connect in some way to competitiveness; it may also connect to Conscientiousness, although this relationship has so far been difficult to reliably establish (e.g., Bönte et al., 2017; Fletcher & Nusbaum, 2008; Graziano et al., 1997; Perry et al., 2010; Ross et al., 2003). Intrasexual competitiveness also seems to have some connection to the five factors, although differently for men and women. For women, intrasexual competitiveness is mainly related to Agreeableness, whereas for men Extraversion and Neuroticism are the more important traits (Buunk & Fisher, 2009). Competitiveness has also been investigated in connection to the RIASEC model of personality-based occupational choice, a model which has notable overlap with the five factors (Barrick et al., 2003; Larson et al., 2002). RIASEC identifies six personality types that are thought to influence job choice: Realistic, Investigative, Artistic, Social, Enterprising, and Conventional. Research suggests that trait competitiveness is positively related to the Investigative and Enterprising types, perhaps because the Investigative type values achievement and the Enterprising type values social success and control over others (Houston et al., 2015). As with research on Type A, however, much more work needs to be done to establish reliable connections between competitiveness and broad, overarching traits.

Narcissism has also been suggested as a trait that may correlate with competitiveness, on the grounds that competitiveness motivated by self-aggrandizement shares with narcissism an inflated sense of self-worth. Narcissism is thought to take two forms: (1) overt narcissism, under which the person externalizes inflated self-perceptions through arrogance and grandiosity; and (2) covert narcissism, under which self-perceptions are internalized resulting in hypersensitivity, vulnerability, and fear of being perceived as a failure (Wink, 1991). Luchner and colleagues (2011) found both forms of narcissism to correlate positively with hypercompetitiveness. However, simple competitiveness was positively related to overt narcissism but negatively related to covert narcissism. That a covert narcissist would be negative about competition but positive about hypercompetition is likely a function of the covert narcissist's fear of failure: the person prefers to avoid competitive situations to eliminate risk of failure, but if the person must compete, then they will take a "win at all costs" approach. For our purposes, this suggests that hypercompetition may be a controllable quality; in other words, it is not a trait that necessarily pervades every aspect of the person's life (although as we will see, there is evidence that hypercompetition can indeed be all-pervasive).

Finally, competitiveness may have a connection to social dominance orientation (SDO), a trait which influences one's degree of preference for social inequality between groups (Pratto et al., 1994). Research finds that people who see the world as a chronically competitive environment tend to be high on SDO (Perry et al., 2013; Van Hiel et al., 2007). Whether this indicates a connection between SDO and trait competitiveness versus a perception of a specific situation is unclear, as researchers have not used global measures of competitiveness in their studies, but it is a possibility worth investigating.

Evolutionary psychologists have proposed that there are individual differences in intrasexual competitiveness as well as general competitiveness. This intrasexual competitiveness is characterized by a desire to outperform others, a desire to see oneself as better than others, negative feelings toward others who are doing better than oneself, and feelings of schadenfreude when successful others stumble (Buunk & Massar, 2012). Buunk and Massar (2012) found good fidelity between their measure of intrasexual competitiveness and the decomposed games technique. An intriguing issue is the nature of the relationship between general competitiveness and intrasexual competitiveness. It is possible that the latter is simply a situation-specific manifestation of the former, but it may also be that intrasexual competitiveness is the root trait which then gets generalized to other social situations. They may, of course, also be independent processes.

Behavioral Benefits of Competitiveness

Much research suggests that competitiveness, properly expressed, offers advantages for personal growth and development. Education researchers have long known that pitting students against each other in friendly competition fosters engagement with the topic material, confidence, and a desire to learn more (Plass et al., 2015). Beyond the classroom, competitiveness can result in enhanced self-knowledge and feelings of personal accomplishment. (Interestingly, it is unclear whether it is beneficial in the realm in which it is stereotypically seen as an asset, namely athletic contests [Allen et al., 2013].) In this section, we review the key findings in each of these areas.

Self-Knowledge

The expression of trait competitiveness provides opportunities for a person to gain self-knowledge and can serve as a motivator of self-improvement. Those high on competitiveness often seek new challenges to discover the range of their abilities and their maximum skill levels on those abilities. Consider, for example, a marathon runner who enters a race with a goal not of winning, but of setting a personal best time or achieving some milestone. Much research documents how competitiveness motivates and promotes self-awareness. High-achieving students consistently score highly on competitiveness (e.g., Goclowska et al., 2017; King et al., 2012) and there is evidence that it induces deep and extended effort to learn and master skills and new information (Wang & Netemeyer, 2002). Those who are motivated to serve in leadership positions espouse competitiveness as a quality that they value in themselves and in others (Chan & Drasgow, 2001). Those high on competitiveness tend to have strong self-esteem (Eime et al., 2013; Hibbard & Buhrmester, 2010) and optimism (Tjosvold et al., 2008). They emphasize forgiveness (Collier et al., 2010) and concern for others (Choi et al., 2014; Ryckman et al., 1997).

The personal benefits of competitiveness speak to the larger issue of the psychological impact of competitive activity on children. If the task environment is healthy and supportive; that is, if it emphasizes personal development and skill acquisition, competitive activity holds many benefits for youth and can help instill a growth mindset (Eime et al., 2013). If on the other hand the environment is oriented around winning and emphasizes relative outcomes, avoidance of defeat, and success however possible, the child is at risk for burnout, anxiety, loss of confidence, and a low sense of control over their environment (Kanters et al., 2008). Interestingly, the current "trophy culture" ethos of recognizing all participants in a competition regardless of performance may have the long-term effect of discouraging competitiveness as a tool for growth. Treating clearly different ability levels as equally praiseworthy may send a signal that competition is not useful for learning about oneself, and lead those who desire self-knowledge to acquire it through other means (see Dickhaus et al., 2019).

Personal Accomplishment

Related to the desire to learn about oneself is the accomplishment of personal goals. While self-knowledge and goal setting are often related, it is sometimes the case that a goal exists for a more concrete reason. For example, a person who is recovering from major surgery may set a goal of returning to work within a certain number of months, the goal serving to keep the person focused on the recovery routine. Trait competitiveness is potentially beneficial for the striving toward these goals. Murayama and Elliot (2012) hypothesized and documented a direct effect of competition on goal setting, although competitiveness can induce two quite different types of goals. Those directed toward pursuing a challenge (Murayama and Elliot refer to these as "performance-approach" goals), and those directed toward avoiding a threat ("performance-avoidance" goals). Complications can arise when the person formulates both types of goals at once. Consider, for example, a competitive student who wants to finish top-five in a course (an approach goal) and fears being so nondescript that the instructor refuses to provide a letter of recommendation (an avoidance goal). Murayama and Elliot (2012) showed that, in such situations, competitiveness will be, at best, a weak influence on performance.

In those situations in which the individual is only approach-oriented, competitiveness offers many benefits. We have already noted that education theorists consider competition an effective tool for learning. Its impact in two other realms, the workplace and health maintenance, has received less attention but there are some important findings in each.

IN THE WORKPLACE

Much research on competitiveness and accomplishment has examined workplace behavior. Kanfer and Ackerman (2000) found trait competitiveness to exist as a largely independent influence on workplace motivation, correlating only with social potency (positively), a facet of extraversion that captures visibility, dominance, and a desire to be in charge, and negatively with age. Workers high in trait competitiveness tend to show stronger levels of organizational commitment and greater dedication to their jobs (Diefendorff & Mehta, 2007; Fletcher et al., 2008). This is especially true if the competitive employee is also coachable and open to leadership intervention (Shannahan et al., 2013). However, people high on trait competitiveness are also more likely to feel time pressure on tasks and be unwilling to assist coworkers when such pressure is felt (Connelly et al., 2014), and those who equate competitiveness with winning may actively sabotage the efforts of their coworkers (Jelinek & Ahearne, 2010). Trait competitiveness applied to workplace accomplishment thus seems to be a double-edged sword. Competitive workers are dedicated, especially if they are open to being led, but they are also susceptible to feeling time pressures, even if in truth the pressure is minimal.

HEALTH MAINTENANCE

Some of the research on competitiveness and accomplishment has been conducted on physical wellbeing. This research shows that trait competitiveness is positively related to benefit from exercise (e.g., Anderson-Hanley et al., 2011) and physical rehabilitation (Novak et al., 2014) programs. It is a contributing factor to perseverance in rehabilitation for post-stroke patients (Navarro et al., 2020). Competitiveness is possibly a positive contributor to successful management of type 1 diabetes because a high level of trait competitiveness is associated with reduction in inflammatory processes (Chauvet-Gélinier et al., 2019). Competitive people treat improvement of nutritional quality as a challenge and success as an accomplishment, a mindset that promotes long-term commitment to healthy eating; by contrast, noncompetitive people tend to treat it as a change necessary to avoid disappointing others, a mindset that does not encourage perseverance (Orji et al., 2019).

Behavioral Impacts of Hypercompetitiveness

Earlier we introduced Horney's (1937) notion of hypercompetitiveness. To recap, a hypercompetitive person treats every situation as a critical competition, never expects to do well, never feels compassion or support for the opponent, and will be dissatisfied with even a dominant performance. Hypercompetitiveness has been implicated as an influence on some pathological behaviors. It is often a factor in gambling addiction (Harris et al., 2015; Lloyd et al., 2010; Parke et al., 2004). It can motivate body dissatisfaction, eating disorders, and extensive plastic surgery in women (Schrick et al., 2012; Sides-Moore & Tochkov, 2011; Thornton et al., 2013a), although whether it has a similar effect on men is less clear (see Fabris et al., 2018, and Thornton et al., 2013b, for opposing evidence). Hypercompetitiveness may have an indirect effect on depression through both chronic fear of inferiority (Basran et al., 2019) and unrelenting emphasis on perfectionism (Flett et al., 2003). Hypercompetitive individuals tend to be deceptive and controlling of romantic partners (Ryckman et al., 2002). While not a truly pathological behavior, hypercompetitive people are also vulnerable to dogmatic thinking and authoritarianism (Dru, 2003). Evolution of the higher education environment to one of hypercompetitiveness among students—for grades, status, recognition, attention—has been cited as the dominant influence on increased college student stress, anxiety, and depression (Posselt & Lipson, 2016).

Despite these worrisome qualities, hypercompetitiveness is considered a desirable quality in some sectors of industry, specifically, those that operate under the philosophy that one's sector operates in a state of chronic disequilibrium, advantage is always temporary and fleeting, advantage is gained by moving more quickly and nimbly than one's competitors, and individuals who seek operational stability should be cast aside (Chen et al., 2010).[4] As such, it is important to understand how hypercompetitiveness impacts behavior, particularly behaviors of relevance in the workplace. In this section, we briefly summarize its impact on productivity, ethical choice, and leadership.

Workplace Productivity

In his classic study of bureaucracy, Merton (1940) asked why teams of skilled, trained workers would nonetheless make poor-quality products. He attributed poor performance to the presence of workers with competitive personalities who are more focused on standing out relative to coworkers than on helping to make the best possible product. Merton's point was that sometimes, competitive workers will direct their trait competitiveness inward and compete with colleagues at the expense of product quality.

What would prompt a person with high trait competitiveness to see coworkers rather than other work teams as the basis for performance comparison? Some research on compensation schemes suggests one answer. This work has examined how trait competitiveness influences reaction to pay-for-performance incentive structures and finds that such a structure induces those high on trait competitiveness to engage in social comparison and hence active undermining of coworkers (Gläser et al., 2017). However, there is some evidence that undermining does not occur if the person perceives the pay-for-performance structure as a personal challenge (Parker et al., 2019). This suggests that whether pay-for-performance is destructive or facilitating depends on whether the high-competitiveness person conceives of competition in terms of victory or challenge.

Related to the question of when trait competitiveness is beneficial versus harmful for worker productivity is the notion of a "bottom-line mentality" personality trait. Greenbaum and colleagues (2012) have shown that people who are high on this trait focus only on accomplishment of a specified final objective, while those low on the trait take a more wholistic view of the task. Greenbaum et al. (2012) argue that a high bottom-line mentality individual tends to see tasks through a competitive lens and focuses not only on achievement of the objective, but also on being the person who contributes the most to the achievement. This can in turn lead to active undermining of coworkers. While this is not a direct demonstration that trait competitiveness can lead to sabotaging of coworkers, it is certainly suggestive of such.

Research on trait competitiveness in the workplace has also addressed to what extent the trait is a contributor to gender differences in workplace achievement (Niederle & Vesterlund, 2011). To date the research has been correlational but suggestive. Buser (2016) found that women scored lower than men on a measure of trait competitiveness and also selected less challenging tasks following a performance setback, whereas men chose more challenging tasks. Bönte and Piegeler (2013) observed a positive connection between competitiveness and willingness to start a new business. They also found a gender difference on competitiveness scores, which they suggest helps explain why women are less willing to engage in entrepreneurship. Some research suggests that this effect may be limited to tasks that are stereotypically male (Apicella & Dreber, 2015) and may be a function of how males and females differentially respond to the stress that often accompanies workplace competition (Cahliková et al., 2020).

Unethical Decision-Making

Hypercompetitiveness has been implicated as a motivator of unethical decision-making, although establishing a clear connection between the two is difficult because of the need to either simulate unethical decisions or analyze them after the fact. For example, a number of studies have found undergraduate business majors who equate competitiveness with winning to be more willing to endorse unethical resolution of business dilemmas than students who equate it with challenge (Mudrack et al., 2012; Sankaran & Bui, 2003; Westbrook et al., 2011). Similarly, Sobral and Islam (2013) had participants in executive education workshops engage in simulated negotiations under favorable or unfavorable conditions and found that individuals high on trait competitiveness were willing to resort to ethically ambiguous negotiating tactics when conditions were not in their favor.

More direct evidence of the influence of competitiveness on ethical behavior can be found in work on response faking on written assessments. This research shows that people who are high on trait competitiveness are relatively likely to provide inaccurate responses that present themselves in a positive light (Tett et al., 2006; Tett & Simonet, 2011). This is likely due to the person perceiving the assessment as a win-lose situation ("If I do not present outstanding qualities, I will be harmed socially") rather than as a simple description of self. To date this research has focused on personality measurement, but it is starting to be extended to falsification of job applicant information (Roulin & Krings, 2016; see also Buehl & Melchers, 2017).

Leadership

Some leadership theorists have decried hypercompetitiveness as a barrier to needed collaboration and ultimately destructive to a company (Gandz et al., 2013). Empirical data backs this claim. Hypercompetitive leaders tend to promote an antisocial work environment, characterized by lack of collaboration among team members, an absence of compassion, and an emphasis on avoiding failure rather than pursuing excellence. The leaders themselves tend to present work team goals that are self-rather than group-or organization-beneficial, and they are poor at interacting with and providing guidance to subordinates (Basran et al., 2019).

It is not hard to envision the exhausting impact of an intensely driven, single-minded, and nonstop leader on a task group. But what about a leader who is merely high on trait competitiveness? Surely this must be a critical quality for leadership success. Interestingly, the evidence for this not clear. Some leadership theorists do not isolate competitiveness as a stand-alone characteristic of successful leaders, and instead treat it as a facet of a broader trait, for example *surgency*, which includes ambitiousness and decisiveness along with competitiveness (Hughes et al., 2006). Thus, a leader who is low on trait competitiveness could nonetheless be quite effective if he/she is decisive and ambitious. Further, research on leader narcissism has found narcissistic leaders to often have a competitive orientation. Narcissistic leaders often prove to be manipulative, ruthless, and exploitative (De Hoogh et al., 2015). This certainly does not mean that a leader who is merely competitive will demonstrate these qualities, but the possibility is there, and there seems to be no research testing whether competitive (as opposed to hypercompetitive) leaders have the potential to behave in these ways.

Summary and Conclusions

Competitiveness clearly exists as a trait. Its development is well-charted, although how best to assess it remains an issue. Considerable effort has been invested in creating measures of competitiveness but attempts to compare and triangulate these measures have been less than thorough. Competitiveness may be correlated with certain other traits, but systematic study of possible links is surprisingly limited. Hypercompetitiveness can be harmful personally and interpersonally, but a more temperate expression of trait competitiveness, especially competitiveness that emphasizes challenge rather than victory, can deepen self-knowledge and encourages persistence toward goal accomplishment.

Given the historic popularity of the notion that some people are "naturally competitive," it is surprising to find prominent gaps in our understanding of the trait. This may well be the result of an assumption that there is no need to test for competitiveness because we know from anecdote that some people have the trait, and that it has value in certain specific realms like athletics and business leadership. A parallel type of assumption can be found in the literature on group decision-making. For decades it was assumed that there is no need to study the quality of group decisions because of course they will be better than decisions made by any one individual. Groups contain a broader range of expertise and multiple points of view and provide the opportunity to discuss and examine task-related evidence, whereas an individual must act in isolation and rely upon his/her interpretation of the evidence. When this notion was finally tested by Stasser and colleagues (see Stasser & Titus, 2003) the data revealed how flawed this assumption was. Groups perform only about as well as their most capable member and are susceptible to a host of process biases that undercut the advantages inherent in multiple people working together. Further, these biases have proven to be resistant to intervention and correction. Thus, the supposition that there is no need to systematically study trait competitiveness because "everyone knows" it exists and what it does is very likely flawed.

A full understanding of the dynamic of trait competitiveness would present many practical advantages. For example, might it be that someone with apparently low competitiveness in fact has dormant competitiveness that can be activated and put to benefit? There is some indirect evidence from education to suggest this might be possible (Papaioannou et al., 2004). Can hypercompetitiveness be modulated down to a more reasonable level? Is it possible to redirect the target of hypercompetition away from other people and toward the task? More generally, how can we take maximal advantage of the positive aspects of trait competitiveness and reduce the negative impacts?

An issue in leadership research that has apparently not been investigated is how competitive leaders who are oriented toward winning compare to those who are oriented toward challenge. This is an important oversight. It is not at all clear that competitiveness is a necessary or even desirable quality in a leader. At the same time, in most countries commerce is inarguably competitive, and it seems paradoxical that a company could thrive in such an environment if none of its leaders have a competitive orientation. It may be that the distinction between victory and challenge is especially critical here. A focus on challenge could encourage the leader to focus on overseeing a "better" work team than other leaders in the company, and as such be largely unwilling to take risks, be flexible, or tolerate worker variability. This leader is most likely to succeed by developing a work team that does one small thing very well. By contrast, a victory-oriented leader would want his/her team to contribute toward creation of the best collective product that the organization can make and will have his/her group do whatever is necessary to make that happen. Some evidence for this prediction may already exist in the distinction between leader competitiveness and leader ambition within the research on surgency, if "competitiveness" is taken to refer to challenge and "ambition" to winning. If this is so, a line of inquiry would then open up contrasting the efficacy of the two views of competitiveness in leadership situations.

Competitiveness is a personality trait that has considerable potential to contribute to human growth and thriving. It is my position that the trait is mostly seen through a stereotypic lens that engenders negativity or at best a grudging respect. As with any trait, extreme and chronic application of competitiveness, in the form of hypercompetitiveness, does indeed seem to be problematic unless applied in a very specific domain. Hopefully this review has convinced the reader that competitiveness can potentially be a positive and beneficial trait and requires much more study to understand how to fully and consistently unlock those benefits.

Notes

1. The wren is disqualified from the competition, and thereafter refuses to again attempt to fly high. Whether Aesop intended the fable as a caution against deviousness as a means of winning, or as a scolding of those who fail to recognize ingenuity, remains a point of debate among philosophers.
2. Whether one's culture is individualistic or collectivistic has historically been thought to also influence the development of competitive orientation. However, more recent research has found no real difference in prevalence of competitiveness between the two types (Oyserman et al., 2002) and current theoretical frameworks do not include competitiveness as a distinguishing characteristic of a culture (Brewer & Chen, 2007).
3. A *cooperative* or *prosocial* person would tend to favor the first option because it produces the greatest total gain. An *individualist* would tend to favor the second option because it produces the greatest personal gain. This method of assessment is typically coupled with the social value orientation approach to interpersonal traits mentioned earlier.
4. It is worth noting that one such industry that fits the hypercompetitive profile is research-intensive higher education (Edwards & Roy, 2017).

References

Allen, M. S., Greenlees, I., & Jones, M. V. (2013). Personality in sport: A comprehensive review. *International Review of Sport and Exercise Psychology 6*, 184–208.

Almås, I., Cappelen, A. W., Salvanes, K. G., Sørensen, E. Ø., & Tungodden, B. (2016). Willingness to compete: Family matters. *Management Science 62*, 2149–2155.

Anderson-Hanley, C., Snyder, A. L., Nimon, J. P., & Arciero, P. J. (2011). Social facilitation in virtual reality-enhanced exercise: Competitiveness moderates exercise effort of older adults. *Clinical Interventions in Aging 6*, 275–280.

Apicella, C. L., & Dreber, A. (2015). Sex differences in competitiveness: Hunter-gatherer women and girls compete less in gender-neutral and male-centric tasks. *Adaptive Human Behavior and Physiology 1*, 247–269.

Balliet, D. P., Parks, C. D., & Joireman, A. (2009). Social value orientation and cooperation: A meta-analysis. *Group Processes and Intergroup Relations 12*, 533–547.

Barrick, M. R., Mount, M. K., & Gupta, R. (2003). Meta-analysis of the relationship between the five-factor theory of personality and Holland's occupational types. *Personnel Psychology 56*, 45–74.

Bartkus, K. R., Peterson, M. F., & Bellenger, D. N. (1989). Type A behavior, experience, and salesperson performance. *Journal of Personal Selling and Sales Management 9*, 11–18.

Basabe, N., & Ros, M. (2005). Cultural dimensions and social behavior correlates: Individualism-collectivism and power distance. *International Journal of Social Psychology 18*, 189–225.

Basran, J., Pires, C., Matos, M., McEwan, K., & Gilbert, P. (2019). Styles of leadership, fears of compassion, and competing to avoid inferiority. *Frontiers in Psychology 9*, 2460.

Bond, M. H., Leung, K., Au, A., Tong, K.-K., & Chemonges-Nielson, Z. (2004). Combining social axioms with values in predicting social behaviours. *European Journal of Personality 18*, 177–191.

Bönte, W., Lombardo, S., & Urbig, D. (2017). Economics meets psychology: Experimental and self-reported measures of individual competitiveness. *Personality and Individual Differences 116*, 179–185.

Bönte, W., & Piegeler, M. (2013). Gender gap in latent and nascent entrepreneurship: Driven by competitiveness. *Small Business Economics 41*, 961–987.

Brewer, M. B., & Chen, Y.-R. (2007). Where (who) are collectives in collectivism? Toward conceptual clarification of individualism and collectivism. *Psychological Review 114*, 133–151.

Brown, S. P., Cron, W. L., & Slocum, J. W. (1998). Effects of trait competitiveness and perceived intraorganizational competition on salesperson goal setting and performance. *Journal of Marketing 64*, 88–98.

Buehl, A.-K., & Melchers, K. G. (2017). Individual difference variables and the occurrence and effectiveness of faking behavior in interviews. *Frontiers in Psychology 8*, 686.

Buser, T. (2016). The impact of losing in a competition on the willingness to seek further challenges. *Management Science 62*, 3439–3449.

Buss, D. M. (1988). The evolution of human intrasexual competition: Tactics of mate attraction. *Journal of Personality and Social Psychology 54*, 616–628.

Buunk, A. P., & Fisher, M. (2009). Individual differences in intrasexual competition. *Journal of Evolutionary Psychology 7*, 37–48.

Buunk, A. P., & Massar, K. (2012). Intrasexual competition among males: Competitive towards men, prosocial towards women. *Personality and Individual Differences 52*, 818–821.

Cahlikova, J., Cingl, L., & Levely, I. (2020). How stress affects performance and competitiveness across gender. *Management Science 66*, 3295–3310.

Chan, K.-Y., & Drasgow, F. (2001). Toward a theory of individual differences and leadership: Understanding the motivation to lead. *Journal of Applied Psychology 86*, 481–498.

Charlesworth, W. R. (1996). Co-operation and competition: Contributions to an evolutionary and developmental model. *International Journal of Behavioral Development 19*, 25–39.

Chauvet-Gélinier, J.-C., Mosca-Boidron, A.-L., Lemogne, C., Ragot, S., Forestier, N., Callegarin, D., Allard, C., Rebaï, A., Bouillet, B., Ponavoy, E., Simoneau, I., Petit, J. M., Bondolfi, G., Callier, P., Trojak, B., Bonin, B., Vergès, B. (2019). Type A competitiveness traits correlate with downregulation of *c-Fos* expression in patients with type 1 diabetes. *Diabetes and Metabolism 45*, 582–585.

Chen, M.-J., Lin, H.-C., & Michel, J. G. (2010). Navigating in a hypercompetitive environment: The roles of action aggressiveness and TMT integration. *Strategic Management Journal 31*, 1410–1430.

Chesney, M. A., Black, G. W., Chadwick, J. H., & Rosenman, R. H. (1981). Psychological correlates of the type A behavior pattern. *Journal of Behavioral Medicine 4*, 217–229.

Choi, H.-S., Johnson, B., & Kim, Y. K. (2014). Children's development through sports competition: Derivative, adjustive, generative, and maladaptive approaches. *Quest 66*, 191–202.

Collier, S. A., Ryckman, R. M., Thornton, B., & Gold, J. A. (2010). Competitive personality attitudes and forgiveness of others. *Journal of Psychology 144*, 535–543.

Connelly, C. E., Ford, D. P., Turel, O., Gallupe, R. B., & Zweig, D. (2014). "I'm busy (and competitive)!" Antecedents of knowledge sharing under pressure. *Knowledge Management Research and Practice 12*, 74–85.

De Hoogh, A. H. B., Den Hartog, D. N., & Nevicka, B. (2015). Gender differences in the perceived effectiveness of narcissistic leaders. *Applied Psychology 64*, 473–498.

Dickhaus, J., Brown, K. A., Ferrucci, P., & Anderson, M. L. (2019). And the award goes to: Examining the effects of the "trophy culture" on millennials. *Journal of Contemporary Athletics 13*, 39–51.

Diefendorff, J. M., & Mehta, K. (2007). The relations of motivational traits with workplace deviance. *Journal of Applied Psychology 92*, 967–977.

Dru, V. (2003). Relationships between an ego orientation scale and a hypercompetitive scale: Their correlates with dogmatism and authoritarianism factors. *Personality and Individual Differences 35*, 1509–1524.

Edwards, M. A., & Roy, S. (2017). Academic research in the 21st century: Maintaining scientific integrity in a climate of perverse incentives and hypercompetition. *Environmental Engineering Science 34*, 51–61.

Eime, R. M., Young, J. A., Harvey, J. T., Charity, M. J., & Payne, W. R. (2013). A systematic review of the psychological and social benefits of participation in sport for children and adolescents: Informing development of a conceptual model of health through sport. *International Journal of Behavioral Nutrition and Physical Activity 10*, 98.

Fabris, M. A., Longobardi, C., Prino, L. E., & Settanni, M. (2018). Attachment style and risk of muscle dysmorphia in a sample of male bodybuilders. *Psychology of Men and Masculinity 19*, 273–281.

Fisher, N., & van Wees, H. (2011). *Competition in the ancient world*. Classical Press of Wales.

Fletcher, T. D., Major, D. A., & Davis, D. D. (2008). The interactive relationship of competitive climate and trait competitiveness with workplace attitudes, stress, and performance. *Journal of Organizational Behavior 29*, 899–922.

Fletcher, T. D., & Nusbaum, D. N. (2008). Trait competitiveness as a composite variable: Linkages with facets of the big-five. *Personality and Individual Differences 45*, 312–317.

Flett, G. L., Besser, A., Davis, R. A., & Hewitt, P. L. (2003). Dimensions of perfectionism, unconditional self-acceptance, and depression. *Journal of Rational-Emotive and Cognitive-Behavior Therapy 21*, 119–138.

Frank, S. A. (2003). Repression of competition and the evolution of cooperation. *Evolution 57*, 693–705.

Friedman, M., & Rosenman, R. H. (1959). Association of specific overt behavior pattern with blood and cardiovascular findings: Blood cholesterol level, blood clotting time, incidence of arcus senilis, and clinical coronary artery disease. *Journal of the American Medical Association 169*, 1286–1296.

Gandz, J., Crossan, M., Seijts, G., & Reno, M. (2013). Leadership character and corporate governance. *Journal of the Institute of Corporate Directors 167*, 15–21.

Gill, D. L., & Deeter, T. E. (1988). Development of the Sports Orientation Questionnaire. *Research Quarterly for Exercise and Sport 59*, 191–202.

Gläser, D., van Gils, S., & van Quaquebeke, N. (2017). Pay-for-performance and interpersonal deviance: Competitiveness as the match that lights the fire. *Journal of Personnel Psychology 16*, 77–90.

Goclowska, M. A., Aldhobaiban, N., Elliot, A. J., Murayama, K., Kobeisy, A., & Abdelaziz, A. (2017). Temperament and self-based correlates of cooperative, competitive, and individualistic learning preferences. *International Journal of Psychology 52*, 180–188.

Graziano, W. G., Hair, E. C., & Finch, J. F. (1997). Competitiveness mediates the link between personality and group performance. *Journal of Personality and Social Psychology 73*, 1394–1408.

Green, E. G. T., Deschamps, J.-C., & Paez, D. (2005). Variation of individualism and collectivism within and between 20 countries: A typological analysis. *Journal of Cross-Cultural Psychology 36*, 321–339.

Greenbaum, R. L., Mawritz, M. B., & Eissa, G. (2012). Bottom-line mentality as an antecedent of social undermining and the moderating role of core self-evaluations and conscientiousness. *Journal of Applied Psychology 97*, 343–359.

Harris, N., Newby, J., & Klein, R. G. (2015). Competitiveness facets and sensation seeking as predictors of problem gambling among a sample of university student gamblers. *Journal of Gambling Studies 31*, 385–396.

Helmreich, R. L., & Spence, J. T. (1978). The Work and Family Orientation Questionnaire: An objective instrument to assess components of achievement motivation and attitudes toward family and career. *JSAS Catalog of Selected Documents in Psychology 8*, 35.

Hibbard, D. R., & Buhrmester, D. (2010). Competitiveness, gender, and adjustment among adolescents. *Sex Roles 63*, 412–424.

Horney, K. (1937). *The neurotic personality of our time*. W. W. Norton.

Houston, J. M., Farese, D. M., & La Du, T. J. (1992). Assessing competitiveness: A validation study of the Competitiveness Index. *Personality and Individual Differences 13*, 1153–1156.

Houston, J. M., Harris, P. B., Howansky, K., & Houston, S. M. (2015). Winning at work: Trait competitiveness, personality types, and occupational interests. *Personality and Individual Differences 76*, 49–51.

Houston, J. M., McIntire, S. A., Kinnie, J., & Terry, C. (2002). A factorial analysis of scales measuring competitiveness. *Educational and Psychological Measurement 62*, 284–298.

Hughes, R. L., Ginnett, R. C., & Curphy, G. R. (2006). *Leadership: Enhancing the lessons of experience*. McGraw-Hill.

Hunsberger, B., & Jackson, L. M. (2005). Religion, meaning, and prejudice. *Journal of Social Issues 61*, 807–826.

Isaac, M. (2017). Uber tallies the costs of its leader's drive to win at any price. *New York Times*, April 23, A1.

Jelinek, R., & Ahearne, M. (2010). Be careful what you look for: The effect of trait competitiveness and long hours on salesperson deviance and whether meaningfulness of work matters. *Journal of Marketing Theory and Practice 18*, 303–321.

Jenkins, C. D., Zyzanski, S. J., & Rosenman, R. H. (1979). *Jenkins Activity Survey*. The Psychological Corporation.

Kanfer, R., & Ackerman, P. L. (2000). Individual differences in work motivation: Further explorations of a trait framework. *Applied Psychology 49*, 470–482.

Kanters, M. A., Boccaro, J., & Casper, J. (2008). Supported or pressured? An examination of agreement among parents and children on parent's role in youth sports. *Journal of Sport Behavior 31*, 64–80.

Kasser, T., Cohn, S., Kanner, A. D., & Ryan, R. M. (2007). Some costs of American corporate capitalism: A psychological exploration of value and goal conflicts. *Psychological Inquiry 18*, 1–22.

King, R. B., McInerney, D. M., & Watkins, D. A. (2012). Competitiveness is not all that bad . . . at least in the East: Testing the hierarchical model of achievement motivation in the Asian setting. *International Journal of Intercultural Relations 36*, 446–457.

Knight, G. P., Cota, M. K., & Bernal, M. E. (1993). The socialization of cooperative, competitive, and individualistic preferences among Mexican American children: The mediating role of ethnic identity. *Hispanic Journal of Behavioral Sciences 15*, 291–309.

Larson, L. M., Rottinghaus, P. J., & Borgen, F. H. (2002). Meta-analysis of the Big Six interests and Big Five factors. *Journal of Vocational Behavior 61*, 217–239.

Leary, T., & Coffey, H. S. (1955). Interpersonal diagnosis: Some problems of methodology and validation. *Journal of Abnormal and Social Psychology 50*, 110–124.

Leibbrandt, A., Gneezy, U., & List, J. A. (2013). Rise and fall of competitiveness in individualistic and collectivistic societies. *PNAS 110*, 9305–9308.

Lloyd, J., Doll, H., Hawton, K., Dutton, W. H., Geddes, J. R., Goodwin, G. M., & Rogers, R. D. (2010). How psychological symptoms relate to different motivations for gambling: An online study of internet gamblers. *Biological Psychiatry 68*, 733–740.

Luchner, A. F., Houston, J. M., Walker, C., & Houston, M. A. (2011). Exploring the relationship between two forms of narcissism and competitiveness. *Personality and Individual Differences 51*, 779–782.

Matthews, K. A., & Angulo, J. (1980). Measurement of the Type A behavior pattern in children: Assessment of children's competitiveness, impatience-anger, and aggression. *Child Development 51*, 466–475.

McDonald, M. M., Navarrete, C. D., & Van Vugt, M. (2012). Evolution and the psychology of intergroup conflict: The male warrior hypothesis. *Philosophical Transactions of the Royal Society B 367*, 670–679.

Merton, R. K. (1940). Bureaucratic structure and personality. *Social Forces 18*, 560–568.

Mudrack, P. E., Bloodgood, J. M., & Turnley, W. H. (2012). Some ethical implications of individual competitiveness. *Journal of Business Ethics 108*, 347–359.

Murayama, K., & Elliot, A. J. (2012). The competition-performance relation: A meta-analytic review and test of the opposing processes model of competition and performance. *Psychological Bulletin 138*, 1035–1070.

Murphy, R. O., & Ackermann, K. A. (2014). Social value orientation: Theoretical and measurement issues in the study of social preferences. *Personality and Social Psychology Review 18*, 13–41.

Murphy, R. O., Ackermann, K. A., & Handgraaf, M. J. J. (2011). Measuring social value orientation. *Judgment and Decision Making 6*, 771–781.

Navarro, M. D., Llorens, R., Borrego, A., Alcañiz, M., Noé, E., & Ferri, J. (2020). Competition enhances the effectiveness and motivation of attention rehabilitation after stroke: A randomized controlled trial. *Frontiers in Human Neuroscience 14*, 575403.

Niederle, M., & Vesterlund, L. (2011). Gender and competition. *Annual Review of Economics 3*, 601–630.

Novak, D., Nagle, A., Keller, U., & Riener, R. (2014). Increasing motivation in robot-aided arm rehabilitation with competitive and cooperative gameplay. *Journal of NeuroEngineering and Rehabilitation 11*, 64.

Orji, R., Oyibo, K., Lomotey, R. K., & Orji, F. A. (2019). Socially-driven persuasive health intervention design: Competition, social comparison, and cooperation. *Health Informatics Journal 25*, 1451–1484.

Oyserman, D., Coon, H. M., & Kemmelmeier, M. (2002). Rethinking individualism and collectivism: Evaluation of theoretical assumptions and meta-analyses. *Psychological Bulletin 128*, 3–72.

Papagelopoulos, P. J., Mavrogenis, A. F., & Soucacos, P. N. (2004). Doping in ancient and modern Olympic Games. *Orthopedics 27*, 1226–1231.

Papaioannou, A., Marsh, H. W., & Theodorakis, Y. (2004). A multilevel approach to motivational climate in physical education and sport settings: An individual or a group level construct? *Journal of Sport and Exercise Psychology 26*, 90–118.

Parke, A., Griffiths, M., & Irwing, P. (2004). Personality traits in pathological gambling: Sensation seeking, deferment of gratification and competitiveness as risk factors. *Addictions Research and Theory 12*, 201–212.

Parker, S. L., Bell, K., Gagné, M., Carey, C., & Hilpert, T. (2019). Collateral damage associated with performance-based pay: The role of stress appraisals. *European Journal of Work and Organizational Psychology 28*, 691–707.

Parks, C. D., Joireman, J., & Van Lange, P. A. M. (2013). Cooperation, trust, and antagonism: How public goods are promoted. *Psychological Science in the Public Interest 14*, 119–165.

Perry, R., Sibley, C. G., & Duckitt, J. (2013). Dangerous and competitive worldviews: A meta-analysis of their associations with Social Dominance Orientation and right-wing authoritarianism. *Journal of Research in Personality 47*, 116–127.

Perry, S. J., Hunter, E. M., Witt, L. A., & Harris, K. J. (2010). P = *f*(conscientiousness x ability): Examining the facets of conscientiousness. *Human Performance 23*, 343–360.

Plass, J. L., Homer, B. D., & Kinzer, C. K. (2015). Foundations of game-based learning. *Educational Psychologist 50*, 258–283.

Posselt, J. R., & Lipson, S. K. (2016). Competition, anxiety, and depression in the college classroom: Variations by student identity and field of study. *Journal of College Student Development 57*, 973–989.

Pratto, F., Sidanius, J., Stallworth, L. M., & Malle, B. F. (1994). Social dominance orientation: A personality variable predicting social and political attitudes. *Journal of Personality and Social Psychology 67*, 741–763.

Riech, K. B. (2014). Psycho lawyer, qu'est-ce que c'est: The high incidence of psychopaths in the legal profession and why they thrive. *Law and Psychology Review 39*, 287–299.

Ross, S. R., Rausch, M. K., & Canada, K. E. (2003). Competition and cooperation in the five-factor model: Individual differences in achievement orientation. *Journal of Psychology 137*, 323–337.

Roulin, N., & Krings, F. (2016). When winning is everything: The relationship between competitive worldviews and job applicant faking. *Applied Psychology 65*, 643–670.

Ryckman, R. M., Hammer, M., Kaczor, L. M., & Gold, J. A. (1990). Construction of a Hypercompetitive Attitude Scale. *Journal of Personality Assessment 55*, 630–639.

Ryckman, R. M., Hammer, M., Kaczor, L. M., & Gold, J. A. (1996). Construction of a Personal Development Competitive Attitude Scale. *Journal of Personality Assessment 66*, 374–385.

Ryckman, R. M., Libby, C. R., van den Borne, B., Gold, J. A., & Lindner, M. A. (1997). Values of hypercompetitive and personal development competitive individuals. *Journal of Personality Assessment 69*, 271–283.

Ryckman, R. M., Thornton, B., Gold, J. A., & Burckle, M. A. (2002). Romantic relationships of hypercompetitive individuals. *Journal of Social and Clinical Psychology 21*, 517–530.

Sankaran, S., & Bui, T. (2003). Ethical attitudes among accounting majors: An empirical study. *Journal of the American Academy of Business 3*, 71–76.

Schmidt, M. F. H., Hardecker, S., & Tomasello, M. (2016). Preschoolers understand the normativity of cooperatively structured competition. *Journal of Experimental Child Psychology 143*, 34–47.

Schrick, B. H., Sharp, E. A., Zvonkovic, A., & Reifman, A. (2012). Never let them see you sweat: Silencing and striving to appear perfect among U.S. college women. *Sex Roles 67*, 591–604.

Shannahan, K. L. J., Bush, A. J., & Shannahan, R. J. (2013). Are your salespeople coachable? How salesperson coachability, trait competitiveness, and transformational leadership enhance sales performance. *Journal of the Academy of Marketing Science 41*, 40–54.

Sides-Moore, L., & Tochkov, K. (2011). The thinner the better? Competitiveness, depression and body image among college student women. *College Student Journal 45*, 439–448.

Smither, R. D., & Houston, J. M. (1992). The nature of competitiveness: The development and validation of the Competitiveness Index. *Educational and Psychological Measurement 52*, 407–418.

Sobral, F., & Islam, G. (2013). Ethically questionable negotiating: The interactive effects of trust, competitiveness, and situation favorability on ethical decision making. *Journal of Business Ethics 117*, 281–296.

Spence, J. T., & Helmreich, R. L. (1983). Achievement-related motives and behavior. In J. T. Spence (Ed.), *Achievement and achievement motives* (pp. 7–74). Freeman.

Spence, J. T., Helmreich, R. L., & Pred, R. S. (1987). Impatience versus achievement strivings in the Type A behavior pattern: Differential effects on students' health and academic achievement. *Journal of Applied Psychology 72*, 522–528.

Stasser, G., & Titus, W. (2003). Hidden profiles: A brief history. *Psychological Inquiry 14*, 304–313.

Swab, R. G., & Johnson, P. D. (2019). Steel sharpens steel: A review of multilevel competition and competitiveness in organizations. *Journal of Organizational Behavior 40*, 147–165.

Tett, R. P., Anderson, M. G., Ho, C.-L., Yang, T. S., Huang, L., & Hanvongse, A. (2006). Seven nested questions about faking on personality tests: An overview and interactionist model of item-level response distortion. In R. L. Griffith & M. H. Peterson (Eds.), *A closer examination of applicant faking behavior* (pp. 43–83). Information Age Publishing.

Tett, R. P., & Simonet, D. V. (2011). Faking in personality assessment: A "multisaturation" perspective on faking as performance. *Human Performance 24*, 302–321.

Thornton, B., Ryckman, R. M., & Gold, J. A. (2013a). Competitive orientations and women's acceptance of cosmetic surgery. *Psychology 4*, 67–72.

Thornton, B., Ryckman, R. M., & Gold, J. A. (2013b). Competitive orientations and men's acceptance of cosmetic surgery. *Psychology 4*, 950–955.

Tjosvold, D., XueHuang, Y., Johnson, D. W., & Johnson, R. T. (2008). Is the way you resolve conflicts related to your psychological health? An empirical investigation. *Peace and Conflict 14*, 395–428.

Udvari, S. J., & Schneider, B. H. (2000). Competition and the adjustment of gifted children: A matter of motivation. *Roeper Review 22*, 212–216.

Van Heil, A., Cornelis, I., & Roets, A. (2007). The intervening role of social worldviews in the relationship between the five-factor model of personality and social attitudes. *European Journal of Personality 21*, 131–148.

Van Lange, P. A. M. (1999). The pursuit of joint outcomes and equality in outcomes: An integrative model of social value orientation. *Journal of Personality and Social Psychology 77*, 337–349.

Van Lange, P. A. M., De Bruin, E. M. N., Otten, W., & Joireman, J. A. (1997). Development of prosocial, individualistic, and competitive orientations: Theory and preliminary evidence. *Journal of Personality and Social Psychology 73*, 733–746.

Veldhuijen van Zanten, J. J. C. S., De Boer, D., Harrison, L. K., Ring, C., Carroll, D., Willemsen, G., & De Geus, E. J. C. (2002). Competitiveness and hemodynamic reactions to competition. *Psychophysiology 39*, 759–766.

Wang, G., & Netemeyer, R. G. (2002). The effects of job autonomy, customer demandingness, and trait competitiveness on salesperson learning, self-efficacy, and performance. *Journal of the Academy of Marketing Science 30*, 217–228.

Westbrook, K. W., Arendall, C. S., & Padelford, W. M. (2011). Gender, competitiveness, and unethical negotiation strategies. *Gender in Management 26*, 289–310.

White, R. W. (1937). Two types of hypnotic trance and their personality correlates. *Journal of Psychology 3*, 279–289.

Wink, P. (1991). Two faces of narcissism. *Journal of Personality and Social Psychology 61*, 590–597.

Gender Differences in the Psychology of Competition

Kathrin J. Hanek

Abstract

Drawing primarily on the literature in experimental economics and social psychology, this article reviews key findings on gender differences for two aspects of competitiveness and competition: entry preferences and performance. Although women, relative to men, have been shown to shy away from competition and underperform in competitive environments, this article also discusses boundary conditions for these effects, such as the nature of the task or gender composition of the group, and highlights manifestations of these effects in applied domains, including in negotiations, the labor market, educational settings, and sports. Adopting social psychological frameworks of prescriptive norms and stereotypes, particularly social role theory, this article examines ways in which gender-incongruencies may underpin gender gaps in competition and gender-congruencies may alleviate them. Finally, this article considers implications for individuals and institutions as well as future directions in the field to continue finding ways to close gaps.

Key Words: gender, competition, preferences, entry decisions, performance, social role theory

Introduction

In the past few decades, women's participation in the workplace and educational institutions has seen some gains (Haines et al., 2016). In the United States, for instance, women comprise nearly half of the labor force (46.7 percent), more than half of the college-educated adult population (57 percent), and, for the first time in 2019, the majority of the college-educated labor force (50.2 percent; Fry, 2019). Yet, gender disparities continue to persist. Women's median earnings across nearly all occupations, for which comparisons were possible, were lower than men's, amounting to a gender wage gap of 18.5 percent for weekly earnings (Hegewisch & Barsi, 2020). Furthermore, the highest-paid occupations also had the largest gender wage gaps (Hegewisch & Barsi, 2020). Women also continue to be underrepresented in the highest positions of power in politics and business. Women serve as Heads of State or Government in only twenty-one countries (UN Women, 2021) and hold only thirty-seven CEO positions among Fortune 500 companies (Hinchliffe, 2020). Although various factors can contribute to these gender disparities, over the last two decades, social scientists have devoted substantial research attention to understanding the role psychological gender differences in competition might play (Croson & Gneezy, 2009; Niederle & Vesterlund, 2011). As Niederle and Vesterlund (2011) note: "If women are more reluctant to compete, they may be less likely to seek promotions or to enter male-dominated and competitive fields" (p. 602). Focusing primarily (though not exclusively) on the experimental economics and social psychological literatures, this chapter provides a review of some of the ways in which gender differences in competition operate and manifest.

A Brief Note on Gender versus Sex Differences

Whereas the term "sex" is typically used to refer to biological differences between females and males, gender is a social construct that is learned through socialization over time and within one's cultural context (e.g., Bem, 1993; Fine, 2017). Even when referring to women versus men (i.e., the two sexes), researchers tend to adopt the term "gender" to connote differences associated with social influences on behavior (Bowles & McGinn, 2008; Mazei et al., 2015). In keeping with this tradition and consistent with the literature reviewed (e.g., Niederle & Vesterlund, 2011), diverging behavioral patterns among women and men are referred to as "gender differences" in this chapter.

Defining and Measuring Competition and Competitiveness

At the core, a *competition* can be defined as an environment in which an individual's goals are at odds with those of others in the same environment, such as in a tournament in which the winner takes all or an office in which the employee with the most sales receives the promotion (e.g., Deutsch, 1949; see also Bönte et al., 2017). *Competitiveness*, by extension, can then be conceived as an individual preference for these types of environments (Bönte et al., 2017; Croson & Gneezy, 2009; Niederle & Vesterlund, 2007). Although some broader definitions of competitiveness encompass competitive motivations or drives such as a "desire to win in interpersonal situations" (e.g., Houston et al., 2002; Smither & Houston, 1992), scholars across disciplines often share in the notion that competitiveness involves self-selecting into competitive environments (Bönte et al., 2017; Croson & Gneezy, 2009; Gupta et al., 2013; Mayr et al., 2012; Niederle & Vesterlund, 2007, 2011).

Disciplines which have grappled with gender differences in competition—particularly experimental economics and social psychology—differ traditionally, however, in how competitiveness is measured. For economists, competitive preferences are typically ascertained through incentivized behavioral choices such as selecting a tournament payoff scheme that rewards an individual based on their performance relative to others over a piece-rate scheme that rewards their individual performance (e.g., Croson & Gneezy, 2009). For psychologists, these preferences are frequently assessed via self-report scales (e.g., Smither & Houston, 1992). Consequently, these different traditions have focused on different research areas, with examinations of gender differences in competition (rather than related concepts like risk attitudes) concentrated primarily in the experimental economics literature (e.g., Niederle & Vesterlund, 2007, 2011).

More recently, however, research suggests that these disparate disciplines may be integrated fruitfully, and that the economics literature can be supplemented successfully with psychological approaches. For instance, a recent study of undergraduate students in Germany has shown that behavioral self-selection into a tournament is positively associated with self-reported competitiveness (i.e., agreement with items such as "I enjoy competing against others"; Bönte et al., 2017), suggesting that both types of assessments may capture a similar and agreed-upon notion of competitiveness. Researchers have also combined individual difference and economic approaches such as by studying the personalities and beliefs of those who select into competition (Kesebir et al., 2019; Müller & Schwieren, 2012). For instance, Kesebir et al. (2019) assessed women's and men's lay beliefs about the positive outcomes of competition via a self-report scale and demonstrated that gender differences in these self-reported lay beliefs partially accounted for gender gaps in behavioral entry choices. Other work has also studied gender differences in behavioral choices for competition through psychological lenses (e.g., aging; Mayr et al., 2012). Moreover, some of the underpinnings of gender differences in competition fit logically into and can be at least in part explained by social psychological frameworks (e.g., Hanek et al., 2016).

Defining competitiveness as a preference for entering competitive environments, scholarship over the past two decades has made important strides in identifying gender differences in the choices for competition and performance gaps in these environments (i.e., the differential effects of competition on women and men). Starting from these foundational findings in entry into and performance under competition, this chapter outlines some of the key gender differences in competition as well as their boundary conditions, and highlights how they manifest in applied contexts such as negotiations and educational settings. Bringing a social psychological lens to these findings, this chapter then discusses the role of prescriptive gender norms and stereotypes as a potential mechanism underlying these gender differences in competition, concluding with implications for alleviating gender disparities and potential considerations for the future study of gender differences in competition.

Entry into Competition

In an experimental study that subsequently shaped the field, Niederle and Vesterlund (2007) asked: "Do women shy away from competition?" Women's distaste for competition has since been well-documented through experimental work in economics in which participants are typically asked to choose how they would like to be compensated for their performance on simple tasks such as adding two-digit numbers (see Niederle & Vesterlund, 2011). Participants effectively enter a competition by selecting a tournament payment scheme in which monetary rewards are given based on relative performance compared to other participants and the top performer receives the payoff while those who do not win typically do not receive a reward. Shying away from competition is measured as a choice of a piece-rate payment scheme instead in which a participant earns a monetary reward based on their individual performance on the task independent of others' performance. Typically, entry into either scheme is presented as roughly equally attractive. For example, a tournament with four competitors may pay the winner $2 whereas a non-competitive piece-rate scheme may offer $0.50 for each correctly solved task (Niederle & Vesterlund, 2007). In this set-up, Niederle and Vesterlund (2007) documented a significant gender gap in entry preferences such that only 35 percent of women, compared to 73 percent of men, chose the tournament over the piece-rate scheme. Putting this gap into perspective, even the worst-performing men were more likely to self-select into the competition than the best-performing women (Niederle & Vesterlund, 2007).

Similar differences in entry preferences have been replicated in other lab settings. For example, Gupta et al. (2013) showed that when women and men were offered a choice to solve a series of mazes under a piece-rate or tournament payment scheme, only 34 percent of women, compared to 60 percent of men, preferred the competition. Even when additional incentives were added to increase the attractiveness of the tournament, the gender gap in entry preferences persisted (Gupta et al., 2013). Women have also been shown to prefer a piece-rate over a tournament scheme in their compensation choices across various tasks such as when answering math puzzles and shooting basketball hoops (see Croson & Gneezy, 2009; Shurchkov, 2012). In general, these gender differences in competition entry preferences have been repeatedly documented (e.g., Balafoutas & Sutter, 2012; Cason et al., 2010; Reuben et al., 2015) and there is consensus that women appear to prefer to eschew competition when possible (Niederle & Vesterlund, 2011), despite occasional non-findings (e.g., Eriksson et al., 2009). Given these gender differences in preferences for entering competitions, it follows logically that women's and men's performances under competition may also differ substantially.

Performance under Competition

To address the question of whether competitive environments differentially affect women's and men's performance, Gneezy et al. (2003) provided the first empirical examination using experimental economics of gender differences in performance under a piece-rate (non-competitive) and a tournament (competitive) compensation scheme. Participants were randomly assigned to one compensation scheme and tasked to solve a series of mazes under time constraints. Whereas women's and men's performance, as assessed via the number of correctly solved mazes, did not differ under a piece-rate scheme, the performance gap under a tournament scheme was significant (Gneezy et al., 2003). Although both women and men appeared to perform better under competition, interestingly, only men's performance improved significantly compared to the non-competitive environment

(Gneezy et al., 2003). Another experimental study using the same task replicated these findings when comparing performance under a piece-rate versus a tournament scheme. Significant gender gaps emerged under competition as men's performance improved significantly relative to the piece-rate scheme (Günther et al., 2010). Using a task similar to Niederle and Vesterlund (2007), Shurchkov (2012) also replicated the finding that competition differentially affects women's and men's performance. When solving math puzzles that required simple addition under time constraints, women and men did not differ in their performance under a piece-rate compensation scheme; under a tournament scheme, however, men significantly outperformed women (Shurchkov, 2012). Interestingly, the gender performance gap was driven not by men's improved competitive performance but by women underperforming relative to their baseline (i.e., no competition; Shurchkov, 2012; see also Niederle & Vesterlund, 2011).

Given that competitive performance naturally follows selection into these environments and performance can be informative for one's future choices of entry, it might be expected that these two sets of findings are interdependent. The evidence on these relationships, however, is decidedly mixed. While some studies control for performance and still find differences in entry preferences (e.g., Shurchkov, 2012), others do not (e.g., Kamas & Preston, 2009; see Niederle & Vesterlund, 2011). Furthermore, although Croson and Gneezy (2009) note that "women who choose competitive environments perform just as well as men in those settings" (p. 465), more work is needed to better grasp these interrelationships between gender differences in entry and performance.

Part of the puzzle arises from the various aspects of competitions and competitiveness that create boundary conditions for both effects. Factors in the competitive environment—such as the task or the gender of one's competitors—as well as person-centered aspects—such as personality and age—can have moderating effects on the general patterns described above.

Competitive Contexts

Types of Tasks

Many of the foundational studies establishing gender differences in competition relied on what can reasonably be construed as "masculine" tasks, such as arithmetic (Niederle & Vesterlund, 2007) and spatial mazes (Gneezy et al., 2003). Although these empirical findings also demonstrate that women and men do not differ generally in their abilities to solve these tasks (i.e., no performance differences under non-competition), people still perceive them to be gendered (e.g., Günther et al., 2010; Shurchkov, 2012; Steele, 1997; Spencer et al., 1999). Therefore, whether or not gender differences exist in entry and performance may depend to a large extent on the nature of the task—as stereotypically feminine or masculine.

Indeed, several studies have documented this moderating effect. In a partial replication of Gneezy et al.'s (2003) study, Günther et al. (2010) examined competitive performance not only in the original maze task (masculine), but also in a word-generating task (neutral), and a pattern matching and memory task (feminine). Whereas results for the masculine task matched prior findings (Gneezy et al., 2003), there were no gender performance gaps in the neutral task as both women and men increased their performance significantly compared to baseline (i.e., under a non-competitive piece-rate scheme; Günther et al., 2010). For the feminine task, there were also no gender gaps in competitive performance, but women, unlike men (for whom performance remained unchanged), significantly increased their performance under competition compared to non-competition (Günther et al., 2010). Similar conclusions emerge from Shurchkov (2012), who replicated prior findings for a time-constrained math task (masculine), but, for a time-constrained verbal task (feminine), found neither differences in competitive performance nor competition entry preferences for women and men. Comparing masculine (e.g., math) and feminine (e.g., verbal) tasks, empirical evidence appears to bolster the notion that gender differences in entry preferences are unique to masculine tasks (Große & Riener, 2010; see Niederle & Vesterlund, 2011). Other studies using gender-neutral tasks, such as creativity tasks (e.g., generating unusual uses for objects), also did not show gender differences in competition entry preferences (Bradler, 2015). Therefore, it appears that women's distaste for entering competitions and their underperformance relative to men in these environments are confined to tasks that are stereotypically masculine; neutral and feminine tasks seem to alleviate these gender gaps.

Gender Composition

The gender composition of the competition—as mixed-sex or same-sex—has also been shown to moderate gender differences in competition (Gneezy et al., 2003; Niederle & Vesterlund, 2011). Whereas many studies typically examine entry preferences and performance in mixed-sex (i.e., an equal number of female and male competitors) environments where participants can see their opponents (although gender is never made specifically salient; e.g., Niederle & Vesterlund, 2007), some have tested the influence of varying the gender composition among competitors and generally found that women's distaste for competition and poorer performance under competition are limited to competitions that also involve men (Burow et al., 2017; Geraldes, 2020; Gneezy et al., 2003; Gneezy & Rustichini, 2004; Kuhnen & Tymula, 2012; Saccardo et al., 2018). In one of the original studies in this literature, Gneezy et al. (2003) varied the gender composition of tournaments such that participants were either competing in a mixed-sex group (consisting of three women and three men) or in a same-sex group (consisting of either six women or six men). Findings indicated that the gender gap in performance was only evident for the mixed-sex tournaments but disappeared in same-sex tournaments and under a non-competitive piece-rate scheme (Gneezy et al., 2003). While these results suggest that competition against men specifically suppresses women's performance, women were also found to be able to be competitive (i.e., their performance increased significantly under a same-sex tournament compared to their piece-rate performance; Gneezy et al., 2003). This suggests that women are not generally uncompetitive or unresponsive to competitive incentives; rather, their responses depend on the environmental context. Other studies have lent further support to the notion that women's performance suffers in mixed-sex competitions and appears to decline the more male competitors they face (Gneezy & Rustichini, 2004; Kuhnen & Tymula, 2012). A similar picture has emerged for entry preferences with women shying away from competitions with men but not with other women and people showing a preference for more competitive payments in groups with more women (Burow et al., 2017; Geraldes, 2020; Saccardo et al., 2018). The gender composition of the group, therefore, appears to play an important moderating role for gender differences in both competition entry preferences and competitive performance.

Other Exogenous and Endogenous Factors

In addition to the variables outlined above, there are several other external aspects of competitions that can shape the gender dynamics of entry and performance. Perhaps some of the ones most readily associated with lay notions of a "competitive" environment are time pressures and the stress these situations can engender. Research has demonstrated that both of these factors can alter the gender effects typically observed. First, Shurchkov (2012) demonstrated that time pressure—the difference between two minutes (high pressure) and ten minutes (low pressure)—can alter the relationship between gender and competitive performance and competition entry preferences. Even for masculine tasks (i.e., a math puzzle), gender differences in performance and entry preferences disappeared under low pressure such that women performed as well as men under a tournament compensation scheme and were just as likely as men to self-select into a competitive tournament (36 percent vs. 44 percent, respectively) over a non-competitive piece-rate scheme (Shurchkov, 2012). Notably, reducing the time pressure nearly doubled women's propensity to select into the competitive compensation scheme (Shurchkov, 2012). For a low-pressure feminine task (i.e., verbal puzzle), the results were even more striking, showing that gender gaps in competitive performance existed in the opposite direction (i.e., women significantly outperformed men under a tournament but not a piece-rate scheme) and were also more likely to choose the tournament than men (57 percent vs. 43 percent, respectively; Shurchkov, 2012). These findings suggest that the time pressures typically associated with competitive environments can be especially detrimental to women's performance and propensity to engage in competition.

In a similar vein, competition can be stressful (e.g., Buckert et al., 2017), and this pressure may differentially impact women's and men's competition entry choices and competitive performance. Indeed, research supports these differential gender effects, showing that, although stress increases during competition for both women and men, men's stress responses to competition do not impact their entry preferences (Buser et al., 2017a). A high cortisol response to competition (i.e., higher stress) among women, however, significantly increases their propensity for choosing to enter subsequent competitions, suggesting that these women may be more "ready to fight" and therefore more prone to facing the competition (Buser et al., 2017a). As another proxy for stress response, higher heart rate variability among women, but not men, has been associated with preference for choosing a competitive tournament over a non-competitive piece-rate scheme (Halko & Sääksvuori, 2017). Although these findings suggest that, for women, individual differences in stress responses may shape their entry preferences, they cannot account for aggregate gender differences in competition entry (Buser et al., 2017a; Halko & Sääksvuori, 2017). In terms of performance, research has shown that the combination of induced stress and competition (compared to no competition) decreases women's, but not men's, performance, widening gender performance gaps (Cahlíková et al., 2020). Interestingly, inducing stress did not appear to widen gender gaps in entry preferences (Cahlíková et al., 2020). Given the often stressful nature of competitions, these studies, and others in this recently developing area that connects stress and competitive behavior (e.g., Zhong et al., 2018), create an important avenue for further investigations into the exogenous as well as endogenous factors that may shape gender differences in competition. Indeed, studying individual characteristics (e.g., stress response; Buser et al., 2017a; Halko & Sääksvuori, 2017) may add to a more complete understanding of what makes someone competitive and drives their competitive performance.

Researchers have increasingly focused on examining the many individual characteristics of the person that may shape the commonly found gender differences in competition. From establishing and evaluating measures of the willingness to compete (Bönte et al., 2017; Jung & Vranceanu, 2019) to studying the family context (Almås et al., 2016), factors unique to the person have been shown to matter for gender differences in competition. For example, Almås et al. (2016) found gender gaps in competition entry preferences only for children from high, but not low, socioeconomic status families. And Müller and Schwieren (2012), for instance, showed that, unlike men, lower levels of Neuroticism (or an anxious disposition) among women was associated with a greater preference for entering competitions. As person-centered perspectives continue to spur further research and synergies between economics and psychology (e.g., Bönte et al., 2017), much of the existing work on endogenous factors has taken a developmental approach and examined gender differences in competition across the lifespan.

Perhaps the two most pressing questions about age and gender differences in competition can be summarized as: First, when do these differences emerge? And second, how long do they persist? Generally, gender differences in competition have been shown to emerge in childhood and persist into older age. Compared to the latter, the former question has received considerably more research attention, as several studies have examined competitiveness among children and adolescents (e.g., Andersen et al., 2013; Cárdenas et al., 2012; Dreber et al., 2011, 2014; Gneezy & Rustichini, 2004; Samak, 2013; Sutter & Glätzle-Rützler, 2015). Nonetheless, there is considerable variability in findings. Some research among children and adolescents in specific cultures, such as Colombia and a matrilineal village in India, has found no gender differences in entry preferences or competitive performance (Andersen et al., 2013; Cárdenas et al., 2012). Other studies of children and adolescents in Sweden have also found no gender differences in competitive performance for a variety of tasks but did report significant gender differences in preference for entry into competition, though only for math tasks (Dreber et al., 2011; 2014). These patterns, however, only partially replicated in a separate sample of Swedish children (Cárdenas et al., 2012). At very young ages (three- to five-year-olds), children have also been shown to not vary in their preferences for competition by gender but do show performance differences such that girls underperform boys (Samak, 2013). In a physical education class in Israel, Gneezy and Rustichini (2004) also observed performance gaps in running speed between nine- to ten-year-old boys and girls under competition (when running against an opponent), but not under non-competition (when running alone). Among Austrian children and adolescents, Sutter and Glätzle-Rützler (2015) found evidence that gender gaps in competition entry preferences start early (among three- to five-year-olds) and persist throughout adolescence (through eighteen years of age). In contrast, examining a patriarchal society in India, Andersen et al. (2013) showed that the gender gap in the propensity to enter competitions emerged in puberty, finding gender differences at age fifteen, but not age seven. Given these mixed findings, many scholars view the development of gender differences in competition as possibly indicative of both socialization and biological processes that ultimately solidify into the well-documented gender differences in entry and performance for adults (e.g., Andersen et al., 2013; Dreber et al., 2014).

Regarding the second question, although there is consensus that the gender gap in competition persists throughout adulthood, there are diverging findings after age fifty. In what they have termed the "feisty fifties," Mayr et al. (2012), in a sample of twenty-five- to seventy-five-year-old adults, found that people's preferences for a competitive compensation scheme increased with age until about fifty and declined thereafter. Gender differences, with women shying away from competition, however, were evident across all ages (Mayr et al., 2012). On the other hand, Flory et al. (2018), found that the gender gap in entry preferences is limited to younger adults. Among participants over the age of forty-nine, women were just as likely as men to choose a competitive tournament payment scheme (Flory et al., 2018). Differences in samples, methods, and control variables may account for these discrepancies (see Flory et al., 2018), but more research on mid and late adulthood in this domain is needed to better understand changes or stability in gender differences not only in entry preferences but also performance.

Applications of Gender Differences in Competition

Outside the realm of experimental economics, much of the evidence for gender differences in competition entry and performance stems from the field or other applied contexts.

Furthermore, the findings in the lab can also inform and inspire additional work in more applied contexts. Given these synergies, the sections below highlight some of the connections between gender differences in competition and various applied settings. Note that these sections are not intended to be comprehensive reviews of the fields they reference, but rather, first, provide additional empirical support for the findings described above and, second, highlight the importance of the study of gender differences in competition for a range of everyday life domains.

Negotiations

Negotiating is an important activity in many domains from organizations and markets to households and families, and can have important downstream economic consequences for earnings and career advancements (Babcock et al., 2006; Leibbrandt & List, 2015; Reif et al., 2019; Säve-Söderbergh, 2019; Stuhlmacher & Linnabery, 2013). It also shares important overlaps with competitiveness and competing and, by extension, gender differences in the preference for and performance under competition. In fact, Niederle and Vesterlund (2008) note that "a negotiation can be viewed as competition over scarce resources" and that, therefore, the general findings that women tend to shy away from competitions and underperform under competition (e.g., Gneezy et al., 2003; Niederle & Vesterlund, 2007) are "very much in line with that of the negotiation literature" (p. 449).

Gender differences in negotiations have received considerable research attention both in terms of entry preferences and performance (Kugler et al., 2018; Kolb, 2009; Mazei et al., 2015; Stuhlmacher & Walters, 1999). Findings suggest that women, compared to men, tend to shy away from negotiations, recognizing fewer opportunities to negotiate and displaying a lower propensity to initiate negotiations (Babcock et al., 2006; Babcock & Laschever, 2003). A recent meta-analysis confirmed this notion, finding that women were less likely than men to initiate negotiations, though these gender gaps also appeared to be sensitive to historical time (diminishing across recent decades) and situational cues (narrowing in less ambiguous and more feminine contexts; Kugler et al., 2018). In terms of performance, meta-analyses have shown that women tend to achieve worse economic negotiation outcomes than men (Mazei et al., 2015; Stuhlmacher & Walters, 1999). Women's underperformance in negotiations, however, also appears to be subject to situational factors such as the gendered nature of the context (Bowles et al., 2005; Mazei et al., 2015). As with competing more generally, negotiating thus appears to show similar gender gaps in entry preferences for and performance under competition and is comparably bound by moderating factors in the competitive context.

Labor Market Outcomes

Similar to negotiations, if women are more likely to shy away from and do less well under competition, they may experience poorer labor market outcomes. Particularly, women may self-select into less competitive work environments in terms of jobs or industries and may, partly because of this self-selection, experience lower pay, which could help account for well-documented wage gaps (Blau & Kahn, 2017). The literature in this vein is rich and growing, though given the complex dynamics of labor markets, gender differences in competition are difficult to tease apart from other confounding forces (e.g., differences in educational tracks or educational achievement; Buser et al., 2014; Jurajda & Münich, 2011; Kleinjans, 2009; Niederle & Vesterlund, 2011). Because labor market outcomes can have a lasting and dramatic impact on the quality of people's lives, continued research in this area to better understand the role of gender differences in competition is critical. Current findings do suggest that gender differences in entry preferences and competitive performance seem to matter for labor market outcomes.

For one, women are underrepresented in stereotypically competitive professions and positions such as business, management, entrepreneurship, law, corporate leadership, and elected public office (Bertrand, 2011; Bertrand & Hallock, 2001; Fox & Lawless, 2004; Fox et al., 2001; Kleinjans, 2009; Shepherd et al., 2015). Research suggests that these gaps may exist in part because women, unlike men, are less likely to choose to enter these fields or seek these positions—in other words, shy away from competition. For instance, Fox et al. (2001) found that even among eligible candidates (in New York State), women were less likely to run for public office than their male counterparts. Assessing entrepreneurship across thirty-six countries, Bönte and Piegeler (2013) found that gender differences in competitiveness accounted for a significant part of the gender gap in likelihood to take steps to start a new business. Field experiments have also supported the notion that women shy away from competition in the labor market by showing that varying the compensation scheme of jobs to be more competitive disproportionately deterred women from applying to those jobs (Flory et al., 2015; Samek, 2019). And among academics in France and Italy, studies have shown that female professors shy away from applying to competitions that could lead to promotions to associate or full professor (Bosquet et al., 2014; De Paola et al., 2015). These patterns of findings seem to support the notion that gender gaps in preferences for entering competitions may at least in part account for some of the job segregation (and its payoff consequences) observed in the labor market.

A gender wage gap has been persistently documented over the last decades and remains prevalent especially at the top of the distribution (Blau & Kahn, 2017). Because choice of industry, competitiveness of the job, and advancements on the job such as promotions can contribute to earnings, women's lower likelihood to negotiate, apply for promotions, or choose jobs with competitive compensation schemes could be a detriment to their earnings (e.g., Babcock & Laschever, 2003; De Paola et al., 2015; Flory et al., 2015). To the extent that some of these gaps may reflect gender differences in competitive entry preferences and performance, it seems plausible that gender wage gaps may in part be traced back to gender differences in competition. Indeed, in their examination of the gender wage gap, Blau and Kahn (2017) noted that gender segregation in occupations and industries remain important factors contributing to earnings differentials between women and men. Testing these relationships in a study of MBA graduates from a top business school in the United States, Reuben et al. (2015) found that female MBAs earned around 15 percent less and were more likely to work in low-paying industries upon graduation than their male counterparts. These gaps also persisted over time, with more competitive people more likely and women less likely to work in high-paying jobs several years later (Reuben et al., 2015). Importantly, gender differences in competition entry preferences accounted for a substantial part of the earnings gap (Reuben et al., 2015). Although at least a part of the wage gap may be attributable to the various manifestations of gender differences in competitive preferences (e.g., Blau & Kahn, 2017; Flory et al., 2015; Reuben et al., 2015), researchers also caution against sweeping conclusions in such a highly complex environment in which factors are interrelated and competitive behavior is difficult to tease apart (Niederle & Vesterlund, 2011).

Educational Settings

Educational settings can be rife with competition as students may compete against peers in the classroom, in applications, and on exams. Generally, in these settings, similar findings for gender differences in competition emerge, though entry preferences have been less well-studied (Hoyer et al., 2020). Nonetheless, some studies have shown that women tend to shy away from competition in educational settings. For example, when undergraduate students were given the option of applying a non-competitive absolute or a competitive tournament grading scheme to a set of bonus questions at the end of a final exam, women, compared to men, were significantly less likely to select the tournament (Hoyer et al., 2020). Examining the rates of female applicants to colleges and universities in the United States, Hanek et al. (2016) found that smaller schools attracted more female applicants, suggesting that women may shy away from larger competitions. Gender differences in competitive preferences have also been linked to men's preference for math-intensive specializations and more prestigious tracks in school (Buser et al., 2014; Buser et al., 2017b). Finally, although a more competitive inclination among middle school students was shown to predict taking a competitive high school entrance exam, girls and boys were not found to differ in their competitive inclinations (Zhang, 2013).

Compared to entry preferences, competition performance gaps appear to be more pervasive and better-documented with women and girls lagging behind, particularly in math-focused fields (Guiso et al., 2008; Niederle & Vesterlund, 2010; Spencer et al., 1999). Despite this, female students do not necessarily perform worse in school generally or for verbal-focused fields specifically. Grade point averages in high school and college for women often surpass those of their male counterparts when accounting for SAT scores, and girls tend to score higher than boys on reading performance tests and perform better in competitive verbal tasks (e.g., Gindi et al., 2019; Guiso et al., 2008; Rothstein, 2004). The gender gap in competitive performance for math (and related fields) has therefore been frequently attributed to differences in how women and men respond to competition

(Niederle & Vesterlund, 2010, 2011). Indeed, Ors et al. (2013) found that, among applicants to a highly selective French business school, women underperformed relative to men on the entry exam. But, in other less competitive contexts (i.e., on the national high school exam and during their first year in the Master of Science program), these gaps reversed (Ors et al., 2013). Other work, in different educational contexts and using different exams, also suggests that gender gaps widen for more competitive tests (Attali et al., Neeman, & Schlosser, 2011; Jurajda & Münich, 2011; Niederle & Vesterlund, 2010). In a similar vein, Price (2008) showed that, as a result of the introduction of a competitive fellowship program (the Mellon Foundation's Graduate Education Initiative), eligible men's, but not eligible women's, performance in graduate school (measured as time to candidacy) improved significantly, suggesting that men perform more favorably in response to increasing competition.

Despite these various findings pointing to gender differences in competitive performance (and entry preferences) in educational settings, there are also notable exceptions. Not only do gender performance gaps disappear or even reverse with more feminine tasks (e.g., Guiso et al., 2008), other contextual factors have also been shown to matter. For instance, gender gaps in competitive math performance have been shown to disappear in cultures with greater gender equality (Guiso et al., 2008), with multiple rounds of contests (Cotton et al., 2013), and with reduced time pressure (Cotton et al., 2013). Though a debated topic, evidence from single-sex schooling also suggests that these educational settings improve female students' math performance (Eisenkopf et al., 2015) and that girls from single-sex schools may be just as likely as boys to enter into competitions (Booth & Nolen, 2012). Same-sex competitions, therefore, appear to diminish gender gaps in performance and entry (e.g., Gneezy et al., 2003). Perhaps not surprisingly, many of these factors that shape gender differences in educational settings mirror those found to moderate gender gaps in competition more generally (see earlier discussion of competitive contexts), strengthening the notion that gender differences in competition are bound by contextual factors.

Sports

One domain in which competitions are ubiquitous is sports. Nonetheless, gender differences in competition may not be as robust (or even existent) for sporting competitions for several reasons. For one, professional competitions are typically same-sex, which could dampen gender gaps in entry and performance (e.g., Gneezy et al., 2003). Furthermore, athletes receive regular feedback about their relative performance and therefore may be less prone to errors of entry (e.g., Wozniak, 2012). Finally, being an athlete may also reflect a self-selection into a competitive profession, which could diminish gender differences in competitiveness (e.g., Comeig et al., 2016; Rosenqvist, 2019). Given these limitations and the multiple other factors that are at play in sports competitions (e.g., prize money, prestige, etc.; Frick, 2011), findings of gender differences in competition in this domain may be non-existent (e.g., Rosenqvist, 2019) or may be highly context- or measure-dependent (e.g., Comeig et al., 2016). For example, using data from professional tennis players, Wozniak (2012) found that women and men are differentially affected by previous performance—such that having done well in a competition increases women's likelihood to enter the next tournament only but shapes men's entry preferences further into the future—and Paserman (2007) found that competitive performance in Grand Slam tournaments, when assessed via crucial points but not aggregate set-level data, varies by gender with women, but not men, more likely to make unforced errors during important (potentially match outcome-altering) points. Among distance runners, for instance, Frick (2011) has shown that gender gaps in performance have been shrinking (and increasingly so) over the past decades, and the greatest gender gaps in entry preferences have been shown among runners unlikely to win a race, with young top-performing women unanimously preferring competition entry (Garratt et al., 2013). And for professional golfers, Rosenqvist (2019) has shown that subsequent competitive performance suffers equally for women and men from prior failure in a tournament. In the more complex and dynamic world of sports, then, gender differences in competition (although evident to some extent) appear to be more difficult to track and require additional considerations before (and if) any general conclusions about women's and men's competitive preferences and performance can be made.

Social Psychological Mechanisms for Gender Differences in Competition

To better understand not only when and why gender differences in competition emerge but also to find avenues for alleviating gender disparities, research has sought to pinpoint the mechanisms for these gender gaps. Several factors such as confidence or risk and feedback aversions have played a role but typically cannot fully account for the observed gender gaps in competition (Buser et al., 2017b; Niederle & Vesterlund, 2011). As such, much of the literature has considered the role of social psychological underpinnings related to prescriptive gender norms and stereotypes as part of the puzzle for explaining gender differences in competition (e.g., Bowles, 2013; Cahlíková et al., 2020; Günther et al., 2010; Hanek et al., 2016; Kugler et al., 2018; Mazei et al., 2015; Niederle & Vesterlund, 2008; Reif et al., 2019; Shurchkov, 2012; Stuhlmacher & Linnabery, 2013).

Specifically, social role theory posits that gender roles entail socially sanctioned norms for behavior expected of women and men (Eagly, 1987; Eagly & Wood, 2012). These shared beliefs about how women and men behave—or gender stereotypes—are not only descriptive, but also prescriptive (or injunctive), prescribing how women and men ought to behave (Eagly & Karau, 2002; Eagly & Steffen, 1984; Heilman, 2001; Koenig & Eagly, 2014; Wood & Eagly, 2010). As such, they exert internal and external pressures as people seek to be congruent or in line with the prescriptive norms associated with their gender roles (Eagly & Wood, 2012; Kugler et al., 2018; Wood & Eagly, 2010). Enacting one's gender role in stereotypical and prescriptive ways can be a way to express an internalized identity (Kugler et al., 2018; Wood & Eagly, 2015) and can intuitively feel more comfortable (Hanek et al., 2016). Not adhering to prescriptive gender norms, on the other hand, can incur social punishment from others, including in the form of backlash (Amanatullah & Morris, 2010; Bowles et al., 2007; Dannals et al., 2021; Heilman & Okimoto, 2007; Heilman et al., 2004; Rudman & Glick, 2001).

The female gender role is stereotypically characterized as *communal*, encompassing selfless, supportive, caring, warm, and generally other-oriented traits and behaviors. On the other hand, the male gender role is stereotypically perceived to be *agentic*, entailing competitive, assertive, ambitious, and generally task-oriented traits and behaviors (Bem, 1974; Eagly & Karau, 2002; Eagly & Steffen, 1994; Eagly & Wood, 2012). In line with these prescriptive gender norms, agentic behavior, including competing, is gender-incongruent for women (Eagly & Karau, 2002). Thus, because women ought not to act agentically, women often avoid or struggle in environments and social roles that require these stereotypically masculine behaviors (i.e., gender-incongruent contexts; Bem & Lenney, 1976; Eagly & Karau, 2002). From this perspective, social roles like that of negotiator, entrepreneur, manager, and so on, are stereotypically perceived to require assertive, task-oriented (i.e., agentic) behaviors and therefore are stereotypically masculine roles, which could account for women's underrepresentation in and avoidance of these fields or situations (e.g., Bear, 2011; Bendell et al., 2020; Eagly & Karau, 2002; Kray & Thompson, 2004; Kray et al., 2001).

Indeed, many other patterns observed for women's and men's diverging responses to competition align with this gender role congruity perspective. For one, when prescriptive gender norms for women and men differ from those described above or are reversed (e.g., in matriarchal societies in which women are expected to be agentic), women's distaste for and underperformance under competition have not been observed. Indeed, in matriarchal societies, women and girls have been shown to be as likely or even more likely to enter competitions than men and do not differ in their performance under competition (Andersen et al., 2013; Gneezy et al., 2009). And gender differences in competitive performance have been attenuated in egalitarian cultures, where gender roles for women and men do not differ as starkly along communal and agentic lines (Berdahl et al., 2015; Guiso et al., 2008; Shan et al., 2019).

Secondly, in line with the notion that more stereotypically masculine contexts are more gender-incongruent (and therefore detrimental) for women, gender differences in competition have typically been shown to be exacerbated in these environments. For instance, women tend to shy away from and underperform in competitions involving tasks or topics that are more stereotypically masculine such as those requiring mathematical or spatial abilities (e.g., Bear, 2011; Bear & Babcock, 2012; Günther et al., 2010; Shurchkov, 2012). To some extent, gender stereotypes in these domains can also impair women's ability to perform as they may fear confirming a negative stereotype (Steele, 1997; Spencer et al., 1999). As mixed-sex environments may also present a more masculine competitive context for women and likely make their (incongruent) gender more salient, women's distaste for and lower performance in mixed-sex competitions could also be accounted for by responses to prescriptive gender norms and stereotypes (Niederle & Vesterlund, 2008).

On the flip side, gender differences in competition should be alleviated by more feminine (i.e., gender-congruent) contexts. Even though competing itself is still a stereotypically masculine behavior (e.g., Eagly & Karau, 2002), doing so in more "feminine" ways should alleviate the pressures of gender-incongruence and enable women to more readily engage in and perform better under competition. Consistent with this rationale, and mirroring the findings described above, women have been shown to be less likely to avoid competition and perform on par with men when the task or topic is stereotypically feminine, such as those requiring verbal abilities (e.g., Bear, 2011; Bear & Babcock, 2012; Günther et al., 2010; Shurchkov, 2012). And same-sex competitions, which may represent a more feminine context, have also been shown to alleviate gender gaps in entry and performance (Burow et al., 2017; Geraldes, 2020; Gneezy et al., 2003; Saccardo et al., 2018).

Furthermore, by applying a gender congruity framework, research has also been able to identify additional factors that have been shown to diminish gender gaps in competition. In general, factors that make competitions more "feminine" (i.e., allow women to enact prescriptive gender norms of being communal) even while engaging in the generally gender-incongruent act of competing, should alleviate barriers to competition for women. For instance, factors related to caring for others such as competing in teams, negotiating on behalf of others, and competing for the benefit of one's child have been linked to increased propensity to compete and better competitive performance for women (Amanatullah & Morris, 2010; Babcock et al., 2006; Cassar et al., 2016; Healy & Pate, 2011). Recently, the size of the competition—or the number of competitors—has also been shown to moderate gender differences in entry preferences (Hanek et al., 2016). Using field and experimental data, Hanek et al. (2016) showed that women, compared to men, were more likely to enter smaller competitions with fewer competitors, compared to larger competitions with more competitors. From a gender congruity perspective, smaller competitions may appear and enable more communal behaviors and fall more closely in line with prescriptive gender norms for women that require selflessness and caring for others (Hanek et al., 2016).

Although not the only account, social psychological perspectives of prescriptive gender norms and stereotypes may be able to provide a unifying framework for at least some of the various findings in the fields relevant to gender differences in competition (Mazei et al., 2015; Stuhlmacher & Linnabery, 2013). And as the literature on gender differences in competition continues to grow, social psychological underpinnings for these effects may additionally help pave the way for future research directions and avenues for mitigating gender gaps.

Implications and Future Directions

Person- versus Institution-Focused Approaches to Closing Gender Gaps

Given that gender differences in competition may in part explain why women have historically been disadvantaged in earnings and remained underrepresentation in certain fields (e.g., Kleinjans, 2009) and that these costs are not only borne by women but also by society that forfeits talent (Niederle & Vesterlund, 2011), research in this domain has also focused on finding ways to close these gender gaps. With popular notions of encouraging women to be more competitive and to "lean in" (Sandberg, 2013), one avenue for closing gaps may be via encouraging women to compete. These person-centered—or "fix-the-women" (Recalde & Vesterlund, 2020)—approaches have typically been criticized as placing the onus of change on individuals who are already disadvantaged by the situation as well as being, for the most part, ineffective (Recalde & Vesterlund, 2020). In fact, recent experimental work in negotiations suggests that having to compete (rather than choosing to do so) can leave women worse off (Exley et al., 2020). Furthermore, encouraging women to be more competitive also does not take into consideration the potential for backlash, which, again, can outweigh any benefits gained from competing (Amanatullah & Morris, 2010; Recalde & Vesterlund, 2020). Keeping in mind that men may be hurt, too, by overcompeting (Niederle & Vesterlund, 2007), institutional changes, rather than person-focused approaches, may also be more balanced in creating a more equitable and advantageous playing field for both women and men.

In line with this approach, several studies have shown that feedback can diminish gender gaps in tournament entry. Specifically, feedback can alleviate issues of self-confidence and, to the extent that these shape competitive preferences, mitigate gender gaps (Niederle & Vesterlund, 2011). Studies have shown that providing feedback about the performance of the tournament winner as well as relative piece-rate performances reduces gender gaps in preference for tournament entry (Ertac & Szentes; 2010; Wozniak et al., 2014). However, gaps may not always disappear with feedback (Cason et al., 2010) and research has shown that, even with feedback, high-performing women tend to be less likely to enter competitions than their male counterparts (Wozniak et al., 2014). General caution is also warranted in providing feedback, as women, but not men, have been shown to focus more on feedback about their own performance (rather than that of their competitors) and also assume negative feedback reflects their overall fixed ability (with no room for improvement), which may more permanently and incorrectly deter them from competitions (Berlin & Dargnies, 2016).

Another institution-based avenue for closing gender gaps that has received some research attention is affirmative action. These types of policies have not been without controversy as providing an advantage to women may incur efficiency losses if such an action passes over better-performing men (Balafoutas & Sutter, 2012; Holzer & Neumark, 2000). Alternatively, affirmative action may produce efficiency gains and help both women and organizations by encouraging high-performing women, who may otherwise shy away from competition, to compete, enabling organizations to select among a more complete representation of the best talent (Balafoutas & Sutter, 2012; Niederle et al., 2013). Research has lent some support to the latter notion. Specifically, with the introduction of a quota (such that there were two winners per tournament, one of which was the highest-performing woman) into the typical competition entry choice (tournament vs. piece-rate) paradigm, women were significantly more likely to enter the tournament than they were without the quota (Niederle et al., 2013). Importantly, although some high-performing men may choose to avoid competition in this case, the influx of women, including high performers, has been shown to leave the overall number of high-performers in the entry pool relatively unchanged, suggesting that the implementation of this type of quota comes at little cost, as long as it is known to potential entrants (Niederle et al., 2013). Similarly, Balafoutas and Sutter (2012) tested the impact of four affirmative action interventions—quotas (one of the two tournament winners had to be a woman), weak preferential treatment (women received one additional correct answer), strong preferential treatment (women received two additional correct answers), and repetition of competition (the competition would be repeated if a woman was not among one of the winners)—on competition entry preferences. Findings indicated that women's preference for entry into competition increased significantly for the preferential treatment interventions and marginally for the quota intervention, compared to their preferences in a standard piece-rate versus tournament (without affirmative action) choice (Balafoutas & Sutter, 2012). Repetition of competition was the only intervention that was not found to have a significant effect on women's entry preferences (Balafoutas & Sutter, 2012). No significant differences in entry preferences for men across the different interventions compared to the standard entry preference were found (Balafoutas & Sutter, 2012). Furthermore, addressing performance under competition, the average performance of winners (among those who entered the competition) in any of the four affirmative action interventions did not differ statistically from the performance of winners under a standard tournament (i.e., top two performers win, regardless of gender), suggesting that affirmative action interventions do not produce efficiency losses (Balafoutas & Sutter, 2012). Taken together, these experimental studies suggest that affirmative action interventions that target the supply side (i.e., potential entrants and competitors) may potentially have more benefits than drawbacks, as they could encourage more (high-performing) women to enter competitions. Controversy about affirmative action policies, nonetheless, remains high and long-term consequences, such as the stigma of being a woman hired through affirmation action creates further potential for negative outcomes (Brandts et al., 2015). Thus, although some of these findings provide interesting implications for closing gender gaps, more work across different contexts is needed to better understand how, where, and in what forms such institutional interventions are indeed beneficial.

Other institutional approaches point to the other people already in the organizations—such as advisors and role models—as potential sources for mitigating gender gaps in competition. Providing people with advice (a recommendation to select the piece-rate or tournament payment scheme) given by a participant from a previous experimental round (i.e., experienced) who has information about performance levels of their competitors and of their advisee (i.e., knowledgeable) has been shown to improve the entry preferences of both high-performing women (more competition entry) and low-performing men (less competition entry; Brandts et al., 2015). Although gender gaps in entry preferences remained in general, they disappeared among low and high performers, creating more efficient outcomes for these groups (Brandts et al., 2015). Observing a role model has also had some effect on making women more competitive, especially after observing a female role model (Schier, 2020). Interestingly, endorsement by a sponsor—as either a vote of confidence by the sponsor or linking payoffs between the protégé and sponsor—was ineffective in closing gender gaps in competition entry as it only increased men's, but not women's, propensity to compete (Baldiga & Coffman, 2018). This set of findings suggests that the roles of more senior people, who are already part of a particular institution, and their behaviors, may play at least a small part in the institutional approaches that could alleviate gender gaps in competition. Overall, however, future research is necessary to present a clearer picture of how institutional practices can close gaps in equitable ways.

Sociobiological Mechanisms

Although social psychological mechanisms (as outlined earlier) can offer some explanation for the observed gender differences in competition, they may not tell the whole story. Several scholars have highlighted the influence of biological factors, especially hormones, on gender differences in competition (e.g., Apicella et al., 2011; Buser, 2012; Buser et al., 2017b; Casto & Prasad, 2017; Croson & Gneezy, 2009; Wozniak et al., 2014). Although testosterone has not been linked to competition entry preferences for men (Apicella et al., 2011), women's preferences have been linked to their hormonal cycles (Buser, 2012; Wozniak et al., 2014). For example, Buser (2012) found that women's propensity to enter competitions varies as a function of their menstrual cycle and hormonal contraceptives such that heightened levels of progesterone are negatively associated with preferring competition. Other findings, such as the onset of gender gaps during adolescence when humans experience hormonal surges and their decline at an age when women typically experience menopause with its related hormonal changes (Andersen et al., 2013; Flory et al., 2018), further suggest that hormonal—and, in general, biological factors—can play a role in gender differences in competition.

Importantly, social and biological underpinnings do not have to act in isolation. Indeed, researchers have increasingly called for an integration of these perspectives (Casto & Prasad, 2017; van Anders et al., 2015; van Anders & Watson, 2006) and shown that gendered socialization can impact physiological responses, including in the context of competition as more broadly defined (van Anders et al., 2015). As van Anders et al. (2015) note: "Gender-related sociocultural experiences related to femininity (sociocultural habits and norms tied to women and girls, usually promoting communality and nurturance) and masculinity (sociocultural habits and norms tied to men and boys, usually promoting agency and competition) may affect physiological parameters such as testosterone" (p. 13805). Therefore, in a continued effort to integrate diverse research streams in this field, future research may find it particularly insightful to consider both social and biological explanations for gender differences in competition simultaneously.

Furthermore, by jointly considering social and biological factors, more research attention may also be devoted to an understanding of *both* women's and men's psychology. Whereas many (but not all) biological approaches have tended to foreground men's behavior (Casto & Prasad, 2017), social approaches, though examining gender differences, have been more (but not exclusively) inclined to focus on and explain women's behavior (Niederle & Vesterlund, 2011). However, gender differences are by definition a consequence of women's and men's behaviors simultaneously and both merit study to fully understand the drivers behind gender gaps. In this vein, as part of their original query into gender differences in competition, Niederle and Vesterlund (2007) not only wondered if women shy away from competition but also asked: "Do men compete too much?" Their results showed that even low-performing men displayed a(n) (irrational) preference for competition, hurting their payoffs. These findings suggest that men's behavior may be explained via similar avenues as women's. Indeed, a growing body of research has shown that men are subject to social processes to ensure conformity to masculine stereotypes (e.g., Berdahl et al., 1996) and that certain competitive environments, such as the workplace and negotiations, create pressure for men to signal their masculinity and prove themselves to be "real men" (Berdahl et al., 2018; Mazei et al., 2021). In addition to shedding light on gender differences in competition, a better understanding of men's competitive behavior can also provide potential avenues for improving outcomes for both women and men under competition and continue to close these gaps (Berdahl et al., 2018; see also Berdahl et al., 2015).

Cross-Cultural Findings

Research with children on gender differences in competition has highlighted the role cultural contexts may play in moderating these effects (Andersen et al., 2013; Cárdenas et al., 2012). Furthermore, given that these gender differences can in part be explained by socialization and reversed in matriarchal societies in which gender roles are switched (Gneezy et al., 2009), it seems reasonable that culture should moderate the established relationships between gender and competition. Surprisingly, not much systematic research has examined cultural differences in this domain, though recent research has begun to address this gap in the literature. Specifically, several studies have investigated these gender differences in China, which can be considered a patriarchal society (Booth et al., 2019; Carlsson et al., 2020; Zhang, 2019). Replicating Niederle and Vesterlund's (2007) findings that women shy away from competition, Carlsson et al. (2020) found that Han Chinese women were less likely than their male counterparts to choose a tournament over a piece-rate payment scheme (20 percent vs. 43 percent, respectively). However, in terms of performance, women outperformed men under the tournament scheme (Carlsson et al., 2020), making their competition aversion particularly costly. The difference in entry preferences among Han Chinese women and men, however, has not been replicated in another study, which did show a significant gender gap for minority ethnic groups in China (Zhang, 2019). And, studying different cohorts in China and Taiwan, Booth et al. (2019) found that women and men who grew up in Beijing under a communist regime differed significantly in their propensity to enter competitions; these women were in fact more prone to enter competitions compared to their male counterparts as well as later Beijing cohorts who grew up under a mixed or market regime. None of the other cohorts in Beijing or Taipei exhibited significant gender differences in entry preferences (Booth et al., 2019). Taken together, these findings may suggest that more nuanced sociopolitical or socioeconomic contexts (see also Almås et al., 2016), rather than (or in addition to) national culture per se, may differentially affect gender differences in competition across different societies. A recent examination of Olympic medal winners also supports this notion (Berdahl et al., 2015). Both female and male athletes from more egalitarian countries—operationalized as economic, political, health, and educational equality between women and men—were more likely to win Olympic medals (i.e., performed better under competition; Berdahl et al., 2015), suggesting that socioeconomic and sociopolitical contexts matter for gender differences in competitive performance (see also Guiso et al., 2008).

Other insights into cross-cultural gender differences in competition can be garnered from research in negotiations. A recent meta-analysis of 185 studies measuring gender differences in performance in intracultural negotiations has found that men were more likely to outperform women in cultures with the following characteristics taken from Hofstede's and GLOBE measures of national cultural dimensions: high individualism, low in-group collectivism practices, and high assertiveness practices (Shan et al., 2019). As the authors note, these cultural attributes are consistent with valuing agentic and competitive behavior and with stereotyping men as such (Shan et al., 2019). These findings suggest that dimensions of national cultures—particularly those tapping into norms and stereotypes for agentic behavior—can have the potential to matter for gender differences in competition. In an effort to unify these various findings related to culture and gender differences in competition, future research may benefit from considering the multiple cultural (broadly defined as national, historical, political, economic, and so on) contexts that may shape both a person's propensity to enter and do well in competitions.

Changing Contexts

One pressing question in the field of gender differences in competition is to what extent the observed gaps in entry into and performance under competition are enduring rather than an artefact of a certain time and place. The previously described cross-cultural findings as well as cohort studies suggest that, at the individual level, time and place do matter to some extent. At a broader societal level, however, researchers have speculated about how much has changed for women's and men's roles and the prescriptive gender norms that may underpin their competitive behavior. Some recent non-findings—for instance, Clot et al. (2020) showed that female and male professionals working in generally competitive consulting firms in the United Kingdom did not differ in their propensity to enter competitions or their performance under competition—may suggest that gender equity (and closing gender gaps for competition) has seen recent advances.

To address this possibility, researchers have examined the flexibility of stereotypes for women and men over time and suggested that rather than representing fixed mental schema, stereotypes respond to changes in social roles (Eagly et al., 2020; Koenig & Eagly, 2014). Specifically, with women's increased representation in the labor force over the past decades and social movements such as feminist activism, gender stereotypes may have become less socially acceptable and beliefs in gender equality more prevalent (Eagly, 2018). However, some research has also suggested that, despite increases of women in more agentic roles such as manager, internal resegregation may have relegated women to versions of these roles that require more communal rather than agentic behavior (Levanon & Grusky, 2016; Skuratowicz & Hunter, 2004), preserving stereotypical gender roles. In the context of negotiations, others have also speculated about gains versus losses for gender equality from recent social movements (e.g., #MeToo) and sociopolitical climates (e.g., the Trump presidency; Kolb, 2019). A recent meta-analysis covering sixteen nationally representative U.S. public opinion polls from the 1940s to 2018 found that stereotypes of women have made gains in communion and competence, but not agency (Eagly et al., 2020). That is, although women may be perceived to be more competent today than in the past, perhaps because of an increase in their representation in male-dominated professions (Hegewisch & Hartmann, 2014), they are still not expected to act agentically (e.g., competitively; Eagly et al., 2020; see also Haines et al., 2016). To the extent that prescriptive gender norms and stereotypes underlie gender differences in competition, these findings suggest that, unless addressed otherwise, gaps between women and men in their preferences for and performance under competition may continue to persist. Continued research in this field is therefore invaluable.

Conclusions

A large body of research on gender differences in competition has documented gender gaps in both entry preferences and performance. Compared to men, women tend to be more likely to shy away from and perform worse under competition (Croson & Gneezy, 2009;

Gneezy et al., 2003; Niederle & Vesterlund, 2007, 2011). These general patterns have also been observed in applied contexts such as negotiations, labor markets, educational settings, and sports (Niederle & Vesterlund, 2011). However, gender gaps in competition also appear to be context-dependent and, in line with social psychological frameworks of prescriptive gender norms and stereotypes, may be attenuated by less gender-incongruent (i.e., more feminine) contexts for women (Eagly, 1987; Eagly & Karau, 2002; Eagly & Wood, 2012; Kugler et al., 2018; Mazei et al., 2015). Given the potential impact of gender differences in competition for gender inequities across life domains, from education to earnings, it is critical that future research continues building our understanding of when and where gender gaps exist and persist in order for individuals and institutions to continue finding avenues to close them.

References

Almås, I., Cappelen, A. W., Salvanes, K. G., Sørensen, E. O., & Tungodden, B. (2016). Willingness to compete: Family matters. *Management Science, 62*(8), 2149–2162.

Amanatullah, E. T., & Morris, M. W. (2010). Negotiating gender roles: Gender differences in assertive negotiating are mediated by women's fear of backlash and attenuated when negotiating on behalf of others. *Journal of Personality and Social Psychology, 98*, 256–267.

Andersen, S., Ertac, S., Gneezy, U., List, J. A., & Maximiano, S. (2013). Gender, competitiveness, and socialization at a young age: Evidence from a matrilineal and a patriarchal society. *The Review of Economics and Statistics, 95*(4), 1438–1443.

Apicella, C. L., Dreber, A., Gray, P. B., Hoffman, M., Little, A. C., & Campbell, B. C. (2011). Androgens and competitiveness in men. *Journal of Neuroscience, Psychology, and Economics, 4*(1), 54–62.

Attali, Y., Neeman, Z., & Schlosser, A. (2011). Rise to the challenge or not give a damn: Differential performance in high vs. low stakes tests. IZA Discussion Paper 5693.

Babcock, L., Gelfand, M. J., Small, D., & Stayn, H. (2006). Gender differences in the propensity to initiate negotiations. In D. Cremer, M. Zeelenberg, & J. K. Murnighan (Eds.), *Social psychology and economics* (pp. 239–260). Erlbaum.

Babcock, L., & Laschever, S. (2003). *Women don't ask: Negotiation and the gender divide.* Princeton University Press.

Balafoutas, L., & Sutter, M. (2012). Affirmative action policies promote women and do not harm efficiency in the laboratory. *Science, 335*, 579–581.

Baldiga, N. R., & Coffman, K. B. (2018). Laboratory evidence on the effects of sponsorship on the competitive preferences of men and women. *Management Science, 64*(2), 888–901.

Bear, J. (2011). "Passing the buck": Incongruence between gender role and topic leads to avoidance of negotiation. *Negotiation and Conflict Management Research, 4*, 47–72.

Bear, J. B., & Babcock, L. (2012). Negotiation topic as a moderator of gender differences in negotiation. *Psychological Science, 23*, 743–744.

Bem, S. L. (1974). The measurement of psychological androgyny. *Journal of Consulting and Clinical Psychology, 42*, 155–162.

Bem, S. L. (1993). *The lenses of gender: Transforming the debate on sexual inequality.* Yale University Press.

Bem, S. L., & Lenney, E. (1976). Sex typing and the avoidance of cross-sex behavior. *Journal of Personality and Social Psychology, 33*, 48–54.

Bendell, B. L., Sullivan, D. M., & Hanek, K. J. (2020). Gender, technology, and decision-making: Insights from an experimental conjoint analysis. *Journal of Entrepreneurial Behavior and Research, 26*(4), 647–670.

Berdahl, J. L., Cooper, M., Glick, P., Livingston, R. W., & Williams, J. C. (2018). Work as a masculinity contest. *Journal of Social Issues, 74*(3), 422–448.

Berdahl, J. L., Magley, V. J., & Waldo, C. R. (1996). The sexual harassment of men: Exploring the concept with theory and data. *Psychology of Women Quarterly, 20*, 527–547.

Berdahl, J. L., Uhlmann, E. L., & Bai, F. (2015). Win–win: Female and male athletes from more gender equal nations perform better in international sports competitions. *Journal of Experimental Social Psychology*, *56*, 1–3.

Berlin, N., & Dargnies, M.-P. (2016). Gender differences in reaction to feedback and willingness to compete. *Journal of Economic Behavior and Organization*, *130*, 320–336.

Bertrand, M. (2011). New perspectives on gender. In D. Card & O. Ashenfelter (Eds.), *Handbook of labor economics* (Vol. 4, pp. 1543–1590). Elsevier.

Bertrand, M., & Hallock, K. (2001). The gender gap in top corporate jobs. *Industrial and Labor Relations Review*, *55*(1), 3–21.

Blau, F. D., & Kahn, L. M. (2017). The gender wage gap: Extent, trends, and explanations. *Journal of Economic Literature*, *55*(3), 789–865.

Bönte, W., Lombardo, S., & Urbig, D. (2017). Economics meets psychology: Experimental and self-reported measures of individual competitiveness. *Personality and Individual Differences*, *116*, 179–185.

Bönte, W., & Piegeler, M. (2013). Gender gap in latent and nascent entrepreneurship: Driven by competitiveness. *Small Business Economics*, *41*(4), 961–987.

Booth, A., Fan, E., Meng, X., & Zhang, D. (2019). Gender differences in willingness to compete: The role of culture and institutions. *The Economic Journal*, *129*, 734–764.

Booth, A., & Nolen, P. (2012). Choosing to compete: How different are girls and boys? *Journal of Economic Behavior & Organization*, *81*(2), 542–555.

Bosquet, C., Combes, P.-P., & Garcia-Peñalosa, C. (2014). Gender and competition: Evidence from academic promotions in France. CEPR Discussion Paper DP9711.

Bowles, H. R. (2013). Psychological perspectives on gender in negotiation. In M. K. Ryan & N. R. Branscombe (Eds.), *The Sage handbook of gender and psychology* (pp. 465–483). Sage.

Bowles, H. R., Babcock, L., & Lai, L. (2007). Social incentives for gender differences in the propensity to initiate negotiations: Sometimes it does hurt to ask. *Organizational Behavior and Human Decision Processes*, *103*, 84–103.

Bowles, H. R., Babcock, L., & McGinn, K. L. (2005). Constraints and triggers: Situational mechanics of gender in negotiation. *Journal of Personality and Social Psychology*, *89*(6), 951–965.

Bowles, H. R., & McGinn, K. L. (2008). Gender in job negotiations: A two-level game. *Negotiation Journal*, *24*, 393–410.

Bradler, C. (2015). How creative are you? An experimental study on self-selection in a competitive incentive scheme for creative performance. ZEW Discussion Paper 15-021.

Brandts, J., Groenert, V., & Rott, C. (2015). The impact of advice on women's and men's selection into competition. *Management Science*, *61*(5), 1018–1035.

Buckert, M., Schwieren, C., Kudielka, B. M., & Fiebach, C. J. (2017). How stressful are economic competitions in the lab? An investigation with physiological measures. *Journal of Economic Psychology*, *62*, 231–245.

Burow, N., Beblo, M., Beninger, D., & Schröder, M. (2017). Why do women favor same-gender competition? Evidence from a choice experiment. DIW Berlin Discussion Paper 1662.

Buser, T. (2012). The impact of the menstrual cycle and hormonal contraceptives on competitiveness. *Journal of Economic Behavior and Organization*, *83*(1), 1–10.

Buser, T., Dreber, A., & Mollerstrom, J. (2017a). The impact of stress on tournament entry. *Experimental Economics*, *20*(2), 506–530.

Buser, T., Niederle, M., & Ooserbeek, H. (2014). Gender, competitiveness, and career choices. *The Quarterly Journal of Economics*, *129*(3), 1409–1447.

Buser, T., Peter, N., & Wolter, S. C. (2017b). Gender, competitiveness, and study choices in high school: Evidence from Switzerland. *The American Economic Review*, *107*(5), 125–130.

Cahlíková, J., Cingl, L., & Levely, I. (2020). How stress affects performance and competitiveness across gender. *Management Science*, *66*(8), 3295–3310.

Cárdenas, J.-C., Dreber, A., von Essen, E., & Ranehill, E. (2012). Gender differences in competitiveness and risk taking: Comparing children in Colombia and Sweden. *Journal of Economic Behavior and Organization*, *83*, 11–23.

Carlsson, F., Lampi, E., Martinsson, P., & Yang, X. (2020). Replication: Do women shy away from competition? Experimental evidence from China. *Journal of Economic Psychology*. Advance online publication.

Cason, T. N., Masters, W. A., & Sheremeta, R. M. (2010). Entry into winner-take-all and proportional-prize contests: An experimental study. *Journal of Public Economics*, *98*, 15–31.

Cassar, A., Wordofa, F., & Zhang, Y. J. (2016). Competing for the benefit of offspring eliminates the gender gap in competitiveness. *Proceedings of the National Academy of Sciences, 113*(19), 5201–5205.

Casto, K. V., & Prasad, S. (2017). Recommendations for the study of women in hormones and competition research. *Hormones and Behavior, 92*, 190–194.

Clot, S., Giusta, M. D., & Razzu, G. (2020). Gender gaps in competition: New experimental evidence from UK professionals. IZA Discussion Paper 13323.

Comeig, I., Grau-Grau, A., Jaramillo-Gutiérrez, A., & Ramírez, F. (2016). Gender, self-confidence, sports, and preferences for competition. *Journal of Business Research, 69*, 1418–1422.

Cotton, C., McIntyre, F., & Price, J. (2013). Gender differences in repeated competition: Evidence from school math contests. *Journal of Economic Behavior and Organization, 86*, 52–66.

Croson, R., & Gneezy, U. (2009). Gender differences in preferences. *Journal of Economic Literature, 47*, 448–474.

Dannals, J. E., Zlatev, J. J., Halevy, N., & Neale, M. A. (2021). The dynamics of gender and alternatives in negotiation. *Journal of Applied Psychology.* Advance online publication.

De Paola, M., Ponzo, M., & Scoppa, V. (2015). Gender differences in attitudes towards competition: Evidence from the Italian Scientific Qualification. IZA Discussion Paper 8859.

Deutsch, M. (1949). A theory of co-operation and competition. *Human Relations, 2*(3), 129–152.

Dreber, A., von Essen, E., & Ranehill, E. (2011). Outrunning the gender gap—boys and girls compete equally. *Experimental Economics, 14*(4), 567–582.

Dreber, A., von Essen, E., & Ranehill, E. (2014). Gender and competition in adolescence: Tasks matter. *Experimental Economics, 17*(1), 154–172.

Eagly, A. H. (1987). *Sex differences in social behavior: A social-role interpretation.* Erlbaum.

Eagly, A. H. (2018). The shaping of science by ideology: How feminism inspired, led, and constrained scientific understanding of sex and gender. *Journal of Social Issues, 74*(4), 871–888.

Eagly, A. H., & Karau, S. J. (2002). Role congruity theory of prejudice toward female leaders. *Psychological Review, 109*, 573–598.

Eagly, A. H., Nater, C., Miller, D. I., Kaufmann, M., & Sczesny, S. (2020). Gender stereotypes have changed: A cross-temporal meta-analysis of U.S. public opinion polls from 1946 to 2018. *American Psychologist, 75*(3), 301–315.

Eagly, A. H., & Steffen, V. J. (1984). Gender stereotypes stem from the distribution of women and men into social roles. *Journal of Personality and Social Psychology, 46*(4), 735–754.

Eagly, A. H., & Wood, W. (2012). Social role theory. In P. M. Van Lange, A. W. Kruglanski, & E. T. Higgins (Eds.), *Handbook of theories of social psychology* (Vol. 2, pp. 458–476). Sage.

Eisenkopf, G., Hessami, Z., Fischbacher, U., & Ursprung, H. W. (2015). Academic performance and single-sex schooling: Evidence from a natural experiment in Switzerland. *Journal of Economic Behavior and Organization, 115*, 123–143.

Ertac, S., & Szentes, B. (2010). The effect of performance feedback on gender differences in competitiveness: Experimental evidence. Working Paper, Koc University, Turkey.

Eriksson, T., Teyssier, S., & Villeval, M.-C. (2009). Self-selection and the efficiency of tournaments. *Economic Inquiry, 47*(3), 530–548.

Exley, C. L., Niederle, M., & Vesterlund, L. (2020). Knowing when to ask: The cost of leaning-in. *Journal of Political Economy, 128*(3), 816–854.

Fine, C. (2017). *Testosterone rex: Unmaking the myths of our gendered minds.* Norton.

Flory, J. A., Gneezy, U., Leonard, K. L., & List, J. A. (2018). Gender, age, and competition: A disappearing gap? *Journal of Economic Behavior and Organization, 150*, 256–276.

Flory, J. A., Leibbrandt, A., & List, J. A. (2015). Do competitive workplaces deter female workers? A large-scale natural field experiment on job entry decisions. *Review of Economic Studies, 82*(1), 122–155.

Fox, R. L., & Lawless, J. L. (2004). Entering the arena? Gender and the decision to run for office. *American Journal of Political Science, 48*(2), 264–280.

Fox, R. L., Lawless, J. L., & Feeley, C. (2001). Gender and the decision to run for office. *Legislative Studies Quarterly, 26*(3), 411–435.

Frick, B. (2011). Gender differences in competitiveness: Empirical evidence from professional distance running. *Labour Economics, 18*, 389–398.

Fry, R. (2019, June 20). *U.S. women near milestone in the college-educated labor force.* Pew Research Center. https://www.pewresearch.org/fact-tank/2019/06/20/u-s-women-near-milestone-in-the-college-educated-labor-force/

Garratt, R. J., Weinberger, C., & Johnson, N. (2013). The state street mile: Age and gender differences in competition aversion in the field. *Economic Inquiry, 51*(1), 806–815.

Geraldes, D. (2020). Women dislike competing against men. Working Paper, Utrecht School of Economics. https://ssrn.com/abstract=3741649

Gindi, S., Kohan-Mass, J., & Pilpel, A. (2019). Gender differences in competition among gifted students: The role of single-sex versus co-ed classrooms. *Roeper Review, 41*, 199–211.

Gneezy, U., Leonard, K. L., & List, J. A. (2009). Gender differences in competition: Evidence from a matrilineal and patriarchal society. *Econometrica, 77*, 1637–1664.

Gneezy, U., Niederle, M., & Rustichini, A. (2003). Performance in competitive environments: Gender differences. *Quarterly Journal of Economics, 118*, 1049–1074.

Gneezy, U., & Rustichini, A. (2004). Gender and competition at a young age. *The American Economic Review, 94*(2), 377–381.

Große, N. D., & Riener G. (2010). Explaining gender differences in competitiveness: Gender-task stereotypes. Working Paper, Jena Economic Research Papers 2010-017.

Guiso, L., Monte, F., Sapienza, P., & Zingales, L. (2008). Culture, gender, and math. *Science, 320*, 1164–1165.

Günther, C., Ekinci, N. A., Schwieren, C., & Strobel, M. (2010). Women can't jump? An experiment on competitive attitudes and stereotype threat. *Journal of Economic Behavior and Organization, 75*, 395–401.

Gupta, N. D., Poulsen, A., & Villeval, M.-C. (2013). Gender matching and competitiveness: Experimental evidence. *Economic Inquiry, 51*(1), 816–835.

Haines, E. L., Deaux, K., & Lofaro, N. (2016). The times they are a-changing. . . or are they not? A comparison of gender stereotypes, 1983-2014. *Psychology of Women Quarterly, 40*(3), 353–363.

Halko, M. L., & Sääksvuori, L. (2017). Competitive behavior, stress, and gender. *Journal of Economic Behavior and Organization, 141*, 96–109.

Hanek, K. J., Garcia, S. M., & Tor, A. (2016). Gender and competitive preferences: The role of competition size. *Journal of Applied Psychology, 101*(8), 1122–1133.

Healy, A., & Pate, J. (2011). Can teams help close the gender competition gap? *The Economic Journal, 121*, 1192–1204.

Hegewisch, A., & Barsi, Z. (2020, March 24). *The gender wage gap by occupation 2019*. Institute for Women's Policy Research. https://iwpr.org/iwpr-issues/employment-and-earnings/the-gender-wage-gap-by-occupation-2019/

Hegewisch, A., & Hartmann, H. (2014, January 23). *Occupational segregation and the gender wage gap: A job half done*. Institute for Women's Policy Research. https://iwpr.org/iwpr-issues/employment-and-earnings/occupational-segregation-and-the-gender-wage-gap-a-job-half-done/

Heilman, M. E. (2001). Description and prescription: How gender stereotypes prevent women's ascent up the organizational ladder. *Journal of Social Issues, 57*(4), 657–674.

Heilman, M. E., & Okimoto, T. G. (2007). Why are women penalized for success at male tasks?: The implied communality deficit. *Journal of Applied Psychology, 92*, 81–92.

Heilman, M. E., Wallen, A. S., Fuchs, D., & Tamkins, M. M. (2004). Penalties for success: Reactions to women who succeed at male gender-typed tasks. *Journal of Applied Psychology, 89*, 416–427.

Hinchliffe, E. (2020, May 18). The number of female CEOs in the Fortune 500 hits an all-time record. *Fortune*. https://fortune.com/2020/05/18/women-ceos-fortune-500-2020/

Holzer, H., & Neumark, D. (2000). Assessing affirmative action. *Journal of Economic Literature, 38*(3), 483–568.

Houston, J., Harris, P., McIntire, S., & Francis, D. (2002). Revising the competitiveness index using factor analysis. *Psychological Reports, 90*, 31–34.

Hoyer, B., van Huizen, T., Keijzer, L., Rezaei, S., Rosenkranz, S., & Westbrock, B. (2020). Gender, competitiveness, and task difficulty: Evidence from the field. *Labour Economics*. Advance online publication.

Jung, S., & Vranceanu, R. (2019). Willingness to compete: Between- and within-gender comparisons. *Managerial and Decision Economics, 40*(3), 321–335.

Jurajda, Š., & Münich, D. (2011). Gender gap in performance under competitive pressure: Admissions to Czech universities. *The American Economic Review, 101*(3), 514–518.

Kamas, L., & Preston, A. (2009). Social preferences, competitiveness and compensation: Are there gender differences. Working Paper, Santa Clara University.

Kesebir, S., Lee, S. Y., Elliot, A. J., & Pillutla, M. M. (2019). Lay beliefs about competition: Scale development and gender differences. *Motivation and Emotion, 43*, 719–739.

Kleinjans, K. J. (2009). Do gender differences in preferences for competition matter for occupational expectations? *Journal of Economic Psychology, 30,* 701–710.

Koenig, A. M., & Eagly, A. H. (2014). Evidence for the social role theory of stereotype content: Observations of groups' roles shape stereotypes. *Journal of Personality and Social Psychology, 107*(3), 371–392.

Kolb, D. M. (2009). Too bad for the women or does it have to be? Gender and negotiation research over the past twenty-five years. *Negotiation Journal, 25*(4), 515–531.

Kolb, D. M. (2019). Her place at the table: Gender and negotiation after Trump. *Negotiation Journal, 35*(1), 185–189.

Kray, L. J., & Thompson, L. (2004). Gender stereotypes and negotiation performance: An examination of theory and research. *Research in Organizational Behavior, 26,* 103–182.

Kray, L. J., Thompson, L., & Galinsky, A. (2001). Battle of the sexes: Gender stereotype confirmation and reactance in negotiations. *Journal of Personality and Social Psychology, 80*(6), 942–958.

Kugler, K. G., Reif, J. A. M., Kaschner, T., & Brodbeck, F. C. (2018). Gender differences in the initiation of negotiations: A meta-analysis. *Psychological Bulletin, 144*(2), 198–222.

Kuhnen, C. M., & Tymula, A. (2012). Feedback, self-esteem, and performance in organizations. *Management Science, 58*(1), 94–113.

Leibbrandt, A., & List, J. A. (2015). Do women avoid salary negotiations? Evidence from a large-scale natural field experiment. *Management Science, 61*(9), 2016–2024.

Levanon, A., & Grusky, D. B. (2016). The persistence of extreme gender segregation in the twenty-first century. *American Journal of Sociology, 122*(2), 573–619.

Mayr, U., Wozniak, D., Davidson, C., Kuhns, D., & Harbaugh, W. T. (2012). Competitiveness across the lifespan: The feisty fifties. *Psychology and Aging, 27*(2), 278–285.

Mazei, J., Hüffmeier, J., Freund, P. A., Stuhlmacher, A. F., Bilke, L., & Hertel, G. (2015). A meta-analysis of gender differences in negotiation outcomes and their moderators. *Psychological Bulletin, 141*(1), 85–104.

Mazei, J., Zerres, A., & Hüffmeier, J. (2021). Masculinity at the negotiation table: A theory of men's negotiation behaviors and outcomes. *Academy of Management Review, 46*(1), 108–127.

Müller, J., & Schwieren, C. (2012). Can personality explain what is underlying women's unwillingness to compete? *Journal of Economic Psychology, 33*(3), 448–460.

Niederle, M., Segal, C., & Vesterlund, L. (2013). How costly is diversity? Affirmative action in light of gender differences in competitiveness. *Management Science, 59*(1), 1–16.

Niederle, M., & Vesterlund, L. (2007). Do women shy away from competition? Do men compete too much? *Quarterly Journal of Economics, 122*(3), 1067–1101.

Niederle, M., & Vesterlund, L. (2008). Gender differences in competition. *Negotiation Journal, 24,* 447–465.

Niederle, M., & Vesterlund, L. (2010). Explaining the gender gap in math test scores: The role of competition. *Journal of Economic Perspectives, 24*(2), 129–144.

Niederle, M., & Vesterlund, L. (2011). Gender and competition. *Annual Review of Economics, 3,* 601–630.

Ors, E., Palomino, F., & Peyrache, E. (2013). Performance gender gap: Does competition matter? *Journal of Labor Economics, 31*(2), 443–499.

Paserman, M. D. 2007. Gender differences in performance in competitive environments: Evidence from professional tennis players. IZA Discussion Paper 2834.

Price, J. (2008). Gender differences in the response to competition. *Industrial and Labor Relations Review, 61*(3), 320–333.

Recalde, M., & Vesterlund, L. (2020). Gender differences in negotiation and policy for improvement. NBER Working Paper 28183.

Reif, J. A. M., Kunz, F. A., Kugler, K. G., & Brodbeck, F. C. (2019). Negotiation contexts: How and why they shape women's and men's decision to negotiate. *Negotiation and Conflict Management Research, 12*(4), 322–342.

Reuben, E., Sapienza, P., & Zingales, L. (2015). Taste for competition and the gender gap among young business professionals. NBER Working Paper 21695.

Rosenqvist, O. (2019). Are the most competitive men more resilient to failures than the most competitive women? Evidence from professional golf tournaments. *Social Science Quarterly, 100*(3), 578–591.

Rothstein, J. (2004). College performance predictions and the SAT. *Journal of Econometrics, 121,* 297–317.

Rudman, L. A., & Glick, P. (2001). Prescriptive gender stereotypes and backlash toward agentic women. *Journal of Social Issues, 57,* 743–762.

Saccardo, S., Pietrasz, A., & Gneezy, U. (2018). On the size of the gender difference in competitiveness. *Management Science, 64*(4), 1477–1973.

Samak, A. S. (2013). Is there a gender gap in preschoolers' competitiveness? An experiment in the U.S. *Journal of Economic Behavior and Organization, 92*, 22–31.

Samek, A. (2019). Gender differences in job entry decisions: A university-wide field experiment. *Management Science, 65*(7), 3272–3281.

Sandberg, S. (2013). *Lean in: Women, work, and the will to lead.* Knopf.

Säve-Söderbergh, J. (2019). Gender gaps in salary negotiations: Salary requests and starting salaries in the field. *Journal of Economic Behavior and Organization, 161*, 35–51.

Schier, U. K. (2020). Female and male role models and competitiveness. *Journal of Economic Behavior and Organization, 173*, 55–67.

Shan, W., Keller, J., & Joseph, D. (2019). Are men better negotiators everywhere? A meta-analysis of how gender differences in negotiation performance vary across cultures. *Journal of Organizational Behavior, 40*, 651–675.

Shepherd, D. A., Williams, T. A., & Patzelt, H. (2015). Thinking about entrepreneurial decision making: Review and research agenda. *Journal of Management, 41*(1), 11–46.

Shurchkov, O. (2012). Under pressure: Gender differences in output quality and quantity under competition and time constraints. *Journal of the European Economic Association, 10*(5), 1189–1213.

Skuratowicz, E., & Hunter, L. W. (2004). Where do women's jobs come from? Job resegregation in an American bank. *Work and Occupations, 31*(1), 73–110.

Smither, R. D., & Houston, J. M. (1992). The nature of competitiveness: The development and validation of the Competitiveness Index. *Educational and Psychological Measurement, 52*, 407–418.

Spencer, S. J., Steele, C. M., & Quinn, D. M. (1999). Stereotype threat and women's math performance. *Journal of Experimental Social Psychology, 35*(1), 4–28.

Steele, C. M. (1997). A threat in the air: How stereotypes shape intellectual identity and performance. *American Psychologist, 52*, 613–629.

Stuhlmacher, A. F., & Linnabery, E. (2013). Gender and negotiation: A social role analysis. In M. Olekalns & W. Adair (Eds.), *Handbook of negotiation research* (pp. 221–248). Edward Elgar.

Stuhlmacher, A. F., & Walters, A. E. (1999). Gender differences in negotiation outcome: A meta-analysis. *Personnel Psychology, 52*, 653–677.

Sutter, M., & Glätzle-Rützler, D. (2015). Gender differences in the willingness to compete emerge early in life and persist. *Management Science, 61*(10), 2339–2354.

UN Women (2021, January 15). *Facts and figures: Women's leadership and political participation.* https://www.unwomen.org/en/what-we-do/leadership-and-political-participation/facts-and-figures

van Anders, S. M., Steiger, J., & Goldey, K. L. (2015). Effects of gendered behavior on testosterone in women and men. *Proceedings of the National Academy of Sciences, 112*(45), 13805–13810.

van Anders, S. M., & Watson, N. V. (2006). Social neuroendocrinology: Effects of social contexts and behaviors on sex steroids in humans. *Human Nature, 17*(2), 212–237.

Wood, W., & Eagly, A. H. (2010). Gender. In S. T. Fiske, D. T. Gilbert, & G. Lindzey (Eds.), *Handbook of social psychology* (5th ed., Vol. 1, pp. 629–667). Wiley.

Wood, W., & Eagly, A. H. (2015). Two traditions of research on gender identity. *Sex Roles, 73*, 461–473.

Wozniak, D. (2012). Gender differences in a market with relative performance feedback: Professional tennis players. *Journal of Economic Behavior and Organization, 83*, 158–171.

Wozniak, D., Harbaugh, W. T., & Mayr, U. (2014). The menstrual cycle and performance feedback alter gender differences in competitive choices. *Journal of Labor Economics, 32*(1), 161–198.

Zhang, Y. J. (2013). Can experimental economics explain competitive behavior outside the lab? Working Paper, Hong Kong University of Science and Technology. https://ssrn.com/abstract=2292929

Zhang, Y. J. (2019). Culture, institutions and the gender gap in competitive inclination: Evidence from the communist experiment in China. *The Economic Journal, 129*(617), 509–552.

Zhong, S., Shalev, I., Koh, D., Ebstein, R. P., & Chew, S. H. (2018). Competitiveness and stress. *International Economic Review, 59*(3), 1263–1281.

PART VI

Competition in Context

Ready, Steady, Go: Competition in Sport

Maria Kavussanu, Andrew Cooke, *and* Marc Jones

Abstract

Competition is an integral part of sport. In this chapter, the authors discuss some of the research conducted in the context of sport that is directly relevant to competition. First, the authors briefly introduce the different types of competition and "appropriate" competition. Then, they discuss the effects of sport competition on select athlete outcomes, specifically performance, enjoyment, anxiety, choking, prosocial behavior, and antisocial behavior. In this discussion, the authors consider the mechanisms that explain the effects of competition on performance, with particular attention to team competition, how extreme anxiety can lead to choking, the theoretical explanations of choking under pressure, and how certain sports could facilitate some types of prosocial behavior. Next, the authors discuss challenge and threat states in sport competition and continue with an overview of how certain personality traits and motivational orientations could influence psychological and behavioral outcomes in sport competition. The authors conclude the chapter with a section on how to create an optimal competitive environment in sport.

Key Words: sport performance, enjoyment, competitive anxiety, choking, prosocial behavior, cheating, challenge and threat states, narcissism, goal orientation, motivational climate

Competition, a feature of many aspects of day-to-day life, is core feature of sport. Sport and competition are so intertwined that the *Oxford English Dictionary* defines sport as "an activity involving physical exertion and skill in which an individual or team *competes* against another or others." Thus, by its very nature, sport involves competition, and as such, it is the ideal context in which to study this phenomenon.

Many of us will recognize being in competitive situations (e.g., job interview, examinations), but for most people formal competition is relatively infrequent. In contrast, for sport performers, formal competition takes place regularly. During regular seasons, in many sports (e.g., basketball, baseball, soccer) this can be every few days, with varying intensity depending on competition importance, crowd size, and opponent quality. The constant evaluation inherent in competition brings with it psychological challenges that athletes must deal with on a regular basis (e.g., criticism from others), and intense negative emotions when losing matches, as the following quote from former Wales rugby international Martyn Williams illustrates: "However much the supporters are hurting, we are hurting just as much when we lose. You are as frustrated as anyone and you take it more personally than anyone. It's just a horrible experience . . . when you get back home, you don't want to go out anywhere" (Williams & Thomas, 2008, p. 7). Other potential negative consequences of sport competition are aggression, cheating, and, in extreme cases, using performance-enhancing substances, which could have harmful consequences for one's health.

Despite some of the challenges, sport competition has several benefits. First, it drives performance excellence, in some instances leading to spectacular achievements. Competitors need to push their limits to win the contest, and this underpins the breathtaking performances that we witness at the top level of sport competition. Contests such as Olympic Games, World Cups, and World Series produce outstanding performances that capture the attention of competitors and spectators the world over. Sport competition can also have psychological benefits. Take soccer, the most popular sport in the United Kingdom. The beautiful game (a colloquial phrase used to refer to soccer in the United Kingdom) is reportedly played as organized competition by over 11 million people in England alone, with the English Football Association having over 119,000 teams on its books, competing across over 1,200 leagues (FA, 2015). At the amateur level, players have no financial incentives or rewards to play. In many cases the opposite is true, as players pay match fees, travel costs, and equipment costs (e.g., kit) to compete. It is difficult to imagine so many individuals voluntarily engaging in regular competition if they do not experience some psychological benefits from taking part.

In this chapter, we discuss competition in sport. First, we briefly introduce the different types of competition and "appropriate" competition. Then, we discuss the effects of sport competition on select athlete outcomes, specifically performance, enjoyment, anxiety, choking, prosocial behavior, and antisocial behavior. We consider the mechanisms underlying the effects of competition on performance, paying particular attention to team competition. We also consider how extreme anxiety can lead to choking, the theoretical explanations of choking under pressure, and how certain sports could facilitate prosocial behavior. Next, we discuss challenge and threat states in sport competition. We continue with an overview of how certain personality traits and motivational orientations could influence psychological and behavioral outcomes in sport competition. We conclude the chapter with guidelines on how to create an optimal competitive environment in sport.

Types of Sport Competition

The typology of competition developed by Johnson and Johnson (1989) is highly relevant to some of the research discussed in this chapter. In this section, we outline different types of competition based on the concepts of outcome and means interdependence. We also describe appropriate competition.

In their typology of competition, Johnson and Johnson (1989) introduced the concepts of outcome and means interdependence. *Outcome* interdependence concerns how one individual achieving his or her desired outcome (e.g., winning the match) impacts the outcome achievement of others and this can be positive or negative. When outcome interdependence is positive, one's goal can be achieved when others also achieve their goal; this occurs when we cooperate with others to achieve a group goal. In contrast, when outcome interdependence is negative, one person achieving his/her goals precludes others from achieving their goals. The most extreme form of negative outcome interdependence is zero-sum or winner-takes-all competition, in which all competitors have a single outcome goal: to be the winner. Examples of this can be found in individual sport competitions such as athletics and swimming, where the first individual to cross the finish line is deemed the winner, and where all other competitors fall short of their victory goal. By its very nature, much individual sport *is* zero-sum competition as it involves negative outcome interdependence.

Means interdependence pertains to the actions required by the participants to achieve their goals and it exists when a task is structured so that two or more people are required to complete it. For example, in a rugby team, coordination of actions between the players is necessary for the team to complete the task of moving the ball across the field and scoring a try. In contrast, in tasks high on means independence, one person can complete the task without help or involvement of another person. An example in sport is when two athletes race against each other in separate lanes of a running track. Individual sports such as running, cycling, swimming, golf, and others are high in means independence, whereas team sports such as basketball, soccer, and rugby are high in means interdependence. The terms pure or individual competition have also been used to refer to tasks that are high on means independence.

A special case of competition that combines outcome and means interdependence is inter-group or team competition. This involves a combination of zero-sum competition, where only one team can be the winner, and cooperation, where the chances of achieving the goal are maximized when performers cooperate. In team competition, the performers work together as a team and their common goal is to defeat other teams, while cooperating with their teammates. Team competition is very common in sport with some of the most popular sports around the world (e.g., soccer, cricket, hockey) being team-based. As we will see later in this chapter, team competition produces distinct psychological responses compared to individual competition.

Johnson and Johnson (1989) also outlined the conditions of "appropriate" competition. In this type of competition, all participants have a reasonable chance of winning, participants can monitor each other's progress, the procedures and criteria for winning are specific and clear, and winning is relatively unimportant. In these cases, physical or mental exercise, fun and enjoyment, or relief from boredom motivate participation (Stanne et al., 1999). It could be argued that conditions of appropriate competition are more likely at the recreational level of sport, such as when participants meet to play a tennis match or a football game for fun. In these instances, winning and losing are not associated with extrinsic rewards, and individuals' own motivational orientations or approaches to competition would determine psychological outcomes. However, in organized sport competition (i.e., when sport clubs are part of a league), which is the focus of this chapter, winning is associated with scoring points in the league, and in some cases, this leads to medals and external recognition, thereby potentially increasing its importance. Consequently, organized sport competition would not meet all the conditions of appropriate competition outlined by Johnson and Johnson (1989).

In sum, there are different types of competition in sport. Some of the research discussed in the next section—which deals with the effects of sport competition on behavioral and psychological outcomes—has examined pure or individual and inter-group or team competition, typically comparing them with a practice condition. In addition, in some experiments, competition has been structured so that it meets most of the conditions of appropriate competition.

Effects of Sport Competition on Behavioral and Psychological Outcomes

Sport competition research has been diverse and has been conducted in the field and the laboratory using a variety of tasks and skill levels. In this section, we discuss the effects of competition on performance, discrete emotions, antisocial behavior, and prosocial behavior.

Performance

The effects of competition on performance in sport is one of the most important research questions in the sport psychology literature and has been examined in both the field and the lab. In this section, we discuss the mechanisms that explain these effects, considering the effects of competition on psychological outcomes. In laboratory studies, performance has been investigated using different tasks, ranging from basketball free-throw shooting and golf-putting (i.e., tasks that involve motor skills) to maintaining the grip in a handgrip dynamometer (i.e., tasks that require muscular endurance). In field studies, performance has been assessed both objectively (i.e., swimming race time) and subjectively using self-report measures. The skill level of study participants has also been varied ranging from beginners to elite performers. In this chapter, we use the term motor performance when we discuss studies that involved motor skills and have been conducted in the lab; in contrast, we use the term sport performance when we discuss field studies or refer to performance in a variety of tasks.

The study of the effects of sport competition on performance has its roots in the nineteenth century. In what is proclaimed as the very first sport competition study, Norman Triplett (1898) observed that cyclists rode faster when competing with others than when performing this task alone. This led Triplett to conclude that "the bodily presence of another contestant participating simultaneously in the race serves to liberate latent energy not ordinarily available" (p. 533). The beneficial effects of competition on sport performance have continued to spark considerable research interest ever since.

In a meta-analysis of 64 studies, Stanne et al. (1999) examined the effects of competition on motor performance relative to cooperative or individualistic "do-your-best" situational goal structures. The competition studies had employed "zero-sum" or "winner-takes-all" competition and a wide range of motor tasks, such as assembling cardboard houses, dropping marbles, and navigating mazes. Many of the studies focused on sports such as tennis, basketball, golf, swimming, and athletics. The results of this meta-analysis showed that individual competition led to better motor performance than the non-competitive or "do-your-best" conditions. However, competition was outperformed by cooperation, which resulted in even better motor performance (effect sizes were 0.53 for cooperation and 0.36 for competitive or individualistic efforts). One limitation of this meta-analysis is that it did not consider the cooperative competitive situations, which characterize team sport.

Interestingly, studies employing tasks high in means independence showed no difference in performance between competitive and cooperative goal structures. However, for tasks high in means interdependence, cooperative goal-structured activities led to better performance than activities performed in individual competition. Stanne et al. (1999) argued that if competition is to support better performance than cooperation, it will most likely need to be structured such that all participants have a reasonable chance of winning (i.e., evenly balanced), and the outcome (i.e., winning versus losing) should be relatively unimportant, thereby outlining the conditions of what they consider "appropriate" competition. However, it is hard to imagine many situations where the competition outcome is of little importance to participants in organized sport!

TEAM COMPETITION

Stanne et al. (1999) clearly showed that different social climates can have a powerful influence upon sports performance, and their data favor cooperation over individual competition as the goal structure that supports optimal outcomes. However, they did not separate the effects of individual versus team competition. In fact, studies of team competition were classified as "cooperation," somewhat clouding the applicability of their conclusions for sport. Analyses of interpersonal variables suggested that cooperation supported better performance than individual competition because it fostered more positive relationships among group members, elevated social support, and increased self-esteem (Tjosvold et al., 2019). As studies of team competition contributed to these findings, it is possible that compared to individual competition, team competition could be especially likely to lead to better performance. A number of studies have examined the effects of team competition on performance, while also investigating enjoyment and effort as mechanisms explaining these effects. Some of these studies compared intergroup competition with pure (or individual) competition, cooperation, or a do-your-best condition.

Tauer and Harackiewicz (2004) were the first to investigate the effects of team competition relative to individual (or pure) competition and cooperation on motor performance. They used a basketball free-throw shooting task performed by mixed-ability adolescent participants during a basketball sports camp. Basketball free-throw shooting is a means-independence task, and the competition created by Tauer and Harackiewicz was structured as "appropriate" competition: clear rules, challenging goal, no pressure on participants to meet their goal, and feedback regarding performance throughout the activity. Players scored more baskets when competing in a team of two and trying to score more baskets than a rival pair than when they were shooting in an individual head-to-head contest or in a cooperative condition, where members of the pair were given a combined target score to work towards. The number of baskets scored in the cooperation versus pure competition conditions did not differ. In addition, enjoyment was consistently higher in the team competition than in pure competition and cooperation, and this variable partially mediated the effects of competition type on performance. Importantly, the effects on both enjoyment and performance were robust across three studies.

Similar effects were observed in studies employing an endurance handgrip task, which has demands akin to those placed by many endurance sports, where participants compete within a team (e.g., rowing, cycling, cross-country skiing, etc.). Specifically, Cooke et al. (2011) measured the amount of time participants could sustain a grip force exceeding 40 percent of their maximum handgrip strength during "do-your-best" versus a team competition condition, where in teams of six they were vying for the greatest team endurance score. Compared to the "do-your-best" condition, during the team competition participants enjoyed the activity more and their endurance time on the task was approximately 20 percent longer. They also reported higher effort, and this was confirmed by the higher electro-myographic activity in the flexor muscle of the active forearm, during the final stages of the isometric contraction. This activity reflects the amount of additional conscious effort applied to maintain the contraction. Both enjoyment and effort partially mediated the beneficial effects of team competition on endurance. These findings were replicated in a second study, using the same task, but this time comparing team with individual competition (Cooke et al., 2013).

Taken together with the findings of Tauer and Harackiewicz (2004), the studies by Cooke et al. (2011, 2013) clearly show that team competition has the potential to lead to more enjoyment, thereby mobilizing effort and leading to better performance. Although these studies did not examine the reasons for the enjoyment in team competition, one potential explanation is the social connection between members of the team, which is an important aspect of many team sports. This is nicely illustrated by a quote from American tennis player John McEnroe, who achieved great success in tennis as an individual and as part of a team: "I always enjoyed being part of a team. I loved the camaraderie. It's what I loved about Davis Cup. It's what made doubles so important to me. If you're on a team, and you're angry or upset at something that happened in a game, you have people to share it with. It's the same thing when you win (McEnroe & Kaplan, 2002, p. 29)." Being able to share sport competition with others could strengthen social connections between group members, thereby leading to more enjoyment, effort, and performance.

The beneficial effects of team versus individual competition are also evident when comparing psychological responses of individual and team sport athletes. In one study (van de Pol & Kavussanu, 2012), athletes taking part in team sports reported both higher effort and greater enjoyment in competition compared to training during the season than did athletes from individual sports. Thus, compared to training, the experience of competition appears to be more enjoyable for team than individual sport athletes. Although performance was not examined in this study, this is an interesting finding that exemplifies the power of team competition to elicit positive psychological responses and mobilize effort. These results are in line with the findings of Tauer and Harackewicz (2004), who showed that competing in a team of two on a basketball free-throw shooting task increased enjoyment more so than competing on a head-to-head contest.

INDIVIDUAL COMPETITION AND GOLF-PUTTING

In a laboratory experiment using a golf-putting task, individual competition was examined compared to a non-competitive practice condition (van de Pol et al., 2012a). Competition led to higher effort and enjoyment compared to the practice condition, but not to better performance. It is possible that the novice sample and/or task employed (i.e., golf putting) stifled any beneficial effects of increased effort or enjoyment on performance. Indeed, studies supporting effort and enjoyment mechanisms as explaining the positive effects of competition on performance have used physical endurance tasks (e.g., Cooke et al., 2011), where the beneficial effects of effort are more easily detected, or they have recruited participants who were reasonably well practiced at performing the competition task, such as basketball players recruited from a sports camp (Tauer & Harackiewicz, 2004). Nevertheless, a robust finding across several studies is that competition is associated with greater enjoyment and effort compared to training or a practice condition (e.g., Cooke et al., 2011; van de Pol et al., 2012b).

In sum, there is convincing evidence from studies employing both skill and endurance tasks that competition and, in particular, team competition can benefit sport performance. This type of competition can promote enjoyment and effort, both of which appear to act as mechanisms that explain the beneficial effects of team competition on performance in sport. However, competition can also increase tension and anxiety, which in some cases can lead to choking. It is to this literature we now turn.

Competitive Anxiety and Choking

Sport competition generates a range of affective, cognitive, and behavioral responses. In this section, we focus on two responses that are typically associated with sport competition, and that are related to each other, namely competitive anxiety and choking. We also discuss how increased anxiety during sport competition could facilitate or impede performance, and we offer theoretical explanations for why choking occurs in sport competition.

COMPETITIVE ANXIETY

Anxiety, an emotion characterized by feelings of worry (Eysenck & Calvo, 1992), is one of the most widely studied emotions in sport, goes hand-in-hand with sport competition, is typically termed competitive anxiety, and is commonly experienced before or during sport competition. In a study of male athletes, Hanton et al. (2004) found that competitive anxiety increased progressively during the week preceding a team competition (i.e., a league fixture), with a peak just before the competition started. In another study, elite middle-distance runners reported elevations in anxiety just before a competition (Jones et al., 1990); the anxiety was specifically directed towards competition-relevant factors, such as competition preparedness and the possible competition outcome. Research in football players has also shown that compared to training, competition increases anxiety (e.g., van de Pol et al., 2012b). Similarly, in experiments that involve tasks requiring muscular endurance or a combination of speed and accuracy, anxiety increased in competition compared to a practice or do-your-best condition (e.g., Cooke et al., 2011; Dewar et al., 2013). Thus, there is unequivocal evidence across a number of studies that competition in sport elicits anxiety.

Moderate levels of anxiety experienced by most performers tend to facilitate performance. In their studies examining the effects of competition on endurance in a handgrip dynamometer, Cooke et al. (2011, 2013) showed that compared to a non-competitive condition, competition increased not only effort and performance (as indicated by longer endurance times) but also anxiety. In addition, mediation analyses revealed that increased anxiety was partially responsible for increased effort, which in turn partially explained the positive effects of competition on performance (Cooke et al., 2013). It has been suggested that mild anxiety that does not overwhelm working memory has a motivational function, which can be particularly powerful in mobilizing spare resources that would not ordinarily be devoted to the task (Eysenck et al., 2007), thereby facilitating performance in sport.

In another experiment, Cooke et al. (2010) examined self-reported anxiety measured immediately before a non-competitive and a competitive golf-putting condition. In the latter condition, participants were presented with an accuracy score that they were told had been (ostensibly) achieved by a rival, and which they were instructed to beat. Anxiety increased by 25 percent from the non-competitive to the competition condition, while performance was impaired, with a significant reduction in the number of putts holed. Thus, competition can intensify anxiety and may also impair performance in some circumstances. This tends to happen when participants experience pressure to perform. Such occurrences of inferior performance during competition are often referred to as choking, and anxiety is cited as a key variable leading to choking.

CHOKING

Coined by the famous psychologist Roy Baumeister (1984), the term choking under pressure refers to the manifestation of inferior performance, despite the performer striving to perform well and the situation demanding superior performance. It is not difficult to think of instances of choking in sport. At the United States Masters Golf championship, Greg Norman (in 1996), Rory McIlroy (in 2011), and Jordan Spieth (in 2016) have all shot uncharacteristically bad scores to squander sizable leads during the final hours of the four-day tournament; all were ranked in the Top 10 players in the world at the time. In tennis, the late Jana Novotna led Steffi Graf 4–1 and 40–30 in the decisive set of the 1993 Ladies Singles final at Wimbledon, meaning she was theoretically just five points away from winning the championship. She followed with a double fault on her serve, and then two unforced errors to hand the game to Graf. Within 15 minutes, Graf reeled off the next four games to defeat her opponent 6–4.

As these examples illustrate, choking occurs in sport, and this is not surprising as sport competition creates pressure and demands for superior performance particularly at the elite level. The significance of choking in sport competition has led several researchers to conduct empirical studies aiming to understand choking and develop theoretical explanations of this phenomenon. Below we briefly discuss two theories used to explain choking in sport competition and the empirical support they have received in sport research: attentional control theory and reinvestment theory.

Attentional Control Theory

Attentional control theory has attention at its heart. Attention refers to the focus of our thoughts on a particular stimulus or set of stimuli, out of the countless stimuli that are present in one's immediate environment, at any given time. Two types or systems of attention have been described (Corbetta & Shulman, 2002): goal driven and stimulus driven. Goal-driven attention pertains to focusing on stimuli relevant to our goals, expectations, and knowledge, while stimulus-driven attention is concerned with the identification of relevant sensory events, such as unexpected stimuli that may appear in the environment. For instance, in sport competition, a soccer player may use goal-driven attention to focus on performance targets (e.g., aim to hit at least 10 crosses into the penalty area per game), but stimulus-driven attention could draw her attention towards threatening behavior demonstrated by one of the opposition defenders or distractions from the crowd.

In normal circumstances, these two systems are said to run simultaneously, with the goal-driven system prevailing. However, when experiencing high levels of anxiety, as it often happens in sport competition, stimulus-driven attention increases at the expense of goal-driven attention (Eysenck et al., 2007). In cases of extreme anxiety, this increase can make it difficult to maintain goal-driven attention and can result in impaired performance due to insufficient attention towards crucial goal-relevant stimuli. In this case, our soccer player might not think about her plan to make runs and hit crosses because her attention is consumed by thoughts about the threatening opposition defender, thus leading her to choke. Thus, according to attentional control theory, the decline in performance associated with anxiety in sport competition occurs when anxiety levels are extremely high, thereby diverting almost all attention away from important goal-related processes.

Several studies have supported the predictions of attentional control theory when examining the relationship between anxiety and performance in sport competition (for review see Eysenck & Wilson, 2016). These studies use insights from eye movements recorded via eye-tracking goggles to code the stimuli that individuals fixate upon during performance of motor skills. In one such study, Wilson et al. (2009) recorded the eye movements of 14 university soccer players, while they kicked penalties at a soccer goal guarded by a goalkeeper, during a practice and during a competition condition. Compared to the practice condition, anxiety increased during competition, and participants spent more time looking at the goalkeeper; moreover, shooting performance was impaired with shots being placed significantly closer to the goalkeeper. Anxiety induced by competition seems to have disrupted the balance between goal-driven attention (i.e., it reduced focus on shooting the ball into the corner of the goal) and stimulus-driven attention (i.e., it increased awareness of the goalkeeper) thereby contributing to impaired performance.

Reinvestment Theory

An alternative anxiety-based explanation of choking during competition is offered by reinvestment theory (Masters, 1992), which describes the relationship between conscious motor control and motor performance. The theory is underpinned by classic models of motor learning (e.g., Fitts & Posner, 1967), which argue that with sufficient repetition, the control of motor skills evolves from cognitive (e.g., attention demanding; rules to guide movement are manipulated in the working memory) to automatic (e.g., movements controlled with minimal conscious awareness). Increased anxiety, which occurs during competition can lead anyone who has evolved beyond the initial stages of learning, to "reinvest" the verbal-analytic rules that they used to support movement when they were a complete beginner. Due to the importance placed on sport competition, individuals may attempt to focus attention on their movements as a strategy designed to help them win. However, this well-intentioned strategy can lead to the de-automatization of well-learned skills, resulting in regression to a more primitive and less efficient forms of motor control (Masters & Maxwell, 2008). Such de-automatization is theorized to result in a substantial decline in performance, with experts reverting back to their novice-like ways, as happens during the relatively rare but spectacular cases of elite athletes choking during competition.

Support for reinvestment theory has been provided by several experiments showing that competition increases one's propensity to consciously control movement. For example, Vine et al. (2013) found that self-reported anxiety and conscious control increased significantly, while performance deteriorated from a practice to an individual competition condition in a golf-putting task among golfers who had received some coaching in golf. In a recent laboratory experiment, anxiety increased and pitching baseball accuracy decreased from practice to an individual competition (Gray et al., 2017). The decline in performance was accompanied by increased variability in the lead foot landing location and pitching elbow flexion angle; these changes were deemed uncharacteristic of automatic execution, and were thereby interpreted as objective behavioral evidence of increased conscious motor control during competition being responsible for this decline in performance.

In sum, anxiety evoked by sport competition can have positive effects on performance, but it can also impair performance. Although most studies indicate that sport performance during competition increases, in some cases choking can occur. Attentional control and reinvestment theories are two viable explanations of choking in sport.

Cheating Aggression, and Antisocial Behavior

As well as eliciting a variety of affective responses, sport competition in some instances can lead to cheating, aggression, and antisocial behavior. Examples of such behaviors in sport are the boxer Mike Tyson biting off part of Evander Holyfield's ear in response to repeated head butting in a heavyweight world title fight, racial abuse of opponents by professional footballer Louis Suarez, and the Australian cricket player Cameron Bancroft tampering with the ball during a match to give his team an unfair advantage in 2018. In some cases, cheating can be extreme and involves the use of banned substances and methods to enhance performance, also known as doping. These examples notwithstanding, as discussed below, some sport competition can also lead to prosocial behavior toward one's teammates.

In sport research, the term antisocial behavior has been used to broadly refer to behaviors intended to harm or disadvantage another, such as trying to injure an opponent and faking an injury (see Kavussanu, 2019). One of the most commonly investigated antisocial behaviors is aggression, which refers to overt behavior (verbal or physical) that is purposeful (i.e., non-accidental), chosen with the intent of causing injury, and has the capacity to cause psychological or physical harm to another person; examples in sport are when an athlete verbally abuses, physically intimidates, or tries to injure an opponent in the pursuit of victory. The number of years of participation in sport has been positively associated with aggression and cheating particularly in males (e.g., Conroy et al., 2001; Kavussanu & Ntoumanis, 2003). Another aspect of antisocial sport behavior is gamesmanship (i.e., behavior that is within the rules of sport but violates its spirit), for example when a player intentionally distracts an opponent. Antisocial behavior can also be directed at teammates, such as swearing at, verbally abusing, and arguing with a teammate.

One line of research has examined whether the frequency of antisocial behavior (toward opponents and teammates) while participants compete for their team differs from the frequency of this behavior in regular interactions with one's fellow students at university, or classmates at secondary (i.e., high) school. Across two independent samples of athletes from a variety of team sports, antisocial behavior toward opponents in matches during the season was more frequent than it was in interactions with fellow students at university (Kavussanu et al., 2013), while antisocial behavior toward teammates did not differ between the two contexts. In another study of adolescent football players (Kavussanu & Ring, 2021), antisocial behavior was more frequent toward one's opponents while competing in sport than toward one's classmates at school. However, contrary to the findings in university athletes (i.e., young adults), late adolescents reported lower antisocial behavior toward teammates in sport than toward classmates at school.

This research also attempted to explain differences in antisocial sport behavior between sport and university contexts (Kavussanu et al., 2013; Kavussanu & Ring, 2021). One variable which partially accounted for the more frequent antisocial behavior toward opponents in sport was moral disengagement, which was higher in sport than university and school. Moral disengagement refers to a set of psychological mechanisms that individuals use to minimize negative emotional reactions, which typically arise when engaging in harmful conduct that runs contrary to one's moral standards (Bandura, 1991). During sport competition, in the pursuit of victory, coaches may ask players to cheat or injure their opponents, and players may receive pressure from their teammates to do so. Thus, in sport, responsibility for one's antisocial behavior can be more easily displaced onto others. The more frequent antisocial behavior toward opponents in sport than toward one's fellow students at university and school may be, in part, due to the higher moral disengagement elicited by sport competition. However, it is worth noting that these two studies (Kavussanu et al., 2013; Kavussanu & Ring, 2021) were cross-sectional, providing weak evidence for causal relationships.

Prosocial Behavior

Researchers have also examined prosocial behavior, defined as voluntary behavior intended to help or benefit another individual or group of individuals (Eisenberg & Fabes, 1998); similar to antisocial behavior, the distinction has been made between behavior directed at opponents and teammates (Kavussanu & Boardley, 2009). Examples of prosocial behavior in sport are helping a player off the floor, helping an injured opponent, and congratulating, supporting, and encouraging a teammate. When directed at teammates, prosocial behaviors could have achievement-related consequences, thus there may be a personal benefit in engaging in these behaviors. For example, by encouraging a teammate after a mistake, one could help the teammate perform better, which would in turn benefit one's team.

The studies examining antisocial behavior in sport have also typically investigated prosocial behavior toward teammates and opponents. In one study (Kavussanu et al., 2013), university student-athletes were asked to indicate how often they engaged in prosocial behavior toward their teammates, for example encouraging their teammates after a mistake, giving them positive and constructive feedback, and supporting them; participants also indicated the frequency of engaging in these behaviors toward their fellow students at university. Prosocial behavior was more frequent toward one's teammates while playing sport than it was toward one's fellow students at university, and these findings were replicated in a second study of high school athletes (Kavussanu & Ring, 2021). Team sport appears to have the power to elicit prosocial behavior toward one's teammates. However, no context difference emerged when comparing lending equipment to an opponent versus notes to a student, two prosocial behaviors described in hypothetical scenarios to which team-sport student-athletes were asked to respond (Kavussanu & Ring, 2016). It is likely that the type of prosocial behavior in which one engages moderates the effects of context on prosocial behavior.

In sum, sport competition can have consequences for participants' prosocial and antisocial behaviors toward opponents and teammates. There is a large body of literature (e.g., Hewstone et al., 2002) indicating that individuals tend to respond differently to others depending on whether these others are members of their own group (the in-group) or members of a different group (the out-group). Sport is a unique context, where one is typically part of a team (the in-group) competing against others (the out-group). This classification appears to influence prosocial and antisocial behavior in sport.

Competition in Sport: Challenge or Threat?

Competition elicits both positive and negative psychological and behavioral responses. Various explanations have been forwarded for the differential responses to competition in sport. In this section, we discuss the role of challenge and threat appraisals in determining how individuals respond to sport competition.

Drawing on the biopsychosocial model of challenge and threat (e.g., Blascovich et al., 2004), sport-specific theories of challenge and threat have been developed (e.g., Jones et al., 2009; Meijen et al., 2020). These approaches theorize that when individuals face a motivated performance situation, such as competition, they appraise first the demands of the competition (e.g., danger, uncertainty, required effort) and then their resources to cope with these demands. If the resources outweigh the demands, a challenge appraisal occurs, whereas if the demands outweigh the resources, a threat appraisal ensues. These states are reflected in two distinct cardiovascular reactivity patterns. In a challenge state, heart rate and cardiac output increase and total peripheral resistance decreases. In a threat state, there is increased sympathetic-adrenomedullary activity accompanied by increased pituitary-adreno-cortical activity, and subsequent cortisol release reflected in increased heart rate, a small increase or stabilization in cardiac output, and an increase or stabilization in total peripheral resistance. A recent meta-analysis (Behnke & Kaczmarek, 2018) found support for the performance benefits of a challenge state as evidenced by cardiovascular reactivity.

The emotions experienced by athletes in challenge and threat states are also likely to differ. Moore et al. (2013) explored appraisals and emotions prior to an individual golf-putting competition, where golfers were assigned to either a challenge or a threat group. In the challenge group, participants were reassured that they were very capable of doing well, that most participants like them handle the task well, and that even participants with limited experience have done well on the task. In contrast, golfers in the threat group were told that the researchers expected them to struggle, that most participants like them find the task very difficult, and that even participants with extensive experience had failed on this task. Thus, challenge and threat states were experimentally manipulated in this study. Results showed that the challenge group perceived higher resources, lower demands, and lower anxiety, and performed better than the threat group.

In another study, college athletes taking part in a variety of sports (e.g., cricket, football, hockey, netball, tennis) completed a questionnaire within 30 minutes of the commencement of a trial, in which they competed for a place in a university team (Kavussanu et al., 2014). Participants were asked to indicate whether they perceived the forthcoming trial as a challenge (i.e., challenge appraisal) or threat (i.e., threat appraisal) and the emotions they experienced at that point in time. Challenge appraisal positively predicted pre-competition excitement and hope, whereas threat appraisal positively predicted anxiety. These findings offer support for the notion that challenge versus threat appraisals might lead performers to experience positive emotions, whereas threat appraisal may lead individuals to experience negative emotions prior to competition.

Effects of Personality and Motivation on Psychological and Behavioral Outcomes

As we have discussed so far, competition in sport can have a variety of cognitive, affective, and behavioral consequences. Performance, effort, enjoyment, prosocial behavior, and antisocial behavior all seem to be influenced by sport competition. However, not everyone responds in the same way to competition. In this section, we discuss how certain personality characteristics influence individuals' responses to sport competition. We will pay particular attention to motivational orientations and how the goals we adopt in competition could be beneficial or detrimental for a variety of outcomes. With a few exceptions, we will consider the same outcomes that were discussed in the previous section.

Personality

The effects of personality have been investigated primarily in relation to performance. Some research shows that certain personality characteristics augment the positive effects of competition on performance. That is, sport competition seems to bring out the best in some people, motivating them to produce superior performance, while others appear to be performing their worst in competition. In this section, we discuss how certain personality characteristics may predispose individuals positively or negatively toward individual versus team competition in sport, and the effects of these personality characteristics on performance. We discuss three personality traits: narcissism, sensitivity to reward, and sensitivity to punishment.

Individuals high in narcissism consider themselves superior to others and are said to be highly motivated by self-enhancement opportunities, such as individual competition, because these provide a platform to demonstrate superiority over others and reaffirm the narcissists' inflated self-beliefs (Wallace & Baumeister, 2002). Highly narcissistic individuals would be expected to thrive in conditions that provide them with an opportunity for glory, and therefore may be particularly likely to try their best and perform well in individual competition. Indeed, Roberts et al. (2019) revealed a positive indirect effect of narcissism on performance via physical effort during individual competition but a negative indirect effect via effort during team competition.

Similar findings were reported by Woodman et al. (2011), who had participants compete in teams of three, requiring them to cover as much distance as possible on the cycle ergometer in a 10-minute cycling task varying the opportunities for glory. Specifically, in one condition, participants were told that the individual scores of all three team members would be published, whereas in the other condition, they were told that only the team score would be published. In both conditions, participants performed the task in screened booths out of sight of their teammates, thus providing no immediate opportunity for recognition, that is, they were unable to see how each member was performing. Highly narcissistic individuals performed exceptionally well during the condition where individual scores were to be published, but they performed less well when only the team score was to be published. Individuals who scored low on narcissism performed equally well in both competitions. Thus, when there is less of a spotlight on members of a team, highly narcissistic individuals are likely to withdraw effort, engage in social loafing, and perform poorly. In contrast, they will thrive during competitions, where a spotlight is placed on their individual performance, as such contests provide the perfect platform for them to showcase their perceived superiority over others.

The relationship between competition and performance in sport could also be influenced by an individual's sensitivity to reward versus punishment. Sensitivity to reward reflects the extent to which one engages in approach behaviors and goals; for example, high reward sensitivity could manifest itself as a cricket batsman playing aggressive shots to try to hit every ball to the boundary. Sensitivity to punishment reflects the extent to which we are able to identify factors that may undermine our ability to achieve our goals; for example, high punishment sensitivity could manifest itself as a cricket batsman playing defensive shots because he recognizes that aggressive shots increase the risk of him losing his wicket (Bell et al., 2013). Reward and punishment sensitivities have been consistently found to interact in predicting performance during competition whereby individuals who are relatively sensitive to punishment and insensitive to reward tend to outperform those who do not possess this personality profile (e.g., Beattie et al., 2017; Bell et al., 2013; Hardy et al., 2014).

In one study, Beattie et al. (2017) examined swimming competition race times and found that individuals who were relatively sensitive to punishment and insensitive to reward produced faster times in swimming competitions than those who were high or low in both of these traits. It may be that athletes with a high punishment and low reward sensitivity personality profile tend to prepare better for competition because their sensitivity to punishment allows them to identify the sorts of threats that could derail them, far in advance of competition and then make plans to deal with these threats (Beattie et al., 2017). For instance, a cricket batsman high in punishment and low in reward sensitivity may recognize the risks of playing aggressive shots and pre-formulate a strategy of how he is going to score his target of 50 runs, choosing to employ aggressive shots only on weak deliveries (e.g., slow full toss), where the risks of an aggressive shot going wrong are low. In contrast, a batsman high in reward and low in punishment sensitivity may find it difficult to inhibit the urge to play aggressive shots at every ball because aggressive shots seem the natural way to score runs, and he has not recognized that this strategy may, in some cases, increase the risk of him getting out early before his 50-run target has been achieved.

Achievement Goals

Sport competition is intertwined with achievement motivation. The Cambridge dictionary defines competition as "a situation in which someone is *trying* to win something or *be more successful* than someone else." Thus, competition is an achievement context with success and achievement motivation at its heart. Achievement goals, which entail our subjective definition of success, and their role in facilitating or hindering a variety of outcomes in competition, have received considerable attention in sport psychology. In this section, we discuss some of this work focusing on how achievement goal pursuit influences individuals' affective, cognitive, and behavioral responses during competition.

Achievement goals are a central construct of achievement goal theory; a few theoretical frameworks exist with some variation in their conceptualization (e.g., Ames, 1992; Dweck, 1986; Elliot & McGregor, 2001 Nicholls, 1989). The research we discuss in this chapter has adopted the conceptualization of John Nicholls (1989), who proposed that two major achievement goals operate in sport and involve variation in the criteria one uses to judge competence and evaluate success (i.e., self or other referenced). The term task involvement has been used to refer to a goal in which an individual strives to *develop* competence and evaluates success using self-referenced criteria (e.g., learning, task mastery). Ego involvement refers to an achievement goal where one strives to *demonstrate* competence and evaluates success using other-referenced criteria (e.g., winning a contest). The propensity to be task or ego-involved in achievement contexts is known as goal orientation. Ego orientation is typically higher in competition compared to training, whereas task orientation tends to be stable between the two contexts (e.g., van de Pol et al., 2012a, 2012b; van de Pol & Kavussanu, 2012).

The terms mastery and performance goals are primarily used in educational psychology (e.g., Ames, 1992; Dweck, 1986), where achievement goal theory originated. These are also the terms used by Elliot and his colleagues in the hierarchical model of approach-avoidance motivation and subsequent 2 x 2 and 3 x 2 models of achievement goals (Elliot et al., 2011; Elliot & Church, 1997; Elliot & McGregor, 2001). For competition research relevant to approach-avoidance goals, see Murayama, Elliot, & Jury, this volume. In this section, we discuss research on sport competition that has adopted the dichotomous conceptualization of achievement goals (e.g., Nicholls, 1989).

EFFECTS OF ACHIEVEMENT GOALS ON EFFORT, EMOTIONS, AND PERFORMANCE

One of the central questions in this area of research is how the achievement goals we pursue in competition shape our emotional experiences, the amount of effort we exert, and how well we perform when competing in sport. In studies of tennis and football players, task orientation positively predicted both effort and enjoyment (van de Pol et al., 2012a; van de Pol & Kavussanu, 2011), whereas ego orientation was positively linked to effort, *only* when athletes reported low or average levels of task orientation; this goal was unrelated to effort when athletes' task orientation was high (van de Pol & Kavussanu, 2011). Thus, athletes, who tend to evaluate success using self-referenced criteria are also more likely to try hard when they compete. However, being ego oriented may be beneficial for effort in competition in individual sports, such as tennis, when one's task orientation is low or average. It is worth noting though that this effect did not emerge in football, a discrepancy which could be attributed to sport type. Ego-oriented athletes may find it easier to link their normative goal striving (i.e., striving to outperform others) to a concrete personal success in individual sports, as these sports provide exact individual performance information, unlike team sports where personal success is intertwined with the overall team achievement. A more concrete prospect of a gain in normative competence (i.e., being better than others) may lead ego-oriented athletes to put more effort in their achievement striving when competing in individual sports relative to team sports.

The effects of task and ego involvement were also examined in a golf-putting experiment, where "training" and "competition" conditions were created (van de Pol et al., 2012a). Tested in pairs, participants were told that the purpose of the (training) session was to learn and improve the skill of golf putting. They were given instructions on how to putt a golf ball and practiced six blocks of 10 putts each prior to performing 10 putts in a zero-sum competition. Task and ego involvement experienced during golf putting were measured at the end of each condition. The two achievement goals interacted such that high levels of both goals were associated with the highest levels of effort and enjoyment. In fact, under conditions of low task involvement, ego involvement was not associated with enjoyment and had a weaker relationship with effort. Thus, ego involvement could be beneficial for both effort and enjoyment as long as task involvement is maintained at high levels. If one derives feelings of success from improvement, effort, and task mastery, then using also normative criteria to evaluate one's competence during competition could lead to the highest levels of effort and enjoyment in this context.

Mediating and Moderating Variables

Achievement goals can also influence discrete emotions, which are defined as "relatively brief but intense experiences activated by cognitive appraisal of situational factors" (Lane & Terry, 2000, p. 17). In one study, adult male golfers with a mean handicap of 13.37 indicated the emotions they experienced and the degree of their task and ego involvement and perceived performance during the round of golf they had just played (Dewar & Kavussanu, 2011). When golfers' task involvement was high, they were more likely to experience happiness and excitement and less likely to feel dejection while playing golf. The relationship between ego involvement and emotions was more complex: this goal was a positive predictor of happiness only when the golfers perceived that they had performed well. In contrast, when the golfers performed poorly, ego involvement was a negative predictor of happiness and a positive predictor of dejection and anxiety. These findings suggest that the effects of ego involvement on emotions during golf competition *depend* on perceived performance. Ego involvement could lead to positive emotions such as happiness when one performs well but is likely to lead to negative emotions when one performs poorly.

These results were replicated and extended in an independent sample of athletes from a variety of team sports, who were recruited from university and local teams, and reported on their experiences during the match they had just played (Dewar & Kavussanu, 2012). Task involvement was positively related to happiness, pride, and hope, and negatively associated with dejection and shame *regardless* of one's level of perceived performance. In contrast, ego involvement was positively related to hope only when athletes perceived they had performed well during the match. When perceived performance was low, ego involvement negatively predicted hope and positively predicted dejection. These athletes may have felt dejected because they believed that they failed to achieve their goal of performing well relative to others. Thus, although ego involvement is unavoidably expected to increase during competition (van de Pol et al., 2012a, 2012b), too much increase appears to be risky, as it may lead to negative emotions when performance is low. Due to the uncertainty of sport competition and its zero-sum nature, this is not a wise strategy as the outcome of competition is not under our control and performance is also influenced by uncontrollable factors.

The relationship between ego involvement and emotions was also moderated by the outcome of competition. Specifically, in athletes who won the match, ego involvement was positively related to pride and hope and unrelated to dejection, whereas in athletes who lost the match, ego involvement was negatively associated with hope, positively related to dejection, and unrelated to pride. It is likely that ego-involved athletes used outcome of the match to inform themselves whether they had achieved beyond their goal (Uphill & Jones, 2007). Immediately after losing a match, athletes who were ego involved during the match may not have thought that improvement was possible and experienced a loss; these thoughts may have triggered negative emotions (Uphill & Jones, 2007), leading to dejection and reduced hope.

These findings clearly show that task involvement is a robust predictor of positive emotions, whereas the relationship between ego involvement and emotions depends on athletes' performance, regardless of whether this is perceived performance or normative performance reflected on the outcome of the match. Thus, being task involved during a sport competition may lead athletes to experience positive emotions during the competition. Maintaining task involvement in an achievement context that values normative success is a challenge shared by performers and coaches alike. However, being able to maintain such a focus can lead athletes to fulfill their athletic potential and perform their best during competition while minimizing the likelihood of choking.

The effects of achievement goals on emotions experienced before, during, and after competition were examined in an experiment (Dewar et al., 2013). Matched with an opponent of the same sex, and tested in pairs, university student athletes performed a speed-agility task known as the tango drill under conditions of task involvement, ego involvement, or neutral. Participants were instructed to complete the drill as fast as possible while making as few errors as possible. After a practice session, they competed against each other over three trials, and they received feedback on their performance. Pre-competition excitement was higher in the ego-involved group than in the task-involved and control groups, and pre-competition anxiety was higher in the ego-involved group than the task-involved group. There was no difference in post-competition happiness among the three groups. Interestingly, both the task-involved and the ego-involved groups perceived their post-competition performance to be superior to the control group, although the three groups did not differ in objective performance. In sum, the emotions experienced just before competition vary depending on one's achievement goals with ego involvement eliciting both positive and negative emotions.

EFFECTS OF GOALS ON CHEATING, PROSOCIAL BEHAVIOR, AND ANTISOCIAL BEHAVIOR

Achievement goals also have implications for cheating during sport competition. Ring and Kavussanu (2018) revealed a positive relationship between ego orientation and acceptance of cheating. They also showed that athletes who illegitimately improved their times in a race to enhance their chances of winning scored higher in ego orientation and lower in task orientation than those who did not illegitimately improve their race times; task orientation was inversely associated with acceptance of cheating. These findings provide strong evidence for the motivation-cheating relationship thereby supporting predictions of achievement goal theory (Nicholls, 1989) regarding the role of ego orientation in the context of sport. As Nicholls (1989) has put it, "when winning is everything, it is worth doing anything to win." The findings regarding task orientation were mixed and inconclusive, suggesting that promoting task involvement in sport is unlikely to prevent cheating. Instead, it is the focus on ego involvement that appears to make a difference for cheating in sport.

Research investigating achievement goals in relation to prosocial and antisocial behaviors has revealed more consistent findings. Across a number of studies, task orientation has been positively associated with prosocial behavior toward teammates and opponents (for a review see Kavussanu & Al-Yaaribi, 2021) with a stronger link evidenced with prosocial teammate behavior. In contrast, ego orientation has been consistently linked to antisocial behavior in sport, with stronger relationships evidenced with behavior directed at opponents. The stronger link of ego orientation with opponent compared to teammate antisocial behavior makes sense, if one considers that athletes high in ego orientation typically strive to outperform their opponents rather than their teammates when taking part in sport, and antisocial behavior toward opponents could be the outcome of these efforts. The positive link between ego involvement and antisocial behavior has also been supported in an experimental study, which involved a table-football competition, whereby the two achievement goals were manipulated (Sage & Kavussanu, 2007). Participants in the ego-involved group were observed to display more antisocial behaviors during the table football competition than did participants in the control group.

In summary, narcissism, sensitivity to reward and punishment, and task and ego achievement goals have been associated with distinct outcomes during competition, including effort, performance, positive and negative emotions, cheating, and prosocial and antisocial behaviors. It is clear that competition could lead to certain psychological and behavioral responses; however, individual personality characteristics play an important role on one's behavior and emotions during competition.

Creating an Optimal Environment in Sport

As our discussion has illustrated so far, sport competition can drive superior performance and can enable millions of people of all ages worldwide to experience a variety of psychological benefits. However, it can also lead to anxiety and choking, leaving participants devastated by their poor performance in competitions that matter. In addition, it can promote antisocial behavior toward one's opponents, while team competition can facilitate prosocial behavior toward one's teammates. In this section, we discuss how sport competition can be a positive force that brings out the best in sport participants.

Sport competition unavoidably increases anxiety, which beyond certain levels can impair performance. One way to manage anxiety is training in anxiety-inducing environments. Adopting this approach, Bell et al. (2013) conducted an intervention that provided exposure to some anxiety in training in elite under-18 male cricketers. The intervention, which was delivered over 46 days at a national team training camp, involved introducing consequences for failure to meet strict performance (e.g., competition scores) or disciplinary (e.g., punctuality, tidiness) standards. It was explained that these consequences were crucial to help prepare cricketers for professional-level international cricket, where any slips in performance or discipline could be very damaging and potentially career-ending. The coaches delivering the intervention clearly communicated their belief that all the players could meet the standards if they worked hard, and they helped them become aware of the consequences ahead of time, thus affording the opportunity for diligent preparation. Performance and fitness significantly improved from pre- to post-intervention, exceeding the improvements recorded by a control group of regional squad under-18 cricketers, who undertook a similar duration training camp without routine consequences in their training environment. Thus, training with consequences could be a useful intervention to help athletes flourish in sport competition.

As the research discussed in this chapter suggests, how athletes approach sport competition is important, with a focus on task involvement yielding optimal benefits. This approach to sport competition was exemplified in the coaching practices of legendary UCLA basketball coach John Wooden, one of the most successful basketball coaches in the US college history (Wooden & Carty, 2010). A religious and thoughtful man, passionate about basketball, John Wooden inspired generations of athletes to be "the best they can be." Known as "the coach," Wooden differentiated between "succeeding" and "winning" and defined success as "peace of mind attained only through self-satisfaction in knowing you made the effort to do the best of which you're capable." Wooden's advice was to not try to be better than someone else (i.e., ego involvement); instead, learn from others (i.e., akin to task involvement), and always try to be the best you can be (i.e., task involvement) as this is under one's control.

Wooden's reflections on the definition of success coincide with the focus on self-referenced criteria used to evaluate success when one is task involved. The situational equivalent of the construct of achievement goals is the motivational climate, which involves the criteria of success prevalent in the achievement context, and communicated to athletes by significant others such as coaches (Ames, 1992). These individuals determine the evaluation procedures and distribution of rewards, and, via their behavior, convey to athletes what is valued in that context. For example, coaches can create a mastery motivational climate—in which personal progress is valued—by rewarding individual effort and improvement and creating opportunities for everyone to succeed, or a performance climate in which normative success is valued. Mastery motivational climate has been positively associated with numerous positive achievement-related outcomes in sport (e.g., Roberts, 2012). It is also more likely to promote prosocial and reduce antisocial behavior (see Kavussanu & Al-Yaaribi, 2021).

Performance motivational climate is also created by significant others, such as coaches, who convey to the athletes that normative ability and doing better than others are valued within the team. In this type of climate, coaches reward only the top athletes and give normative feedback, thus communicating to their athletes that they value winning over personal progress (Ames, 1992). Performance motivational climate has been associated with numerous maladaptive achievement and moral outcomes (Kavussanu & Al-Yaaribi, 2021; Roberts, 2012). The normative nature of competition is bound to increase ego involvement, thus, there is no need for additional pressure placed on sport participants by coaches. Instead, we need to teach athletes to focus on, and derive satisfaction from, success that is self-referenced, learning to see competition as an opportunity that will allow them to realize their own athletic potential. Sport competition enables performers to be the best they can be. It pushes their limits. Following the example of inspirational coach John Wooden, practitioners can structure the sport environment in a manner that enables each and every participant to feel valued and given the opportunity to succeed.

References

Ames, C. (1992). Classrooms: Goals, structures, and student motivation. *Journal of Educational Psychology 84*, 261–271. doi:10.1037/0022-0663.84.3.261.

Bandura, A. (1991). Social cognitive theory of moral thought and action. In W. M. Kurtines & J. L. Gewirtz (Eds.), *Handbook of moral behavior and development* (pp. 45–103). Erlbaum.

Baumeister, R. F. (1984). Choking under pressure: Self-consciousness and paradoxical effects of incentives on skillful performance. *Journal of Personality and Social Psychology 46*(3), 610–620. https://doi.org/10.1037/0022-3514.46.3.610.

Beattie, S., Alqallaf, A., & Hardy, L. (2017). The effects of punishment and reward sensitivities on mental toughness and performance in swimming. *International Journal of Sport Psychology 48*(3), 246–261.

Behnke, M., & Kaczmarek, L. D. (2018). Successful performance and cardiovascular markers of challenge and threat: A meta-analysis. *International Journal of Psychophysiology 130*, 73–79.

Bell, J. J., Hardy, L., & Beattie, S. (2013). Enhancing mental toughness and performance under pressure in elite young cricketers: A 2-year longitudinal intervention. *Sport, Exercise, and Performance Psychology 2*(4), 281–297.

Blascovich, J., Seery, M. D., Mugridge, C. A., Norris, R. K., & Weisbuch, M. (2004). Predicting athletic performance from cardiovascular indexes of challenge and threat. *Journal of Experimental Social Psychology 40*(5), 683–688.

Conroy, D. E., Silva, J. M., Newcomer, R. R., Walker, B. W., & Johnson, M. S. (2001). Personal and participatory socializers of the perceived legitimacy of aggressive behavior in sport. *Aggressive Behavior 27*, 405–418.

Cooke, A., Kavussanu, M., McIntyre, D., & Ring, C. (2010). Psychological, muscular and kinematic factors mediate performance under pressure. *Psychophysiology 47*(6), 1109–1118.

Cooke, A., Kavussanu, M., McIntyre, D., & Ring, C. (2011). Effects of competition on endurance performance and the underlying psychological and physiological mechanisms. *Biological Psychology 86*, 370–378.

Cooke, A., Kavussanu, M., McIntyre, D., & Ring, C. (2013). Effects of individual and team competitions on performance, emotions, and effort. *Journal of Sport & Exercise Psychology 35*, 132–143.

Corbetta, M., & Shulman, G. L. (2002). Control of goal-directed and stimulus-driven attention in the brain. *Nature Reviews Neuroscience 3*(3), 201–215.

Dewar, A. J., Kavussanu, M., & Ring, C. (2013). The effect of achievement goals on emotions and performance in a competitive agility task. *Sport, Exercise, and Performance Psychology 2*, 250–264.

Dewar, A., & Kavussanu, M. (2011). Achievement goals and emotions in golf: The mediating and moderating role of perceived performance. *Psychology of Sport and Exercise 12*, 525–532.

Dewar, A., & Kavussanu, M. (2012). Achievement goals and emotions in team sport athletes. *Sport, Exercise, and Performance Psychology 1*, 254–267.

Dweck, C. S. (1986). Motivational processes affecting learning. *American Psychologist 41*(10), 1040–1048.

Eisenberg, N., & Fabes, R. A. (1998). Prosocial development. In N. Eisenberg (Ed.), *Handbook of child psychology, Vol 3: Social, emotional, and personality development* (pp. 701–778). Wiley.

Elliot, A. J., & Church, M. A. (1997). A hierarchical model of approach and avoidance achievement motivation. *Journal of Personality and Social Psychology 72*, 218–232.

Elliot, A. J., & McGregor, H. A. (2001). A 2 × 2 achievement goal framework. *Journal of Personality and Social Psychology 80*(3), 501–519.

Elliot, A. J., Murayama, K., & Pekrun, R. (2011). A 3 × 2 achievement goal model. *Journal of Educational Psychology 103*(3), 632–648.

Eysenck, M. W., & Calvo, M. G. (1992). Anxiety and performance: The processing efficiency theory. *Cognition & Emotion 6*(6), 409–434.

Eysenck, M. W., Derakshan, N., Santos, R., & Calvo, M. G. (2007). Anxiety and cognitive performance: Attentional control theory. *Emotion 7*(2), 336–353.

Eysenck, M. W., & Wilson, M. R. (2016). Sporting performance, pressure and cognition: Introducing Attentional Control Theory in Sport. In D. Groome & M. Eysenck (Eds.), *An introduction to applied cognitive psychology* (pp. 329–350). Psychology Press.

Fitts, P. M., & Posner, M. I. (1967). *Human performance.* Brooks/Cole.

Football Association. (2015). 11 Million footballers in England cannot be wrong! http://www.thefa.com/news/2015/jun/10/11-million-playing-football-in-england.

Gray, R., Orn, A., & Woodman, T. (2017). Ironic and reinvestment effects in baseball pitching: How information about an opponent can influence performance under pressure. *Journal of Sport & Exercise Psychology 39*(1), 3–12.

Hanton, S., Thomas, O., & Maynard, I. (2004). Competitive anxiety responses in the week leading up to competition: The role of intensity, direction and frequency dimensions. *Psychology of Sport and Exercise 5*(2), 169–181.

Hardy, L., Bell, J., & Beattie, S. (2014). A neuropsychological model of mentally tough behavior. *Journal of Personality 82*(1), 69–81.

Hewstone, M., Rubin, M., & Willis, H. (2002). Intergroup bias. *Annual Review of Psychology 53*, 575–604.

Johnson, D. W., & Johnson, R. T. (1989). *Cooperation and competition: Theory and research.* Interaction Book Company.

Jones, J. G., Swain, A., & Cale, A. (1990). Antecedents of multidimensional competitive state anxiety and self-confidence in elite intercollegiate middle-distance runners. *The Sport Psychologist 4*(2), 107–118.

Jones, M., Meijen, C., McCarthy, P. J., & Sheffield, D. (2009). A theory of challenge and threat states in athletes. *International Review of Sport and Exercise Psychology 2*(2), 161–180.

Kavussanu, M. (2019). Toward an understanding of transgressive behavior in sport: Progress and prospects. Special issue of *Psychology of Sport & Exercise 42*, 33–39.

Kavussanu, M., & Al-Yaaribi, A. (2021). Prosocial and antisocial behavior in sport. *International Journal of Sport and Exercise Psychology 19*, 179–202.

Kavussanu, M., & Boardley, I. D. (2009). The prosocial and antisocial behavior in sport scale. *Journal of Sport & Exercise Psychology 31*, 97–117.

Kavussanu, M., Boardley, I. D., Sagar, S., & Ring, C. M. (2013). Bracketed morality revisited: How do athletes behave in two contexts? *Journal of Sport & Exercise Psychology 35*, 449–463.

Kavussanu, M., Dewar, A. J., & Boardley, I. D. (2014). Achievement goals and emotions in athletes: The mediating role of challenge and threat appraisals. *Motivation and Emotion 38*, 589–599.

Kavussanu, M., & Ntoumanis, N. (2003). Participation in sport and moral functioning: Does ego orientation mediate their relationship? *Journal of Sport & Exercise Psychology 25*(4), 1–18.

Kavussanu, M., & Ring, C. (2016). Moral thought and action in sport and student life: A study of bracketed morality. *Ethics and Behavior 26*, 267–276.

Kavussanu, M., & Ring, C. (2021). Bracketed morality in adolescent football players: A tale of two contexts. *Psychology of Sport and Exercise 53*, 101835. https://doi.org/10.1016/j.psychsport.2020.101835.

Lane, A. M., & Terry, P. C. (2000). The nature of mood: Development of a conceptual model with a focus on depression. *Journal of Applied Sport Psychology 12*, 16–33.

Masters, R. S. (1992). Knowledge, knerves and know-how: The role of explicit versus implicit knowledge in the breakdown of a complex motor skill under pressure. *British Journal of Psychology 83*(3), 343–358.

Masters, R., & Maxwell, J. (2008). The theory of reinvestment. *International Review of Sport and Exercise Psychology 1*(2), 160–183.

McEnroe, J., & Kaplan, J. (2002). *Serious*. Little, Brown.

Meijen, C., Turner, M., Jones, M. V., Sheffield, D., & McCarthy, P. (2020). A theory of challenge and threat states in athletes: A revised conceptualization. *Frontiers in Psychology 11*, 126. doi: 10.3389/fpsyg.2020.00126.

Moore, L. J., Wilson, M. R., Vine, S. J., Coussens, A. H., & Freeman, P. (2013). Champ or chump? Challenge and threat states during pressurized competition. *Journal of Sport & Exercise Psychology 35*(6), 551–562.

Nicholls, J. G. (1989). *The competitive ethos and democratic education*. Harvard University Press.

Ring, C., & Kavussanu, M. (2018). The impact of achievement goals on cheating in sport. *Psychology of Sport and Exercise 35*, 98–103.

Roberts, G. C. (2012). Motivation in sport and exercise from an achievement goal theory perspective: After 30 years, where are we? In G. C. Roberts & D. C. Treasure (Eds.), *Advances in motivation in sport and exercise* (pp. 5–58). Human Kinetics.

Roberts, R., Cooke, A., Woodman, T., Hupfeld, H., Barwood, C., & Manley, H. (2019). When the going gets tough, who gets going? An examination of the relationship between narcissism, effort, and performance. *Sport, Exercise, and Performance Psychology 8*(1), 93–105.

Sage, L., & Kavussanu, M. (2007). The effects of goal involvement on moral behavior in an experimentally manipulated competitive setting. *Journal of Sport & Exercise Psychology 29*, 190–207.

Stanne, M. B., Johnson, D. W., & Johnson, R. T. (1999). Does competition enhance or inhibit motor performance: A meta-analysis. *Psychological Bulletin 125*(1), 133–154.

Tauer, J. M., & Harackiewicz, J. M. (2004). The effects of cooperation and competition on intrinsic motivation and performance. *Journal of Personality and Social Psychology 86*(6), 849–861.

Tjosvold, D., Zhang, X., Li, W. Chen, Y., & Zhang, H. (2019). Open-minded discussion: A meta-analytic evaluation of cooperation and competition theory. *Academy of Management*, Proceedings, 1. https://doi.org/10.5465/AMBPP.2019.16186abstract.

Triplett, N. (1898). The dynamogenic factors in pace-making and competition. *The American Journal of Psychology 9*(4), 507–533.

Uphill, M. A., & Jones, M. V. (2007). Antecedents of emotions in elite athletes: A cognitive motivational relational theory perspective. *Research Quarterly for Exercise and Sport 78*, 79–89.

van de Pol, P. K. C., & Kavussanu, M. (2011). Achievement goals and motivational consequences in tennis: Does the context matter? *Psychology of Sport and Exercise 12*, 176–183.

van de Pol, P. K. C., & Kavussanu, M. (2012). Achievement motivation across training and competition in individual and team sports. *Sport, Exercise, and Performance Psychology 1*, 91–105.

van de Pol, P. K. C., Kavussanu, M., & Ring, C. (2012a). The effects of training and competition on achievement goals, motivational responses, and performance in a golf-putting task. *Journal of Sport & Exercise Psychology 34*, 787–807.

van de Pol, P. K. C., Kavussanu, M., & Ring, C. (2012b). Goal orientations, perceived motivational climate, and motivational responses in football: A comparison between training and competition contexts. *Psychology of Sport and Exercise 13*, 491–499.

Vine, S. J., Moore, L. J., Cooke, A., Ring, C., & Wilson, M. R. (2013). Quiet eye training: A means to implicit motor learning. *International Journal of Sport Psychology 44*(4), 367–386.

Wallace, H. M., & Baumeister, R. F. (2002). The performance of narcissists rises and falls with perceived opportunity for glory. *Journal of Personality and Social Psychology 82*(5), 819–834.

Williams, M., & Thomas, S. (2008). *The magnificent seven*. John Blake Publishing.

Wilson, M. R., Wood, G., & Vine, S. J. (2009). Anxiety, attentional control, and performance impairment in penalty kicks. *Journal of Sport & Exercise Psychology 31*(6), 761–775.

Wooden, J., & Carty, J. (2010). *Coach Wooden's pyramid of success*. McGraw Hill.

Woodman, T., Roberts, R., Hardy, L., Callow, N., & Rogers, C. H. (2011). There is an "I" in TEAM: Narcissism and social loafing. *Research Quarterly for Exercise and Sport 82*(2), 285–290.

Competition in Education

Fabrizio Butera, Wojciech Świątkowski, *and* Benoît Dompnier

Abstract

In this chapter, the authors delineate how competition circulates through education. First, the authors show how competitive ideologies, values, and norms are transmitted from society to educational institutions, in particular ideologies and values such as meritocracy, the belief in a fair free market, and neoliberalism, as well as norms such as productivism and employability. Second, the authors review the competitive structures and climates within educational institutions that shape students' values, goals, and behaviors, in particular structures such as normative assessment, tracking, and *numerus clausus*, as well as climates such as classroom climate, goal structures, and error climate. Third, the authors report research that documents the impact of students' competitive values, goals, and behaviors on educational outcomes, from learning and achievement to social relations. Finally, the authors conclude by reflecting on how such a socialization of students may impact society in a feedback loop, either in terms of maintenance of the status quo or in terms of social change.

Key Words: meritocracy, neoliberalism, normative assessment, tracking, performance goals, socialization

Competition in Education

Competition is a ubiquitous factor in educational institutions, from their organizational values and norms to the socialization of students. In the present chapter we adopt a social influence approach and discuss how competitive values and norms are transmitted from society to educational institutions; how competitive structures within these institutions shape students' values, goals, and behaviors; and how such a socialization of students may impact society in a feedback loop (see Figure 25.1). In doing so, we limit our analysis to mechanisms at work in industrialized countries, as it is in these countries that the vast majority of studies have been conducted.

Competitive Societies

Educational systems (from kindergarten to higher education) are the institutions in charge of the transmission of knowledge and skills through the generations, and as such they are

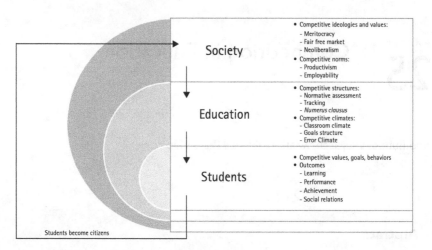

Figure 25.1 A Multi-Level Depiction of Competition in Education

deeply rooted in the social functioning of the societies in which they are embedded. As a matter of fact, the history of modern educational systems has been one of dependency from state-driven policies and specific demands from the economy. In several historical accounts of the development of educational systems, the emergence and rise of generalized education appears to be linked to the development of nation-states (e.g., Archer, 2013). For example, Green (1990) notes that from the nineteenth century onwards, "education system came to assume a primary responsibility for the moral, cultural and political development of the nation" (p. 13), by forging the country's national identity through the promotion of dominant values, habits, language, religion, and political and economic creeds. Such a tight relationship between the development of the nation-state and the formal organization of education is apparent in the training of the ruling class, but also in the expansion of mass education. For example, a study carried out with enrollment data of over 120 countries for the period 1870–1980 revealed that "mass education spread around the world with the spread of the Western system, with its joined principles of national citizenship and state authority" (Meyer et al., 1992, p. 146). Actually, archival data showed that well before the modern organization of educational institutions, during the Middle Ages, higher education was controlled by power-holders (kings, princes, popes) and used as a means to shape the political and administrative organization of a given territory, "by training individuals for specific professional statuses" (Goastellec, 2020, p. 287, our translation).

It is therefore unsurprising that educational systems evolve as a function of the historical, political, cultural, and economic context of a given country, both in terms of the specific policies that lie at the core of its organization and in terms of the dominant culture it vehiculates (e.g., Perry, 2009). Indeed, several authors have noted that education transmits the dominant values and ideologies of a given society (Zajda, 2009) and

FABRIZIO BUTERA, WOJCIECH ŚWIĄTKOWSKI, AND BENOÎT DOMPNIER

socializes children in such values and ideologies (Apple, 2018; Bronfenbrenner, 1977). In particular, as far as competition is concerned, it has been argued that competitive values and ideologies at the societal level spill over into educational policies and practices (Rich & DeVitis, 1992), and that there is a growing call in industrialized countries for increased competitive selection and excellence in education (Van de Werfhorst, 2014). Which are, then, the competitive ideologies and values of industrialized countries that surround their educational systems?

COMPETITIVE IDEOLOGIES AND VALUES

System justification theory posits that people are motivated to justify the existing social order of the society in which they live, both to reduce uncertainty in life and avoid questioning the legitimacy of the social system (Jost et al., 2004). People living in industrialized, capitalist countries are therefore motivated to adhere to a set of interrelated competitive ideologies such as meritocracy and the fairness of free-market economy (Jost & Hunyady, 2005), as well as neoliberalism (Beauvois, 2005).

Meritocracy

The belief that upward social mobility is available to the entire population also called the "American dream," lays its foundations on the ideology of merit: People are rewarded as a function of their effort and ability, and not because they belong to a specific (privileged) social group (e.g., Son Hing et al., 2011). In other words, meritocracy refers to the belief that in a competitive society—where privileged positions in terms of wealth, power, and prestige are scarce—all citizens can potentially access such positions, provided they display greater levels of effort and ability than others (Butera, 2006). This ideology is so pervasive in industrial societies, and the "rhetoric of rising" so widespread, that support spans the entire political spectrum from left to right (Sandel, 2020). However, although democratic societies are in theory permeable and allow upward social mobility, research showed that belonging to an underprivileged or discriminated group represents in fact a disadvantage (McNamee & Miller, 2004), as competition does not take place in a level playing field but rather reproduces existing inequalities (Haney & Hurtado, 1994; Son Hing et al., 2002). Nevertheless, people believe in meritocracy and justify existing inequalities in terms of lack of ability or effort (Son Hing et al., 2011), even when they belong to an underprivileged group (Jost et al., 2003b).

The same applies to educational systems. Merit, and not wealth, has been the basic principle used to assess and promote pupils in schools, ever since the American and French revolutions (Butera et al., 2021). Merit is also the principle that justifies equal access to all children in primary education, following the call for generalized, free, and compulsory education formulated in the Universal Declaration of Human rights: Children are granted equal opportunities, and then relative ability and effort determine the subsequent educational path that they will follow (Batruch et al., 2019a). Again, even though the school system appears to reproduce existing social disparities (Bourdieu & Passeron, 1977; Falcon, 2012), pupils and parents by and large believe in school meritocracy (Darnon et al., 2018a, 2018b; Duru-Bellat & Tenret, 2012; Wiederkehr et al., 2015b), even disadvantaged pupils (Wiederkehr et al., 2015a). According to these authors, belief in school meritocracy plays a palliative role for disadvantaged pupils in dealing with an uncertain future. Indeed, school meritocracy feeds the belief that class boundaries are permeable and that at least some disadvantaged pupils will be able to achieve upward social mobility (a phenomenon also called *tokenism*, cf. Wright, 2001). To conclude this section with a quote from a famous article on merit in education by Deutsch (1979, p. 379), "merit based on individual performance will be the dominant principle of distributive justice in situations where an economic orientation predominates"; that is where competition predominates.

Fair, Free Market

The association between the economy and competition is epitomized by the free-market ideology. Although markets in capitalist countries can be more or less regulated by state institutions (Hall & Gingerich, 2009), the concept of free market has become an ideology. As noted by Piketty (2020), markets, profits, and capital are historical constructs, mainly coined and used for political motives. Importantly, Jost et al. (2003a) have remarked that, although market-driven inequalities have been on the rise for the past four decades (Frank & Cook, 1995; Piketty, 2020), the free-market ideology seems well accepted by the general public. Jost et al. (2003a) even noted that in a large-scale Gallup poll, the majority of American respondents considered that the economic system is fair, including more than a half of the low-income respondents (p. 56). Thus, because free-market ideology represents the *status quo*, people who are motivated to justify the existing social order are likely to accept such an ideology as being fair (Jost & Hunyady, 2005).

Several scholars have noted that, in industrialized countries, the corporate models of the market economy have been used to shape the competitive functioning of, and values transmitted in, public education (e.g., Apple, 2006; Engel, 2000). Entrepreneurial efficiency, unconstrained competition, and the market's permanent quest for performance are metaphors that school managers have adopted to promote the idea that competition in education can boost performance just like it can in the marketplace (Apple, 2006). This state of affairs has produced two intertwined trends of public and scholarly debate. On the one hand, the question of "school choice"—parents' freedom to choose the best school for their children—has fueled the debate on whether or not a market of freely competing schools leads to a more efficient and effective education system (e.g., Dudley-Marling, 2020; Jabbar et al., 2019). On the other hand, the question of merit pay for teachers— paying teachers as a function of their results—has fueled the debate on whether or not paying teachers as a function of performance does indeed promote their performance (e.g., Dee & Keys, 2004; Nathaniel et al., 2016). Whatever the answer to these questions, and the jury is still out, research shows that there is a clear tendency to transfer market-level policies, in particular competitive ones, to education-level practices.

Neoliberalism

"Neoliberalism, originally a loose economic theory, has evolved into a sociopolitical ideology and extended its hegemonic influence to all areas of life (. . .)" (Bettache & Chiu, 2019, p. 9). This quote is taken from the introductory article to a special issue on the social psychology of neoliberalism in the *Journal of Social Issues*, and it summarizes how yet another competitive ideology has spilled over well beyond the political and economic spheres. As noted by Plehwe (2009), since its inception in the 1920s, and through its formalization by the Mont Pélerin Society, neoliberalism promoted the idea that only effective competitive markets and decentralized control can foster individual liberty, via freedom to choose one's employment or means of production, select ways and goods to consume, and manage one's life choices and outcomes. The transfer from the emphasis on the importance of economic exchange in a free marketplace to the entrepreneurialization of all personal activities and social relationships is also a major feature of the depiction of neoliberalism made by several philosophers and psychologists, from Foucault (1984/2010) to Beauvois (2005).

Although neoliberalism has been criticized for having generic political, economic, and philosophical underpinnings, its influence has been steadily growing, with a peak in the 1980s and the advent of the Thatcher–Reagan era (Bettache & Chiu, 2019). If we focus on the psychological consequences of living in a neoliberal environment, research has shown that making neoliberalism salient reduces feelings of bonding with, and trust toward others, both in traditionally capitalistic countries (Hartwich & Becker, 2019) and in a transition economy like China (Zhang & Xin, 2019). Kasser et al. (2007) made a similar analysis and showed how what is called American corporate capitalism—an ideology whose description is similar to that of neoliberalism—promotes a set of goals, namely self-interest, financial success, and competition, that conflict with pro-social goals such as being helpful, honest, loyal, and caring for other. Some authors have even noted that such an influence is also apparent in the way mainstream psychological science has developed: "Neoliberal systems build on and reinforce characteristic psychological tendencies of liberal individualism—including radical abstraction of self from context, an entrepreneurial understanding of self as an ongoing development project, an imperative for personal growth and fulfillment, and an emphasis on affect management for self-regulation" (Adams et al., 2019).

Neoliberalism's "hegemonic influence to all areas of life" extends to education. Two trends of research that have emerged to study such an extension are of interest for the question of competition in education. On the one hand, it has been noted that teachers are increasingly under pressure to abide by the representation of their profession as an entrepreneurial activity, with enhanced accountability as regards their productivity (e.g.,

Attick, 2017). On the other hand, the competitive climate that permeates schools and universities in neoliberal societies has prompted in students a representation of education as a means of prevailing in the struggle for a valuable position in the marketplace, thereby maximizing their future salary (e.g., Busch, 2017). These trends underline that the neoliberal ideology has far-reaching consequences in the educational systems of countries that espouse it, from the representation of what teaching is worth to the representation of what learning is for.

Ideologies and Values

In the above sections, we have discussed the links between competitive ideologies and values on the one hand and educational systems on the other hand. This may have suggested that we treat ideologies and values as interchangeable concepts, and we must now specify the relationship they entertain with each other. Values are defined as higher-order life goals at the individual level (Schwartz et al., 2012), but they are influenced by a country's dominant higher-order social goals that are part of the dominant ideologies in that country. Such a relationship is illustrated in a study on the link between the level of deregulated capitalism in industrialized countries and the adherence of these countries' population to competitive values (Schwartz, 2007). More precisely, this study has correlated the degree to which a set of OECD countries pursue neoliberal free-market capitalism (on an index ranging from strategic to competitive market coordination) with the level of self-enhancement values of power and achievement reported by people living in those countries. The results have shown a positive association between the neoliberal pursuit of competitive market coordination and the adherence to competitive self-enhancement values. In sum, there appears to be a link between ideologies that regulate the political and economic life of a country, and the values that its citizens adopt.

COMPETITIVE NORMS

In addition to the competitive ideologies and values reviewed above, educational systems are also submitted to the influence of competitive norms. Unlike ideologies and values, which provide the cultural context in which educational institutions are embedded, norms provide direct guidance as to the desired outcomes that education should deliver. Most modern industrialized countries have developed tools aimed at monitoring the performance of students, schools, and local authorities, and use those tools as a means to regulate their educational systems. Indeed, several studies have shown that international standardized testing, such as the Programme for International Student Assessment (PISA), has fulfilled this specific role in most OECD countries (Mons, 2009). In this respect, we refer here to injunctive norms, i.e., those that specify the behaviors and outcomes a given society approves or disapproves of, along with the set of measures intended to reward or punish normative and counter-normative behaviors (Cialdini et al., 1991).

Two competitive norms appear to be particularly relevant for educational institutions: productivism and employability.

Productivism

Productivism, also called performativity, refers to the call for schools and universities to train pupils and students to acquire skills needed in the job market (Lyotard, 1984). The development of knowledge is therefore subordinated to the criteria of usefulness, salability, and efficiency of the training (Segal, 2014). Productivism has been identified as a fundamental norm in modern societies because the production of useful skills in pupils and students is seen as a guarantee of economic growth (Anderson, 2008). As a consequence, the evaluation of schools, teachers, and students is based on the same competitive criteria as in the job market, in particular their potential economic worth.

Employability

Parallel to productivism, employability is an indicator of performance for educational institutions, in particular vocational training (e.g., Kratz et al., 2019) and higher education (e.g., Morley, 2001). Employability is to be considered as a norm because it exerts pressure on the educational system to produce individuals that will be useful and adaptable to the job market (Masdonati et al., in press). Human capital is "the stock of individual skills, competencies and qualifications" (Morley, 2001, p. 132), and in industrialized countries higher education is meant to provide these skills, competencies, and qualifications, following an input-output logic. In this respect, employability is an end for higher education, but also a means for society, to the extent that higher employability is seen as competitive advantage in the global market (Knight & Yorke, 2004).

COMPETITION FROM SOCIETY TO EDUCATIONAL SYSTEMS

In this section we have discussed the competitive ideologies and values—in particular, meritocracy, free market, and neoliberalism—that constitute the backbone of most capitalist countries. Given their pervasive nature and the need for system justification that they induce (Jost & Hunyady, 2005), they appear to permeate all areas of activity in a given society, including education. We have also discussed the competitive norms—in particular, productivism and employability—that define the quality of an educational system as a function of its ability to produce outcomes that will serve the competitive nature of the marketplace. But how does competition flow from society to education?

The link between competition at the social and educational levels has been well documented in a comparative study with more than thirty countries. The higher the economic competition and the influence of diplomas on salary, the stronger the implementation of competitive structures in the educational system (Dubet et al., 2010). Two major features of educational systems account for such a transfer of competition: competitive selection structures and competitive climates. On the one hand, competitive ideologies and norms promote a hierarchical representation of society whereby some individuals and groups are seen as having higher worth than others. For instance, meritocracy requires that some individuals receive greater rewards because of their higher level of effort and ability (Mijs, 2016). As a consequence, educational systems are equipped with tools that allow educators and assessors to measure differential merit and distribute differential rewards. The next section will focus on three such tools, namely normative assessment, tracking, and *numerus clausus*. On the other hand, competitive ideologies and norms are internalized by teachers who transmit them to their classrooms (Pérez Gómez, 1998). Teachers know that students should be able to adapt to a neoliberal economy (Davies & Bansel, 2007), and that their worth will also be judged based on their ability to present themselves as independent, autonomous, and accountable individuals (Pansu et al., 2008). As a consequence, teachers reproduce in their classroom the competitive ethos present in society at large (Nicholls, 1989) by creating a competitive climate. The next section will focus in particular on classroom climate, goal structure, and error climate (see Figure 25.1).

Competitive Educational Systems

In the context of competitive societies, educational systems have developed two intertwined sets of competitive features, namely competitive selection structures and competitive teaching climates.

COMPETITIVE STRUCTURES

The educational function of educational systems—the role of improving the knowledge and skills of pupils and students—is probably their most relevant, salient, and noticeable feature, almost a tautology. However, a number of studies have noted that selection is an equally central feature of educational systems, as it corresponds to the function to "provide a rational means of selecting persons in order that the most able and motivated persons are sorted into the highest status positions" (Dornbusch, 1996, p. 405). In line with the meritocratic principle, such a function is considered to help society match abilities and effort with more or less valued positions in the social hierarchy (e.g., Dubet & Duru-Bellat, 2004). It also acts as a filter that assigns students to the economic roles that they merit, based on their educational performance (Arrow, 1973). Although not advertised as the most desirable function, selection is so well rooted in the educational system that students recognize that pursuing competitive goals is indeed useful to succeed in the system (Darnon et al., 2009; Dompnier et al., 2008). Because selection is a major role of educational systems, several structures have been developed to ensure that selection actually takes place. Here we discuss three such structures, namely normative assessment, tracking, and *numerus clausus*.

Normative Assessment

Educational critic Alfie Kohn recently reported that, according to Harvard political science professor Harvey Mansfield, "the essence of grading is exclusiveness" (Kohn, 2019). This blunt statement summarizes the strong relationship between grades and normative assessment. Grades take different forms in different systems—letters, numbers, percentages—but they all aim at quantifying pupils' and students' performance (Glaser, 1963). Whether or not grading systems that are, and have been, used accurately represent the students' performance is still under debate (e.g., Rom, 2011). In this chapter, however, we focus on the functions of grading, rather than its accuracy, and in particular its contribution to the selection function of educational systems.

Grades can be used to represent the extent to which a student has learned, as compared to a desired standard; this is generally termed "criterion-referenced assessment" (e.g., Glaser, 1963). For example, a grade of seventy-five percent may indicate that three-quarters of a lesson has been learned or that three-quarters of the answers in a test were correct. Grades can also be used to provide a formative feedback, accompanied by detailed comments, aimed at providing the students with useful information as to improve their learning; this is generally termed "formative assessment" (e.g., Black & Wiliam, 2009). However, in the vast majority of systems, grades are used because they make performance easy to compare across students (Knight & Yorke, 2003), which in turn allows teachers to make selective and competitive decisions such as retention, awards, and ranking. In this respect, grades are used most of the time as "norm-referenced" or "normative" assessments (Pulfrey et al., 2011; 2013). In other words, competence is considered as other-based in normative assessment—unlike criterion-referenced and formative assessment, where competence is task-based and self-based, respectively (Elliot et al., 2011)—which encourages and justifies comparison across students (Butera & Darnon, 2017).

The competitive nature of normative assessment has two important consequences on assessment itself. First, if assessment is comparative, teachers' judgment of each of their pupils depends on the average level of the relevant group of pupils, usually the classroom. This phenomenon is known as the "context effect" and is defined as the fact that "after factoring out actual performance, it appears that a pupil is judged better in a classroom in which the average achievement level is low than another pupil in a classroom in which this level is high" (Dompnier et al., 2006, p. 120). The second, related consequence is that such comparative effects can also be found at the school level, whereby "equally able students earned higher grades in lower ability schools" (Marsh, 1987, p. 280). Thus, normative assessment leads evaluators to distribute grades as a function of the need to produce a ranking among students, rather than as a function of actual performance.

This state of affairs explains why "the essence of grading is exclusiveness": As soon as grading is used as a normative assessment tool, and it is most of the time, only some students can get the highest grades and the benefits in terms of academic and social positions that will follow from those grades. Such an association between selection and grades is clearly perceived by students. Autin et al. (2015) showed that the more students believed that the role of the educational system is to select, the more favorable they were toward the use of normative assessment. In a nutshell, normative grading is the tool that facilitates decision-making in a competitive and selective system.

Tracking

Decision-making in a competitive and selective system often implies tracking (also called streaming), which is defined as "the practice of assigning students to instructional groups on the basis of ability" (Hallinan, 1994, p. 79). In other words, students compete to access the more prestigious instructional groups or curricula. All OECD countries implement one type of tracking or another (OECD, 2013). Some countries divide students of the same class, school, or curriculum into ability groups, that is groups in which the same subject is more or less demanding depending on the group. Other countries send students of different ability to different schools or curricula, for instance to vocational or academic programs (Batruch et al., 2019b).

Although it has been argued that tracking allows the provision of a better fit between specific curricula and the students' specific needs and ability (Chmielewski, 2014; Hallinan, 1994), the difference between tracks is not merely descriptive or functional. Different tracks lead to different diplomas that give access to more or less prestigious professional and social positions. And, indeed, research has shown that tracking systems reproduce existing social hierarchies, as students from privileged social classes are overrepresented in more prestigious tracks (e.g., Duru-Bellat, 1996; Van de Werfhorst & Mijs, 2010). It is worth noting that research on tracking reveals a network of strong relationships between meritocracy at the ideological level, and normative grading and tracking at the structural level. In countries where meritocracy is a dominant ideology, more or less prestigious professional and social positions are occupied as a function of more or less prestigious diplomas, earned by attending more or less prestigious curricula whose access is determined by higher or lower grades (a mechanism also called "predictive assessment," assessment that provides information for decisions about admission, cf. Allal, 2010).

Numerus Clausus

Another way to select students is *numerus clausus*, a Latin expression that means "closed number" and refers to a curriculum that accepts only a fixed number or proportion of students (Spence, 1981). In most OECD countries, *numerus clausus* has been mainly used to regulate the number of students that enter medical and nursing training (Moreira & Lafortune, 2016), but it can be found in many high-prestige curricula in higher education, such as Law and Business Administration, as well as in private schools of all levels. Each school and university has its specific rules, but two main types of *numerus clausus* can be found (Sommet et al., 2013). On the one hand, pre-curriculum selection takes place when students must take an exam (and/or must present their past grades) to enter a specific curriculum. As a function of the needs and requirements of that curriculum, only a certain number or proportion of the students will be allowed to enter, selecting those with the highest results on the admission exam. On the other hand, in-curriculum selection takes place when students are evaluated on the basis of the results of their first year. In this case, many institutions standardize grades in order to make comparison and selection easier (Kaufman, 1994).

Interestingly, as far as competition is concerned, the students who are confronted with such systems clearly perceive the competitive pressure, even though quite often—especially in the case of in-curriculum selection—*numerus clausus* is hidden. Indeed, in a series of three studies with university students, Sommet et al. (2013) showed that students in departments with *numerus clausus* developed lower levels of self-efficacy than students in departments without *numerus clausus*. The same was found when comparing students who believed or not that *numerus clausus* was in force in their department (in a department where it was hidden), and when comparing students in an experiment where the presence vs. absence of *numerus clausus* was manipulated. Self-efficacy is an interesting measure because it highlights the effect of *numerus clausus*: Students understand that they are in a relation of negative interdependence with the other (aspirant) students, and their self-efficacy is therefore reduced because their chance of succeeding is not only determined by how much they study, but also by how much their contenders do. A structure that creates objective negative interdependence perfectly fits the classic definition of competition (Deutsch, 1949).

COMPETITIVE CLIMATES

Competitive structures in educational institutions are shaped by democratic deliberation and political decision-making, at least as far as public education is concerned. There is, however, a less institutionalized mechanism that promotes competition in education, namely the implementation of competitive climates in schools and especially classrooms. Teachers are socialized to adopt a competitive ethos and to apply the neoliberal principle of performance accountability in their professional practice (Webb et al., 2009). In this respect, not only do they work in and with the existing competitive structures (normative grading and tracking), but they also create competitive climates. In this section, we discuss how this is done through classroom climate, goals structure, and error climate.

Classroom Climate

Narrative and meta-analytical reviews of work on classroom climate have documented the relationship between this construct and a wealth of academic, behavioral, and socio-emotional outcomes (Fraser, 1989; Wang et al., 2020a). They have also documented the important variations in how classroom climate has been operationalized—for example, teaching quality, classroom organization, teacher–student relationship—although the variability found in the literature can be reduced to three basic components that refer to teacher–student interactions: instructional support, socioemotional support, and classroom organization and management (Wang et al., 2020a). School-level mechanisms have also been identified as important in the development of specific climates (Wang & Degol, 2016), but Wang et al. (2020a, 2020b) have noted that proximal processes, like those occurring in the interaction between teachers and students, are more likely to yield substantial and long-lasting influence, as they are the ones that students experience daily and over an extended period of time.

In their meta-analysis, Wang et al. (2020a) report that performance-based and socially comparative instructional practices appear to negatively affect important psychological needs such as competence and relatedness (Ryan & Deci, 2000; see also Wang, 2012). As noted above when discussing *numerus clausus*, the presence of a competitive structure affects the representation of students' own competence, to the extent that one's competence is negatively interdependent with the competence of others—the same holds for competitive climates.

Goal Structure

Instructional practices also influence the specific goal structure of a given classroom (e.g., Kaplan et al., 2002). The work initiated by Ames and Archer (1988), and formalized by Ames (1992a, 1992b), identified five key dimensions in such practices that are likely to influence the goals of the students socialized in a given class. Her TARGET system proposed that the five organizing dimensions are task assignments (T), authority relations (A), recognition systems (R), grouping procedures (G), evaluation practices (E), and use of time (T). Based on this work, Midgely and colleagues developed an instrument, the Patterns of Adaptive Learning Survey (PALS) that measures how students perceive the goal structure in their classroom (Anderman & Midgely, 2002; Midgely et al., 2000): Their research showed that students concur in their perception of the surrounding goal structure, which also happens to be in line with the goal structure that teachers report about their class (see also Urdan et al., 1998).

Importantly, the literature review conducted by Meece et al. (2006) reveals that there is a consistent relationship between the goal structure in which the students are embedded and the goals they endorse. In particular, they found ample evidence that students who perceive that their teachers promote competition for grades and social comparisons of ability—e.g., "My teacher calls on smart students more than on other students" or "My teacher tells us how we compare with other students"—also develop competitive goals of their own, such as for instance "I want to do better than other students in my class." Thus, the competitive goals that teachers set for students of their class through their instructional practices create a competitive goal structure that the students perceive and recognize, and with which they align their own goals. Actually, subsequent research has shown that classroom goal structure and personal achievement goals may be tied in three different ways: (a) classroom goal structure predict personal achievement goals, as noted above; (b) they can be parallel processes; and (c) they can interact (Murayama & Elliot, 2009). Interestingly, repeated exposure to a competitive structure may create a self-sufficient competitive ethos that requires little additional input from the teachers. Indeed, a recent study has shown that when students have internalized competition (trait competitiveness), they project competition onto their environment (perceived environmental competitiveness): " . . . a highly competitive person may enter an achievement situation, construe it as highly competitive, and behave accordingly, which may lead others in that situation to respond with competitive behavior in reciprocal fashion. In this way, competitiveness projection can be self-fulfilling" (Elliot et al., 2018, p. 361).

Error Climate

Among instructional practices, teachers' interpretation of the nature and consequences of errors appears to be highly important for their students in decoding the possibly competitive climate of a given classroom. Although errors have been described by several scholars as an opportunity for learning (e.g., Kapur, 2008; Zamora et al., 2018), they are used in everyday assessment as a basis for grading, especially in standardized, end-of-the-year or summative tests, as well as in predictive assessment. Thus, students know too well that errors may have far-reaching consequences on their grades and the future of their education. Teachers, however, do not hold uniform attitudes toward errors, and students perceive that errors may be more or less tolerated or even encouraged. This corresponds to what has been called "perceived error climate" (Steuer et al., 2013). These authors have described perceived error climate as a "bundle of interrelated, but nevertheless distinguishable aspects of the learning environment" (p. 198). Four aspects relate to the teacher (Error tolerance by the teacher, Irrelevance of errors for assessment, Teacher support following errors, Absence of negative teacher reactions), two aspects relate to the reactions of classmates (Absence of negative classmate reactions and Taking the error risk), and two aspects relate to the process of learning from errors (Analysis of errors and Functionality of errors for learning). Importantly, their multi-level analysis revealed that these dimensions also appear at the class level, thereby suggesting that such perceptions indeed constitute a climate. Their results also showed that perceived error climate is related to, but separate from perceived classroom goal structure, and uniquely predicts learners' individual reactions to errors.

The role of teachers in the development of the error climate has been documented by several correlational and observational studies (Santagata, 2005; Tulis, 2013), and more recently by an experimental study (Soncini et al., 2021). In the latter, the manipulation of error handling via a fictitious teacher (more punitive vs. more supportive) significantly affected the pupils' perception of the error climate between a pre- and a post-test. In sum, errors are routinely used to rank and select students, as they provide an important basis for grading, but they may be used to promote learning. This line of research shows that students adapt their reaction to errors as a function of the more punitive and selective vs. promotive and supporting view of errors conveyed by their teachers.

In this section we have discussed the educational structures—in particular, normative assessment, tracking, and *numerus clausus*—that promote competition among students. We have also discussed the climates implemented by teachers' instructional practices—in particular, classroom climate, goal structure, and error climate—that encourage more or less competitive reactions in students. Now, how does competition move from the educational environment, with its structures and climates, to the functioning of students? In this section, we have already noted that the environment in which students are embedded (e.g., goal structure) is likely to affect students' functioning (e.g., the goals they endorse).

This is consistent with work on educational socialization. In particular, regarding socialization with competitive ideologies, a cross-sectional study showed that people who have studied business are more likely than those who have studied social sciences to endorse the dominant ideology (Baer, 1990). Moreover, a longitudinal study showed that university students enrolled in a commerce department (but not students in social sciences) became more favorable to capitalism and more prone to attribute poverty to internal dispositions over the course of their curriculum (Guimond & Palmer, 1996; see also Guimond, 2001). Such socialization processes also concern other constructs, for example competitive goals (Świątkowski & Dompnier, 2017), and in fact any other individual factor. Indeed, the Social Comparison Model of Competition holds that individual factors (e.g., individual differences in competitiveness) are embedded in contextual factors (e.g., incentive structures such as grading), and together they elicit social comparison concerns and competitive behavior (Garcia et al., 2013). In line with such a socialization approach, four studies revealed that competitive goals are effectively transmitted from leaders (coaches, PhD supervisors, team leaders, and teachers) to followers (soccer players, PhD students, video-games players, and pupils) over time (Sommet et al., 2017). The next section will focus on individual-level competitive values, goals, and behaviors (see Figure 25.1).

Competitive Students

In a complex and integrated system such as the circulation of competition within society, it is important to consider the role of individual-level variables such as values, goals, and behaviors. On the one hand, they are influenced by the surrounding ideologies and structures through the socialization of students, as noted above. On the other hand, they represent sometimes stable dispositions that ensure long-lasting consequences of the socialization or contextual effects.

COMPETITIVE VALUES

The study of values has a long history in psychology; here we will only focus on the Schwartz (1992) theory of basic human values because it is by far the most widespread framework, and because it organizes values in a structure that explicitly identifies competitive values.

In this framework, values are defined as "trans-situational goals, varying in importance, that serve as guiding principles in the life of a person or group. (. . .) basic values are organized into a coherent system that underlies and can help to explain individual decision making, attitudes, and behavior" (Schwartz et al., 2012, p. 664). Schwartz and colleagues have shown that the structure of values is the same across situations and cultures (Schwartz et al., 2001), and that it comprises nineteen values (in the latest version of the model, Schwartz et al., 2012). These values are organized in a circumplex that opposes four higher-order goals: openness to change values are opposed to conservation values, and self-transcendence values are opposed to self-enhancement values. The latter is the most relevant category for the present chapter. Self-enhancement higher-order values refer to the pursuit of one's own interest, and their core basic values are achievement and power. In this respect, not only are self-enhancement values individualistic values, but they are also competitive values in that power implies domination over others.

The stable structure of values notwithstanding, their relative importance varies across individuals, situations, and countries. Actually, the theory holds that it is the relative importance of values that guides behavior (Schwartz, 1992). For example, self-enhancement values are present in all value systems, but it is the prioritization of these values over the others that accounts for competitive behaviors. Interestingly, and as noted above, Schwartz (2007) showed that self-enhancement values are endorsed to a higher extent in countries adhering to neoliberal free-market capitalism. A recent study tested the idea that in all fields of study in higher education self-enhancement values are predominant, which is at odds with values prioritized by female students, thereby reducing their feelings of belonging (Aelenei et al., 2020). The results indeed showed that if success was defined in terms of self-enhancement values, female—more than male—students expressed a lower sense of belonging, reported lower self-efficacy, and were less likely to pursue a given academic opportunity, whatever the field of study. In sum, competitive ideologies lead educational systems to prioritize self-enhancement values, which creates unequal chances between students who prioritize these values to a lower or higher extent.

COMPETITIVE GOALS

Goals are crucial in guiding individuals toward a specific action, given their dispositional tendencies and situational constraints (Elliot & Niesta, 2009). This area of research is vast, and here we focus on achievement goals, defined as the "purpose (. . .) or cognitive-dynamic focus (. . .) of competence-relevant behavior" (Elliot & McGregor, 2001, p. 501). These goals vary as a function of their definition—whether they are mastery goals, focusing on intra-individual standards of competence, or performance goals, focusing on normative and comparative standards. They also vary as a function of their valence— whether they are directed toward approaching success or avoiding failure. Performance goals, be they approach- or avoidance-oriented, are relevant in competitive situations, especially in educational contexts (Darnon et al., 2012), as they focus on relative competence and seek to position one's competence within a pertinent social hierarchy (i.e., outperform other students vs. being outperformed, respectively). Accordingly, a meta-analysis by Murayama and Elliot (2012) has shown that competition—structural, perceived, or dispositional—predicts the endorsement of both performance-approach and performance-avoidance goals.

We have already noted that competitive goals, in particular performance-approach goals, are considered as useful to succeed at university by students (e.g., Dompnier et al., 2008). Moreover, it has been shown that utility judgments made by teachers are particularly favorable in the appreciation of students (Dompnier et al., 2007). It is therefore unsurprising that students express performance-approach goals to a higher extent when the selection function of the educational system is salient (Jury et al., 2017). Moreover, the second study presented by these authors revealed that students endorsed performance-approach goals when selection was at stake because they considered that these goals were useful, in that they allow them to show teachers that they are students "who possess all the qualities to succeed at university" (Jury et al., 2017, p. 244). Performance-avoidance goals are also endorsed to a higher extent in selective contexts, but for different reasons. A study by Pulfrey et al. (2011) manipulated the presence or absence of normative grading for an academic task, and observed that performance-avoidance goals were more adopted when grades were present. This effect appeared to be mediated by a reduction in autonomous motivation; in other words, grading—because it is an extrinsic incentive—reduces the students' feelings of being in control of their engagement in a task, and results in higher strivings to avoid failure. Performance goals thus clearly proceed, for different reasons, from competitive and selective environments.

COMPETITIVE BEHAVIORS

Several competitive behaviors, relevant to education, have been shown to proceed from competitive ideologies, structures, and goals.

Cheating

Cheating at school and at university is an extremely prevalent behavior. For example, Teixeira and Rocha (2010), in an international study with students from more than twenty countries, found that ninety percent of the respondents had observed others cheating at least once. Cheating is a competitive behavior to the extent that it amounts to increasing one's performance or achievement without paying the price that the educational community has set for recognizing competence (e.g., studying). And indeed, numerous lines of research have shown that several factors related to competition do predict individual cheating. Murdock and Anderman (2006) have reviewed a great deal of such studies on cheating and have summarized the results in a motivational framework (p. 130). These authors observed that pressure for grades (from teachers, parents, and peers), competitive social comparison in classrooms, and performance-oriented classroom goal structures all concur in eliciting extrinsic and performance-oriented personal goals, which in turn result in a greater propensity to cheat. In line with this framework, Pulfrey and Butera (2013) showed that self-enhancement goals predicted leniency towards cheating through performance-approach goals, and directly predicted cheating behavior. It is noteworthy that all the above studies focus on individual cheating. Collective cheating appears to be predicted by a different set of values, namely benevolence values, which refer to the defense and promotion of one's group (Pulfrey et al., 2018). Interestingly for the present chapter, benevolence can be a competitive set of values when the defense and promotion of one's own group occur in an intergroup context.

Sabotage

Sabotage resembles cheating in that it is also an unethical behavior based on succeeding without paying the set price. However, while cheating entails unduly increasing one's performance, sabotage aims at reducing the others' performance. Research has shown that sabotage is also predicted by competition, for example by status-seeking (Charness et al., 2014) and the need to protect one's status (Garcia et al., 2010).

Exploitation

Exploitation of others' work is another anti-social behavior that is reinforced by competitive factors. Poortvliet et al. (2007) showed that performance goals predicted exploitation of others in information sharing (see also Poortvliet et al., 2009); Sommet et al. (2019) found that this effect is stronger when selection is salient, and it is explained by controlled reasons connected to performance goals. Thus, selection as a competitive structure and performance goals as competitive strivings contribute to the emergence of exploitation behaviors.

Bullying

Finally, moving from covert anti-social behaviors to explicit aggression, bullying has also been described as a consequence of competitive environments. Bullying refers to the repeated physical, verbal, or social (ostracism) aggressions performed by one or several persons on a chosen victim. Di Stasio et al. (2016), for example, modeled the teaching practices in dozens of classrooms and measured bullying outcomes at the student level. Their results revealed that classroom-level social comparison and competition predicted student-level self-reported bullying. In another study, Sutton and Keogh (2000) showed that competitive tendencies in the classroom, in particular the desire for social success, are related to a self-report measure of bullying. Moreover, as far as competitive values are concerned, a study by Menesini et al. (2013) showed that self-enhancement values predicted both cyber and traditional bullying in high-school students. In sum, a series of anti-social behaviors—here, cheating, sabotage, exploitation, and bullying—appear to be the result of competitive ideologies, competitive classroom structures and climates, and competitive values.

OUTCOMES OF A COMPETITIVE EDUCATION

The above review leaves unanswered the question of the educational outcomes of a competitive education. This section will summarize the links that the reviewed literature has established between competition at various levels (society, educational systems, and intra-individual variables in students) and educational outcomes. The term educational outcomes may seem rather generic, but we use it here to highlight that both Psychology and the Educational Sciences have used a very large array of measures to assess what results from education.

Learning, Performance, and Achievement

Learning is probably the gold standard of what the outcome of education is expected to be. However, studying learning requires educators (and researchers) to measure a difference in competence (before and after), and to define the depth of learning that one wants to assess, from surface learning (reciting, naming) to deep learning (analyzing, generalizing; see for instance Bloom, 1956; Butera et al., 2021). This is why many studies instead assess performance (e.g., to a test) or collect specific or end-of-the-year grades from schools as a measure of achievement. In this respect, many comprehensive reviews collapse learning, performance, and achievement. We will be no exception.

A thorough meta-analysis of the relation between competition and performance did not find any notable effect (Murayama & Elliot, 2012), and a meta-analysis of four meta-analyses that specifically focused on student learning found a small positive effect that does not exceed developmental and teacher effects (Hattie, 2009). Interestingly, however, a second meta-analysis by Murayama and Elliot (2012) revealed that the null relation between competition and performance hides two opposing processes. Competition predicts performance-approach goals that favor performance, and at the same time performance-avoidance goals that inhibit performance. Thus, not all competitive structures or dispositions lead to increased performance, but this link depends on the performance goals that are prompted by competition (cf. Murayama, Elliot, & Jury, in this volume).

In addition to these comprehensive results, the question of the relation between performance-approach goals and performance, learning, or achievement has been abundantly debated. Some authors have argued that performance-approach goals predict task performance when there is a delay between the measure of performance-approach goals and that of task performance, but performance is impaired in experiments where the measure immediately follows the manipulation (Crouzevialle & Butera, 2013, 2017). This work is in line with studies that showed that evaluative pressure to perform impairs executive functions (e.g., working memory) that are crucial in learning (Beilock et al., 2004). Others have argued that performance-approach goals have a deleterious effect on

FABRIZIO BUTERA, WOJCIECH ŚWIĄTKOWSKI, AND BENOÎT DOMPNIER

performance when measured through their appearance ("demonstrate one's competences") rather than normative ("outperform others") component (Hulleman et al., 2010). Some authors have suggested that these two types of performance-approach goals each relate to different kinds of reasons that sustain their endorsement—controlled reasons for appearance and autonomous reasons for normative—which in turn account for the difference in predictive validity of performance-approach goals (Senko & Tropiano, 2016). A parallel effort has focused on uncovering the mechanisms that make performance-approach goals predictive of performance. For instance, Senko et al. (2013) argued that performance-approach goals promote a vigilant state in students, which leads them to look for factors that their teachers seem to find important for succeeding and invest in those; when students correctly spotted the right factors, their achievement was increased. Similarly, Dompnier et al. (2013) found that performance-approach goals positively predicted achievement when students thought that these goals were useful to succeed; however, these goals negatively predicted achievement when students thought that they helped convey a desirable image of themselves in the eyes of their teachers. Finally, a small-scale meta-analysis recently showed that performance-approach goals positively predict performance when students pursue a promotion regulatory focus, that is when they are particularly attentive to the gains that their actions may entail, and focus on positive results (Świątkowski & Dompnier, 2020).

The above debate is mainly concerned with the question of the effect of performance-approach goals on performance/achievement. Regarding their effects on other important educational outcomes, the picture is more homogeneous. Performance-approach goals have been found to predict surface—rather than deep—study strategies, to impair task interest and resistance to failure, and to promote self-handicapping (for a review, see Darnon et al., 2012).

Social Relations

At the relational level, we have already noted that performance-approach goals predict cheating and exploitation behaviors; moreover, they reduce the ability to take into account and learn from a partner's diverging point of view (Darnon et al., 2006, 2007; Sommet et al., 2014; see Butera et al., 2019, for a review). Even when a cooperative structure is in place, a competitive regulation of disagreement between partners leads to reduced peer learning (Buchs et al., 2010).

Moving to more structural variables, it has been shown that competitive settings (negative interdependence) lead to reduced information exchange with partners (Toma & Butera, 2009). In particular, several studies have shown that the presence of normative grading leads students to withholding useful information during cooperative work (Hayek et al., 2015), and to impaired coordination in a collective task (Hayek et al., 2017). Finally, in terms of intergroup relations, the pursuit of performance-approach goals impaired the academic performance of students who experienced low (as compared with high) relative social class (Crouzevialle & Darnon, 2019). Moreover, the use of grading as a selective tool—and more generally, the salience of the selection function of education—were associated with an increase in the achievement gap between higher and lower socioeconomic status (SES) students (Smeding et al. 2013), as well as between boys and girls on a science subject (Souchal et al., 2014). The contribution of assessment contexts to the achievement gap is massive (see Easterbrook & Hadden, 2021, for a recent review), but these effects are not limited to students. Recent research has shown that normative grading also leads evaluators to artificially increase the achievement gap between higher and lower SES students (Autin et al., 2019; Batruch et al., 2019b).

To summarize, competition appears to have a null effect on performance, whereas performance-approach goals have a positive effect, under certain conditions that we have reviewed, while performance-avoidance goals have a consistent negative effect. Ideological, structural, and dispositional competition, however, results in an overall impairment of other educational outcomes, be these at the individual level—from task interest to study strategies—or at the level of social relations—from cheating to exploitation, and from information sharing to coordination.

Conclusions: Education as a Feedback Loop

In this chapter we aimed to show that education is an integrated system that resonates with the society in which it is embedded, and that socializes its students to adopt its values and practices. We have shown that, as far as competition is concerned, it is possible to trace an influence pathway that leads from dominant competitive ideologies, values, and norms to the implementation of competitive structures and climates in schools and universities. These educational institutions, in turn, lead students to adopt competitive values, goals, and behaviors. Is this the end of the story?

At some point, students become adults, begin to vote, take up professional positions, and become active agents of society. In this respect, they begin to contribute to shaping their society's ideologies, values, and norms. What then is the nature of the influence students may yield upon society when they become citizens? At least two scenarios are possible. The first amounts to social reproduction, whereby society perpetuates itself in terms of values and structures because educational institutions socialize students to those values and structures. A few years ago, Attick (2017) wrote: "Teachers today are held responsible for developing in students the skills that the neoliberal economic system requires for its ongoing survival" (p. 42; see also Rikowski, 2001, for a similar idea). Whether it is skills or values and norms, this idea is in line with the theory of social reproduction, and the observation that school perpetuates the social hierarchies that can be found in society (Bourdieu & Passeron, 1977). It is also consistent with system justification theory, and the observation that people tend to comply with dominant ideologies and norms, even when they are members of an underprivileged group (Jost et al., 2004). Thus, according to the social reproduction scenario, students socialized at school with values derived from the dominant ideologies in society will later contribute to those same ideologies by perpetuating them.

The second possible scenario is that of minority influence, whereby students develop values and norms that are not the dominant ones, and they engage in social activism to replace the *status quo*. The mechanism through which minorities may produce individual and social change are well known (e.g., Butera et al., 2017, for a review), but this second scenario begs the question of how students can be socialized with non-dominant values and norms. On the one hand, educational institutions maintain a sufficient degree of freedom, and in some cases instill values that are at odds with those of the surrounding society. Students may be inspired by a Marxist teacher or attend a school that promotes degrowth in their practices. Moreover, at the level of school systems, it should be noted that in the past century a number of schools have been established on the basis of non-competitive ideologies and values. The most well-known and widespread around the world are probably the Steiner-Waldorf, the Freinet, and the Montessori schools, but many other progressive schools can be found at a more local level. The specifics of their pedagogies may differ, but they share a focus of the peculiar development of every child—thereby reducing the weight of social comparison and competition—the encouragement of critical thinking, the promotion of cooperation, and the equal importance given to the cognitive, moral, spiritual, social, and physical aspects of development (e.g., Carnie, 2003). Interestingly, these schools are based on the philosophy of their initiators—as well as many other intellectuals such as John Dewey and Jean Piaget—who were equally interested in the promotion of child development and the reform of the overly strict and competitive educational systems in force in their respective countries (for an overview of progressive education systems on the five continents, see Röhrs & Lenhart, 1995). In other words, these theoretical and educational frameworks have been conceived as much as pedagogical systems as levers intended to promote different, less competitive forms of society (or even revolutionize society, as in the work by Paulo Freire, 1970). However, the number and liveliness of these methods notwithstanding, they remain a very small minority within educational practices (e.g., Pianta et al., 2007). In sum, the possibility for schools to transmit alternative values currently relies on the dissident action of some schools or teachers.

On the other hand, it is possible to consider that socialization takes place not only in the family and at school, but also in other circles. Political scientists have long studied political socialization, and several models are currently debated. The important point here is that some scholars consider it possible that political socialization takes place outside of school and family, for example, in local or global social movements (e.g., Filleule, 2013). Social media have rendered distant social movements immediately available (Wray-Lake, 2019); the case of Greta Thunberg and the Fridays for Future movement is a clear example of sudden engagement of thousands of adolescents (and beyond) in a movement in stark contrast with dominant ideologies and values. Therefore, it is possible. Which path—of social reproduction or minority influence—will be followed by students in their contribution to society, and in which contexts and through which mechanisms, is left to future research.

Acknowledgments

The preparation of this work was supported by the Swiss National Science Foundation. We wish to thank Gaële Goastellec for her invaluable suggestions on a previous draft.

References

Adams, G., Estrada-Villalta, S., Sullivan, D., & Markus, H. R. (2019). The psychology of neoliberalism and the neoliberalism of psychology. *Journal of Social Issues, 75,* 189–216. https://doi.org/10.1111/josi.12305

Aelenei, C., Martinot, D., Sicard, A., & Darnon, C. (2020). When an academic culture based on self-enhancement values undermines female students' sense of belonging, self-efficacy, and academic choices. *The Journal of Social Psychology, 160,* 373–389. https://doi.org/10.1080/00224545.2019.1675576

Ames, C. (1992a). Classrooms: Goals, structures, and student motivation. *Journal of Educational Psychology, 84,* 261–271. https://doi.org/10.1037/0022-0663.84.3.261

Ames C. (1992b). Achievement goals and the classroom climate. In D. H. Schunk & J. L. Meece (Eds.), *Student Perceptions in the Classroom* (pp. 327–48). Erlbaum.

Ames, C., & Archer, J. (1988). Achievement goals in the classroom: Students' learning strategies and motivation processes. *Journal of Educational Psychology, 80,* 260–267. https://doi.org/10.1037/0022-0663.80.3.260

Anderman, E. M., & Midgley, C. (2002). Methods for studying goals, goal structures, and patterns of adaptive learning. In C. Midgley (Ed.), *Goals, goal structures, and patterns of adaptive learning* (1–20). Erlbaum

Anderson, D. (2008). Productivism, vocational and professional education, and the ecological question. *Vocations and Learning, 1,* 105–129. https://doi.org/10.1007/s12186-008-9007-0

Apple, M. W. (2006). *Educating the "right" way: Markets, standards, God, and inequality.* Taylor & Francis.

Apple, M. W. (2018). Ideology and cultural and economic reproduction. In M. Apple & M. W. Apple (Eds.), *Ideology and curriculum* (pp. 26–44). Routledge.

Allal, L. (2010). Assessment and the regulation of learning. *International Encyclopedia of Education, 3,* 348–352.

Archer, M. S. (2013). *Social origins of educational systems.* Routledge.

Arrow, K. (1973). Higher education as a filter. *Journal of Public Economics, 2,* 193–216. https://doi.org/10.1016/0047-2727(73)90013-3

Attick, D. (2017). Homo economicus at school: Neoliberal education and teacher as economic being. *Educational Studies, 53,* 37–48. https://doi.org/10.1080/00131946.2016.1258362

Autin, F., Batruch, A., & Butera, F. (2015). Social justice in education: How the function of selection in educational institutions predicts support for (non)egalitarian assessment practices. *Frontiers in Psychology, 6,* 707. https://doi.org/10.3389/fpsyg.2015.00707

Autin, F., Batruch, A., & Butera, F. (2019). The function of selection of assessment leads evaluators to artificially create the social class achievement gap. *Journal of Educational Psychology, 111,* 717–735.

Baer, D. E. (1990). Socialization into dominant vs. counter ideology among university-educated Canadians. *Canadian Review of Sociology/Revue Canadienne de Sociologie, 27,* 487–504. https://doi.org/10.1111/j.1755-618X.1990.tb00136.x

Batruch, A., Autin, F., & Butera, F. (2019a). The paradoxical role of meritocratic selection in the perpetuation of social inequalities at school. In J. Jetten & K. Peters (Eds.), *The social psychology of inequality* (pp. 123–137). Springer Nature.

Batruch, A., Autin, F., Bataillard, F., & Butera, F. (2019b). School selection and the social class divide: How tracking contributes to the reproduction of inequalities. *Personality and Social Psychology Bulletin, 45,* 477–490. https://doi.org/10.1177/0146167218791804

Beauvois, J. L. (2005). *Les illusions libérales: individualisme et pouvoir social (Liberal illusions: individualism and social power).* Presses Universitaires de Grenoble.

Beilock, S. L., Kulp, C. A., Holt, L. E., & Carr, T. H. (2004). More on the fragility of performance: Choking under pressure in mathematical problem solving. *Journal of Experimental Psychology: General, 133*, 584–600. https://doi.org/10.1037/0096-3445.133.4.584

Bettache, K., & Chiu, C. Y. (2019). The invisible hand is an ideology: Toward a social psychology of neoliberalism. *Journal of Social Issues, 75*, 8–19. https://doi.org/10.1111/josi.12308

Black, P., & Wiliam, D. (2009). Developing the theory of formative assessment. *Educational Assessment, Evaluation and Accountability, 21*, 5–31. https://doi.org/10.1007/s11092-008-9068-5

Bloom, B. S. (Ed.). (1956). *Taxonomy of educational objectives, Handbook I: Cognitive domain.* David McKay Company.

Bourdieu, P., & Passeron, J. C. (1977). *Reproduction in education, society and culture.* Sage.

Bronfenbrenner, U. (1977). Toward an experimental ecology of human development. *American Psychologist, 32*, 513–531. https://doi.org/10.1037/0003-066X.32.7.513

Buchs, C., Pulfrey, C., Gabarrot, F., & Butera, F. (2010). Competitive conflict regulation and informational dependence in peer learning. *European Journal of Social Psychology, 40*, 418–435. https://doi.org/10.1002/ejsp.631

Busch, L. (2017). *Knowledge for sale: The neoliberal takeover of higher education.* MIT Press.

Butera, F. (2006). La meritocrazia a scuola: Un serio ostacolo all'apprendimento (Meritocracy at school: a serious obstacle to learning). *Psicologia Sociale, 1*, 431–448.

Butera, F., & Darnon, C. (2017). Competence assessment, social comparison and conflict regulation. In A. Elliot, C. Dweck & D. Yaeger (Eds.), *Handbook of Competence and Motivation (2nd Edition: Theory and Application*, pp. 192–213). Guilford Press.

Butera, F., Falomir-Pichastor, J. M., Mugny, G., & Quiamzade, A. (2017). Minority influence. In S. Harkins, K. D. Williams & J. Burger (Eds.), *The Oxford Handbook of Social Influence* (pp. 317–337). Oxford University Press.

Butera, F., Sommet, N., & Darnon, C. (2019). Sociocognitive conflict regulation: How to make sense of diverging ideas. *Current Direction in Psychological Science, 28*, 145–151. https://doi.org/10.1177/09637 21418813986

Butera, F., Batruch, A., Autin, F., Mugny, G., Quiamzade, A., & Pulfrey, C. (2021). Teaching as social influence: Empowering teachers to become agents of social change. *Social Issues and Policy Review, 15*(1), 323–355. https://doi.org/10.1111/sipr.12072

Carnie, F. (2003). *Alternative approaches to education: A guide for parents and teachers.* Psychology Press.

Charness, G., Masclet, D., & Villeval, M. C. (2014). The dark side of competition for status. *Management Science, 60*, 38–55. https://doi.org/10.1287/mnsc.2013.1747

Chmielewski, A. K. (2014). An international comparison of achievement inequality in within- and between-school tracking systems. *American Journal of Education, 120*, 293–324. doi: 10.1086/675529

Cialdini, R. B., Kallgren, C. A., & Reno, R. R. (1991). A focus theory of normative conduct: A theoretical refinement and reevaluation of the role of norms in human behavior. In M. P. Zanna (Ed.), *Advances in experimental social psychology* (Vol. 24, pp. 201–234). Academic Press. https://doi.org/10.1016/S0065-2601(08)60330-5

Crouzevialle, M., & Butera, F. (2013). Performance-approach goals deplete working memory and impair cognitive performance. *Journal of Experimental Psychology: General, 142*, 666–678. https://doi.org/10.1037/a0029632

Crouzevialle, M., & Butera, F. (2017). Performance goals and task performance: Integrative considerations on the distraction hypothesis. *European Psychologist, 22*, 73–82. https://doi.org/10.1027/1016-9040/a000281

Crouzevialle, M., & Darnon, C. (2019). On the academic disadvantage of low social class individuals: Pursuing performance goals fosters the emergence of the achievement gap. *Journal of Educational Psychology, 111*, 1261–1272. http://dx.doi.org/10.1037/edu0000349

Darnon, C., Butera, F., & Harackiewicz, J. M. (2007). Achievement goals in social interactions: Learning with mastery vs. performance goals. *Motivation and Emotion, 31*, 61–70.

Darnon, C., Dompnier, B., Delmas, F., Pulfrey, C., & Butera F. (2009). Achievement goal promotion at university: Social desirability and social utility of mastery and performance goals. *Journal of Personality and Social Psychology, 96*, 119–134. https://doi.org/10.1037/a0012824

Darnon, C., Dompnier, B., & Poortvliet, M. (2012). Achievement goals in educational contexts: A social psychology perspective. *Social and Personality Psychology Compass, 6*, 760–771. https://doi.org/10.1111/j.1751-9004.2012.00457.x

Darnon, C., Muller, D., Schrager, S. M., Pannuzzo, N., & Butera, F. (2006). Mastery and performance goals predict epistemic and relational conflict regulation. *Journal of Educational Psychology, 98*, 766–776. https://doi.org/10.1037/0022-0663.98.4.766

Darnon, C., Smeding, A., & Redersdorff, S. (2018a). Belief in school meritocracy as an ideological barrier to the promotion of equality. *European Journal of Social Psychology, 48*, 523–534. https://doi.org/10.1002/ejsp.2347

Darnon, C., Wiederkehr, V., Dompnier, B., & Martinot, D. (2018b). "Where there is a will, there is a way": Belief in school meritocracy and the social-class achievement gap. *British Journal of Social Psychology, 57*, 250–262. https://doi.org/10.1111/bjso.12214

Davies, B., & Bansel, P. (2007). Neoliberalism and education. *International Journal of Qualitative Studies in Education, 20*, 247–259. https://doi.org/10.1080/09518390701281751

Dee, T. S., & Keys, B. J. (2004). Does merit pay reward good teachers? Evidence from a randomized experiment. *Journal of Policy Analysis and Management, 23*, 471–488. https://doi.org/10.1002/pam.20022

Deutsch, M. (1949). A theory of co-operation and competition. *Human Relations, 2*, 129–152.

Deutsch, M. (1979). Education and distributive justice: Some reflections on grading systems. *American Psychologist, 34*, 301–401.

Di Stasio, M. R., Savage, R., & Burgos, G. (2016). Social comparison, competition and teacher–student relationships in junior high school classrooms predicts bullying and victimization. *Journal of Adolescence, 53*, 207–216. https://doi.org/10.1016/j.adolescence.2016.10.002

Dompnier, B., Pansu, P., & Bressoux, P. (2006). An integrative model of scholastic judgments: Pupils' characteristics, class context, halo effect and internal attributions. *European Journal of Psychology of Education, 21*, 119–133.

Dompnier, B., Pansu, P., & Bressoux, P. (2007). Social utility, social desirability and scholastic judgments: Toward a personological model of academic evaluation. *European Journal of Psychology of Education, 22*, 333–350. https://doi.org/10.1007/BF03173431

Dompnier, B., Darnon, C., Delmas, F., & Butera, F. (2008). Achievement goals and social judgment: The performance-approach paradox. *International Review of Social Psychology, 21*, 247–271. https://doi.org/10.1111/bjso.12025

Dompnier, B., Darnon, C., & Butera, F. (2013). When performance-approach goals predict academic achievement and when they do not: A social value approach. *British Journal of Social Psychology, 52*, 587–596. https://doi.org/10.1111/bjso.12025

Dornbusch, S. M., Glasgow, K. L., & Lin, I. C. (1996). The social structure of schooling. *Annual Review of Psychology, 47*, 401–429. https://doi.org/10.1146/annurev.psych.47.1.401

Dubet, F., & Duru-Bellat, M. (2004). Qu'est-ce qu'une école juste? (What is a fair school?) *Revue Française de Pédagogie, 146*, 105–114.

Dubet, F., Duru-Bellat, M., & Vérétout, A. (2010). *Les sociétés et leur école. Emprise du diplôme et cohésion sociale (Societies and their schools: influence of diplomas and social cohesion).* Le Seuil.

Dudley-Marling, C. (2020). School choice and inclusive education. In *Oxford Research Encyclopedia of Education.* https://doi.org/10.1093/acrefore/9780190264093.013.1241

Duru-Bellat, M. (1996). Social inequalities in French secondary schools: From figures to theories. *British Journal of Sociology of Education, 17*, 341–351. https://doi.org/10.1080/0142569960170307

Duru-Bellat, M., & Tenret, E. (2012). Who's for meritocracy? Individual and contextual variations in the faith. *Comparative Education Review, 56*, 223–247. https://www.jstor.org/stable/10.1086/661290

Easterbrook, M. J., & Hadden, I. R. (2021). Tackling educational inequalities with social psychology: Identities, contexts, and interventions. *Social Issues and Policy Review, 15*, 180–236. https://doi.org/10.1111/sipr.12070

Elliot, A. J., & McGregor, H. A. (2001). A 2× 2 achievement goal framework. *Journal of Personality and Social Psychology, 80*, 501–519. http://dx.doi.org/10.1037/0022-3514.80.3.501

Elliot, A. J., & Niesta, D. (2009). Goals in the context of the hierarchical model of approach-avoidance motivation. In G. Moskowitz & H. Grant (Eds.), *The psychology of goals* (pp. 56–76). Guilford Press.

Elliot, A. J., Murayama, K., & Pekrun, R. (2011). A 3× 2 achievement goal model. *Journal of Educational Psychology, 103*, 632–648. http://dx.doi.org/10.1037/a0023952

Elliot, A. J., Jury, M., & Murayama, K. (2018). Trait and perceived environmental competitiveness in achievement situations. *Journal of Personality, 86*(3), 353–367. https://doi.org/10.1111/jopy.12320

Engel, M. (2000). *The struggle for control of public education: Market ideology vs. democratic values.* Temple University Press.

Falcon, J. (2012). Temporal trends in intergenerational social mobility in Switzerland: A cohort study of men and women born between 1912 and 1974. *Swiss Journal of Sociology, 38,* 153–175.

Fillieule, O. (2013). Political socialization and social movements. *The Wiley-Blackwell Encyclopedia of Social and Political Movements* (pp. 1–7). Blackwell. https://doi.org/10.1002/9780470674871.wbespm199

Foucault, M. (2010). *The birth of biopolitics: Lectures at the College de France, 1978–1979* (G. Burchell, Trans.). Picador. (Original work published 1984).

Frank, R. H., & Cook, P. J. (1995). *The winner-take-all society: Why the few at the top get so much more than the rest of us.* Penguin Books.

Fraser, B. J. (1989). Twenty years of classroom climate work: Progress and prospect. *Journal of Curriculum studies, 21*(4), 307–327. https://doi.org/10.1080/0022027890210402

Freire, P. (1970). *Pedagogia do oprimido [Pedagogy of the oppressed]* (11th ed.). Paz e Terra.

Garcia, S. M., Song, H., & Tesser, A. (2010). Tainted recommendations: The social comparison bias. *Organizational Behavior and Human Decision Processes, 113,* 97–101. https://doi.org/10.1016/j.obhdp.2010.06.002

Garcia, S. M., Tor, A., & Schiff, T. M. (2013). The psychology of competition: A social comparison perspective. *Perspectives on Psychological Science, 8,* 634–650. https://doi.org/10.1177/1745691613504114

Glaser, R. (1963). Instructional technology and the measurement of learning outcomes: Some questions. *American Psychologist, 18,* 519–521. https://doi.org/10.1037/h0049294

Goastellec, G. (2020). Le sens de la justice dans l'accès à l'université: les apports de la longue durée (Sense of justice in access to university: the contribution of a long-term perspective). *L'Annee Sociologique, 70,* 283–312.

Green, A. (1990). *Education and state formation.* Palgrave Macmillan.

Guimond, S. (2001). Epistemic authorities in higher education: The relative influence of peers, faculty and courses on attitude formation and change. In F. Butera & G. Mugny (Eds.), *Social influence in social reality* (pp. 211–223). Hogrefe & Huber.

Guimond, S., & Palmer, D. L. (1996). The political socialization of commerce and social science students: Epistemic authority and attitude change. *Journal of Applied Social Psychology, 26,* 1985–2013. https://doi.org/10.1111/j.1559-1816.1996.tb01784.x

Hall, P. A., & Gingerich, D. W. (2009). Varieties of capitalism and institutional complementarities in the political economy: An empirical analysis. *British Journal of Political Science, 39,* 449–482. https://doi.org/10.1017/S0007123409000672

Hallinan, M. T. (1994). Tracking: From theory to practice. *Sociology of Education, 67,* 79–84. https://doi.org/10.2307/2112697

Haney, C., & Hurtado, A. (1994). The jurisprudence of race and meritocracy: Standardized testing and "race neutral" racism in the workplace. *Law and Human Behavior, 18,* 223–248. https://doi.org/10.1007/BF01499586

Hartwich, L., & Becker, J. C. (2019). Exposure to neoliberalism increases resentment of the elite via feelings of anomie and negative psychological reactions. *Journal of Social Issues, 75,* 113–133. https://doi.org/10.1111/josi.12311

Hattie, J. (2009). *Visible learning: A synthesis of over 800 meta-analyses relating to achievement.* Routledge.

Hayek, A.S., Toma, C., Oberlé, D., & Butera, F. (2015). Grading hampers cooperative information sharing in group problem solving. *Social Psychology, 46,* 121–131.

Hayek, A.S., Toma, C., Guidotti, S., Oberlé, D., & Butera, F. (2017). Grades degrade group coordination: deteriorated interactions and performance in a cooperative motor task. *European Journal of Psychology of Education, 32,* 97–112.

Hulleman, C. S., Schrager, S. M., Bodmann, S. M., & Harackiewicz, J. M. (2010). A meta-analytic review of achievement goal measures: Different labels for the same constructs or different constructs with similar labels? *Psychological Bulletin, 136,* 422–449. https://doi.org/10.1037/a0018947

Jabbar, H., Fong, C. J., Germain, E., Li, D., Sanchez, J., Sun, W. L., & Devall, M. (2019). The competitive effects of school choice on student achievement: A systematic review. *Educational Policy.* Advance online publication. https://doi.org/10.1177/0895904819874756

Jost, J. T., & Hunyady, O. (2005). Antecedents and consequences of system-justifying ideologies. *Current Directions in Psychological Science, 14,* 260–265. https://doi.org/10.1111/j.0963-7214.2005.00377.x

Jost, J.T., Blount, S., Pfeffer, J., & Hunyady, G. (2003a). Fair market ideology: Its cognitive-motivational under-pinnings. *Research in Organizational Behavior, 25*, 53–91. https://doi.org/10.1016/S0191-3085(03)25002-4

Jost, J.T., Pelham, B.W., Sheldon, O., & Sullivan, B.N. (2003b). Social inequality and the reduction of ideo-logical dissonance on behalf of the system: Evidence of enhanced system justification among the disadvan-taged. *European Journal of Social Psychology, 33*, 13–36. https://doi.org/10.1002/ejsp.127

Jost, J.T., Banaji, M.R., & Nosek, B.A. (2004). A decade of system justification theory: Accumulated evidence of conscious and unconscious bolstering of the status quo. *Political Psychology, 25*, 881–919. https://doi.org/10.1111/j.1467-9221.2004.00402.x

Jury, M., Darnon, C., Dompnier, B., & Butera, F. (2017). The social utility of performance-approach goals in a selective educational environment. *Social Psychology of Education, 20*(1), 215–235. https://doi.org/10.1007/s11218-016-9354-x

Kaplan, A., Middleton, M. J., Urdan, T., & Midgley, C. (2002). Achievement goals and goal structures. In C. Midgley (Ed.), *Goals, goal structures, and patterns of adaptive learning* (pp. 21–53). Erlbaum.

Kapur, M. (2008) Productive failure. *Cognition and Instruction, 26*, 379–424. https://doi.org/10.1080/07370000802212669

Kasser, T., Cohn, S., Kanner, A. D., & Ryan, R. M. (2007). Some costs of American corporate capitalism: A psychological exploration of value and goal conflicts. *Psychological Inquiry, 18*, 1–22. https://doi.org/10.1080/10478400701386579

Kratz, F., Patzina, A., Kleinert, C., & Dietrich, H. (2019). Vocational education and employment: Explaining cohort variations in life course patterns. *Social Inclusion, 7*, 224–253. http://dx.doi.org/10.17645/si.v7i3.2045

Kaufman, N. H. (1994). A survey of law school grading practices. *Journal of Legal Education, 44*, 415–423.

Kohn, A. (2019). Can everyone be excellent? https://www.alfiekohn.org/article/excellence/

Knight, P., & Yorke, M. (2003). *Assessment, learning and employability*. Open University Press.

Knight, P., & Yorke, M. (2004). *Learning, curriculum and employability in higher education*. RoutledgeFalmer.

Lyotard, J. F. (1984). *The postmodern condition: A report on knowledge*. University of Minnesota Press.

Marsh, H. W. (1987). The big-fish-little-pond effect on academic self-concept. *Journal of Educational Psychology, 79*, 280–295. https://doi.org/10.1037/0022-0663.79.3.280

Masdonati, J., Massoudi, K., Blustein, D. L., & Duffy, R. (in press). Moving toward decent work: Application of the Psychology of Working Theory to the school-to-work transition. *Journal of Career Development*. DOI: 10.1177/0894845321991681

McNamee, S. J., & Miller, R. K. (2004). *The meritocracy myth*. Rowan & Littlefield.

Meece, J. L., Anderman, E. M., & Anderman, L. H. (2006). Classroom goal structure, student motivation, and academic achievement. *Annual Review of Psychology, 57*, 487–503. https://doi.org/10.1146/annurev.psych.56.091103.070258

Menesini, E., Nocentini, A., & Camodeca, M. (2013). Morality, values, traditional bullying, and cyber-bullying in adolescence. *British Journal of Developmental Psychology, 31*, 1–14. https://doi.org/10.1111/j.2044-835X.2011.02066.x

Meyer, J. W., Ramirez, F. O., & Soysal, Y. N. (1992). World expansion of mass education, 1870–1980. *Sociology of Education, 65*, 128–149. https://doi.org/10.2307/2112679

Midgley, C., Maehr, M. L., Hruda, L. Z., Anderman, E., Anderman, L., Freeman, K. E., Gheen, M., Kaplan, A., Kumar, R., Middleton, M.J., Nelson, J., Roeser. R., & Urdan, T. (2000). *Manual for the patterns of adaptive learning scales*. The University of Michigan Press.

Mijs, J. J. (2016). The unfulfillable promise of meritocracy: Three lessons and their implications for justice in education. *Social Justice Research, 29*, 14–34. https://doi.org/10.1007/s11211-014-0228-0

Mons, N. (2009). Effets théoriques et réels des politiques d'évaluation standardisée (Theoretical and real effects of standardized assessment policies). *Revue Française de Pédagogie, 169*, 99–140. https://doi.org/10.4000/rfp.1531

Moreira, L., & Lafortune, G. (2016). Education and training for doctors and nurses: what's happening with *numerus clausus* policies? In OECD (Ed.), *Health Workforce Policies in OECD Countries: Right Jobs, Right Skills, Right Places* (pp. 63–102). OECD.

Morley, L. (2001). Producing new workers: Quality, equality and employability in higher education. *Quality in Higher Education, 7*, 131–138. https://doi.org/10.1080/13538320120060024

Murayama, K., & Elliot, A. J. (2009). The joint influence of personal achievement goals and classroom goal structures on achievement-relevant outcomes. *Journal of Educational Psychology, 101*, 432–447. https://doi.org/10.1037/a0014221

Murayama, K., & Elliot, A. J. (2012). The competition–performance relation: A meta-analytic review and test of the opposing processes model of competition and performance. *Psychological Bulletin, 138*, 1035–1070. https://doi.org/10.1037/a0028324

Murdock, T. B., & Anderman, E. M. (2006). Motivational perspectives on student cheating: Toward an integrated model of academic dishonesty. *Educational Psychologist, 41*, 129–145. https://doi.org/10.1207/s15326985ep4103_1

Nathaniel, P., Pendergast, L. L., Segool, N., Saeki, E., & Ryan, S. (2016). The influence of test-based accountability policies on school climate and teacher stress across four states. *Teaching and Teacher Education, 59*, 492–502. https://doi.org/10.1016/j.tate.2016.07.013

Nicholls, J. G. (1989). *The competitive ethos and democratic education.* Harvard University Press.

OECD. (2013). *PISA 2012 results: What makes schools successful? Resources, policies and practices* (volume IV). OECD.

Pansu, P., Dubois, N., & Dompnier, B. (2008). Internality-norm theory in educational contexts. *European Journal of Psychology of Education, 23*, 385–397. https://doi.org/10.1007/BF03172748

Pérez Gómez, Á. I. (1998). *La cultura escolar en la sociedad neoliberal (School culture in a neoliberal society).* Ediciones Morata.

Perry, L. B. (2009). Conceptualizing education policy in democratic societies. *Educational Policy, 23*, 423–450. https://doi.org/10.1177/0895904807310032

Pianta, R. C., Belsky, J., Houts, R., & Morrison, F. (2007). Opportunities to learn in America's elementary classrooms. *Science, 315*, 1795–1796. https://doi.org/10.1126/science.1139719

Piketty, T. (2020). *Capital and ideology.* Harvard University Press.

Plehwe, D. (2009). Introduction. In P. Mirowski & D. Plehwe (Eds.), *The road from Mont Pelerin: The making of the neoliberal thought collective* (pp. 1–42). Harvard University Press.

Poortvliet, P. M., Janssen, O., Van Yperen, N. W., & Van de Vliert, E. (2007). Achievement goals and interpersonal behavior: How mastery and performance goals shape information exchange. *Personality and Social Psychology Bulletin, 33*, 1435–1447. https://doi.org/10.1177/0146167207305536

Poortvliet, P. M., Janssen, O., Van Yperen, N. W., & Vliert, E. V. D. (2009). The joint impact of achievement goals and performance feedback on information giving. *Basic and Applied Social Psychology, 31*, 197–209. https://doi.org/10.1080/01973530903058276

Pulfrey, C., & Butera, F. (2013). Why neoliberal values of self-enhancement lead to cheating in higher education: A motivational account. *Psychological Science, 24*, 2153–2162. https://doi.org/10.1177/0956797613487221

Pulfrey, C., Buchs, C., & Butera, F. (2011). Why grades engender performance avoidance goals: The mediating role of autonomous motivation. *Journal of Educational Psychology, 103*, 683–700. https://doi.org/10.1037/a0023911

Pulfrey, C., Darnon, C., & Butera, F. (2013). Autonomy and task performance: Explaining the impact of grades on intrinsic motivation. *Journal of Educational Psychology, 105*, 39–57. https://doi.org/10.1037/a0029376

Pulfrey, C., Durussel, K., & Butera, F. (2018). The good cheat: Benevolence and the justification of collective cheating. *Journal of Educational Psychology, 110*, 764–784. https://doi.org/10.1037/edu0000247

Rich, J. M., & DeVitis, J. L. (1992). *Competition in education.* Charles C. Thomas Publisher.

Rikowski, G. (2001). Education for industry: A complex technicism. *Journal of Education and Work, 14*, 29–49.

Röhrs, H., & Lenhart, V. (Eds.). (1995). *Progressive education across the continents: A handbook* (Heidelberger Studien Zur Erziehungswissenschaft, Vol. 44). Peter Lang.

Rom, M. C. (2011). Grading more accurately. *Journal of Political Science Education, 7*, 208–223. https://doi.org/10.1080/15512169.2011.564916

Ryan, R. M., & Deci, E. L. (2000). Self-determination theory and the facilitation of intrinsic motivation, social development, and well-being. *American Psychologist, 55*, 68–78. https://doi.org/10.1037110003-066X.55.1.68

Sandel, M. (2020). *The tyranny of merit: What's become of the common good.* Farrar, Straus and Giroux.

Santagata, R. (2005). Practices and beliefs in mistake-handling activities: A video study of Italian and US mathematics lessons. *Teaching and Teacher Education, 21*, 491–508. https://doi.org/10.1016/j.tate.2005.03.004

Schwartz, S. H. (1992). Universals in the content and structure of values: Theory and empirical tests in 20 countries. In M. Zanna (Ed.), *Advances in experimental social psychology* (Vol. 25, pp. 1–65). Academic Press.

Schwartz, S. H. (2007). Cultural and individual value correlates of capitalism: A comparative analysis. *Psychological Inquiry*, *18*, 52–57. https://doi.org/10.1080/10478400701388963

Schwartz, S. H., Melech, G., Lehmann, A., Burgess, S., Harris, M., & Owens, V. (2001). Extending the cross-cultural validity of the theory of basic human values with a different method of measurement. *Journal of Cross-Cultural Psychology*, *32*, 519–542. https://doi.org/10.1177/0022022101032005001

Schwartz, S. H., Cieciuch, J., Vecchione, M., Davidov, E., Fischer, R., Beierlein, C., Ramos, A., Verkasalo, M., Lönnqvist, J.-E., Demirutku, K., Dirilen-Gumus, O., & Konty, M. (2012). Refining the theory of basic individual values. *Journal of Personality and Social Psychology*, *103*, 663–688. https://doi.org/10.1037/a0029393

Segal, J. (2014). Ideology and the reform of public higher education. *New Political Science*, *36*(4), 489–503. https://doi.org/10.1080/07393148.2014.954804

Senko, C., & Tropiano, K. L. (2016). Comparing three models of achievement goals: Goal orientations, goal standards, and goal complexes. *Journal of Educational Psychology*, *108*, 1178–1192. https://doi.org/10.1037/edu0000114

Senko, C., Hama, H., & Belmonte, K. (2013). Achievement goals, study strategies, and achievement: A test of the "learning agenda" framework. *Learning and Individual Differences*, *24*, 1–10. https://doi.org/10.1016/j.lindif.2012.11.003

Sommet, N., Pulfrey, C., & Butera, F. (2013). Did my M.D. really go to university to learn? Detrimental effects of *numerus clausus* on self-efficacy, mastery goals and learning. *PLoS ONE*, *8*(12), e84178. https://doi.org/10.1371/journal.pone.0084178

Sommet, N., Darnon, C., Mugny, G., Quiamzade, A., Pulfrey, C., Dompnier, B., & Butera, F. (2014). Performance goals in conflictual social interactions: Towards the distinction between two modes of relational conflict regulation. *British Journal of Social Psychology*, *53*, 134–153.

Sommet, N., Pillaud, V., Meuleman, B., & Butera, F. (2017). The socialization of performance goals. *Contemporary Educational Psychology*, *49*, 337–354. https://doi.org/10.1016/j.cedpsych.2017.03.008

Sommet, N., Nguyen, D., Fahrni, K., Jobin, M., Nguyen, H. P., Sehaqui, H., & Butera, F. (2019). When and why performance goals predict exploitation behaviors: An achievement goal complex analysis of the selection function of assessment. *Motivation and Emotion*, *43*, 266–284. https://doi.org/10.1007/s11031-018-9742-y

Son Hing, L. S., Bobocel, D. R., & Zanna, M. P. (2002). Meritocracy and opposition to affirmative action: Making concessions in the face of discrimination. *Journal of Personality and Social Psychology*, *83*, 493–509. https://doi.org/10.1037/0022-3514.83.3.493

Son Hing, L. S., Bobocel, D. R., Zanna, M. P., Garcia, D. M., Gee, S. S., & Orazietti, K. (2011). The merit of meritocracy. *Journal of Personality and Social Psychology*, *101*, 433–50. https://doi.org/10.1037/a0024618

Soncini, A., Matteucci, M. C., & Butera, F. (2021). Error handling in the classroom: An experimental study of teachers' strategies to foster positive error climate. *European Journal of Psychology of Education*, *36*, 719–738. https://doi.org/10.1007/s10212-020-00494-1

Souchal, C., Toczek-Capelle, M. C., Darnon, C., Smeding, A., Butera, F., & Martinot, D. (2014). Assessing does not mean threatening: Assessment as a key determinant of girls' and boys' performance in a science class. *British Journal of Educational Psychology*, *84*, 125–136.

Spence, J. (1981). Access to higher education in the Federal Republic of Germany: The *numerus clausus* issue. *Comparative Education*, *17*, 285–292. https://doi.org/10.1080/0305006810170305

Smeding, A., Darnon, C., Souchal, C., Toczeck-Capelle, M.C., & Butera, F. (2013). Reducing the socio-economic status achievement gap at university by promoting mastery-oriented assessment. *PLoS ONE*, *8*(8), e71678. doi:10.1371/journal.pone.0071678

Steuer, G., Rosentritt-Brunn, G., & Dresel, M. (2013). Dealing with errors in mathematics classrooms: Structure and relevance of perceived error climate. *Contemporary Educational Psychology*, *38*, 196–210. https://doi.org/10.1016/j.cedpsych.2013.03.002

Sutton, J., & Keogh, E. (2000). Social competition in school: Relationships with bullying, Machiavellianism and personality. *British Journal of Educational Psychology*, *70*, 443–456. https://doi.org/10.1348/000709900158227

Świątkowski, W., & Dompnier, B. (2017). La compétition à l'Université: Perspectives individuelles et sociétales (Competition at University: individual and societal perspectives). In C. Staerklé & F. Butera (Eds.), *Conflits constructifs, conflits destructifs: Regards psychosociaux* (pp. 101–117). Antipodes.

Świątkowski, W., & Dompnier, B. (2020). A regulatory focus perspective on performance goals' effects on achievement: A small-scale meta-analytical approach. *Learning and Individual Differences, 78*, 101840. https://doi.org/10.1016/j.lindif.2020.101840

Teixeira, A. A., & Rocha, M. F. (2010). Cheating by economics and business undergraduate students: an exploratory international assessment. *Higher Education, 59*, 663–701. https://doi.org/10.1007/s10734-009-9274-1

Toma, C., & Butera, F. (2009). Hidden profiles and concealed information: Strategic information sharing and use in group decision making. *Personality and Social Psychology Bulletin, 35*, 793–806.

Tulis, M. (2013). Error management behavior in classrooms: Teachers' responses to student mistakes. *Teaching and Teacher Education, 33*, 56–68. https://doi.org/10.1016/j.tate.2013.02.003

Urdan, T., Midgley, C., & Anderman, E. M. (1998). The role of classroom goal structure in students' use of self-handicapping strategies. *American Educational Research Journal, 35*, 101–122. https://doi.org/10.3102/00028312035001101

Van de Werfhorst, H. G. (2014). Changing societies and four tasks of schooling: Challenges for strongly differentiated educational systems. *International Review of Education, 60*, 123–144. https://doi.org/10.1007/s11159-014-9410-8

Van de Werfhorst, H. G., & Mijs, J. J. B. (2010). Achievement inequality and the institutional structure of educational systems: A comparative perspective. *Annual Review of Sociology, 36*, 407–428. https://doi.org/10.1146/annurev.soc.012809.102538

Wang, M. T. (2012). Educational and career interests in math: A longitudinal examination of the links between classroom environment, motivational beliefs, and interests. *Developmental Psychology, 48*, 1643–1657. https://doi.org/10.1146/10.1037/a0027247

Wang, M. T., & Degol, J. L. (2016). School climate: A review of the construct, measurement, and impact on student outcomes. *Educational Psychology Review, 28*, 315–352. https://doi.org/10.1007/s10648-015-9319-1

Wang, M. T., Degol, J. L., Amemiya, J., Parr, A., & Guo, J. (2020a). Classroom climate and children's academic and psychological wellbeing: A systematic review and meta-analysis. *Developmental Review, 57*, 100912. https://doi.org/10.1016/j.dr.2020.100912

Wang, M. T., Hofkens, T., & Ye, F. (2020b). Classroom quality and adolescent student engagement and performance in mathematics: A multi-method and multi-informant approach. *Journal of Youth and Adolescence, 49*, 1987–2002. https://doi.org/10.1007/s10964-020-01195-0

Webb, P. T., Briscoe, F. M., & Mussman, M. P. (2009). Preparing teachers for the neoliberal panopticon. *Educational Foundations, 23*, 3–18.

Wiederkehr, V., Bonnot, V., Krauth-Gruber, S., & Darnon, C. (2015a). Belief in school meritocracy as a system-justifying tool for low status students. *Frontiers in Psychology, 6*, 1053. https://doi.org/10.3389/fpsyg.2015.01053

Wiederkehr, V., Darnon, C., Chazal, S., Guimond, S., & Martinot, D. (2015b). From social class to self-efficacy: Internalization of low social status pupils' school performance. *Social Psychology of Education: An International Journal, 18*, 769–784. https://doi.org/10.1007/s11218-015-9308-8

Wray-Lake, L. (2019). How do young people become politically engaged? *Child Development Perspectives, 13*, 127–132. https://doi.org/10.1111/cdep.12324

Wright, S. (2001). Restricted intergroup boundaries: Tokenism, ambiguity, and the tolerance of injustice. In J. Jost & B. Major (Eds.), *The psychology of legitimacy* (pp. 223–254). Cambridge University Press.

Zajda, J. (2009). Values education and multiculturalism. In J. Zajda & D. Holger (Eds.), *Global values education* (pp. 13–23). Springer.

Zamora, A., Súarez, J. M., & Ardura, D. (2018) A model of the role of error detection and self-regulation in academic performance. *The Journal of Educational Research, 111*, 595–602. https://doi.org/10.1080/00220671.2017.349072

Zhang, Y., & Xin, Z. (2019). Rule comes first: The influences of market-attributes on interpersonal trust in the marketization process. *Journal of Social Issues, 75*, 286–313. https://doi.org/10.1111/josi.12306

Mindfulness, Competition, and Sports Psychology: A Phenomenological Perspective

Ramaswami Mahalingam

Abstract

Mindfulness is defined as the awareness of our present, recognizing the changing nature of our thoughts, feelings, and emotions and the interdependent nature of human existence. This chapter provides an overview of existing research on mindfulness with a specific focus on sports psychology. Mindfulness-based interventions, in general, were found to improve athletic performance, flow experiences and emotional regulation. Although mindfulness-based interventions are beneficial to athletes, there is a significant gap in research on the impact of mindfulness practices in shaping the subjective experiences of athletes on the process of competition. This chapter proposes a phenomenological approach to mindful competition, outlining four critical interrelated avenues for research. First, we need more qualitative studies examining how mindfulness training helps athletes make sense of competition. Second, it is crucial to investigate the potential benefits of mindfulness during three stages of competition: (1) preparation, (2) performance, and (3) reflection. Because each step of the competition has unique demands, it is vital to investigate the usefulness of mindfulness beyond flow experiences and athletic performance. Third, sympathetic joy, our capacity to feel happy for other people's happiness, is an essential mindfulness skill that will help athletes in group sports to rejoice with the success of their teammates. Finally, the mindfulness-based interventions also call for ethical behavior, emphasizing compassion and kindness with the potential to reduce cheating in sports.

Key Words: ACT, sports psychology, sympathetic joy, ethical mindfulness, qualitative research

While the psychology of competition is studied from various perspectives, this chapter focuses on the psychology of competition using psychological research on mindfulness in sports psychology. Because mindfulness is an emerging area of research in psychology, its application to the psychology of competition has recently gained attention in sports psychology (Kaufman, Glass & Arnkoff, 2009; Kee & Wang, 2008). The chapter is structured in three sections. The first section will briefly overview relevant psychological research on mindfulness. The second section will focus on how mindfulness is conceptualized and operationalized in empirical research in sports psychology. The last section identifies potential new avenues for future research on the psychology of competition in sports psychology.

Mindfulness: A Brief Overview

A search on Google for "mindfulness" returns with several million hits revealing its popularity. It has gained increasingly more scholarly attention in disparate fields from Creative Consciousness to Cognitive Neuroscience. Growing research interest in the art and science of mindfulness from various subfields of psychology illustrates that psychological science recognizes mindfulness as an important area of research to understand the beneficial effects of mindfulness in improving mental and physical well-being. Several empirical studies investigated the usefulness of mindfulness practices in enhancing attention, resilience, coping with pain, and social anxiety. For instance, there is an emerging interest in the role of mindfulness-awareness in reducing the social anxiety of students suffering from Asperger's syndrome. There is also a growing body of research on the usefulness of mindfulness in emotional regulation, coping with stress, depression, and PTSD (Post Traumatic Stress Disorder Follette, Vijay, & Didonna, 2009, also see Shapiro & Carlson, 2017).

While there is a growing interest in mindfulness, defining mindfulness has been challenging (Baer, 2019). What is mindfulness? Each scholarly discipline defines the term within its intellectual lineage and discourse. Buddhist meditation teachers, such as Jack Kornfield (2003), inspired by the *Vipassana* tradition, emphasize cultivating compassion and kindness as the major goals of mindfulness practices. Often mindfulness is reduced to meditation practices. Salzberg (2009) argues that mindfulness should not merely be confined to the practice of meditation. Rather, it should help us to have compassion toward ourselves and others. Mindfulness practices help us strengthen our connection to our communities in the process.

There is some broad consensus among researchers within social sciences about a secular definition of mindfulness. Mindfulness is viewed as an *awareness* and a *process* (Brown & Ryan, 2003; Kabat-Zinn, 2005; Shapiro & Carlson, 2017). Mindfulness is an awareness—a way of being in the present and inhabiting our body in a moment-by-moment awareness or bare attention. Shapiro and Carlson (2017) define mindfulness as a way of being in the present, inhabiting our body and mind in a moment-by-moment and nonjudgmental awareness of the present. Mindfulness is a process or practice where we intentionally cultivate a habit of being fully present in all our daily endeavors with acceptance and compassion toward ourselves and others cultivated by various mindfulness practices, including meditation and contemplative art. Mindfulness intervention studies focus on the cultivation and skillful practice of mindfulness in workshops over six to eight weeks (typically meeting once a week) or five-to-ten-day-long mindfulness retreats to learn and practice mindfulness under the guidance of a certified or experienced mindfulness teacher.

Mindfulness practice has two components: formal and applied. The formal mindful practices include systemic meditation. The applied component calls for an expansion of mindful awareness to all aspects of our everyday lives, including mundane things like walking, eating, and social interactions. Researchers developed several scales to measure mindfulness (see Baer, Walsh & Lykins, 2009, for a review). Some of the unifying themes in these definitions of mindfulness are nonjudging, openness, nonreactivity, curiosity, changing nature of our emotions, and compassion (Shapiro & Carlson, 2017; Walsh & Shapiro, 2006).

Psychological Research on Mindfulness

Research in mindfulness in psychology and education spreads over many subareas of psychology. Cognitive neuroscientists have studied the neurological basis of mindfulness by comparing Tibetan monks and people with varying degrees of experience in meditation (Davidson et al., 2003). They also looked at the neurological changes resulting from participation in a mindfulness-based stress reduction program. Social psychological researchers have examined whether mindfulness training affects emotional regulation and negative affect (Fredrickson et al., 2008) and stereotype reduction (Djikic et al., 2008). Clinical psychologists have investigated the effect of mindfulness on depression (Baer et al., 2009). Organizational psychologists have looked at mindfulness practices at the organizational level and their beneficial effect on organizational climate and the well-being of employees (Dutton et al., 2006). Educational psychologists also examined whether mindfulness practices improve teaching and pedagogical practices (see Kabat-Zinn, 2003) and creativity (Langer, 2009). All these research reports positive (and some very robust) effects of mindfulness practices in improving psychological well-being. For example, participating in a mindfulness-based stress reduction (MBSR) program augments participants' ability to cope with stress.

Cultivating mindfulness (a nonjudgmental moment-to-moment awareness) also improves self-regulation and eating behavior. For example, participants who went through a MBSR program were more successful in following their diet plans (Didonna & Didonna, 2009; Wolver & Best, 2009). Mindfulness practitioners scored high on measures of cognitive and emotional regulation. One of the cornerstones of mindfulness research has been to explore how mindfulness practices have enhanced psychological resilience by improving compassion towards the self and others. Neff (2003) found a significant association between self-compassion and academic achievement, positive body image, hope, and self-esteem in a study investigating the impact of cultivating self-compassion (also see Neff et al., 2018). A review of kindness-based interventions also documents the beneficial effects of cultivating compassion and kindness in lowering stress and improving happiness (Galante et al., 2014).

Recent clinical research examining the relationship between mindfulness and emotional regulation shows that participating in a MBSR program alleviates anxiety and promotes positive emotions. For example, in a study conducted by Fredrickson et al. (2008), participants who were recruited for an eight-week loving-kindness (a form of compassion meditation) program reported more positive emotions than those who were in the control condition. Gross and John (2003) proposed a process model with two distinct strategies for emotional regulation: reappraisal and suppression. Reappraisal consists of how we think of a situation to minimize its emotional impact. Suppression, which comes later, is the process that involves the managing of emotion through inhibition. Mindfulness interventions improve reappraisal (Garland et al., 2009) and lower emotional suppression scores (Mahalingam & Rabelo, 2019). By contrast, suppression was positively associated with negative emotions and negatively related to the experience and expression of negative emotions. Because suppression involves effort, it adversely affected memory and was negatively associated with closeness and diminished social support. In a six-week mindfulness intervention study, Mahalingam and Rabelo (2019) found that practicing mindfulness meditation twice a week for 20 minutes in a mindfulness class significantly lowered the participants' emotional suppression scores.

Several criticisms have been leveled against psychological research on mindfulness. There is a lack of consensus in defining mindfulness and the various measures used in measuring mindfulness. In addition, lack of sufficient attention to standardizing procedures in intervention studies in terms of dosage or optimal length of practice to achieve the positive efforts of mindfulness (van Dam et al., 2018). Mindfulness research is also criticized for using self-reported measures of mindfulness. Baer (2019) responded to these criticisms by pointing out that mindfulness is conceptualized as a multidimensional construct. By monitoring one's self-awareness of their moment-to-moment experience of their thinking and feeling, self-reported measures provide a window to understanding participants' mindfulness awareness. Baer (2019) also pointed out that those who score high on dispositional mindfulness benefit greatly by practicing mindfulness regularly. The empirical findings are robust, documenting the beneficial effects of mindfulness practices. Even 15 minutes of mindfulness practice every day improves attention and the ability to deal with negative emotions, stress, and anxiety while positively contributing to resilience, social connectedness, and self-esteem (Basso et al., 2019).

Mindfulness, Competition, and Sports Psychology

Sports events exemplify competition because they are public dramas performed with winners and losers. Any sports event is stressful because there is a clear winner where participants are rank ordered. Sports psychologists have recognized the usefulness of mindfulness practices. Particularly, a mindfulness-based clinical approach to augment well-being, Acceptance and Commitment Therapy (ACT), has garnered the scholarly attention of sports psychologists (Gardner & Moore, 2012). Drawing on Buddhist psychology and cognitive behavioral therapy, Hayes et al. (2004) developed ACT as a clinical perspective that requires no meditation practices. The main emphasis is on helping clients to see "self as a process" by consciously bringing attention to the moment-to-moment awareness of experiencing the now with openness, curiosity, and acceptance. ACT has six core dimensions: (1) diffusion, (2) acceptance, (3) contact with the present moment, (4) the observing self, (5) values, and (6) committed action (Harris, 2006). According to ACT, the moment-to-moment awareness of our thoughts and emotions and the changing nature of self improves metacognitive skills fostering more self-compassion and acceptance.

In traditional approaches to sports psychology, most of the emphasis has been on the therapeutic aspects of skill training, such as motivation, imagery, goal setting, and pre-competitive self-talk, to control one's emotional and physical state to achieve an optimal performance state (Gardner & Moore, 2004, 2012). By contrast, mindfulness-based approaches emphasize an openness to present, without any discomfort with the changing nature of self, cognitions, and emotions, and with an open mind, instead of listening to the inner voice that is judging and controlling one's ability to compete. According to Gardner and Moore (2012, p. 309), "the mindfulness and acceptance-based models suggest that optimal performance does not require the reduction or volitional control of internal states at all, but rather, requires (a) a nonjudging (i.e., not good, not bad, not right, not wrong) moment-to-moment awareness and acceptance of one's internal state, whatever that may be; (b) an attentional focus on task-relevant external stimuli, instead of a focus on internal processes that include judgment and direct efforts at control/modulation; and (c) a consistent and effortful personal values-driven commitment to behavioral actions/ choices that support one's athletic endeavor." Mindfulness and acceptance commitment (MAC) interventions help athletes and players reframe their internal experiences instead of needing control or suppressing their emotions and cognitions (either their frequency or valence) to reach a perfect performance state.

Drawing on ACT principles, MAC is the most researched and systemic integration of mindfulness principles in sports psychology (Gardner & Moore, 2006). MAC has seven modules of intervention that can be adapted to the individual needs of the athletes: (1) psychoeducation, (2) mindfulness training and cognitive diffusion, (3) values identification and values-driven behavior, (4) cognitive and emotional acceptance, (5) behavioral commitment, (6) skill consolidation and poise, and (7) skill maintenance. The MAC model differs from ACT in its explicit commitment to mindfulness practices, including meditation as part of its training model while incorporating the six core principles of ACT to the specific context of athletic training. It also emphasizes mindful awareness of the relationship between skill development, emotional regulation, and value-driven behavior in and outside of sports with a commitment to mindful engagement to find meaning in life. While MAC is the most influential model of mindfulness, other researchers have adapted MAC principles to specific training contexts of athletes (e.g., Thompson et al., 2011).

How do MAC interventions help athletes' ability to compete? Based on empirical research on mindfulness, sports psychologists predict that MAC applications will benefit athletes in several ways (Birrer et al., 2012). MAC improves athletic performance by nine mechanisms: (1) improving bare attention, (2) experiential acceptance, (3) values clarifications, (4) self-regulation/negative affect, (5) clarity about one's inner life, (6) exposure, (7) flexibility, (8) non-attachment, and (9) lowering rumination (Birrer et al., 2012). In a meta-analysis of mindfulness-based interventions for a wide range of participants (e.g., cyclists, dart throwers, hammer throwers, hockey players, hurdlers, judo fighters, rugby players), Buhlmayer et al. (2017) found that mindfulness practices improved physiological surrogates (i.e., salivary cortisol level, immune response, resting heart rate, maximal oxygen uptake), and psychological performance surrogates (i.e., flow, goal-directed energy, anxiety/apprehension, anxiety).

MAC interventions enhance performance by enhancing *mental efficiency* because of their efficacy in improving attention, as evidenced by many neurological studies on mindfulness (Davidson et al., 2003; Jha et al., 2010, 2007). Neural plasticity and efficient uses of cortical resources enhance athletic performance (Bertollo et al., 2016; Gardner & Moore, 2020). MAC interventions also improve athletes' awareness of their internal cognitive and emotional states. In a review of research on mindfulness-based interventions on long-distance runners, Corbally et al. (2020) found tentative support for the benefits of mindfulness practices in attenuating immune responses, lowering performance anxiety, and increased trait mindfulness. In a meta-analytic study examining the relationship between mindfulness and burnout, Li et al. (2019) found that mindfulness interventions also lowered athletic burnout.

Another central area of exploration of mindfulness is the usefulness of mindfulness for experiencing flow states. Correlational studies found that dispositional flow was positively associated with peak performance and mindfulness was a significant predictor of dispositional flow (Gardner & Moore, 2020). According to Noetel et al. (2019, pp. 155–156), in sports, "flow is defined as an intense, rewarding, undistracted absorption in the activity which has been found to be a mediator of success in performance. It can reflect a moment-to-moment experience (state flow) or the tendency of an athlete to experience these states." In a systemic review of 66 studies of mindful and acceptance-based intervention on a broader range of athletes and team sports, Noetel et al. (2019) found support for the claim that mindfulness-based practices promote the flow state of athletes.

In sum, mindfulness-based interventions improve the attention and mental efficiency of athletes. MAC lowers performance anxiety by enhancing the emotional regulation skills of athletes. Mindfulness-based practices promote the flow states of athletes. While these results are promising, the researchers warn us to interpret the results with caution for potential bias and flaws in research designs (Buhlmayer et al., 2017; Gardner & Moore, 2020; Noetel et al., 2019; Li et al., 2019). Gardner and Moore (2020) point out that while the efficacy of mindfulness-based interventions improves athletes' performance, more research is needed to ascertain the usefulness of mindfulness in sports contexts. Gardner and Moore (2020) identified five critical issues on mindfulness-based approaches to the competition: (1) we need more RCT studies with a large sample; (2) we need more studies comparing multiple sports, sports types, and sports levels (e.g., individual vs. team sports); (3) research studies need to incorporate multiple measures of athletic performance; (4) we also need to explore the role of cultural contexts in shaping the effectiveness of mindfulness-based interventions in cross-cultural comparative studies; and (5) we need to conduct more multi-site studies of mindfulness-interventions.

Although mindfulness-based acceptance practices help athletes improve athletic performance, more research is necessary to ascertain the effectiveness of mindfulness across sports contexts and in different cultures.

Phenomenology of Mindfulness and Sports Psychology: New Possibilities

Mindfulness interventions, especially acceptance-based interventions, are effective in helping athletes enhance flow experiences, improve focus with openness and curiosity, and lower levels of performance anxiety. More than two decades of mindfulness research in sports psychology have demonstrated the efficacy of mindfulness practices. However, there are few critical gaps in research on mindfulness in sports psychology.

Qualitative Research on Mindfulness and the Phenomenology of Competition

Most mindfulness-based studies in sports psychology are correlational or intervention studies using RCT or convenience samples. While the growing body of mindfulness-based studies in sports captures the positive change in cognitions and emotional regulations, most studies do not sufficiently explore the effects of prior mindfulness practice experiences. For example, years of mindfulness practice play a significant role in facilitating various cognitive processes, emotional regulation, and creativity. Because mindful awareness is cultivated through rigorous practice, it will be helpful to examine whether years of mindfulness practice are a critical factor in improving performance and experiencing affect peak performance, attention, and emotional regulation (Colzato & Kibele, 2017). Longitudinal studies need to analyze how athletes use various mindfulness practices (e.g., breath meditation, loving kindness meditation) to fine-tune specific skills, such as focus, performance anxiety, and rumination, during the three stages of the competition. Such a longitudinal study will help us understand the individual differences in athletes' flexibility in using mindfulness practices and greater integration of mindfulness in finding meaning and joy while playing their favorite sport.

Another significant gap in mindfulness research in sports psychology is the lack of attention to the qualitative research on mindfulness that focuses on the experiential aspects of mindfulness (Khong & Mruk, 2009). Only a handful of qualitative studies provide a phenomenological lens to understand the subjective experiences of practicing mindfulness to compete. In a qualitative study of the mindfulness experiences of the Division I women's soccer team after a six-week and a 12-session of mindfulness training, Baltzell et al. (2014) found that several participants cultivated a different relationship with their emotions. However, some participants found it hard to practice meditation and did not see the point of meditation in playing soccer. Baltzell et al. (2014) found that athletes carried a caring thought for the self and the team on and off the field. Participants' interview responses reveal their everyday struggles and triumphs in practicing mindfulness. Another qualitative study of a mindfulness intervention of Division III Lacrosse players also found players' positive reflective understanding of mindfulness practices in their everyday life (Minkler et al., 2021). Qualitative studies provide new insights into the challenges athletes face in developing effective mindfulness practices to help athletes. Holistic mindfulness practices, including contemplative art and journaling, may help those who struggle during meditation. For example, Gussak (2007) found that holistic mindfulness intervention that includes contemplative arts improved psychological well-being and sense of agency. Including a wide range of contemplative practices, such as art, poetry, and mindfulness journaling using photovoice (Mahalingam & Rabelo, 2019), may help athletes who find it challenging to find time to sit and meditate.

Sympathetic Joy and Sports Psychology

Interestingly most of the MAC approaches in sports psychology focus on improving psychological resilience and performance at the individual level. How mindfulness affects the athletes at the intersubjective level, such as whether mindfulness practices improve compassion and a deeper connection to their teammates, is not fully explored in mindfulness-based intervention studies in sports psychology. For example, one of the core pillars of Buddhist psychology is the notion of sympathetic joy, our capacity to rejoice or genuinely feel happy for others' happiness. Interestingly, most of the research on mindfulness focused on compassion; that is, our ability to respond to other people's suffering. Only a handful of studies examined the significance of sympathetic joy in our lives (Royzman & Rozin, 2006). Our capacity to feel happy from the happiness of others, and if we can diligently work toward promoting sympathetic joy, will improve our psychological well-being.

It is ubiquitous in many team sports events to witness moments of joy in rooting for teammates. Players openly display their joy and happiness while rejoicing with the success of their teammates, which has an infectious effect on the fans. Sympathetic joy is one of the most common shared experiences in the sports arena. Despite being one of the critical pillars of Buddhist psychology, sympathetic joy is rarely examined in sports psychology. Mindfulness intervention programs in sports psychology primarily focus on individual performance. The moments of experiencing sympathetic joy from the spontaneous display of happiness in witnessing the success of their friends and fellow players have been rarely studied in sports psychology. Intentional cultivation of sympathetic joy will help athletes, and players will also allow athletes to authentically connect to their positive emotions in seeing the success of others. Over time, sympathetic joy will improve athletes' psychological well-being and help them overcome jealousy over the success of others.

Efficacy of Mindfulness and the Contexts of Competition

Mindfulness-based interventions in sports psychology could expand its theoretical perspective to more *explicitly* address the contextual demands of the athletes. Every competition involves three phases: preparation, performance, and reflection (see Figure 26.1). The preparation stage consists of the conditioning of the mind and body to the demands of the competition. Players must go through rigorous training with goal setting, focusing on specific strategies for the competition. Professional rivalries, such as the University of Michigan vs. the Ohio State football games, add additional layers of pressure for the athletes if it is a team sport. Mindfulness practices that enhance focus and emotional regulation while lowering performance anxiety will benefit the athletes.

The athletes must perform during the *performance* stage while feeling the pressure, and mindfulness practices help them in at least three significant ways. It will help them enjoy their performance and improve the chances of creating or assisting innovative plays, a form of being in the zone simultaneously improving their teammates' level of performance. Mindfulness practices also help them overcome rumination (Jain et al., 2007) on their mistakes at a critical moment in the game. By cultivating self-compassion, they can overcome the spiraling of their negative emotions stemming from their failure, which could undermine their performance. Experiencing sympathetic joy at the success of their teammates will help them more authentically connect and care for their team's success.

After the performance is over, the next stage of the competition is the *reflection* to prepare for improved future performance irrespective of the results. Reflecting on their performance is the hallmark of great athletes. After a loss or failure, it is difficult to overcome the adverse effects of personal disappointments and frustrations in not reaching one's goals and standards. Suppressing negative emotions hampers honest performance evaluation in planning future improvements. Equanimity and self-compassion will help us deal with our imperfections with sublime empathy (Mahalingam, 2019). Mindfulness practices can help athletes have the courage and openness to confront their imperfections and shortcomings. Research on mindfulness and pain management (e.g., Gardner-Nix & Didonna, 2009; Sephton et al., 2007) suggests that mindfulness will also help athletes cope with their pain and injuries.

Mapping the usefulness of mindfulness at various stages of the competition will help athletes develop a toolbox approach to mindfulness to effectively apply their mindfulness practices at different stages of the competition with intention and purpose. Such

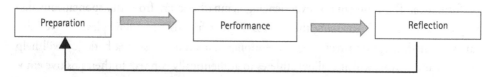

Figure 26.1 Mindfulness during the three stages of the competition

engagement with mindfulness improves their performance, which is the focus of most research in sports psychology, and will improve their psychological and physical well-being while fostering deeper connection and genuine kindness to their teammates.

Right Mindfulness and the Ethics of Competition

One of the core emphases of ACT is a commitment to value-guided behavior. Mindfulness-based acceptance programs incorporate values as the core of their training program. Keeping value-guided behavior as the core of MAC programs will also help athletes explore ethical aspects of their behavior. For Greenberg and Mitra (2015), practicing mindfulness to lead a value-driven life is the right way of practicing mindfulness (right mindfulness). Interestingly there is a lack of research on the effect of mindfulness practices on the ethical behavior of athletes. Do athletes who practice mindfulness cheat? Do they play the games according to the rules? Future research on mindfulness in sports psychology needs to explore these critical questions. It will be helpful to document that mindfulness practices improve performance and well-being and foster ethical behavior during competition.

Conclusion

Mindfulness has been gaining well deserved attention in sports psychology, and the results have been promising, despite the need for more research (Bondár et al., 2021; Gardner & Moore, 2020). Mindfulness helps athletes to focus and experience more peak performance with low levels of performance anxiety. Mindfulness-based interventions improve emotion regulation and reduce burnout of athletes. Future research needs to explore how mindfulness practices improve performance concerning specific demands of the team sport (e.g., soccer, lacrosse, basketball) and the particular needs of different kinds of athletes (e.g., sprinter, long-distance runners). Such explorations will develop context-specific guidelines for mindfulness intervention programs to optimize their benefits for athletes who play different sports. In addition, expanding the theoretical orientation of the various aspects of mindfulness that will be useful at different competition stages can help athletes develop a fine-tuned strategic use of mindfulness while competing. Athletes will be more motivated to continue their mindfulness practice because they can adapt to the specific demands of the competition phase. Mindfulness practices will also help athletes to cope with pain management. They will also allow athletes to build an ethical vision for competing, and thus reduce cheating, which is a chronic problem in sports.

References

Baer, R. (2019). Assessment of mindfulness by self-report. *Current Opinion in Psychology 28*, 42–48.

Baer R. A., Walsh, E., & Lykins, E. (2009). Assessment of mindfulness. In F. Didonna (Ed.). *Clinical handbook of mindfulness* (pp. 153–168). Springer.

Baltzell, A., Caraballo, N., Chipman, K., & Hayden, L. (2014). A qualitative study of the mindfulness meditation training for sport: Division I female soccer players' experience. *Journal of Clinical Sport Psychology, 8*(3), 221–244.

Basso, J. C., McHale, A., Ende, V., Oberlin, D. J., & Suzuki, W. A. (2019). Brief, daily meditation enhances attention, memory, mood, and emotional regulation in non-experienced meditators. *Behavioral Brain Research 356*, 208–220.

Bertollo, M., di Fronso, S., Filho, E., Conforto, S., Schmid, M., Bortoli, L., Comani, S., Robazza, C. (2016). Proficient brain for optimal performance: The MAP model perspective. *PeerJ 4*, e2082. https://doi.org/10.7717/peerj.2082.

Birrer, D., Rothlin, P., & Morgan, G. (2012). Mindfulness to enhance athletic performance: Theoretical considerations and possible impact mechanisms. *Mindfulness 3*(3), 235–246.

Bondár, R. Z., Bertollo, M., di Fronso, S., & Robazza, C. (2021). Mindfulness to performance enhancement: A systematic review of neural correlates. *International Review of Sport and Exercise Psychology*, 1–29.

Brown, K. W., & Ryan, R. M. (2003) The benefits of being present: mindfulness and its role in psychological well-being. *Journal of Personality and Social Psychology 84*(4), 822–848.

Buhlmayer, L., Birrer, D., Rothlin, P., Faude, O., & Donath, L. (2017). Effects of mindfulness practice on performance-relevant parameters and performance outcomes in sports: A meta-analytical review. *Sports Medicine 47*(11), 2309–2321.

Colzato, L. S., & Kibele, A. (2017). How different types of meditation can enhance athletic performance depending on the specific sport skills. *Journal of Cognitive Enhancement 1*(2), 122–126.

Corbally, L., Wilkinson, M., & Fothergill, M. A. (2020). Effects of mindfulness practice on performance and factors related to performance in long-distance running: A systematic review. *Journal of Clinical Sport Psychology 14*(4), 376–398.

Davidson, R. J., Kabat-Zinn, J., Schumacher, J., Rosenkranz, M., Muller, D., Santorelli, S. F., Urbanowski, F., Harrington, A., Bonus, K., & Sheridan, J. F. (2003). Alterations in brain and immune function produced by mindfulness meditation. *Psychosomatic Medicine 65*, 564–570.

Didonna, F., & Didonna, F. (2009). Mindfulness and obsessive-compulsive disorder: Developing a way to trust and validate one's an internal experience. In F. Didonna (Ed.), *Clinical handbook of mindfulness* (pp. 189–219). Springer Science + Business Media.

Djikic, M., Langer, E. J., & Stapleton, S. F. (2008). Reducing stereotyping through mindfulness: Effects on automatic stereotype-activated behaviors. *Journal of Adult Development 15*(2), 106–111.

Dutton, J., M. Worline, P. Frost, and J. Lilius. (2006) Explaining compassion organizing. *Administrative Science Quarterly 51*(1), 59–96.

Follette, V. M., Vijay, A., & Didonna, F. (2009). Mindfulness for trauma and posttraumatic stress disorder. In F. Didonna (Ed.), *Clinical handbook of mindfulness* (pp. 299–317). Springer Science + Business Media.

Fredrickson, B. L., Cohn, M. A., Coffey, K. A., Pek, J., & Finkel, S. M. (2008). Open hearts build lives: Positive emotions, induced through loving-kindness meditation, build consequential personal resources. *Journal of Personality and Social Psychology 95*, 1045–1062.

Galante, J., Galante, I., Bekkers, M. J., & Gallacher, J. (2014). Effect of kindness-based meditation on health and well-being: a systematic review and meta-analysis. *Journal of Consulting and Clinical Psychology 82*(6), 1101–1114.

Gardner, F. L., & Moore, Z. E. (2004). A mindfulness-acceptance-commitment (MAC) based approach to athletic performance enhancement: Theoretical considerations. *Behavior Therapy 35*, 707–723. doi:10.1016/S0005-7894(04)80016-9.

Gardner, F. L., & Moore, Z. E. (2006). *Clinical sport psychology*. Human Kinetics.

Gardner, F. L., & Moore, Z. E. (2012). Mindfulness and acceptance models in sport psychology: A decade of scientific advancements. *Canadian Psychology 53*(4), 309–318. doi:10.1037/a0030220.

Gardner, F. L., & Moore, Z. E. (2020). Mindfulness in sports contexts. In G. Tenenbaum and R. C. Eklund (Eds.), *Handbook of sport psychology* (pp. 738–750). John Wiley & Sons.

Gardner-Nix, J., & Didonna, F. (2009). Mindfulness-based stress reduction for chronic pain management. In F. Didonna (Ed.), *Clinical handbook of mindfulness* (pp. 369–381). Springer Science + Business Media.

Garland, E., Gaylord, S., & Park, J. (2009) The role of mindfulness in positive reappraisal. *Explore (N.Y.) 5*, 37–44.

Greenberg, M. T., & Mitra, J. L. (2015). From mindfulness to right mindfulness: The intersection of awareness and ethics. *Mindfulness 6*(1), 74–78.

Gross, J. J., & John, O. P. (2003). Individual differences in two emotion regulation processes: Implications for affect, relationships, and well-being. *Journal of Personality and Social Psychology 85*, 348–362.

Gussak, D. (2007). The effectiveness of art therapy in reducing depression in prison populations. *International Journal of Offender Therapy and Comparative Criminology 51*(4), 444–460.

Harris, R. (2006). Embracing your demons: An overview of acceptance and commitment therapy. *Psychotherapy in Australia 12*, 1–8.

Hayes, S. C., Strosahl, K. D., Bunting, K., Twohig, M., & Wilson, K. G. (2004). What is acceptance and commitment therapy? In S. C. Hayes and K. D. Strosahl (Eds.), *A practical guide to acceptance and commitment therapy* (pp. 3–29). Springer.

Jain, S., Shapiro, S., Swanick, S., Roesch, S., Mills, P., Bell, I., & Schwartz, G. (2007). A randomized controlled trial of mindfulness meditation versus relaxation training: Effects on distress, positive states of mind, rumination, and distraction. *Annals of Behavioral Medicine 33*(1), 11–21. doi:10.1207/sl5324796abm3301.

Jha, A. P., Stanley, E. A., Kiyaonga, A., Wong, L., & Gelfand, L. (2010). Examining protective effects of mindfulness training on working memory capacity and affective experience. *Emotion 10*(1), 54–64.

Jha, A. P., Krompinger, J., & Baime, M. J. (2007). Mindfulness training modifies subsystems of attention. *Cognitive, Affective, & Behavioral Neuroscience 7*, 109–119. doi:10.3758/CABN.7.2.109.

Kabat-Zinn, J. (2003). Mindfulness-based interventions, past, present and future. *Clinical Psychology: Science and Practice 10*(2), 144–156.

Kabat-Zinn, J. (2005). *Healing ourselves through mindfulness*. Hyperion

Kaufman, K., Glass, C., & Arnkoff, D. (2009). Evaluation of mindful sport performance enhancement (MSPE): A new approach to promote flow in athletes. *Journal of Clinical Sports Psychology 4*, 334–356.

Kee, Y. H., & Wang, C. K. J. (2008). Relationship between mindfulness, flow dispositions and mental skill adoptions: A cluster analytic approach. *Psychology of Sport and Exercise 9*, 393–411. doi:10.1016/j.psychsport.2007.07.001.

Khong, B. S. L., & Mruk, C. J. (2009). Editor's introduction to the special issue on mindfulness in psychology. The *Humanistic Psychologist 37*, 109–116.

Kornfield, J. (2003). *The art of forgiveness, loving-kindness, and peace*. Bantam.

Langer, E. (2009). *Counterclockwise and the power of possibility*. Ballentine.

Li, C., Zhu, Y., Zhang, M., Gustafsson, H., & Chen, T. (2019). Mindfulness and athlete burnout: A systematic review and meta-analysis. *International Journal of Environmental Research and Public Health 16*(3), 449, 1–13.

Mahalingam, R. (2019). Mindful mindset, interconnectedness and dignity. *Youth and Globalization 1*(2), 230–253.

Mahalingam, R., & Rabelo, V. C. (2019). Teaching mindfulness to undergraduates: A survey and photovoice Study. *Journal of Transformative Education 17*(1), 51–70.

Minkler, T. O., Glass, C. R., & Hut, M. (2021). Mindfulness training for a college team: Feasibility, acceptability, and effectiveness from within an athletic department. *Journal of Applied Sport Psychology 33*(6), 609–626.

Neff, K. D., Long, P., Knox, M. C., Davidson, O., Kuchar, A., Costigan, A., Williamson, Z., Rohleder, N., Tóth-Király, I. & Breines, J. G. (2018). The forest and the trees: Examining the association of self-compassion and its positive and negative components with psychological functioning. *Self and Identity 17*(6), 627–645.

Neff, K. D. (2003). The development and validation of a scale to measure self-compassion. *Self and Identity 2*, 223–250.

Noetel, M., Ciarrochi, J., Van Zanden, B., & Lonsdale, C. (2019). Mindfulness and acceptance approaches to sporting performance enhancement: A systematic review. *International Review of Sport and Exercise Psychology 12*(1), 139–175. doi:10.1080/1750984X.2017.1387803.

Royzman, E. B., & Rozin, P. (2006). Limits of symhedonia: The differential role of prior emotional attachment in sympathy and sympathetic joy. *Emotion 6*(1), 82–89.

Salzberg, S. (2009). *The kindness handbook: A practical companion*. Sounds True Inc.

Sephton, S. E., Salmon P., Weissbecker, I., Ulmer, C., Floyd, A., Hoover, K., & Studts, J.L. (2007). Mindfulness meditation alleviates depressive symptoms in women with fibromyalgia: Results of a randomized clinical trial. *Arthritis Rheumatology 57*, 77–85.

Shapiro, S. L., & Carlson, L. E. (2017). *The art and science of mindfulness: Integrating mindfulness into psychology and the helping professions*. American Psychological Association.

Thompson, R. W., Kaufman, K. A., De Petrillo, L. A., Glass, C. R., & Arnkoff, D. B. (2011). One-year follow-up of mindful sport performance enhancement (MSPE) with archers, golfers, and runners. *Journal of Clinical Sport Psychology 5*, 99–116.

van Dam, N. T., van Vugt, M. K., Vago, D. R., Schmalzl, L., Saron, C. D., Olendzki, A., Meissner, T., Lazar, S.W., Kerr, C.E., Gorchov, J., Fox, K.C.R., Field, B.A., Britton, W.B., Brefczynski-Lewis, J.A., & Meyer, D.E. (2018). Mind the hype: A critical evaluation and prescriptive agenda for research on mindfulness and meditation. *Perspectives on Psychological Science 13*, 36–61. doi:1745691617709589.

Walsh R., & Shapiro S. L. (2006). The meeting of meditative disciplines and Western psychology: A mutually enriching dialogue. *American Psychologist 61*, 227–239.

Wolver, R. Q., & Best, J. L. (2009). Mindfulness-based approaches to eating disorders. In F. Didonna (Ed.), *Clinical handbook of mindfulness* (pp. 259–288). Springer.

Hide a Dagger Behind a Smile: A Review of How Collectivistic Cultures Compete More Than Individualistic Cultures

Kaidi Wu *and* Thomas Talhelm

Abstract

In this chapter, we review cultural differences in people's attitudes about competition, why cultures differ in competition, and how they compete in different ways. Researchers have long associated collectivistic culture with harmony and cooperation. However, the bulk of the evidence suggests that collectivistic cultures compete more, and more intensely, than individualistic cultures. Collectivists are more likely to see competition as zero-sum, engage in social comparison, and base their self-worth on common standards rather than self-defined goals. This raises a paradox: where does the popular conception of harmony in collectivism come from? In reviewing prior studies, we find that people in collectivistic cultures tend to use indirect, hidden methods to compete against others. This allows for an outward harmony, without negating competition. We ask whether competition in collectivistic cultures is only stronger when competing with outsiders. Studies reject this speculation. Rather, people in collectivistic cultures compete more with in-group members and are more vigilant toward classmates and co-workers. Next, we explore how people from different cultures decide to enter into competition. We find that collectivists' tendency to enter into prestigious competitive environments might end up harming them. Finally, we discuss whether there can be versions of collectivistic groups without competition or whether this is a utopian dream.

Key Words: culture, collectivism, competition, sabotage, social comparison, zero-sum belief

Hide a dagger behind a smile.

—*The Thirty-Six Stratagems (Taylor, 2013)*

On April 1, 2013, Yang Huang, a medical student from prestigious Fudan University in Shanghai, drank from a water dispenser in his dormitory and fell violently ill. Two weeks later, Huang died of poisoning. The culprit was none other than his roommate, a fellow medical student who held a held a grudge against him and laced the water with thallium

(Zhuang, 2013). Within the same year, Zijie Wang, a 26-year-old graduate student at Queen's University was caught on camera dosing his co-worker with a carcinogenic chemical NDMA (Faris, 2018).

These were far from isolated incidents amid the competitive landscape of higher education in China. Students have committed similar crimes against their fellow classmates at Tsinghua University, Peking University, and the China University of Mining and Technology (Pan, 2013). Overseas, a 22-year-old Chinese student at Lehigh University admitted to sickening his roommate by sprinkling thallium over his food over an extended period of time (Swenson, 2018).

The tacit ill will directed at close others stands in stark contrast to the cultural ideals of collectivism. Cultural psychology has long been highlighting the idea that people in East Asia attune to a collective self, placing high values on interdependence and social harmony. In contrast, Westerners tend to focus on an individual self, emphasizing independence and personal agency (Markus & Kitayama, 1991, 2010; Triandis et al., 1988). Much literature on competition and cooperation tends to associate collectivism with cooperation and individualism with competition (Bonta, 1997; C. C. Chen et al., 1998).

However, accumulating empirical evidence has suggested otherwise. Compared to people in individualistic cultures, people in collectivistic cultures place just as much importance on the role of competition (Watkins, 2006), are more likely to subscribe to zero-sum beliefs (Różycka-Tran et al., 2015), and are more suspicious of in-group members (S. S. Liu et al., 2019). For example, one study asked people in the United States and China to anticipate what aspiring actors would do when they were trying out for a leading role. People in China were more likely to anticipate that other people would compete unethically, such as by "poisoning other actresses' food."

Why is there so much competition in seemingly harmonious societies? We could find no comprehensive review on this question, except for one overview on the topic of culture and competition, focusing on China (H. Leung & Au, 2010). In this chapter, we connect different veins of research on cultural differences in competition. We first review cultural variation in people's attitudes about competition. Next, we discuss why and how people from different cultures compete. We argue that, in cultures that demand social harmony, people use tacit strategies to compete against others. This social vigilance is a consequence of collectivism,[1] rather than the exception. Next, we explore how people from different cultures enter competitions and how it affects them afterwards. We end with a discussion of whether there can be versions of collectivistic societies without competition or whether this is a utopian dream.

Views of Competition Across Cultures

There is broad consensus about what competition means for different cultures. People in East Asia and the West alike associate competition with the goal of outperforming others, and they view cooperation as working with others to achieve collective goals (Keller & Loewenstein, 2011). People across Europe, North America, and East Asia also generally agree about *where* competition often takes place, such as in the world economy, personal finance, work, education, politics, sports, science, military, fashion, beauty, and entertainment (Fülöp, 1999, 2000). However, there are distinct ways in which cultures differ in what they think about that competition.

Fülöp (2005) argues that there are systematic differences between stable, wealthy Western countries and developing, post-socialist countries like Hungary. Fülöp asked people to describe their thoughts on competition in open-ended responses, contrasting (1) countries with stable democracies and capitalist economies, such as the United States, Canada, and the United Kingdom, and (2) countries with emerging economies and less democratic governments. In more democratic nations, people tended to acknowledge that they live in competitive societies but felt neutral about the role of competition in society. They tended to describe competition with non-emotional words, focusing on its mechanistic aspects, with little detail of its negative consequences (Fülöp, 2000). This is similar to studies finding that French adolescents hold meritocratic beliefs about competition—it stimulates hard work and brings success (Fülöp et al., 2004).

This contrasts with respondents from Hungary, a country transitioning from a socialist society to a free enterprise economy. Participants from Hungary tended to think competition was negative. They associated it with cheating, bribery, jealousy, aggression, and survival (Fülöp & Sándor, 2006; Watkins, 2010). Similarly, people from post-communist countries such as Armenia, Georgia, and Ukraine described a more pessimistic, social-Darwinist view of competition (Fülöp et al., 2004; Roberts et al., 2000).

Much like their North American and Western European counterparts, people in Japan and Hong Kong view competition as an important driving force for individual improvement and societal advancement (Watkins, 2006). However, people in East Asia report enjoying competition less than North Americans (Houston et al., 2005). This research suggests it is important to separate people's views on competition's role in society from whether they *like* competition.

There are also differences in whether people see competition and cooperation as opposites. One study found that North Americans view competition and cooperation as opposing processes, whereas people in East Asia see competition co-existing with cooperation (Keller & Loewenstein, 2011). Researchers presented different work situations to participants in China and the United States and asked them whether each situation was cooperative or not. Some scenarios involved work groups with little competition, such as "Members don't try to perform better or faster than other members." In those cases, Americans assumed that situation was cooperative. The lack of competition meant cooperation. In contrast, people in China did not think that scenario implied cooperation. In other words, Americans assumed "low competition" means "cooperative," whereas participants in China did not.

This fits with other findings of how people interpret the intentions of people being helpful. Participants in America viewed going out of one's way to help others with their work as a signal of cooperation (Keller & Loewenstein, 2011). People in China considered it to be uncooperative. To explain this counterintuitive finding, Keller and Loewenstein (2011) suggested that people in China would sense ulterior motives if a co-worker is over-eager to help; they would see unsolicited help as a way of gaining trust and information from them—information they would otherwise not be willing to share. In another study, people in China were far more likely than Americans to perceive overt friendliness and help as sabotage in disguise (S. S. Liu et al., 2019).

Some Research Has Defined Competitiveness as a Part of Individualism

Studies in cultural psychology have explicitly defined competition as a part of individual-ism and cooperativeness as a central feature of collectivism (Grimm et al., 1999; Singelis et al., 1995; Triandis & Gelfand, 1998). For example, the Horizontal-Vertical Collectivism scale gives people more points on individualism if they agree with items like "winning is everything" and "it is important that I do my job better than others." In contrast, it gives people points for collectivism if they agree with cooperation: "I feel good when I cooper-ate with others" (Triandis & Gelfand, 1998).

A meta-analysis of individual–collectivism scales found four different scales that included competition as a part of individualism (Oyserman et al., 2002). A more recent review similarly found individualism scales that measured competitiveness rather than inde-pendence per se (Vignoles et al., 2016). This assumption is evident in people's reactions to data that find the opposite. For example, when researchers found evidence that collectivistic cultures score higher competition, they called it "the most surprising result" (Różycka-Tran et al., 2015). This reaction is understandable given the prior theorizing on competition. In short, research on competition tends to associate competitive behavior with individualism and cooperative behavior with collectivism (C. C. Chen et al., 1998; Domino, 1992).

Studies Find Collectivistic Cultures More Competitive Than Individualistic Cultures

Despite this theorizing, evidence for the association between individualism and compe-tition is mostly in the opposite direction. Most studies have found either no difference or that collectivistic cultures compete more. On self-reported measures of competitive-ness, American college students scored no higher than students in China; nor did they score any lower on cooperativeness (Tang, 1999). Among fourth- through sixth-graders, European Americans (who tend to score higher on individualism) were no more competi-tive at social motive games than Mexican Americans (who tend to score higher on col-lectivism) (Knight et al., 1981).

More definitive data comes from a large research project that compared 12,000 stu-dents in 41 countries across the globe (Furnham et al., 1994). Researchers found that

Asian countries (e.g., China, Japan, Korea, Singapore, India) actually score the highest on self-reported competitiveness. Data from the Programme for International Student Assessment (PISA) showed that students from Asian countries (e.g., Hong Kong, Korea, Singapore) report the highest level of competitiveness, whereas those from northern and central European countries (e.g., Denmark, Iceland, Austria) report the highest level of cooperativeness. Students in Asia were more likely to rate their school environment as competitive, agreeing with the statement that "Students are competing with each other." Students in Europe were more likely to agree with the statement, "It seems that students are co-operating with others" (OECD, 2018). Similarly, in a study of zero-sum beliefs in 37 countries, people from collectivistic cultures reported a stronger belief that the world is zero-sum than people in individualistic cultures (Różycka-Tran et al., 2015).

Studies that measure competitiveness through social games align with these findings. In one study, researchers had second-, fourth-, and sixth- graders in Belgium, Greece, the United States (including European Americans and Mexican Americans), and Japan play the Maximizing Difference Game (Toda et al., 1978). In this game, two players played 100 trials. During each trial, both players could choose either option A or B. If both players chose A, they each win six points. This outcome maximizes joint gain and personal gain. But if one player chooses B, they get five points and stick their partner with zero points. This outcome maximizes *relative* gain. The instructions did not give the children any explicit goals during the game. They were simply told to play a game in which they could win points.

The researchers measured competitiveness by the number of B choices—the number of times a participant chose relative gain over the possibility of joint and personal gain. They found that children in Japan made more competitive choices than children from any other culture (Table 27.1).

Another study had three- to five-year-old children in Taiwan and United States play a modified Marble-Pull Game (Sparkes, 1991; Figure 27.1). In the game, two children sit on opposite sides of a game board. At each end of the board, there is a hole the size of a disc. At the center of the board are two half-blocks held together by magnets. At the center of the half-blocks is a hollow space containing a disc. If both children choose to pull their half-block towards themselves, the block pulls apart and the disc stays at the

Table 27.1 Maximizing difference game matrix. Within each cell, Player I gains the number of points on the left; Player II gains the number of points on the right.

Maximizing Difference Game		Player I	
		A	B
Player II	A	6, 6	0, 5
	B	5, 0	0, 0

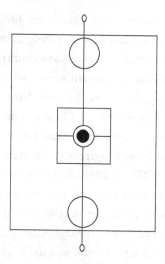

Figure 27.1 Gameboard for the modified marble-pull game.

center of the game board. This is a competitive choice. However, if one child pulls the disc and the other child lets him do so, then the disc is carried to that side and falls into the hole. This is a cooperative choice. The game ends when the children have cooperated 10 times and a total of 10 discs have fallen into one hole or the other. The study found that children in Taiwan spent more time pulling against each other rather than taking turns to win the game together. These findings suggest that people from collectivistic cultures are more competitive, and that this competitive assumption may paradoxically lead people from collectivistic cultures to achieve fewer joint gains.

Still, why do some studies find that collectivists cooperate to a greater extent than individualists (Domino, 1992)? Several studies point to the importance of monitoring and reputation. Some researchers have suggested that people in collectivistic cultures are not inherently more cooperative; they do so when there is a sanctioning system in place (H. Leung & Au, 2010). They default to acting in the interest of the group when doing otherwise would incur reputational cost (Yamagishi et al., 2008).

For example, (Yamagishi, 1988, 2003) put participants from America and Japan into groups to play a public goods game. Participants were given 50 cents and asked how much of the 50 cents they would give to other members of the group. The contributions would then be doubled and distributed equally among everyone. There was no public sanctioning in the game, which meant no group member would be punished if they contributed less than others. Participants in Japan showed lower social trust and cooperated less than the Americans. Similarly, another study found that people in China make less cooperative business decisions than Australians in the absence of a sanction system (X. P. Chen & Li, 2005).

In sum, we think the data fits better with the theory that competition is not necessary for individualism (Oyserman et al., 2002). Individualism is often independent of competition. Individualism emphasizes striving to stand on one's own instead of out-doing others (Schneider et al., 2011). Furthermore, collectivism can underpin uncooperative behaviors. For example, people in China show vigilance towards their coworkers in competition (S. S. Liu et al., 2019).

Is Collectivistic Competition Just an In-Group–Out-Group Phenomenon?

If the finding that collectivists compete more is a puzzle, one reasonable explanation might be that this increased competition only applies to outsiders. For example, later in this chapter we describe the finding that negotiators from collectivistic cultures are more likely to withhold information in their negotiations. Perhaps this is to be expected. Perhaps people in collectivistic cultures are withholding information because their negotiation counterparts are outsiders. They're opponents. In many negotiation practice cases, the two sides are opposing companies. If it's really about in-group versus out-group, people in collectivistic cultures should tone down their competitiveness with people inside their group.

Although this explanation sounds plausible, it does not fit the data. For example, other research has found that people in China withhold knowledge even from in-group members. In-depth interviews among employees have found competition and antagonism among Chinese co-workers, but not among Brazilian and Russian co-workers (Ardichvili et al., 2006). For example, Chinese interviewees expressed vigilance toward their coworkers: "If we are in the same line of work, we are enemies." Employees in China also tended to think of outcomes as zero-sum: "In China there are too many people for 'one cake' and so the competition is high." In addition, they expressed hesitance about sharing information: "Many people do not want to share the expertise they get through many years of hard working. The reason for this situation is competition."

But perhaps coworkers are not considered in-group members in China? Not so. In another study, participants in China rated colleagues and classmates as more of in-group members than participants in the United States (S. S. Liu et al., 2019). Yet despite calling coworkers in-group members, participants in China still expressed more suspicion toward them. Thus, a general in-group favoritism does not seem to explain the difference. Suspicion and competition pervade even within the group in collectivistic cultures.

Is The Collectivism–Competition Link Just Corruption?

In this chapter, we argue that intense competition is a part of collectivistic culture. Yet one alternative theory could be that this is an artifact of corruption or simple resource scarcity. If collectivistic cultures tend to be poorer, the competition might be a consequence of scarce resources. Similarly, living in a corrupt political system could create suspicion and vying behind the scenes.

These are plausible alternative explanations. They are plausible because it is true that collectivistic cultures are poorer on average (Hofstede, 2003; Talhelm, 2015). It is also true that collectivistic cultures have more corruption on average (Mazar & Aggarwal, 2011). What's more, temporarily putting people in a more collectivistic mindset made them more willing to offer a bribe (Mazar & Aggarwal, 2011). Thus, it's important to pull apart competition from poverty and corruption.

One way to tackle this question is to compare differences within the same country. Researchers did this by comparing northern and southern China (S. S. Liu et al., 2019). Although China is generally collectivistic, research has found evidence that rice-farming areas of southern China are more collectivistic than the wheat-farming north (Talhelm et al., 2014, 2018). In the south, paddy rice relied on irrigation networks that bound villages together to maintain and regulate water use. Paddy rice also required about twice as much labor as wheat, which pushed rice farmers to form cooperative labor exchanges (Talhelm & Oishi, 2018). Thus, China offers a unique test case to compare regions that vary on collectivism within the same country. This helps rule out many of the variables that confound East–West comparisons, such as language, religion, and national political system.

Using the same competition scenarios from the study comparing the United States and China, researchers gave the scenarios to people from different parts of China (Talhelm & Oishi, 2018). Although they were living under the same national political system, people from rice areas of China anticipated more unethical behaviors than people from wheat areas (Figure 27.2). Rice–wheat differences were just as strong after taking into account provincial measures of corruption and good governance (p. 5).

What about poverty and resource scarcity? It is true that collectivistic countries tend to be poorer. But within China, rice-farming provinces are actually wealthier on average (Talhelm et al., 2014). Thus, modern-day wealth could not explain the rice–wheat differences. In fact, provincial development (GDP per capita) did not significantly predict people's vigilance ($p = .640$).

In sum, collectivism was a better explanation of the intense competition than corruption and resource scarcity. The idea that interdependence causes suspicion and intense competition apart from resource scarcity also fits with studies that have found differences between Hong Kong and the United States (Lam et al., 2004; L. M. W. Li et al., 2015). Hong Kong has a GDP per capita on par with the UK and other wealthy European countries. Yet the intense competition persists.

The case of rice farming suggests how it is possible to have both cooperation and intense competition in the same culture. For example, anthropologists observing traditional Japanese rice villages saw that farmers competed intensely with each other over water (Yoshida, 1984). This coexistence of cooperation and competition seems to be living on beyond the rice fields. In modern offices, employees in China saw their relationships with coworkers as both more cooperative and more competitive than Americans (Keller & Loewenstein, 2011). In short, cooperation does not exclude competition. Interdependence only requires interdependence—not that that dependence be pleasant.

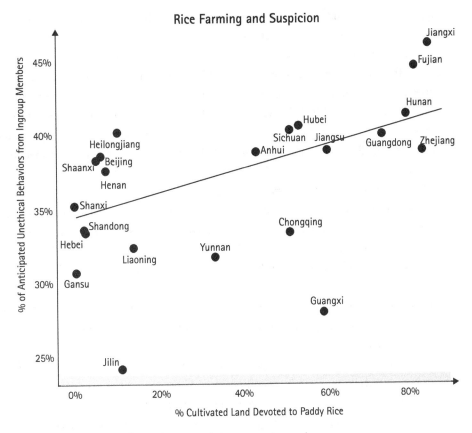

Figure 27.2 Rice farming predicts vigilance toward classmates and co-workers.

Collectivistic Cultures Compete Covertly

Humans around the world compete with each other. But *how* people compete depends on the social structure they live in. The *how* question can help resolve the paradox of why cultures that emphasize harmony still manage to harbor so much competition (Hsu, 1981). In collectivistic cultures, competition often gets channeled from direct, overt conflict into covert, tacit competition.

Withholding Information

One tacit competition strategy is withholding information. Withholding information is less direct and harder to detect than outright lying. Withholding also offers some amount of plausible deniability—a mechanism that saves face and minimizes conflict.

One study asked managers from China and the United States to imagine a contact seeking advice about it was like to work in their industry in an attempt to gain entry into that industry. In one condition, participants were told this contact was trustworthy and had successfully worked with them in the past. In another condition, participants were told this contact was merely an acquaintance and had only met with them once or twice.

Participants in China did not differ from Americans in sharing knowledge about the industry with a work partner they trust. However, participants in China withheld knowledge from an acquaintance more than Americans (Chow et al., 2000).

People from collectivistic cultures also withhold information during negotiations. In a series of studies, researchers had people from 10 cultures negotiate the same business deal (W. Adair et al., 2004; W. L. Adair & Brett, 2005). While they were negotiating, researchers audiotaped their conversations and coded their behaviors. Negotiators from the traditionally individualistic cultures of the United States, Germany, Israel, and Sweden spent far more time communicating directly—sharing their priorities and giving feedback on their counterpart's offers.

In contrast, participants from traditionally collectivistic cultures Japan, Hong Kong, India, and Thailand shared far less information with their counterpart (Gunia et al., 2011). Rather than sharing information, they spent more time making offers back and forth. Withholding information may be a good strategy in simple negotiations, where two people haggle about a single price. But this negotiation had win–win tradeoffs that participants could find if they shared information about their true priorities. Because they had a harder time gathering this information, cultures that withheld information won fewer points on average.

This international study offers important data from countries that appear less often in the cultural psychology research on competition. Cross-cultural psychology research is not balanced across parts of the world. According to one calculation, there are six times as many studies about China, Korea, and Japan as there are about the three most-populous nations in Africa and South America (Talhelm & Oishi, 2019). Much of the research we discuss in this chapter also comes from Mainland China and Hong Kong. That raises an important question: is the link between collectivism and competition unique to collectivism in China? Perhaps China is an aberration, and there are other "flavors" of collectivism more common around the world that really are harmonious.

One reason these negotiation studies are valuable is that they extend the sample to Thailand, India, and Japan, as well as other less-studied individualistic cultures. Russia also offers a useful datapoint. Negotiators in Russia withheld information similar to participants in other collectivistic cultures. Although Russia is a "middle culture" between East and West, studies have found that people in Russia score higher on collectivism and lower on individualism than people in Western Europe and North America (Gelfand et al., 2004; Grossmann & Varnum, 2011; Hofstede, 2003; Suh et al., 1998). In sum, these studies suggest the link between collectivism and competition is not just a China phenomenon. It seems to extend to other less-studied collectivistic cultures.

Covert Competition Among Frenemies and In-group Vigilance

In addition to withholding information as a form of covert competition, collectivists also harbor more vigilance towards people in their social group. Research in another less-frequently studied culture, Ghana, described competition among the in-group in a novel way (Adams, 2005). According to Adams, it is common in Ghana for people to be fearful of having an enemy among their friends or family—a "frenemy." Adams profiled cultural artifacts like bumper stickers that reflect a caution toward frenemies. For example, one local proverb warns, "if an insect bites you, it comes from inside your clothes" (p. 949).

Interviews backed up the cultural products. In Ghana, 71 percent of people reported being the target of an enemy versus 26 percent of Americans. Participants in America weren't just less likely to report having an enemy; they were doubtful of the idea itself. Many Americans were skeptical that frenemies really exist. As one American participant put it, if someone thought they had enemies among their friends, "I would think they were paranoid" (p. 953). In fact, 20 percent of Americans used the word "paranoid" to describe the fear of frenemies.

A study comparing students in Hong Kong and the United States found similar results (L. M. W. Li et al., 2015). Students in Hong Kong were more suspicious of their friends than Americans. For example, Hong Kongers were more likely to agree that "There are likely to be people in my close social network (relatives and friends) who feel hatred and ill will toward me."

In another study, researchers asked people in the United States and China to imagine competing for a scholarship or for an acting role (S. S. Liu et al., 2019). Then they asked people to write what they thought the other students, actors, or work colleagues would do. Research assistants coded their responses as ethical (such as ethical "do research on the role"), unethical (such as "poison other actresses' food"), or gray area (such as "become buddy–buddy with the director"). In the U.S., 16 percent of imagined behaviors were unethical or gray area versus 38 percent in China. In short, people in collectivistic cultures report more suspicion and vigilance toward friends, colleagues, and even family.

Why Would Collectivism Breed Competition and Suspicion?

Why have some studies found that people in collectivistic cultures compete more? Here we discuss the beliefs that underpin competition. We entertain the explanation that differences in competition are based on people's basic beliefs about how the world is structured.

Zero-Sum Beliefs

Perhaps the most logical place to start is zero-sum beliefs. Zero-sum beliefs describe the idea that there is only a finite amount of resources, so one person's gains are another person's loss. If people in collectivistic cultures tend to believe that resources are finite, it would be rational to compete more as a result.

Researchers tested people's zero-sum beliefs in over 40 countries (Różycka-Tran et al., 2015, 2018). They found that people in collectivistic cultures and lower-income nations were more likely to endorse zero-sum beliefs. In these societies, people have to navigate tight social relationships and manage interpersonal obligations, all of which could exacerbate zero-sum beliefs. Recent research highlights the role of zero-sum beliefs as the culprit behind cultural differences in how vigilant people are towards in-group others. For example, people in more collectivistic regions in China believed more in the idea of zero sum, which in turn predicted greater in-group vigilance (S. S. Liu et al., 2019).

In perhaps the most convincing demonstration, researchers manipulated zero-sum beliefs and found that it changed people's expectations about competition (S. S. Liu et al., 2019). In the baseline condition, participants imagined working on an important project in the office, when a coworker comes by to offer help. Without any sort of priming, 21 percent of participants in China predicted that the coworker was secretly trying to sabotage them. In the US, just four percent predicted sabotage.

Next, researchers explicitly defined the company environment as zero-sum. In that condition, more people in the U.S. (25 percent) and China (35 percent) predicted sabotage. Then, when researchers explicitly defined the office as a win-win environment, predictions of sabotage fell (five to eight percent). It is interesting to note that the United States results were nearly identical when the situation was ambiguous and when the situation was explicitly win–win. These results suggest that (1) perceptions of the environment as zero-sum cause people to be suspicious and (2) the baseline situation in China is similar to the explicitly zero-sum condition.

Social Comparison

Another process that shapes competition is social comparison (Garcia et al., 2020). Baldwin & Mussweiler (2018) found two cultural dimensions that explain variation in social comparison tendencies within the United States: tightness–looseness and individualism–collectivism. They used Google Correlate search data—a database of millions of search queries since 2003 in the United States—to obtain search frequencies of emotions related to social comparison, such as envy and resentment. They found that US states with more social comparison had tighter cultural norms and more relational self-construal. People in these states tended to Google more emotion words related to social comparison.

Cross-cultural comparisons also show that people in collectivistic cultures spend more time on social comparison (Chung & Mallery, 1999; Sasaki et al., 2014). For example, researchers had European Canadian and Asian Canadian students complete a test. Afterwards, they gave them options to seek out as many of other students' rankings as they wished. They found that Asian Canadians sought out more social comparisons than Canadians of European descent, especially upward comparisons and comparisons after failure. These tendencies were explained by higher self-reported collectivism (White & Lehman, 2005).

There is also neural imaging research finding a link between culture and social comparison. One study measured people's sensitivity towards social comparison by having participants play a gambling game while researchers recorded activity in brain regions sensitive to reward (ventral striatum and the ventromedial prefrontal cortex; Kang et al., 2013). Americans showed greater neural activity in response to their *absolute* financial gain, whereas participants in Korea showed greater neural activity in response to financial gain relative to their partner in the game. This suggests that participants in Korea were more sensitive to social comparison, even without the potential confound of self-report surveys.

Research has found that giving participants social comparison information makes them more competitive in social games. However, this effect is particularly pronounced in Japan compared to the United States and Belgium (Toda et al., 1978). This is not surprising, given research showing that people's motivation to succeed in collectivistic cultures is often driven by social approval and upward comparison rather than internal standards (Niles, 1995; Sasaki et al., 2014). Qualitative accounts aptly illustrate the pressure to excel through social comparison. Asian American children report that their parents constantly compare their children to other people's children, berating their children for "only having a 4.0 GPA [when others] have a 4.3" (Becerra, 2008; Yang, 2011). In one qualitative interview study, an Asian American student described the "Asian scale" in relation to the immense pressure of social comparison at school: "A is for average; B is for bad; C is for crap; and F is find another a family" (Zhou & Lee, 2017).

Asian and Asian Americans are also more likely to base their self-esteem on competition than White and Black Americans (Cheng & Kwan, 2008; Crocker et al., 2003; C.-H. Liu et al., 2016). They agree more with scale items such as "my self-worth is affected by how well I do when I am competing with others" (Crocker et al., 2003). Because people from interdependent cultures base their self-worth more on outperforming other people, underperformance has worse consequences for them. For example, one study found that participants who were more interdependent reported lower self-esteem after witnessing a close friend's success (Sasaki et al., 2014).

In another study, European American and Asian American participants were asked to imagine themselves as a university student whose sister was either the valedictorian or on academic probation. The valedictorian situation represented upward social comparison, whereas the probation situation represented downward social comparison. Even though upward social comparison is potentially damaging, European Americans actually reported feeling better when they imagined their sister performing well. In contrast, Asian Americans reported feeling worse about themselves after upward social comparison and feeling better after downward social comparison (Sasaki et al., 2014).

Several studies have found that people from East Asia report lower subjective well-being than European Americans (Diener et al., 1995; Kitayama et al., 2000; Oishi et al., 1999). Comparing different nations, the East Asian "happiness gap" remains even when comparing happiness between East Asia and other countries that are just as wealthy (Diener et al., 1995). These contingencies of self-worth can partly explain cultural differences in well-being. People from East Asia are more likely to base their sense of self-worth on the approval of others, which is linked to an overall lower sense of well-being (C.-H. Liu et al., 2016). Similarly, social comparison can sometimes make people happy and sometimes make people unhappy. But research suggests that the costs are bigger than the benefits. The overall effect is that social comparison makes people unhappy (Fujita, 2008). This seems to be true across cultures—despite the fact that some social comparison is upward and some is downward, the overall effect is that social comparison is linked to less happiness in the United States and in China (Lee & Talhelm, 2021).

Common Standard versus Self-Defined Goals

Another plausible cause of competition is whether people have a commonly defined or self-defined goals. People in interdependent cultures often define people's self-worth based on common standards and objective metrics such as grades, income, and awards. In cultures that define the self as independent, people have more latitude to define their worth based on their own standards.

In one study, we asked participants in United States and China to rate what characteristics (e.g., reading widely, having a logical mind) best describe an intelligent person (Wu & Dunning, 2021a). Americans showed varying standards of what they think qualifies as intelligence, based on what characteristics of intelligence they have themselves. For instance, for American participants who read widely, their definition of intelligence tended to include the characteristic of reading widely. However, participants in China showed more of a common standard for what being intelligent entailed, regardless of what characteristics they have themselves.

In other words, people in the United States tend to have more fluid and idiosyncratic definitions of what they consider to be intelligent, creative, a good leader, and so on (Dunning et al., 1991; Dunning & Cohen, 1992; Hayes & Dunning, 1997). If people are not an avid reader but good at math, they simply adjust the standard of intelligence to being good at math. There would be little reason for them to compete with a person who is an avid reader. Yet, people in China share a common trait prototype. If being an avid reader is what is commonly acknowledged as intelligent (more so than being a math whiz), a person who is good at math would see herself as being less intelligent than a person who reads widely and have more incentive to compete.

Objective metrics of status also have more impact on well-being in East Asian cultures. In nationally representative surveys conducted in Japan and the United States, objective markers of status (e.g., education attainment) more strongly predicted psychological well-being such as life satisfaction and self-acceptance in Japan than in the United States. However, subjective markers of status (where people *think* they stand relative to others in their community) more strongly predicted psychological well-being in United States than in Japan (Curhan et al., 2014).

A recent study found similar differences comparing more collectivistic rice-farming regions of China to more individualistic wheat-farming regions (Lee & Talhelm, 2021).

In two large, nationally representative surveys, people's income and social status were stronger predictors of people's happiness in rice-farming areas than wheat-farming areas. Although wealthier people were happy all over China, income was more than twice as predictive in rice areas. This is consistent with the idea that people in interdependent cultures define happiness based on commonly shared markers—income and job status in this case. To the extent that people in a society are all striving for the same thing, social comparison and competition are more integral to success.

This tendency to strive for a common standard provides a path to understanding the "surprising" finding that people in collectivistic cultures tend to believe more that the world is zero-sum (Różycka-Tran et al., 2015). If people have more latitude to define their own self-worth, then one person's success does not have to reflect upon another person's success. When people have flexibility to define their self-worth, the son who makes a modest salary helping children as a public-school teacher has less impetus to begrudge his older brother who earns big money as a Wall Street consultant. Likewise, the American student with a middling SAT score but outstanding extracurriculars has far less reason to begrudge a classmate with a perfect SAT than a similar student in China. Because college admission in China hinges on a single test score, students have less wiggle room to resist being defined in a clear way to everyone.

The Social Ecology of Competition: Relational Mobility

So far, we have made a simple empirical claim: people in collectivistic cultures compete more intensely and endorse competition more than people in individualistic cultures. Yet it seems like a contradiction to say that we should find *more* competition in cultures that prioritize connectedness and relationships. Why would collectivism predict more competition?

One promising explanation to explain this seemingly paradoxical link is relational mobility. Relational mobility describes whether relationships in a society tend to be open, flexible, and easy to find (Thomson et al., 2018). A study of 39 countries found that countries in Western Europe and the Americas tend to be relationally mobile (Thomson et al., 2018). In contrast, countries in the Middle East and Asia tended to have fixed, stable relationships.

Interdependent cultures tend to be low in relational mobility, $r = .72$ (Thomson et al., 2018). Thus, low relational mobility describes most (but not all) interdependent cultures. Relational mobility helps set out the payoffs for different behaviors. If relationships tend to be fixed, and if it is hard to replace damaged relationships with new ones, it makes strategic sense to avoid open conflict. It also makes it more likely that two people who do not get along will have to still be around each other.

In other words, relational mobility changes the payoffs for taking social risks in conflicts. When mobility is low, it is riskier to damage relationships. Researchers tested this idea by asking people to rate how willing they would be to take social risks (L. M. W.

Li et al., 2015). For example, how willing would you be to speak "your mind about an unpopular issue in a meeting at work?" Low relational mobility predicted less willingness to take social risks.

However, relational mobility did *not* mean people were simply risk-takers in general. They were no more likely to take ethical or financial risks, such as gambling a day's income. Instead, risk-taking was specific to the social world.

Results were similar when researchers experimentally manipulated people's perception of the social environment. When researchers asked participants to imagine being in a low-mobility social group, they saw social behaviors as riskier. In short, social environments with low relational mobility seem to make people more hesitant to take social risks.

At the same time, low relational mobility makes it harder for people to exit relationships after conflict arises. In social environments with lots of flexibility and choice, people have an easier time leaving people they have conflict with. For example, in the interviews about frenemies, 48 percent of Americans mentioned having choice in their relationships compared to just six percent of people in Ghana (Adams, 2005). One American interviewee couldn't understand "why one would continue to interact with somebody who one did not like" (p. 956). Yet in many collectivistic cultures, people do not see relationships as free to choose and dispose of.

The low mobility makes it so that people cannot easily get away from people they have grudges with. When people have more freedom of choice, they can simply separate from each other, like boxers going into their own corners. But low-mobility societies essentially force those boxers back together, round after round.

It would be naïve to think that collectivism makes conflict disappear. If some amount of conflict is inevitable, then that conflict paired with social risk aversion makes *open conflict* less likely. Studies suggest that people channel the conflict "underground" (S. S. Liu et al., 2021). Instead of competing directly, collectivists tend to compete covertly more often.

We bring together candidates for the causes of competition in collectivism in Figure 27.3. This model links foundational conditions (relational mobility and interdependence) to intermediate mechanisms (such as the difficulty of distancing oneself from rivals) to specific behaviors and outcomes (such as vigilance). While speculative, this model is rooted in the research we review here, and it provides testable hypotheses for future researchers to explore.

Cultures Differ in the Types of Competition They Choose

Besides the question of how people compete after competition has started, there is also the question of how people *enter* conflict. Consider this: Would you rather be a stellar student in a mid-ranked university, or a below-average student in an Ivy League? We asked 273 students of East Asian and European American backgrounds if they preferred to be the metaphorical "big frog in a small pond" or the "small frog in a big pond" (Wu

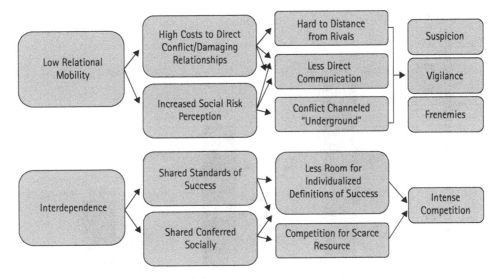

Figure 27.3 Theoretical model explaining causes of cultural differences in competition.

et al., 2018). Seventy-five percent of East Asian students chose to the "big pond"; only 59 percent of European American students chose so.

This competition entry preference translates to making decisions about which school to attend. We asked adults in the United States and China to choose between two college offers (Wu et al., 2018). They could accept an offer from a top-10 college, but their academic performance would be below average. Alternatively, they could accept an offer from a top-100 college, where their academic performance would be above average. People in China were much more likely (58 percent) than European Americans (29 percent) to choose the top-10 college despite being below average on academic performance.

These differences are not just for school. Similar cultural differences appeared for work (Wu et al., 2018). More people in China said they would prefer working at one of the top-10 companies in the world, even though their performance would be below average. In contrast, more Americans said they would prefer to work at a top-100 company, where their performance would be above average (Figure 27.4).

Desire for Prestige

Why would East Asians prefer the "big pond" more than European Americans? One possibility is that frog-pond entry depends on self-construal. European Americans tend to focus on the self as independent from others, whereas East Asians tend to attune to a collective self embedded in social groups (Markus & Kitayama, 2010). Given their emphasis on a collective self, East Asians may put more weight on intergroup comparisons ("I belong to a big pond") more than comparison within groups ("I am a big frog in this pond"). That emphasis on the group would logically cause people to prefer entering the "big pond" even at the expense of being a "small frog."

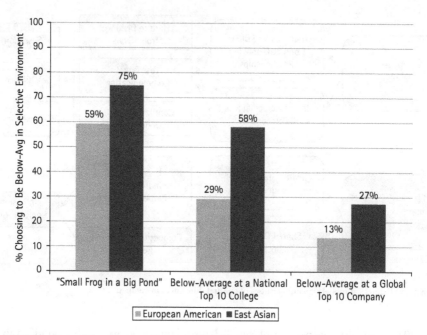

Figure 27.4 Percentage of European Americans versus East Asians choosing to be below-average in a selective environment rather than above-average in a less selective environment.

Yet when tested, people's tendencies to compare groups failed to explain cultural differences in entry decisions. Rather, the decision to vie for the "big pond" was driven by a greater desire for prestige (Wu et al., 2018). Why? East Asian countries are not just collectivistic. They share a *face* culture, wherein people gain face or respectability by attaining a position in the social hierarchy (Ho, 1976; Kim et al., 2010). The problem with face is that it is socially conferred, which means people cannot gain face by themselves. In a social hierarchy, people can only claim as much status as other people will grant them.

In contrast, researchers have described mainstream American culture as a *dignity* culture (Kim & Cohen, 2010; A. K.-Y. Leung & Cohen, 2011). To have dignity is to hold the conviction that each individual is born with a level of inherent worth equal to everyone else. People's self-worth is intrinsic, inalienable, and independent of others' judgments and approval.

With this backdrop of face versus dignity, the "big pond" decision starts to make cultural sense. The "big pond" is prestigious, but it does not define people's sense of self-worth in dignity cultures. Going to a prestigious university does not guarantee success and going to a mid-tier university does not equal failure. However, things change in face cultures. If success and failure depend on what other people think, coming from a "big pond" sends a strong signal of one's social worth.

In line with this theory, an additional set of studies suggest that there is a social reward system in East Asian cultures that reinforces the "big pond" premium. East Asian employers place a premium on candidates coming from prestigious competition environments, even if their performance is subpar (Y. B. Li, 2018). Compared to Americans, people in China more strongly preferred to hire job applicants who had graduated from a top-10 college rather than a top-100 college, even when their academic performance was below average. In other words, it seems that employers' desires help motivate collectivists' choice to enter the "big pond."

Consequence of Competition

People from different cultures have varying perceptions about the consequences of competition. One study found that people in Hungary, for example, thought that competition may lead to sabotage and aggression (Watkins, 2006). In contrast, participants in the United States and Japan saw competition as contributing to individual improvement. But what are the actual consequences of competition?

The Perils of Choosing a Competitive Environment

Many students from East Asia go to great lengths to vie for elite schools. The past decade witnessed increasing frenzy of Chinese students attempting to get into elite universities in the West (Larmer, 2014). Along with it came "ghost" SAT testers and cheating scandals. Education consulting agencies proliferated in China, manufacturing application essays for students hungry for an elite Western education. Some agencies go so far as to groom children for an Ivy League education by sending them overseas at an age as early as nine (Qing et al., 2016).

Is entry into a prestigious competition environment worth it? This is a legitimate empirical question. Perhaps getting into elite schools is worth it because society will later reward the students for it. This is true in certain academic fields. One study looked at the United States academic job market in the disciplines of computer science, business, and history (Clauset et al., 2015). The prestige of a job candidate's doctoral program alone predicted job placement, such that the more prestigious the doctoral program, the more likely the student would get a job, and the more likely the job would be at a prestigious institution. In history, for example, top 10 universities produce three times the number of future faculty than universities ranked from 11 to 20.

However, do the benefits of prestigious schools carry over to job prospects outside of academia? Research suggests not. Dale and Krueger (Dale & Krueger, 2014) tracked groups of college students for more than two decades. The students were from a variety of public and private universities and liberal arts colleges in the United States and went on to different career paths. The researchers found that all else equal, the prestige of a university or college had no impact on future earnings. For students with similar SAT scores, whether they attended a selective college made no difference on how much money they made in their careers.

Worse yet, studies point to psychological costs associated with attending elite schools. Correlational and longitudinal studies have found that high-performing students in less-selective schools ("big frog in a small pond") feel more competent, achieve higher grade point averages, and have greater career aspirations than low-performing students in more selective schools (Marsh et al., 2000, 2014). This is known as the "frog-pond effect," which suggests that being in the "big pond" as a "small frog" can harm students (Davis, 1966). It can make them feel lost and incapable, lagging behind their high achieving peers, even when they are doing well objectively.

Alicke, Zell, and Bloom (2010) tested this idea out in an experiment. They divided each group of 10 people into two five-person groups. They had participants complete a lie-detection task and told them they ranked either fifth or sixth out of 10 people. For half of the participants, they told them an additional piece of information about their relative ranking: for people who ranked fifth, researchers told them they also ranked the worst in their five-person group ("small frog in a big pond"); for people who ranked sixth, they told them they also ranked the best in their five-person group ("big frog in a small pond").

Participants who were only told about their absolute ranking evaluated themselves similarly. Those ranked fifth did not think they performed significantly better on the lie detection test than those ranked sixth. However, when told about their relative ranking, people who ranked fifth and worst in their group evaluated their performance significantly worse than people who ranked sixth and best in their group. Being a small frog in a big pond makes people devalue themselves, even when they were performing better objectively.

So far, the evidence suggests that being in a prestigious environment comes with more costs than benefits. But most of these studies were conducted with Western samples. Do consequences of competing for the "big pond" carry over to non-Western cultures? Studies have replicated the "frog-pond effect" in 41 culturally and economically diverse countries across the globe (Marsh & Hau, 2003; Seaton et al., 2009). Students across cultures evaluate themselves more negatively if they are under-performing in a selective school than if they are performing well in a less-selective school.

Effects of Competition on Performance

One large, open question in the field of culture and competition is the consequences. There is little research on the consequences of competition in non-Western cultures. We could find only one study that directly examined the effect of competition on performance and motivation outside the West. The researchers studied seventh graders in Hong Kong taking a course on Chinese typewriting (Lam et al., 2004). Researchers assigned the students to either a competition condition or a non-competition condition. In the competition condition, the students received a course certificate with their relative performance ranking printed on it. In the non-competition condition, the students just received a certificate. The study found that competition did boost performance. However, it only helped for easy tasks, not difficult tasks. Further, students evaluated themselves more negatively after failure.

At the end of the experiment, all students were told to complete one more test. They could choose an easy test which they would likely get a good score on or a difficult one which would help them learn more. More students in the competition condition chose the easy test on which they could perform well rather than the test that is better for learning.

This study speaks to the adverse consequence of competition in East Asian culture. However, research competition and performance across cultures is in its early stages. A meta-analysis of studies conducted with Western samples found no overall relationship between competition and performance (Murayama & Elliot, 2012). The researchers found evidence of both competition prompting the motivation to do better than others and competition increasing the tendency to avoid doing worse than others. The former predicted better performance and the latter predicted worse performance. As the literature grows around the influence of culture on competition and performance, it is important to keep in mind that competition may be beneficial or detrimental to performance under different circumstances.

Are There Collectivistic Societies Without Competition?

We started this chapter by describing how researchers have connected collectivism to harmony and therefore low competition. The data collected since then has not only found that this idea was wrong. It was in the wrong direction. Collectivistic cultures tend to endorse competition and zero-sum beliefs *more* (S. S. Liu et al., 2019; Różycka-Tran et al., 2015). So where did that intuition come from? Are non-competitive collectivistic societies a figment of our imagination, or is it possible to have truly non-competitive collectivistic societies?

There are hints in anthropology research on traditional societies suggesting that they strongly oppose competition (Bonta, 1997). The Piaroa indigenous people in Venezuela identify competition with cannibalism and view it as highly destructive (Overing, 1986). Many Westerners consider activities like hunting to be competitive, yet this was not the case for the Chewong, a hunter-gatherer group living in the tropical rain forest of the Malay Peninsula (Howell, 1989). They also do not have words for "compete."

The ethnography suggests that competition may be a "hypocognized" concept in Chewong society. In other words, Chewong people may have few ideas about what competition entails and how competition can be interwoven into the fabric of their social relations and everyday activities (Howell, 1989; Levy, 1973). Without a societally established framework for a concept, people tend not to form associations around that concept (Levy, 1973; Wu & Dunning, 2018a, 2018b). Nor can they readily recognize, identify, interpret, or remember instances and behaviors related to that concept (Wu & Dunning, 2019, 2020, 2021b; Wu, 2021). For example, the Chewong people may have difficulty perceiving the activity *hunting* as associated with the concept "competition" because no conceptual schema of "competition" is engrained in their culture in the first place. Rather than saying the Chewong have no capacity for feeling competitive, it is probably more accurate to say that they reside in a culture where there is little need or motivation to develop principles and practices related to competition.

However, it would be a mistake to see traditional societies as uniformly collectivistic. In fact, inhabitants of what are termed "peaceful" societies focus strongly on individual autonomy (but not individual achievement or overshadowing others), egalitarianism, and voluntary relationships (Bonta, 1997). For example, the Buid people living on Mindoro Island in the Philippines place little value on kinship and dependence—hallmarks of many collectivistic cultures (Gibson, 1985). The Buid also minimize dyadic relationships, which they believe can lead to aggression and competition. Thus, some traditional societies may be peaceful, but not because they are collectivistic. Rather, they strongly embrace individualistic values to the extent that they eschew competition all together.

Instead of collectivism, ethnographies point to another dimension that separates societies that are highly competitive or not: flexibility of power hierarchy (Mead, 1937). If the status hierarchy is stable and consensually accepted, there is little competition. The military is a clear example of a clear power hierarchy that is relatively stable and where advancement is clearly defined. In that environment, competition is unlikely to change the status of an individual or a group.

But when status is changeable, competition becomes a means of attaining higher status. Animal research bears this out. Conflict increases and incurs more damage between similar-sized animals than animals with a large size or dominance discrepancy (Enquist & Leimar, 1983; Reddon et al., 2019). When ambiguity exists in who holds the power, the likelihood of competition increases (Gould, 2003).

Note that the flexibility of power is a different dimension from the flexibility of finding friends and mates, as in relational mobility. Societies can have flexible interpersonal relationships but stable hierarchy. Across 37 societies, relational mobility is not significantly correlated with power distance $r(35) = -.27$, $p = .116$ (Thomson et al., 2018). For example, Mexico scores high on relational mobility and power distance.

Finally, we speculate that there is another condition that can create non-competitive collectivistic groups. In war and other competitions *at the group level*, individuals may unite to defeat other groups. For example, after the 9/11 terror attacks, opposing political parties in the United States voted together more frequently. Polls found Americans' pride in being American increased from 55 percent to 70 percent (Petrecca, 2017). Similarly, in his book *Bowling Alone*, sociologist Robert Putnam speculated that America's high social capital in the 1950s and 1960s stemmed from the unity of World War II (Putnam, 2000). Perhaps it is no accident that militaries seem to combine both elements—a common enemy and a well-defined hierarchy.

Research in sociology and economics has tested this "common enemy effect"—the idea that facing a common enemy increases group solidarity (De Jaegher & Hoyer, 2012,

2016; McLauchlin & Pearlman, 2012). Having to confront a common enemy, people from different social groups no longer think of things as "our group" versus "their group." Rather, they come to recategorize themselves as an inclusive "we" against their common enemy (Dovidio et al., 1993). Although the research on the common enemy effect does find that conflict with an enemy group can promote unity within the group, there are exceptions. External enemies fail to bring unity when there is already significant discord among group members. At times, common enemies can even strengthen disagreements and incite more conflict within the group (DeNardo, 1985; Olson, 1965).

Summary and Future Directions

Across decades of studies, research has documented consistent differences in competition across cultures. One broad theme in those findings is that collectivistic cultures experience more intense competition than individualistic cultures. It is clear that the classic notion that collectivistic cultures emphasize "harmony" is only partly true. There is certainly evidence that people in collectivistic cultures avoid open conflict (Morris et al., 1998). However, people in collectivistic cultures tend to see the world as a competitive place, and they are more likely to suspect that people around them—even their friends—are competing with them beneath the surface.

We set out a model wherein these differences start not with abstract values, religious heritage, or language (Figure 27.3). Rather, we see these differences as stemming primarily from the social ecology. Environments with fixed relationships and few choices for meeting new people raise the costs of direct conflict. Similarly, strongly collectivistic societies share norms and definitions about what is valuable in life. When there is strong agreement about a narrow set of goals, it becomes harder for people to set their own goals and succeed in different, individual ways.

Areas in Need of Future Research

Much work is still undone. Few psychological studies have explored competition in Africa, Latin America, and the Middle East. Although we highlighted studies in collectivistic cultures outside East Asia, it is true that most of the studies on culture and competition have sampled collectivistic cultures in East Asia. It is important to understand whether the relationships between collectivism and competition here are general or unique to East Asia's type of collectivism.

A second area for future research is how competition could affect underrepresented groups. For example, competition is a part of college admissions, and getting into an elite college might influence people's earnings. Dale and Krueger (2014) found that university prestige did not matter for later income for students who had similar SAT scores. However, university prestige did make a difference for Black and Hispanic students, as well as first-generation students. A degree from an elite university predicted higher earnings later in life.

However, this elite status advantage only holds if the students finished their degrees in the first place. If students from underrepresented groups enter a "big pond" as the "small frog," they face the risk of feeling out of place in the competitive environment and failing to graduate altogether. One study found that Black and Hispanic students are less likely to complete STEM degrees at more prestigious universities (Elliott et al., 1996). These findings suggest that it is important that universities encourage students from underrepresented groups to pursue an elite college education; however, once they enter a selective environment, universities have to foster a welcoming enough environment to encourage them to stay (Phillips et al., 2020).

Another area ripe for research is cultural change. It is difficult to look in the cultural psychology research on competition and pull out any concrete guidance for how to change a culture of competition. For example, if a company or school finds that competition is undermining student achievement or mental health, what steps can cultural psychologists suggest to reduce competition or to channel it in a more productive direction? Similarly, if a company or sports team is finding performance and motivation lagging, what could they do to instill a more competitive culture? These areas are wide open for future research.

Finally, few psychology studies have looked at how the institutions that cultures create might reinforce competition. For example, perhaps people in China believe in the idea of competition in the first place and therefore create institutions based on competition. University admissions are certainly a human-created institution, and that institution is more explicitly based on competition (a single test score) in China than in the United States. This belief in competition and meritocracy goes back to the Tang Dynasty and the Imperial Exam system (Powers, 2020). If some cultures create systems that focus on competition, it could reinforce people's belief that competition is an inherent part of the world.

Competition Exists ≠ Liking Competition

There is a phrase that appears frequently on Twitter: "retweet does not equal endorsement." Putting content on one's feed does not necessarily mean the person likes that content. Throughout the research we have covered here, even though we found that people in collectivistic cultures compete more, there is no evidence that they like competition. Nor did we find evidence that they think competition is good for people. Instead, the evidence simply says that competition is more common and more intense.

We think it is more likely that people in collectivistic cultures see competition simply as a part of how the world works. There are some hints of this if you look at specific questions about competition. For example, we analyzed questions given to 3,799 participants from the United States and Asia from the research website YourMorals.org. Participants from Asia agreed more with the item, "It is important to me that I do my job better than others" ($d = 0.36$, $p = .003$; Figure 27.5a). However, they did *not* agree more with the item saying they enjoy that competition: "I enjoy working in situations involving competition

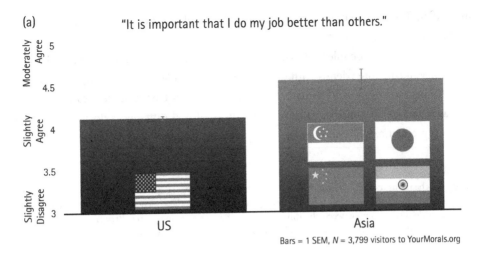

(a) "It is important that I do my job better than others."

Bars = 1 SEM, *N* = 3,799 visitors to YourMorals.org

Figure 27.5a Agreement with the statement "It is important that I do my job better than others" in the United States versus Asia (China, Japan, Korea, India).

with others" ($d = 0.08$, $p = .392$; Figure 27.5b). A comparison of World Values Survey data across 56 countries found that people East Asia agreed the most with the statement "I hate to compete with people" (Minkov, 2018).

It is perhaps no wonder that some Chinese parents bemoan the fierce competition in Chinese education and choose to send their children overseas to study (Yan, 2015). One study conducted focus group interviews with Chinese parents about their view of Chinese education and *Gaokao*, a national college entrance exam similar to the SAT in the United States. Most Chinese parents viewed the entrance exam as overly competitive

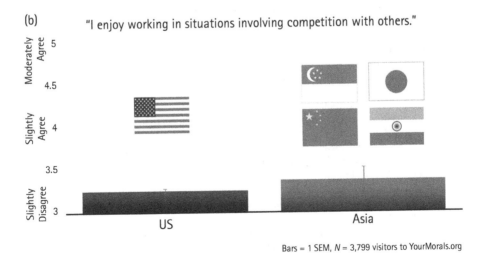

(b) "I enjoy working in situations involving competition with others."

Bars = 1 SEM, *N* = 3,799 visitors to YourMorals.org

Figure 27.5b Agreement with the statement "I enjoy working in situations involving competition with others" in the United States versus Asia (China, Japan, Korea, India).

and unfair. They also expressed their wish for their children not to have to compete (Hu & Hagedorn, 2014).

Similarly, many people in Ghana reported believing in enemies, but this does not mean they liked being friends with enemies. Rather, people in Ghana simply said that to deny having enemies would be naïve. Similarly, people in East Asia seem to see competition as a part of life—prevalent yet unpleasant. Cultural differences do not always boil down to preferences. For collectivists, competition is simply a part of life.

Note

1. We use the terms "collectivism" and "individualism" throughout this paper. However, cultural psychologists have used other similar terms, such as "interdependence" and "independence." Although some researchers have made distinctions between the different terms (Brewer & Chen, 2007; Brewer & Gardner, 1996), researchers generally use the terms interchangeably (Oyserman et al., 2002).

References

Adair, W., Brett, J., Lempereur, A., Okumura, T., Shikhirev, P., Tinsley, C., & Lytle, A. (2004). Culture and negotiation strategy. *Negotiation Journal, 20*(1), 87–111. https://doi.org/10.1111/j.1571-9979.2004.00008.x.

Adair, W. L., & Brett, J. M. (2005). The negotiation dance: Time, culture, and behavioral sequences in negotiation. *Organization Science, 16*(1), 33–51. https://doi.org/10.1287/orsc.1040.0102.

Adams, G. (2005). The cultural grounding of personal relationship: Enemyship in North American and West African worlds. *Journal of Personality and Social Psychology, 88*(6), 948–968. https://doi.org/10.1037/0022-3514.88.6.948.

Alicke, M. D., Zell, E., & Bloom, D. L. (2010). Mere categorization and the Frog-Pond Effect. *Psychological Science, 21*(2), 174–177. https://doi.org/10.1177/0956797609357718.

Ardichvili, A., Maurer, M., Li, W., Wentling, T., & Stuedemann, R. (2006). Cultural influences on knowledge sharing through online communities of practice. *Journal of Knowledge Management, 10*(1), 94–107. https://doi.org/10.1108/13673270610650139.

Baldwin, M., & Mussweiler, T. (2018). The culture of social comparison. *Proceedings of the National Academy of Sciences of the United States of America 115*(39), E9067–E9074. https://doi.org/10.1073/pnas.1721555115.

Becerra, H. (2008, July 16). Trying to bridge the grade divide. *Los Angeles Times.*

Bonta, B. D. (1997). Cooperation and competition in peaceful societies. *Psychological Bulletin, 121*(2), 299. https://doi.org/10.1037/0033-2909.121.2.299.

Brewer, M. B., & Chen, Y.-R. (2007). Where (who) are collectives in collectivism? Toward conceptual clarification of individualism and collectivism. *Psychological Review, 114*(1), 133–151. https://doi.org/10.1037/0033-295X.114.1.133.

Brewer, M. B., & Gardner, W. (1996). Who is this "We"? Levels of collective identity and self representations. *Journal of Personality and Social Psychology, 71*(1), 83–93. https://doi.org/10.1037//0022-3514.71.1.83.

Chen, C. C., Chen, X., & Meindl, J. R. (1998). How can cooperation be fostered? The cultural effects of individualism-collectivism. *Academy of Management Review, 23*(2), 285–304. https://doi.org/10.5465/amr.1998.533227.

Chen, X. P., & Li, S. (2005). Cross-national differences in cooperative decision-making in mixed-motive business contexts: The mediating effect of vertical and horizontal individualism. *Journal of International Business Studies, 36*(6), 622–636. https://doi.org/10.1057/palgrave.jibs.8400169.

Cheng, S. T., & Kwan, K. W. K. (2008). Attachment dimensions and contingencies of self-worth: The moderating role of culture. *Personality and Individual Differences, 45*(6), 509–514. https://doi.org/10.1016/j.paid.2008.06.003.

Chow, C. W., Deng, F. J., & Ho, J. L. (2000). The openness of knowledge sharing within organizations: A comparative study of the United States and the People's Republic of China. *Journal of Management Accounting Research, 12*(1), 65–95. https://doi.org/10.2308/jmar.2000.12.1.65.

Chung, T., & Mallery, P. (1999). Social comparison, individualism-collectivism, and self-esteem in China and the United States. *Current Psychology, 18*(4), 340–352. https://doi.org/10.1007/s12144-999-1008-0.

Clauset, A., Arbesman, S., & Larremore, D. B. (2015). Systematic inequality and hierarchy in faculty hiring networks. *Science Advances, 1*(1), 1–6. https://doi.org/10.1126/sciadv.1400005.

Crocker, J., Luhtanen, R. K., Cooper, M. L., & Bouvrette, A. (2003). Contingencies of self-worth in college students: Theory and measurement. *Journal of Personality and Social Psychology, 85*(5), 894–908. https://doi.org/10.1037/0022-3514.85.5.894.

Curhan, K. B., Levine, C. S., Markus, H. R., Kitayama, S., Park, J., Karasawa, M., Kawakami, N., Love, G. D., Coe, C. L., Miyamoto, Y., & Ryff, C. D. (2014). Subjective and objective hierarchies and their relations to psychological well-being. *Social Psychological and Personality Science, 5*(8), 855–864. https://doi.org/10.1177/1948550614538461.

Dale, S. B., & Krueger, A. B. (2014). Estimating the effects of college characteristics over the career using administrative earnings data. *Journal of Human Resources, 49*(2), 323–358. https://doi.org/10.3368/jhr.49.2.323.

Davis, J. A. (1966). The campus as a frog pond: An application of the theory of relative deprivation to career decisions of college men. *American Journal of Sociology, 72*(1), 17–31. https://doi.org/10.1086/224257.

De Jaegher, K., & Hoyer, B. (2012). Cooperation and the common enemy effect. Discussion Paper Series nr: 12-24. *Koopmans Research Institute, 12*(24), 12–24.

De Jaegher, K., & Hoyer, B. (2016). Collective action and the common enemy effect. *Defence and Peace Economics, 27*(5), 644–664. https://doi.org/10.1080/10242694.2014.925676.

DeNardo, J. (1985). *Power in numbers.* Princeton University Press.

Diener, E., Diener, M., & Diener, C. (1995). Factors predicting the subjective well-being of nations. *Journal of Personality and Social Psychology, 69*(5), 851–864. https://doi.org/10.1037/0022-3514.69.5.851.

Domino, G. (1992). Cooperation and competition in Chinese and American children. *Journal of Cross-Cultural Psychology, 23*(4), 456–467. https://doi.org/10.1177/0022022192234003.

Dovidio, J. F., Gaertner, S. L., Anastasio, P. A., Bachman, B. A., & Rust, M. C. (1993). The common ingroup identity model: Recategorization and the reduction of intergroup bias. *European Review of Social Psychology, 4*(1), 1–26. https://doi.org/10.1080/14792779343000004.

Dunning, D., & Cohen, G. L. (1992). Egocentric definitions of traits and abilities in social judgment. *Journal of Personality and Social Psychology, 63*(3), 341–355. https://doi.org/10.1037/0022-3514.63.3.341.

Dunning, D., Perie, M., & Story, A. L. (1991). Self-serving prototypes of social categories. *Journal of Personality and Social Psychology, 61*(6), 957–968. https://doi.org/10.1037/0022-3514.61.6.957.

Elliott, R., Strenta, A. C., Adair, R., Matier, M., & Scott, J. (1996). The role of ethnicity in choosing and leaving science in highly selective institutions. *Research in Higher Education, 37*(6), 681–709. https://doi.org/10.1007/BF01792952.

Enquist, M., & Leimar, O. (1983). Evolution of fighting behaviour: Decision rules and assessment of relative strength. *Journal of Theoretical Biology, 102*(3), 387–410. https://doi.org/10.1016/0022-5193(83)90376-4.

Faris, N. (2018, October 26). Researcher at Queen's University, caught on video, admits to poisoning coworker. *National Post.*

Fujita, F. (2008). The frequency of social comparison and its relation to subjective well-being. In M. Eid & R. J. Larsen (Eds.), *The Science of subjective well-being* (pp. 239–257). Guilford Press.

Fülöp, M. (1999). Students' perception of the role of competition in their respective countries: Hungary, Japan, USA. In: A. Ross (Red.) *Young citizens in Europe.* University of North London, 195–219.

Fülöp, M. (2000). Teachers' perception of the role of competition in their country: Hungary, Japan and the USA. *Citizenship, Social and Economics Education, 4*(3), 142–158. https://doi.org/10.2304/csee.2000.4.3.142.

Fülöp, M. (2005). The development of social, economical, political identity among adolescents in the post-socialist countries of Europe. *Growing up in Europe Today: Developing Identities among Adolescents,* January, 11–39.

Fülöp, M., Roland-Lévy, C., & Berkics, M. (2004). Economic competition perceived by French and Hungarian adolescents. In Ross, A. (Eds.) *The Experience of Citizenship* (pp. 325–331). London: Metropolitan University.

Fülöp, M., & Sándor, M. (2006). Cross-cultural understandings from social psychology on cooperation and competition. In A. Ross (Ed.), *Citizenship education: Europe and the world* (pp. 75–88). CiCe.

Furnham, A., Kirkcaldy, B. D., & Lynn, R. (1994). National attitudes to competitiveness, money, and work among young people: First, second, and third world differences. *Human Relations, 47*(1), 119–132. https://doi.org/10.1177/001872679404700106.

Garcia, S. M., Reese, Z. A., & Tor, A. (2020). Social comparison before, during, and after the competition. In J. Suls, R. L. Collins, & L. Wheeler (Eds.), *Social comparison, judgment, and behavior* (pp. 105–142). Oxford University Press. https://doi.org/10.1093/oso/9780190629113.003.0005.

Gelfand, M. J., Bhawuk, D. P., Nishii, L. H., & Bechtold, D. J. (2004). Individualism and collectivism. In R. J. House, P. J. Hanges, M. Javidan, P. W. Dorfman, & V. Gupta (Eds.), *Culture, leadership and organizations: The GLOBE study of 62 societies* (pp. 473–512). Sage.

Gibson, T. (1985). The sharing of substance versus the sharing of activity among the Buid. *Man, 20*(3), 391. https://doi.org/10.2307/2802438.

Gould, R. V. (2003). *Collision of wills: How ambiguity about social rank breeds conflict.* University of Chicago Press.

Grimm, S. D., Church, A. T., Katigbak, M. S., & Reyes, J. A. S. (1999). Self-described traits, values, and moods associated with individualism and collectivism: Testing I-C theory in an individualistic (U.S.) and a collectivistic (Philippine) culture. *Journal of Cross-Cultural Psychology, 30*(4), 466–500. https://doi.org/10.1177/0022022199030004005.

Grossmann, I., & Varnum, M. E. W. (2011). Social class, culture, and cognition. *Social Psychological and Personality Science, 2*(1), 81–89. https://doi.org/10.1177/1948550610377119.

Gunia, B. C., Brett, J. M., Nandkeolyar, A. K., & Kamdar, D. (2011). Paying a price: Culture, trust, and negotiation consequences. *Journal of Applied Psychology, 96*(4), 774–789. https://doi.org/10.1037/a0021986.

Hayes, A. F., & Dunning, D. (1997). Construal processes and trait ambiguity: Implications for self-peer agreement in personality judgment. *Journal of Personality and Social Psychology, 72*(3), 664–677. https://doi.org/10.1037/0022-3514.72.3.664

Ho, D. Y. (1976). On the concept of face. *American Journal of Sociology, 81*(4), 867–884.

Hofstede, G. (2003). *Culture's consequences: Comparing values, behaviors, institutions and organizations across nations.* Sage.

Houston, J. M., Harris, P. B., Moore, R., Brummett, R., & Kametani, H. (2005). Competitiveness among Japanese, Chinese, and American undergraduate students. *Psychological Reports, 97*(1), 205–212. https://doi.org/10.2466/pr0.97.1.205-212.

Howell, S. (1989). "To be angry is not to be Human, but to be fearful is": Chewong concepts of human nature. In S. Howell & R. Willis (Eds.), *Societies at Peace: Anthropological Perspectives* (pp. 45–59). Taylor & Frances/Routledge.

Hsu, F. L. K. (1981). *Americans and Chinese: Passages to differences.* University of Hawaii Press.

Hu, J., & Hagedorn, L. S. (2014). Chinese parents' hopes for their only children: A transition program case study. *Journal of College Admission, 223*, 34–42.

Kang, P., Lee, Y., Choi, I., & Kim, H. (2013). Neural evidence for individual and cultural variability in the social comparison effect. *Journal of Neuroscience, 33*(41), 16200–16208. https://doi.org/10.1523/JNEUROSCI.5084-12.2013.

Keller, J., & Loewenstein, J. (2011). The cultural category of cooperation: A cultural consensus model analysis for China and the United States. *Organization Science, 22*(2), 299–319. https://doi.org/10.1287/orsc.1100.0530.

Kim, Y.-H., & Cohen, D. (2010). Information, perspective, and judgments about the self in face and dignity cultures. *Personality and Social Psychology Bulletin, 36*, 537–550. https://doi.org/10.1177/0146167210362398.

Kim, Y.-H., Cohen, D., & Au, W.-T. (2010). The jury and abjury of my peers: The self in face and dignity cultures. *Journal of Personality and Social Psychology, 98*(6), 904–916. https://doi.org/10.1037/a0017936.

Kitayama, S., Markus, H. R., & Kurokawa, M. (2000). Culture, emotion, and well-being: Good feelings in Japan and the United States. *Cognition and Emotion, 14*(1), 93–124. https://doi.org/10.1080/026999300379003.

Knight, G. P., Kagan, S., & Buriel, R. (1981). Confounding effects of individualism in children's cooperation—Competition social motive measures. *Motivation and Emotion, 5*(2), 167–178. https://doi.org/10.1007/BF00993895.

Lam, S. F., Yim, P. S., Law, J. S. F., & Cheung, R. W. Y. (2004). The effects of competition on achievement motivation in Chinese classrooms. *British Journal of Educational Psychology, 74*(2), 281–296. https://doi.org/10.1348/000709904773839888.

Larmer, B. (2014, December 31). Inside a Chinese test-prep factory. *The New York Times.*

Lee, C.-S., & Talhelm, T. (2021). *History of rice farming may explain lower happiness and more intense social comparison in East Asia than West.* Manuscript under review.

Leung, A. K.-Y., & Cohen, D. (2011). Within- and between-culture variation: Individual differences and the cultural logics of honor, face, and dignity cultures. *Journal of Personality and Social Psychology, 100*(3), 507–526. https://doi.org/10.1037/a0022151.

Leung, H., & Au, W. T. (2010). Chinese cooperation and competition. In M. H. Bond (Ed.), *The Oxford handbook of Chinese psychology* (pp. 499–514). Oxford University Press. https://doi.org/10.1093/oxfordhb/9780199541850.013.0030.

Levy, R. I. (1973). *Tahitians: Mind and experience in the Society Islands.* University of Chicago Press. http://dx.doi.org/10.1016/j.cmet.2014.03.003.

Li, L. M. W., Adams, G., Kurtiş, T., & Hamamura, T. (2015). Beware of friends: The cultural psychology of relational mobility and cautious intimacy. *Asian Journal of Social Psychology, 18* (2), 124–133. https://doi.org/10.1111/ajsp.12091.

Li, Y. B. (2018). *Post-frog pond: Cultural variations in hiring decisions.* University of Michigan.

Liu, C.-H., Chiu, Y.-H. C., & Chang, J.-H. (2016). Why do Easterners have lower well-being than Westerners? The role of others' approval contingencies of self-worth in the cross-cultural differences in subjective well-being. *Journal of Cross-Cultural Psychology, 48* (2), 0022022116677580. https://doi.org/10.1177/0022022116677580.

Liu, S. S., Morris, M. W., Talhelm, T., & Yang, Q. (2019). Ingroup vigilance in collectivistic cultures. *Proceedings of the National Academy of Sciences of the United States of America, 116*(29), 14538–14547. https://doi.org/10.1073/pnas.1817588116.

Liu, S. S., Morris, M. W., Talhelm, T., & Yang, Q. (2021). *Covert competition in collectivistic cultures: The role of relational mobility.* Manuscript under review.

Markus, H. R., & Kitayama, S. (1991). Culture and the self: Implications for cognition, emotion, and motivation. *Psychological Review, 98*(2), 224–253. https://doi.org/10.1037/0033-295X.98.2.224.

Markus, H. R., & Kitayama, S. (2010). Cultures and Selves: A cycle of mutual constitution. *Perspectives on Psychological Science, 5*(4), 420–430. https://doi.org/10.1177/1745691610375557.

Marsh, H. W., & Hau, K.-T. (2003). Big-fish–little-pond effect on academic self-concept: A cross-cultural (26-country) test of the negative effects of academically selective schools. *American Psychologist, 58*(5), 364–376. https://doi.org/10.1037/0003-066X.58.5.364.

Marsh, H. W., Kong, C.-K., & Hau, K.-T. (2000). Longitudinal multilevel models of the big-fish-little-pond effect on academic self-concept: Counterbalancing contrast and reflected-glory effects in Hong Kong schools. *Journal of Personality and Social Psychology, 78*(2), 337–349. https://doi.org/10.1037/0022-3514.78.2.337.

Marsh, H. W., Kuyper, H., Morin, A. J. S., Parker, P. D., & Seaton, M. (2014). Big-fish-little-pond social comparison and local dominance effects: Integrating new statistical models, methodology, design, theory and substantive implications. *Learning and Instruction, 33*, 50–66. https://doi.org/10.1016/j.learninstruc.2014.04.002.

Mazar, N., & Aggarwal, P. (2011). Greasing the palm: Can collectivism promote bribery? *Psychological Science, 22*(7), 843–848. https://doi.org/10.1177/0956797611412389.

McLauchlin, T., & Pearlman, W. (2012). Out-group conflict, in-group unity? Exploring the effect of repression on intramovement cooperation. *Journal of Conflict Resolution, 56*(1), 41–66. https://doi.org/10.1177/0022002711429707.

Mead, M. (1937). *Cooperation and competition among primitive peoples.* McGraw-Hill.

Minkov, M. (2018). A revision of Hofstede's model of national culture: Old evidence and new data from 56 countries. *Cross Cultural and Strategic Management, 25*(2), 231–256. https://doi.org/10.1108/CCSM-03-2017-0033.

Morris, M. W., Williams, K. Y., Leung, K., Larrick, R., Mendoza, M. T., Bhatnagar, D., Li, J., Kondo, M., Luo, J., & Hu, J. (1998). Conflict management style: Accounting for cross-national differences. *Journal of International Business Studies, 29*(4), 729–747. https://doi.org/10.1057/palgrave.jibs.8490050.

Murayama, K., & Elliot, A. J. (2012). The competition-performance relation: A meta-analytic review and test of the opposing processes model of competition and performance. *Psychological Bulletin, 138*(6), 1035–1070. https://doi.org/10.1037/a0028324.

Niles, F. S. (1995). Cultural differences in learning motivation and learning strategies: A comparison of overseas and Australian students at an Australian university. *International Journal of Intercultural Relations 19*(3), 369–385. https://doi.org/10.1016/0147-1767(94)00025-S.

OECD. (2018). Student co-operation and competition. In *PISA 2018 results: What school life means for students' lives: Vol. III* (pp. 119–128). OECD Publishing. https://doi.org/10.1787/19963777.

Oishi, S., Diener, E., Suh, E., & Lucas, R. E. (1999). Value as a moderator in subjective well-being. *Journal of Personality, 67*(1), 157–184. https://doi.org/10.1111/1467-6494.00051.

Olson, M. (1965). *The logic of collective action.* Harvard University.

Overing, J. (1986). Images of cannibalism, death and domination in a "non-violent" society. *Journal de La Société Des Américanistes, 72*(1), 133–156. https://doi.org/10.3406/jsa.1986.1001.

Oyserman, D., Coon, H. M., & Kemmelmeier, M. (2002). Rethinking individualism and collectivism: Evaluation of theoretical assumptions and meta-analyses. *Psychological Bulletin, 128*(1), 3–72. https://doi.org/10.1037/0033-2909.128.1.3.

Pan, L. (2013, April). What can we learn from China's college murders? *The Atlantic.*

Petrecca, L. (2017, September 11). America's division: We united in the wake of 9/11, then partisanship re-emerged. *USA Today.*

Phillips, L. T., Stephens, N. M., Townsend, S. S. M., & Goudeau, S. (2020). Access is not enough: Cultural mismatch persists to limit first-generation students' opportunities for achievement throughout college. *Journal of Personality and Social Psychology, 119*(5), 1112–1131. https://doi.org/10.1037/pspi0000234.

Powers, M. (2020). *China and England: The preindustrial struggle for justice in word and image.* Routledge.

Putnam, R. D. (2000). *Bowling alone: The collapse and revival of American community.* Simon and Schuster.

Qing, K. G., Harney, A., Stecklow, S., & Pomfret, J. (2016, May 25). How an industry helps Chinese cheat their way into and through US colleges. *Reuters.*

Reddon, A. R., Dey, C. J., & Balshine, S. (2019). Submissive behaviour is mediated by sex, social status, relative body size and shelter availability in a social fish. *Animal Behaviour, 155*, 131–139. https://doi.org/10.1016/j.anbehav.2019.06.026.

Roberts, K., Clark, S. C., Fagan, C., Adibekian, A., Tholen, J., Nemiria, G., & Tarkhnishvili, L. (2000). *Surviving post-communism: Young people in the former Soviet.* Edward Elgar Publishing.

Różycka-Tran, J., Alessandri, G., Jurek, P., & Olech, M. (2018). A test of construct isomorphism of the belief in a zero-Sum game scale: A multilevel 43-nation study. *PLoS ONE, 13*(9), 1–15. https://doi.org/10.1371/journal.pone.0203196.

Różycka-Tran, J., Boski, P., & Wojciszke, B. (2015). Belief in a zero-sum game as a social axiom: A 37-nation study. *Journal of Cross-Cultural Psychology, 46*(4), 525–548. https://doi.org/10.1177/0022022115572226.

Sasaki, J. Y., Ko, D., & Kim, H. S. (2014). Culture and self-worth: Implications for social comparison processes and coping with threats to self-worth. In F. Gibbons & Z. Križan (Eds.), *Communal functions of social comparison* (pp. 231–251). Cambridge University Press.

Schneider, B. H., Benenson, J., & Berkics, M. (2011). Cooperation and competition. In P. K. Smith & C. H. Hart (Eds.), *The Wiley-Blackwell handbook of childhood social development* (2nd ed., pp. 472–490). Blackwell Publishing Ltd.

Seaton, M., Marsh, H. W., & Craven, R. G. (2009). Earning its place as a pan-human theory: Universality of the big-fish-little-pond effect across 41 culturally and economically diverse countries. *Journal of Educational Psychology, 101*(2), 403–419. https://doi.org/10.1037/a0013838.

Singelis, T. M., Triandis, H. C., Bhawuk, D. P. S., & Gelfand, M. J. (1995). Horizontal and vertical dimensions of individualism and collectivism: A theoretical and measurement refinement. *Cross-Cultural Research, 29*(3), 240–275. https://doi.org/10.1177/106939719502900302.

Sparkes, K. K. (1991). Cooperative and competitive behavior in dyadic game-playing: A comparison of Anglo-American and Chinese children. *Early Child Development and Care, 68*(1), 37–47. https://doi.org/10.1080/0300443910680105.

Suh, E., Diener, E., Oishi, S., & Triandis, H. C. (1998). The shifting basis of life satisfaction judgments across cultures: Emotions versus norms. *Journal of Personality and Social Psychology, 74*(2), 482–493. https://doi.org/10.1037/0022-3514.74.2.482.

Swenson, K. (2018, December 21). He suspected his roommate left the racist graffiti. He didn't know about the poison. *The Washington Post.*

Talhelm, T. (2015). *The rice theory of culture.* University of Virginia.

Talhelm, T., & Oishi, S. (2018). How rice farming shaped culture in Southern China. In A. K. Uskul & S. Oishi (Eds.), *Socioeconomic environment and human psychology* (pp. 53–76). New York, NY: Oxford University Press.

Talhelm, T., & Oishi, S. (2019). Culture and ecology. In D. Cohen & S. Kitayama (Eds.), *Handbook of cultural psychology* (pp. 119–143). The Guilford Press.

Talhelm, T., Zhang, X., & Oishi, S. (2018). Moving chairs in Starbucks: Observational studies find rice-wheat cultural differences in daily life in China. *Science Advances, 4*(4), 1–10. https://doi.org/10.1126/sciadv.aap8469.

Talhelm, T., Zhang, X., Oishi, S., Shimin, C., Duan, D., Lan, X., & Kitayama, S. (2014). Large-scale psychological differences within China explained by rice versus wheat agriculture. *Science, 344*(6184), 603–608. https://doi.org/10.1126/science.1246850.

Tang, S. (1999). Cooperation or competition: A comparison of U.S. and Chinese college students. *Journal of Psychology: Interdisciplinary and Applied, 133*(4), 413–423. https://doi.org/10.1080/00223989909599752.

Taylor, P. (2013). *The thirty-six stratagems: A modern interpretation of a strategy classic.* Infinite Ideas.

Thomson, R., Yuki, M., Talhelm, T., Schug, J., Kito, M., Ayanian, A. H., Becker, J. C., Becker, M., Chiu, C., Choi, H.-S., Ferreira, C. M., Fülöp, M., Gul, P., Houghton-Illera, A. M., Joasoo, M., Jong, J., Kavanagh, C. M., Khutkyy, D., Manzi, C., . . . Visserman, M. L. (2018). Relational mobility predicts social behaviors in 39 countries and is tied to historical farming and threat. *Proceedings of the National Academy of Sciences, 115*(29), 7521–7526. https://doi.org/10.1073/pnas.1713191115.

Toda, M., Shinotsuka, H., McClintock, C. G., & Stech, F. J. (1978). Development of competitive behavior as a function of culture, age, and social comparison. *Journal of Personality and Social Psychology, 36*(8), 825–839. https://doi.org/10.1037/0022-3514.36.8.825.

Triandis, H. C., Bontempo, R., Villareal, M. J., Asai, M., & Lucca, N. (1988). Individualism and collectivism: Cross-cultural perspectives on self-ingroup relationships. *Journal of Personality and Social Psychology, 54*(2), 323–338. https://doi.org/10.1037/0022-3514.54.2.323.

Triandis, H. C., & Gelfand, M. J. (1998). Converging measurement of horizontal and vertical individualism and collectivism. *Journal of Personality and Social Psychology, 74*(1), 118–128. https://doi.org/10.1037/0022-3514.74.1.118.

Vignoles, V. L., Owe, E., Becker, M., Smith, P. B., Easterbrook, M. J., Brown, R., González, R., Didier, N., Carrasco, D., Cadena, M. P., Lay, S., Schwartz, S. J., Des Rosiers, S. E., Villamar, J. A., Gavreliuc, A., Zinkeng, M., Kreuzbauer, R., Baguma, P., Martin, M., . . . Bond, M. H. (2016). Beyond the "East–West" dichotomy: Global variation in cultural models of selfhood. *Journal of Experimental Psychology: General, 145*(8), 966–1000. https://doi.org/10.1037/xge0000175.

Watkins, D. A. (2006). The role of competition in today's Hong Kong: The views of Hong Kong Chinese adolescents in comparative perspective. *Journal of Social Sciences, 2*(3), 85–88. https://doi.org/10.3844/jssp.2006.85.88.

Watkins, D. A. (2010). Motivation and competition in Hong Kong secondary schools: The students' perspective. In C. K. K. Chan & N. Rao (Eds.), *Revisiting the Chinese learner* (pp. 71–88). Springer. https://doi.org/10.1007/978-90-481-3840-1

White, K., & Lehman, D. R. (2005). Culture and social comparison seeking: The role of self-motives. *Personality & Social Psychology Bulletin, 31*(2), 232–242. https://doi.org/10.1177/0146167204271326.

Wu, K. (2021). Invisibility of social privilege to those who have it. *Academy of Management Proceedings 2021* (1). https://doi.org/10.5465/AMBPP.2021.27

Wu, K., & Dunning, D. (2018a). Unknown unknowns: The problem of hypocognition. *Scientific American Mind, 29*(6), 42–45. https://doi.org/10.1038/scientificamericanmind1118-42.

Wu, K., & Dunning, D. (2018b). Hypocognition: Making sense of the landscape beyond one's conceptual reach. *Review of General Psychology, 22*(1), 25–35. https://doi.org/10.1037/gpr0000126.

Wu, K., & Dunning, D. (2019). *Hypocognitive mind: How lack of conceptual knowledge confines what people see and remember.* https://doi.org/10.31234/osf.io/29ryz.

Wu, K., & Dunning, D. (2020). Hypocognition and the invisibility of social privilege. In S. R. Thye & E. J. Lawler (Eds.), *Advances in group processes* (Vol. 37, pp. 1–23). Emerald Publishing Limited. https://doi.org/10.1108/S0882-614520200000037001.

Wu, K., & Dunning, D. (2021a). *Culture and self-view: Variation in trait conceptions.* Manuscript in preparation.

Wu, K., & Dunning, D. (2021b). *Invisibility of social privilege to those who have it.* https://doi.org/10.31234/osf.io/tuy8m.

Wu, K., Garcia, S. M., & Kopelman, S. (2018). Frogs, ponds, and culture: Variations in entry decisions. *Social Psychological and Personality Science, 9*(1), 99–106. https://doi.org/10.1177/1948550617706731.

Yamagishi, T. (1988). The provision of a sanctioning system in the United States and Japan. *Social Psychology Quarterly, 51*(3), 265. https://doi.org/10.2307/2786924.

Yamagishi, T. (2003). Cross-societal experimentation on trust: A comparison of the United States and Japan. In E. Ostrom & J. Walker (Eds.), *Trust and reciprocity: Interdisciplinary lessons from experimental research* (pp. 352–370). Russell Sage Foundation.

Yamagishi, T., Hashimoto, H., & Schug, J. (2008). Preferences versus strategies as explanations for culture-specific behavior. *Psychological Science, 19*(6), 579–584. https://doi.org/10.1111/j.1467-9280.2008.02126.x.

Yan, A. (2015, March 25). Why Chinese parents are sending their children abroad to study at a younger age. *South China Morning Post.*

Yang, W. (2011). Paper Tigers. *New York Magazine.*

Yoshida, T. (1984). Spirit possession and village conflict. In E. Krauss, T. Rohlen, & P. Steinhoff (Eds.), *Conflict in Japan* (pp. 85–104). University of Hawaii Press.

Zhou, M., & Lee, J. (2017). Hyper-selectivity and the remaking of culture: Understanding the Asian American achievement paradox. *Asian American Journal of Psychology, 8*(1), 7–15. https://doi.org/10.1037/aap0000069.

Zhuang, P. (2013, April 21). Poisoning, death of Fudan student recalls disturbing case of Zhu Ling. *South China Morning Post.*

INDEX

Tables and figures are indicated by *t* and *f* following the page number

A

ability-based risk-taking, 375–376, 391
Abramson, L. Y., 425
acceptance and commitment therapy, 601–602, 607
accomplishment, personal, from trait competitiveness, 503–504
achievement
  education outcomes, 586–587
  gap, grading on, 588
achievement goals
  education, 583–584
  on sport performance, 560–562
    effort, emotions, and performance, 561–562
achievement goal theory, 190
  performance, sports, 560–562
  task- *vs.* ego-involvement, 561
Ackerman, J. M., 384
Ackerman, P. L., 503
Acquiring a Company problem, 27–31
Adachi, P. J. C., 254, 258–259
Adam, M. T. P., 125, 169, 170–171, 173, 174, 176, 178–179
adolescent-limited delinquency, 386
adolescents, gender differences, 521–522
adrenaline (rush), 16, 163–164, 165, 184
adrenarche, 66–67
adverse selection problem, 25, 27
advisors, on gender differences, 532
affect-as-information theory, 311
affective sex differences, 74–76
affirmative action, on gender differences, 530–531
age, on gender differences, 521–522

agency, personal
  conception, culture on, 299
  conjoint, 299
  disjoint, 299
  impact, overweighting, 292–294
agentic role, 528
aggression/aggressive behavior. *See also* male–male competition
  androgens on, 77–78
  cheating and, sports, 555–556
  from competition, perceived, 629
  post-competition, 258–259
  rela4tional, 146–148
  sex differences, 77–78
  testosterone dynamics and, 40–42
    pharmacological challenge, 45–46
  reactive, 39–40, 107
Akerlof, G., 28
Alacreu-Crespo, A., 92
Alexander, G. M., 76
Alicke, M. D., 333, 334, 335, 337, 338, 340, 341, 342, 343, 344, 630
all-pay auctions, 16
Almås, I., 521
Amado, D., 253
Amaldoss, W., 20–21
Ames, C., 580
amotivation, 243, 244, 247, 249–250, 251, 252, 255, 260
Anderman, E. M., 584
Andersen, S., 522
Anderson, C., 382
Anderson, M. S., 255
androgenicity, phenotypic, 108
androgen receptors, 62, 63
  polymorphism, on testosterone reactivity, 108

androgens, 59–64. *See also* sex hormones; testosterone dynamics, competition-induced
  on aggression, 77–78
  aromatization, 38, 60, 61, 63, 64, 69
  synthesis, 60
Angulo, J., 500
anisogamy, 57
anteroventral periventricular nucleus, 69
antisocial behavior
  gamesmanship, 556
  sports on, 555–556
anxiety
  competitive arousal, 167 n3, 172–173, 177, 182
  sports, 552–553, 564–565
Apicella, C. L., 42
Appraisal Tendency Framework, 311
"appropriate" sport competition, 547–548, 549, 550
Archer, M. S., 580
ardent male–coy female hypothesis, 57
aromatase, 61, 102
aromatization, androgens, 38, 60, 61, 63, 64, 69
Arora, P., 313, 316, 322
arousal, 165
  adrenaline (rush), 16, 163–164, 165, 184
  autonomic nervous system, 165
  competitive (*see* competitive arousal)
  definition, 165
  measuring, 167, 168t
  overbidding, 164
ascending (clock) auction, 169, 170, 176, 178
aspiration levels, 390

assertiveness, testosterone on, 78
assessment
    competence, flawed, 296–298
    education
        criterion-referenced, 577
        formative, 577
        normative, 577–578
        Programme for International
            Student Assessment,
            574
attachment
    styles, 191–192
    on testosterone reactivity, 107
Attari, S. Z., 314
attention
    definition, 553
    goal-driven, 553–554
    status, 451
    stimulus-driven, 553–554
    sustained selective attention
        joint task, 118–120
attentional control theory,
    553–554
Attick, D., 588
attributional process, competitive
    arousal on, 174
attributional uncertainty, 432
auction(s), 12
    all-pay, 16
    ascending (clock), 169, 170,
        176, 178
    bidding
        competitive arousal, 16, 164,
            164f, 175, 175 n2, 178,
            179, 181, 183–184
        feedback on, full, 29
        hormones on, 109
        for money vs. points, 169
        social psychology, 14
    common value, 24–30, 175
        n2 (see also common value
        auction)
    descending, 24, 169, 170, 176
    Dutch, 12, 24
    economic approaches, 12
    English, 12, 24
    fairness and unfairness,
        perceived, 170
    fever, 164, 174, 181, 184
    first-price, 12, 24, 175 n2
    games, 12
    live, on competitive arousal,
        173
    payoffs, 169
    sealed-bid, 168t

    first-price, 168t, 175 n2, 176
    second-price, 12, 24, 168t
    winner's curse, 25
    time pressure, 170–171
    valuations, 169
    winning and losing, 169
audience, on competitive arousal,
    172–173
Autin, F., 578
autonomic indices, 120
    physiological linkage
        measurement, 125–126
autonomic nervous system,
    arousal, 165
autonomous engagement,
    competition in, 201–203
autonomy, 242, 243
    cognitive evaluation theory,
        242–247, 250–258, 256f, 260
awareness, 599. See also
    mindfulness, competition,
    and sports psychology

B

Baer, R., 601
Balafoutas, L., 531
Balanced Emotional Empathy
    Scale, 120
Balconi, M., 126, 127
Baldwin, M., 622
Ball, S., 28, 29
Baltzell, A., 604–605
Bandura, A., 213, 377
Barclay, P., 382
Barsi, Z., 514
Bartkus, K. R., 500
Bartling, B., 322
basic psychological needs theory, 260
Basking in Reflected Glory, 484
Bateman, A. J., 57
Bateman gradient, 57
Bateman's principle, 57
Bateup, H. S., 82
Baumeister, R. F., 200–201, 553
Bazerman, M. H., 25, 27, 30
"beat the other," 245
Beattie, S., 560
Beauvois, J. L., 573
bed nucleus of the stria terminals,
    69, 71t
behavior
    competitions, determinants,
        14–18
    competitive arousal on,
        174–178

    attributional process, 174
    auction bidding, 175, 175 n2
    general performance,
        177–178
    as help and hindrance, 174
    negotiation performance,
        176–177
    risky decisions, 175–176
    confirmation, 355, 358
    flexibility, 58, 352, 356, 357, 358,
        362, 366, 367
    hormonal effects on
        activational, 65, 66, 72,
            73, 92
        organizational, 64–65, 92
    from intention to, 322–323
    intergroup, 477
    models, descriptive, 11
    reading, 354
    testosterone dynamics and,
        competition-induced, 38–44,
        104
        aggressive behavior, 40–42
        athletic performance, 44
        competitive behavior, 39–40
        mating psychology and
            behavior, 42–43
        risk-taking, 42
        utility maximization, 11
behavior, competitive
    competitive phenomenon
        preceding and following, 402
    social comparison and, 402
    testosterone dynamics and,
        39–40
        pharmacological challenge,
            44–45
behavior, student, 584–586
    bullying, 585–586
    cheating, 584–585
    exploitation, 585
    sabotage, 585
behavioral beliefs, gender
    difference cooperation, 308f,
        309–312
    individually motivated, 310–311
    socially motivated, 311–312
behavioral economics, 11
Behaviors from Intergroup Affect
    and Stereotypes, 273–274
Behavioural Activation System
    scale score, 124
Belavadi, S., 487–488, 489
belief structures, subjective,
    482–483

Bell, J. J., 565
Benign and Malicious Envy Scale, 275
benign envy, 202, 266–269, 271–279
Bereby-Meyer, Y., 29
Berthold, A. A., 101
between-group violence, 135, 141–142, 149, 150, 151
Betzig, L., 143
Bezos, Jeff, 150, 152
bias
  agency and intention, overweighting, 292–294
  in-group, cooperation, 311
  survivorship, 298
bidding. *See also* overbidding
  competitive arousal on, 16, 164, 164*f*, 175, 175 n2, 178, 179, 183–184
  feedback on, full, 29
  hormones on, 109
  for money *vs.* points, 169
  social psychology, 14
Biesanz, J. C., 363
big-fish–little-pond effect, 338, 339–340
biopsychology approaches, 5
Biosocial Model of Status, 84, 103
Biosocial Status Hypothesis, 79
bipolar disorder, sex differences, 75
Bird, B., 104
Bird, B. M., 47
BIRGing, 485
BIS/BAS questionnaire, 120
Blau, F. D., 524–525
Bless, H., 365
Bloom, D. L., 630
bonding, team sports, 89
Bönte, W., 505–506, 524
Booth, A., 534
bottom-line mentality, 505
bounded functionalist account, 450
Bounded Reciprocity Theory, 311
Bowling Alone (Putnam), 632
Braun, S., 274
Brooks, A. W., 274
Brown, A. D., 173, 176, 177
Brown, S. P., 10
Buhlmayer, L., 603
bulbocavernous spinal nucleus, 69–70
Bull, C., 13, 15
bullying, education, 585–586

Burton-Chellew, M. N., 20
Buser, T., 505, 532
Buss, D. M., 386
Butera, F., 585
Butler, R., 202
Buunk, A. P., 501–502

C

Cain, D. M., 17
Callan, M. J., 381
Campbell, A., 384
Campbell, B., 151
Capen, E. C., 25
capital
  embodied, 376, 377–378
  monetary, 377
  social, 377, 632
Capra, C. M., 322
Carlson, L. E., 599
Carlsson, F., 534
Carpenter, J., 24
Carré, J. M., 39, 40, 87
Carroll, J. S., 27
Casto, K. V., 40, 83*t*, 87
causality orientation theory, 260
Chagnon, N. A., 141–142, 143
challenge
  cognitive evaluation theory, 248–249
  opposing processes model of competition and performance, 199–200
  sports, 557–558
  sympathetic-adrenomedullary axis, 199
Challenge Hypothesis, 79, 102–103, 105
challenge-related pattern, 200
"Challenging Darwin's Theory of Sexual Selection" (Roughgarden), 58
Chan, E. Y., 386
characterization
  efforts, 352
  target's perspective, 352–353
characterization and predictions
  choking under pressure, 364–365
  negative, inviting, 365
  positive, avoiding, 364–365
  unpredictability, target, 364
  well-adjusted persona and self–other agreement, 363
characterization of self, reactions to perceiver attempts to, 355–359

  reactions to being characterized and predicted, 356
  (over) sensitivity to being noticed, 356–357
  paranoid cognition, 356
  spotlight effect, 357
  transparent, feeling, 357
  strategic disclosure, 358–359
  strategic legibility, 357–358
Charness, G., 28
cheating
  acceptance of, 257
  college scandals, Chinese students, 629
  competitive arousal in, 176
  cost-benefit calculation, 437
  education, 584–585, 587, 588
  rivalry and, 437
  for scholarship, 273
  social comparison on, 23
  sports, 546, 555
    aggression and, 555–556
    ethical vision on, athletes', 607
  goals on, 563–564
  status concerns, 452, 454, 457
  in winners, 23, 408
Chen, P., 412
children, gender differences, 521–522
China
  competitiveness, 611–612
  gender differences, 534
choices of others, control over, 322
choking (under pressure), 200–201, 364–365, 553, 564
  reinvestment theory and, 554–555
classroom climate, 579–580
climates, educational, 579–582
  classroom, 579–580
  error, 581–582
  goal structure, 580–581
Clot, S., 535
coaction, social comparison, 411–412
co-actors, on physiological arousal, 171–172
coalitional value, 148–149
coalitions, male, 148
  competition, 138, 140–141
  empires, early, 142
  food stores of other groups, raiding, 142
  intrasexual competition, 138
  male-on-male violence, 141–142
  Yanomamö, 141–142

Coffee, H. S., 497
Coffman, L. C., 322
cognitive approaches, 6
cognitive dimorphism, 73–74
cognitive evaluation theory,
    241–253
  experimental studies, 243–244
    free choice behavior, 243,
      244
    methodology, 244
  intrinsic motivation, 242, 243
    (see also intrinsic motivation)
    predictive power, hypothesis-
      driven, 243
  pressure, 243
  proposition 1, 245–247
    competitive set and pressure
      to win, 245
    rewards, competitively
      contingent, 245–247
  proposition 2
    challenge, 248–249
    feedback and competitive
      outcome, 247–248
  proposition 3, 249–250
  proposition 4, leader's
    motivating style, 250–251
  proposition 5
    ego-involvement as
      "internally controlling"
      states, 252
    self-talk - informational or
      controlling, 253
  psychological needs, 191,
    242–243
    autonomy, 242, 243
    competence, 242
    relatedness, 242
  social environments and
    relationships, 243
cognitive mechanisms, illusory
  superiority, 290, 294–298
  competence, flawed
    assessments, 296–298
  reference group neglect,
    294–295
cognitive reappraisal, 278
collaborate to compete, 18–21
collective self, social identity
  and, 481
collectivism. See also
    interdependence
  terminology, 612 n1
collectivist cultures,
    competitiveness, 611–636

causes, competition and
    suspicion, 621–626
  common standard vs. self-
    defined goals, 624–625
  social comparison, 622–624
  social ecology, relational
    mobility, 625–626, 627f
  zero-sum beliefs, 621–622
China, 611–612
  on competitive orientation,
    498 n2
consequences, 629–631
  choosing competitive
    environment, perils,
    629–630
  performance, 630–631
corruption, collectivism–
    competition link, 617–618, 619f
covert, 619–621
  frenemies and in-group
    vigilance, 620–621
  information, withholding,
    619–620
future directions
  competitions exists ≠ liking
    competition, 634–636,
    635f
  research areas, 633–634
  vs. individualistic cultures, 614–
    617, 615t, 617f
  as in-group–out-group
    phenomenon, 617
  societies without competition,
    631–633
  types, cultural differences,
    626–629
    competitions entered,
      choice, 626–627, 628f
    prestige, desire for, 627–629
  views, across cultures, 612–614
college application, gender
  differences, 525
collusion, 23, 24, 179
commitment, to goals
  specific and challenging
    on task performance, 211–212
    value of goal and expectancy
      of attainment on,
      212–213
  valence on, 212
common enemy effect, 632–633
common standard, vs. self-defined
  goals, 624–625
common value auction, 24–30,
  175 n2

adverse selection problem,
    25, 27
  definition, 25
  winner's curse and, 24
communal role, 528
Comparing and Being Compared
  Framework, 411–412
comparison referent, 333
comparisons
  convenience, 339
  upwards, 335–336, 402
competence, 242
  assessments, flawed, 296–298
  competitive outcome, 247–248
  Dunning-Kruger effect, 295,
    300
  on envy, 273–274
  feedback/satisfaction, 244
  perceived, 197f, 198, 200–201,
    246, 248, 452
  on social judgments, 273–274
competence-relevant engagement,
  190
competition, 240–260
  autonomous engagement and,
    201–203
  conceptualizing, 10
  to cooperation, 305–307
  cooperation and, cultural
    views, 613
  definition, 4–5, 241, 373, 515,
    560
  effect, 81, 82, 84, 85, 86, 91, 93
  entry into, gender differences,
    516–517
  markets, 11
  measurement, 515–516
  outcomes, behavioral and
    psychological, 5
  perceived environmental, 10
  perfect, deviations from, 12
  performance and, 189–204
    (see also opposing processes
      model of competition and
      performance)
  structural, 10
  study of
    psychological, 4, 5–7
    in psychology vs. economics,
      11–13
  subjective nature, 4–5
  testosterone dynamics induced
    by, 37–47, 104 (see also
      testosterone dynamics,
      competition-induced)

competition characteristics
and, 105
zero-sum interaction, 4
competition and suspicion,
collectivist cultures, 621–626
common standard *vs.* self-
defined goals, 624–625
social comparison, 622–624
social ecology, relational
mobility, 625–626, 627*f*
zero-sum beliefs, 621–622
competition pool
definition, 335
leaving/exiting, 345
competition pools, self-
evaluation, 332–346
big-fish-little-pond effect,
339–340
comparison processes, 335–336
competition, 335
social *vs.* temporal
comparisons, 335–336
future directions, 345–346
huge-fish–little-pond effect, 343
implications, broader, 344–345
local and global, 338–344
local dominance, 340–344
referents, 336–338
genius effect, 336–337
referent status, selective use,
337–338
social comparison
theory, 332, 334–335 (*see also*
social comparison)
transitivity, 338
status in pool on, 345
competitive advantage,
judgmental biases on
perception of, 287–301
exceptions, 298–301
comparison, object of, 299
culture, 299
methodological note, 298
self-views, negative, 299–300
top performers, plight,
300–301
illusory superiority, 288–289
illusory superiority mechanisms,
cognitive, 290, 294–298
competence, flawed
assessments, 296–298
reference group neglect,
294–295
illusory superiority mechanisms,
motivational, 290–294

intentions, overweighting,
292–294
optimistic, overweighting,
291–292
predictions, preference-
driven, 290
skill, self-flattering
definitions, 290–291
position, self-perception of, 288
positional rewards, 287–288
competitive altruism hypothesis,
447–448
competitive anxiety, sports, 552–
553, 564–565
competitive arousal, 16, 120,
163–185
adrenaline (rush), 16, 163–164,
165, 184
anxiety, 167 n3, 172–173, 177,
182
arousal, 165
empirical
operationalizations, 182
measuring, 167
on attributional process, 174
auctions on, live, 173
audience on, 172–173
in cheating, 176
clarifying and redefining,
181–183
construct interrelationships,
179–180
on decision making and
behavior, 174–178
attributional process, 174
auction bidding, 175, 175 n2
general performance,
177–178
as help and hindrance, 174
negotiation performance,
176–177
risky decisions, 175–176
definition, 181–182
domains of interactions, 179
effects, full range, 179
existence, reasons for, 181
framework, 164–165, 164*f*,
183–184
fundamentals, 163–165
incidentally induced, 183
integral factors
audience, 172–173
co-actors and counterparts
on, 171–172
competitors, number of, 172

fairness and unfairness on,
perceived, 170
time pressure, 170–171
trash-talking, 172
winning and losing auctions,
169–170
knowledge gaps and future
research directions, 179–181
moderating influences, 180
emotion regulation, 178–179
integral factors, 178
task complexity, 178
overbidding/auction bidding,
16, 164, 164*f*, 175, 175 n2, 178,
179, 181, 183–184
practical implications, 184
sources, 166–174
research articles, context
and, 167, 168*t*
research articles, integral and
incidental, 166–167,
167*t*
sources, incidental, 166
sources, integral, 166
competition audience,
172–173
interaction partner, 171–172
stimuli outside competition,
173–174
task, 169–171
temporal study, 182
unique factors, 180–181
valence, 165, 182
Yerkes Dodson law, 180
competitive expansion schema,
rivalry, 423–424
competitive field, tournaments,
15–16, 23, 24
competitive history, shared,
cognitive elaboration, 427*f*,
429–433
contributory causes, social-
comparison concerns,
430–433
personal factors, 431
relational factors, 431–432
schema formation and
"instant" rivalries, 433
situational factors, 432–433
as origin, 427*f*, 430
competitiveness
Aesop on, 497, 497 n1
child understanding of, 497
definition, 90, 497, 515–516
gender differences, 505–506

competitiveness (*cont.*)
  intrasexual, individual
      differences, 501–502
  measurement, 499, 515–516
  social dominance orientation,
      501
  social value orientation, 498
  trait, 10, 496–508 (*see also* trait
      competitiveness)
  Type A behavior, 219, 498, 500
Competitiveness Index, 499
competitive set, cognitive
    evaluation theory, 245
competitor reactions, speed of,
    167 n3
competitors, number of
  competitive advantage,
      judgmental biases, 295
  competitive arousal, 172
  gender differences, 529
  social comparison, 405, 410,
      414
conjoint agency, 299
connectedness, team sports, 89
Connolly, T., 311
constructive competition, 197–198
contest competition, 91
contested hierarchies, properties
  individual, 461–462
  relational, 459–461
  structural, 454–456
  temporal, 457–459
context
  competitive arousal, 167, 168t
  on gender differences, 535
  status and, 446
context effect, 577
Contrary to Dual Envy Theory,
    266–267
control
  illusion of, overweighting, 293
  over actions, 307, 321, 322, 323
  over choices
    one's own, 322, 323
    others, 322–323
  over negative behavior, 322
controlling aspect/elements, 249–
    253, 254
controlling elements, 243, 244,
    255–259, 256f
controlling self-talk, cognitive
    evaluation theory, 253
convenience comparisons, 339
Cook, C. J., 44
Cook, T. R., 379, 381

Cooke, A., 550, 552
cooperation, 352
  competition and, cultural
      views, 613
  from competition to, 305–307
  as constructed choice, 308f,
      322–323
    positively, 313–314, 314t
  definition, 307–308
  identity vis-à-vis others who
      benefit from, 311
  as individual difference, 307
  in-group bias, 311
  in-group identification/group
      norms, 319–320
  ongoing, 321
  proselfs, 310, 312
  prosocial individuals/tactics,
      312, 316
  research approaches, 306
  self-interested elements, 375
  situational motivations, 307
  status, 319
  subjective norms, 315–320
    motivation to comply with
        cooperative norms,
        316–320
      external, 317–319
      internal, 319–320
    normative beliefs, 315–316
  tapering off, temporally
      dynamic goal pursuit model,
      implicit competitions, 228
  trust, 321
  visibility, 319
cooperation, theory of planned
    behavior
  attitudes towards, 308f, 309–314
    affective reactions, 310
    behavioral beliefs, 308f,
        309–312
    behavioral beliefs,
        individually motivated,
        310–311
    behavioral beliefs, socially
        motivated, 311–312
    behavioral outcomes,
        evaluations, 313–315,
        314t
    social value orientation, 307,
        310, 311
  as constructed choice, 322–323
cooperative interactions, 351
cooperative person, defined,
    499 n3

cooperative social dilemmas, 306
cooperative *vs.* competitive
    contexts, moderating role,
    359–362
  social connections and
      reduction of feeling
      scrutinized, 360–361
  social connections and
      reductions in prediction
      avoidance, 361–362
Coping Competition Model,
    80–81, 81f, 85, 87, 88, 92
coping style, on testosterone
    reactivity, 107
Corbally, L., 603
core gender identity, 77
corruption, collectivism–
    competition link as, 617–618,
    619f
cortisol
  in gender differences,
      520–521
  on testosterone reactivity,
      109–110
cosmopolitanism, 148
Costa, R., 85
Costello, P., 435–436
counterparts, on competitive
    arousal, 171–172
covert collectivist competition,
    619–621
  frenemies and in-group
      vigilance, 620–621
  information, withholding,
      619–620
Crawford, B., 27, 28
Crewther, B. T., 44
criterion-referenced assessment,
    577
Crivelli, D., 126
Croson, R., 518
cross-level effects, status striving
    hierarchical competition,
    464
Cruise, J., 269
Crusius, J., 271, 275
Cuddy, A. J. C., 273–274
Cui, F., 123
Cui, X., 121
culture
  collectivist, 611–636 (*see
      also* collectivist cultures,
      competitiveness)
  competition across, views of,
      612–614

on competitiveness, 498, 498
n2
on gender differences, 533–534
illusory superiority, 299
Cumming, S. P., 251
Curhan, J. R., 173, 176, 177
cytosine-adenine-guanine (CAG)
repeats, androgen receptor,
46, 108

D

Dale, S. B., 633
Daly, M., 386
Darnon, C., 202
Darwin, C., 57, 135, 144, 152
*Descent of Man and Selection in
Relation to Sex, The,* 57
Darwin-Bateman-Trivers
Paradigm, 57, 58
Darwinian perspective, 134–153
human competition, 139–148
developed nations, 146–147
empires, early, 142–143
evolutionary history, 141
female–female competition,
139, 144
male–male competition, 57,
137–138, 140–141
coalitions, 138
empires, early, 142
mate competition, 382
reproductive skew, 144
WEIRD societies, 148, 152
polygynous societies, 145–146
reproductive skew, 143–144
traditional societies, 141–142
sexual selection, 57–59, 135–137
female choice, 57–58
intersexual choice, 136–137,
137f
intrasexual competition, 136,
137–138, 138f
social selection, 135, 138–139
sports, 134–135
WEIRD societies, competition
in, 148–152
dominance, prestige, and
competition, 149–152
violence, decline, 148–149
de-automatization, 554–555
deception, economics on, 11
Decety, J., 122
Deci, E. L., 245, 246, 248
decision making
approaches, 6

competitive arousal on,
174–178
attributional process, 174
auction bidding, 175, 175 n2
general performance,
177–178
as help and hindrance, 174
negotiation performance,
176–177
risky decisions, 175–176
under risk, 374
sex differences, 73
unethical,
hypercompetitiveness and,
506
decomposed games approach,
499–500, 499 n3, 502
De Cremer, D., 311
dejection, upward comparisons
on, 408
Delgado, M. R., 171
delinquency, adolescent-limited,
386
De Lisle, S. P., 59
de Melo, C. M., 311
Deminchuk, J., 382
depression
hopelessness depression model,
423, 425
sex differences, 75
deprivation, personal relative,
388–389
descending auctions, 24, 169,
170, 176
*Descent of Man and Selection
in Relation to Sex, The*
(Darwin), 57
Deutsch, M., 572
deviance, generality, 387
dimorphism, sexual. *See* sexual
dimorphism
disadvantage
perceived, 389–390
personal relative deprivation,
388–389
dis/advantage, risk-taking and,
375–376
competitive, relative state and,
determinants, 376–379
embodied capital, 376,
377–378
situational/environmental
factors, 376, 378–379
proximate psychology, 388–391
disclosure, strategic, 358–359

discrepancy feedback
from goal attainment
early, 214
on effort exertion to specific
and challenging goals,
213–214
temporally dynamic goal
pursuit model
explicit competitions,
220–221
implicit competitions, 226–227
dishonesty, behavioral, envy and,
270
disjoint agency, 299
disparagement, envy, 270
dispositional envy scale, 265,
272, 275
Di Stasio, M. R., 585
distinctiveness, positive, 481–482
dominance, 385
achieving and maintaining,
141, 149
local, defined, 341
local dominance effect, 341–
344, 415
male competition, 140–141
traditional societies, 141–142
WEIRD societies, 149–152
Dompnier, B., 587
Donahue, E. G., 258
doping, 257–258, 497
downward comparisons, post-
competition, 408
"do-your-best" goal structures,
549, 551
Drea, C. M., 58
Dual Envy Theory, 266
dual-hormone hypothesis,
109–110
Dumas, T. L., 456
Dunning, D., 293
Dunning-Kruger effect, 295, 300
Durocher, Leo, 496
Dutch auction, 12, 24

E

ECD theory, 59
ecological character
displacement, 59
ecological sexual dimorphisms,
58–59
economic inequality
homicide rates, 381
need-based risk-taking, 375–
376, 391

economics
  on deception, 11
  incentive structure, 11
  preferences, rational
    maximization, 11
  psychology *vs.*, 10–13
  study of competition, 11–13
education, 569–590
  achievement gap, assessments
    on, 588
  from educational systems to
    student characteristics, 582
  feedback loop, education as,
    569, 570f, 588–590
  settings, gender differences,
    525–526
  social class, 578, 588
  societies, 569–575 (*see also*
    education societies)
  from society to educational
    systems, 575–576
  students, 582–588
    (*see also* students)
    behaviors, 584–586
    goals, 583–584
    information exchange, 587
    outcomes, 586–588
    socioeconomic status, 588
    values, 582–583
  systems, 576–582 (*see also*
    education systems)
  terms, defined, 574
  Universal Declaration of
    Human Rights, 571
educational performance, gender
  differences, 525–526
education societies, 569–575
  history, 570
  ideologies and values, 571–574
    definitions, 571, 574
    fair, free market, 572–573
    meritocracy, 571–572
    neoliberalism, 573–574
    transmission of dominant,
      570–571
  norms, 574–575
    employability, 575
    productivism, 575
education systems, 576–582
  climates, 579–582
    classroom, 579–580
    error, 581–582
    goal structure, 580–581
  structures, 576–579
    normative assessment, 577–578

numerus clausus, 578–579,
      580, 582
    tracking, 578
Edwards, D. A., 40, 83t, 84
effectance, 242, 243
  feedback relevant, 244, 247,
    249, 255
effort
  achievement goals on, sports,
    561–562
  exertion of, over time, 212–213
effort-based competitions,
    13–14. *See also* rank-order
    tournaments and effort-
    based competitions
ego goals, 191
ego orientation/involvement
  on achievement, 561
  achievement goals and
    performance
    effort, 561–562
    emotions, 562–563
  as "internally controlling"
    state, 252
Ehrhart, K.-M., 170
electroencephalogram,
  hyperscanning research,
    123–125
Elliot, A. J., 192, 193, 194–196,
    502, 584, 586
embeddedness, rivalry, 434
embodied capital, 376, 377–378
emotional approaches, 6
emotions
  achievement goals on, sports,
    561–562
  competitive arousal on, 178–179,
    182
  expressed, 311
  regulation
    on envy, 278
    mindfulness for, 607
    reappraisal and suppression
      model, 601
    strategies, 278
empathy, prenatal testosterone
  on, 78
employability norms, 575
English auction, 12, 24
enhanced brain effect, 122
enjoyment, competitive situations
  on, 241
entity theory, 277
entrepreneurship, gender
  differences, 524

environmental competition,
  perceived, 10
environmental competitiveness,
  perceived, 192–193, 193f
environmental factors, 376, 378–379
envy, 202, 265–279
  benign, 202, 266–269, 271–279
    competence on, 273–274
    competition and, 267–268, 268f
    conceptualizations, varying,
      266–267
    conditions, 266
    consequences, 268–272
      cognitive, 268–269
      intentional and behavioral,
        269–272
      well-being, 272
  definition, qualities, and
    impacts, 265–266
  determinants, 272–276
    envy target, 273–274
    individual, 274–276
    situational, 273
  dispositional, 275
  from fear of failure, 275
  intentional and behavioral
    consequences
    constructive, 271–272
    covert hostility, 270
    covert victimization, 270–271
    dishonest behaviors, 270
    disparagement, 270
    help, dependence-producing,
      271
    schadenfreude, 270, 275
    social undermining, 270
  interventions, potential, 276–278
    emotion regulation, 278
    enactment costs and benefits,
      moderating, 277
    incremental implicit theory,
      277
    pay transparency, 276–277
    self-regulation, 278
  vs. jealousy, 266
  malicious, 202, 266–267,
    269–279
  narcissism, 274, 275–276
  pain, 266–267
  pride on, 274
  proneness, 274–275
  prosocial tendencies, 275
  schadenfreude, 270, 275
  self-esteem, 276
  success, hope for, 275

unfairness beliefs, 275
upward comparisons on, 408
warmth on, 273–274
equilibrium levels, theoretic, 13
Erev, I., 19
error climate, 581–582
errors
of omission *vs.* commission, 297
spotting own *vs.* others',
asymmetry, 296–297
Esses, V. M., 487
estradiol, from testosterone, 38,
61, 63, 102
estrogens, 59–64. *See also* sex
hormones
receptors, 62, 63
synthesis, 61
ethics, 259
behavior, hypercompetitiveness
and, 506
doping, 257–258
right mindfulness and, 607
sportspersonship, 259
unethical behavior, rivalry and,
436–437
evaluation
apprehension, rivalry, 402,
411–412
competition pools, defined, 335
excitement, competitive arousal,
165, 166, 167 n3, 170, 172, 182
Exline, J. J., 22
expansion/expansiveness, rivalry,
427, 433–434, 436, 438, 439
expectancy beliefs, 212–213
attainment, on commitment to
specific and challenging goal,
212–213
temporally dynamic goal
pursuit model
explicit competitions, 220
implicit competitions, 226
explicit competitions
goal pursuit, 211
temporally dynamic goal
pursuit model, 217–224, 217f
discrepancy feedback, 220–221
expectancy beliefs, 220
goal, 218
goal setting, 218–219
over course of competition,
221–224, 222f, 224f, 225f
winning, value of, 219
exploitation, 320, 449, 498
education, 585, 587, 588

exposure, social comparisons
model, 432
expressive suppression, 278
extremism, intergroup, 486–488
Eyster, E., 26–27, 28

F
Facebook, social comparison, 413
fair, free market, 572–573
fairness
perceived, on competitive
arousal, 170
social comparison and
competition frameworks, 415
sustainability, 415–416
violation, 322
Fang, H., 248–249
fear
competitive arousal, 165, 166
of failure, envy from, 275
Federico, C. M., 487
feedback
on bidding, 29
cognitive evaluation theory,
247–248
competence, 244
on gender differences, 530
negative, 247
negativity related to, 249
positive, 247
feedback, discrepancy
from goal attainment
early, 214
on effort exertion to specific
and challenging goals,
213–214
temporally dynamic goal
pursuit model, 216–217, 217f
explicit competitions, 220–221
implicit competitions, 226–227
feedback loops
education, 569, 570f, 588–590
rivalry, 439
Feiler, L., 322
female. *See also* gender differences,
psychology of competition
choice, 57
female–female competition, 139,
144, 146–148, 153
Fershtman, C., 22, 322
Festinger, L., 332, 333–334,
335–336, 338, 388, 402, 416
fight-or-flight response, 78–79
Filaire, E., 83t
Finke, M. S., 382

first-price auction, 12, 24, 175 n2
first-price sealed-bid auctions,
168t, 175 n2, 176
Fischbacher, U., 322
Fiske, S. T., 273
fitness
biological
natural selection, 374–375
proxies, risk-taking, 375, 387
relative state, 376
protection system, 104
five-factor model of personality,
500–501
flexibility, behavioral, 58, 352, 356,
357, 358, 362, 366, 367
Flory, J. A., 522
flow states, mindfulness on, 607
follicle-stimulating hormone, 38,
61, 62–63
Fong, M., 16
Foreman, P., 29
formative assessment, 577
Foucault, M., 572
Fox, R. L., 524
Fredrickson, B. L., 601
free choice behavior, 243, 244
free-market ideology, 572
frenemies, covert competition,
620–621
Frick, B., 527
Friedman, M., 500
Fülöp, M., 613
hyperscanning research, 121–123

G
gain frame, 316
Galinsky, A. D., 382
Gallaway, T., 253
gamesmanship, 556
gamification, 415
Garcia, S. M., 16–17, 430–431
Gardner, F. L., 602–603
Gates, Bill, 150, 152
gender. *See also* sex
gender congruity framework, 529
gender differences, psychology of
competition, 514–536
applications, 522–527
education, 525–526
labor markets, 523–525
negotiations, 523
sports, 526–527
competition and
competitiveness, defining
and measuring, 515–516

gender differences, psychology of
    competition (*cont.*)
    contexts, 518–522
        exogenous/endogenous
            factors, other, 520–522
        gender composition, 519–520
        types of tasks, 518–519
    entry into competition, 516–517
    gender *vs.* sex differences, 515
    implications and future
        directions, 530–535
        contexts, 535
        cross-cultural, 533–534
        gender gaps, person *vs.*
            institution-focused,
            530–532
        sociobiological mechanisms,
            532–533
    performance under
        competition, 517–518
    piece-rate *vs.* tournament
        compensation, 517–518,
        520.530–532, 534
    social psychological
        mechanisms, 527–529
    wage gap, 514, 524–525
    women
        in labor force, 514
        in power, political and
            business, 514
gender identity, core, 77
gender *vs.* sex differences, 515
generality of deviance, 387
Geniole, S. N., 45, 81, 85
genius effect, 336–337
genomic actions, 62, 102
Giardini, F., 318
Gilovich, T., 357
Gino, F., 270
Give and Take (Grant), 449
Glätzle-Rützler, D., 522
glucocorticoids, 60
    on testosterone reactivity, 109–110
Gneezy, U., 22, 322, 517–520, 522
goal(s)
    attainment
        discrepancy feedback from,
            on effort exertion to
            specific and challenging
            goals, 213–214
        expectancy of, commitment
            to specific and
            challenging goals on,
            212–213
    definition, 211

education
    climates, structure, 580–581
    student, 583–584
gradients, 191
mastery (learning), 190–191
performance (ego), 191
pursuit, 210
    explicit competitions, 211
    implicit competitions, 211
    interdependent, 218
    motivation, 211–214 (*see also*
        temporally dynamic
        goal pursuit model)
    rivalry, 434–436
    temporally dynamic goal
        pursuit model, 210–235
        (*see also* temporally
        dynamic goal pursuit
        model)
self-defined
    collectivist culture
        competitiveness,
        624–625
    vs. common standard, 624–625
setting, temporally dynamic
    goal pursuit model
    explicit competitions, 218–219
    implicit competitions, 226
success, interdependent, 221
temporally dynamic goal
    pursuit model
    explicit competitions, 218
    implicit competitions, 226
"winning is the goal," 245
goal content theory, 260
goal-driven attention, 553–554
Goal Framing Theory, 316
goal-setting theory, classic, 211–214
    specific and challenging goals
        commitment to, goal value
            and expectancy of
            attainment in, 212–213
        effort exertion to,
            discrepancy feedback
            from goal attainment
            on, 213–214
        higher task performance
            from, 211–212
goal-transformation hypothesis,
    311
golf-putting, 551
Gollwitzer, P. M., 212
gonadotropin-releasing hormone,
    37–38, 61
gonadotropins, 61

gossip, women's competition,
    146–147, 153
grading, exclusiveness, 577–578
Granger causality, 127
Grant, A. M., *Give and Take,* 449
greater male variability
    hypothesis, 57
Green, A., 570
Greenbaum, R. L., 505
Greenberg, M. T., 607
Griskevicius, V., 319
Gross, J. J., 278, 601
Grosskopf, B., 29, 30
Grossman, Z. J., 322
group
    centrism, drive for, 487
    competition, 18–21
    definition, 477
    identification
        motives for, 488
        status and status threats,
            487–488
    memberships
        depersonalization, 483
        as prototypes, 483–484
Groysberg, B., 456
Günther, C., 518–519
Gupta, N. D., 517
Gussak, D., 605

H

Hadrian, Emperor, 150
Hamilton, L. D., 82
Hamman, J. R., 322
Hancock, M., 357
Hanek, K. J., 525, 529
Hangen, E. J., 196, 199–200
Hanton, S., 552
Harackiewicz, J. M., 550, 551
Haran, U., 17, 172
Harbring, C., 23, 24
Hardy, C. L., 448
Hargadon, A., 463
hatred, intergroup, 485–491. *See
    also* violence and hatred,
    intergroup
Häubl, G., 167 n3
Haugen, J. A., 361
Hayes, S. C., 601
health maintenance, from trait
    competitiveness, 503
heart rate
    physiological linkage, 125–126
    variability, gender differences,
        521

hedonic frame, 316
hegemonic masculinity, 151, 153
Hegewisch, A., 514
help, dependence-producing,
envy and, 271
helpful, being
cultural views, 614
goal pursuit on, 228
prosocial goals, 573
sports, task mastery, 219
Helzer, E. G., 293
hierarchies
contested, properties
individual, 461–462
relational, 459–461
structural, 454–456
temporal, 457–459
social, 129
stability, on testosterone
reactivity, 105–106
status
coordination benefits, 446–447
perceptions, lay, 465
value, perceptions of, 455
higher education profession
gender differences, 524
research-intensive programs, as
hypercompetitive, 505 n4
high explicit self-esteem, 276
Hill, S. E., 386
Hobbes, T., 140
Hodge, K., 254, 258
Hoffman, P. J., 336
Hogg, M. A., 487–488, 489
Hohman, Z. P., 490
hopelessness depression model,
423, 425
Horizontal-Vertical Collectivism
scale, 614
hormone-binding globulins, 61
Horney, K., 497, 504
hostility, covert, envy and, 270
hot sauce paradigm, 40–41
Houston, J. M., 499
Huang, S.-C., 214, 222, 222f
Huberman, G., 295
huge-fish–little-pond effect, 343
Huguet, P., 342
Human, L. J., 363
Huston, S. J., 382
Hypercompetitive Attitude
Scale, 499
hypercompetitiveness, 201
behavioral impacts, 504–507,
505 n4

decision-making, unethical,
506
leadership, 506–507
productivity, workplace,
505–506
definition, 504
as desirable, 504–505
higher education, research-
intensive, 505 n4
narcissism, 501
pay-for-performance incentive
structures, 505
personality traits, 497
hyperscanning
as social neuroscience
paradigm, 117–118
studies, 121–126
autonomic indices,
physiological linkage
measurement, 125–126
EEG-based, 123–125
fNIRS-based, 121–123
hypothalamic-pituitary-adrenal
axis, threat, 199
hypothalamic-pituitary-gonadal
axis, 109
function and activation, 37
testosterone physiology and,
37–38
hypothalamus, suprachiasmatic
nucleus, 70

I

Ickes, W., 357
identity
leaders
as entrepreneurs of, 490
provoking uncertainty, 490
rivalry
maintenance, 436
salience, 437
social
collective self and, 481
intergroup competition
and, 476–492 (see
also social identity,
intergroup competition
and)
uncertainty, 432, 485, 486, 487,
490
ideologies, defined, 574
ideologies and values, 570–574
competitive, 571–574
definitions, 571, 574
fair, free market, 572–573

meritocracy, 571–572
neoliberalism, 573–574
education system, 571–574
definitions, 571, 574
dominant, transmission, 570–571
fair, free market, 572–573
meritocracy, 571–572
neoliberalism, 573–574
Idson, L. C., 30
ignorance, strategic, 322
illusory superiority. See
superiority, illusory
immunocompetence, 109
implicit competitions, goal
pursuit, 211
implicit competitions, temporally
dynamic goal pursuit model,
224–232
discrepancy feedback, 226–227
goal setting, 226
individual goal pursuit
consequences of competition
on, 230–232
shifting goals on, 225–226
over course of competition,
228–230
cooperation tapering off, 228
sabotage, 229–230, 230f
vigilance of others, 228–229
value and expectancy of goal,
226
implicit power motivation, 87, 107
incentives, competitive, harmful
behavior from, 21–24
counterproductive and
harmful, 22–24
motivation reduction, 21–22
incentive structure, 11
homicide rates, 381
on motivation, 374
performance-approach goals,
406–407
risk-taking and, 380
Social Comparison Model of
Competition, 406–407
tournaments, 407
incidental factors, competitive
arousal, 166
incidental uncertainty, 433
inconsistency, perceivers not
liking, 355
incremental implicit theory, 277
independence. See also
individualism
terminology, 612 n1

individual
    contested hierarchies, 461–462
    sports, performance, 551
individual–collectivism scales, 614
individual differences
    Comparing and Being
        Compared Framework, 412
    cooperation, 307
    Social Comparison Cycle of
        Competition, 407
individual goal pursuit, temporally
        dynamic goal pursuit model,
        implicit competitions
    consequences of competition
        on, 230–232
    shifting goals, 225–226
individualism. *See also*
        independence
    independence from
        competition, 616–617
    research, 614
    terminology, 612 n1
individualist, defined, 499 n3
individualistic cultures
    competitiveness, *vs.* collectivist
        cultures, 614–617, 615t, 617f
    on competitive orientation,
        498 n2
individual performance-rank
        appraisals, 455–456
industrial organization, 12
inequality, economic
    homicide rates, 381
    need-based risk-taking, 381–382,
        391
influential sociometer hypothesis,
        389
information
    affect-as-information theory, 311
    competitive set,
        self-determination
        theory, 255–256, 256f
    elements, 243, 244, 246,
        247–253, 255–257, 256f,
        259, 260 (*see also* cognitive
        mechanisms, illusory
        superiority)
        Dunning-Kruger effect, 295,
        300
    exchange, education
        competition, 587
    withholding, covert collectivist
        competition, 619–620
informational self-talk, 253
Inglehart, R. F., 151

in-group
    bias, cooperation and, 311
    leaders, intergroup competition
        and, 489–491
    preference for, 366
in-group–out-group
        phenomenon, collectivist
        competition and, 617
Instagram, social comparison, 413
"instant" rivalries, 433
institution-focused approaches,
        on gender gaps, 530–532
instrumentality belief, 212
instrumental self-analysis, 334
integral factors, competitive
        arousal and, 166, 178
    competition audience, 172–173
    context, measurement, and,
        167, 168t
    factor, source of arousal, and
        article, 166, 167t
    interaction partner, 171–172
    stimuli outside competition,
        173–174
    task, 169–171
intelligence, Dunning-Kruger
        effect, 295, 300
intention(s)
    behavior from, 322–323
    overweighting, 292–294
inter-brain neural
        synchronization, 121,
        122–124
interdependence. *See also*
        collectivism
    goal pursuit, 218
    goal success, 221
    social dilemmas
        decisions, 305
        definition, 305
        incentive structure, 305–306
    terminology, 612 n1
intergroup behavior, 477
intergroup competition
    beneficial, 476–477
    destructive, 477
    examples, 476
    groups, defined, 477
    ingroup leaders and, 489–491
    social category fault lines, 406,
        414–415
    social identity and, 476–492
        (*see also* social identity,
        intergroup competition and)
    sports, 547

intergroup violence and hatred,
        485–491
    threat, uncertainty, and
        extremism, 486–488
    victimhood, collective and
        competitive, 488–489
inter-/intra-hemispheric
        connectivity, sex differences, 73
"internally controlling" states,
        cognitive evaluation theory,
        252
interpersonal comparison, 334–335
interpersonal contexts, 250–251
Interpersonal Relational Index, 120
interpersonal success, 499
intersexual choice, 136–137, 137f
intersexual competition,
        risk-taking, 382–384
interstitial nuclei of the anterior
        hypothalamus, 70, 71t
intertemporal variability, Social
        Comparison Model of
        Competition, 404
intractable conflicts, 436
intragroup competition, social
        category fault lines, 406
intrapersonal comparison, 334–335
intrasexual competition, 136, 137–
        138, 138f, 146
    definition, 382
    female–female, 139, 144, 146–148
    male–male, 57, 137–138,
        140–141 (*see also* male–male
        competition)
    risk-taking, 382–384
intrasexual competitiveness,
        individual differences,
        501–502
intrinsic motivation, 240–260.
        See also self-determination
        theory
    cognitive evaluation theory,
        242, 243
        predictive power, hypothesis-
        driven, 243
    competitive situations on, 241,
        244
    feedback and competitive
        outcome on, 248
intuitive thought processes, 388
Iowa Gambling Task, 46
Iriberri, N., 27, 28
Irlenbusch, B., 24
Irons, W., 140
Islam, G., 506

J

jealousy, *vs.* envy, 266
Jiménez, M., 83*t*, 84, 88
Jogia, J., 75
John, L. K., 23
John, O. P., 601
Johnson, C. S., 364–365
Johnson, D. W., 546–548
Johnson, P. D., 499
Johnson, R. T., 546–548
Josephs, R., 39, 91, 109
Jost, J. T., 572
Jost Hypothesis, 65–66
joy, sympathetic, sports
    psychology and, 605
Jury, M., 193, 202

K

Kagel, J. H., 26
Kahn, L. M., 524–525
Kalanick, Travis, 496
Kanfer, R., 503
Kaplan, H. B., 125
Karau, S. J., 316
Kasser, T., 573
Kavussanu, M., 563–564
Keeley, L. H., 142
Keller, J., 365, 614
Kelley, H. H., 313
Kenrick, D. T., 389–391
Keogh, E., 585
Kesebir, S., 516
Kilduff, G. J., 425–426, 431–432
Kim, H. Y., 448
Kim, S. H., 267, 278
Kimura, D., 72
Kivlighan, K. T., 83*t*, 84
Klinesmith, J., 40
Knight, E. L., 110
knowledge acquisition, reward-
    learning framework, 203
Koch, C., 28
Kocher, M. G., 314
Kohn, A., 577
Kornfield, J., 599
Krueger, A. B., 633
Krupp, D. B., 379, 381
Ku, G., 16, 164, 172, 173, 182, 183
Kudu horn, 138*f*, 139
Kugler, T., 311
!Kung san, 143

L

laboratory competitions, sex
    differences, 85–87
labor markets, gender differences
    competition, 523–525
    wage gap, 514, 524–525
    women, increased
        participation, 535
Lalumière, M. L., 382
Lam, S. S. K., 271
Lamb, T. A., 85
Lange, J., 269, 271, 275
Larson, T., 322
Lazear, E. P., 13, 21
leaders
    as entrepreneurs of identity, 490
    hypercompetitiveness, 506–507
    ingroup, intergroup
        competition and, 489–491
    intergroup division, healing, 490
    intergroup relational identity,
        encouraging, 491
    leadership patterns,
        testosterone on, 78
    motivating style, cognitive
        evaluation theory, 250–251
    trait competitiveness and, 502
learning. *See also* education
    education, 586, 587
    goals, 190–191
Leary, T., 497
legibility, strategic, 357–358
Le Panse, B., 83*t*
Lesick, T. L., 340, 343
Levin, D., 26, 28
Leydig cells, 60, 61, 65
Li, C., 603
Lieberman, J. D., 41
life course persistent offending,
    386–387
life history
    theory, 59, 103–104, 105,
        377–378, 390
    tradeoffs, 103, 377–378
Liu, T., 121, 124
Lobel, M., 22
local dominance
    definition, 341
    effect, 341–344, 415
    sustainability, 415
Locke, E. A., 213
Locke, K. D., 17
Lonsdale, C., 254
losing
    auctions, on competitive
        arousal, 169–170
    feedback from, 247
    objective and subjective, 248
loss–win difference wave, 249
lotteries, 12
Lowenstein, J., 614
Luchner, A. F., 501
Lugovskyy, V., 23
luteinizing hormone, 38, 61, 62,
    63

M

Mahalingam, R., 601
male–male competition, 57, 137–
    138, 140–141, 565–566
    coalitions, 138
    empires, early, 142
    mate competition, 382
    reproductive skew, 144
    WEIRD societies, 148, 152
males, risk-taking *vs.* females,
    383–384
Malhotra, D., 172
malicious envy, 202, 266–267,
    269–279
management, gender differences,
    524
Maner, J. K., 87, 107, 384
Manning, J., 151
Marble-Pull Game, 615–616, 616*f*
markets
    competition and, 11–12
    definition, 11–12
Marr, J. C., 457
masculinity, hegemonic, 151, 153
Maslow, A. H., 390–391
Maslow's hierarchy of needs,
    390–391
Massar, K., 501–502
mastery goals, 190–191, 211
    competitive context, 202–203
    definition, 202
    performance criterion from,
        internal, 203
    task performance and, 202–203
mastery motivational climate,
    565–566
mastery-performance model, 191
mating
    competition, risk-taking, 382–384
    effort, *vs.* parenting effort,
        103–104
    propensity, sex differences, 57
    psychology and behavior,
        testosterone dynamics and,
        42–43
    pharmacological challenge,
        47

Matthews, K. A., 500
Matthey, A., 322
maximization, utility, 11
Maximizing Difference Game,
    615, 615*t*
Mayr, U., 522
Mazur, A., 85
McCarthy, M. M., 69
McCaul, K. D., 85
McCormick, C. M., 39
means interdependence, sports,
    547, 549
medial prefrontal cortex, fNIRS-
    based hyperscanning studies,
    121–122
Meece, J. L., 580
Mehta, P. H., 39, 44–45, 91–92,
    109, 110
menarche, 66, 67
Menesini, E., 585
men's sociobiology, on
    competition, 533
menstrual cycle, on women
    entering competition, 532
mental efficiency, mindfulness
    on, 603
mental health disorders, sex
    differences, 75–76
meritocracy, 462, 571–572
Merton, R. K., 505
message framing, 192
meta-correlation matrix, 195
microaggressions, 152
Midgely, C., 580
Miller, S. L., 106
mindfulness
    definition, secular, 599
    empirical studies, 599–600
    formal and applied, 600
    on mental efficiency, 603
    overview, 599–600
    psychological research, 600–601
mindfulness, competition, and
    sports psychology, 601–607
    acceptance and commitment
        therapy, 601–602, 607
    critical issues, 603–604
    emotion regulation, 607
    for flow states, 607
    mindfulness and acceptance
        commitment, 602–603, 605,
        607
    new possibilities, 604–607
    mindfulness efficacy,
        competition contexts,
        606–607, 606*f*

qualitative research,
    mindfulness and
    phenomenology of
    competition, 604–605
    right, ethics of competition,
        607
    sympathetic joy and sports
        psychology, 605
mindfulness and acceptance
    commitment, 602–603, 605,
    607
mindfulness-based stress
    reduction, 600–601
mind readers
    attempts, culturally universal, 353
    mixed-motive landscape, 353–355
    inconsistency, perceivers not
        liking, 355
    others' predictions, being
        constrained by, 355
    predicting others, incessant
        tendency, 354
mineralocorticoids, 60
minimal acceptable thresholds,
    390
minimal categorization effect,
    480–481
minimal group paradigm, 480
mirror neuron system, 354
Mishra, S., 378, 381, 382, 389
Mitra, J. L., 607
mixed-sex groups *vs.* same-sex
    groups, on competition
    performance, 519–520, 528–529
mobility, social, 482
Molho, C., 322
monetary capital, 377
Montal-Rosenberg, R., 271, 273,
    277
Monty Hall problem, 30
Moore, L. J., 249, 558
Moore, Z. E., 602–603
moral disengagement, 556
moral wiggle room, 322, 323
Moran, S., 270, 271, 273, 274, 277
Moskowitz, G. B., 212
motivating style, leader's
    cognitive evaluation theory,
        250–251
    Wooden, John, 565–566
motivation
    competitive, 14, 21–22, 88,
        189–190, 241
    testosterone and, 39
    cooperative norms, complying
        with

external, 317–319
internal, 319–320
goal pursuit, 211–214 (*see also*
    temporally dynamic goal
    pursuit model)
    commitment to specific and
        challenging goal occurs
        as function of value of
        goal and expectancy of
        attainment, 212–213
    discrepancy feedback from
        goal attainment affects
        effort exertion to
        specific and challenging
        goals, 213–214
    specific and challenging
        goals lead to higher task
        performance, 211–212
group-oriented, 463
incentives/incentive structures
    on, 21–22, 374
power, 87, 91, 107
rivalry on, 18, 200
Social Comparison Cycle of
    Competition, 407
status and, 450–451
motivational approaches, 6
motivational climate
    mastery, 565–566
    performance, 566
    Wooden, John, 565–566
motivational dynamics, 189–204.
    See also opposing processes
    model of competition and
    performance
motivational mechanisms,
    illusory superiority, 290–294
    intentions, overweighting,
        292–294
    optimistic, overweighting,
        291–292
    predictions, preference-driven,
        290
    skill, self-flattering definitions,
        290–291
Mulder, L. B., 321
Müller, J., 521
Müllerian ducts, 65–66
multi-level depiction, 569, 570*f*
multi-method studies,
    neuroscientific, 120
Multiparty Ultimatum game, 30
multiperson dilemmas, 306
Murayama, K., 192, 193, 194–196,
    502, 584, 586
Murdock, T. B., 584

Murnighan, J. K., 29, 164
Murphy, R. O., 500
Murray, N. P., 172–173
Mussweiler, T., 622

N

Nadler, A., 19
Nalbantian, B. H. R., 20
narcissism, 559, 564
    competitiveness, 501, 507
    envy, 274, 275–276
    hypercompetitiveness, 501
    on sports performance, 559
    trait competitiveness, 501
NASA Task Load Index, 120
Nash equilibrium, 16, 20, 26,
    313
natural selection, 56–57
    as competition, 56
    fitness, 374–375
    risk-taking, 374–375
nature, rivalry in, 425–426
near-misses, 433
need-based risk-taking, 375–376,
    391
needs
    basic psychological needs
        theory, 260
    psychological, 191, 242–243
        autonomy, 242, 243
        competence, 242
        competitive situations on, 241
        Maslow's hierarchy, 390–391
        relatedness, 242
        vs. wants, 390, 391
Neeley, T. B., 456
Neff, K. D., 600
N-Effect, 405
negative feedback control model,
    212–213
negotiations
    gender differences, 523
        cross-cultural, 534
    performance, competitive
        arousal on, 176–177
neoliberalism, 573–574
neuromanagement, 128
neuropsychiatric disorders, sex
    differences, 75–76
neuroscience, 5, 117–129
    experimental task and
        measures, 118–120
    multimethod, 120
    sustained selective attention
        joint task, 118–120
    future areas of interest, 128–129

hyperscanning, as social
    neuroscience paradigm,
    117–118
hyperscanning studies, 121–126
    autonomic indices,
        physiological linkage
        measurement, 125–126
    EEG-based, 123–125
    fNIRS-based, 121–123
    intra-brain and inter-brain
        functional connectivity
        analysis, methodological
        note, 126–128
    frequency-domain data,
        127–128
    time-domain data, 127
neuroticism, on gender
    differences, 521
Nicholls, J. G., 564
Niederle, M., 515, 516–517, 518,
    523, 533, 534
Noetel, M., 603
Nolen-Hoeksema, S., 75
non-genomic actions, 62, 110
normative assessment, education,
    577–578
normative frame, 316
norms
    cooperative, complying with
        external motivation, 317–319
        internal motivation, 319–320
    education, 574–575
        employability, 575
        productivism, 575
    theory of planned behavior,
        social dilemmas, 309
    noticed, being, (over) sensitivity
        to, 356–357
    paranoid cognition, 356
    spotlight effect, 357
    transparency, feelings of, 357
numerus clausus, 578–579, 580,
    582

O

Obama, Barack, 152
object of comparison, illusory
    superiority, 299
obsessive-compulsive disorder, sex
    differences, 76
Oettingen, G., 212, 227
Oexl, R., 322
offending, life course persistent,
    386–387
Oliver, E. J., 253
Onuf's nucleus, 70–71, 71t

opposing processes model
    of competition and
    performance, 189–204
    autonomous engagement,
        201–203
    competitive reward structure,
        192–193, 193f
    conceptual model, 192–194,
        193f
    empirical support, 194–196
    perceived environmental
        competitiveness, 192–193,
        193f
    performance-approach &
        performance-avoidance
        achievement goals, 190–192
    social comparison process, 193
    theories, 196–201
        challenge and threat,
            199–200
        choking under pressure, 200–
            201, 364–365, 553, 564
        performance-approach &
            performance-avoidance
            goals, downstream
            processes, 197, 197f
        rivalry, 200
        social facilitation and
            inhibition, 198–199
        social interdependence
            theory, 197–198
        trait competitiveness, 192–193,
            193f
opposing process model
    mediation, inconsistent, 194
    performance-approach vs.
        performance-avoidance
        goals, 192–194
optimism
    overweighting, 291–292
    trait competitiveness and, 502
Ordóñez, L. D., 311
organismic integration theory, 260
organizational psychology
    approaches, 6–7
Oris aries, 139
Orosz, G., 200
Orrison, A., 15
Ors, E., 526
ostracism, 152, 315, 318, 320, 585
other-oriented concerns, status
    striving, 450–452
other schema, defined, 428
outcome
    cognitive evaluation theory,
        247–248

outcome (*cont.*)
  competitive, 247–248
  expectation, 212
  interdependence, 346, 547
outcome pay transparency, 276–277
outgroups, preference against, 366
outward-orientation, 451
overbidding. *See also* bidding
  arousal in, 164
  competitive arousal, 16, 164,
    164*f*, 175, 178, 179, 183–184
    (*see also* competitive arousal)
  feedback on, full, 29
  hormones on, 109
  Olympic games auction, 16
  social psychology, 14
(over) sensitivity to being noticed,
    356–357
  paranoid cognition, 356
  spotlight effect, 357
  transparency, feelings of, 357
overweighting, in illusory
    superiority mechanisms
    of intentions, 292–294
    of optimism, 291–292

P

Pain of Envy Theory, 266–267
Pan, Y., 128
paranoid cognition, 356
parasympathetic nervous system,
    165
parental investment
  intersexual choice and, 136
  males, 136
  by sex, 57
parenting effort *vs.* mating effort,
    103–104
Paserman, M. D., 527
Patterns of Adaptive Learning
    Survey, 580
pay-for-performance, 13, 267, 505
Payne, B. K., 381–382
payoffs, auctions, 169
payoff structures, two-person,
    306–307
pay transparency, on envy, 276–277
Penczynski, S. P., 28
Peng, W., 250
perceived competence, 197*f*, 198,
    200–201, 246, 248, 452
perceived disadvantage, 389–390
perceived environmental
    competitiveness, 10, 192–193,
    193*f*

perceived error climate, 581
perceived value
  status and, 446, 448–449, 452
  of winning, 217, 219, 220, 338
perceiver *vs.* target, 350–367. *See
    also* predicting and being
    predicted
performance, 189. *See also* top
    performers
  achievement goals on, sports,
    561–562
  ambiguity on, 198
  athletic, testosterone dynamics
    and, 44
  competition and, 189–204
    (*see also* opposing processes
    model of competition and
    performance)
    collectivist cultures, 630–631
    education, 586
    gender differences, 517–518
  competitive arousal on, 177–178
  education, 586–588
  internal criterion, from mastery
    goals, 203
  pay-for-performance, 13, 267,
    505
  rivalry on, 200
  sports on, 548–551
    fundamentals, 548–549
    individual competition and
    golf-putting, 551
    team competition, 549–551
  task, commitment to specific
    and challenging goals on,
    211–212
performance-approach goals,
    211, 503
  achievement, 190–192
  definition, 406
  downstream processes, 197, 197*f*
  education, 583–584, 585,
    586–588
  social comparison, 406–407
performance-avoidance goals,
    211, 503
  achievement, 190–192
  downstream processes, 197,
    197*f*
  education, 583–584, 586, 588
performance goals, 561
  education, 583–584, 585, 586
    (*see also* education)
  effectance/ineffectance, 255
  ego-involvement, 252

incentive structure studies,
    406–407
  motivational, 190–192, 193, 211
performance motivational
    climate, 566
performance-rank appraisals,
    individual, 455–456, 463
personal
  agency (*see* agency, personal)
  concerns, status striving, 450,
    452–454
  factors, Social Comparison
    Model of Competition, 403
personal-development
  competitive attitude,
    201–202
Personal Development
    Competitive Attitude Scale,
    499
personality, on sports
    performance, 559–560
personality psychology
    approaches, 6
personal relative deprivation,
    388–389
person-focused approaches, on
    gender gaps, 530–532
Peterson, B. S., 76
Pettit, N. C., 457
phenotypic androgenicity, 108
physiological linkage, autonomic
    indices, 125–126
Piegeler, M., 505–506, 524
Pierce, L., 270
Pike, B. E., 435
Piketty, T., 572
Pinker, S., 149
planum temporale, 70–71, 71*t*
Plehwe, D., 573
Point Subtraction Aggression
    Paradigm, 39–41
polygyny
  Darwinian competition, 145–146
  social power, 143
polygyny, male–male
    competition, 141, 142
  resource-based, 142–143
  Yanomamö, 143
Poortvliet, P. M., 585
Popkowski Leszcyc, P. L. L., 167 n3
positional rewards, 287–288
positive orientation personality
    trait, 199
posttraumatic stress disorder, sex
    differences, 75–76

Potters, J., 379
power
    hierarchy, flexibility, 632
    motivation, 87, 91, 107
        implicit, 87, 107
        on testosterone reactivity,
            107
    on predicting and being
        predicted, 366
    status and control over other's
        choices, 322–323
pre-conceptions, 355
predicting and being predicted,
    350–367
    analysis and implications,
        362–365
    choking under pressure, 200–
        201, 364–365, 553, 564
    negative predictions and
        characterizations,
        inviting, 365
    positive character
        predictions, avoiding,
        364–365
    targets being unpredictable,
        364
    well-adjusted persona and
        self–other agreement,
        363
    characterization efforts, 352
    cooperation, 352
    cooperative vs. competitive
        contexts, moderating role,
        359–362
        social connections and
            reduction of feeling
            scrutinized, 360–361
        social connections and
            reductions in prediction
            avoidance, 361–362
    future research, 365–367
    as human behavior, 350–351
    mind readers, mixed-motive
        landscape, 353–355
        inconsistency, perceivers do
            not like, 355
        others' predictions, being
            constrained by, 355
        predicting others, incessant
            tendency, 354
    social coordination, 351, 352
    as social motive, 350
    social navigation model, 351–353
        being characterized, target's
            perspective, 352–353

framework, 352–353
    social cognitive processing,
        perceiver, 352
    targets, people as, 351
    target's reactions, to perceiver
        attempts to predict and
        characterize self, 355–359
        reactions to being
            characterized and
            predicted, 356
        (over) sensitivity to being
            noticed, 356–357
        (over) sensitivity to being
            noticed: feeling
            transparent, 357
        (over) sensitivity to being
            noticed: paranoid
            cognition, 356
        (over) sensitivity to being
            noticed: spotlight effect,
            357
        strategic disclosure, 358–359
        strategic legibility, 357–358
prediction(s)
    avoidance, reduction, 361–362
    others', being constrained by,
        355
    of others, incessant tendency, 354
prefrontal cortex, fNIRS-based
    hyperscanning studies,
    121–122
pressure
    choking under, 200–201,
        364–365, 553, 564
    cognitive evaluation theory,
        243, 245
    time, 170–171
    to win, 245
prestige, 385
    desire for, collectivist cultures,
        627–629
    intergroup competition, 482
    male competition, 140–141
    WEIRD societies, 148, 149–152
prevention concerns, 435
Price, J., 526
pride, on envy, 274
prize spread, tournaments, 15–16,
    379
process pay transparency, 277
productivism norms, 575
productivity, 189
    workplace,
        hypercompetitiveness and,
        505–506

progesterone level, on women
    entering competition, 532
progestins, 60
Programme for International
    Student Assessment, 574
Proietti, V., 45
promotion concerns, 435
proselfs, 310, 312
prosocial behavior, 128
    definition, 556
    other-concern, 450
    sports, 556–557
    status and
        dispersion, 456
        striving, 449, 450, 453
        visibility, 453
prosocial individuals/tactics, 312,
    316
prosocial person/tendencies
    definition, 499 n3
    envy and, 275
prototypes, 483–484
proxies of fitness, 387
proximate psychology, dis/
    advantage and risk-taking,
    388–391
Przyylski, A. K., 258
pseudo-losses, 167t, 170
psychological needs, 191,
    240–260. See also self-
    determination theory
    autonomy, 242, 243
    competence, 242
    competitive situations
        on, 241
    Maslow's hierarchy, 390–391
    relatedness, 242
psychology
    economics vs., 10–13
    studies of competition, 11–13
psychology and experimentation
    economics, 9–31
    auction types, 24
    common value auctions, 24–
        30, 175 n2 (see also common
        value auction)
    conceptualizing, 10
    psychology vs. economics,
        10–13
    study of competition, 11–13
    rank-order tournaments and
        effort-based competitions,
        13–24
        behavior, determinants,
            14–18

psychology and experimentation
  economics (*cont.*)
    incentives, harmful behavior
      from, 21–24 (*see also*
      incentives, competitive,
      harmful behavior from)
    incentive system, 13–14
    team competitions, 18–21
  winner's curse, 12, 24–30
    common value auctions
      and, 24
    mechanism and Acquiring
      a Company problem,
      27–28
    overcoming, learning, 28–30
    as real, 25–26
    theoretical explanations,
      26–27
psychology of competition,
  defined, 3–7
public office, elected, gender
  differences, 524
Pulfrey, C., 584, 585
punishment, cooperation
  dilemmas, 315, 317–319, 321
Putnam, R., *Bowling Alone,* 632

R
Rabelo, V. C., 601
Rabin, M., 11, 26–27, 28
Raedeke, T. D., 172–173
ranking effects, proximity to,
  social comparison, 404–405,
  410
rank-order tournaments and
  effort-based competitions,
  13–24
  behavior, determinants, 14–18
  incentives, harmful behavior
    from, 21–24 (*see also*
    incentives, competitive,
    harmful behavior from)
  incentive system, 13–14
  team competitions, 18–21
Rational Choice Theory, 306
"Rationality in Psychology and
  Economics" (Simon), 30
rational maximization
  preferences, 11
realist conflict theory, 478–480
Reeve, J., 245
Refaie, N., 378, 382
reference group neglect, 294–295
referent
  comparison, 333

status
  neglect, 337–338
  selective use, 337–338
Régner, I., 202
Regner, T., 322
regulatory focus, 192
reinvestment theory, 554–555
relatedness, 242
  cognitive evaluation theory, 242
  self-determination theory,
    253–255
    competition between/
      cooperation with
      groups/teams, 254
    competition between
      individuals, 253–254
    competition within groups,
      254–255
relational intergroup identity, 491
relational mobility, 625–626, 627*f*
relational model, rivalry, 409–410
relational schema
  definition, 428
  rivalry, 423, 427–429, 427*f*
relationship motivation theory, 260
relationships/relational factors
  aggression, 146–148
  closeness, social comparison, 432
  cognitive evaluation theory, 243
  contested hierarchies, 459–461
  dynamics, rivalry model
    expansion, 438–439
  rivalry, 409–410, 439
  Social Comparison Model of
    Competition, 403–404
  status striving, 450–452
  terminology, 428
relative state, 376
  model, 375–376, 379, 380, 390,
    391
  status competition, 385
Relief Nursery, 215
reproduction
  effort, 107, 377–378, 390
  opportunities, on testosterone
    reactivity, 106–107
  skew, 138
    Darwinian competition,
      143–144
  success, by sex, 136
reputation, cooperation
  dilemmas, 312, 317–319, 320,
    321, 322
resource competition, 59, 380–381,
  382, 627*f*

realist conflict theory and
  battle, 478–480
risk-taking, 380–382
scarcity (*see* scarcity, resource)
social selection, 138–139
sustainability, 414
resources
  physical, 380–381
  tangible and intangible, 373
Reuben, E., 525
reward-learning framework,
  knowledge acquisition, 203
rewards
  competitively contingent,
    245–247
  pay-for-performance, 13, 267,
    505
  positional, 287–288
  sensitivity to, on sports
    performance, 559–560
  structure, 10, 192–193, 193*f*
RIASEC model of personality-
  based occupational choice,
    501
Ring, C., 563–564
risk-taking, 373–391
  ability-based, 375–376, 391
  asocial/antisocial, 385–387
  aspiration levels, 390
  competitive arousal on, 175–176
  current–desired status,
    perceived mismatch, 108
  decision-making, 374
  definition, 42, 374
  dis/advantage and, 375–376
    proximate psychology,
      388–391
  domains, 380–387
    incentives to compete, 380
    mate competition, 382–384
    proxies of fitness, 375, 387
    resource competition,
      380–382
    status competition, 385–387
  dominance and, 150
  example, 374
  factors, 374
  intuitive thought processes, 388
  minimal acceptable thresholds,
    390
  natural selection, competition,
    and motivation, 373–375
  need-based, 375–376, 391
  personal relative deprivation,
    388–389

prosocial, 387
reference points, actor, 390
relative state and competitive
   dis/advantage, determinants,
   376–379
   embodied capital, 376,
      377–378
   situational/environmental
      factors, 376, 378–379
relative state model, 375–376,
   379, 380, 390, 391
sex differences, 383–384
testosterone dynamics and, 42
   pharmacological challenge,
      46–47
utility maximization, 374
risk-tolerance, 382
risky decisions, competitive
   arousal on, 175–176
Ritov, I., 17, 23, 172
rivalry, 200, 232, 461
   cheating and, 437
   competition, view of, 4
   on competitive arousal and
      bidding, 166, 173–174, 176
   conceptualizations, 424
   contributory events, causal,
      429–430
   definition, 409
   embeddedness, 434
   envy, 266 (see also envy)
   evaluation apprehension and
      competition, 402, 411–412
   expansion/expansiveness, 427,
      433–434, 436, 438, 439
   factors, 172
   feedback loops and auxiliary
      connections, 439
   formation, 18
   history, 426
   identity salience, 437
   "instant," 433
   intractable conflicts, 436
   on motivation, 18, 200
   operationalization, 426–427
   relational model, 409–410
   on relationships, other, 439
   repeated competition, 232
   self-reinforcing, 439
   social-cognitive approach, 410–
      411, 426
   social comparison, 409–411,
      430–433
   as social-psychological
      construct, 423

social relations model, 425–426
sportspersonship, 437
terminology, 428
trash-talking on, 177
rivalry, psychology of, 422–440
   causes, contributory, 424
   competitive expansion schema,
      423–424
   competitive relational
      dynamics, model expansion,
      438–439
   competitive relational schema,
      423, 427–429, 427f
   empirical caveat, 426–427
   example, 422–423
   formation, cognitive
      elaboration of shared
      competitive history, 429–433
      origin, 427f, 430
      social-comparison concerns,
         430–433
      social-comparison concerns,
         personal factors, 431
      social-comparison concerns,
         relational factors,
         431–432
      social-comparison concerns,
         schema formation and
         "instant" rivalries, 433
      social-comparison concerns,
         situational factors,
         432–433
   hopelessness depression model,
      423, 425
   individual/group in, specific, 423
   in nature, 425–426
   psychosocial consequences,
      433–438
      distal and proximal, linking,
         438
      expansiveness, 427, 433–434,
         436, 438, 439
      goal pursuit, 434–436
      identity maintenance, 436
      unethical behavior, 436–437
   social-cognitive approach, 410–
      411, 426
   symptom profile, 424
   tension, 423
   terminology, 424
Robbers Cave field experiment,
   479
Roberts, G. C., 559
Rocha, M. F., 584–585
Rodin, J., 270

Rohde, W., 107
role models, on gender
   differences, 532
Ronay, T., 108
Roney, J. R., 42–43, 108
Rosen, S., 13
Rosenman, R. H., 500
Rosenqvist, O., 527
Roughgarden, J., "Challenging
   Darwin's Theory of Sexual
   Selection," 58
Rubinstein, A., 295
Rubinstein games, 176
Rustichini, A., 522
Ryckman, R. M., 201

S
sabotage
   from competition, perceived,
      629
   education, 585
   temporally dynamic goal
      pursuit model
      implicit competitions, 229–
         230, 230f
      implicit competitions, on
         individual goal pursuit,
         231–232
      tournament settings on, 23–24
Salerno, A., 271–272
Salovey, P., 270
Salvador, A., 85
Salzberg, S., 599
same-sex groups vs. mixed-sex
   groups, on performance,
   519–520
Samuelson, W. F., 25, 27
scale of competition, 378–379,
   381, 385, 391
scarcity, resource, 498
   auctions, 183
   collectivism–competition link,
      617, 618
   corruption, 618
   embodied capital, 378
   group solidarity, 151
   poverty, 618
   on pressures, 383, 384, 398
   prize value, 169
   situational/environmental
      factors, 376–377
   social competition and, 180
Schachter, S., 174
schadenfreude, 270, 275
Schaubroeck, J., 271

schema formation, rivalry, 433
Schotter, A., 20
Schultheiss, O. C., 87, 91, 107
Schurr, A., 23
Schwartz, S. H., 582–583
Schweitzer, M. E., 270
Schwieren, C., 521
scramble competition, 91
scrutinized, feeling, 360–361
sealed-bid auctions, 168*t*
  first-price, 168*t*, 175 n2, 176
  second-price, 12, 24, 168*t*
second-price sealed-bid auctions,
  12, 24, 168*t*
Sedickes, C., 338, 344
self-aggrandizement, 499
self-analysis
  instrumental, 334
  social, 334
self-appraisal
  personal relative deprivation
    and socioemotional
    comparisons, 389
  on testosterone reactivity,
    107–108
  underestimation, top
    performers, 300–301
self-categorization
  intergroup relations and,
    483–484
  theory, 483
self-concept
  social interactions verifying and
    confirming, 436
  status competitions on, 447
self-concern, status striving, 450,
  452–454
self-construal, 42, 622, 627
self-defined goals
  collectivist culture
    competitiveness, 624–625
  common standard *vs.*, 624–625
self-determination theory
  analysis, 240–260
  basic psychological needs
    theory and, 260
  causality orientation theory
    and, 260
  cognitive evaluation theory,
    241–253 (*see also* cognitive
    evaluation theory)
  competition in, defined, 241
  competitive set, initial -
    informational *vs.* controlling,
    255–256, 256*f*

competitive situations, 241
  dark side, 257–259
    aggression, post-
      competition, 258–259
    cheating, acceptance, 257
    competitive ethics and
      sportspersonship, 259
    doping, 257–258
  goal content theory and, 260
  organismic integration theory
    and, 260
  relatedness, 253–255
    competition between/
      cooperation with
      groups/teams, 254
    competition between
      individuals, 253–254
    competition within groups,
      254–255
  relationship motivation theory
    and, 260
self-developmental competitive
  orientation, 201
self-disclosure, 359
self-efficacy
  beliefs, 212, 213
  perception, 88–89, 93
self-enhancement, 338, 481–482
  assertive, 276
  competitive values and goals,
    583, 585
  intergroup competition, 482
  narcissists, 559
  OCD countries, neoliberal
    free-market capitalist, 574
  social comparison transitivity, 338
  societies emphasizing, trait
    competitiveness, 498
  strategies, 344–345
self-enhancement higher-order
  values, 583
self-esteem. *See also* motivational
  mechanisms, illusory
  superiority
  downward comparisons on, 408
  envy and, 276
  high explicit, 276
  maintaining, self-centered and
    self-flattering definitions, 291
  pursuit of, 481
  trait competitiveness and, 502
self-evaluation
  competition pools, 332–346
    competition pools, defined,
      335

social comparison theory,
  332, 334–335 (*see also*
  social comparison)
  fundamental need for, 407
self-expression, 151, 244
self-interest, status concerns and
  behaviors, drivers, 454–462
  contested hierarchies,
    properties
    individual, 461–462
    relational, 459–461
    structural, 454–456
    temporal, 457–459
  status striving, 450, 452–454
self-judgment, 366
self-knowledge, from trait
  competitiveness, 502–503
self–other agreement, 363
self-protection, 391
  antagonistic, 276
  strategies, 344–345
self-schema, defined, 428
self-signaling research, 351
self-talk, cognitive evaluation
  theory, 253
self-uncertainty reduction,
  484–485
self-verification, 365
self-views
  envy on, malicious, 278
  high explicit self-esteem, 276
  negative, 299–300
  referent status neglect, 338
  relationships, seeking, 351
Selten, R., 29
seminiferous tubules, 60
Senko, C., 587
(over) sensitivity to being noticed,
  356–357
  paranoid cognition, 356
  spotlight effect, 357
  transparency, feelings of, 357
senso-perceptive abilities, sex
  differences, 73
Sertoli cells, 60, 61, 62
set, competitive, cognitive
  evaluation theory, 245
sex. *See also* gender
sex determination and
  differentiation,
  morphological and
  physiological levels, 64–68
sex differences, biological, 55–93
  competitive contexts, 79–92,
  80*f*

Biosocial Status Hypothesis, 79
Challenge Hypothesis, 79, 102–103, 105
cognitive appraisal and moderating variables, 88–91
Coping Competition Model, 80–81, 81*f*, 85, 87, 88, 92
effects, short- and long-term, 91–92
fundamentals, 79–81, 80*f*
laboratory competitions, 85–87
sports competition, 80, 82–84, 83*t*
Darwin-Bateman-Trivers Paradigm, 57, 58
ecological character displacement, 59
evolutionary and ontogenetic forces, 56
life history theory, 59, 103–104, 105, 377, 390
life span development, 56
natural selection, 56–57
physical and mental health differences, socially acknowledged, 55
resource competition, 59, 380–381, 382, 627*f*
sex determination and differentiation, morphological and physiological levels, 64–68
sex hormones, 59–64
sexual dimorphism and, 68–79 (*see also* sexual dimorphism)
anisogamy, 57
ecological, 58–59
sexual selection, 57–59
social selection, 58, 59, 79, 135, 138–139, 140, 152
sex differences, sexual dimorphism and, 68–79
affective, 74–76
behavior, 77–79
brain, 69–72, 71*t*
cognitive, 72–74
sex hormone-binding globulin, 61, 63
sex hormones. *See also* androgens; estrogens; testosterone dynamics, competition-induced

aromatization, 63
binding globulins and circulation, 61, 63
characteristics and functioning, 59–64
definition, 59
receptors, 62, 63
synthesis, 60–61
sex roles, 58, 59, 78
sexual dimorphism, 57
anisogamy, 57
causal models, non-exclusivity, 59
ecological, 58–59
sex differences and, 68–79
affective, 74–76
behavior, 77–79
brain, 69–72, 71*t*
cognitive, 72–74
sexually dimorphic nucleus of the preoptic area, 69, 70, 71*t*
sexual orientation, 77
sexual selection, 57–59, 135–137
"Challenging Darwin's Theory of Sexual Selection" (Roughgarden), 58
intersexual choice, 136–137, 137*f*
intrasexual competition, 136, 137–138, 138*f*
social selection and, 138–139
sex *vs.* gender differences, 515
Shapiro, S. L., 599
shared realities, 351, 483, 484
Sharma, A., 147
Sheldon, K. M., 246
Sheremeta, R. M., 15
Sherif, M., 479
shifting goals, individual goal pursuit, implicit competitions, 225–226
Showers, C. J., 200–201
Shurchkov, O., 518, 519, 520
Simmons, Z. L., 43, 108
Simon, H., "Rationality in Psychology and Economics," 30
Singer, J. E., 174
situational/environmental factors, 376, 378–379
Comparing and Being Compared Framework, 412
Social Comparison Model of Competition, 404–407
competitors, number of, 405, 410

definition, 404
incentive structure, 406–407
social category fault lines, 406, 414–415
standard and ranking effects, proximity to, 404–405, 410
situation envy, 273
situations, 241
competence feedback/satisfaction, 244
evaluative feedback, negative, 244
as gate closers, 241
on intrinsic motivation, 241, 244 (*see also* intrinsic motivation; self-determination theory)
skills
definitions of, self-flattering and egocentric, 290–291
of others, flawed evaluation, 297
own, confidence in *vs.* others', 294–295
skin conductance response, physiological linkage, 125–126, 129
slope of competition, 378–379, 381, 383, 384, 385, 386, 391
Smallets, S., 276
Smith, D. M., 358
Smith, H. J., 388–389
Smith, J. L., 364–365
Smith, R. H., 267, 278
Sniehotta, F. F., 309
Snyder, M., 361
Soay sheep, 139
Sobral, F., 506
social acceptance, 352
social anxiety, on testosterone reactivity, 107
social behavior
definition, 77
study of, 9
social capital, 377, 632
social category fault lines, 406, 414–415
social change belief structure, 482
social cognition, sex differences, 73
social cognitive approach, rivalry, 410–411, 426
competitive relational schema, 423, 427–429, 427*f*
social cognitive processing, perceiver, 352

social cognitive theory, 377
social comparison (theory), 10, 14,
        16–18, 332, 334–335, 401–416
    antecedents and consequences,
        333–334
    collectivist culture
        competitiveness, 622–624
    comparison referent, 333
    competition and suspicion,
        collectivist cultures, 622–624
    competition as catalyst of,
        267, 401
    competitive behavior and, 402
        as antecedent, 402
        as consequence, 267–268, 402
    convenience comparisons, 338
    as counterproductive and
        harmful, 22–23
    Festinger, 402
    focused models, 409–412
        Comparing and Being
            Compared Framework,
            411–412
        specific competitive context,
            coaction and evaluation
            apprehension, 402,
            411–412
        specific competitive
            relationships, rivalry,
            409–411
    frameworks, general, 403–409
        Social Comparison Cycle
            of Competition, 404,
            407–409, 410, 412,
            414 (see also Social
            Comparison Cycle of
            Competition)
        Social Comparison Model
            of Competition, 403–
            407, 408, 410–411,
            412, 413, 416, 431, 432,
            439, 581 (see also Social
            Comparison Model of
            Competition)
    functions, 335
    instrumental self-analysis, 334
    intensifiers, 267
    intergroup behavior, 477
    interpersonal vs. intrapersonal
        comparisons, 334–335
    on motivation, 19
    origins, 332
    personal relative deprivation,
        388–389
    relationship closeness, 432

    rivalry, 430–433
    social networks, 413–414
    social self-analysis, 334
    social vs. temporal comparison,
        334
    sustainability, 414–416
    target for, perception of self as, 22
    vs. temporal comparisons, 334,
        335–336
    temporal comparison with, 202
    transitivity, 338
    upwards comparisons, 335–336,
        402
Social Comparison Cycle of
        Competition, 404, 407–409,
        410, 412, 414
    after competition
        downward comparisons, 408
        upward comparison, 408–409
    before competition
        individual differences, 407
        motives, 407
    during competition, 408
    dynamic, 407, 410, 412, 414
    individual differences, 407
    motives, 407
Social Comparison Model of
        Competition, 403–407, 408,
        410–411, 412, 413, 416, 431,
        432, 439, 581
    dynamic, 402
    individual factors
        intertemporal variability, 404
        personal, 403
        relational, 403–404
    situational factors
        competitors, number of, 405,
            410, 414
        incentive structure, 406–407
        social category fault lines,
            406, 414–415
        standard and ranking effects,
            proximity to, 404–405,
            410
social competition
    adolescence, 386
    human, 139–148
    neuroscience, 123, 125
    scarcity, resource, 180
    sex similarities, 69, 92–93
    strategies, 483
social connections
    prediction avoidance,
        reduction, 361–362
    primate life, 351

    scrutinized, feeling, 360–361
social coordination, 351, 352
social creativity strategies, 482–483
social cues, 193
social dilemmas, 305–324
    competition to cooperation,
        305–307
    competitive vs. cooperative
        options, 306
    cooperation
        as individual difference, 307
        research approaches, 306
        situational motivations, 307
    interdependent
        decisions, 305
        defined, 305
        incentive structure, 305–306
    mixed-motive, 306
    multiperson, 306
    Rational Choice Theory, 306
    theory of planned behavior,
        307–323 (see also theory of
        planned behavior)
    two-person dilemmas, 306
    two-person payoff structures,
        306–307
social dominance orientation, 501
social ecology, 625–626, 627f
social environments, cognitive
        evaluation theory, 243
social exchange theories, status
        conferral, 450
social facilitation, 174
    competitive arousal, 177
    opposing process model, 198–199
social hierarchy, 129
    coordination benefits, 446–447
social identity, collective self and,
        481
social identity, intergroup
        competition and, 476–492
    fundamentals, 476–478
    intergroup violence and hatred,
        485–491
        ingroup leaders, 489–491
        threat, uncertainty, and
            extremism, intergroup,
            486–488
        victimhood, collective and
            competitive, 488–489
    realist conflict theory and
        battle for scarce resources,
        478–480
    self-categorization and
        intergroup relations, 483–484

social identity theory and
   intergroup competitive
   relations, 477, 480–483 (*see
   also* social identity theory)
uncertainty reduction and
   intergroup distinctiveness,
   484–485
social identity theory, 311, 477
   intergroup competitive
      relations and, 477, 480–483
   collective self and social
      identity, 481
   minimal categorization
      effect, 480–481
   self-enhancement and
      positive distinctiveness,
      481–482
   subjective belief structures,
      482–483
social inferences, 354
social inhibition, opposing
   process model, 198–199
social interdependence theory,
   197–198
socialization hypothesis, 258–259
social judgments, competence
   and warmth on, 273–274
social mobility, 482
social navigation model, 351–353
   being characterized, target's
      perspective, 352–353
   framework, 352–353
   social cognitive processing,
      perceiver, 352
social networks, social
   comparison theory, 413–414
social neuroendocrinology,
   testosterone dynamics,
   37–47, 104. *See also*
   testosterone dynamics,
   competition-induced
social-personality approaches, 6–7
social prediction. *See* predicting
   and being predicted
social psychology
   on competition, 12
   decisions, 11
   gender differences, 527–529
   communal *vs.* agentic role,
      528
   competitors, number of, 529
   gender congruity framework,
      529
   social role theory, 527–529
   on rank-order competitions, 16

social relations.
   See also relationships/
      relational factors
rivalry
   analysis, 431–432
   model, 425–426
   students, 587–588
social role theory, 527–529
social selection, 58, 59, 79, 135,
   138–139, 140, 152
   sexual selection and, 138–139
social self-analysis, 334
social standing
   competitive motivation, 461
   on competitive motivations
      and behaviors, 461
   group centrism, 487
   group identification, 488
   protecting, helping for, 453
   support, withholding, 460
social undermining, envy and, 270
social value orientation, 307, 310,
   311, 498
societies, competitive, education
   and, 569–575
   history, 570
   ideologies and values, 571–574
      definitions, 571, 574
      dominant, transmission,
         570–571
      fair, free market, 572–573
      meritocracy, 571–572
      neoliberalism, 573–574
   norms, 574–575
      employability, 575
      productivism, 575
sociobiological mechanisms,
   gender differences, 532–533
socioeconomic status
   on education, 588
   on gender differences, 521
somatic effort, 377
somatic marker hypothesis, 174
Sommet, N., 196, 579, 585
Spadoni, L., 379
spatial analysis, sex differences, 73
spillover effects, status striving
   hierarchical competition,
   464
sport competition, 545–566
   behavioral and psychological
      outcomes, 548–557
      anxiety, 552–553, 564–565
      attentional control theory,
         553–554

cheating aggression and
      antisocial behavior,
      555–556
   choking, 553, 564
   performance, 548–551
      competitive *vs.* cooperative
         goal structures, 549–550
      fundamentals, 548–549
      individual competition
         and golf-putting, 551
      self-report measures, 548
      team competition, 549–551
   prosocial behavior, 556–557
   reinvestment theory, 554–555
behavioral and psychological
   outcomes, personality and
   motivation on, 558–564
   achievement goals, 560–562
   achievement goals, on
      effort, emotions, and
      performance, 561–562
   personality, 559–560
   variables, mediating and
      moderating, 562–563
   variables, mediating and
      moderating: goals on
      cheating, prosocial
      behavior, and antisocial
      behavior, 563–564
benefits, 546
competition as challenge or
   threat?, 557–558
competitive nature, 545
gamesmanship, 556
gender differences, 80, 82–84,
   83t, 526–527
harmful consequences, 545–546
moral disengagement, 556
optimal environment, creating,
   564–566
personality, 559–560
sport, defined, 545
types, 546–548
   "appropriate," 547–548, 549,
      550
   inter-group/team
      competition, 547
   means interdependence,
      547, 549
   outcome interdependence, 547
variables, mediating and
   moderating, 562–563
   goals on cheating, prosocial
      behavior, and antisocial
      behavior, 563–564

sportspersonship, 259, 437
sports psychology, mindfulness,
    competition and, 598–
    607. *See also* mindfulness,
    competition, and sports
    psychology
spotlight effect, 357
stacked ranking systems, 455–456,
    463
Standage, M., 252
standard effects, proximity to, social
    comparison, 404–405, 410
Stanne, M. B., 549
Stasser, G., 507
status
    attention, 451
    Biosocial Model of Status, 84, 103
    Biosocial Status Hypothesis, 79
    bounded functionalist account,
        450
    competition, risk-taking, 385–387
    conferral, social exchange
        theories, other-concern, 450
    context-dependent, 446
    cooperation, 319
    definition, 446
    dimensions, 465
    dominance-based, 150 (*see also*
        dominance)
    extraverts *vs.* intraverts, 462
    flexibility, 632
    hierarchies, 385
    intergroup competition, 482
    leakage, 453
    losing, 457–458
    motivation and, 450–451
    others, managing impression
        of, 461–462
    outward-orientation, 451
    perception, others', 446
    power and, 322–323
    as relational, 446
    self-interested, 450, 452–454
        drivers, 454–462 (*see
            also under* status
            competitions, within
            organizations)
    subjectivity, 446
    takers, givers, and matchers,
        449
    testosterone on, 78
    threatened, 87, 92
    value, perceived, 446, 448–449,
        452
    value signaling, 456

status change
    contested hierarchies, 454,
        457–459
    direction, 457–458
    fairness, perceptions of, 459
    hierarchical instability, 105
    proximity, two individuals', 460
    speed or magnitude, 458–459
status competitions, within
    organizations, 444–466
    attention, 445
    coordination
        benefits, 446–447
        harm, 447
    examples, 444–445
    future research directions,
        464–466
    individual + collective benefits,
        463
    intra-team, 447
    outcomes, 445
    perceptions, others', 445
    practice implications, 462–464
    re-negotiation, 447
    self-interested status concerns
        and behaviors, drivers,
        454–462 (*see also* status
        hierarchies)
    status attainment behaviors,
        447–448
    status moves, 447, 462
    status striving psychology,
        social dilemma, 449–454
        fundamentals, 449–450
        personal and self-oriented
            concerns, 450, 452–454
        relational and other-oriented
            concerns, 450–452
    workgroups, status pursuit and
        conferral, 446–449
status dispersion, 454–455, 456, 464
status distance, interpersonal, 460
status hierarchies
    contested, properties, 454–461
        individual, 461–462
        relational, 459–461
        structural, 454–456
        temporal, 457–459
    coordination
        benefits, 446–447
        harm, 447
    cultural background on,
        465–466
    perceptions, lay, 465
    value, perceptions of, 455

status homophily, 460
status instability hypothesis, 106
status jolts, 456
status moves, 447, 462
status striving
    hierarchical competition, cross-
        level or spillover effects, 464
    motivation, person-centered,
        464
    prosocial behavior, 449, 450, 453
    psychology, as social dilemma,
        449–454
        fundamentals, 449–450
        personal and self-oriented
            concerns, 450, 452–454
        relational and other-oriented
            concerns, 450–452
    takers, givers, and matchers,
        449
status threat, 87, 453, 460
status trajectory, 458–460
Stereotype Content Model, 273
stereotype flexibility, gender
    differences, 535
Sterling, C. M., 271
steroid hormones, 60
    genomic actions, 62, 102
    non-genomic actions, 62, 110
stimulus-driven attention, 553–554
Stouten, J., 311
strategic disclosure, 358–359
strategic ignorance, 322
strategic legibility, 357–358
streaming, 578
stress responses
    challenge and threat, 199–200
    on gender differences, 520–521
    sex differences, 78–79
Strickhouser, J. E., 17, 334–335
structural competition, 10, 192–
    193, 193*f*
structures
    contested hierarchies, 454–456
    educational, 576–579
        normative assessment,
            577–578
        numerus clausus, 578–579,
            580, 582
        tracking, 578
students, 582–588
    behaviors, 584–586
        bullying, 585–586
        cheating, 584–585
        exploitation, 585
        sabotage, 585

goals, 583–584
  information exchange, 587
  outcomes, educational, 586–588
    learning, performance, and
      achievement, 586–587
    social relations, 587–588
  socioeconomic status, 588
  values, 582–583
subjective belief structures,
    482–483
subject pool, 26
success
  goals, interdependent, 221
  hope for, envy and, 275
  interpersonal, 499
  reproductive, by sex, 136
superiority, illusory
  definition, 288
    position, self-perception of, 288
  examples, 288–289
  exceptions
    comparison, object of, 299
    culture, 299
    self-views, negative, 299–300
  mechanisms, cognitive, 290,
    294–298
    competence, flawed
      assessments, 296–298
    reference group neglect,
      294–295
  mechanisms, motivational,
    290–294
    intentions, overweighting,
      292–294
    optimistic, overweighting,
      291–292
    predictions, preference-
      driven, 290
    skill, self-flattering
      definitions, 290–291
suprachiasmatic nucleus, 70, 71t
surgency, 507, 508
survivorship bias, 298
suspicion and competition,
    collectivist cultures, 621–626
  common standard vs. self-
    defined goals, 624–625
  social comparison, 622–624
  social ecology, relational
    mobility, 625–626, 627f
  zero-sum beliefs, 621–622
sustainability, social comparison
    theory, 414–416
sustained selective attention joint
    task, 118–120

Sutter, M., 522, 531
Sutton, J., 585
Sutton, R. I., 463
Swab, R. G., 499
Swann, W. B., 365
sympathetic-adrenomedullary
    axis, 199
sympathetic joy, sports
    psychology, 605
sympathetic nervous system, 165
system justification theory, 571, 588

T
Tamir, Y., 19
targets
  (over) sensitivity to being
    noticed, 356–357
    paranoid cognition, 356
    spotlight effect, 357
    transparency, feelings
      of, 357
  perceivers characterizing, 354
targets, prediction
  people as, 351
  reactions, to perceiver attempts
    to predict and characterize
    self, 355–359
    reactions to being
      characterized and
      predicted, 356
    (over) sensitivity to being
      noticed, 356–357
    (over) sensitivity to being
      noticed: feeling
      transparent, 357
    (over) sensitivity to being
      noticed: paranoid
      cognition, 356
    (over) sensitivity to being
      noticed: spotlight effect,
      357
    strategic disclosure, 358–359
    strategic legibility, 357–358
TARGET system, 580
task
  complexity, competitive arousal
    on, 178
  orientation/involvement
    on achievement, 561
    achievement goals, effort and
      performance, 561–562
    achievement goals, emotions,
      562–563
  performance, mastery goals
    and, 202–203

type, on gender differences,
    518–519
Tauer, J. M., 550, 551
Taylor, S. E., 78
team competitions, 18–21
team sports, 547
  performance, 549–551
Tedeschi, G. A., 322
Teixeira, A. A., 584–585
temperaments, 192
temporal comparison
  vs. social comparisons, 334, 335–336
  social comparison with, 202
temporally dynamic goal pursuit
    model, 210–235
  action phase, 214
  competition in goal pursuit, 210
  discrepancy feedback on, 216–
    217, 217f
    explicit competitions, 220–221
    implicit competitions, 226–227
  explicit competitions, 217–224
    expectancy beliefs, 220
    goal, 218
    goal setting, 218–219
    over course of competition,
      221–224, 222f, 224f, 225f
    winning, value of, 219
  fundamentals, 214–217, 215f
  future directions, 232–235
  goal's attainability, early stage,
    214
  implicit competitions, 224–232
    goal setting, 226
    individual goal pursuit,
      consequences of
      competition on, 230–232
    individual goal pursuit,
      shifting goals on, 225–226
    over course of competition,
      228–230
    over course of competition,
      cooperation tapering
      off, 228
    over course of competition,
      sabotage, 229–230, 230f
    over course of competition,
      vigilance of others,
      228–229
    value and expectancy of goal,
      226
  motivation in competitions,
    evolution of, 216, 217f
  Relief Nursery experiment,
    215–216, 215f

temporal properties, contested hierarchies, 457–459
temporary standing, contestants', 221
tend-and-befriend, 78–79, 89
Terada, K., 311
testosterone
  on competition, 110–111
  discovery and Berthold's work, 101
  on empathy, prenatal, 78
  fitness protection system, 104
  on leadership patterns, 78
  mating effort *vs.* parenting effort, 103–104
  mechanisms of action, 102
  release and functions, 101–102
  on status and assertiveness, 78
testosterone dynamics, competition-induced, 37–47, 104
  cytosine-adenine-guanine repeats, androgen receptor, 46
  human behavior and, 38–44
    aggressive behavior, 40–42
    athletic performance, 44
    competitive behavior, 39–40
    mating psychology and behavior, 42–43
    risk-taking, 42
  hypothalamic-pituitary-gonadal axis, 37–38
  pharmacological challenge, 44–47
    aggressive behavior, 45–46
    competitive behavior, 44–45
    mating psychology and behavior, 47
    risk-taking, 46–47
  reproduction, 38
  survival, 38
testosterone dynamics, men's endogenous, 101–111
  Biosocial Model of Status, 103
  Challenge Hypothesis, 102–103
  exogenous testosterone and competition, 110–111
  integrated models, 104–105
  life history theory, 103–104, 105
  reactivity, moderators, 105–110
    motivational, 107–108
    motivational: appraisal, 107–108
    motivational: personality factors, 107
    physiological, 108–110

physiological: androgen receptor polymorphism, 108
physiological: hormones, 109–110
physiological: physical condition, 109
situational, 105–107
situational: competition characteristics, 105
situational: hierarchical stability, 105–106
situational: reproductive opportunities, 106–107
Teubner, T., 176
Thau, S., 457
theca cells, 61, 63
theoretic equilibrium levels, 13
theories of competitions, opposing processes model of competition and performance, 196–201
  challenge and threat, 199–200
  choking under pressure, 200–201, 364–365, 553, 564
  performance-approach & performance-avoidance goals, downstream processes, 197, 197f
  rivalry, 200
  social facilitation and inhibition, 198–199
  social interdependence theory, 197–198
theory of mind, child development, 354
theory of planned behavior, 307–323
  behavioral intention, 320–321
  cooperation, as constructed choice, 322–323
  cooperation, attitudes towards, 308f, 309–314
    behavioral beliefs, gender difference, 308f, 309–312
    behavioral beliefs, gender difference, individually motivated, 310–311
    behavioral beliefs, gender difference, socially motivated, 311–312
    behavioral outcomes, evaluations, 313–315, 314t
  cooperation, defined, 307–308

criticisms, 309
fundamentals, 307–309, 308f
from intention to behavior, 322–323
social dilemmas
  attitudes, norms, and perceived control, 309
  decision-make process building blocks, 309
  motivation to cooperate, sources, 309
subjective cooperative norms, 315–320
  motivation to comply with cooperative norms, 316–320
    external, 317–319
    internal, 319–320
  normative beliefs, gender difference cooperations, 315–316
Thibaut, J. W., 313
threat
  hypothalamic-pituitary-adrenal axis, 199
  intergroup, 486–488
  opposing processes model of competition and performance, 199–200
  sports, 557–558
  status, 87, 92, 453, 460
  stress responses, 199–200
  sympathetic-adrenomedullary axis, 199
  theories, 199–200
threatened status, 87, 92
threat premium, 45
threat-related pattern, 200
time pressure, 170–171, 520
Titus, W., 507
To, C., 435
tokenism, 572
top performers
  evaluation of, flawed, 297–298
  plight, 300–301
Tor, A., 16–17, 30
tournaments, 12–16
  behavior, determinants, 14–18
  competitive field, 15–16, 23, 24
  definition, 12, 13
  inequality and hierarchy from, 22–24
  on motivation, 22
  prize spread, 15–16, 379
  rank-order, 13–24

behavior, determinants,
14–18
incentives, harmful behavior
from, 21–24 (*see also*
incentives, competitive,
harmful behavior from)
incentive system, 13–14
team competitions, 18–21
setting, 13
tournament theory, 13–15
tracking, education, 578
tradeoffs
life history, 103, 377–378
win–win, 620
trait competitiveness, 10,
496–508
behavioral benefits, 502–504
personal accomplishment,
502–503
personal accomplishment,
health maintenance, 503
personal accomplishment,
workplace, 502–503
self-knowledge, 502–503
belief elicitation measurement,
499
benefits and drawbacks,
496–497
bottom-line mentality, 505
decomposed games approach,
499–500, 499 n3, 502
evolutionary value, 497
five-factor model of personality,
500–501
goal accomplishment, 503
hypercompetitiveness
definition, 504
as desirable, 504–505
hypercompetitiveness,
behavioral impacts, 504–507
decision-making, unethical,
506
leadership, 506–507
productivity, workplace,
505–506
interpersonal diagnosis
approach, 497–498
intrasexual competitiveness,
individual differences,
501–502
on mental health, children,
502–503
narcissism, 501
opposing process model, 192–
193, 193*f*

autonomous engagement,
201
empirical support, 194–195
other traits and, 500–502
pay-for-performance incentive
structures, 505
RIASEC model of personality-
based occupational choice,
501
structure, 497–500
development, 498
measurement, 498–500
Type A behavior, 498
transparency, feelings of, 357
trash-talking, on competitive
arousal
negotiation performance, 176
relationship intensification, 172
Triplett, N., 190, 548–549
Trivers, R. L., 57–58, 351
Tseng, S., 219
Turchin, P., 151
Twitter, social comparison, 413
two-person
dilemmas, 306
payoff structures, 306–307
Type A behavior, trait
competitiveness, 219, 498,
500

U

Ultimatum Game, 110–111, 168*t*,
170, 171, 176
Ultimatum Game, Multiparty, 30
uncertainty
attributional, 432
identity, 432, 485, 486, 487, 490
incidental, 433
intergroup, 486–488
leaders provoking, 490
reduction, intergroup
distinctiveness and, 484–485
uncertainty-identity theory, 478,
484
undermining, social, envy and,
270
unethical behavior, rivalry and,
436–437
unfairness
beliefs, envy and, 275
perceived, 388–389
on competitive arousal, 170
unidirectional drive upward, 402
universal drive upwards, 335–336,
402

unpredictability, target, 360, 364,
366. *See also* predicting and
being predicted
upwards comparison, 335–336,
402
post-competition, 408–409
utility maximization, 11
risk-taking, 374
Uziel, L., 199

V

Vaillancourt, T., 147
valence, 165, 182, 212
valuations, auctions, 169
value, perceived
status and, 446, 448–449, 452
status hierarchies, 455
of winning, 217, 219, 220, 338
values
definition, 574, 583
self-enhancement higher-order,
583
student, education, 582–583
van Anders, S. M., 86, 107, 533
van der Meij, L., 43, 89, 106
van der Weele, J. J., 322
Van de Ven, N., 271, 272, 273
Van Dijk, F., 21–22
van Honk, J., 46
Vansteenkiste, M., 219, 246, 248,
259
Vanutelli, M. E., 127
Van Vugt, M., 448
variability hypothesis, 57
Vecchio, R., 270
Veldhuijen van Zanten, J. J. C.
S., 500
Vermeer, A. B. L., 110
Vermeer, A. L., 45
Vesterlund, L., 515, 516–517, 518,
523, 533, 534
victimhood
collective and competitive,
488–489
culture, 151–152
narrative, identity-defining,
489
victimization covert, envy and,
270–271
vigilance
in-group, collectivists,
620–621
of others, temporally dynamic
goal pursuit model, implicit
competitions, 228–229

Vine, S. J., 555
violence
    between-group, 135, 141–142,
        149, 150, 151
    decline, WEIRD societies,
        148–149
    between-group, 150
violence and hatred, intergroup,
        485–491
    ingroup leaders, 489–491
    threat, uncertainty, and
        extremism, 486–488
    victimhood, collective and
        competitive, 488–489
visibility
    cooperation, 319
    female tactics, 148
    status and, group-oriented
        behaviors, 453
    workplace, personal
        accomplishment, 503
visuospatial perception, sex
        differences, 73
vitamin D, 60
vocal control regions, 70
vomeronasal organ, 70
von Hippel, W., 108

W
wage gap, gender, 514, 524–525
Wang, M. T., 580
wants vs. needs, 390, 391
warmth, on social judgments,
        273–274
Watson, N. V., 40, 86, 92
WEIRD societies, 148–152
    dominance, prestige, and
        competition, 149–152
    microaggressions and wokeism,
        152
    violence, decline, 148–149
Weissman, D., 196

Welker, K. M., 42
well-adjusted persona, 363
well-being
    competition on, 241
    from envy, 272
    trait competitiveness on, 504
West-Eberhard, M. J., 135, 138–
        139, 152
White, M. H., 246
White, R. W., 498
wiggle room, moral, 322, 323
Willer, R., 450
Williams, K. D., 316
Willoughby, T., 258–259
Wilson, M., 386
Wilson, M. R., 554
Winegard, B., 152
winner effect, 81, 82, 85, 93
winner-loser effect, 103, 105, 106
winner's curse, 12, 24–30
    adverse selection problem,
        25, 27
    common value auctions and, 24
    definition, 25
    mechanism and Acquiring a
        Company problem, 27–28
    overcoming, learning, 28–30
    as real, 25–26
    theoretical explanations, 26–27
"winner takes all," 246, 381, 515,
        547
winning
    feedback from, 247
    objective and subjective, 248
    perceived value, 217, 219, 220,
        338
    temporally dynamic goal
        pursuit model, explicit
        competitions, 219
winning auctions, on competitive
        arousal, 169–170
"winning is the goal," 245

win–win tradeoffs, 620
Wirth, M. M., 91
Wohl, M. J. A., 381
wokeism, 152
Wolffian ducts, 65–66
women, 139, 144, 146–148,
        153
    gossip, 146–147, 153
    in labor force, 514
    in power, political and
        business, 514
    wage gaps, 514, 524–525
Wood, J. V., 389
Wooden, J., 565
Woodman, T., 559
workgroups, status pursuit and
        conferral, 446–449
Wozniak, D., 527
Wu, Y., 106
Wubben, M., 311

X
Xavante, 143

Y
Yamagishi, T., 316
Yanomamö, 141–142,
        143
Yerkes Dodson law, 178
Yip, J. A., 172
Yomat, 143
young male syndrome, 386

Z
Zajonc, R. B., 177, 178
Zell, E., 17, 333, 334–335, 336, 337,
        340, 341, 343, 630
zero-sum beliefs, collectivist
        culture competitiveness,
        621–622
zero-sum interaction, 4
Zilioli, S., 40, 87, 92, 104